DATE DUE

PRESENTED

_____

TO

_____

BY

_____

ON

_____

THE NIV
QUIET TIME
BIBLE

New Testament & Psalms

NEW
INTERNATIONAL
VERSION

A L I F E G U I D E ®

B I B L E

INTERVARSITY PRESS
DOWNERS GROVE, ILLINOIS 60515

InterVarsity Press® is the book-publishing division of InterVarsity Christian Fellowship®, a student movement active on campus at hundreds of universities, colleges and schools of nursing in the United States of America, and a member movement of the International Fellowship of Evangelical Students. For information about local and regional activities, write Public Relations Dept., InterVarsity Christian Fellowship, 6400 Schroeder Rd., P.O. Box 7895, Madison, WI 53707-7895.

Cover photograph: J. C. Leacock
ISBN 0-8308-2101-5 (cloth)
ISBN 0-8308-2102-3 (paper)

Printed in the United States of America ∞

Library of Congress Cataloging-in-Publication Data

Bible. N.T. English. New International. 1994.
  The NIV quiet time Bible: New Testament & Psalms: New
International Version.
    p.   cm.—(A Life guide Bible)
  Includes index.
  ISBN 0-8308-2101-5 (hard).—ISBN 0-8308-2102-3 (pbk.)
  I. Bible. O.T. Psalms. English. New International. 1994.
II. Title.   III. Series: Lifeguide Bible study.
  BS 2095.N37   1994
  225.5′208—dc20   94-18631
                                             CIP

18	17	16	15	14	13	12	11	10	9	8	7	6	5	4	3	2	1
09	08	07	06	05	04	03	02	01	00	99	98	97	96	95	94		

CONTENTS

ABBREVIATIONS

Books of the Bible

Matthew	Mt	1 Timothy	1Ti
Mark	Mk	2 Timothy	2Ti
Luke	Lk	Titus	Tit
John	Jn	Philemon	Phm
Acts	Ac	Hebrews	Heb
Romans	Ro	James	Jas
1 Corinthians	1Co	1 Peter	1Pe
2 Corinthians	2Co	2 Peter	2Pe
Galatians	Gal	1 John	1Jn
Ephesians	Eph	2 John	2Jn
Philippians	Php	3 John	3Jn
Colossians	Col	Jude	Jude
1 Thessalonians	1Th	Revelation	Rev
2 Thessalonians	2Th	Psalms	Ps

THE NIV QUIET TIME BIBLE
STAFF & CONTRIBUTORS

QUIET TIME WRITERS

Matthew: Stephen and Jacalyn Eyre
Mark: James Hoover
Luke: Ada Lum
John: Douglas Connelly
Acts: Phyllis J. Le Peau
Romans: Jack Kuhatschek
1 Corinthians: Paul Stevens and Dan Williams
2 Corinthians: Paul Stevens
Galatians: Jack Kuhatschek
Ephesians: Andrew T. and Phyllis J. Le Peau
Philippians: Donald Baker
Colossians: Martha Reapsome
1 & 2 Thessalonians: Donald Baker
1 & 2 Timothy: Pete Sommer
Titus: Pete Sommer
Philemon: Martha Reapsome
Hebrews: James Reapsome
James: Andrew T. and Phyllis J. Le Peau
1 & 2 Peter: Carolyn Nystrom
1, 2, 3 John: Ron Blankley
Jude: Carolyn Nystrom
Revelation: Paul Stevens and Scott Hotaling
Psalms: Cindy Bunch, Isaac Canales, Stephen Eyre, Mary Fisher, Linda Gehrs, Dietrich Gruen, Dan Harrison, Jack Kuhatschek, Phyllis J. Le Peau, Carolyn Nystrom, Hazel Offner, Dale Ryan, Juanita Ryan, Bill Syrios and Brian Wallace

GENERAL EDITOR

Cindy Bunch

EDITORIAL TEAM

Ken DeRuiter, James Hoover, Nancy Iglesias, Andrew T. Le Peau and Don Stephenson

GRAPHIC DESIGN

Kathy Lay Burrows

DESIGN ASSISTANT

Carla Sonheim

WORD PROCESSING

Gloria Duncan-Bevilacqua

PROOFREADING

Michele Pelton

PRODUCTION

Nancy Fox, Don Frye, Marjorie Sire

TYPESETTING

Auto-graphics: Jerry Fincher and Kam Cheng

BIBLE READING PLAN 1

Check off the boxes as you go to keep track of your reading. You may proceed in any order. Each psalm is listed whether or not there is a quiet time.

☐ Mt 1—2	☐ Lk 8:1-21	☐ Acts 8	☐ 2Co 1:1-11	☐ Col 4:2-18
☐ Mt 3	☐ Lk 8:22-56	☐ Acts 9:1-31	☐ 2Co 1:12—2:11	
☐ Mt 4	☐ Lk 9:1-50	☐ Acts 9:32—10:48	☐ 2Co 2:12—3:6	☐ 1Th 1
☐ Mt 5:1—6:18	☐ Lk 9:51—10:24	☐ Acts 11	☐ 2Co 3:7-18	☐ 1Th 2:1-16
☐ Mt 6:19—7:29	☐ Lk 10:25—11:13	☐ Acts 12	☐ 2Co 4:1—5:10	☐ 1Th 2:17—3:13
☐ Mt 8:1—9:34	☐ Lk 11:14—12:12	☐ Acts 13—14	☐ 2Co 5:11—6:13	☐ 1Th 4:1-12
☐ Mt 9:35—11:30	☐ Lk 12:13—13:21	☐ Acts 15	☐ 2Co 6:14—7:16	☐ 1Th 4:13—5:11
☐ Mt 12	☐ Lk 13:22—14:35	☐ Acts 16	☐ 2Co 8—9	☐ 1Th 5:12-28
☐ Mt 13	☐ Lk 15	☐ Acts 17	☐ 2Co 10	
☐ Mt 14	☐ Lk 16	☐ Acts 18	☐ 2Co 11	☐ 2Th 1
☐ Mt 15:1—16:20	☐ Lk 17:1—18:14	☐ Acts 19:1—20:12	☐ 2Co 12	☐ 2Th 2
☐ Mt 16:21—17:27	☐ Lk 18:15—19:10	☐ Acts 20:13-38	☐ 2Co 13	☐ 2Th 3
☐ Mt 18	☐ Lk 19:11-48	☐ Acts 21:1—22:21		
☐ Mt 19—20	☐ Lk 20:1—21:4	☐ Acts 22:22—23:35	☐ Gal 1:1-10	☐ 1Ti 1
☐ Mt 21:1-27	☐ Lk 21:5-38	☐ Acts 24:1—25:12	☐ Gal 1:11—2:10	☐ 1Ti 2
☐ Mt 21:28—22:46	☐ Lk 22:1-46	☐ Acts 25:13—26:32	☐ Gal 2:11-21	☐ 1Ti 3
☐ Mt 23	☐ Lk 22:47—23:56	☐ Acts 27—28	☐ Gal 3:1-14	☐ 1Ti 4
☐ Mt 24	☐ Lk 24		☐ Gal 3:15-29	☐ 1Ti 5:1—6:2
☐ Mt 25		☐ Rm 1:1-17	☐ Gal 4:1-20	☐ 1Ti 6:3-20
☐ Mt 26	☐ Jn 1	☐ Rm 1:18-32	☐ Gal 4:21—5:1	
☐ Mt 27	☐ Jn 2	☐ Rm 2:1-29	☐ Gal 5:2-15	☐ 2Ti 1
☐ Mt 28	☐ Jn 3	☐ Rm 3:1-20	☐ Gal 5:13-26	☐ 2Ti 2
	☐ Jn 4	☐ Rm 3:21-31	☐ Gal 6:1-10	☐ 2Ti 3
☐ Mk 1:1-15	☐ Jn 5	☐ Rm 4	☐ Gal 6:11-18	☐ 2Ti 4
☐ Mk 1:16-39	☐ Jn 6	☐ Rm 5		
☐ Mk 1:40—2:17	☐ Jn 7:1-52	☐ Rm 6:1—7:6	☐ Eph 1:1-14	☐ Tit
☐ Mk 2:18—3:35	☐ Jn 7:53—8:11	☐ Rm 7:7-25	☐ Eph 1:15-23	
☐ Mk 4:1-34	☐ Jn 8:12-59	☐ Rm 8:1-17	☐ Eph 2:1-10	☐ Phm
☐ Mk 4:35—6:6	☐ Jn 9	☐ Rm 8:18-39	☐ Eph 2:11-22	
☐ Mk 6:6-56	☐ Jn 10	☐ Rm 9:1-29	☐ Eph 3	☐ Heb 1
☐ Mk 7	☐ Jn 11	☐ Rm 9:30—10:21	☐ Eph 4:1-16	☐ Heb 2
☐ Mk 8:1—9:1	☐ Jn 12	☐ Rm 11	☐ Eph 4:17-32	☐ Heb 3
☐ Mk 9:2-32	☐ Jn 13:1-17	☐ Rm 12	☐ Eph 5:1-21	☐ Heb 4:1-13
☐ Mk 9:33-50	☐ Jn 13:18-38	☐ Rm 13	☐ Eph 5:21-33	☐ Heb 4:14—5:10
☐ Mk 10:1-31	☐ Jn 14	☐ Rm 14	☐ Eph 6:1-9	☐ Heb 5:11—6:20
☐ Mk 10:32-52	☐ Jn 15:1-17	☐ Rm 15:1-13	☐ Eph 6:10-24	☐ Heb 7
☐ Mk 11:1-25	☐ Jn 15:18—16:4	☐ Rm 15:14—16:27		☐ Heb 8
☐ Mk 11:27—12:27	☐ Jn 16:5-33		☐ Php 1:1-11	☐ Heb 9
☐ Mk 12:28-44	☐ Jn 17	☐ 1Co 1	☐ Php 1:12-30	☐ Heb 10
☐ Mk 13	☐ Jn 18:1-27	☐ 1Co 2	☐ Php 2:1-18	☐ Heb 11
☐ Mk 14:1-42	☐ Jn 18:28—19:16	☐ 1Co 3	☐ Php 2:19-30	☐ Heb 12
☐ Mk 14:43-72	☐ Jn 19:17-42	☐ 1Co 4	☐ Php 3	☐ Heb 13
☐ Mk 15—16	☐ Jn 20	☐ 1Co 5:1—6:20	☐ Php 4:1-9	
	☐ Jn 21	☐ 1Co 7	☐ Php 4:10-23	☐ Jas 1:1-18
☐ Lk 1		☐ 1Co 8—9		☐ Jas 1:19-27
☐ Lk 2	☐ Acts 1	☐ 1Co 10:1—11:1	☐ Col 1:1-14	☐ Jas 2:1-13
☐ Lk 3:1-20	☐ Acts 2	☐ 1Co 11:2-34	☐ Col 1:15-23	☐ Jas 2:14-26
☐ Lk 3:21—4:13	☐ Acts 3	☐ 1Co 12	☐ Col 1:24—2:5	☐ Jas 3:1-12
☐ Lk 4:14—5:16	☐ Acts 4:1-31	☐ 1Co 13	☐ Col 2:6-23	☐ Jas 3:13—4:10
☐ Lk 5:17—6:11	☐ Acts 4:32—5:16	☐ 1Co 14	☐ Col 3:1-11	☐ Jas 4:11-17
☐ Lk 6:12-49	☐ Acts 5:17—6:7	☐ 1Co 15—16	☐ Col 3:12-17	☐ Jas 5:1-11
☐ Lk 7	☐ Acts 6:8—7:60		☐ Col 3:18—4:1	☐ Jas 5:12-20

☐ 1Pe 1:1-12	☐ Rev 13	☐ Ps 32	☐ Ps 72	☐ Ps 112
☐ 1Pe 1:13-25	☐ Rev 14—15	☐ Ps 33	☐ Ps 73	☐ Ps 113
☐ 1Pe 2:1-12	☐ Rev 16	☐ Ps 34	☐ Ps 74	☐ Ps 114
☐ 1Pe 2:13—3:7	☐ Rev 17—18	☐ Ps 35	☐ Ps 75	☐ Ps 115
☐ 1Pe 3:8-22	☐ Rev 19	☐ Ps 36	☐ Ps 76	☐ Ps 116
☐ 1Pe 4	☐ Rev 20	☐ Ps 37:1-17	☐ Ps 77	☐ Ps 117
☐ 1Pe 5	☐ Rev 21	☐ Ps 37:18-40	☐ Ps 78	☐ Ps 118
		☐ Ps 38	☐ Ps 79	☐ Ps 119:1-24
☐ 2Pe 1:1-11	☐ Ps 1	☐ Ps 39	☐ Ps 80	☐ Ps 119:25-40
☐ 2Pe 1:12-21	☐ Ps 2	☐ Ps 40	☐ Ps 81	☐ Ps 119:41-176
☐ 2Pe 2	☐ Ps 3	☐ Ps 41	☐ Ps 82	☐ Ps 120
☐ 2Pe 3	☐ Ps 4	☐ Ps 42—43	☐ Ps 83	☐ Ps 121
	☐ Ps 5	☐ Ps 44	☐ Ps 84	☐ Ps 122
☐ 1Jn 1	☐ Ps 6	☐ Ps 45	☐ Ps 85	☐ Ps 123
☐ 1Jn 2:1-11	☐ Ps 7	☐ Ps 46	☐ Ps 86	☐ Ps 124
☐ 1Jn 2:12-17	☐ Ps 8	☐ Ps 47	☐ Ps 87	☐ Ps 125
☐ 1Jn 2:18-27	☐ Ps 9	☐ Ps 48	☐ Ps 88	☐ Ps 126
☐ 1Jn 2:28—3:10	☐ Ps 10	☐ Ps 49	☐ Ps 89	☐ Ps 127
☐ 1Jn 3:11-24	☐ Ps 11	☐ Ps 50	☐ Ps 90	☐ Ps 128
☐ 1Jn 4:1-12	☐ Ps 12	☐ Ps 51	☐ Ps 91	☐ Ps 129
☐ 1Jn 4:13-21	☐ Ps 13	☐ Ps 52	☐ Ps 92	☐ Ps 130
☐ 1Jn 5:1-12	☐ Ps 14	☐ Ps 53	☐ Ps 93	☐ Ps 131
☐ 1Jn 5:13-21	☐ Ps 15	☐ Ps 54	☐ Ps 94	☐ Ps 132
	☐ Ps 16	☐ Ps 55	☐ Ps 95	☐ Ps 133
☐ 2Jn	☐ Ps 17	☐ Ps 56	☐ Ps 96	☐ Ps 134
	☐ Ps 18:1-24	☐ Ps 57	☐ Ps 97	☐ Ps 135
☐ 3Jn	☐ Ps 18:25-50	☐ Ps 58	☐ Ps 98	☐ Ps 136
	☐ Ps 19	☐ Ps 59	☐ Ps 99	☐ Ps 137
☐ Jude	☐ Ps 20	☐ Ps 60	☐ Ps 100	☐ Ps 138
	☐ Ps 21	☐ Ps 61	☐ Ps 101	☐ Ps 139
☐ Rev 1:1-8	☐ Ps 22	☐ Ps 62	☐ Ps 102	☐ Ps 140
☐ Rev 1:9-20	☐ Ps 23	☐ Ps 63	☐ Ps 103	☐ Ps 141
☐ Rev 2	☐ Ps 24	☐ Ps 64	☐ Ps 104	☐ Ps 142
☐ Rev 3	☐ Ps 25	☐ Ps 65	☐ Ps 105	☐ Ps 143
☐ Rev 4—5	☐ Ps 26	☐ Ps 66	☐ Ps 106	☐ Ps 144
☐ Rev 6	☐ Ps 27	☐ Ps 67	☐ Ps 107	☐ Ps 145
☐ Rev 7	☐ Ps 28	☐ Ps 68	☐ Ps 108	☐ Ps 146
☐ Rev 8—9	☐ Ps 29	☐ Ps 69	☐ Ps 109	☐ Ps 147
☐ Rev 10—11	☐ Ps 30	☐ Ps 70	☐ Ps 110	☐ Ps 148
☐ Rev 12	☐ Ps 31	☐ Ps 71	☐ Ps 111	☐ Ps 149
				☐ Ps 150

BIBLE READING PLAN 2

The plan outlined below offers some variety in reading. The psalms that do not have individual quiet times are included here, so you can read them along with or in between the other quiet times.

☐ Luke 1—9	☐ 2 Thessalonians	☐ 1 Timothy	☐ Psalms 85—91	☐ Matthew 1:1—16:20
☐ Psalms 1—5	☐ Mark 1—9	☐ Titus	☐ John 13—25	☐ Psalms 116—124
☐ Luke 10—19	☐ Psalms 30—35	☐ 2 Timothy	☐ 1 John	☐ Matthew 16:21—28:20
☐ Psalms 6—13	☐ Mark 10—16	☐ Psalms 51—61	☐ 2 John	
☐ Luke 20—24	☐ Psalms 36—41	☐ Hebrews	☐ 3 John	☐ Psalms 125—138
☐ Acts 1—12	☐ Galatians	☐ Psalms 62—72	☐ Psalms 92—106	☐ James
☐ Psalms 14—20	☐ Romans	☐ 1 Peter	☐ Philippians	☐ 2 Peter
☐ Acts 13—28	☐ Psalms 42—50	☐ Ephesians	☐ Psalms 107—115	☐ Jude
☐ Psalms 21—29	☐ 1 Corinthians	☐ Psalms 73—84	☐ Colossians	☐ Psalms 139—150
☐ 1 Thessalonians	☐ 2 Corinthians	☐ John 1—12	☐ Philemon	☐ Revelation

Getting the Most Out of
The NIV Quiet Time Bible

Cindy Bunch & Andrew T. Le Peau

Quiet time can seem like an impossible dream to many of us. We face so many demands—work, family, friends, maintaining a home, schoolwork, church obligations each day—that we have little time left for peaceful reflection. Yet this can be one of the most renewing and vitalizing experiences of our Christian lives.

Whether you call it quiet time, devotions, or Bible study and prayer, what we are talking about is a portion of your day that is set aside to be in solitude. It is a time to connect with God and to hear what he has to say to you, to study Scripture, to apply the Word to your life, to offer praise and worship to God, and to pray. This may also be a time when you record what you are learning in a spiritual journal.

God is calling us to be with him. We cannot neglect this honor.

Why a Quiet Time Bible?

The NIV Quiet Time Bible puts us in direct touch with God's Word. It leads us to discover what the Bible says rather than simply telling us what it says. In the same way, this Bible does not tell you how to apply the Word to your life; rather it guides us with God's help to apply the Scripture ourselves. It uncovers the questions we have, the issues we face and the challenges that lie ahead. In this way, God's Word becomes as current as this morning's breakfast conversations.

How does *The NIV Quiet Time Bible* accomplish all this? Not by giving you study notes, extensive background notes or cross-references. Instead, it helps you discover for yourself the meaning of Scripture by asking thought-provoking questions. This question format is known as *inductive Bible study.*

We tend to remember very little of what others tell us. But we remember a large percentage of what we discover ourselves. As it has been said, "Tell me, and I will forget. Show me, and I may remember.

Involve me, and I will understand." This is why inductive study works so well. Even if other sources of spiritual nourishment are hard to find, if we learn how to feed ourselves from the Word of God, we will never go hungry.

The quiet times in this Bible are personal. The questions expose us to the promises, assurances, exhortations and challenges of God's Word. They are designed to allow the Scriptures to renew our minds so that we can be transformed by the Spirit of God. Our goal as Christians is not just to know *about* God, but to actually know him as one person knows another. He is our Friend, our Father, our Comforter, our Helper, our Guide and our Lord. Knowing him in this way, talking with him in this way calls for responses of joy, of worship, of repentance and sorrow, of hope and expectation. Loving God more. That's what this Bible is all about.

How to Use *The NIV Quiet Time Bible*

Because you will be making discoveries about yourself and about God, you may want to keep a special notebook to record what you are learning each day. You may want to note commitments that you make and keep a list of prayer concerns so that you can look back and discover how God has been working in your life.

At the beginning of each book of the Bible you will find a brief introduction which provides important information on who wrote the book, who it was written to and why it was written. It will also include historical background. All of this is important to understanding each book.

Each quiet time has several components:

Warming Up to God. Sometimes a question that draws you into the theme for the day, sometimes a topic to reflect on or pray about, this portion is designed to help you prepare your heart and mind for what you will be learning from Scripture.

Daily Scripture Reading. Read and reread the assigned Bible passage to familiarize yourself with what the author is saying. When you begin a new section you may want to read the entire book along with the introduction to that book. This will give you a helpful overview of its contents. It might be good to have a Bible dictionary handy. You could use it to look up any unfamiliar words, names or places.

Discovering the Word. The studies ask three different kinds of questions. *Observation* questions help us to understand the content of the passage by asking about the basic facts: who, what, when, where and how. *Interpretation* questions delve into the meaning of the passage. *Application* questions help us discover its implications for growing in Christ. These three keys unlock the treasures of the biblical writings and help us live them out.

Applying the Word. This is your opportunity to make the study personal. How has God's Word spoken to you? What actions do you need to take as a result of what you have learned?

Responding in Prayer. The suggestion here is to help you begin to seek God's wisdom in the area you've studied. You will also want to pray about your daily concerns, for family and friends, and about national and world events.

The introductory articles that follow will help you to better understand each of the parts of the study and show you how to get the most out of them.

The studies are designed to take fifteen or twenty minutes. You'll want to set aside additional time for prayer. Feel free to work at your own pace. Sometimes you may want to spend two days on one quiet time; other times you might want to do two in one day (one psalm and one New Testament study, for example). There are a total of 365 quiet times, which will allow you to complete the New Testament and the Psalms in one year. However, this schedule should not be something you feel bound to. Go at your own pace and as the Spirit leads you. Not all of the psalms are covered in the quiet times, but you may want to read them all as you go along.

Two plans are provided at the front of the Bible so that you can move around according to your needs and interests and keep track of what you have covered. An index is at the end of the Bible so that you can locate particular topics. Generally, you'll find that you gain the best grasp of each Bible book if you work through the book from beginning to end, rather than skipping around.

If you are in a Bible study group, you may be interested in knowing that our LifeGuide® Bible Study Series includes companion guides on each New Testament book and the Psalms. You may want to double up on your learning by using those guides, which provide studies forty-five to sixty minutes long and include leader's notes, in a group context.

It is our hope that these quiet times will be an encouragement and a source of growth for your life with Christ. May the Holy Spirit be with you as you meet God each day.

Why Have a Quiet Time?

John White

Quiet times work. Regular sessions of prayer and Bible study produce changes —changes in us and changes in people around us.

Our values alter once we start meeting regularly with God. Some things that once seemed important shrivel and lose their fascination, while others swell in significance.

We will see people differently. We will pity people we once feared, and pray for people who once enraged us. The changes do not result because we mechanically follow rules, but because we have our new way of seeing, a new way of savoring life on earth.

We will, to be sure, approach problems differently, feel different about our work, our studies, our job, our future. Our goals will have changed so that life slowly takes on new meaning. The changes are understandable since we are influenced by those we associate with. It follows that if we spend time daily in the company of our Creator God, it will have a profound impact on our existence.

But do I recommend that we have a daily quiet time solely for these reasons? As a matter of fact, no. There's much more to be gained.

To commune with God is to touch both infinity and eternity. We have opened a window to both a beyondness and an immediacy which time and space are powerless to provide and which we can experience in no other way.

We are limited too in our contact with ideas and truth. The most widely read person among us has only rubbed shoulders with a few obscurity-bound professors or dipped into a selection of "the world's great books"—a contradictory jumble of finite perspectives. Yet we are invited to private tutorials with the fountain of ultimate wisdom.

We are invited to collaborate in the creation of destiny, not to be a mere spectator but a coauthor. God does not want to determine all things in splendid solitude by the word of his power. He wants the painting of the future to be a family project in which we all play a part under his benign direction. Earth's policymakers are but actors in a drama written in heaven, and we are offered a pen to do some of the writing. Can we imagine anything better?

For Love's Sake

Yet not even for any of these reasons but for love's sake would I urge us to meet God daily!

As the deer pants for streams of water,
  so my soul pants for you, O God.

My soul thirsts for God, for the living God.
  When can I go and meet with God?
  (Ps 42:1-2)

For love's sake we must seek him. For what he is, not for any advantage we may gain. Our quest must be that of a suitor too blinded by beauty to descend to calculating self-interest, too intoxicated with love to care about the cost or the consequences of his suit.

It must be the love of Mary, sitting at Jesus' feet, enchanted by his words and grace, but deaf and blind to the frustration and fuss of her resentful sister (Lk 10:38-42). An enchantment of that sort will not be broken, nor its pleasures denied. It is time we forgot about our spiritual performance and our spiritual needs and gave ourselves up to passion.

"Beautiful!" you sigh. "I wish I felt that way. But I don't love God like that. So what can I do? How can I love when my heart is cold, when all I experience is the nagging guilt of knowing my love is a sorry thing not worth offering?"

But wait. A moment ago when you read the words of the psalmist, wasn't there a faint stirring of envy in you, an echo of the longing the psalmist expressed? If there was—and it matters not how feeble or faint—then your love is not absent but suppressed. It lies dormant beneath the weight of unbelief and discouragement.

Our love for God lies within many of us like a coiled spring, inactive but straining for release. It is a potential volcano, a dangerous thing that we fear to set free lest we shall have to cope with raging fire. Unless we take the risk of loving, we will only be half alive. But we should not be afraid of the longing within; it is more than matched by the greater longing of a God who planted it there.

Come, then, for love's sake. Come boldly defying fears. Enter into a love-pact to meet Christ daily. Come trembling to confess inadequacies. He is gentle and will understand. He will not force us or hurry the pace beyond what we are able to tolerate.

Come to his footstool. Come trusting. And come for love of him.

How to Have a Quiet Time

Stephen D. Eyre

One of the questions I frequently ask in counseling and discipling is "How is your quiet time?" If the person is having one, usually there is a slight pause and then the answer "I am having it regularly." Or, "I have been studying the Scriptures diligently."

Both responses are good, but not what I am after. I want to know more than just frequency or diligence in Scripture. What I want to know is, What is happening in your personal encounter with God?

Only as I get a glimpse of what's happening in the heart in touch with God can I give helpful spiritual guidance. Is there a sense of worship, or a sense of deadness? Perhaps so many concerns come to mind that we can't focus on the Scriptures. Or our prayer may be jumbled and distracted. All these things mean something, indicating both our needs and what God may be doing in our hearts.

I also want to know what is happening in a quiet time because I have found that it is possible to be blind to the presence of God and not even know it. When this happens, quiet times become merely an empty formality. Scripture becomes a book of principles to be applied. Prayer is a shopping list of things God is supposed to do. Difficulties in life are problems God is supposed to solve.

When we are blind to God, what God is doing in us in the midst of difficulties is overlooked. That God might want us to listen rather than do all the talking in prayer never occurs to us. And that God might want to meet us in Scripture is lost in our search for principles.

The Presence of God

The Lord's presence is the birthright of every believer and the heart of every quiet time. Before Jesus was born he was named *Immanuel*—God with us. During his discipling of the apostles, Jesus promised them, and us, that he would not leave us as orphans but make his home with us (Jn 14:15-21). His last words in the Gospel of Matthew were his promise to be with us to the end of the age (Mt 28:20).

This is more than an abstract promise or an intellectual idea. Nor is it an exotic mystical experience. It is merely a matter of relationship. God intends for us to know that he is with us. Meeting with God is very similar to being with a friend when you know each other well. There is a sense of connection that is much deeper than what we say to each other or the things we do together.

Sometimes you can know the presence of the Lord as a warm, quiet affection that wells up as you sit quietly before him. At other times the sense of his presence may come as a deep sense of heaviness and grief over your sinfulness. Or perhaps you know the Lord is with you as you read the Scriptures—a sense of inner nourishment as you read about God's work in the lives of people in the Old and New Testaments.

God's presence gives strength for living. And, we should note, the presence of God with us is not merely for our benefit. Others too will sense a depth about our lives that stirs spiritual hunger within them.

Using Your Emotions

All relationships involve our emotions, and our relationship with God is no different. Just as ignoring our emotions will leave us feeling separate and distant from people, the same will be true of our relationship with God if we ignore its emotional dimension.

So if we are to grow in spiritual perception, then we need to understand that emotions play an important role. With my emotions I sense God's affection for me, embrace his Word and react to his commands.

I realize that to bring in emotions is to invite controversy. Talking about emotions among Christians can be, well, emotional. Some pride themselves on their emotional restraint. Others take pride in their ability to display emotion. For those who value emotional restraint, let me say that, while I am suggesting that we must open ourselves up to emotion, I am not necessarily advocating outward displays of emotion. For those who have found great benefit in the feeling side of faith, you should keep in mind that emotions are natural responses that vary from time to time and should not be forced or manipulated.

Both in Scripture and in history we see godly people whose emotions were central in their encounters with God. David, as many psalms testify, experienced tremendous heights and great depths. Elijah, Jeremiah, Jonah and Habakkuk, to mention a few, had their times of ups and lots of downs.

Our emotions are more than mere reactions. They mean something. The writer of Psalm 42 begins, "As the deer pants for streams of water, so my soul pants for you, O God." He continues, "Why are you downcast, O my soul? Why so disturbed within me?" (vv. 5, 11). Today we would just consider ourselves depressed. The psalmist, in contrast, knew that his soul was "downcast" for a reason; he was thirsty for a fresh encounter with God.

This is not to say that strong emotions are a guarantee that God's Spirit is at work. Satan can duplicate almost anything. The way to discern true spiritual affection is in our love for God. Are we growing in appreciation of God's might, majesty and beauty? And when we are emotionally down, are we pitying ourselves or are we reaching out to seek God's consolation?

Once we are open to our emotions before the Lord, fresh springs of spiritual life can open up. And there is no better place to embrace our emotions than in our quiet times.

Quiet Time Phases

Because knowing God is a dynamic personal relationship, just like any other relationship, it tends to shift and vary with time and circumstances. If we are unaware of this dynamic, we may expect the same thing to happen each time we sit down to enjoy time with God. But the reality is that our quiet times are full of variety. Sometimes they are rich and sweet, other times dry and boring. Sometimes they require great determination, and other times they seem fresh and spontaneous. Sometimes we may go for long periods in which we do not consistently have quiet times, while at other times we are easily able to maintain the discipline of meeting God regularly.

We should not feel guilty about these ebbs and flows. If we think of quiet times as merely something we do, a method to be followed, then this variety will bother us. But if we know that our quiet times are always changing because our relationship with God is always growing and developing, then we can view these changes in our quiet times with deeper spiritual insight.

Personality and Spiritual Disciplines

Our temperaments have a great deal to do with our spiritual disciplines. I have observed that people who are methodical and detail oriented—accountants and engineers, for example—may have a hard time getting beyond staying in a routine, focusing on rigorously doing one's spiritual duty. On the other hand, those who tend to be spontaneous—say, artists, musicians and designers—may struggle to maintain a routine, but meet God on a more intimate level.

I am of the spontaneous temperament. I don't like to settle into one way of doing things for very long. I have a natural inclination to avoid set daily quiet times. I deal with this tendency in two ways. Sometimes I find it necessary to be very determined on a daily basis. At other times, I make it a goal to have four or five quiet times during the week and feel good about it if I have three or four.

Whatever our quiet time experience, there is no place for self-condemnation or pride. When we do well, it is surely a gift of God's grace to us. When we do poorly, being either irregular or legalistic, we shouldn't be surprised. God isn't. I don't condemn myself when I miss the mark. I am grateful for what times I have. I know the Lord is glad to be with me, and I determine to do better next time.

Each person has to move through the spiritual journey in his or her own way. Wherever we are in our spiritual lives, we should keep in mind that our goal in having a quiet time is to live with a heart-sense of devotion in the presence of God.

Inexpressible Joy

Quiet times are so much more than a duty. A quiet time is a divine encounter. God is with us. The purpose of a quiet time is to meet with him. If we are not listening for him, if we are not looking for him, we may miss the meeting.

On the other hand, if we are looking and listening through carefully developed spiritual disciplines, we will, in the words of Peter, be "filled with an inexpressible and glorious joy" (1Pe 1:8).

The Lord is present in his world, and all creation declares his glory. In our work, our family, our recreation, whatever we do, we can be filled with a sense of his presence.

However, unless we practice the discipline of a quiet time, we will be apt to miss his glory that swirls and sings around us. A fruitful quiet time will allow us to be before him in such a way that we sense his presence in everything we do.

How to Study the Bible

James F. Nyquist & Jack Kuhatschek

Sherlock Holmes was known for his brilliant powers of observation. One day a stranger came into Holmes's study. The detective looked over the gentleman carefully and then remarked to Watson: "Beyond the obvious facts that he has at some time done manual labour, that he takes snuff, that he is a Freemason, that he has been in China, and that he has done considerable amount of writing lately, I can deduce nothing else."[1]

Watson was so astounded by his abilities that he commented: "I could not help laughing at the ease with which he explained his process of deduction. 'When I hear you give your reasons,' I remarked, 'the thing always appears to me to be so ridiculously simple that I could easily do it myself, though at each successive instance of your reasoning I am baffled, until you explain your process. And yet I believe that my eyes are as good as yours.'

" 'Quite so,' he answered . . . throwing himself down into an armchair. 'You see, but you do not observe.' "[2]

Step One: Observation

The first step in personal Bible study is to make several *observations* about the passage or book you are studying. Like a good detective, we must train our eyes to see the obvious and the not so obvious. We can learn to do this by bombarding the book or passage with questions. Rudyard Kipling once wrote:

I have six faithful serving men
Who taught me all I know,
Their names are *What* and *Where* and *When*
And *How* and *Why* and *Who*.

[1] *Who*—Who is the author of the book? To whom is he writing? Who are the major and minor characters?

[2] *Where*—Where do the events occur? Are there any references to towns, cities, provinces? If you are reading a letter, where do the recipients live?

[3] *When*—Are there any references to the time, day, month or year, or to when events took place in relation to other events?

[4] *What*—What actions or events are taking place? What words or ideas are repeated or are central to the passage? What is the mood (joyous, somber)?

[5] *Why*—Does the passage offer any reasons, explanations, statements of purpose?

[6] *How*—How is the passage written? Is it a letter, speech, poem, parable? Does the author use any figures of speech (similes, metaphors)? How is it organized (around ideas, people, geography)?

The observation questions in the quiet times (which often begin with one of these six words) help us probe a book or passage and uncover many important facts. *Writing down* our observations in a notebook helps us make sure we are observing clearly and allows us to refer to these facts later in our study.

The importance of careful observation cannot be

overstressed since your observations will form the basis for your interpretations. In one of his most baffling cases, Sherlock Holmes commented to Watson: "I had . . . come to an entirely erroneous conclusion, which shows, my dear Watson, how dangerous it always is to reason from insufficient data."[3]

Sometimes observation may seem simplistic and dull. But it is extremely important. As Holmes suggests, faulty or inadequate data could lead us to wrong conclusions about what the passage means, which is the next step in the process.

Step Two: Interpretation

When we interpret we seek to understand those facts discovered through careful observation.

Were there any words you didn't understand? Define them.

Did the author use figurative language? This needs to be unraveled.

Were major ideas presented? Try to grasp their meaning and significance.

Did you encounter any difficulties? Seek to resolve them.

Meaning, significance, explanation—these are the goals of the interpreter. How do you reach these goals? And once you have reached them, how do you know you are not mistaken?

For example, have you ever been discussing a passage of Scripture with someone when suddenly he or she says, "That's just *your* interpretation," as if to say, "You have your interpretation and I have mine, and mine is just as good as yours!"

The person is half right. People often disagree on how the Bible should be interpreted. But just because there are many different interpretations of a passage doesn't mean they are all *good* interpretations. A good interpretation must pass one crucial test—it must conform to the *author's* intended meaning. You may have a seemingly wonderful interpretation of Scripture, but if it is different from what the author intended, it is incorrect.

How then can we discover the author's meaning? By following five steps:

1. Discover the historical context of the book. The events described in the Bible took place thousands of years ago. Therefore, we often lack important information regarding the background or context in which these events took place. For example, almost every New Testament letter was written to address a particular problem or set of problems: the Galatians were seeking to be justified by law; the Corinthians wanted answers to questions about marriage, spiritual gifts, meat offered to idols and so on; Timothy needed to know how to restore order to a church.

Sometimes the background or context of a psalm, prophetic book or New Testament letter can be found within the book or passage itself. For example, in 1 John we read, "I am writing these things to you about those who are trying to lead you astray" (1Jn 2:26). The introductions to each book in *The NIV Quiet Time Bible* also give you much of the basic information you'll need. If you want more, you can always consult a good reference work like the *New Bible Dictionary.*

2. Identify the type of literature you are studying. The biblical authors communicated in a variety of ways—through stories, letters, poems, proverbs, parables and symbols. The *way* they say things adds richness and beauty to *what* they say.

The literature of the Bible has been classified into various types. These include discourse (for example, the New Testament letters), prose narrative (the style used in the Gospels re-creating scenes and events from biblical history), poetry (the Psalms), proverbs (wise sayings such as those in the book of Proverbs), parables (Jesus used parables to explain a spiritual truth by means of a story or analogy), prophetic literature (for example, Isaiah) and apocalyptic literature (Revelation, which makes heavy use of symbolism, fits here).

3. Get an overview of the book. In Bible study it is helpful to get an overview of the book you are studying. And you may want to do this before starting on the quiet times in any given book. The parts of the book only take on their true significance in light of the whole. But remember that the way a book is put together will be closely related to its literary type. An epistle such as Romans is organized around ideas. Historical narratives are put together in a variety of ways. Genesis (after chapter 11) is organized around people: Abraham, Isaac, Jacob and Joseph. The Gospel of John focuses primarily on several "signs" which Jesus did. Psalm 119 is structured around the letters of the Hebrew alphabet!

Begin by reading quickly through the book. As you read, try to discover its overall theme. Next, look for major sections or divisions within the book. Look for connections or relationships between the sections, subsections and paragraphs. Look also for contracts, for cause and effect, for movement from general to specific and so on. Continually ask yourself how these paragraphs, subsections and sections contribute to the overall theme of the book.

4. *Study the book passage by passage.* Once you have an overview of the structure and contents of a book, begin studying it passage by passage, which are already clearly divided for you in this Bible. Many of the questions you will find in the quiet times will help you identify the main *subject* of the passage, what the author is *saying* about it, the *context* of the passage you are studying and its *atmosphere* or *mood.*

5. *Compare your interpretation with a good commentary.* Once you feel you have understood the main subject of the passage and what the author is saying about it, compare your interpretation with that of a good commentary, such as the *New Bible Commentary,* which can give you additional insights that you might have missed. It can also serve as a corrective if you have misunderstood something the author has said. But do your best to understand the passage on your own before consulting a commentary.

Step Three: Application

To properly apply the Scriptures, we must remember the nature of Scripture. We mentioned earlier that almost every book of the Bible was written to address specific problems, needs and questions of the people living *at that time.*

We face many of these same problems and questions today. It is still possible to take a fellow believer to court, and we still have questions about marriage. In fact there are hundreds of ways in which our problems and needs correspond to those faced by the people in the Bible. This is natural since we share a common humanity.

This leads us to the first principle of application:

Rule #1: *Whenever our situation corresponds to that faced by the original readers, God's Word to us is exactly the same as it was to them.*

But there are also situations from their day which do not have an exact counterpart today. This, too, is to be expected because of the differences between modern and biblical culture. In such cases we should follow the second principle of application:

Rule #2: *Whenever our situation does not correspond to that faced by the original readers, we should look for the* principle *underlying God's Word to them. We can then apply that principle to comparable situations today.*

For example, what was the principle underlying Paul's words about food sacrificed to idols? He was concerned that the Corinthians not do anything that would lead someone with a weak conscience to sin: "Therefore, if what I eat causes my brother to fall into sin, I will never eat meat again, so that I will not cause him to fall" (1Co 8:13). This principle might be applicable to many situations today, such as whether a Christian should drink alcoholic beverages around someone who is a former alcoholic—or drink at all.

Once we understand these principles of application, we can think of unlimited ways in which God's Word applies today.

Practice Makes Perfect (Well, Almost)

Learning to study the Bible is like learning any other skill—the more you do it, the easier it becomes. One of the side benefits of using *The NIV Quiet Time Bible* regularly is that you will be trained to better observe, interpret and apply Scripture. At first, it may seem mechanical, like learning how to type. And remember, you are not alone in Bible study. The Holy Spirit did not write Scripture in order to confuse us. He will help you to understand and apply the Bible as you pray, study diligently and make use of many of the study aids available today. Bon appetit!

---

[1] *The Illustrated Sherlock Holmes Treasury* (New York: Avenel Books, 1976), p. 17.
[2] Ibid., p. 2 (emphasis added).
[3] Ibid., p. 112.

Prayer and Journaling

Bill Hybels

According to a well-known business axiom, "if you want to know something, ask an expert." If you want to learn about sailboat racing, ask Dennis Connor. If you want to know about broadcast journalism, ask Diane Sawyer. If you want to find out how to turn around a large corporation, ask Lee Iacocca.

It makes sense, then, if you want to learn how to pray, to ask the number-one expert—Jesus Christ himself. Jesus' disciples recognized his expertise. Once they stumbled upon him while he was praying privately (see Lk 11:1). They were so moved by his earnestness and intensity that when he finally got up from his knees, one of them timidly asked, "Would you teach us to pray?" They knew that in comparison to their Master, they were mere neophytes—first-graders in the school of prayer.

Jesus did not object to their question. Instead, he took the opportunity to teach them how to pray. This is what he said:

When you pray, do not be like the hypocrites, for they love to pray standing in the synagogues and on the street corners to be seen by men. . . . When you pray, go into your room, close the door and pray to your Father, who is unseen. Then your Father, who sees what is done in secret, will reward you. And when you pray, do not keep on babbling like pagans, for they think they will be heard because of their many words. Do not be like them, for your Father knows what you need before you ask him.

This, then, is how you should pray:

"Our Father in heaven, hallowed be your name, your kingdom come, your will be done on earth as it is in heaven. Give us today our daily bread. Forgive us our debts, as we also have forgiven our debtors. And lead us not into temptation, but deliver us from the evil one." (Mt 6:5-13)

No other passage in Scripture tells so straightforwardly how to pray, and the advice Jesus offered his disciples two thousand years ago applies to all of us today: (1) pray secretly, (2) pray sincerely and (3) pray specifically.

Getting Away from Distractions

Some people pray in public places, at social gatherings and at mealtimes, just so they can be seen and heard and assumed to be religious. But prayer, Jesus says, is not a spectator sport. It is not something we are to engage in to give off signals of spirituality. Forget that idea, says Jesus. When you pray, go into your room and shut the door. Find a closet, an empty office, the workshop out in the garage, some secret place away from people and alone with God. That's where you can pray most effectively.

Why the emphasis on privacy? Why shut the door? First, there is an obvious, practical reason. A private place ensures a minimum of distractions, and most people find distractions deadly when it comes to making connection with God. Almost any kind of noise—voices, music, a ringing phone, kids, dogs, birds—can cause me to lose my concentration during a time of prayer. Even a ticking clock can catch me up in its rhythm until I'm tapping my foot and singing a country song to its beat. Jesus knows how our minds are put together, and he counsels, "Don't bother fighting distractions, because you'll lose. Avoid them. Find a quiet place where you can pray without interruption."

The practical reasons for privacy are important, but I think there is also a more subtle wisdom in Jesus' advice to pray in a secret place. Once you identify such a place and begin to use it regularly, a kind of aura surrounds it. Your prayer room becomes to you what the garden of Gethsemane became to Jesus—a holy place, the place where God meets with you.

I created such a prayer room near the credenza in a corner of my former office. In my prayer place I put an open Bible, a sign that says "God is able," a crown of thorns to remind me of the suffering

Savior and a shepherd's staff that I often hold up while making requests.

That office corner became a holy place for me. I arrived there around six o'clock in the morning when no one was around and the phone was unlikely to ring, and there I communed with the Lord. I poured out my heart to him, worshiped him, prayed for members of my congregation and received remarkable answers to my prayer.

My office has recently been relocated, and I now have a new prayer corner. But I miss the old one—not because there is anything holy about the corner itself, but because of what happened there. Every morning for several years I met with the Lord, and he met faithfully with me. Thinking of that corner is like thinking of home.

If you want to learn how to pray, find yourself a quiet place, free of distractions. It doesn't have to be a chapel. It can be the utility room, the kitchen pantry, the barn, your office or the front seat of your pickup truck, as long as the surroundings are familiar and quiet.

Meaning What We Say

Not only did Jesus tell his disciples to pray secretly; he also told them to pray sincerely. "Do not keep on babbling," he said. Be careful of clichés. Don't fall into the habit of using meaningless repetition.

How easy it is to use sanctified jargon while praying! Certain phrases sound so appropriate, so spiritual, so pious, that many believers learn to string them together and call that prayer. They may not even think of the implications of what they are saying.

For example, I sometimes hear a mature believer say very earnestly, "Dear Lord, please be with me as I go on this new job interview," or "Please be with me as I go on this trip." When you first hear it, this request sounds holy. Unfortunately, it doesn't make sense. I'm often tempted to ask the one doing the praying, "Why do you ask God to do what he is already doing?" We don't need to ask God to be with us if we are members of his family. Instead, we need to pray that we will be *aware* of his presence, that we will be confident because of it. Asking God to be with us when he is already there is one kind of "babbling."

Another kind of meaningless repetition is often heard at the dinner table. A believer sits down to a meal that is a nutritional nightmare. The grease is bubbling, the salt is glistening, the sugared drink stands ready to slosh the stuff down. "Dear Lord," the person prays, "bless this food to our bodies, and grant us strength and nourishment from it so that we may do your will." God's will might be for the believer to say, "Amen," push back from the table and give the meal to the dog—except that dogs matter to God too!

The apostle Paul tells us God's will in 1 Corinthians 6:20: "Honor God with your body." That means putting the right things into your body. Don't ask God to bless junk food and miraculously transform it so that it has nutritional value. Doing that is acting like the fifth-grader who, after taking the geography test, prayed, "Dear God, please make Detroit the capital of Michigan." That's not how God works.

Praying Specifically

God-honoring prayers are not simply shopping lists. They are more than cries for help, strength, mercy and miracles. Authentic prayer should include worship: "Our Father in heaven, hallowed be your name" (Mt 6:9). It should include submission: "Your will be done on earth as it is in heaven" (v. 10). Requests are certainly appropriate: "Give us today our daily bread" (v. 11); as are confessions: "Forgive us our debts, as we also have forgiven our debtors" (v. 12).

The Lord's Prayer is an excellent model, but it was never intended to be a magical incantation to get God's attention. Jesus didn't give this prayer as a paragraph to be recited; in fact, he had just warned against using repetitious phrases. Instead, he gave it as a pattern to suggest the variety of elements that should be included when we pray.

Putting Prayers on Paper

A good way to learn to pray specifically is to write out your prayers and then read them to God. Many people find they are better able to concentrate if they put pen to paper and arrange their assorted thoughts into an organized format. I've been doing this for several years, and I find that it helps me in several ways. It forces me to be specific; broad generalities don't look good on paper. It keeps my mind from wandering. And it helps me see when

God answers prayers.

At the end of each month, I read over my prayer journal and see where God has done miraculous things. Whenever my faith feels weak, I turn to my journal and see evidence that God is answering my prayers. If I can list a number of answers to specific prayers in January, I feel better prepared to trust God in February.

I write out my prayers every day; I have not been able to grow in my prayer life any other way. Experiment and see what works best for you. Try writing out your prayers once a week at first. If you find it helpful, do it more often. If it cramps your style and makes you uncomfortable, find another way that is more effective for you. But however you do it, pray Jesus' way: make your prayers private, sincere and specific.

Remember that God's prevailing power is released through prayer. He is interested in you and your needs. He is able to meet any need, and he has invited you to pray. His Son, Jesus, the expert on prayer, has given instructions so that you know just how to pray.

Here's an assignment to get your prayer routine started. Take a sheet of paper and draw three horizontal lines across it, dividing it into four sections. Label the sections A, C, T and S.

In the first section, write a paragraph of adoration. List God's characteristics that especially move you today. In the second, write a paragraph of confession. Specifically identify the sins that are on your conscience. (You can burn this paper when you're done with it!) In the third, list God's blessings for which you are thankful. And in the fourth, make your requests, whatever they may be.

Do this again tomorrow, and the next day. Experiment with the ACTS routine. Adapt the categories to fit your situation, but be sure to include each category each time you pray. Experience the blessings of balance.

And see what God does in your life.

PREFACE

The New International Version of the Holy Bible is a completely new translation made by over a hundred scholars working directly from the best available Greek texts. It had its beginning in 1965 when, after several years of exploratory study by committees from the Christian Reformed Church and the National Association of Evangelicals, a group of scholars met at Palos Heights, Illinois, and concurred in the need for a new translation of the Bible in contemporary English. This group, though not made up of official church representatives, was transdenominational. Its conclusion was endorsed by a large number of leaders from many denominations who met in Chicago in 1966.

Responsibility for the new version was delegated by the Palos Heights group to a self-governing body of fifteen, the Committee on Bible Translation, composed for the most part of biblical scholars from colleges, universities and seminaries. In 1967 the New York Bible Society (now the International Bible Society) generously undertook the financial sponsorship of the project—a sponsorship that made it possible to enlist the help of many distinguished scholars. The fact that participants from the United States, Great Britain, Canada, Australia and New Zealand worked together gave the project its international scope. That they were from many denominations—including Anglican, Assemblies of God, Baptist, Brethren, Christian Reformed, Church of Christ, Evangelical Free, Lutheran, Mennonite, Methodist, Nazarene, Presbyterian, Wesleyan and other churches helped to safeguard the translation from sectarian bias.

How it was made helps to give the New International Version its distinctiveness. The translation of each book was assigned to a team of scholars. Next, one of the Intermediate Editorial Committees revised the initial translation, with constant reference to the Hebrew, Aramaic or Greek. Their work then went to one of the General Editorial Committees, which checked it in detail and made another thorough revision. This revision in turn was carefully reviewed by the Committee on Bible Translation, which made further changes and then released the final version for publication. In this way the entire Bible underwent three revisions, during each of which the translation was examined for its faithfulness to the original languages and for its English style.

All this involved many thousands of hours of research and discussion regarding the meaning of the texts and the precise way of putting them into English. It may well be that no other translation has been made by a more thorough process of review and revision from committee to committee than this one.

From the beginning of the project, the Committee on Bible Translation held to certain goals for the New International Version: that it would be an accurate translation and one that would have clarity and literary quality and so prove suitable for public and private reading, teaching, preaching, memorizing and liturgical use. The Committee also sought to preserve some measure of continuity with the long tradition of translating the Scriptures into English.

In working toward these goals, the translators were united in their commitment to the authority and infallibility of the Bible as God's Word in written form. They believe that it contains the divine answer to the deepest needs of humanity, that it sheds unique light on our path in a dark world, and that it sets forth the way to our eternal well-being.

The first concern of the translators has been the accuracy of the translation and its fidelity to the thought of the biblical writers. They have striven for more than a word-for-word translation. Because thought patterns and syntax differ from language to language, faithful communication of the meaning of the writers of the Bible demands frequent modifications in sentence structure and constant regard for the contextual meanings of words.

The Committee on Bible Translation submitted the developing version to a number of stylistic consultants. Samples of the translation were tested for clarity and ease of reading by various kinds of people—young and old, highly educated and less well educated, ministers and laymen. Concern for clear and natural English motivated the translators and consultants. In view of the international use of English, the translators sought to avoid obvious Americanisms on the one hand and obvious Anglicisms on the other. A British edition reflects the comparatively few differences of significant idiom and of spelling.

As for the traditional pronouns "thou," "thee" and "thine" in reference to the Deity, the translators judged that to use these archaisms (along with the old verb forms such as "doest," "wouldest" and "hadst") would violate accuracy in translation. Greek does not use special pronouns for the persons of the Godhead. A present-day translation is not enhanced by forms that in the time of the King James Version were used in everyday speech, whether referring to God or man.

The Greek text used in translating the New Testament was an eclectic one. No other piece of ancient literature has such an abundance of manuscript witnesses as does the New Testament. Where existing manuscripts differ, the translators made their choice of readings according to accepted principles of New Testament textual criticism. Footnotes call attention to places where there was uncertainty about what the original text was. The best current printed texts of the Greek New Testament were used.

There is a sense in which the work of translation is never wholly finished. This applies to all great literature and uniquely so to the Bible. In 1973 the New Testament in the New International Version was published. Since then, suggestions for corrections and revisions have been received from various sources. The Committee on Bible Translation carefully considered the suggestions and adopted a number of them. These were incorporated in the first printing of the entire Bible in 1978. Additional revisions were made by the Committee on Bible Translation in 1983 and appear in printings after that date.

As in other ancient documents, the precise meaning of the biblical texts is sometimes uncertain. This is more often the case with the Hebrew and Aramaic texts than with the Greek text. Although archaeological and linguistic discoveries in this century aid in understanding difficult passages, some uncertainties remain. The more significant of these have been called to the reader's attention in the footnotes.

In regard to the divine name *YHWH,* commonly referred to as the *Tetragrammaton,* the translators adopted the device used in most English versions of rendering that name as "Lord" in capital letters to distinguish it from *Adonai,* another Hebrew word rendered "Lord," for which small letters are used. Wherever the two names stand together in the Old Testament as a compound name of God, they are rendered "Sovereign Lord."

Because for most readers today the phrases "the Lord of hosts" and "God of hosts" have little meaning, this version renders them "the Lord Almighty" and "God Almighty." These renderings convey the sense of the Hebrew, namely, "he who is sovereign over all the 'hosts' (powers) in heaven and on earth, especially over the 'hosts' (armies) of Israel." For readers unacquainted with Hebrew this does not make clear the distinction between *Sabaoth* ("hosts" or "Almighty") and *Shaddai* (which can also be translated "Almighty"), but the latter occurs infrequently and is always footnoted. When *Adonai* and *YHWH Sabaoth* occur together, they are rendered "the Lord, the Lord Almighty."

As for other proper nouns, the familiar spellings of the King James Version are generally retained. Names traditionally spelled with "ch," except where it is final, are usually spelled in this translation with "k" or "c," since the biblical languages do not have the sound that "ch" frequently indicates in English—for example, in *chant.* For well-known names such as Zechariah, however, the traditional spelling has been retained. Variation in the spelling of names in the original languages has usually not been indicated. Where a person or place has two or more different names in the Hebrew, Aramaic or Greek texts, the more familiar one has generally been used, with footnotes where needed.

To achieve clarity the translators sometimes supplied words not in the original texts but required by the context. If there was uncertainty about such material, it is enclosed in brackets. Also for the sake of clarity or style, nouns, including some proper nouns, are sometimes substituted for pronouns, and vice versa. As an aid to the reader, italicized sectional headings are inserted in most of the books. They are not to be regarded as part of the NIV text, are not for oral reading, and are not intended to dictate the interpretation of the sections they head.

The footnotes in this version are of several kinds, most of which need no explanation. Those giving alternative translations begin with "Or" and generally introduce the alternative with the last word preceding it in the text, except when it is a single-word alternative; in poetry quoted in a footnote a slant mark indicates a line division. Footnotes introduced by "Or" do not have uniform significance. In some cases two possible translations were considered to have about equal validity. In other cases, though the translators were convinced that the translation in the text was correct, they judged that another interpretation was possible and of sufficient importance to be represented in a footnote.

In the New Testament, footnotes that refer to uncertainty regarding the original text are introduced by "Some manuscripts" or similar expressions. In the Old Testament, evidence for the reading chosen is given first and evidence for the alternative is added after a semicolon (for example: Septuagint; Hebrew *father*). In such notes the term "Hebrew" refers to the Masoretic Text.

It should be noted that minerals, flora and fauna, architectural details, articles of clothing and jewelry, musical instruments and other articles cannot always be identified with precision. Also measures of capacity in the biblical period are particularly uncertain.

Like all translations of the Bible, made as they are by imperfect man, this one undoubtedly falls short of its goals. Yet we are grateful to God for the extent to which he has enabled us to realize these goals and for the strength he has given us and our colleagues to complete our task. We offer this version of the Bible to him in whose name and for whose glory it has been made. We pray that it will lead many into a better understanding of the Holy Scriptures and a fuller knowledge of Jesus Christ the incarnate Word, of whom the Scriptures so faithfully testify.

The Committee on Bible Translation

June 1978
(Revised August 1983)

Names of the translators and editors
may be secured
from the International Bible Society,
translation sponsors of the
New International Version,
P.O. Box 62970,
Colorado Springs, Colorado
80962-2970 U.S.A.

TABLE OF WEIGHTS AND MEASURES

Biblical Unit		Approximate American Equivalent	Approximate Metric Equivalent
WEIGHTS			
talent	(60 minas)	75 pounds	34 kilograms
mina	(50 shekels)	1¼ pounds	0.6 kilogram
shekel	(2 bekas)	³/₅ ounce	11.5 grams
pim	(²/₃ shekel)	¹/₃ ounce	7.6 grams
beka	(10 gerahs)	¹/₅ ounce	5.5 grams
gerah		¹/₅₀ ounce	0.6 gram
LENGTH			
cubit		18 inches	0.5 meter
span		9 inches	23 centimeters
handbreadth		3 inches	8 centimeters
CAPACITY Dry Measure			
cor [homer]	(10 ephahs)	6 bushels	220 liters
lethek	(5 ephahs)	3 bushels	110 liters
ephah	(10 omers)	³/₅ bushel	22 liters
seah	(¹/₃ ephah)	7 quarts	7.3 liters
omer	(¹/₁₀ ephah)	2 quarts	2 liters
cab	(¹/₁₈ ephah)	1 quart	1 liter
Liquid Measure			
bath	(1 ephah)	6 gallons	22 liters
hin	(¹/₆ bath)	4 quarts	4 liters
log	(¹/₇₂ bath)	¹/₃ quart	0.3 liter

The figures of the table are calculated on the basis of a shekel equaling 11.5 grams, a cubit equaling 18 inches and an ephah equaling 22 liters. The quart referred to is either a dry quart (slightly larger than a liter) or a liquid quart (slightly smaller than a liter), whichever is applicable. The ton referred to in the footnotes is the American ton of 2,000 pounds.

This table is based on the best available information, but it is not intended to be mathematically precise; like the measurement equivalents in the footnotes, it merely gives approximate amounts and distances. Weights and measures differed somewhat at various times and places in the ancient world. There is uncertainty particularly about the ephah and the bath; further discoveries may give more light on these units of capacity.

Matthew

What does it mean to be a disciple of Jesus Christ? How can we effectively disciple others? Christian bookstores are full of "how-to" manuals that seek to answer these questions. The early church had a discipling manual too—the book of Matthew. It was written to teach us how to be a disciple of Jesus Christ and how to disciple others. Before looking at current discipling manuals, why not go back to one of the originals?

Discipleship is the application of Christian truth to the present. "What does God want me to do about this relationship?" "How can I deal with anxiety?" We need to know what God expects of us on a daily basis. Discipleship is a very practical matter.

Practical questions are a concern of Matthew's as he writes his book. Matthew is a tax collector, so he knows how important it is to be practical. A tax collector has to know things like how much tax you owe, where you pay and who is authorized to collect it. And when a tax is paid, it must be recorded exactly. Otherwise government authorities tend to become hostile. Very practical stuff.

Matthew draws on all his background as he writes. Your most important need as a disciple is to know what the Lord is like. Matthew will help you. Through his work you will get to know Jesus better as he responds to needy people, handles conflict and faces opposition. You will also see what Jesus is like as a king. How does he handle authority? What type of laws does he give? How does he provide for his subjects?

For your daily living you will discover how to handle anger and envy. You will learn how to strengthen your faith, how to pray and how to grow in humility. You will gain insights into a biblical approach to evangelism. You will find out what attitudes the Lord thinks are important. And you will learn how to handle suffering and grief.

In short, a study of Matthew will help you become a better disciple and disciplemaker.

The contents of Matthew will be covered by dividing it into two equal sections, 1:1—16:20 and 16:21—28:20. The first half is entitled "Discovering the King." It focuses on the identity and authority of Jesus. The second half is entitled "The Rejection and Resurrection of the King." It focuses on Jesus as he encounters opposition and persecution culminating in the cross and resurrection.

From beginning to end Matthew is an exciting and challenging Gospel. Get ready for an adventure!

Outline

Part 1: Discovering the King

Part 2: The Rejection and Resurrection of the King

1 / *Matthew 1—2*
In Search of the King

HAVE YOU EVER waited with anticipation for something only to find that when it came it was not what you wanted at all?

The long-awaited birth of the Messiah is recorded in Matthew 1—2. The nation of Israel waited for centuries for God's anointed King to be born. What a wonderful day that was to be. Jesus' birth, however, was not greeted with royal gladness by the nation and its leaders. Instead, there was intrigue and conflict. The political and religious establishment felt threatened by the coming of the Messiah. It was left to foreign leaders to welcome the newborn King.

 Warming Up to God Think of something you once strongly desired (a car, TV, stereo, a special relationship or whatever). When you got it, did it fulfill your expectations? Why or why not?

 Read Matthew 1—2.

1 A record of the genealogy of Jesus Christ the son of David, the son of Abraham:

²Abraham was the father of Isaac,
Isaac the father of Jacob,
Jacob the father of Judah and his brothers,
³Judah the father of Perez and Zerah, whose mother was Tamar,
Perez the father of Hezron,
Hezron the father of Ram,
⁴Ram the father of Amminadab,
Amminadab the father of Nahshon,
Nahshon the father of Salmon,
⁵Salmon the father of Boaz, whose mother was Rahab,
Boaz the father of Obed, whose mother was Ruth,
Obed the father of Jesse,
⁶and Jesse the father of King David.

David was the father of Solomon, whose mother had been Uriah's wife,
⁷Solomon the father of Rehoboam,
Rehoboam the father of Abijah,
Abijah the father of Asa,
⁸Asa the father of Jehoshaphat,
Jehoshaphat the father of Jehoram,
Jehoram the father of Uzziah,
⁹Uzziah the father of Jotham,
Jotham the father of Ahaz,
Ahaz the father of Hezekiah,
¹⁰Hezekiah the father of Manasseh,
Manasseh the father of Amon,
Amon the father of Josiah,
¹¹and Josiah the father of Jeconiah[a] and his brothers at the time of the exile to Babylon.

¹²After the exile to Babylon:
Jeconiah was the father of Shealtiel,
Shealtiel the father of Zerubbabel,
¹³Zerubbabel the father of Abiud,
Abiud the father of Eliakim,
Eliakim the father of Azor,
¹⁴Azor the father of Zadok,
Zadok the father of Akim,
Akim the father of Eliud,
¹⁵Eliud the father of Eleazar,
Eleazar the father of Matthan,
Matthan the father of Jacob,
¹⁶and Jacob the father of Joseph, the husband of Mary, of whom was born Jesus, who is called Christ.

¹⁷Thus there were fourteen generations in all from Abraham to David, fourteen from David to the exile to Babylon, and fourteen from the exile to the Christ.[b]

¹⁸This is how the birth of Jesus Christ came about: His mother Mary was pledged to be married to Joseph, but before they came together, she was found to be with child through the Holy Spirit. ¹⁹Because Joseph her husband was a righteous man and did not want to expose her to public disgrace, he had in mind to divorce her quietly.

²⁰But after he had considered this, an angel of the Lord appeared to him in a dream and said, "Joseph son of David, do not be afraid to take

a11 That is, Jehoiachin; also in verse 12   *b17* Or *Messiah.* "The Christ" (Greek) and "the Messiah" (Hebrew) both mean "the Anointed One."

Mary home as your wife, because what is conceived in her is from the Holy Spirit. 21She will give birth to a son, and you are to give him the name Jesus,*c* because he will save his people from their sins."

22All this took place to fulfill what the Lord had said through the prophet: 23"The virgin will be with child and will give birth to a son, and they will call him Immanuel"*d*—which means, "God with us."

24When Joseph woke up, he did what the angel of the Lord had commanded him and took Mary home as his wife. 25But he had no union with her until she gave birth to a son. And he gave him the name Jesus.

2 After Jesus was born in Bethlehem in Judea, during the time of King Herod, Magi*e* from the east came to Jerusalem 2and asked, "Where is the one who has been born king of the Jews? We saw his star in the east*f* and have come to worship him."

3When King Herod heard this he was disturbed, and all Jerusalem with him. 4When he had called together all the people's chief priests and teachers of the law, he asked them where the Christ*g* was to be born. 5"In Bethlehem in Judea," they replied, "for this is what the prophet has written:

6" 'But you, Bethlehem, in the land of Judah,
      are by no means least among the rulers of
         Judah;
   for out of you will come a ruler
      who will be the shepherd of my people
         Israel.'*h* "

7Then Herod called the Magi secretly and found out from them the exact time the star had appeared. 8He sent them to Bethlehem and said, "Go and make a careful search for the child. As soon as you find him, report to me, so that I too may go and worship him."

9After they had heard the king, they went on their way, and the star they had seen in the east*i* went ahead of them until it stopped over the place where the child was. 10When they saw the star, they were overjoyed. 11On coming to the house, they saw the child with his mother Mary, and they bowed down and worshiped him. Then

they opened their treasures and presented him with gifts of gold and of incense and of myrrh. 12And having been warned in a dream not to go back to Herod, they returned to their country by another route.

13When they had gone, an angel of the Lord appeared to Joseph in a dream. "Get up," he said, "take the child and his mother and escape to Egypt. Stay there until I tell you, for Herod is going to search for the child to kill him."

14So he got up, took the child and his mother during the night and left for Egypt, 15where he stayed until the death of Herod. And so was fulfilled what the Lord had said through the prophet: "Out of Egypt I called my son."*j*

16When Herod realized that he had been outwitted by the Magi, he was furious, and he gave orders to kill all the boys in Bethlehem and its vicinity who were two years old and under, in accordance with the time he had learned from the Magi. 17Then what was said through the prophet Jeremiah was fulfilled:

18"A voice is heard in Ramah,
      weeping and great mourning,
   Rachel weeping for her children
      and refusing to be comforted,
   because they are no more."*k*

19After Herod died, an angel of the Lord appeared in a dream to Joseph in Egypt 20and said, "Get up, take the child and his mother and go to the land of Israel, for those who were trying to take the child's life are dead."

21So he got up, took the child and his mother and went to the land of Israel. 22But when he heard that Archelaus was reigning in Judea in place of his father Herod, he was afraid to go there. Having been warned in a dream, he withdrew to the district of Galilee, 23and he went and lived in a town called Nazareth. So was fulfilled what was said through the prophets: "He will be called a Nazarene."

---

c21 Jesus is the Greek form of *Joshua,* which means *the* Lord *saves.*
d23 Isaiah 7:14   *e1* Traditionally *Wise Men*   *f2* Or *star when it rose*   *g4* Or *Messiah*   *h6* Micah 5:2   *i9* Or *seen when it rose*
j15 Hosea 11:1   *k18* Jer. 31:15

Discovering the Word 1. Considering Matthew's purpose to portray Jesus as a heavenly king, why would Matthew include a lineage at the very beginning of his book (1:1–17)? 2. Matthew highlights Jesus' birth in 1:18–25. What do these verses tell us about his origin and destiny? 3. In chapter 2, Matthew portrays Jesus' initial reception by the world. How does Jesus the heavenly king contrast with Herod the earthly king? 4. How are the Magi different from the religious leaders in this passage? 5. God is the unseen actor throughout chapter 2. In what ways can we see his "behind-the-scenes" actions (vv. 6, 15, 18 and 23)?

 Applying the Word 1. How has knowing Jesus involved you in a search or journey? 2. The responses of the Magi and Herod are typical of the ways people respond to Jesus today. What factors might cause people to respond to Jesus in such radically different ways? 3. The Magi not only found Jesus, but they worshiped him and witnessed to the entire city of Jerusalem concerning his birth (2:2–3). In what ways has your search for the Lord resulted in worshiping him and telling others about him?

 Responding in Prayer Spend time worshiping the King of kings. Then ask God to help you tell others about him.

2 / *Matthew 3*
Preparing for the King

IN ANCIENT TIMES the coming of a king required special preparation. A herald was sent ahead to prepare the road on which the king would be traveling. Holes were filled, rough places made smooth and crooked sections straightened. The same thing happened in recent times when Queen Elizabeth II visited the Bahamas. In preparation for her coming, the roads she would be traveling on were completely resurfaced. In Matthew 3, John the Baptist is sent to prepare the way for the coming of the Lord. But his arrival required a very different kind of preparation.

Warming Up to God Spend some time in preparation for meeting the Lord by confessing your sins and listening for God's assurance of forgiveness.

Read Matthew 3.

3 In those days John the Baptist came, preaching in the Desert of Judea ²and saying, "Repent, for the kingdom of heaven is near." ³This is he who was spoken of through the prophet Isaiah:

"A voice of one calling in the desert,
'Prepare the way for the Lord,
    make straight paths for him.' "¹

⁴John's clothes were made of camel's hair, and he had a leather belt around his waist. His food was locusts and wild honey. ⁵People went out to him from Jerusalem and all Judea and the whole region of the Jordan. ⁶Confessing their sins, they were baptized by him in the Jordan River.

⁷But when he saw many of the Pharisees and Sadducees coming to where he was baptizing, he said to them: "You brood of vipers! Who warned you to flee from the coming wrath? ⁸Produce fruit in keeping with repentance. ⁹And do not think you can say to yourselves, 'We have Abraham as our father.' I tell you that out of these stones God can raise up children for Abraham. ¹⁰The ax is already at the root of the trees, and every tree that does not produce good fruit will be cut down and thrown into the fire.

¹¹"I baptize you with^m water for repentance. But after me will come one who is more powerful than I, whose sandals I am not fit to carry. He will baptize you with the Holy Spirit and with fire. ¹²His winnowing fork is in his hand, and he will clear his threshing floor, gathering his wheat into the barn and burning up the chaff with unquenchable fire."

¹³Then Jesus came from Galilee to the Jordan to be baptized by John. ¹⁴But John tried to deter him, saying, "I need to be baptized by you, and do you come to me?"

¹⁵Jesus replied, "Let it be so now; it is proper

¹3 Isaiah 40:3   ᵐ11 Or in

for us to do this to fulfill all righteousness." Then John consented.

[16]As soon as Jesus was baptized, he went up out of the water. At that moment heaven was opened, and he saw the Spirit of God descending like a dove and lighting on him. [17]And a voice from heaven said, "This is my Son, whom I love; with him I am well pleased."

Discovering the Word 1. For Israel the desert was a place of both punishment and renewal (recall the wilderness wanderings). How does John's ministry convey both concepts (vv. 1–12)? 2. The religious leaders considered themselves children of Abraham (v. 9). According to verses 7–10, how were they abusing this privilege? 3. John calls us to produce "fruit in keeping with repentance" (v. 8). Give examples of the kind of fruit you think he has in mind. 4. Both John and Jesus have ministries of baptism (vv. 11–12). How are their baptisms similar and different? 5. What does Jesus' willingness to be baptized suggest about him (v. 15)?

Applying the Word 1. The coming of Christ either demands repentance or brings judgment. In what ways do you need to better prepare for his return? 2. Think of people around you who have rough places or valleys in their lives. How can you help them smooth out the rough places or fill in the valleys in preparation for Jesus' coming?

Responding in Prayer Ask God to help you show others how to prepare for Jesus.

---

3 / *Matthew 4*
The Beginning of the Kingdom

"IS IT TIME yet?" "How much longer?" Those are the questions children ask repeatedly as Christmas approaches. It's hard on them (and their parents) to wait. But when Christmas day comes, it's full of fun and surprises. After weeks of waiting, we all get to open our new gifts. The beginning of Jesus' ministry was like the coming of Christmas. After a long wait, the wrappings came off and the world got to see God's greatest gift.

Warming Up to God All of us have experienced something new—starting a new job, going to a new school, moving to a new community. What did it feel like?

Read Matthew 4.

---

4 Then Jesus was led by the Spirit into the desert to be tempted by the devil. [2]After fasting forty days and forty nights, he was hungry. [3]The tempter came to him and said, "If you are the Son of God, tell these stones to become bread."

[4]Jesus answered, "It is written: 'Man does not live on bread alone, but on every word that comes from the mouth of God.'[n]"

[5]Then the devil took him to the holy city and had him stand on the highest point of the temple. [6]"If you are the Son of God," he said, "throw yourself down. For it is written:

" 'He will command his angels concerning you,
and they will lift you up in their hands,
so that you will not strike your foot against a stone.'[o]"

[7]Jesus answered him, "It is also written: 'Do not put the Lord your God to the test.'[p]"

[8]Again, the devil took him to a very high mountain and showed him all the kingdoms of the world and their splendor. [9]"All this I will give you," he said, "if you will bow down and worship me."

[10]Jesus said to him, "Away from me, Satan! For it is written: 'Worship the Lord your God, and serve him only.'[q]"

[11]Then the devil left him, and angels came and attended him.

[n]4 Deut. 8:3   [o]6 Psalm 91:11,12   [p]7 Deut. 6:16   [q]10 Deut. 6:13

[12]When Jesus heard that John had been put in prison, he returned to Galilee. [13]Leaving Nazareth, he went and lived in Capernaum, which was by the lake in the area of Zebulun and Naphtali— [14]to fulfill what was said through the prophet Isaiah:

[15]"Land of Zebulun and land of Naphtali,
    the way to the sea, along the Jordan,
    Galilee of the Gentiles—
[16]the people living in darkness
    have seen a great light;
on those living in the land of the shadow of
        death
    a light has dawned."[r]

[17]From that time on Jesus began to preach, "Repent, for the kingdom of heaven is near."

[18]As Jesus was walking beside the Sea of Galilee, he saw two brothers, Simon called Peter and his brother Andrew. They were casting a net into the lake, for they were fishermen. [19]"Come, follow me," Jesus said, "and I will make you fishers of men." [20]At once they left their nets and followed him.

[21]Going on from there, he saw two other brothers, James son of Zebedee and his brother John. They were in a boat with their father Zebedee, preparing their nets. Jesus called them, [22]and immediately they left the boat and their father and followed him.

[23]Jesus went throughout Galilee, teaching in their synagogues, preaching the good news of the kingdom, and healing every disease and sickness among the people. [24]News about him spread all over Syria, and people brought to him all who were ill with various diseases, those suffering severe pain, the demon-possessed, those having seizures, and the paralyzed, and he healed them. [25]Large crowds from Galilee, the Decapolis,[s] Jerusalem, Judea and the region across the Jordan followed him.

[r]16 Isaiah 9:1,2   [s]25 That is, the Ten Cities

Discovering the Word 1. Look over the entire chapter to discover the locations mentioned. What do they tell us about Jesus' ministry? 2. The prerequisite for Jesus' ministry was his ability to resist temptation. What can we discover about Jesus from his encounter with Satan (vv. 1–11)? 3. Look specifically at each temptation (vv. 3–4, 5–7, 8–10). What was Satan trying to accomplish with each of them? 4. How does Jesus demonstrate his message "The kingdom of heaven is near" in verses 18–25? 5. One of Jesus' first functions as heavenly king is calling disciples. From verses 18–22 develop a brief definition of discipleship.

Applying the Word 1. What can we learn about temptation and how to resist it from Jesus' example? 2. Discipleship for the first disciples meant leaving job and family and following Jesus wherever he went. How has discipleship affected your life? 3. Imagine the excitement of the first disciples as they watched Jesus healing and teaching among the crowds. Put yourself in their place and describe how you would feel.

Responding in Prayer Recall the qualities of discipleship you saw. Pray that you will be made a faithful disciple.

---

4 / Matthew 5:1—6:18
The Law of the King (Part 1)

C. S. LEWIS was once criticized for not caring for the Sermon on the Mount. He replied, "As to 'caring for' the Sermon on the Mount, if 'caring for' here means 'liking' or enjoying, I suppose no one 'cares for' it. Who can like being knocked flat on his face by a sledge hammer? I can hardly imagine a more deadly spiritual condition than that of a man who can read that passage with tranquil pleasure" (*God in the Dock* [Grand Rapids, Mich.: Eerdmans, 1970], pp. 181–82).

Lewis was right. Studying the Sermon on the Mount can be a devastating experience. It exposes the depth of our sin and the shallowness of our commitment. But the pain it inflicts is meant to heal, not destroy, us. In fact, the Sermon on the Mount could be called the Christian's job description. It is the most complete summary we have of

Jesus' ethical expectations for his followers. Throughout church history it has been a helpful guide and a convincing challenge.

 Warming Up to God When is it hard for you to follow God's law? Talk to God about your struggles with sin.

 Read Matthew 5:1—6:18.

---

5 Now when he saw the crowds, he went up on a mountainside and sat down. His disciples came to him, ²and he began to teach them, saying:

³"Blessed are the poor in spirit,
for theirs is the kingdom of heaven.
⁴Blessed are those who mourn,
for they will be comforted.
⁵Blessed are the meek,
for they will inherit the earth.
⁶Blessed are those who hunger and thirst for
righteousness,
for they will be filled.
⁷Blessed are the merciful,
for they will be shown mercy.
⁸Blessed are the pure in heart,
for they will see God.
⁹Blessed are the peacemakers,
for they will be called sons of God.
¹⁰Blessed are those who are persecuted because
of righteousness,
for theirs is the kingdom of heaven.

¹¹"Blessed are you when people insult you, persecute you and falsely say all kinds of evil against you because of me. ¹²Rejoice and be glad, because great is your reward in heaven, for in the same way they persecuted the prophets who were before you.

¹³"You are the salt of the earth. But if the salt loses its saltiness, how can it be made salty again? It is no longer good for anything, except to be thrown out and trampled by men.

¹⁴"You are the light of the world. A city on a hill cannot be hidden. ¹⁵Neither do people light a lamp and put it under a bowl. Instead they put it on its stand, and it gives light to everyone in the house. ¹⁶In the same way, let your light shine before men, that they may see your good deeds and praise your Father in heaven.

¹⁷"Do not think that I have come to abolish the Law or the Prophets; I have not come to abolish them but to fulfill them. ¹⁸I tell you the truth, until heaven and earth disappear, not the smallest letter, not the least stroke of a pen, will by any means disappear from the Law until everything is accomplished. ¹⁹Anyone who breaks one of the least of these commandments and teaches others to do the same will be called least in the kingdom of heaven, but whoever practices and teaches these commands will be called great in the kingdom of heaven. ²⁰For I tell you that unless your righteousness surpasses that of the Pharisees and the teachers of the law, you will certainly not enter the kingdom of heaven.

²¹"You have heard that it was said to the people long ago, 'Do not murder,ᵗ and anyone who murders will be subject to judgment.' ²²But I tell you that anyone who is angry with his brotherᵘ will be subject to judgment. Again, anyone who says to his brother, 'Raca,ᵛ' is answerable to the Sanhedrin. But anyone who says, 'You fool!' will be in danger of the fire of hell.

²³"Therefore, if you are offering your gift at the altar and there remember that your brother has something against you, ²⁴leave your gift there in front of the altar. First go and be reconciled to your brother; then come and offer your gift.

²⁵"Settle matters quickly with your adversary who is taking you to court. Do it while you are still with him on the way, or he may hand you over to the judge, and the judge may hand you over to the officer, and you may be thrown into prison. ²⁶I tell you the truth, you will not get out until you have paid the last penny.ʷ

²⁷"You have heard that it was said, 'Do not commit adultery.'ˣ ²⁸But I tell you that anyone who looks at a woman lustfully has already committed adultery with her in his heart. ²⁹If your right eye causes you to sin, gouge it out and throw it away. It is better for you to lose one part of your body than for your whole body to be thrown into hell. ³⁰And if your right hand causes you to sin, cut it off and throw it away. It is better for you to lose one part of your body than for your whole body to go into hell.

ᵗ21 Exodus 20:13   ᵘ22 Some manuscripts *brother without cause*
ᵛ22 An Aramaic term of contempt   ʷ26 Greek *kodrantes*
ˣ27 Exodus 20:14

31"It has been said, 'Anyone who divorces his wife must give her a certificate of divorce.'ʸ 32But I tell you that anyone who divorces his wife, except for marital unfaithfulness, causes her to become an adulteress, and anyone who marries the divorced woman commits adultery.

33"Again, you have heard that it was said to the people long ago, 'Do not break your oath, but keep the oaths you have made to the Lord.' 34But I tell you, Do not swear at all: either by heaven, for it is God's throne; 35or by the earth, for it is his footstool; or by Jerusalem, for it is the city of the Great King. 36And do not swear by your head, for you cannot make even one hair white or black. 37Simply let your 'Yes' be 'Yes,' and your 'No,' 'No'; anything beyond this comes from the evil one.

38"You have heard that it was said, 'Eye for eye, and tooth for tooth.'ᶻ 39But I tell you, Do not resist an evil person. If someone strikes you on the right cheek, turn to him the other also. 40And if someone wants to sue you and take your tunic, let him have your cloak as well. 41If someone forces you to go one mile, go with him two miles. 42Give to the one who asks you, and do not turn away from the one who wants to borrow from you.

43"You have heard that it was said, 'Love your neighborᵃ and hate your enemy.' 44But I tell you: Love your enemiesᵇ and pray for those who persecute you, 45that you may be sons of your Father in heaven. He causes his sun to rise on the evil and the good, and sends rain on the righteous and the unrighteous. 46If you love those who love you, what reward will you get? Are not even the tax collectors doing that? 47And if you greet only your brothers, what are you doing more than others? Do not even pagans do that? 48Be perfect, therefore, as your heavenly Father is perfect.

6 "Be careful not to do your 'acts of righteousness' before men, to be seen by them. If you do, you will have no reward from your Father in heaven.

2"So when you give to the needy, do not announce it with trumpets, as the hypocrites do in the synagogues and on the streets, to be honored by men. I tell you the truth, they have received their reward in full. 3But when you give to the needy, do not let your left hand know what your right hand is doing, 4so that your giving may be in secret. Then your Father, who sees what is done in secret, will reward you.

5"And when you pray, do not be like the hypocrites, for they love to pray standing in the synagogues and on the street corners to be seen by men. I tell you the truth, they have received their reward in full. 6But when you pray, go into your room, close the door and pray to your Father, who is unseen. Then your Father, who sees what is done in secret, will reward you. 7And when you pray, do not keep on babbling like pagans, for they think they will be heard because of their many words. 8Do not be like them, for your Father knows what you need before you ask him.

9"This, then, is how you should pray:

" 'Our Father in heaven,
hallowed be your name,
10your kingdom come,
your will be done
on earth as it is in heaven.
11Give us today our daily bread.
12Forgive us our debts,
as we also have forgiven our debtors.
13And lead us not into temptation,
but deliver us from the evil one.ᶜ'

14For if you forgive men when they sin against you, your heavenly Father will also forgive you. 15But if you do not forgive men their sins, your Father will not forgive your sins.

16"When you fast, do not look somber as the hypocrites do, for they disfigure their faces to show men they are fasting. I tell you the truth, they have received their reward in full. 17But when you fast, put oil on your head and wash your face, 18so that it will not be obvious to men that you are fasting, but only to your Father, who is unseen; and your Father, who sees what is done in secret, will reward you.

ʸ31 Deut. 24:1   ᶻ38 Exodus 21:24; Lev. 24:20; Deut. 19:21
ᵃ43 Lev. 19:18   ᵇ44 Some late manuscripts *enemies, bless those who curse you, do good to those who hate you*   ᶜ13 Or *from evil*; some late manuscripts *one, / for yours is the kingdom and the power and the glory forever. Amen.*

Discovering the Word 1. The Beatitudes describe the qualities Jesus desires in each of his disciples (5:3–12). Give a brief definition of each quality. 2. Jesus compares his followers to salt and light (5:13–16). What do these metaphors suggest about our role in society? 3. In the rest of chapter 5 Jesus discusses various misconceptions we might have about the Law (Old Testament Scriptures). Why do you think that Jesus stresses that he did not come to abolish the Law (5:17–20)? 4. How does Jesus' teaching on murder and adultery (5:21–30) differ from the traditional understanding? 5. How does Jesus want us to respond to evil people and enemies (5:38–47)? 6. What do we learn about proper and improper motives from Jesus' examples about giving, praying and fasting (6:1–18)?

 Applying the Word 1. Why are our motives just as important as our religious acts? 2. What does this reveal to you about your motives? 3. In what way do you need to experience Christ's blessing?

Responding in Prayer Pray for Christ's blessing in the areas in which you feel needy.

---

5 / *Matthew 6:19—7:29*
The Law of the King (Part 2)

JIM ELLIOT, A missionary killed by the Auca Indians, once wrote: "He is no fool who gives what he cannot keep to gain what he cannot lose." His words echo this portion of the Sermon on the Mount. Jesus asks us to choose between two treasures, two masters, two roads and two destinies. But he clearly explains why following him is the only wise choice.

 Warming Up to God When are earthly treasures more tempting to you than heavenly ones?

 Read Matthew 6:19—7:29.

---

¹⁹"Do not store up for yourselves treasures on earth, where moth and rust destroy, and where thieves break in and steal. ²⁰But store up for yourselves treasures in heaven, where moth and rust do not destroy, and where thieves do not break in and steal. ²¹For where your treasure is, there your heart will be also.

²²"The eye is the lamp of the body. If your eyes are good, your whole body will be full of light. ²³But if your eyes are bad, your whole body will be full of darkness. If then the light within you is darkness, how great is that darkness!

²⁴"No one can serve two masters. Either he will hate the one and love the other, or he will be devoted to the one and despise the other. You cannot serve both God and Money.

²⁵"Therefore I tell you, do not worry about your life, what you will eat or drink; or about your body, what you will wear. Is not life more important than food, and the body more important than clothes? ²⁶Look at the birds of the air; they do not sow or reap or store away in barns, and yet your heavenly Father feeds them. Are you not much more valuable than they? ²⁷Who of you by worrying can add a single hour to his life^d?

²⁸"And why do you worry about clothes? See how the lilies of the field grow. They do not labor or spin. ²⁹Yet I tell you that not even Solomon in all his splendor was dressed like one of these. ³⁰If that is how God clothes the grass of the field, which is here today and tomorrow is thrown into the fire, will he not much more clothe you, O you of little faith? ³¹So do not worry, saying, 'What shall we eat?' or 'What shall we drink?' or 'What shall we wear?' ³²For the pagans run after all these things, and your heavenly Father knows that you need them. ³³But seek first his kingdom and his righteousness, and all these things will be given to you as well. ³⁴Therefore do not worry about tomorrow, for tomorrow will worry about itself. Each day has enough trouble of its own.

^{d}27 Or *single cubit to his height*

7 "Do not judge, or you too will be judged. ²For in the same way you judge others, you will be judged, and with the measure you use, it will be measured to you.

³"Why do you look at the speck of sawdust in your brother's eye and pay no attention to the plank in your own eye? ⁴How can you say to your brother, 'Let me take the speck out of your eye,' when all the time there is a plank in your own eye? ⁵You hypocrite, first take the plank out of your own eye, and then you will see clearly to remove the speck from your brother's eye.

⁶"Do not give dogs what is sacred; do not throw your pearls to pigs. If you do, they may trample them under their feet, and then turn and tear you to pieces.

⁷"Ask and it will be given to you; seek and you will find; knock and the door will be opened to you. ⁸For everyone who asks receives; he who seeks finds; and to him who knocks, the door will be opened.

⁹"Which of you, if his son asks for bread, will give him a stone? ¹⁰Or if he asks for a fish, will give him a snake? ¹¹If you, then, though you are evil, know how to give good gifts to your children, how much more will your Father in heaven give good gifts to those who ask him! ¹²So in everything, do to others what you would have them do to you, for this sums up the Law and the Prophets.

¹³"Enter through the narrow gate. For wide is the gate and broad is the road that leads to destruction, and many enter through it. ¹⁴But small is the gate and narrow the road that leads to life, and only a few find it.

¹⁵"Watch out for false prophets. They come to you in sheep's clothing, but inwardly they are ferocious wolves. ¹⁶By their fruit you will recognize them. Do people pick grapes from thornbushes, or figs from thistles? ¹⁷Likewise every good tree bears good fruit, but a bad tree bears bad fruit. ¹⁸A good tree cannot bear bad fruit, and a bad tree cannot bear good fruit. ¹⁹Every tree that does not bear good fruit is cut down and thrown into the fire. ²⁰Thus, by their fruit you will recognize them.

²¹"Not everyone who says to me, 'Lord, Lord,' will enter the kingdom of heaven, but only he who does the will of my Father who is in heaven. ²²Many will say to me on that day, 'Lord, Lord, did we not prophesy in your name, and in your name drive out demons and perform many miracles?' ²³Then I will tell them plainly, 'I never knew you. Away from me, you evildoers!'

²⁴"Therefore everyone who hears these words of mine and puts them into practice is like a wise man who built his house on the rock. ²⁵The rain came down, the streams rose, and the winds blew and beat against that house; yet it did not fall, because it had its foundation on the rock. ²⁶But everyone who hears these words of mine and does not put them into practice is like a foolish man who built his house on sand. ²⁷The rain came down, the streams rose, and the winds blew and beat against that house, and it fell with a great crash."

²⁸When Jesus had finished saying these things, the crowds were amazed at his teaching, ²⁹because he taught as one who had authority, and not as their teachers of the law.

Discovering the Word 1. In 6:19–24 Jesus talks about treasures, eyes and masters. What common themes tie these verses together? 2. Worry is a dominant theme in 6:25–34. How can we escape worrying about such things as food and clothes? 3. What is the difference between judging others and being properly discerning (7:1–6)? 4. How should our knowledge of the Father affect our prayers (7:7–11)? 5. In the final section of the Sermon (7:13–27) Jesus talks about narrow and wide gates, good and bad trees, and wise and foolish builders. How do these three metaphors work together to make a common point?

Applying the Word 1. What does seeking first God's kingdom and righteousness (6:33) mean practically for your life? 2. Putting Jesus' words in practice is the way to build a lasting foundation against the day of judgment (7:24–27). What will the practice of Jesus' Sermon require of you?

  Responding in Prayer Pray that you will be a person of wisdom and discernment and not of judgment.

6 / *Matthew 8:1—9:34*
The Powers of the King

SOMEONE ONCE COMMENTED about a U.S. president: "I don't know where he is going, but I sure like the way he leads."

Leaders must demonstrate authority. But wise leaders know they must not abuse their authority. They know people follow leaders who also demonstrate integrity and compassion. In chapters 8 and 9 Jesus demonstrates that he is a worthy king, one in whom we can safely put our trust.

 Warming Up to God How has Jesus' authority been a guide to you in recent days?

 Read Matthew 8:1—9:34.

---

8 When he came down from the mountainside, large crowds followed him. ²A man with leprosy*ᵉ* came and knelt before him and said, "Lord, if you are willing, you can make me clean."

³Jesus reached out his hand and touched the man. "I am willing," he said. "Be clean!" Immediately he was cured*ᶠ* of his leprosy. ⁴Then Jesus said to him, "See that you don't tell anyone. But go, show yourself to the priest and offer the gift Moses commanded, as a testimony to them."

⁵When Jesus had entered Capernaum, a centurion came to him, asking for help. ⁶"Lord," he said, "my servant lies at home paralyzed and in terrible suffering."

⁷Jesus said to him, "I will go and heal him."

⁸The centurion replied, "Lord, I do not deserve to have you come under my roof. But just say the word, and my servant will be healed. ⁹For I myself am a man under authority, with soldiers under me. I tell this one, 'Go,' and he goes; and that one, 'Come,' and he comes. I say to my servant, 'Do this,' and he does it."

¹⁰When Jesus heard this, he was astonished and said to those following him, "I tell you the truth, I have not found anyone in Israel with such great faith. ¹¹I say to you that many will come from the east and the west, and will take their places at the feast with Abraham, Isaac and Jacob in the kingdom of heaven. ¹²But the subjects of the kingdom will be thrown outside, into the darkness, where there will be weeping and gnashing of teeth."

¹³Then Jesus said to the centurion, "Go! It will be done just as you believed it would." And his servant was healed at that very hour.

¹⁴When Jesus came into Peter's house, he saw Peter's mother-in-law lying in bed with a fever. ¹⁵He touched her hand and the fever left her, and she got up and began to wait on him.

¹⁶When evening came, many who were demon-possessed were brought to him, and he drove out the spirits with a word and healed all the sick. ¹⁷This was to fulfill what was spoken through the prophet Isaiah:

> "He took up our infirmities
> and carried our diseases."*ᵍ*

¹⁸When Jesus saw the crowd around him, he gave orders to cross to the other side of the lake. ¹⁹Then a teacher of the law came to him and said, "Teacher, I will follow you wherever you go."

²⁰Jesus replied, "Foxes have holes and birds of the air have nests, but the Son of Man has no place to lay his head."

²¹Another disciple said to him, "Lord, first let me go and bury my father."

²²But Jesus told him, "Follow me, and let the dead bury their own dead."

²³Then he got into the boat and his disciples followed him. ²⁴Without warning, a furious storm came up on the lake, so that the waves swept over the boat. But Jesus was sleeping. ²⁵The disciples went and woke him, saying, "Lord, save us! We're going to drown!"

²⁶He replied, "You of little faith, why are you so afraid?" Then he got up and rebuked the winds and the waves, and it was completely calm.

²⁷The men were amazed and asked, "What kind of man is this? Even the winds and the waves obey him!"

²⁸When he arrived at the other side in the re-

ᵉ2 The Greek word was used for various diseases affecting the skin—not necessarily leprosy.   ᶠ3 Greek made clean   ᵍ17 Isaiah 53:4

gion of the Gadarenes,[h] two demon-possessed men coming from the tombs met him. They were so violent that no one could pass that way. [29]"What do you want with us, Son of God?" they shouted. "Have you come here to torture us before the appointed time?"

[30]Some distance from them a large herd of pigs was feeding. [31]The demons begged Jesus, "If you drive us out, send us into the herd of pigs."

[32]He said to them, "Go!" So they came out and went into the pigs, and the whole herd rushed down the steep bank into the lake and died in the water. [33]Those tending the pigs ran off, went into the town and reported all this, including what had happened to the demon-possessed men. [34]Then the whole town went out to meet Jesus. And when they saw him, they pleaded with him to leave their region.

9 Jesus stepped into a boat, crossed over and came to his own town. [2]Some men brought to him a paralytic, lying on a mat. When Jesus saw their faith, he said to the paralytic, "Take heart, son; your sins are forgiven."

[3]At this, some of the teachers of the law said to themselves, "This fellow is blaspheming!"

[4]Knowing their thoughts, Jesus said, "Why do you entertain evil thoughts in your hearts? [5]Which is easier: to say, 'Your sins are forgiven,' or to say, 'Get up and walk'? [6]But so that you may know that the Son of Man has authority on earth to forgive sins. . . ." Then he said to the paralytic, "Get up, take your mat and go home." [7]And the man got up and went home. [8]When the crowd saw this, they were filled with awe; and they praised God, who had given such authority to men.

[9]As Jesus went on from there, he saw a man named Matthew sitting at the tax collector's booth. "Follow me," he told him, and Matthew got up and followed him.

[10]While Jesus was having dinner at Matthew's house, many tax collectors and "sinners" came and ate with him and his disciples. [11]When the Pharisees saw this, they asked his disciples, "Why does your teacher eat with tax collectors and 'sinners'?"

[12]On hearing this, Jesus said, "It is not the healthy who need a doctor, but the sick. [13]But go and learn what this means: 'I desire mercy, not sacrifice.'[i] For I have not come to call the righteous, but sinners."

[14]Then John's disciples came and asked him, "How is it that we and the Pharisees fast, but your disciples do not fast?"

[15]Jesus answered, "How can the guests of the bridegroom mourn while he is with them? The time will come when the bridegroom will be taken from them; then they will fast.

[16]"No one sews a patch of unshrunk cloth on an old garment, for the patch will pull away from the garment, making the tear worse. [17]Neither do men pour new wine into old wineskins. If they do, the skins will burst, the wine will run out and the wineskins will be ruined. No, they pour new wine into new wineskins, and both are preserved."

[18]While he was saying this, a ruler came and knelt before him and said, "My daughter has just died. But come and put your hand on her, and she will live." [19]Jesus got up and went with him, and so did his disciples.

[20]Just then a woman who had been subject to bleeding for twelve years came up behind him and touched the edge of his cloak. [21]She said to herself, "If I only touch his cloak, I will be healed."

[22]Jesus turned and saw her. "Take heart, daughter," he said, "your faith has healed you." And the woman was healed from that moment.

[23]When Jesus entered the ruler's house and saw the flute players and the noisy crowd, [24]he said, "Go away. The girl is not dead but asleep." But they laughed at him. [25]After the crowd had been put outside, he went in and took the girl by the hand, and she got up. [26]News of this spread through all that region.

[27]As Jesus went on from there, two blind men followed him, calling out, "Have mercy on us, Son of David!"

[28]When he had gone indoors, the blind men came to him, and he asked them, "Do you believe that I am able to do this?"

"Yes, Lord," they replied.

[29]Then he touched their eyes and said, "According to your faith will it be done to you"; [30]and their sight was restored. Jesus warned them sternly, "See that no one knows about this." [31]But they went out and spread the news about him all over that region.

---

[h]28 Some manuscripts *Gergesenes*; others *Gerasenes*   [i]13 Hosea 6:6

³²While they were going out, a man who was demon-possessed and could not talk was brought to Jesus. ³³And when the demon was driven out, the man who had been mute spoke. The crowd was amazed and said, "Nothing like this has ever been seen in Israel."

³⁴But the Pharisees said, "It is by the prince of demons that he drives out demons."

Discovering the Word 1. In chapters 8—9 Jesus' miracles occur in three groups, followed by a response, or reaction. Briefly describe how Jesus demonstrates his authority in 8:1–22. 2. In 8:18–22 Jesus begins to attract would-be followers. What do these verses teach us about the cost and urgency of following him? 3. What do we learn about the extent of Jesus' authority in 8:23—9:17? 4. What is the relationship between Jesus' claim to have authority to forgive sins and his healing of the paralytic (9:1–8)? 5. In 9:9–17 Jesus compares himself to a doctor and a bridegroom. Then he discusses garments and wineskins. What do these illustrations teach us about his ministry? 6. How do people respond to Jesus in 9:18–34?

Applying the Word 1. Look back over chapters 8—9. How does Jesus want us to respond to his power and authority? 2. How can a knowledge of Jesus' power and authority strengthen your faith?

Responding in Prayer Spend time praising God for Jesus' leadership.

7 / *Matthew 9:35—11:30*
The Messengers of the King

DURING THE LATE 1800s a wealthy philanthropist decided to give away all his money. He announced he would give five hundred dollars to anyone with a legitimate need. The response was overwhelming! People lined up day after day to receive their gift.

The gospel is a priceless treasure. But as we offer it to people, their response is not always enthusiastic. In this passage Jesus warns us about those who oppose his message and his messengers. But he also encourages us as we reach out to blind and needy people.

Warming Up to God Have you ever known someone who seemed to like you only for what you could give them? What did it feel like?

Read Matthew 9:35—11:30.

³⁵Jesus went through all the towns and villages, teaching in their synagogues, preaching the good news of the kingdom and healing every disease and sickness. ³⁶When he saw the crowds, he had compassion on them, because they were harassed and helpless, like sheep without a shepherd. ³⁷Then he said to his disciples, "The harvest is plentiful but the workers are few. ³⁸Ask the Lord of the harvest, therefore, to send out workers into his harvest field."

10 He called his twelve disciples to him and gave them authority to drive out evil ʲ spirits and to heal every disease and sickness.

²These are the names of the twelve apostles: first, Simon (who is called Peter) and his brother Andrew; James son of Zebedee, and his brother John; ³Philip and Bartholomew; Thomas and Matthew the tax collector; James son of Alphaeus, and Thaddaeus; ⁴Simon the Zealot and Judas Iscariot, who betrayed him.

⁵These twelve Jesus sent out with the following instructions: "Do not go among the Gentiles or enter any town of the Samaritans. ⁶Go rather to the lost sheep of Israel. ⁷As you go, preach this message: 'The kingdom of heaven is near.' ⁸Heal the sick, raise the dead, cleanse those who have leprosy,ᵏ drive out demons. Freely you have received, freely give. ⁹Do not take along any gold or silver or copper in your belts; ¹⁰take no bag for

ʲ1 Greek unclean   ᵏ8 The Greek word was used for various diseases affecting the skin—not necessarily leprosy.

the journey, or extra tunic, or sandals or a staff; for the worker is worth his keep.

[11]"Whatever town or village you enter, search for some worthy person there and stay at his house until you leave. [12]As you enter the home, give it your greeting. [13]If the home is deserving, let your peace rest on it; if it is not, let your peace return to you. [14]If anyone will not welcome you or listen to your words, shake the dust off your feet when you leave that home or town. [15]I tell you the truth, it will be more bearable for Sodom and Gomorrah on the day of judgment than for that town. [16]I am sending you out like sheep among wolves. Therefore be as shrewd as snakes and as innocent as doves.

[17]"Be on your guard against men; they will hand you over to the local councils and flog you in their synagogues. [18]On my account you will be brought before governors and kings as witnesses to them and to the Gentiles. [19]But when they arrest you, do not worry about what to say or how to say it. At that time you will be given what to say, [20]for it will not be you speaking, but the Spirit of your Father speaking through you.

[21]"Brother will betray brother to death, and a father his child; children will rebel against their parents and have them put to death. [22]All men will hate you because of me, but he who stands firm to the end will be saved. [23]When you are persecuted in one place, flee to another. I tell you the truth, you will not finish going through the cities of Israel before the Son of Man comes.

[24]"A student is not above his teacher, nor a servant above his master. [25]It is enough for the student to be like his teacher, and the servant like his master. If the head of the house has been called Beelzebub,[l] how much more the members of his household!

[26]"So do not be afraid of them. There is nothing concealed that will not be disclosed, or hidden that will not be made known. [27]What I tell you in the dark, speak in the daylight; what is whispered in your ear, proclaim from the roofs. [28]Do not be afraid of those who kill the body but cannot kill the soul. Rather, be afraid of the One who can destroy both soul and body in hell. [29]Are not two sparrows sold for a penny[m]? Yet not one of them will fall to the ground apart from the will of your Father. [30]And even the very hairs of your head are all numbered. [31]So don't be afraid; you are worth more than many sparrows.

[32]"Whoever acknowledges me before men, I will also acknowledge him before my Father in heaven. [33]But whoever disowns me before men, I will disown him before my Father in heaven.

[34]"Do not suppose that I have come to bring peace to the earth. I did not come to bring peace, but a sword. [35]For I have come to turn

" 'a man against his father,
    a daughter against her mother,
  a daughter-in-law against her mother-in-
      law—
[36] a man's enemies will be the members of his
      own household.'[n]

[37]"Anyone who loves his father or mother more than me is not worthy of me; anyone who loves his son or daughter more than me is not worthy of me; [38]and anyone who does not take his cross and follow me is not worthy of me. [39]Whoever finds his life will lose it, and whoever loses his life for my sake will find it.

[40]"He who receives you receives me, and he who receives me receives the one who sent me. [41]Anyone who receives a prophet because he is a prophet will receive a prophet's reward, and anyone who receives a righteous man because he is a righteous man will receive a righteous man's reward. [42]And if anyone gives even a cup of cold water to one of these little ones because he is my disciple, I tell you the truth, he will certainly not lose his reward."

11

After Jesus had finished instructing his twelve disciples, he went on from there to teach and preach in the towns of Galilee.[o]

[2]When John heard in prison what Christ was doing, he sent his disciples [3]to ask him, "Are you the one who was to come, or should we expect someone else?"

[4]Jesus replied, "Go back and report to John what you hear and see: [5]The blind receive sight, the lame walk, those who have leprosy[p] are cured, the deaf hear, the dead are raised, and the good news is preached to the poor. [6]Blessed is the man who does not fall away on account of me."

[7]As John's disciples were leaving, Jesus began to speak to the crowd about John: "What did you go out into the desert to see? A reed swayed by the wind? [8]If not, what did you go out to see? A man dressed in fine clothes? No, those who wear

---

[l]25 Greek *Beezeboul* or *Beelzeboul*   [m]29 Greek *an assarion*
[n]36 Micah 7:6   [o]1 Greek *in their towns*   [p]5 The Greek word was used for various diseases affecting the skin—not necessarily leprosy.

fine clothes are in kings' palaces. [9]Then what did
you go out to see? A prophet? Yes, I tell you, and
more than a prophet. [10]This is the one about
whom it is written:

" 'I will send my messenger ahead of you,
who will prepare your way before you.'[q]

[11]I tell you the truth: Among those born of
women there has not risen anyone greater than
John the Baptist; yet he who is least in the kingdom of heaven is greater than he. [12]From the days
of John the Baptist until now, the kingdom of
heaven has been forcefully advancing, and forceful men lay hold of it. [13]For all the Prophets and
the Law prophesied until John. [14]And if you are
willing to accept it, he is the Elijah who was to
come. [15]He who has ears, let him hear.

[16]"To what can I compare this generation?
They are like children sitting in the marketplaces
and calling out to others:

[17]" 'We played the flute for you,
and you did not dance;
we sang a dirge,
and you did not mourn.'

[18]For John came neither eating nor drinking, and
they say, 'He has a demon.' [19]The Son of Man
came eating and drinking, and they say, 'Here is a
glutton and a drunkard, a friend of tax collectors
and "sinners." ' But wisdom is proved right by her
actions."

[20]Then Jesus began to denounce the cities in
which most of his miracles had been performed,
because they did not repent. [21]"Woe to you, Korazin! Woe to you, Bethsaida! If the miracles that
were performed in you had been performed in
Tyre and Sidon, they would have repented long
ago in sackcloth and ashes. [22]But I tell you, it will
be more bearable for Tyre and Sidon on the day of
judgment than for you. [23]And you, Capernaum,
will you be lifted up to the skies? No, you will go
down to the depths.[r] If the miracles that were
performed in you had been performed in Sodom,
it would have remained to this day. [24]But I tell
you that it will be more bearable for Sodom on
the day of judgment than for you."

[25]At that time Jesus said, "I praise you, Father,
Lord of heaven and earth, because you have hidden these things from the wise and learned, and
revealed them to little children. [26]Yes, Father, for
this was your good pleasure.

[27]"All things have been committed to me by my
Father. No one knows the Son except the Father,
and no one knows the Father except the Son and
those to whom the Son chooses to reveal him.

[28]"Come to me, all you who are weary and burdened, and I will give you rest. [29]Take my yoke
upon you and learn from me, for I am gentle and
humble in heart, and you will find rest for your
souls. [30]For my yoke is easy and my burden is
light."

[q]10 Mal. 3:1 [r]23 Greek *Hades*

Discovering the Word 1. How and why does Jesus demonstrate compassion for the crowds (9:35–38)? 2. As a result of his compassion, Jesus sends out the Twelve (10:1–15). Describe their mission. 3. Jesus warns the disciples that their compassionate ministry will not be warmly received (10:16–25). What will they experience? 4. In 10:26–33 Jesus prepares his present and future disciples for opposition. Why shouldn't we be afraid of those who oppose us? 5. What does Jesus promise to those who are receptive to our message (10:40–42)? 6. What does 11:7–19 tell us about John and those who heard his message?

Applying the Word 1. In what ways have you found rest in your life by coming to Jesus? 2. What have you learned about Jesus and the nature of discipleship from this study?

Responding in Prayer Pray for the gift of rest in Jesus.

8 / *Matthew 12*
The Leaders and the King

POWER OVER PEOPLE is not easily shared. Wars have been fought, people assassinated and elections rigged in order to gain or maintain power.

The leaders of Israel were becoming concerned over the growing reputation and following of Jesus. Like ripples in a pool of water, the ministry of Jesus and his disciples continued to have a widening impact on the Jewish nation. If Jesus' followers became too numerous, the leaders would end up losing their positions of authority. In Matthew 12 they formulate a strategy to discredit him.

 Warming Up to God How would you feel if untrue rumors about you were being spread around?

 Read Matthew 12.

---

12 At that time Jesus went through the grainfields on the Sabbath. His disciples were hungry and began to pick some heads of grain and eat them. ²When the Pharisees saw this, they said to him, "Look! Your disciples are doing what is unlawful on the Sabbath."

³He answered, "Haven't you read what David did when he and his companions were hungry? ⁴He entered the house of God, and he and his companions ate the consecrated bread—which was not lawful for them to do, but only for the priests. ⁵Or haven't you read in the Law that on the Sabbath the priests in the temple desecrate the day and yet are innocent? ⁶I tell you that one[s] greater than the temple is here. ⁷If you had known what these words mean, 'I desire mercy, not sacrifice,'[t] you would not have condemned the innocent. ⁸For the Son of Man is Lord of the Sabbath."

⁹Going on from that place, he went into their synagogue, ¹⁰and a man with a shriveled hand was there. Looking for a reason to accuse Jesus, they asked him, "Is it lawful to heal on the Sabbath?"

¹¹He said to them, "If any of you has a sheep and it falls into a pit on the Sabbath, will you not take hold of it and lift it out? ¹²How much more valuable is a man than a sheep! Therefore it is lawful to do good on the Sabbath."

¹³Then he said to the man, "Stretch out your hand." So he stretched it out and it was completely restored, just as sound as the other. ¹⁴But the Pharisees went out and plotted how they might kill Jesus.

¹⁵Aware of this, Jesus withdrew from that place. Many followed him, and he healed all their sick, ¹⁶warning them not to tell who he was. ¹⁷This was to fulfill what was spoken through the prophet Isaiah:

¹⁸"Here is my servant whom I have chosen,
    the one I love, in whom I delight;
I will put my Spirit on him,
    and he will proclaim justice to the nations.
¹⁹He will not quarrel or cry out;
    no one will hear his voice in the streets.
²⁰A bruised reed he will not break,
    and a smoldering wick he will not snuff
        out,
till he leads justice to victory.
²¹   In his name the nations will put their
        hope."[u]

²²Then they brought him a demon-possessed man who was blind and mute, and Jesus healed him, so that he could both talk and see. ²³All the people were astonished and said, "Could this be the Son of David?"

²⁴But when the Pharisees heard this, they said, "It is only by Beelzebub,[v] the prince of demons, that this fellow drives out demons."

²⁵Jesus knew their thoughts and said to them, "Every kingdom divided against itself will be ruined, and every city or household divided against itself will not stand. ²⁶If Satan drives out Satan, he is divided against himself. How then can his kingdom stand? ²⁷And if I drive out demons by Beelzebub, by whom do your people drive them out? So then, they will be your judges. ²⁸But if I drive

[s]6 Or *something*; also in verses 41 and 42   [t]7 Hosea 6:6
[u]21 Isaiah 42:1-4   [v]24 Greek *Beezeboul* or *Beelzeboul*; also in verse 27

out demons by the Spirit of God, then the kingdom of God has come upon you.

²⁹"Or again, how can anyone enter a strong man's house and carry off his possessions unless he first ties up the strong man? Then he can rob his house.

³⁰"He who is not with me is against me, and he who does not gather with me scatters. ³¹And so I tell you, every sin and blasphemy will be forgiven men, but the blasphemy against the Spirit will not be forgiven. ³²Anyone who speaks a word against the Son of Man will be forgiven, but anyone who speaks against the Holy Spirit will not be forgiven, either in this age or in the age to come.

³³"Make a tree good and its fruit will be good, or make a tree bad and its fruit will be bad, for a tree is recognized by its fruit. ³⁴You brood of vipers, how can you who are evil say anything good? For out of the overflow of the heart the mouth speaks. ³⁵The good man brings good things out of the good stored up in him, and the evil man brings evil things out of the evil stored up in him. ³⁶But I tell you that men will have to give account on the day of judgment for every careless word they have spoken. ³⁷For by your words you will be acquitted, and by your words you will be condemned."

³⁸Then some of the Pharisees and teachers of the law said to him, "Teacher, we want to see a miraculous sign from you."

³⁹He answered, "A wicked and adulterous generation asks for a miraculous sign! But none will be given it except the sign of the prophet Jonah. ⁴⁰For as Jonah was three days and three nights in the belly of a huge fish, so the Son of Man will be three days and three nights in the heart of the earth. ⁴¹The men of Nineveh will stand up at the judgment with this generation and condemn it; for they repented at the preaching of Jonah, and now one^w greater than Jonah is here. ⁴²The Queen of the South will rise at the judgment with this generation and condemn it; for she came from the ends of the earth to listen to Solomon's wisdom, and now one greater than Solomon is here.

⁴³"When an evil^x spirit comes out of a man, it goes through arid places seeking rest and does not find it. ⁴⁴Then it says, 'I will return to the house I left.' When it arrives, it finds the house unoccupied, swept clean and put in order. ⁴⁵Then it goes and takes with it seven other spirits more wicked than itself, and they go in and live there. And the final condition of that man is worse than the first. That is how it will be with this wicked generation."

⁴⁶While Jesus was still talking to the crowd, his mother and brothers stood outside, wanting to speak to him. ⁴⁷Someone told him, "Your mother and brothers are standing outside, wanting to speak to you."^{y}

⁴⁸He replied to him, "Who is my mother, and who are my brothers?" ⁴⁹Pointing to his disciples, he said, "Here are my mother and my brothers. ⁵⁰For whoever does the will of my Father in heaven is my brother and sister and mother."

^{w}41 Or *something*; also in verse 42 ^{x}43 Greek *unclean*
^{y}47 Some manuscripts do not have verse 47.

 Discovering the Word 1. Consider the ways that religious leaders attacked Jesus in verses 1–14. What was their strategy? 2. As you compare the Pharisees' second accusation against Jesus (v. 10) with their own response (v. 14), what irony do you see? 3. Notice the startling contrast between the religious leaders' attitude toward Jesus and God's attitude (vv. 15–21). How do they differ? 4. In verses 43–45 Jesus tells the Pharisees and teachers of the law a story. What does it reveal about them? 5. Look back over chapter 12. What factors led to the hardness and unbelief of the Pharisees and teachers of the law?

 Applying the Word 1. How can we avoid being like the Pharisees and teachers of the law? 2. What area of change in your life does this suggest you consider?

Responding in Prayer Ask God to teach you how to read and understand his Word so that you can use it to his glory.

9 / *Matthew 13*
The Parables of the King

CROWDS ARE FICKLE. One moment they follow with enthusiasm, the next they turn hostile and angry. In Matthew 13 Jesus speaks to a mixed and fickle crowd. Some are hungry to hear his message. Others are suspicious and hostile. In this setting Jesus begins to speak in parables. These stories test our spiritual sight and hearing. They also expose the condition of our hearts.

 Warming Up to God Prepare for this study by asking God to open your mind and heart to what is here for you.

 Read Matthew 13.

---

13 That same day Jesus went out of the house and sat by the lake. ²Such large crowds gathered around him that he got into a boat and sat in it, while all the people stood on the shore. ³Then he told them many things in parables, saying: "A farmer went out to sow his seed. ⁴As he was scattering the seed, some fell along the path, and the birds came and ate it up. ⁵Some fell on rocky places, where it did not have much soil. It sprang up quickly, because the soil was shallow. ⁶But when the sun came up, the plants were scorched, and they withered because they had no root. ⁷Other seed fell among thorns, which grew up and choked the plants. ⁸Still other seed fell on good soil, where it produced a crop—a hundred, sixty or thirty times what was sown. ⁹He who has ears, let him hear."

¹⁰The disciples came to him and asked, "Why do you speak to the people in parables?"

¹¹He replied, "The knowledge of the secrets of the kingdom of heaven has been given to you, but not to them. ¹²Whoever has will be given more, and he will have an abundance. Whoever does not have, even what he has will be taken from him. ¹³This is why I speak to them in parables:

"Though seeing, they do not see;
  though hearing, they do not hear or
    understand.

¹⁴In them is fulfilled the prophecy of Isaiah:

" 'You will be ever hearing but never
    understanding;
  you will be ever seeing but never
    perceiving.
¹⁵For this people's heart has become calloused;
  they hardly hear with their ears,
  and they have closed their eyes.

Otherwise they might see with their eyes,
  hear with their ears,
  understand with their hearts
  and turn, and I would heal them.'ᶻ

¹⁶But blessed are your eyes because they see, and your ears because they hear. ¹⁷For I tell you the truth, many prophets and righteous men longed to see what you see but did not see it, and to hear what you hear but did not hear it.

¹⁸"Listen then to what the parable of the sower means: ¹⁹When anyone hears the message about the kingdom and does not understand it, the evil one comes and snatches away what was sown in his heart. This is the seed sown along the path. ²⁰The one who received the seed that fell on rocky places is the man who hears the word and at once receives it with joy. ²¹But since he has no root, he lasts only a short time. When trouble or persecution comes because of the word, he quickly falls away. ²²The one who received the seed that fell among the thorns is the man who hears the word, but the worries of this life and the deceitfulness of wealth choke it, making it unfruitful. ²³But the one who received the seed that fell on good soil is the man who hears the word and understands it. He produces a crop, yielding a hundred, sixty or thirty times what was sown."

²⁴Jesus told them another parable: "The kingdom of heaven is like a man who sowed good seed in his field. ²⁵But while everyone was sleeping, his enemy came and sowed weeds among the wheat, and went away. ²⁶When the wheat sprouted and formed heads, then the weeds also appeared.

²⁷"The owner's servants came to him and said,

ᶻ15 Isaiah 6:9,10

'Sir, didn't you sow good seed in your field? Where then did the weeds come from?'

²⁸" 'An enemy did this,' he replied.

"The servants asked him, 'Do you want us to go and pull them up?'

²⁹" 'No,' he answered, 'because while you are pulling the weeds, you may root up the wheat with them. ³⁰Let both grow together until the harvest. At that time I will tell the harvesters: First collect the weeds and tie them in bundles to be burned; then gather the wheat and bring it into my barn.' "

³¹He told them another parable: "The kingdom of heaven is like a mustard seed, which a man took and planted in his field. ³²Though it is the smallest of all your seeds, yet when it grows, it is the largest of garden plants and becomes a tree, so that the birds of the air come and perch in its branches."

³³He told them still another parable: "The kingdom of heaven is like yeast that a woman took and mixed into a large amount^a of flour until it worked all through the dough."

³⁴Jesus spoke all these things to the crowd in parables; he did not say anything to them without using a parable. ³⁵So was fulfilled what was spoken through the prophet:

"I will open my mouth in parables,
    I will utter things hidden since the creation
        of the world."^{b}

³⁶Then he left the crowd and went into the house. His disciples came to him and said, "Explain to us the parable of the weeds in the field."

³⁷He answered, "The one who sowed the good seed is the Son of Man. ³⁸The field is the world, and the good seed stands for the sons of the kingdom. The weeds are the sons of the evil one, ³⁹and the enemy who sows them is the devil. The harvest is the end of the age, and the harvesters are angels.

⁴⁰"As the weeds are pulled up and burned in the fire, so it will be at the end of the age. ⁴¹The Son of Man will send out his angels, and they will weed out of his kingdom everything that causes sin and all who do evil. ⁴²They will throw them into the fiery furnace, where there will be weep-ing and gnashing of teeth. ⁴³Then the righteous will shine like the sun in the kingdom of their Father. He who has ears, let him hear.

⁴⁴"The kingdom of heaven is like treasure hidden in a field. When a man found it, he hid it again, and then in his joy went and sold all he had and bought that field.

⁴⁵"Again, the kingdom of heaven is like a merchant looking for fine pearls. ⁴⁶When he found one of great value, he went away and sold everything he had and bought it.

⁴⁷"Once again, the kingdom of heaven is like a net that was let down into the lake and caught all kinds of fish. ⁴⁸When it was full, the fishermen pulled it up on the shore. Then they sat down and collected the good fish in baskets, but threw the bad away. ⁴⁹This is how it will be at the end of the age. The angels will come and separate the wicked from the righteous ⁵⁰and throw them into the fiery furnace, where there will be weeping and gnashing of teeth.

⁵¹"Have you understood all these things?" Jesus asked.

"Yes," they replied.

⁵²He said to them, "Therefore every teacher of the law who has been instructed about the kingdom of heaven is like the owner of a house who brings out of his storeroom new treasures as well as old."

⁵³When Jesus had finished these parables, he moved on from there. ⁵⁴Coming to his hometown, he began teaching the people in their synagogue, and they were amazed. "Where did this man get this wisdom and these miraculous powers?" they asked. ⁵⁵"Isn't this the carpenter's son? Isn't his mother's name Mary, and aren't his brothers James, Joseph, Simon and Judas? ⁵⁶Aren't all his sisters with us? Where then did this man get all these things?" ⁵⁷And they took offense at him.

But Jesus said to them, "Only in his hometown and in his own house is a prophet without honor."

⁵⁸And he did not do many miracles there because of their lack of faith.

^{a}33 Greek *three satas* (probably about 1/2 bushel or 22 liters)
^{b}35 Psalm 78:2

Discovering the Word 1. According to the parable of the sower, what responses does Jesus expect as he preaches his message of the kingdom (vv. 1–9, 18–23)? 2. In verse 10 the disciples ask Jesus why he speaks to the people in parables. Explain his reply (vv. 11–17). 3. Wheat and weeds look similar until the harvest. How does this parable explain God's delayed judgment of the wicked (vv. 24–30, 36–43)? 4. What do the parables of the mustard seed and yeast suggest about the way the kingdom grows (vv. 31–35)? 5. What do the parables of the hidden treasure and the pearl teach us about the value of the kingdom (vv. 44–46)?

 Applying the Word 1. Jesus wants his disciples to understand the parables. How have they enlarged your understanding of the kingdom of heaven? 2. Jesus also wants us to respond to what we have heard and understood. Throughout this chapter, what types of responses does he desire?

 Responding in Prayer Ask the Lord to help you respond to him in the ways you observed.

---

10 / *Matthew 14*
The Revelation of the King (Part 1)

CRISES ARE UNCOMFORTABLE. They force us to make painful decisions, even when we don't want to decide. In Matthew 14 Jesus places the disciples in tough situations where they must act on what they have learned about him. The focus shifts from parables about the kingdom to the identity of the king.

Warming Up to God Teachers use tests during our school years. But tests are not limited to school; God also uses tests throughout our lives. How do you think you've been tested lately?

Read Matthew 14.

---

14 At that time Herod the tetrarch heard the reports about Jesus, ²and he said to his attendants, "This is John the Baptist; he has risen from the dead! That is why miraculous powers are at work in him."

³Now Herod had arrested John and bound him and put him in prison because of Herodias, his brother Philip's wife, ⁴for John had been saying to him: "It is not lawful for you to have her." ⁵Herod wanted to kill John, but he was afraid of the people, because they considered him a prophet.

⁶On Herod's birthday the daughter of Herodias danced for them and pleased Herod so much ⁷that he promised with an oath to give her whatever she asked. ⁸Prompted by her mother, she said, "Give me here on a platter the head of John the Baptist." ⁹The king was distressed, but because of his oaths and his dinner guests, he ordered that her request be granted ¹⁰and had John beheaded in the prison. ¹¹His head was brought in on a platter and given to the girl, who carried it to her mother. ¹²John's disciples came and took his body and buried it. Then they went and told Jesus.

¹³When Jesus heard what had happened, he withdrew by boat privately to a solitary place. Hearing of this, the crowds followed him on foot from the towns. ¹⁴When Jesus landed and saw a large crowd, he had compassion on them and healed their sick.

¹⁵As evening approached, the disciples came to him and said, "This is a remote place, and it's already getting late. Send the crowds away, so they can go to the villages and buy themselves some food."

¹⁶Jesus replied, "They do not need to go away. You give them something to eat."

¹⁷"We have here only five loaves of bread and two fish," they answered.

¹⁸"Bring them here to me," he said. ¹⁹And he directed the people to sit down on the grass. Taking the five loaves and the two fish and looking up to heaven, he gave thanks and broke the loaves. Then he gave them to the disciples, and the disciples gave them to the people. ²⁰They all ate and were satisfied, and the disciples picked up twelve basketfuls of broken pieces that were left over. ²¹The number of those who ate was about five thousand men, besides women and children.

²²Immediately Jesus made the disciples get into the boat and go on ahead of him to the other side, while he dismissed the crowd. ²³After he had dismissed them, he went up on a mountainside by himself to pray. When evening came, he was there alone, ²⁴but the boat was already a considerable distance^c from land, buffeted by the waves because the wind was against it.

²⁵During the fourth watch of the night Jesus went out to them, walking on the lake. ²⁶When the disciples saw him walking on the lake, they were terrified. "It's a ghost," they said, and cried out in fear.

²⁷But Jesus immediately said to them: "Take courage! It is I. Don't be afraid."

²⁸"Lord, if it's you," Peter replied, "tell me to come to you on the water."

²⁹"Come," he said.

Then Peter got down out of the boat, walked on the water and came toward Jesus. ³⁰But when he saw the wind, he was afraid and, beginning to sink, cried out, "Lord, save me!"

³¹Immediately Jesus reached out his hand and caught him. "You of little faith," he said, "why did you doubt?"

³²And when they climbed into the boat, the wind died down. ³³Then those who were in the boat worshiped him, saying, "Truly you are the Son of God."

³⁴When they had crossed over, they landed at Gennesaret. ³⁵And when the men of that place recognized Jesus, they sent word to all the surrounding country. People brought all their sick to him ³⁶and begged him to let the sick just touch the edge of his cloak, and all who touched him were healed.

^c24 Greek *many stadia*

Discovering the Word 1. In verses 1–2 Herod speculates about Jesus' identity. What led him to believe that Jesus is John the Baptist (vv. 3–12)? 2. How is the feeding of the five thousand (vv. 13–21) a test for the disciples? 3. Herod and Jesus, the two kings in this passage, both serve banquets. What does each king's banquet reveal about his character and authority? 4. Imagine you are in the boat with the anxious disciples (vv. 22–26). Describe what you would see, hear and feel. 5. How is Peter's trying experience on the water a vivid picture of faith and doubt (vv. 28–31)?

Applying the Word 1. When are you most tempted to take your eyes off the Lord and to sink in doubt? 2. In verse 33 the disciples worship Jesus and declare, "Truly you are the Son of God." What do you see in this incident that leads you to worship Jesus? 3. How can these things help you to trust Jesus the next time you are tempted to doubt?

Responding in Prayer Spend a few minutes worshiping Jesus, the Son of God.

---

11 / *Matthew 15:1—16:20*
The Revelation of the King (Part 2)

EUREKA! WHAT A relief and pleasure it is when something we have not quite understood becomes clear to us. In this section of Matthew the disciples come to a supernatural understanding of Jesus. What they thought they knew becomes a new and deeper knowledge. Peter, speaking for the disciples, declares who Jesus really is. Peter's words bring us to the climax of the first half of Matthew.

Warming Up to God When you first recognized who Jesus is and what he offers to you, what were your thoughts and feelings?

Read Matthew 15:1—16:20.

15 Then some Pharisees and teachers of the law came to Jesus from Jerusalem and asked, 2"Why do your disciples break the tradition of the elders? They don't wash their hands before they eat!"

3Jesus replied, "And why do you break the command of God for the sake of your tradition? 4For God said, 'Honor your father and mother'*d* and 'Anyone who curses his father or mother must be put to death.'*e* 5But you say that if a man says to his father or mother, 'Whatever help you might otherwise have received from me is a gift devoted to God,' 6he is not to 'honor his father*f*' with it. Thus you nullify the word of God for the sake of your tradition. 7You hypocrites! Isaiah was right when he prophesied about you:

8" 'These people honor me with their lips,
    but their hearts are far from me.
9They worship me in vain;
    their teachings are but rules taught by
        men.'*g*"

10Jesus called the crowd to him and said, "Listen and understand. 11What goes into a man's mouth does not make him 'unclean,' but what comes out of his mouth, that is what makes him 'unclean.' "

12Then the disciples came to him and asked, "Do you know that the Pharisees were offended when they heard this?"

13He replied, "Every plant that my heavenly Father has not planted will be pulled up by the roots. 14Leave them; they are blind guides.*h* If a blind man leads a blind man, both will fall into a pit."

15Peter said, "Explain the parable to us."

16"Are you still so dull?" Jesus asked them. 17"Don't you see that whatever enters the mouth goes into the stomach and then out of the body? 18But the things that come out of the mouth come from the heart, and these make a man 'unclean.' 19For out of the heart come evil thoughts, murder, adultery, sexual immorality, theft, false testimony, slander. 20These are what make a man 'unclean'; but eating with unwashed hands does not make him 'unclean.' "

21Leaving that place, Jesus withdrew to the region of Tyre and Sidon. 22A Canaanite woman from that vicinity came to him, crying out, "Lord, Son of David, have mercy on me! My daughter is suffering terribly from demon-possession."

23Jesus did not answer a word. So his disciples came to him and urged him, "Send her away, for she keeps crying out after us."

24He answered, "I was sent only to the lost sheep of Israel."

25The woman came and knelt before him. "Lord, help me!" she said.

26He replied, "It is not right to take the children's bread and toss it to their dogs."

27"Yes, Lord," she said, "but even the dogs eat the crumbs that fall from their masters' table."

28Then Jesus answered, "Woman, you have great faith! Your request is granted." And her daughter was healed from that very hour.

29Jesus left there and went along the Sea of Galilee. Then he went up on a mountainside and sat down. 30Great crowds came to him, bringing the lame, the blind, the crippled, the mute and many others, and laid them at his feet; and he healed them. 31The people were amazed when they saw the mute speaking, the crippled made well, the lame walking and the blind seeing. And they praised the God of Israel.

32Jesus called his disciples to him and said, "I have compassion for these people; they have already been with me three days and have nothing to eat. I do not want to send them away hungry, or they may collapse on the way."

33His disciples answered, "Where could we get enough bread in this remote place to feed such a crowd?"

34"How many loaves do you have?" Jesus asked.

"Seven," they replied, "and a few small fish."

35He told the crowd to sit down on the ground. 36Then he took the seven loaves and the fish, and when he had given thanks, he broke them and gave them to the disciples, and they in turn to the people. 37They all ate and were satisfied. Afterward the disciples picked up seven basketfuls of broken pieces that were left over. 38The number of those who ate was four thousand, besides women and children. 39After Jesus had sent the crowd away, he got into the boat and went to the vicinity of Magadan.

16 The Pharisees and Sadducees came to Jesus and tested him by asking him to show them a sign from heaven.

2He replied,*i* "When evening comes, you say,

d4 Exodus 20:12; Deut. 5:16   *e4* Exodus 21:17; Lev. 20:9
f6 Some manuscripts *father or his mother*   *g9* Isaiah 29:13
h14 Some manuscripts *guides of the blind*   *i2* Some early manuscripts do not have the rest of verse 2 and all of verse 3.

'It will be fair weather, for the sky is red,' ³and in the morning, 'Today it will be stormy, for the sky is red and overcast.' You know how to interpret the appearance of the sky, but you cannot interpret the signs of the times. ⁴A wicked and adulterous generation looks for a miraculous sign, but none will be given it except the sign of Jonah." Jesus then left them and went away.

⁵When they went across the lake, the disciples forgot to take bread. ⁶"Be careful," Jesus said to them. "Be on your guard against the yeast of the Pharisees and Sadducees."

⁷They discussed this among themselves and said, "It is because we didn't bring any bread."

⁸Aware of their discussion, Jesus asked, "You of little faith, why are you talking among yourselves about having no bread? ⁹Do you still not understand? Don't you remember the five loaves for the five thousand, and how many basketfuls you gathered? ¹⁰Or the seven loaves for the four thousand, and how many basketfuls you gathered? ¹¹How is it you don't understand that I was not talking to you about bread? But be on your guard against the yeast of the Pharisees and Sadducees." ¹²Then they understood that he was not telling them to guard against the yeast used in bread, but

against the teaching of the Pharisees and Sadducees.

¹³When Jesus came to the region of Caesarea Philippi, he asked his disciples, "Who do people say the Son of Man is?"

¹⁴They replied, "Some say John the Baptist; others say Elijah; and still others, Jeremiah or one of the prophets."

¹⁵"But what about you?" he asked. "Who do you say I am?"

¹⁶Simon Peter answered, "You are the Christ,ʲ the Son of the living God."

¹⁷Jesus replied, "Blessed are you, Simon son of Jonah, for this was not revealed to you by man, but by my Father in heaven. ¹⁸And I tell you that you are Peter,ᵏ and on this rock I will build my church, and the gates of Hadesˡ will not overcome it.ᵐ ¹⁹I will give you the keys of the kingdom of heaven; whatever you bind on earth will beⁿ bound in heaven, and whatever you loose on earth will beⁿ loosed in heaven." ²⁰Then he warned his disciples not to tell anyone that he was the Christ.

ʲ16 Or *Messiah*; also in verse 20   ᵏ18 *Peter means rock.*   ˡ18 Or *hell*   ᵐ18 Or *not prove stronger than it*   ⁿ19 Or *have been*

 Discovering the Word 1. Top religious leaders from Jerusalem oppose Jesus by attacking the disciples (15:1–2). What is their complaint, and what does it suggest about Jesus? 2. How does Jesus respond to their accusation (15:3–20)? 3. How would you account for the unusual interaction between Jesus, the woman and the disciples (15:21–28)? 4. After Jesus heals the sick and feeds the four thousand, the religious leaders ask him for a sign from heaven (16:1). Why do you think Jesus resists them (16:2–4)? 5. In 16:5–12 the disciples misunderstand Jesus' allusion to yeast. How is their misunderstanding related to a lack of faith? 6. In 16:5–12 the disciples couldn't even grasp a simple figure of speech. How then does Peter have enough insight to confess that Jesus is the Christ, the Son of God (16:13–17)?

Applying the Word 1. Are there religious practices in your life that are in danger of becoming outward, empty forms? Explain. 2. How can you avoid this tendency? 3. Jesus' question to Peter is one that everyone will have to respond to at some point. Who do you say Jesus is, and why?

Responding in Prayer Offer praise to Jesus Christ for who he is.

---

12 / *Matthew 16:21—17:27*
The Work of the King

ONE OF THE rules of good management is "No surprises." While surprises can be fun, they can also be upsetting. Good corporate leadership seeks to eliminate surprises so that everything runs according to plan.

Now that the disciples have been with Jesus for a while, he must prepare them for the true nature of his kingdom. They are shocked at the cost of his mission and his requirements for discipleship.

 Warming Up to God Recall an unpleasant surprise you received. How did you handle it?

 Read Matthew 16:21—17:27.

21From that time on Jesus began to explain to his disciples that he must go to Jerusalem and suffer many things at the hands of the elders, chief priests and teachers of the law, and that he must be killed and on the third day be raised to life.

22Peter took him aside and began to rebuke him. "Never, Lord!" he said. "This shall never happen to you!"

23Jesus turned and said to Peter, "Get behind me, Satan! You are a stumbling block to me; you do not have in mind the things of God, but the things of men."

24Then Jesus said to his disciples, "If anyone would come after me, he must deny himself and take up his cross and follow me. 25For whoever wants to save his life*o* will lose it, but whoever loses his life for me will find it. 26What good will it be for a man if he gains the whole world, yet forfeits his soul? Or what can a man give in exchange for his soul? 27For the Son of Man is going to come in his Father's glory with his angels, and then he will reward each person according to what he has done. 28I tell you the truth, some who are standing here will not taste death before they see the Son of Man coming in his kingdom."

17 After six days Jesus took with him Peter, James and John the brother of James, and led them up a high mountain by themselves. 2There he was transfigured before them. His face shone like the sun, and his clothes became as white as the light. 3Just then there appeared before them Moses and Elijah, talking with Jesus.

4Peter said to Jesus, "Lord, it is good for us to be here. If you wish, I will put up three shelters—one for you, one for Moses and one for Elijah."

5While he was still speaking, a bright cloud enveloped them, and a voice from the cloud said, "This is my Son, whom I love; with him I am well pleased. Listen to him!"

6When the disciples heard this, they fell face-down to the ground, terrified. 7But Jesus came and touched them. "Get up," he said. "Don't be afraid." 8When they looked up, they saw no one except Jesus.

9As they were coming down the mountain, Jesus instructed them, "Don't tell anyone what you have seen, until the Son of Man has been raised from the dead."

10The disciples asked him, "Why then do the teachers of the law say that Elijah must come first?"

11Jesus replied, "To be sure, Elijah comes and will restore all things. 12But I tell you, Elijah has already come, and they did not recognize him, but have done to him everything they wished. In the same way the Son of Man is going to suffer at their hands." 13Then the disciples understood that he was talking to them about John the Baptist.

14When they came to the crowd, a man approached Jesus and knelt before him. 15"Lord, have mercy on my son," he said. "He has seizures and is suffering greatly. He often falls into the fire or into the water. 16I brought him to your disciples, but they could not heal him."

17"O unbelieving and perverse generation," Jesus replied, "how long shall I stay with you? How long shall I put up with you? Bring the boy here to me." 18Jesus rebuked the demon, and it came out of the boy, and he was healed from that moment.

19Then the disciples came to Jesus in private and asked, "Why couldn't we drive it out?"

20He replied, "Because you have so little faith. I tell you the truth, if you have faith as small as a mustard seed, you can say to this mountain, 'Move from here to there' and it will move. Nothing will be impossible for you.*p*"

22When they came together in Galilee, he said to them, "The Son of Man is going to be betrayed into the hands of men. 23They will kill him, and on the third day he will be raised to life." And the disciples were filled with grief.

24After Jesus and his disciples arrived in Caper-

*o*25 The Greek word means either *life* or *soul*; also in verse 26.
*p*20 Some manuscripts *you. 21But this kind does not go out except by prayer and fasting.*

naum, the collectors of the two-drachma tax came to Peter and asked, "Doesn't your teacher pay the temple tax*q*?"

25"Yes, he does," he replied.

When Peter came into the house, Jesus was the first to speak. "What do you think, Simon?" he asked. "From whom do the kings of the earth collect duty and taxes—from their own sons or from others?"

26"From others," Peter answered.

"Then the sons are exempt," Jesus said to him. 27"But so that we may not offend them, go to the lake and throw out your line. Take the first fish you catch; open its mouth and you will find a four-drachma coin. Take it and give it to them for my tax and yours."

q24 Greek the two drachmas

 Discovering the Word 1. What were some of the surprises the disciples received? 2. Peter and Jesus seem to be at cross purposes in 16:22–23. Why do you think Jesus addresses Peter as Satan? 3. What does Jesus reveal about the cost and rewards of following him (16:24–28)? 4. What would the disciples learn about Jesus by his transformed appearance, his conversation with Moses and Elijah, and the voice from heaven (17:1–8)? 5. How might this help resolve their confusion about Jesus' impending death? 6. As a result of their powerlessness, what do the disciples learn about faith?

 Applying the Word 1. How has following Jesus produced times of confusion for you? 2. We don't always understand life from a heavenly perspective. How can this passage reorient your thinking?

Responding in Prayer Ask God to help you understand his ways so that you can be a better disciple.

---

13 / *Matthew 18*
The Greatest in the Kingdom

WHO IS GREATEST in the kingdom of God? How can a subject of the kingdom earn true wealth? When should we forgive? These questions dominate the thoughts of the disciples as they approach Jerusalem. They are also important questions for us. How we answer them will directly affect the quality of our discipleship.

 Warming Up to God When has someone sinned against you? How did it affect you?

 Read Matthew 18.

---

18 At that time the disciples came to Jesus and asked, "Who is the greatest in the kingdom of heaven?"

2He called a little child and had him stand among them. 3And he said: "I tell you the truth, unless you change and become like little children, you will never enter the kingdom of heaven. 4Therefore, whoever humbles himself like this child is the greatest in the kingdom of heaven.

5"And whoever welcomes a little child like this in my name welcomes me. 6But if anyone causes one of these little ones who believe in me to sin, it would be better for him to have a large mill-

stone hung around his neck and to be drowned in the depths of the sea.

7"Woe to the world because of the things that cause people to sin! Such things must come, but woe to the man through whom they come! 8If your hand or your foot causes you to sin, cut it off and throw it away. It is better for you to enter life maimed or crippled than to have two hands or two feet and be thrown into eternal fire. 9And if your eye causes you to sin, gouge it out and throw it away. It is better for you to enter life with one eye than to have two eyes and be thrown into the fire of hell.

¹⁰"See that you do not look down on one of these little ones. For I tell you that their angels in heaven always see the face of my Father in heaven.ʳ

¹²"What do you think? If a man owns a hundred sheep, and one of them wanders away, will he not leave the ninety-nine on the hills and go to look for the one that wandered off? ¹³And if he finds it, I tell you the truth, he is happier about that one sheep than about the ninety-nine that did not wander off. ¹⁴In the same way your Father in heaven is not willing that any of these little ones should be lost.

¹⁵"If your brother sins against you,ˢ go and show him his fault, just between the two of you. If he listens to you, you have won your brother over. ¹⁶But if he will not listen, take one or two others along, so that 'every matter may be established by the testimony of two or three witnesses.'ᵗ ¹⁷If he refuses to listen to them, tell it to the church; and if he refuses to listen even to the church, treat him as you would a pagan or a tax collector.

¹⁸"I tell you the truth, whatever you bind on earth will beᵘ bound in heaven, and whatever you loose on earth will beᵘ loosed in heaven.

¹⁹"Again, I tell you that if two of you on earth agree about anything you ask for, it will be done for you by my Father in heaven. ²⁰For where two or three come together in my name, there am I with them."

²¹Then Peter came to Jesus and asked, "Lord, how many times shall I forgive my brother when he sins against me? Up to seven times?"

²²Jesus answered, "I tell you, not seven times, but seventy-seven times.ᵛ

²³"Therefore, the kingdom of heaven is like a king who wanted to settle accounts with his servants. ²⁴As he began the settlement, a man who owed him ten thousand talentsʷ was brought to him. ²⁵Since he was not able to pay, the master ordered that he and his wife and his children and all that he had be sold to repay the debt.

²⁶"The servant fell on his knees before him. 'Be patient with me,' he begged, 'and I will pay back everything.' ²⁷The servant's master took pity on him, canceled the debt and let him go.

²⁸"But when that servant went out, he found one of his fellow servants who owed him a hundred denarii.ˣ He grabbed him and began to choke him. 'Pay back what you owe me!' he demanded.

²⁹"His fellow servant fell to his knees and begged him, 'Be patient with me, and I will pay you back.'

³⁰"But he refused. Instead, he went off and had the man thrown into prison until he could pay the debt. ³¹When the other servants saw what had happened, they were greatly distressed and went and told their master everything that had happened.

³²"Then the master called the servant in. 'You wicked servant,' he said, 'I canceled all that debt of yours because you begged me to. ³³Shouldn't you have had mercy on your fellow servant just as I had on you?' ³⁴In anger his master turned him over to the jailers to be tortured, until he should pay back all he owed.

³⁵"This is how my heavenly Father will treat each of you unless you forgive your brother from your heart."

ʳ10 Some manuscripts *heaven.* ¹¹*The Son of Man came to save what was lost.*   ˢ15 Some manuscripts do not have *against you.*   ᵗ16 Deut. 19:15   ᵘ18 Or *have been*   ᵛ22 Or *seventy times seven* ʷ24 That is, millions of dollars   ˣ28 That is, a few dollars

---

Discovering the Word 1. The disciples want to know who is the greatest in the kingdom of heaven (v. 1). How does Jesus' appeal to little children answer their question (vv. 2–5)? 2. Spiritually speaking, the "little ones" are those who humble themselves ("become like little children") and believe in Jesus. What is Jesus' attitude toward those who cause the little ones to sin (vv. 6–7)? 3. How do verses 10–14 further emphasize the value Jesus places on his "little ones"? 4. Greatness in the kingdom is also dependent on living a life of forgiveness and mercy. What guidelines does Jesus give for dealing with those who sin against us (vv. 15–20)? 5. Forgiving someone once does not always guarantee he or she will not offend us again. How can the parable of the unmerciful servant help us to keep on forgiving (vv. 21–35)?

Applying the Word 1. Children have little status in the eyes of adults. How can we assume the status of children in our circle of friends and coworkers? 2. How should the value Jesus places on his "little ones" affect the way we view ourselves and other believers? 3. How does this chapter challenge your ideas of value and greatness?

Responding in Prayer Ask God to help you forgive those who have hurt you.

---

14 / *Matthew 19—20*
Life in the Kingdom

WHAT IS REALLY important to you? What makes you feel important? Money? Success? Recognition? These are common answers. The values that Jesus teaches, however, have little to do with such things. In the previous study we learned that to be great in the kingdom, we must become "small." In this study we will see how the values of the kingdom conflict with the world's approach to wealth and leadership.

Warming Up to God What does success mean to you? How does that compare to what our culture says about success?

Read Matthew 19—20.

---

19 When Jesus had finished saying these things, he left Galilee and went into the region of Judea to the other side of the Jordan. ²Large crowds followed him, and he healed them there.

³Some Pharisees came to him to test him. They asked, "Is it lawful for a man to divorce his wife for any and every reason?"

⁴"Haven't you read," he replied, "that at the beginning the Creator 'made them male and female,'ʸ ⁵and said, 'For this reason a man will leave his father and mother and be united to his wife, and the two will become one flesh'ᶻ? ⁶So they are no longer two, but one. Therefore what God has joined together, let man not separate."

⁷"Why then," they asked, "did Moses command that a man give his wife a certificate of divorce and send her away?"

⁸Jesus replied, "Moses permitted you to divorce your wives because your hearts were hard. But it was not this way from the beginning. ⁹I tell you that anyone who divorces his wife, except for marital unfaithfulness, and marries another woman commits adultery."

¹⁰The disciples said to him, "If this is the situation between a husband and wife, it is better not to marry."

¹¹Jesus replied, "Not everyone can accept this word, but only those to whom it has been given. ¹²For some are eunuchs because they were born that way; others were made that way by men; and others have renounced marriageᵃ because of the kingdom of heaven. The one who can accept this should accept it."

¹³Then little children were brought to Jesus for him to place his hands on them and pray for them. But the disciples rebuked those who brought them.

¹⁴Jesus said, "Let the little children come to me, and do not hinder them, for the kingdom of heaven belongs to such as these." ¹⁵When he had placed his hands on them, he went on from there.

¹⁶Now a man came up to Jesus and asked, "Teacher, what good thing must I do to get eternal life?"

¹⁷"Why do you ask me about what is good?" Jesus replied. "There is only One who is good. If you want to enter life, obey the commandments."

¹⁸"Which ones?" the man inquired.

Jesus replied, " 'Do not murder, do not commit adultery, do not steal, do not give false testimony, ¹⁹honor your father and mother,'ᵇ and 'love your neighbor as yourself.'ᶜ "

²⁰"All these I have kept," the young man said. "What do I still lack?"

²¹Jesus answered, "If you want to be perfect, go, sell your possessions and give to the poor, and you will have treasure in heaven. Then come, follow me."

²²When the young man heard this, he went away sad, because he had great wealth.

²³Then Jesus said to his disciples, "I tell you the truth, it is hard for a rich man to enter the king-

ʸ4 Gen. 1:27   ᶻ5 Gen. 2:24   ᵃ12 Or *have made themselves eunuchs*   ᵇ19 Exodus 20:12-16; Deut. 5:16-20   ᶜ19 Lev. 19:18

dom of heaven. ²⁴Again I tell you, it is easier for a camel to go through the eye of a needle than for a rich man to enter the kingdom of God."

²⁵When the disciples heard this, they were greatly astonished and asked, "Who then can be saved?"

²⁶Jesus looked at them and said, "With man this is impossible, but with God all things are possible."

²⁷Peter answered him, "We have left everything to follow you! What then will there be for us?"

²⁸Jesus said to them, "I tell you the truth, at the renewal of all things, when the Son of Man sits on his glorious throne, you who have followed me will also sit on twelve thrones, judging the twelve tribes of Israel. ²⁹And everyone who has left houses or brothers or sisters or father or mother^d or children or fields for my sake will receive a hundred times as much and will inherit eternal life. ³⁰But many who are first will be last, and many who are last will be first.

20 "For the kingdom of heaven is like a landowner who went out early in the morning to hire men to work in his vineyard. ²He agreed to pay them a denarius for the day and sent them into his vineyard.

³"About the third hour he went out and saw others standing in the marketplace doing nothing. ⁴He told them, 'You also go and work in my vineyard, and I will pay you whatever is right.' ⁵So they went.

"He went out again about the sixth hour and the ninth hour and did the same thing. ⁶About the eleventh hour he went out and found still others standing around. He asked them, 'Why have you been standing here all day long doing nothing?'

⁷"'Because no one has hired us,' they answered.

"He said to them, 'You also go and work in my vineyard.'

⁸"When evening came, the owner of the vineyard said to his foreman, 'Call the workers and pay them their wages, beginning with the last ones hired and going on to the first.'

⁹"The workers who were hired about the eleventh hour came and each received a denarius. ¹⁰So when those came who were hired first, they expected to receive more. But each one of them also received a denarius. ¹¹When they received it, they began to grumble against the landowner.

¹²'These men who were hired last worked only one hour,' they said, 'and you have made them equal to us who have borne the burden of the work and the heat of the day.'

¹³"But he answered one of them, 'Friend, I am not being unfair to you. Didn't you agree to work for a denarius? ¹⁴Take your pay and go. I want to give the man who was hired last the same as I gave you. ¹⁵Don't I have the right to do what I want with my own money? Or are you envious because I am generous?'

¹⁶"So the last will be first, and the first will be last."

¹⁷Now as Jesus was going up to Jerusalem, he took the twelve disciples aside and said to them, ¹⁸"We are going up to Jerusalem, and the Son of Man will be betrayed to the chief priests and the teachers of the law. They will condemn him to death ¹⁹and will turn him over to the Gentiles to be mocked and flogged and crucified. On the third day he will be raised to life!"

²⁰Then the mother of Zebedee's sons came to Jesus with her sons and, kneeling down, asked a favor of him.

²¹"What is it you want?" he asked.

She said, "Grant that one of these two sons of mine may sit at your right and the other at your left in your kingdom."

²²"You don't know what you are asking," Jesus said to them. "Can you drink the cup I am going to drink?"

"We can," they answered.

²³Jesus said to them, "You will indeed drink from my cup, but to sit at my right or left is not for me to grant. These places belong to those for whom they have been prepared by my Father."

²⁴When the ten heard about this, they were indignant with the two brothers. ²⁵Jesus called them together and said, "You know that the rulers of the Gentiles lord it over them, and their high officials exercise authority over them. ²⁶Not so with you. Instead, whoever wants to become great among you must be your servant, ²⁷and whoever wants to be first must be your slave— ²⁸just as the Son of Man did not come to be served, but to serve, and to give his life as a ransom for many."

²⁹As Jesus and his disciples were leaving Jericho, a large crowd followed him. ³⁰Two blind

d29 Some manuscripts *mother or wife*

men were sitting by the roadside, and when they heard that Jesus was going by, they shouted, "Lord, Son of David, have mercy on us!"

³¹The crowd rebuked them and told them to be quiet, but they shouted all the louder, "Lord, Son of David, have mercy on us!"

³²Jesus stopped and called them. "What do you want me to do for you?" he asked.

³³"Lord," they answered, "we want our sight."

³⁴Jesus had compassion on them and touched their eyes. Immediately they received their sight and followed him.

Discovering the Word 1. How do Jesus' teachings on divorce and remarriage contrast with the values and practices of our culture (19:1–12)? 2. In 19:16–22 a young man struggles between choosing wealth or eternal life. Why do you think Jesus required him to choose? 3. What wealth does Jesus offer those who follow him (vv. 27–30)? 4. What does the parable of the workers teach us about greatness and wealth in the kingdom of God (20:1–16)? 5. In what ways is Jesus a model of the values he teaches in 20:25–28? 6. How does Jesus' interaction with the two blind men illustrate the values he has just taught?

Applying the Word 1. How have you experienced what Jesus describes in 19:29? 2. In what ways has Jesus' teaching on greatness and wealth (Mt 18—20) challenged you?

Responding in Prayer Ask God to give you strength to stand against the world and to make his values your values.

---

15 / *Matthew 21:1–27*
The King Occupies His Capital

IT IS FASHIONABLE to believe in Jesus. Surveys reveal that millions profess to be Christians. Celebrities claim miraculous, overnight conversions. Politicians boast they are "born again." Religion has become big business.

In Matthew 21 Jesus' popularity reaches its zenith. In the midst of public acclamation he occupies Jerusalem, the capital of the Jewish nation. His clash with the religious leaders reveals the difference between genuine faith and empty profession.

Warming Up to God Today we will see Jesus enter Jerusalem to the praise and acclamation of the crowd. Imagine you have an opportunity to see Jesus. How do you feel? Express your feelings to the Lord.

Read Matthew 21:1–27.

---

21 As they approached Jerusalem and came to Bethphage on the Mount of Olives, Jesus sent two disciples, ²saying to them, "Go to the village ahead of you, and at once you will find a donkey tied there, with her colt by her. Untie them and bring them to me. ³If anyone says anything to you, tell him that the Lord needs them, and he will send them right away."

⁴This took place to fulfill what was spoken through the prophet:

⁵"Say to the Daughter of Zion,
    'See, your king comes to you,
gentle and riding on a donkey,
    on a colt, the foal of a donkey.' "ᵉ

⁶The disciples went and did as Jesus had instructed them. ⁷They brought the donkey and the colt, placed their cloaks on them, and Jesus sat on them. ⁸A very large crowd spread their cloaks on the road, while others cut branches from the trees and spread them on the road. ⁹The crowds that went ahead of him and those that followed shouted,

"Hosannaᶠ to the Son of David!"

"Blessed is he who comes in the name of the Lord!"ᵍ

"Hosannaᶠ in the highest!"

ᵉ5 Zech. 9:9   ᶠ9 A Hebrew expression meaning "Save!" which became an exclamation of praise; also in verse 15   ᵍ9 Psalm 118:26

[10]When Jesus entered Jerusalem, the whole city was stirred and asked, "Who is this?"

[11]The crowds answered, "This is Jesus, the prophet from Nazareth in Galilee."

[12]Jesus entered the temple area and drove out all who were buying and selling there. He overturned the tables of the money changers and the benches of those selling doves. [13]"It is written," he said to them, " 'My house will be called a house of prayer,'[h] but you are making it a 'den of robbers.'[i]"

[14]The blind and the lame came to him at the temple, and he healed them. [15]But when the chief priests and the teachers of the law saw the wonderful things he did and the children shouting in the temple area, "Hosanna to the Son of David," they were indignant.

[16]"Do you hear what these children are saying?" they asked him.

"Yes," replied Jesus, "have you never read,

" 'From the lips of children and infants
    you have ordained praise'[j]?"

[17]And he left them and went out of the city to Bethany, where he spent the night.

[18]Early in the morning, as he was on his way back to the city, he was hungry. [19]Seeing a fig tree by the road, he went up to it but found nothing on it except leaves. Then he said to it, "May you never bear fruit again!" Immediately the tree withered.

[20]When the disciples saw this, they were amazed. "How did the fig tree wither so quickly?" they asked.

[21]Jesus replied, "I tell you the truth, if you have faith and do not doubt, not only can you do what was done to the fig tree, but also you can say to this mountain, 'Go, throw yourself into the sea,' and it will be done. [22]If you believe, you will receive whatever you ask for in prayer."

[23]Jesus entered the temple courts, and, while he was teaching, the chief priests and the elders of the people came to him. "By what authority are you doing these things?" they asked. "And who gave you this authority?"

[24]Jesus replied, "I will also ask you one question. If you answer me, I will tell you by what authority I am doing these things. [25]John's baptism—where did it come from? Was it from heaven, or from men?"

They discussed it among themselves and said, "If we say, 'From heaven,' he will ask, 'Then why didn't you believe him?' [26]But if we say, 'From men'—we are afraid of the people, for they all hold that John was a prophet."

[27]So they answered Jesus, "We don't know."

Then he said, "Neither will I tell you by what authority I am doing these things.

[h]13 Isaiah 56:7   [i]13 Jer. 7:11   [j]16 Psalm 8:2

 Discovering the Word   1. Excitement is building and emotions are intense. What words or phrases communicate something of the electrifying atmosphere?   2. What different perceptions does the crowd have of Jesus (vv. 9–11)?   3. Jesus clears the temple in verses 12–17. How does the condition of the temple contrast with what God intended?   4. A fig tree with leaves usually had fruit. How does Jesus' cursing of the fig tree relate to his clearing the temple (vv. 18–22)?   5. How does Jesus' encounter with the Pharisees (vv. 23–27) illustrate the danger of not responding to the light God gives us?

 Applying the Word   1. In what ways do you see the modern church "buying and selling" like those in the temple?   2. Identify one area in which your actions need to be more consistent with your beliefs.

Responding in Prayer   Praise God for who Jesus is and what you have seen about him in this passage.

16 / *Matthew 21:28—22:46*
The King Silences the Opposition

CONFRONTATION IS NEVER easy. Yet there are times when the situation demands it. The religious leaders refused to acknowledge that Jesus was God's Messiah sent to rule. Skillfully, Jesus seeks to expose their hardness of heart and bring them to repentance. They respond not in repentance but by plotting a trap for him.

 Warming Up to God From time to time we all have been involved in confrontations. How do you feel in these situations?

 Read Matthew 21:28—22:46.

28"What do you think? There was a man who had two sons. He went to the first and said, 'Son, go and work today in the vineyard.'

29" 'I will not,' he answered, but later he changed his mind and went.

30"Then the father went to the other son and said the same thing. He answered, 'I will, sir,' but he did not go.

31"Which of the two did what his father wanted?"

"The first," they answered.

Jesus said to them, "I tell you the truth, the tax collectors and the prostitutes are entering the kingdom of God ahead of you. 32For John came to you to show you the way of righteousness, and you did not believe him, but the tax collectors and the prostitutes did. And even after you saw this, you did not repent and believe him.

33"Listen to another parable: There was a landowner who planted a vineyard. He put a wall around it, dug a winepress in it and built a watchtower. Then he rented the vineyard to some farmers and went away on a journey. 34When the harvest time approached, he sent his servants to the tenants to collect his fruit.

35"The tenants seized his servants; they beat one, killed another, and stoned a third. 36Then he sent other servants to them, more than the first time, and the tenants treated them the same way. 37Last of all, he sent his son to them. 'They will respect my son,' he said.

38"But when the tenants saw the son, they said to each other, 'This is the heir. Come, let's kill him and take his inheritance.' 39So they took him and threw him out of the vineyard and killed him.

40"Therefore, when the owner of the vineyard comes, what will he do to those tenants?"

41"He will bring those wretches to a wretched end," they replied, "and he will rent the vineyard to other tenants, who will give him his share of the crop at harvest time."

42Jesus said to them, "Have you never read in the Scriptures:

" 'The stone the builders rejected
    has become the capstone*k*;
the Lord has done this,
    and it is marvelous in our eyes'*l*?

43"Therefore I tell you that the kingdom of God will be taken away from you and given to a people who will produce its fruit. 44He who falls on this stone will be broken to pieces, but he on whom it falls will be crushed."*m*

45When the chief priests and the Pharisees heard Jesus' parables, they knew he was talking about them. 46They looked for a way to arrest him, but they were afraid of the crowd because the people held that he was a prophet.

22 Jesus spoke to them again in parables, saying: 2"The kingdom of heaven is like a king who prepared a wedding banquet for his son. 3He sent his servants to those who had been invited to the banquet to tell them to come, but they refused to come.

4"Then he sent some more servants and said, 'Tell those who have been invited that I have prepared my dinner: My oxen and fattened cattle have been butchered, and everything is ready. Come to the wedding banquet.'

5"But they paid no attention and went off—one to his field, another to his business. 6The rest seized his servants, mistreated them and killed them. 7The king was enraged. He sent his army and destroyed those murderers and burned their city.

*k*42 Or *cornerstone*   *l*42 Psalm 118:22,23   *m*44 Some manuscripts do not have verse 44.

8"Then he said to his servants, 'The wedding banquet is ready, but those I invited did not deserve to come. 9Go to the street corners and invite to the banquet anyone you find.' 10So the servants went out into the streets and gathered all the people they could find, both good and bad, and the wedding hall was filled with guests.

11"But when the king came in to see the guests, he noticed a man there who was not wearing wedding clothes. 12'Friend,' he asked, 'how did you get in here without wedding clothes?' The man was speechless.

13"Then the king told the attendants, 'Tie him hand and foot, and throw him outside, into the darkness, where there will be weeping and gnashing of teeth.'

14"For many are invited, but few are chosen."

15Then the Pharisees went out and laid plans to trap him in his words. 16They sent their disciples to him along with the Herodians. "Teacher," they said, "we know you are a man of integrity and that you teach the way of God in accordance with the truth. You aren't swayed by men, because you pay no attention to who they are. 17Tell us then, what is your opinion? Is it right to pay taxes to Caesar or not?"

18But Jesus, knowing their evil intent, said, "You hypocrites, why are you trying to trap me? 19Show me the coin used for paying the tax." They brought him a denarius, 20and he asked them, "Whose portrait is this? And whose inscription?"

21"Caesar's," they replied.

Then he said to them, "Give to Caesar what is Caesar's, and to God what is God's."

22When they heard this, they were amazed. So they left him and went away.

23That same day the Sadducees, who say there is no resurrection, came to him with a question. 24"Teacher," they said, "Moses told us that if a man dies without having children, his brother must marry the widow and have children for him. 25Now there were seven brothers among us. The first one married and died, and since he had no children, he left his wife to his brother. 26The same thing happened to the second and third brother, right on down to the seventh. 27Finally, the woman died. 28Now then, at the resurrection, whose wife will she be of the seven, since all of them were married to her?"

29Jesus replied, "You are in error because you do not know the Scriptures or the power of God. 30At the resurrection people will neither marry nor be given in marriage; they will be like the angels in heaven. 31But about the resurrection of the dead—have you not read what God said to you, 32'I am the God of Abraham, the God of Isaac, and the God of Jacob'[n]? He is not the God of the dead but of the living."

33When the crowds heard this, they were astonished at his teaching.

34Hearing that Jesus had silenced the Sadducees, the Pharisees got together. 35One of them, an expert in the law, tested him with this question: 36"Teacher, which is the greatest commandment in the Law?"

37Jesus replied: " 'Love the Lord your God with all your heart and with all your soul and with all your mind.'[o] 38This is the first and greatest commandment. 39And the second is like it: 'Love your neighbor as yourself.'[p] 40All the Law and the Prophets hang on these two commandments."

41While the Pharisees were gathered together, Jesus asked them, 42"What do you think about the Christ[q]? Whose son is he?"

"The son of David," they replied.

43He said to them, "How is it then that David, speaking by the Spirit, calls him 'Lord'? For he says,

44" 'The Lord said to my Lord:
   "Sit at my right hand
until I put your enemies
   under your feet." '[r]

45If then David calls him 'Lord,' how can he be his son?" 46No one could say a word in reply, and from that day on no one dared to ask him any more questions.

[n]32 Exodus 3:6   [o]37 Deut. 6:5   [p]39 Lev. 19:18   [q]42 Or Messiah   [r]44 Psalm 110:1

Discovering the Word 1. What does the parable of the two sons reveal about the chief priests and the elders (21:28–32)? 2. How does the parable of the tenants illustrate the character of the Father, the Son and the religious leaders (21:33–46)? 3. How is the kingdom of heaven like the banquet described in 22:1–14? 4. In 22:23–28 the Sadducees tell Jesus a story designed to refute the resurrection. How does the story illustrate their ignorance of Scripture and God's power (22:29–33)? 5. Love was the foundation of the Old Testament law (22:34–40). Why do you think we have so much trouble equating God's laws with love? 6. Jesus poses a dilemma to the Pharisees that silences them: "How can the Christ be both the son of David and his Lord?" (22:41–46). What does this paradox reveal about the Lord?

 Applying the Word 1. What guidance does Jesus give for fulfilling our obligations to God and the government? 2. How can these accounts of Jesus in conflict strengthen our faith in him? 3. What do they teach you about handling conflict?

 Responding in Prayer Ask for the help you need for whatever conflict you face today.

---

17 / *Matthew 23*
The King Condemns the Rebels

INFLUENCE IS A powerful force. Those who influence others are able to change minds and to direct actions. The religious leaders in Israel possessed the power of influence. After they decided to oppose Jesus, they tried to lead others to do the same. In Matthew 23 Jesus condemns them point-blank. They should have been the first to enter the kingdom of God because of their knowledge of Scripture and their standing in the Jewish community. Because they refused, Jesus calls them to judgment. This passage exposes the guilt of those who do not practice what they preach.

Warming Up to God When have you been hurt by inconsistency in the life or teaching of an influential person you respected? Talk to God about any feelings of hurt you still have.

Read Matthew 23.

---

23 Then Jesus said to the crowds and to his disciples: 2"The teachers of the law and the Pharisees sit in Moses' seat. 3So you must obey them and do everything they tell you. But do not do what they do, for they do not practice what they preach. 4They tie up heavy loads and put them on men's shoulders, but they themselves are not willing to lift a finger to move them.

5"Everything they do is done for men to see: They make their phylacteries⁵ wide and the tassels on their garments long; 6they love the place of honor at banquets and the most important seats in the synagogues; 7they love to be greeted in the marketplaces and to have men call them 'Rabbi.'

8"But you are not to be called 'Rabbi,' for you have only one Master and you are all brothers. 9And do not call anyone on earth 'father,' for you have one Father, and he is in heaven. 10Nor are you to be called 'teacher,' for you have one Teacher, the Christ.ᵗ 11The greatest among you will be your servant. 12For whoever exalts himself will be humbled, and whoever humbles himself will be exalted.

13"Woe to you, teachers of the law and Pharisees, you hypocrites! You shut the kingdom of heaven in men's faces. You yourselves do not enter, nor will you let those enter who are trying to.ᵘ

15"Woe to you, teachers of the law and Pharisees, you hypocrites! You travel over land and sea to win a single convert, and when he becomes one, you make him twice as much a son of hell as you are.

16"Woe to you, blind guides! You say, 'If any-

⁵5 That is, boxes containing Scripture verses, worn on forehead and arm ᵗ10 Or *Messiah* ᵘ13 Some manuscripts *to.* ¹⁴*Woe to you, teachers of the law and Pharisees, you hypocrites! You devour widows' houses and for a show make lengthy prayers. Therefore you will be punished more severely.*

one swears by the temple, it means nothing; but if anyone swears by the gold of the temple, he is bound by his oath.' [17]You blind fools! Which is greater: the gold, or the temple that makes the gold sacred? [18]You also say, 'If anyone swears by the altar, it means nothing; but if anyone swears by the gift on it, he is bound by his oath.' [19]You blind men! Which is greater: the gift, or the altar that makes the gift sacred? [20]Therefore, he who swears by the altar swears by it and by everything on it. [21]And he who swears by the temple swears by it and by the one who dwells in it. [22]And he who swears by heaven swears by God's throne and by the one who sits on it.

[23]"Woe to you, teachers of the law and Pharisees, you hypocrites! You give a tenth of your spices—mint, dill and cummin. But you have neglected the more important matters of the law—justice, mercy and faithfulness. You should have practiced the latter, without neglecting the former. [24]You blind guides! You strain out a gnat but swallow a camel.

[25]"Woe to you, teachers of the law and Pharisees, you hypocrites! You clean the outside of the cup and dish, but inside they are full of greed and self-indulgence. [26]Blind Pharisee! First clean the inside of the cup and dish, and then the outside also will be clean.

[27]"Woe to you, teachers of the law and Pharisees, you hypocrites! You are like whitewashed tombs, which look beautiful on the outside but on the inside are full of dead men's bones and everything unclean. [28]In the same way, on the outside you appear to people as righteous but on the inside you are full of hypocrisy and wickedness.

[29]"Woe to you, teachers of the law and Pharisees, you hypocrites! You build tombs for the prophets and decorate the graves of the righteous. [30]And you say, 'If we had lived in the days of our forefathers, we would not have taken part with them in shedding the blood of the prophets.' [31]So you testify against yourselves that you are the descendants of those who murdered the prophets. [32]Fill up, then, the measure of the sin of your forefathers!

[33]"You snakes! You brood of vipers! How will you escape being condemned to hell? [34]Therefore I am sending you prophets and wise men and teachers. Some of them you will kill and crucify; others you will flog in your synagogues and pursue from town to town. [35]And so upon you will come all the righteous blood that has been shed on earth, from the blood of righteous Abel to the blood of Zechariah son of Berekiah, whom you murdered between the temple and the altar. [36]I tell you the truth, all this will come upon this generation.

[37]"O Jerusalem, Jerusalem, you who kill the prophets and stone those sent to you, how often I have longed to gather your children together, as a hen gathers her chicks under her wings, but you were not willing. [38]Look, your house is left to you desolate. [39]For I tell you, you will not see me again until you say, 'Blessed is he who comes in the name of the Lord.'[v]"

v39 Psalm 118:26

Discovering the Word 1. What attitude does Jesus teach the people to have toward the religious leaders, and why (vv. 1–4)? 2. Compare the motives of the religious leaders (vv. 5–7) with the motives and attitudes Jesus requires of his followers (vv. 8–12). 3. Jesus pronounces seven woes (judgments) against the teachers of the law and the Pharisees (vv. 13–32). Summarize each one. 4. The entire generation to whom Jesus is speaking is held accountable for the "righteous blood" shed in all previous generations (vv. 33–36). Why do you think they received such a terrible sentence? 5. What responses do you have as you observe Jesus as a judge? 6. In the midst of this overwhelming condemnation, how is the tender compassion of Jesus also evident (vv. 33–39)?

Applying the Word 1. Jesus condemns the religious leaders for confusing inward and outward righteousness (vv. 25–28). In what ways are we inclined to do that today? 2. Where does this point out a place that needs to change in your life?

 Responding in Prayer Ask God to make your Christian life consistent with your beliefs.

18 / *Matthew 24*
The Return of the King

WE ALL WANT to be safe and secure. Yet many things can threaten our security—losing our job, our income, our health, our loved ones. Our ability to handle these threats will depend on the source of our security. Matthew 24 focuses on the destruction of Jerusalem and the return of Christ. The true issue of Christ's return is not the "hows" or "whens" that fascinate us. Rather we must learn to live in the present in light of the future. We must learn the true source of our security.

 Warming Up to God   What gives you a sense of security?

 Read Matthew 24.

---

24 Jesus left the temple and was walking away when his disciples came up to him to call his attention to its buildings. ²"Do you see all these things?" he asked. "I tell you the truth, not one stone here will be left on another; every one will be thrown down."

³As Jesus was sitting on the Mount of Olives, the disciples came to him privately. "Tell us," they said, "when will this happen, and what will be the sign of your coming and of the end of the age?"

⁴Jesus answered: "Watch out that no one deceives you. ⁵For many will come in my name, claiming, 'I am the Christ,'ʷ and will deceive many. ⁶You will hear of wars and rumors of wars, but see to it that you are not alarmed. Such things must happen, but the end is still to come. ⁷Nation will rise against nation, and kingdom against kingdom. There will be famines and earthquakes in various places. ⁸All these are the beginning of birth pains.

⁹"Then you will be handed over to be persecuted and put to death, and you will be hated by all nations because of me. ¹⁰At that time many will turn away from the faith and will betray and hate each other, ¹¹and many false prophets will appear and deceive many people. ¹²Because of the increase of wickedness, the love of most will grow cold, ¹³but he who stands firm to the end will be saved. ¹⁴And this gospel of the kingdom will be preached in the whole world as a testimony to all nations, and then the end will come.

¹⁵"So when you see standing in the holy place 'the abomination that causes desolation,'ˣ spoken of through the prophet Daniel—let the reader understand— ¹⁶then let those who are in Judea flee to the mountains. ¹⁷Let no one on the roof of his house go down to take anything out of the house. ¹⁸Let no one in the field go back to get his cloak. ¹⁹How dreadful it will be in those days for pregnant women and nursing mothers! ²⁰Pray that your flight will not take place in winter or on the Sabbath. ²¹For then there will be great distress, unequaled from the beginning of the world until now—and never to be equaled again. ²²If those days had not been cut short, no one would survive, but for the sake of the elect those days will be shortened. ²³At that time if anyone says to you, 'Look, here is the Christ!' or, 'There he is!' do not believe it. ²⁴For false Christs and false prophets will appear and perform great signs and miracles to deceive even the elect—if that were possible. ²⁵See, I have told you ahead of time.

²⁶"So if anyone tells you, 'There he is, out in the desert,' do not go out; or, 'Here he is, in the inner rooms,' do not believe it. ²⁷For as lightning that comes from the east is visible even in the west, so will be the coming of the Son of Man. ²⁸Wherever there is a carcass, there the vultures will gather.

²⁹"Immediately after the distress of those days

" 'the sun will be darkened,
    and the moon will not give its light;
the stars will fall from the sky,
    and the heavenly bodies will be shaken.'ʸ

³⁰"At that time the sign of the Son of Man will appear in the sky, and all the nations of the earth will mourn. They will see the Son of Man coming on the clouds of the sky, with power and great glory. ³¹And he will send his angels with a loud

ʷ5 Or *Messiah*; also in verse 23   ˣ15 Daniel 9:27; 11:31; 12:11
ʸ29 Isaiah 13:10; 34:4

trumpet call, and they will gather his elect from the four winds, from one end of the heavens to the other.

³²"Now learn this lesson from the fig tree: As soon as its twigs get tender and its leaves come out, you know that summer is near. ³³Even so, when you see all these things, you know that it*z* is near, right at the door. ³⁴I tell you the truth, this generation*a* will certainly not pass away until all these things have happened. ³⁵Heaven and earth will pass away, but my words will never pass away.

³⁶"No one knows about that day or hour, not even the angels in heaven, nor the Son,*b* but only the Father. ³⁷As it was in the days of Noah, so it will be at the coming of the Son of Man. ³⁸For in the days before the flood, people were eating and drinking, marrying and giving in marriage, up to the day Noah entered the ark; ³⁹and they knew nothing about what would happen until the flood came and took them all away. That is how it will be at the coming of the Son of Man. ⁴⁰Two men will be in the field; one will be taken and the other left. ⁴¹Two women will be grinding with a hand mill; one will be taken and the other left.

⁴²"Therefore keep watch, because you do not know on what day your Lord will come. ⁴³But understand this: If the owner of the house had known at what time of night the thief was coming, he would have kept watch and would not have let his house be broken into. ⁴⁴So you also must be ready, because the Son of Man will come at an hour when you do not expect him.

⁴⁵"Who then is the faithful and wise servant, whom the master has put in charge of the servants in his household to give them their food at the proper time? ⁴⁶It will be good for that servant whose master finds him doing so when he returns. ⁴⁷I tell you the truth, he will put him in charge of all his possessions. ⁴⁸But suppose that servant is wicked and says to himself, 'My master is staying away a long time,' ⁴⁹and he then begins to beat his fellow servants and to eat and drink with drunkards. ⁵⁰The master of that servant will come on a day when he does not expect him and at an hour he is not aware of. ⁵¹He will cut him to pieces and assign him a place with the hypocrites, where there will be weeping and gnashing of teeth.

*z*33 Or he   *a*34 Or *race*   *b*36 Some manuscripts do not have *nor the Son.*

Discovering the Word 1. Following Jesus' statement about the temple's destruction, the disciples ask two questions (v. 3). Look through chapter 24, briefly noting ways that Jesus answers these questions. 2. Throughout history people have set dates for Christ's return and have been mistaken. What events might deceive the disciples into thinking the end is at hand (vv. 4–8)? 3. Before the end comes, what dangers will believers face, and how are we to handle them (vv. 9–14)? 4. In 167 B.C. Antiochus Epiphanes attacked Jerusalem and set up a pagan altar in the temple—an event that anticipated "the abomination that causes desolation" spoken of by Jesus (v. 15). What occurs in the aftermath of this abomination (vv. 15–22)? 5. How will we be able to distinguish false Christs from the true (vv. 23–31)? 6. How do the parables of the thief and the wise and wicked servants (vv. 42–51) emphasize the importance of living in light of Christ's return?

Applying the Word 1. Few of us have ever faced deadly peril for our faith. What types of pressure do you face for your faith in Christ? 2. In what ways do you have need of greater watchfulness and perseverance?

Responding in Prayer Praise God for giving you an unfailing source of security.

19 / *Matthew 25*
Preparation for the King's Return

ACCOUNTABILITY can be uncomfortable and inconvenient. Our desires and preferences are subject to the demands of another. Most of us would prefer to do things our own way. A rule of thumb in management is that people don't do what you expect; they do what you inspect. Jesus is coming back to inspect our lives. He holds us accountable for how we conduct ourselves in his absence. In Matthew 25 he urges us to prepare for his coming.

 Warming Up to God Have you ever been in a situation where your work did not meet up to standards when it was reviewed or inspected? How did it affect you?

 Read Matthew 25.

---

25 "At that time the kingdom of heaven will be like ten virgins who took their lamps and went out to meet the bridegroom. ²Five of them were foolish and five were wise. ³The foolish ones took their lamps but did not take any oil with them. ⁴The wise, however, took oil in jars along with their lamps. ⁵The bridegroom was a long time in coming, and they all became drowsy and fell asleep.

⁶"At midnight the cry rang out: 'Here's the bridegroom! Come out to meet him!'

⁷"Then all the virgins woke up and trimmed their lamps. ⁸The foolish ones said to the wise, 'Give us some of your oil; our lamps are going out.'

⁹" 'No,' they replied, 'there may not be enough for both us and you. Instead, go to those who sell oil and buy some for yourselves.'

¹⁰"But while they were on their way to buy the oil, the bridegroom arrived. The virgins who were ready went in with him to the wedding banquet. And the door was shut.

¹¹"Later the others also came. 'Sir! Sir!' they said. 'Open the door for us!'

¹²"But he replied, 'I tell you the truth, I don't know you.'

¹³"Therefore keep watch, because you do not know the day or the hour.

¹⁴"Again, it will be like a man going on a journey, who called his servants and entrusted his property to them. ¹⁵To one he gave five talents*c* of money, to another two talents, and to another one talent, each according to his ability. Then he went on his journey. ¹⁶The man who had received the five talents went at once and put his money to work and gained five more. ¹⁷So also, the one with the two talents gained two more. ¹⁸But the man who had received the one talent went off,

dug a hole in the ground and hid his master's money.

¹⁹"After a long time the master of those servants returned and settled accounts with them. ²⁰The man who had received the five talents brought the other five. 'Master,' he said, 'you entrusted me with five talents. See, I have gained five more.'

²¹"His master replied, 'Well done, good and faithful servant! You have been faithful with a few things; I will put you in charge of many things. Come and share your master's happiness!'

²²"The man with the two talents also came. 'Master,' he said, 'you entrusted me with two talents; see, I have gained two more.'

²³"His master replied, 'Well done, good and faithful servant! You have been faithful with a few things; I will put you in charge of many things. Come and share your master's happiness!'

²⁴"Then the man who had received the one talent came. 'Master,' he said, 'I knew that you are a hard man, harvesting where you have not sown and gathering where you have not scattered seed. ²⁵So I was afraid and went out and hid your talent in the ground. See, here is what belongs to you.'

²⁶"His master replied, 'You wicked, lazy servant! So you knew that I harvest where I have not sown and gather where I have not scattered seed? ²⁷Well then, you should have put my money on deposit with the bankers, so that when I returned I would have received it back with interest.

²⁸" 'Take the talent from him and give it to the one who has the ten talents. ²⁹For everyone who has will be given more, and he will have an abundance. Whoever does not have, even what he has will be taken from him. ³⁰And throw that worth-

c15 A talent was worth more than a thousand dollars.

less servant outside, into the darkness, where there will be weeping and gnashing of teeth.'

³¹"When the Son of Man comes in his glory, and all the angels with him, he will sit on his throne in heavenly glory. ³²All the nations will be gathered before him, and he will separate the people one from another as a shepherd separates the sheep from the goats. ³³He will put the sheep on his right and the goats on his left.

³⁴"Then the King will say to those on his right, 'Come, you who are blessed by my Father; take your inheritance, the kingdom prepared for you since the creation of the world. ³⁵For I was hungry and you gave me something to eat, I was thirsty and you gave me something to drink, I was a stranger and you invited me in, ³⁶I needed clothes and you clothed me, I was sick and you looked after me, I was in prison and you came to visit me.'

³⁷"Then the righteous will answer him, 'Lord, when did we see you hungry and feed you, or thirsty and give you something to drink? ³⁸When did we see you a stranger and invite you in, or needing clothes and clothe you? ³⁹When did we see you sick or in prison and go to visit you?'

⁴⁰"The King will reply, 'I tell you the truth, whatever you did for one of the least of these brothers of mine, you did for me.'

⁴¹"Then he will say to those on his left, 'Depart from me, you who are cursed, into the eternal fire prepared for the devil and his angels. ⁴²For I was hungry and you gave me nothing to eat, I was thirsty and you gave me nothing to drink, ⁴³I was a stranger and you did not invite me in, I needed clothes and you did not clothe me, I was sick and in prison and you did not look after me.'

⁴⁴"They also will answer, 'Lord, when did we see you hungry or thirsty or a stranger or needing clothes or sick or in prison, and did not help you?'

⁴⁵"He will reply, 'I tell you the truth, whatever you did not do for one of the least of these, you did not do for me.'

⁴⁶"Then they will go away to eternal punishment, but the righteous to eternal life."

 Discovering the Word 1. How does the parable of the ten virgins illustrate the need to prepare for the groom's delayed return (vv. 1–13)? 2. A talent was a vast sum of money. In the parable of the talents, what were the master's expectations of his servants (vv. 14–30)? 3. How does the master demonstrate his approval or disapproval? 4. In the parable of the sheep and the goats, identify the King, the sheep, the goats and the "brothers" of the King (vv. 31–46). 5. What criteria does the King use to separate the sheep from the goats? 6. According to Jesus' teaching in this chapter, what should we be doing until he returns?

Applying the Word 1. What resources and responsibilities has Jesus given you? 2. How can you handle them in a good and faithful manner? 3. How should the material in this chapter affect your current priorities?

Responding in Prayer Ask God to show you how to serve him.

---

20 / *Matthew 26*
The Betrayal of the King

ON THE DRIZZLY day of October 16, 1555, Hugh Latimer and Nicholas Ridley, two influential English reformers, were tied to the stake and bundles of sticks were piled at their feet. The crowd strained to hear what the two men were saying. Would they recant or would they persist in dying as heretics? As the executioner pushed a torch into the wood, Latimer said, "Be of good comfort, Master Ridley, and play the man; we shall this day light such a candle, by God's grace, in England, as I trust shall never be put out." Suffering and temptation reveal the quality of our discipleship. Nowhere is this more evident than in Matthew 26, as we move into the climax of the book.

 Warming Up to God Have you ever been tempted to stop following Christ? Explain.

Read Matthew 26.

26 When Jesus had finished saying all these things, he said to his disciples, [2]"As you know, the Passover is two days away—and the Son of Man will be handed over to be crucified."

[3]Then the chief priests and the elders of the people assembled in the palace of the high priest, whose name was Caiaphas, [4]and they plotted to arrest Jesus in some sly way and kill him. [5]"But not during the Feast," they said, "or there may be a riot among the people."

[6]While Jesus was in Bethany in the home of a man known as Simon the Leper, [7]a woman came to him with an alabaster jar of very expensive perfume, which she poured on his head as he was reclining at the table.

[8]When the disciples saw this, they were indignant. "Why this waste?" they asked. [9]"This perfume could have been sold at a high price and the money given to the poor."

[10]Aware of this, Jesus said to them, "Why are you bothering this woman? She has done a beautiful thing to me. [11]The poor you will always have with you, but you will not always have me. [12]When she poured this perfume on my body, she did it to prepare me for burial. [13]I tell you the truth, wherever this gospel is preached throughout the world, what she has done will also be told, in memory of her."

[14]Then one of the Twelve—the one called Judas Iscariot—went to the chief priests [15]and asked, "What are you willing to give me if I hand him over to you?" So they counted out for him thirty silver coins. [16]From then on Judas watched for an opportunity to hand him over.

[17]On the first day of the Feast of Unleavened Bread, the disciples came to Jesus and asked, "Where do you want us to make preparations for you to eat the Passover?"

[18]He replied, "Go into the city to a certain man and tell him, 'The Teacher says: My appointed time is near. I am going to celebrate the Passover with my disciples at your house.' " [19]So the disciples did as Jesus had directed them and prepared the Passover.

[20]When evening came, Jesus was reclining at the table with the Twelve. [21]And while they were eating, he said, "I tell you the truth, one of you will betray me."

[22]They were very sad and began to say to him one after the other, "Surely not I, Lord?"

[23]Jesus replied, "The one who has dipped his hand into the bowl with me will betray me. [24]The Son of Man will go just as it is written about him. But woe to that man who betrays the Son of Man! It would be better for him if he had not been born."

[25]Then Judas, the one who would betray him, said, "Surely not I, Rabbi?"

Jesus answered, "Yes, it is you."[d]

[26]While they were eating, Jesus took bread, gave thanks and broke it, and gave it to his disciples, saying, "Take and eat; this is my body."

[27]Then he took the cup, gave thanks and offered it to them, saying, "Drink from it, all of you. [28]This is my blood of the[e] covenant, which is poured out for many for the forgiveness of sins. [29]I tell you, I will not drink of this fruit of the vine from now on until that day when I drink it anew with you in my Father's kingdom."

[30]When they had sung a hymn, they went out to the Mount of Olives.

[31]Then Jesus told them, "This very night you will all fall away on account of me, for it is written:

" 'I will strike the shepherd,
    and the sheep of the flock will be
        scattered.'[f]

[32]But after I have risen, I will go ahead of you into Galilee."

[33]Peter replied, "Even if all fall away on account of you, I never will."

[34]"I tell you the truth," Jesus answered, "this very night, before the rooster crows, you will disown me three times."

[35]But Peter declared, "Even if I have to die with you, I will never disown you." And all the other disciples said the same.

[36]Then Jesus went with his disciples to a place called Gethsemane, and he said to them, "Sit here while I go over there and pray." [37]He took Peter and the two sons of Zebedee along with him, and he began to be sorrowful and troubled. [38]Then he said to them, "My soul is overwhelmed with sor-

[d]25 Or "You yourself have said it"   [e]28 Some manuscripts the new
[f]31 Zech. 13:7

row to the point of death. Stay here and keep watch with me."

39Going a little farther, he fell with his face to the ground and prayed, "My Father, if it is possible, may this cup be taken from me. Yet not as I will, but as you will."

40Then he returned to his disciples and found them sleeping. "Could you men not keep watch with me for one hour?" he asked Peter. **41**"Watch and pray so that you will not fall into temptation. The spirit is willing, but the body is weak."

42He went away a second time and prayed, "My Father, if it is not possible for this cup to be taken away unless I drink it, may your will be done."

43When he came back, he again found them sleeping, because their eyes were heavy. **44**So he left them and went away once more and prayed the third time, saying the same thing.

45Then he returned to the disciples and said to them, "Are you still sleeping and resting? Look, the hour is near, and the Son of Man is betrayed into the hands of sinners. **46**Rise, let us go! Here comes my betrayer!"

47While he was still speaking, Judas, one of the Twelve, arrived. With him was a large crowd armed with swords and clubs, sent from the chief priests and the elders of the people. **48**Now the betrayer had arranged a signal with them: "The one I kiss is the man; arrest him." **49**Going at once to Jesus, Judas said, "Greetings, Rabbi!" and kissed him.

50Jesus replied, "Friend, do what you came for."*g*

Then the men stepped forward, seized Jesus and arrested him. **51**With that, one of Jesus' companions reached for his sword, drew it out and struck the servant of the high priest, cutting off his ear.

52"Put your sword back in its place," Jesus said to him, "for all who draw the sword will die by the sword. **53**Do you think I cannot call on my Father, and he will at once put at my disposal more than twelve legions of angels? **54**But how then would the Scriptures be fulfilled that say it must happen in this way?"

55At that time Jesus said to the crowd, "Am I leading a rebellion, that you have come out with swords and clubs to capture me? Every day I sat in the temple courts teaching, and you did not arrest me. **56**But this has all taken place that the writings of the prophets might be fulfilled." Then all the disciples deserted him and fled.

57Those who had arrested Jesus took him to Caiaphas, the high priest, where the teachers of the law and the elders had assembled. **58**But Peter followed him at a distance, right up to the courtyard of the high priest. He entered and sat down with the guards to see the outcome.

59The chief priests and the whole Sanhedrin were looking for false evidence against Jesus so that they could put him to death. **60**But they did not find any, though many false witnesses came forward.

Finally two came forward **61**and declared, "This fellow said, 'I am able to destroy the temple of God and rebuild it in three days.' "

62Then the high priest stood up and said to Jesus, "Are you not going to answer? What is this testimony that these men are bringing against you?" **63**But Jesus remained silent.

The high priest said to him, "I charge you under oath by the living God: Tell us if you are the Christ,*h* the Son of God."

64"Yes, it is as you say," Jesus replied. "But I say to all of you: In the future you will see the Son of Man sitting at the right hand of the Mighty One and coming on the clouds of heaven."

65Then the high priest tore his clothes and said, "He has spoken blasphemy! Why do we need any more witnesses? Look, now you have heard the blasphemy. **66**What do you think?"

"He is worthy of death," they answered.

67Then they spit in his face and struck him with their fists. Others slapped him **68**and said, "Prophesy to us, Christ. Who hit you?"

69Now Peter was sitting out in the courtyard, and a servant girl came to him. "You also were with Jesus of Galilee," she said.

70But he denied it before them all. "I don't know what you're talking about," he said.

71Then he went out to the gateway, where another girl saw him and said to the people there, "This fellow was with Jesus of Nazareth."

72He denied it again, with an oath: "I don't know the man!"

73After a little while, those standing there went up to Peter and said, "Surely you are one of them, for your accent gives you away."

74Then he began to call down curses on himself and he swore to them, "I don't know the man!"

Immediately a rooster crowed. **75**Then Peter remembered the word Jesus had spoken: "Before the rooster crows, you will disown me three times." And he went outside and wept bitterly.

g50 Or "Friend, why have you come?"   *h63 Or Messiah; also in verse 68*

Discovering the Word 1. How do verses 1–16 set the stage for Jesus' betrayal and death? 2. In verses 17–30 Jesus celebrates the Passover with his disciples. How is this occasion both ominous and hopeful? 3. What insights can we gain about Jesus during his time in Gethsemane (vv. 36–45)? 4. Jesus' betrayal comes at the hand of one of his own disciples (vv. 47–50). As you look over the role of Judas in this chapter, why do you think the religious leaders used him? 5. Why do you think Jesus remained silent during the first part of his trial (vv. 57–63)? 6. In answer to the high priest's question (v. 63), Jesus declares that he is the Christ (alluding to Dan 7:13–14). Describe the immediate—and ultimate—impact of Jesus' words on those present (vv. 65–68).

 Applying the Word 1. When have you been confronted with the weakness of your commitment to the Lord? 2. Both Jesus and the disciples faced temptation in this chapter. How can Jesus' example and the disciples' failures help us withstand temptation and testing?

 Responding in Prayer Ask God to give you the courage to claim allegiance to Christ.

21 / *Matthew 27*
The Crucifixion of the King

MY GOD, MY God, why have you forsaken me?
Why are you so far from saving me, so far from the words of my groaning?
O my God, I cry out by day, but you do not answer, by night, and am not silent. (Ps 22:1–2)
Do you ever feel that God is absent when you need him most? You pray but receive no answer. You cry but no one seems to care. As Pilate and the religious leaders condemn, mock and crucify God's Son, God himself seems strangely absent. Those who trust in the midst of roaring silence will in the end discover that God was there all along.

Warming Up to God When have you felt as though God were absent when you needed him? Talk to God about how you felt.

Read Matthew 27.

27 Early in the morning, all the chief priests and the elders of the people came to the decision to put Jesus to death. ²They bound him, led him away and handed him over to Pilate, the governor.

³When Judas, who had betrayed him, saw that Jesus was condemned, he was seized with remorse and returned the thirty silver coins to the chief priests and the elders. ⁴"I have sinned," he said, "for I have betrayed innocent blood."

"What is that to us?" they replied. "That's your responsibility."

⁵So Judas threw the money into the temple and left. Then he went away and hanged himself.

⁶The chief priests picked up the coins and said, "It is against the law to put this into the treasury, since it is blood money." ⁷So they decided to use

the money to buy the potter's field as a burial place for foreigners. ⁸That is why it has been called the Field of Blood to this day. ⁹Then what was spoken by Jeremiah the prophet was fulfilled: "They took the thirty silver coins, the price set on him by the people of Israel, ¹⁰and they used them to buy the potter's field, as the Lord commanded me."ⁱ

¹¹Meanwhile Jesus stood before the governor, and the governor asked him, "Are you the king of the Jews?"

"Yes, it is as you say," Jesus replied.

¹²When he was accused by the chief priests and the elders, he gave no answer. ¹³Then Pilate asked him, "Don't you hear the testimony they are bringing against you?" ¹⁴But Jesus made no reply,

ⁱ10 See Zech. 11:12,13; Jer. 19:1-13; 32:6-9.

not even to a single charge—to the great amazement of the governor.

15Now it was the governor's custom at the Feast to release a prisoner chosen by the crowd. 16At that time they had a notorious prisoner, called Barabbas. 17So when the crowd had gathered, Pilate asked them, "Which one do you want me to release to you: Barabbas, or Jesus who is called Christ?" 18For he knew it was out of envy that they had handed Jesus over to him.

19While Pilate was sitting on the judge's seat, his wife sent him this message: "Don't have anything to do with that innocent man, for I have suffered a great deal today in a dream because of him."

20But the chief priests and the elders persuaded the crowd to ask for Barabbas and to have Jesus executed.

21"Which of the two do you want me to release to you?" asked the governor.

"Barabbas," they answered.

22"What shall I do, then, with Jesus who is called Christ?" Pilate asked.

They all answered, "Crucify him!"

23"Why? What crime has he committed?" asked Pilate.

But they shouted all the louder, "Crucify him!"

24When Pilate saw that he was getting nowhere, but that instead an uproar was starting, he took water and washed his hands in front of the crowd. "I am innocent of this man's blood," he said. "It is your responsibility!"

25All the people answered, "Let his blood be on us and on our children!"

26Then he released Barabbas to them. But he had Jesus flogged, and handed him over to be crucified.

27Then the governor's soldiers took Jesus into the Praetorium and gathered the whole company of soldiers around him. 28They stripped him and put a scarlet robe on him, 29and then twisted together a crown of thorns and set it on his head. They put a staff in his right hand and knelt in front of him and mocked him. "Hail, king of the Jews!" they said. 30They spit on him, and took the staff and struck him on the head again and again. 31After they had mocked him, they took off the robe and put his own clothes on him. Then they led him away to crucify him.

32As they were going out, they met a man from Cyrene, named Simon, and they forced him to carry the cross. 33They came to a place called Gol-

gotha (which means The Place of the Skull). 34There they offered Jesus wine to drink, mixed with gall; but after tasting it, he refused to drink it. 35When they had crucified him, they divided up his clothes by casting lots.j 36And sitting down, they kept watch over him there. 37Above his head they placed the written charge against him: THIS IS JESUS, THE KING OF THE JEWS. 38Two robbers were crucified with him, one on his right and one on his left. 39Those who passed by hurled insults at him, shaking their heads 40and saying, "You who are going to destroy the temple and build it in three days, save yourself! Come down from the cross, if you are the Son of God!"

41In the same way the chief priests, the teachers of the law and the elders mocked him. 42"He saved others," they said, "but he can't save himself! He's the King of Israel! Let him come down now from the cross, and we will believe in him. 43He trusts in God. Let God rescue him now if he wants him, for he said, 'I am the Son of God.'" 44In the same way the robbers who were crucified with him also heaped insults on him.

45From the sixth hour until the ninth hour darkness came over all the land. 46About the ninth hour Jesus cried out in a loud voice, *"Eloi, Eloi,k lama sabachthani?"*—which means, "My God, my God, why have you forsaken me?"l

47When some of those standing there heard this, they said, "He's calling Elijah."

48Immediately one of them ran and got a sponge. He filled it with wine vinegar, put it on a stick, and offered it to Jesus to drink. 49The rest said, "Now leave him alone. Let's see if Elijah comes to save him."

50And when Jesus had cried out again in a loud voice, he gave up his spirit.

51At that moment the curtain of the temple was torn in two from top to bottom. The earth shook and the rocks split. 52The tombs broke open and the bodies of many holy people who had died were raised to life. 53They came out of the tombs, and after Jesus' resurrection they went into the holy city and appeared to many people.

54When the centurion and those with him who were guarding Jesus saw the earthquake and all that had happened, they were terrified, and exclaimed, "Surely he was the Sonm of God!"

55Many women were there, watching from a

j35 A few late manuscripts *lots that the word spoken by the prophet might be fulfilled: "They divided my garments among themselves and cast lots for my clothing"* (Psalm 22:18)   k46 Some manuscripts *Eli, Eli*   l46 Psalm 22:1   m54 Or *a son*

distance. They had followed Jesus from Galilee to care for his needs. ⁵⁶Among them were Mary Magdalene, Mary the mother of James and Joses, and the mother of Zebedee's sons.

⁵⁷As evening approached, there came a rich man from Arimathea, named Joseph, who had himself become a disciple of Jesus. ⁵⁸Going to Pilate, he asked for Jesus' body, and Pilate ordered that it be given to him. ⁵⁹Joseph took the body, wrapped it in a clean linen cloth, ⁶⁰and placed it in his own new tomb that he had cut out of the rock. He rolled a big stone in front of the entrance to the tomb and went away. ⁶¹Mary Magdalene and the other Mary were sitting there opposite the tomb.

⁶²The next day, the one after Preparation Day, the chief priests and the Pharisees went to Pilate. ⁶³"Sir," they said, "we remember that while he was still alive that deceiver said, 'After three days I will rise again.' ⁶⁴So give the order for the tomb to be made secure until the third day. Otherwise, his disciples may come and steal the body and tell the people that he has been raised from the dead. This last deception will be worse than the first."

⁶⁵"Take a guard," Pilate answered. "Go, make the tomb as secure as you know how." ⁶⁶So they went and made the tomb secure by putting a seal on the stone and posting the guard.

Discovering the Word 1. After the religious leaders hand Jesus over to Pilate, Judas feels remorse (vv. 1–5). How is remorse different from repentance? 2. Jesus stands before Pilate in verses 11–26. How and why does Pilate seek to avoid sentencing Jesus? 3. The soldiers viciously mock Jesus in verses 27–31. What does their mockery reveal about their knowledge of Jesus? 4. As Jesus hangs on the cross, he is repeatedly mocked and insulted (vv. 32–44). How do these insults reveal the spiritual choices these people have made? 5. As death begins to engulf him, Jesus cries out to God (vv. 45–46). What does his cry, and the overshadowing darkness, reveal about his relationship to the Father during this torment? 6. Observe the role Jesus' followers play during the events of his crucifixion and burial (vv. 55–61). How do you think they felt?

Applying the Word 1. This chapter is filled with irony. Satan's "triumph" is actually his defeat. Christ's "defeat" is actually his triumph. How should this challenge our views about the way God works in our lives?

Responding in Prayer Pray for protection so that you won't succumb to social pressure.

---

22 / *Matthew 28*
The Resurrection of the King

VICTORY REQUIRES PROCLAMATION! Once a battle has been won, it's time to spread the word. Matthew 28 focuses on the messengers of Jesus' resurrection—the angel tells the women, the women tell the disciples, the disciples tell the nations, even the guards tell the religious leaders. As Matthew concludes his Gospel, we are invited to join with those who throughout history have been witnesses and messengers of Jesus, the victorious resurrected Lord.

Warming Up to God To prepare for this study, recall the joy of an Easter celebration you have experienced. What elements made that joyful for you?

Read Matthew 28.

---

28 After the Sabbath, at dawn on the first day of the week, Mary Magdalene and the other Mary went to look at the tomb.

²There was a violent earthquake, for an angel of the Lord came down from heaven and, going to the tomb, rolled back the stone and sat on it. ³His appearance was like lightning, and his clothes were white as snow. ⁴The guards were so afraid of him that they shook and became like dead men.

[5]The angel said to the women, "Do not be afraid, for I know that you are looking for Jesus, who was crucified. [6]He is not here; he has risen, just as he said. Come and see the place where he lay. [7]Then go quickly and tell his disciples: 'He has risen from the dead and is going ahead of you into Galilee. There you will see him.' Now I have told you."

[8]So the women hurried away from the tomb, afraid yet filled with joy, and ran to tell his disciples. [9]Suddenly Jesus met them. "Greetings," he said. They came to him, clasped his feet and worshiped him. [10]Then Jesus said to them, "Do not be afraid. Go and tell my brothers to go to Galilee; there they will see me."

[11]While the women were on their way, some of the guards went into the city and reported to the chief priests everything that had happened. [12]When the chief priests had met with the elders and devised a plan, they gave the soldiers a large sum of money, [13]telling them, "You are to say, 'His disciples came during the night and stole him away while we were asleep.' [14]If this report gets to the governor, we will satisfy him and keep you out of trouble." [15]So the soldiers took the money and did as they were instructed. And this story has been widely circulated among the Jews to this very day.

[16]Then the eleven disciples went to Galilee, to the mountain where Jesus had told them to go. [17]When they saw him, they worshiped him; but some doubted. [18]Then Jesus came to them and said, "All authority in heaven and on earth has been given to me. [19]Therefore go and make disciples of all nations, baptizing them in[n] the name of the Father and of the Son and of the Holy Spirit, [20]and teaching them to obey everything I have commanded you. And surely I am with you always, to the very end of the age."

[n]19 Or *into*; see Acts 8:16; 19:5; Romans 6:3; 1 Cor. 1:13; 10:2 and Gal. 3:27.

 Discovering the Word   1. The angel is the first messenger of the resurrection (vv. 2–7). What is the significance of his appearance and words?   2. Consider the mission of the women (vv. 1–9). How does it undergo a radical change?   3. The Roman guard and the Jewish leaders are confronted with a miracle. How do they respond, and why?   4. The disciples go to Galilee where they meet with Jesus. Describe the commission he gives to them and us (vv. 16–20).   5. How does Jesus equip them and future disciples to carry out his commission?

Applying the Word   1. What keeps people today from believing that Jesus is the resurrected Lord?   2. As you conclude this study of Matthew, how can you be more involved in making disciples and fulfilling the Great Commission?

Responding in Prayer   Pray that God will help you to be faithful to this task.

Mark

F ew Americans put much stock in royalty. We have been raised to treasure the spirit of democracy. But democracy, at least on any large scale, is a recent development in human history.

People in other eras were most accustomed to kings. For good or evil, kings and emperors left their mark on daily life. Thus when a new king came to power, whether through natural succession or through victory in battle, questions clamored in people's minds. What would the new king be like? Would he be kind and compassionate or selfish and ruthless? Would he use his power to serve his own ends, or would he seek the welfare of all his subjects?

The Jews of Jesus' day, long oppressed by foreign rulers, yearned for a new king—one whom God himself would anoint and use to establish his own rule of justice and peace, not only over Israel but over all the earth. Imagine the excitement as John the Baptist came announcing the coming of the Lord as king and as Jesus himself announced, "The time has come. The kingdom of God is near." Yet as Jesus continued his ministry, he met a growing wave of opposition. Not everyone was pleased with the kind of kingdom he seemed to be announcing or with who he proclaimed himself to be. The religious rulers especially opposed him, but the common people heard him gladly.

New Testament scholars, with few exceptions, agree that Mark's Gospel is the earliest written account of Jesus' life and ministry. Composed between A.D. 60 and 70, it likely served as the basis for the Gospels of Matthew and Luke. Mark himself, though not one of the Twelve, was probably an early convert (Acts 12:12) and a companion to both Peter (1 Pe 5:13) and Paul. Though Mark had an early falling out with Paul (Acts 15:36–41), the two were clearly reconciled later on (Co 4:10; 2Ti 4:11; Phm 24). Thus Mark is linked to two of the most prominent apostles.

More and more, scholars are coming to believe that Mark was not just a collector of stories about Jesus but that he gave form and shape to these stories to counteract some dangerous distortions of the gospel message. Apparently some Christians so focused on Jesus' deity and glorious resurrection that they began to ignore his humanity and suffering. As a result they expected to be spared suffering in this life and to quickly join Jesus in the glories of heaven. You can well imagine how their faith may have been shaken when Nero took to using some of them as torches!

Mark theologically and pastorally sets out to retell the story of Jesus, showing that the kingdom in its glory comes at the end of the path of suffering and service. While Matthew focuses on Jesus as the teacher from whom we should learn (Mt 11:29; 28:20) and John focuses on him as the Son of God in whom we should believe (Jn 20:31), Mark portrays Jesus principally as the servant-king whom we should follow (Mk 1:17). Thus, if we are to enjoy the glories of the kingdom, we too must follow the road of suffering and service.

May the Lord himself increase your understanding of who he is and the life to which he has called you.

Outline

1/ Mark 1:1–15 ———————————— *Gospel Beginnings*

2/ Mark 1:16–39 ———————————— *Four Portraits*

3/ Mark 1:40—2:17 ———————————— *The Clean and the Unclean*

4/ Mark 2:18—3:35 ———————————— *Conflict in Galilee*

5/ Mark 4:1–34 ———————————— *Kingdom Parables*

6/ Mark 4:35—6:6 ———————————— *Desperate Straits*

7/ Mark 6:6–56 ———————————— *Beyond Burnout*

8/ Mark 7 ———————————— *Violating Tradition*

9/ Mark 8:1—9:1 ———————————— *Who Do You Say I Am?*

10/ Mark 9:2–32 ———————————— *Suffering and Glory*

11/ Mark 9:33–50 ———————————— *The First and the Last*

12/ Mark 10:1–31 ———————————— *Divorce, Children and Eternal Life*

13/ Mark 10:32–52 ———————————— *Blindness and Sight*

14/ Mark 11:1–25 ———————————— *Palm Sunday*

15/ Mark 11:27—12:27 ———————————— *Tempting Questions*

16/ Mark 12:28–44 ———————————— *An End to Questions*

17/ Mark 13 ———————————— *Keep Watch*

18/ Mark 14:1–42 ———————————— *The Betrayer Approaches*

19/ Mark 14:43–72 ———————————— *Betrayed!*

20/ Mark 15:1—16:8 ———————————— *Victory Snatched from Defeat*

1 / *Mark 1:1–15*
Gospel Beginnings

DO YOU HAVE any friends who begin mystery novels at the back? Like endings, beginnings tell us a lot. In them writers set the context for what is to come and often drop hints which later prove to be important. The beginning of Mark's Gospel is no exception. This passage introduces several important themes which will be developed in the following chapters.

 Warming Up to God   What does it mean to you that Jesus is King? What images and feelings does that bring to mind? Meditate on Jesus as King for a while in preparation for reading Mark's Gospel.

 Read Mark 1:1–15.

1 The beginning of the gospel about Jesus Christ, the Son of God.[a]

²It is written in Isaiah the prophet:

"I will send my messenger ahead of you,
who will prepare your way"[b]—
³"a voice of one calling in the desert,
'Prepare the way for the Lord,
make straight paths for him.' "[c]

⁴And so John came, baptizing in the desert region and preaching a baptism of repentance for the forgiveness of sins. ⁵The whole Judean countryside and all the people of Jerusalem went out to him. Confessing their sins, they were baptized by him in the Jordan River. ⁶John wore clothing made of camel's hair, with a leather belt around his waist, and he ate locusts and wild honey. ⁷And this was his message: "After me will come one more powerful than I, the thongs of whose sandals I am not worthy to stoop down and untie. ⁸I baptize you with[d] water, but he will baptize you with the Holy Spirit."

⁹At that time Jesus came from Nazareth in Galilee and was baptized by John in the Jordan. ¹⁰As Jesus was coming up out of the water, he saw heaven being torn open and the Spirit descending on him like a dove. ¹¹And a voice came from heaven: "You are my Son, whom I love; with you I am well pleased."

¹²At once the Spirit sent him out into the desert, ¹³and he was in the desert forty days, being tempted by Satan. He was with the wild animals, and angels attended him.

¹⁴After John was put in prison, Jesus went into Galilee, proclaiming the good news of God. ¹⁵"The time has come," he said. "The kingdom of God is near. Repent and believe the good news!"

---

[a]1 Some manuscripts do not have *the Son of God.*   [b]2 Mal. 3:1   [c]3 Isaiah 40:3   [d]8 Or *in*

 Discovering the Word   1. Verses 2 and 3 combine quotations from Malachi and Isaiah. What do these two quotations have in common?   2. How does John's ministry prepare the way for Jesus?   3. How does John emphasize the greatness of the one who will come after him (vv. 7–8)?   4. Despite his greatness, Jesus came to John for baptism. What does this tell us about Jesus' relationship to us?   5. How do the events surrounding Jesus' baptism prepare him for his temptation in the desert?   6. How does Jesus summarize his mission at the beginning of his ministry?

 Applying the Word   1. What temptations are you currently struggling with?   2. What encouragement do you find here for facing your own temptations?

Responding in Prayer   Ask God to help you find the encouragement and strength you need to face temptation.

2 / *Mark 1:16–39*
Four Portraits

WE ALL LIVE with authority—whether supervisors, professors, parents or police. And depending on how that authority is exercised, we feel either put upon, trapped and used, or we feel secure, free and useful.

In 1:1–15 Mark has told us that Jesus has come as king to fulfill the Old Testament longings for the Lord's rule over all the earth. But what kind of king is he? Mark, it seems, knows that a picture is worth a thousand words. So, rather than offering an abstract character analysis, he paints four verbal portraits of Jesus in action.

 Warming Up to God In this passage we see Jesus going to a solitary place to pray after a busy day of ministry. But even here he is interrupted with more needs. When have you been in that kind of situation? Ask God to help you balance your need to be with him with the needs of others.

 Read Mark 1:16–39.

---

¹⁶As Jesus walked beside the Sea of Galilee, he saw Simon and his brother Andrew casting a net into the lake, for they were fishermen. ¹⁷"Come, follow me," Jesus said, "and I will make you fishers of men." ¹⁸At once they left their nets and followed him.

¹⁹When he had gone a little farther, he saw James son of Zebedee and his brother John in a boat, preparing their nets. ²⁰Without delay he called them, and they left their father Zebedee in the boat with the hired men and followed him.

²¹They went to Capernaum, and when the Sabbath came, Jesus went into the synagogue and began to teach. ²²The people were amazed at his teaching, because he taught them as one who had authority, not as the teachers of the law. ²³Just then a man in their synagogue who was possessed by an evil*ᶜ* spirit cried out, ²⁴"What do you want with us, Jesus of Nazareth? Have you come to destroy us? I know who you are—the Holy One of God!"

²⁵"Be quiet!" said Jesus sternly. "Come out of him!" ²⁶The evil spirit shook the man violently and came out of him with a shriek.

²⁷The people were all so amazed that they asked each other, "What is this? A new teaching—and with authority! He even gives orders to evil spirits and they obey him." ²⁸News about him spread quickly over the whole region of Galilee.

²⁹As soon as they left the synagogue, they went with James and John to the home of Simon and Andrew. ³⁰Simon's mother-in-law was in bed with a fever, and they told Jesus about her. ³¹So he went to her, took her hand and helped her up. The fever left her and she began to wait on them.

³²That evening after sunset the people brought to Jesus all the sick and demon-possessed. ³³The whole town gathered at the door, ³⁴and Jesus healed many who had various diseases. He also drove out many demons, but he would not let the demons speak because they knew who he was.

³⁵Very early in the morning, while it was still dark, Jesus got up, left the house and went off to a solitary place, where he prayed. ³⁶Simon and his companions went to look for him, ³⁷and when they found him, they exclaimed: "Everyone is looking for you!"

³⁸Jesus replied, "Let us go somewhere else—to the nearby villages—so I can preach there also. That is why I have come." ³⁹So he traveled throughout Galilee, preaching in their synagogues and driving out demons.

ᶜ23 Greek unclean; also in verses 26 and 27

Discovering the Word 1. What different factors contributed to the ready response of Simon, Andrew, James and John to Jesus' invitation (vv. 16–20)? (Don't forget 1:1–15!) 2. What might be some of the reasons that Jesus silences the demon about who he is (vv. 21–28)? 3. What impression of Jesus do you get from the portrait of his visit to the home of Simon and Andrew (vv. 29–34)? 4. Thus far we have looked at three portraits of Jesus. What aspects of Jesus' character do we see in them? 5. How does Jesus exercise his authority differently from kings and dictators and other human authorities? 6. The quiet and solitude of verses 35–39 are quite a contrast from the previous events. What do these verses reveal about Jesus' priorities?

Applying the Word 1. How do you respond to Jesus' authority? 2. Jesus' priorities are clear in this passage. What steps do you need to take to bring your priorities more closely in line with his?

Responding in Prayer Ask God to help you reevaluate your priorities in light of Jesus' kingship.

3 / Mark 1:40—2:17
The Clean and the Unclean

"UNCLEAN! UNCLEAN!" THE man shouted, and everyone scattered to avoid contact with the leper—everyone except Jesus.

The religious wisdom of the day demanded that a holy man keep away from the common people, the "sinners." So Jesus was bound to encounter resistance as he openly welcomed them. This passage focuses on Christ's compassion toward those we normally avoid.

Warming Up to God What is it about yourself that you feel is "unclean"? Confess your sins to God and hear him declare you to be clean once again.

Read Mark 1:40—2:17.

---

⁴⁰A man with leprosy*ᶠ* came to him and begged him on his knees, "If you are willing, you can make me clean."

⁴¹Filled with compassion, Jesus reached out his hand and touched the man. "I am willing," he said. "Be clean!" ⁴²Immediately the leprosy left him and he was cured.

⁴³Jesus sent him away at once with a strong warning: ⁴⁴"See that you don't tell this to anyone. But go, show yourself to the priest and offer the sacrifices that Moses commanded for your cleansing, as a testimony to them." ⁴⁵Instead he went out and began to talk freely, spreading the news. As a result, Jesus could no longer enter a town openly but stayed outside in lonely places. Yet the people still came to him from everywhere.

2 A few days later, when Jesus again entered Capernaum, the people heard that he had come home. ²So many gathered that there was no room left, not even outside the door, and he preached the word to them. ³Some men came, bringing to him a paralytic, carried by four of them. ⁴Since they could not get him to Jesus because of the crowd, they made an opening in the roof above Jesus and, after digging through it, lowered the mat the paralyzed man was lying on. ⁵When Jesus saw their faith, he said to the paralytic, "Son, your sins are forgiven."

⁶Now some teachers of the law were sitting there, thinking to themselves, ⁷"Why does this fellow talk like that? He's blaspheming! Who can forgive sins but God alone?"

⁸Immediately Jesus knew in his spirit that this was what they were thinking in their hearts, and he said to them, "Why are you thinking these things? ⁹Which is easier: to say to the paralytic, 'Your sins are forgiven,' or to say, 'Get up, take your mat and walk'? ¹⁰But that you may know that the Son of Man has authority on earth to forgive sins . . . ." He said to the paralytic, ¹¹"I tell you, get up, take your mat and go home." ¹²He got up, took his mat and walked out in full view of them all. This amazed everyone and they praised God, saying, "We have never seen anything like this!"

¹³Once again Jesus went out beside the lake. A large crowd came to him, and he began to teach them. ¹⁴As he walked along, he saw Levi son of Alphaeus sitting at the tax collector's booth. "Follow me," Jesus told him, and Levi got up and followed him.

¹⁵While Jesus was having dinner at Levi's house, many tax collectors and "sinners" were eating with him and his disciples, for there were many who followed him. ¹⁶When the teachers of the law who were Pharisees saw him eating with

ᶠ40 The Greek word was used for various diseases affecting the skin—not necessarily leprosy.

the "sinners" and tax collectors, they asked his disciples: "Why does he eat with tax collectors and 'sinners'?"

[17]On hearing this, Jesus said to them, "It is not the healthy who need a doctor, but the sick. I have not come to call the righteous, but sinners."

 Discovering the Word 1. Leviticus 13:45–46 states that a leper "must wear torn clothes, let his hair be unkempt, cover the lower part of his face and cry out, 'Unclean! Unclean!' As long as he has the infection he remains unclean. He must live alone; he must live outside the camp." What risks did the leper take in coming to Jesus (1:40–45)? 2. What risks did Jesus take in responding to him as he did? 3. How does Jesus respond to the man's total need? 4. Imagine that you are the paralytic being lowered before Jesus (2:1–12). How do you feel, especially when Jesus announces, "Son, your sins are forgiven"? 5. Contrast the Pharisees' attitude toward tax collectors and "sinners" with that of Jesus.

 Applying the Word 1. Who do you consider to be some of the "unlovely" or "unreachable" for God's kingdom? 2. What steps can you take to bring your thoughts and actions toward them into line with those of Jesus?

 Responding in Prayer Ask Jesus to help you see people as he does and act toward them as he would.

---

4 / *Mark 2:18—3:35*
Conflict in Galilee

"A TRULY RELIGIOUS person wouldn't do such a thing!"
  "Religion is fine, but you're becoming a fanatic!"
  Such accusations are commonly leveled at Christians. They are difficult to bear under any circumstances. But when they come from family and friends, the pain is even greater. This passage looks at some of the pressures and privileges of following Jesus.

Warming Up to God In what area of your life are you currently facing pressure or conflict? Ask God to provide you with the strength you need in that situation through his Word and the Holy Spirit.

Read Mark 2:18—3:35.

---

[18]Now John's disciples and the Pharisees were fasting. Some people came and asked Jesus, "How is it that John's disciples and the disciples of the Pharisees are fasting, but yours are not?"

[19]Jesus answered, "How can the guests of the bridegroom fast while he is with them? They cannot, so long as they have him with them. [20]But the time will come when the bridegroom will be taken from them, and on that day they will fast.

[21]"No one sews a patch of unshrunk cloth on an old garment. If he does, the new piece will pull away from the old, making the tear worse. [22]And no one pours new wine into old wineskins. If he does, the wine will burst the skins, and both the wine and the wineskins will be ruined. No, he pours new wine into new wineskins."

[23]One Sabbath Jesus was going through the grainfields, and as his disciples walked along, they began to pick some heads of grain. [24]The Pharisees said to him, "Look, why are they doing what is unlawful on the Sabbath?"

[25]He answered, "Have you never read what David did when he and his companions were hungry and in need? [26]In the days of Abiathar the high priest, he entered the house of God and ate the consecrated bread, which is lawful only for priests to eat. And he also gave some to his companions."

[27]Then he said to them, "The Sabbath was made for man, not man for the Sabbath. [28]So the Son of Man is Lord even of the Sabbath."

3 Another time he went into the synagogue, and a man with a shriveled hand was there. ²Some of them were looking for a reason to accuse Jesus, so they watched him closely to see if he would heal him on the Sabbath. ³Jesus said to the man with the shriveled hand, "Stand up in front of everyone."

⁴Then Jesus asked them, "Which is lawful on the Sabbath: to do good or to do evil, to save life or to kill?" But they remained silent.

⁵He looked around at them in anger and, deeply distressed at their stubborn hearts, said to the man, "Stretch out your hand." He stretched it out, and his hand was completely restored. ⁶Then the Pharisees went out and began to plot with the Herodians how they might kill Jesus.

⁷Jesus withdrew with his disciples to the lake, and a large crowd from Galilee followed. ⁸When they heard all he was doing, many people came to him from Judea, Jerusalem, Idumea, and the regions across the Jordan and around Tyre and Sidon. ⁹Because of the crowd he told his disciples to have a small boat ready for him, to keep the people from crowding him. ¹⁰For he had healed many, so that those with diseases were pushing forward to touch him. ¹¹Whenever the evil*g* spirits saw him, they fell down before him and cried out, "You are the Son of God." ¹²But he gave them strict orders not to tell who he was.

¹³Jesus went up on a mountainside and called to him those he wanted, and they came to him. ¹⁴He appointed twelve—designating them apostles*h*—that they might be with him and that he might send them out to preach ¹⁵and to have authority to drive out demons. ¹⁶These are the twelve he appointed: Simon (to whom he gave the name Peter); ¹⁷James son of Zebedee and his brother John (to them he gave the name Boanerges, which means Sons of Thunder); ¹⁸Andrew, Philip, Bartholomew, Matthew, Thomas, James son of Alphaeus, Thaddaeus, Simon the Zealot ¹⁹and Judas Iscariot, who betrayed him.

²⁰Then Jesus entered a house, and again a crowd gathered, so that he and his disciples were not even able to eat. ²¹When his family heard about this, they went to take charge of him, for they said, "He is out of his mind."

²²And the teachers of the law who came down from Jerusalem said, "He is possessed by Beelzebub*i*! By the prince of demons he is driving out demons."

²³So Jesus called them and spoke to them in parables: "How can Satan drive out Satan? ²⁴If a kingdom is divided against itself, that kingdom cannot stand. ²⁵If a house is divided against itself, that house cannot stand. ²⁶And if Satan opposes himself and is divided, he cannot stand; his end has come. ²⁷In fact, no one can enter a strong man's house and carry off his possessions unless he first ties up the strong man. Then he can rob his house. ²⁸I tell you the truth, all the sins and blasphemies of men will be forgiven them. ²⁹But whoever blasphemes against the Holy Spirit will never be forgiven; he is guilty of an eternal sin."

³⁰He said this because they were saying, "He has an evil spirit."

³¹Then Jesus' mother and brothers arrived. Standing outside, they sent someone in to call him. ³²A crowd was sitting around him, and they told him, "Your mother and brothers are outside looking for you."

³³"Who are my mother and my brothers?" he asked.

³⁴Then he looked at those seated in a circle around him and said, "Here are my mother and my brothers! ³⁵Whoever does God's will is my brother and sister and mother."

g11 Greek unclean; also in verse 30   h14 Some manuscripts do not have designating them apostles.   i22 Greek Beezeboul or Beelzeboul

---

 Discovering the Word 1. On what grounds are Jesus and his disciples criticized in 2:18—3:6? 2. How are Jesus' and the Pharisees' attitudes toward the Sabbath different? 3. While the Pharisees and the Herodians are plotting to kill Jesus, how are the common people responding to him (3:7–12)? 4. What charge do the teachers of the law bring against Jesus in 3:20–30? 5. How does Jesus refute it?

Applying the Word 1. What types of opposition have you encountered as a Christian? 2. How have you dealt with experiences of opposition? 3. When you are opposed or rejected by those who are closest to you, what comfort can you receive from Jesus' words in verses 33–35?

Responding in Prayer Ask God to give you courage to follow him even when others stand against you.

5 / *Mark 4:1–34*
Kingdom Parables

SOME STORIES WEAR their points on their sleeves, as it were. Others, to borrow from P. G. Wodehouse's definition of a parable, keep something up their sleeves "which suddenly pops up and knocks you flat." Among Jesus' stories we find a variety—from those that are easy to understand to those that are so difficult they invite our thought and reflection again and again. The stories in this passage contain vital information about God's kingdom and its subjects—for those who have ears to hear!

 Warming Up to God What aspect in your life makes it difficult for you to hear the voice of Christ? Talk to Jesus about the barriers you face and ask him to show you how to remove them.

 Read Mark 4:1–34.

4Again Jesus began to teach by the lake. The crowd that gathered around him was so large that he got into a boat and sat in it out on the lake, while all the people were along the shore at the water's edge. ²He taught them many things by parables, and in his teaching said: ³"Listen! A farmer went out to sow his seed. ⁴As he was scattering the seed, some fell along the path, and the birds came and ate it up. ⁵Some fell on rocky places, where it did not have much soil. It sprang up quickly, because the soil was shallow. ⁶But when the sun came up, the plants were scorched, and they withered because they had no root. ⁷Other seed fell among thorns, which grew up and choked the plants, so that they did not bear grain. ⁸Still other seed fell on good soil. It came up, grew and produced a crop, multiplying thirty, sixty, or even a hundred times."

⁹Then Jesus said, "He who has ears to hear, let him hear."

¹⁰When he was alone, the Twelve and the others around him asked him about the parables. ¹¹He told them, "The secret of the kingdom of God has been given to you. But to those on the outside everything is said in parables ¹²so that,

" 'they may be ever seeing but never
        perceiving,
    and ever hearing but never understanding;
  otherwise they might turn and be
        forgiven!'ʲ"

¹³Then Jesus said to them, "Don't you understand this parable? How then will you understand any parable? ¹⁴The farmer sows the word. ¹⁵Some people are like seed along the path, where the word is sown. As soon as they hear it, Satan comes and takes away the word that was sown in them. ¹⁶Others, like seed sown on rocky places, hear the word and at once receive it with joy. ¹⁷But since they have no root, they last only a short time. When trouble or persecution comes because of the word, they quickly fall away. ¹⁸Still others, like seed sown among thorns, hear the word; ¹⁹but the worries of this life, the deceitfulness of wealth and the desires for other things come in and choke the word, making it unfruitful. ²⁰Others, like seed sown on good soil, hear the word, accept it, and produce a crop—thirty, sixty or even a hundred times what was sown."

²¹He said to them, "Do you bring in a lamp to put it under a bowl or a bed? Instead, don't you put it on its stand? ²²For whatever is hidden is meant to be disclosed, and whatever is concealed is meant to be brought out into the open. ²³If anyone has ears to hear, let him hear."

²⁴"Consider carefully what you hear," he continued. "With the measure you use, it will be measured to you—and even more. ²⁵Whoever has will be given more; whoever does not have, even what he has will be taken from him."

²⁶He also said, "This is what the kingdom of God is like. A man scatters seed on the ground. ²⁷Night and day, whether he sleeps or gets up, the seed sprouts and grows, though he does not know how. ²⁸All by itself the soil produces grain—first the stalk, then the head, then the full kernel in the head. ²⁹As soon as the grain is ripe, he puts the sickle to it, because the harvest has come."

³⁰Again he said, "What shall we say the kingdom of God is like, or what parable shall we use to describe it? ³¹It is like a mustard seed, which is the smallest seed you plant in the ground. ³²Yet

ʲ12 Isaiah 6:9,10

when planted, it grows and becomes the largest of all garden plants, with such big branches that the birds of the air can perch in its shade."

33With many similar parables Jesus spoke the word to them, as much as they could understand. 34He did not say anything to them without using a parable. But when he was alone with his own disciples, he explained everything.

Discovering the Word 1. Watch especially for words and phrases that are repeated in verses 1–25. What idea or ideas seem to dominate these verses? 2. Jesus explains the parable of the sower, or the parable of the soils (vv. 3–8), in verses 14–20. Put this explanation in your own words, describing from your own experience examples of each kind of soil-seed combination. 3. On what grounds are people included or excluded from the secret of the kingdom? 4. How do verses 21–25 help explain verses 11–12? 5. What insights into kingdom growth do the parables of the growing seed and the mustard seed give us (vv. 26–34)?

Applying the Word 1. What kind of soil are you? 2. What can you do to become the kind of soil Jesus is looking for? 3. In this passage we see Jesus both spreading the message of the kingdom and teaching about how the kingdom grows. What lessons can we learn about evangelism both from his example and from his teaching?

Responding in Prayer Ask Jesus to work in you to make you receptive soil.

6 / Mark 4:35—6:6
Desperate Straits

"DON'T BE AFRAID; just believe." These words may ring rather hollow when we, and not someone else, face a fearful or life-threatening situation. Yet in the face of real danger we discover just how much faith we have. In this study we find a number of different people in desperate straits. Their experiences with Jesus can help us to trust him with the fearful areas of our own lives.

Warming Up to God When do you feel afraid? Reflect on these words from Isaiah 12:2: "Surely God is my salvation; I will trust and not be afraid." Allow God to comfort you.

Read Mark 4:35—6:6.

35That day when evening came, he said to his disciples, "Let us go over to the other side." 36Leaving the crowd behind, they took him along, just as he was, in the boat. There were also other boats with him. 37A furious squall came up, and the waves broke over the boat, so that it was nearly swamped. 38Jesus was in the stern, sleeping on a cushion. The disciples woke him and said to him, "Teacher, don't you care if we drown?"

39He got up, rebuked the wind and said to the waves, "Quiet! Be still!" Then the wind died down and it was completely calm.

40He said to his disciples, "Why are you so afraid? Do you still have no faith?"

41They were terrified and asked each other,

"Who is this? Even the wind and the waves obey him!"

5 They went across the lake to the region of the Gerasenes.k 2When Jesus got out of the boat, a man with an evill spirit came from the tombs to meet him. 3This man lived in the tombs, and no one could bind him any more, not even with a chain. 4For he had often been chained hand and foot, but he tore the chains apart and broke the irons on his feet. No one was strong enough to subdue him. 5Night and day among the tombs and in the hills he would cry out and cut himself with stones.

6When he saw Jesus from a distance, he ran and fell on his knees in front of him. 7He shouted

---

k1 Some manuscripts *Gadarenes*; other manuscripts *Gergesenes*
l2 Greek *unclean*; also in verses 8 and 13

at the top of his voice, "What do you want with me, Jesus, Son of the Most High God? Swear to God that you won't torture me!" 8For Jesus had said to him, "Come out of this man, you evil spirit!"

9Then Jesus asked him, "What is your name?"

"My name is Legion," he replied, "for we are many." 10And he begged Jesus again and again not to send them out of the area.

11A large herd of pigs was feeding on the nearby hillside. 12The demons begged Jesus, "Send us among the pigs; allow us to go into them." 13He gave them permission, and the evil spirits came out and went into the pigs. The herd, about two thousand in number, rushed down the steep bank into the lake and were drowned.

14Those tending the pigs ran off and reported this in the town and countryside, and the people went out to see what had happened. 15When they came to Jesus, they saw the man who had been possessed by the legion of demons, sitting there, dressed and in his right mind; and they were afraid. 16Those who had seen it told the people what had happened to the demon-possessed man—and told about the pigs as well. 17Then the people began to plead with Jesus to leave their region.

18As Jesus was getting into the boat, the man who had been demon-possessed begged to go with him. 19Jesus did not let him, but said, "Go home to your family and tell them how much the Lord has done for you, and how he has had mercy on you." 20So the man went away and began to tell in the Decapolis^m how much Jesus had done for him. And all the people were amazed.

21When Jesus had again crossed over by boat to the other side of the lake, a large crowd gathered around him while he was by the lake. 22Then one of the synagogue rulers, named Jairus, came there. Seeing Jesus, he fell at his feet 23and pleaded earnestly with him, "My little daughter is dying. Please come and put your hands on her so that she will be healed and live." 24So Jesus went with him.

A large crowd followed and pressed around him. 25And a woman was there who had been subject to bleeding for twelve years. 26She had suffered a great deal under the care of many doctors and had spent all she had, yet instead of getting better she grew worse. 27When she heard about Jesus, she came up behind him in the crowd and touched his cloak, 28because she

thought, "If I just touch his clothes, I will be healed." 29Immediately her bleeding stopped and she felt in her body that she was freed from her suffering.

30At once Jesus realized that power had gone out from him. He turned around in the crowd and asked, "Who touched my clothes?"

31"You see the people crowding against you," his disciples answered, "and yet you can ask, 'Who touched me?' "

32But Jesus kept looking around to see who had done it. 33Then the woman, knowing what had happened to her, came and fell at his feet and, trembling with fear, told him the whole truth. 34He said to her, "Daughter, your faith has healed you. Go in peace and be freed from your suffering."

35While Jesus was still speaking, some men came from the house of Jairus, the synagogue ruler. "Your daughter is dead," they said. "Why bother the teacher any more?"

36Ignoring what they said, Jesus told the synagogue ruler, "Don't be afraid; just believe."

37He did not let anyone follow him except Peter, James and John the brother of James. 38When they came to the home of the synagogue ruler, Jesus saw a commotion, with people crying and wailing loudly. 39He went in and said to them, "Why all this commotion and wailing? The child is not dead but asleep." 40But they laughed at him.

After he put them all out, he took the child's father and mother and the disciples who were with him, and went in where the child was. 41He took her by the hand and said to her, *"Talitha koum!"* (which means, "Little girl, I say to you, get up!"). 42Immediately the girl stood up and walked around (she was twelve years old). At this they were completely astonished. 43He gave strict orders not to let anyone know about this, and told them to give her something to eat.

6 Jesus left there and went to his hometown, accompanied by his disciples. 2When the Sabbath came, he began to teach in the synagogue, and many who heard him were amazed.

"Where did this man get these things?" they asked. "What's this wisdom that has been given him, that he even does miracles! 3Isn't this the carpenter? Isn't this Mary's son and the brother of

m20 That is, the Ten Cities

James, Joseph,ⁿ Judas and Simon? Aren't his sisters here with us?" And they took offense at him.

⁴Jesus said to them, "Only in his hometown, among his relatives and in his own house is a prophet without honor." ⁵He could not do any

miracles there, except lay his hands on a few sick people and heal them. ⁶And he was amazed at their lack of faith.

ⁿ3 Greek *Joses,* a variant of *Joseph*

Discovering the Word 1. In the first incident the disciples are quite naturally afraid of the storm and disturbed that Jesus seems not to be concerned about their drowning. Once Jesus calms the storm, however, they are still terrified. How does their fear after the storm differ from their previous fears? 2. Who in the next incident is afraid and why (5:1–20)? 3. Many people find it hard to understand why Jesus allowed the demons to destroy the pigs. It could have been to prevent a violent exit from the man or to show him visibly that he was now free. Even if we can't pin down exactly why Jesus allowed this, what does the fate of the pigs show about what the demons were trying to do to the man? 4. In 5:21–43 two stories are woven together—that of Jairus's daughter and the woman with a hemorrhage. What sorts of fears are involved in these two incidents? 5. What are the relationships between fear and faith in each of these incidents?

Applying the Word 1. Fear can be a very powerful emotion. What kinds of fear keep you from doing some things you think you should? 2. What keeps you from turning your fears into faith? 3. How can Jesus' authority as shown here calm your fears and strengthen your faith?

Responding in Prayer Pray for your fears to become increased faith.

---

7 / *Mark 6:6–56*
Beyond Burnout

BURNOUT IS ALL too common an experience among Christians today. One of its most disastrous consequences is a hardened heart that keeps us from being refreshed by our Lord. In this study we see the disciples suffering from burnout and catch a vision of how Jesus can help us to counteract its effects.

Warming Up to God What is pressing on you and taking away your energy? Ask God to refresh your spirit and renew your commitment. Then consider how you could better handle your responsibilities.

Read Mark 6:6–56.

Then Jesus went around teaching from village to village. ⁷Calling the Twelve to him, he sent them out two by two and gave them authority over evilᵒ spirits.

⁸These were his instructions: "Take nothing for the journey except a staff—no bread, no bag, no money in your belts. ⁹Wear sandals but not an extra tunic. ¹⁰Whenever you enter a house, stay there until you leave that town. ¹¹And if any place will not welcome you or listen to you, shake the dust off your feet when you leave, as a testimony against them."

¹²They went out and preached that people should repent. ¹³They drove out many demons

and anointed many sick people with oil and healed them.

¹⁴King Herod heard about this, for Jesus' name had become well known. Some were saying,ᵖ "John the Baptist has been raised from the dead, and that is why miraculous powers are at work in him."

¹⁵Others said, "He is Elijah."

And still others claimed, "He is a prophet, like one of the prophets of long ago."

¹⁶But when Herod heard this, he said, "John, the man I beheaded, has been raised from the dead!"

¹⁷For Herod himself had given orders to have

ᵒ7 Greek *unclean*   ᵖ14 Some early manuscripts *He was saying*

John arrested, and he had him bound and put in prison. He did this because of Herodias, his brother Philip's wife, whom he had married. 18For John had been saying to Herod, "It is not lawful for you to have your brother's wife." 19So Herodias nursed a grudge against John and wanted to kill him. But she was not able to, 20because Herod feared John and protected him, knowing him to be a righteous and holy man. When Herod heard John, he was greatly puzzled*q*; yet he liked to listen to him.

21Finally the opportune time came. On his birthday Herod gave a banquet for his high officials and military commanders and the leading men of Galilee. 22When the daughter of Herodias came in and danced, she pleased Herod and his dinner guests.

The king said to the girl, "Ask me for anything you want, and I'll give it to you." 23And he promised her with an oath, "Whatever you ask I will give you, up to half my kingdom."

24She went out and said to her mother, "What shall I ask for?"

"The head of John the Baptist," she answered.

25At once the girl hurried in to the king with the request: "I want you to give me right now the head of John the Baptist on a platter."

26The king was greatly distressed, but because of his oaths and his dinner guests, he did not want to refuse her. 27So he immediately sent an executioner with orders to bring John's head. The man went, beheaded John in the prison, 28and brought back his head on a platter. He presented it to the girl, and she gave it to her mother. 29On hearing of this, John's disciples came and took his body and laid it in a tomb.

30The apostles gathered around Jesus and reported to him all they had done and taught. 31Then, because so many people were coming and going that they did not even have a chance to eat, he said to them, "Come with me by yourselves to a quiet place and get some rest."

32So they went away by themselves in a boat to a solitary place. 33But many who saw them leaving recognized them and ran on foot from all the towns and got there ahead of them. 34When Jesus landed and saw a large crowd, he had compassion on them, because they were like sheep without a shepherd. So he began teaching them many things.

35By this time it was late in the day, so his disciples came to him. "This is a remote place," they said, "and it's already very late. 36Send the people away so they can go to the surrounding countryside and villages and buy themselves something to eat."

37But he answered, "You give them something to eat."

They said to him, "That would take eight months of a man's wages*r*! Are we to go and spend that much on bread and give it to them to eat?"

38"How many loaves do you have?" he asked. "Go and see."

When they found out, they said, "Five—and two fish."

39Then Jesus directed them to have all the people sit down in groups on the green grass. 40So they sat down in groups of hundreds and fifties. 41Taking the five loaves and the two fish and looking up to heaven, he gave thanks and broke the loaves. Then he gave them to his disciples to set before the people. He also divided the two fish among them all. 42They all ate and were satisfied, 43and the disciples picked up twelve basketfuls of broken pieces of bread and fish. 44The number of the men who had eaten was five thousand.

45Immediately Jesus made his disciples get into the boat and go on ahead of him to Bethsaida, while he dismissed the crowd. 46After leaving them, he went up on a mountainside to pray.

47When evening came, the boat was in the middle of the lake, and he was alone on land. 48He saw the disciples straining at the oars, because the wind was against them. About the fourth watch of the night he went out to them, walking on the lake. He was about to pass by them, 49but when they saw him walking on the lake, they thought he was a ghost. They cried out, 50because they all saw him and were terrified.

Immediately he spoke to them and said, "Take courage! It is I. Don't be afraid." 51Then he climbed into the boat with them, and the wind died down. They were completely amazed, 52for they had not understood about the loaves; their hearts were hardened.

53When they had crossed over, they landed at Gennesaret and anchored there. 54As soon as they got out of the boat, people recognized Jesus. 55They ran throughout that whole region and carried the sick on mats to wherever they heard he was. 56And wherever he went—into villages,

q20 Some early manuscripts he did many things   *r37 Greek take two hundred denarii*

towns or countryside—they placed the sick in the marketplaces. They begged him to let them touch even the edge of his cloak, and all who touched him were healed.

 Discovering the Word 1. What do Jesus' instructions to the Twelve tell us about the kind of ministry they were to have (vv. 6–13)? 2. What kind of man was Herod (vv. 14–29)? 3. This flashback to the execution of John the Baptist interrupts the account of Jesus' sending out the Twelve to preach and heal. Why do you suppose Mark recounts it here? 4. What differences are there between Jesus' approach to the crowd and that of his disciples (vv. 30–44)? 5. Jesus and Herod, the two kings in this passage, both serve banquets. Compare the two.

 Applying the Word 1. When has tiredness blunted your desire to care for others? 2. Recognizing the contributing factors, what steps can you take to counteract burnout and a hardened heart?

Responding in Prayer Ask God to help you to give of yourself while maintaining balance in your life so that you don't burn out.

---

8 / *Mark 7*
Violating Tradition

ALL OF US are influenced by traditions of one sort or another—even those of us who *by tradition* don't put much stock in them! But at what point do traditions lose their value or even become counterproductive? When do religious practices become a substitute for really obeying God? In this study Jesus has some rather harsh words for the Pharisees and the traditions they choose to observe.

 Warming Up to God Consider your spiritual life. Are there any aspects of your devotional practices that you feel bound to? Consider before God whether you are putting unrealistic expectations on yourself.

 Read Mark 7.

---

7 The Pharisees and some of the teachers of the law who had come from Jerusalem gathered around Jesus and ²saw some of his disciples eating food with hands that were "unclean," that is, unwashed. ³(The Pharisees and all the Jews do not eat unless they give their hands a ceremonial washing, holding to the tradition of the elders. ⁴When they come from the marketplace they do not eat unless they wash. And they observe many other traditions, such as the washing of cups, pitchers and kettles.ˢ)

⁵So the Pharisees and teachers of the law asked Jesus, "Why don't your disciples live according to the tradition of the elders instead of eating their food with 'unclean' hands?"

⁶He replied, "Isaiah was right when he prophesied about you hypocrites; as it is written:

" 'These people honor me with their lips,
    but their hearts are far from me.
⁷They worship me in vain;

their teachings are but rules taught by
    men.'ᵗ

⁸You have let go of the commands of God and are holding on to the traditions of men."

⁹And he said to them: "You have a fine way of setting aside the commands of God in order to observeᵘ your own traditions! ¹⁰For Moses said, 'Honor your father and your mother,'ᵛ and, 'Anyone who curses his father or mother must be put to death.'ʷ ¹¹But you say that if a man says to his father or mother: 'Whatever help you might otherwise have received from me is Corban' (that is, a gift devoted to God), ¹²then you no longer let him do anything for his father or mother. ¹³Thus you nullify the word of God by your tradition that you have handed down. And you do many things like that."

¹⁴Again Jesus called the crowd to him and said,

ˢ4 Some early manuscripts *pitchers, kettles and dining couches*
ᵗ6,7 Isaiah 29:13   ᵘ9 Some manuscripts *set up*   ᵛ10 Exodus 20:12; Deut. 5:16   ʷ10 Exodus 21:17; Lev. 20:9

"Listen to me, everyone, and understand this. 15Nothing outside a man can make him 'unclean' by going into him. Rather, it is what comes out of a man that makes him 'unclean.'*x*"

17After he had left the crowd and entered the house, his disciples asked him about this parable. 18"Are you so dull?" he asked. "Don't you see that nothing that enters a man from the outside can make him 'unclean'? 19For it doesn't go into his heart but into his stomach, and then out of his body." (In saying this, Jesus declared all foods "clean.")

20He went on: "What comes out of a man is what makes him 'unclean.' 21For from within, out of men's hearts, come evil thoughts, sexual immorality, theft, murder, adultery, 22greed, malice, deceit, lewdness, envy, slander, arrogance and folly. 23All these evils come from inside and make a man 'unclean.' "

24Jesus left that place and went to the vicinity of Tyre.*y* He entered a house and did not want anyone to know it; yet he could not keep his presence secret. 25In fact, as soon as she heard about him, a woman whose little daughter was possessed by an evil*z* spirit came and fell at his feet. 26The woman was a Greek, born in Syrian Phoenicia. She begged Jesus to drive the demon out of her daughter.

27"First let the children eat all they want," he told her, "for it is not right to take the children's bread and toss it to their dogs."

28"Yes, Lord," she replied, "but even the dogs under the table eat the children's crumbs."

29Then he told her, "For such a reply, you may go; the demon has left your daughter."

30She went home and found her child lying on the bed, and the demon gone.

31Then Jesus left the vicinity of Tyre and went through Sidon, down to the Sea of Galilee and into the region of the Decapolis.*a* 32There some people brought to him a man who was deaf and could hardly talk, and they begged him to place his hand on the man.

33After he took him aside, away from the crowd, Jesus put his fingers into the man's ears. Then he spit and touched the man's tongue. 34He looked up to heaven and with a deep sigh said to him, *"Ephphatha!"* (which means, "Be opened!"). 35At this, the man's ears were opened, his tongue was loosened and he began to speak plainly.

36Jesus commanded them not to tell anyone. But the more he did so, the more they kept talking about it. 37People were overwhelmed with amazement. "He has done everything well," they said. "He even makes the deaf hear and the mute speak."

x15 Some early manuscripts *'unclean.'* 16*If anyone has ears to hear, let him hear.*   y24 Many early manuscripts *Tyre and Sidon*   z25 Greek *unclean*   a31 That is, the Ten Cities

---

Discovering the Word 1. What are the Pharisees concerned about (vv. 1–5)? 2. What specific complaints does Jesus raise against the Pharisees' approach to tradition (vv. 6–13)? 3. How does Jesus' view of becoming "unclean" differ from that of the Pharisees (vv. 14–23)? 4. Jesus responds to the Syrophoenician woman's request with a miniparable about children, bread and dogs (vv. 24–27). What is he actually saying? 5. What does the woman's response reveal about her? 6. The healing of the deaf man takes place in the Decapolis, where Jesus had exorcised the demons from the Gerasene man at the tombs (5:1–20). How do the events here demonstrate that man's success in telling about what Jesus had done for him (vv. 31–37)?

Applying the Word 1. What religious traditions influence your life? Is that influence good or bad? Explain. 2. What sorts of traditions do we observe today that get in the way of really honoring God? 3. In what ways do you sometimes emphasize appearance over internal reality?

Responding in Prayer Now, as then, those who are spiritually deaf—whether through hardness of heart or through substituting traditions for true obedience—can be healed by Jesus. Pray for yourself and others who need Jesus' healing touch.

9 / *Mark 8:1—9:1*
Who Do You Say I Am?

"WHO DO YOU say I am?" The whole Gospel of Mark so far has been supplying evidence for answering this question. It's a question Jesus asks each of us, and the answer we give ultimately determines our destiny. But our answer involves more than what we say with our lips. Our real answer is to be found in the way we live our lives.

 Warming Up to God What need in your life has God met recently? Spend time praising God and thanking him for meeting your needs.

 Read Mark 8:1—9:1.

---

8 During those days another large crowd gathered. Since they had nothing to eat, Jesus called his disciples to him and said, ²"I have compassion for these people; they have already been with me three days and have nothing to eat. ³If I send them home hungry, they will collapse on the way, because some of them have come a long distance."

⁴His disciples answered, "But where in this remote place can anyone get enough bread to feed them?"

⁵"How many loaves do you have?" Jesus asked.

"Seven," they replied.

⁶He told the crowd to sit down on the ground. When he had taken the seven loaves and given thanks, he broke them and gave them to his disciples to set before the people, and they did so. ⁷They had a few small fish as well; he gave thanks for them also and told the disciples to distribute them. ⁸The people ate and were satisfied. Afterward the disciples picked up seven basketfuls of broken pieces that were left over. ⁹About four thousand men were present. And having sent them away, ¹⁰he got into the boat with his disciples and went to the region of Dalmanutha.

¹¹The Pharisees came and began to question Jesus. To test him, they asked him for a sign from heaven. ¹²He sighed deeply and said, "Why does this generation ask for a miraculous sign? I tell you the truth, no sign will be given to it." ¹³Then he left them, got back into the boat and crossed to the other side.

¹⁴The disciples had forgotten to bring bread, except for one loaf they had with them in the boat. ¹⁵"Be careful," Jesus warned them. "Watch out for the yeast of the Pharisees and that of Herod."

¹⁶They discussed this with one another and said, "It is because we have no bread."

¹⁷Aware of their discussion, Jesus asked them: "Why are you talking about having no bread? Do you still not see or understand? Are your hearts hardened? ¹⁸Do you have eyes but fail to see, and ears but fail to hear? And don't you remember? ¹⁹When I broke the five loaves for the five thousand, how many basketfuls of pieces did you pick up?"

"Twelve," they replied.

²⁰"And when I broke the seven loaves for the four thousand, how many basketfuls of pieces did you pick up?"

They answered, "Seven."

²¹He said to them, "Do you still not understand?"

²²They came to Bethsaida, and some people brought a blind man and begged Jesus to touch him. ²³He took the blind man by the hand and led him outside the village. When he had spit on the man's eyes and put his hands on him, Jesus asked, "Do you see anything?"

²⁴He looked up and said, "I see people; they look like trees walking around."

²⁵Once more Jesus put his hands on the man's eyes. Then his eyes were opened, his sight was restored, and he saw everything clearly. ²⁶Jesus sent him home, saying, "Don't go into the village.ᵇ"

²⁷Jesus and his disciples went on to the villages around Caesarea Philippi. On the way he asked them, "Who do people say I am?"

²⁸They replied, "Some say John the Baptist; others say Elijah; and still others, one of the prophets."

²⁹"But what about you?" he asked. "Who do you say I am?"

ᵇ26 Some manuscripts *Don't go and tell anyone in the village*

Peter answered, "You are the Christ.*c*"

³⁰Jesus warned them not to tell anyone about him.

³¹He then began to teach them that the Son of Man must suffer many things and be rejected by the elders, chief priests and teachers of the law, and that he must be killed and after three days rise again. ³²He spoke plainly about this, and Peter took him aside and began to rebuke him.

³³But when Jesus turned and looked at his disciples, he rebuked Peter. "Get behind me, Satan!" he said. "You do not have in mind the things of God, but the things of men."

³⁴Then he called the crowd to him along with his disciples and said: "If anyone would come after me, he must deny himself and take up his cross and follow me. ³⁵For whoever wants to save his life*d* will lose it, but whoever loses his life for me and for the gospel will save it. ³⁶What good is it for a man to gain the whole world, yet forfeit his soul? ³⁷Or what can a man give in exchange for his soul? ³⁸If anyone is ashamed of me and my words in this adulterous and sinful generation, the Son of Man will be ashamed of him when he comes in his Father's glory with the holy angels."

9 And he said to them, "I tell you the truth, some who are standing here will not taste death before they see the kingdom of God come with power."

c29 Or Messiah. "The Christ" (Greek) and "the Messiah" (Hebrew) both mean "the Anointed One."   d35 The Greek word means either life or soul; also in verse 36.

Discovering the Word 1. Why do you suppose the disciples, having witnessed the feeding of the 5,000, have such a hard time believing Jesus can supply the needs of 4,000 here (8:1–13)? 2. What do the disciples fail to understand in verses 14–21 and why? 3. What unusual thing happens while Jesus is curing the blind man (vv. 22–26)? 4. How is Peter in verses 27–33 like the blind man in verses 22–26? 5. What does Jesus say it means to acknowledge him as the Christ and to follow him?

Applying the Word 1. When have you acted like the disciples in verses 1–13, not expecting God to work just after he has met a need in your life? 2. Is your life characterized more by seeking to lose your life or to save it? Explain. 3. In what way do you need to "lose your life"?

Responding in Prayer Ask Jesus to help you see more clearly those areas where you are not yet following him.

---

10 / *Mark 9:2–32*
Suffering and Glory

IN A FAMOUS short story, the main character is given the choice of opening one of two doors. Behind one is a beautiful maiden; behind the other, a ferocious tiger. It is easy to identify with the hero of the story, hoping for joy rather than suffering, pleasure rather than pain. But what if we cannot have one without the other? This passage examines the relationship between suffering and glory, human weakness and divine power.

Warming Up to God In this passage God tells the disciples to "listen to" his Son. What does Christ want to say to you today?

Read Mark 9:2–32.

---

²After six days Jesus took Peter, James and John with him and led them up a high mountain, where they were all alone. There he was transfigured before them. ³His clothes became dazzling white, whiter than anyone in the world could bleach them. ⁴And there appeared before them Elijah and Moses, who were talking with Jesus.

⁵Peter said to Jesus, "Rabbi, it is good for us to be here. Let us put up three shelters—one for you, one for Moses and one for Elijah." ⁶(He did not know what to say, they were so frightened.)

⁷Then a cloud appeared and enveloped them, and a voice came from the cloud: "This is my Son, whom I love. Listen to him!"

⁸Suddenly, when they looked around, they no longer saw anyone with them except Jesus.

⁹As they were coming down the mountain, Jesus gave them orders not to tell anyone what they had seen until the Son of Man had risen from the dead. ¹⁰They kept the matter to themselves, discussing what "rising from the dead" meant.

¹¹And they asked him, "Why do the teachers of the law say that Elijah must come first?"

¹²Jesus replied, "To be sure, Elijah does come first, and restores all things. Why then is it written that the Son of Man must suffer much and be rejected? ¹³But I tell you, Elijah has come, and they have done to him everything they wished, just as it is written about him."

¹⁴When they came to the other disciples, they saw a large crowd around them and the teachers of the law arguing with them. ¹⁵As soon as all the people saw Jesus, they were overwhelmed with wonder and ran to greet him.

¹⁶"What are you arguing with them about?" he asked.

¹⁷A man in the crowd answered, "Teacher, I brought you my son, who is possessed by a spirit that has robbed him of speech. ¹⁸Whenever it seizes him, it throws him to the ground. He foams at the mouth, gnashes his teeth and becomes rigid. I asked your disciples to drive out the spirit, but they could not."

¹⁹"O unbelieving generation," Jesus replied, "how long shall I stay with you? How long shall I put up with you? Bring the boy to me."

²⁰So they brought him. When the spirit saw Jesus, it immediately threw the boy into a convul-sion. He fell to the ground and rolled around, foaming at the mouth.

²¹Jesus asked the boy's father, "How long has he been like this?"

"From childhood," he answered. ²²"It has often thrown him into fire or water to kill him. But if you can do anything, take pity on us and help us."

²³" 'If you can'?" said Jesus. "Everything is possible for him who believes."

²⁴Immediately the boy's father exclaimed, "I do believe; help me overcome my unbelief!"

²⁵When Jesus saw that a crowd was running to the scene, he rebuked the evil*ᵉ* spirit. "You deaf and mute spirit," he said, "I command you, come out of him and never enter him again."

²⁶The spirit shrieked, convulsed him violently and came out. The boy looked so much like a corpse that many said, "He's dead." ²⁷But Jesus took him by the hand and lifted him to his feet, and he stood up.

²⁸After Jesus had gone indoors, his disciples asked him privately, "Why couldn't we drive it out?"

²⁹He replied, "This kind can come out only by prayer.*ᶠ*"

³⁰They left that place and passed through Galilee. Jesus did not want anyone to know where they were, ³¹because he was teaching his disciples. He said to them, "The Son of Man is going to be betrayed into the hands of men. They will kill him, and after three days he will rise." ³²But they did not understand what he meant and were afraid to ask him about it.

ᵉ25 Greek *unclean*   ᶠ29 Some manuscripts *prayer and fasting*

Discovering the Word 1. What is the significance of the presence of Elijah and Moses with Jesus on the mount? 2. In verse 7 God's voice is heard for a second time in Mark's Gospel, the first being in 1:11. What purposes are accomplished by God's affirmation here? 3. Jesus descends the mountain and returns to his other disciples, only to find them in hot debate with the teachers of the law over their failure to exorcise a young boy robbed of speech (vv. 14–18). Why do you suppose Jesus is so harsh in verse 19? 4. At the end of this account, Jesus again tells his disciples about his death and resurrection (vv. 30–32). Why do you suppose the disciples failed to understand what he meant? 5. What details in the account of the boy's healing parallel those in Jesus' prediction of his coming suffering and victory?

Applying the Word 1. Which do you struggle with more—believing that Jesus *can* or that he *wants* to answer your prayers? Explain. 2. How can the dialogue between Jesus and the boy's father encourage you when your faith is weak? 3. How can this passage encourage you in the midst of pain and suffering? 4. The statement in verse 7, "Listen to him!" probably alludes to Deuteronomy 18:15–19. Explain how we can listen to Jesus today.

Responding in Prayer Ask God to provide you with the encouragement you need in your life and to make you a channel of his grace to others.

11 / *Mark 9:33–50*
The First and the Last

ALL OF US, I imagine, struggle with the question of status and identity within a group. Where do I fit? How important am I to this group? Who is on our side? Who isn't? In this study we find out how Jesus turns conventional wisdom about status and group identity on its ear.

 Warming Up to God When have you put yourself before others? Be vulnerable before God as you consider your selfishness. Let him show you your sin.

 Read Mark 9:33–50.

---

³³They came to Capernaum. When he was in the house, he asked them, "What were you arguing about on the road?" ³⁴But they kept quiet because on the way they had argued about who was the greatest.

³⁵Sitting down, Jesus called the Twelve and said, "If anyone wants to be first, he must be the very last, and the servant of all."

³⁶He took a little child and had him stand among them. Taking him in his arms, he said to them, ³⁷"Whoever welcomes one of these little children in my name welcomes me; and whoever welcomes me does not welcome me but the one who sent me."

³⁸"Teacher," said John, "we saw a man driving out demons in your name and we told him to stop, because he was not one of us."

³⁹"Do not stop him," Jesus said. "No one who does a miracle in my name can in the next moment say anything bad about me, ⁴⁰for whoever is not against us is for us. ⁴¹I tell you the truth, anyone who gives you a cup of water in my name because you belong to Christ will certainly not lose his reward.

⁴²"And if anyone causes one of these little ones who believe in me to sin, it would be better for him to be thrown into the sea with a large millstone tied around his neck. ⁴³If your hand causes you to sin, cut it off. It is better for you to enter life maimed than with two hands to go into hell, where the fire never goes out.[g] ⁴⁵And if your foot causes you to sin, cut it off. It is better for you to enter life crippled than to have two feet and be thrown into hell.[h] ⁴⁷And if your eye causes you to sin, pluck it out. It is better for you to enter the kingdom of God with one eye than to have two eyes and be thrown into hell, ⁴⁸where

" 'their worm does not die,
    and the fire is not quenched.'[i]

⁴⁹Everyone will be salted with fire.

⁵⁰"Salt is good, but if it loses its saltiness, how can you make it salty again? Have salt in yourselves, and be at peace with each other."

g43 Some manuscripts *out,* ⁴⁴*where* / " *'their worm does not die,* / *and the fire is not quenched.'*   h45 Some manuscripts *hell,* ⁴⁶*where* / " *'their worm does not die,* / *and the fire is not quenched.'*   i48 Isaiah 66:24

 Discovering the Word 1. In verses 33–37, what is Jesus trying to get across to the disciples? 2. Why is a child so appropriate an illustration for Jesus' point (vv. 36–37)? 3. What perspective governs Jesus' response to John in verses 39–41? 4. Christian history has known some individuals to take Jesus' words in verses 43–47 quite literally. Why is cutting off a hand or foot or plucking out an eye not radical enough a way to deal with sin? 5. How are Jesus' attitudes about greatness and personal worth radically different from attitudes we often adopt from society?

Applying the Word 1. What individuals or groups are you tempted to silence because they are not one of us? 2. When should you oppose someone in Jesus' name (if ever)? 3. What attitudes and actions does this passage suggest should govern our relationships with rival individuals or groups who act in Jesus' name?

Responding in Prayer Look to God for his wisdom as you consider how to deal with groups and individuals you know who don't uphold the truth as you understand it.

12 / *Mark 10:1–31*
Divorce, Children and Eternal Life

FOR MANY OF us preachin' becomes meddlin' when it impinges on how we live. But Jesus and the New Testament, like the Old Testament before them, never allow religion to be divorced from family life and social relationships. This passage exposes some of the ways the gospel ought to transform these areas of our life.

 Warming Up to God Think about a child you know and how that child trusts his or her parents. Compare that picture to how you regard God. Talk to God about what you discover about yourself.

 Read Mark 10:1–31.

10 Jesus then left that place and went into the region of Judea and across the Jordan. Again crowds of people came to him, and as was his custom, he taught them.

2Some Pharisees came and tested him by asking, "Is it lawful for a man to divorce his wife?"

3"What did Moses command you?" he replied.

4They said, "Moses permitted a man to write a certificate of divorce and send her away."

5"It was because your hearts were hard that Moses wrote you this law," Jesus replied. 6"But at the beginning of creation God 'made them male and female.'^j 7'For this reason a man will leave his father and mother and be united to his wife,^k 8and the two will become one flesh.'^l So they are no longer two, but one. 9Therefore what God has joined together, let man not separate."

10When they were in the house again, the disciples asked Jesus about this. 11He answered, "Anyone who divorces his wife and marries another woman commits adultery against her. 12And if she divorces her husband and marries another man, she commits adultery."

13People were bringing little children to Jesus to have him touch them, but the disciples rebuked them. 14When Jesus saw this, he was indignant. He said to them, "Let the little children come to me, and do not hinder them, for the kingdom of God belongs to such as these. 15I tell you the truth, anyone who will not receive the kingdom of God like a little child will never enter it." 16And he took the children in his arms, put his hands on them and blessed them.

17As Jesus started on his way, a man ran up to him and fell on his knees before him. "Good teacher," he asked, "what must I do to inherit eternal life?"

18"Why do you call me good?" Jesus answered. "No one is good—except God alone. 19You know the commandments: 'Do not murder, do not commit adultery, do not steal, do not give false testimony, do not defraud, honor your father and mother.'^m"

20"Teacher," he declared, "all these I have kept since I was a boy."

21Jesus looked at him and loved him. "One thing you lack," he said. "Go, sell everything you have and give to the poor, and you will have treasure in heaven. Then come, follow me."

22At this the man's face fell. He went away sad, because he had great wealth.

23Jesus looked around and said to his disciples, "How hard it is for the rich to enter the kingdom of God!"

24The disciples were amazed at his words. But Jesus said again, "Children, how hard it is^n to enter the kingdom of God! 25It is easier for a camel to go through the eye of a needle than for a rich man to enter the kingdom of God."

26The disciples were even more amazed, and said to each other, "Who then can be saved?"

27Jesus looked at them and said, "With man this is impossible, but not with God; all things are possible with God."

28Peter said to him, "We have left everything to follow you!"

29"I tell you the truth," Jesus replied, "no one who has left home or brothers or sisters or mother or father or children or fields for me and the gospel 30will fail to receive a hundred times as much in this present age (homes, brothers, sis-

j6 Gen. 1:27   k7 Some early manuscripts do not have *and be united to his wife.*   l8 Gen. 2:24   m19 Exodus 20:12-16; Deut. 5:16-20   n24 Some manuscripts *is for those who trust in riches*

ters, mothers, children and fields—and with
them, persecutions) and in the age to come, eternal life. ³¹But many who are first will be last, and
the last first."

Discovering the Word 1. What differences in approach to the question of divorce seem evident between Jesus and the Pharisees? 2. On the basis of verses 6–9, some Christian churches have refused to recognize divorce even when a couple has obtained a civil dissolution of their marriage. Do you think this is the intent of Jesus' statement? Why or why not? 3. In verses 13–16 we find that Jesus has used a child or children for the second time to illustrate a spiritual principle. What does it mean to receive the kingdom like a little child? 4. What kind of answer does the rich man expect from Jesus in response to his question (v. 17)? 5. How have the Pharisees (vv. 2–9) and the rich man (vv. 17–25) failed to receive the kingdom like a child (v. 15)?

Applying the Word 1. What obstacles were or are hardest for you to overcome in entering the kingdom? 2. What evidence has there been of God's help in your overcoming these obstacles? 3. In what areas of your life do you most need to express more childlike faith in God? 4. How have you experienced the truth of Jesus' words, "No one who has left home . . . will fail to receive a hundred times as much"?

Responding in Prayer Ask God to make you like a child.

---

13 / *Mark 10:32–52*
Blindness and Sight

THE BLIND SOMETIMES have uncanny "sight," and the deaf sometimes "hear" what others miss. Spiritual insight and alertness arise from the heart rather than from status or position. In this passage Mark seems to delight in the irony of a blind man who perceives what the sighted cannot see.

Warming Up to God What does God want you to "see" or know? Sit quietly before him and listen for his voice.

Read Mark 10:32–52.

---

³²They were on their way up to Jerusalem, with Jesus leading the way, and the disciples were astonished, while those who followed were afraid. Again he took the Twelve aside and told them what was going to happen to him. ³³"We are going up to Jerusalem," he said, "and the Son of Man will be betrayed to the chief priests and teachers of the law. They will condemn him to death and will hand him over to the Gentiles, ³⁴who will mock him and spit on him, flog him and kill him. Three days later he will rise."

³⁵Then James and John, the sons of Zebedee, came to him. "Teacher," they said, "we want you to do for us whatever we ask."

³⁶"What do you want me to do for you?" he asked.

³⁷They replied, "Let one of us sit at your right and the other at your left in your glory."

³⁸"You don't know what you are asking," Jesus said. "Can you drink the cup I drink or be baptized with the baptism I am baptized with?"

³⁹"We can," they answered.

Jesus said to them, "You will drink the cup I drink and be baptized with the baptism I am baptized with, ⁴⁰but to sit at my right or left is not for me to grant. These places belong to those for whom they have been prepared."

⁴¹When the ten heard about this, they became indignant with James and John. ⁴²Jesus called them together and said, "You know that those who are regarded as rulers of the Gentiles lord it over them, and their high officials exercise authority over them. ⁴³Not so with you. Instead, whoever wants to become great among you must be your servant, ⁴⁴and whoever wants to be first must be slave of all. ⁴⁵For even the Son of Man did not come to be served, but to serve, and to give his life as a ransom for many."

⁴⁶Then they came to Jericho. As Jesus and his disciples, together with a large crowd, were leaving the city, a blind man, Bartimaeus (that is, the Son of Timaeus), was sitting by the roadside begging. ⁴⁷When he heard that it was Jesus of Nazareth, he began to shout, "Jesus, Son of David, have mercy on me!"

⁴⁸Many rebuked him and told him to be quiet, but he shouted all the more, "Son of David, have mercy on me!"

⁴⁹Jesus stopped and said, "Call him."

So they called to the blind man, "Cheer up! On your feet! He's calling you." ⁵⁰Throwing his cloak aside, he jumped to his feet and came to Jesus.

⁵¹"What do you want me to do for you?" Jesus asked him.

The blind man said, "Rabbi, I want to see."

⁵²"Go," said Jesus, "your faith has healed you." Immediately he received his sight and followed Jesus along the road.

Discovering the Word 1. Given what Jesus has just said in verses 33–34, what is ironic about James and John's request (vv. 35–37)? 2. What seems to motivate James and John's request? 3. When the other ten apostles hear about this status request, they become indignant. In response, what principle does Jesus bring out again (see 9:35, 10:31 and 10:42–45)? 4. From the brief account in verses 46–52, what kind of man does Bartimaeus seem to be? 5. Why do you suppose Jesus asked Bartimaeus what he wanted him to do for him?

Applying the Word 1. How can your life better conform to Jesus' view of greatness? (Consider what motivates your actions as well as what you do.) 2. Jesus is indeed on the road to glory, but that road will not bypass Jerusalem. Self-sacrifice and service mark the way. What are some present opportunities for you to follow him? 3. What may be some of the costs?

Responding in Prayer Tell God how you want to sacrifice for him.

---

14 / *Mark 11:1–25*
Palm Sunday

THE TROUBLE WITH righteous anger is that it is so much easier to be angry than righteous. But it is possible to be both. This passage provides an example of how our emotions and attitudes can work toward God's purposes instead of against them.

 Warming Up to God When have your emotions "gotten the better of you" lately? Evaluate that experience prayerfully.

 Read Mark 11:1–25.

---

11 As they approached Jerusalem and came to Bethphage and Bethany at the Mount of Olives, Jesus sent two of his disciples, ²saying to them, "Go to the village ahead of you, and just as you enter it, you will find a colt tied there, which no one has ever ridden. Untie it and bring it here. ³If anyone asks you, 'Why are you doing this?' tell him, 'The Lord needs it and will send it back here shortly.' "

⁴They went and found a colt outside in the street, tied at a doorway. As they untied it, ⁵some people standing there asked, "What are you doing, untying that colt?" ⁶They answered as Jesus had told them to, and the people let them go. ⁷When they brought the colt to Jesus and threw their cloaks over it, he sat on it. ⁸Many people spread their cloaks on the road, while others spread branches they had cut in the fields. ⁹Those who went ahead and those who followed shouted,

"Hosanna!ᵒ"

"Blessed is he who comes in the name of the
        Lord!"ᵖ

⁰9 A Hebrew expression meaning "Save!" which became an exclamation of praise; also in verse 10   ᵖ9 Psalm 118:25,26

10“Blessed is the coming kingdom of our father
David!”

“Hosanna in the highest!”

11Jesus entered Jerusalem and went to the temple. He looked around at everything, but since it was already late, he went out to Bethany with the Twelve.

12The next day as they were leaving Bethany, Jesus was hungry. 13Seeing in the distance a fig tree in leaf, he went to find out if it had any fruit. When he reached it, he found nothing but leaves, because it was not the season for figs. 14Then he said to the tree, “May no one ever eat fruit from you again.” And his disciples heard him say it.

15On reaching Jerusalem, Jesus entered the temple area and began driving out those who were buying and selling there. He overturned the tables of the money changers and the benches of those selling doves, 16and would not allow anyone to carry merchandise through the temple courts. 17And as he taught them, he said, “Is it not written:

“ ‘My house will be called
a house of prayer for all nations’[q]?
But you have made it ‘a den of robbers.’[r]”

18The chief priests and the teachers of the law heard this and began looking for a way to kill him, for they feared him, because the whole crowd was amazed at his teaching.

19When evening came, they[s] went out of the city.

20In the morning, as they went along, they saw the fig tree withered from the roots. 21Peter remembered and said to Jesus, “Rabbi, look! The fig tree you cursed has withered!”

22“Have[t] faith in God,” Jesus answered. 23“I tell you the truth, if anyone says to this mountain, ‘Go, throw yourself into the sea,’ and does not doubt in his heart but believes that what he says will happen, it will be done for him. 24Therefore I tell you, whatever you ask for in prayer, believe that you have received it, and it will be yours. 25And when you stand praying, if you hold anything against anyone, forgive him, so that your Father in heaven may forgive you your sins.[u]”

[q]17 Isaiah 56:7 [r]17 Jer. 7:11 [s]19 Some early manuscripts *he* [t]22 Some early manuscripts *If you have* [u]25 Some manuscripts *sins.* 26*But if you do not forgive, neither will your Father who is in heaven forgive your sins.*

Discovering the Word 1. What progression of moods do you see in this passage? 2. In what ways is the significance of Jesus' entry into Jerusalem reinforced? 3. Why is Jesus so angry with what is taking place in the temple (vv. 15–17)? 4. Why do you suppose Mark has sandwiched this account of Jesus' clearing out of the temple within that of the cursing of the fig tree? 5. What does Jesus teach us about prayer in verses 22–25?

Applying the Word 1. When is anger righteous? 2. Are there activities or attitudes in your church or fellowship which get in the way of God's purposes? 3. What can you do to help eliminate them?

Responding in Prayer Respond to this passage in prayer, praising the King of peace and asking that his kingdom might be established.

15 / *Mark 11:27—12:27*
Tempting Questions

SOME PEOPLE ASK questions because they want to know the answers. Others take malicious delight in posing unanswerable questions or in trying to trip up an opponent. Jesus often asked questions to get his hearers to think deeply for themselves. Learning to look behind questions to motives and learning to pose effective questions can help us all to be better evangelists and servants.

Warming Up to God When is Jesus most real to you? Spend some time meditating on the privilege of having Christ present with you.

Read Mark 11:27—12:27.

²⁷They arrived again in Jerusalem, and while Jesus was walking in the temple courts, the chief priests, the teachers of the law and the elders came to him. ²⁸"By what authority are you doing these things?" they asked. "And who gave you authority to do this?"

²⁹Jesus replied, "I will ask you one question. Answer me, and I will tell you by what authority I am doing these things. ³⁰John's baptism—was it from heaven, or from men? Tell me!"

³¹They discussed it among themselves and said, "If we say, 'From heaven,' he will ask, 'Then why didn't you believe him?' ³²But if we say, 'From men' . . . ." (They feared the people, for everyone held that John really was a prophet.)

³³So they answered Jesus, "We don't know."

Jesus said, "Neither will I tell you by what authority I am doing these things."

12 He then began to speak to them in parables: "A man planted a vineyard. He put a wall around it, dug a pit for the winepress and built a watchtower. Then he rented the vineyard to some farmers and went away on a journey. ²At harvest time he sent a servant to the tenants to collect from them some of the fruit of the vineyard. ³But they seized him, beat him and sent him away empty-handed. ⁴Then he sent another servant to them; they struck this man on the head and treated him shamefully. ⁵He sent still another, and that one they killed. He sent many others; some of them they beat, others they killed.

⁶"He had one left to send, a son, whom he loved. He sent him last of all, saying, 'They will respect my son.'

⁷"But the tenants said to one another, 'This is the heir. Come, let's kill him, and the inheritance will be ours.' ⁸So they took him and killed him, and threw him out of the vineyard.

⁹"What then will the owner of the vineyard do? He will come and kill those tenants and give the vineyard to others. ¹⁰Haven't you read this scripture:

" 'The stone the builders rejected
   has become the capstoneᵛ;
¹¹the Lord has done this,
   and it is marvelous in our eyes'ʷ?"

¹²Then they looked for a way to arrest him because they knew he had spoken the parable against them. But they were afraid of the crowd; so they left him and went away.

¹³Later they sent some of the Pharisees and Herodians to Jesus to catch him in his words. ¹⁴They came to him and said, "Teacher, we know you are a man of integrity. You aren't swayed by men, because you pay no attention to who they are; but you teach the way of God in accordance with the truth. Is it right to pay taxes to Caesar or not? ¹⁵Should we pay or shouldn't we?"

But Jesus knew their hypocrisy. "Why are you trying to trap me?" he asked. "Bring me a denarius and let me look at it." ¹⁶They brought the coin, and he asked them, "Whose portrait is this? And whose inscription?"

"Caesar's," they replied.

¹⁷Then Jesus said to them, "Give to Caesar what is Caesar's and to God what is God's."

And they were amazed at him.

¹⁸Then the Sadducees, who say there is no resurrection, came to him with a question. ¹⁹"Teacher," they said, "Moses wrote for us that if a man's brother dies and leaves a wife but no children, the man must marry the widow and have children for his brother. ²⁰Now there were seven brothers. The first one married and died without leaving any children. ²¹The second one married the widow, but he also died, leaving no child. It was the same with the third. ²²In fact, none of the seven left any children. Last of all, the woman died too. ²³At the resurrectionˣ whose wife will she be, since the seven were married to her?"

²⁴Jesus replied, "Are you not in error because you do not know the Scriptures or the power of God? ²⁵When the dead rise, they will neither marry nor be given in marriage; they will be like the angels in heaven. ²⁶Now about the dead rising—have you not read in the book of Moses, in the account of the bush, how God said to him, 'I am the God of Abraham, the God of Isaac, and the God of Jacob'ʸ? ²⁷He is not the God of the dead, but of the living. You are badly mistaken!"

ᵛ10 Or *cornerstone*   ʷ11 Psalm 118:22,23   ˣ23 Some manuscripts *resurrection, when men rise from the dead,*   ʸ26 Exodus 3:6

Discovering the Word 1. In 11:27 the chief priests, the elders and the teachers of the law come asking a seemingly straightforward question about Jesus' authority. What does Jesus' reply and the subsequent discussion reveal about their motives? 2. The parable of the tenants is rich in meaning. If the tenants are Israel and its religious leaders, who are the owner, the servants and the son? 3. A common enemy can often draw together people who are not otherwise on good terms. In 12:13–17 we find Herodians (supporters of the puppet monarchy) and the Pharisees (ardent nationalists and opponents of Roman rule) joining forces. How does the question they pose to Jesus reflect their conflicting interests? 4. The Sadducees differed from their Jewish contemporaries because they rejected the idea of resurrection. What motives lie behind their question to Jesus (12:18–23)? 5. How do the Sadducees display ignorance of the Scriptures and the power of God?

 Applying the Word 1. How are you experiencing the truth of the Scriptures and the power of God? 2. How can we get to know the Scriptures and the power of God better? 3. As we seek to share the good news of Christ and his kingdom, we will meet people with a wide variety of questions and motives. What can we learn about answering and asking questions from this passage?

 Responding in Prayer Pray that you will be ready to answer questions about your beliefs.

16 / *Mark 12:28–44*
An End to Questions

PEOPLE ARE MOTIVATED by many things—ambition, money, power, recognition, the desire to please God. In this passage Jesus encounters or comments on a variety of people whose lives are governed by different goals. In so doing he exposes our own motivations to his searching glance.

Warming Up to God What motivates your daily life and future plans? List each motivating factor. Reflect on your list before God.

Read Mark 12:28–44.

²⁸One of the teachers of the law came and heard them debating. Noticing that Jesus had given them a good answer, he asked him, "Of all the commandments, which is the most important?"

²⁹"The most important one," answered Jesus, "is this: 'Hear, O Israel, the Lord our God, the Lord is one.ᶻ ³⁰Love the Lord your God with all your heart and with all your soul and with all your mind and with all your strength.'ᵃ ³¹The second is this: 'Love your neighbor as yourself.'ᵇ There is no commandment greater than these."

³²"Well said, teacher," the man replied. "You are right in saying that God is one and there is no other but him. ³³To love him with all your heart, with all your understanding and with all your strength, and to love your neighbor as yourself is more important than all burnt offerings and sacrifices."

³⁴When Jesus saw that he had answered wisely, he said to him, "You are not far from the kingdom of God." And from then on no one dared ask him any more questions.

³⁵While Jesus was teaching in the temple courts, he asked, "How is it that the teachers of the law say that the Christᶜ is the son of David? ³⁶David himself, speaking by the Holy Spirit, declared:

" 'The Lord said to my Lord:
  "Sit at my right hand
until I put your enemies
  under your feet." 'ᵈ

³⁷David himself calls him 'Lord.' How then can he be his son?"

The large crowd listened to him with delight.

³⁸As he taught, Jesus said, "Watch out for the teachers of the law. They like to walk around in flowing robes and be greeted in the marketplaces, ³⁹and have the most important seats in the syna-

ᶻ29 Or *the Lord our God is one Lord*   ᵃ30 Deut. 6:4,5   ᵇ31 Lev. 19:18   ᶜ35 Or *Messiah*   ᵈ36 Psalm 110:1

gogues and the places of honor at banquets. ⁴⁰They devour widows' houses and for a show make lengthy prayers. Such men will be punished most severely."

⁴¹Jesus sat down opposite the place where the offerings were put and watched the crowd putting their money into the temple treasury. Many rich people threw in large amounts. ⁴²But a poor widow came and put in two very small copper coins,ᵉ worth only a fraction of a penny.ᶠ

⁴³Calling his disciples to him, Jesus said, "I tell you the truth, this poor widow has put more into the treasury than all the others. ⁴⁴They all gave out of their wealth; but she, out of her poverty, put in everything—all she had to live on."

ᵉ42 Greek *two lepta*   ᶠ42 Greek *kodrantes*

 Discovering the Word 1. Like the chief priests, elders, Pharisees and Sadducees of 11:27—12:27, another teacher of the law comes to Jesus with a pointed question (v. 28). What evidence is there that he is not out to trap Jesus? 2. Though Jesus is only asked for one commandment, in good rabbinic fashion he responds by adding a second to his reply. What relationship does this second commandment bear to the first? 3. To a Jew in Jesus' day a descendant was always inferior to an ancestor. A son might call his father or grandfather "lord," but never vice versa. How *can* Christ be both David's Lord and his descendant (vv. 35–37)? 4. In contrast to the teachers of the law and the rich, what motivates the widow's religious behavior?

 Applying the Word 1. If you were to evaluate your daily activities on the basis of love for God and neighbor, how would you fare? Explain. 2. What steps can you take to make the love of God and love of neighbor a higher priority in your life? 3. What implications does the example of the widow have for our giving to the Lord's work?

 Responding in Prayer Ask God to give you the attitude of the widow both in your love for him and toward others.

---

17 / *Mark 13*
Keep Watch

WAITING FOR CHRISTMAS can keep some children excited and on their best behavior for weeks. But what if Christmas never came? To many of us the Second Coming may seem like a Christmas that never comes. In this passage, Jesus answers some questions about the future, both near and far off, but above all he encourages an attitude we all need to develop.

Warming Up to God When is it hard for you to wait for God? Ask him to give you insight and courage as you watch and wait.

Read Mark 13.

---

13 As he was leaving the temple, one of his disciples said to him, "Look, Teacher! What massive stones! What magnificent buildings!"

²"Do you see all these great buildings?" replied Jesus. "Not one stone here will be left on another; every one will be thrown down."

³As Jesus was sitting on the Mount of Olives opposite the temple, Peter, James, John and Andrew asked him privately, ⁴"Tell us, when will these things happen? And what will be the sign that they are all about to be fulfilled?"

⁵Jesus said to them: "Watch out that no one deceives you. ⁶Many will come in my name, claiming, 'I am he,' and will deceive many. ⁷When you hear of wars and rumors of wars, do not be alarmed. Such things must happen, but the end is still to come. ⁸Nation will rise against nation, and kingdom against kingdom. There will be earthquakes in various places, and famines. These are the beginning of birth pains.

⁹"You must be on your guard. You will be handed over to the local councils and flogged in the synagogues. On account of me you will stand

before governors and kings as witnesses to them. [10]And the gospel must first be preached to all nations. [11]Whenever you are arrested and brought to trial, do not worry beforehand about what to say. Just say whatever is given you at the time, for it is not you speaking, but the Holy Spirit.

[12]"Brother will betray brother to death, and a father his child. Children will rebel against their parents and have them put to death. [13]All men will hate you because of me, but he who stands firm to the end will be saved.

[14]"When you see 'the abomination that causes desolation'[g] standing where it[h] does not belong—let the reader understand—then let those who are in Judea flee to the mountains. [15]Let no one on the roof of his house go down or enter the house to take anything out. [16]Let no one in the field go back to get his cloak. [17]How dreadful it will be in those days for pregnant women and nursing mothers! [18]Pray that this will not take place in winter, [19]because those will be days of distress unequaled from the beginning, when God created the world, until now—and never to be equaled again. [20]If the Lord had not cut short those days, no one would survive. But for the sake of the elect, whom he has chosen, he has shortened them. [21]At that time if anyone says to you, 'Look, here is the Christ[i]!' or, 'Look, there he is!' do not believe it. [22]For false Christs and false prophets will appear and perform signs and miracles to deceive the elect—if that were possible. [23]So be on your guard; I have told you everything ahead of time.

[24]"But in those days, following that distress,

" 'the sun will be darkened,
     and the moon will not give its light;
[25]the stars will fall from the sky,
     and the heavenly bodies will be shaken.'[j]

[26]"At that time men will see the Son of Man coming in clouds with great power and glory. [27]And he will send his angels and gather his elect from the four winds, from the ends of the earth to the ends of the heavens.

[28]"Now learn this lesson from the fig tree: As soon as its twigs get tender and its leaves come out, you know that summer is near. [29]Even so, when you see these things happening, you know that it is near, right at the door. [30]I tell you the truth, this generation[k] will certainly not pass away until all these things have happened. [31]Heaven and earth will pass away, but my words will never pass away.

[32]"No one knows about that day or hour, not even the angels in heaven, nor the Son, but only the Father. [33]Be on guard! Be alert[l]! You do not know when that time will come. [34]It's like a man going away: He leaves his house and puts his servants in charge, each with his assigned task, and tells the one at the door to keep watch.

[35]"Therefore keep watch because you do not know when the owner of the house will come back—whether in the evening, or at midnight, or when the rooster crows, or at dawn. [36]If he comes suddenly, do not let him find you sleeping. [37]What I say to you, I say to everyone: 'Watch!' "

[g]14 Daniel 9:27; 11:31; 12:11   [h]14 Or he; also in verse 29
[i]21 Or Messiah   [j]25 Isaiah 13:10; 34:4   [k]30 Or race
[l]33 Some manuscripts alert and pray

Discovering the Word 1. Jesus doesn't seem to answer the disciples' question directly, at least not at first. What is he concerned about (vv. 5–8)? 2. How would Jesus' warnings and encouragements (vv. 5–13) have helped the disciples in the early years of the church? 3. Christians have sometimes disagreed about how to interpret Jesus' words in verses 14–23. Some think Jesus is talking about the destruction of the temple in A.D. 70 and the events leading up to that. Others think these events are still future. What evidence is there to support each view? 4. How is the distress described in verses 24–27 different from that described in verses 5–23? 5. Many people throughout the ages have tried to make precise predictions about the return of Jesus. How does watching as Jesus urges differ from making such predictions?

Applying the Word 1. What relevance do the warnings and encouragements in verses 5–13 have for us today? 2. In what area of your life do you need to "be on guard"? 3. In what practical ways can we be alert for Jesus' return?

 Responding in Prayer Spend some time in praise and thanksgiving for the promises in this passage.

18 / *Mark 14:1–42*
The Betrayer Approaches

IF YOU'VE EVER caught yourself yawning at a critical moment or felt spiritually asleep when the Lord was calling you to a task, you'll have little difficulty in empathizing with the disciples in this account. We now enter into the last few days of Jesus' earthly ministry. The mood is somber as more and more people begin to fail and desert him.

 Warming Up to God What task has God been calling you to? Spend some time prayerfully considering what God has for you.

 Read Mark 14:1–42.

14 Now the Passover and the Feast of Unleavened Bread were only two days away, and the chief priests and the teachers of the law were looking for some sly way to arrest Jesus and kill him. ²"But not during the Feast," they said, "or the people may riot."

³While he was in Bethany, reclining at the table in the home of a man known as Simon the Leper, a woman came with an alabaster jar of very expensive perfume, made of pure nard. She broke the jar and poured the perfume on his head.

⁴Some of those present were saying indignantly to one another, "Why this waste of perfume? ⁵It could have been sold for more than a year's wages[m] and the money given to the poor." And they rebuked her harshly.

⁶"Leave her alone," said Jesus. "Why are you bothering her? She has done a beautiful thing to me. ⁷The poor you will always have with you, and you can help them any time you want. But you will not always have me. ⁸She did what she could. She poured perfume on my body beforehand to prepare for my burial. ⁹I tell you the truth, wherever the gospel is preached throughout the world, what she has done will also be told, in memory of her."

¹⁰Then Judas Iscariot, one of the Twelve, went to the chief priests to betray Jesus to them. ¹¹They were delighted to hear this and promised to give him money. So he watched for an opportunity to hand him over.

¹²On the first day of the Feast of Unleavened Bread, when it was customary to sacrifice the Passover lamb, Jesus' disciples asked him, "Where do you want us to go and make preparations for you to eat the Passover?"

¹³So he sent two of his disciples, telling them, "Go into the city, and a man carrying a jar of water will meet you. Follow him. ¹⁴Say to the owner of the house he enters, 'The Teacher asks: Where is my guest room, where I may eat the Passover with my disciples?' ¹⁵He will show you a large upper room, furnished and ready. Make preparations for us there."

¹⁶The disciples left, went into the city and found things just as Jesus had told them. So they prepared the Passover.

¹⁷When evening came, Jesus arrived with the Twelve. ¹⁸While they were reclining at the table eating, he said, "I tell you the truth, one of you will betray me—one who is eating with me."

¹⁹They were saddened, and one by one they said to him, "Surely not I?"

²⁰"It is one of the Twelve," he replied, "one who dips bread into the bowl with me. ²¹The Son of Man will go just as it is written about him. But woe to that man who betrays the Son of Man! It would be better for him if he had not been born."

²²While they were eating, Jesus took bread, gave thanks and broke it, and gave it to his disciples, saying, "Take it; this is my body."

²³Then he took the cup, gave thanks and offered it to them, and they all drank from it.

²⁴"This is my blood of the[n] covenant, which is poured out for many," he said to them. ²⁵"I tell you the truth, I will not drink again of the fruit of the vine until that day when I drink it anew in the kingdom of God."

²⁶When they had sung a hymn, they went out to the Mount of Olives.

²⁷"You will all fall away," Jesus told them, "for it is written:

" 'I will strike the shepherd,
    and the sheep will be scattered.'[o]

[m]5 Greek *than three hundred denarii*   [n]24 Some manuscripts *the new*
[o]27 Zech. 13:7

²⁸But after I have risen, I will go ahead of you into Galilee."

²⁹Peter declared, "Even if all fall away, I will not."

³⁰"I tell you the truth," Jesus answered, "today—yes, tonight—before the rooster crows twice*P* you yourself will disown me three times."

³¹But Peter insisted emphatically, "Even if I have to die with you, I will never disown you." And all the others said the same.

³²They went to a place called Gethsemane, and Jesus said to his disciples, "Sit here while I pray." ³³He took Peter, James and John along with him, and he began to be deeply distressed and troubled. ³⁴"My soul is overwhelmed with sorrow to the point of death," he said to them. "Stay here and keep watch."

³⁵Going a little farther, he fell to the ground and prayed that if possible the hour might pass from him. ³⁶"*Abba*,*q* Father," he said, "every-

thing is possible for you. Take this cup from me. Yet not what I will, but what you will."

³⁷Then he returned to his disciples and found them sleeping. "Simon," he said to Peter, "are you asleep? Could you not keep watch for one hour? ³⁸Watch and pray so that you will not fall into temptation. The spirit is willing, but the body is weak."

³⁹Once more he went away and prayed the same thing. ⁴⁰When he came back, he again found them sleeping, because their eyes were heavy. They did not know what to say to him.

⁴¹Returning the third time, he said to them, "Are you still sleeping and resting? Enough! The hour has come. Look, the Son of Man is betrayed into the hands of sinners. ⁴²Rise! Let us go! Here comes my betrayer!"

P30 Some early manuscripts do not have *twice*.   *q36* Aramaic for *Father*

 Discovering the Word 1. What different motives are present in the conflict that arises at the home of Simon the Leper? 2. During the Passover feast Jesus tells the Twelve that one of them will betray him. What do you think they were feeling as they responded to his announcement (v. 19)? 3. Few words have spawned as much debate regarding their meaning as those Jesus spoke in verses 22–24. Regardless of how literally we take them, what are the bread and cup of the Lord's Supper to symbolize for us? 4. How might verses 32–36 help those who struggle with the question of whether Jesus is the only way to God?

Applying the Word 1. How can the exhortations in verses 34 and 38 make the difference in your own life between resisting or falling into temptation? 2. When have you felt like the disciples must have felt in verse 40? 3. What consolation and encouragement can you draw from the disciples' experience?

Responding in Prayer Thank God for his wonderful provision of forgiveness in Christ.

---

19 / *Mark 14:43–72*
Betrayed!

THE PERSECUTION OF enemies is one thing, the abandonment of friends another. In this study we find Jesus not only betrayed by one of his disciples but abandoned by all the others and ruefully denied by one of his closest friends. All this added to the cruel and unlawful treatment by the Sanhedrin. This account reveals how intense pressures can test the quality of our discipleship.

 Warming Up to God We all betray Christ in the things we say or do. How have you betrayed him recently? Spend time in sincere confession. Hear the words of forgiveness.

 Read Mark 14:43–72.

43Just as he was speaking, Judas, one of the Twelve, appeared. With him was a crowd armed with swords and clubs, sent from the chief priests, the teachers of the law, and the elders.

44Now the betrayer had arranged a signal with them: "The one I kiss is the man; arrest him and lead him away under guard." 45Going at once to Jesus, Judas said, "Rabbi!" and kissed him. 46The men seized Jesus and arrested him. 47Then one of those standing near drew his sword and struck the servant of the high priest, cutting off his ear.

48"Am I leading a rebellion," said Jesus, "that you have come out with swords and clubs to capture me? 49Every day I was with you, teaching in the temple courts, and you did not arrest me. But the Scriptures must be fulfilled." 50Then everyone deserted him and fled.

51A young man, wearing nothing but a linen garment, was following Jesus. When they seized him, 52he fled naked, leaving his garment behind.

53They took Jesus to the high priest, and all the chief priests, elders and teachers of the law came together. 54Peter followed him at a distance, right into the courtyard of the high priest. There he sat with the guards and warmed himself at the fire.

55The chief priests and the whole Sanhedrin were looking for evidence against Jesus so that they could put him to death, but they did not find any. 56Many testified falsely against him, but their statements did not agree.

57Then some stood up and gave this false testimony against him: 58"We heard him say, 'I will destroy this man-made temple and in three days will build another, not made by man.' " 59Yet even then their testimony did not agree.

60Then the high priest stood up before them and asked Jesus, "Are you not going to answer? What is this testimony that these men are bringing against you?" 61But Jesus remained silent and gave no answer.

Again the high priest asked him, "Are you the Christ,ʳ the Son of the Blessed One?"

62"I am," said Jesus. "And you will see the Son of Man sitting at the right hand of the Mighty One and coming on the clouds of heaven."

63The high priest tore his clothes. "Why do we need any more witnesses?" he asked. 64"You have heard the blasphemy. What do you think?"

They all condemned him as worthy of death. 65Then some began to spit at him; they blindfolded him, struck him with their fists, and said, "Prophesy!" And the guards took him and beat him.

66While Peter was below in the courtyard, one of the servant girls of the high priest came by. 67When she saw Peter warming himself, she looked closely at him.

"You also were with that Nazarene, Jesus," she said.

68But he denied it. "I don't know or understand what you're talking about," he said, and went out into the entryway.ˢ

69When the servant girl saw him there, she said again to those standing around, "This fellow is one of them." 70Again he denied it.

After a little while, those standing near said to Peter, "Surely you are one of them, for you are a Galilean."

71He began to call down curses on himself, and he swore to them, "I don't know this man you're talking about."

72Immediately the rooster crowed the second time.ᵗ Then Peter remembered the word Jesus had spoken to him: "Before the rooster crows twiceᵘ you will disown me three times." And he broke down and wept.

ʳ61 Or Messiah   ˢ68 Some early manuscripts entryway and the rooster crowed   ᵗ72 Some early manuscripts do not have the second time.   ᵘ72 Some early manuscripts do not have twice.

Discovering the Word 1. How does Jesus respond to his betrayal? 2. What aspects of Jesus' trial before the Sanhedrin (vv. 53–65) does Mark emphasize? 3. Up until this point Jesus has regularly disguised his identity, but in verse 62 he openly confesses his identity as the Christ. Why do you think he does this now? 4. How is the charge against Jesus both justifiable and unjustifiable? 5. What mix of motives brings Peter into the high priest's courtyard yet keeps him from acknowledging his relationship to Jesus (vv. 66–72)?

Applying the Word 1. How are your motives mixed in following Jesus? 2. In what circumstances are you most tempted to be ashamed of Jesus or to deny him? 3. What warnings and encouragement can you draw from Peter's experience?

Responding in Prayer Ask God to keep you from betrayal.

20 / *Mark 15:1—16:8*
Victory Snatched from Defeat

TRUE GREATNESS, JESUS taught, is found in being a servant: "Whoever wants to be first must be slave of all. For even the Son of Man did not come to be served, but to serve, and to give his life as a ransom for many." Recorded here is the vivid testimony to Jesus' greatness and glory.

 Warming Up to God What about death is intimidating to you? Reflect on how Jesus would have felt going to the cross. Spend time responding in prayer.

 Read Mark 15:1—16:8.

15 Very early in the morning, the chief priests, with the elders, the teachers of the law and the whole Sanhedrin, reached a decision. They bound Jesus, led him away and handed him over to Pilate.

²"Are you the king of the Jews?" asked Pilate.

"Yes, it is as you say," Jesus replied.

³The chief priests accused him of many things. ⁴So again Pilate asked him, "Aren't you going to answer? See how many things they are accusing you of."

⁵But Jesus still made no reply, and Pilate was amazed.

⁶Now it was the custom at the Feast to release a prisoner whom the people requested. ⁷A man called Barabbas was in prison with the insurrectionists who had committed murder in the uprising. ⁸The crowd came up and asked Pilate to do for them what he usually did.

⁹"Do you want me to release to you the king of the Jews?" asked Pilate, ¹⁰knowing it was out of envy that the chief priests had handed Jesus over to him. ¹¹But the chief priests stirred up the crowd to have Pilate release Barabbas instead.

¹²"What shall I do, then, with the one you call the king of the Jews?" Pilate asked them.

¹³"Crucify him!" they shouted.

¹⁴"Why? What crime has he committed?" asked Pilate.

But they shouted all the louder, "Crucify him!"

¹⁵Wanting to satisfy the crowd, Pilate released Barabbas to them. He had Jesus flogged, and handed him over to be crucified.

¹⁶The soldiers led Jesus away into the palace (that is, the Praetorium) and called together the whole company of soldiers. ¹⁷They put a purple robe on him, then twisted together a crown of thorns and set it on him. ¹⁸And they began to call out to him, "Hail, king of the Jews!" ¹⁹Again and again they struck him on the head with a staff and spit on him. Falling on their knees, they paid homage to him. ²⁰And when they had mocked him, they took off the purple robe and put his own clothes on him. Then they led him out to crucify him.

²¹A certain man from Cyrene, Simon, the father of Alexander and Rufus, was passing by on his way in from the country, and they forced him to carry the cross. ²²They brought Jesus to the place called Golgotha (which means The Place of the Skull). ²³Then they offered him wine mixed with myrrh, but he did not take it. ²⁴And they crucified him. Dividing up his clothes, they cast lots to see what each would get.

²⁵It was the third hour when they crucified him. ²⁶The written notice of the charge against him read: THE KING OF THE JEWS. ²⁷They crucified two robbers with him, one on his right and one on his left.ᵛ ²⁹Those who passed by hurled insults at him, shaking their heads and saying, "So! You who are going to destroy the temple and build it in three days, ³⁰come down from the cross and save yourself!"

³¹In the same way the chief priests and the teachers of the law mocked him among themselves. "He saved others," they said, "but he can't save himself! ³²Let this Christ,ʷ this King of Israel, come down now from the cross, that we may see and believe." Those crucified with him also heaped insults on him.

³³At the sixth hour darkness came over the whole land until the ninth hour. ³⁴And at the ninth hour Jesus cried out in a loud voice, *"Eloi, Eloi, lama sabachthani?"*—which means, "My God, my God, why have you forsaken me?"ˣ

³⁵When some of those standing near heard this, they said, "Listen, he's calling Elijah."

³⁶One man ran, filled a sponge with wine vinegar, put it on a stick, and offered it to Jesus to drink. "Now leave him alone. Let's see if Elijah comes to take him down," he said.

³⁷With a loud cry, Jesus breathed his last.

ᵛ27 Some manuscripts *left,* ²⁸*and the scripture was fulfilled which says,* *"He was counted with the lawless ones"* (Isaiah 53:12)   ʷ32 Or *Messiah*   ˣ34 Psalm 22:1

38The curtain of the temple was torn in two from top to bottom. 39And when the centurion, who stood there in front of Jesus, heard his cry and[y] saw how he died, he said, "Surely this man was the Son[z] of God!"

40Some women were watching from a distance. Among them were Mary Magdalene, Mary the mother of James the younger and of Joses, and Salome. 41In Galilee these women had followed him and cared for his needs. Many other women who had come up with him to Jerusalem were also there.

42It was Preparation Day (that is, the day before the Sabbath). So as evening approached, 43Joseph of Arimathea, a prominent member of the Council, who was himself waiting for the kingdom of God, went boldly to Pilate and asked for Jesus' body. 44Pilate was surprised to hear that he was already dead. Summoning the centurion, he asked him if Jesus had already died. 45When he learned from the centurion that it was so, he gave the body to Joseph. 46So Joseph bought some linen cloth, took down the body, wrapped it in the linen, and placed it in a tomb cut out of rock. Then he rolled a stone against the entrance of the tomb. 47Mary Magdalene and Mary the mother of Joses saw where he was laid.

16 When the Sabbath was over, Mary Magdalene, Mary the mother of James, and Salome bought spices so that they might go to anoint Jesus' body. 2Very early on the first day of the week, just after sunrise, they were on their way to the tomb 3and they asked each other, "Who will roll the stone away from the entrance of the tomb?"

4But when they looked up, they saw that the stone, which was very large, had been rolled away. 5As they entered the tomb, they saw a young man dressed in a white robe sitting on the right side, and they were alarmed.

6"Don't be alarmed," he said. "You are looking for Jesus the Nazarene, who was crucified. He has risen! He is not here. See the place where they laid him. 7But go, tell his disciples and Peter, 'He is going ahead of you into Galilee. There you will see him, just as he told you.' "

8Trembling and bewildered, the women went out and fled from the tomb. They said nothing to anyone, because they were afraid.

[The earliest manuscripts and some other
ancient witnesses do not have
Mark 16:9–20.]

9When Jesus rose early on the first day of the week, he appeared first to Mary Magdalene, out of whom he had driven seven demons. 10She went and told those who had been with him and who were mourning and weeping. 11When they heard that Jesus was alive and that she had seen him, they did not believe it.

12Afterward Jesus appeared in a different form to two of them while they were walking in the country. 13These returned and reported it to the rest; but they did not believe them either.

14Later Jesus appeared to the Eleven as they were eating; he rebuked them for their lack of faith and their stubborn refusal to believe those who had seen him after he had risen.

15He said to them, "Go into all the world and preach the good news to all creation. 16Whoever believes and is baptized will be saved, but whoever does not believe will be condemned. 17And these signs will accompany those who believe: In my name they will drive out demons; they will speak in new tongues; 18they will pick up snakes with their hands; and when they drink deadly poison, it will not hurt them at all; they will place their hands on sick people, and they will get well."

19After the Lord Jesus had spoken to them, he was taken up into heaven and he sat at the right hand of God. 20Then the disciples went out and preached everywhere, and the Lord worked with them and confirmed his word by the signs that accompanied it.

y39 Some manuscripts do not have heard his cry and   z39 Or a son

---

Discovering the Word 1. What kind of man is Pilate (vv. 1–15)? 2. What keeps him from doing what is right? 3. What ironies are present in the charges and jeers directed toward Jesus on the cross (vv. 25–32)? 4. Why do you think it was Joseph and the women who had followed Jesus, and not the eleven, who were present when Jesus died and his body needed a tomb (15:42—16:8)? 5. Why is it significant that Peter is mentioned by name in 16:7?

Applying the Word 1. How can we keep from succumbing to the temptation Pilate faced? 2. How can this passage reinforce our commitment to sharing the good news of Christ with others?

Responding in Prayer Spend time in praise and thanksgiving for Christ's sacrifice and for his resurrection over death.

Luke

A t coffee break in a Paris conference, a third-year law student approached me with a good question. "You were talking about me when you spoke of church people who are respectfully bored with Jesus. You talk about him as if he's fascinating. How can I see Jesus this way?"

That opener with Jacques led to a fruitful discussion about the basic need to know the earthly life of Jesus Christ. Apart from Revelation 14:4, all references to "following Jesus" are of him as a man living in this world. The Son of God—*yes!* But just as emphatically we must say he is the Son of Humanity, authentically human!

How can we better know and follow Jesus Christ? Master the facts and implications of his earthly life and mission. That is how the first disciples gradually were dispelled of their wrong notions and came to see who Jesus of Nazareth really was—a divine Messiah, the Son of God, the universal Savior. They left behind historical records of his life. You have chosen to study the most comprehensive record of that life, *Luke's good news of new hope and new joy.*

The Uniqueness of Luke
Of the four Gospels, Luke's is the longest. It includes material not found elsewhere—for example, Jesus' childhood, his parables in chapters 10—19, his one-year ministry through Samaria and Berea during his final journey to Jerusalem. It includes unique characters—for instance, Zechariah and Elizabeth, Simeon and Anna, Simon the Pharisee and the prostitute, the Emmaus disciples (note the coupling) and Zaccheus.

Of the four Gospel writers, Luke was the only Gentile. As an initial outsider to God's chosen community, he was intrigued by Jesus' compassionate attention to foreigners (Syrians, Romans, Greeks, Africans) and social outcasts (tax collectors, lepers, prostitutes, beggars).

No other biblical author includes as many women—or as sympathetically as Luke does. No other writer talks about children and describes family life as he does. This is delightfully surprising for one who was apparently a bachelor.

Luke made a rich contribution to apostolic history, the period when the gospel was established in the Roman Empire. As a cosmopolitan traveler, he was admirably suited to become a coworker and "beloved doctor" of Paul, the apostle to the Gentiles. Acts and Paul's letters hint that this companionship had a tempering effect on the fiery apostle who became Christianity's foremost church planter, theologian and statesman.

The Writing of Luke

Luke's Gospel is accurate and well organized. Its formal introduction reflects the writer's Greek literary background (1:1–4). Here he claims to follow the principles for writing dependable history: (1) acquaintance with similar accounts, (2) interviews with primary sources—eyewitnesses and leading personages, (3) investigation of reported events, (4) orderliness in arranging materials, and (5) a stated aim.

Most scholars think that Luke (like Matthew) probably used Mark's older Gospel as the structural basis of his Gospel. When, however, he does use Mark's stories, he often touches them lightly with an extra personal detail. For example, compare the openings of the Jairus story in Mark 5:21–23 and Luke 8:40–42.

Luke addresses his Gospel (and Acts) to Theophilus. We know nothing else about this man. His name, "lover of God," was an aristocratic Roman one, and not uncommon among government officials. He could have been an actual person or a literary representative of this upper class of Gentile readers. According to Luke 1:4, he was either a seeker or a new Christian in need of historical substantiation of the good news.

Characteristics of Luke

Luke writes history like an artist. He employs prose and poetry, dialogue and description. In his choice of events and people he uses rhythm of emphasis, comparisons and contrasts. He uses this last teaching technique especially well with broad subjects—for example, Jesus' compassion for outcasts and his condemnation of the Pharisees, and Jesus' teachings on freedom of life with God and the cost of discipleship.

In transitions Luke is especially artistic. Note how the change of persons and locations in chapter 1 is smoothened by moving from one pregnancy to another. Likewise, his summaries of events also serve as links to the next train of events (for example, 2:39–40 or 5:15–16).

His book overflows with worship, prayer and praise, hope and joy. It begins with Old Testament believers in the temple, worshiping in messianic hope. It ends with New Testament believers also in the temple, rejoicing in resurrection hope. In between we see Jesus interacting personally with the widest range of human beings found in any book of the Bible (or any book in the world)—the old and the young, the very poor and the very rich, Jews and foreigners, national/international leaders and the rejects of society, the highly articulate and the nonarticulate.

Watch for bits of humor (for example, in Jesus' parables and in the Zaccheus story), the role of the Holy Spirit, medical terms, Jesus' habits of prayer, and the "divine necessity" Jesus felt (2:49; 4:43; 13:16, 33; 17:25; 24:26). Luke's portrait of Jesus is strong, warm, compassionate and cosmopolitan—like the writer himself.

My prayer for you as you study comes from Paul the apostle, Luke's friend:

May the God of hope fill you with all joy and peace as you trust in him, so that you may overflow with hope by the power of the Holy Spirit. (Ro 15:13)

Outline

Part 1: Mission in Galilee

1/ Luke 1 ———————————————— *People of Hope*

Part 2: Mission in Samaria, Berea and Judea

1 / *Luke 1*
People of Hope

LUKE BEGINS HIS story of the extraordinary Christ by introducing some very ordinary people. They live in a small, second-rate country occupied by imperial Rome. It is around 4 B.C. For over 400 years their nation, Israel, has had no prophetic voice from God. Has God forgotten his chosen people? Has he left them to be the perennial pawns of aggressive neighbors? Is he going back on his many promises to send his Messiah to save them?

No. God is about to break into Israel's dark history with new light, and he chooses to do this through an elderly childless couple and a teenaged village girl.

 Warming Up to God How do you feel when you are part of a hopeful minority among pessimistic people on a committee or in a group?

 Read Luke 1.

1 Many have undertaken to draw up an account of the things that have been fulfilled*a* among us, ²just as they were handed down to us by those who from the first were eyewitnesses and servants of the word. ³Therefore, since I myself have carefully investigated everything from the beginning, it seemed good also to me to write an orderly account for you, most excellent Theophilus, ⁴so that you may know the certainty of the things you have been taught.

⁵In the time of Herod king of Judea there was a priest named Zechariah, who belonged to the priestly division of Abijah; his wife Elizabeth was also a descendant of Aaron. ⁶Both of them were upright in the sight of God, observing all the Lord's commandments and regulations blamelessly. ⁷But they had no children, because Elizabeth was barren; and they were both well along in years.

⁸Once when Zechariah's division was on duty and he was serving as priest before God, ⁹he was chosen by lot, according to the custom of the priesthood, to go into the temple of the Lord and burn incense. ¹⁰And when the time for the burning of incense came, all the assembled worshipers were praying outside.

¹¹Then an angel of the Lord appeared to him, standing at the right side of the altar of incense. ¹²When Zechariah saw him, he was startled and was gripped with fear. ¹³But the angel said to him: "Do not be afraid, Zechariah; your prayer has been heard. Your wife Elizabeth will bear you a son, and you are to give him the name John. ¹⁴He will be a joy and delight to you, and many will rejoice because of his birth, ¹⁵for he will be great

in the sight of the Lord. He is never to take wine or other fermented drink, and he will be filled with the Holy Spirit even from birth.*b* ¹⁶Many of the people of Israel will he bring back to the Lord their God. ¹⁷And he will go on before the Lord, in the spirit and power of Elijah, to turn the hearts of the fathers to their children and the disobedient to the wisdom of the righteous—to make ready a people prepared for the Lord."

¹⁸Zechariah asked the angel, "How can I be sure of this? I am an old man and my wife is well along in years."

¹⁹The angel answered, "I am Gabriel. I stand in the presence of God, and I have been sent to speak to you and to tell you this good news. ²⁰And now you will be silent and not able to speak until the day this happens, because you did not believe my words, which will come true at their proper time."

²¹Meanwhile, the people were waiting for Zechariah and wondering why he stayed so long in the temple. ²²When he came out, he could not speak to them. They realized he had seen a vision in the temple, for he kept making signs to them but remained unable to speak.

²³When his time of service was completed, he returned home. ²⁴After this his wife Elizabeth became pregnant and for five months remained in seclusion. ²⁵"The Lord has done this for me," she said. "In these days he has shown his favor and taken away my disgrace among the people."

²⁶In the sixth month, God sent the angel Gabriel to Nazareth, a town in Galilee, ²⁷to a virgin pledged to be married to a man named Joseph, a descendant of David. The virgin's name was

a1 Or been surely believed   *b15 Or from his mother's womb*

Mary. 28The angel went to her and said, "Greetings, you who are highly favored! The Lord is with you."

29Mary was greatly troubled at his words and wondered what kind of greeting this might be. 30But the angel said to her, "Do not be afraid, Mary, you have found favor with God. 31You will be with child and give birth to a son, and you are to give him the name Jesus. 32He will be great and will be called the Son of the Most High. The Lord God will give him the throne of his father David, 33and he will reign over the house of Jacob forever; his kingdom will never end."

34"How will this be," Mary asked the angel, "since I am a virgin?"

35The angel answered, "The Holy Spirit will come upon you, and the power of the Most High will overshadow you. So the holy one to be born will be called^c the Son of God. 36Even Elizabeth your relative is going to have a child in her old age, and she who was said to be barren is in her sixth month. 37For nothing is impossible with God."

38"I am the Lord's servant," Mary answered. "May it be to me as you have said." Then the angel left her.

39At that time Mary got ready and hurried to a town in the hill country of Judea, 40where she entered Zechariah's home and greeted Elizabeth. 41When Elizabeth heard Mary's greeting, the baby leaped in her womb, and Elizabeth was filled with the Holy Spirit. 42In a loud voice she exclaimed: "Blessed are you among women, and blessed is the child you will bear! 43But why am I so favored, that the mother of my Lord should come to me? 44As soon as the sound of your greeting reached my ears, the baby in my womb leaped for joy. 45Blessed is she who has believed that what the Lord has said to her will be accomplished!"

46And Mary said:

"My soul glorifies the Lord
47   and my spirit rejoices in God my Savior,
48for he has been mindful
    of the humble state of his servant.
  From now on all generations will call me
      blessed,
49   for the Mighty One has done great things
      for me—
    holy is his name.
50His mercy extends to those who fear him,
    from generation to generation.

51He has performed mighty deeds with his arm;
    he has scattered those who are proud in
        their inmost thoughts.
52He has brought down rulers from their
        thrones
    but has lifted up the humble.
53He has filled the hungry with good things
    but has sent the rich away empty.
54He has helped his servant Israel,
    remembering to be merciful
55to Abraham and his descendants forever,
    even as he said to our fathers."

56Mary stayed with Elizabeth for about three months and then returned home.

57When it was time for Elizabeth to have her baby, she gave birth to a son. 58Her neighbors and relatives heard that the Lord had shown her great mercy, and they shared her joy.

59On the eighth day they came to circumcise the child, and they were going to name him after his father Zechariah, 60but his mother spoke up and said, "No! He is to be called John."

61They said to her, "There is no one among your relatives who has that name."

62Then they made signs to his father, to find out what he would like to name the child. 63He asked for a writing tablet, and to everyone's astonishment he wrote, "His name is John." 64Immediately his mouth was opened and his tongue was loosed, and he began to speak, praising God. 65The neighbors were all filled with awe, and throughout the hill country of Judea people were talking about all these things. 66Everyone who heard this wondered about it, asking, "What then is this child going to be?" For the Lord's hand was with him.

67His father Zechariah was filled with the Holy Spirit and prophesied:

68"Praise be to the Lord, the God of Israel,
    because he has come and has redeemed his
        people.
69He has raised up a horn^d of salvation for us
    in the house of his servant David
70(as he said through his holy prophets of long
        ago),
71salvation from our enemies
    and from the hand of all who hate us—
72to show mercy to our fathers
    and to remember his holy covenant,

c 35 Or So the child to be born will be called holy,   d 69 Horn here symbolizes strength.

73 the oath he swore to our father Abraham:
74to rescue us from the hand of our enemies,
    and to enable us to serve him without fear
75 in holiness and righteousness before him all
        our days.

76And you, my child, will be called a prophet of
        the Most High;
    for you will go on before the Lord to
        prepare the way for him,
77to give his people the knowledge of salvation

through the forgiveness of their sins,
78because of the tender mercy of our God,
    by which the rising sun will come to us
        from heaven
79to shine on those living in darkness
    and in the shadow of death,
    to guide our feet into the path of peace."

80And the child grew and became strong in
spirit; and he lived in the desert until he appeared
publicly to Israel.

Discovering the Word 1. Gabriel announces some astounding facts to Zechariah about his son who is to be born (vv. 11–17). Do you find yourself sympathetic or critical of Zechariah's response of unbelief (vv. 18–22)? Explain. 2. Luke 1:26–56 has Gabriel's second birth announcement. How is it even more extraordinary than the first? 3. The visit to her cousin Elizabeth bolsters Mary's faith for the stupendous event to come. As expressed in her song of response, what kind of God does she believe in (vv. 46–55)? 4. Note the effects of John's birth on neighbors and relatives (vv. 57–66). What might be Luke's purpose in describing their response in such detail? 5. In Zechariah's inspired prophecy he sees (1) the great acts that God's Redeemer will do (vv. 68–75), and (2) his child's unique relation to this Redeemer (vv. 76–79). Suppose you were one of Zechariah's neighbors or relatives listening to him. Which part would have stirred you as a devout Jew? Explain.

Applying the Word 1. When is it difficult for you to hope in God? 2. Zechariah and Mary expressed their hope in God differently. What in their interaction with God gives you hope as you also seek to trust God totally?

Responding in Prayer Thank God for being the only source of true hope.

---

2 / *Luke 2*
Child of Hope

DID YOU HEAR the one about the woman shopper at Christmas who came upon a nativity scene in the store window? In disgust she exclaimed, "Now look what they're dragging into Christmas. Religion!"

Warming Up to God For you, what is most meaningful at Christmas?

Read Luke 2.

---

2 In those days Caesar Augustus issued a decree that a census should be taken of the entire Roman world. 2(This was the first census that took place while Quirinius was governor of Syria.) 3And everyone went to his own town to register.

4So Joseph also went up from the town of Nazareth in Galilee to Judea, to Bethlehem the town of David, because he belonged to the house and line of David. 5He went there to register with

Mary, who was pledged to be married to him and was expecting a child. 6While they were there, the time came for the baby to be born, 7and she gave birth to her firstborn, a son. She wrapped him in cloths and placed him in a manger, because there was no room for them in the inn.

8And there were shepherds living out in the fields nearby, keeping watch over their flocks at night. 9An angel of the Lord appeared to them, and the glory of the Lord shone around them, and they were terrified. [10]But the angel said to them, "Do not be afraid. I bring you good news of great joy that will be for all the people. [11]Today in the town of David a Savior has been born to you; he is Christ[e] the Lord. [12]This will be a sign to you: You will find a baby wrapped in cloths and lying in a manger."

[13]Suddenly a great company of the heavenly host appeared with the angel, praising God and saying,

[14]"Glory to God in the highest,
and on earth peace to men on whom his
favor rests."

[15]When the angels had left them and gone into heaven, the shepherds said to one another, "Let's go to Bethlehem and see this thing that has happened, which the Lord has told us about."

[16]So they hurried off and found Mary and Joseph, and the baby, who was lying in the manger. [17]When they had seen him, they spread the word concerning what had been told them about this child, [18]and all who heard it were amazed at what the shepherds said to them. [19]But Mary treasured up all these things and pondered them in her heart. [20]The shepherds returned, glorifying and praising God for all the things they had heard and seen, which were just as they had been told.

[21]On the eighth day, when it was time to circumcise him, he was named Jesus, the name the angel had given him before he had been conceived.

[22]When the time of their purification according to the Law of Moses had been completed, Joseph and Mary took him to Jerusalem to present him to the Lord [23](as it is written in the Law of the Lord, "Every firstborn male is to be consecrated to the Lord"[f]), [24]and to offer a sacrifice in keeping with what is said in the Law of the Lord: "a pair of doves or two young pigeons."[g]

[25]Now there was a man in Jerusalem called Simeon, who was righteous and devout. He was waiting for the consolation of Israel, and the Holy Spirit was upon him. [26]It had been revealed to him by the Holy Spirit that he would not die before he had seen the Lord's Christ. [27]Moved by the Spirit, he went into the temple courts. When the parents brought in the child Jesus to do for him what the custom of the Law required, [28]Simeon took him in his arms and praised God, saying:

[29]"Sovereign Lord, as you have promised,
you now dismiss[h] your servant in peace.
[30]For my eyes have seen your salvation,
[31]   which you have prepared in the sight of all
people,
[32]a light for revelation to the Gentiles
and for glory to your people Israel."

[33]The child's father and mother marveled at what was said about him. [34]Then Simeon blessed them and said to Mary, his mother: "This child is destined to cause the falling and rising of many in Israel, and to be a sign that will be spoken against, [35]so that the thoughts of many hearts will be revealed. And a sword will pierce your own soul too."

[36]There was also a prophetess, Anna, the daughter of Phanuel, of the tribe of Asher. She was very old; she had lived with her husband seven years after her marriage, [37]and then was a widow until she was eighty-four.[i] She never left the temple but worshiped night and day, fasting and praying. [38]Coming up to them at that very moment, she gave thanks to God and spoke about the child to all who were looking forward to the redemption of Jerusalem.

[39]When Joseph and Mary had done everything required by the Law of the Lord, they returned to Galilee to their own town of Nazareth. [40]And the child grew and became strong; he was filled with wisdom, and the grace of God was upon him.

[41]Every year his parents went to Jerusalem for the Feast of the Passover. [42]When he was twelve years old, they went up to the Feast, according to the custom. [43]After the Feast was over, while his parents were returning home, the boy Jesus stayed behind in Jerusalem, but they were unaware of it. [44]Thinking he was in their company, they traveled on for a day. Then they began looking for him among their relatives and friends. [45]When they did not find him, they went back to Jerusalem to look for him. [46]After three days they found him in the temple courts, sitting among the teachers, listening to them and asking them questions. [47]Everyone who heard him was amazed at his understanding and his answers. [48]When his parents saw him, they were astonished. His mother said to him, "Son, why have you treated

e11 Or Messiah. "The Christ" (Greek) and "the Messiah" (Hebrew) both mean "the Anointed One"; also in verse 26.   f23 Exodus 13:2,12   g24 Lev. 12:8   h29 Or promised, / now dismiss   i37 Or widow for eighty-four years

us like this? Your father and I have been anxiously searching for you."

⁴⁹"Why were you searching for me?" he asked. "Didn't you know I had to be in my Father's house?" ⁵⁰But they did not understand what he was saying to them.

⁵¹Then he went down to Nazareth with them and was obedient to them. But his mother treasured all these things in her heart. ⁵²And Jesus grew in wisdom and stature, and in favor with God and men.

 Discovering the Word 1. As with other strategic events, Luke gives the historical setting of the birth of Jesus (vv. 1–4). What implications does this setting suggest about the world into which Jesus came? 2. Luke gives us few details of Jesus' birth in verses 6–7. But what impression does he leave with you? 3. We like shepherds on Christmas cards. But back then they were an outcast group. So what in the angels' message would be incredible to them (vv. 9–14)? 4. The second and third prophetic events (note that the naming of Jesus was a prophetic event) are closely tied together (2:22–28). In what ways are Simeon and Anna similar? 5. How are their prophetic messages about Jesus similar yet different?

 Applying the Word 1. Compare yourself with Jesus' development (vv. 40, 49, 51–52). In which area do you think you need more growth? 2. What can you begin to do to experience that growth?

Responding in Prayer Ask God to mold you into the person he wants you to be.

---

3 / *Luke 3:1–20*
Public Preparation

SEVERAL YEARS AGO, before Queen Elizabeth arrived in a British Commonwealth country, its people feverishly prepared a royal welcome. They gave special attention to the highway running from the airport to the capital. Each house along the way received from the government a fresh coat of paint—but only on the front of the house!

Superficial changes that people can notice—that's all some Christian leaders seem to ask for. Not so the preaching of John the Baptizer. He asked for radical moral changes, reversals of lifestyle.

 Warming Up to God In what way are you likely to be satisfied with superficial changes in your own life?

 Read Luke 3:1–20.

---

3 In the fifteenth year of the reign of Tiberius Caesar—when Pontius Pilate was governor of Judea, Herod tetrarch of Galilee, his brother Philip tetrarch of Iturea and Traconitis, and Lysanias tetrarch of Abilene— ²during the high priesthood of Annas and Caiaphas, the word of God came to John son of Zechariah in the desert. ³He went into all the country around the Jordan, preaching a baptism of repentance for the forgiveness of sins. ⁴As is written in the book of the words of Isaiah the prophet:

"A voice of one calling in the desert,
'Prepare the way for the Lord,
    make straight paths for him.

⁵Every valley shall be filled in,
    every mountain and hill made low.
The crooked roads shall become straight,
    the rough ways smooth.
⁶And all mankind will see God's salvation.' "ʲ

⁷John said to the crowds coming out to be baptized by him, "You brood of vipers! Who warned you to flee from the coming wrath? ⁸Produce fruit in keeping with repentance. And do not begin to say to yourselves, 'We have Abraham as our father.' For I tell you that out of these stones God can raise up children for Abraham. ⁹The ax is already at the root of the trees, and every tree that

ʲ6 Isaiah 40:3-5

does not produce good fruit will be cut down and thrown into the fire."

¹⁰"What should we do then?" the crowd asked.

¹¹John answered, "The man with two tunics should share with him who has none, and the one who has food should do the same."

¹²Tax collectors also came to be baptized. "Teacher," they asked, "what should we do?"

¹³"Don't collect any more than you are required to," he told them.

¹⁴Then some soldiers asked him, "And what should we do?"

He replied, "Don't extort money and don't accuse people falsely—be content with your pay."

¹⁵The people were waiting expectantly and were all wondering in their hearts if John might possibly be the Christ.ᵏ ¹⁶John answered them all, "I baptize you withˡ water. But one more powerful than I will come, the thongs of whose sandals I am not worthy to untie. He will baptize you with the Holy Spirit and with fire. ¹⁷His winnowing fork is in his hand to clear his threshing floor and to gather the wheat into his barn, but he will burn up the chaff with unquenchable fire." ¹⁸And with many other words John exhorted the people and preached the good news to them.

¹⁹But when John rebuked Herod the tetrarch because of Herodias, his brother's wife, and all the other evil things he had done, ²⁰Herod added this to them all: He locked John up in prison.

ᵏ15 Or Messiah ˡ16 Or in

Discovering the Word 1. Reflect on John's dominant preaching theme in verses 3–9. How would you paraphrase this theme with contemporary relevance? 2. John gladly answers three distinct groups asking about the practical fruits of repentance. What basic sin does John attack in each case (vv. 8–14)? 3. In verses 15–20 John introduces Jesus the Christ. He has been uncompromising about the need for repentance. Now he also refuses to let the crowds think he is the expected Christ. In warning them, what picture of the Christ does he paint? 4. Like repentance, judgment is not a popular topic today among many Christians. Yet how is this also part of "the good news" (v. 18)?

Applying the Word 1. What injustices in your society would John attack? 2. John's message and ministry show what repentance should be. How would you explain repentance to inquirers in terms that make sense to them?

Responding in Prayer Pray for a friend who needs this explanation.

---

4 / *Luke 3:21—4:13*
Personal Preparation

"THE BEST WAY to get rid of temptation is to give in to it," said Oscar Wilde. He was the brilliant, flamboyant Irish writer of the second half of the nineteenth century. He died young, gifted and dissipated by his unbridled passions.

Jesus also died young and gifted, but disciplined by his passion for God. His discipline began in childhood where we have already observed an early consciousness of his life mission. Now, at thirty, he submits himself to more tests to prepare him further for this goal.

Warming Up to God What would you like to have achieved ten years from now?

Read Luke 3:21—4:13.

---

²¹When all the people were being baptized, Jesus was baptized too. And as he was praying, heaven was opened ²²and the Holy Spirit descended on him in bodily form like a dove. And a voice came from heaven: "You are my Son, whom I love; with you I am well pleased."

23Now Jesus himself was about thirty years old when he began his ministry. He was the son, so it was thought, of Joseph,

the son of Heli, 24the son of Matthat,
the son of Levi, the son of Melki,
the son of Jannai, the son of Joseph,
25the son of Mattathias, the son of Amos,
the son of Nahum, the son of Esli,
the son of Naggai, 26the son of Maath,
the son of Mattathias, the son of Semein,
the son of Josech, the son of Joda,
27the son of Joanan, the son of Rhesa,
the son of Zerubbabel, the son of Shealtiel,
the son of Neri, 28the son of Melki,
the son of Addi, the son of Cosam,
the son of Elmadam, the son of Er,
29the son of Joshua, the son of Eliezer,
the son of Jorim, the son of Matthat,
the son of Levi, 30the son of Simeon,
the son of Judah, the son of Joseph,
the son of Jonam, the son of Eliakim,
31the son of Melea, the son of Menna,
the son of Mattatha, the son of Nathan,
the son of David, 32the son of Jesse,
the son of Obed, the son of Boaz,
the son of Salmon,m the son of Nahshon,
33the son of Amminadab, the son of Ram,n
the son of Hezron, the son of Perez,
the son of Judah, 34the son of Jacob,
the son of Isaac, the son of Abraham,
the son of Terah, the son of Nahor,
35the son of Serug, the son of Reu,
the son of Peleg, the son of Eber,
the son of Shelah, 36the son of Cainan,
the son of Arphaxad, the son of Shem,
the son of Noah, the son of Lamech,
37the son of Methuselah, the son of Enoch,
the son of Jared, the son of Mahalalel,

the son of Kenan, 38the son of Enosh,
the son of Seth, the son of Adam,
the son of God.

4 Jesus, full of the Holy Spirit, returned from the Jordan and was led by the Spirit in the desert, 2where for forty days he was tempted by the devil. He ate nothing during those days, and at the end of them he was hungry.

3The devil said to him, "If you are the Son of God, tell this stone to become bread."

4Jesus answered, "It is written: 'Man does not live on bread alone.'o"

5The devil led him up to a high place and showed him in an instant all the kingdoms of the world. 6And he said to him, "I will give you all their authority and splendor, for it has been given to me, and I can give it to anyone I want to. 7So if you worship me, it will all be yours."

8Jesus answered, "It is written: 'Worship the Lord your God and serve him only.'p"

9The devil led him to Jerusalem and had him stand on the highest point of the temple. "If you are the Son of God," he said, "throw yourself down from here. 10For it is written:

" 'He will command his angels concerning you
    to guard you carefully;
11they will lift you up in their hands,
    so that you will not strike your foot against
    a stone.'q"

12Jesus answered, "It says: 'Do not put the Lord your God to the test.'r"

13When the devil had finished all this tempting, he left him until an opportune time.

m32 Some early manuscripts Sala   n33 Some manuscripts
Amminadab, the son of Admin, the son of Arni; other manuscripts vary
widely.   o4 Deut. 8:3   p8 Deut. 6:13   q11 Psalm 91:11,12
r12 Deut. 6:16

Discovering the Word 1. Jesus did not have to be baptized for the forgiveness of his sins (v. 3). But by this public act he identified with our human race in need of repentance and forgiveness. What do Luke's details emphasize about Jesus' baptism? 2. Luke's genealogy of Jesus begins with his father, Joseph, and passing Abraham moves all the way back to "Adam, the son of God" (3:23–38). What does Luke want to bring out about Jesus? 3. Temptations are strong appeals to satisfy legitimate desires in wrong circumstances or by wrong means. What natural desire is the devil trying to get Jesus to satisfy in each appeal? 4. God created these desires. Why then would it become sin if Jesus were to satisfy each desire in his circumstances then?

Applying the Word 1. What do you learn from Jesus about dealing with temptations? 2. If we want to serve God wholeheartedly, we too must undergo tough training. In which area do you feel the greatest need for discipline? 3. What should be your first step in that direction?

 Responding in Prayer Pray that God would work in your life to prepare you for the ministry he has for you.

5 / *Luke 4:14—5:16*
Promising Yet Dangerous Beginnings

SOMETIMES PEOPLE SAY, "Everything has been going so well that I feel something awful coming." They know enough about life not to expect good things to continue forever. But we need not be fatalistic. We can be both realistic and positive about expectations in life. We have seen how well Jesus began. We shall also see how realistic he was about fickle human nature and how he drew out the best in people who wanted to follow him.

 Warming Up to God When you've felt rejection (on any level), what was your greatest fear?

 Read Luke 4:14—5:16.

---

¹⁴Jesus returned to Galilee in the power of the Spirit, and news about him spread through the whole countryside. ¹⁵He taught in their synagogues, and everyone praised him.

¹⁶He went to Nazareth, where he had been brought up, and on the Sabbath day he went into the synagogue, as was his custom. And he stood up to read. ¹⁷The scroll of the prophet Isaiah was handed to him. Unrolling it, he found the place where it is written:

¹⁸"The Spirit of the Lord is on me,
  because he has anointed me
  to preach good news to the poor.
He has sent me to proclaim freedom for the
     prisoners
  and recovery of sight for the blind,
to release the oppressed,
¹⁹ to proclaim the year of the Lord's favor."ˢ

²⁰Then he rolled up the scroll, gave it back to the attendant and sat down. The eyes of everyone in the synagogue were fastened on him, ²¹and he began by saying to them, "Today this scripture is fulfilled in your hearing."

²²All spoke well of him and were amazed at the gracious words that came from his lips. "Isn't this Joseph's son?" they asked.

²³Jesus said to them, "Surely you will quote this proverb to me: 'Physician, heal yourself! Do here in your hometown what we have heard that you did in Capernaum.' "

²⁴"I tell you the truth," he continued, "no prophet is accepted in his hometown. ²⁵I assure you that there were many widows in Israel in Elijah's time, when the sky was shut for three and a half years and there was a severe famine throughout the land. ²⁶Yet Elijah was not sent to any of them, but to a widow in Zarephath in the region of Sidon. ²⁷And there were many in Israel with leprosyᵗ in the time of Elisha the prophet, yet not one of them was cleansed—only Naaman the Syrian."

²⁸All the people in the synagogue were furious when they heard this. ²⁹They got up, drove him out of the town, and took him to the brow of the hill on which the town was built, in order to throw him down the cliff. ³⁰But he walked right through the crowd and went on his way.

³¹Then he went down to Capernaum, a town in Galilee, and on the Sabbath began to teach the people. ³²They were amazed at his teaching, because his message had authority.

³³In the synagogue there was a man possessed by a demon, an evilᵘ spirit. He cried out at the top of his voice, ³⁴"Ha! What do you want with us, Jesus of Nazareth? Have you come to destroy us? I know who you are—the Holy One of God!"

³⁵"Be quiet!" Jesus said sternly. "Come out of him!" Then the demon threw the man down before them all and came out without injuring him.

³⁶All the people were amazed and said to each other, "What is this teaching? With authority and power he gives orders to evil spirits and they come out!" ³⁷And the news about him spread throughout the surrounding area.

³⁸Jesus left the synagogue and went to the home of Simon. Now Simon's mother-in-law was suffering from a high fever, and they asked Jesus to help her. ³⁹So he bent over her and rebuked the fever, and it left her. She got up at once and began to wait on them.

⁴⁰When the sun was setting, the people brought to Jesus all who had various kinds of sickness, and laying his hands on each one, he

ˢ19 Isaiah 61:1,2   ᵗ27 The Greek word was used for various diseases affecting the skin—not necessarily leprosy.   ᵘ33 Greek *unclean*; also in verse 36

healed them. ⁴¹Moreover, demons came out of many people, shouting, "You are the Son of God!" But he rebuked them and would not allow them to speak, because they knew he was the Christ.ᵛ

⁴²At daybreak Jesus went out to a solitary place. The people were looking for him and when they came to where he was, they tried to keep him from leaving them. ⁴³But he said, "I must preach the good news of the kingdom of God to the other towns also, because that is why I was sent." ⁴⁴And he kept on preaching in the synagogues of Judea.ʷ

5 One day as Jesus was standing by the Lake of Gennesaret,ˣ with the people crowding around him and listening to the word of God, ²he saw at the water's edge two boats, left there by the fishermen, who were washing their nets. ³He got into one of the boats, the one belonging to Simon, and asked him to put out a little from shore. Then he sat down and taught the people from the boat.

⁴When he had finished speaking, he said to Simon, "Put out into deep water, and let downʸ the nets for a catch."

⁵Simon answered, "Master, we've worked hard all night and haven't caught anything. But because you say so, I will let down the nets."

⁶When they had done so, they caught such a large number of fish that their nets began to break. ⁷So they signaled their partners in the other boat to come and help them, and they came and filled both boats so full that they began to sink.

⁸When Simon Peter saw this, he fell at Jesus' knees and said, "Go away from me, Lord; I am a sinful man!" ⁹For he and all his companions were astonished at the catch of fish they had taken, ¹⁰and so were James and John, the sons of Zebedee, Simon's partners.

Then Jesus said to Simon, "Don't be afraid; from now on you will catch men." ¹¹So they pulled their boats up on shore, left everything and followed him.

¹²While Jesus was in one of the towns, a man came along who was covered with leprosy.ᶻ When he saw Jesus, he fell with his face to the ground and begged him, "Lord, if you are willing, you can make me clean."

¹³Jesus reached out his hand and touched the man. "I am willing," he said. "Be clean!" And immediately the leprosy left him.

¹⁴Then Jesus ordered him, "Don't tell anyone, but go, show yourself to the priest and offer the sacrifices that Moses commanded for your cleansing, as a testimony to them."

¹⁵Yet the news about him spread all the more, so that crowds of people came to hear him and to be healed of their sicknesses. ¹⁶But Jesus often withdrew to lonely places and prayed.

ᵛ41 Or *Messiah*   ʷ44 Or *the land of the Jews*; some manuscripts *Galilee*   ˣ1 That is, Sea of Galilee   ʸ4 The Greek verb is plural.
ᶻ12 The Greek word was used for various diseases affecting the skin—not necessarily leprosy.

Discovering the Word 1. What link do you see between Jesus' temptations and the beginning of his mission (4:14–15)? 2. Watch the people's changing attitudes to Jesus (vv. 14–15, 20–22, 28–29). What has caused the radical change? 3. What prejudices can make people today object to Jesus' good news or perhaps to Jesus himself? How would you respond to these objections? 4. Having been rejected by Nazareth, Jesus now makes Capernaum his base of operations. Here Luke describes what may be a typical work day for Jesus. Identify his activities during that period (4:31–44). 5. Read Luke 5:1–16. Note the progressive steps by which Jesus persuades Simon Peter to leave everything and follow him. When you met Jesus, what tensions arose as you recognized the need to leave everything to follow him?

Applying the Word 1. What can you learn from Jesus' example of dealing with rejection? 2. In its context Jesus' healing of the leper appears to be a personal encounter, typical of his opening ministry. As such then, what do you observe about Jesus as a people helper? 3. Think of your ministry to others. Which of Jesus' ministering qualities do you want to have added to or reinforced in your life?

 Responding in Prayer Praise God for such a practical Teacher and Lord!

6 / *Luke 5:17—6:11*
Radical Authority

GOD IS ALWAYS full of surprises. Those who know him delight in this. This, however, upsets people who feel secure only with neatly structured beliefs that are left untouched. One problem for them is that every now and then God chooses to do something new and fresh. Then packaged religions and secure traditions fall apart! This often happened when Jesus came on Israel's religious scene with surprising teaching and authority.

 Warming Up to God Do you wish you had more or less authority in your life? Why?

 Read Luke 5:17—6:11.

---

¹⁷One day as he was teaching, Pharisees and teachers of the law, who had come from every village of Galilee and from Judea and Jerusalem, were sitting there. And the power of the Lord was present for him to heal the sick. ¹⁸Some men came carrying a paralytic on a mat and tried to take him into the house to lay him before Jesus. ¹⁹When they could not find a way to do this because of the crowd, they went up on the roof and lowered him on his mat through the tiles into the middle of the crowd, right in front of Jesus.

²⁰When Jesus saw their faith, he said, "Friend, your sins are forgiven."

²¹The Pharisees and the teachers of the law began thinking to themselves, "Who is this fellow who speaks blasphemy? Who can forgive sins but God alone?"

²²Jesus knew what they were thinking and asked, "Why are you thinking these things in your hearts? ²³Which is easier: to say, 'Your sins are forgiven,' or to say, 'Get up and walk'? ²⁴But that you may know that the Son of Man has authority on earth to forgive sins. . . ." He said to the paralyzed man, "I tell you, get up, take your mat and go home." ²⁵Immediately he stood up in front of them, took what he had been lying on and went home praising God. ²⁶Everyone was amazed and gave praise to God. They were filled with awe and said, "We have seen remarkable things today."

²⁷After this, Jesus went out and saw a tax collector by the name of Levi sitting at his tax booth. "Follow me," Jesus said to him, ²⁸and Levi got up, left everything and followed him.

²⁹Then Levi held a great banquet for Jesus at his house, and a large crowd of tax collectors and others were eating with them. ³⁰But the Pharisees and the teachers of the law who belonged to their sect complained to his disciples, "Why do you eat and drink with tax collectors and 'sinners'?"

³¹Jesus answered them, "It is not the healthy who need a doctor, but the sick. ³²I have not come to call the righteous, but sinners to repentance."

³³They said to him, "John's disciples often fast and pray, and so do the disciples of the Pharisees, but yours go on eating and drinking."

³⁴Jesus answered, "Can you make the guests of the bridegroom fast while he is with them? ³⁵But the time will come when the bridegroom will be taken from them; in those days they will fast."

³⁶He told them this parable: "No one tears a patch from a new garment and sews it on an old one. If he does, he will have torn the new garment, and the patch from the new will not match the old. ³⁷And no one pours new wine into old wineskins. If he does, the new wine will burst the skins, the wine will run out and the wineskins will be ruined. ³⁸No, new wine must be poured into new wineskins. ³⁹And no one after drinking old wine wants the new, for he says, 'The old is better.' "

6 One Sabbath Jesus was going through the grainfields, and his disciples began to pick some heads of grain, rub them in their hands and eat the kernels. ²Some of the Pharisees asked, "Why are you doing what is unlawful on the Sabbath?"

³Jesus answered them, "Have you never read what David did when he and his companions were hungry? ⁴He entered the house of God, and taking the consecrated bread, he ate what is lawful only for priests to eat. And he also gave some to his companions." ⁵Then Jesus said to them, "The Son of Man is Lord of the Sabbath."

⁶On another Sabbath he went into the syna-

gogue and was teaching, and a man was there whose right hand was shriveled. 7The Pharisees and the teachers of the law were looking for a reason to accuse Jesus, so they watched him closely to see if he would heal on the Sabbath. 8But Jesus knew what they were thinking and said to the man with the shriveled hand, "Get up and stand in front of everyone." So he got up and stood there.

9Then Jesus said to them, "I ask you, which is lawful on the Sabbath: to do good or to do evil, to save life or to destroy it?"

10He looked around at them all, and then said to the man, "Stretch out your hand." He did so, and his hand was completely restored. 11But they were furious and began to discuss with one another what they might do to Jesus.

Discovering the Word 1. Imagine yourself a part of the religious establishment mentioned in 5:17. How would you have viewed Jesus' growing popularity? 2. Compare the Pharisees' questions in 5:21, 30, 33; 6:2, 7—criticisms which climax in 6:11. What pattern(s) do you observe? 3. What skills in answering religious critics can you learn from Jesus?

Applying the Word 1. Jesus was relentless in his battle with the religious legalists of his day. He clearly saw that in distorting God's laws they also distorted God's image. What religious legalisms can keep you from enjoying the Lord and his true sabbath? 2. Over which area of your life do you see Jesus exercising authority? 3. Over which area of your life do you sense an absence of Jesus' authority?

Responding in Prayer Ask Jesus to rule over your *whole* life.

7 / *Luke 6:12–49*
Radical Lifestyle

MAHATMA MOHANDAS GANDHI was India's revered leader in the fight for national independence from British colonialism. As a child in India, a student in England and a lawyer in South Africa, he was exposed to Christianity—and racism. He admired the teachings of Jesus, especially the Sermon on the Mount. He admired the life of Jesus, and indeed was inspired to follow his example. But after years of observing Christians, he sadly concluded, "For me to believe in their Redeemer, their lives must show they are redeemed." He never became a Christian.

A Christian's lifestyle matters—not only correct words. The total teaching and example of Jesus demands a lifestyle that is noticeably different from the average person's.

Warming Up to God Describe someone you know who has a truly Christlike lifestyle.

Read Luke 6:12–49.

12One of those days Jesus went out to a mountainside to pray, and spent the night praying to God. 13When morning came, he called his disciples to him and chose twelve of them, whom he also designated apostles: 14Simon (whom he named Peter), his brother Andrew, James, John, Philip, Bartholomew, 15Matthew, Thomas, James son of Alphaeus, Simon who was called the Zealot, 16Judas son of James, and Judas Iscariot, who became a traitor.

17He went down with them and stood on a level place. A large crowd of his disciples was there and a great number of people from all over Judea, from Jerusalem, and from the coast of Tyre and Sidon, 18who had come to hear him and to be healed of their diseases. Those troubled by evil*a* spirits were cured, 19and the people all tried to touch him, because power was coming from him and healing them all.

20Looking at his disciples, he said:

*a*18 Greek *unclean*

"Blessed are you who are poor,
   for yours is the kingdom of God.
21Blessed are you who hunger now,
   for you will be satisfied.
Blessed are you who weep now,
   for you will laugh.
22Blessed are you when men hate you,
   when they exclude you and insult you
   and reject your name as evil,
      because of the Son of Man.

23"Rejoice in that day and leap for joy, because great is your reward in heaven. For that is how their fathers treated the prophets.

24"But woe to you who are rich,
   for you have already received your comfort.
25Woe to you who are well fed now,
   for you will go hungry.
Woe to you who laugh now,
   for you will mourn and weep.
26Woe to you when all men speak well of you,
   for that is how their fathers treated the
      false prophets.

27"But I tell you who hear me: Love your enemies, do good to those who hate you, 28bless those who curse you, pray for those who mistreat you. 29If someone strikes you on one cheek, turn to him the other also. If someone takes your cloak, do not stop him from taking your tunic. 30Give to everyone who asks you, and if anyone takes what belongs to you, do not demand it back. 31Do to others as you would have them do to you.

32"If you love those who love you, what credit is that to you? Even 'sinners' love those who love them. 33And if you do good to those who are good to you, what credit is that to you? Even 'sinners' do that. 34And if you lend to those from whom you expect repayment, what credit is that to you? Even 'sinners' lend to 'sinners,' expecting to be repaid in full. 35But love your enemies, do good to them, and lend to them without expecting to get anything back. Then your reward will be great, and you will be sons of the Most High, because he is kind to the ungrateful and wicked. 36Be merciful, just as your Father is merciful.

37"Do not judge, and you will not be judged. Do not condemn, and you will not be condemned. Forgive, and you will be forgiven. 38Give, and it will be given to you. A good measure, pressed down, shaken together and running over, will be poured into your lap. For with the measure you use, it will be measured to you."

39He also told them this parable: "Can a blind man lead a blind man? Will they not both fall into a pit? 40A student is not above his teacher, but everyone who is fully trained will be like his teacher.

41"Why do you look at the speck of sawdust in your brother's eye and pay no attention to the plank in your own eye? 42How can you say to your brother, 'Brother, let me take the speck out of your eye,' when you yourself fail to see the plank in your own eye? You hypocrite, first take the plank out of your eye, and then you will see clearly to remove the speck from your brother's eye.

43"No good tree bears bad fruit, nor does a bad tree bear good fruit. 44Each tree is recognized by its own fruit. People do not pick figs from thornbushes, or grapes from briers. 45The good man brings good things out of the good stored up in his heart, and the evil man brings evil things out of the evil stored up in his heart. For out of the overflow of his heart his mouth speaks.

46"Why do you call me, 'Lord, Lord,' and do not do what I say? 47I will show you what he is like who comes to me and hears my words and puts them into practice. 48He is like a man building a house, who dug down deep and laid the foundation on rock. When a flood came, the torrent struck that house but could not shake it, because it was well built. 49But the one who hears my words and does not put them into practice is like a man who built a house on the ground without a foundation. The moment the torrent struck that house, it collapsed and its destruction was complete."

Discovering the Word   1. In verses 17–19 Luke has carefully given us the setting for the "Sermon on the Plain." What kinds of people are in Jesus' audience?   2. Jesus begins with kingdom attitudes that shape one's lifestyle. What contrasts does he draw between his way of personal fulfillment and the world's way (vv. 20–26)?   3. Jesus knows that loving one's enemies is impossible without strong motivation. How does he argue that his disciples can have that motivation (vv. 31–36)?   4. In verse 37 Jesus is probably being facetious, for he knows it is impossible not to judge others. Rather we are to judge with good sense. What guidelines does he give to judge in this way (vv. 37b–42)?   5. Jesus concludes by warning his listeners of the long-term results of their present choice of lifestyle (vv. 43–49). How do his logic and illustrations sharpen his argument?

 Applying the Word   1. In what ways have you found Jesus' road to happiness the right one? Or an unsatisfactory one?   2. Loving one's enemies is another aspect of a radical Christian lifestyle. In what ways does your enemy make it hard for you to love him/her?   3. What in this study gives you hope that you can maintain the kind of radical lifestyle Jesus expects of his followers?

 Responding in Prayer   Pray for the strength and wisdom you need to love your enemies.

8 / *Luke 7*
Five People of Faith

AN ARTIST FRIEND struggled over the exclusive claim of the Christian faith. Is Jesus really the only way to God? Growing up in a pluralistic society had conditioned her to resist such an intolerant position. Because she was still interested, some Christians pressured her to "accept Jesus as your Savior and Lord." She could not. But she privately pursued the Gospels. She began to note how differently people approached Jesus and how personally he treated each of them. Gradually she saw a distinction: There is indeed only one way to God—through Jesus Christ—but there are many ways to Jesus Christ. Today we meet five persons with diverse backgrounds and varying approaches to Jesus—all different in expressing faith in Jesus.

 Warming Up to God   When is it hard for you to accept the idea that there is only one way to God?

Read Luke 7.

7 When Jesus had finished saying all this in the hearing of the people, he entered Capernaum. ²There a centurion's servant, whom his master valued highly, was sick and about to die. ³The centurion heard of Jesus and sent some elders of the Jews to him, asking him to come and heal his servant. ⁴When they came to Jesus, they pleaded earnestly with him, "This man deserves to have you do this, ⁵because he loves our nation and has built our synagogue." ⁶So Jesus went with them.

He was not far from the house when the centurion sent friends to say to him: "Lord, don't trouble yourself, for I do not deserve to have you come under my roof. ⁷That is why I did not even consider myself worthy to come to you. But say the word, and my servant will be healed. ⁸For I myself am a man under authority, with soldiers under me. I tell this one, 'Go,' and he goes; and that one, 'Come,' and he comes. I say to my servant, 'Do this,' and he does it."

⁹When Jesus heard this, he was amazed at him, and turning to the crowd following him, he said, "I tell you, I have not found such great faith even in Israel." ¹⁰Then the men who had been sent returned to the house and found the servant well.

¹¹Soon afterward, Jesus went to a town called Nain, and his disciples and a large crowd went along with him. ¹²As he approached the town gate, a dead person was being carried out—the only son of his mother, and she was a widow. And a large crowd from the town was with her. ¹³When the Lord saw her, his heart went out to her and he said, "Don't cry."

¹⁴Then he went up and touched the coffin, and those carrying it stood still. He said, "Young man, I say to you, get up!" ¹⁵The dead man sat up and began to talk, and Jesus gave him back to his mother.

¹⁶They were all filled with awe and praised God. "A great prophet has appeared among us," they said. "God has come to help his people." ¹⁷This news about Jesus spread throughout Judea*ᵇ* and the surrounding country.

¹⁸John's disciples told him about all these things. Calling two of them, ¹⁹he sent them to the

ᵇ17 Or the land of the Jews

Lord to ask, "Are you the one who was to come, or should we expect someone else?"

20When the men came to Jesus, they said, "John the Baptist sent us to you to ask, 'Are you the one who was to come, or should we expect someone else?' "

21At that very time Jesus cured many who had diseases, sicknesses and evil spirits, and gave sight to many who were blind. 22So he replied to the messengers, "Go back and report to John what you have seen and heard: The blind receive sight, the lame walk, those who have leprosy*c* are cured, the deaf hear, the dead are raised, and the good news is preached to the poor. 23Blessed is the man who does not fall away on account of me."

24After John's messengers left, Jesus began to speak to the crowd about John: "What did you go out into the desert to see? A reed swayed by the wind? 25If not, what did you go out to see? A man dressed in fine clothes? No, those who wear expensive clothes and indulge in luxury are in palaces. 26But what did you go out to see? A prophet? Yes, I tell you, and more than a prophet. 27This is the one about whom it is written:

" 'I will send my messenger ahead of you,
  who will prepare your way before you.'*d*

28I tell you, among those born of women there is no one greater than John; yet the one who is least in the kingdom of God is greater than he."

29(All the people, even the tax collectors, when they heard Jesus' words, acknowledged that God's way was right, because they had been baptized by John. 30But the Pharisees and experts in the law rejected God's purpose for themselves, because they had not been baptized by John.)

31"To what, then, can I compare the people of this generation? What are they like? 32They are like children sitting in the marketplace and calling out to each other:

" 'We played the flute for you,
  and you did not dance;
we sang a dirge,
  and you did not cry.'

33For John the Baptist came neither eating bread nor drinking wine, and you say, 'He has a demon.' 34The Son of Man came eating and drinking, and

you say, 'Here is a glutton and a drunkard, a friend of tax collectors and "sinners." ' 35But wisdom is proved right by all her children."

36Now one of the Pharisees invited Jesus to have dinner with him, so he went to the Pharisee's house and reclined at the table. 37When a woman who had lived a sinful life in that town learned that Jesus was eating at the Pharisee's house, she brought an alabaster jar of perfume, 38and as she stood behind him at his feet weeping, she began to wet his feet with her tears. Then she wiped them with her hair, kissed them and poured perfume on them.

39When the Pharisee who had invited him saw this, he said to himself, "If this man were a prophet, he would know who is touching him and what kind of woman she is—that she is a sinner."

40Jesus answered him, "Simon, I have something to tell you."

"Tell me, teacher," he said.

41"Two men owed money to a certain moneylender. One owed him five hundred denarii,*e* and the other fifty. 42Neither of them had the money to pay him back, so he canceled the debts of both. Now which of them will love him more?"

43Simon replied, "I suppose the one who had the bigger debt canceled."

"You have judged correctly," Jesus said.

44Then he turned toward the woman and said to Simon, "Do you see this woman? I came into your house. You did not give me any water for my feet, but she wet my feet with her tears and wiped them with her hair. 45You did not give me a kiss, but this woman, from the time I entered, has not stopped kissing my feet. 46You did not put oil on my head, but she has poured perfume on my feet. 47Therefore, I tell you, her many sins have been forgiven—for she loved much. But he who has been forgiven little loves little."

48Then Jesus said to her, "Your sins are forgiven."

49The other guests began to say among themselves, "Who is this who even forgives sins?"

50Jesus said to the woman, "Your faith has saved you; go in peace."

---

*c*22 The Greek word was used for various diseases affecting the skin—not necessarily leprosy.   *d*27 Mal. 3:1   *e*41 A denarius was a coin worth about a day's wages.

Discovering the Word 1. Note the distinctive background of each of the five individuals who met Jesus. How are their backgrounds different? 2. What do they all have in common as they relate to Jesus? 3. Picture the two processions in verses 11–13 meeting just outside the town gate. There is no request for help, no sign of faith from the widow. But look at Jesus himself in verses 13–15. What does this focus suggest about another dimension of faith in God's power? 4. Despite the Pharisees' public rejection of Jesus, one of them invites him to dinner. A drama unfolds (vv. 36–50). The woman's faith in Jesus is obvious. But Simon shows signs of some kind of faith in Jesus (vv. 36a, 39, 40b). How does Jesus proceed to draw out his faith? 5. Jesus' interaction with the woman is vastly different from his interaction with Simon. What does this indicate about his understanding of each?

Applying the Word 1. It was physically easy for Jesus to touch the dead man. But in doing so, he ritualistically contaminated himself. In our society what comparable risks might we have to take to help needy people? 2. Of the five people you have looked at, with whom can you more readily identify? How does she/he challenge your faith in Jesus as Friend and Lord?

Responding in Prayer Pray for courage to take risks in reaching out to those around you who are open to learning about Christ.

---

9 / *Luke 8:1–21*
Taking Care How You Listen

WHEN THE BERLIN Wall fell in 1989, the West rejoiced. For Christians it symbolized evangelistic opportunities in East Europe. At first we heard much of "tremendous openness," "thousands accepting Christ," "demand for Bibles." This was probably true. Then we began hearing about growing materialism and power struggles among some Christian leaders. Journalists began to report that many who came to meetings were mainly eager for Western contacts to worldly opportunities. Wherever the gospel is preached, results vary, because people have different motives for listening and responding. Jesus knew this about his contemporary audience, and he dealt with it in a graphic way.

Warming Up to God What were the two most significant factors that influenced your response to the Christian gospel?

Read Luke 8:1–21.

---

8 After this, Jesus traveled about from one town and village to another, proclaiming the good news of the kingdom of God. The Twelve were with him, ²and also some women who had been cured of evil spirits and diseases: Mary (called Magdalene) from whom seven demons had come out; ³Joanna the wife of Cuza, the manager of Herod's household; Susanna; and many others. These women were helping to support them out of their own means.

⁴While a large crowd was gathering and people were coming to Jesus from town after town, he told this parable: ⁵"A farmer went out to sow his seed. As he was scattering the seed, some fell along the path; it was trampled on, and the birds of the air ate it up. ⁶Some fell on rock, and when it came up, the plants withered because they had no moisture. ⁷Other seed fell among thorns,

which grew up with it and choked the plants. ⁸Still other seed fell on good soil. It came up and yielded a crop, a hundred times more than was sown."

When he said this, he called out, "He who has ears to hear, let him hear."

⁹His disciples asked him what this parable meant. ¹⁰He said, "The knowledge of the secrets of the kingdom of God has been given to you, but to others I speak in parables, so that,

" 'though seeing, they may not see;
    though hearing, they may not
        understand.'ᶠ

¹¹"This is the meaning of the parable: The seed is the word of God. ¹²Those along the path are the ones who hear, and then the devil comes and

ᶠ10 Isaiah 6:9

takes away the word from their hearts, so that they may not believe and be saved. 13Those on the rock are the ones who receive the word with joy when they hear it, but they have no root. They believe for a while, but in the time of testing they fall away. 14The seed that fell among thorns stands for those who hear, but as they go on their way they are choked by life's worries, riches and pleasures, and they do not mature. 15But the seed on good soil stands for those with a noble and good heart, who hear the word, retain it, and by persevering produce a crop.

16"No one lights a lamp and hides it in a jar or puts it under a bed. Instead, he puts it on a stand, so that those who come in can see the light. 17For there is nothing hidden that will not be disclosed, and nothing concealed that will not be known or brought out into the open. 18Therefore consider carefully how you listen. Whoever has will be given more; whoever does not have, even what he thinks he has will be taken from him."

19Now Jesus' mother and brothers came to see him, but they were not able to get near him because of the crowd. 20Someone told him, "Your mother and brothers are standing outside, wanting to see you."

21He replied, "My mother and brothers are those who hear God's word and put it into practice."

 Discovering the Word 1. Luke's description of the women followers in verses 2–3 is unique among the Gospels. What do these verses tell you about the changing nature of Jesus' ministry? 2. In Jesus' first parable the seeds sown are the same, but the soils are different. How are they different? 3. Jesus himself interprets this opening parable. What is his main point (vv. 11–15)? 4. As the crowds grow, Jesus increasingly teaches in parables. He gives his reason for this in verses 8b–10. How is the use of parables effective in testing a listener's sincerity? 5. Luke uses the family episode as a live illustration of listening to God (vv. 19–21). What does Jesus highlight by this illustration?

Applying the Word 1. Think over 8:15, where Jesus spells out what good soil is. How do you aim to cultivate your good soil? 2. Reflecting on the parable of the lighted lamp (vv. 16–18), consider your habits of listening to God's truth. How can you be more open to God?

Responding in Prayer Ask God to guide you to his truth and make you always open to what he has to say to you.

---

10 / *Luke 8:22–56*
Four Signs of Power and Identity

WHEN IS GOD present among people? Worshipers in a village in Portugal, in a village in Yugoslavia and more recently in an Illinois town all said he was present in a unique way. They claimed the Virgin Mary appeared to them, sometimes instructing or comforting and sometimes healing them. These locations drew thousands of people, either seeking the physical reality of God or simply curious. Visions, healing and deliverance services easily draw crowds all over the world. Whether people are believers or skeptics, they want to see, and perhaps experience, God's power—if it's there.

 Warming Up to God To what extent do we today need unusual displays of God's power?

 Read Luke 8:22–56.

22One day Jesus said to his disciples, "Let's go over to the other side of the lake." So they got into a boat and set out. 23As they sailed, he fell asleep. A squall came down on the lake, so that the boat was being swamped, and they were in great danger.

24The disciples went and woke him, saying, "Master, Master, we're going to drown!"

He got up and rebuked the wind and the raging waters; the storm subsided, and all was calm. 25"Where is your faith?" he asked his disciples.

In fear and amazement they asked one another, "Who is this? He commands even the winds and the water, and they obey him."

26They sailed to the region of the Gerasenes,ᵍ which is across the lake from Galilee. 27When Jesus stepped ashore, he was met by a demon-possessed man from the town. For a long time this man had not worn clothes or lived in a house, but had lived in the tombs. 28When he saw Jesus, he cried out and fell at his feet, shouting at the top of his voice, "What do you want with me, Jesus, Son of the Most High God? I beg you, don't torture me!" 29For Jesus had commanded the evilʰ spirit to come out of the man. Many times it had seized him, and though he was chained hand and foot and kept under guard, he had broken his chains and had been driven by the demon into solitary places.

30Jesus asked him, "What is your name?"

"Legion," he replied, because many demons had gone into him. 31And they begged him repeatedly not to order them to go into the Abyss.

32A large herd of pigs was feeding there on the hillside. The demons begged Jesus to let them go into them, and he gave them permission. 33When the demons came out of the man, they went into the pigs, and the herd rushed down the steep bank into the lake and was drowned.

34When those tending the pigs saw what had happened, they ran off and reported this in the town and countryside, 35and the people went out to see what had happened. When they came to Jesus, they found the man from whom the demons had gone out, sitting at Jesus' feet, dressed and in his right mind; and they were afraid. 36Those who had seen it told the people how the demon-possessed man had been cured. 37Then all the people of the region of the Gerasenes asked Jesus to leave them, because they were overcome with fear. So he got into the boat and left.

38The man from whom the demons had gone out begged to go with him, but Jesus sent him away, saying, 39"Return home and tell how much God has done for you." So the man went away and told all over town how much Jesus had done for him.

40Now when Jesus returned, a crowd welcomed him, for they were all expecting him. 41Then a man named Jairus, a ruler of the synagogue, came and fell at Jesus' feet, pleading with him to come to his house 42because his only daughter, a girl of about twelve, was dying.

As Jesus was on his way, the crowds almost crushed him. 43And a woman was there who had been subject to bleeding for twelve years,ⁱ but no one could heal her. 44She came up behind him and touched the edge of his cloak, and immediately her bleeding stopped.

45"Who touched me?" Jesus asked.

When they all denied it, Peter said, "Master, the people are crowding and pressing against you."

46But Jesus said, "Someone touched me; I know that power has gone out from me."

47Then the woman, seeing that she could not go unnoticed, came trembling and fell at his feet. In the presence of all the people, she told why she had touched him and how she had been instantly healed. 48Then he said to her, "Daughter, your faith has healed you. Go in peace."

49While Jesus was still speaking, someone came from the house of Jairus, the synagogue ruler. "Your daughter is dead," he said. "Don't bother the teacher any more."

50Hearing this, Jesus said to Jairus, "Don't be afraid; just believe, and she will be healed."

51When he arrived at the house of Jairus, he did not let anyone go in with him except Peter, John and James, and the child's father and mother. 52Meanwhile, all the people were wailing and mourning for her. "Stop wailing," Jesus said. "She is not dead but asleep."

53They laughed at him, knowing that she was dead. 54But he took her by the hand and said, "My child, get up!" 55Her spirit returned, and at once she stood up. Then Jesus told them to give her something to eat. 56Her parents were astonished, but he ordered them not to tell anyone what had happened.

ᵍ26 Some manuscripts *Gadarenes*; other manuscripts *Gergesenes*; also in verse 37   ʰ29 Greek *unclean*   ⁱ43 Many manuscripts *years, and she had spent all she had on doctors*

Discovering the Word 1. Jesus' Galilean disciples were used to sudden, violent storms on their sea, but this one was ferocious. What emotions do they experience from the beginning to the end of this event (vv. 22–25)? 2. Luke 8:26–39 is the second power encounter—this time in foreign territory. What unusual elements do you observe in the interchange between the man and Jesus? 3. We should not get morbidly curious about the subject of demons. But from this text what can you know about them? 4. Jesus and his disciples are back in home territory, where two more astonishing events take place. How is the healing of the woman different from other Bible healings you know of (vv. 40–56)? 5. What signs of God's power in your world move you most to worship and obey Jesus Christ as Lord of the universe?

Applying the Word 1. Jesus insists on knowing who touched him. How has it helped to witness publicly to what God has done for you? 2. What signs of God's power in your world move you most to worship and obey Jesus Christ as Lord of the universe?

Responding in Prayer Be thankful that you may worship God, who is both all-powerful and all-loving.

11 / *Luke 9:1–50*
Training for the Twelve

"IT HAS BEEN my experience that superior people are attracted only by challenge. By setting our standards low and making our life soft we have, quite automatically and unconsciously, assured ourselves of mediocre people" (Ambassador MacWhite in *The Ugly American*, referring to his observations in the diplomatic corps). Looking at Jesus' diplomatic corps of twelve, we might wonder about his standards. The Gospels tell us little about their backgrounds, but they tell us much about how Jesus trained them. This is useful for us.

 Warming Up to God In what area of your Christian life do you feel that you are growing?

 Read Luke 9:1–50.

9 When Jesus had called the Twelve together, he gave them power and authority to drive out all demons and to cure diseases, ²and he sent them out to preach the kingdom of God and to heal the sick. ³He told them: "Take nothing for the journey—no staff, no bag, no bread, no money, no extra tunic. ⁴Whatever house you enter, stay there until you leave that town. ⁵If people do not welcome you, shake the dust off your feet when you leave their town, as a testimony against them." ⁶So they set out and went from village to village, preaching the gospel and healing people everywhere.

⁷Now Herod the tetrarch heard about all that was going on. And he was perplexed, because some were saying that John had been raised from the dead, ⁸others that Elijah had appeared, and still others that one of the prophets of long ago had come back to life. ⁹But Herod said, "I beheaded John. Who, then, is this I hear such things about?" And he tried to see him.

¹⁰When the apostles returned, they reported to Jesus what they had done. Then he took them with him and they withdrew by themselves to a town called Bethsaida, ¹¹but the crowds learned about it and followed him. He welcomed them and spoke to them about the kingdom of God, and healed those who needed healing.

¹²Late in the afternoon the Twelve came to him and said, "Send the crowd away so they can go to the surrounding villages and countryside and find food and lodging, because we are in a remote place here."

¹³He replied, "You give them something to eat."

They answered, "We have only five loaves of bread and two fish—unless we go and buy food for all this crowd." ¹⁴(About five thousand men were there.)

But he said to his disciples, "Have them sit down in groups of about fifty each." ¹⁵The disciples did so, and everybody sat down. ¹⁶Taking the five loaves and the two fish and looking up to heaven, he gave thanks and broke them. Then he gave them to the disciples to set before the people. ¹⁷They all ate and were satisfied, and the disciples picked up twelve basketfuls of broken pieces that were left over.

¹⁸Once when Jesus was praying in private and his disciples were with him, he asked them, "Who do the crowds say I am?"

¹⁹They replied, "Some say John the Baptist; others say Elijah; and still others, that one of the prophets of long ago has come back to life."

²⁰"But what about you?" he asked. "Who do you say I am?"

Peter answered, "The Christ^j of God."

²¹Jesus strictly warned them not to tell this to anyone. ²²And he said, "The Son of Man must suffer many things and be rejected by the elders, chief priests and teachers of the law, and he must be killed and on the third day be raised to life."

²³Then he said to them all: "If anyone would come after me, he must deny himself and take up his cross daily and follow me. ²⁴For whoever wants to save his life will lose it, but whoever loses his life for me will save it. ²⁵What good is it for a man to gain the whole world, and yet lose or forfeit his very self? ²⁶If anyone is ashamed of me and my words, the Son of Man will be ashamed of him when he comes in his glory and in the glory of the Father and of the holy angels. ²⁷I tell you the truth, some who are standing here will not taste death before they see the kingdom of God."

²⁸About eight days after Jesus said this, he took Peter, John and James with him and went up onto a mountain to pray. ²⁹As he was praying, the appearance of his face changed, and his clothes became as bright as a flash of lightning. ³⁰Two men, Moses and Elijah, ³¹appeared in glorious splendor, talking with Jesus. They spoke about his departure, which he was about to bring to fulfillment at Jerusalem. ³²Peter and his companions were very sleepy, but when they became fully awake, they saw his glory and the two men standing with him. ³³As the men were leaving Jesus, Peter said to him, "Master, it is good for us to be here. Let us put up three shelters—one for you, one for Moses and one for Elijah." (He did not know what he was saying.)

³⁴While he was speaking, a cloud appeared and enveloped them, and they were afraid as they entered the cloud. ³⁵A voice came from the cloud, saying, "This is my Son, whom I have chosen; listen to him." ³⁶When the voice had spoken, they found that Jesus was alone. The disciples kept this to themselves, and told no one at that time what they had seen.

³⁷The next day, when they came down from the mountain, a large crowd met him. ³⁸A man in the crowd called out, "Teacher, I beg you to look at my son, for he is my only child. ³⁹A spirit seizes him and he suddenly screams; it throws him into convulsions so that he foams at the mouth. It scarcely ever leaves him and is destroying him. ⁴⁰I begged your disciples to drive it out, but they could not."

⁴¹"O unbelieving and perverse generation," Jesus replied, "how long shall I stay with you and put up with you? Bring your son here."

⁴²Even while the boy was coming, the demon threw him to the ground in a convulsion. But Jesus rebuked the evil^k spirit, healed the boy and gave him back to his father. ⁴³And they were all amazed at the greatness of God.

While everyone was marveling at all that Jesus did, he said to his disciples, ⁴⁴"Listen carefully to what I am about to tell you: The Son of Man is going to be betrayed into the hands of men." ⁴⁵But they did not understand what this meant. It was hidden from them, so that they did not grasp it, and they were afraid to ask him about it.

⁴⁶An argument started among the disciples as to which of them would be the greatest. ⁴⁷Jesus, knowing their thoughts, took a little child and had him stand beside him. ⁴⁸Then he said to them, "Whoever welcomes this little child in my name welcomes me; and whoever welcomes me welcomes the one who sent me. For he who is least among you all—he is the greatest."

⁴⁹"Master," said John, "we saw a man driving out demons in your name and we tried to stop him, because he is not one of us."

⁵⁰"Do not stop him," Jesus said, "for whoever is not against you is for you."

^{j}20 Or Messiah ^{k}42 Greek unclean

Discovering the Word 1. For two years Jesus has been teaching, training and testing the Twelve. In what important ways has Jesus prepared them for this first short-term mission without him (vv. 1–9)? 2. The apostles have just returned from an intense and successful evangelistic mission. Their reluctance to help the crowd is understandable. But Jesus is insistent. What progressive steps do you see him take to involve them in feeding the people (vv. 10–17)? 3. Peter's "Great Confession" of Jesus' true identity is followed by two hard teachings—the first prediction of his ignominious death (vv. 21–22) and the costs of commitment to him as Lord (vv. 23–27). But what does Jesus say are the long-term benefits of these short-term costs? 4. Luke links Jesus' transfiguration to his final trip to Jerusalem, where death awaits (9:30–32, 51ff.). How then is the transfiguration important to Jesus himself and to the disciples? 5. On the plain with the mixed crowd we can sense Jesus' deep feelings. How can he be at once both compassionate and impatient?

 Applying the Word 1. When have you felt both God's compassion and impatience? 2. What is one blind spot, or area of spiritual immaturity, that you need to work on?

Responding in Prayer Talk to God about how you want to grow into spiritual maturity.

12 / *Luke 9:51—10:24*
Short-Term Costs for Long-Term Benefits

I THOUGHT ALL my problems would be solved when I became a Christian. But they have increased. Cost? Pain? Sacrifice? These elements don't fit into the American way of life of avoiding discomfort and inconvenience. Instant gratification is the order of the day. No goal could be further from Jesus' way of life for his disciples while here on earth.

 Warming Up to God What has been costly for you in following Jesus?

 Read Luke 9:51—10:24.

---

[51]As the time approached for him to be taken up to heaven, Jesus resolutely set out for Jerusalem. [52]And he sent messengers on ahead, who went into a Samaritan village to get things ready for him; [53]but the people there did not welcome him, because he was heading for Jerusalem. [54]When the disciples James and John saw this, they asked, "Lord, do you want us to call fire down from heaven to destroy them[l]?" [55]But Jesus turned and rebuked them, [56]and[m] they went to another village.

[57]As they were walking along the road, a man said to him, "I will follow you wherever you go."

[58]Jesus replied, "Foxes have holes and birds of the air have nests, but the Son of Man has no place to lay his head."

[59]He said to another man, "Follow me."

But the man replied, "Lord, first let me go and bury my father."

[60]Jesus said to him, "Let the dead bury their own dead, but you go and proclaim the kingdom of God."

[61]Still another said, "I will follow you, Lord; but first let me go back and say good-by to my family."

[62]Jesus replied, "No one who puts his hand to the plow and looks back is fit for service in the kingdom of God."

10 After this the Lord appointed seventy-two[n] others and sent them two by two ahead of him to every town and place where he was about to go. [2]He told them, "The harvest is plentiful, but the workers are few. Ask the Lord of the harvest, therefore, to send out workers into his harvest field. [3]Go! I am sending you out like lambs among wolves. [4]Do not take a purse or bag or sandals; and do not greet anyone on the road.

[l]54 Some manuscripts *them, even as Elijah did*   [m]55,56 Some manuscripts *them. And he said, "You do not know what kind of spirit you are of, for the Son of Man did not come to destroy men's lives, but to save them." [56]And*   [n]1 Some manuscripts *seventy*; also in verse 17

⁵"When you enter a house, first say, 'Peace to this house.' ⁶If a man of peace is there, your peace will rest on him; if not, it will return to you. ⁷Stay in that house, eating and drinking whatever they give you, for the worker deserves his wages. Do not move around from house to house.

⁸"When you enter a town and are welcomed, eat what is set before you. ⁹Heal the sick who are there and tell them, 'The kingdom of God is near you.' ¹⁰But when you enter a town and are not welcomed, go into its streets and say, ¹¹'Even the dust of your town that sticks to our feet we wipe off against you. Yet be sure of this: The kingdom of God is near.' ¹²I tell you, it will be more bearable on that day for Sodom than for that town.

¹³"Woe to you, Korazin! Woe to you, Bethsaida! For if the miracles that were performed in you had been performed in Tyre and Sidon, they would have repented long ago, sitting in sackcloth and ashes. ¹⁴But it will be more bearable for Tyre and Sidon at the judgment than for you. ¹⁵And you, Capernaum, will you be lifted up to the skies? No, you will go down to the depths.°

¹⁶"He who listens to you listens to me; he who rejects you rejects me; but he who rejects me rejects him who sent me."

¹⁷The seventy-two returned with joy and said, "Lord, even the demons submit to us in your name."

¹⁸He replied, "I saw Satan fall like lightning from heaven. ¹⁹I have given you authority to trample on snakes and scorpions and to overcome all the power of the enemy; nothing will harm you. ²⁰However, do not rejoice that the spirits submit to you, but rejoice that your names are written in heaven."

²¹At that time Jesus, full of joy through the Holy Spirit, said, "I praise you, Father, Lord of heaven and earth, because you have hidden these things from the wise and learned, and revealed them to little children. Yes, Father, for this was your good pleasure.

²²"All things have been committed to me by my Father. No one knows who the Son is except the Father, and no one knows who the Father is except the Son and those to whom the Son chooses to reveal him."

²³Then he turned to his disciples and said privately, "Blessed are the eyes that see what you see. ²⁴For I tell you that many prophets and kings wanted to see what you see but did not see it, and to hear what you hear but did not hear it."

°15 Greek *Hades*

Discovering the Word 1. This is the beginning of Jesus' final, year-long journey to Jerusalem. What impressions of Jesus do the opening statements (9:51–53) leave with you? 2. In 9:56–62 Jesus interviews three would-be disciples. Each encounter reveals the person's inadequate understanding of what it means to follow Jesus. What issues are at stake for each of these people? 3. From Jesus' response to each what do you learn about some specific costs of discipleship in his kingdom? 4. How is the mission of the seventy-two in Luke 10:1–16 different from the mission of the Twelve in 9:1–6? 5. Verses 17–24 record a postmission report and evaluation. Of course celebration is in order! For Jesus the success of the seventy-two is a preview of the ultimate overthrow of Satan. But as one of them, how would you have felt on hearing Jesus' words in verse 20?

Applying the Word 1. Jesus' every instruction reveals a deep sense of urgency. How do we develop an urgency for mission and evangelism? 2. Jesus' demands in discipleship and mission are indeed serious (9:57–62; 10:2–12). But he accompanies them with positive appeals—explicit and implicit (9:60b, 62b; 10:2, 16, 18–24). Which of his appeals inspires you to pursue discipleship on his terms?

 Responding in Prayer Ask for strength to bear the real cost of discipleship.

13 / *Luke 10:25—11:13*
Marks of Jesus' True Disciples

IT IS SOMETIMES hard to tell who is a real Christian. This is not necessarily because people indiscriminately claim to be Christian. One reason is that many people sincerely live by inherited Christian values and even show fruit of the Spirit. But they have no personal relationship with God. On the other hand, some claim such a relationship to God but do not live by his standards. Among the many who followed Jesus were those who also were not clear about true discipleship. So Jesus makes it absolutely clear what marks a true follower of his.

 Warming Up to God If you are not told, how can you tell if a person is a Christian?

 Read Luke 10:25—11:13.

---

²⁵On one occasion an expert in the law stood up to test Jesus. "Teacher," he asked, "what must I do to inherit eternal life?"

²⁶"What is written in the Law?" he replied. "How do you read it?"

²⁷He answered: " 'Love the Lord your God with all your heart and with all your soul and with all your strength and with all your mind'*p*; and, 'Love your neighbor as yourself.'*q*"

²⁸"You have answered correctly," Jesus replied. "Do this and you will live."

²⁹But he wanted to justify himself, so he asked Jesus, "And who is my neighbor?"

³⁰In reply Jesus said: "A man was going down from Jerusalem to Jericho, when he fell into the hands of robbers. They stripped him of his clothes, beat him and went away, leaving him half dead. ³¹A priest happened to be going down the same road, and when he saw the man, he passed by on the other side. ³²So too, a Levite, when he came to the place and saw him, passed by on the other side. ³³But a Samaritan, as he traveled, came where the man was; and when he saw him, he took pity on him. ³⁴He went to him and bandaged his wounds, pouring on oil and wine. Then he put the man on his own donkey, took him to an inn and took care of him. ³⁵The next day he took out two silver coins*r* and gave them to the innkeeper. 'Look after him,' he said, 'and when I return, I will reimburse you for any extra expense you may have.'

³⁶"Which of these three do you think was a neighbor to the man who fell into the hands of robbers?"

³⁷The expert in the law replied, "The one who had mercy on him."

Jesus told him, "Go and do likewise."

³⁸As Jesus and his disciples were on their way, he came to a village where a woman named Martha opened her home to him. ³⁹She had a sister called Mary, who sat at the Lord's feet listening to what he said. ⁴⁰But Martha was distracted by all the preparations that had to be made. She came to him and asked, "Lord, don't you care that my sister has left me to do the work by myself? Tell her to help me!"

⁴¹"Martha, Martha," the Lord answered, "you are worried and upset about many things, ⁴²but only one thing is needed.*s* Mary has chosen what is better, and it will not be taken away from her."

11 One day Jesus was praying in a certain place. When he finished, one of his disciples said to him, "Lord, teach us to pray, just as John taught his disciples."

²He said to them, "When you pray, say:

" 'Father,*t*
hallowed be your name,
your kingdom come.*u*
³Give us each day our daily bread.
⁴Forgive us our sins,
    for we also forgive everyone who sins
        against us.*v*
And lead us not into temptation.*w*' "

⁵Then he said to them, "Suppose one of you has a friend, and he goes to him at midnight and says, 'Friend, lend me three loaves of bread, ⁶be-

*p*27 Deut. 6:5   *q*27 Lev. 19:18   *r*35 Greek *two denarii*
*s*42 Some manuscripts *but few things are needed—or only one*
*t*2 Some manuscripts *Our Father in heaven*   *u*2 Some manuscripts
come. May your will be done on earth as it is in heaven.   *v*4 Greek
everyone who is indebted to us   *w*4 Some manuscripts *temptation but
deliver us from the evil one*

cause a friend of mine on a journey has come to me, and I have nothing to set before him.'

7"Then the one inside answers, 'Don't bother me. The door is already locked, and my children are with me in bed. I can't get up and give you anything.' 8I tell you, though he will not get up and give him the bread because he is his friend, yet because of the man's boldness× he will get up and give him as much as he needs.

9"So I say to you: Ask and it will be given to you; seek and you will find; knock and the door will be opened to you. 10For everyone who asks receives; he who seeks finds; and to him who knocks, the door will be opened.

11"Which of you fathers, if your son asks forʸ a fish, will give him a snake instead? 12Or if he asks for an egg, will give him a scorpion? 13If you then, though you are evil, know how to give good gifts to your children, how much more will your Father in heaven give the Holy Spirit to those who ask him!"

×8 Or *persistence*   ʸ11 Some manuscripts *for bread, will give him a stone; or if he asks for*

 Discovering the Word 1. The conversation begins with a man who "stood up," indicating he had been sitting with others listening to Jesus teach. What other facts about this man can you pick up in 10:25–29? 2. What does Jesus perceive about his understanding of the Law (10:25–28)? 3. To challenge the expert Jesus portrays the hero in his parable as a Samaritan. This despised outsider proves obedience to God's law of love by his actions (first mark). Note the specific ways that he "took pity" on the victim (10:33–35). What could be Jesus' reasons for including such details? 4. In verse 36 Jesus reverses the expert's original question in verse 29. If you were the expert, what effect would this have on you? 5. Martha displays both positive and negative qualities (10:38–42). What (second) mark does her sister Mary show? 6. Look at 11:1–13 for the third mark of Jesus' true disciples—praying. In verses 2–4 Jesus is not giving a prayer merely to be recited. Rather, he is giving prayer headings. What basic needs do these headings cover?

 Applying the Word 1. What qualities do you observe in people who, like Mary, "choose what is better"? 2. By parable and commentary Jesus urges his disciples to pray with boldness. We can dare to be bold because of who God is—our Father and our King (vv. 2, 13). How should trust in such a God radicalize your praying?

 Responding in Prayer Speak to God boldly and with trust.

---

14 / *Luke 11:14—12:12*
Jesus the Controversialist

WHEN I THINK of controversialists, Al comes to mind. He was one of the most effective missionaries I've known. Yet he stirred up controversy with almost everyone near him—his board, his colleagues, the local church leaders. They didn't know what to do with him, or what to do without him. But those he was evangelizing loved him!

Some people seem to be born controversialists. They're happiest when arguing with others, only half alive when the atmosphere is congenial. Jesus was a controversialist. But it was not for his ego that he engaged in fierce debates with the most highly trained Bible scholars of his day. He engaged in controversy because he loved the truth and hated lies.

Warming Up to God How do you respond to controversies? Why?

Read Luke 11:14—12:12.

14Jesus was driving out a demon that was mute. When the demon left, the man who had been mute spoke, and the crowd was amazed. 15But

some of them said, "By Beelzebub,ᶻ the prince of

ᶻ15 Greek *Beezeboul* or *Beelzeboul*; also in verses 18 and 19 demons, he is driving out demons." ¹⁶Others tested him by asking for a sign from heaven.

¹⁷Jesus knew their thoughts and said to them: "Any kingdom divided against itself will be ruined, and a house divided against itself will fall. ¹⁸If Satan is divided against himself, how can his kingdom stand? I say this because you claim that I drive out demons by Beelzebub. ¹⁹Now if I drive out demons by Beelzebub, by whom do your followers drive them out? So then, they will be your judges. ²⁰But if I drive out demons by the finger of God, then the kingdom of God has come to you.

²¹"When a strong man, fully armed, guards his own house, his possessions are safe. ²²But when someone stronger attacks and overpowers him, he takes away the armor in which the man trusted and divides up the spoils.

²³"He who is not with me is against me, and he who does not gather with me, scatters.

²⁴"When an evil[a] spirit comes out of a man, it goes through arid places seeking rest and does not find it. Then it says, 'I will return to the house I left.' ²⁵When it arrives, it finds the house swept clean and put in order. ²⁶Then it goes and takes seven other spirits more wicked than itself, and they go in and live there. And the final condition of that man is worse than the first."

²⁷As Jesus was saying these things, a woman in the crowd called out, "Blessed is the mother who gave you birth and nursed you."

²⁸He replied, "Blessed rather are those who hear the word of God and obey it."

²⁹As the crowds increased, Jesus said, "This is a wicked generation. It asks for a miraculous sign, but none will be given it except the sign of Jonah. ³⁰For as Jonah was a sign to the Ninevites, so also will the Son of Man be to this generation. ³¹The Queen of the South will rise at the judgment with the men of this generation and condemn them; for she came from the ends of the earth to listen to Solomon's wisdom, and now one[b] greater than Solomon is here. ³²The men of Nineveh will stand up at the judgment with this generation and condemn it; for they repented at the preaching of Jonah, and now one greater than Jonah is here.

³³"No one lights a lamp and puts it in a place where it will be hidden, or under a bowl. Instead he puts it on its stand, so that those who come in may see the light. ³⁴Your eye is the lamp of your body. When your eyes are good, your whole body also is full of light. But when they are bad, your body also is full of darkness. ³⁵See to it, then, that the light within you is not darkness. ³⁶Therefore, if your whole body is full of light, and no part of it dark, it will be completely lighted, as when the light of a lamp shines on you."

³⁷When Jesus had finished speaking, a Pharisee invited him to eat with him; so he went in and reclined at the table. ³⁸But the Pharisee, noticing that Jesus did not first wash before the meal, was surprised.

³⁹Then the Lord said to him, "Now then, you Pharisees clean the outside of the cup and dish, but inside you are full of greed and wickedness. ⁴⁰You foolish people! Did not the one who made the outside make the inside also? ⁴¹But give what is inside ⌐the dish⌐[c] to the poor, and everything will be clean for you.

⁴²"Woe to you Pharisees, because you give God a tenth of your mint, rue and all other kinds of garden herbs, but you neglect justice and the love of God. You should have practiced the latter without leaving the former undone.

⁴³"Woe to you Pharisees, because you love the most important seats in the synagogues and greetings in the marketplaces.

⁴⁴"Woe to you, because you are like unmarked graves, which men walk over without knowing it."

⁴⁵One of the experts in the law answered him, "Teacher, when you say these things, you insult us also."

⁴⁶Jesus replied, "And you experts in the law, woe to you, because you load people down with burdens they can hardly carry, and you yourselves will not lift one finger to help them.

⁴⁷"Woe to you, because you build tombs for the prophets, and it was your forefathers who killed them. ⁴⁸So you testify that you approve of what your forefathers did; they killed the prophets, and you build their tombs. ⁴⁹Because of this, God in his wisdom said, 'I will send them prophets and apostles, some of whom they will kill and others they will persecute.' ⁵⁰Therefore this generation will be held responsible for the blood of all the prophets that has been shed since the beginning of the world, ⁵¹from the blood of Abel to the blood of Zechariah, who was killed between the altar and the sanctuary. Yes, I tell you, this generation will be held responsible for it all.

⁵²"Woe to you experts in the law, because you

[a]24 Greek unclean   [b]31 Or something; also in verse 32   [c]41 Or what you have

have taken away the key to knowledge. You yourselves have not entered, and you have hindered those who were entering."

⁵³When Jesus left there, the Pharisees and the teachers of the law began to oppose him fiercely and to besiege him with questions, ⁵⁴waiting to catch him in something he might say.

12 Meanwhile, when a crowd of many thousands had gathered, so that they were trampling on one another, Jesus began to speak first to his disciples, saying: "Be on your guard against the yeast of the Pharisees, which is hypocrisy. ²There is nothing concealed that will not be disclosed, or hidden that will not be made known. ³What you have said in the dark will be heard in the daylight, and what you have whispered in the ear in the inner rooms will be proclaimed from the roofs.

⁴"I tell you, my friends, do not be afraid of those who kill the body and after that can do no more. ⁵But I will show you whom you should fear: Fear him who, after the killing of the body,

has power to throw you into hell. Yes, I tell you, fear him. ⁶Are not five sparrows sold for two pennies^d? Yet not one of them is forgotten by God. ⁷Indeed, the very hairs of your head are all numbered. Don't be afraid; you are worth more than many sparrows.

⁸"I tell you, whoever acknowledges me before men, the Son of Man will also acknowledge him before the angels of God. ⁹But he who disowns me before men will be disowned before the angels of God. ¹⁰And everyone who speaks a word against the Son of Man will be forgiven, but anyone who blasphemes against the Holy Spirit will not be forgiven.

¹¹"When you are brought before synagogues, rulers and authorities, do not worry about how you will defend yourselves or what you will say, ¹²for the Holy Spirit will teach you at that time what you should say."

---

^{d}6 Greek *two assaria*

Discovering the Word 1. In what two ways do Jesus' critics attack him (11:15–16)? 2. In 11:17–20 Jesus answers the first attack. How does he point out their illogical position? 3. Jesus answers his critics' second attack in 11:29–36. In what way is Jesus comparing himself to Jonah and Solomon? 4. In 11:37–38 the host is surprised that Jesus has not ritually washed his hands after contact with public "uncleanness." Jesus counters that criticism, then adds six more attacks on their religious practices! Of these accusations (11:42, 43, 44, 46, 47, 52), which reminds you of a contemporary practice? In what ways? 5. Jesus must now prepare his disciples for persecution by these same leaders (12:1–12). First, he deals with the fear of these men. How does he help them to distinguish between the wrong kind of fear and the proper kind (12:4–7)?

Applying the Word 1. Few of us would engage in public religious controversy as Jesus did. But we all have occasions when we need to stand against lies and speak the truth. What are your opportunities to do this? 2. In what ways is it difficult for you?

Responding in Prayer Ask the Lord Jesus to give you the help you need to take a stand.

---

15 / *Luke 12:13—13:21*
Greed, Need & Judgment

A CHRISTIAN YUPPIE? Is it possible to be Jesus' disciple on his terms and at the same time be a yuppie, for whom material values and the latest exotica are priorities? Some try to have it both ways and don't make it—either way. One such Christian yuppie described her experience. "For ten years I skillfully juggled both sets of values—Jesus' and Madison Avenue's. Then I collapsed." We are constantly tested in our value system, because we live between earth and heaven, time and eternity. Jesus gives us guidelines and solemn warnings on how to live productively in this creative tension.

Warming Up to God Think about the past few days. In what ways have you been enticed by the material values of the world? Confess them before the Lord.

Read Luke 12:13—13:21.

13Someone in the crowd said to him, "Teacher, tell my brother to divide the inheritance with me."

14Jesus replied, "Man, who appointed me a judge or an arbiter between you?" 15Then he said to them, "Watch out! Be on your guard against all kinds of greed; a man's life does not consist in the abundance of his possessions."

16And he told them this parable: "The ground of a certain rich man produced a good crop. 17He thought to himself, 'What shall I do? I have no place to store my crops.'

18"Then he said, 'This is what I'll do. I will tear down my barns and build bigger ones, and there I will store all my grain and my goods. 19And I'll say to myself, "You have plenty of good things laid up for many years. Take life easy; eat, drink and be merry." '

20"But God said to him, 'You fool! This very night your life will be demanded from you. Then who will get what you have prepared for yourself?'

21"This is how it will be with anyone who stores up things for himself but is not rich toward God."

22Then Jesus said to his disciples: "Therefore I tell you, do not worry about your life, what you will eat; or about your body, what you will wear. 23Life is more than food, and the body more than clothes. 24Consider the ravens: They do not sow or reap, they have no storeroom or barn; yet God feeds them. And how much more valuable you are than birds! 25Who of you by worrying can add a single hour to his life*e*? 26Since you cannot do this very little thing, why do you worry about the rest?

27"Consider how the lilies grow. They do not labor or spin. Yet I tell you, not even Solomon in all his splendor was dressed like one of these. 28If that is how God clothes the grass of the field, which is here today, and tomorrow is thrown into the fire, how much more will he clothe you, O you of little faith! 29And do not set your heart on what you will eat or drink; do not worry about it. 30For the pagan world runs after all such things, and your Father knows that you need them. 31But seek his kingdom, and these things will be given to you as well.

32"Do not be afraid, little flock, for your Father has been pleased to give you the kingdom. 33Sell your possessions and give to the poor. Provide purses for yourselves that will not wear out, a treasure in heaven that will not be exhausted, where no thief comes near and no moth destroys. 34For where your treasure is, there your heart will be also.

35"Be dressed ready for service and keep your lamps burning, 36like men waiting for their master to return from a wedding banquet, so that when he comes and knocks they can immediately open the door for him. 37It will be good for those servants whose master finds them watching when he comes. I tell you the truth, he will dress himself to serve, will have them recline at the table and will come and wait on them. 38It will be good for those servants whose master finds them ready, even if he comes in the second or third watch of the night. 39But understand this: If the owner of the house had known at what hour the thief was coming, he would not have let his house be broken into. 40You also must be ready, because the Son of Man will come at an hour when you do not expect him."

41Peter asked, "Lord, are you telling this parable to us, or to everyone?"

42The Lord answered, "Who then is the faithful and wise manager, whom the master puts in charge of his servants to give them their food allowance at the proper time? 43It will be good for that servant whom the master finds doing so when he returns. 44I tell you the truth, he will put him in charge of all his possessions. 45But suppose the servant says to himself, 'My master is taking a long time in coming,' and he then begins to beat the menservants and maidservants and to eat and drink and get drunk. 46The master of that servant will come on a day when he does not expect him and at an hour he is not aware of. He will cut him to pieces and assign him a place with the unbelievers.

47"That servant who knows his master's will and does not get ready or does not do what his master wants will be beaten with many blows. 48But the one who does not know and does things deserving punishment will be beaten with few blows. From everyone who has been given much, much will be demanded; and from the one who

e25 Or single cubit to his height

has been entrusted with much, much more will be asked.

⁴⁹"I have come to bring fire on the earth, and how I wish it were already kindled! ⁵⁰But I have a baptism to undergo, and how distressed I am until it is completed! ⁵¹Do you think I came to bring peace on earth? No, I tell you, but division. ⁵²From now on there will be five in one family divided against each other, three against two and two against three. ⁵³They will be divided, father against son and son against father, mother against daughter and daughter against mother, mother-in-law against daughter-in-law and daughter-in-law against mother-in-law."

⁵⁴He said to the crowd: "When you see a cloud rising in the west, immediately you say, 'It's going to rain,' and it does. ⁵⁵And when the south wind blows, you say, 'It's going to be hot,' and it is. ⁵⁶Hypocrites! You know how to interpret the appearance of the earth and the sky. How is it that you don't know how to interpret this present time?

⁵⁷"Why don't you judge for yourselves what is right? ⁵⁸As you are going with your adversary to the magistrate, try hard to be reconciled to him on the way, or he may drag you off to the judge, and the judge turn you over to the officer, and the officer throw you into prison. ⁵⁹I tell you, you will not get out until you have paid the last penny.ʃ"

13 Now there were some present at that time who told Jesus about the Galileans whose blood Pilate had mixed with their sacrifices. ²Jesus answered, "Do you think that these Galileans were worse sinners than all the other Galileans because they suffered this way? ³I tell you, no! But unless you repent, you too will all perish. ⁴Or those eighteen who died when the tower in Siloam fell on them—do you think they were more guilty than all the others living in Jerusalem? ⁵I tell you, no! But unless you repent, you too will all perish."

⁶Then he told this parable: "A man had a fig tree, planted in his vineyard, and he went to look for fruit on it, but did not find any. ⁷So he said to the man who took care of the vineyard, 'For three years now I've been coming to look for fruit on this fig tree and haven't found any. Cut it down! Why should it use up the soil?'

⁸" 'Sir,' the man replied, 'leave it alone for one more year, and I'll dig around it and fertilize it. ⁹If it bears fruit next year, fine! If not, then cut it down.' "

¹⁰On a Sabbath Jesus was teaching in one of the synagogues, ¹¹and a woman was there who had been crippled by a spirit for eighteen years. She was bent over and could not straighten up at all. ¹²When Jesus saw her, he called her forward and said to her, "Woman, you are set free from your infirmity." ¹³Then he put his hands on her, and immediately she straightened up and praised God.

¹⁴Indignant because Jesus had healed on the Sabbath, the synagogue ruler said to the people, "There are six days for work. So come and be healed on those days, not on the Sabbath."

¹⁵The Lord answered him, "You hypocrites! Doesn't each of you on the Sabbath untie his ox or donkey from the stall and lead it out to give it water? ¹⁶Then should not this woman, a daughter of Abraham, whom Satan has kept bound for eighteen long years, be set free on the Sabbath day from what bound her?"

¹⁷When he said this, all his opponents were humiliated, but the people were delighted with all the wonderful things he was doing.

¹⁸Then Jesus asked, "What is the kingdom of God like? What shall I compare it to? ¹⁹It is like a mustard seed, which a man took and planted in his garden. It grew and became a tree, and the birds of the air perched in its branches."

²⁰Again he asked, "What shall I compare the kingdom of God to? ²¹It is like yeast that a woman took and mixed into a large amountᵍ of flour until it worked all through the dough."

ʃ59 Greek *lepton*   ᵍ21 Greek *three satas* (probably about 1/2 bushel or 22 liters)

Discovering the Word 1. Nowhere does Jesus condemn possessions. But he has much to say about how to use them. From 12:15, 22–23 and 31, how could you summarize Jesus' teaching about life and material goods? 2. What view of God do worrying Christians apparently have? 3. The parable in 12:35–48 illustrates priorities Christians should have in view of Jesus' return after his departure—or in any crisis situation. (That Jesus was referring to his Second Coming would not be obvious to his listeners, as it is to us.) What are these priorities that apply to all servant disciples? 4. All three parables above speak or hint of God's judgment on the choices we make (12:20, 40, 46–48). The language and imagery of our present text also point to that judgment. In the midst of these warnings, what hope does Jesus offer to the wise (12:57–59)? **5.** Provoked by Jesus' teaching on judgment (13:1–9), some people raise a question about a well-known atrocity. In reply, how does Jesus both correct their wrong assumption and still extend hope? **6.** This is the last time we see Jesus teaching in a synagogue (13:10–21). In what ways does this sabbath conflict with the synagogue ruler summarize the priorities and values of Jesus' total ministry?

 Applying the Word **1.** The obviously rich are not the only ones in danger of being fools. How do poor and middle-class people also face the same dangers? **2.** Recall again your past week's activities and personal concerns. To what extent do they reflect the priorities and values of God's kingdom?

Responding in Prayer Ask God to mold your values and priorities into his own.

16 / *Luke 13:22—14:35*
Are Only a Few People Going to Be Saved?

STILL ANOTHER NEW group has come to our town, attracting scores of disaffected members of other churches. The leaders have convinced them that they alone have the right interpretation of "who is really saved." People in Jesus' day also wanted to be sure about salvation. They asked the question in different ways—"What must I do to inherit eternal life?" "How can a man be born again to enter the kingdom of God?" "Who then can be saved?" Even secular people ask, "Which life goal is right?" No matter the form, it is still an essential question for anyone to ask.

 Warming Up to God When are you likely to question your salvation?

 Read Luke 13:22—14:35.

22Then Jesus went through the towns and villages, teaching as he made his way to Jerusalem. 23Someone asked him, "Lord, are only a few people going to be saved?"

He said to them, 24"Make every effort to enter through the narrow door, because many, I tell you, will try to enter and will not be able to. 25Once the owner of the house gets up and closes the door, you will stand outside knocking and pleading, 'Sir, open the door for us.'

"But he will answer, 'I don't know you or where you come from.'

26"Then you will say, 'We ate and drank with you, and you taught in our streets.'

27"But he will reply, 'I don't know you or where you come from. Away from me, all you evildoers!'

28"There will be weeping there, and gnashing of teeth, when you see Abraham, Isaac and Jacob and all the prophets in the kingdom of God, but you yourselves thrown out. 29People will come from east and west and north and south, and will take their places at the feast in the kingdom of God. 30Indeed there are those who are last who will be first, and first who will be last."

31At that time some Pharisees came to Jesus and said to him, "Leave this place and go somewhere else. Herod wants to kill you."

32He replied, "Go tell that fox, 'I will drive out demons and heal people today and tomorrow, and on the third day I will reach my goal.' 33In any case, I must keep going today and tomorrow and the next day—for surely no prophet can die outside Jerusalem!

34"O Jerusalem, Jerusalem, you who kill the prophets and stone those sent to you, how often I have longed to gather your children together, as a hen gathers her chicks under her wings, but you were not willing! 35Look, your house is left to you desolate. I tell you, you will not see me again until you say, 'Blessed is he who comes in the name of the Lord.'*h*"

14 One Sabbath, when Jesus went to eat in the house of a prominent Pharisee, he was being carefully watched. 2There in front of him was a man suffering from dropsy. 3Jesus asked the Pharisees and

*h*35 Psalm 118:26

experts in the law, "Is it lawful to heal on the Sabbath or not?" ⁴But they remained silent. So taking hold of the man, he healed him and sent him away.

⁵Then he asked them, "If one of you has a sonⁱ or an ox that falls into a well on the Sabbath day, will you not immediately pull him out?" ⁶And they had nothing to say.

⁷When he noticed how the guests picked the places of honor at the table, he told them this parable: ⁸"When someone invites you to a wedding feast, do not take the place of honor, for a person more distinguished than you may have been invited. ⁹If so, the host who invited both of you will come and say to you, 'Give this man your seat.' Then, humiliated, you will have to take the least important place. ¹⁰But when you are invited, take the lowest place, so that when your host comes, he will say to you, 'Friend, move up to a better place.' Then you will be honored in the presence of all your fellow guests. ¹¹For everyone who exalts himself will be humbled, and he who humbles himself will be exalted."

¹²Then Jesus said to his host, "When you give a luncheon or dinner, do not invite your friends, your brothers or relatives, or your rich neighbors; if you do, they may invite you back and so you will be repaid. ¹³But when you give a banquet, invite the poor, the crippled, the lame, the blind, ¹⁴and you will be blessed. Although they cannot repay you, you will be repaid at the resurrection of the righteous."

¹⁵When one of those at the table with him heard this, he said to Jesus, "Blessed is the man who will eat at the feast in the kingdom of God."

¹⁶Jesus replied: "A certain man was preparing a great banquet and invited many guests. ¹⁷At the time of the banquet he sent his servant to tell those who had been invited, 'Come, for everything is now ready.'

¹⁸"But they all alike began to make excuses. The first said, 'I have just bought a field, and I must go and see it. Please excuse me.'

¹⁹"Another said, 'I have just bought five yoke of oxen, and I'm on my way to try them out. Please excuse me.'

²⁰"Still another said, 'I just got married, so I can't come.'

²¹"The servant came back and reported this to his master. Then the owner of the house became angry and ordered his servant, 'Go out quickly into the streets and alleys of the town and bring in the poor, the crippled, the blind and the lame.'

²²"'Sir,' the servant said, 'what you ordered has been done, but there is still room.'

²³"Then the master told his servant, 'Go out to the roads and country lanes and make them come in, so that my house will be full. ²⁴I tell you, not one of those men who were invited will get a taste of my banquet.' "

²⁵Large crowds were traveling with Jesus, and turning to them he said: ²⁶"If anyone comes to me and does not hate his father and mother, his wife and children, his brothers and sisters—yes, even his own life—he cannot be my disciple. ²⁷And anyone who does not carry his cross and follow me cannot be my disciple.

²⁸"Suppose one of you wants to build a tower. Will he not first sit down and estimate the cost to see if he has enough money to complete it? ²⁹For if he lays the foundation and is not able to finish it, everyone who sees it will ridicule him, ³⁰saying, 'This fellow began to build and was not able to finish.'

³¹"Or suppose a king is about to go to war against another king. Will he not first sit down and consider whether he is able with ten thousand men to oppose the one coming against him with twenty thousand? ³²If he is not able, he will send a delegation while the other is still a long way off and will ask for terms of peace. ³³In the same way, any of you who does not give up everything he has cannot be my disciple.

³⁴"Salt is good, but if it loses its saltiness, how can it be made salty again? ³⁵It is fit neither for the soil nor for the manure pile; it is thrown out.

"He who has ears to hear, let him hear."

ⁱ5 Some manuscripts *donkey*

Discovering the Word 1. Jesus' journeying to Jerusalem gives the setting of our title question (13:22–23). What in Jesus' parable answer would startle his Jewish listeners or perhaps you? 2. The Pharisees' motive for warning Jesus is not clear. They are now allied with the Herodians, their political enemies, against Jesus. But he is fearless (13:31–33). Then he expresses other emotions (vv. 34–35). Why do you think Jesus is so deeply passionate about Jerusalem? 3. What explains the Pharisees' double silence to Jesus' questions (14:4,6)? 4. How does this third parable climax Jesus' answer to our study question of who ultimately will be saved

(14:15–24)? **5.** Travelers nearing Jerusalem passed old wooden crosses along the way. Everyone knew their use—for criminal execution. So how would Jesus' fellow travelers understand his words in 14:27?

 Applying the Word **1.** With two parables he teaches the guests about true honor (14:7–11) and his host about true hospitality (14:12–14). How should Jesus' lessons affect your social life? **2.** Jesus lays down his conditions for discipleship by calling into question powerful loyalties—to family and to self. What would be a contemporary example of Christians "hating" their family? **3.** Try counting the cost of not following Jesus on his terms. What to you is most sobering?

 Responding in Prayer Talk openly with God about how you are experiencing the cost of discipleship.

17 / *Luke 15*
The God Who Likes to Throw Parties

THE TITLE OF Rembrandt's famous painting "Return of the Prodigal Son" focuses on the father's younger son in Jesus' well-known parable. But by composition and lighting, the artist causes us to focus on the father—his face weathered by suffering, his hands lovingly embracing the ragged boy, his whole body bent to his returned son. Some people focus more on the sin and repentance of the young man than on God's compassion and purposes. Repentance is necessary. But Jesus' rejoicing Father completes, indeed dominates, the picture.

 Warming Up to God How have you recently experienced the joyful side of God's nature? Praise God for who he is.

Read Luke 15.

15 Now the tax collectors and "sinners" were all gathering around to hear him. ²But the Pharisees and the teachers of the law muttered, "This man welcomes sinners and eats with them."

³Then Jesus told them this parable: ⁴"Suppose one of you has a hundred sheep and loses one of them. Does he not leave the ninety-nine in the open country and go after the lost sheep until he finds it? ⁵And when he finds it, he joyfully puts it on his shoulders ⁶and goes home. Then he calls his friends and neighbors together and says, 'Rejoice with me; I have found my lost sheep.' ⁷I tell you that in the same way there will be more rejoicing in heaven over one sinner who repents than over ninety-nine righteous persons who do not need to repent.

⁸"Or suppose a woman has ten silver coinsʲ and loses one. Does she not light a lamp, sweep the house and search carefully until she finds it? ⁹And when she finds it, she calls her friends and neighbors together and says, 'Rejoice with me; I have found my lost coin.' ¹⁰In the same way, I tell you, there is rejoicing in the presence of the angels of God over one sinner who repents."

¹¹Jesus continued: "There was a man who had two sons. ¹²The younger one said to his father, 'Father, give me my share of the estate.' So he divided his property between them.

¹³"Not long after that, the younger son got together all he had, set off for a distant country and there squandered his wealth in wild living. ¹⁴After he had spent everything, there was a severe famine in that whole country, and he began to be in need. ¹⁵So he went and hired himself out to a citizen of that country, who sent him to his fields to feed pigs. ¹⁶He longed to fill his stomach with the pods that the pigs were eating, but no one gave him anything.

¹⁷"When he came to his senses, he said, 'How many of my father's hired men have food to spare, and here I am starving to death! ¹⁸I will set out and go back to my father and say to him: Father, I have sinned against heaven and against you. ¹⁹I am no longer worthy to be called your son; make me like one of your hired men.' ²⁰So he got up and went to his father.

"But while he was still a long way off, his father

j8 Greek ten drachmas, each worth about a day's wages

saw him and was filled with compassion for him; he ran to his son, threw his arms around him and kissed him.

²¹"The son said to him, 'Father, I have sinned against heaven and against you. I am no longer worthy to be called your son.ᵏ'

²²"But the father said to his servants, 'Quick! Bring the best robe and put it on him. Put a ring on his finger and sandals on his feet. ²³Bring the fattened calf and kill it. Let's have a feast and celebrate. ²⁴For this son of mine was dead and is alive again; he was lost and is found.' So they began to celebrate.

²⁵"Meanwhile, the older son was in the field. When he came near the house, he heard music and dancing. ²⁶So he called one of the servants and asked him what was going on. ²⁷'Your brother has come,' he replied, 'and your father has killed the fattened calf because he has him back safe and sound.'

²⁸"The older brother became angry and refused to go in. So his father went out and pleaded with him. ²⁹But he answered his father, 'Look! All these years I've been slaving for you and never disobeyed your orders. Yet you never gave me even a young goat so I could celebrate with my friends. ³⁰But when this son of yours who has squandered your property with prostitutes comes home, you kill the fattened calf for him!'

³¹" 'My son,' the father said, 'you are always with me, and everything I have is yours. ³²But we had to celebrate and be glad, because this brother of yours was dead and is alive again; he was lost and is found.' "

ᵏ21 Some early manuscripts son. *Make me like one of your hired men.*

 Discovering the Word 1. What provoked Jesus' parables (vv. 1–2)? 2. In the first two parables the theme of an owner searching for something lost and rejoicing when it is found begins to answer Jesus' critics. The third parable repeats the basic theme. But how is it different from the first two? 3. What steps do you perceive in the young man's 180-degree turnabout? 4. The drama grows as Jesus describes the father in verses 20–24. In the light of verse 2, what does he want his critics to see about this man? 5. In the interaction with his older son, what other dimensions of the father's character and motives appear (vv. 28–32)? 6. The rejoicing nature of God is still foreign if not downright offensive to some religious people (see vv. 2, 6–7, 9–10, 22–24, 32 and 14:16–17). Why?

 Applying the Word 1. How do these parables move you to believe in the possibilities of new or fresh changes in your relationship to family members and to God? 2. Which of your friends have like the older son an inadequate or wrong view of God?

 Responding in Prayer Pray for an opportunity to share with your friends this appealing portrait of God.

18 / Luke 16
Managing Your Money

WE HAVE SUPPOSEDLY left the high-flying 1980s decade of greed. In 1985 Ivan Boesky was commencement speaker at a prestigious school of business administration in California. He said to the graduating class, "Greed is all right, by the way. I want you to know that I think greed is healthy. You can be greedy and still feel good about yourself." Sad, yes. And the response of those young men and women was just as sad. They laughed and applauded. A year and a half later Boesky was in prison for his runaway greed. The two parables in our present chapter show Jesus' judgment on the proper use of money.

Warming Up to God Why do you like money?

Read Luke 16.

16

Jesus told his disciples: "There was a rich man whose manager was accused of wasting his possessions. ²So he called him in and asked him, 'What is this I hear about you? Give an account of your management, because you cannot be manager any longer.'

³"The manager said to himself, 'What shall I do now? My master is taking away my job. I'm not strong enough to dig, and I'm ashamed to beg— ⁴I know what I'll do so that, when I lose my job here, people will welcome me into their houses.'

⁵"So he called in each one of his master's debtors. He asked the first, 'How much do you owe my master?'

⁶" 'Eight hundred gallons¹ of olive oil,' he replied.

"The manager told him, 'Take your bill, sit down quickly, and make it four hundred.'

⁷"Then he asked the second, 'And how much do you owe?'

" 'A thousand bushels^m of wheat,' he replied.

"He told him, 'Take your bill and make it eight hundred.'

⁸"The master commended the dishonest manager because he had acted shrewdly. For the people of this world are more shrewd in dealing with their own kind than are the people of the light. ⁹I tell you, use worldly wealth to gain friends for yourselves, so that when it is gone, you will be welcomed into eternal dwellings.

¹⁰"Whoever can be trusted with very little can also be trusted with much, and whoever is dishonest with very little will also be dishonest with much. ¹¹So if you have not been trustworthy in handling worldly wealth, who will trust you with true riches? ¹²And if you have not been trustworthy with someone else's property, who will give you property of your own?

¹³"No servant can serve two masters. Either he will hate the one and love the other, or he will be devoted to the one and despise the other. You cannot serve both God and Money."

¹⁴The Pharisees, who loved money, heard all this and were sneering at Jesus. ¹⁵He said to them, "You are the ones who justify yourselves in the eyes of men, but God knows your hearts. What is highly valued among men is detestable in God's sight.

¹⁶"The Law and the Prophets were proclaimed until John. Since that time, the good news of the kingdom of God is being preached, and everyone is forcing his way into it. ¹⁷It is easier for heaven and earth to disappear than for the least stroke of a pen to drop out of the Law.

¹⁸"Anyone who divorces his wife and marries another woman commits adultery, and the man who marries a divorced woman commits adultery.

¹⁹"There was a rich man who was dressed in purple and fine linen and lived in luxury every day. ²⁰At his gate was laid a beggar named Lazarus, covered with sores ²¹and longing to eat what fell from the rich man's table. Even the dogs came and licked his sores.

²²"The time came when the beggar died and the angels carried him to Abraham's side. The rich man also died and was buried. ²³In hell,^n where he was in torment, he looked up and saw Abraham far away, with Lazarus by his side. ²⁴So he called to him, 'Father Abraham, have pity on me and send Lazarus to dip the tip of his finger in water and cool my tongue, because I am in agony in this fire.'

²⁵"But Abraham replied, 'Son, remember that in your lifetime you received your good things, while Lazarus received bad things, but now he is comforted here and you are in agony. ²⁶And besides all this, between us and you a great chasm has been fixed, so that those who want to go from here to you cannot, nor can anyone cross over from there to us.'

²⁷"He answered, 'Then I beg you, father, send Lazarus to my father's house, ²⁸for I have five brothers. Let him warn them, so that they will not also come to this place of torment.'

²⁹"Abraham replied, 'They have Moses and the Prophets; let them listen to them.'

³⁰" 'No, father Abraham,' he said, 'but if someone from the dead goes to them, they will repent.'

³¹"He said to him, 'If they do not listen to Moses and the Prophets, they will not be convinced even if someone rises from the dead.' "

---

¹6 Greek *one hundred batous* (probably about 3 kiloliters)   ^m7 Greek *one hundred korous* (probably about 35 kiloliters)   ^n23 Greek *Hades*

Discovering the Word 1. Jesus' parable in verses 1–18 is quite straightforward. His application, however, seems not as clear (vv. 8b–9). At first reading, how does he seem to be applying the parable to his disciples? 2. Where in the context could you show that Jesus is not condoning greed and dishonesty? 3. According to Jesus in verses 10–15, what does our management of money have to do with our standing before God? 4. In the first part of the parable in verses 19–31 Jesus contrasts the earthly status of Lazarus and the rich man, and then their different eternal states. What does Jesus want the Pharisees to see about the relationship of money in this life and in the life after death? 5. In the second part of the parable we learn more about life after death (vv. 26–31). What facts and implications do you observe about this dimension of existence?

Applying the Word 1. How should these parables affect your present use of money? 2. What practical actions would help you to use your money more effectively?

Responding in Prayer Our relatives and friends are not all skeptics. Pray that Jesus' teaching on life after death may spur you to more personal evangelism with those who are still open.

19 / Luke 17:1—18:14
How to Grow Mustard-Seed Faith

AS JESUS, HIS disciples and the crowds draw near Jerusalem, he knows disillusion will set in for them. No one understands his repeated predictions of death by the hands of the nation's leaders. They all expect political glory. Their faith is in a nationalistic, political Messiah come to overthrow the Roman rulers and reinstate their national independence. They had to learn what we also have to learn: Faith is not a complete package one receives at conversion. Our trust is not to be in a set program but in a dynamic Person. Faith is a growing response to God, and grows best in the adversities of life.

Warming Up to God Since you first met Jesus, what disillusionments have you had about him and his way of life?

Read Luke 17:1—18:14

17 Jesus said to his disciples: "Things that cause people to sin are bound to come, but woe to that person through whom they come. ²It would be better for him to be thrown into the sea with a millstone tied around his neck than for him to cause one of these little ones to sin. ³So watch yourselves.

"If your brother sins, rebuke him, and if he repents, forgive him. ⁴If he sins against you seven times in a day, and seven times comes back to you and says, 'I repent,' forgive him."

⁵The apostles said to the Lord, "Increase our faith!"

⁶He replied, "If you have faith as small as a mustard seed, you can say to this mulberry tree, 'Be uprooted and planted in the sea,' and it will obey you.

⁷"Suppose one of you had a servant plowing or looking after the sheep. Would he say to the servant when he comes in from the field, 'Come along now and sit down to eat'? ⁸Would he not

rather say, 'Prepare my supper, get yourself ready and wait on me while I eat and drink; after that you may eat and drink'? ⁹Would he thank the servant because he did what he was told to do? ¹⁰So you also, when you have done everything you were told to do, should say, 'We are unworthy servants; we have only done our duty.' "

¹¹Now on his way to Jerusalem, Jesus traveled along the border between Samaria and Galilee. ¹²As he was going into a village, ten men who had leprosy° met him. They stood at a distance ¹³and called out in a loud voice, "Jesus, Master, have pity on us!"

¹⁴When he saw them, he said, "Go, show yourselves to the priests." And as they went, they were cleansed.

¹⁵One of them, when he saw he was healed, came back, praising God in a loud voice. ¹⁶He

---

°12 The Greek word was used for various diseases affecting the skin—not necessarily leprosy.

threw himself at Jesus' feet and thanked him—
and he was a Samaritan.

¹⁷Jesus asked, "Were not all ten cleansed?
Where are the other nine? ¹⁸Was no one found to
return and give praise to God except this foreigner?" ¹⁹Then he said to him, "Rise and go;
your faith has made you well."

²⁰Once, having been asked by the Pharisees
when the kingdom of God would come, Jesus replied, "The kingdom of God does not come with
your careful observation, ²¹nor will people say,
'Here it is,' or 'There it is,' because the kingdom of
God is within*p* you."

²²Then he said to his disciples, "The time is
coming when you will long to see one of the days
of the Son of Man, but you will not see it. ²³Men
will tell you, 'There he is!' or 'Here he is!' Do not
go running off after them. ²⁴For the Son of Man
in his day*q* will be like the lightning, which
flashes and lights up the sky from one end to the
other. ²⁵But first he must suffer many things and
be rejected by this generation.

²⁶"Just as it was in the days of Noah, so also
will it be in the days of the Son of Man. ²⁷People
were eating, drinking, marrying and being given
in marriage up to the day Noah entered the ark.
Then the flood came and destroyed them all.

²⁸"It was the same in the days of Lot. People
were eating and drinking, buying and selling,
planting and building. ²⁹But the day Lot left
Sodom, fire and sulfur rained down from heaven
and destroyed them all.

³⁰"It will be just like this on the day the Son of
Man is revealed. ³¹On that day no one who is on
the roof of his house, with his goods inside,
should go down to get them. Likewise, no one in
the field should go back for anything. ³²Remem-
ber Lot's wife! ³³Whoever tries to keep his life
will lose it, and whoever loses his life will preserve it. ³⁴I tell you, on that night two people will
be in one bed; one will be taken and the other
left. ³⁵Two women will be grinding grain together; one will be taken and the other left.*r*"

³⁷"Where, Lord?" they asked.

He replied, "Where there is a dead body, there
the vultures will gather."

18 Then Jesus told his disciples a parable to show them that they should
always pray and not give up. ²He
said: "In a certain town there was a judge who
neither feared God nor cared about men. ³And
there was a widow in that town who kept coming
to him with the plea, 'Grant me justice against my
adversary.'

⁴"For some time he refused. But finally he said
to himself, 'Even though I don't fear God or care
about men, ⁵yet because this widow keeps bothering me, I will see that she gets justice, so that
she won't eventually wear me out with her coming!' "

⁶And the Lord said, "Listen to what the unjust
judge says. ⁷And will not God bring about justice
for his chosen ones, who cry out to him day and
night? Will he keep putting them off? ⁸I tell you,
he will see that they get justice, and quickly.
However, when the Son of Man comes, will he
find faith on the earth?"

⁹To some who were confident of their own
righteousness and looked down on everybody
else, Jesus told this parable: ¹⁰"Two men went up
to the temple to pray, one a Pharisee and the
other a tax collector. ¹¹The Pharisee stood up and
prayed about*s* himself: 'God, I thank you that I
am not like other men—robbers, evildoers, adulterers—or even like this tax collector. ¹²I fast
twice a week and give a tenth of all I get.'

¹³"But the tax collector stood at a distance. He
would not even look up to heaven, but beat his
breast and said, 'God, have mercy on me, a sinner.'

¹⁴"I tell you that this man, rather than the
other, went home justified before God. For everyone who exalts himself will be humbled, and he
who humbles himself will be exalted."

p21 Or *among*   *q24* Some manuscripts do not have *in his day.*
r35 Some manuscripts *left.* *36Two men will be in the field; one will be*
taken and the other left.   *s11* Or *to*

Discovering the Word 1. Consider the strong reaction of the disciples in 17:1–5. What has caused this
reaction? 2. In the story of the lepers Jesus seems surprised that only one of the ten returned in gratitude
for his healing. What relation can you see between faith and gratitude in his final words (17:17–19)? 3. For the
Pharisees, what emphasis about the kingdom of God does Jesus make (17:20–21)? Why? 4. To his disciples
Jesus stresses the need to be prepared for the coming of the Son of Man (himself). He uses two examples of
warning in the Old Testament. Why were those people unprepared for God's judgment (17:22–37)? 5. To encourage us to persist in praying Jesus draws a portrait of a certain judge as a contrast to God. In what ways is God

different from the judge (18:6–8)? **6.** Persistence in praying is balanced by the caution in the second parable not to be presumptuous about God (18:9–14). Both men address "God." But how do their prayers reveal different concepts of God and their relation to him?

 Applying the Word **1.** What might your prayers reveal about your concept of God and how you relate to him? **2.** Faith often seems abstract and elusive. How has Jesus in this study made it more concrete and attainable for your daily living?

 Responding in Prayer Pray from your heart to the God who desires to hear you.

20 / *Luke 18:15—19:10*
The Nobodies God Wants

"ONLY THE LITTLE people pay taxes." This quote comes from the very rich hotel "queen," Leona Helmsley, who is now paying dearly for tax evasion. What a contrast of attitude with God's compassion for "the little people." Our study introduces us to three groups or individuals whom society considered insignificant—little children, a blind beggar and a tax collector. They represent the kind of people he wants in his messianic community.

 Warming Up to God Reflect on the past week. Is it possible that you have treated someone as insignificant? If so, confess your sin to the Lord.

Read Luke 18:15—19:10.

---

¹⁵People were also bringing babies to Jesus to have him touch them. When the disciples saw this, they rebuked them. ¹⁶But Jesus called the children to him and said, "Let the little children come to me, and do not hinder them, for the kingdom of God belongs to such as these. ¹⁷I tell you the truth, anyone who will not receive the kingdom of God like a little child will never enter it."

¹⁸A certain ruler asked him, "Good teacher, what must I do to inherit eternal life?"

¹⁹"Why do you call me good?" Jesus answered. "No one is good—except God alone. ²⁰You know the commandments: 'Do not commit adultery, do not murder, do not steal, do not give false testimony, honor your father and mother.'ᵗ"

²¹"All these I have kept since I was a boy," he said.

²²When Jesus heard this, he said to him, "You still lack one thing. Sell everything you have and give to the poor, and you will have treasure in heaven. Then come, follow me."

²³When he heard this, he became very sad, because he was a man of great wealth. ²⁴Jesus looked at him and said, "How hard it is for the rich to enter the kingdom of God! ²⁵Indeed, it is

easier for a camel to go through the eye of a needle than for a rich man to enter the kingdom of God."

²⁶Those who heard this asked, "Who then can be saved?"

²⁷Jesus replied, "What is impossible with men is possible with God."

²⁸Peter said to him, "We have left all we had to follow you!"

²⁹"I tell you the truth," Jesus said to them, "no one who has left home or wife or brothers or parents or children for the sake of the kingdom of God ³⁰will fail to receive many times as much in this age and, in the age to come, eternal life."

³¹Jesus took the Twelve aside and told them, "We are going up to Jerusalem, and everything that is written by the prophets about the Son of Man will be fulfilled. ³²He will be handed over to the Gentiles. They will mock him, insult him, spit on him, flog him and kill him. ³³On the third day he will rise again."

³⁴The disciples did not understand any of this. Its meaning was hidden from them, and they did not know what he was talking about.

³⁵As Jesus approached Jericho, a blind man was

*20 Exodus 20:12-16; Deut. 5:16-20

sitting by the roadside begging. ³⁶When he heard the crowd going by, he asked what was happening. ³⁷They told him, "Jesus of Nazareth is passing by."

³⁸He called out, "Jesus, Son of David, have mercy on me!"

³⁹Those who led the way rebuked him and told him to be quiet, but he shouted all the more, "Son of David, have mercy on me!"

⁴⁰Jesus stopped and ordered the man to be brought to him. When he came near, Jesus asked him, ⁴¹"What do you want me to do for you?"

"Lord, I want to see," he replied.

⁴²Jesus said to him, "Receive your sight; your faith has healed you." ⁴³Immediately he received his sight and followed Jesus, praising God. When all the people saw it, they also praised God.

19 Jesus entered Jericho and was passing through. ²A man was there by the name of Zacchaeus; he was a chief tax collector and was wealthy. ³He wanted to see who Jesus was, but being a short man he could not, because of the crowd. ⁴So he ran ahead and climbed a sycamore-fig tree to see him, since Jesus was coming that way.

⁵When Jesus reached the spot, he looked up and said to him, "Zacchaeus, come down immediately. I must stay at your house today." ⁶So he came down at once and welcomed him gladly.

⁷All the people saw this and began to mutter, "He has gone to be the guest of a 'sinner.' "

⁸But Zacchaeus stood up and said to the Lord, "Look, Lord! Here and now I give half of my possessions to the poor, and if I have cheated anybody out of anything, I will pay back four times the amount."

⁹Jesus said to him, "Today salvation has come to this house, because this man, too, is a son of Abraham. ¹⁰For the Son of Man came to seek and to save what was lost."

Discovering the Word 1. The disciples represent their society's attitude to children—they're insignificant (18:15). How does Jesus give significance to them? 2. In contrast, 18:18–30 is about a "somebody" who disqualifies himself from the kingdom. He has everything society considers admirable and desirable. But what condition for eternal life does he lack (18:22)? 3. In Luke 18:31–34 Jesus' fourth prediction to the Twelve about his coming violent death again meets with lack of understanding. Their presuppositions about riches and their political agenda (19:11) deafens them to Jesus' intent. Then in 18:35–45 Luke introduces us to someone who represents another group of nobodies. What is unusual about the beggar's attitude and title that catches Jesus' attention? 4. Jericho was a rich agricultural town, a popular resort for royalty and priests. What kind of character would a chief tax collector in such a town likely develop? 5. What other side of Zaccheus surfaces in 19:3–6 and 8?

 Applying the Word 1. How does Jesus' example with Zaccheus show you how you might share the gospel? 2. Which outsider or nobody from your circle of acquaintances could you introduce to Jesus?

 Responding in Prayer Pray for those who are considered insignificant in your community.

---

21 / *Luke 19:11–48*
False Hopes About the Kingdom of God

MOST OF MY bosses have been hard drivers who regularly exasperated me. But in the long run we worked together productively. If we respect and like our bosses, we are often willing to work hard and even overtime. If we don't respect or like them, we usually are not willing. Then we probably become unproductive. Likewise our personal view of God affects our working relationship to him. In this case productivity has not just temporal but eternal consequences.

 Warming Up to God How has work been for you this week? Talk to God about any frustrations you have experienced.

Read Luke 19:11—48.

¹¹While they were listening to this, he went on to tell them a parable, because he was near Jerusalem and the people thought that the kingdom of God was going to appear at once. ¹²He said: "A man of noble birth went to a distant country to have himself appointed king and then to return. ¹³So he called ten of his servants and gave them ten minas.ᵘ 'Put this money to work,' he said, 'until I come back.'

¹⁴"But his subjects hated him and sent a delegation after him to say, 'We don't want this man to be our king.'

¹⁵"He was made king, however, and returned home. Then he sent for the servants to whom he had given the money, in order to find out what they had gained with it.

¹⁶"The first one came and said, 'Sir, your mina has earned ten more.'

¹⁷" 'Well done, my good servant!' his master replied. 'Because you have been trustworthy in a very small matter, take charge of ten cities.'

¹⁸"The second came and said, 'Sir, your mina has earned five more.'

¹⁹"His master answered, 'You take charge of five cities.'

²⁰"Then another servant came and said, 'Sir, here is your mina; I have kept it laid away in a piece of cloth. ²¹I was afraid of you, because you are a hard man. You take out what you did not put in and reap what you did not sow.'

²²"His master replied, 'I will judge you by your own words, you wicked servant! You knew, did you, that I am a hard man, taking out what I did not put in, and reaping what I did not sow? ²³Why then didn't you put my money on deposit, so that when I came back, I could have collected it with interest?'

²⁴"Then he said to those standing by, 'Take his mina away from him and give it to the one who has ten minas.'

²⁵" 'Sir,' they said, 'he already has ten!'

²⁶"He replied, 'I tell you that to everyone who has, more will be given, but as for the one who has nothing, even what he has will be taken away. ²⁷But those enemies of mine who did not want me to be king over them—bring them here and kill them in front of me.' "

²⁸After Jesus had said this, he went on ahead, going up to Jerusalem. ²⁹As he approached Bethphage and Bethany at the hill called the Mount of Olives, he sent two of his disciples, saying to them, ³⁰"Go to the village ahead of you, and as you enter it, you will find a colt tied there, which no one has ever ridden. Untie it and bring it here. ³¹If anyone asks you, 'Why are you untying it?' tell him, 'The Lord needs it.' "

³²Those who were sent ahead went and found it just as he had told them. ³³As they were untying the colt, its owners asked them, "Why are you untying the colt?"

³⁴They replied, "The Lord needs it."

³⁵They brought it to Jesus, threw their cloaks on the colt and put Jesus on it. ³⁶As he went along, people spread their cloaks on the road.

³⁷When he came near the place where the road goes down the Mount of Olives, the whole crowd of disciples began joyfully to praise God in loud voices for all the miracles they had seen:

³⁸"Blessed is the king who comes in the name
       of the Lord!"ᵛ

"Peace in heaven and glory in the highest!"

³⁹Some of the Pharisees in the crowd said to Jesus, "Teacher, rebuke your disciples!"

⁴⁰"I tell you," he replied, "if they keep quiet, the stones will cry out."

⁴¹As he approached Jerusalem and saw the city, he wept over it ⁴²and said, "If you, even you, had only known on this day what would bring you peace—but now it is hidden from your eyes. ⁴³The days will come upon you when your enemies will build an embankment against you and encircle you and hem you in on every side. ⁴⁴They will dash you to the ground, you and the children within your walls. They will not leave one stone on another, because you did not recognize the time of God's coming to you."

⁴⁵Then he entered the temple area and began driving out those who were selling. ⁴⁶"It is written," he said to them, " 'My house will be a house of prayer'ʷ; but you have made it 'a den of robbers.'ˣ "

⁴⁷Every day he was teaching at the temple. But

ᵘ13 A mina was about three months' wages.   ᵛ38 Psalm 118:26
ʷ46 Isaiah 56:7   ˣ46 Jer. 7:11

the chief priests, the teachers of the law and the leaders among the people were trying to kill him.

⁴⁸Yet they could not find any way to do it, because all the people hung on his words.

Discovering the Word 1. Jesus' key words in verse 10 have inflamed the crowd's messianic expectations. Jesus' parable aims to counter any false hopes. In verses 12–15 what comparisons between the nobleman and himself does Jesus highlight? 2. Consider the hour of accountability when the master returns as king (vv. 15–26). The reward of the first two (representative) servants is simple. But the king's dialogue with the third servant is detailed. With this emphasis, what point is Jesus making (keep in mind v. 11)? 3. The adversaries of the nobleman-made-king are mentioned only at the beginning and the end (vv. 14, 27). Whom does Jesus intend them to represent? 4. How does he smash the false hopes of this group? 5. In verses 28–40 we see Jesus in various aspects of his messianic role. In a descriptive word or phrase, what concern of Jesus' do you see as he approaches Jerusalem? 6. What concern of Jesus' do you note as he reflects on Jerusalem (vv. 41–44)?

Applying the Word 1. In this panoramic view of Jesus the Messiah, what do you find hard to understand about him? 2. What about Jesus here can you positively respond to? Why?

Responding in Prayer Worship Jesus the Messiah king with praise, awe and thanksgiving.

---

22 / *Luke 20:1—21:4*
Final Debates—Clear Rejection

I CAN REMEMBER when a humanist on campus branded the Christians a bunch of losers. He claimed he did not need religion for a crutch as they did. I was reduced to wordlessness by his hostile tone. Then I thought of three perfect answers—late that night in bed.

Most of us are not quick to think on our feet, and certainly not as quick and sharp as Jesus. We have seen him as a fearless controversialist in Galilee. Now we will see him in the capital, taking on four distinct authority groups as each mounts attacks on him.

Warming Up to God When have you felt humiliated because you could not defend your faith?

Read Luke 20:1—21:4.

---

20 One day as he was teaching the people in the temple courts and preaching the gospel, the chief priests and the teachers of the law, together with the elders, came up to him. ²"Tell us by what authority you are doing these things," they said. "Who gave you this authority?"

³He replied, "I will also ask you a question. Tell me, ⁴John's baptism—was it from heaven, or from men?"

⁵They discussed it among themselves and said, "If we say, 'From heaven,' he will ask, 'Why didn't you believe him?' ⁶But if we say, 'From men,' all the people will stone us, because they are persuaded that John was a prophet."

⁷So they answered, "We don't know where it was from."

⁸Jesus said, "Neither will I tell you by what authority I am doing these things."

⁹He went on to tell the people this parable: "A man planted a vineyard, rented it to some farmers and went away for a long time. ¹⁰At harvest time he sent a servant to the tenants so they would give him some of the fruit of the vineyard. But the tenants beat him and sent him away empty-handed. ¹¹He sent another servant, but that one also they beat and treated shamefully and sent away empty-handed. ¹²He sent still a third, and they wounded him and threw him out.

¹³"Then the owner of the vineyard said, 'What

shall I do? I will send my son, whom I love; perhaps they will respect him.'

14"But when the tenants saw him, they talked the matter over. 'This is the heir,' they said. 'Let's kill him, and the inheritance will be ours.' 15So they threw him out of the vineyard and killed him.

"What then will the owner of the vineyard do to them? 16He will come and kill those tenants and give the vineyard to others."

When the people heard this, they said, "May this never be!"

17Jesus looked directly at them and asked, "Then what is the meaning of that which is written:

" 'The stone the builders rejected
   has become the capstone[y]'[z]?

18Everyone who falls on that stone will be broken to pieces, but he on whom it falls will be crushed."

19The teachers of the law and the chief priests looked for a way to arrest him immediately, because they knew he had spoken this parable against them. But they were afraid of the people.

20Keeping a close watch on him, they sent spies, who pretended to be honest. They hoped to catch Jesus in something he said so that they might hand him over to the power and authority of the governor. 21So the spies questioned him: "Teacher, we know that you speak and teach what is right, and that you do not show partiality but teach the way of God in accordance with the truth. 22Is it right for us to pay taxes to Caesar or not?"

23He saw through their duplicity and said to them, 24"Show me a denarius. Whose portrait and inscription are on it?"

25"Caesar's," they replied.

He said to them, "Then give to Caesar what is Caesar's, and to God what is God's."

26They were unable to trap him in what he had said there in public. And astonished by his answer, they became silent.

27Some of the Sadducees, who say there is no resurrection, came to Jesus with a question. 28"Teacher," they said, "Moses wrote for us that if a man's brother dies and leaves a wife but no children, the man must marry the widow and have children for his brother. 29Now there were seven brothers. The first one married a woman

and died childless. 30The second 31and then the third married her, and in the same way the seven died, leaving no children. 32Finally, the woman died too. 33Now then, at the resurrection whose wife will she be, since the seven were married to her?"

34Jesus replied, "The people of this age marry and are given in marriage. 35But those who are considered worthy of taking part in that age and in the resurrection from the dead will neither marry nor be given in marriage, 36and they can no longer die; for they are like the angels. They are God's children, since they are children of the resurrection. 37But in the account of the bush, even Moses showed that the dead rise, for he calls the Lord 'the God of Abraham, and the God of Isaac, and the God of Jacob.'[a] 38He is not the God of the dead, but of the living, for to him all are alive."

39Some of the teachers of the law responded, "Well said, teacher!" 40And no one dared to ask him any more questions.

41Then Jesus said to them, "How is it that they say the Christ[b] is the Son of David? 42David himself declares in the Book of Psalms:

" 'The Lord said to my Lord:
   "Sit at my right hand
43until I make your enemies
   a footstool for your feet." '[c]

44David calls him 'Lord.' How then can he be his son?"

45While all the people were listening, Jesus said to his disciples, 46"Beware of the teachers of the law. They like to walk around in flowing robes and love to be greeted in the marketplaces and have the most important seats in the synagogues and the places of honor at banquets. 47They devour widows' houses and for a show make lengthy prayers. Such men will be punished most severely."

21 As he looked up, Jesus saw the rich putting their gifts into the temple treasury. 2He also saw a poor widow put in two very small copper coins.[d] 3"I tell you the truth," he said, "this poor widow has put in more than all the others. 4All these people gave their gifts out of their wealth; but she out of her poverty put in all she had to live on."

y17 Or cornerstone   z17 Psalm 118:22   a37 Exodus 3:6
b41 Or Messiah   c43 Psalm 110:1   d2 Greek two lepta

Discovering the Word 1. By the end of the debate on Jesus' authority, what has each side achieved (20:1–8)? 2. By parable and commentary Jesus pronounces final judgment on the leaders (20:9–18). How do you respond to his stern characterization of God? 3. The Sadducees accepted only the first five Old Testament books, which they (wrongly) presumed said nothing about life after death. What, therefore, do they expect their hypothetical story to do to belief in the resurrection (20:27–47)? 4. Again Jesus points to wrong assumptions behind their question. What error does he identify in their view of life after death (vv. 34–36)? 5. How refreshing this widow must have been to Jesus after the controversies! What does this tell you about the kind of faith Jesus values (21:1–4)?

 Applying the Word 1. All four groups totally reject Jesus as God's Messiah king. After this, there are no more debates on the truth—only arrest and death. Besides valid debates, how can we maintain biblical truth against the enemies of Christianity? 2. What is a political/religious tension for you as a Christian? 3. In what way would you like to be more bold in defending your faith?

 Responding in Prayer Pray now for faith like the widow's.

23 / *Luke 21:5–38*
Getting Ready for the End

THE "EVIL EMPIRE" of the once-powerful USSR has disappeared, and its former allies are left dangling for military aid. We praise God for this. But some "scholars" of biblical prophecy have to rewrite their books about who the antichrist is and who the nations that will meet for battle in Magog are. Sensational interpretations of "the last days" can stir up some people, especially when the Middle East is in the news. Others react against what they perceive as scare tactics by avoiding any consideration of biblical prophecies. In today's chapter the Lord Jesus shows us how to keep a balance by being properly informed and obedient to his instructions.

Warming Up to God What feelings does talk about the last days create in you?

Read Luke 21:5–38.

---

⁵Some of his disciples were remarking about how the temple was adorned with beautiful stones and with gifts dedicated to God. But Jesus said, ⁶"As for what you see here, the time will come when not one stone will be left on another; every one of them will be thrown down."

⁷"Teacher," they asked, "when will these things happen? And what will be the sign that they are about to take place?"

⁸He replied: "Watch out that you are not deceived. For many will come in my name, claiming, 'I am he,' and, 'The time is near.' Do not follow them. ⁹When you hear of wars and revolutions, do not be frightened. These things must happen first, but the end will not come right away."

¹⁰Then he said to them: "Nation will rise against nation, and kingdom against kingdom. ¹¹There will be great earthquakes, famines and pestilences in various places, and fearful events and great signs from heaven.

¹²"But before all this, they will lay hands on you and persecute you. They will deliver you to synagogues and prisons, and you will be brought before kings and governors, and all on account of my name. ¹³This will result in your being witnesses to them. ¹⁴But make up your mind not to worry beforehand how you will defend yourselves. ¹⁵For I will give you words and wisdom that none of your adversaries will be able to resist or contradict. ¹⁶You will be betrayed even by parents, brothers, relatives and friends, and they will put some of you to death. ¹⁷All men will hate you because of me. ¹⁸But not a hair of your head will perish. ¹⁹By standing firm you will gain life.

²⁰"When you see Jerusalem being surrounded by armies, you will know that its desolation is near. ²¹Then let those who are in Judea flee to the

mountains, let those in the city get out, and let those in the country not enter the city. ²²For this is the time of punishment in fulfillment of all that has been written. ²³How dreadful it will be in those days for pregnant women and nursing mothers! There will be great distress in the land and wrath against this people. ²⁴They will fall by the sword and will be taken as prisoners to all the nations. Jerusalem will be trampled on by the Gentiles until the times of the Gentiles are fulfilled.

²⁵"There will be signs in the sun, moon and stars. On the earth, nations will be in anguish and perplexity at the roaring and tossing of the sea. ²⁶Men will faint from terror, apprehensive of what is coming on the world, for the heavenly bodies will be shaken. ²⁷At that time they will see the Son of Man coming in a cloud with power and great glory. ²⁸When these things begin to take place, stand up and lift up your heads, because your redemption is drawing near."

²⁹He told them this parable: "Look at the fig tree and all the trees. ³⁰When they sprout leaves,

you can see for yourselves and know that summer is near. ³¹Even so, when you see these things happening, you know that the kingdom of God is near.

³²"I tell you the truth, this generationᵉ will certainly not pass away until all these things have happened. ³³Heaven and earth will pass away, but my words will never pass away.

³⁴"Be careful, or your hearts will be weighed down with dissipation, drunkenness and the anxieties of life, and that day will close on you unexpectedly like a trap. ³⁵For it will come upon all those who live on the face of the whole earth. ³⁶Be always on the watch, and pray that you may be able to escape all that is about to happen, and that you may be able to stand before the Son of Man."

³⁷Each day Jesus was teaching at the temple, and each evening he went out to spend the night on the hill called the Mount of Olives, ³⁸and all the people came early in the morning to hear him at the temple.

ᵉ32 Or *race*

Discovering the Word 1. What are your general impressions of Jesus' discourse on the end of the age? 2. At least three important events are evident. The first is Jesus' delivering this discourse to his disciples in A.D. 30 in Jerusalem. What are the other two (vv. 20–24 and vv. 27–28)? 3. But Jesus also says some positive things will happen during this time (vv. 12–19). (These activities can also be applied between the second and third events.) What in Jesus' message gives you hope for an otherwise uncertain future? 4. In verses 8–9 Jesus has said that certain activities are not signs of the end. But what does he say will be signs of the end when he returns (vv. 25–28, and probably vv. 10–11)? 5. How is Jesus' parable of the fig tree (vv. 29–31) related to his preceding teachings (for example, 19:41–44; 20:16)?

Applying the Word 1. Earthly preoccupation can keep us insensitive to spiritual realities and unprepared "to stand before the Son of Man" (vv. 5, 34–36). What aspects of modern living tempt you this way? 2. Which one of Jesus' promises gives you strong incentive to be well prepared (vv. 14–15, 19, 24, 28, 31, 33)?

Responding in Prayer Pray that you would be made ready.

---

24 / Luke 22:1–46
Jesus' New Passover

NOW WE ENTER deeply into the saddest days of history. With Judas' help the religious leaders, considered the most enlightened men in their nation, complete their plot to kill the Son of God. But these days are also the greatest days on earth for Jesus. He is about to complete his life mission, and he confirms to the eleven remaining that they will carry on that mission. So with them he privately establishes his new Passover to supersede the old Passover.

Warming Up to God Recall your most moving celebration of the Lord's Supper. What made it so?

Read Luke 22:1–46.

22 Now the Feast of Unleavened Bread, called the Passover, was approaching, ²and the chief priests and the teachers of the law were looking for some way to get rid of Jesus, for they were afraid of the people. ³Then Satan entered Judas, called Iscariot, one of the Twelve. ⁴And Judas went to the chief priests and the officers of the temple guard and discussed with them how he might betray Jesus. ⁵They were delighted and agreed to give him money. ⁶He consented, and watched for an opportunity to hand Jesus over to them when no crowd was present.

⁷Then came the day of Unleavened Bread on which the Passover lamb had to be sacrificed. ⁸Jesus sent Peter and John, saying, "Go and make preparations for us to eat the Passover."

⁹"Where do you want us to prepare for it?" they asked.

¹⁰He replied, "As you enter the city, a man carrying a jar of water will meet you. Follow him to the house that he enters, ¹¹and say to the owner of the house, 'The Teacher asks: Where is the guest room, where I may eat the Passover with my disciples?' ¹²He will show you a large upper room, all furnished. Make preparations there."

¹³They left and found things just as Jesus had told them. So they prepared the Passover.

¹⁴When the hour came, Jesus and his apostles reclined at the table. ¹⁵And he said to them, "I have eagerly desired to eat this Passover with you before I suffer. ¹⁶For I tell you, I will not eat it again until it finds fulfillment in the kingdom of God."

¹⁷After taking the cup, he gave thanks and said, "Take this and divide it among you. ¹⁸For I tell you I will not drink again of the fruit of the vine until the kingdom of God comes."

¹⁹And he took bread, gave thanks and broke it, and gave it to them, saying, "This is my body given for you; do this in remembrance of me."

²⁰In the same way, after the supper he took the cup, saying, "This cup is the new covenant in my blood, which is poured out for you. ²¹But the hand of him who is going to betray me is with mine on the table. ²²The Son of Man will go as it has been decreed, but woe to that man who betrays him." ²³They began to question among themselves which of them it might be who would do this.

²⁴Also a dispute arose among them as to which of them was considered to be greatest. ²⁵Jesus said to them, "The kings of the Gentiles lord it over them; and those who exercise authority over them call themselves Benefactors. ²⁶But you are not to be like that. Instead, the greatest among you should be like the youngest, and the one who rules like the one who serves. ²⁷For who is greater, the one who is at the table or the one who serves? Is it not the one who is at the table? But I am among you as one who serves. ²⁸You are those who have stood by me in my trials. ²⁹And I confer on you a kingdom, just as my Father conferred one on me, ³⁰so that you may eat and drink at my table in my kingdom and sit on thrones, judging the twelve tribes of Israel.

³¹"Simon, Simon, Satan has asked to sift you[f] as wheat. ³²But I have prayed for you, Simon, that your faith may not fail. And when you have turned back, strengthen your brothers."

³³But he replied, "Lord, I am ready to go with you to prison and to death."

³⁴Jesus answered, "I tell you, Peter, before the rooster crows today, you will deny three times that you know me."

³⁵Then Jesus asked them, "When I sent you without purse, bag or sandals, did you lack anything?"

"Nothing," they answered.

³⁶He said to them, "But now if you have a purse, take it, and also a bag; and if you don't have a sword, sell your cloak and buy one. ³⁷It is written: 'And he was numbered with the transgressors'[g]; and I tell you that this must be fulfilled in me. Yes, what is written about me is reaching its fulfillment."

³⁸The disciples said, "See, Lord, here are two swords."

"That is enough," he replied.

³⁹Jesus went out as usual to the Mount of Olives, and his disciples followed him. ⁴⁰On reaching the place, he said to them, "Pray that you will not fall into temptation." ⁴¹He withdrew about a stone's throw beyond them, knelt down and prayed, ⁴²"Father, if you are willing, take this cup from me; yet not my will, but yours be done."

f31 The Greek is plural.   g37 Isaiah 53:12

⁴³An angel from heaven appeared to him and strengthened him. ⁴⁴And being in anguish, he prayed more earnestly, and his sweat was like drops of blood falling to the ground.ʰ

⁴⁵When he rose from prayer and went back to the disciples, he found them asleep, exhausted from sorrow. ⁴⁶"Why are you sleeping?" he asked them. "Get up and pray so that you will not fall into temptation."

ʰ44 Some early manuscripts do not have verses 43 and 44.

 Discovering the Word 1. What do verses 1–6 tell you about the authorities? 2. Look at verses 7–23, comparing Jesus' plans with the authorities' plans. As you examine his plans, what impresses you about Jesus himself? 3. Jesus chides the disciples for their preoccupation with power and prestige. What lesson does he teach about the kind of leaders he wants to carry on his work (vv. 26–27)? 4. Jesus further prepares them for coming tests. The first preparation is for Peter immediately ahead. The second is for all the apostles in the long run. Like him they would have to face official hostility (vv. 36–38). In either testing what should help them to persevere (vv. 28, 29–30, 31, 32, 35)? 5. What guidelines for praying do you see in each verse of 39–46, showing Jesus' example?

Applying the Word 1. Jesus' institution of his new Passover was interspersed with human weakness and failure. In redeeming his disciples, he used their shortcomings. What weaknesses and failures do you want to acknowledge as you contemplate afresh eating Jesus' new Passover? 2. What new, or renewed, truths about prayer do you discover in Jesus' example (22:39–46)?

Responding in Prayer Follow the guidelines for prayer in Jesus' example.

---

25 / Luke 22:47—23:56
The Message of the Cross

THE SYMBOL OF the cross is used in many ways—on and in Christian churches, by the Red Cross, on many European flags. It is used as jewelry even by non-Christians. But they would never think of wearing a burnished gold miniature of an electric chair around their necks. In the first century the wooden cross meant capital punishment for criminals. Jesus died as a criminal to be the substitute for us sinners. Some old hymns have well retained this essential truth of Jesus' cross. Not many contemporary songs about his death do that. Approach this study with prayer for a deeper understanding of the cross of Jesus.

 Warming Up to God What was your first understanding of the Christian cross?

 Read Luke 22:47—23:56.

---

⁴⁷While he was still speaking a crowd came up, and the man who was called Judas, one of the Twelve, was leading them. He approached Jesus to kiss him, ⁴⁸but Jesus asked him, "Judas, are you betraying the Son of Man with a kiss?"

⁴⁹When Jesus' followers saw what was going to happen, they said, "Lord, should we strike with our swords?" ⁵⁰And one of them struck the servant of the high priest, cutting off his right ear.

⁵¹But Jesus answered, "No more of this!" And he touched the man's ear and healed him.

⁵²Then Jesus said to the chief priests, the officers of the temple guard, and the elders, who had come for him, "Am I leading a rebellion, that you have come with swords and clubs? ⁵³Every day I was with you in the temple courts, and you did not lay a hand on me. But this is your hour—when darkness reigns."

⁵⁴Then seizing him, they led him away and took him into the house of the high priest. Peter followed at a distance. ⁵⁵But when they had kindled a fire in the middle of the courtyard and had

sat down together, Peter sat down with them. ⁵⁶A servant girl saw him seated there in the firelight. She looked closely at him and said, "This man was with him."

⁵⁷But he denied it. "Woman, I don't know him," he said.

⁵⁸A little later someone else saw him and said, "You also are one of them."

"Man, I am not!" Peter replied.

⁵⁹About an hour later another asserted, "Certainly this fellow was with him, for he is a Galilean."

⁶⁰Peter replied, "Man, I don't know what you're talking about!" Just as he was speaking, the rooster crowed. ⁶¹The Lord turned and looked straight at Peter. Then Peter remembered the word the Lord had spoken to him: "Before the rooster crows today, you will disown me three times." ⁶²And he went outside and wept bitterly.

⁶³The men who were guarding Jesus began mocking and beating him. ⁶⁴They blindfolded him and demanded, "Prophesy! Who hit you?" ⁶⁵And they said many other insulting things to him.

⁶⁶At daybreak the council of the elders of the people, both the chief priests and teachers of the law, met together, and Jesus was led before them. ⁶⁷"If you are the Christ,ⁱ" they said, "tell us."

Jesus answered, "If I tell you, you will not believe me, ⁶⁸and if I asked you, you would not answer. ⁶⁹But from now on, the Son of Man will be seated at the right hand of the mighty God."

⁷⁰They all asked, "Are you then the Son of God?"

He replied, "You are right in saying I am."

⁷¹Then they said, "Why do we need any more testimony? We have heard it from his own lips."

23 Then the whole assembly rose and led him off to Pilate. ²And they began to accuse him, saying, "We have found this man subverting our nation. He opposes payment of taxes to Caesar and claims to be Christ,ʲ a king."

³So Pilate asked Jesus, "Are you the king of the Jews?"

"Yes, it is as you say," Jesus replied.

⁴Then Pilate announced to the chief priests and the crowd, "I find no basis for a charge against this man."

⁵But they insisted, "He stirs up the people all over Judeaᵏ by his teaching. He started in Galilee and has come all the way here."

⁶On hearing this, Pilate asked if the man was a Galilean. ⁷When he learned that Jesus was under Herod's jurisdiction, he sent him to Herod, who was also in Jerusalem at that time.

⁸When Herod saw Jesus, he was greatly pleased, because for a long time he had been wanting to see him. From what he had heard about him, he hoped to see him perform some miracle. ⁹He plied him with many questions, but Jesus gave him no answer. ¹⁰The chief priests and the teachers of the law were standing there, vehemently accusing him. ¹¹Then Herod and his soldiers ridiculed and mocked him. Dressing him in an elegant robe, they sent him back to Pilate. ¹²That day Herod and Pilate became friends—before this they had been enemies.

¹³Pilate called together the chief priests, the rulers and the people, ¹⁴and said to them, "You brought me this man as one who was inciting the people to rebellion. I have examined him in your presence and have found no basis for your charges against him. ¹⁵Neither has Herod, for he sent him back to us; as you can see, he has done nothing to deserve death. ¹⁶Therefore, I will punish him and then release him.ˡ"

¹⁸With one voice they cried out, "Away with this man! Release Barabbas to us!" ¹⁹(Barabbas had been thrown into prison for an insurrection in the city, and for murder.)

²⁰Wanting to release Jesus, Pilate appealed to them again. ²¹But they kept shouting, "Crucify him! Crucify him!"

²²For the third time he spoke to them: "Why? What crime has this man committed? I have found in him no grounds for the death penalty. Therefore I will have him punished and then release him."

²³But with loud shouts they insistently demanded that he be crucified, and their shouts prevailed. ²⁴So Pilate decided to grant their demand. ²⁵He released the man who had been thrown into prison for insurrection and murder, the one they asked for, and surrendered Jesus to their will.

²⁶As they led him away, they seized Simon from Cyrene, who was on his way in from the country, and put the cross on him and made him carry it behind Jesus. ²⁷A large number of people followed him, including women who mourned and wailed for him. ²⁸Jesus turned and said to

---

ⁱ67 Or *Messiah*   ʲ2 Or *Messiah; also in verses 35 and 39*   ᵏ5 Or *over the land of the Jews*   ˡ16 Some manuscripts *him." ¹⁷Now he was obliged to release one man to them at the Feast.*

them, "Daughters of Jerusalem, do not weep for me; weep for yourselves and for your children. ²⁹For the time will come when you will say, 'Blessed are the barren women, the wombs that never bore and the breasts that never nursed!' ³⁰Then

" 'they will say to the mountains, "Fall on us!"
and to the hills, "Cover us!" '*m*

³¹For if men do these things when the tree is green, what will happen when it is dry?"

³²Two other men, both criminals, were also led out with him to be executed. ³³When they came to the place called the Skull, there they crucified him, along with the criminals—one on his right, the other on his left. ³⁴Jesus said, "Father, forgive them, for they do not know what they are doing."*n* And they divided up his clothes by casting lots.

³⁵The people stood watching, and the rulers even sneered at him. They said, "He saved others; let him save himself if he is the Christ of God, the Chosen One."

³⁶The soldiers also came up and mocked him. They offered him wine vinegar ³⁷and said, "If you are the king of the Jews, save yourself."

³⁸There was a written notice above him, which read: THIS IS THE KING OF THE JEWS.

³⁹One of the criminals who hung there hurled insults at him: "Aren't you the Christ? Save yourself and us!"

⁴⁰But the other criminal rebuked him. "Don't you fear God," he said, "since you are under the same sentence? ⁴¹We are punished justly, for we are getting what our deeds deserve. But this man has done nothing wrong."

⁴²Then he said, "Jesus, remember me when you come into your kingdom.*o*"

⁴³Jesus answered him, "I tell you the truth, today you will be with me in paradise."

⁴⁴It was now about the sixth hour, and darkness came over the whole land until the ninth hour, ⁴⁵for the sun stopped shining. And the curtain of the temple was torn in two. ⁴⁶Jesus called out with a loud voice, "Father, into your hands I commit my spirit." When he had said this, he breathed his last.

⁴⁷The centurion, seeing what had happened, praised God and said, "Surely this was a righteous man." ⁴⁸When all the people who had gathered to witness this sight saw what took place, they beat their breasts and went away. ⁴⁹But all those who knew him, including the women who had followed him from Galilee, stood at a distance, watching these things.

⁵⁰Now there was a man named Joseph, a member of the Council, a good and upright man, ⁵¹who had not consented to their decision and action. He came from the Judean town of Arimathea and he was waiting for the kingdom of God. ⁵²Going to Pilate, he asked for Jesus' body. ⁵³Then he took it down, wrapped it in linen cloth and placed it in a tomb cut in the rock, one in which no one had yet been laid. ⁵⁴It was Preparation Day, and the Sabbath was about to begin.

⁵⁵The women who had come with Jesus from Galilee followed Joseph and saw the tomb and how his body was laid in it. ⁵⁶Then they went home and prepared spices and perfumes. But they rested on the Sabbath in obedience to the commandment.

m30 Hosea 10:8   *n34* Some early manuscripts do not have this sentence.   *o42* Some manuscripts *come with your kingly power*

Discovering the Word   1. In a word or phrase, what describes the way Jesus relates to each individual or group during his arrest (22:47–62)?   2. Only a few hours after Peter swore loyalty to Jesus, he makes an about-face (vv. 57–60). In what kind of situation are you tempted to avoid identification with Jesus and his cause?   3. Three times Pilate says he finds no valid charge against Jesus, and seeks to release him (23:4, 13–16 and 22). Why then does he ultimately pronounce the death penalty on Jesus?   4. Luke gives few details of Jesus' physical death. Instead he focuses on people's attitudes. What attitude to the man on the center cross does each group or individual reveal (23:32–49)?   5. Throughout his six hours on the cross, Jesus is in touch with his Father. What do his brief words to the Father reflect about their relationship (23:34,46)?

Applying the Word   1. What can you do to make the message of the cross relevant to your needy world?   2. How can the cross become more relevant to you as an individual?

Responding in Prayer   Praise God for giving his Son over to this horrible death on the cross for your sake.

26 / Luke 24
God Has the Last Word

HOW MIGHT YOU destroy Christianity? Explain away Jesus' resurrection. For instance, you could say the overemotional women at the tomb were deluded. Or argue that they went to the wrong tomb. You might insist that the resurrection was spiritual, not physical, or that the disciples had hallucinations. From that first Easter till now the enemies of the church have tried to get rid of the historical facts (Mt 28:11–15). None has succeeded.

 Warming Up to God What does Christ's resurrection mean to you? What would the world lose if Jesus did not rise from death?

 Read Luke 24.

24 On the first day of the week, very early in the morning, the women took the spices they had prepared and went to the tomb. ²They found the stone rolled away from the tomb, ³but when they entered, they did not find the body of the Lord Jesus. ⁴While they were wondering about this, suddenly two men in clothes that gleamed like lightning stood beside them. ⁵In their fright the women bowed down with their faces to the ground, but the men said to them, "Why do you look for the living among the dead? ⁶He is not here; he has risen! Remember how he told you, while he was still with you in Galilee: ⁷'The Son of Man must be delivered into the hands of sinful men, be crucified and on the third day be raised again.'" ⁸Then they remembered his words.

⁹When they came back from the tomb, they told all these things to the Eleven and to all the others. ¹⁰It was Mary Magdalene, Joanna, Mary the mother of James, and the others with them who told this to the apostles. ¹¹But they did not believe the women, because their words seemed to them like nonsense. ¹²Peter, however, got up and ran to the tomb. Bending over, he saw the strips of linen lying by themselves, and he went away, wondering to himself what had happened.

¹³Now that same day two of them were going to a village called Emmaus, about seven miles*p* from Jerusalem. ¹⁴They were talking with each other about everything that had happened. ¹⁵As they talked and discussed these things with each other, Jesus himself came up and walked along with them; ¹⁶but they were kept from recognizing him.

¹⁷He asked them, "What are you discussing together as you walk along?"

They stood still, their faces downcast. ¹⁸One of them, named Cleopas, asked him, "Are you only a visitor to Jerusalem and do not know the things that have happened there in these days?"

¹⁹"What things?" he asked.

"About Jesus of Nazareth," they replied. "He was a prophet, powerful in word and deed before God and all the people. ²⁰The chief priests and our rulers handed him over to be sentenced to death, and they crucified him; ²¹but we had hoped that he was the one who was going to redeem Israel. And what is more, it is the third day since all this took place. ²²In addition, some of our women amazed us. They went to the tomb early this morning ²³but didn't find his body. They came and told us that they had seen a vision of angels, who said he was alive. ²⁴Then some of our companions went to the tomb and found it just as the women had said, but him they did not see."

²⁵He said to them, "How foolish you are, and how slow of heart to believe all that the prophets have spoken! ²⁶Did not the Christ*q* have to suffer these things and then enter his glory?" ²⁷And beginning with Moses and all the Prophets, he explained to them what was said in all the Scriptures concerning himself.

²⁸As they approached the village to which they were going, Jesus acted as if he were going farther. ²⁹But they urged him strongly, "Stay with us, for it is nearly evening; the day is almost over." So he went in to stay with them.

³⁰When he was at the table with them, he took bread, gave thanks, broke it and began to give it to them. ³¹Then their eyes were opened and they recognized him, and he disappeared from their sight. ³²They asked each other, "Were not our

p 13 Greek *sixty stadia* (about 11 kilometers)   *q 26* Or *Messiah*; also in verse 46

hearts burning within us while he talked with us on the road and opened the Scriptures to us?"

³³They got up and returned at once to Jerusalem. There they found the Eleven and those with them, assembled together ³⁴and saying, "It is true! The Lord has risen and has appeared to Simon." ³⁵Then the two told what had happened on the way, and how Jesus was recognized by them when he broke the bread.

³⁶While they were still talking about this, Jesus himself stood among them and said to them, "Peace be with you."

³⁷They were startled and frightened, thinking they saw a ghost. ³⁸He said to them, "Why are you troubled, and why do doubts rise in your minds? ³⁹Look at my hands and my feet. It is I myself! Touch me and see; a ghost does not have flesh and bones, as you see I have."

⁴⁰When he had said this, he showed them his hands and feet. ⁴¹And while they still did not believe it because of joy and amazement, he asked them, "Do you have anything here to eat?" ⁴²They gave him a piece of broiled fish, ⁴³and he took it and ate it in their presence.

⁴⁴He said to them, "This is what I told you while I was still with you: Everything must be fulfilled that is written about me in the Law of Moses, the Prophets and the Psalms."

⁴⁵Then he opened their minds so they could understand the Scriptures. ⁴⁶He told them, "This is what is written: The Christ will suffer and rise from the dead on the third day, ⁴⁷and repentance and forgiveness of sins will be preached in his name to all nations, beginning at Jerusalem. ⁴⁸You are witnesses of these things. ⁴⁹I am going to send you what my Father has promised; but stay in the city until you have been clothed with power from on high."

⁵⁰When he had led them out to the vicinity of Bethany, he lifted up his hands and blessed them. ⁵¹While he was blessing them, he left them and was taken up into heaven. ⁵²Then they worshiped him and returned to Jerusalem with great joy. ⁵³And they stayed continually at the temple, praising God.

Discovering the Word 1. The women are a personal link between the cross and the empty tomb. Suppose you are one of them. How do you feel when the men respond with "Nonsense!" (vv. 1–12)? 2. What strikes you about the stranger's dialogue with the disciples (vv. 13–35)? 3. We can sympathize with the disciples' struggle between despair and hope. In his rebuke Jesus identifies the cause of their despair—reluctance to believe the Scriptures about a suffering Messiah (v. 25). How have the Scriptures ever moved you from despair to new hope? 4. Look at verses 36–53 as a seeker inquiring about Jesus' resurrection. Which facts and implications help you to believe his personal reality? 5. For three or so years Jesus has been preparing his disciples to carry on his world mission. He climaxes this mission training by stressing systematic, in-depth Bible understanding (vv. 25–27, 32, 44–47). In what ways can you testify to this importance?

Applying the Word 1. We have been carefully studying the life and mission of Jesus. What would you say are your three greatest incentives to be his "witness of these things"? 2. What a message we have! The Lord Jesus has come to bring new hope and new joy to the world! How can you (and your church or fellowship group) take Jesus' message of new hope and new joy to your community?

Responding in Prayer Pray that you will be a source of joy to many as you bring Jesus' message.

John

The most significant fact in history can be summed up in four words: *Jesus Christ is God!* The great declaration of the Bible is that God in human flesh was born in Bethlehem. It was God in the person of Jesus Christ who astonished the people of his day with his miracles and amazed them with his teaching. It was God who lived a perfect life and then allowed himself to be put to death on a Roman cross for humanity's sins. It was God who three days after he died broke the bonds of death and came out of the grave alive. The deity of Jesus—the fact that he was God in human flesh—is the bottom line of the Christian faith.

When the apostle John sat down to write his Gospel, he was not interested simply in adding one more biography of Jesus to the three already in existence. John wrote his book with a very specific purpose in mind. He tells us in 20:30–31:

> Jesus did many other miraculous signs in the presence of his disciples, which are not recorded in this book. But these are written that you may believe that Jesus is the Christ, the Son of God, and that by believing you may have life in his name.

John's book is not a biography; it's a theological argument. John wants to convince us that Jesus of Nazareth is God the Son. Then he wants to show us how that fact will change our lives in some rather amazing ways. It is by believing in Jesus Christ as the Son of God that we find life—real life, eternal life, a whole new kind of life!

Every event John records is designed to show us that Jesus is God. John pulls from the life of Jesus specific incidents that demonstrate his majesty and deity. Of particular interest to John are the sign miracles of Jesus. In the first twelve chapters of his book, John records seven miracles. These miracles were not performed simply to alleviate human suffering or to meet human need. The miracles were "signs." They pointed to the truth of Jesus' claim to be the Son of God.

John was the last Gospel writer. The best evidence points to a date around A.D. 90 for the composition of his Gospel. The other Gospels had been in circulation for some time. John wrote to add his unique perspective and to fill in some of the details not recorded by the other writers. He assumes his readers are familiar with the other Gospels. John does not mention, for example, the anguish of Jesus in the Garden of Gethsemane. The other writers had adequately described that incident. John does give us the details of Jesus' conversation with his disciples in the upper room. The other writers mention it only briefly.

John never mentions himself by name in the Gospel. He refers to himself simply as "the disciple whom Jesus loved." We have in this Gospel the memories of an intimate friend about the Lord Jesus. Jesus Christ had transformed John's life. I hope you are prepared to have that happen to you! You are about to begin a fascinating study focused on the greatest person who ever lived—Jesus Christ. If you will respond to what John writes in faith and obedience, you, like John, will experience a whole new kind of life.

Outline

Part 1: Jesus, the Living Word of God

Part 2: Jesus, the Living Way to God

1 / *John 1*
The Master & Five Who Followed

IT WAS A great day in our history when a man first walked on the moon. But the Bible declares that a far greater event took place two thousand years ago. God walked on the earth in the person of Jesus Christ. John opens his Gospel with a beautiful hymn of exaltation to Christ. It is one of the most profound passages in all the Bible. It is written in simple, straightforward language, yet in studying the depths of its meaning, it is a passage where we never reach bottom. It is an ocean-sized truth, and we have to be content to paddle around in shallow water.

 Warming Up to God   Consider the miracle of God becoming human. Give him your praise and worship for what he has done for you.

 Read John 1.

1 In the beginning was the Word, and the Word was with God, and the Word was God. ²He was with God in the beginning. ³Through him all things were made; without him nothing was made that has been made. ⁴In him was life, and that life was the light of men. ⁵The light shines in the darkness, but the darkness has not understood[a] it.

⁶There came a man who was sent from God; his name was John. ⁷He came as a witness to testify concerning that light, so that through him all men might believe. ⁸He himself was not the light; he came only as a witness to the light. ⁹The true light that gives light to every man was coming into the world.[b]

¹⁰He was in the world, and though the world was made through him, the world did not recognize him. ¹¹He came to that which was his own, but his own did not receive him. ¹²Yet to all who received him, to those who believed in his name, he gave the right to become children of God— ¹³children born not of natural descent,[c] nor of human decision or a husband's will, but born of God.

¹⁴The Word became flesh and made his dwelling among us. We have seen his glory, the glory of the One and Only,[d] who came from the Father, full of grace and truth. ¹⁵John testifies concerning him. He cries out, saying, "This was he of whom I said, 'He who comes after me has surpassed me because he was before me.' " ¹⁶From the fullness of his grace we have all received one blessing after another. ¹⁷For the law was given through Moses; grace and truth came through Jesus Christ. ¹⁸No one has ever seen God, but God the One and Only,[d,e] who is at the Father's side, has made him known.

¹⁹Now this was John's testimony when the Jews of Jerusalem sent priests and Levites to ask him who he was. ²⁰He did not fail to confess, but confessed freely, "I am not the Christ.[f]"

²¹They asked him, "Then who are you? Are you Elijah?"

He said, "I am not."

"Are you the Prophet?"

He answered, "No."

²²Finally they said, "Who are you? Give us an answer to take back to those who sent us. What do you say about yourself?"

²³John replied in the words of Isaiah the prophet, "I am the voice of one calling in the desert, 'Make straight the way for the Lord.' "[g]

²⁴Now some Pharisees who had been sent ²⁵questioned him, "Why then do you baptize if you are not the Christ, nor Elijah, nor the Prophet?"

²⁶"I baptize with[h] water," John replied, "but among you stands one you do not know. ²⁷He is the one who comes after me, the thongs of whose sandals I am not worthy to untie."

²⁸This all happened at Bethany on the other side of the Jordan, where John was baptizing.

²⁹The next day John saw Jesus coming toward him and said, "Look, the Lamb of God, who takes away the sin of the world! ³⁰This is the one I meant when I said, 'A man who comes after me has surpassed me because he was before me.' ³¹I myself did not know him, but the reason I came

---

[a]5 Or *darkness, and the darkness has not overcome*   [b]9 Or *This was the true light that gives light to every man who comes into the world*   [c]13 Greek *of bloods*   [d]14,18 Or *the Only Begotten*   [e]18 Some manuscripts *but the only (or only begotten) Son*   [f]20 Or *Messiah.* "The Christ" (Greek) and "the Messiah" (Hebrew) both mean "the Anointed One"; also in verse 25.   [g]23 Isaiah 40:3   [h]26 Or *in*; also in verses 31 and 33

baptizing with water was that he might be revealed to Israel."

³²Then John gave this testimony: "I saw the Spirit come down from heaven as a dove and remain on him. ³³I would not have known him, except that the one who sent me to baptize with water told me, 'The man on whom you see the Spirit come down and remain is he who will baptize with the Holy Spirit.' ³⁴I have seen and I testify that this is the Son of God."

³⁵The next day John was there again with two of his disciples. ³⁶When he saw Jesus passing by, he said, "Look, the Lamb of God!"

³⁷When the two disciples heard him say this, they followed Jesus. ³⁸Turning around, Jesus saw them following and asked, "What do you want?"

They said, "Rabbi" (which means Teacher), "where are you staying?"

³⁹"Come," he replied, "and you will see."

So they went and saw where he was staying, and spent that day with him. It was about the tenth hour.

⁴⁰Andrew, Simon Peter's brother, was one of the two who heard what John had said and who had followed Jesus. ⁴¹The first thing Andrew did was to find his brother Simon and tell him, "We have found the Messiah" (that is, the Christ). ⁴²And he brought him to Jesus.

Jesus looked at him and said, "You are Simon son of John. You will be called Cephas" (which, when translated, is Peterⁱ).

⁴³The next day Jesus decided to leave for Galilee. Finding Philip, he said to him, "Follow me."

⁴⁴Philip, like Andrew and Peter, was from the town of Bethsaida. ⁴⁵Philip found Nathanael and told him, "We have found the one Moses wrote about in the Law, and about whom the prophets also wrote—Jesus of Nazareth, the son of Joseph."

⁴⁶"Nazareth! Can anything good come from there?" Nathanael asked.

"Come and see," said Philip.

⁴⁷When Jesus saw Nathanael approaching, he said of him, "Here is a true Israelite, in whom there is nothing false."

⁴⁸"How do you know me?" Nathanael asked.

Jesus answered, "I saw you while you were still under the fig tree before Philip called you."

⁴⁹Then Nathanael declared, "Rabbi, you are the Son of God; you are the King of Israel."

⁵⁰Jesus said, "You believeʲ because I told you I saw you under the fig tree. You shall see greater things than that." ⁵¹He then added, "I tell youᵏ the truth, youᵏ shall see heaven open, and the angels of God ascending and descending on the Son of Man."

ⁱ42 Both *Cephas* (Aramaic) and *Peter* (Greek) mean *rock.*   ʲ50 Or *Do you believe . . . ?*   ᵏ51 The Greek is plural.

Discovering the Word 1. John records more than a dozen names or descriptions of Jesus in this chapter. What are some of these? 2. In verses 1–3 what facts does John declare to be true of the Word? 3. According to verses 14–18, what specific aspects of God's character are revealed to us through Jesus? 4. What steps did John take to guarantee that people would not look at him but at Christ? 5. In verses 35–51 we are introduced to five men: Andrew, Simon, Philip, Nathanael and one unnamed disciple (John). How did each man respond to the testimony he heard about Jesus?

 Applying the Word 1. Which of the names of Jesus has the most significance to you personally? Explain why. 2. What do you hope will happen in your life as a result of studying the Gospel of John?

 Responding in Prayer Ask God to bring the light and life of Jesus to you as you study his Word.

---

2 / *John 2*
Wine & a Whip

AFTER I HAD given a presentation on the claims of Christ, a skeptical student asked: "What proof do you have that Jesus really was who he claimed to be?" People have been asking that question for two thousand years! For John the convincing proof of Jesus' deity was found in his words and deeds. No one but God could say the things Jesus said, and no one but God could do the things Jesus did. In this chapter are two signs that demonstrate that Jesus was the fullness of God clothed in humanity.

 Warming Up to God Thank God for revealing himself to you personally.

 Read John 2.

2 On the third day a wedding took place at Cana in Galilee. Jesus' mother was there, ²and Jesus and his disciples had also been invited to the wedding. ³When the wine was gone, Jesus' mother said to him, "They have no more wine."

⁴"Dear woman, why do you involve me?" Jesus replied. "My time has not yet come."

⁵His mother said to the servants, "Do whatever he tells you."

⁶Nearby stood six stone water jars, the kind used by the Jews for ceremonial washing, each holding from twenty to thirty gallons.^{l}

⁷Jesus said to the servants, "Fill the jars with water"; so they filled them to the brim.

⁸Then he told them, "Now draw some out and take it to the master of the banquet."

They did so, ⁹and the master of the banquet tasted the water that had been turned into wine. He did not realize where it had come from, though the servants who had drawn the water knew. Then he called the bridegroom aside ¹⁰and said, "Everyone brings out the choice wine first and then the cheaper wine after the guests have had too much to drink; but you have saved the best till now."

¹¹This, the first of his miraculous signs, Jesus performed at Cana in Galilee. He thus revealed his glory, and his disciples put their faith in him.

¹²After this he went down to Capernaum with his mother and brothers and his disciples. There they stayed for a few days.

¹³When it was almost time for the Jewish Passover, Jesus went up to Jerusalem. ¹⁴In the temple courts he found men selling cattle, sheep and doves, and others sitting at tables exchanging money. ¹⁵So he made a whip out of cords, and drove all from the temple area, both sheep and cattle; he scattered the coins of the money changers and overturned their tables. ¹⁶To those who sold doves he said, "Get these out of here! How dare you turn my Father's house into a market!"

¹⁷His disciples remembered that it is written: "Zeal for your house will consume me." ^{m}

¹⁸Then the Jews demanded of him, "What miraculous sign can you show us to prove your authority to do all this?"

¹⁹Jesus answered them, "Destroy this temple, and I will raise it again in three days."

²⁰The Jews replied, "It has taken forty-six years to build this temple, and you are going to raise it in three days?" ²¹But the temple he had spoken of was his body. ²²After he was raised from the dead, his disciples recalled what he had said. Then they believed the Scripture and the words that Jesus had spoken.

²³Now while he was in Jerusalem at the Passover Feast, many people saw the miraculous signs he was doing and believed in his name.^{n} ²⁴But Jesus would not entrust himself to them, for he knew all men. ²⁵He did not need man's testimony about man, for he knew what was in a man.

^{l}6 Greek *two to three metretes* (probably about 75 to 115 liters)
^{m}17 Psalm 69:9 ^{n}23 Or *and believed in him*

 Discovering the Word 1. When the groom's parents ran out of wine for their guests, Jesus' mother asked him to help (v. 3). What do you think Mary expected Jesus to do? (Remember, according to verse 11 Jesus had not yet performed any miracles.) 2. What did Jesus mean by his reply to Mary in verse 4? 3. According to verse 11, the purpose of Jesus' miracle was not to save the groom from embarrassment but to display Christ's glory. What aspects of Christ's glory does this miracle reveal to you? 4. How does John's picture of Jesus in verses 15–16 fit with today's popular concept of him? 5. Only the Messiah had the authority to cleanse the temple. The people recognized that and asked Jesus for a miraculous sign to confirm his identify (v. 18). To what "sign" did Jesus point them (vv. 19–22)? Why do you think that particular sign was so significant in Jesus' mind?

Applying the Word 1. In what practical ways can you demonstrate the same concern that Jesus does toward the holy character of God? 2. How do Jesus' presence and actions at this party serve as a model for you?

Responding in Prayer Ask God to help you to be his representative in everything you do.

3 / *John 3*
The New Birth

I TALKED TODAY to a junior in college who is only one month old. No, she isn't a child genius. Recently a friend explained to her the claims of Christ. As she responded in simple faith, she experienced the joys of spiritual birth.

The most beautiful explanation of the new birth is found here in John 3. It's a passage that children can understand, and one that the greatest saints of God have never fully grasped. It's a message not so much to be analyzed and dissected as it is to be received with joy.

Warming Up to God Do you remember your spiritual birthday? Reflect on what that time meant for you.

Read John 3.

3 Now there was a man of the Pharisees named Nicodemus, a member of the Jewish ruling council. 2 He came to Jesus at night and said, "Rabbi, we know you are a teacher who has come from God. For no one could perform the miraculous signs you are doing if God were not with him."

3 In reply Jesus declared, "I tell you the truth, no one can see the kingdom of God unless he is born again.[o]"

4 "How can a man be born when he is old?" Nicodemus asked. "Surely he cannot enter a second time into his mother's womb to be born!"

5 Jesus answered, "I tell you the truth, no one can enter the kingdom of God unless he is born of water and the Spirit. 6 Flesh gives birth to flesh, but the Spirit[p] gives birth to spirit. 7 You should not be surprised at my saying, 'You[q] must be born again.' 8 The wind blows wherever it pleases. You hear its sound, but you cannot tell where it comes from or where it is going. So it is with everyone born of the Spirit."

9 "How can this be?" Nicodemus asked.

10 "You are Israel's teacher," said Jesus, "and do you not understand these things? 11 I tell you the truth, we speak of what we know, and we testify to what we have seen, but still you people do not accept our testimony. 12 I have spoken to you of earthly things and you do not believe; how then will you believe if I speak of heavenly things? 13 No one has ever gone into heaven except the one who came from heaven—the Son of Man.[r] 14 Just as Moses lifted up the snake in the desert, so the Son of Man must be lifted up, 15 that everyone who believes in him may have eternal life.[s]

16 "For God so loved the world that he gave his one and only Son,[t] that whoever believes in him shall not perish but have eternal life. 17 For God did not send his Son into the world to condemn the world, but to save the world through him. 18 Whoever believes in him is not condemned, but whoever does not believe stands condemned already because he has not believed in the name of God's one and only Son.[u] 19 This is the verdict: Light has come into the world, but men loved darkness instead of light because their deeds were evil. 20 Everyone who does evil hates the light, and will not come into the light for fear that his deeds will be exposed. 21 But whoever lives by the truth comes into the light, so that it may be seen plainly that what he has done has been done through God."[v]

22 After this, Jesus and his disciples went out into the Judean countryside, where he spent some time with them, and baptized. 23 Now John also was baptizing at Aenon near Salim, because there was plenty of water, and people were constantly coming to be baptized. 24 (This was before John was put in prison.) 25 An argument developed between some of John's disciples and a certain Jew[w] over the matter of ceremonial washing.

[o] *3* Or *born from above*; also in verse 7 [p] *6* Or *but spirit* [q] *7* The Greek is plural. [r] *13* Some manuscripts *Man, who is in heaven* [s] *15* Or *believes may have eternal life in him* [t] *16* Or *his only begotten Son* [u] *18* Or *God's only begotten Son* [v] *21* Some interpreters end the quotation after verse 15. [w] *25* Some manuscripts *and certain Jews*

²⁶They came to John and said to him, "Rabbi, that man who was with you on the other side of the Jordan—the one you testified about—well, he is baptizing, and everyone is going to him."

²⁷To this John replied, "A man can receive only what is given him from heaven. ²⁸You yourselves can testify that I said, 'I am not the Christ^x but am sent ahead of him.' ²⁹The bride belongs to the bridegroom. The friend who attends the bridegroom waits and listens for him, and is full of joy when he hears the bridegroom's voice. That joy is mine, and it is now complete. ³⁰He must become greater; I must become less.

³¹"The one who comes from above is above all; the one who is from the earth belongs to the earth, and speaks as one from the earth. The one who comes from heaven is above all. ³²He testifies to what he has seen and heard, but no one accepts his testimony. ³³The man who has accepted it has certified that God is truthful. ³⁴For the one whom God has sent speaks the words of God, for God^y gives the Spirit without limit. ³⁵The Father loves the Son and has placed everything in his hands. ³⁶Whoever believes in the Son has eternal life, but whoever rejects the Son will not see life, for God's wrath remains on him."^{z}

$^x28$ Or *Messiah* $^y34$ Greek *he* $^z36$ Some interpreters end the quotation after verse 30.

Discovering the Word 1. What is your impression of Nicodemus (vv. 1–21)? 2. Why do you suppose Nicodemus responds to Jesus' explanation of new birth with such amazement (v. 9)? 3. How does the story of Moses lifting up the snake in the desert (vv. 14–15; see Nu 21:4–9) illustrate our need and Christ's offer? 4. How and why does our response to God's Son determine our destiny (vv. 18–21)? 5. How would you summarize John's view of the character and ministry of Jesus (vv. 22–36)?

Applying the Word 1. John made it clear that Jesus was superior to him. What is one way you can demonstrate Christ's superiority in your life? 2. Who do you know that needs to know the truth about God? 3. How can you help that person see God?

Responding in Prayer Ask God to make you ready to testify of the role of Jesus in your life.

4 / *John 4*
Soul & Body—Saving & Healing

"I LOVE HUMANITY; it's people I can't stand!" Those well-known words from a member of the "Peanuts" gang still make us chuckle. But our smiles hide the fact that we sometimes feel exactly like that. John says very little about Jesus' contact with the multitudes. But long sections of the Gospel are devoted to conversations Jesus had with individuals. In John 4 we see Jesus reach out first to a woman, then to his disciples, and finally to a grieving father. Watching Jesus give himself to people with love and compassion will help us care for those God puts in our paths.

Warming Up to God When have you recently felt that you were being mobbed by the multitudes? Ask God to help you take care of yourself even as you try to help others.

Read John 4.

4 The Pharisees heard that Jesus was gaining and baptizing more disciples than John, ²although in fact it was not Jesus who baptized, but his disciples. ³When the Lord learned of this, he left Judea and went back once more to Galilee.

⁴Now he had to go through Samaria. ⁵So he came to a town in Samaria called Sychar, near the plot of ground Jacob had given to his son Joseph. ⁶Jacob's well was there, and Jesus, tired as he was from the journey, sat down by the well. It was about the sixth hour.

⁷When a Samaritan woman came to draw water, Jesus said to her, "Will you give me a drink?" ⁸(His disciples had gone into the town to buy food.)

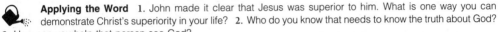

⁹The Samaritan woman said to him, "You are a Jew and I am a Samaritan woman. How can you ask me for a drink?" (For Jews do not associate with Samaritans.ᵃ)

¹⁰Jesus answered her, "If you knew the gift of God and who it is that asks you for a drink, you would have asked him and he would have given you living water."

¹¹"Sir," the woman said, "you have nothing to draw with and the well is deep. Where can you get this living water? ¹²Are you greater than our father Jacob, who gave us the well and drank from it himself, as did also his sons and his flocks and herds?"

¹³Jesus answered, "Everyone who drinks this water will be thirsty again, ¹⁴but whoever drinks the water I give him will never thirst. Indeed, the water I give him will become in him a spring of water welling up to eternal life."

¹⁵The woman said to him, "Sir, give me this water so that I won't get thirsty and have to keep coming here to draw water."

¹⁶He told her, "Go, call your husband and come back."

¹⁷"I have no husband," she replied.

Jesus said to her, "You are right when you say you have no husband. ¹⁸The fact is, you have had five husbands, and the man you now have is not your husband. What you have just said is quite true."

¹⁹"Sir," the woman said, "I can see that you are a prophet. ²⁰Our fathers worshiped on this mountain, but you Jews claim that the place where we must worship is in Jerusalem."

²¹Jesus declared, "Believe me, woman, a time is coming when you will worship the Father neither on this mountain nor in Jerusalem. ²²You Samaritans worship what you do not know; we worship what we do know, for salvation is from the Jews. ²³Yet a time is coming and has now come when the true worshipers will worship the Father in spirit and truth, for they are the kind of worshipers the Father seeks. ²⁴God is spirit, and his worshipers must worship in spirit and in truth."

²⁵The woman said, "I know that Messiah" (called Christ) "is coming. When he comes, he will explain everything to us."

²⁶Then Jesus declared, "I who speak to you am he."

²⁷Just then his disciples returned and were surprised to find him talking with a woman. But no one asked, "What do you want?" or "Why are you talking with her?"

²⁸Then, leaving her water jar, the woman went back to the town and said to the people, ²⁹"Come, see a man who told me everything I ever did. Could this be the Christᵇ?" ³⁰They came out of the town and made their way toward him.

³¹Meanwhile his disciples urged him, "Rabbi, eat something."

³²But he said to them, "I have food to eat that you know nothing about."

³³Then his disciples said to each other, "Could someone have brought him food?"

³⁴"My food," said Jesus, "is to do the will of him who sent me and to finish his work. ³⁵Do you not say, 'Four months more and then the harvest'? I tell you, open your eyes and look at the fields! They are ripe for harvest. ³⁶Even now the reaper draws his wages, even now he harvests the crop for eternal life, so that the sower and the reaper may be glad together. ³⁷Thus the saying 'One sows and another reaps' is true. ³⁸I sent you to reap what you have not worked for. Others have done the hard work, and you have reaped the benefits of their labor."

³⁹Many of the Samaritans from that town believed in him because of the woman's testimony, "He told me everything I ever did." ⁴⁰So when the Samaritans came to him, they urged him to stay with them, and he stayed two days. ⁴¹And because of his words many more became believers.

⁴²They said to the woman, "We no longer believe just because of what you said; now we have heard for ourselves, and we know that this man really is the Savior of the world."

⁴³After the two days he left for Galilee. ⁴⁴(Now Jesus himself had pointed out that a prophet has no honor in his own country.) ⁴⁵When he arrived in Galilee, the Galileans welcomed him. They had seen all that he had done in Jerusalem at the Passover Feast, for they also had been there.

⁴⁶Once more he visited Cana in Galilee, where he had turned the water into wine. And there was a certain royal official whose son lay sick at Capernaum. ⁴⁷When this man heard that Jesus had arrived in Galilee from Judea, he went to him and begged him to come and heal his son, who was close to death.

⁴⁸"Unless you people see miraculous signs and

ᵃ9 Or *do not use dishes Samaritans have used*   ᵇ29 Or *Messiah* wonders," Jesus told him, "you will never believe."

⁴⁹The royal official said, "Sir, come down before my child dies."

⁵⁰Jesus replied, "You may go. Your son will live."

The man took Jesus at his word and departed. ⁵¹While he was still on the way, his servants met him with the news that his boy was living. ⁵²When he inquired as to the time when his son got better, they said to him, "The fever left him yesterday at the seventh hour."

⁵³Then the father realized that this was the exact time at which Jesus had said to him, "Your son will live." So he and all his household believed.

⁵⁴This was the second miraculous sign that Jesus performed, having come from Judea to Galilee.

 Discovering the Word 1. What is surprising about Jesus' question to the Samaritan woman (vv. 8–9)? 2. Why does the woman suddenly change the subject and begin talking about the controversy over the proper place of worship (vv. 16–20)? 3. From verses 27–42, do you think the Samaritan woman genuinely believed? What do you see in the passage that supports your position? 4. After his encounter with the Samaritan woman, what specific lessons does Jesus apply to his disciples and to us (vv. 34–38)? 5. What does the "second miraculous sign" Jesus performs (vv. 43–54) reveal about him?

Applying the Word 1. What has Jesus taught you in this chapter about meeting the specific needs of those around you? 2. What present-day situations might arouse the same racial, religious and sexual prejudices as the Samaritan woman did? 3. How could you reach someone who has been rejected by the world, as Jesus did?

Responding in Prayer Ask God to help you be aware of the "Samaritans" around you. Ask him to help you reach out to them.

---

5 / *John 5*
Deity on Trial

IN MY HIGH-SCHOOL years, I was hooked on television lawyer programs. Those intrepid men and women always found the missing piece of evidence that would rescue the innocent and convict the guilty. I've learned since high-school days that sometimes judges and juries are wrong.

In John chapter five Jesus is on trial. A group of people are forced to make a decision about Jesus in their hearts. They hear all the evidence but make a disastrously wrong decision. Judgments are still made for and against Jesus. Whenever he is presented as Savior and Lord, people decide in their hearts to believe his claims or to turn and walk away.

 Warming Up to God How has God recently revealed the truth of his claims as Savior to you? Thank him for his powerful works in your life.

 Read John 5.

---

5 Some time later, Jesus went up to Jerusalem for a feast of the Jews. ²Now there is in Jerusalem near the Sheep Gate a pool, which in Aramaic is called Bethesda*ᶜ* and which is surrounded by five covered colonnades. ³Here a great number of disabled people used to lie—the blind, the lame, the paralyzed.*ᵈ* ⁵One who was there had been an invalid for thirty-eight years.

⁶When Jesus saw him lying there and learned that he had been in this condition for a long time, he asked him, "Do you want to get well?"

⁷"Sir," the invalid replied, "I have no one to help me into the pool when the water is stirred.

ᶜ2 Some manuscripts Bethzatha; other manuscripts Bethsaida
ᵈ3 Some less important manuscripts paralyzed—and they waited for the moving of the waters. ⁴From time to time an angel of the Lord would come down and stir up the waters. The first one into the pool after each such disturbance would be cured of whatever disease he had.

While I am trying to get in, someone else goes down ahead of me."

[8]Then Jesus said to him, "Get up! Pick up your mat and walk." [9]At once the man was cured; he picked up his mat and walked.

The day on which this took place was a Sabbath, [10]and so the Jews said to the man who had been healed, "It is the Sabbath; the law forbids you to carry your mat."

[11]But he replied, "The man who made me well said to me, 'Pick up your mat and walk.' "

[12]So they asked him, "Who is this fellow who told you to pick it up and walk?"

[13]The man who was healed had no idea who it was, for Jesus had slipped away into the crowd that was there.

[14]Later Jesus found him at the temple and said to him, "See, you are well again. Stop sinning or something worse may happen to you." [15]The man went away and told the Jews that it was Jesus who had made him well.

[16]So, because Jesus was doing these things on the Sabbath, the Jews persecuted him. [17]Jesus said to them, "My Father is always at his work to this very day, and I, too, am working." [18]For this reason the Jews tried all the harder to kill him; not only was he breaking the Sabbath, but he was even calling God his own Father, making himself equal with God.

[19]Jesus gave them this answer: "I tell you the truth, the Son can do nothing by himself; he can do only what he sees his Father doing, because whatever the Father does the Son also does. [20]For the Father loves the Son and shows him all he does. Yes, to your amazement he will show him even greater things than these. [21]For just as the Father raises the dead and gives them life, even so the Son gives life to whom he is pleased to give it. [22]Moreover, the Father judges no one, but has entrusted all judgment to the Son, [23]that all may honor the Son just as they honor the Father. He who does not honor the Son does not honor the Father, who sent him.

[24]"I tell you the truth, whoever hears my word and believes him who sent me has eternal life and will not be condemned; he has crossed over from death to life. [25]I tell you the truth, a time is coming and has now come when the dead will hear the voice of the Son of God and those who hear

will live. [26]For as the Father has life in himself, so he has granted the Son to have life in himself. [27]And he has given him authority to judge because he is the Son of Man.

[28]"Do not be amazed at this, for a time is coming when all who are in their graves will hear his voice [29]and come out—those who have done good will rise to live, and those who have done evil will rise to be condemned. [30]By myself I can do nothing; I judge only as I hear, and my judgment is just, for I seek not to please myself but him who sent me.

[31]"If I testify about myself, my testimony is not valid. [32]There is another who testifies in my favor, and I know that his testimony about me is valid.

[33]"You have sent to John and he has testified to the truth. [34]Not that I accept human testimony; but I mention it that you may be saved. [35]John was a lamp that burned and gave light, and you chose for a time to enjoy his light.

[36]"I have testimony weightier than that of John. For the very work that the Father has given me to finish, and which I am doing, testifies that the Father has sent me. [37]And the Father who sent me has himself testified concerning me. You have never heard his voice nor seen his form, [38]nor does his word dwell in you, for you do not believe the one he sent. [39]You diligently study[e] the Scriptures because you think that by them you possess eternal life. These are the Scriptures that testify about me, [40]yet you refuse to come to me to have life.

[41]"I do not accept praise from men, [42]but I know you. I know that you do not have the love of God in your hearts. [43]I have come in my Father's name, and you do not accept me; but if someone else comes in his own name, you will accept him. [44]How can you believe if you accept praise from one another, yet make no effort to obtain the praise that comes from the only God[f]?

[45]"But do not think I will accuse you before the Father. Your accuser is Moses, on whom your hopes are set. [46]If you believed Moses, you would believe me, for he wrote about me. [47]But since you do not believe what he wrote, how are you going to believe what I say?"

[e]39 Or *Study diligently* (the imperative)   [f]44 Some early manuscripts *the Only One*

Discovering the Word 1. Based on the scene and conversation around the pool, how would you describe the feelings and attitudes of the invalid (vv. 1–15)? 2. The seventh commandment said: "Remember the Sabbath day by keeping it holy" (see Ex 20:8–11). In their zeal to apply this command, what were the Jews failing to see (vv. 9–15)? 3. What insights do verses 19–23 give us into (a) the Father's devotion to the Son and (b) the Son's dependence on the Father? 4. What "witnesses" does Jesus call forward to testify on his behalf (vv. 31–47)? 5. What counter-accusations does Jesus make against those who are attacking him? 6. According to this chapter, what really influences our verdict for or against Jesus?

 Applying the Word 1. When have you been more concerned about a religious activity than the reality behind it? Explain. 2. How can you avoid the kind of religion that is outwardly pious but inwardly bankrupt?

Responding in Prayer Ask God to help you discover true religion.

6 / *John 6*
Jesus, the Bread of Life

DO YOU REALIZE that during your lifetime you will probably spend over thirty-five thousand hours eating? That's the equivalent of eight years of nonstop meals, twelve hours a day! The problem, of course, is that even after a big meal we get hungry again. At best, food only satisfies us for a few hours.

Yet in this chapter, Jesus offers us food that satisfies our hunger forever. You can't buy it in a grocery store. It is found only in Jesus himself.

 Warming Up to God How do you usually respond to an "impossible" situation—a problem in your life that doesn't seem to have a solution?

 Read John 6.

6 Some time after this, Jesus crossed to the far shore of the Sea of Galilee (that is, the Sea of Tiberias), ²and a great crowd of people followed him because they saw the miraculous signs he had performed on the sick. ³Then Jesus went up on a mountainside and sat down with his disciples. ⁴The Jewish Passover Feast was near.

⁵When Jesus looked up and saw a great crowd coming toward him, he said to Philip, "Where shall we buy bread for these people to eat?" ⁶He asked this only to test him, for he already had in mind what he was going to do.

⁷Philip answered him, "Eight months' wages⁸ would not buy enough bread for each one to have a bite!"

⁸Another of his disciples, Andrew, Simon Peter's brother, spoke up, ⁹"Here is a boy with five small barley loaves and two small fish, but how far will they go among so many?"

¹⁰Jesus said, "Have the people sit down." There was plenty of grass in that place, and the men sat down, about five thousand of them. ¹¹Jesus then took the loaves, gave thanks, and distributed to those who were seated as much as they wanted. He did the same with the fish.

¹²When they had all had enough to eat, he said to his disciples, "Gather the pieces that are left over. Let nothing be wasted." ¹³So they gathered them and filled twelve baskets with the pieces of the five barley loaves left over by those who had eaten.

¹⁴After the people saw the miraculous sign that Jesus did, they began to say, "Surely this is the Prophet who is to come into the world." ¹⁵Jesus, knowing that they intended to come and make him king by force, withdrew again to a mountain by himself.

¹⁶When evening came, his disciples went down to the lake, ¹⁷where they got into a boat and set off across the lake for Capernaum. By now it was dark, and Jesus had not yet joined them. ¹⁸A

⁸7 Greek *two hundred denarii*

strong wind was blowing and the waters grew rough. ¹⁹When they had rowed three or three and a half miles,ʰ they saw Jesus approaching the boat, walking on the water; and they were terrified. ²⁰But he said to them, "It is I; don't be afraid." ²¹Then they were willing to take him into the boat, and immediately the boat reached the shore where they were heading.

²²The next day the crowd that had stayed on the opposite shore of the lake realized that only one boat had been there, and that Jesus had not entered it with his disciples, but that they had gone away alone. ²³Then some boats from Tiberias landed near the place where the people had eaten the bread after the Lord had given thanks. ²⁴Once the crowd realized that neither Jesus nor his disciples were there, they got into the boats and went to Capernaum in search of Jesus.

²⁵When they found him on the other side of the lake, they asked him, "Rabbi, when did you get here?"

²⁶Jesus answered, "I tell you the truth, you are looking for me, not because you saw miraculous signs but because you ate the loaves and had your fill. ²⁷Do not work for food that spoils, but for food that endures to eternal life, which the Son of Man will give you. On him God the Father has placed his seal of approval."

²⁸Then they asked him, "What must we do to do the works God requires?"

²⁹Jesus answered, "The work of God is this: to believe in the one he has sent."

³⁰So they asked him, "What miraculous sign then will you give that we may see it and believe you? What will you do? ³¹Our forefathers ate the manna in the desert; as it is written: 'He gave them bread from heaven to eat.'ⁱ "

³²Jesus said to them, "I tell you the truth, it is not Moses who has given you the bread from heaven, but it is my Father who gives you the true bread from heaven. ³³For the bread of God is he who comes down from heaven and gives life to the world."

³⁴"Sir," they said, "from now on give us this bread."

³⁵Then Jesus declared, "I am the bread of life. He who comes to me will never go hungry, and he who believes in me will never be thirsty. ³⁶But as I told you, you have seen me and still you do not believe. ³⁷All that the Father gives me will come to me, and whoever comes to me I will never drive away. ³⁸For I have come down from

heaven not to do my will but to do the will of him who sent me. ³⁹And this is the will of him who sent me, that I shall lose none of all that he has given me, but raise them up at the last day. ⁴⁰For my Father's will is that everyone who looks to the Son and believes in him shall have eternal life, and I will raise him up at the last day."

⁴¹At this the Jews began to grumble about him because he said, "I am the bread that came down from heaven." ⁴²They said, "Is this not Jesus, the son of Joseph, whose father and mother we know? How can he now say, 'I came down from heaven'?"

⁴³"Stop grumbling among yourselves," Jesus answered. ⁴⁴"No one can come to me unless the Father who sent me draws him, and I will raise him up at the last day. ⁴⁵It is written in the Prophets: 'They will all be taught by God.'ʲ Everyone who listens to the Father and learns from him comes to me. ⁴⁶No one has seen the Father except the one who is from God; only he has seen the Father. ⁴⁷I tell you the truth, he who believes has everlasting life. ⁴⁸I am the bread of life. ⁴⁹Your forefathers ate the manna in the desert, yet they died. ⁵⁰But here is the bread that comes down from heaven, which a man may eat and not die. ⁵¹I am the living bread that came down from heaven. If anyone eats of this bread, he will live forever. This bread is my flesh, which I will give for the life of the world."

⁵²Then the Jews began to argue sharply among themselves, "How can this man give us his flesh to eat?"

⁵³Jesus said to them, "I tell you the truth, unless you eat the flesh of the Son of Man and drink his blood, you have no life in you. ⁵⁴Whoever eats my flesh and drinks my blood has eternal life, and I will raise him up at the last day. ⁵⁵For my flesh is real food and my blood is real drink. ⁵⁶Whoever eats my flesh and drinks my blood remains in me, and I in him. ⁵⁷Just as the living Father sent me and I live because of the Father, so the one who feeds on me will live because of me. ⁵⁸This is the bread that came down from heaven. Your forefathers ate manna and died, but he who feeds on this bread will live forever." ⁵⁹He said this while teaching in the synagogue in Capernaum.

⁶⁰On hearing it, many of his disciples said, "This is a hard teaching. Who can accept it?"

ʰ19 Greek *rowed twenty-five or thirty stadia* (about 5 or 6 kilometers)
ⁱ31 Exodus 16:4; Neh. 9:15; Psalm 78:24,25   ʲ45 Isaiah 54:13

⁶¹Aware that his disciples were grumbling about this, Jesus said to them, "Does this offend you? ⁶²What if you see the Son of Man ascend to where he was before! ⁶³The Spirit gives life; the flesh counts for nothing. The words I have spoken to you are spirit^k and they are life. ⁶⁴Yet there are some of you who do not believe." For Jesus had known from the beginning which of them did not believe and who would betray him. ⁶⁵He went on to say, "This is why I told you that no one can come to me unless the Father has enabled him."

⁶⁶From this time many of his disciples turned back and no longer followed him.

⁶⁷"You do not want to leave too, do you?" Jesus asked the Twelve.

⁶⁸Simon Peter answered him, "Lord, to whom shall we go? You have the words of eternal life. ⁶⁹We believe and know that you are the Holy One of God."

⁷⁰Then Jesus replied, "Have I not chosen you, the Twelve? Yet one of you is a devil!" ⁷¹(He meant Judas, the son of Simon Iscariot, who, though one of the Twelve, was later to betray him.)

ᵏ63 Or *Spirit*

 Discovering the Word 1. How would you characterize Philip's and Andrew's responses to the problem of feeding this enormous crowd (vv. 5–9)? 2. Imagine that you are one of the disciples, rowing the boat in dark, rough waters (vv. 16–21). How would your concept of Jesus have been altered by seeing him walk on water? 3. The next day the people were hungry again, so they came seeking Jesus (vv. 22–25). How does he try to redirect their thinking (vv. 26–33)? 4. Based on the remarks of some in the crowd (vv. 41–42), do you think they finally understood what Jesus was saying? Explain. 5. When Jesus said, "This bread is my flesh," the crowd could think only of cannibalism (v. 52). What do you think it means to eat Jesus' flesh and drink his blood (vv. 53–59)? Is this something we do once for all time, or is it an ongoing process? Explain. 6. In verses 60–71 Jesus turns away from the crowd and focuses on his disciples. How would you describe their responses to his "hard teaching"?

Applying the Word 1. Which response in question 6 best describes your present attitude toward Jesus? Explain. 2. Jesus has contrasted the two appetites found in every person—the appetite for food that perishes and the appetite for food that endures. In what ways has Jesus satisfied the spiritual hunger in your heart?

Responding in Prayer Praise God for satisfying all your needs.

---

7 / *John 7:1–52*
Confusion over Christ

NOT LONG AGO I had a series of conversations with a young man about Jesus Christ and why faith in him is so important. At first, the young man was interested. He was open to listen to God's Word and to consider Christ's claims. As time went on, however, he became more and more hostile to Christ. Finally, he told me that he didn't want to pursue his investigation any further. He had decided to reject Christ and his offer of salvation.

That is precisely the pattern that John traces in his Gospel. In the early chapters, men and women responded to Jesus with belief. Then some of those who were following him turned away. Now open warfare breaks out between Jesus and his enemies—and yet, some still seek the truth. This chapter will help you respond positively to the wide variety of attitudes toward Jesus today.

Warming Up to God "If anyone is thirsty, let him come to me and drink." These are Jesus' words to us today. In what way do you need Jesus' spiritual refreshment? Be quiet before him and experience the "streams of living water."

 Read John 7:1–52.

7After this, Jesus went around in Galilee, purposely staying away from Judea because the Jews there were waiting to take his life. 2But when the Jewish Feast of Tabernacles was near, 3Jesus' brothers said to him, "You ought to leave here and go to Judea, so that your disciples may see the miracles you do. 4No one who wants to become a public figure acts in secret. Since you are doing these things, show yourself to the world." 5For even his own brothers did not believe in him.

6Therefore Jesus told them, "The right time for me has not yet come; for you any time is right. 7The world cannot hate you, but it hates me because I testify that what it does is evil. 8You go to the Feast. I am not yet[l] going up to this Feast, because for me the right time has not yet come." 9Having said this, he stayed in Galilee.

10However, after his brothers had left for the Feast, he went also, not publicly, but in secret. 11Now at the Feast the Jews were watching for him and asking, "Where is that man?"

12Among the crowds there was widespread whispering about him. Some said, "He is a good man."

Others replied, "No, he deceives the people." 13But no one would say anything publicly about him for fear of the Jews.

14Not until halfway through the Feast did Jesus go up to the temple courts and begin to teach. 15The Jews were amazed and asked, "How did this man get such learning without having studied?"

16Jesus answered, "My teaching is not my own. It comes from him who sent me. 17If anyone chooses to do God's will, he will find out whether my teaching comes from God or whether I speak on my own. 18He who speaks on his own does so to gain honor for himself, but he who works for the honor of the one who sent him is a man of truth; there is nothing false about him. 19Has not Moses given you the law? Yet not one of you keeps the law. Why are you trying to kill me?"

20"You are demon-possessed," the crowd answered. "Who is trying to kill you?"

21Jesus said to them, "I did one miracle, and you are all astonished. 22Yet, because Moses gave you circumcision (though actually it did not come from Moses, but from the patriarchs), you circumcise a child on the Sabbath. 23Now if a child can be circumcised on the Sabbath so that the law of Moses may not be broken, why are you angry with me for healing the whole man on the Sabbath? 24Stop judging by mere appearances, and make a right judgment."

25At that point some of the people of Jerusalem began to ask, "Isn't this the man they are trying to kill? 26Here he is, speaking publicly, and they are not saying a word to him. Have the authorities really concluded that he is the Christ[m]? 27But we know where this man is from; when the Christ comes, no one will know where he is from."

28Then Jesus, still teaching in the temple courts, cried out, "Yes, you know me, and you know where I am from. I am not here on my own, but he who sent me is true. You do not know him, 29but I know him because I am from him and he sent me."

30At this they tried to seize him, but no one laid a hand on him, because his time had not yet come. 31Still, many in the crowd put their faith in him. They said, "When the Christ comes, will he do more miraculous signs than this man?"

32The Pharisees heard the crowd whispering such things about him. Then the chief priests and the Pharisees sent temple guards to arrest him.

33Jesus said, "I am with you for only a short time, and then I go to the one who sent me. 34You will look for me, but you will not find me; and where I am, you cannot come."

35The Jews said to one another, "Where does this man intend to go that we cannot find him? Will he go where our people live scattered among the Greeks, and teach the Greeks? 36What did he mean when he said, 'You will look for me, but you will not find me,' and 'Where I am, you cannot come'?"

37On the last and greatest day of the Feast, Jesus stood and said in a loud voice, "If anyone is thirsty, let him come to me and drink. 38Whoever believes in me, as[n] the Scripture has said, streams of living water will flow from within him." 39By this he meant the Spirit, whom those who believed in him were later to receive. Up to that time the Spirit had not been given, since Jesus had not yet been glorified.

40On hearing his words, some of the people said, "Surely this man is the Prophet."

41Others said, "He is the Christ."

Still others asked, "How can the Christ come from Galilee? 42Does not the Scripture say that

l8 Some early manuscripts do not have yet.   m26 Or Messiah; also in verses 27, 31, 41 and 42   n37,38 Or / If anyone is thirsty, let him come to me. / And let him drink, 38who believes in me. / As

the Christ will come from David's family° and from Bethlehem, the town where David lived?" 43Thus the people were divided because of Jesus. 44Some wanted to seize him, but no one laid a hand on him.

45Finally the temple guards went back to the chief priests and Pharisees, who asked them, "Why didn't you bring him in?"

46"No one ever spoke the way this man does," the guards declared.

47"You mean he has deceived you also?" the Pharisees retorted. 48"Has any of the rulers or of the Pharisees believed in him? 49No! But this mob that knows nothing of the law—there is a curse on them."

50Nicodemus, who had gone to Jesus earlier and who was one of their own number, asked, 51"Does our law condemn anyone without first hearing him to find out what he is doing?"

52They replied, "Are you from Galilee, too? Look into it, and you will find that a prophet^p does not come out of Galilee."

[The earliest manuscripts and many other ancient witnesses do not have John 7:53–8:11.]

°42 Greek *seed*   ^p52 Two early manuscripts *the Prophet*

 Discovering the Word 1. The first blast of hostility against Jesus comes from his own family (vv. 1–13). How would you characterize the statements made by Jesus' brothers (vv. 3–5)? 2. When Jesus makes his presence in Jerusalem known, people begin to challenge the origin (and, therefore, the authority) of his teaching. According to Jesus, how can we verify the truth of his teaching (vv. 16–18)? 3. What other opinions or questions do people have about Jesus in verses 20–36? 4. How does Jesus respond to each one? 5. On the last day of the Feast of Tabernacles, large vats of water were poured out on the pavement of the temple court as a reminder of God's provision of water in the wilderness. With that custom in mind, how would you explain the significance of Jesus' remarks in verses 37–39?

Applying the Word 1. What counsel would you give a believer who faces spiritual opposition from his or her family? 2. Which of the opinions about Jesus you have identified in this chapter are still expressed today, and in what way? 3. Based on Jesus' example, what should our response be to such reactions?

Responding in Prayer Pray for wisdom as you face various reactions to Jesus.

---

8 / *John 7:53—8:11*
Caught in Adultery

NOTHING IS MORE humiliating than being caught in an act of disobedience! Whether it's a child with his hand in the cookie jar or an adult driving over the speed limit, we all know the sinking feeling of being caught. In John 8, a woman is caught in the most awkward of situations—in the very act of adultery. The way Jesus responds to her may surprise you.

 Warming Up to God Think of a time when you hurt someone and that person was willing to forgive you. How did it feel to be forgiven? Thank God for extending forgiveness to you.

 Read John 7:53—8:11.

53Then each went to his own home.

8 But Jesus went to the Mount of Olives. 2At dawn he appeared again in the temple courts, where all the people gathered around him, and he sat down to teach them. 3The

teachers of the law and the Pharisees brought in a woman caught in adultery. They made her stand before the group 4and said to Jesus, "Teacher, this woman was caught in the act of adultery. 5In the Law Moses commanded us to stone such women.

Now what do you say?" 6They were using this question as a trap, in order to have a basis for accusing him.

But Jesus bent down and started to write on the ground with his finger. 7When they kept on questioning him, he straightened up and said to them, "If any one of you is without sin, let him be the first to throw a stone at her." 8Again he stooped down and wrote on the ground.

9At this, those who heard began to go away one at a time, the older ones first, until only Jesus was left, with the woman still standing there. 10Jesus straightened up and asked her, "Woman, where are they? Has no one condemned you?"

11"No one, sir," she said.

"Then neither do I condemn you," Jesus declared. "Go now and leave your life of sin."

 Discovering the Word 1. What do we know about the character and motives of those who bring this woman to Jesus? 2. While it is obvious that the woman is guilty, what elements of injustice can you find in this situation? 3. The Pharisees and teachers were often very self-righteous. Why do you think they went away rather than stoning the woman (vv. 7–9)? 4. How would you describe Jesus' attitude toward the woman (vv. 10–11)?

 Applying the Word 1. What can we learn from this passage about Christ's attitude toward us—even when we feel awful about ourselves? 2. What does it teach us about forgiving and accepting others? 3. Who do you need to offer your forgiveness to?

 Responding in Prayer Ask God to show you what it means to forgive.

9 / *John 8:12–59*
Jesus, the Light of the World

JESUS NEVER SPOKE in public without creating controversy. In fact, he was constantly in trouble! Rather than retreating behind the safety of a pulpit, Jesus spoke in settings where people were bold enough to talk back. In this portion of John's story, Jesus makes a series of claims about himself. Each claim is met by a challenge from his enemies. Each challenge is then answered, and the answer leads to the next claim. Throughout this interchange, Jesus shows us how to speak the truth in the face of hostility. He also reveals some amazing things about himself.

Warming Up to God Have you ever tried to talk about Christ with a family member or coworker who was hostile to your message? How did you feel at the time? Thank God for giving you a Savior who understands everything we experience.

Read John 8:12–59.

12When Jesus spoke again to the people, he said, "I am the light of the world. Whoever follows me will never walk in darkness, but will have the light of life."

13The Pharisees challenged him, "Here you are, appearing as your own witness; your testimony is not valid."

14Jesus answered, "Even if I testify on my own behalf, my testimony is valid, for I know where I came from and where I am going. But you have no idea where I come from or where I am going.

15You judge by human standards; I pass judgment on no one. 16But if I do judge, my decisions are right, because I am not alone. I stand with the Father, who sent me. 17In your own Law it is written that the testimony of two men is valid. 18I am one who testifies for myself; my other witness is the Father, who sent me."

19Then they asked him, "Where is your father?"

"You do not know me or my Father," Jesus replied. "If you knew me, you would know my

Father also." 20He spoke these words while teaching in the temple area near the place where the offerings were put. Yet no one seized him, because his time had not yet come.

21Once more Jesus said to them, "I am going away, and you will look for me, and you will die in your sin. Where I go, you cannot come."

22This made the Jews ask, "Will he kill himself? Is that why he says, 'Where I go, you cannot come'?"

23But he continued, "You are from below; I am from above. You are of this world; I am not of this world. 24I told you that you would die in your sins; if you do not believe that I am ∟the one I claim to be⌐,q you will indeed die in your sins."

25"Who are you?" they asked.

"Just what I have been claiming all along," Jesus replied. 26"I have much to say in judgment of you. But he who sent me is reliable, and what I have heard from him I tell the world."

27They did not understand that he was telling them about his Father. 28So Jesus said, "When you have lifted up the Son of Man, then you will know that I am ∟the one I claim to be⌐ and that I do nothing on my own but speak just what the Father has taught me. 29The one who sent me is with me; he has not left me alone, for I always do what pleases him." 30Even as he spoke, many put their faith in him.

31To the Jews who had believed him, Jesus said, "If you hold to my teaching, you are really my disciples. 32Then you will know the truth, and the truth will set you free."

33They answered him, "We are Abraham's descendantsr and have never been slaves of anyone. How can you say that we shall be set free?"

34Jesus replied, "I tell you the truth, everyone who sins is a slave to sin. 35Now a slave has no permanent place in the family, but a son belongs to it forever. 36So if the Son sets you free, you will be free indeed. 37I know you are Abraham's descendants. Yet you are ready to kill me, because you have no room for my word. 38I am telling you what I have seen in the Father's presence, and you do what you have heard from your father.s"

39"Abraham is our father," they answered.

"If you were Abraham's children," said Jesus, "then you wouldt do the things Abraham did. 40As it is, you are determined to kill me, a man who has told you the truth that I heard from God. Abraham did not do such things. 41You are doing the things your own father does."

"We are not illegitimate children," they protested. "The only Father we have is God himself."

42Jesus said to them, "If God were your Father, you would love me, for I came from God and now am here. I have not come on my own; but he sent me. 43Why is my language not clear to you? Because you are unable to hear what I say. 44You belong to your father, the devil, and you want to carry out your father's desire. He was a murderer from the beginning, not holding to the truth, for there is no truth in him. When he lies, he speaks his native language, for he is a liar and the father of lies. 45Yet because I tell the truth, you do not believe me! 46Can any of you prove me guilty of sin? If I am telling the truth, why don't you believe me? 47He who belongs to God hears what God says. The reason you do not hear is that you do not belong to God."

48The Jews answered him, "Aren't we right in saying that you are a Samaritan and demon-possessed?"

49"I am not possessed by a demon," said Jesus, "but I honor my Father and you dishonor me. 50I am not seeking glory for myself; but there is one who seeks it, and he is the judge. 51I tell you the truth, if anyone keeps my word, he will never see death."

52At this the Jews exclaimed, "Now we know that you are demon-possessed! Abraham died and so did the prophets, yet you say that if anyone keeps your word, he will never taste death. 53Are you greater than our father Abraham? He died, and so did the prophets. Who do you think you are?"

54Jesus replied, "If I glorify myself, my glory means nothing. My Father, whom you claim as your God, is the one who glorifies me. 55Though you do not know him, I know him. If I said I did not, I would be a liar like you, but I do know him and keep his word. 56Your father Abraham rejoiced at the thought of seeing my day; he saw it and was glad."

57"You are not yet fifty years old," the Jews said to him, "and you have seen Abraham!"

58"I tell you the truth," Jesus answered, "before Abraham was born, I am!" 59At this, they picked up stones to stone him, but Jesus hid himself, slipping away from the temple grounds.

q24 Or I am he; also in verse 28   r33 Greek seed; also in verse 37
s38 Or presence. Therefore do what you have heard from the Father.
t39 Some early manuscripts "If you are Abraham's children," said Jesus, "then

Discovering the Word 1. The Pharisees challenge the validity of Jesus' claim (v. 13). How does Jesus answer their challenge (vv. 14–18)? 2. Jesus' reference to his Father leads to his second claim—that he came from God. How does this claim heighten the tension between Jesus and the Jews (vv. 19–30)? 3. Jesus makes another startling claim in verses 31–32: "If you hold to my teaching . . . then you will know the truth, and the truth will set you free." Why does holding to Jesus' teaching lead to true knowledge and freedom? 4. Jesus' opponents also claim to have both Abraham and God as their father. According to Jesus, how does their conduct contradict their claim (vv. 39–47)?

 Applying the Word 1. Why is our conduct the truest test of our beliefs? 2. In what ways does your lifestyle validate (or invalidate) your claim to be a follower of Christ?

 Responding in Prayer Ask God to help you change the parts of your life that don't match your beliefs.

10 / *John 9*
A Blind Man Sees the Light

OUR SIGHT IS a wonderful gift from God. We marvel at the fiery colors of a sunset, the rich pastels of spring and the delicate beauty of a flower. How tragic it must be to never see the light of day. Yet there is a far greater tragedy than physical blindness. In this passage Jesus meets a man who has been blind from birth. The man illustrates that those who are blind often see clearly, while those with sight see nothing at all.

 Warming Up to God Before you begin this chapter about various kinds of blindness and sight, ask God to open your eyes so that you can see what he has for you.

Read John 9.

9 As he went along, he saw a man blind from birth. [2]His disciples asked him, "Rabbi, who sinned, this man or his parents, that he was born blind?"

[3]"Neither this man nor his parents sinned," said Jesus, "but this happened so that the work of God might be displayed in his life. [4]As long as it is day, we must do the work of him who sent me. Night is coming, when no one can work. [5]While I am in the world, I am the light of the world."

[6]Having said this, he spit on the ground, made some mud with the saliva, and put it on the man's eyes. [7]"Go," he told him, "wash in the Pool of Siloam" (this word means Sent). So the man went and washed, and came home seeing.

[8]His neighbors and those who had formerly seen him begging asked, "Isn't this the same man who used to sit and beg?" [9]Some claimed that he was.

Others said, "No, he only looks like him."

But he himself insisted, "I am the man."

[10]"How then were your eyes opened?" they demanded.

[11]He replied, "The man they call Jesus made some mud and put it on my eyes. He told me to go to Siloam and wash. So I went and washed, and then I could see."

[12]"Where is this man?" they asked him.

"I don't know," he said.

[13]They brought to the Pharisees the man who had been blind. [14]Now the day on which Jesus had made the mud and opened the man's eyes was a Sabbath. [15]Therefore the Pharisees also asked him how he had received his sight. "He put mud on my eyes," the man replied, "and I washed, and now I see."

[16]Some of the Pharisees said, "This man is not from God, for he does not keep the Sabbath."

But others asked, "How can a sinner do such miraculous signs?" So they were divided.

[17]Finally they turned again to the blind man, "What have you to say about him? It was your eyes he opened."

The man replied, "He is a prophet."

[18]The Jews still did not believe that he had been blind and had received his sight until they

sent for the man's parents. [19]"Is this your son?" they asked. "Is this the one you say was born blind? How is it that now he can see?"

[20]"We know he is our son," the parents answered, "and we know he was born blind. [21]But how he can see now, or who opened his eyes, we don't know. Ask him. He is of age; he will speak for himself." [22]His parents said this because they were afraid of the Jews, for already the Jews had decided that anyone who acknowledged that Jesus was the Christ[u] would be put out of the synagogue. [23]That was why his parents said, "He is of age; ask him."

[24]A second time they summoned the man who had been blind. "Give glory to God,[v]" they said. "We know this man is a sinner."

[25]He replied, "Whether he is a sinner or not, I don't know. One thing I do know. I was blind but now I see!"

[26]Then they asked him, "What did he do to you? How did he open your eyes?"

[27]He answered, "I have told you already and you did not listen. Why do you want to hear it again? Do you want to become his disciples, too?"

[28]Then they hurled insults at him and said, "You are this fellow's disciple! We are disciples of Moses! [29]We know that God spoke to Moses, but as for this fellow, we don't even know where he comes from."

[30]The man answered, "Now that is remarkable! You don't know where he comes from, yet he opened my eyes. [31]We know that God does not listen to sinners. He listens to the godly man who does his will. [32]Nobody has ever heard of opening the eyes of a man born blind. [33]If this man were not from God, he could do nothing."

[34]To this they replied, "You were steeped in sin at birth; how dare you lecture us!" And they threw him out.

[35]Jesus heard that they had thrown him out, and when he found him, he said, "Do you believe in the Son of Man?"

[36]"Who is he, sir?" the man asked. "Tell me so that I may believe in him."

[37]Jesus said, "You have now seen him; in fact, he is the one speaking with you."

[38]Then the man said, "Lord, I believe," and he worshiped him.

[39]Jesus said, "For judgment I have come into this world, so that the blind will see and those who see will become blind."

[40]Some Pharisees who were with him heard him say this and asked, "What? Are we blind too?"

[41]Jesus said, "If you were blind, you would not be guilty of sin; but now that you claim you can see, your guilt remains."

[u]22 Or *Messiah*   [v]24 A solemn charge to tell the truth (see Joshua 7:19)

 Discovering the Word 1. Based on the question the disciples ask Jesus (v. 2), how do they view the relation between sickness and sin? 2. What is Jesus' view of the same issue (vv. 3–5)? 3. Why do you think Jesus goes through the process of making mud and instructing the man to go wash, instead of simply healing him instantly? 4. On what grounds do the Pharisees object to this miracle (vv. 16, 22, 24, 29)? 5. How do the Pharisees react when the genuineness of the miracle becomes undeniable (vv. 28–34)?

 Applying the Word 1. When might Christians today exhibit the Pharisees' attitude to a marvelous work of God's grace or power? 2. What principles in this chapter could help you improve your spiritual eyesight?

Responding in Prayer Ask God to strengthen your faith so that you might respond as the man did, "Lord, I believe."

11 / *John 10*
The Shepherd & His Sheep

JESUS WAS A master at using simple, everyday objects or events to illustrate profound spiritual truths. The farmer scattering seed, the vine sustaining the branches, and sparrows falling to the earth all took on a new dimension in Jesus' eyes. In John 10, Jesus uses the scene of a shepherd enclosing his sheep in a sheepfold to give us one of the most moving pictures of our salvation and security in Christ found anywhere in the Bible. If you've ever doubted the love of Christ, Jesus will give you a healthy dose of assurance in this chapter.

 Warming Up to God What usually prompts you to have doubts about your salvation or your walk with Christ—your own sin? feelings of unworthiness? personal failures? Be honest with Christ about your doubts.

 Read John 10.

---

10 "I tell you the truth, the man who does not enter the sheep pen by the gate, but climbs in by some other way, is a thief and a robber. ²The man who enters by the gate is the shepherd of his sheep. ³The watchman opens the gate for him, and the sheep listen to his voice. He calls his own sheep by name and leads them out. ⁴When he has brought out all his own, he goes on ahead of them, and his sheep follow him because they know his voice. ⁵But they will never follow a stranger; in fact, they will run away from him because they do not recognize a stranger's voice." ⁶Jesus used this figure of speech, but they did not understand what he was telling them.

⁷Therefore Jesus said again, "I tell you the truth, I am the gate for the sheep. ⁸All who ever came before me were thieves and robbers, but the sheep did not listen to them. ⁹I am the gate; whoever enters through me will be saved.ʷ He will come in and go out, and find pasture. ¹⁰The thief comes only to steal and kill and destroy; I have come that they may have life, and have it to the full.

¹¹"I am the good shepherd. The good shepherd lays down his life for the sheep. ¹²The hired hand is not the shepherd who owns the sheep. So when he sees the wolf coming, he abandons the sheep and runs away. Then the wolf attacks the flock and scatters it. ¹³The man runs away because he is a hired hand and cares nothing for the sheep.

¹⁴"I am the good shepherd; I know my sheep and my sheep know me— ¹⁵just as the Father knows me and I know the Father—and I lay down my life for the sheep. ¹⁶I have other sheep that are not of this sheep pen. I must bring them

also. They too will listen to my voice, and there shall be one flock and one shepherd. ¹⁷The reason my Father loves me is that I lay down my life— only to take it up again. ¹⁸No one takes it from me, but I lay it down of my own accord. I have authority to lay it down and authority to take it up again. This command I received from my Father."

¹⁹At these words the Jews were again divided. ²⁰Many of them said, "He is demon-possessed and raving mad. Why listen to him?"

²¹But others said, "These are not the sayings of a man possessed by a demon. Can a demon open the eyes of the blind?"

²²Then came the Feast of Dedicationˣ at Jerusalem. It was winter, ²³and Jesus was in the temple area walking in Solomon's Colonnade. ²⁴The Jews gathered around him, saying, "How long will you keep us in suspense? If you are the Christ,ʸ tell us plainly."

²⁵Jesus answered, "I did tell you, but you do not believe. The miracles I do in my Father's name speak for me, ²⁶but you do not believe because you are not my sheep. ²⁷My sheep listen to my voice; I know them, and they follow me. ²⁸I give them eternal life, and they shall never perish; no one can snatch them out of my hand. ²⁹My Father, who has given them to me, is greater than allᶻ; no one can snatch them out of my Father's hand. ³⁰I and the Father are one."

³¹Again the Jews picked up stones to stone him, ³²but Jesus said to them, "I have shown you many great miracles from the Father. For which of these do you stone me?"

ʷ9 Or *kept safe*   ˣ22 That is, Hanukkah   ʸ24 Or *Messiah*
ᶻ29 Many early manuscripts *What my Father has given me is greater than all*

³³"We are not stoning you for any of these," replied the Jews, "but for blasphemy, because you, a mere man, claim to be God."

³⁴Jesus answered them, "Is it not written in your Law, 'I have said you are gods'ᵃ? ³⁵If he called them 'gods,' to whom the word of God came—and the Scripture cannot be broken— ³⁶what about the one whom the Father set apart as his very own and sent into the world? Why then do you accuse me of blasphemy because I said, 'I am God's Son'? ³⁷Do not believe me unless I do what my Father does. ³⁸But if I do it, even though you do not believe me, believe the mira-

cles, that you may know and understand that the Father is in me, and I in the Father." ³⁹Again they tried to seize him, but he escaped their grasp.

⁴⁰Then Jesus went back across the Jordan to the place where John had been baptizing in the early days. Here he stayed ⁴¹and many people came to him. They said, "Though John never performed a miraculous sign, all that John said about this man was true." ⁴²And in that place many believed in Jesus.

ᵃ34 Psalm 82:6

Discovering the Word   1. What spiritual truths is Jesus trying to convey in verses 1–5?   2. In verses 11–15 Jesus talks about the shepherd's care for his sheep. What can you learn from those verses about Jesus' care and relationship with you?   3. According to Jesus, how are the Jews in this passage different from his sheep (vv. 22–27)?   4. When Jesus claims that he and the Father are one, the Jews pick up stones to stone him (vv. 30–33). Do you think his defense is a denial of his deity (vv. 33–36)? Explain.

Applying the Word   1. How do you respond to promises and assurances Jesus gives his sheep in verses 28–29?   2. Which promise from Jesus in this chapter is most encouraging to you?   3. How can Jesus' promise help you when you have doubts?

Responding in Prayer   Praise God for giving you such a Good Shepherd.

---

12 / *John 11*
Resurrection & Life

EVER SINCE GOD judged Adam and Eve, death has plagued humanity. It separates us from those we love and looms over our own lives like a menacing spirit. In this chapter Jesus reaches out to a family struggling with the pain of death. He shows us why we need never fear death again.

Warming Up to God   When is it difficult for you to feel that God is with you? Talk to God about your feelings of abandonment.

Read John 11.

---

11 Now a man named Lazarus was sick. He was from Bethany, the village of Mary and her sister Martha. ²This Mary, whose brother Lazarus now lay sick, was the same one who poured perfume on the Lord and wiped his feet with her hair. ³So the sisters sent word to Jesus, "Lord, the one you love is sick."

⁴When he heard this, Jesus said, "This sickness will not end in death. No, it is for God's glory so

that God's Son may be glorified through it." ⁵Jesus loved Martha and her sister and Lazarus. ⁶Yet when he heard that Lazarus was sick, he stayed where he was two more days.

⁷Then he said to his disciples, "Let us go back to Judea."

⁸"But Rabbi," they said, "a short while ago the Jews tried to stone you, and yet you are going back there?"

⁹Jesus answered, "Are there not twelve hours of

daylight? A man who walks by day will not stumble, for he sees by this world's light. [10]It is when he walks by night that he stumbles, for he has no light."

[11]After he had said this, he went on to tell them, "Our friend Lazarus has fallen asleep; but I am going there to wake him up."

[12]His disciples replied, "Lord, if he sleeps, he will get better." [13]Jesus had been speaking of his death, but his disciples thought he meant natural sleep.

[14]So then he told them plainly, "Lazarus is dead, [15]and for your sake I am glad I was not there, so that you may believe. But let us go to him."

[16]Then Thomas (called Didymus) said to the rest of the disciples, "Let us also go, that we may die with him."

[17]On his arrival, Jesus found that Lazarus had already been in the tomb for four days. [18]Bethany was less than two miles[b] from Jerusalem, [19]and many Jews had come to Martha and Mary to comfort them in the loss of their brother. [20]When Martha heard that Jesus was coming, she went out to meet him, but Mary stayed at home.

[21]"Lord," Martha said to Jesus, "if you had been here, my brother would not have died. [22]But I know that even now God will give you whatever you ask."

[23]Jesus said to her, "Your brother will rise again."

[24]Martha answered, "I know he will rise again in the resurrection at the last day."

[25]Jesus said to her, "I am the resurrection and the life. He who believes in me will live, even though he dies; [26]and whoever lives and believes in me will never die. Do you believe this?"

[27]"Yes, Lord," she told him, "I believe that you are the Christ,[c] the Son of God, who was to come into the world."

[28]And after she had said this, she went back and called her sister Mary aside. "The Teacher is here," she said, "and is asking for you." [29]When Mary heard this, she got up quickly and went to him. [30]Now Jesus had not yet entered the village, but was still at the place where Martha had met him. [31]When the Jews who had been with Mary in the house, comforting her, noticed how quickly she got up and went out, they followed her, supposing she was going to the tomb to mourn there.

[32]When Mary reached the place where Jesus was and saw him, she fell at his feet and said,

"Lord, if you had been here, my brother would not have died."

[33]When Jesus saw her weeping, and the Jews who had come along with her also weeping, he was deeply moved in spirit and troubled. [34]"Where have you laid him?" he asked.

"Come and see, Lord," they replied.

[35]Jesus wept.

[36]Then the Jews said, "See how he loved him!"

[37]But some of them said, "Could not he who opened the eyes of the blind man have kept this man from dying?"

[38]Jesus, once more deeply moved, came to the tomb. It was a cave with a stone laid across the entrance. [39]"Take away the stone," he said.

"But, Lord," said Martha, the sister of the dead man, "by this time there is a bad odor, for he has been there four days."

[40]Then Jesus said, "Did I not tell you that if you believed, you would see the glory of God?"

[41]So they took away the stone. Then Jesus looked up and said, "Father, I thank you that you have heard me. [42]I knew that you always hear me, but I said this for the benefit of the people standing here, that they may believe that you sent me."

[43]When he had said this, Jesus called in a loud voice, "Lazarus, come out!" [44]The dead man came out, his hands and feet wrapped with strips of linen, and a cloth around his face.

Jesus said to them, "Take off the grave clothes and let him go."

[45]Therefore many of the Jews who had come to visit Mary, and had seen what Jesus did, put their faith in him. [46]But some of them went to the Pharisees and told them what Jesus had done. [47]Then the chief priests and the Pharisees called a meeting of the Sanhedrin.

"What are we accomplishing?" they asked. "Here is this man performing many miraculous signs. [48]If we let him go on like this, everyone will believe in him, and then the Romans will come and take away both our place[d] and our nation."

[49]Then one of them, named Caiaphas, who was high priest that year, spoke up, "You know nothing at all! [50]You do not realize that it is better for you that one man die for the people than that the whole nation perish."

[51]He did not say this on his own, but as high priest that year he prophesied that Jesus would die for the Jewish nation, [52]and not only for that

[b]18 Greek *fifteen stadia* (about 3 kilometers)   [c]27 Or *Messiah*
[d]48 Or *temple*

nation but also for the scattered children of God, to bring them together and make them one. ⁵³So from that day on they plotted to take his life.

⁵⁴Therefore Jesus no longer moved about publicly among the Jews. Instead he withdrew to a region near the desert, to a village called Ephraim, where he stayed with his disciples.

⁵⁵When it was almost time for the Jewish Passover, many went up from the country to Jerusa-lem for their ceremonial cleansing before the Passover. ⁵⁶They kept looking for Jesus, and as they stood in the temple area they asked one another, "What do you think? Isn't he coming to the Feast at all?" ⁵⁷But the chief priests and Pharisees had given orders that if anyone found out where Jesus was, he should report it so that they might arrest him.

 Discovering the Word 1. How can we resolve the apparent conflict between Jesus' love for Lazarus and his deliberate delay in helping him (vv. 4–6)? 2. What additional insight into God's purposes can we gain from Jesus' statement in verse 15? 3. What elements of doubt and faith do you see in Martha's statements to Jesus (vv. 17–27)? 4. How should Christ's statement in verses 25–26 radically alter our views of life and death? 5. Why do you think John emphasizes that Jesus was deeply moved by Mary's grief and the anguish of those with her (vv. 28–38)? 6. How would you explain the fact that the people who see the same miracle respond in two totally different ways (vv. 45–57)?

 Applying the Word 1. How can those verses help us when we feel abandoned by God in a time of great need? 2. In what ways will this chapter change the way you respond to personal difficulty or the apparent delay of God?

 Responding in Prayer Thank God for his personal presence with you.

---

13 / John 12
The King's Last Acts

IF YOU HAVE ever felt rejected or misunderstood, you know how Jesus felt as his public ministry came to an end. The hostility against him had risen to a fever pitch. His gentle compassion and abundant miracles were met with oppression and violence. Jesus knew what none of his friends knew—that he was about to die. In spite of the fleeting attempts of the crowd to make him King, Jesus chose the way of the cross.

 Warming Up to God If you knew for sure that you had only one week to live, what would you do with that week?

Read John 12.

---

12 Six days before the Passover, Jesus arrived at Bethany, where Lazarus lived, whom Jesus had raised from the dead. ²Here a dinner was given in Jesus' honor. Martha served, while Lazarus was among those reclining at the table with him. ³Then Mary took about a pint*ᵉ* of pure nard, an expensive perfume; she poured it on Jesus' feet and wiped his feet with her hair. And the house was filled with the fragrance of the perfume.

⁴But one of his disciples, Judas Iscariot, who was later to betray him, objected, ⁵"Why wasn't this perfume sold and the money given to the poor? It was worth a year's wages.ᶠ" ⁶He did not say this because he cared about the poor but because he was a thief; as keeper of the money bag, he used to help himself to what was put into it.

⁷"Leave her alone," Jesus replied. "⌐It was intended⌐ that she should save this perfume for the day of my burial. ⁸You will always have the poor among you, but you will not always have me."

⁹Meanwhile a large crowd of Jews found out

ᵉ3 Greek a litra (probably about 0.5 liter)   *ᶠ5 Greek three hundred denarii*

that Jesus was there and came, not only because of him but also to see Lazarus, whom he had raised from the dead. ¹⁰So the chief priests made plans to kill Lazarus as well, ¹¹for on account of him many of the Jews were going over to Jesus and putting their faith in him.

¹²The next day the great crowd that had come for the Feast heard that Jesus was on his way to Jerusalem. ¹³They took palm branches and went out to meet him, shouting,

"Hosanna!ᵍ"

"Blessed is he who comes in the name of the Lord!"ʰ

"Blessed is the King of Israel!"

¹⁴Jesus found a young donkey and sat upon it, as it is written,

¹⁵"Do not be afraid, O Daughter of Zion;
see, your king is coming,
seated on a donkey's colt."ⁱ

¹⁶At first his disciples did not understand all this. Only after Jesus was glorified did they realize that these things had been written about him and that they had done these things to him.

¹⁷Now the crowd that was with him when he called Lazarus from the tomb and raised him from the dead continued to spread the word. ¹⁸Many people, because they had heard that he had given this miraculous sign, went out to meet him. ¹⁹So the Pharisees said to one another, "See, this is getting us nowhere. Look how the whole world has gone after him!"

²⁰Now there were some Greeks among those who went up to worship at the Feast. ²¹They came to Philip, who was from Bethsaida in Galilee, with a request. "Sir," they said, "we would like to see Jesus." ²²Philip went to tell Andrew; Andrew and Philip in turn told Jesus.

²³Jesus replied, "The hour has come for the Son of Man to be glorified. ²⁴I tell you the truth, unless a kernel of wheat falls to the ground and dies, it remains only a single seed. But if it dies, it produces many seeds. ²⁵The man who loves his life will lose it, while the man who hates his life in this world will keep it for eternal life. ²⁶Whoever serves me must follow me; and where I am, my servant also will be. My Father will honor the one who serves me.

²⁷"Now my heart is troubled, and what shall I say? 'Father, save me from this hour'? No, it was

for this very reason I came to this hour. ²⁸Father, glorify your name!"

Then a voice came from heaven, "I have glorified it, and will glorify it again." ²⁹The crowd that was there and heard it said it had thundered; others said an angel had spoken to him.

³⁰Jesus said, "This voice was for your benefit, not mine. ³¹Now is the time for judgment on this world; now the prince of this world will be driven out. ³²But I, when I am lifted up from the earth, will draw all men to myself." ³³He said this to show the kind of death he was going to die.

³⁴The crowd spoke up, "We have heard from the Law that the Christ ʲ will remain forever, so how can you say, 'The Son of Man must be lifted up'? Who is this 'Son of Man'?"

³⁵Then Jesus told them, "You are going to have the light just a little while longer. Walk while you have the light, before darkness overtakes you. The man who walks in the dark does not know where he is going. ³⁶Put your trust in the light while you have it, so that you may become sons of light." When he had finished speaking, Jesus left and hid himself from them.

³⁷Even after Jesus had done all these miraculous signs in their presence, they still would not believe in him. ³⁸This was to fulfill the word of Isaiah the prophet:

"Lord, who has believed our message
and to whom has the arm of the Lord been
revealed?"ᵏ

³⁹For this reason they could not believe, because, as Isaiah says elsewhere:

⁴⁰"He has blinded their eyes
and deadened their hearts,
so they can neither see with their eyes,
nor understand with their hearts,
nor turn—and I would heal them."ˡ

⁴¹Isaiah said this because he saw Jesus' glory and spoke about him.

⁴²Yet at the same time many even among the leaders believed in him. But because of the Pharisees they would not confess their faith for fear they would be put out of the synagogue; ⁴³for they loved praise from men more than praise from God.

⁴⁴Then Jesus cried out, "When a man believes

ᵍ13 A Hebrew expression meaning "Save!" which became an exclamation of praise ʰ13 Psalm 118:25, 26 ⁱ15 Zech. 9:9 ʲ34 Or Messiah ᵏ38 Isaiah 53:1 ˡ40 Isaiah 6:10

in me, he does not believe in me only, but in the one who sent me. ⁴⁵When he looks at me, he sees the one who sent me. ⁴⁶I have come into the world as a light, so that no one who believes in me should stay in darkness.

⁴⁷"As for the person who hears my words but does not keep them, I do not judge him. For I did not come to judge the world, but to save it.

⁴⁸There is a judge for the one who rejects me and does not accept my words; that very word which I spoke will condemn him at the last day. ⁴⁹For I did not speak of my own accord, but the Father who sent me commanded me what to say and how to say it. ⁵⁰I know that his command leads to eternal life. So whatever I say is just what the Father has told me to say."

Discovering the Word 1. What motivates Mary to pour expensive perfume on Jesus' feet? 2. Judas objects to Mary's extravagance. What motives and wrong thinking lie behind his objection (vv. 4–8)? 3. What do the shouts of the crowd tell us about their expectations of Jesus (vv. 12–13)? 4. How do Christ's statements about his mission clash with the crowd's expectations (vv. 23–28)? 5. When we stubbornly refuse to believe, what happens to our spiritual senses, and why (vv. 37–41)? 6. Jesus' last public message to his people is recorded in verses 44–50. What indications do you find that he is still reaching out in love and grace to those who have rejected him?

Applying the Word 1. In what ways should we be extravagant in our devotion to Jesus? 2. How can you apply the example of Jesus to people who reject you or your testimony about Christ?

Responding in Prayer In your own life are you more interested in earthly acclaim and glory or are you willing to lose your life for Christ's sake? Examine your direction and life goals in the light of Jesus' commitment to do the will of the Father.

14 / *John 13:1–17*
The Son as a Slave

THERE WERE TWO things on Jesus' heart the night before his crucifixion—his Father and his disciples. In John 13—17, we have the privilege of listening to his conversations with them both. However, before Jesus can instruct his disciples about his death, he has to act out a lesson in servitude. Jesus also shows us the spirit he expects in those who follow him. Greatness in Christ's eyes does not come from having many servants but from being the servant of many.

Warming Up to God Have you ever been asked to do a demeaning, lowly job? What thoughts went through your mind at that time? Praise God for a Savior who was willing to take on the lowliest task of all.

Read John 13:1–17.

13 It was just before the Passover Feast. Jesus knew that the time had come for him to leave this world and go to the Father. Having loved his own who were in the world, he now showed them the full extent of his love.ᵐ

²The evening meal was being served, and the devil had already prompted Judas Iscariot, son of Simon, to betray Jesus. ³Jesus knew that the Father had put all things under his power, and that he had come from God and was returning to God; ⁴so he got up from the meal, took off his outer clothing, and wrapped a towel around his waist. ⁵After that, he poured water into a basin and began to wash his disciples' feet, drying them with the towel that was wrapped around him.

⁶He came to Simon Peter, who said to him, "Lord, are you going to wash my feet?"

⁷Jesus replied, "You do not realize now what I am doing, but later you will understand."

⁸"No," said Peter, "you shall never wash my feet."

ᵐ1 Or *he loved them to the last*

Jesus answered, "Unless I wash you, you have no part with me."

⁹"Then, Lord," Simon Peter replied, "not just my feet but my hands and my head as well!"

¹⁰Jesus answered, "A person who has had a bath needs only to wash his feet; his whole body is clean. And you are clean, though not every one of you." ¹¹For he knew who was going to betray him, and that was why he said not every one was clean.

¹²When he had finished washing their feet, he put on his clothes and returned to his place. "Do you understand what I have done for you?" he asked them. ¹³"You call me 'Teacher' and 'Lord,' and rightly so, for that is what I am. ¹⁴Now that I, your Lord and Teacher, have washed your feet, you also should wash one another's feet. ¹⁵I have set you an example that you should do as I have done for you. ¹⁶I tell you the truth, no servant is greater than his master, nor is a messenger greater than the one who sent him. ¹⁷Now that you know these things, you will be blessed if you do them.

Discovering the Word 1. According to John, what did Jesus know about himself (vv. 1–3)? In light of that knowledge, what is remarkable about what Jesus did next (vv. 4–5)? 2. Footwashing was normally done by servants or slaves. Why do you think that Jesus washed his disciples' feet instead of simply talking to them about love? 3. Was Peter simply being humble when he refused to allow Jesus to serve him (vv. 6–8)? Explain. 4. What spiritual truth was Jesus trying to communicate to Peter (and to us) in verses 8–11? 5. Based on Jesus' words in verse 17, how would you describe the relationship between knowledge, action and joy in the Christian life?

Applying the Word 1. What has this chapter revealed to you about your attitude toward serving? 2. In what specific ways can you model the humility of Jesus toward those with whom you live or work?

Responding in Prayer Ask God to give you a humble spirit.

---

15 / *John 13:18–38*
The Betrayer & the Boaster

THERE ARE SOME people we just don't like to be around! They aren't necessarily our enemies. They simply have the uncanny ability to irritate us. If we had been one of Jesus' disciples, we would probably have found it difficult to be around Peter. He was blunt and, at times, arrogant. On the other hand, we might have regarded Judas with trust and respect. The only one who saw deeply enough to discern the true character of these men was Jesus.

Warming Up to God Has someone in your life ever hurt you deeply? How have you responded to that hurt? Tell God how you feel about what happened. Allow him to speak to your pain.

Read John 13:18–38.

---

¹⁸"I am not referring to all of you; I know those I have chosen. But this is to fulfill the scripture: 'He who shares my bread has lifted up his heel against me.'ⁿ

¹⁹"I am telling you now before it happens, so that when it does happen you will believe that I am He. ²⁰I tell you the truth, whoever accepts anyone I send accepts me; and whoever accepts me accepts the one who sent me."

²¹After he had said this, Jesus was troubled in spirit and testified, "I tell you the truth, one of you is going to betray me."

²²His disciples stared at one another, at a loss to know which of them he meant. ²³One of them, the disciple whom Jesus loved, was reclining next to him. ²⁴Simon Peter motioned to this disciple and said, "Ask him which one he means."

²⁵Leaning back against Jesus, he asked him, "Lord, who is it?"

ⁿ18 Psalm 41:9

²⁶Jesus answered, "It is the one to whom I will give this piece of bread when I have dipped it in the dish." Then, dipping the piece of bread, he gave it to Judas Iscariot, son of Simon. ²⁷As soon as Judas took the bread, Satan entered into him.

"What you are about to do, do quickly," Jesus told him, ²⁸but no one at the meal understood why Jesus said this to him. ²⁹Since Judas had charge of the money, some thought Jesus was telling him to buy what was needed for the Feast, or to give something to the poor. ³⁰As soon as Judas had taken the bread, he went out. And it was night.

³¹When he was gone, Jesus said, "Now is the Son of Man glorified and God is glorified in him. ³²If God is glorified in him,ᵒ God will glorify the Son in himself, and will glorify him at once.

³³"My children, I will be with you only a little longer. You will look for me, and just as I told the Jews, so I tell you now: Where I am going, you cannot come.

³⁴"A new command I give you: Love one another. As I have loved you, so you must love one another. ³⁵By this all men will know that you are my disciples, if you love one another."

³⁶Simon Peter asked him, "Lord, where are you going?"

Jesus replied, "Where I am going, you cannot follow now, but you will follow later."

³⁷Peter asked, "Lord, why can't I follow you now? I will lay down my life for you."

³⁸Then Jesus answered, "Will you really lay down your life for me? I tell you the truth, before the rooster crows, you will disown me three times!

ᵒ32 Many early manuscripts do not have *If God is glorified in him.*

 Discovering the Word 1. Jesus takes this opportunity to predict his betrayal. How would his prediction dispel any doubts the disciples might have and strengthen their faith (v. 19)? 2. Evidently, the disciples did not know who would betray Jesus (v. 22). What does this tell us about how Jesus had treated Judas? 3. Why does the kind of love Jesus describes convince all of humanity that we are Jesus' disciples (v. 35)? 4. Do you think Peter's declaration in verse 37 comes from pride or from sincerity? Explain. 5. Three people stand out in this passage—Jesus, Judas and Peter. What one character quality of each—good or evil—impresses you the most?

 Applying the Word 1. How would you have treated Judas if you knew he would eventually betray you? 2. John later wrote: "This is how we know what love is: Jesus Christ laid down his life for us. And we ought to lay down our lives for our brothers" (1 Jn 3:16). In what practical ways can you exhibit this sacrificial love?

 Responding in Prayer Pray for a strong faith that won't lead you into betrayal when times are tough.

---

16 / *John 14*
Comfort for a Troubled Heart

THE CALL CAME late at night. A broken sob was followed by these words: "Our son is dying. Will you please come to the hospital?" As I made the trip through darkened streets, I wondered what I could say to bring comfort to these heartbroken parents. Jesus faced that challenge too. In this chapter he comforts eleven disciples who feel like their world is coming unglued.

Warming Up to God What is troubling you? Give it to God, and wait before him to receive his comfort.

Read John 14.

14

"Do not let your hearts be troubled. Trust in God*p*; trust also in me. ²In my Father's house are many rooms; if it were not so, I would have told you. I am going there to prepare a place for you. ³And if I go and prepare a place for you, I will come back and take you to be with me that you also may be where I am. ⁴You know the way to the place where I am going."

⁵Thomas said to him, "Lord, we don't know where you are going, so how can we know the way?"

⁶Jesus answered, "I am the way and the truth and the life. No one comes to the Father except through me. ⁷If you really knew me, you would know*q* my Father as well. From now on, you do know him and have seen him."

⁸Philip said, "Lord, show us the Father and that will be enough for us."

⁹Jesus answered: "Don't you know me, Philip, even after I have been among you such a long time? Anyone who has seen me has seen the Father. How can you say, 'Show us the Father'? ¹⁰Don't you believe that I am in the Father, and that the Father is in me? The words I say to you are not just my own. Rather, it is the Father, living in me, who is doing his work. ¹¹Believe me when I say that I am in the Father and the Father is in me; or at least believe on the evidence of the miracles themselves. ¹²I tell you the truth, anyone who has faith in me will do what I have been doing. He will do even greater things than these, because I am going to the Father. ¹³And I will do whatever you ask in my name, so that the Son may bring glory to the Father. ¹⁴You may ask me for anything in my name, and I will do it.

¹⁵"If you love me, you will obey what I command. ¹⁶And I will ask the Father, and he will give you another Counselor to be with you forever— ¹⁷the Spirit of truth. The world cannot accept him, because it neither sees him nor knows him. But you know him, for he lives with you and will be*r* in you. ¹⁸I will not leave you as orphans; I will come to you. ¹⁹Before long, the world will not see me anymore, but you will see me. Because I live, you also will live. ²⁰On that day you will realize that I am in my Father, and you are in me, and I am in you. ²¹Whoever has my commands and obeys them, he is the one who loves me. He who loves me will be loved by my Father, and I too will love him and show myself to him."

²²Then Judas (not Judas Iscariot) said, "But, Lord, why do you intend to show yourself to us and not to the world?"

²³Jesus replied, "If anyone loves me, he will obey my teaching. My Father will love him, and we will come to him and make our home with him. ²⁴He who does not love me will not obey my teaching. These words you hear are not my own; they belong to the Father who sent me.

²⁵"All this I have spoken while still with you. ²⁶But the Counselor, the Holy Spirit, whom the Father will send in my name, will teach you all things and will remind you of everything I have said to you. ²⁷Peace I leave with you; my peace I give you. I do not give to you as the world gives. Do not let your hearts be troubled and do not be afraid.

²⁸"You heard me say, 'I am going away and I am coming back to you.' If you loved me, you would be glad that I am going to the Father, for the Father is greater than I. ²⁹I have told you now before it happens, so that when it does happen you will believe. ³⁰I will not speak with you much longer, for the prince of this world is coming. He has no hold on me, ³¹but the world must learn that I love the Father and that I do exactly what my Father has commanded me.

"Come now; let us leave."

p1 Or You trust in God   q7 Some early manuscripts If you really have known me, you will know   r17 Some early manuscripts and is

---

Discovering the Word 1. How would the promises Jesus makes in verses 1–4 bring comfort to his disciples? 2. In light of verses 5–14, why is it crucial for our focus to be on Jesus himself? 3. According to Jesus, how will the Spirit bring comfort and help to his followers (vv. 15–27)? 4. What is the relationship between our love and obedience to Jesus and his love and presence in our lives (vv. 15–24)? 5. How does the peace Christ offers differ from that which the world offers (vv. 25–31)?

Applying the Word 1. Think of a friend who is going through a personal crisis. How could this chapter help you to minister to that person? 2. How can Jesus' words help you in a personal crisis or when you have a troubled heart?

Responding in Prayer Ask God to comfort someone you know who is troubled.

17 / *John 15:1–17*
The Secret of Remaining

THE FINAL WEEKEND before Christmas is not the time to visit a shopping mall. If you are fortunate enough to find a parking spot, the press of people inside makes shopping almost impossible. I overheard one mother giving these final instructions to her young son before plunging into the crowd: "Stay close to me and hold my hand all the time. We won't get separated if we hold on to each other."

As Jesus prepared his disciples to face life without his visible presence, he impressed on them the importance of staying close to him spiritually. He said, "Remain in me." If you've ever longed to understand the secret of spiritual growth, you will find it in Jesus' words to us in John 15.

 Warming Up to God Have you ever felt far from Christ since becoming a Christian? What circumstances made you feel that way? Be still before God and feel his presence with you now.

 Read John 15:1–17.

15 "I am the true vine, and my Father is the gardener. ²He cuts off every branch in me that bears no fruit, while every branch that does bear fruit he prunes⁵ so that it will be even more fruitful. ³You are already clean because of the word I have spoken to you. ⁴Remain in me, and I will remain in you. No branch can bear fruit by itself; it must remain in the vine. Neither can you bear fruit unless you remain in me.

⁵"I am the vine; you are the branches. If a man remains in me and I in him, he will bear much fruit; apart from me you can do nothing. ⁶If anyone does not remain in me, he is like a branch that is thrown away and withers; such branches are picked up, thrown into the fire and burned. ⁷If you remain in me and my words remain in you, ask whatever you wish, and it will be given you. ⁸This is to my Father's glory, that you bear much fruit, showing yourselves to be my disciples.

⁹"As the Father has loved me, so have I loved you. Now remain in my love. ¹⁰If you obey my commands, you will remain in my love, just as I have obeyed my Father's commands and remain in his love. ¹¹I have told you this so that my joy may be in you and that your joy may be complete. ¹²My command is this: Love each other as I have loved you. ¹³Greater love has no one than this, that he lay down his life for his friends. ¹⁴You are my friends if you do what I command. ¹⁵I no longer call you servants, because a servant does not know his master's business. Instead, I have called you friends, for everything that I learned from my Father I have made known to you. ¹⁶You did not choose me, but I chose you and appointed you to go and bear fruit—fruit that will last. Then the Father will give you whatever you ask in my name. ¹⁷This is my command: Love each other.

⁵2 The Greek for *prunes* also means *cleans.*

Discovering the Word 1. Jesus' instructions to his disciples in this passage revolve around three symbols—the vine, the gardener and the branches. What is Jesus trying to communicate by calling himself the *true vine*? 2. What does it mean to remain in Christ (v. 4)? 3. The Father prunes fruitful branches to make them more fruitful (v. 2). In what ways have you experienced the Father's "pruning"? 4. What spiritual benefits result from remaining in Christ (vv. 7–11)? 5. What are the requirements and benefits of friendship with Christ (vv. 14–17)?

Applying the Word 1. There are three categories of branches described in this passage—those bearing no fruit, those bearing some fruit, and those bearing much fruit. In which category would you place yourself and why? 2. If you are not bearing much fruit, what is Jesus' counsel to you in these verses?

Responding in Prayer Picture yourself as a tree laden with plump, healthy fruit. Ask God to help you become the person he wants you to be.

---

18 / *John 15:18—16:4*
The Cost of Friendship with Jesus

WHILE ON EARTH, Jesus did not surround himself with a group of students or even a group of followers. He placed himself in the company of friends. To admit that we need friends is a sign of maturity, not immaturity. Close relationships are Christlike! In this passage Jesus shows us what friendship with him is really like. There's both comfort and cost.

 Warming Up to God Are you ready to face the cost of following Christ? Talk openly with God about your fears—and excitement.

 Read John 15:18—16:4.

---

¹⁸"If the world hates you, keep in mind that it hated me first. ¹⁹If you belonged to the world, it would love you as its own. As it is, you do not belong to the world, but I have chosen you out of the world. That is why the world hates you. ²⁰Remember the words I spoke to you: 'No servant is greater than his master.'[t] If they persecuted me, they will persecute you also. If they obeyed my teaching, they will obey yours also. ²¹They will treat you this way because of my name, for they do not know the One who sent me. ²²If I had not come and spoken to them, they would not be guilty of sin. Now, however, they have no excuse for their sin. ²³He who hates me hates my Father as well. ²⁴If I had not done among them what no one else did, they would not be guilty of sin. But now they have seen these miracles, and yet they have hated both me and my Father. ²⁵But this is to fulfill what is written in their Law: 'They hated me without reason.'[u]

²⁶"When the Counselor comes, whom I will send to you from the Father, the Spirit of truth who goes out from the Father, he will testify about me. ²⁷And you also must testify, for you have been with me from the beginning.

16 "All this I have told you so that you will not go astray. ²They will put you out of the synagogue; in fact, a time is coming when anyone who kills you will think he is offering a service to God. ³They will do such things because they have not known the Father or me. ⁴I have told you this, so that when the time comes you will remember that I warned you. I did not tell you this at first because I was with you.

t20 John 13:16   u25 Psalms 35:19; 69:4

 Discovering the Word 1. If love is to characterize our relationship with other believers, hate will characterize our relationships with the world. What reasons does Jesus give for the world's hatred? 2. What does Jesus mean when he says that without his coming, his words and his miracles, the world "would not be guilty of sin" (15:22–25)? 3. In what specific ways will the Counselor and the disciples themselves continue the ministry begun by Jesus (15:26–27)? 4. What kind of treatment can the disciples expect from those who do not know Christ (16:1–4)?

Applying the Word 1. What kinds of persecution are more probable for us in our society? Explain. 2. If we as Christians are not persecuted in some way, what might that imply about our spiritual commitment? 3. How are you experiencing the world's hatred as a Christian?

Responding in Prayer Pray for those around the world who face persecution for their faith.

19 / *John 16:5–33*
Secrets of the Spirit

A LOVELY WOMAN in our church died not long ago. She knew for almost a year that, unless the Lord intervened, the cancer in her brain would kill her. That year gave her time of wonderful interaction with her husband and family. Her family had the opportunity to express their love for her, and the dying woman had the privilege of passing on her godly wisdom.

In John 16 Jesus knows that he will die in less than twenty-four hours. When his disciples are faced with that reality, Jesus responds to their concerns by talking about the coming Holy Spirit.

 Warming Up to God Think about the people in your life who are important to you. What would you want to tell them if you knew that you had only a short time to live? Ask God to make you ready to hear what Jesus had to say in his last days.

 Read John 16:5–33.

---

⁵"Now I am going to him who sent me, yet none of you asks me, 'Where are you going?' ⁶Because I have said these things, you are filled with grief. ⁷But I tell you the truth: It is for your good that I am going away. Unless I go away, the Counselor will not come to you; but if I go, I will send him to you. ⁸When he comes, he will convict the world of guilt[v] in regard to sin and righteousness and judgment: ⁹in regard to sin, because men do not believe in me; ¹⁰in regard to righteousness, because I am going to the Father, where you can see me no longer; ¹¹and in regard to judgment, because the prince of this world now stands condemned.

¹²"I have much more to say to you, more than you can now bear. ¹³But when he, the Spirit of truth, comes, he will guide you into all truth. He will not speak on his own; he will speak only what he hears, and he will tell you what is yet to come. ¹⁴He will bring glory to me by taking from what is mine and making it known to you. ¹⁵All that belongs to the Father is mine. That is why I said the Spirit will take from what is mine and make it known to you.

¹⁶"In a little while you will see me no more, and then after a little while you will see me."

¹⁷Some of his disciples said to one another, "What does he mean by saying, 'In a little while you will see me no more, and then after a little while you will see me,' and 'Because I am going to the Father'?" ¹⁸They kept asking, "What does he mean by 'a little while'? We don't understand what he is saying."

¹⁹Jesus saw that they wanted to ask him about this, so he said to them, "Are you asking one another what I meant when I said, 'In a little while you will see me no more, and then after a little while you will see me'? ²⁰I tell you the truth, you will weep and mourn while the world rejoices. You will grieve, but your grief will turn to joy. ²¹A woman giving birth to a child has pain because her time has come; but when her baby is born she forgets the anguish because of her joy that a child is born into the world. ²²So with you: Now is your time of grief, but I will see you again and you will rejoice, and no one will take away your joy. ²³In that day you will no longer ask me anything. I tell you the truth, my Father will give you whatever you ask in my name. ²⁴Until now you have not asked for anything in my name. Ask and you will receive, and your joy will be complete.

²⁵"Though I have been speaking figuratively, a time is coming when I will no longer use this kind of language but will tell you plainly about my Father. ²⁶In that day you will ask in my name. I am not saying that I will ask the Father on your behalf. ²⁷No, the Father himself loves you because you have loved me and have believed that I came from God. ²⁸I came from the Father and entered the world; now I am leaving the world and going back to the Father."

²⁹Then Jesus' disciples said, "Now you are speaking clearly and without figures of speech. ³⁰Now we can see that you know all things and that you do not even need to have anyone ask you questions. This makes us believe that you came from God."

³¹"You believe at last!"[w] Jesus answered.

[v]8 Or *will expose the guilt of the world*   [w]31 Or *"Do you now believe?"*

32"But a time is coming, and has come, when you will be scattered, each to his own home. You will leave me all alone. Yet I am not alone, for my Father is with me.

33"I have told you these things, so that in me you may have peace. In this world you will have trouble. But take heart! I have overcome the world."

Discovering the Word 1. Jesus said that it was for the disciples' good that he go away and that the Counselor come. Why was the Spirit's presence more profitable to the disciples than Jesus' presence? 2. What did Jesus say the Spirit's ministry would be toward the world (vv. 8–11)? 3. The Spirit's ministry is one of communication. What specific things did Jesus say the Spirit would communicate to the disciples (vv. 13–15)? 4. Jesus answers the questions the disciples ask in verses 17–18, not by giving them an explanation but by making them a promise (vv. 19–22). What was the promise? 5. Why would Jesus' promise bring them joy in the midst of their grief and confusion? 6. How would Jesus' assurance of the Father's love help the disciples in the days just ahead of them (vv. 25–33)?

Applying the Word 1. How can this incident help us when our questions to the Lord seemingly go unanswered? 2. How do you respond to the promise in verses 23–24?

Responding in Prayer Give God the desires of your heart, knowing that he wants to make your joy complete.

---

20 / *John 17*
The Master's Final Prayer

THE APPROACH OF death has a way of bringing our priorities into focus. People who know death is imminent also know what is really important in life and who they really care about. In Jesus' final prayer with his disciples, he prays for himself, for them and for you! Every believer is on Jesus' mind as he faces the greatest trial of his life—the cross.

Warming Up to God Spend some time reflecting on God's glory. To what extent is God's glory foremost in your mind on a daily basis? Explain.

Read John 17.

17 After Jesus said this, he looked toward heaven and prayed:

"Father, the time has come. Glorify your Son, that your Son may glorify you. 2For you granted him authority over all people that he might give eternal life to all those you have given him. 3Now this is eternal life: that they may know you, the only true God, and Jesus Christ, whom you have sent. 4I have brought you glory on earth by completing the work you gave me to do. 5And now, Father, glorify me in your presence with the glory I had with you before the world began.

6"I have revealed youˣ to those whom you gave me out of the world. They were yours; you gave them to me and they have obeyed your word. 7Now they know that ev-

erything you have given me comes from you. 8For I gave them the words you gave me and they accepted them. They knew with certainty that I came from you, and they believed that you sent me. 9I pray for them. I am not praying for the world, but for those you have given me, for they are yours. 10All I have is yours, and all you have is mine. And glory has come to me through them. 11I will remain in the world no longer, but they are still in the world, and I am coming to you. Holy Father, protect them by the power of your name—the name you gave me—so that they may be one as we are one. 12While I was with them, I protected them and kept them safe by that name you gave me. None

ˣ6 Greek *your name*; also in verse 26

has been lost except the one doomed to destruction so that Scripture would be fulfilled.

¹³"I am coming to you now, but I say these things while I am still in the world, so that they may have the full measure of my joy within them. ¹⁴I have given them your word and the world has hated them, for they are not of the world any more than I am of the world. ¹⁵My prayer is not that you take them out of the world but that you protect them from the evil one. ¹⁶They are not of the world, even as I am not of it. ¹⁷Sanctifyʸ them by the truth; your word is truth. ¹⁸As you sent me into the world, I have sent them into the world. ¹⁹For them I sanctify myself, that they too may be truly sanctified.

²⁰"My prayer is not for them alone. I pray also for those who will believe in me through their message, ²¹that all of them may be one, Father, just as you are in me and I am in you. May they also be in us so that the world may believe that you have sent me. ²²I have given them the glory that you gave me, that they may be one as we are one: ²³I in them and you in me. May they be brought to complete unity to let the world know that you sent me and have loved them even as you have loved me.

²⁴"Father, I want those you have given me to be with me where I am, and to see my glory, the glory you have given me because you loved me before the creation of the world.

²⁵"Righteous Father, though the world does not know you, I know you, and they know that you have sent me. ²⁶I have made you known to them, and will continue to make you known in order that the love you have for me may be in them and that I myself may be in them."

ʸ17 Greek *hagiazo* (*set apart for sacred use* or *make holy*); also in verse 19

 Discovering the Word 1. Jesus makes only one request for himself—that the Father would glorify him so that he might glorify the Father. In what way would each one glorify the other (vv. 1–5)? Why do you think that was so important to Jesus? 2. According to verses 6–19, what specific ministries did Jesus have toward his disciples? 3. Twice Jesus asked the Father to protect his disciples from the evil one (vv. 11, 15). Why would that protection have been so important in Jesus' mind as he faced the cross? 4. Jesus prayed that those who believe in him would be one "so that the world may believe that you have sent me" (vv. 21, 23)? Why is our unity a powerful argument for the reality of Jesus?

Applying the Word 1. Jesus also asked the Father to sanctify his disciples through his word (v. 17). How can we allow God's Word to have that kind of effect on our lives? 2. Jesus obviously prayed this prayer out loud to bring comfort and assurance to his disciples. In what particular ways do Jesus' words encourage or assure you?

Responding in Prayer Ask God to bring unity to your church or fellowship.

---

21 / *John 18:1–27*
"Jesus, You're Under Arrest!"

MOST OF US would hate the thought of being arrested and brought to trial. If we were guilty of a crime, being arrested would be humiliating. But if we were innocent, it would be devastating. Yet in what should have been a demeaning experience for Jesus, we see again his majesty and glory. Jesus uses an experience of attack, betrayal and abandonment to demonstrate his confident trust in the Father. His calm assurance will help us face life's hurts and injustices with the same trust in the same Father.

 Warming Up to God Think about a time when you realized you had committed a deep sin. How did you feel when you took it before Christ? Thank him for his grace to you then and now.

Read John 18:1–27.

18 When he had finished praying, Jesus left with his disciples and crossed the Kidron Valley. On the other side there was an olive grove, and he and his disciples went into it.

²Now Judas, who betrayed him, knew the place, because Jesus had often met there with his disciples. ³So Judas came to the grove, guiding a detachment of soldiers and some officials from the chief priests and Pharisees. They were carrying torches, lanterns and weapons.

⁴Jesus, knowing all that was going to happen to him, went out and asked them, "Who is it you want?"

⁵"Jesus of Nazareth," they replied.

"I am he," Jesus said. (And Judas the traitor was standing there with them.) ⁶When Jesus said, "I am he," they drew back and fell to the ground.

⁷Again he asked them, "Who is it you want?"

And they said, "Jesus of Nazareth."

⁸"I told you that I am he," Jesus answered. "If you are looking for me, then let these men go." ⁹This happened so that the words he had spoken would be fulfilled: "I have not lost one of those you gave me."ᶻ

¹⁰Then Simon Peter, who had a sword, drew it and struck the high priest's servant, cutting off his right ear. (The servant's name was Malchus.) ¹¹Jesus commanded Peter, "Put your sword away! Shall I not drink the cup the Father has given me?"

¹²Then the detachment of soldiers with its commander and the Jewish officials arrested Jesus. They bound him ¹³and brought him first to Annas, who was the father-in-law of Caiaphas, the high priest that year. ¹⁴Caiaphas was the one who had advised the Jews that it would be good if one man died for the people.

¹⁵Simon Peter and another disciple were fol-lowing Jesus. Because this disciple was known to the high priest, he went with Jesus into the high priest's courtyard, ¹⁶but Peter had to wait outside at the door. The other disciple, who was known to the high priest, came back, spoke to the girl on duty there and brought Peter in.

¹⁷"You are not one of his disciples, are you?" the girl at the door asked Peter.

He replied, "I am not."

¹⁸It was cold, and the servants and officials stood around a fire they had made to keep warm. Peter also was standing with them, warming him-self.

¹⁹Meanwhile, the high priest questioned Jesus about his disciples and his teaching.

²⁰"I have spoken openly to the world," Jesus replied. "I always taught in synagogues or at the temple, where all the Jews come together. I said nothing in secret. ²¹Why question me? Ask those who heard me. Surely they know what I said."

²²When Jesus said this, one of the officials nearby struck him in the face. "Is this the way you answer the high priest?" he demanded.

²³"If I said something wrong," Jesus replied, "testify as to what is wrong. But if I spoke the truth, why did you strike me?" ²⁴Then Annas sent him, still bound, to Caiaphas the high priest.ᵃ

²⁵As Simon Peter stood warming himself, he was asked, "You are not one of his disciples, are you?"

He denied it, saying, "I am not."

²⁶One of the high priest's servants, a relative of the man whose ear Peter had cut off, challenged him, "Didn't I see you with him in the olive grove?" ²⁷Again Peter denied it, and at that moment a rooster began to crow.

ᶻ9 John 6:39   ᵃ24 Or (Now Annas had sent him, still bound, to Caiaphas the high priest.)

 Discovering the Word 1. Why would Jesus go to a place where Judas knew he might be found (vv. 1–3)? 2. When the soldiers say they are seeking Jesus of Nazareth, Jesus replies, "I am he" (literally, "I am"; v. 5). How would you explain the reaction of the soldiers (v. 6)? 3. What insight do Peter's action and Jesus' rebuke (v. 11) give you about our attempts at times to "help God out" in our own strength and wisdom? 4. Think back to the deepest sin of your life. How does a look at your own sin change your attitude toward Peter's denial of Jesus? 5. What specific events in this passage display (a) Jesus' courage, (b) his power and (c) his obedience to the Father?

Applying the Word 1. What can we learn from Peter's failure about being ready to stand against the world's challenges? 2. How will this study change the way you will face a time of testing in your own life?

Responding in Prayer Ask God to make you ready to face difficulties with grace.

22 / *John 18:28—19:16*
Pilate on Trial

"CHRIST KILLERS!" THE words made my stomach tighten. Someone had spray-painted the words and a series of swastikas on the Jewish synagogue in our city. Anti-Semitism had raised its ugly head again.

The New Testament does blame the Jewish leaders for condemning Jesus to die. But they weren't acting alone. The Roman governor, Pontius Pilate, also condemned Jesus to die. There is a sense, too, in which we killed Jesus. He died for *our* sins. The most amazing answer to the question of who killed Jesus is that no one did! Jesus said, "No one takes my life from me. I lay it down of my own choice."

 Warming Up to God What temptation to compromise your Christian faith or witness are you facing? Ask the One who has faced deep trials to give you strength.

 Read John 18:28—19:16.

²⁸Then the Jews led Jesus from Caiaphas to the palace of the Roman governor. By now it was early morning, and to avoid ceremonial uncleanness the Jews did not enter the palace; they wanted to be able to eat the Passover. ²⁹So Pilate came out to them and asked, "What charges are you bringing against this man?"

³⁰"If he were not a criminal," they replied, "we would not have handed him over to you."

³¹Pilate said, "Take him yourselves and judge him by your own law."

"But we have no right to execute anyone," the Jews objected. ³²This happened so that the words Jesus had spoken indicating the kind of death he was going to die would be fulfilled.

³³Pilate then went back inside the palace, summoned Jesus and asked, "Are you the king of the Jews?"

³⁴"Is that your own idea," Jesus asked, "or did others talk to you about me?"

³⁵"Am I a Jew?" Pilate replied. "It was your people and your chief priests who handed you over to me. What is it you have done?"

³⁶Jesus said, "My kingdom is not of this world. If it were, my servants would fight to prevent my arrest by the Jews. But now my kingdom is from another place."

³⁷"You are a king, then!" said Pilate.

Jesus answered, "You are right in saying I am a king. In fact, for this reason I was born, and for this I came into the world, to testify to the truth. Everyone on the side of truth listens to me."

³⁸"What is truth?" Pilate asked. With this he went out again to the Jews and said, "I find no basis for a charge against him. ³⁹But it is your custom for me to release to you one prisoner at the time of the Passover. Do you want me to release 'the king of the Jews'?"

⁴⁰They shouted back, "No, not him! Give us Barabbas!" Now Barabbas had taken part in a rebellion.

19 Then Pilate took Jesus and had him flogged. ²The soldiers twisted together a crown of thorns and put it on his head. They clothed him in a purple robe ³and went up to him again and again, saying, "Hail, king of the Jews!" And they struck him in the face.

⁴Once more Pilate came out and said to the Jews, "Look, I am bringing him out to you to let you know that I find no basis for a charge against him." ⁵When Jesus came out wearing the crown of thorns and the purple robe, Pilate said to them, "Here is the man!"

⁶As soon as the chief priests and their officials saw him, they shouted, "Crucify! Crucify!"

But Pilate answered, "You take him and crucify him. As for me, I find no basis for a charge against him."

⁷The Jews insisted, "We have a law, and according to that law he must die, because he claimed to be the Son of God."

⁸When Pilate heard this, he was even more afraid, ⁹and he went back inside the palace.

"Where do you come from?" he asked Jesus, but Jesus gave him no answer. ¹⁰"Do you refuse to speak to me?" Pilate said. "Don't you realize I have power either to free you or to crucify you?"

¹¹Jesus answered, "You would have no power over me if it were not given to you from above. Therefore the one who handed me over to you is guilty of a greater sin."

¹²From then on, Pilate tried to set Jesus free, but the Jews kept shouting, "If you let this man go, you are no friend of Caesar. Anyone who claims to be a king opposes Caesar."

¹³When Pilate heard this, he brought Jesus out and sat down on the judge's seat at a place known as the Stone Pavement (which in Aramaic is Gabbatha). ¹⁴It was the day of Preparation of Passover Week, about the sixth hour.

"Here is your king," Pilate said to the Jews.

¹⁵But they shouted, "Take him away! Take him away! Crucify him!"

"Shall I crucify your king?" Pilate asked.

"We have no king but Caesar," the chief priests answered.

¹⁶Finally Pilate handed him over to them to be crucified.

 Discovering the Word 1. A Roman trial included four basic elements: the accusation (18:29–31), the interrogation (search for evidence) (18:32–35), the defense (18:36–37) and the verdict (18:38). What events or statements from the text are included in each? 2. Pilate obviously was trying to release Jesus. What specific attempts did he make (18:39; 19:4, 6, 10, 12, 15)? 3. The Jews' true charge against Jesus comes out in verse 7—"He claimed to be the Son of God." Why do you think Pilate reacted to that statement as he did (vv. 8–9)? 4. Why didn't Jesus say more to Pilate (vv. 9–11)? Shouldn't he have defended himself more vigorously? 5. What can you conclude about Pilate's character after reading this passage? What kind of man was he?

 Applying the Word 1. How can you respond appropriately to Christ's grace to you? 2. What does this passage tell you about how you should respond when you are treated unjustly?

 Responding in Prayer Ask God to help you follow his example of grace when you are under pressure.

---

23 / John 19:17–42
Obedient to Death

THERE IS NOTHING pleasant or attractive about an execution. The only one I've ever seen was in a televised news report from Vietnam. A captured soldier was shot. It left a knot in my stomach for days.

In Jesus' day execution was designed to be public and painful. The account of the crucifixion is not easy to read. You may be tempted to think that Jesus' death was a cruel mistake. It wasn't. Jesus' life was not taken from him; he laid it down willingly. It was part of his plan—a plan that included you and me. His cross was in a very real sense our cross.

 Warming Up to God When you think about death, what feelings and thoughts come to mind?

Read John 19:17–42.

So the soldiers took charge of Jesus. ¹⁷Carrying his own cross, he went out to the place of the Skull (which in Aramaic is called Golgotha). ¹⁸Here they crucified him, and with him two others—one on each side and Jesus in the middle.

¹⁹Pilate had a notice prepared and fastened to the cross. It read: JESUS OF NAZARETH, THE KING OF THE JEWS. ²⁰Many of the Jews read this sign, for the place where Jesus was crucified was near the city, and the sign was written in Aramaic, Latin and Greek. ²¹The chief priests of the Jews protested to Pilate, "Do not write 'The King of the Jews,' but that this man claimed to be king of the Jews."

²²Pilate answered, "What I have written, I have written."

²³When the soldiers crucified Jesus, they took his clothes, dividing them into four shares, one for each of them, with the undergarment remaining. This garment was seamless, woven in one piece from top to bottom.

²⁴"Let's not tear it," they said to one another. "Let's decide by lot who will get it."

This happened that the scripture might be fulfilled which said,

> "They divided my garments among them
>   and cast lots for my clothing."[b]

So this is what the soldiers did.

²⁵Near the cross of Jesus stood his mother, his mother's sister, Mary the wife of Clopas, and Mary Magdalene. ²⁶When Jesus saw his mother there, and the disciple whom he loved standing nearby, he said to his mother, "Dear woman, here is your son," ²⁷and to the disciple, "Here is your mother." From that time on, this disciple took her into his home.

²⁸Later, knowing that all was now completed, and so that the Scripture would be fulfilled, Jesus said, "I am thirsty." ²⁹A jar of wine vinegar was there, so they soaked a sponge in it, put the sponge on a stalk of the hyssop plant, and lifted it to Jesus' lips. ³⁰When he had received the drink, Jesus said, "It is finished." With that, he bowed his head and gave up his spirit.

³¹Now it was the day of Preparation, and the next day was to be a special Sabbath. Because the Jews did not want the bodies left on the crosses during the Sabbath, they asked Pilate to have the legs broken and the bodies taken down. ³²The soldiers therefore came and broke the legs of the first man who had been crucified with Jesus, and then those of the other. ³³But when they came to Jesus and found that he was already dead, they did not break his legs. ³⁴Instead, one of the soldiers pierced Jesus' side with a spear, bringing a sudden flow of blood and water. ³⁵The man who saw it has given testimony, and his testimony is true. He knows that he tells the truth, and he testifies so that you also may believe. ³⁶These things happened so that the scripture would be fulfilled: "Not one of his bones will be broken,"[c] ³⁷and, as another scripture says, "They will look on the one they have pierced."[d]

³⁸Later, Joseph of Arimathea asked Pilate for the body of Jesus. Now Joseph was a disciple of Jesus, but secretly because he feared the Jews. With Pilate's permission, he came and took the body away. ³⁹He was accompanied by Nicodemus, the man who earlier had visited Jesus at night. Nicodemus brought a mixture of myrrh and aloes, about seventy-five pounds.[e] ⁴⁰Taking Jesus' body, the two of them wrapped it, with the spices, in strips of linen. This was in accordance with Jewish burial customs. ⁴¹At the place where Jesus was crucified, there was a garden, and in the garden a new tomb, in which no one had ever been laid. ⁴²Because it was the Jewish day of Preparation and since the tomb was nearby, they laid Jesus there.

b24 Psalm 22:18   c36 Exodus 12:46; Num. 9:12; Psalm 34:20
d37 Zech. 12:10   e39 Greek *a hundred litrai* (about 34 kilograms)

Discovering the Word 1. Three groups were involved in Jesus' death—the soldiers, the Jewish leaders and Pilate. How would you characterize each one's attitude toward Jesus? In what ways do their attitudes toward Jesus parallel those of men and women today? 2. How is Jesus' tender care for Mary evident even while he is dying (vv. 26–27)? 3. What was the significance of Jesus' cry "It is finished" (v. 30; see Jn 17:4)? 4. What evidence does John give that Jesus really died? 5. Why was it so important for John to establish the certainty of Jesus' death?

Applying the Word 1. The disciples are not mentioned at the crucifixion; they were probably not there. When it comes to public identification with Jesus, under what circumstances are you tempted to respond in the same way? 2. What aspect of Jesus' death has made the deepest impression on you, and why?

Responding in Prayer Thank God for providing salvation to you through Christ's death.

24 / *John 20*
The Son Is Up!

THE STORY CIRCULATED for days in the hospital where my brother worked. An orderly was told to take a body to the morgue. Simply out of habit, the orderly felt the man's wrist for a pulse. When he realized his mistake, the orderly quickly dropped the arm, but not before his sensitive fingers told him something his mind struggled to believe. There was a pulse! The doctors were called, and the man revived.

That story may or may not be true. But I know of one account of a man coming back to life that is true. The man lived for years after the event. In fact, he is still alive.

 Warming Up to God Imagine being with Joseph of Arimathea and Nicodemus preparing Jesus' body for burial. What thoughts and feelings would have gone through your mind?

 Read John 20.

20 Early on the first day of the week, while it was still dark, Mary Magdalene went to the tomb and saw that the stone had been removed from the entrance. ²So she came running to Simon Peter and the other disciple, the one Jesus loved, and said, "They have taken the Lord out of the tomb, and we don't know where they have put him!"

³So Peter and the other disciple started for the tomb. ⁴Both were running, but the other disciple outran Peter and reached the tomb first. ⁵He bent over and looked in at the strips of linen lying there but did not go in. ⁶Then Simon Peter, who was behind him, arrived and went into the tomb. He saw the strips of linen lying there, ⁷as well as the burial cloth that had been around Jesus' head. The cloth was folded up by itself, separate from the linen. ⁸Finally the other disciple, who had reached the tomb first, also went inside. He saw and believed. ⁹(They still did not understand from Scripture that Jesus had to rise from the dead.)

¹⁰Then the disciples went back to their homes, ¹¹but Mary stood outside the tomb crying. As she wept, she bent over to look into the tomb ¹²and saw two angels in white, seated where Jesus' body had been, one at the head and the other at the foot.

¹³They asked her, "Woman, why are you crying?"

"They have taken my Lord away," she said, "and I don't know where they have put him." ¹⁴At this, she turned around and saw Jesus standing there, but she did not realize that it was Jesus.

¹⁵"Woman," he said, "why are you crying? Who is it you are looking for?"

Thinking he was the gardener, she said, "Sir, if you have carried him away, tell me where you have put him, and I will get him."

¹⁶Jesus said to her, "Mary."

She turned toward him and cried out in Aramaic, "Rabboni!" (which means Teacher).

¹⁷Jesus said, "Do not hold on to me, for I have not yet returned to the Father. Go instead to my brothers and tell them, 'I am returning to my Father and your Father, to my God and your God.' "

¹⁸Mary Magdalene went to the disciples with the news: "I have seen the Lord!" And she told them that he had said these things to her.

¹⁹On the evening of that first day of the week, when the disciples were together, with the doors locked for fear of the Jews, Jesus came and stood among them and said, "Peace be with you!" ²⁰After he said this, he showed them his hands and side. The disciples were overjoyed when they saw the Lord.

²¹Again Jesus said, "Peace be with you! As the Father has sent me, I am sending you." ²²And with that he breathed on them and said, "Receive the Holy Spirit. ²³If you forgive anyone his sins, they are forgiven; if you do not forgive them, they are not forgiven."

²⁴Now Thomas (called Didymus), one of the Twelve, was not with the disciples when Jesus came. ²⁵So the other disciples told him, "We have seen the Lord!"

But he said to them, "Unless I see the nail marks in his hands and put my finger where the nails were, and put my hand into his side, I will not believe it."

²⁶A week later his disciples were in the house again, and Thomas was with them. Though the

doors were locked, Jesus came and stood among them and said, "Peace be with you!" ²⁷Then he said to Thomas, "Put your finger here; see my hands. Reach out your hand and put it into my side. Stop doubting and believe."

²⁸Thomas said to him, "My Lord and my God!"

²⁹Then Jesus told him, "Because you have seen me, you have believed; blessed are those who have not seen and yet have believed."

³⁰Jesus did many other miraculous signs in the presence of his disciples, which are not recorded in this book. ³¹But these are written that you mayʄ believe that Jesus is the Christ, the Son of God, and that by believing you may have life in his name.

f31 Some manuscripts may continue to

Discovering the Word 1. John records three witnesses to the empty tomb: Mary Magdalene, Peter and "the other disciple" (John himself). What important details do we learn from each one (vv. 1–9)? 2. John also records three appearances of the risen Christ: to Mary, to his disciples and to Thomas. Why do you think Mary doesn't immediately recognize Jesus (vv. 10–15)? 3. After she does recognize him, what impresses you most about their encounter (vv. 16–18)? 4. When Jesus appears to his disciples, what specific gifts and promises does he give them (vv. 19–23)? 5. Finally, Jesus appears to Thomas (vv. 24–29). How does Thomas's attitude—both before and after Jesus appears to him—add credibility to the resurrection?

Applying the Word 1. What do you learn from Jesus' encounter with Thomas about dealing with people who have doubts about Christianity? 2. Who could you help to understand and believe the claims of Christ? 3. John tells us why he has written his Gospel in verses 30–31. Of all the "miraculous signs" John has included, which have been most convincing to you? Why?

Responding in Prayer Praise God for what he has done in Christ.

---

25 / John 21
A Walk with a Resurrected Man

MOST OF US find it easier to forgive than to forget. We may be ready to forgive someone who has hurt us deeply, but we have a hard time trusting that person again. Peter failed Jesus miserably. He promised to give up his life if necessary to protect Jesus, but denied him a few hours later. Peter knew Jesus had forgiven him. But would Jesus still trust him? Could Jesus still use him to bring glory to God? Will Christ still use us after we've failed?

Warming Up to God How do you feel when someone you have hurt refuses to forgive you?

Read John 21.

21 Afterward Jesus appeared again to his disciples, by the Sea of Tiberias.ᵍ It happened this way: ²Simon Peter, Thomas (called Didymus), Nathanael from Cana in Galilee, the sons of Zebedee, and two other disciples were together. ³"I'm going out to fish," Simon Peter told them, and they said, "We'll go with you." So they went out and got into the boat, but that night they caught nothing.

⁴Early in the morning, Jesus stood on the shore, but the disciples did not realize that it was Jesus.

⁵He called out to them, "Friends, haven't you any fish?"

"No," they answered.

⁶He said, "Throw your net on the right side of the boat and you will find some." When they did, they were unable to haul the net in because of the large number of fish.

⁷Then the disciple whom Jesus loved said to

g1 That is, Sea of Galilee

Peter, "It is the Lord!" As soon as Simon Peter heard him say, "It is the Lord," he wrapped his outer garment around him (for he had taken it off) and jumped into the water. ⁸The other disciples followed in the boat, towing the net full of fish, for they were not far from shore, about a hundred yards.ʰ ⁹When they landed, they saw a fire of burning coals there with fish on it, and some bread.

¹⁰Jesus said to them, "Bring some of the fish you have just caught."

¹¹Simon Peter climbed aboard and dragged the net ashore. It was full of large fish, 153, but even with so many the net was not torn. ¹²Jesus said to them, "Come and have breakfast." None of the disciples dared ask him, "Who are you?" They knew it was the Lord. ¹³Jesus came, took the bread and gave it to them, and did the same with the fish. ¹⁴This was now the third time Jesus appeared to his disciples after he was raised from the dead.

¹⁵When they had finished eating, Jesus said to Simon Peter, "Simon son of John, do you truly love me more than these?"

"Yes, Lord," he said, "you know that I love you."

Jesus said, "Feed my lambs."

¹⁶Again Jesus said, "Simon son of John, do you truly love me?"

He answered, "Yes, Lord, you know that I love you."

Jesus said, "Take care of my sheep."

¹⁷The third time he said to him, "Simon son of John, do you love me?"

Peter was hurt because Jesus asked him the third time, "Do you love me?" He said, "Lord, you know all things; you know that I love you."

Jesus said, "Feed my sheep. ¹⁸I tell you the truth, when you were younger you dressed yourself and went where you wanted; but when you are old you will stretch out your hands, and someone else will dress you and lead you where you do not want to go." ¹⁹Jesus said this to indicate the kind of death by which Peter would glorify God. Then he said to him, "Follow me!"

²⁰Peter turned and saw that the disciple whom Jesus loved was following them. (This was the one who had leaned back against Jesus at the supper and had said, "Lord, who is going to betray you?") ²¹When Peter saw him, he asked, "Lord, what about him?"

²²Jesus answered, "If I want him to remain alive until I return, what is that to you? You must follow me." ²³Because of this, the rumor spread among the brothers that this disciple would not die. But Jesus did not say that he would not die; he only said, "If I want him to remain alive until I return, what is that to you?"

²⁴This is the disciple who testifies to these things and who wrote them down. We know that his testimony is true.

²⁵Jesus did many other things as well. If every one of them were written down, I suppose that even the whole world would not have room for the books that would be written.

ʰ8 Greek *about two hundred cubits* (about 90 meters)

Discovering the Word   1. What was Jesus trying to show the disciples by allowing them to catch such a large number of fish (vv. 4–6; see Lk 5:4–11)?   2. When Peter hears that "it is the Lord" (vv. 7–8), he jumps into the water and begins swimming ahead of the boat. What does this reveal about Peter and his relationship with Jesus?   3. What subtle differences do you notice in Jesus' three questions and Peter's responses (vv. 15–17)?   4. Why do you think Jesus chose this particular time to predict the kind of death Peter would die (vv. 18–19)?   5. What does Jesus' rebuke to Peter (v. 22) reveal about the danger of comparing ourselves with other Christians?

Applying the Word   1. What can we learn from this passage about the steps involved in restoring a Christian who has sinned?   2. How does it help to know that you can still serve and glorify God no matter what your past failures have been?

Responding in Prayer   Respond to God with your heart and life for what you have learned about Jesus in your study of John.

Acts

The book of Acts should come with a warning label reading, "If you are open to God, this book will call you to new life."

Acts is an extraordinary work. In essence, it is the story of transformed lives—and the difference these lives made in the world.

Just before Acts begins, we see the disciples behind closed doors wallowing in the mire of their fear, self-doubt and personal shame. Apart from their master, they were a pathetic group indeed (Lk 24:11; Jn 20:19). However, by the second chapter of Acts, the same men who abandoned Jesus at Gethsemane have become irrepressible dynamos, preaching with utter conviction—and at great personal risk—"the mighty acts of God."

What changed them? And what impact did they make upon their generation and all subsequent ones? *This* is the story of Acts.

Acts is an important book for us today because it confirms that the power which transformed the disciples' lives is the same power that can transform our lives today! That power is, of course, God himself—coming to us through the Holy Spirit.

There are many benefits to studying Acts:

☐ *Acts serves as a distant mirror.* We will see the dynamics of the earliest church, the nature of their fellowship, the intensity of their prayer life and their out-and-out zeal to declare the saving gospel of Jesus Christ. Through this example, our own situation will be called into question. What does it mean to be the church today—and what are we to be doing?

☐ *Acts emphasizes the primary task of the church—evangelization.* Speaking the gospel is only part of the task. It is the formative process that we see in these earliest communities. In Acts we see the entire process of calling, healing, empowering and sending people forth to love and obey Jesus Christ. Acts will challenge us to a holistic-community spirituality that can renew our churches today.

☐ *Acts calls us to a vital experience with the Holy Spirit.* Jesus promised power to the disciples *after* the Holy Spirit came upon them. And the book of Acts reveals the Holy Spirit as the driving force behind all meaningful ministry in Jesus' name. Where do we look for spiritual power today? Education? Work? Religious heritage? Acts calls us to a Spirit-filled life.

☐ *Acts forges a new sense of identity.* The disciples gradually realized they were no longer Jews (at least from the confessional and ceremonial points of view). They slowly began to understand that they were part of that new community of the Spirit which was prophesied in the Hebrew Scriptures. And they saw the need to call all people—Jews and Gentiles—to repentance and fellowship with this new community—the church. Baptism in the name of the Father, the Son and the Holy Spirit, and the Lord's Supper became the outward signs of the inward grace. The emphasis is on relationships.

The explosive power of this living document will touch you. As you work through these quiet times, may you experience the calling, healing, empowering and sending dynamic of the Holy Spirit.

Outline

Part 1: God's Power in Jerusalem and Judea

Part 2: God's Power at the Ends of the Earth

1 / *Acts 1*
You Will Be My Witnesses

I REMEMBER TELLING a friend, "If I were dying, what I would most need would be confidence that all I had believed about Jesus was true. I would want you to read Scripture to me, pray with me, and talk to me about Jesus and heaven." This confidence is what I need most not only when I am dying, but also when I am living.

During the days between his resurrection and ascension, Jesus built the confidence of his disciples. He demonstrated and spoke truth about himself. And then he left them with a clearly defined task and the promise of the power to carry out that task. Thus, Luke was able to write with confidence to Theophilus about Jesus.

 Warming Up to God Have you had days when you did not feel confident, but fearful? Let God encourage you this day with the power and strength contained in his Word.

 Read Acts 1.

In my former book, Theophilus, I wrote about all that Jesus began to do and to teach ²until the day he was taken up to heaven, after giving instructions through the Holy Spirit to the apostles he had chosen. ³After his suffering, he showed himself to these men and gave many convincing proofs that he was alive. He appeared to them over a period of forty days and spoke about the kingdom of God. ⁴On one occasion, while he was eating with them, he gave them this command: "Do not leave Jerusalem, but wait for the gift my Father promised, which you have heard me speak about. ⁵For John baptized with*a* water, but in a few days you will be baptized with the Holy Spirit."

⁶So when they met together, they asked him, "Lord, are you at this time going to restore the kingdom to Israel?"

⁷He said to them: "It is not for you to know the times or dates the Father has set by his own authority. ⁸But you will receive power when the Holy Spirit comes on you; and you will be my witnesses in Jerusalem, and in all Judea and Samaria, and to the ends of the earth."

⁹After he said this, he was taken up before their very eyes, and a cloud hid him from their sight.

¹⁰They were looking intently up into the sky as he was going, when suddenly two men dressed in white stood beside them. ¹¹"Men of Galilee," they said, "why do you stand here looking into the sky? This same Jesus, who has been taken from you into heaven, will come back in the same way you have seen him go into heaven."

¹²Then they returned to Jerusalem from the hill called the Mount of Olives, a Sabbath day's walk*b* from the city. ¹³When they arrived, they went upstairs to the room where they were staying. Those present were Peter, John, James and Andrew; Philip and Thomas, Bartholomew and Matthew; James son of Alphaeus and Simon the Zealot, and Judas son of James. ¹⁴They all joined together constantly in prayer, along with the women and Mary the mother of Jesus, and with his brothers.

¹⁵In those days Peter stood up among the believers*c* (a group numbering about a hundred and twenty) ¹⁶and said, "Brothers, the Scripture had to be fulfilled which the Holy Spirit spoke long ago through the mouth of David concerning Judas, who served as guide for those who arrested Jesus— ¹⁷he was one of our number and shared in this ministry."

¹⁸(With the reward he got for his wickedness, Judas bought a field; there he fell headlong, his body burst open and all his intestines spilled out. ¹⁹Everyone in Jerusalem heard about this, so they called that field in their language Akeldama, that is, Field of Blood.)

²⁰"For," said Peter, "it is written in the book of Psalms,

" 'May his place be deserted;
    let there be no one to dwell in it,'*d*

and,

" 'May another take his place of leadership.'*e*

²¹Therefore it is necessary to choose one of the men who have been with us the whole time the Lord Jesus went in and out among us, ²²beginning from John's baptism to the time when Jesus

*a5 Or in   b12 That is, about 3/4 mile (about 1,100 meters)
c15 Greek brothers   d20 Psalm 69:25   e20 Psalm 109:8*

was taken up from us. For one of these must become a witness with us of his resurrection."

²³So they proposed two men: Joseph called Barsabbas (also known as Justus) and Matthias. ²⁴Then they prayed, "Lord, you know everyone's heart. Show us which of these two you have chosen ²⁵to take over this apostolic ministry, which Judas left to go where he belongs." ²⁶Then they cast lots, and the lot fell to Matthias; so he was added to the eleven apostles.

 Discovering the Word 1. What did Luke, the author of Acts, report to Theophilus about Jesus' last days on earth (vv. 1–11)? 2. Put yourself in the shoes of the apostles. How would you feel if you were the first to be given the task described in verse 8? 3. How are we equipped for this task, according to the passage? 4. How did the disciples respond to all that they had seen and heard (vv. 12–26)? 5. Peter goes to Scripture immediately when he speaks. How do these words of David affect their confidence as well as give them direction (v. 20)?

Applying the Word 1. When has your faith in Jesus Christ been encouraged by the words of others? 2. How is your hope and confidence in Jesus affected by what you learn about him in the passage? 3. How are you affected when you pray with other believers—especially as you consider your part in God's mission for the church (v. 14)?

Responding in Prayer Thank God for giving you a task to carry out, and tell him about the fears and joys you feel as his servant.

2 / Acts 2
Receiving the Power

AT MY SCHOOL a group of upperclassmen wanted to communicate the message of Jesus to the incoming class of freshmen. They realized that there was only one source to accomplish this task—the power of the Holy Spirit. So they decided to pray for all the new students by name weeks before they arrived on campus. As a result, many who did not know Jesus when they arrived graduated as maturing Christians.

 Warming Up to God The Holy Spirit, although at times we do not sense him, is always there to help us. Let him quiet you now and open your heart to what he wants to tell you about himself.

 Read Acts 2.

2 When the day of Pentecost came, they were all together in one place. ²Suddenly a sound like the blowing of a violent wind came from heaven and filled the whole house where they were sitting. ³They saw what seemed to be tongues of fire that separated and came to rest on each of them. ⁴All of them were filled with the Holy Spirit and began to speak in other tongues*ᶠ* as the Spirit enabled them.

⁵Now there were staying in Jerusalem God-fearing Jews from every nation under heaven. ⁶When they heard this sound, a crowd came together in bewilderment, because each one heard them speaking in his own language. ⁷Utterly amazed, they asked: "Are not all these men who are speaking Galileans? ⁸Then how is it that each of us hears them in his own native language? ⁹Parthians, Medes and Elamites; residents of Mesopotamia, Judea and Cappadocia, Pontus and Asia, ¹⁰Phrygia and Pamphylia, Egypt and the parts of Libya near Cyrene; visitors from Rome ¹¹(both Jews and converts to Judaism); Cretans and Arabs—we hear them declaring the wonders of God in our own tongues!" ¹²Amazed and perplexed, they asked one another, "What does this mean?"

¹³Some, however, made fun of them and said, "They have had too much wine.*ᵍ*"

¹⁴Then Peter stood up with the Eleven, raised his voice and addressed the crowd: "Fellow Jews and all of you who live in Jerusalem, let me ex-

ᶠ4 Or languages; also in verse 11   ᵍ13 Or sweet wine

plain this to you; listen carefully to what I say. [15]These men are not drunk, as you suppose. It's only nine in the morning! [16]No, this is what was spoken by the prophet Joel:

[17]" 'In the last days, God says,
   I will pour out my Spirit on all people.
   Your sons and daughters will prophesy,
     your young men will see visions,
     your old men will dream dreams.
[18]Even on my servants, both men and women,
   I will pour out my Spirit in those days,
     and they will prophesy.
[19]I will show wonders in the heaven above
     and signs on the earth below,
     blood and fire and billows of smoke.
[20]The sun will be turned to darkness
     and the moon to blood
   before the coming of the great and glorious
     day of the Lord.
[21]And everyone who calls
   on the name of the Lord will be saved.'[h]

[22]"Men of Israel, listen to this: Jesus of Nazareth was a man accredited by God to you by miracles, wonders and signs, which God did among you through him, as you yourselves know. [23]This man was handed over to you by God's set purpose and foreknowledge; and you, with the help of wicked men,[i] put him to death by nailing him to the cross. [24]But God raised him from the dead, freeing him from the agony of death, because it was impossible for death to keep its hold on him. [25]David said about him:

" 'I saw the Lord always before me.
   Because he is at my right hand,
   I will not be shaken.
[26]Therefore my heart is glad and my tongue
     rejoices;
   my body also will live in hope,
[27]because you will not abandon me to the
     grave,
   nor will you let your Holy One see decay.
[28]You have made known to me the paths of life;
   you will fill me with joy in your
     presence.'[j]

[29]"Brothers, I can tell you confidently that the patriarch David died and was buried, and his tomb is here to this day. [30]But he was a prophet and knew that God had promised him on oath

that he would place one of his descendants on his throne. [31]Seeing what was ahead, he spoke of the resurrection of the Christ,[k] that he was not abandoned to the grave, nor did his body see decay. [32]God has raised this Jesus to life, and we are all witnesses of the fact. [33]Exalted to the right hand of God, he has received from the Father the promised Holy Spirit and has poured out what you now see and hear. [34]For David did not ascend to heaven, and yet he said,

" 'The Lord said to my Lord:
   "Sit at my right hand
[35]until I make your enemies
   a footstool for your feet." '[l]

[36]"Therefore let all Israel be assured of this: God has made this Jesus, whom you crucified, both Lord and Christ."

[37]When the people heard this, they were cut to the heart and said to Peter and the other apostles, "Brothers, what shall we do?"

[38]Peter replied, "Repent and be baptized, every one of you, in the name of Jesus Christ for the forgiveness of your sins. And you will receive the gift of the Holy Spirit. [39]The promise is for you and your children and for all who are far off—for all whom the Lord our God will call."

[40]With many other words he warned them; and he pleaded with them, "Save yourselves from this corrupt generation." [41]Those who accepted his message were baptized, and about three thousand were added to their number that day.

[42]They devoted themselves to the apostles' teaching and to the fellowship, to the breaking of bread and to prayer. [43]Everyone was filled with awe, and many wonders and miraculous signs were done by the apostles. [44]All the believers were together and had everything in common. [45]Selling their possessions and goods, they gave to anyone as he had need. [46]Every day they continued to meet together in the temple courts. They broke bread in their homes and ate together with glad and sincere hearts, [47]praising God and enjoying the favor of all the people. And the Lord added to their number daily those who were being saved.

[h]21 Joel 2:28-32   [i]23 Or of those not having the law (that is, Gentiles)   [j]28 Psalm 16:8-11   [k]31 Or Messiah. "The Christ" (Greek) and "the Messiah" (Hebrew) both mean "the Anointed One"; also in verse 36.   [l]35 Psalm 110:1

Discovering the Word 1. How do the Jews respond to the power of the Spirit which they witness (vv. 5–12)? 2. Here we see Peter as a dynamic leader and preacher. It is the power of the Holy Spirit that has changed this man who was once a coward who denied Jesus three times. Scripture, again, is the foundation of Peter's proclamation of truth. What message does the Old Testament book of Joel have for the bewildered crowd (vv. 17–21)? 3. What is there in Peter's sermon that would reassure Theophilus about his faith and help him "know the certainty of the things" that he'd been taught? 4. What does Peter have to offer to those who are responsive to his message (vv. 37–39)? 5. Describe the fellowship of the believers in this young church (vv. 42–47).

 Applying the Word 1. Imagine you were there on the day of Pentecost. What do you think it would have been like for you as one of the crowd looking on? 2. How has your life been affected by the gift of the Holy Spirit? 3. How does the life and purpose of your church or Christian fellowship group compare to that of this group?

 Responding in Prayer Ask God to make the power of the Holy Spirit come alive in your life, and pray that God will use you through that power.

---

3 / Acts 3
Healing Power

I MET ANNE at the hospital where I was working one evening. She was in an isolation room. She had hepatitis from using contaminated needles to take drugs. In time our relationship grew, and Anne came to know Jesus. She recovered from hepatitis and went off drugs. She worked at healing her relationship with her parents. Later, she married and established a Christian home. Anne's story makes it clear that the power of the Holy Spirit is demonstrated not only through physical healing, but also in the "complete healing" that includes every aspect of our lives.

 Warming Up to God Recall a time when you felt broken and in need of healing. Thank God for the ways that he has transformed and healed you since then.

Read Acts 3.

---

3 One day Peter and John were going up to the temple at the time of prayer—at three in the afternoon. ²Now a man crippled from birth was being carried to the temple gate called Beautiful, where he was put every day to beg from those going into the temple courts. ³When he saw Peter and John about to enter, he asked them for money. ⁴Peter looked straight at him, as did John. Then Peter said, "Look at us!" ⁵So the man gave them his attention, expecting to get something from them.

⁶Then Peter said, "Silver or gold I do not have, but what I have I give you. In the name of Jesus Christ of Nazareth, walk." ⁷Taking him by the right hand, he helped him up, and instantly the man's feet and ankles became strong. ⁸He jumped to his feet and began to walk. Then he went with them into the temple courts, walking and jumping, and praising God. ⁹When all the people saw him walking and praising God, ¹⁰they recognized him as the same man who used to sit begging at

the temple gate called Beautiful, and they were filled with wonder and amazement at what had happened to him.

¹¹While the beggar held on to Peter and John, all the people were astonished and came running to them in the place called Solomon's Colonnade. ¹²When Peter saw this, he said to them: "Men of Israel, why does this surprise you? Why do you stare at us as if by our own power or godliness we had made this man walk? ¹³The God of Abraham, Isaac and Jacob, the God of our fathers, has glorified his servant Jesus. You handed him over to be killed, and you disowned him before Pilate, though he had decided to let him go. ¹⁴You disowned the Holy and Righteous One and asked that a murderer be released to you. ¹⁵You killed the author of life, but God raised him from the dead. We are witnesses of this. ¹⁶By faith in the name of Jesus, this man whom you see and know was made strong. It is Jesus' name and the faith

that comes through him that has given this complete healing to him, as you can all see.

17"Now, brothers, I know that you acted in ignorance, as did your leaders. 18But this is how God fulfilled what he had foretold through all the prophets, saying that his Christ[m] would suffer. 19Repent, then, and turn to God, so that your sins may be wiped out, that times of refreshing may come from the Lord, 20and that he may send the Christ, who has been appointed for you—even Jesus. 21He must remain in heaven until the time comes for God to restore everything, as he promised long ago through his holy prophets. 22For Moses said, 'The Lord your God will raise up for you a prophet like me from among your own people; you must listen to everything he tells you. 23Anyone who does not listen to him will be completely cut off from among his people.'[n]

24"Indeed, all the prophets from Samuel on, as many as have spoken, have foretold these days. 25And you are heirs of the prophets and of the covenant God made with your fathers. He said to Abraham, 'Through your offspring all peoples on earth will be blessed.'[o] 26When God raised up his servant, he sent him first to you to bless you by turning each of you from your wicked ways."

[m]18 Or Messiah; also in verse 20   [n]23 Deut. 18:15,18,19
[o]25 Gen. 22:18; 26:4

 Discovering the Word 1. How does the response of the people to the miracle in verses 6–8 contrast with the beggar's response (vv. 8 and 11–12)? 2. When Peter noticed how the crowd reacted, he saw his opportunity and talked to them about Jesus. According to Peter's message, what had God done to Jesus (vv. 13–15)? What had the Jews done to him? 3. How is the authority of Jesus demonstrated in this miracle (v. 16)? 4. How did Peter explain that all that had happened to Jesus was a part of God's plan (vv. 17–26)?

Applying the Word 1. What healing do you need in your life? 2. How do you respond when you have opportunities like Peter's to talk about Jesus? 3. The "completely" healed man was a powerful testimony to the power of God and the truth of Peter's words. How have you seen the power of God demonstrated in your life and in the lives of others?

Responding in Prayer Thank God for working so powerfully to change your life, and ask him to give you the opportunity to talk about Jesus to one person this week.

---

4 / Acts 4:1–31
Called into Question

A DISABLED PERSON becomes abled! And a one-time burden to society, a beggar, becomes a contributing citizen! How do the religious leaders respond to these miraculous events? Instead of expressing gratitude, they become extremely upset. The two men responsible for the healing are arrested.

Warming Up to God Today, in this new day that God has created, your Savior wants to come to you. With calmness, let the distractions around you—the voices and restless thoughts—slip away. As the spirit of God comes to dwell with you, allow yourself to enjoy his presence in quietness and gratitude.

 Read Acts 4:1–31.

---

4 The priests and the captain of the temple guard and the Sadducees came up to Peter and John while they were speaking to the people. 2They were greatly disturbed because the apostles were teaching the people and proclaiming in Jesus the resurrection of the dead. 3They seized Peter and John, and because it was evening, they put them in jail until the next day.

4But many who heard the message believed, and the number of men grew to about five thousand.

5The next day the rulers, elders and teachers of the law met in Jerusalem. 6Annas the high priest was there, and so were Caiaphas, John, Alexander and the other men of the high priest's family. 7They had Peter and John brought before them and began to question them: "By what power or what name did you do this?"

⁸Then Peter, filled with the Holy Spirit, said to them: "Rulers and elders of the people! ⁹If we are being called to account today for an act of kindness shown to a cripple and are asked how he was healed, ¹⁰then know this, you and all the people of Israel: It is by the name of Jesus Christ of Nazareth, whom you crucified but whom God raised from the dead, that this man stands before you healed. ¹¹He is

" 'the stone you builders rejected,
　　which has become the capstone.ᵖ'�q

¹²Salvation is found in no one else, for there is no other name under heaven given to men by which we must be saved."

¹³When they saw the courage of Peter and John and realized that they were unschooled, ordinary men, they were astonished and they took note that these men had been with Jesus. ¹⁴But since they could see the man who had been healed standing there with them, there was nothing they could say. ¹⁵So they ordered them to withdraw from the Sanhedrin and then conferred together. ¹⁶"What are we going to do with these men?" they asked. "Everybody living in Jerusalem knows they have done an outstanding miracle, and we cannot deny it. ¹⁷But to stop this thing from spreading any further among the people, we must warn these men to speak no longer to anyone in this name."

¹⁸Then they called them in again and commanded them not to speak or teach at all in the name of Jesus. ¹⁹But Peter and John replied, "Judge for yourselves whether it is right in God's sight to obey you rather than God. ²⁰For we can-

not help speaking about what we have seen and heard."

²¹After further threats they let them go. They could not decide how to punish them, because all the people were praising God for what had happened. ²²For the man who was miraculously healed was over forty years old.

²³On their release, Peter and John went back to their own people and reported all that the chief priests and elders had said to them. ²⁴When they heard this, they raised their voices together in prayer to God. "Sovereign Lord," they said, "you made the heaven and the earth and the sea, and everything in them. ²⁵You spoke by the Holy Spirit through the mouth of your servant, our father David:

" 'Why do the nations rage
　　and the peoples plot in vain?
²⁶The kings of the earth take their stand
　　and the rulers gather together
　against the Lord
　　and against his Anointed One.ʳ'ˢ

²⁷Indeed Herod and Pontius Pilate met together with the Gentiles and the peopleᵗ of Israel in this city to conspire against your holy servant Jesus, whom you anointed. ²⁸They did what your power and will had decided beforehand should happen. ²⁹Now, Lord, consider their threats and enable your servants to speak your word with great boldness. ³⁰Stretch out your hand to heal and perform miraculous signs and wonders through the name of your holy servant Jesus." ³¹After they prayed, the place where they were meeting was shaken. And they were all filled with the Holy Spirit and spoke the word of God boldly.

ᵖ11 Or *cornerstone*　�q11 Psalm 118:22　ʳ26 That is, Christ or Messiah　ˢ26 Psalm 2:1,2　ᵗ27 The Greek is plural.

Discovering the Word　1. What has upset the religious leaders (vv. 1–2)?　2. What action did they take (vv. 3–7)?　3. Just a few weeks have passed since Annas and Caiaphas had been involved in the condemnation of Jesus. In his response to their question "By what power or what name did you do this?" Peter is forcing them to encounter Jesus again. What does Peter say about him (vv. 10–12)?　4. In verses 13–22 what made it so difficult for the opposing religious leaders to bring this unacceptable behavior to a halt?　5. What was the reaction of the believers to John and Peter's account (vv. 24–30)?　6. What does their prayer tell you about their faith in the character, power and faithfulness of God (vv. 24–30)?

Applying the Word　1. When has your faith been challenged by others?　2. Imagine that you had been in a group of believers John and Peter returned to and told of what had happened. What would have been your reaction?　3. "After they prayed, the place where they were meeting was shaken. And they were all filled with the Holy Spirit and spoke the word of God boldly." In what ways do you need the power of the Holy Spirit to face the world today?

Responding in Prayer Ask God to fill you with the Spirit as you face constant challenge to the power for and the task of experiencing and communicating the gospel.

5 / *Acts 4:32—5:16*
Oneness of Heart

IT WAS WITH a heavy feeling of dread and pain that I read name after name engraved on the Vietnam Memorial in Washington, D.C. Then I saw that next to the memorial was a statue of three men—a black, a Hispanic and a white soldier. They were standing very close together. The tour guide, a former soldier who fought in Nam, explained the significance of the statue. He said that there were more minorities fighting for the U.S. than ever before. And the reason that they were standing so close together was that in Vietnam they learned, like never before, how very much they needed each other. In this study we will see that when the battle is spiritual, our need for each other is even more critical.

 Warming Up to God Who has God given you that meets a need in your life? Thank God for giving you such a valuable and loving gift.

 Read Acts 4:32—5:16.

³²All the believers were one in heart and mind. No one claimed that any of his possessions was his own, but they shared everything they had. ³³With great power the apostles continued to testify to the resurrection of the Lord Jesus, and much grace was upon them all. ³⁴There were no needy persons among them. For from time to time those who owned lands or houses sold them, brought the money from the sales ³⁵and put it at the apostles' feet, and it was distributed to anyone as he had need.

³⁶Joseph, a Levite from Cyprus, whom the apostles called Barnabas (which means Son of Encouragement), ³⁷sold a field he owned and brought the money and put it at the apostles' feet.

5 Now a man named Ananias, together with his wife Sapphira, also sold a piece of property. ²With his wife's full knowledge he kept back part of the money for himself, but brought the rest and put it at the apostles' feet.

³Then Peter said, "Ananias, how is it that Satan has so filled your heart that you have lied to the Holy Spirit and have kept for yourself some of the money you received for the land? ⁴Didn't it belong to you before it was sold? And after it was sold, wasn't the money at your disposal? What made you think of doing such a thing? You have not lied to men but to God."

⁵When Ananias heard this, he fell down and died. And great fear seized all who heard what had happened. ⁶Then the young men came for-

ward, wrapped up his body, and carried him out and buried him.

⁷About three hours later his wife came in, not knowing what had happened. ⁸Peter asked her, "Tell me, is this the price you and Ananias got for the land?"

"Yes," she said, "that is the price."

⁹Peter said to her, "How could you agree to test the Spirit of the Lord? Look! The feet of the men who buried your husband are at the door, and they will carry you out also."

¹⁰At that moment she fell down at his feet and died. Then the young men came in and, finding her dead, carried her out and buried her beside her husband. ¹¹Great fear seized the whole church and all who heard about these events.

¹²The apostles performed many miraculous signs and wonders among the people. And all the believers used to meet together in Solomon's Colonnade. ¹³No one else dared join them, even though they were highly regarded by the people. ¹⁴Nevertheless, more and more men and women believed in the Lord and were added to their number. ¹⁵As a result, people brought the sick into the streets and laid them on beds and mats so that at least Peter's shadow might fall on some of them as he passed by. ¹⁶Crowds gathered also from the towns around Jerusalem, bringing their sick and those tormented by evilᵘ spirits, and all of them were healed.

ᵘ 16 Greek *unclean*

Discovering the Word 1. How is oneness of heart and mind demonstrated in 4:32–37? 2. What have Ananias and Sapphira done that is not consistent with Christian community (5:1–2)? 3. Pretend you are watching the interaction between Peter and Ananias and Sapphira (5:3–9). How would you report this incident? 4. Verse 11 states that "great fear seized the whole church and all who heard about these events." How do you think the church was affected by this fear? 5. What are the tangible evidences of the power of the Holy Spirit in this community in 5:12–16?

Applying the Word 1. How does this story demonstrate the high value that God places on truth and unity within the body of Christ? 2. In what ways do we lie to each other today within our Christian communities? 3. How could you begin to help others in your church or fellowship understand what Christian community is about?

Responding in Prayer Ask God to uphold truth in his church and to help you speak the truth before others.

---

6 / Acts 5:17—6:7
Persecution and Expansion

IN 1956 TRAGIC news spread across the world. Five American men—sons, husbands and fathers—were massacred by a tribe of Auca Indians. Their purpose was to take the good news of Jesus Christ to the Aucas. The opposition to this endeavor cost them their lives.

That agonizing loss, which seemed at the time to be such a waste, has turned into great fruit for the kingdom of God. Over the years that same tribe of Indians has been transformed by the power of God. The message of Jesus was taken to them by the loved ones of those five young men. Another visible fruit of this great loss is the many who have gone into the world with the gospel, having been inspired by the lives and deaths of these missionaries. The church of Jesus Christ continues to expand today in spite of great persecution, even as it did in the day of the apostles.

 Warming Up to God Although we know that God is in complete control of the universe, we often forget that he also has specific plans for our individual lives. Thank him for being sovereign everywhere, including the secrecy of your own heart.

 Read Acts 5:17—6:7.

17Then the high priest and all his associates, who were members of the party of the Sadducees, were filled with jealousy. 18They arrested the apostles and put them in the public jail. 19But during the night an angel of the Lord opened the doors of the jail and brought them out. 20"Go, stand in the temple courts," he said, "and tell the people the full message of this new life."

21At daybreak they entered the temple courts, as they had been told, and began to teach the people.

When the high priest and his associates arrived, they called together the Sanhedrin—the full assembly of the elders of Israel—and sent to the jail for the apostles. 22But on arriving at the jail, the officers did not find them there. So they went back and reported, 23"We found the jail securely locked, with the guards standing at the

doors; but when we opened them, we found no one inside." 24On hearing this report, the captain of the temple guard and the chief priests were puzzled, wondering what would come of this.

25Then someone came and said, "Look! The men you put in jail are standing in the temple courts teaching the people." 26At that, the captain went with his officers and brought the apostles. They did not use force, because they feared that the people would stone them.

27Having brought the apostles, they made them appear before the Sanhedrin to be questioned by the high priest. 28"We gave you strict orders not to teach in this name," he said. "Yet you have filled Jerusalem with your teaching and are determined to make us guilty of this man's blood."

29Peter and the other apostles replied: "We must obey God rather than men! 30The God of our fathers raised Jesus from the dead—whom you had killed by hanging him on a tree. ³¹God exalted him to his own right hand as Prince and Savior that he might give repentance and forgiveness of sins to Israel. ³²We are witnesses of these things, and so is the Holy Spirit, whom God has given to those who obey him."

³³When they heard this, they were furious and wanted to put them to death. ³⁴But a Pharisee named Gamaliel, a teacher of the law, who was honored by all the people, stood up in the Sanhedrin and ordered that the men be put outside for a little while. ³⁵Then he addressed them: "Men of Israel, consider carefully what you intend to do to these men. ³⁶Some time ago Theudas appeared, claiming to be somebody, and about four hundred men rallied to him. He was killed, all his followers were dispersed, and it all came to nothing. ³⁷After him, Judas the Galilean appeared in the days of the census and led a band of people in revolt. He too was killed, and all his followers were scattered. ³⁸Therefore, in the present case I advise you: Leave these men alone! Let them go! For if their purpose or activity is of human origin, it will fail. ³⁹But if it is from God, you will not be able to stop these men; you will only find yourselves fighting against God."

⁴⁰His speech persuaded them. They called the apostles in and had them flogged. Then they ordered them not to speak in the name of Jesus, and let them go.

⁴¹The apostles left the Sanhedrin, rejoicing because they had been counted worthy of suffering disgrace for the Name. ⁴²Day after day, in the temple courts and from house to house, they never stopped teaching and proclaiming the good news that Jesus is the Christ. ᵛ

6 In those days when the number of disciples was increasing, the Grecian Jews among them complained against the Hebraic Jews because their widows were being overlooked in the daily distribution of food. ²So the Twelve gathered all the disciples together and said, "It would not be right for us to neglect the ministry of the word of God in order to wait on tables. ³Brothers, choose seven men from among you who are known to be full of the Spirit and wisdom. We will turn this responsibility over to them ⁴and will give our attention to prayer and the ministry of the word."

⁵This proposal pleased the whole group. They chose Stephen, a man full of faith and of the Holy Spirit; also Philip, Procorus, Nicanor, Timon, Parmenas, and Nicolas from Antioch, a convert to Judaism. ⁶They presented these men to the apostles, who prayed and laid their hands on them.

⁷So the word of God spread. The number of disciples in Jerusalem increased rapidly, and a large number of priests became obedient to the faith.

ᵛ42 Or *Messiah*

 Discovering the Word 1. List the expressions and causes of emotion throughout verses 5:17–42. 2. Describe the apostles' response, motivation and source of strength throughout this whole episode. 3. What was Gamaliel's message to the religious leaders (5:34–39)? 4. How was his influence in saving the apostles' lives an example of that truth which he spoke? 5. As the number of disciples increased, what practical needs began to present themselves (6:1–6)? 6. How did the Twelve respond to those needs (6:2–6)?

Applying the Word 1. When have you encountered internal and/or external opposition when you have attempted to proclaim the message of Jesus? 2. Is it more difficult for you to deal with internal or external opposition? Why? 3. As you observe the work of the Holy Spirit throughout this passage, what actions do you think you and/or your church should take to ensure his ministry among you?

Responding in Prayer Tell God about the difficulties and struggles you have been facing as a believer in him. Ask him to give you strength and to remind you that his ways are higher than your own.

7 / *Acts 6:8—7:60*
Stephen, Full of Spirit and Wisdom

I AM GLAD for those people in my life who make me long to know God better. God's character in them makes me hunger and thirst for him. That is what happens to me when I am exposed to Stephen. I read about him and I want to know God.

Stephen is described as "full of the Holy Spirit and wisdom, full of God's grace and power." He was a gift to the early church but could not be tolerated by her enemies.

 Warming Up to God Think of a person that makes you want to know God better. Reflect on the qualities you see in him or her.

 Read Acts 6:8—7:60.

---

⁸Now Stephen, a man full of God's grace and power, did great wonders and miraculous signs among the people. ⁹Opposition arose, however, from members of the Synagogue of the Freedmen (as it was called)—Jews of Cyrene and Alexandria as well as the provinces of Cilicia and Asia. These men began to argue with Stephen, ¹⁰but they could not stand up against his wisdom or the Spirit by whom he spoke.

¹¹Then they secretly persuaded some men to say, "We have heard Stephen speak words of blasphemy against Moses and against God."

¹²So they stirred up the people and the elders and the teachers of the law. They seized Stephen and brought him before the Sanhedrin. ¹³They produced false witnesses, who testified, "This fellow never stops speaking against this holy place and against the law. ¹⁴For we have heard him say that this Jesus of Nazareth will destroy this place and change the customs Moses handed down to us."

¹⁵All who were sitting in the Sanhedrin looked intently at Stephen, and they saw that his face was like the face of an angel.

7 Then the high priest asked him, "Are these charges true?"

²To this he replied: "Brothers and fathers, listen to me! The God of glory appeared to our father Abraham while he was still in Mesopotamia, before he lived in Haran. ³'Leave your country and your people,' God said, 'and go to the land I will show you.'ʷ

⁴"So he left the land of the Chaldeans and settled in Haran. After the death of his father, God sent him to this land where you are now living. ⁵He gave him no inheritance here, not even a foot of ground. But God promised him that he and his descendants after him would possess the land, even though at that time Abraham had no child. ⁶God spoke to him in this way: 'Your descendants will be strangers in a country not their own, and they will be enslaved and mistreated four hundred years. ⁷But I will punish the nation they serve as slaves,' God said, 'and afterward they will come out of that country and worship me in this place.'ˣ ⁸Then he gave Abraham the covenant of circumcision. And Abraham became the father of Isaac and circumcised him eight days after his birth. Later Isaac became the father of Jacob, and Jacob became the father of the twelve patriarchs.

⁹"Because the patriarchs were jealous of Joseph, they sold him as a slave into Egypt. But God was with him ¹⁰and rescued him from all his troubles. He gave Joseph wisdom and enabled him to gain the goodwill of Pharaoh king of Egypt; so he made him ruler over Egypt and all his palace.

¹¹"Then a famine struck all Egypt and Canaan, bringing great suffering, and our fathers could not find food. ¹²When Jacob heard that there was grain in Egypt, he sent our fathers on their first visit. ¹³On their second visit, Joseph told his brothers who he was, and Pharaoh learned about Joseph's family. ¹⁴After this, Joseph sent for his father Jacob and his whole family, seventy-five in all. ¹⁵Then Jacob went down to Egypt, where he and our fathers died. ¹⁶Their bodies were brought back to Shechem and placed in the tomb that Abraham had bought from the sons of Hamor at Shechem for a certain sum of money.

¹⁷"As the time drew near for God to fulfill his promise to Abraham, the number of our people in Egypt greatly increased. ¹⁸Then another king, who knew nothing about Joseph, became ruler of

ʷ3 Gen. 12:1   ˣ7 Gen. 15:13,14

Egypt. [19]He dealt treacherously with our people and oppressed our forefathers by forcing them to throw out their newborn babies so that they would die.

[20]"At that time Moses was born, and he was no ordinary child.[y] For three months he was cared for in his father's house. [21]When he was placed outside, Pharaoh's daughter took him and brought him up as her own son. [22]Moses was educated in all the wisdom of the Egyptians and was powerful in speech and action.

[23]"When Moses was forty years old, he decided to visit his fellow Israelites. [24]He saw one of them being mistreated by an Egyptian, so he went to his defense and avenged him by killing the Egyptian. [25]Moses thought that his own people would realize that God was using him to rescue them, but they did not. [26]The next day Moses came upon two Israelites who were fighting. He tried to reconcile them by saying, 'Men, you are brothers; why do you want to hurt each other?'

[27]"But the man who was mistreating the other pushed Moses aside and said, 'Who made you ruler and judge over us? [28]Do you want to kill me as you killed the Egyptian yesterday?'[z] [29]When Moses heard this, he fled to Midian, where he settled as a foreigner and had two sons.

[30]"After forty years had passed, an angel appeared to Moses in the flames of a burning bush in the desert near Mount Sinai. [31]When he saw this, he was amazed at the sight. As he went over to look more closely, he heard the Lord's voice: [32]'I am the God of your fathers, the God of Abraham, Isaac and Jacob.'[a] Moses trembled with fear and did not dare to look.

[33]"Then the Lord said to him, 'Take off your sandals; the place where you are standing is holy ground. [34]I have indeed seen the oppression of my people in Egypt. I have heard their groaning and have come down to set them free. Now come, I will send you back to Egypt.'[b]

[35]"This is the same Moses whom they had rejected with the words, 'Who made you ruler and judge?' He was sent to be their ruler and deliverer by God himself, through the angel who appeared to him in the bush. [36]He led them out of Egypt and did wonders and miraculous signs in Egypt, at the Red Sea[c] and for forty years in the desert.

[37]"This is that Moses who told the Israelites, 'God will send you a prophet like me from your own people.'[d] [38]He was in the assembly in the desert, with the angel who spoke to him on Mount Sinai, and with our fathers; and he received living words to pass on to us.

[39]"But our fathers refused to obey him. Instead, they rejected him and in their hearts turned back to Egypt. [40]They told Aaron, 'Make us gods who will go before us. As for this fellow Moses who led us out of Egypt—we don't know what has happened to him!'[e] [41]That was the time they made an idol in the form of a calf. They brought sacrifices to it and held a celebration in honor of what their hands had made. [42]But God turned away and gave them over to the worship of the heavenly bodies. This agrees with what is written in the book of the prophets:

" 'Did you bring me sacrifices and offerings
    forty years in the desert, O house of Israel?
[43]You have lifted up the shrine of Molech
    and the star of your god Rephan,
    the idols you made to worship.
Therefore I will send you into exile'[f] beyond
    Babylon.

[44]"Our forefathers had the tabernacle of the Testimony with them in the desert. It had been made as God directed Moses, according to the pattern he had seen. [45]Having received the tabernacle, our fathers under Joshua brought it with them when they took the land from the nations God drove out before them. It remained in the land until the time of David, [46]who enjoyed God's favor and asked that he might provide a dwelling place for the God of Jacob.[g] [47]But it was Solomon who built the house for him.

[48]"However, the Most High does not live in houses made by men. As the prophet says:

[49]" 'Heaven is my throne,
    and the earth is my footstool.
What kind of house will you build for me?
                                    says the Lord.
    Or where will my resting place be?
[50]Has not my hand made all these things?'[h]

[51]"You stiff-necked people, with uncircumcised hearts and ears! You are just like your fathers: You always resist the Holy Spirit! [52]Was there ever a prophet your fathers did not persecute? They even killed those who predicted the coming of the Righteous One. And now you have betrayed and murdered him— [53]you who have

y20 Or was fair in the sight of God   z28 Exodus 2:14
a32 Exodus 3:6   b34 Exodus 3:5,7,8,10   c36 That is, Sea of Reeds
d37 Deut. 18:15   e40 Exodus 32:1   f43 Amos 5:25-27
g46 Some early manuscripts the house of Jacob   h50 Isaiah 66:1,2

received the law that was put into effect through angels but have not obeyed it."

⁵⁴When they heard this, they were furious and gnashed their teeth at him. ⁵⁵But Stephen, full of the Holy Spirit, looked up to heaven and saw the glory of God, and Jesus standing at the right hand of God. ⁵⁶"Look," he said, "I see heaven open and the Son of Man standing at the right hand of God."

⁵⁷At this they covered their ears and, yelling at the top of their voices, they all rushed at him, ⁵⁸dragged him out of the city and began to stone him. Meanwhile, the witnesses laid their clothes at the feet of a young man named Saul.

⁵⁹While they were stoning him, Stephen prayed, "Lord Jesus, receive my spirit." ⁶⁰Then he fell on his knees and cried out, "Lord, do not hold this sin against them." When he had said this, he fell asleep.

 Discovering the Word 1. What do you learn about Stephen throughout this passage? 2. What do the accusations against Stephen tell us about why the Jewish religious leaders were so upset (6:13–14)? 3. Sometimes the speech in chapter 7 is called "Stephen's defense," although it is actually a defense of pure Christianity as God's appointed way to worship. What are the main points of this defense? 4. What did God tell Abraham would happen to his descendants, the Hebrews (7:1–7)? 5. What direct application does Stephen make concerning the religious leaders from 7:39–43 (see 7:51–53)?

 Applying the Word 1. God told Abraham what would happen to the Hebrews years before it all happened, even before he had a son. How are you affected when you see all that unfolds in history? 2. Throughout this whole passage, we see in Stephen the evidence of being full of the Spirit and wisdom. What are the evidences today of being full of the Spirit and wisdom? 3. In what aspect of your life would you like to reflect more of the Spirit and wisdom?

 Responding in Prayer Ask God to fill you with the Spirit and with wisdom.

---

8 / *Acts 8*
The Power of Suffering

STEPHEN IS DEAD. When he is buried, the people mourn deeply. The church has experienced the tragedy of her first martyr. In this study we meet Philip and Saul. Saul approves of Stephen's death. He is putting all his energy into destroying the rest of Jesus' followers. In contrast, Philip is one of the seven, full of the Spirit and wisdom. His energy goes into the proclamation of the truth about Jesus. People respond. And so both the persecution and the expansion of the church continue.

 Warming Up to God Has there been a time recently that you were confused about God's intentions behind the events that he placed in your life? Ask him to give you his understanding and peace.

 Read Acts 8.

---

8 And Saul was there, giving approval to his death.

On that day a great persecution broke out against the church at Jerusalem, and all except the apostles were scattered throughout Judea and Samaria. ²Godly men buried Stephen and mourned deeply for him. ³But Saul began to destroy the church. Going from house to house, he dragged off men and women and put them in prison.

⁴Those who had been scattered preached the word wherever they went. ⁵Philip went down to a city in Samaria and proclaimed the Christⁱ there. ⁶When the crowds heard Philip and saw the miraculous signs he did, they all paid close attention to what he said. ⁷With shrieks, evilʲ spirits came

ⁱ5 Or *Messiah*   ʲ7 Greek *unclean*

out of many, and many paralytics and cripples were healed. [8]So there was great joy in that city.

[9]Now for some time a man named Simon had practiced sorcery in the city and amazed all the people of Samaria. He boasted that he was someone great, [10]and all the people, both high and low, gave him their attention and exclaimed, "This man is the divine power known as the Great Power." [11]They followed him because he had amazed them for a long time with his magic. [12]But when they believed Philip as he preached the good news of the kingdom of God and the name of Jesus Christ, they were baptized, both men and women. [13]Simon himself believed and was baptized. And he followed Philip everywhere, astonished by the great signs and miracles he saw.

[14]When the apostles in Jerusalem heard that Samaria had accepted the word of God, they sent Peter and John to them. [15]When they arrived, they prayed for them that they might receive the Holy Spirit, [16]because the Holy Spirit had not yet come upon any of them; they had simply been baptized into[k] the name of the Lord Jesus. [17]Then Peter and John placed their hands on them, and they received the Holy Spirit.

[18]When Simon saw that the Spirit was given at the laying on of the apostles' hands, he offered them money [19]and said, "Give me also this ability so that everyone on whom I lay my hands may receive the Holy Spirit."

[20]Peter answered: "May your money perish with you, because you thought you could buy the gift of God with money! [21]You have no part or share in this ministry, because your heart is not right before God. [22]Repent of this wickedness and pray to the Lord. Perhaps he will forgive you for having such a thought in your heart. [23]For I see that you are full of bitterness and captive to sin."

[24]Then Simon answered, "Pray to the Lord for me so that nothing you have said may happen to me."

[25]When they had testified and proclaimed the word of the Lord, Peter and John returned to Jerusalem, preaching the gospel in many Samaritan villages.

[26]Now an angel of the Lord said to Philip, "Go south to the road—the desert road—that goes down from Jerusalem to Gaza." [27]So he started out, and on his way he met an Ethiopian[l] eunuch, an important official in charge of all the treasury of Candace, queen of the Ethiopians. This man had gone to Jerusalem to worship, [28]and on his way home was sitting in his chariot reading the book of Isaiah the prophet. [29]The Spirit told Philip, "Go to that chariot and stay near it."

[30]Then Philip ran up to the chariot and heard the man reading Isaiah the prophet. "Do you understand what you are reading?" Philip asked.

[31]"How can I," he said, "unless someone explains it to me?" So he invited Philip to come up and sit with him.

[32]The eunuch was reading this passage of Scripture:

"He was led like a sheep to the slaughter,
and as a lamb before the shearer is silent,
so he did not open his mouth.
[33]In his humiliation he was deprived of justice.
Who can speak of his descendants?
For his life was taken from the earth."[m]

[34]The eunuch asked Philip, "Tell me, please, who is the prophet talking about, himself or someone else?" [35]Then Philip began with that very passage of Scripture and told him the good news about Jesus.

[36]As they traveled along the road, they came to some water and the eunuch said, "Look, here is water. Why shouldn't I be baptized?"[n] [38]And he gave orders to stop the chariot. Then both Philip and the eunuch went down into the water and Philip baptized him. [39]When they came up out of the water, the Spirit of the Lord suddenly took Philip away, and the eunuch did not see him again, but went on his way rejoicing. [40]Philip, however, appeared at Azotus and traveled about, preaching the gospel in all the towns until he reached Caesarea.

[k]16 Or in   [l]27 That is, from the upper Nile region   [m]33 Isaiah 53:7,8   [n]36 Some late manuscripts baptized?" [37]Philip said, "If you believe with all your heart, you may." The eunuch answered, "I believe that Jesus Christ is the Son of God."

Discovering the Word 1. In this passage the command to be witnesses in all of Judea and Samaria (Ac 1:8) is fulfilled. What are the causes and extent of the spread of the gospel at this time? 2. Look at the story of Simon the Sorcerer (vv. 9–25). How does he attempt to get spiritual power? What is his motivation for wanting this power (vv. 18–19)? 3. In contrast, what is God's way for his people to receive spiritual power (vv.

20–23)? **4.** What are the factors involved in the eunuch's coming to know the Lord (vv. 26–39)? **5.** How was Philip's ministry to the eunuch the beginning of the witness "to the ends of the earth" (Ac 1:8)?

 Applying the Word **1.** The story of Simon the Sorcerer demonstrates that becoming a Christian does not instantly resolve all problems and character flaws. What do you learn from Peter concerning nurturing young believers? **2.** What principles of evangelism have you observed throughout this passage? **3.** What have you learned from Acts 8 that might make you a more effective witness for Jesus?

 Responding in Prayer Ask God for the guidance of his Holy Spirit, and ask him to help you follow the model of evangelism that Philip provides.

9 / *Acts 9:1–31*
Saul's Conversion

WHEN CHUCK COLSON became a Christian in prison, the whole nation reacted with skepticism—Christians and non-Christians alike. Of all the leading characters in the Watergate scandal, he was one of the most notorious. Could such a calculating man sincerely come to God?

 Warming Up to God Think back to what your life was like before you met Christ. Thank God for the transformation that he has made in your life—both your instant rebirth into his kingdom and the gradual remolding of your character since then.

Read Acts 9:1–31.

9 Meanwhile, Saul was still breathing out murderous threats against the Lord's disciples. He went to the high priest ²and asked him for letters to the synagogues in Damascus, so that if he found any there who belonged to the Way, whether men or women, he might take them as prisoners to Jerusalem. ³As he neared Damascus on his journey, suddenly a light from heaven flashed around him. ⁴He fell to the ground and heard a voice say to him, "Saul, Saul, why do you persecute me?"

⁵"Who are you, Lord?" Saul asked.

"I am Jesus, whom you are persecuting," he replied. ⁶"Now get up and go into the city, and you will be told what you must do."

⁷The men traveling with Saul stood there speechless; they heard the sound but did not see anyone. ⁸Saul got up from the ground, but when he opened his eyes he could see nothing. So they led him by the hand into Damascus. ⁹For three days he was blind, and did not eat or drink anything.

¹⁰In Damascus there was a disciple named Ananias. The Lord called to him in a vision, "Ananias!"

"Yes, Lord," he answered.

¹¹The Lord told him, "Go to the house of Judas on Straight Street and ask for a man from Tarsus named Saul, for he is praying. ¹²In a vision he has seen a man named Ananias come and place his hands on him to restore his sight."

¹³"Lord," Ananias answered, "I have heard many reports about this man and all the harm he has done to your saints in Jerusalem. ¹⁴And he has come here with authority from the chief priests to arrest all who call on your name."

¹⁵But the Lord said to Ananias, "Go! This man is my chosen instrument to carry my name before the Gentiles and their kings and before the people of Israel. ¹⁶I will show him how much he must suffer for my name."

¹⁷Then Ananias went to the house and entered it. Placing his hands on Saul, he said, "Brother Saul, the Lord—Jesus, who appeared to you on the road as you were coming here—has sent me so that you may see again and be filled with the Holy Spirit." ¹⁸Immediately, something like scales fell from Saul's eyes, and he could see again. He got up and was baptized, ¹⁹and after taking some food, he regained his strength.

Saul spent several days with the disciples in Damascus. ²⁰At once he began to preach in the synagogues that Jesus is the Son of God. [21]All those who heard him were astonished and asked, "Isn't he the man who raised havoc in Jerusalem among those who call on this name? And hasn't he come here to take them as prisoners to the chief priests?" [22]Yet Saul grew more and more powerful and baffled the Jews living in Damascus by proving that Jesus is the Christ.[o]

[23]After many days had gone by, the Jews conspired to kill him, [24]but Saul learned of their plan. Day and night they kept close watch on the city gates in order to kill him. [25]But his followers took him by night and lowered him in a basket through an opening in the wall.

[26]When he came to Jerusalem, he tried to join the disciples, but they were all afraid of him, not believing that he really was a disciple. [27]But Bar-nabas took him and brought him to the apostles. He told them how Saul on his journey had seen the Lord and that the Lord had spoken to him, and how in Damascus he had preached fearlessly in the name of Jesus. [28]So Saul stayed with them and moved about freely in Jerusalem, speaking boldly in the name of the Lord. [29]He talked and debated with the Grecian Jews, but they tried to kill him. [30]When the brothers learned of this, they took him down to Caesarea and sent him off to Tarsus.

[31]Then the church throughout Judea, Galilee and Samaria enjoyed a time of peace. It was strengthened; and encouraged by the Holy Spirit, it grew in numbers, living in the fear of the Lord.

[o]22 Or Messiah

Discovering the Word 1. Review what you know about Saul (7:58—8:3). What further insights do you get about him from 9:1–2? 2. Describe Saul's encounter with Jesus Christ in verses 3–9. (What is the emotional, spiritual, physical and social climate?) 3. Ananias is the second person within three days to have a direct encounter with the Lord. Compare and contrast his encounter (vv. 10–16) with that of Saul. 4. What is the significance of Ananias addressing Saul as "Brother" (v. 17)? 5. What is the response of both believers and nonbelievers to Saul and his ministry (vv. 19–30)? 6. What role does Barnabas play in Saul's life and ministry?

Applying the Word 1. What do you learn about obedience to God through Saul and Ananias? 2. What does Saul's conversion teach us about those in our lives who are most likely not to believe? 3. Consider the people in your life who are most antagonistic to Christianity. How might God use you to bring them to Christ?

Responding in Prayer Pray for the salvation of someone you consider an unlikely convert. Ask God to increase your faith.

---

10 / *Acts 9:32—10:48*
Salvation for Every Nation

ONCE THE BERLIN Wall seemed impenetrable, and communism powerful and indestructible. For seventy years Christians wondered if Christmas would ever be openly celebrated in Russia. Then, dramatically, the wall fell. Communism collapsed. Nations that had been closed to the gospel for years began to welcome Christians, their help and their message with open arms. The historic breakthrough was like the one the early Christians experienced in this passage. A seemingly impenetrable spiritual wall was broken down. In both situations we see that from God's perspective there is always the potential for reaching every person in all the corners of the world with the wonderful news of Jesus Christ.

Warming Up to God Think of an impossible feat that you have seen God accomplish. Thank him and allow him to show you again that he truly is almighty.

Read Acts 9:32—10:48.

³²As Peter traveled about the country, he went to visit the saints in Lydda. ³³There he found a man named Aeneas, a paralytic who had been bedridden for eight years. ³⁴"Aeneas," Peter said to him, "Jesus Christ heals you. Get up and take care of your mat." Immediately Aeneas got up. ³⁵All those who lived in Lydda and Sharon saw him and turned to the Lord.

³⁶In Joppa there was a disciple named Tabitha (which, when translated, is Dorcas*P*), who was always doing good and helping the poor. ³⁷About that time she became sick and died, and her body was washed and placed in an upstairs room. ³⁸Lydda was near Joppa; so when the disciples heard that Peter was in Lydda, they sent two men to him and urged him, "Please come at once!"

³⁹Peter went with them, and when he arrived he was taken upstairs to the room. All the widows stood around him, crying and showing him the robes and other clothing that Dorcas had made while she was still with them.

⁴⁰Peter sent them all out of the room; then he got down on his knees and prayed. Turning toward the dead woman, he said, "Tabitha, get up." She opened her eyes, and seeing Peter she sat up. ⁴¹He took her by the hand and helped her to her feet. Then he called the believers and the widows and presented her to them alive. ⁴²This became known all over Joppa, and many people believed in the Lord. ⁴³Peter stayed in Joppa for some time with a tanner named Simon.

10 At Caesarea there was a man named Cornelius, a centurion in what was known as the Italian Regiment. ²He and all his family were devout and God-fearing; he gave generously to those in need and prayed to God regularly. ³One day at about three in the afternoon he had a vision. He distinctly saw an angel of God, who came to him and said, "Cornelius!"

⁴Cornelius stared at him in fear. "What is it, Lord?" he asked.

The angel answered, "Your prayers and gifts to the poor have come up as a memorial offering before God. ⁵Now send men to Joppa to bring back a man named Simon who is called Peter. ⁶He is staying with Simon the tanner, whose house is by the sea."

⁷When the angel who spoke to him had gone, Cornelius called two of his servants and a devout soldier who was one of his attendants. ⁸He told them everything that had happened and sent them to Joppa.

⁹About noon the following day as they were on their journey and approaching the city, Peter went up on the roof to pray. ¹⁰He became hungry and wanted something to eat, and while the meal was being prepared, he fell into a trance. ¹¹He saw heaven opened and something like a large sheet being let down to earth by its four corners. ¹²It contained all kinds of four-footed animals, as well as reptiles of the earth and birds of the air. ¹³Then a voice told him, "Get up, Peter. Kill and eat."

¹⁴"Surely not, Lord!" Peter replied. "I have never eaten anything impure or unclean."

¹⁵The voice spoke to him a second time, "Do not call anything impure that God has made clean."

¹⁶This happened three times, and immediately the sheet was taken back to heaven.

¹⁷While Peter was wondering about the meaning of the vision, the men sent by Cornelius found out where Simon's house was and stopped at the gate. ¹⁸They called out, asking if Simon who was known as Peter was staying there.

¹⁹While Peter was still thinking about the vision, the Spirit said to him, "Simon, three*q* men are looking for you. ²⁰So get up and go downstairs. Do not hesitate to go with them, for I have sent them."

²¹Peter went down and said to the men, "I'm the one you're looking for. Why have you come?"

²²The men replied, "We have come from Cornelius the centurion. He is a righteous and God-fearing man, who is respected by all the Jewish people. A holy angel told him to have you come to his house so that he could hear what you have to say." ²³Then Peter invited the men into the house to be his guests.

The next day Peter started out with them, and some of the brothers from Joppa went along. ²⁴The following day he arrived in Caesarea. Cornelius was expecting them and had called together his relatives and close friends. ²⁵As Peter entered the house, Cornelius met him and fell at his feet in reverence. ²⁶But Peter made him get up. "Stand up," he said, "I am only a man myself."

²⁷Talking with him, Peter went inside and found a large gathering of people. ²⁸He said to

---

P36 Both *Tabitha* (Aramaic) and *Dorcas* (Greek) mean *gazelle.*
q19 One early manuscript *two*; other manuscripts do not have the number.

them: "You are well aware that it is against our law for a Jew to associate with a Gentile or visit him. But God has shown me that I should not call any man impure or unclean. ²⁹So when I was sent for, I came without raising any objection. May I ask why you sent for me?"

³⁰Cornelius answered: "Four days ago I was in my house praying at this hour, at three in the afternoon. Suddenly a man in shining clothes stood before me ³¹and said, 'Cornelius, God has heard your prayer and remembered your gifts to the poor. ³²Send to Joppa for Simon who is called Peter. He is a guest in the home of Simon the tanner, who lives by the sea.' ³³So I sent for you immediately, and it was good of you to come. Now we are all here in the presence of God to listen to everything the Lord has commanded you to tell us."

³⁴Then Peter began to speak: "I now realize how true it is that God does not show favoritism ³⁵but accepts men from every nation who fear him and do what is right. ³⁶You know the message God sent to the people of Israel, telling the good news of peace through Jesus Christ, who is Lord of all. ³⁷You know what has happened throughout Judea, beginning in Galilee after the baptism that John preached— ³⁸how God anointed Jesus of Nazareth with the Holy Spirit and power, and how he went around doing good and healing all who were under the power of the devil, because God was with him.

³⁹"We are witnesses of everything he did in the country of the Jews and in Jerusalem. They killed him by hanging him on a tree, ⁴⁰but God raised him from the dead on the third day and caused him to be seen. ⁴¹He was not seen by all the people, but by witnesses whom God had already chosen—by us who ate and drank with him after he rose from the dead. ⁴²He commanded us to preach to the people and to testify that he is the one whom God appointed as judge of the living and the dead. ⁴³All the prophets testify about him that everyone who believes in him receives forgiveness of sins through his name."

⁴⁴While Peter was still speaking these words, the Holy Spirit came on all who heard the message. ⁴⁵The circumcised believers who had come with Peter were astonished that the gift of the Holy Spirit had been poured out even on the Gentiles. ⁴⁶For they heard them speaking in tongues_r_ and praising God.

Then Peter said, ⁴⁷"Can anyone keep these people from being baptized with water? They have received the Holy Spirit just as we have." ⁴⁸So he ordered that they be baptized in the name of Jesus Christ. Then they asked Peter to stay with them for a few days.

_r_46 Or other languages

Discovering the Word   1. How is God's power demonstrated in 9:32–43?   2. This is the first time Peter has been involved in raising someone from the dead. How might this prepare him for what happens in chapter 10?   3. How did God prepare Cornelius for Peter (10:1–8)?   4. In what ways did God prepare Peter for Cornelius (10:9–33)?   5. What evidence is there that Cornelius expected God to work (10:24–26)?

Applying the Word   1. What lessons do we learn from Cornelius's life?   2. In summary, how do you see God's purpose, as stated in Acts 1:8, "You will receive power when the Holy Spirit comes on you; and you will be my witnesses in Jerusalem, and in all Judea and Samaria, and to the ends of the earth," being fulfilled in this passage?   3. In what ways could you grow in relating to people of other cultures and races?

 Responding in Prayer   Ask God to use your experiences in life and knowledge of him to bring others to Christ.

---

11 / *Acts 11*
The First Jewish-Gentile Church

LUKE SET UP the stories of Peter and Cornelius and Ananias with amazing symmetry. The Holy Spirit simultaneously prepared the hearts of Ananias and of Saul—as he simultaneously prepared those of Peter and Cornelius. Peter questioned and hesitated, as did Ananias. Peter doubted whether he could be friends with the Gentiles,

Ananias whether he could approach the enemy of the church. Both obey without hesitation when God makes his divine will known. These stories come together in today's study. Peter defends his ministry to Cornelius to the church at Jerusalem. He convinces them of God's work in the Gentiles. It is also here that Saul, the one-time enemy of the church, reappears as a minister to the church in Antioch, a church filled with both Jewish and Gentile Christians.

 Warming Up to God In the face of change, how do you handle the need for a new perspective? Resistance? Excitement? Uncertainty? Do you face a change now? Take time to put your response, whatever it is, in God's hands.

Read Acts 11.

11 The apostles and the brothers throughout Judea heard that the Gentiles also had received the word of God. ²So when Peter went up to Jerusalem, the circumcised believers criticized him ³and said, "You went into the house of uncircumcised men and ate with them."

⁴Peter began and explained everything to them precisely as it had happened: ⁵"I was in the city of Joppa praying, and in a trance I saw a vision. I saw something like a large sheet being let down from heaven by its four corners, and it came down to where I was. ⁶I looked into it and saw four-footed animals of the earth, wild beasts, reptiles, and birds of the air. ⁷Then I heard a voice telling me, 'Get up, Peter. Kill and eat.'

⁸"I replied, 'Surely not, Lord! Nothing impure or unclean has ever entered my mouth.'

⁹"The voice spoke from heaven a second time, 'Do not call anything impure that God has made clean.' ¹⁰This happened three times, and then it was all pulled up to heaven again.

¹¹"Right then three men who had been sent to me from Caesarea stopped at the house where I was staying. ¹²The Spirit told me to have no hesitation about going with them. These six brothers also went with me, and we entered the man's house. ¹³He told us how he had seen an angel appear in his house and say, 'Send to Joppa for Simon who is called Peter. ¹⁴He will bring you a message through which you and all your household will be saved.'

¹⁵"As I began to speak, the Holy Spirit came on them as he had come on us at the beginning. ¹⁶Then I remembered what the Lord had said: 'John baptized withˢ water, but you will be baptized with the Holy Spirit.' ¹⁷So if God gave them the same gift as he gave us, who believed in the Lord Jesus Christ, who was I to think that I could oppose God?"

¹⁸When they heard this, they had no further objections and praised God, saying, "So then, God has granted even the Gentiles repentance unto life."

¹⁹Now those who had been scattered by the persecution in connection with Stephen traveled as far as Phoenicia, Cyprus and Antioch, telling the message only to Jews. ²⁰Some of them, however, men from Cyprus and Cyrene, went to Antioch and began to speak to Greeks also, telling them the good news about the Lord Jesus. ²¹The Lord's hand was with them, and a great number of people believed and turned to the Lord.

²²News of this reached the ears of the church at Jerusalem, and they sent Barnabas to Antioch. ²³When he arrived and saw the evidence of the grace of God, he was glad and encouraged them all to remain true to the Lord with all their hearts. ²⁴He was a good man, full of the Holy Spirit and faith, and a great number of people were brought to the Lord.

²⁵Then Barnabas went to Tarsus to look for Saul, ²⁶and when he found him, he brought him to Antioch. So for a whole year Barnabas and Saul met with the church and taught great numbers of people. The disciples were called Christians first at Antioch.

²⁷During this time some prophets came down from Jerusalem to Antioch. ²⁸One of them, named Agabus, stood up and through the Spirit predicted that a severe famine would spread over the entire Roman world. (This happened during the reign of Claudius.) ²⁹The disciples, each according to his ability, decided to provide help for the brothers living in Judea. ³⁰This they did, sending their gift to the elders by Barnabas and Saul.

ˢ16 Or *in*

Discovering the Word 1. What kind of reception was awaiting Peter when he went back up to Jerusalem (vv. 1–3)? 2. What seemed to be the final and most convincing proof to Peter of God's working in the Gentiles (vv. 15–17)? Why? 3. In the meantime the gospel is spreading to Gentiles at a tremendous rate in Antioch. What kind of care is provided for new believers (vv. 22–30)? 4. What was the reason for, and what were the results of, Barnabas's trip to Antioch (vv. 22–30)?

 Applying the Word 1. What can we learn from the way Peter responded to his critics? 2. How does our care for new believers compare and contrast to the care given here? 3. How do you see in this passage the true meaning of "Christian" being more fully discovered and lived out in a multicultural church?

 Responding in Prayer Ask God to help you be more open and flexible to the changes that he desires to bring about in your life.

12 / *Acts 12*
Miraculous Escape

HUDSON TAYLOR, FAMOUS missionary to China, said, "Man is moved by God through prayer alone." We see the power of God demonstrated in this passage in response to the prayers of his people.

Warming Up to God Recall a time when God answered one of your prayers. Thank him for the joy and encouragement you received from his gracious blessing upon you.

Read Acts 12.

12 It was about this time that King Herod arrested some who belonged to the church, intending to persecute them. ²He had James, the brother of John, put to death with the sword. ³When he saw that this pleased the Jews, he proceeded to seize Peter also. This happened during the Feast of Unleavened Bread. ⁴After arresting him, he put him in prison, handing him over to be guarded by four squads of four soldiers each. Herod intended to bring him out for public trial after the Passover.

⁵So Peter was kept in prison, but the church was earnestly praying to God for him.

⁶The night before Herod was to bring him to trial, Peter was sleeping between two soldiers, bound with two chains, and sentries stood guard at the entrance. ⁷Suddenly an angel of the Lord appeared and a light shone in the cell. He struck Peter on the side and woke him up. "Quick, get up!" he said, and the chains fell off Peter's wrists. ⁸Then the angel said to him, "Put on your clothes and sandals." And Peter did so. "Wrap your cloak around you and follow me," the angel told him. ⁹Peter followed him out of the prison, but he had no idea that what the angel was doing was really happening; he thought he was seeing a vision. ¹⁰They passed the first and second guards and came to the iron gate leading to the city. It opened for them by itself, and they went through it. When they had walked the length of one street, suddenly the angel left him.

¹¹Then Peter came to himself and said, "Now I know without a doubt that the Lord sent his angel and rescued me from Herod's clutches and from everything the Jewish people were anticipating."

¹²When this had dawned on him, he went to the house of Mary the mother of John, also called Mark, where many people had gathered and were praying. ¹³Peter knocked at the outer entrance, and a servant girl named Rhoda came to answer the door. ¹⁴When she recognized Peter's voice, she was so overjoyed she ran back without opening it and exclaimed, "Peter is at the door!"

¹⁵"You're out of your mind," they told her. When she kept insisting that it was so, they said, "It must be his angel."

¹⁶But Peter kept on knocking, and when they opened the door and saw him, they were astonished. ¹⁷Peter motioned with his hand for them to be quiet and described how the Lord had brought him out of prison. "Tell James and the brothers

about this," he said, and then he left for another place.

¹⁸In the morning, there was no small commotion among the soldiers as to what had become of Peter. ¹⁹After Herod had a thorough search made for him and did not find him, he cross-examined the guards and ordered that they be executed.

Then Herod went from Judea to Caesarea and stayed there a while. ²⁰He had been quarreling with the people of Tyre and Sidon; they now joined together and sought an audience with him. Having secured the support of Blastus, a trusted personal servant of the king, they asked for peace, because they depended on the king's country for their food supply.

²¹On the appointed day Herod, wearing his royal robes, sat on his throne and delivered a public address to the people. ²²They shouted, "This is the voice of a god, not of a man." ²³Immediately, because Herod did not give praise to God, an angel of the Lord struck him down, and he was eaten by worms and died.

²⁴But the word of God continued to increase and spread.

²⁵When Barnabas and Saul had finished their mission, they returned from' Jerusalem, taking with them John, also called Mark.

ᶠ25 Some manuscripts to

Discovering the Word 1. Describe the main characters in this passage. How do they respond to what is happening to and around them? 2. What seems to motivate Herod's actions (vv. 1–5)? 3. What does the church's response to James's death and Peter's being in prison (vv. 5 and 12) demonstrate about prayer? 4. Why was Herod struck down (vv. 21–23)? 5. Contrast Herod's end with what happened with the Word of God (vv. 19–24).

Applying the Word 1. How have you seen God respond to a group of people who were earnestly praying? 2. Why do you think the praying Christians reacted as they did to Peter's return? 3. The earnest prayer of the church significantly affected the outcome of the events of this chapter. How is your motivation to pray influenced by this truth?

Responding in Prayer Think of an "impossible" prayer request or need that you have. Place it before God and ask him to give you the faith to believe that he will answer your prayer and give you "the desires of your heart."

---

13 / Acts 13—14
Paul's First Missionary Journey

PETER HAS DISAPPEARED. We do not know where he is hiding. Luke is ushering Peter from the stage while Paul steps to the forefront. Peter, the apostle to the Jews, has played his part well and prepared the way for Paul, the apostle to the Gentiles. Paul and Barnabas have completed their mission of mercy in Jerusalem on behalf of the church in Antioch (11:29) and have returned to Antioch with John Mark. In this study we will look at Paul's first missionary journey—the beginning of his master plan of evangelism.

Warming Up to God Do you feel distant from God as you try to approach the Scriptures? Remember that God in his great mercy has come to us first and wants to meet us here. He longs to care for us, his little sheep, and capture us in his arms.

 Read Acts 13—14.

---

13 In the church at Antioch there were prophets and teachers: Barnabas, Simeon called Niger, Lucius of Cyrene, Manaen (who had been brought up with Herod the tetrarch) and Saul. ²While they were worshiping the Lord and fasting, the Holy Spirit said, "Set apart for me Barnabas and Saul for the work to which I have called them." ³So after they had fasted and prayed, they placed their hands on them and sent them off.

⁴The two of them, sent on their way by the Holy Spirit, went down to Seleucia and sailed from there to Cyprus. ⁵When they arrived at Salamis, they proclaimed the word of God in the Jewish synagogues. John was with them as their helper.

⁶They traveled through the whole island until they came to Paphos. There they met a Jewish sorcerer and false prophet named Bar-Jesus, ⁷who was an attendant of the proconsul, Sergius Paulus. The proconsul, an intelligent man, sent for Barnabas and Saul because he wanted to hear the word of God. ⁸But Elymas the sorcerer (for that is what his name means) opposed them and tried to turn the proconsul from the faith. ⁹Then Saul, who was also called Paul, filled with the Holy Spirit, looked straight at Elymas and said, ¹⁰"You are a child of the devil and an enemy of everything that is right! You are full of all kinds of deceit and trickery. Will you never stop perverting the right ways of the Lord? ¹¹Now the hand of the Lord is against you. You are going to be blind, and for a time you will be unable to see the light of the sun."

Immediately mist and darkness came over him, and he groped about, seeking someone to lead him by the hand. ¹²When the proconsul saw what had happened, he believed, for he was amazed at the teaching about the Lord.

¹³From Paphos, Paul and his companions sailed to Perga in Pamphylia, where John left them to return to Jerusalem. ¹⁴From Perga they went on to Pisidian Antioch. On the Sabbath they entered the synagogue and sat down. ¹⁵After the reading from the Law and the Prophets, the synagogue rulers sent word to them, saying, "Brothers, if you have a message of encouragement for the people, please speak."

¹⁶Standing up, Paul motioned with his hand and said: "Men of Israel and you Gentiles who worship God, listen to me! ¹⁷The God of the people of Israel chose our fathers; he made the people prosper during their stay in Egypt, with mighty power he led them out of that country, ¹⁸he endured their conduct[u] for about forty years in the desert, ¹⁹he overthrew seven nations in Canaan and gave their land to his people as their inheritance. ²⁰All this took about 450 years.

"After this, God gave them judges until the time of Samuel the prophet. ²¹Then the people asked for a king, and he gave them Saul son of Kish, of the tribe of Benjamin, who ruled forty years. ²²After removing Saul, he made David their king. He testified concerning him: 'I have found David son of Jesse a man after my own heart; he will do everything I want him to do.'

²³"From this man's descendants God has brought to Israel the Savior Jesus, as he promised. ²⁴Before the coming of Jesus, John preached repentance and baptism to all the people of Israel. ²⁵As John was completing his work, he said: 'Who do you think I am? I am not that one. No, but he is coming after me, whose sandals I am not worthy to untie.'

²⁶"Brothers, children of Abraham, and you God-fearing Gentiles, it is to us that this message of salvation has been sent. ²⁷The people of Jerusalem and their rulers did not recognize Jesus, yet in condemning him they fulfilled the words of the prophets that are read every Sabbath. ²⁸Though they found no proper ground for a death sentence, they asked Pilate to have him executed. ²⁹When they had carried out all that was written about him, they took him down from the tree and laid him in a tomb. ³⁰But God raised him from the dead, ³¹and for many days he was seen by those who had traveled with him from Galilee to Jerusalem. They are now his witnesses to our people.

³²"We tell you the good news: What God promised our fathers ³³he has fulfilled for us, their children, by raising up Jesus. As it is written in the second Psalm:

" 'You are my Son;
        today I have become your Father.'[v][w]

³⁴The fact that God raised him from the dead, never to decay, is stated in these words:

" 'I will give you the holy and sure blessings
        promised to David.'[x]

³⁵So it is stated elsewhere:

" 'You will not let your Holy One see decay.'[y]

³⁶"For when David had served God's purpose in his own generation, he fell asleep; he was buried with his fathers and his body decayed. ³⁷But the one whom God raised from the dead did not see decay.

³⁸"Therefore, my brothers, I want you to know that through Jesus the forgiveness of sins is pro-

---

u18 Some manuscripts *and cared for them*   v33 Or *have begotten you*
w33 Psalm 2:7   x34 Isaiah 55:3   y35 Psalm 16:10

claimed to you. 39Through him everyone who believes is justified from everything you could not be justified from by the law of Moses. 40Take care that what the prophets have said does not happen to you:

41" 'Look, you scoffers,
    wonder and perish,
for I am going to do something in your days
    that you would never believe,
    even if someone told you.'z "

42As Paul and Barnabas were leaving the synagogue, the people invited them to speak further about these things on the next Sabbath. 43When the congregation was dismissed, many of the Jews and devout converts to Judaism followed Paul and Barnabas, who talked with them and urged them to continue in the grace of God.

44On the next Sabbath almost the whole city gathered to hear the word of the Lord. 45When the Jews saw the crowds, they were filled with jealousy and talked abusively against what Paul was saying.

46Then Paul and Barnabas answered them boldly: "We had to speak the word of God to you first. Since you reject it and do not consider yourselves worthy of eternal life, we now turn to the Gentiles. 47For this is what the Lord has commanded us:

" 'I have made youa a light for the Gentiles,
    that youa may bring salvation to the ends
        of the earth.'b "

48When the Gentiles heard this, they were glad and honored the word of the Lord; and all who were appointed for eternal life believed.

49The word of the Lord spread through the whole region. 50But the Jews incited the God-fearing women of high standing and the leading men of the city. They stirred up persecution against Paul and Barnabas, and expelled them from their region. 51So they shook the dust from their feet in protest against them and went to Iconium. 52And the disciples were filled with joy and with the Holy Spirit.

14 At Iconium Paul and Barnabas went as usual into the Jewish synagogue. There they spoke so effectively that a great number of Jews and Gentiles believed. 2But the Jews who refused to believe stirred up the Gentiles and poisoned their minds against the brothers. 3So Paul and Barnabas spent consider-

able time there, speaking boldly for the Lord, who confirmed the message of his grace by enabling them to do miraculous signs and wonders. 4The people of the city were divided; some sided with the Jews, others with the apostles. 5There was a plot afoot among the Gentiles and Jews, together with their leaders, to mistreat them and stone them. 6But they found out about it and fled to the Lycaonian cities of Lystra and Derbe and to the surrounding country, 7where they continued to preach the good news.

8In Lystra there sat a man crippled in his feet, who was lame from birth and had never walked. 9He listened to Paul as he was speaking. Paul looked directly at him, saw that he had faith to be healed 10and called out, "Stand up on your feet!" At that, the man jumped up and began to walk.

11When the crowd saw what Paul had done, they shouted in the Lycaonian language, "The gods have come down to us in human form!" 12Barnabas they called Zeus, and Paul they called Hermes because he was the chief speaker. 13The priest of Zeus, whose temple was just outside the city, brought bulls and wreaths to the city gates because he and the crowd wanted to offer sacrifices to them.

14But when the apostles Barnabas and Paul heard of this, they tore their clothes and rushed out into the crowd, shouting: 15"Men, why are you doing this? We too are only men, human like you. We are bringing you good news, telling you to turn from these worthless things to the living God, who made heaven and earth and sea and everything in them. 16In the past, he let all nations go their own way. 17Yet he has not left himself without testimony: He has shown kindness by giving you rain from heaven and crops in their seasons; he provides you with plenty of food and fills your hearts with joy." 18Even with these words, they had difficulty keeping the crowd from sacrificing to them.

19Then some Jews came from Antioch and Iconium and won the crowd over. They stoned Paul and dragged him outside the city, thinking he was dead. 20But after the disciples had gathered around him, he got up and went back into the city. The next day he and Barnabas left for Derbe.

21They preached the good news in that city and won a large number of disciples. Then they returned to Lystra, Iconium and Antioch,

z41 Hab. 1:5   a47 The Greek is singular.   b47 Isaiah 49:6

²²strengthening the disciples and encouraging them to remain true to the faith. "We must go through many hardships to enter the kingdom of God," they said. ²³Paul and Barnabas appointed elders*c* for them in each church and, with prayer and fasting, committed them to the Lord, in whom they had put their trust. ²⁴After going through Pisidia, they came into Pamphylia, ²⁵and when they had preached the word in Perga, they went down to Attalia.

²⁶From Attalia they sailed back to Antioch, where they had been committed to the grace of God for the work they had now completed. ²⁷On arriving there, they gathered the church together and reported all that God had done through them and how he had opened the door of faith to the Gentiles. ²⁸And they stayed there a long time with the disciples.

c23 Or Barnabas ordained elders; or Barnabas had elders elected

---

 Discovering the Word 1. Antioch was the second greatest metropolis of the church and the mother of Gentile Christianity. What role did the church of Antioch play in Paul's first missionary journey (13:1–3; 14:26–28)? 2. Review Paul's message in the synagogue in Pisidian Antioch (13:16–41). What truths of the gospel are communicated? 3. How does Paul's message show sensitivity to his audience and the context? 4. List the different responses to the gospel (13:7–8, 13, 42–45, 48, 52; 14:1–5) that you see throughout this passage. 5. How did Paul respond to those who rejected the gospel (13:9–11, 46, 51)? to those who believed (14:9–10, 21–23)?

Applying the Word 1. People today are not apt to offer sacrifices to those who bring the good news of Jesus. However, in what ways are we faced with the temptation to be "God" in another's life or to take credit for what God has done? 2. How can we help one another when in the midst of such temptations? 3. Consider the qualities you see in Paul and Barnabas that made them effective in their ministry. Which of these qualities do you want God to develop in you to make you more effective in communicating the gospel?

Responding in Prayer Is there a way God wants to change you? Talk to God about it.

---

14 / *Acts 15*
Conflict in the Church

IN MOST AREAS of life, I think I am pretty realistic. When it comes to conflict among believers, however, I tend to be an idealist. I believe that unity is something that God requires of us. Believers should be able to talk, pray and work through conflict—just the way it was worked through by the church at Jerusalem. However, I am becoming a little more realistic about this. I have been in several situations in which I felt like I did everything within my power to bring about reconciliation—but failed.

This seems to be the case with Paul and Barnabas. These two men who were used by God to keep a church from splitting could not resolve their own differences and ended up going separate ways. The late Kenneth Strachan of Latin American Mission said, "We all need to live and serve in the constant recognition of our own humanity."

 Warming Up to God Has there been a time recently when you were in conflict with someone? Tell God about it and let his peace and compassion wash over you as he teaches you.

 Read Acts 15.

---

15 Some men came down from Judea to Antioch and were teaching the brothers: "Unless you are circumcised, according to the custom taught by Moses, you cannot be saved." ²This brought Paul and Barnabas into sharp dispute and debate with them. So Paul and Barnabas were appointed, along with some other believers, to go up to Jerusalem to see the apostles and elders about this question. ³The church sent them on their way, and as they traveled through Phoenicia and Samaria, they told how the Gentiles had been converted. This news made all the brothers very glad. [4]When they came to Jerusalem, they were welcomed by the church and the apostles and elders, to whom they reported everything God had done through them.

[5]Then some of the believers who belonged to the party of the Pharisees stood up and said, "The Gentiles must be circumcised and required to obey the law of Moses."

[6]The apostles and elders met to consider this question. [7]After much discussion, Peter got up and addressed them: "Brothers, you know that some time ago God made a choice among you that the Gentiles might hear from my lips the message of the gospel and believe. [8]God, who knows the heart, showed that he accepted them by giving the Holy Spirit to them, just as he did to us. [9]He made no distinction between us and them, for he purified their hearts by faith. [10]Now then, why do you try to test God by putting on the necks of the disciples a yoke that neither we nor our fathers have been able to bear? [11]No! We believe it is through the grace of our Lord Jesus that we are saved, just as they are."

[12]The whole assembly became silent as they listened to Barnabas and Paul telling about the miraculous signs and wonders God had done among the Gentiles through them. [13]When they finished, James spoke up: "Brothers, listen to me. [14]Simon[d] has described to us how God at first showed his concern by taking from the Gentiles a people for himself. [15]The words of the prophets are in agreement with this, as it is written:

[16]" 'After this I will return
    and rebuild David's fallen tent.
Its ruins I will rebuild,
    and I will restore it,
[17]that the remnant of men may seek the Lord,
    and all the Gentiles who bear my name,
says the Lord, who does these things'[e]
[18]   that have been known for ages.[f]

[19]"It is my judgment, therefore, that we should not make it difficult for the Gentiles who are turning to God. [20]Instead we should write to them, telling them to abstain from food polluted by idols, from sexual immorality, from the meat of strangled animals and from blood. [21]For Moses has been preached in every city from the earliest times and is read in the synagogues on every Sabbath."

[22]Then the apostles and elders, with the whole church, decided to choose some of their own men and send them to Antioch with Paul and Barnabas. They chose Judas (called Barsabbas) and Silas, two men who were leaders among the brothers. [23]With them they sent the following letter:

The apostles and elders, your brothers,

To the Gentile believers in Antioch, Syria and Cilicia:

Greetings.

[24]We have heard that some went out from us without our authorization and disturbed you, troubling your minds by what they said. [25]So we all agreed to choose some men and send them to you with our dear friends Barnabas and Paul— [26]men who have risked their lives for the name of our Lord Jesus Christ. [27]Therefore we are sending Judas and Silas to confirm by word of mouth what we are writing. [28]It seemed good to the Holy Spirit and to us not to burden you with anything beyond the following requirements: [29]You are to abstain from food sacrificed to idols, from blood, from the meat of strangled animals and from sexual immorality. You will do well to avoid these things.

Farewell.

[30]The men were sent off and went down to Antioch, where they gathered the church together and delivered the letter. [31]The people read it and were glad for its encouraging message. [32]Judas and Silas, who themselves were prophets, said much to encourage and strengthen the brothers. [33]After spending some time there, they were sent off by the brothers with the blessing of peace to return to those who had sent them.[g] [35]But Paul and Barnabas remained in Antioch, where they and many others taught and preached the word of the Lord.

[36]Some time later Paul said to Barnabas, "Let us go back and visit the brothers in all the towns where we preached the word of the Lord and see how they are doing." [37]Barnabas wanted to take John, also called Mark, with them, [38]but Paul did not think it wise to take him, because he had deserted them in Pamphylia and had not contin-

[d]14 Greek *Simeon*, a variant of *Simon*; that is, Peter   [e]17 Amos 9:11,12   [f]17,18 Some manuscripts *things'—* / [18]*known to the Lord for ages is his work*   [g]33 Some manuscripts *them,* [34]*but Silas decided to remain there*

ued with them in the work. ³⁹They had such a sharp disagreement that they parted company. Barnabas took Mark and sailed for Cyprus, ⁴⁰but Paul chose Silas and left, commended by the brothers to the grace of the Lord. ⁴¹He went through Syria and Cilicia, strengthening the churches.

Discovering the Word 1. Describe the conflict that arises between the Christians (vv. 1–35). 2. Describe the spirit of those involved and the steps that were taken to resolve this conflict. 3. What were the results? 4. In what ways do you see (or can you assume) unity between Paul and Barnabas (vv. 36–41)? 5. Paul and Barnabas came to the point of "agreeing to disagree" and going their separate ways. What were the benefits of this temporary solution?

Applying the Word 1. What principles do you observe that are vital to follow as we face conflict with others in our Christian community? 2. Which of these principles do you struggle with implementing the most? 3. Both Paul and Barnabas seemed to have strong cases for their points of view. Under what kinds of circumstances should we surrender deep convictions when they are challenged by another? 4. No matter how strongly we feel about an issue, we do not see the whole picture. How should that affect the way we respond to people with whom we are in conflict?

Responding in Prayer Ask God to give you discernment as you face conflict in both the church and in your personal life.

---

15 / Acts 16
What Must I Do?

THE MEMORY IS still vivid. The event was InterVarsity's Urbana Missionary Conference. The place, a dormitory room. The person, a young lady from the Bible study group that I led. I sensed the prompting of the Holy Spirit to stop by Susan's room. As I walked in to say "hi" she looked up from the booklet she was reading and said, "I would like to become a Christian. Will you help me?" This dormitory setting was not quite as dramatic as the Philippian jail. But it was just as exciting to hear Susan's words, as it was for Paul and Silas to hear the jailer's cry, "Sirs, what must I do to be saved?"

Warming Up to God Think back to the time you uttered those words, either to a friend or to God himself. Praise God for creating a desire for him in you and thank him for giving his precious salvation to you.

Read Acts 16.

---

16 He came to Derbe and then to Lystra, where a disciple named Timothy lived, whose mother was a Jewess and a believer, but whose father was a Greek. ²The brothers at Lystra and Iconium spoke well of him. ³Paul wanted to take him along on the journey, so he circumcised him because of the Jews who lived in that area, for they all knew that his father was a Greek. ⁴As they traveled from town to town, they delivered the decisions reached by the apostles and elders in Jerusalem for the people to obey. ⁵So the churches were strengthened in the faith and grew daily in numbers.

⁶Paul and his companions traveled throughout the region of Phrygia and Galatia, having been kept by the Holy Spirit from preaching the word in the province of Asia. ⁷When they came to the border of Mysia, they tried to enter Bithynia, but the Spirit of Jesus would not allow them to. ⁸So they passed by Mysia and went down to Troas. ⁹During the night Paul had a vision of a man of Macedonia standing and begging him, "Come over to Macedonia and help us." ¹⁰After Paul had seen the vision, we got ready at once to leave for Macedonia, concluding that God had called us to preach the gospel to them.

¹¹From Troas we put out to sea and sailed

straight for Samothrace, and the next day on to Neapolis. ¹²From there we traveled to Philippi, a Roman colony and the leading city of that district of Macedonia. And we stayed there several days.

¹³On the Sabbath we went outside the city gate to the river, where we expected to find a place of prayer. We sat down and began to speak to the women who had gathered there. ¹⁴One of those listening was a woman named Lydia, a dealer in purple cloth from the city of Thyatira, who was a worshiper of God. The Lord opened her heart to respond to Paul's message. ¹⁵When she and the members of her household were baptized, she invited us to her home. "If you consider me a believer in the Lord," she said, "come and stay at my house." And she persuaded us.

¹⁶Once when we were going to the place of prayer, we were met by a slave girl who had a spirit by which she predicted the future. She earned a great deal of money for her owners by fortune-telling. ¹⁷This girl followed Paul and the rest of us, shouting, "These men are servants of the Most High God, who are telling you the way to be saved." ¹⁸She kept this up for many days. Finally Paul became so troubled that he turned around and said to the spirit, "In the name of Jesus Christ I command you to come out of her!" At that moment the spirit left her.

¹⁹When the owners of the slave girl realized that their hope of making money was gone, they seized Paul and Silas and dragged them into the marketplace to face the authorities. ²⁰They brought them before the magistrates and said, "These men are Jews, and are throwing our city into an uproar ²¹by advocating customs unlawful for us Romans to accept or practice."

²²The crowd joined in the attack against Paul and Silas, and the magistrates ordered them to be stripped and beaten. ²³After they had been severely flogged, they were thrown into prison, and the jailer was commanded to guard them carefully. ²⁴Upon receiving such orders, he put them in the inner cell and fastened their feet in the stocks.

²⁵About midnight Paul and Silas were praying and singing hymns to God, and the other prisoners were listening to them. ²⁶Suddenly there was such a violent earthquake that the foundations of the prison were shaken. At once all the prison doors flew open, and everybody's chains came loose. ²⁷The jailer woke up, and when he saw the prison doors open, he drew his sword and was about to kill himself because he thought the prisoners had escaped. ²⁸But Paul shouted, "Don't harm yourself! We are all here!"

²⁹The jailer called for lights, rushed in and fell trembling before Paul and Silas. ³⁰He then brought them out and asked, "Sirs, what must I do to be saved?"

³¹They replied, "Believe in the Lord Jesus, and you will be saved—you and your household." ³²Then they spoke the word of the Lord to him and to all the others in his house. ³³At that hour of the night the jailer took them and washed their wounds; then immediately he and all his family were baptized. ³⁴The jailer brought them into his house and set a meal before them; he was filled with joy because he had come to believe in God—he and his whole family.

³⁵When it was daylight, the magistrates sent their officers to the jailer with the order: "Release those men." ³⁶The jailer told Paul, "The magistrates have ordered that you and Silas be released. Now you can leave. Go in peace."

³⁷But Paul said to the officers: "They beat us publicly without a trial, even though we are Roman citizens, and threw us into prison. And now do they want to get rid of us quietly? No! Let them come themselves and escort us out."

³⁸The officers reported this to the magistrates, and when they heard that Paul and Silas were Roman citizens, they were alarmed. ³⁹They came to appease them and escorted them from the prison, requesting them to leave the city. ⁴⁰After Paul and Silas came out of the prison, they went to Lydia's house, where they met with the brothers and encouraged them. Then they left.

Discovering the Word   1. In verses 6–10 how is Paul directed concerning where he should go?   2. What principles of guidance do you see in verses 6–10?   3. Paul responded immediately to God's message. How was his obedience confirmed on arriving in Macedonia (vv. 11–15)?   4. The slaveowners had Paul and Silas jailed. Their response to being in jail and being beaten was to pray and sing hymns. Describe the events that led up to the jailer's question "What must I do to be saved?" (vv. 23–30).   5. It is clear in the book of Acts that God is concerned about the world and the nations being reached with the gospel. But he is also concerned about reaching individuals. What individuals were affected by Paul's obedience to God's leading (vv. 14, 18, 30–31)? How?

Applying the Word 1. How does your response to opposition to and suffering for the gospel compare and contrast to that of Paul and Silas (v. 25)? 2. Paul and Silas speak the truth of the gospel as well as living it out. How do you give both a verbal and a living witness to Jesus? 3. Is there a person or task to which God is calling you? What steps do you need to take for immediate and unreserved obedience?

Responding in Prayer Ask God to give you courage as you step in faith to obey him, to tell those around you about the good news that has transformed your life.

16 / *Acts 17*
An Unknown God

ONLY A FEW short decades ago, Christians in the West could assume that most people they met belonged to a church or at least based their lives on Judeo-Christian values. Today, Christians in the West face what Christians in the East have had to cope with for centuries—a wide variety of religious beliefs and practices that often have little in common with Christianity. The world's major religions, Hinduism, Buddhism and Islam, are making inroads as are a variety of cults, New Age philosophies, occultic activities and even traditional paganism. How do we cope with a world that knows or cares so little about the truth of Jesus Christ? Paul left us a helpful model when he visited the world center of pagan philosophy and religion—Athens.

Warming Up to God Do you often feel overwhelmed by the dismal spiritual conditions of this world? Remember and even savor the knowledge that Jesus is Lord over it all—the sin, deceit and pain around us are all subject to his will.

Read Acts 17.

17 When they had passed through Amphipolis and Apollonia, they came to Thessalonica, where there was a Jewish synagogue. ²As his custom was, Paul went into the synagogue, and on three Sabbath days he reasoned with them from the Scriptures, ³explaining and proving that the Christ[h] had to suffer and rise from the dead. "This Jesus I am proclaiming to you is the Christ,[h]" he said. ⁴Some of the Jews were persuaded and joined Paul and Silas, as did a large number of God-fearing Greeks and not a few prominent women.

⁵But the Jews were jealous; so they rounded up some bad characters from the marketplace, formed a mob and started a riot in the city. They rushed to Jason's house in search of Paul and Silas in order to bring them out to the crowd.[i] ⁶But when they did not find them, they dragged Jason and some other brothers before the city officials, shouting: "These men who have caused trouble all over the world have now come here, ⁷and Jason has welcomed them into his house. They are all defying Caesar's decrees, saying that there is another king, one called Jesus." ⁸When they heard this, the crowd and the city officials were

thrown into turmoil. ⁹Then they made Jason and the others post bond and let them go.

¹⁰As soon as it was night, the brothers sent Paul and Silas away to Berea. On arriving there, they went to the Jewish synagogue. ¹¹Now the Bereans were of more noble character than the Thessalonians, for they received the message with great eagerness and examined the Scriptures every day to see if what Paul said was true. ¹²Many of the Jews believed, as did also a number of prominent Greek women and many Greek men.

¹³When the Jews in Thessalonica learned that Paul was preaching the word of God at Berea, they went there too, agitating the crowds and stirring them up. ¹⁴The brothers immediately sent Paul to the coast, but Silas and Timothy stayed at Berea. ¹⁵The men who escorted Paul brought him to Athens and then left with instructions for Silas and Timothy to join him as soon as possible.

¹⁶While Paul was waiting for them in Athens, he was greatly distressed to see that the city was full of idols. ¹⁷So he reasoned in the synagogue with the Jews and the God-fearing Greeks, as well as in the marketplace day by day with those who

h3 Or *Messiah*   i5 Or *the assembly of the people*

happened to be there. [18]A group of Epicurean and Stoic philosophers began to dispute with him. Some of them asked, "What is this babbler trying to say?" Others remarked, "He seems to be advocating foreign gods." They said this because Paul was preaching the good news about Jesus and the resurrection. [19]Then they took him and brought him to a meeting of the Areopagus, where they said to him, "May we know what this new teaching is that you are presenting? [20]You are bringing some strange ideas to our ears, and we want to know what they mean." [21](All the Athenians and the foreigners who lived there spent their time doing nothing but talking about and listening to the latest ideas.)

[22]Paul then stood up in the meeting of the Areopagus and said: "Men of Athens! I see that in every way you are very religious. [23]For as I walked around and looked carefully at your objects of worship, I even found an altar with this inscription: TO AN UNKNOWN GOD. Now what you worship as something unknown I am going to proclaim to you.

[24]"The God who made the world and everything in it is the Lord of heaven and earth and does not live in temples built by hands. [25]And he is not served by human hands, as if he needed anything, because he himself gives all men life and breath and everything else. [26]From one man he made every nation of men, that they should inhabit the whole earth; and he determined the times set for them and the exact places where they should live. [27]God did this so that men would seek him and perhaps reach out for him and find him, though he is not far from each one of us. [28]'For in him we live and move and have our being.' As some of your own poets have said, 'We are his offspring.'

[29]"Therefore since we are God's offspring, we should not think that the divine being is like gold or silver or stone—an image made by man's design and skill. [30]In the past God overlooked such ignorance, but now he commands all people everywhere to repent. [31]For he has set a day when he will judge the world with justice by the man he has appointed. He has given proof of this to all men by raising him from the dead."

[32]When they heard about the resurrection of the dead, some of them sneered, but others said, "We want to hear you again on this subject." [33]At that, Paul left the Council. [34]A few men became followers of Paul and believed. Among them was Dionysius, a member of the Areopagus, also a woman named Damaris, and a number of others.

Discovering the Word 1. In this chapter Paul interacts with three cities and three different cultures. Compare and contrast Paul's ministry in Thessalonica and Berea. (What approach did he take? How was his message received by the people? What kind of results did he have?) 2. In Thessalonica and Berea, as in most places, Paul makes his contacts in the synagogues and speaks almost exclusively from Scripture. How does his ministry in Athens differ from this? 3. How do the people respond to his teaching in Athens? 4. Though Paul approaches people differently, some points in the content of his message are very consistent. Identify these (vv. 3, 18, 24–28, 30–31).

Applying the Word 1. In his lecture in Athens, Paul mentions "the objects of your worship." What are some of the objects of worship for people in our culture? 2. In Athens Paul begins to tell them about the living God with an inscription from one of their altars—"to an unknown god." What are the "points of truth" from which you can start to communicate the gospel to those in your world? 3. What are ways that you might be tempted to compromise the message of the gospel as you communicate it to certain people? 4. How do you need to better prepare yourself to effectively communicate the gospel of Jesus Christ to those to whom God has called you to minister?

Responding in Prayer Ask God to show you what you have in common with the non-Christians in your life.

17 / *Acts 18*
Companions in Ministry

JUST RECENTLY, I visited my childhood pastor and his wife. As I left them, my heart was full of gratitude. Gratitude not only for the Wrights, but also for the others past and present who have prepared me for outreach. I am thankful for those who have prayed for me, been my friends, walked along with me, listened to me, loved me and cared about my walk with God and my service to others, who have encouraged me and corrected me. I enjoy thinking about the people who have touched my life and who have been companions in ministry. I am not alone in this need for companionship. In this study we will look at some of the people in Paul's life who were his companions in ministry.

 Warming Up to God Close your eyes and think about one person who profoundly affects your life. Tell God how grateful you are to know such a wonderful friend and thank God for loving you through that person.

 Read Acts 18.

18 After this, Paul left Athens and went to Corinth. ²There he met a Jew named Aquila, a native of Pontus, who had recently come from Italy with his wife Priscilla, because Claudius had ordered all the Jews to leave Rome. Paul went to see them, ³and because he was a tentmaker as they were, he stayed and worked with them. ⁴Every Sabbath he reasoned in the synagogue, trying to persuade Jews and Greeks.

⁵When Silas and Timothy came from Macedonia, Paul devoted himself exclusively to preaching, testifying to the Jews that Jesus was the Christ.ʲ ⁶But when the Jews opposed Paul and became abusive, he shook out his clothes in protest and said to them, "Your blood be on your own heads! I am clear of my responsibility. From now on I will go to the Gentiles."

⁷Then Paul left the synagogue and went next door to the house of Titius Justus, a worshiper of God. ⁸Crispus, the synagogue ruler, and his entire household believed in the Lord; and many of the Corinthians who heard him believed and were baptized.

⁹One night the Lord spoke to Paul in a vision: "Do not be afraid; keep on speaking, do not be silent. ¹⁰For I am with you, and no one is going to attack and harm you, because I have many people in this city." ¹¹So Paul stayed for a year and a half, teaching them the word of God.

¹²While Gallio was proconsul of Achaia, the Jews made a united attack on Paul and brought him into court. ¹³"This man," they charged, "is persuading the people to worship God in ways contrary to the law."

¹⁴Just as Paul was about to speak, Gallio said to the Jews, "If you Jews were making a complaint about some misdemeanor or serious crime, it would be reasonable for me to listen to you. ¹⁵But since it involves questions about words and names and your own law—settle the matter yourselves. I will not be a judge of such things." ¹⁶So he had them ejected from the court. ¹⁷Then they all turned on Sosthenes the synagogue ruler and beat him in front of the court. But Gallio showed no concern whatever.

¹⁸Paul stayed on in Corinth for some time. Then he left the brothers and sailed for Syria, accompanied by Priscilla and Aquila. Before he sailed, he had his hair cut off at Cenchrea because of a vow he had taken. ¹⁹They arrived at Ephesus, where Paul left Priscilla and Aquila. He himself went into the synagogue and reasoned with the Jews. ²⁰When they asked him to spend more time with them, he declined. ²¹But as he left, he promised, "I will come back if it is God's will." Then he set sail from Ephesus. ²²When he landed at Caesarea, he went up and greeted the church and then went down to Antioch.

²³After spending some time in Antioch, Paul set out from there and traveled from place to place throughout the region of Galatia and Phrygia, strengthening all the disciples.

²⁴Meanwhile a Jew named Apollos, a native of Alexandria, came to Ephesus. He was a learned man, with a thorough knowledge of the Scriptures. ²⁵He had been instructed in the way of the Lord, and he spoke with great fervorᵏ and taught

ʲ5 Or *Messiah;* also in verse 28   ᵏ25 Or *with fervor in the Spirit* about Jesus accurately, though he knew only the baptism of John. ²⁶He began to speak boldly in the synagogue. When Priscilla and Aquila heard him, they invited him to their home and explained to him the way of God more adequately.

²⁷When Apollos wanted to go to Achaia, the brothers encouraged him and wrote to the disciples there to welcome him. On arriving, he was a great help to those who by grace had believed. ²⁸For he vigorously refuted the Jews in public debate, proving from the Scriptures that Jesus was the Christ.

Discovering the Word 1. List the people in Paul's life that you see in this passage. 2. What did Silas and Timothy contribute to Paul's life and ministry (v. 5)? 3. In verses 18–23 what do you learn about Paul's relationships? 4. Describe Apollos (vv. 24–26). 5. How was Apollos's ministry affected by his relationship with Aquila and Priscilla (vv. 27–28)?

Applying the Word 1. When has someone encouraged you with good news of God's work elsewhere, entered into your ministry, shared themselves or their home with you, or supported you financially or in other ways? 2. What keeps you from allowing others to enter into your life and ministry in such ways? 3. As you review this passage, what ways do you recognize in which you need to develop, build and nurture relationships that will contribute to your spiritual growth and outreach?

Responding in Prayer Who are your companions in ministry? Thank God for their presence in your life as good gifts from him.

---

18 / *Acts 19:1—20:12*
In the Name of Jesus

WE LEFT PAUL in chapter 18 traveling throughout Galatia and Phrygia "strengthening all the disciples." In this chapter he returns to Ephesus, where he settles for two and a half years. Great work is done there during this time, and it radiates out to other cities in the province of Asia. Luke vividly portrays the effect of Paul's ministry in just a few scenes in this chapter.

Warming Up to God Often we feel that reading the Bible is our time to give to God. But he dearly wants to come to us as we study Scripture and pray. Lay aside your effort right now and commit yourself to accepting God's grace. Let God be your companion while you study the Word.

Read Acts 19:1—20:12.

---

19 While Apollos was at Corinth, Paul took the road through the interior and arrived at Ephesus. There he found some disciples ²and asked them, "Did you receive the Holy Spirit when¹ you believed?"

They answered, "No, we have not even heard that there is a Holy Spirit."

³So Paul asked, "Then what baptism did you receive?"

"John's baptism," they replied.

⁴Paul said, "John's baptism was a baptism of repentance. He told the people to believe in the one coming after him, that is, in Jesus." ⁵On hearing this, they were baptized into^m the name of the Lord Jesus. ⁶When Paul placed his hands on

them, the Holy Spirit came on them, and they spoke in tongues^n and prophesied. ⁷There were about twelve men in all.

⁸Paul entered the synagogue and spoke boldly there for three months, arguing persuasively about the kingdom of God. ⁹But some of them became obstinate; they refused to believe and publicly maligned the Way. So Paul left them. He took the disciples with him and had discussions daily in the lecture hall of Tyrannus. ¹⁰This went on for two years, so that all the Jews and Greeks who lived in the province of Asia heard the word of the Lord.

¹¹God did extraordinary miracles through Paul,

¹2 Or *after*   ^m5 Or *in*   ^n6 Or *other languages*

¹²so that even handkerchiefs and aprons that had touched him were taken to the sick, and their illnesses were cured and the evil spirits left them.

¹³Some Jews who went around driving out evil spirits tried to invoke the name of the Lord Jesus over those who were demon-possessed. They would say, "In the name of Jesus, whom Paul preaches, I command you to come out." ¹⁴Seven sons of Sceva, a Jewish chief priest, were doing this. ¹⁵ᴸOne dayᴶ the evil spirit answered them, "Jesus I know, and I know about Paul, but who are you?" ¹⁶Then the man who had the evil spirit jumped on them and overpowered them all. He gave them such a beating that they ran out of the house naked and bleeding.

¹⁷When this became known to the Jews and Greeks living in Ephesus, they were all seized with fear, and the name of the Lord Jesus was held in high honor. ¹⁸Many of those who believed now came and openly confessed their evil deeds. ¹⁹A number who had practiced sorcery brought their scrolls together and burned them publicly. When they calculated the value of the scrolls, the total came to fifty thousand drachmas.ᵒ ²⁰In this way the word of the Lord spread widely and grew in power.

²¹After all this had happened, Paul decided to go to Jerusalem, passing through Macedonia and Achaia. "After I have been there," he said, "I must visit Rome also." ²²He sent two of his helpers, Timothy and Erastus, to Macedonia, while he stayed in the province of Asia a little longer.

²³About that time there arose a great disturbance about the Way. ²⁴A silversmith named Demetrius, who made silver shrines of Artemis, brought in no little business for the craftsmen. ²⁵He called them together, along with the workmen in related trades, and said: "Men, you know we receive a good income from this business. ²⁶And you see and hear how this fellow Paul has convinced and led astray large numbers of people here in Ephesus and in practically the whole province of Asia. He says that man-made gods are no gods at all. ²⁷There is danger not only that our trade will lose its good name, but also that the temple of the great goddess Artemis will be discredited, and the goddess herself, who is worshiped throughout the province of Asia and the world, will be robbed of her divine majesty."

²⁸When they heard this, they were furious and began shouting: "Great is Artemis of the Ephesians!" ²⁹Soon the whole city was in an uproar. The people seized Gaius and Aristarchus, Paul's traveling companions from Macedonia, and rushed as one man into the theater. ³⁰Paul wanted to appear before the crowd, but the disciples would not let him. ³¹Even some of the officials of the province, friends of Paul, sent him a message begging him not to venture into the theater.

³²The assembly was in confusion: Some were shouting one thing, some another. Most of the people did not even know why they were there. ³³The Jews pushed Alexander to the front, and some of the crowd shouted instructions to him. He motioned for silence in order to make a defense before the people. ³⁴But when they realized he was a Jew, they all shouted in unison for about two hours: "Great is Artemis of the Ephesians!"

³⁵The city clerk quieted the crowd and said: "Men of Ephesus, doesn't all the world know that the city of Ephesus is the guardian of the temple of the great Artemis and of her image, which fell from heaven? ³⁶Therefore, since these facts are undeniable, you ought to be quiet and not do anything rash. ³⁷You have brought these men here, though they have neither robbed temples nor blasphemed our goddess. ³⁸If, then, Demetrius and his fellow craftsmen have a grievance against anybody, the courts are open and there are proconsuls. They can press charges. ³⁹If there is anything further you want to bring up, it must be settled in a legal assembly. ⁴⁰As it is, we are in danger of being charged with rioting because of today's events. In that case we would not be able to account for this commotion, since there is no reason for it." ⁴¹After he had said this, he dismissed the assembly.

20 When the uproar had ended, Paul sent for the disciples and, after encouraging them, said good-by and set out for Macedonia. ²He traveled through that area, speaking many words of encouragement to the people, and finally arrived in Greece, ³where he stayed three months. Because the Jews made a plot against him just as he was about to sail for Syria, he decided to go back through Macedonia. ⁴He was accompanied by Sopater son of Pyrrhus from Berea, Aristarchus and Secundus from Thessalonica, Gaius from Derbe, Timothy also, and Tychicus and Trophimus from the province of Asia. ⁵These men went on ahead and waited for us at Troas. ⁶But we sailed from Philippi after the

ᵒ19 A drachma was a silver coin worth about a day's wages.

Feast of Unleavened Bread, and five days later joined the others at Troas, where we stayed seven days.

⁷On the first day of the week we came together to break bread. Paul spoke to the people and, because he intended to leave the next day, kept on talking until midnight. ⁸There were many lamps in the upstairs room where we were meeting. ⁹Seated in a window was a young man named Eutychus, who was sinking into a deep sleep as Paul talked on and on. When he was sound asleep, he fell to the ground from the third story and was picked up dead. ¹⁰Paul went down, threw himself on the young man and put his arms around him. "Don't be alarmed," he said. "He's alive!" ¹¹Then he went upstairs again and broke bread and ate. After talking until daylight, he left. ¹²The people took the young man home alive and were greatly comforted.

Discovering the Word 1. Scan chapter 19. Where do you see God's power revealed? 2. In 19:1–7 Paul encounters some disciples. What did he do to interact with them effectively? 3. Throughout this entire passage it is evident that Paul has a strategy for communicating the gospel. Specifically, what strategy does Paul have for his ministry in Ephesus (19:8–10)? 4. What is the cause of the riot in Ephesus (19:23–41)? How was it settled? 5. Paul continued to travel and encourage believers as he preached the gospel. What effect did the episode in 20:7–12 have on the crowd?

Applying the Word 1. What do you see in Paul's relationship with the disciples that might help you in relating to young Christians or your non-Christian friends? 2. What kind of plan for communicating the gospel would be helpful in your world? 3. How can you prepare yourself for both positive and negative responses as you are a part of communicating the gospel of Christ?

Responding in Prayer Thank God for the amazing fact that he uses us, sinful humanity, to spread the gospel and advance his kingdom. Thank him for using you.

19 / *Acts 20:13–38*
Paul's Farewell

"I WILL SEE you in heaven." I nodded, gave him a hug and a kiss and walked away from his bedside. When I left the room, I wept. Although it was twenty years ago that I said goodbye to Pop Z, the memory is still deep in my heart. In this chapter we will enter into weeping as Paul says his final goodbye to the elders at Ephesus. He knows that more hardship and prison await him in Jerusalem. And he will never see the faces of these elders again.

Warming Up to God Is the busyness of the world around you crowding you as you seek the face of God? Thank God that he has given you the grace that brought you to his Word right now, and ask him to still your restless heart as he comes to sit with you.

Read Acts 20:13–38.

¹³We went on ahead to the ship and sailed for Assos, where we were going to take Paul aboard. He had made this arrangement because he was going there on foot. ¹⁴When he met us at Assos, we took him aboard and went on to Mitylene. ¹⁵The next day we set sail from there and arrived off Kios. The day after that we crossed over to Samos, and on the following day arrived at Miletus. ¹⁶Paul had decided to sail past Ephesus to avoid spending time in the province of Asia, for he was in a hurry to reach Jerusalem, if possible, by the day of Pentecost.

¹⁷From Miletus, Paul sent to Ephesus for the elders of the church. ¹⁸When they arrived, he said to them: "You know how I lived the whole time I was with you, from the first day I came into the province of Asia. ¹⁹I served the Lord with great humility and with tears, although I was severely tested by the plots of the Jews. ²⁰You know that I have not hesitated to preach anything that would

be helpful to you but have taught you publicly and from house to house. [21]I have declared to both Jews and Greeks that they must turn to God in repentance and have faith in our Lord Jesus.

[22]"And now, compelled by the Spirit, I am going to Jerusalem, not knowing what will happen to me there. [23]I only know that in every city the Holy Spirit warns me that prison and hardships are facing me. [24]However, I consider my life worth nothing to me, if only I may finish the race and complete the task the Lord Jesus has given me—the task of testifying to the gospel of God's grace.

[25]"Now I know that none of you among whom I have gone about preaching the kingdom will ever see me again. [26]Therefore, I declare to you today that I am innocent of the blood of all men. [27]For I have not hesitated to proclaim to you the whole will of God. [28]Keep watch over yourselves and all the flock of which the Holy Spirit has made you overseers.[p] Be shepherds of the church of God,[q] which he bought with his own blood. [29]I know that after I leave, savage wolves will come in among you and will not spare the flock. [30]Even from your own number men will arise and distort the truth in order to draw away disciples after them. [31]So be on your guard! Remember that for three years I never stopped warning each of you night and day with tears.

[32]"Now I commit you to God and to the word of his grace, which can build you up and give you an inheritance among all those who are sanctified. [33]I have not coveted anyone's silver or gold or clothing. [34]You yourselves know that these hands of mine have supplied my own needs and the needs of my companions. [35]In everything I did, I showed you that by this kind of hard work we must help the weak, remembering the words the Lord Jesus himself said: 'It is more blessed to give than to receive.' "

[36]When he had said this, he knelt down with all of them and prayed. [37]They all wept as they embraced him and kissed him. [38]What grieved them most was his statement that they would never see his face again. Then they accompanied him to the ship.

[p]28 Traditionally *bishops* [q]28 Many manuscripts *of the Lord*

Discovering the Word 1. What does Paul say about his ministry to the Ephesians (vv. 18–21, 26–27, 31, 33–35)? 2. What are Paul's priorities (vv. 22–25)? 3. What instructions did Paul give to the leaders of the church at Ephesus (vv. 28–31)? 4. According to verse 32, why can Paul leave them with confidence? 5. In summary, according to this passage, why would Paul be able to say with integrity and humility to these leaders, "Follow my example. Do as I have done"?

Applying the Word 1. Who is in your spiritual care? 2. How are you preparing those that you nurture spiritually so that you can leave them with this same confidence? 3. Paul and the Ephesian elders were given the rare and special gift of being able to say goodby. What would you want to say to those in your spiritual care if you knew that you were going to die? Take time to express your hope and your love to that person in the near future.

Responding in Prayer Ask God for the courage to say these most important words to those you love and for whom you care deeply.

---

20 / *Acts 21:1—22:21*
Facing Opposition

AS THEY WENT to their death, taking the gospel of Jesus Christ to the Auca Indians, five young men sang:

We go in faith, our own great weakness feeling,
And needing more each day Thy grace to know:
Yet from our hearts a song of triumph pealing;
We rest on Thee, and in Thy name we go.

We rest on Thee our Shield and our Defender!
Thine is the battle, thine shall be the praise
When passing through the gates of pearly splendor,
Victors—we rest with Thee, through endless days.
Like Paul, knowing that death was a very real possibility, they did not turn aside from what they knew God wanted them to do.

 Warming Up to God There are times when we do not feel courageous about our faith, but question it. However, God is just as real when we doubt or fear as when our faith is strong. Let him come to you now in the midst of your fear and allow him to stretch your vision of how powerful he truly is.

 Read Acts 21:1—22:21.

21 After we had torn ourselves away from them, we put out to sea and sailed straight to Cos. The next day we went to Rhodes and from there to Patara. ²We found a ship crossing over to Phoenicia, went on board and set sail. ³After sighting Cyprus and passing to the south of it, we sailed on to Syria. We landed at Tyre, where our ship was to unload its cargo. ⁴Finding the disciples there, we stayed with them seven days. Through the Spirit they urged Paul not to go on to Jerusalem. ⁵But when our time was up, we left and continued on our way. All the disciples and their wives and children accompanied us out of the city, and there on the beach we knelt to pray. ⁶After saying good-by to each other, we went aboard the ship, and they returned home.

⁷We continued our voyage from Tyre and landed at Ptolemais, where we greeted the brothers and stayed with them for a day. ⁸Leaving the next day, we reached Caesarea and stayed at the house of Philip the evangelist, one of the Seven. ⁹He had four unmarried daughters who prophesied.

¹⁰After we had been there a number of days, a prophet named Agabus came down from Judea. ¹¹Coming over to us, he took Paul's belt, tied his own hands and feet with it and said, "The Holy Spirit says, 'In this way the Jews of Jerusalem will bind the owner of this belt and will hand him over to the Gentiles.' "

¹²When we heard this, we and the people there pleaded with Paul not to go up to Jerusalem. ¹³Then Paul answered, "Why are you weeping and breaking my heart? I am ready not only to be bound, but also to die in Jerusalem for the name of the Lord Jesus." ¹⁴When he would not be dissuaded, we gave up and said, "The Lord's will be done."

¹⁵After this, we got ready and went up to Jerusalem. ¹⁶Some of the disciples from Caesarea accompanied us and brought us to the home of Mnason, where we were to stay. He was a man from Cyprus and one of the early disciples.

¹⁷When we arrived at Jerusalem, the brothers received us warmly. ¹⁸The next day Paul and the rest of us went to see James, and all the elders were present. ¹⁹Paul greeted them and reported in detail what God had done among the Gentiles through his ministry.

²⁰When they heard this, they praised God. Then they said to Paul: "You see, brother, how many thousands of Jews have believed, and all of them are zealous for the law. ²¹They have been informed that you teach all the Jews who live among the Gentiles to turn away from Moses, telling them not to circumcise their children or live according to our customs. ²²What shall we do? They will certainly hear that you have come, ²³so do what we tell you. There are four men with us who have made a vow. ²⁴Take these men, join in their purification rites and pay their expenses, so that they can have their heads shaved. Then everybody will know there is no truth in these reports about you, but that you yourself are living in obedience to the law. ²⁵As for the Gentile believers, we have written to them our decision that they should abstain from food sacrificed to idols, from blood, from the meat of strangled animals and from sexual immorality."

²⁶The next day Paul took the men and purified himself along with them. Then he went to the temple to give notice of the date when the days of purification would end and the offering would be made for each of them.

²⁷When the seven days were nearly over, some Jews from the province of Asia saw Paul at the temple. They stirred up the whole crowd and seized him, ²⁸shouting, "Men of Israel, help us! This is the man who teaches all men everywhere

against our people and our law and this place. And besides, he has brought Greeks into the temple area and defiled this holy place." 29(They had previously seen Trophimus the Ephesian in the city with Paul and assumed that Paul had brought him into the temple area.)

30The whole city was aroused, and the people came running from all directions. Seizing Paul, they dragged him from the temple, and immediately the gates were shut. 31While they were trying to kill him, news reached the commander of the Roman troops that the whole city of Jerusalem was in an uproar. 32He at once took some officers and soldiers and ran down to the crowd. When the rioters saw the commander and his soldiers, they stopped beating Paul.

33The commander came up and arrested him and ordered him to be bound with two chains. Then he asked who he was and what he had done. 34Some in the crowd shouted one thing and some another, and since the commander could not get at the truth because of the uproar, he ordered that Paul be taken into the barracks. 35When Paul reached the steps, the violence of the mob was so great he had to be carried by the soldiers. 36The crowd that followed kept shouting, "Away with him!"

37As the soldiers were about to take Paul into the barracks, he asked the commander, "May I say something to you?"

"Do you speak Greek?" he replied. 38"Aren't you the Egyptian who started a revolt and led four thousand terrorists out into the desert some time ago?"

39Paul answered, "I am a Jew, from Tarsus in Cilicia, a citizen of no ordinary city. Please let me speak to the people."

40Having received the commander's permission, Paul stood on the steps and motioned to the crowd. When they were all silent, he said to them in Aramaic[r]: 1"Brothers and fathers, listen now to my defense."

2When they heard him speak to them in Aramaic, they became very quiet.

Then Paul said: 3"I am a Jew, born in Tarsus of Cilicia, but brought up in this city. Under Gamaliel I was thoroughly trained in the law of our fathers and was just as zealous for God as any of you are today. 4I persecuted the followers of this

Way to their death, arresting both men and women and throwing them into prison, 5as also the high priest and all the Council can testify. I even obtained letters from them to their brothers in Damascus, and went there to bring these people as prisoners to Jerusalem to be punished.

6"About noon as I came near Damascus, suddenly a bright light from heaven flashed around me. 7I fell to the ground and heard a voice say to me, 'Saul! Saul! Why do you persecute me?'

8" 'Who are you, Lord?' I asked.

" 'I am Jesus of Nazareth, whom you are persecuting,' he replied. 9My companions saw the light, but they did not understand the voice of him who was speaking to me.

10" 'What shall I do, Lord?' I asked.

" 'Get up,' the Lord said, 'and go into Damascus. There you will be told all that you have been assigned to do.' 11My companions led me by the hand into Damascus, because the brilliance of the light had blinded me.

12"A man named Ananias came to see me. He was a devout observer of the law and highly respected by all the Jews living there. 13He stood beside me and said, 'Brother Saul, receive your sight!' And at that very moment I was able to see him.

14"Then he said: 'The God of our fathers has chosen you to know his will and to see the Righteous One and to hear words from his mouth. 15You will be his witness to all men of what you have seen and heard. 16And now what are you waiting for? Get up, be baptized and wash your sins away, calling on his name.'

17"When I returned to Jerusalem and was praying at the temple, I fell into a trance 18and saw the Lord speaking. 'Quick!' he said to me. 'Leave Jerusalem immediately, because they will not accept your testimony about me.'

19" 'Lord,' I replied, 'these men know that I went from one synagogue to another to imprison and beat those who believe in you. 20And when the blood of your martyr[s] Stephen was shed, I stood there giving my approval and guarding the clothes of those who were killing him.'

21"Then the Lord said to me, 'Go; I will send you far away to the Gentiles.' "

[r]40 Or possibly Hebrew; also in 22:2   [s]20 Or witness

Discovering the Word 1. Describe the warnings to Paul concerning going to Jerusalem (21:4, 10–12). 2. How did Paul respond to these warnings (21:5, 13)? 3. Paul arrives in Jerusalem, is greeted by the elders and reports what God has done through his ministry. What are the elders concerned about for Paul (21:20–25)? 4. How does Paul demonstrate his desire to be at one with the Jewish Christians (21:26)? 5. Note how Paul was treated with mob hysteria, assumption and false evidence (21:27–36, 38). How does he respond to all of this (21:37—22:21)?

 Applying the Word 1. Think of a person you know who is focused on obeying God. How are you affected by his/her obedience? 2. How do you usually respond when you find yourself in conflict with others as a result of your obedience to God? 3. What have you seen in this passage that will help you become more single-minded in your obedience to God's will?

 Responding in Prayer Tell God of your desire to be obedient, but admit the difficulties you face because of your sin. Ask him again to cleanse you and help you run the race with fervor.

---

21 / *Acts 22:22—23:35*
God at Work

BEING UNDER GOD'S protection is not a guarantee of physical safety. Being under his protection does guarantee that our Father is with us and has a purpose for us and that nothing happens to us that does not come through his hands. We can live with confidence that our life on earth will not end until that purpose for us is complete. And that ultimately we will end up safe and protected in heaven. Paul was so sure of God's hand in his life that he continued to move out boldly with the message of Jesus Christ in spite of physical danger intensifying.

Warming Up to God The protection of the Father's strong arms is always around us. Thank him for his mighty but unseen acts that keep you safe and secure as you walk through this life.

Read Acts 22:22—23:35.

---

²²The crowd listened to Paul until he said this. Then they raised their voices and shouted, "Rid the earth of him! He's not fit to live!"

²³As they were shouting and throwing off their cloaks and flinging dust into the air, ²⁴the commander ordered Paul to be taken into the barracks. He directed that he be flogged and questioned in order to find out why the people were shouting at him like this. ²⁵As they stretched him out to flog him, Paul said to the centurion standing there, "Is it legal for you to flog a Roman citizen who hasn't even been found guilty?"

²⁶When the centurion heard this, he went to the commander and reported it. "What are you going to do?" he asked. "This man is a Roman citizen."

²⁷The commander went to Paul and asked, "Tell me, are you a Roman citizen?"

"Yes, I am," he answered.

²⁸Then the commander said, "I had to pay a big price for my citizenship."

"But I was born a citizen," Paul replied.

²⁹Those who were about to question him withdrew immediately. The commander himself was alarmed when he realized that he had put Paul, a Roman citizen, in chains.

³⁰The next day, since the commander wanted to find out exactly why Paul was being accused by the Jews, he released him and ordered the chief priests and all the Sanhedrin to assemble. Then he brought Paul and had him stand before them.

23 Paul looked straight at the Sanhedrin and said, "My brothers, I have fulfilled my duty to God in all good conscience to this day." ²At this the high priest Ananias ordered those standing near Paul to strike him on the mouth. ³Then Paul said to him, "God will strike you, you whitewashed wall! You sit there to judge me according to the law, yet you yourself violate the law by commanding that I be struck!"

⁴Those who were standing near Paul said, "You dare to insult God's high priest?"

⁵Paul replied, "Brothers, I did not realize that

he was the high priest; for it is written: 'Do not speak evil about the ruler of your people.'*"

⁶Then Paul, knowing that some of them were Sadducees and the others Pharisees, called out in the Sanhedrin, "My brothers, I am a Pharisee, the son of a Pharisee. I stand on trial because of my hope in the resurrection of the dead." ⁷When he said this, a dispute broke out between the Pharisees and the Sadducees, and the assembly was divided. ⁸(The Sadducees say that there is no resurrection, and that there are neither angels nor spirits, but the Pharisees acknowledge them all.)

⁹There was a great uproar, and some of the teachers of the law who were Pharisees stood up and argued vigorously. "We find nothing wrong with this man," they said. "What if a spirit or an angel has spoken to him?" ¹⁰The dispute became so violent that the commander was afraid Paul would be torn to pieces by them. He ordered the troops to go down and take him away from them by force and bring him into the barracks.

¹¹The following night the Lord stood near Paul and said, "Take courage! As you have testified about me in Jerusalem, so you must also testify in Rome."

¹²The next morning the Jews formed a conspiracy and bound themselves with an oath not to eat or drink until they had killed Paul. ¹³More than forty men were involved in this plot. ¹⁴They went to the chief priests and elders and said, "We have taken a solemn oath not to eat anything until we have killed Paul. ¹⁵Now then, you and the Sanhedrin petition the commander to bring him before you on the pretext of wanting more accurate information about his case. We are ready to kill him before he gets here."

¹⁶But when the son of Paul's sister heard of this plot, he went into the barracks and told Paul. ¹⁷Then Paul called one of the centurions and said, "Take this young man to the commander; he has something to tell him." ¹⁸So he took him to the commander.

The centurion said, "Paul, the prisoner, sent for me and asked me to bring this young man to you because he has something to tell you."

¹⁹The commander took the young man by the hand, drew him aside and asked, "What is it you want to tell me?"

²⁰He said: "The Jews have agreed to ask you to bring Paul before the Sanhedrin tomorrow on the pretext of wanting more accurate information about him. ²¹Don't give in to them, because more than forty of them are waiting in ambush for him. They have taken an oath not to eat or drink until they have killed him. They are ready now, waiting for your consent to their request."

²²The commander dismissed the young man and cautioned him, "Don't tell anyone that you have reported this to me."

²³Then he called two of his centurions and ordered them, "Get ready a detachment of two hundred soldiers, seventy horsemen and two hundred spearmenᵘ to go to Caesarea at nine tonight. ²⁴Provide mounts for Paul so that he may be taken safely to Governor Felix."

²⁵He wrote a letter as follows:

²⁶Claudius Lysias,

To His Excellency, Governor Felix:

Greetings.

²⁷This man was seized by the Jews and they were about to kill him, but I came with my troops and rescued him, for I had learned that he is a Roman citizen. ²⁸I wanted to know why they were accusing him, so I brought him to their Sanhedrin. ²⁹I found that the accusation had to do with questions about their law, but there was no charge against him that deserved death or imprisonment. ³⁰When I was informed of a plot to be carried out against the man, I sent him to you at once. I also ordered his accusers to present to you their case against him.

³¹So the soldiers, carrying out their orders, took Paul with them during the night and brought him as far as Antipatris. ³²The next day they let the cavalry go on with him, while they returned to the barracks. ³³When the cavalry arrived in Caesarea, they delivered the letter to the governor and handed Paul over to him. ³⁴The governor read the letter and asked what province he was from. Learning that he was from Cilicia, ³⁵he said, "I will hear your case when your accusers get here." Then he ordered that Paul be kept under guard in Herod's palace.

*5 Exodus 22:28   ᵘ23 The meaning of the Greek for this word is uncertain.

Discovering the Word 1. Throughout this passage, we can see God's hand in the circumstances of Paul's life, protecting and directing him. In Acts 22:22–29 what is the source of the conflict? What is it that protects Paul? 2. In 23:1–10 what is the source of the conflict? How is Paul protected? 3. Why was Paul struck on the mouth for saying, "My brothers, I have fulfilled my duty to God in all good conscience to this day" (23:1)? 4. In Acts 23:12–25 the Jews are frustrated because they cannot get rid of Paul through the law, so they decide to ambush and kill him on their own. How is Paul protected? 5. We have observed God's protection of Paul. How do we see God's care for Paul in a more direct and supernatural way in 23:11?

Applying the Word 1. Think about God's hand in your life and ministry. How have you seen him work to protect and direct you toward his will? 2. In what ways do you need to grow in humbly acknowledging God's hand in your life? 3. How has your hope for God's will to be done in you been affected by looking at God's hand in Paul's life?

Responding in Prayer Ask God to show you his active hand in your life.

---

22 / *Acts 24:1—25:12*
Falsely Accused

OUR DEAR FRIEND George was falsely accused and on trial for heresy. My husband prayed fervently that God would shut the accusers' mouths, that he would bind their efforts, and that truth would prevail and bring freedom. He asked God to confound their actions so that their own words would bring out the truth and show up their false accusations. God chose to do what Andy asked for, and George was exonerated in a dramatic fashion. The words of the accusers brought condemnation on them. The defense did not even have to present their case. The pain, however, of being falsely accused is great. And the damage was not easily repaired. But George's consistent godly response throughout the whole ordeal reminded me of Jesus and Paul when they were falsely accused.

Warming Up to God Remember that today has been given to you by God, and he desires to be with you as you walk through it. Let him come to you now, knowing that he will show you more of himself through his Word.

Read Acts 24:1—25:12.

---

24 Five days later the high priest Ananias went down to Caesarea with some of the elders and a lawyer named Tertullus, and they brought their charges against Paul before the governor. ²When Paul was called in, Tertullus presented his case before Felix: "We have enjoyed a long period of peace under you, and your foresight has brought about reforms in this nation. ³Everywhere and in every way, most excellent Felix, we acknowledge this with profound gratitude. ⁴But in order not to weary you further, I would request that you be kind enough to hear us briefly.

⁵"We have found this man to be a troublemaker, stirring up riots among the Jews all over the world. He is a ringleader of the Nazarene sect ⁶and even tried to desecrate the temple; so we seized him. ⁸By* examining him yourself you

will be able to learn the truth about all these charges we are bringing against him."

⁹The Jews joined in the accusation, asserting that these things were true.

¹⁰When the governor motioned for him to speak, Paul replied: "I know that for a number of years you have been a judge over this nation; so I gladly make my defense. ¹¹You can easily verify that no more than twelve days ago I went up to Jerusalem to worship. ¹²My accusers did not find me arguing with anyone at the temple, or stirring up a crowd in the synagogues or anywhere else in the city. ¹³And they cannot prove to you the charges they are now making against me. ¹⁴However, I admit that I worship the God of our fathers

*v 6-8 Some manuscripts *him and wanted to judge him according to our law.* ⁷*But the commander, Lysias, came and with the use of much force snatched him from our hands* ⁸*and ordered his accusers to come before you. By*

as a follower of the Way, which they call a sect. I believe everything that agrees with the Law and that is written in the Prophets, 15and I have the same hope in God as these men, that there will be a resurrection of both the righteous and the wicked. 16So I strive always to keep my conscience clear before God and man.

17"After an absence of several years, I came to Jerusalem to bring my people gifts for the poor and to present offerings. 18I was ceremonially clean when they found me in the temple courts doing this. There was no crowd with me, nor was I involved in any disturbance. 19But there are some Jews from the province of Asia, who ought to be here before you and bring charges if they have anything against me. 20Or these who are here should state what crime they found in me when I stood before the Sanhedrin— 21unless it was this one thing I shouted as I stood in their presence: 'It is concerning the resurrection of the dead that I am on trial before you today.' "

22Then Felix, who was well acquainted with the Way, adjourned the proceedings. "When Lysias the commander comes," he said, "I will decide your case." 23He ordered the centurion to keep Paul under guard but to give him some freedom and permit his friends to take care of his needs.

24Several days later Felix came with his wife Drusilla, who was a Jewess. He sent for Paul and listened to him as he spoke about faith in Christ Jesus. 25As Paul discoursed on righteousness, self-control and the judgment to come, Felix was afraid and said, "That's enough for now! You may leave. When I find it convenient, I will send for you." 26At the same time he was hoping that Paul would offer him a bribe, so he sent for him frequently and talked with him.

27When two years had passed, Felix was succeeded by Porcius Festus, but because Felix wanted to grant a favor to the Jews, he left Paul in prison.

25 Three days after arriving in the province, Festus went up from Caesarea to Jerusalem, 2where the chief priests and Jewish leaders appeared before him and presented the charges against Paul. 3They urgently requested Festus, as a favor to them, to have Paul transferred to Jerusalem, for they were preparing an ambush to kill him along the way. 4Festus answered, "Paul is being held at Caesarea, and I myself am going there soon. 5Let some of your leaders come with me and press charges against the man there, if he has done anything wrong."

6After spending eight or ten days with them, he went down to Caesarea, and the next day he convened the court and ordered that Paul be brought before him. 7When Paul appeared, the Jews who had come down from Jerusalem stood around him, bringing many serious charges against him, which they could not prove.

8Then Paul made his defense: "I have done nothing wrong against the law of the Jews or against the temple or against Caesar."

9Festus, wishing to do the Jews a favor, said to Paul, "Are you willing to go up to Jerusalem and stand trial before me there on these charges?"

10Paul answered: "I am now standing before Caesar's court, where I ought to be tried. I have not done any wrong to the Jews, as you yourself know very well. 11If, however, I am guilty of doing anything deserving death, I do not refuse to die. But if the charges brought against me by these Jews are not true, no one has the right to hand me over to them. I appeal to Caesar!"

12After Festus had conferred with his council, he declared: "You have appealed to Caesar. To Caesar you will go!"

Discovering the Word 1. What are the accusations brought against Paul by the Jews (24:1–27)? 2. How would you describe Paul's defense? (Consider the content and the attitude and tone.) 3. What do you think is the significance of the fact that Felix was well acquainted with the Way (v. 22)? 4. In Acts 25:1–12 two years have passed since his trial, and Festus has become the new governor. The Jews have not given up. They continue to plot to kill Paul and ask Festus to have him transferred to Jerusalem. Festus refuses and tells the Jewish leaders to come to Caesarea for the trial. What evidence is there in this passage that Festus knows that Paul is innocent? 5. Why does Festus suggest that Paul go back to Jerusalem to be on trial?

Applying the Word 1. When have you known someone to respond to the proclamation of the gospel as Felix did? What might this mean? 2. Describe a time you have been falsely accused because of your faith. 3. What can you learn about how to respond to accusers from the way Paul responded to his accusers?

Responding in Prayer Ask God to give you patience and a heart of love for the people who surround you—your coworkers, family—people you can show the example of Christ.

23 / *Acts 25:13—26:32*
Testimony Before Agrippa

THOUGH HIS INNOCENCE has been clearly stated many times, Paul remains a prisoner. He repeatedly has to face the unfair charges of the Jewish leaders. He has made his defense with integrity and power, and in return he gets only threats of death. In it all Paul's witness remains consistent. His greatest desire is that his accusers and those in judgment over him will become Christians.

Warming Up to God How do you respond to the unfairness in the world around you—poverty, homeless-ness, the unfairness in your own life? It is difficult to assume an attitude like Paul's in the face of injustice. But God sees and knows what is right, and he understands the anger we feel. Express your thoughts and feelings to him. Let him calm the stirring in your heart with his gentle words.

Read Acts 25:13—26:32.

¹³A few days later King Agrippa and Bernice arrived at Caesarea to pay their respects to Festus. ¹⁴Since they were spending many days there, Festus discussed Paul's case with the king. He said: "There is a man here whom Felix left as a prisoner. ¹⁵When I went to Jerusalem, the chief priests and elders of the Jews brought charges against him and asked that he be condemned.

¹⁶"I told them that it is not the Roman custom to hand over any man before he has faced his accusers and has had an opportunity to defend himself against their charges. ¹⁷When they came here with me, I did not delay the case, but convened the court the next day and ordered the man to be brought in. ¹⁸When his accusers got up to speak, they did not charge him with any of the crimes I had expected. ¹⁹Instead, they had some points of dispute with him about their own religion and about a dead man named Jesus who Paul claimed was alive. ²⁰I was at a loss how to investigate such matters; so I asked if he would be willing to go to Jerusalem and stand trial there on these charges. ²¹When Paul made his appeal to be held over for the Emperor's decision, I ordered him held until I could send him to Caesar."

²²Then Agrippa said to Festus, "I would like to hear this man myself."

He replied, "Tomorrow you will hear him."

²³The next day Agrippa and Bernice came with great pomp and entered the audience room with the high ranking officers and the leading men of the city. At the command of Festus, Paul was brought in. ²⁴Festus said: "King Agrippa, and all who are present with us, you see this man! The whole Jewish community has petitioned me about him in Jerusalem and here in Caesarea, shouting that he ought not to live any longer. ²⁵I found he had done nothing deserving of death, but because he made his appeal to the Emperor I decided to send him to Rome. ²⁶But I have nothing definite to write to His Majesty about him. Therefore I have brought him before all of you, and especially before you, King Agrippa, so that as a result of this investigation I may have something to write. ²⁷For I think it is unreasonable to send on a prisoner without specifying the charges against him."

26 Then Agrippa said to Paul, "You have permission to speak for yourself."

So Paul motioned with his hand and began his defense: ²"King Agrippa, I consider myself fortunate to stand before you today as I make my defense against all the accusations of the Jews, ³and especially so because you are well acquainted with all the Jewish customs and controversies. Therefore, I beg you to listen to me patiently.

⁴"The Jews all know the way I have lived ever since I was a child, from the beginning of my life in my own country, and also in Jerusalem. ⁵They have known me for a long time and can testify, if they are willing, that according to the strictest

sect of our religion, I lived as a Pharisee. 6And now it is because of my hope in what God has promised our fathers that I am on trial today. 7This is the promise our twelve tribes are hoping to see fulfilled as they earnestly serve God day and night. O king, it is because of this hope that the Jews are accusing me. 8Why should any of you consider it incredible that God raises the dead?

9"I too was convinced that I ought to do all that was possible to oppose the name of Jesus of Nazareth. 10And that is just what I did in Jerusalem. On the authority of the chief priests I put many of the saints in prison, and when they were put to death, I cast my vote against them. 11Many a time I went from one synagogue to another to have them punished, and I tried to force them to blaspheme. In my obsession against them, I even went to foreign cities to persecute them.

12"On one of these journeys I was going to Damascus with the authority and commission of the chief priests. 13About noon, O king, as I was on the road, I saw a light from heaven, brighter than the sun, blazing around me and my companions. 14We all fell to the ground, and I heard a voice saying to me in Aramaic,w 'Saul, Saul, why do you persecute me? It is hard for you to kick against the goads.'

15"Then I asked, 'Who are you, Lord?'

" 'I am Jesus, whom you are persecuting,' the Lord replied. 16'Now get up and stand on your feet. I have appeared to you to appoint you as a servant and as a witness of what you have seen of me and what I will show you. 17I will rescue you from your own people and from the Gentiles. I am sending you to them 18to open their eyes and turn them from darkness to light, and from the power of Satan to God, so that they may receive forgiveness of sins and a place among those who are sanctified by faith in me.'

19"So then, King Agrippa, I was not disobedient to the vision from heaven. 20First to those in Damascus, then to those in Jerusalem and in all Judea, and to the Gentiles also, I preached that they should repent and turn to God and prove their repentance by their deeds. 21That is why the Jews seized me in the temple courts and tried to kill me. 22But I have had God's help to this very day, and so I stand here and testify to small and great alike. I am saying nothing beyond what the prophets and Moses said would happen— 23that the Christx would suffer and, as the first to rise from the dead, would proclaim light to his own people and to the Gentiles."

24At this point Festus interrupted Paul's defense. "You are out of your mind, Paul!" he shouted. "Your great learning is driving you insane."

25"I am not insane, most excellent Festus," Paul replied. "What I am saying is true and reasonable. 26The king is familiar with these things, and I can speak freely to him. I am convinced that none of this has escaped his notice, because it was not done in a corner. 27King Agrippa, do you believe the prophets? I know you do."

28Then Agrippa said to Paul, "Do you think that in such a short time you can persuade me to be a Christian?"

29Paul replied, "Short time or long—I pray God that not only you but all who are listening to me today may become what I am, except for these chains."

30The king rose, and with him the governor and Bernice and those sitting with them. 31They left the room, and while talking with one another, they said, "This man is not doing anything that deserves death or imprisonment."

32Agrippa said to Festus, "This man could have been set free if he had not appealed to Caesar."

w14 Or Hebrew   x23 Or Messiah

Discovering the Word 1. Describe the nature and content of Festus's report to Agrippa (25:13–22). 2. What are the main points about himself that Paul presents in his defense (26:1–23)? 3. Why does Paul say he is on trial (26:6–8)? 4. Contrast the commission of the Sanhedrin (26:9–11) to the commission of Christ (26:15–18). 5. Describe Paul's final interaction with King Agrippa (26:26–29).

Applying the Word 1. What motivates you to tell non-Christians about Jesus? 2. How does Paul's desire for King Agrippa compare or contrast with your desire for those around you who do not know Christ? 3. How might you move closer to where Paul was in this desire?

Responding in Prayer Ask God to give you the proper response to injustice and a heart that is soft toward those who do not know him.

24 / Acts 27—28
Paul in Rome!

ROME AT LAST! Paul was innocent. He could have been a free man. But he had appealed to Caesar—and to Caesar he was to go. As we look at these last two chapters of Acts and complete our study of the life of this marvelous servant of God, it might be worthwhile to ask the questions "Who was really free, and who were the real prisoners?"

 Warming Up to God Sit quietly for a few moments, without trying to force your thoughts to move in any direction. Let silence reign in your heart before you look to Scripture.

 Read Acts 27—28.

27 When it was decided that we would sail for Italy, Paul and some other prisoners were handed over to a centurion named Julius, who belonged to the Imperial Regiment. ²We boarded a ship from Adramyttium about to sail for ports along the coast of the province of Asia, and we put out to sea. Aristarchus, a Macedonian from Thessalonica, was with us.

³The next day we landed at Sidon; and Julius, in kindness to Paul, allowed him to go to his friends so they might provide for his needs. ⁴From there we put out to sea again and passed to the lee of Cyprus because the winds were against us. ⁵When we had sailed across the open sea off the coast of Cilicia and Pamphylia, we landed at Myra in Lycia. ⁶There the centurion found an Alexandrian ship sailing for Italy and put us on board. ⁷We made slow headway for many days and had difficulty arriving off Cnidus. When the wind did not allow us to hold our course, we sailed to the lee of Crete, opposite Salmone. ⁸We moved along the coast with difficulty and came to a place called Fair Havens, near the town of Lasea.

⁹Much time had been lost, and sailing had already become dangerous because by now it was after the Fast.ʸ So Paul warned them, ¹⁰"Men, I can see that our voyage is going to be disastrous and bring great loss to ship and cargo, and to our own lives also." ¹¹But the centurion, instead of listening to what Paul said, followed the advice of the pilot and of the owner of the ship. ¹²Since the harbor was unsuitable to winter in, the majority decided that we should sail on, hoping to reach Phoenix and winter there. This was a harbor in Crete, facing both southwest and northwest.

¹³When a gentle south wind began to blow, they thought they had obtained what they wanted; so they weighed anchor and sailed along the shore of Crete. ¹⁴Before very long, a wind of hurricane force, called the "northeaster," swept down from the island. ¹⁵The ship was caught by the storm and could not head into the wind; so we gave way to it and were driven along. ¹⁶As we passed to the lee of a small island called Cauda, we were hardly able to make the lifeboat secure. ¹⁷When the men had hoisted it aboard, they passed ropes under the ship itself to hold it together. Fearing that they would run aground on the sandbars of Syrtis, they lowered the sea anchor and let the ship be driven along. ¹⁸We took such a violent battering from the storm that the next day they began to throw the cargo overboard. ¹⁹On the third day, they threw the ship's tackle overboard with their own hands. ²⁰When neither sun nor stars appeared for many days and the storm continued raging, we finally gave up all hope of being saved.

²¹After the men had gone a long time without food, Paul stood up before them and said: "Men, you should have taken my advice not to sail from Crete; then you would have spared yourselves this damage and loss. ²²But now I urge you to keep up your courage, because not one of you will be lost; only the ship will be destroyed. ²³Last night an angel of the God whose I am and whom I serve stood beside me ²⁴and said, 'Do not be afraid, Paul. You must stand trial before Caesar; and God has graciously given you the lives of all who sail with you.' ²⁵So keep up your courage, men, for I have faith in God that it will happen just as he told me. ²⁶Nevertheless, we must run aground on some island."

²⁷On the fourteenth night we were still being

*y*9 That is, the Day of Atonement (Yom Kippur)

driven across the Adriatic^z Sea, when about midnight the sailors sensed they were approaching land. ^{28}They took soundings and found that the water was a hundred and twenty feet^a deep. A short time later they took soundings again and found it was ninety feet^b deep. ^{29}Fearing that we would be dashed against the rocks, they dropped four anchors from the stern and prayed for daylight. ^{30}In an attempt to escape from the ship, the sailors let the lifeboat down into the sea, pretending they were going to lower some anchors from the bow. ^{31}Then Paul said to the centurion and the soldiers, "Unless these men stay with the ship, you cannot be saved." ^{32}So the soldiers cut the ropes that held the lifeboat and let it fall away.

^{33}Just before dawn Paul urged them all to eat. "For the last fourteen days," he said, "you have been in constant suspense and have gone without food—you haven't eaten anything. ^{34}Now I urge you to take some food. You need it to survive. Not one of you will lose a single hair from his head." ^{35}After he said this, he took some bread and gave thanks to God in front of them all. Then he broke it and began to eat. ^{36}They were all encouraged and ate some food themselves. ^{37}Altogether there were 276 of us on board. ^{38}When they had eaten as much as they wanted, they lightened the ship by throwing the grain into the sea.

^{39}When daylight came, they did not recognize the land, but they saw a bay with a sandy beach, where they decided to run the ship aground if they could. ^{40}Cutting loose the anchors, they left them in the sea and at the same time untied the ropes that held the rudders. Then they hoisted the foresail to the wind and made for the beach. ^{41}But the ship struck a sandbar and ran aground. The bow stuck fast and would not move, and the stern was broken to pieces by the pounding of the surf.

^{42}The soldiers planned to kill the prisoners to prevent any of them from swimming away and escaping. ^{43}But the centurion wanted to spare Paul's life and kept them from carrying out their plan. He ordered those who could swim to jump overboard first and get to land. ^{44}The rest were to get there on planks or on pieces of the ship. In this way everyone reached land in safety.

28 Once safely on shore, we found out that the island was called Malta. ^{2}The islanders showed us unusual kindness. They built a fire and welcomed us all because it was raining and cold. ^{3}Paul gathered a pile of brushwood and, as he put it on the fire, a viper, driven out by the heat, fastened itself on his hand. ^{4}When the islanders saw the snake hanging from his hand, they said to each other, "This man must be a murderer; for though he escaped from the sea, Justice has not allowed him to live." ^{5}But Paul shook the snake off into the fire and suffered no ill effects. ^{6}The people expected him to swell up or suddenly fall dead, but after waiting a long time and seeing nothing unusual happen to him, they changed their minds and said he was a god.

^{7}There was an estate nearby that belonged to Publius, the chief official of the island. He welcomed us to his home and for three days entertained us hospitably. ^{8}His father was sick in bed, suffering from fever and dysentery. Paul went in to see him and, after prayer, placed his hands on him and healed him. ^{9}When this had happened, the rest of the sick on the island came and were cured. ^{10}They honored us in many ways and when we were ready to sail, they furnished us with the supplies we needed.

^{11}After three months we put out to sea in a ship that had wintered in the island. It was an Alexandrian ship with the figurehead of the twin gods Castor and Pollux. ^{12}We put in at Syracuse and stayed there three days. ^{13}From there we set sail and arrived at Rhegium. The next day the south wind came up, and on the following day we reached Puteoli. ^{14}There we found some brothers who invited us to spend a week with them. And so we came to Rome. ^{15}The brothers there had heard that we were coming, and they traveled as far as the Forum of Appius and the Three Taverns to meet us. At the sight of these men Paul thanked God and was encouraged. ^{16}When we got to Rome, Paul was allowed to live by himself, with a soldier to guard him.

^{17}Three days later he called together the leaders of the Jews. When they had assembled, Paul said to them: "My brothers, although I have done nothing against our people or against the customs of our ancestors, I was arrested in Jerusalem and handed over to the Romans. ^{18}They examined me and wanted to release me, because I was not guilty of any crime deserving death. ^{19}But when the Jews objected, I was compelled to appeal to Caesar—not that I had any charge to bring

^{z}27 In ancient times the name referred to an area extending well south of Italy. ^{a}28 Greek *twenty orguias* (about 37 meters) ^{b}28 Greek *fifteen orguias* (about 27 meters)

against my own people. ²⁰For this reason I have asked to see you and talk with you. It is because of the hope of Israel that I am bound with this chain."

²¹They replied, "We have not received any letters from Judea concerning you, and none of the brothers who have come from there has reported or said anything bad about you. ²²But we want to hear what your views are, for we know that people everywhere are talking against this sect."

²³They arranged to meet Paul on a certain day, and came in even larger numbers to the place where he was staying. From morning till evening he explained and declared to them the kingdom of God and tried to convince them about Jesus from the Law of Moses and from the Prophets. ²⁴Some were convinced by what he said, but others would not believe. ²⁵They disagreed among themselves and began to leave after Paul had made this final statement: "The Holy Spirit spoke the truth to your forefathers when he said through Isaiah the prophet:

²⁶" 'Go to this people and say,
    "You will be ever hearing but never
        understanding;
    you will be ever seeing but never
        perceiving."
²⁷For this people's heart has become calloused;
    they hardly hear with their ears,
    and they have closed their eyes.
Otherwise they might see with their eyes,
    hear with their ears,
    understand with their hearts
and turn, and I would heal them.'ᶜ

²⁸"Therefore I want you to know that God's salvation has been sent to the Gentiles, and they will listen!"ᵈ

³⁰For two whole years Paul stayed there in his own rented house and welcomed all who came to see him. ³¹Boldly and without hindrance he preached the kingdom of God and taught about the Lord Jesus Christ.

ᶜ27 Isaiah 6:9,10   ᵈ28 Some manuscripts *listen!" ²⁹After he said this, the Jews left, arguing vigorously among themselves.*

 Discovering the Word 1. Though Paul had every reason by this time to become very self-centered, how do you see him continuing to minister to others throughout these two chapters (27:9–10, 21–25, 31–38, 42–43; 28:3, 8–9, 17–20, 23–31)? 2. What do you see of Paul's compassion as he ministers? 3. What do you think it says about Paul that Julius let him go see his friends (27:3)? 4. What do you see of Paul's confidence in God throughout this passage? 5. In conclusion, what from the book of Acts motivates and equips you to be a witness "to the ends of the earth" (1:8)?

Applying the Word 1. What are the situations or relationships in your life with non-Christians in which you are tempted to give up on your proclamation of the gospel? 2. What truths from this study of Acts encourage you to not give up? 3. The words "Boldly and without hindrance he preached the kingdom of God and taught about the Lord Jesus Christ" (28:31) summarize not only Paul's two years in Rome, but his whole Christian life. To what degree would you like this to be a summary of your life? Explain.

Responding in Prayer Thank God for the ways that he has taught you through the book of Acts. Ask him to continue to teach you as you try to live out the lessons you have learned.

Romans

R omans may be the most important letter you will ever read. It is Paul's masterpiece, the clearest and fullest explanation of the gospel in the Bible. John Calvin said that "if a man understands it, he has a sure road opened for him to the understanding of the whole Scripture." William Tyndale, the father of English Bible translators, believed that every Christian should learn it by heart. "The more it is studied," he wrote, "the easier it is; the more it is chewed, the pleasanter it is" (prologue to Romans in his 1534 English New Testament).

But watch out! Those who study Romans are rarely the same afterward. For example, in the summer of A.D. 386 Augustine sat weeping in the garden of his friend Alypius. He wanted to begin a new life but lacked the strength to break with the old. Taking up a scroll of Romans, he read, "Clothe yourselves with the Lord Jesus Christ, and do not think about how to gratify the desires of the sinful nature." "No further would I read," he tells us, "nor had I any need; instantly at the end of this sentence, a clear light flooded my heart and all the darkness of doubt vanished away."

In 1515 Martin Luther began to teach the book of Romans to his students. He wrote, "Night and day I pondered until . . . I grasped the truth that the righteousness of God is that righteousness whereby, through grace and sheer mercy, he justifies us by faith. Thereupon I felt myself to be reborn and to have gone through open doors into paradise. The whole scripture took on new meaning, and whereas before the 'righteousness of God' had filled me with hate, now it became to me inexpressibly sweet in greater love. This passage in Paul became to me a gateway to heaven." Two years later he nailed his ninety-five theses to the door of the castle church in Wittenberg, and the Protestant Reformation began!

The evening of May 24, 1738, John Wesley "went very unwillingly to a society in Aldersgate Street, where one was reading Luther's preface to the Epistle to the Romans. About a quarter before nine," he wrote in his journal, "while he was describing the change which God works in the heart through faith in Christ, I felt my heart strangely warmed. I felt I did trust in Christ, Christ alone, for my salvation; and an assurance was given me that he had taken *my* sins away, even *mine*; and saved me from the law of sin and death." This event in Wesley's life helped to launch the great Evangelical Revival of the eighteenth century.

We need to grasp the message of Romans in our day as well. Many are preaching a gospel that lacks clarity and substance. People are told to "invite Jesus into their heart" or simply to "follow Christ" without understanding the meaning of his death and resurrection.

We cannot correct this problem merely by memorizing gospel outlines or canned presentations. We need to immerse ourselves in Scripture through diligent study and thoughtful reflection. Only when the gospel grips us as it did Augustine, Luther and Wesley will we realize why "it is the power of God for the salvation of everyone who believes" (Ro 1:16).

Romans is different from most of Paul's letters. He did not found the church in Rome; in fact, he had never been there. It has been suggested that the church in Rome was founded by some of those who were present on the day of Pentecost (Acts 2:10). However, Paul had met some of the Roman Christians, such as Priscilla and Aquila (Ro 16), during his missionary journeys to other cities.

Other letters were written to address specific problems within the churches. Romans seems relatively free of problems. Their only major "problem" was that they had never met the apostle. Therefore, Paul felt a need to fully explain to them in a letter what he would have said in person.

Paul probably wrote Romans between A.D. 57–58 while he was at Corinth in the home of his friend and convert Gaius. He planned to go first to Jerusalem to deliver a gift of money from the Gentile churches to the poor in Jerusalem. Then he hoped to visit Rome on his way to Spain. His hopes were later realized, but not as he had expected. When he finally arrived in Rome in early A.D. 60, he was a prisoner under house arrest (Acts 28:11–31).

May you be encouraged and challenged by the new life and the new lifestyle we have in Christ!

Outline

Part 1: A New Life

Part 2: A New Lifestyle

1 / *Romans 1:1–17*
Good News from God

"I'M ENGAGED!"
  "I got a raise!"
  "My wife's having a baby!"
  What is our immediate response to good news? We tell others! We feel we will burst unless we share our joy with those around us.
  Paul felt that way about the gospel, the good news about Jesus Christ. As we read these opening verses in his letter to the Romans, we find his excitement is contagious.

 Warming Up to God Our days and weeks are often filled with bad news. Think of all the *good* news you can, and praise God for it.

 Read Romans 1:1–17.

1 Paul, a servant of Christ Jesus, called to be an apostle and set apart for the gospel of God— ²the gospel he promised beforehand through his prophets in the Holy Scriptures ³regarding his Son, who as to his human nature was a descendant of David, ⁴and who through the Spirit*ᵃ* of holiness was declared with power to be the Son of God*ᵇ* by his resurrection from the dead: Jesus Christ our Lord. ⁵Through him and for his name's sake, we received grace and apostleship to call people from among all the Gentiles to the obedience that comes from faith. ⁶And you also are among those who are called to belong to Jesus Christ.

⁷To all in Rome who are loved by God and called to be saints:

Grace and peace to you from God our Father and from the Lord Jesus Christ.

⁸First, I thank my God through Jesus Christ for all of you, because your faith is being reported all over the world. ⁹God, whom I serve with my whole heart in preaching the gospel of his Son, is my witness how constantly I remember you ¹⁰in my prayers at all times; and I pray that now at last by God's will the way may be opened for me to come to you.

¹¹I long to see you so that I may impart to you some spiritual gift to make you strong— ¹²that is, that you and I may be mutually encouraged by each other's faith. ¹³I do not want you to be unaware, brothers, that I planned many times to come to you (but have been prevented from doing so until now) in order that I might have a harvest among you, just as I have had among the other Gentiles.

¹⁴I am obligated both to Greeks and non-Greeks, both to the wise and the foolish. ¹⁵That is why I am so eager to preach the gospel also to you who are at Rome.

¹⁶I am not ashamed of the gospel, because it is the power of God for the salvation of everyone who believes: first for the Jew, then for the Gentile. ¹⁷For in the gospel a righteousness from God is revealed, a righteousness that is by faith from first to last,*ᶜ* just as it is written: "The righteous will live by faith."*ᵈ*

ᵃ4 Or who as to his spirit   ᵇ4 Or was appointed to be the Son of God with power   ᶜ17 Or is from faith to faith   ᵈ17 Hab. 2:4

Discovering the Word 1. Imagine that verses 1 and 5 are the only information you possess about Paul. Describe everything you would know about him. 2. In verses 1–5 Paul gives a summary of the gospel for which he had been set apart. What do we learn about the gospel from these verses? 3. What do verses 8–13 reveal about Paul's attitude toward the Romans? 4. Paul says we can be eager to preach the gospel or be ashamed of it (vv. 15–16). What might lead us to adopt one attitude or the other?

Applying the Word 1. Because he was an apostle ("one who is sent"), Paul felt obligated to preach the gospel to everyone (v. 14). Whom do you have the greatest opportunity of reaching with the gospel? 2. What steps can you take to reach them?

Responding in Prayer Pray that God will use Romans to give you Paul's attitude toward the gospel and toward those who need its message.

2 / *Romans 1:18–32*
The Wrath of God

"HOW ARE YOU?" someone asks. "I'm fine," we reply. But are we really, or do our words mask our true condition? In this passage Paul tells us that we are not fine—neither we nor our friends nor society. Something is dreadfully wrong.

 Warming Up to God Usually we have to admit we need help before we can be helped. Why do we often find it so difficult to admit a need? Give your needs to God's care.

 Read Romans 1:18–32.

¹⁸The wrath of God is being revealed from heaven against all the godlessness and wickedness of men who suppress the truth by their wickedness, ¹⁹since what may be known about God is plain to them, because God has made it plain to them. ²⁰For since the creation of the world God's invisible qualities—his eternal power and divine nature—have been clearly seen, being understood from what has been made, so that men are without excuse.

²¹For although they knew God, they neither glorified him as God nor gave thanks to him, but their thinking became futile and their foolish hearts were darkened. ²²Although they claimed to be wise, they became fools ²³and exchanged the glory of the immortal God for images made to look like mortal man and birds and animals and reptiles.

²⁴Therefore God gave them over in the sinful desires of their hearts to sexual impurity for the degrading of their bodies with one another. ²⁵They exchanged the truth of God for a lie, and worshiped and served created things rather than the Creator—who is forever praised. Amen.

²⁶Because of this, God gave them over to shameful lusts. Even their women exchanged natural relations for unnatural ones. ²⁷In the same way the men also abandoned natural relations with women and were inflamed with lust for one another. Men committed indecent acts with other men, and received in themselves the due penalty for their perversion.

²⁸Furthermore, since they did not think it worthwhile to retain the knowledge of God, he gave them over to a depraved mind, to do what ought not to be done. ²⁹They have become filled with every kind of wickedness, evil, greed and depravity. They are full of envy, murder, strife, deceit and malice. They are gossips, ³⁰slanderers, God-haters, insolent, arrogant and boastful; they invent ways of doing evil; they disobey their parents; ³¹they are senseless, faithless, heartless, ruthless. ³²Although they know God's righteous decree that those who do such things deserve death, they not only continue to do these very things but also approve of those who practice them.

Discovering the Word 1. John Stott defines God's wrath (v. 18) as "his righteous reaction to evil, his implacable hostility to it, his refusal to condone it, and his judgment upon it" (John R. W. Stott, "God's Judgment," in *Believing and Obeying Jesus Christ*). According to this definition, how would God's wrath differ from the sinful anger or violent temper condemned by Scripture? 2. What does everyone know about God, according to verses 19–20? 3. Verses 21–32 describe the downward spiral of sin experienced by people who rebel against God. How would you summarize each level of their descent? 4. How might each level lead to the next? 5. People often raise the question of how God could condemn those who have never heard of him. How does this passage address this question?

Applying the Word 1. What evidence do you see of this moral and spiritual degeneration today? 2. How might this passage make you less ashamed of the gospel and more eager to preach it?

Responding in Prayer Pray that God would be revealed powerfully to those who are rejecting him.

3 / *Romans 2*
The Judgment of God

PROSTITUTES, DRUG ADDICTS, thieves—it's easy to see why these people need the gospel. But what about "respectable" people: doctors, business executives, the family next door? They seem so contented, so fulfilled, so ... *nice*!

In Romans 1:18–32 Paul described the depravity of those who reject God. Now he imagines someone saying, "You're absolutely right, Paul. Such people are wicked and deserve everything that's coming to them! But of course *we* would never do such things and would be very critical of anyone who did." In this passage Paul shows why even "nice" people need the gospel.

Warming Up to God Have you ever wondered whether some non-Christians really need the gospel? Explain. Ask God to open your heart to understand what place he has in each of our lives.

Read Romans 2.

2 You, therefore, have no excuse, you who pass judgment on someone else, for at whatever point you judge the other, you are condemning yourself, because you who pass judgment do the same things. ²Now we know that God's judgment against those who do such things is based on truth. ³So when you, a mere man, pass judgment on them and yet do the same things, do you think you will escape God's judgment? ⁴Or do you show contempt for the riches of his kindness, tolerance and patience, not realizing that God's kindness leads you toward repentance?

⁵But because of your stubbornness and your unrepentant heart, you are storing up wrath against yourself for the day of God's wrath, when his righteous judgment will be revealed. ⁶God "will give to each person according to what he has done."ᵉ ⁷To those who by persistence in doing good seek glory, honor and immortality, he will give eternal life. ⁸But for those who are self-seeking and who reject the truth and follow evil, there will be wrath and anger. ⁹There will be trouble and distress for every human being who does evil: first for the Jew, then for the Gentile; ¹⁰but glory, honor and peace for everyone who does good: first for the Jew, then for the Gentile. ¹¹For God does not show favoritism.

¹²All who sin apart from the law will also perish apart from the law, and all who sin under the law will be judged by the law. ¹³For it is not those who hear the law who are righteous in God's sight, but it is those who obey the law who will be declared righteous. ¹⁴(Indeed, when Gentiles, who do not have the law, do by nature things required by the law, they are a law for themselves, even though they do not have the law, ¹⁵since they show that the requirements of the law are written on their hearts, their consciences also bearing witness, and their thoughts now accusing, now even defending them.) ¹⁶This will take place on the day when God will judge men's secrets through Jesus Christ, as my gospel declares.

¹⁷Now you, if you call yourself a Jew; if you rely on the law and brag about your relationship to God; ¹⁸if you know his will and approve of what is superior because you are instructed by the law; ¹⁹if you are convinced that you are a guide for the blind, a light for those who are in the dark, ²⁰an instructor of the foolish, a teacher of infants, because you have in the law the embodiment of knowledge and truth— ²¹you, then, who teach others, do you not teach yourself? You who preach against stealing, do you steal? ²²You who

ᵉ6 Psalm 62:12; Prov. 24:12

say that people should not commit adultery, do you commit adultery? You who abhor idols, do you rob temples? ²³You who brag about the law, do you dishonor God by breaking the law? ²⁴As it is written: "God's name is blasphemed among the Gentiles because of you."ᶠ

²⁵Circumcision has value if you observe the law, but if you break the law, you have become as though you had not been circumcised. ²⁶If those who are not circumcised keep the law's requirements, will they not be regarded as though they were circumcised? ²⁷The one who is not circum-

cised physically and yet obeys the law will condemn you who, even though you have theᵍ written code and circumcision, are a lawbreaker.

²⁸A man is not a Jew if he is only one outwardly, nor is circumcision merely outward and physical. ²⁹No, a man is a Jew if he is one inwardly; and circumcision is circumcision of the heart, by the Spirit, not by the written code. Such a man's praise is not from men, but from God.

f24 Isaiah 52:5; Ezek. 36:22   g27 Or who, by means of a

 Discovering the Word   1. When people are judgmental, how do they reveal both an understanding and a misunderstanding of God's judgment (vv. 1–4)?   2. Verses 5–16 describe a future day of judgment known as "the day of God's wrath" (v. 5). What will God consider important and unimportant on that day?   3. How are God's standards of judgment both similar and different for the two groups described in verses 12–16?   4. In verses 17–29 Paul focuses his attention on a hypocritical Jew. How does such a person view himself and others (vv. 17–20)?   5. Jews placed great value on circumcision because it was the visible sign that they were God's people. How had some of them confused the sign with what it signified (vv. 25–29)?

 Applying the Word   1. How has religious hypocrisy hurt the cause of Christ in our day?   2. Many non-Christians have high moral standards. How can we use their own standards to help them see their need of Christ?   3. How can this chapter help you to more effectively share the gospel with respectable, religious or moral non-Christians?

 Responding in Prayer   Ask God to make you bold in talking with a non-Christian.

---

4 / *Romans 3:1–20*
The Verdict

IF YOUR ETERNAL destiny were decided by the quality of your life and the level of your obedience to God, how would you fare? There is one sure way to find out. Take your case to the divine court. The Bible assures us that we will all have our day in court (Ro 2:5–6; 14:10–12). But we need not wait until then to find out the verdict. Paul tells us in advance in this passage.

Warming Up to God   Describe some of the thoughts and feelings you might have if you were on trial for committing a serious crime—and you knew you were guilty. Now consider the fact that Christ has set you free despite your guilt. How do you feel?

Read Romans 3:1–20.

3What advantage, then, is there in being a Jew, or what value is there in circumcision? ²Much in every way! First of all, they have been entrusted with the very words of God.

³What if some did not have faith? Will their lack of faith nullify God's faithfulness? ⁴Not at

all! Let God be true, and every man a liar. As it is written:

"So that you may be proved right when you
          speak
      and prevail when you judge."ʰ

h4 Psalm 51:4

5But if our unrighteousness brings out God's righteousness more clearly, what shall we say? That God is unjust in bringing his wrath on us? (I am using a human argument.) 6Certainly not! If that were so, how could God judge the world? 7Someone might argue, "If my falsehood enhances God's truthfulness and so increases his glory, why am I still condemned as a sinner?" 8Why not say—as we are being slanderously reported as saying and as some claim that we say— "Let us do evil that good may result"? Their condemnation is deserved.

9What shall we conclude then? Are we any better[i]? Not at all! We have already made the charge that Jews and Gentiles alike are all under sin. 10As it is written:

"There is no one righteous, not even one;
11 there is no one who understands,
   no one who seeks God.
12All have turned away,
   they have together become worthless;
there is no one who does good,

not even one."[j]
13"Their throats are open graves;
   their tongues practice deceit."[k]
"The poison of vipers is on their lips."[l]
14 "Their mouths are full of cursing and
      bitterness."[m]
15"Their feet are swift to shed blood;
16 ruin and misery mark their ways,
17and the way of peace they do not know."[n]
18 "There is no fear of God before their
      eyes."[o]

19Now we know that whatever the law says, it says to those who are under the law, so that every mouth may be silenced and the whole world held accountable to God. 20Therefore no one will be declared righteous in his sight by observing the law; rather, through the law we become conscious of sin.

i9 Or *worse*   j12 Psalms 14:1-3; 53:1-3; Eccles. 7:20
k13 Psalm 5:9   l13 Psalm 140:3   m14 Psalm 10:7
n17 Isaiah 59:7,8   o18 Psalm 36:1

Discovering the Word 1. Why might some Jews have accused God of unfaithfulness and injustice (vv. 3–8)? 2. How does Paul respond to these accusations? 3. In the role of prosecutor, Paul has charged that Jews and Gentiles alike are under sin (v. 9). How does Scripture support his charge (vv. 10–18)? 4. In verses 13–18 Paul describes how the various parts of our bodies are involved in sin. How does this figurative language graphically illustrate our condition as fallen people? 5. How would you reconcile the statements in verses 10–18 with the fact that some non-Christians *do* seem to seek after God and lead exemplary lives? 6. Imagine a courtroom scene with God as the judge and the world on trial. From what you have learned in Romans 1:18—3:20, summarize the charges against us, the supporting evidence and the verdict.

Applying the Word 1. Paul does not discuss the grace of God (3:21—5:21) until he has discussed the judgment of God (1:18—3:20). He does not proclaim the good news until we have understood the bad news. Why does he follow this order? 2. How should Paul's example affect our evangelism? (Be as specific as possible.)

Responding in Prayer The letter to the Romans could have ended with 3:20. God would be perfectly just to condemn us all and to leave us fearfully awaiting his wrath. Let this fact sink in for a moment, then take time to thank God for being not only just but also merciful and gracious.

---

5 / *Romans 3:21–31*
The Righteousness from God

LIKE PRISONERS ON death row, people are guilty, condemned and awaiting the execution of God's wrath. They sit silently in the miserable darkness of their cell, all hope extinguished.

Then abruptly, the door swings open and darkness becomes light, death becomes life, and bondage becomes freedom. "You are *pardoned*," a voice tells them. But how? Why? This passage answers these questions.

Warming Up to God Imagine that you are a judge, and someone you love is on trial. Would you be more tempted to compromise your justice or your love? Explain.

 Read Romans 3:21–31.

²¹But now a righteousness from God, apart from law, has been made known, to which the Law and the Prophets testify. ²²This righteousness from God comes through faith in Jesus Christ to all who believe. There is no difference, ²³for all have sinned and fall short of the glory of God, ²⁴and are justified freely by his grace through the redemption that came by Christ Jesus. ²⁵God presented him as a sacrifice of atonement,ᵖ through faith in his blood. He did this to demonstrate his justice, because in his forbearance he had left the sins committed beforehand unpunished— ²⁶he did it to demonstrate his justice at the present time, so as to be just and the one who justifies those who have faith in Jesus.

²⁷Where, then, is boasting? It is excluded. On what principle? On that of observing the law? No, but on that of faith. ²⁸For we maintain that a man is justified by faith apart from observing the law. ²⁹Is God the God of Jews only? Is he not the God of Gentiles too? Yes, of Gentiles too, ³⁰since there is only one God, who will justify the circumcised by faith and the uncircumcised through that same faith. ³¹Do we, then, nullify the law by this faith? Not at all! Rather, we uphold the law.

ᵖ25 *Or as the one who would turn aside his wrath, taking away sin*

 Discovering the Word 1. How is the righteousness from God (3:22–24) different from righteousness by law (2:5–13)? 2. The word *redemption* (v. 24) is borrowed from the slave market. It means to buy someone out of slavery. From what types of slavery has Christ delivered us? 3. The phrase *sacrifice of atonement* (v. 25) is borrowed from the Old Testament. Animal sacrifices turned away God's wrath from the sinner. Why does Christ's death turn away God's wrath from us? 4. How should we respond, emotionally and spiritually, to the fact that Jesus experienced God's wrath for us? 5. Some people find it difficult to understand how God can be perfectly just and gracious at the same time. How do the justice and grace of God meet at the cross (vv. 25–26)? 6. How does boasting about ourselves betray a fundamental misunderstanding of the gospel (vv. 27–31)?

 Applying the Word 1. At times do you still feel unacceptable to God? Explain. 2. In what ways might you feel or act differently if you more fully grasped what Jesus has done for you?

 Responding in Prayer Take time to praise and thank God for Jesus Christ.

6 / *Romans 4*
The Example of Abraham

"IT'S HOPELESS." NO words are more discouraging than these. Yet sometimes situations appear beyond hope, beyond help. Our natural response during such times is despair and depression.

Abraham knew what it meant to face insurmountable obstacles. He too was hopeless, yet somehow he found renewed reason to hope. For this reason he has become a timeless example and encouragement for us.

 Warming Up to God Recall a situation in which you felt hopeless. What restored you to hope?

 Read Romans 4.

4 What then shall we say that Abraham, our
forefather, discovered in this matter? [2]If,
in fact, Abraham was justified by works,
he had something to boast about—but not before
God. [3]What does the Scripture say? "Abraham believed God, and it was credited to him as righteousness."[q]

[4]Now when a man works, his wages are not
credited to him as a gift, but as an obligation.
[5]However, to the man who does not work but
trusts God who justifies the wicked, his faith is
credited as righteousness. [6]David says the same
thing when he speaks of the blessedness of the
man to whom God credits righteousness apart
from works:

[7]"Blessed are they
whose transgressions are forgiven,
whose sins are covered.
[8]Blessed is the man
whose sin the Lord will never count against
him."[r]

[9]Is this blessedness only for the circumcised, or
also for the uncircumcised? We have been saying
that Abraham's faith was credited to him as righteousness. [10]Under what circumstances was it
credited? Was it after he was circumcised, or before? It was not after, but before! [11]And he received the sign of circumcision, a seal of the righteousness that he had by faith while he was still
uncircumcised. So then, he is the father of all
who believe but have not been circumcised, in
order that righteousness might be credited to
them. [12]And he is also the father of the circumcised who not only are circumcised but who also
walk in the footsteps of the faith that our father
Abraham had before he was circumcised.

[13]It was not through law that Abraham and his
offspring received the promise that he would be
heir of the world, but through the righteousness
that comes by faith. [14]For if those who live by law
are heirs, faith has no value and the promise is
worthless, [15]because law brings wrath. And where
there is no law there is no transgression.

[16]Therefore, the promise comes by faith, so
that it may be by grace and may be guaranteed to
all Abraham's offspring—not only to those who
are of the law but also to those who are of the
faith of Abraham. He is the father of us all. [17]As it
is written: "I have made you a father of many
nations."[s] He is our father in the sight of God, in
whom he believed—the God who gives life to the
dead and calls things that are not as though they
were.

[18]Against all hope, Abraham in hope believed
and so became the father of many nations, just as
it had been said to him, "So shall your offspring
be."[t] [19]Without weakening in his faith, he faced
the fact that his body was as good as dead—since
he was about a hundred years old—and that
Sarah's womb was also dead. [20]Yet he did not wa-
ver through unbelief regarding the promise of
God, but was strengthened in his faith and gave
glory to God, [21]being fully persuaded that God
had power to do what he had promised. [22]This is
why "it was credited to him as righteousness."
[23]The words "it was credited to him" were written
not for him alone, [24]but also for us, to whom God
will credit righteousness—for us who believe in
him who raised Jesus our Lord from the dead.
[25]He was delivered over to death for our sins and
was raised to life for our justification.

[q]*3* Gen. 15:6; also in verse 22 [r]*8* Psalm 32:1,2 [s]*17* Gen. 17:5
[t]*18* Gen. 15:5

Discovering the Word 1. According to Paul, how were Old Testament saints, such as Abraham and David, justified (vv. 1–8)? 2. What are some of the differences between justification by faith and by works (vv. 4–8)? 3. It's easy to feel that God accepts us only when we are good. When we feel this way, how can the examples of Abraham and David give us hope? 4. Some people today claim that unless we are baptized, we have no hope of being saved. How might Abraham's experience refute this claim? 5. God promised that Abraham and his offspring would inherit the world (v. 13). Who are Abraham's offspring (vv. 13–17)? 6. How does Abraham illustrate our own hopeless predicament as non-Christians and the solution provided in Jesus Christ (vv. 18–25)?

Applying the Word 1. What situation are you currently facing that requires faith in the God of resurrection and creation? 2. How can you demonstrate faith and hope in that situation?

Responding in Prayer Know that God wants you to have hope. Pray with that assurance.

7 / *Romans 5*
Reasons to Rejoice

WE ALL LONG to be joyful, to experience the pure delight that life sometimes offers. But life's joys are elusive, momentary, gone as quickly as they come. How can we have an abiding, enduring joy—especially when suffering intrudes into our lives? In Romans 5 Paul gives us several firm and lasting reasons to rejoice.

 Warming Up to God What kinds of things make you joyful? If you are in a private place where you feel comfortable, sing a short song of praise to God.

 Read Romans 5.

5 Therefore, since we have been justified through faith, we[u] have peace with God through our Lord Jesus Christ, ²through whom we have gained access by faith into this grace in which we now stand. And we[u] rejoice in the hope of the glory of God. ³Not only so, but we[u] also rejoice in our sufferings, because we know that suffering produces perseverance; ⁴perseverance, character; and character, hope. ⁵And hope does not disappoint us, because God has poured out his love into our hearts by the Holy Spirit, whom he has given us.

⁶You see, at just the right time, when we were still powerless, Christ died for the ungodly. ⁷Very rarely will anyone die for a righteous man, though for a good man someone might possibly dare to die. ⁸But God demonstrates his own love for us in this: While we were still sinners, Christ died for us.

⁹Since we have now been justified by his blood, how much more shall we be saved from God's wrath through him! ¹⁰For if, when we were God's enemies, we were reconciled to him through the death of his Son, how much more, having been reconciled, shall we be saved through his life! ¹¹Not only is this so, but we also rejoice in God through our Lord Jesus Christ, through whom we have now received reconciliation.

¹²Therefore, just as sin entered the world through one man, and death through sin, and in this way death came to all men, because all sinned— ¹³for before the law was given, sin was in the world. But sin is not taken into account when there is no law. ¹⁴Nevertheless, death reigned from the time of Adam to the time of Moses, even over those who did not sin by breaking a command, as did Adam, who was a pattern of the one to come.

¹⁵But the gift is not like the trespass. For if the many died by the trespass of the one man, how much more did God's grace and the gift that came by the grace of the one man, Jesus Christ, overflow to the many! ¹⁶Again, the gift of God is not like the result of the one man's sin: The judgment followed one sin and brought condemnation, but the gift followed many trespasses and brought justification. ¹⁷For if, by the trespass of the one man, death reigned through that one man, how much more will those who receive God's abundant provision of grace and of the gift of righteousness reign in life through the one man, Jesus Christ.

¹⁸Consequently, just as the result of one trespass was condemnation for all men, so also the result of one act of righteousness was justification that brings life for all men. ¹⁹For just as through the disobedience of the one man the many were made sinners, so also through the obedience of the one man the many will be made righteous.

²⁰The law was added so that the trespass might increase. But where sin increased, grace increased all the more, ²¹so that, just as sin reigned in death, so also grace might reign through righteousness to bring eternal life through Jesus Christ our Lord.

[u]1,2,3 Or *let us*

Discovering the Word 1. How has faith in Jesus Christ changed our relationship with God (vv. 1–2)? 2. In verses 2–11 what reasons does Paul give for rejoicing? 3. How does suffering for Christ's sake produce the character changes mentioned in verses 3–4? 4. How do verses 5–8 emphasize the love God has for us? 5. Read verses 12–21. How are Adam and Christ similar (vv. 12, 18–19)? 6. How is Christ's gift different from Adam's trespass (vv. 15–21)?

 Applying the Word 1. In what area of your life are you experiencing suffering? 2. How can a knowledge of the process of character change help us to rejoice in our sufferings?

 Responding in Prayer This passage gives us many reasons for rejoicing. Spend time thanking and praising God for all we have in Christ Jesus.

8 / *Romans 6:1—7:6*
New Life, New Lifestyle

SUBTLE ALLURE, PERSISTENT urges, passionate desires. Sin entices us in many ways. A thought enters our mind that we dare not acknowledge: "If I give in, I can always be forgiven." Sound familiar? Such thinking can become an excuse for immoral practices. But it betrays a fundamental misunderstanding of God's grace in our lives. In Romans 6:1—7:6 Paul explains why the idea of "sinning so that grace may increase" is unthinkable for Christians.

 Warming Up to God When you became a Christian, was the change in your life dramatic, gradual or imperceptible? Explain. Whether it has taken place slowly or quickly, praise God for the change he has worked in your life.

 Read Romans 6:1—7:6.

6 What shall we say, then? Shall we go on sinning so that grace may increase? ²By no means! We died to sin; how can we live in it any longer? ³Or don't you know that all of us who were baptized into Christ Jesus were baptized into his death? ⁴We were therefore buried with him through baptism into death in order that, just as Christ was raised from the dead through the glory of the Father, we too may live a new life.

⁵If we have been united with him like this in his death, we will certainly also be united with him in his resurrection. ⁶For we know that our old self was crucified with him so that the body of sin might be done away with,ᵛ that we should no longer be slaves to sin— ⁷because anyone who has died has been freed from sin.

⁸Now if we died with Christ, we believe that we will also live with him. ⁹For we know that since Christ was raised from the dead, he cannot die again; death no longer has mastery over him. ¹⁰The death he died, he died to sin once for all; but the life he lives, he lives to God.

¹¹In the same way, count yourselves dead to sin but alive to God in Christ Jesus. ¹²Therefore do not let sin reign in your mortal body so that you obey its evil desires. ¹³Do not offer the parts of your body to sin, as instruments of wickedness, but rather offer yourselves to God, as those who have been brought from death to life; and offer the parts of your body to him as instruments of righteousness. ¹⁴For sin shall not be your master, because you are not under law, but under grace.

¹⁵What then? Shall we sin because we are not under law but under grace? By no means! ¹⁶Don't you know that when you offer yourselves to someone to obey him as slaves, you are slaves to the one whom you obey—whether you are slaves to sin, which leads to death, or to obedience, which leads to righteousness? ¹⁷But thanks be to God that, though you used to be slaves to sin, you wholeheartedly obeyed the form of teaching to which you were entrusted. ¹⁸You have been set free from sin and have become slaves to righteousness.

¹⁹I put this in human terms because you are weak in your natural selves. Just as you used to offer the parts of your body in slavery to impurity and to ever-increasing wickedness, so now offer them in slavery to righteousness leading to holiness. ²⁰When you were slaves to sin, you were free from the control of righteousness. ²¹What benefit did you reap at that time from the things

ᵛ6 Or *be rendered powerless*

you are now ashamed of? Those things result in death! ²²But now that you have been set free from sin and have become slaves to God, the benefit you reap leads to holiness, and the result is eternal life. ²³For the wages of sin is death, but the gift of God is eternal life in^w Christ Jesus our Lord.

7 Do you not know, brothers—for I am speaking to men who know the law—that the law has authority over a man only as long as he lives? ²For example, by law a married woman is bound to her husband as long as he is alive, but if her husband dies, she is released from the law of marriage. ³So then, if she marries another man while her husband is still alive, she is called an adulteress. But if her husband dies, she is released from that law and is not an adulteress, even though she marries another man.

⁴So, my brothers, you also died to the law through the body of Christ, that you might belong to another, to him who was raised from the dead, in order that we might bear fruit to God. ⁵For when we were controlled by the sinful nature,^x the sinful passions aroused by the law were at work in our bodies, so that we bore fruit for death. ⁶But now, by dying to what once bound us, we have been released from the law so that we serve in the new way of the Spirit, and not in the old way of the written code.

^w23 Or *through*   ^x5 Or *the flesh*; also in verse 25

Discovering the Word 1. In what sense was our baptism both a funeral and a resurrection? 2. Our "old self" (6:6) refers to everything we were as non-Christians. When our old self was crucified with Christ, in what sense was sin rendered powerless (6:5–7)? 3. What does it mean to "count yourselves dead to sin but alive to God" (6:11)? 4. Paul compares both our old life and our new to slavery. Why is this analogy appropriate in each case (6:15–18)? 5. How is the principle "that the law has authority over a man only as long as he lives" illustrated by marriage (7:1–3)? 6. In 6:1—7:6 Paul uses baptism, slavery and marriage to illustrate the differences between our old life and our new life. What common themes are emphasized in these illustrations?

Applying the Word 1. What sins are you particularly struggling to free yourself of? 2. What assurance and encouragement is Paul giving you in your struggle against sin?

Responding in Prayer Thank God that you are no longer a slave to sin. Pray that you will live as a slave to righteousness.

9 / *Romans 7:7–25*
Our Struggle with Sin

ARE YOU EVER baffled by your behavior? You know the right thing to do, but you fail to do it. You resolve to avoid certain things, and they become even more attractive and enticing. Why? What keeps us from translating our desires into actions? In Romans 7 Paul explores his own inner struggles to do good and avoid evil. As we look into his mind and heart, we see a reflection of ourselves and the power that opposes us.

Warming Up to God Saying no to a piece of pie we don't need *seems* so simple, but is easier said than done. How have you recently struggled to do what you know you should do?

Read Romans 7:7–25.

⁷What shall we say, then? Is the law sin? Certainly not! Indeed I would not have known what sin was except through the law. For I would not have known what coveting really was if the law had not said, "Do not covet."^y ⁸But sin, seizing the opportunity afforded by the commandment, produced in me every kind of covetous desire. For apart from law, sin is dead. ⁹Once I was alive apart from law; but when the commandment came, sin sprang to life and I died. ¹⁰I found that

^y7 Exodus 20:17; Deut. 5:21

the very commandment that was intended to bring life actually brought death. ¹¹For sin, seizing the opportunity afforded by the commandment, deceived me, and through the commandment put me to death. ¹²So then, the law is holy, and the commandment is holy, righteous and good.

¹³Did that which is good, then, become death to me? By no means! But in order that sin might be recognized as sin, it produced death in me through what was good, so that through the commandment sin might become utterly sinful.

¹⁴We know that the law is spiritual; but I am unspiritual, sold as a slave to sin. ¹⁵I do not understand what I do. For what I want to do I do not do, but what I hate I do. ¹⁶And if I do what I do not want to do, I agree that the law is good. ¹⁷As it is, it is no longer I myself who do it, but it is sin living in me. ¹⁸I know that nothing good lives in me, that is, in my sinful nature.ᶻ For I

have the desire to do what is good, but I cannot carry it out. ¹⁹For what I do is not the good I want to do; no, the evil I do not want to do—this I keep on doing. ²⁰Now if I do what I do not want to do, it is no longer I who do it, but it is sin living in me that does it.

²¹So I find this law at work: When I want to do good, evil is right there with me. ²²For in my inner being I delight in God's law; ²³but I see another law at work in the members of my body, waging war against the law of my mind and making me a prisoner of the law of sin at work within my members. ²⁴What a wretched man I am! Who will rescue me from this body of death? ²⁵Thanks be to God—through Jesus Christ our Lord!

So then, I myself in my mind am a slave to God's law, but in the sinful nature a slave to the law of sin.

ᶻ18 Or *my flesh*

Discovering the Word 1. How did the law create in Paul a vivid awareness of sin (vv. 7–12)? 2. Why would it be wrong to blame the law for Paul's spiritual death (vv. 13–14)? 3. According to verses 14–20, why does Paul feel so wretched? 4. In chapter 6 Paul stated that Christians are no longer slaves to sin. Yet here he claims he is a slave to sin (v. 14). How would you explain this difference? 5. How can a person's anguish and frustration with sin be beneficial (vv. 24–25)?

Applying the Word 1. To what extent can you identify with Paul's struggles in these verses? Explain. 2. Why is it important to realize that only Christ can rescue you from the power of your sin?

Responding in Prayer When Paul realized that Jesus could rescue him from his wretched condition, he cried out, "Thanks be to God!" If this is your response too, spend time thanking him.

---

10 / *Romans 8:1–17*
The Spirit Brings Life

IF WE WERE unable to obey God as non-Christians, then how can we as Christians? What has happened to turn our slavery into freedom, our sin into righteousness and our spiritual death into life?

The struggle described in Romans 7 does not end when we become Christians. But there is a new dimension to that struggle that totally changes its outcome. In chapter 8 Paul describes the life-giving effects of the Spirit.

Warming Up to God This chapter is one of celebration. What has the Holy Spirit recently done in you that gives you reason to rejoice?

Read Romans 8:1–17.

8 Therefore, there is now no condemnation for those who are in Christ Jesus,*a* ²because through Christ Jesus the law of the Spirit of life set me free from the law of sin and death. ³For what the law was powerless to do in that it was weakened by the sinful nature,*b* God did by sending his own Son in the likeness of sinful man to be a sin offering.*c* And so he condemned sin in sinful man,*d* ⁴in order that the righteous requirements of the law might be fully met in us, who do not live according to the sinful nature but according to the Spirit.

⁵Those who live according to the sinful nature have their minds set on what that nature desires; but those who live in accordance with the Spirit have their minds set on what the Spirit desires. ⁶The mind of sinful man*e* is death, but the mind controlled by the Spirit is life and peace; ⁷the sinful mind*f* is hostile to God. It does not submit to God's law, nor can it do so. ⁸Those controlled by the sinful nature cannot please God.

⁹You, however, are controlled not by the sinful nature but by the Spirit, if the Spirit of God lives in you. And if anyone does not have the Spirit of Christ, he does not belong to Christ. ¹⁰But if Christ is in you, your body is dead because of sin, yet your spirit is alive because of righteousness. ¹¹And if the Spirit of him who raised Jesus from the dead is living in you, he who raised Christ from the dead will also give life to your mortal bodies through his Spirit, who lives in you.

¹²Therefore, brothers, we have an obligation—but it is not to the sinful nature, to live according to it. ¹³For if you live according to the sinful nature, you will die; but if by the Spirit you put to death the misdeeds of the body, you will live, ¹⁴because those who are led by the Spirit of God are sons of God. ¹⁵For you did not receive a spirit that makes you a slave again to fear, but you received the Spirit of sonship.*g* And by him we cry, "*Abba,*h* Father.*" ¹⁶The Spirit himself testifies with our spirit that we are God's children. ¹⁷Now if we are children, then we are heirs—heirs of God and co-heirs with Christ, if indeed we share in his sufferings in order that we may also share in his glory.

a1 Some later manuscripts *Jesus, who do not live according to the sinful nature but according to the Spirit,* *b3* Or *the flesh*; also in verses 4, 5, 8, 9, 12 and 13 *c3* Or *man, for sin* *d3* Or *in the flesh* *e6* Or *mind set on the flesh* *f7* Or *the mind set on the flesh* *g15* Or *adoption* *h15* Aramaic for *Father*

 Discovering the Word 1. Romans 7 described how the law of sin brought about our spiritual death. What has God done to free us from the law of sin and death (vv. 1–4)? 2. In verses 5–8 Paul divides all of humanity into two categories: those who live according to the sinful nature and those who live according to the Spirit. In your own words, what are some characteristics of each group? 3. There are many professing Christians whose lives seem very different from Paul's description of life in the Spirit. How do you think Paul would account for this fact? 4. In verse 12 Paul concludes that we have an obligation. Describe in your own words the negative and positive aspects of that obligation (vv. 12–14). 5. How do we experience the reality and privileges of being God's children (vv. 15–17)?

 Applying the Word 1. What evidence do you see of your life being controlled by the Spirit? 2. Practically speaking, how can we put to death the misdeeds of the body by the Spirit?

Responding in Prayer Spend time thanking God for the gift of the Spirit and the difference he makes in our lives.

---

11 / *Romans 8:18–39*
Glorious Conquerors

"ROMAN CONQUERORS RETURNING from the wars enjoyed the honor of a triumph, a tumultuous parade. In the procession came trumpeters, musicians and strange animals from the conquered territories, together with carts laden with treasure and captured armaments. The conqueror rode in a triumphal chariot, the dazed prisoners walking in chains before him. Sometimes his children, robed in white, stood with him in the chariot or rode the trace horses. A slave stood behind the conqueror, holding a golden crown and whispering in his ear a warning: that all glory is fleeting." (At the end of the movie *Patton,* these words went through the mind of that famous general.)

In Romans 8 Paul describes Christians as glorious conquerors who by God's grace overcome all forces arrayed against us. But the glory we receive is eternal.

 Warming Up to God Why is it often difficult to feel like a glorious conqueror?

 Read Romans 8:18–39.

---

¹⁸I consider that our present sufferings are not worth comparing with the glory that will be revealed in us. ¹⁹The creation waits in eager expectation for the sons of God to be revealed. ²⁰For the creation was subjected to frustration, not by its own choice, but by the will of the one who subjected it, in hope ²¹that[i] the creation itself will be liberated from its bondage to decay and brought into the glorious freedom of the children of God.

²²We know that the whole creation has been groaning as in the pains of childbirth right up to the present time. ²³Not only so, but we ourselves, who have the firstfruits of the Spirit, groan inwardly as we wait eagerly for our adoption as sons, the redemption of our bodies. ²⁴For in this hope we were saved. But hope that is seen is no hope at all. Who hopes for what he already has? ²⁵But if we hope for what we do not yet have, we wait for it patiently.

²⁶In the same way, the Spirit helps us in our weakness. We do not know what we ought to pray for, but the Spirit himself intercedes for us with groans that words cannot express. ²⁷And he who searches our hearts knows the mind of the Spirit, because the Spirit intercedes for the saints in accordance with God's will.

²⁸And we know that in all things God works for the good of those who love him,[j] who[k] have been called according to his purpose. ²⁹For those God foreknew he also predestined to be conformed to the likeness of his Son, that he might be the firstborn among many brothers. ³⁰And

those he predestined, he also called; those he called, he also justified; those he justified, he also glorified.

³¹What, then, shall we say in response to this? If God is for us, who can be against us? ³²He who did not spare his own Son, but gave him up for us all—how will he not also, along with him, graciously give us all things? ³³Who will bring any charge against those whom God has chosen? It is God who justifies. ³⁴Who is he that condemns? Christ Jesus, who died—more than that, who was raised to life—is at the right hand of God and is also interceding for us. ³⁵Who shall separate us from the love of Christ? Shall trouble or hardship or persecution or famine or nakedness or danger or sword? ³⁶As it is written:

"For your sake we face death all day long;
    we are considered as sheep to be
        slaughtered."[l]

³⁷No, in all these things we are more than conquerors through him who loved us. ³⁸For I am convinced that neither death nor life, neither angels nor demons,[m] neither the present nor the future, nor any powers, ³⁹neither height nor depth, nor anything else in all creation, will be able to separate us from the love of God that is in Christ Jesus our Lord.

[i]20,21 Or subjected it in hope. 21For   [j]28 Some manuscripts And we know that all things work together for good to those who love God   [k]28 Or works together with those who love him to bring about what is good—with those who   [l]36 Psalm 44:22   [m]38 Or nor heavenly rulers

---

 Discovering the Word 1. What words and vivid images in these verses underscore the difficulties of the present time? 2. Explain why these difficulties don't compare with the glory that will be revealed in us (vv. 18–25). 3. How can the Spirit's help encourage us (vv. 26–27)? 4. In verse 28 Paul speaks of "the good" and "his purpose." What is God's good purpose for us (v. 29)? 5. How might trouble, hardship, persecution, famine, nakedness, danger or the threat of death cause us to question God's love for us (vv. 35–36)? 6. In spite of these things, why does Paul proclaim that we are "more than conquerors" (vv. 37–39)?

 Applying the Word 1. How can eager expectation of glory help us cope with our present problems and sufferings? 2. Look again at the powerful words of verses 38–39. How does this give you courage to persevere?

Responding in Prayer Ask God to make you ready for his future glory.

12 / *Romans 9:1–29*
The Potter and His Clay

"I DON'T BELIEVE in Christ." It grieves us to hear these words. But when they come from close friends or family members, the pain can be unbearable. Why doesn't God open their hearts to the gospel? Why did he save us and not them? Paul felt great pain and perplexity over Israel's unbelief. Their Messiah had come, and they had rejected him. In chapters 9—11 Paul wrestles with these questions.

Warming Up to God Whose unbelief grieves you? Talk openly with God about your concerns.

Read Romans 9:1–29.

9 I speak the truth in Christ—I am not lying, my conscience confirms it in the Holy Spirit— [2]I have great sorrow and unceasing anguish in my heart. [3]For I could wish that I myself were cursed and cut off from Christ for the sake of my brothers, those of my own race, [4]the people of Israel. Theirs is the adoption as sons; theirs the divine glory, the covenants, the receiving of the law, the temple worship and the promises. [5]Theirs are the patriarchs, and from them is traced the human ancestry of Christ, who is God over all, forever praised![n] Amen.

[6]It is not as though God's word had failed. For not all who are descended from Israel are Israel. [7]Nor because they are his descendants are they all Abraham's children. On the contrary, "It is through Isaac that your offspring will be reckoned."[o] [8]In other words, it is not the natural children who are God's children, but it is the children of the promise who are regarded as Abraham's offspring. [9]For this was how the promise was stated: "At the appointed time I will return, and Sarah will have a son."[p]

[10]Not only that, but Rebekah's children had one and the same father, our father Isaac. [11]Yet, before the twins were born or had done anything good or bad—in order that God's purpose in election might stand: [12]not by works but by him who calls—she was told, "The older will serve the younger."[q] [13]Just as it is written: "Jacob I loved, but Esau I hated."[r]

[14]What then shall we say? Is God unjust? Not at all! [15]For he says to Moses,

"I will have mercy on whom I have mercy,
and I will have compassion on whom I
have compassion."[s]

[16]It does not, therefore, depend on man's desire or effort, but on God's mercy. [17]For the Scripture says to Pharaoh: "I raised you up for this very purpose, that I might display my power in you and that my name might be proclaimed in all the earth."[t] [18]Therefore God has mercy on whom he wants to have mercy, and he hardens whom he wants to harden.

[19]One of you will say to me: "Then why does God still blame us? For who resists his will?" [20]But who are you, O man, to talk back to God? "Shall what is formed say to him who formed it, 'Why did you make me like this?' "[u] [21]Does not the potter have the right to make out of the same lump of clay some pottery for noble purposes and some for common use?

[22]What if God, choosing to show his wrath and make his power known, bore with great patience the objects of his wrath—prepared for destruction? [23]What if he did this to make the riches of his glory known to the objects of his mercy, whom he prepared in advance for glory— [24]even us, whom he also called, not only from the Jews but also from the Gentiles? [25]As he says in Hosea:

"I will call them 'my people' who are not my
people;

[n]*5* Or *Christ, who is over all. God be forever praised!* Or *Christ. God who is over all be forever praised!* [o]*7* Gen. 21:12
[p]*9* Gen. 18:10,14 [q]*12* Gen. 25:23 [r]*13* Mal. 1:2,3
[s]*15* Exodus 33:19 [t]*17* Exodus 9:16 [u]*20* Isaiah 29:16; 45:9

and I will call her 'my loved one' who is
    not my loved one,"ᵛ

²⁶and,

"It will happen that in the very place where it
    was said to them,
'You are not my people,'
they will be called 'sons of the living God.' "ʷ

²⁷Isaiah cries out concerning Israel:

"Though the number of the Israelites be like
    the sand by the sea,

only the remnant will be saved.
²⁸For the Lord will carry out
    his sentence on earth with speed and
    finality."ˣ

²⁹It is just as Isaiah said previously:

"Unless the Lord Almighty
    had left us descendants,
we would have become like Sodom,
    we would have been like Gomorrah."ʸ

ᵛ25 Hosea 2:23   ʷ26 Hosea 1:10   ˣ28 Isaiah 10:22,23
ʸ29 Isaiah 1:9

 Discovering the Word 1. Why does Paul have great sorrow for the people of Israel? 2. How do verses 6–13 demonstrate that God has not failed in his promises and purposes for Israel? 3. Many people feel it is unjust for God to choose some and not others (v. 14). In reply why does Paul speak of God's mercy rather than his justice or injustice (vv. 15–18)? 4. How does the illustration of the potter and his clay help us gain a proper perspective (vv. 20–23)? 5. How is God's mercy and justice revealed in his treatment of the Gentiles and Jews (vv. 24–29)?

 Applying the Word 1. How do you respond to the idea of election (v. 11), God's choosing certain people to be the objects of his mercy? 2. When do you feel uncertain about your own salvation? 3. What would help you to feel more secure?

 Responding in Prayer Thank God for the fact that although he would have been perfectly just to condemn us all, he mercifully chose to save some.

---

13 / *Romans 9:30—10:21*
Misguided Zeal

THE WORLD IS full of religious people: Jews, Christians, Muslims, Hindus, Buddhists and many others. Islam alone has over 800 million adherents. Many of these people are zealous, dedicated and sincere. But are zeal and sincerity enough? Are there many paths to God, or just one? In this passage Paul continues to wrestle with the problem of Israel's unbelief. He now focuses on Israel's and on our own responsibility to believe the gospel.

Warming Up to God Have you ever known a sincere and devout non-Christian? How did you respond to his or her zeal?

Read Romans 9:30—10:21

---

³⁰What then shall we say? That the Gentiles, who did not pursue righteousness, have obtained it, a righteousness that is by faith; ³¹but Israel, who pursued a law of righteousness, has not attained it. ³²Why not? Because they pursued it not by faith but as if it were by works. They stumbled over the "stumbling stone." ³³As it is written:

"See, I lay in Zion a stone that causes men to
    stumble

and a rock that makes them fall,
and the one who trusts in him will never be
    put to shame."ᶻ

10 Brothers, my heart's desire and prayer to God for the Israelites is that they may be saved. ²For I can testify about them that they are zealous for God, but their zeal is not based on knowledge. ³Since

ᶻ33 Isaiah 8:14; 28:16

they did not know the righteousness that comes from God and sought to establish their own, they did not submit to God's righteousness. ⁴Christ is the end of the law so that there may be righteousness for everyone who believes.

⁵Moses describes in this way the righteousness that is by the law: "The man who does these things will live by them."ᵃ ⁶But the righteousness that is by faith says: "Do not say in your heart, 'Who will ascend into heaven?'ᵇ" (that is, to bring Christ down) ⁷"or 'Who will descend into the deep?'ᶜ" (that is, to bring Christ up from the dead). ⁸But what does it say? "The word is near you; it is in your mouth and in your heart,"ᵈ that is, the word of faith we are proclaiming: ⁹That if you confess with your mouth, "Jesus is Lord," and believe in your heart that God raised him from the dead, you will be saved. ¹⁰For it is with your heart that you believe and are justified, and it is with your mouth that you confess and are saved. ¹¹As the Scripture says, "Anyone who trusts in him will never be put to shame."ᵉ ¹²For there is no difference between Jew and Gentile—the same Lord is Lord of all and richly blesses all who call on him, ¹³for, "Everyone who calls on the name of the Lord will be saved."ᶠ

¹⁴How, then, can they call on the one they have not believed in? And how can they believe in the one of whom they have not heard? And how can they hear without someone preaching to them?

¹⁵And how can they preach unless they are sent? As it is written, "How beautiful are the feet of those who bring good news!"ᵍ

¹⁶But not all the Israelites accepted the good news. For Isaiah says, "Lord, who has believed our message?"ʰ ¹⁷Consequently, faith comes from hearing the message, and the message is heard through the word of Christ. ¹⁸But I ask: Did they not hear? Of course they did:

"Their voice has gone out into all the earth,
    their words to the ends of the world."ⁱ

¹⁹Again I ask: Did Israel not understand? First, Moses says,

"I will make you envious by those who are
    not a nation;
I will make you angry by a nation that has
    no understanding."ʲ

²⁰And Isaiah boldly says,

"I was found by those who did not seek me;
I revealed myself to those who did not ask
    for me."ᵏ

²¹But concerning Israel he says,

"All day long I have held out my hands
    to a disobedient and obstinate people."ˡ

ᵃ5 Lev. 18:5   ᵇ6 Deut. 30:12   ᶜ7 Deut. 30:13   ᵈ8 Deut. 30:14
ᵉ11 Isaiah 28:16   ᶠ13 Joel 2:32   ᵍ15 Isaiah 52:7
ʰ16 Isaiah 53:1   ⁱ18 Psalm 19:4   ʲ19 Deut. 32:21
ᵏ20 Isaiah 65:1   ˡ21 Isaiah 65:2

Discovering the Word 1. Why was Jesus Christ more of a stumbling stone to the Jews than to the Gentiles (9:30–33)? 2. Many people believe religious zeal and sincerity are all a person needs to be saved. How would Paul respond to this belief (10:1–4)? 3. How do verses 6–8 stress the simplicity of righteousness by faith? 4. First-century Christians publicly confessed that "Jesus is Lord" at their baptism. Why is public confession important in addition to the belief in one's heart (vv. 9–13)? 5. William Carey, the father of modern missions, once proposed to a group of ministers that they discuss the implications of the Great Commission. Dr. John C. Ryland retorted: "Young man, sit down. When God pleases to convert the heathen, he will do it without your aid or mine!" How does Dr. Ryland's understanding of God's sovereignty mesh with verses 14–15?

Applying the Word 1. Realizing the implications of verses such as Romans 10:14–15, William Carey responded to God's call and went to India. Where do you feel called to go with the gospel? 2. What steps can you take (or have you taken) to be obedient to that call?

Responding in Prayer Israel's unbelief did not stop Paul from praying for them (10:1). Spend time praying for those with whom you have the opportunity of sharing the gospel.

14 / *Romans 11*
The Future of Israel

FOR CENTURIES THE people of Israel awaited their Messiah. But when he came, very few believed in him. This situation has persisted to the point where Christianity is now considered a Gentile religion. What happened to God's promises and plans for Israel? Has God rejected his people? In this chapter Paul answers these questions.

 Warming Up to God We all have expectations of how God will work in our lives that come out of our desires rather than God's. In what way do you feel that God has failed to follow your plan? Express to God any feelings of disappointment or discouragement you might have.

 Read Romans 11.

11 I ask then: Did God reject his people? By no means! I am an Israelite myself, a descendant of Abraham, from the tribe of Benjamin. ²God did not reject his people, whom he foreknew. Don't you know what the Scripture says in the passage about Elijah—how he appealed to God against Israel: ³"Lord, they have killed your prophets and torn down your altars; I am the only one left, and they are trying to kill me"^m? ⁴And what was God's answer to him? "I have reserved for myself seven thousand who have not bowed the knee to Baal."^n ⁵So too, at the present time there is a remnant chosen by grace. ⁶And if by grace, then it is no longer by works; if it were, grace would no longer be grace.^o

⁷What then? What Israel sought so earnestly it did not obtain, but the elect did. The others were hardened, ⁸as it is written:

"God gave them a spirit of stupor,
   eyes so that they could not see
   and ears so that they could not hear,
to this very day."^p

⁹And David says:

"May their table become a snare and a trap,
   a stumbling block and a retribution for
      them.
¹⁰May their eyes be darkened so they cannot
      see,
   and their backs be bent forever."^q

¹¹Again I ask: Did they stumble so as to fall beyond recovery? Not at all! Rather, because of their transgression, salvation has come to the Gentiles to make Israel envious. ¹²But if their transgression means riches for the world, and

their loss means riches for the Gentiles, how much greater riches will their fullness bring!

¹³I am talking to you Gentiles. Inasmuch as I am the apostle to the Gentiles, I make much of my ministry ¹⁴in the hope that I may somehow arouse my own people to envy and save some of them. ¹⁵For if their rejection is the reconciliation of the world, what will their acceptance be but life from the dead? ¹⁶If the part of the dough offered as firstfruits is holy, then the whole batch is holy; if the root is holy, so are the branches.

¹⁷If some of the branches have been broken off, and you, though a wild olive shoot, have been grafted in among the others and now share in the nourishing sap from the olive root, ¹⁸do not boast over those branches. If you do, consider this: You do not support the root, but the root supports you. ¹⁹You will say then, "Branches were broken off so that I could be grafted in." ²⁰Granted. But they were broken off because of unbelief, and you stand by faith. Do not be arrogant, but be afraid. ²¹For if God did not spare the natural branches, he will not spare you either.

²²Consider therefore the kindness and sternness of God: sternness to those who fell, but kindness to you, provided that you continue in his kindness. Otherwise, you also will be cut off. ²³And if they do not persist in unbelief, they will be grafted in, for God is able to graft them in again. ²⁴After all, if you were cut out of an olive tree that is wild by nature, and contrary to nature were grafted into a cultivated olive tree, how much more readily will these, the natural branches, be grafted into their own olive tree!

²⁵I do not want you to be ignorant of this mys-

^m3 1 Kings 19:10,14   ^n4 1 Kings 19:18   ^o6 Some manuscripts *by grace. But if by works, then it is no longer grace; if it were, work would no longer be work.*   ^p8 Deut. 29:4; Isaiah 29:10
^q10 Psalm 69:22,23

tery, brothers, so that you may not be conceited: Israel has experienced a hardening in part until the full number of the Gentiles has come in. ²⁶And so all Israel will be saved, as it is written:

"The deliverer will come from Zion;
    he will turn godlessness away from Jacob.
²⁷And this is ʳ my covenant with them
    when I take away their sins." ˢ

²⁸As far as the gospel is concerned, they are enemies on your account; but as far as election is concerned, they are loved on account of the patriarchs, ²⁹for God's gifts and his call are irrevocable. ³⁰Just as you who were at one time disobedient to God have now received mercy as a result of their disobedience, ³¹so they too have now become disobedient in order that they too may

now ᵗ receive mercy as a result of God's mercy to you. ³²For God has bound all men over to disobedience so that he may have mercy on them all.

³³Oh, the depth of the riches of the wisdom
        and ᵘ knowledge of God!
    How unsearchable his judgments,
        and his paths beyond tracing out!
³⁴"Who has known the mind of the Lord?
        Or who has been his counselor?" ᵛ
³⁵"Who has ever given to God,
        that God should repay him?" ʷ
³⁶For from him and through him and to him
        are all things.
    To him be the glory forever! Amen.

ʳ27 Or *will be*   ˢ27 Isaiah 59:20,21; 27:9; Jer. 31:33,34   ᵗ31 Some manuscripts do not have *now*.   ᵘ33 Or *riches and the wisdom and the*   ᵛ34 Isaiah 40:13   ʷ35 Job 41:11

Discovering the Word 1. How does Paul know that God has not rejected his people (vv. 1–6)? 2. What were the spiritual consequences for those Israelites who rejected Jesus Christ (vv. 7–10)? 3. Why are these consequences inevitable for anyone who persistently rejects the gospel? 4. Why is Paul convinced that even greater blessings will come from Israel's acceptance of Christ (vv. 11–16)? 5. Why should Paul's illustration of the olive tree prevent Gentiles from feeling superior to unbelieving Israelites (vv. 17–24)? 6. In this chapter Paul has argued that Israel's unbelief is partial (vv. 1–10), purposeful (vv. 11–16) and temporary (vv. 25–32). How does this make him feel about God (vv. 33–36)?

Applying the Word 1. Why is it foolish for Christians today to feel superior to non-Christians? 2. How can Paul's description of God in verses 33–36 also encourage us to trust and praise him?

Responding in Prayer Thank God that his plans are greater than anything we can conceive.

---

15 / *Romans 12*
Living Sacrifices

IN THE FIRST eleven chapters Paul has described God's gift of righteousness. In Christ we who were condemned are justified. We who were sinners are sanctified. And we who had no hope will be glorified. But what is our proper response to God's mercy, love and grace? Paul tells us in this and the following chapters.

Warming Up to God Jesus once told a Pharisee that a person who is forgiven little loves little. But a person who is forgiven much loves much (Lk 7:47). Why do you think this is so?

Read Romans 12.

---

12 Therefore, I urge you, brothers, in view of God's mercy, to offer your bodies as living sacrifices, holy and pleasing to God—this is your spiritual ˣ act of worship. ²Do not conform any longer to the pattern of this world, but be transformed by the re-

newing of your mind. Then you will be able to test and approve what God's will is—his good, pleasing and perfect will.

³For by the grace given me I say to every one of

ˣ1 Or *reasonable*

you: Do not think of yourself more highly than you ought, but rather think of yourself with sober judgment, in accordance with the measure of faith God has given you. ⁴Just as each of us has one body with many members, and these members do not all have the same function, ⁵so in Christ we who are many form one body, and each member belongs to all the others. ⁶We have different gifts, according to the grace given us. If a man's gift is prophesying, let him use it in proportion to his*ʸ* faith. ⁷If it is serving, let him serve; if it is teaching, let him teach; ⁸if it is encouraging, let him encourage; if it is contributing to the needs of others, let him give generously; if it is leadership, let him govern diligently; if it is showing mercy, let him do it cheerfully.

⁹Love must be sincere. Hate what is evil; cling to what is good. ¹⁰Be devoted to one another in brotherly love. Honor one another above yourselves. ¹¹Never be lacking in zeal, but keep your spiritual fervor, serving the Lord. ¹²Be joyful in hope, patient in affliction, faithful in prayer. ¹³Share with God's people who are in need. Practice hospitality.

¹⁴Bless those who persecute you; bless and do not curse. ¹⁵Rejoice with those who rejoice; mourn with those who mourn. ¹⁶Live in harmony with one another. Do not be proud, but be willing to associate with people of low position.*ᶻ* Do not be conceited.

¹⁷Do not repay anyone evil for evil. Be careful to do what is right in the eyes of everybody. ¹⁸If it is possible, as far as it depends on you, live at peace with everyone. ¹⁹Do not take revenge, my friends, but leave room for God's wrath, for it is written: "It is mine to avenge; I will repay,"*ᵃ* says the Lord. ²⁰On the contrary:

"If your enemy is hungry, feed him;
    if he is thirsty, give him something to
    drink.
In doing this, you will heap burning coals on
    his head."*ᵇ*

²¹Do not be overcome by evil, but overcome evil with good.

*ʸ6 Or in agreement with the   ᶻ16 Or willing to do menial work
ᵃ19 Deut. 32:35   ᵇ20 Prov. 25:21,22*

Discovering the Word 1. Why do you think Paul uses the imagery of "living sacrifices" to describe our proper response to God's mercy? 2. Sometimes we view God's will as something to be avoided rather than desired. How can the last part of verse 2 correct this distortion? 3. How can the realization that we are members of a body (vv. 3–8) prevent us from thinking too highly of ourselves (v. 3)? 4. How would the kind of love Paul describes in verses 9–16 transform our relationships with other Christians? 5. How would Paul's advice in verses 17–21 help us to overcome our enemies?

Applying the Word 1. What are some ways we can renew our minds (v. 2) and so be transformed? 2. As you think "with sober judgment" about yourself, what gift (or gifts) do you think God has given you (vv. 3–8)? 3. In what ways do you need to begin living more sacrificially before God, other Christians or the world?

 Responding in Prayer Ask God to use you in serving the body of Christ.

---

16 / *Romans 13*
Submitting to Authorities

THE SERGEANT GLARES at a delinquent recruit whose face is now only inches away.
"That's an order!" he barks. "Do you understand?"
"Yes, sir," replies the recruit.
"I can't *hear* you!" shouts the sergeant.
"YES, SIR!" screams the recruit, who has just had his first lesson in military authority.
For many people the word *authority* conjures up images like the one just described. Those in authority are viewed as oppressors, and too often the impression is correct. Paul was no stranger to the abuses of authority. He had

experienced much persecution at the hands of civil and religious authorities all around the Mediterranean. In light of this, Paul's view of authority may be surprising.

 Warming Up to God What comes into your mind when you hear the word *authority*? Why?

 Read Romans 13.

13 Everyone must submit himself to the governing authorities, for there is no authority except that which God has established. The authorities that exist have been established by God. ²Consequently, he who rebels against the authority is rebelling against what God has instituted, and those who do so will bring judgment on themselves. ³For rulers hold no terror for those who do right, but for those who do wrong. Do you want to be free from fear of the one in authority? Then do what is right and he will commend you. ⁴For he is God's servant to do you good. But if you do wrong, be afraid, for he does not bear the sword for nothing. He is God's servant, an agent of wrath to bring punishment on the wrongdoer. ⁵Therefore, it is necessary to submit to the authorities, not only because of possible punishment but also because of conscience.

⁶This is also why you pay taxes, for the authorities are God's servants, who give their full time to governing. ⁷Give everyone what you owe him: If you owe taxes, pay taxes; if revenue, then revenue; if respect, then respect; if honor, then honor.

⁸Let no debt remain outstanding, except the continuing debt to love one another, for he who loves his fellowman has fulfilled the law. ⁹The commandments, "Do not commit adultery," "Do not murder," "Do not steal," "Do not covet,"ᶜ and whatever other commandment there may be, are summed up in this one rule: "Love your neighbor as yourself."ᵈ ¹⁰Love does no harm to its neighbor. Therefore love is the fulfillment of the law.

¹¹And do this, understanding the present time. The hour has come for you to wake up from your slumber, because our salvation is nearer now than when we first believed. ¹²The night is nearly over; the day is almost here. So let us put aside the deeds of darkness and put on the armor of light. ¹³Let us behave decently, as in the daytime, not in orgies and drunkenness, not in sexual immorality and debauchery, not in dissension and jealousy. ¹⁴Rather, clothe yourselves with the Lord Jesus Christ, and do not think about how to gratify the desires of the sinful nature.ᵉ

ᶜ9 Exodus 20:13-15,17; Deut. 5:17-19,21   ᵈ9 Lev. 19:18   ᵉ14 Or *the flesh*

 Discovering the Word 1. What is Paul's view of authority and those who exercise it (vv. 1–5)? 2. How would Paul's view of governing authorities apply to wicked and perverse rulers such as Nero or Hitler? 3. What are some reasons Paul gives for submitting to those in authority (vv. 1–5)? 4. In verse 8 Paul says, "Let no debt remain outstanding." Does this mean Christians should never incur any type of debts (mortgage, car and so on)? 5. In verses 11–14 Paul uses several vivid images to describe "the present time." How does each one give us a picture of how we should (or shouldn't) live?

Applying the Word 1. In verses 6–7 Paul suggests some practical ways we should submit to those in authority. What other examples can you think of? 2. Do you think it is ever appropriate to resist rather than to submit to the authorities? Explain. 3. Think back over this chapter. In what ways do you need to "clothe yourselves with the Lord Jesus Christ"?

Responding in Prayer Submission does not come to us naturally. Pray that you will learn to submit.

17 / *Romans 14*
To Eat or Not to Eat

IN THE LATE 1800s robed choirs were considered worldly by some Christians. More recently going to movies, watching television and drinking wine or beer have been viewed as sinful.

The Bible contains many clear commands. But it is also silent or ambiguous about many moral issues. These "gray" areas have always been a source of dispute and conflict among Christians, even though the specific areas of dispute change from time to time. What principles should guide us when our actions are criticized by others or when we feel critical toward them? Romans 14 helps us answer these questions.

 Warming Up to God What types of behavior do Christians disagree about today?

 Read Romans 14:1–23.

---

14 Accept him whose faith is weak, without passing judgment on disputable matters. ²One man's faith allows him to eat everything, but another man, whose faith is weak, eats only vegetables. ³The man who eats everything must not look down on him who does not, and the man who does not eat everything must not condemn the man who does, for God has accepted him. ⁴Who are you to judge someone else's servant? To his own master he stands or falls. And he will stand, for the Lord is able to make him stand.

⁵One man considers one day more sacred than another; another man considers every day alike. Each one should be fully convinced in his own mind. ⁶He who regards one day as special, does so to the Lord. He who eats meat, eats to the Lord, for he gives thanks to God; and he who abstains, does so to the Lord and gives thanks to God. ⁷For none of us lives to himself alone and none of us dies to himself alone. ⁸If we live, we live to the Lord; and if we die, we die to the Lord. So, whether we live or die, we belong to the Lord.

⁹For this very reason, Christ died and returned to life so that he might be the Lord of both the dead and the living. ¹⁰You, then, why do you judge your brother? Or why do you look down on your brother? For we will all stand before God's judgment seat. ¹¹It is written:

" 'As surely as I live,' says the Lord,
'every knee will bow before me;
  every tongue will confess to God.' " *f*

¹²So then, each of us will give an account of himself to God.

¹³Therefore let us stop passing judgment on one another. Instead, make up your mind not to put any stumbling block or obstacle in your brother's way. ¹⁴As one who is in the Lord Jesus, I am fully convinced that no food*g* is unclean in itself. But if anyone regards something as unclean, then for him it is unclean. ¹⁵If your brother is distressed because of what you eat, you are no longer acting in love. Do not by your eating destroy your brother for whom Christ died. ¹⁶Do not allow what you consider good to be spoken of as evil. ¹⁷For the kingdom of God is not a matter of eating and drinking, but of righteousness, peace and joy in the Holy Spirit, ¹⁸because anyone who serves Christ in this way is pleasing to God and approved by men.

¹⁹Let us therefore make every effort to do what leads to peace and to mutual edification. ²⁰Do not destroy the work of God for the sake of food. All food is clean, but it is wrong for a man to eat anything that causes someone else to stumble. ²¹It is better not to eat meat or drink wine or to do anything else that will cause your brother to fall.

²²So whatever you believe about these things keep between yourself and God. Blessed is the man who does not condemn himself by what he approves. ²³But the man who has doubts is condemned if he eats, because his eating is not from faith; and everything that does not come from faith is sin.

*f*11 Isaiah 45:23   *g*14 Or *that nothing*

Discovering the Word 1. What are some areas of dispute between the "weak" and the "strong" in verses 1–6? 2. What attitudes do the weak and the strong tend to have toward each other (vv. 1–4)? Why? 3. What types of Christians are you most likely to judge or look down on? Why? 4. Why is it wrong to pass judgment on other Christians (vv. 1–13)? 5. When we are *not* around those whose faith is weak, what principles should govern our Christian liberty (vv. 5–23)? 6. When we *are* around those whose faith is weak, what principles should guide our actions, and why (vv. 13–21)?

Applying the Word 1. What practices offend you? 2. Which of your own practices might distress or destroy another brother or sister in Christ?

Responding in Prayer Ask God for wisdom to know how to respond in areas in which you are causing offense.

---

18 / *Romans 15:1–13*
Unity, Hope and Praise

YOU DESERVE THE best. Look out for number one. Pamper yourself. These are the watchwords of our age. But in this chapter Paul urges us to stop gazing at our own reflection. For the first time in Romans he holds up the example of Christ, the one who embodies all the qualities God desires in us.

 Warming Up to God When is self-concern appropriate, and when does it turn into selfishness?

 Read Romans 15:1–13.

---

15 We who are strong ought to bear with the failings of the weak and not to please ourselves. ²Each of us should please his neighbor for his good, to build him up. ³For even Christ did not please himself but, as it is written: "The insults of those who insult you have fallen on me."ʰ ⁴For everything that was written in the past was written to teach us, so that through endurance and the encouragement of the Scriptures we might have hope.

⁵May the God who gives endurance and encouragement give you a spirit of unity among yourselves as you follow Christ Jesus, ⁶so that with one heart and mouth you may glorify the God and Father of our Lord Jesus Christ.

⁷Accept one another, then, just as Christ accepted you, in order to bring praise to God. ⁸For I tell you that Christ has become a servant of the Jewsⁱ on behalf of God's truth, to confirm the promises made to the patriarchs ⁹so that the Gentiles may glorify God for his mercy, as it is written:

"Therefore I will praise you among the Gentiles;
I will sing hymns to your name."ʲ

¹⁰Again, it says,

"Rejoice, O Gentiles, with his people."ᵏ

¹¹And again,

"Praise the Lord, all you Gentiles,
and sing praises to him, all you peoples."ˡ

¹²And again, Isaiah says,

"The Root of Jesse will spring up,
one who will arise to rule over the nations;
the Gentiles will hope in him."ᵐ

¹³May the God of hope fill you with all joy and peace as you trust in him, so that you may overflow with hope by the power of the Holy Spirit.

ʰ3 Psalm 69:9   ⁱ8 Greek *circumcision*   ʲ9 2 Samuel 22:50;
Psalm 18:49   ᵏ10 Deut. 32:43   ˡ11 Psalm 117:1
ᵐ12 Isaiah 11:10

Discovering the Word 1. What personal attitudes might hinder or help us to bear with the failings of the weak (vv. 1–2)? Explain why. 2. If we follow Christ's example in this and other areas of our lives, why will we need endurance, encouragement and hope (vv. 4–5)? 3. In contrast to the discord and possible verbal abuse hinted at in Romans 14, what does God desire of us (vv. 5–6)? 4. In verses 9–12 Paul quotes from four different Old Testament passages. What words and phrases express the dominant mood of these verses? 5. Why is this mood appropriate for all who hope in Jesus?

 Applying the Word 1. Keeping in mind the context of verses 1–12, how can we become those whose lives overflow with joy, peace and hope (v. 13)? 2. Paul concludes this passage with a vivid prayer (v. 13). Consider these words, and try to picture this reality. How do you feel?

 Responding in Prayer Spend time praising God for the joy, peace and hope we have in Christ.

19 / *Romans 15:14—16:27*
Brothers and Sisters in Christ

IN CHRIST WE have a bond that is stronger than flesh and blood. We are now and will always be brothers and sisters in Christ, members of God's family. This passage introduces us to some of our first-century relatives. As you read about them, notice the care they had for each other.

Warming Up to God What images come to mind when you think of the first-century church?

Read Romans 15:14—16:27.

14I myself am convinced, my brothers, that you yourselves are full of goodness, complete in knowledge and competent to instruct one another. 15I have written you quite boldly on some points, as if to remind you of them again, because of the grace God gave me 16to be a minister of Christ Jesus to the Gentiles with the priestly duty of proclaiming the gospel of God, so that the Gentiles might become an offering acceptable to God, sanctified by the Holy Spirit.

17Therefore I glory in Christ Jesus in my service to God. 18I will not venture to speak of anything except what Christ has accomplished through me in leading the Gentiles to obey God by what I have said and done— 19by the power of signs and miracles, through the power of the Spirit. So from Jerusalem all the way around to Illyricum, I have fully proclaimed the gospel of Christ. 20It has always been my ambition to preach the gospel where Christ was not known, so that I would not be building on someone else's foundation. 21Rather, as it is written:

"Those who were not told about him will see,
  and those who have not heard will
    understand." [n]

22This is why I have often been hindered from coming to you.

23But now that there is no more place for me to work in these regions, and since I have been longing for many years to see you, 24I plan to do so when I go to Spain. I hope to visit you while passing through and to have you assist me on my journey there, after I have enjoyed your company for a while. 25Now, however, I am on my way to Jerusalem in the service of the saints there. 26For Macedonia and Achaia were pleased to make a contribution for the poor among the saints in Jerusalem. 27They were pleased to do it, and indeed they owe it to them. For if the Gentiles have shared in the Jews' spiritual blessings, they owe it to the Jews to share with them their material blessings. 28So after I have completed this task and have made sure that they have received this fruit, I will go to Spain and visit you on the way. 29I know that when I come to you, I will come in the full measure of the blessing of Christ.

[n]21 Isaiah 52:15

³⁰I urge you, brothers, by our Lord Jesus Christ and by the love of the Spirit, to join me in my struggle by praying to God for me. ³¹Pray that I may be rescued from the unbelievers in Judea and that my service in Jerusalem may be acceptable to the saints there, ³²so that by God's will I may come to you with joy and together with you be refreshed. ³³The God of peace be with you all. Amen.

16 I commend to you our sister Phoebe, a servant^o of the church in Cenchrea. ²I ask you to receive her in the Lord in a way worthy of the saints and to give her any help she may need from you, for she has been a great help to many people, including me.

³Greet Priscilla^p and Aquila, my fellow workers in Christ Jesus. ⁴They risked their lives for me. Not only I but all the churches of the Gentiles are grateful to them.

⁵Greet also the church that meets at their house.

Greet my dear friend Epenetus, who was the first convert to Christ in the province of Asia.

⁶Greet Mary, who worked very hard for you.

⁷Greet Andronicus and Junias, my relatives who have been in prison with me. They are outstanding among the apostles, and they were in Christ before I was.

⁸Greet Ampliatus, whom I love in the Lord.

⁹Greet Urbanus, our fellow worker in Christ, and my dear friend Stachys.

¹⁰Greet Apelles, tested and approved in Christ.

Greet those who belong to the household of Aristobulus.

¹¹Greet Herodion, my relative.

Greet those in the household of Narcissus who are in the Lord.

¹²Greet Tryphena and Tryphosa, those women who work hard in the Lord.

Greet my dear friend Persis, another woman who has worked very hard in the Lord.

¹³Greet Rufus, chosen in the Lord, and his mother, who has been a mother to me, too.

¹⁴Greet Asyncritus, Phlegon, Hermes, Patrobas, Hermas and the brothers with them.

¹⁵Greet Philologus, Julia, Nereus and his sister, and Olympas and all the saints with them.

¹⁶Greet one another with a holy kiss.

All the churches of Christ send greetings.

¹⁷I urge you, brothers, to watch out for those who cause divisions and put obstacles in your way that are contrary to the teaching you have learned. Keep away from them. ¹⁸For such people are not serving our Lord Christ, but their own appetites. By smooth talk and flattery they deceive the minds of naive people. ¹⁹Everyone has heard about your obedience, so I am full of joy over you; but I want you to be wise about what is good, and innocent about what is evil.

²⁰The God of peace will soon crush Satan under your feet.

The grace of our Lord Jesus be with you.

²¹Timothy, my fellow worker, sends his greetings to you, as do Lucius, Jason and Sosipater, my relatives.

²²I, Tertius, who wrote down this letter, greet you in the Lord.

²³Gaius, whose hospitality I and the whole church here enjoy, sends you his greetings.

Erastus, who is the city's director of public works, and our brother Quartus send you their greetings.^q

²⁵Now to him who is able to establish you by my gospel and the proclamation of Jesus Christ, according to the revelation of the mystery hidden for long ages past, ²⁶but now revealed and made known through the prophetic writings by the command of the eternal God, so that all nations might believe and obey him— ²⁷to the only wise God be glory forever through Jesus Christ! Amen.

^o1 Or *deaconess*   ^p3 Greek *Prisca*, a variant of *Priscilla*
^q23 Some manuscripts *their greetings.* ²⁴*May the grace of our Lord Jesus Christ be with all of you. Amen.*

 Discovering the Word 1. What do we learn about Paul's apostolic ministry from 15:22? 2. What are Paul's immediate and future plans (15:23–33)? 3. What does 15:23–33 teach us about relationships among first-century Christians? 4. Use your imagination. From what we know about Paul and the Romans, how might the people in verses 1–16 have "risked their lives," "worked very hard" and "been a great help" to Paul and others? 5. How do the final words of this letter summarize the scope of our salvation (vv. 25–27)?

 Applying the Word 1. In what ways can we share material blessings with other Christians? 2. What can you do to strengthen relationships in your spiritual family?

Responding in Prayer Pray for your church and the needs of specific people you know.

1 Corinthians

*I*n 1938, just before World War II, Dietrich Bonhoeffer wrote *Life Together*, a moving little book on the principles of Christian community. Eighteen and a half centuries earlier the apostle Paul wrote what has come to be known as 1 Corinthians, a fascinating commentary on one Christian community that he founded. Why should we bother with either of these books?

Simply because we all have to live together with people, in Christian contexts and otherwise. Whether the situation involves a close friendship, a roommate, a spouse, a small group, a family, an office, a campus club, a neighborhood or a congregation, the challenges of life together will inevitably crop up. Church life is not immune to these problems, and Corinth was particularly susceptible. As a result, we can benefit from Paul's advice to that community.

Are there cliques and power struggles in the communities of which you are a part? Are you plagued by people who think they are spiritually or intellectually superior? How do you handle the immorality that seems so prevalent in the world, especially when it begins to invade the church? What is the proper way to exercise your rights, especially when a friend wrongs you or you feel that a matter of principle is at stake? How do we regulate marriage and singleness in the face of so many attacks on the health of both these life situations? How are we ever going to solve the battle of the sexes? What is the path to respecting one another's personality and gifts? Can eternity make a difference in how we live together today?

If any of these questions are relevant to your life and communities, then 1 Corinthians has something to say to you.

The relationship between Paul and the church at Corinth is a bittersweet chapter in church history. As the apostle traveled down the isthmus joining the two halves of Achaia (Greece) and first spotted the plain surrounding the city and the hill known as the Acrocorinth jutting up behind, he could hardly have imagined the depths and heights that would be reached by the church he left behind eighteen months later (see Acts 18 for the background of this part of Paul's second missionary journey). Nor could Paul have any idea of the depths and heights of emotion to which the members of that church would lead him, their spiritual father, over the next few years of visits and letters.

Both comedy and tragedy are found in the story of the Corinthian church. There was the comedy of a dynamic, gifted Christian community composed of uneducated, uninfluential people. They were plucked out of one of the greatest centers of trade, political authority and pagan religion in the Roman empire. Morals were so bad in that city that its citizens had inspired a word for sexual license—to *Corinthianize!* The existence of a church in such a setting was a reason for comic rejoicing.

However, there was also the tragedy of the Corinthians forgetting their humble roots and placing themselves as kings over one another—even over Paul, their founder and friend. The resulting tensions and schisms would boil over with even greater heartache for Paul in 2 Corinthians.

In the first six chapters of 1 Corinthians Paul begins with the distressing matters he has learned about: factions, incest, court cases and freedom gone wild. In chapters 7—14 he treats a series of topics that the Corinthians have asked him about, from marriage to spiritual gifts, with each new topic signaled by the phrase *Now concerning*. Finally, he sums up the teaching of the book in chapter 15, which is devoted to a theology of the resurrection or "last things."

Understanding why chapter 15 and parts of chapters 1—4 fit into this book is the key to unlocking 1 Corinthians. As always, Paul is not only interested in correcting practice but also in grounding his instruction in theological principles. In fact, the Corinthians had two root problems: premature spirituality (they thought they had everything heaven could offer) and immature spirituality (they forgot that the heart of the gospel is love, servanthood and the cross). Perhaps our communities, too, need correction in both practice and theology.

Outline

1/ 1 Corinthians 1 —————————— Called in Christ

2/ 1 Corinthians 2 —————————— Mind of Christ

3/ 1 Corinthians 3 —————————— Founded on Christ

4/ 1 Corinthians 4 —————————— Servants of Christ

5/ 1 Corinthians 5—6 ————————— Members of Christ

6/ 1 Corinthians 7 —————————— Devoted to Christ

7/ 1 Corinthians 8—9 ————————— Living for Christ

8/ 1 Corinthians 10:1—11:1 ————————— Eating with Christ

9/ 1 Corinthians 11:2–34 ————————— Headship of Christ

10/ 1 Corinthians 12 ————————— Body of Christ

11/ 1 Corinthians 13 ————————— Love of Christ

12/ 1 Corinthians 14 ————————— Speaking for Christ

13/ 1 Corinthians 15—16 ————————— Hope in Christ

1 / *1 Corinthians 1*
Called in Christ

HAVE YOU EVER found a Christian group that doesn't have any problems? If so, don't join it—you'll ruin everything!
The church in Corinth was far from perfect. Paul had heard a long list of complaints about this eager but misguided flock. As he attempted some long-distance pastoring, where would he begin? Paul's starting point is very relevant for problem groups and individuals today.

 Warming Up to God When have you been hurt by division within a church or Christian group you were a part of?

 Read 1 Corinthians 1.

1 Paul, called to be an apostle of Christ Jesus by the will of God, and our brother Sosthenes,

²To the church of God in Corinth, to those sanctified in Christ Jesus and called to be holy, together with all those everywhere who call on the name of our Lord Jesus Christ—their Lord and ours:

³Grace and peace to you from God our Father and the Lord Jesus Christ.

⁴I always thank God for you because of his grace given you in Christ Jesus. ⁵For in him you have been enriched in every way—in all your speaking and in all your knowledge— ⁶because our testimony about Christ was confirmed in you. ⁷Therefore you do not lack any spiritual gift as you eagerly wait for our Lord Jesus Christ to be revealed. ⁸He will keep you strong to the end, so that you will be blameless on the day of our Lord Jesus Christ. ⁹God, who has called you into fellowship with his Son Jesus Christ our Lord, is faithful.

¹⁰I appeal to you, brothers, in the name of our Lord Jesus Christ, that all of you agree with one another so that there may be no divisions among you and that you may be perfectly united in mind and thought. ¹¹My brothers, some from Chloe's household have informed me that there are quarrels among you. ¹²What I mean is this: One of you says, "I follow Paul"; another, "I follow Apollos"; another, "I follow Cephas*ᵃ*"; still another, "I follow Christ."

¹³Is Christ divided? Was Paul crucified for you? Were you baptized into*ᵇ* the name of Paul? ¹⁴I am thankful that I did not baptize any of you except Crispus and Gaius, ¹⁵so no one can say that you were baptized into my name. ¹⁶(Yes, I also baptized the household of Stephanas; beyond that, I don't remember if I baptized anyone else.) ¹⁷For Christ did not send me to baptize, but to preach the gospel—not with words of human wisdom, lest the cross of Christ be emptied of its power.

¹⁸For the message of the cross is foolishness to those who are perishing, but to us who are being saved it is the power of God. ¹⁹For it is written:

"I will destroy the wisdom of the wise;
   the intelligence of the intelligent I will
      frustrate."*ᶜ*

²⁰Where is the wise man? Where is the scholar? Where is the philosopher of this age? Has not God made foolish the wisdom of the world? ²¹For since in the wisdom of God the world through its wisdom did not know him, God was pleased through the foolishness of what was preached to save those who believe. ²²Jews demand miraculous signs and Greeks look for wisdom, ²³but we preach Christ crucified: a stumbling block to Jews and foolishness to Gentiles, ²⁴but to those whom God has called, both Jews and Greeks, Christ the power of God and the wisdom of God. ²⁵For the foolishness of God is wiser than man's wisdom, and the weakness of God is stronger than man's strength.

²⁶Brothers, think of what you were when you were called. Not many of you were wise by human standards; not many were influential; not many were of noble birth. ²⁷But God chose the foolish things of the world to shame the wise; God chose the weak things of the world to shame the strong. ²⁸He chose the lowly things of this world and the despised things—and the things

*ᵃ12 That is, Peter   *ᵇ13 Or in; also in verse 15   *ᶜ19 Isaiah 29:14

that are not—to nullify the things that are, [29]so that no one may boast before him. [30]It is because of him that you are in Christ Jesus, who has become for us wisdom from God—that is, our righteousness, holiness and redemption. [31]Therefore, as it is written: "Let him who boasts boast in the Lord."[d]

[d]31 Jer. 9:24

Discovering the Word 1. Before discussing the problems in Corinth, Paul affirms his readers (vv. 1–9). Why is he thankful for them? 2. Why do you think cliques had formed around Paul, Apollos and Cephas (v. 12)? 3. How did Paul conduct himself in Corinth to avoid, if possible, the problem of a personality cult (vv. 14–17)? 4. The Corinthians boasted in worldly wisdom and those who taught it. How does the message of the cross destroy all such boasting (vv. 18–25)? 5. The Corinthians also felt intellectually and spiritually superior to others. What had they forgotten about their past and the reason God chose them (vv. 26–29)? 6. What does it mean to "boast in the Lord" (vv. 30–31)?

Applying the Word 1. As you reflect on your own past, what reasons do you have for being humble rather than proud? 2. How can genuine humility promote unity in your church or fellowship?

Responding in Prayer Take time to thank the Lord for all he has done for you.

---

2 / *1 Corinthians 2*
Mind of Christ

MANY PEOPLE THINK Christianity is for the mindless and dull. Someone has said, "I feel like unscrewing my head and putting it underneath the pew every time I go to church." Unfortunately, this chapter has been used to support an uneducated, unthinking approach to Christianity. But this misses the point. As Søren Kierkegaard, the Danish philosopher, once said: Christ doesn't destroy reason; he *dethrones* it.

Warming Up to God In what area of your life do you need wisdom?

Read 1 Corinthians 2.

---

2 When I came to you, brothers, I did not come with eloquence or superior wisdom as I proclaimed to you the testimony about God.[e] [2]For I resolved to know nothing while I was with you except Jesus Christ and him crucified. [3]I came to you in weakness and fear, and with much trembling. [4]My message and my preaching were not with wise and persuasive words, but with a demonstration of the Spirit's power, [5]so that your faith might not rest on men's wisdom, but on God's power.

[6]We do, however, speak a message of wisdom among the mature, but not the wisdom of this age or of the rulers of this age, who are coming to nothing. [7]No, we speak of God's secret wisdom, a wisdom that has been hidden and that God destined for our glory before time began. [8]None of the rulers of this age understood it, for if they had, they would not have crucified the Lord of glory. [9]However, as it is written:

"No eye has seen,
　no ear has heard,
no mind has conceived
　what God has prepared for those who love
　　him"[f]—

[10]but God has revealed it to us by his Spirit.

The Spirit searches all things, even the deep things of God. [11]For who among men knows the thoughts of a man except the man's spirit within him? In the same way no one knows the thoughts of God except the Spirit of God. [12]We have not

[e]1 Some manuscripts *as I proclaimed to you God's mystery*
[f]9 Isaiah 64:4

received the spirit of the world but the Spirit who is from God, that we may understand what God has freely given us. ¹³This is what we speak, not in words taught us by human wisdom but in words taught by the Spirit, expressing spiritual truths in spiritual words.ᵍ ¹⁴The man without the Spirit does not accept the things that come from the Spirit of God, for they are foolishness to him, and he cannot understand them, because they are spiritually discerned. ¹⁵The spiritual man makes judgments about all things, but he himself is not subject to any man's judgment:

¹⁶"For who has known the mind of the Lord
    that he may instruct him?"ʰ

But we have the mind of Christ.

ᵍ13 Or *Spirit, interpreting spiritual truths to spiritual men*
ʰ16 Isaiah 40:13

Discovering the Word 1. Greek philosophers were often polished orators whose eloquence and wisdom dazzled their audiences. How does this contrast with Paul's preaching in Corinth (vv. 1–5)? 2. How is God's wisdom different from the wisdom of this age (vv. 6–10)? 3. Why are *secret* and *hidden* appropriate words to describe this wisdom? 4. When it comes to understanding God's wisdom, how does the person without the Spirit contrast with the spiritual person (vv. 14–16)? 5. Based on this passage, how would you define spiritual maturity?

Applying the Word 1. Who has been an example of spiritual maturity to you? 2. What can you do to become more spiritually mature?

Responding in Prayer Ask that you would be given the true wisdom that comes from the Spirit.

---

3 / *1 Corinthians 3*
Founded on Christ

THE DUKE OF Windsor, recalling his childhood discipline by George V, then King of England, said that his father used to daily remind him, "Never forget who you are." As the spiritual father of the Corinthians, Paul reminds them in this chapter, "Never forget *whose* you are."

The Corinthians were worldly and quarrelsome because they misunderstood both the message and the messengers of the cross. In chapters one and two, Paul focused on the message—the true wisdom from God. Now he looks at God's messengers. As he does so, Paul reminds the Corinthians and us of our true identity in Christ.

Warming Up to God Think of a time when someone who really cared for you confronted you with a failure to live up to your values. What qualities of that encounter made it constructive? Praise God for giving you people who care about your spiritual life.

Read 1 Corinthians 3.

---

3 Brothers, I could not address you as spiritual but as worldly—mere infants in Christ. ²I gave you milk, not solid food, for you were not yet ready for it. Indeed, you are still not ready. ³You are still worldly. For since there is jealousy and quarreling among you, are you not worldly? Are you not acting like mere men? ⁴For when one says, "I follow Paul," and another, "I follow Apollos," are you not mere men?

⁵What, after all, is Apollos? And what is Paul? Only servants, through whom you came to believe—as the Lord has assigned to each his task. ⁶I planted the seed, Apollos watered it, but God made it grow. ⁷So neither he who plants nor he who waters is anything, but only God, who makes things grow. ⁸The man who plants and the man who waters have one purpose, and each will be rewarded according to his own labor. ⁹For we are God's fellow workers; you are God's field, God's building.

¹⁰By the grace God has given me, I laid a foun-

dation as an expert builder, and someone else is building on it. But each one should be careful how he builds. ¹¹For no one can lay any foundation other than the one already laid, which is Jesus Christ. ¹²If any man builds on this foundation using gold, silver, costly stones, wood, hay or straw, ¹³his work will be shown for what it is, because the Day will bring it to light. It will be revealed with fire, and the fire will test the quality of each man's work. ¹⁴If what he has built survives, he will receive his reward. ¹⁵If it is burned up, he will suffer loss; he himself will be saved, but only as one escaping through the flames.

¹⁶Don't you know that you yourselves are God's temple and that God's Spirit lives in you? ¹⁷If anyone destroys God's temple, God will de-

stroy him; for God's temple is sacred, and you are that temple.

¹⁸Do not deceive yourselves. If any one of you thinks he is wise by the standards of this age, he should become a "fool" so that he may become wise. ¹⁹For the wisdom of this world is foolishness in God's sight. As it is written: "He catches the wise in their craftiness"ⁱ; ²⁰and again, "The Lord knows that the thoughts of the wise are futile."ʲ ²¹So then, no more boasting about men! All things are yours, ²²whether Paul or Apollos or Cephasᵏ or the world or life or death or the present or the future—all are yours, ²³and you are of Christ, and Christ is of God.

ⁱ19 Job 5:13   ʲ20 Psalm 94:11   ᵏ22 That is, Peter

Discovering the Word 1. Even though the Corinthians had the Spirit, why couldn't they be considered spiritual (vv. 1–4)? 2. What two illustrations does Paul use to describe himself and Apollos (vv. 6–9, 10–15)? 3. In what ways is God's church like a field being planted (vv. 6–9)? 4. In 3:10–15 Paul changes the metaphor from farming to building. Describe the various ways the church is like a building under construction. 5. In verse 3 Paul accused the Corinthians of being worldly. How can he say to the same people, "You are God's temple" and "God's Spirit lives in you" (v. 16)? 6. The Corinthians had initially claimed, "I belong to Paul" or "I belong to Apollos" (1:12 RSV). Paul claims something more important. In what sense do Paul, Apollos and everything else belong to the Corinthians—and to us (vv. 21–23)?

Applying the Word 1. How does this chapter affect your view of your own ministry in the church and that of professional ministers? 2. How does this way of evaluating our lives apply not only to so-called Christian work but also to other aspects of our vocation in Christ: relationships, occupations, avocations, community involvement and so on? 3. In what way are you challenged to "be careful" about how you build?

Responding in Prayer Everything we do must be founded on Christ. Before God, search your attitudes and actions, and pray that this would be true of you.

---

4 / 1 Corinthians 4
Servants of Christ

IN THE LAST study Paul called the Corinthians not to forget that they were God's holy temple. Now he calls them and all Christian communities to experience the power of radical servanthood for Christ's sake. St. Francis of Assisi exhibited this when he walked through Muslim battle lines during the Crusades in order to preach to the Sultan. Mother Teresa also is a "fool for Christ" when she bends down to care for a dying beggar in Calcutta. There is power in such actions, even though the wise ones of this age shake their heads in disbelief or wag their tongues in scorn.

Warming Up to God How do you feel when you hear about people like St. Francis who give away all they have to the poor, or Mother Teresa who live sacrificially?

Read 1 Corinthians 4.

4 So then, men ought to regard us as servants of Christ and as those entrusted with the secret things of God. ²Now it is required that those who have been given a trust must prove faithful. ³I care very little if I am judged by you or by any human court; indeed, I do not even judge myself. ⁴My conscience is clear, but that does not make me innocent. It is the Lord who judges me. ⁵Therefore judge nothing before the appointed time; wait till the Lord comes. He will bring to light what is hidden in darkness and will expose the motives of men's hearts. At that time each will receive his praise from God.

⁶Now, brothers, I have applied these things to myself and Apollos for your benefit, so that you may learn from us the meaning of the saying, "Do not go beyond what is written." Then you will not take pride in one man over against another. ⁷For who makes you different from anyone else? What do you have that you did not receive? And if you did receive it, why do you boast as though you did not?

⁸Already you have all you want! Already you have become rich! You have become kings—and that without us! How I wish that you really had become kings so that we might be kings with you! ⁹For it seems to me that God has put us apostles on display at the end of the procession, like men condemned to die in the arena. We have been made a spectacle to the whole universe, to angels as well as to men. ¹⁰We are fools for Christ, but you are so wise in Christ! We are weak, but you are strong! You are honored, we are dishonored! ¹¹To this very hour we go hungry and thirsty, we are in rags, we are brutally treated, we are homeless. ¹²We work hard with our own hands. When we are cursed, we bless; when we are persecuted, we endure it; ¹³when we are slandered, we answer kindly. Up to this moment we have become the scum of the earth, the refuse of the world.

¹⁴I am not writing this to shame you, but to warn you, as my dear children. ¹⁵Even though you have ten thousand guardians in Christ, you do not have many fathers, for in Christ Jesus I became your father through the gospel. ¹⁶Therefore I urge you to imitate me. ¹⁷For this reason I am sending to you Timothy, my son whom I love, who is faithful in the Lord. He will remind you of my way of life in Christ Jesus, which agrees with what I teach everywhere in every church.

¹⁸Some of you have become arrogant, as if I were not coming to you. ¹⁹But I will come to you very soon, if the Lord is willing, and then I will find out not only how these arrogant people are talking, but what power they have. ²⁰For the kingdom of God is not a matter of talk but of power. ²¹What do you prefer? Shall I come to you with a whip, or in love and with a gentle spirit?

 Discovering the Word 1. In contrast to the hero worship in Corinth, how do Paul and his coworkers wish to be regarded (vv. 1–2)? 2. Paul fears the Corinthians are moving "beyond what was written"—probably a reference to the Old Testament Scriptures. How might going beyond the authority of Scripture result in taking "pride in one man over against another" (v. 6)? 3. Scripture teaches that the suffering of this present age precedes the glory of the age to come. In their own minds, how had the Corinthians taken a shortcut to glory (vv. 8, 10)? 4. How did their "glorious" description of themselves contrast with the experiences of Paul and the other apostles (vv. 9–13)? 5. We receive the first hint in this section that some in Corinth were not only boasting about other leaders but were also putting down Paul. How does the apostle choose to combat these opponents (vv. 18–21)?

 Applying the Word 1. How would imitating Paul's way of life (vv. 16–17) require changes in your thinking and actions? 2. In what ways does this passage challenge you to become a "fool for Christ"?

Responding in Prayer Thank God for the leaders who have formed and impacted your Christian faith and walk.

5 / *1 Corinthians 5—6*
Members of Christ

THE NEW TESTAMENT church has inspired both exciting and disastrous experiments down through history. Hoping to create the perfect New Testament community, some have tried to design groups where all the gifts are expressed, worship is spontaneous and fellowship is deep. But they forget the common element of all New Testament churches—problems!

In chapters 1—4 Paul dealt with divisions in the church. Now he focuses on serious moral problems in Corinth. Incest and drunkenness during Communion are hardly what we hope to find in church. But we must remember that growing churches are not always filled with well-scrubbed Christians, but rather with a motley collection of sinners being saved.

 Warming Up to God How do you react when you hear about serious moral and spiritual problems of people in your church? What about your attitude do you think might be inappropriate or judgmental? Ask God to open your heart to this study.

 Read 1 Corinthians 5—6.

5 It is actually reported that there is sexual immorality among you, and of a kind that does not occur even among pagans: A man has his father's wife. ²And you are proud! Shouldn't you rather have been filled with grief and have put out of your fellowship the man who did this? ³Even though I am not physically present, I am with you in spirit. And I have already passed judgment on the one who did this, just as if I were present. ⁴When you are assembled in the name of our Lord Jesus and I am with you in spirit, and the power of our Lord Jesus is present, ⁵hand this man over to Satan, so that the sinful nature¹ may be destroyed and his spirit saved on the day of the Lord.

⁶Your boasting is not good. Don't you know that a little yeast works through the whole batch of dough? ⁷Get rid of the old yeast that you may be a new batch without yeast—as you really are. For Christ, our Passover lamb, has been sacrificed. ⁸Therefore let us keep the Festival, not with the old yeast, the yeast of malice and wickedness, but with bread without yeast, the bread of sincerity and truth.

⁹I have written you in my letter not to associate with sexually immoral people— ¹⁰not at all meaning the people of this world who are immoral, or the greedy and swindlers, or idolaters. In that case you would have to leave this world. ¹¹But now I am writing you that you must not associate with anyone who calls himself a brother but is sexually immoral or greedy, an idolater or a slanderer, a drunkard or a swindler. With such a man do not even eat.

¹²What business is it of mine to judge those outside the church? Are you not to judge those inside? ¹³God will judge those outside. "Expel the wicked man from among you." ᵐ

6 If any of you has a dispute with another, dare he take it before the ungodly for judgment instead of before the saints? ²Do you not know that the saints will judge the world? And if you are to judge the world, are you not competent to judge trivial cases? ³Do you not know that we will judge angels? How much more the things of this life! ⁴Therefore, if you have disputes about such matters, appoint as judges even men of little account in the church! ⁿ ⁵I say this to shame you. Is it possible that there is nobody among you wise enough to judge a dispute between believers? ⁶But instead, one brother goes to law against another—and this in front of unbelievers!

⁷The very fact that you have lawsuits among you means you have been completely defeated already. Why not rather be wronged? Why not rather be cheated? ⁸Instead, you yourselves cheat and do wrong, and you do this to your brothers.

⁹Do you not know that the wicked will not inherit the kingdom of God? Do not be deceived: Neither the sexually immoral nor idolaters nor adulterers nor male prostitutes nor homosexual offenders ¹⁰nor thieves nor the greedy nor drunkards nor slanderers nor swindlers will inherit the kingdom of God. ¹¹And that is what some of you

⁵ Or that his body; or that the flesh   ᵐ13 Deut. 17:7; 19:19; 21:21; 22:21,24; 24:7   ⁿ4 Or matters, do you appoint as judges men of little account in the church?

were. But you were washed, you were sanctified, you were justified in the name of the Lord Jesus Christ and by the Spirit of our God.

¹²"Everything is permissible for me"—but not everything is beneficial. "Everything is permissible for me"—but I will not be mastered by anything. ¹³"Food for the stomach and the stomach for food"—but God will destroy them both. The body is not meant for sexual immorality, but for the Lord, and the Lord for the body. ¹⁴By his power God raised the Lord from the dead, and he will raise us also. ¹⁵Do you not know that your bodies are members of Christ himself? Shall I then take the members of Christ and unite them with a prostitute? Never! ¹⁶Do you not know that he who unites himself with a prostitute is one with her in body? For it is said, "The two will become one flesh."ᵒ ¹⁷But he who unites himself with the Lord is one with him in spirit.

¹⁸Flee from sexual immorality. All other sins a man commits are outside his body, but he who sins sexually sins against his own body. ¹⁹Do you not know that your body is a temple of the Holy Spirit, who is in you, whom you have received from God? You are not your own; ²⁰you were bought at a price. Therefore honor God with your body.

ᵒ16 Gen. 2:24

Discovering the Word 1. In Greece there was no shame in having sexual relationships before marriage or outside of marriage. What made the sexual problem in this church especially loathsome to Paul? 2. How is Paul's strategy of discipline designed to bring health to both the church and the individual (5:2–5)? 3. Paul compares the Christian life to the Passover and Feast of Unleavened Bread. According to Paul, what do the yeast, the bread without yeast and the Passover lamb symbolize (5:6–8)? 4. Some Christians practice a doctrine of "double separation." First, they separate themselves from the evil influences in the world. Second, they separate themselves from Christians who have not separated themselves from the world. What type of separation is taught in verses 9–13? 5. What commands and guidelines does Paul give for settling disputes between Christians (vv. 1–8)? Explain. 6. Paul calls the body "a temple of the Holy Spirit" (6:18–20). How does the biblical view of the body presented here contrast with the modern view?

Applying the Word 1. Why do you think so few churches today practice discipline of those who commit an immorality? 2. How can we distinguish between the kinds of people who should be put out of the church (5:2, 9–11; 6:9–10) and those who belong in the church even though they are "worldly" and immature (see 3:1)? 3. How can understanding your body as a temple of the Holy Spirit (v. 19) lead to a healthy balance of bodily control and bodily celebration?

Responding in Prayer Ask God to help you take whatever steps are necessary to maintain both personal and corporate purity.

---

6 / 1 Corinthians 7
Devoted to Christ

CORINTH, UNLIKE MOST modern cities today, did not have sex shops, *Playboy* magazines, porn videos and "adult entertainment" centers. But there was so much sexual immorality that the ancients had a word to describe engaging in raw sensual pleasure—to *Corinthianize*. In chapter six Paul dealt with those who justified a permissive lifestyle in the name of Christian freedom. In this chapter he battles on the opposite front. Some Corinthians claimed sex was sinful—or at least a second-class diversion—even in marriage. In response Paul answers questions about marriage, sexuality and singleness.

Warming Up to God How did you learn about sexuality? What attitudes did you learn that have been hurtful to you? Ask God to use this passage to help you better understand marriage and singleness.

Read 1 Corinthians 7.

7 Now for the matters you wrote about: It is good for a man not to marry.ᵖ ²But since there is so much immorality, each man should have his own wife, and each woman her own husband. ³The husband should fulfill his marital duty to his wife, and likewise the wife to her husband. ⁴The wife's body does not belong to her alone but also to her husband. In the same way, the husband's body does not belong to him alone but also to his wife. ⁵Do not deprive each other except by mutual consent and for a time, so that you may devote yourselves to prayer. Then come together again so that Satan will not tempt you because of your lack of self-control. ⁶I say this as a concession, not as a command. ⁷I wish that all men were as I am. But each man has his own gift from God; one has this gift, another has that.

⁸Now to the unmarried and the widows I say: It is good for them to stay unmarried, as I am. ⁹But if they cannot control themselves, they should marry, for it is better to marry than to burn with passion.

¹⁰To the married I give this command (not I, but the Lord): A wife must not separate from her husband. ¹¹But if she does, she must remain unmarried or else be reconciled to her husband. And a husband must not divorce his wife.

¹²To the rest I say this (I, not the Lord): If any brother has a wife who is not a believer and she is willing to live with him, he must not divorce her. ¹³And if a woman has a husband who is not a believer and he is willing to live with her, she must not divorce him. ¹⁴For the unbelieving husband has been sanctified through his wife, and the unbelieving wife has been sanctified through her believing husband. Otherwise your children would be unclean, but as it is, they are holy.

¹⁵But if the unbeliever leaves, let him do so. A believing man or woman is not bound in such circumstances; God has called us to live in peace. ¹⁶How do you know, wife, whether you will save your husband? Or, how do you know, husband, whether you will save your wife?

¹⁷Nevertheless, each one should retain the place in life that the Lord assigned to him and to which God has called him. This is the rule I lay down in all the churches. ¹⁸Was a man already circumcised when he was called? He should not become uncircumcised. Was a man uncircumcised when he was called? He should not be circumcised. ¹⁹Circumcision is nothing and uncircumcision is nothing. Keeping God's commands is what counts. ²⁰Each one should remain in the situation which he was in when God called him. ²¹Were you a slave when you were called? Don't let it trouble you—although if you can gain your freedom, do so. ²²For he who was a slave when he was called by the Lord is the Lord's freedman; similarly, he who was a free man when he was called is Christ's slave. ²³You were bought at a price; do not become slaves of men. ²⁴Brothers, each man, as responsible to God, should remain in the situation God called him to.

²⁵Now about virgins: I have no command from the Lord, but I give a judgment as one who by the Lord's mercy is trustworthy. ²⁶Because of the present crisis, I think that it is good for you to remain as you are. ²⁷Are you married? Do not seek a divorce. Are you unmarried? Do not look for a wife. ²⁸But if you do marry, you have not sinned; and if a virgin marries, she has not sinned. But those who marry will face many troubles in this life, and I want to spare you this.

²⁹What I mean, brothers, is that the time is short. From now on those who have wives should live as if they had none; ³⁰those who mourn, as if they did not; those who are happy, as if they were not; those who buy something, as if it were not theirs to keep; ³¹those who use the things of the world, as if not engrossed in them. For this world in its present form is passing away.

³²I would like you to be free from concern. An unmarried man is concerned about the Lord's affairs—how he can please the Lord. ³³But a married man is concerned about the affairs of this world—how he can please his wife— ³⁴and his interests are divided. An unmarried woman or virgin is concerned about the Lord's affairs: Her aim is to be devoted to the Lord in both body and spirit. But a married woman is concerned about the affairs of this world—how she can please her husband. ³⁵I am saying this for your own good, not to restrict you, but that you may live in a right way in undivided devotion to the Lord.

³⁶If anyone thinks he is acting improperly toward the virgin he is engaged to, and if she is getting along in years and he feels he ought to marry, he should do as he wants. He is not sinning. They should get married. ³⁷But the man who has settled the matter in his own mind, who is under no compulsion but has control over his

ᵖ1 Or "It is good for a man not to have sexual relations with a woman."

own will, and who has made up his mind not to marry the virgin—this man also does the right thing. 38So then, he who marries the virgin does right, but he who does not marry her does even better.q

39A woman is bound to her husband as long as he lives. But if her husband dies, she is free to marry anyone she wishes, but he must belong to the Lord. 40In my judgment, she is happier if she stays as she is—and I think that I too have the Spirit of God.

q36-38 Or 36If anyone thinks he is not treating his daughter properly, and if she is getting along in years, and he feels she ought to marry, he should do as he wants. He is not sinning. He should let her get married. 37But the man who has settled the matter in his own mind, who is under no compulsion but has control over his own will, and who has made up his mind to keep the virgin unmarried—this man also does the right thing. 38So then, he who gives his virgin in marriage does right, but he who does not give her in marriage does even better.

 Discovering the Word   1. Although Paul agrees that celibacy is good (v. 1), why is it impractical for most people (vv. 2, 7)?   **2.** What practical advice does Paul give to the unmarried and the married for avoiding sexual immorality (vv. 2–9)?   **3.** According to Paul, what are some benefits of remaining in a marriage to a non-Christian (vv. 12–16)?   **4.** Under what circumstances would Paul seemingly allow for divorce, and why (vv. 15–16)?   **5.** Paul speaks of God calling us *to* a certain situation (vv. 17, 24) and of God calling us while we were *in* that situation (vv. 18–22). How are these two dimensions of calling different?   **6.** In verses 24–40 Paul addresses *those considering marriage.* Why does Paul call singleness a "better" way (v. 38) and a "happier" way (v. 40) when he has such a high view of marriage?

Applying the Word   1. What principles from this passage could help us care for Christians who are considering separation or divorce?   **2.** Whether you are married or single, in what way do you struggle to be faithful to God's calling?

Responding in Prayer Ask God to show you his calling for you.

---

7 / 1 Corinthians 8—9
Living for Christ

A NOTE TACKED up on a refrigerator had these words: "It is better to be righteous than right!" Today individuals and groups are clamoring and clashing over rights: the right to free speech, the rights of the poor, the right to liberation, women's rights, aboriginal rights, the right not to be bothered by smokers (or nonsmokers), the rights of animals, the rights of blacks, the rights of whites.

So many of the struggles over rights, both legitimate and bogus, seem to revolve around attaining freedom to change the status quo. The apostle Paul, however, appears to be on opposite ground. For him rights and freedoms are unimportant compared to the privilege of living for Christ.

 Warming Up to God In what area are you currently struggling with a person or group in opposition to you? Ask God to use this study to show you how to be righteous.

 Read 1 Corinthians 8—9.

---

8 Now about food sacrificed to idols: We know that we all possess knowledge.r Knowledge puffs up, but love builds up. 2The man who thinks he knows something does not yet know as he ought to know. 3But the man who loves God is known by God.

4So then, about eating food sacrificed to idols: We know that an idol is nothing at all in the world and that there is no God but one. 5For even if there are so-called gods, whether in heaven or on earth (as indeed there are many "gods" and many "lords"), 6yet for us there is but one God, the Father, from whom all things came and for whom we live; and there is but one Lord, Jesus

r1 Or "We all possess knowledge," as you say

Christ, through whom all things came and through whom we live.

⁷But not everyone knows this. Some people are still so accustomed to idols that when they eat such food they think of it as having been sacrificed to an idol, and since their conscience is weak, it is defiled. ⁸But food does not bring us near to God; we are no worse if we do not eat, and no better if we do.

⁹Be careful, however, that the exercise of your freedom does not become a stumbling block to the weak. ¹⁰For if anyone with a weak conscience sees you who have this knowledge eating in an idol's temple, won't he be emboldened to eat what has been sacrificed to idols? ¹¹So this weak brother, for whom Christ died, is destroyed by your knowledge. ¹²When you sin against your brothers in this way and wound their weak conscience, you sin against Christ. ¹³Therefore, if what I eat causes my brother to fall into sin, I will never eat meat again, so that I will not cause him to fall.

9 Am I not free? Am I not an apostle? Have I not seen Jesus our Lord? Are you not the result of my work in the Lord? ²Even though I may not be an apostle to others, surely I am to you! For you are the seal of my apostleship in the Lord.

³This is my defense to those who sit in judgment on me. ⁴Don't we have the right to food and drink? ⁵Don't we have the right to take a believing wife along with us, as do the other apostles and the Lord's brothers and Cephasˢ? ⁶Or is it only I and Barnabas who must work for a living?

⁷Who serves as a soldier at his own expense? Who plants a vineyard and does not eat of its grapes? Who tends a flock and does not drink of the milk? ⁸Do I say this merely from a human point of view? Doesn't the Law say the same thing? ⁹For it is written in the Law of Moses: "Do not muzzle an ox while it is treading out the grain."ᵗ Is it about oxen that God is concerned? ¹⁰Surely he says this for us, doesn't he? Yes, this was written for us, because when the plowman plows and the thresher threshes, they ought to do so in the hope of sharing in the harvest. ¹¹If we have sown spiritual seed among you, is it too much if we reap a material harvest from you? ¹²If

others have this right of support from you, shouldn't we have it all the more?

But we did not use this right. On the contrary, we put up with anything rather than hinder the gospel of Christ. ¹³Don't you know that those who work in the temple get their food from the temple, and those who serve at the altar share in what is offered on the altar? ¹⁴In the same way, the Lord has commanded that those who preach the gospel should receive their living from the gospel.

¹⁵But I have not used any of these rights. And I am not writing this in the hope that you will do such things for me. I would rather die than have anyone deprive me of this boast. ¹⁶Yet when I preach the gospel, I cannot boast, for I am compelled to preach. Woe to me if I do not preach the gospel! ¹⁷If I preach voluntarily, I have a reward; if not voluntarily, I am simply discharging the trust committed to me. ¹⁸What then is my reward? Just this: that in preaching the gospel I may offer it free of charge, and so not make use of my rights in preaching it.

¹⁹Though I am free and belong to no man, I make myself a slave to everyone, to win as many as possible. ²⁰To the Jews I became like a Jew, to win the Jews. To those under the law I became like one under the law (though I myself am not under the law), so as to win those under the law. ²¹To those not having the law I became like one not having the law (though I am not free from God's law but am under Christ's law), so as to win those not having the law. ²²To the weak I became weak, to win the weak. I have become all things to all men so that by all possible means I might save some. ²³I do all this for the sake of the gospel, that I may share in its blessings.

²⁴Do you not know that in a race all the runners run, but only one gets the prize? Run in such a way as to get the prize. ²⁵Everyone who competes in the games goes into strict training. They do it to get a crown that will not last; but we do it to get a crown that will last forever. ²⁶Therefore I do not run like a man running aimlessly; I do not fight like a man beating the air. ²⁷No, I beat my body and make it my slave so that after I have preached to others, I myself will not be disqualified for the prize.

ˢ5 That is, Peter   ᵗ9 Deut. 25:4

Discovering the Word 1. Sacrificial animals offered in temples were dedicated to a pagan god, and most of them were sold in the public market. Understandably, many Christians in Corinth wondered whether they should eat such meat. According to Paul, what do mature Christians know about food sacrificed to idols (8:4–6, 8)? 2. What warning does Paul give about this kind of knowledge (8:1–3)? Explain. 3. What does Paul say is more important than exercising the freedom that comes from knowledge (8:9–13)? 4. Paul moves on from rights and freedoms based on *knowledge* to the topic of rights based on *position*. What apostolic rights has Paul given up (9:4–5, 11–12, 14, 18–19)? 5. How and why has Paul given up the freedom to live whatever lifestyle he prefers (9:19–23)? 6. In giving up the rights mentioned in chapters 8—9, how are we like athletes in training (9:24–27)?

Applying the Word 1. In what situations today might our "knowledge" and freedom destroy a weaker brother? 2. What distinguishes actions that challenge the immature to grow from actions that wound them? 3. How might we adjust our lifestyles in order to reach people in various subcultures?

Responding in Prayer Ask God to help you train more rigorously so you will not be disqualified but will receive the victor's crown.

---

8 / *1 Corinthians 10:1—11:1*
Eating with Christ

SHOULD CHRISTIANS GO to R-rated movies—or any movies, for that matter? Should they drink alcoholic beverages such as beer or wine? Should they wear expensive clothes, makeup and jewelry? Debates over such "questionable" practices are as old as the church. How can we resolve them?

The Corinthians were divided over such issues. Some had overscrupulous consciences. They would not sit down to a meal if the meat had been purchased at a pagan meat market (and therefore offered to a "god"). Others were so "liberated" that they could eat the Lord's Supper and then commit sexual immorality. These liberated Christians regarded baptism and the Eucharist (Communion) as automatic protection against God's judgment. In 1 Corinthians 10 Paul finds a way of reaching both kinds of people: he calls them and us to do everything for the glory of God.

Warming Up to God What "questionable" practices have you wrestled with personally?

Read 1 Corinthians 10:1—11:1.

---

10 For I do not want you to be ignorant of the fact, brothers, that our forefathers were all under the cloud and that they all passed through the sea. ²They were all baptized into Moses in the cloud and in the sea. ³They all ate the same spiritual food ⁴and drank the same spiritual drink; for they drank from the spiritual rock that accompanied them, and that rock was Christ. ⁵Nevertheless, God was not pleased with most of them; their bodies were scattered over the desert.

⁶Now these things occurred as examples[u] to keep us from setting our hearts on evil things as they did. ⁷Do not be idolaters, as some of them were; as it is written: "The people sat down to eat and drink and got up to indulge in pagan revelry."[v] ⁸We should not commit sexual immorality, as some of them did—and in one day twenty-three thousand of them died. ⁹We should not test the Lord, as some of them did—and were killed by snakes. ¹⁰And do not grumble, as some of them did—and were killed by the destroying angel.

¹¹These things happened to them as examples and were written down as warnings for us, on whom the fulfillment of the ages has come. ¹²So, if you think you are standing firm, be careful that you don't fall! ¹³No temptation has seized you except what is common to man. And God is faithful; he will not let you be tempted beyond what you can bear. But when you are tempted, he will also provide a way out so that you can stand up under it.

ᵘ6 Or *types*; also in verse 11   ᵛ7 Exodus 32:6

¹⁴Therefore, my dear friends, flee from idolatry. ¹⁵I speak to sensible people; judge for yourselves what I say. ¹⁶Is not the cup of thanksgiving for which we give thanks a participation in the blood of Christ? And is not the bread that we break a participation in the body of Christ? ¹⁷Because there is one loaf, we, who are many, are one body, for we all partake of the one loaf.

¹⁸Consider the people of Israel: Do not those who eat the sacrifices participate in the altar? ¹⁹Do I mean then that a sacrifice offered to an idol is anything, or that an idol is anything? ²⁰No, but the sacrifices of pagans are offered to demons, not to God, and I do not want you to be participants with demons. ²¹You cannot drink the cup of the Lord and the cup of demons too; you cannot have a part in both the Lord's table and the table of demons. ²²Are we trying to arouse the Lord's jealousy? Are we stronger than he?

²³"Everything is permissible"—but not everything is beneficial. "Everything is permissible"—but not everything is constructive. ²⁴Nobody should seek his own good, but the good of others. ²⁵Eat anything sold in the meat market without raising questions of conscience, ²⁶for, "The earth is the Lord's, and everything in it." ʷ

²⁷If some unbeliever invites you to a meal and you want to go, eat whatever is put before you without raising questions of conscience. ²⁸But if anyone says to you, "This has been offered in sacrifice," then do not eat it, both for the sake of the man who told you and for conscience' sakeˣ— ²⁹the other man's conscience, I mean, not yours. For why should my freedom be judged by another's conscience? ³⁰If I take part in the meal with thankfulness, why am I denounced because of something I thank God for?

³¹So whether you eat or drink or whatever you do, do it all for the glory of God. ³²Do not cause anyone to stumble, whether Jews, Greeks or the church of God— ³³even as I try to please everybody in every way. For I am not seeking my own good but the good of many, so that they may be saved. ¹Follow my example, as I follow the example of Christ.

11

ʷ26 Psalm 24:1   ˣ28 Some manuscripts *conscience' sake, for "the earth is the Lord's and everything in it"*

Discovering the Word 1. What experiences did all the Israelites have in common when they left Egypt and headed for the Promised Land (vv. 1–10)? 2. Why does Paul remind the Corinthians (and us) of these events (vv. 11–13)? 3. Why are some lifestyles incompatible with celebrating the Lord's Supper (vv. 14–22)? 4. According to verses 23–33, what principles should guide our behavior as Christians? 5. How does Paul apply these principles to the subject of eating meat offered to idols?

Applying the Word 1. Think of one or two areas where you are currently experiencing temptation. In which one of these are you least likely to believe that there is a way of escape? 2. In what way has God provided an escape for your temptation? 3. How can the principles discussed in this passage guide your behavior in areas that might be "permissible" but not beneficial?

 Responding in Prayer Ask God to give you courage to flee temptation.

---

9 / *1 Corinthians 11:2–34*
Headship of Christ

TWO TRENDS IN Western society contrive to make us independent people: the trend to blur the differences between the sexes (androgyny) and the human potential movement. In the movie *Tootsie* a male actor impersonating a woman said to a woman with whom he fell in love, "I was a better man with you when I was a woman than I am a woman with you now that I am a man." Such is the sexual confusion produced by the first trend. Fritz Perls verbalized the second trend this way: "I do my thing and you do your thing and if by chance we meet, it's beautiful."

Both trends work against our newness in Christ. Followers of Jesus are neither independent nor dependent but *inter*dependent. We discover interdependence in Christian worship in this passage.

Warming Up to God When you enter a worship service, do you tend to think mainly of your personal relationship to God or your relationship with your fellow worshipers? Explain.

Read 1 Corinthians 11:2–34.

²I praise you for remembering me in everything and for holding to the teachings,ʸ just as I passed them on to you.

³Now I want you to realize that the head of every man is Christ, and the head of the woman is man, and the head of Christ is God. ⁴Every man who prays or prophesies with his head covered dishonors his head. ⁵And every woman who prays or prophesies with her head uncovered dishonors her head—it is just as though her head were shaved. ⁶If a woman does not cover her head, she should have her hair cut off; and if it is a disgrace for a woman to have her hair cut or shaved off, she should cover her head. ⁷A man ought not to cover his head,ᶻ since he is the image and glory of God; but the woman is the glory of man. ⁸For man did not come from woman, but woman from man; ⁹neither was man created for woman, but woman for man. ¹⁰For this reason, and because of the angels, the woman ought to have a sign of authority on her head.

¹¹In the Lord, however, woman is not independent of man, nor is man independent of woman. ¹²For as woman came from man, so also man is born of woman. But everything comes from God. ¹³Judge for yourselves: Is it proper for a woman to pray to God with her head uncovered? ¹⁴Does not the very nature of things teach you that if a man has long hair, it is a disgrace to him, ¹⁵but that if a woman has long hair, it is her glory? For long hair is given to her as a covering. ¹⁶If anyone wants to be contentious about this, we have no other practice—nor do the churches of God.

¹⁷In the following directives I have no praise for you, for your meetings do more harm than good. ¹⁸In the first place, I hear that when you come together as a church, there are divisions among you, and to some extent I believe it. ¹⁹No doubt there have to be differences among you to show which of you have God's approval. ²⁰When you come together, it is not the Lord's Supper you eat, ²¹for as you eat, each of you goes ahead without waiting for anybody else. One remains hungry, another gets drunk. ²²Don't you have homes to eat and drink in? Or do you despise the church of God and humiliate those who have nothing? What shall I say to you? Shall I praise you for this? Certainly not!

²³For I received from the Lord what I also passed on to you: The Lord Jesus, on the night he was betrayed, took bread, ²⁴and when he had given thanks, he broke it and said, "This is my body, which is for you; do this in remembrance of me." ²⁵In the same way, after supper he took the cup, saying, "This cup is the new covenant in my blood; do this, whenever you drink it, in remembrance of me." ²⁶For whenever you eat this bread and drink this cup, you proclaim the Lord's death until he comes.

²⁷Therefore, whoever eats the bread or drinks the cup of the Lord in an unworthy manner will be guilty of sinning against the body and blood of the Lord. ²⁸A man ought to examine himself before he eats of the bread and drinks of the cup. ²⁹For anyone who eats and drinks without recognizing the body of the Lord eats and drinks judgment on himself. ³⁰That is why many among you are weak and sick, and a number of you have fallen asleep. ³¹But if we judged ourselves, we would not come under judgment. ³²When we are judged by the Lord, we are being disciplined so that we will not be condemned with the world.

³³So then, my brothers, when you come together to eat, wait for each other. ³⁴If anyone is hungry, he should eat at home, so that when you meet together it may not result in judgment.

And when I come I will give further directions.

ʸ2 Or *traditions*   ᶻ4-7 Or ⁴*Every man who prays or prophesies with long hair dishonors his head.* ⁵*And every woman who prays or prophesies with no covering ⌐of hair⌐ on her head dishonors her head—she is just like one of the "shorn women."* ⁶*If a woman has no covering, let her be for now with short hair, but since it is a disgrace for a woman to have her hair shorn or shaved, she should grow it again.* ⁷*A man ought not to have long hair*

Discovering the Word 1. What seems to be Paul's major concern for the church in this section? 2. The word *head* in verse 3 could mean either "chief" and "ruler" or "source" and "origin" (like the head of a stream). Which understanding of headship best fits Paul's concern here? Explain. 3. In the culture of Corinth a woman signaled that she was in right relationship with her husband either by wearing a veil which covered her hair or by wearing her hair up (rather than letting it fall loose). What reasons does Paul give for continuing this practice (vv. 4–10, 13–16)? **4.** Paul balances his previous statements by saying that "in the Lord" man is not independent of woman (vv. 11–12). Why is this balance important? **5.** Why would eating and drinking "without recognizing the body of the Lord" be so dangerous (vv. 29–32)? **6.** According to Paul, how can we eat and drink the Lord's Supper in a worthy manner (vv. 28–33)?

 Applying the Word 1. Although we may not have a cultural equivalent for head coverings, how should appropriate relationships between men and women be expressed in Christian community? **2.** What has this chapter taught you about worship that is honoring or dishonoring to God? **3.** How do you need to change your pattern of worship?

 Responding in Prayer Thank God for making you part of a larger body.

10 / *1 Corinthians 12*
Body of Christ

THE CHURCH TODAY has enormous frozen assets. Only when we thaw these assets and release every member for ministry can the work of God be done in the world. After several decades of "gift" teaching, we have made surprisingly little progress. One reason is that gifts have been co-opted by the human potential movement. We view our gifts as part of our development and fulfillment rather than as one more glorious way to be interdependent in Christ. This passage focuses on the true nature and purpose of spiritual gifts.

 Warming Up to God What has God shown you about your gifts and how you should use them in the church?

Read 1 Corinthians 12.

12 Now about spiritual gifts, brothers, I do not want you to be ignorant. ²You know that when you were pagans, somehow or other you were influenced and led astray to mute idols. ³Therefore I tell you that no one who is speaking by the Spirit of God says, "Jesus be cursed," and no one can say, "Jesus is Lord," except by the Holy Spirit.

⁴There are different kinds of gifts, but the same Spirit. ⁵There are different kinds of service, but the same Lord. ⁶There are different kinds of working, but the same God works all of them in all men.

⁷Now to each one the manifestation of the Spirit is given for the common good. ⁸To one there is given through the Spirit the message of wisdom, to another the message of knowledge by means of the same Spirit, ⁹to another faith by the same Spirit, to another gifts of healing by that one Spirit, ¹⁰to another miraculous powers, to another prophecy, to another distinguishing between spirits, to another speaking in different kinds of tongues,ᵃ and to still another the interpretation

of tongues.ᵃ ¹¹All these are the work of one and the same Spirit, and he gives them to each one, just as he determines.

¹²The body is a unit, though it is made up of many parts; and though all its parts are many, they form one body. So it is with Christ. ¹³For we were all baptized byᵇ one Spirit into one body—whether Jews or Greeks, slave or free—and we were all given the one Spirit to drink.

¹⁴Now the body is not made up of one part but of many. ¹⁵If the foot should say, "Because I am not a hand, I do not belong to the body," it would not for that reason cease to be part of the body. ¹⁶And if the ear should say, "Because I am not an eye, I do not belong to the body," it would not for that reason cease to be part of the body. ¹⁷If the whole body were an eye, where would the sense of hearing be? If the whole body were an ear, where would the sense of smell be? ¹⁸But in fact God has arranged the parts in the body, every one

ᵃ10 Or *languages*; also in verse 28   ᵇ13 Or *with*; or *in*

of them, just as he wanted them to be. ¹⁹If they were all one part, where would the body be? ²⁰As it is, there are many parts, but one body.

²¹The eye cannot say to the hand, "I don't need you!" And the head cannot say to the feet, "I don't need you!" ²²On the contrary, those parts of the body that seem to be weaker are indispensable, ²³and the parts that we think are less honorable we treat with special honor. And the parts that are unpresentable are treated with special modesty, ²⁴while our presentable parts need no special treatment. But God has combined the members of the body and has given greater honor to the parts that lacked it, ²⁵so that there should be no division in the body, but that its parts should have equal concern for each other. ²⁶If one part suffers, every part suffers with it; if one part is honored, every part rejoices with it.

²⁷Now you are the body of Christ, and each one of you is a part of it. ²⁸And in the church God has appointed first of all apostles, second prophets, third teachers, then workers of miracles, also those having gifts of healing, those able to help others, those with gifts of administration, and those speaking in different kinds of tongues. ²⁹Are all apostles? Are all prophets? Are all teachers? Do all work miracles? ³⁰Do all have gifts of healing? Do all speak in tongues*c*? Do all interpret? ³¹But eagerly desire*d* the greater gifts.

And now I will show you the most excellent way.

c30 Or other languages   *d31 Or But you are eagerly desiring*

 Discovering the Word 1. What particular problem in the Corinthian church may have led Paul to offer the "test" in verse 3? 2. What clue does Paul's test give us about the ultimate goal of spiritual gifts? 3. What do verses 4–6 reveal about the unity and diversity of spiritual gifts? 4. What might make some members of your church feel useless or envious of other parts of the body (vv. 12–26)? 5. According to Paul, how can we make every part of the body feel special (vv. 21–26)? 6. Paul does not give us a complete list of gifts in this chapter. What might the words *first, second, third* and *then* (v. 28) indicate?

 Applying the Word 1. What can you do to help others in your group or church to discover their giftedness? 2. How would you like to develop and exercise your spiritual gifts?

 Responding in Prayer Pray that both you and those you know would use your gifts to God's glory.

---

11 / *1 Corinthians 13*
Love of Christ

PERHAPS THE MOST abused phrase in the English language is "I love you." Instead of communicating unselfish caring, it often expresses enlightened self-interest, manipulative affection or sheer lust. In 1 Corinthians 13 Paul not only defines love for us but shows us why this is the most excellent way to relate to anyone—especially to members of the family of God.

 Warming Up to God Think of a person who has truly loved you. What were the marks of that person's way of relating to you?

Read 1 Corinthians 13.

13 If I speak in the tongues*e* of men and of angels, but have not love, I am only a resounding gong or a clanging cymbal. ²If I have the gift of prophecy and can fathom all mysteries and all knowledge, and if I have a faith that can move mountains, but have not love, I am nothing. ³If I give all I possess to the poor and surrender my body to the flames,*f* but have not love, I gain nothing.

⁴Love is patient, love is kind. It does not envy, it does not boast, it is not proud. ⁵It is not rude,

e1 Or languages   *f3 Some early manuscripts body that I may boast* it is not self-seeking, it is not easily angered, it keeps no record of wrongs. ⁶Love does not delight in evil but rejoices with the truth. ⁷It always protects, always trusts, always hopes, always perseveres.

⁸Love never fails. But where there are prophecies, they will cease; where there are tongues, they will be stilled; where there is knowledge, it will pass away. ⁹For we know in part and we prophesy in part, ¹⁰but when perfection comes,

the imperfect disappears. ¹¹When I was a child, I talked like a child, I thought like a child, I reasoned like a child. When I became a man, I put childish ways behind me. ¹²Now we see but a poor reflection as in a mirror; then we shall see face to face. Now I know in part; then I shall know fully, even as I am fully known.

¹³And now these three remain: faith, hope and love. But the greatest of these is love.

 Discovering the Word 1. What is so tragic about using our gifts without love (vv. 1–3)? 2. How would you define each of love's qualities (vv. 4–7)? 3. In verses 8–13 Paul summarizes the *supremacy of love.* Compared with love, why do the spiritual gifts have limited value? 4. Some understand the "perfection" in verse 10 as the completed New Testament, thus eliminating the need for tongues or prophecy today. Others understand it as the perfection we will experience when Christ returns. In light of Paul's other comparisons (vv. 11–12), which interpretation seems more likely? Explain. 5. Why is love greater than faith or hope (v. 13)?

Applying the Word 1. How can love lead to healthy interdependence in your relationships rather than unhealthy independence or dependence? 2. Which aspect of love do you most need to develop? 3. Besides telling us what love is, this passage gives us an incidental portrait of Jesus as the ultimate lover. Reread verses 4–7, replacing *love* with *Jesus.* What fresh picture of Jesus' care do you gain through this exercise?

Responding in Prayer Ask Jesus Christ to teach you what it means to love.

---

12 / *1 Corinthians 14*
Speaking for Christ

WORDS ARE CHEAP today. They can be digitized and processed. With one depressed button on a computer we can eliminate words forever, without even a trace remaining in memory. However, the Bible says words have great power, because they are an extension of our personality. God's Word always accomplishes his purposes, because it is spoken with his personal power. In this chapter Paul focuses on the exciting potential of God-inspired speech in the Christian community.

 Warming Up to God Recall a time when something that was shared from the congregation during a worship service (or in a small group) truly encouraged you. What characterized this word ministry?

 Read 1 Corinthians 14.

---

14 Follow the way of love and eagerly desire spiritual gifts, especially the gift of prophecy. ²For anyone who speaks in a tongue*g* does not speak to men but to God. Indeed, no one understands him; he utters mysteries with his spirit.*h* ³But everyone who prophesies speaks to men for their strengthening, encouragement and comfort. ⁴He who speaks in a tongue edifies himself, but he who prophesies edifies the church. ⁵I would like every one of you to

speak in tongues,*i* but I would rather have you prophesy. He who prophesies is greater than one who speaks in tongues,*i* unless he interprets, so that the church may be edified.

⁶Now, brothers, if I come to you and speak in tongues, what good will I be to you, unless I bring you some revelation or knowledge or prophecy or word of instruction? ⁷Even in the case of lifeless

*g*2 Or *another language*; also in verses 4, 13, 14, 19, 26 and 27
*h*2 Or *by the Spirit*   *i*5 Or *other languages*; also in verses 6, 18, 22, 23 and 39

things that make sounds, such as the flute or harp, how will anyone know what tune is being played unless there is a distinction in the notes? [8]Again, if the trumpet does not sound a clear call, who will get ready for battle? [9]So it is with you. Unless you speak intelligible words with your tongue, how will anyone know what you are saying? You will just be speaking into the air. [10]Undoubtedly there are all sorts of languages in the world, yet none of them is without meaning. [11]If then I do not grasp the meaning of what someone is saying, I am a foreigner to the speaker, and he is a foreigner to me. [12]So it is with you. Since you are eager to have spiritual gifts, try to excel in gifts that build up the church.

[13]For this reason anyone who speaks in a tongue should pray that he may interpret what he says. [14]For if I pray in a tongue, my spirit prays, but my mind is unfruitful. [15]So what shall I do? I will pray with my spirit, but I will also pray with my mind; I will sing with my spirit, but I will also sing with my mind. [16]If you are praising God with your spirit, how can one who finds himself among those who do not understand[j] say "Amen" to your thanksgiving, since he does not know what you are saying? [17]You may be giving thanks well enough, but the other man is not edified.

[18]I thank God that I speak in tongues more than all of you. [19]But in the church I would rather speak five intelligible words to instruct others than ten thousand words in a tongue.

[20]Brothers, stop thinking like children. In regard to evil be infants, but in your thinking be adults. [21]In the Law it is written:

"Through men of strange tongues
    and through the lips of foreigners
I will speak to this people,
    but even then they will not listen to me,"[k]
says the Lord.

[22]Tongues, then, are a sign, not for believers but for unbelievers; prophecy, however, is for believers, not for unbelievers. [23]So if the whole church comes together and everyone speaks in tongues, and some who do not understand[l] or some unbelievers come in, will they not say that you are out of your mind? [24]But if an unbeliever or someone who does not understand[m] comes in while everybody is prophesying, he will be convinced by all that he is a sinner and will be judged by all, [25]and the secrets of his heart will be laid bare. So he will fall down and worship God, exclaiming, "God is really among you!"

[26]What then shall we say, brothers? When you come together, everyone has a hymn, or a word of instruction, a revelation, a tongue or an interpretation. All of these must be done for the strengthening of the church. [27]If anyone speaks in a tongue, two—or at the most three—should speak, one at a time, and someone must interpret. [28]If there is no interpreter, the speaker should keep quiet in the church and speak to himself and God.

[29]Two or three prophets should speak, and the others should weigh carefully what is said. [30]And if a revelation comes to someone who is sitting down, the first speaker should stop. [31]For you can all prophesy in turn so that everyone may be instructed and encouraged. [32]The spirits of prophets are subject to the control of prophets. [33]For God is not a God of disorder but of peace.

As in all the congregations of the saints, [34]women should remain silent in the churches. They are not allowed to speak, but must be in submission, as the Law says. [35]If they want to inquire about something, they should ask their own husbands at home; for it is disgraceful for a woman to speak in the church.

[36]Did the word of God originate with you? Or are you the only people it has reached? [37]If anybody thinks he is a prophet or spiritually gifted, let him acknowledge that what I am writing to you is the Lord's command. [38]If he ignores this, he himself will be ignored.[n]

[39]Therefore, my brothers, be eager to prophesy, and do not forbid speaking in tongues. [40]But everything should be done in a fitting and orderly way.

[j]16 Or *among the inquirers*   [k]21 Isaiah 28:11,12   [l]23 Or *some inquirers*   [m]24 Or *or some inquirer*   [n]38 Some manuscripts *If he is ignorant of this, let him be ignorant*

Discovering the Word   1. Evidently, the Corinthians placed great value on the gift of tongues. Why does Paul prefer prophecy to uninterpreted tongues (vv. 1–5)?   2. What illustrations does Paul use to show why uninterpreted tongues do not build up the church (vv. 6–12)?   3. What remedy does Paul suggest (vv. 13–19)? 4. What does Paul say about the *purpose* of tongues and of prophecy (vv. 20–25)?   5. What guidelines does Paul give for when someone should speak in tongues and when he should remain silent (vv. 27–28)? 6. How can Paul's statements in verses 33–35 be harmonized with his teaching about women praying and prophesying (11:5)?

 Applying the Word 1. In what ways might we be guilty of meaningless or mindless worship today? 2. How can Paul's counsel improve the quality of our worship?

 Responding in Prayer Ask that worship in your church might be meaningful and powerful for all who come.

13 / *1 Corinthians 15—16*
Hope in Christ

WHAT HAPPENS AFTER death? Do we live on as disembodied souls, as the Greeks taught? Do we go through countless cycles of reincarnation, as the Hindus believe? Do both body and soul cease to exist, as naturalism maintains?

Because of their Greek heritage, the Corinthians questioned the reality of the resurrection. In this passage Paul challenges their thinking by pointing out the absurd conclusions to which it leads. He reminds us that the resurrection is a crucial aspect of our hope in Christ.

 Warming Up to God Have you ever pondered what death will be like for you? How do you feel about it? Express your feelings to Christ. Allow him to prepare you for this study.

 Read 1 Corinthians 15—16.

15 Now, brothers, I want to remind you of the gospel I preached to you, which you received and on which you have taken your stand. ²By this gospel you are saved, if you hold firmly to the word I preached to you. Otherwise, you have believed in vain.

³For what I received I passed on to you as of first importance⁰: that Christ died for our sins according to the Scriptures, ⁴that he was buried, that he was raised on the third day according to the Scriptures, ⁵and that he appeared to Peter,ᵖ and then to the Twelve. ⁶After that, he appeared to more than five hundred of the brothers at the same time, most of whom are still living, though some have fallen asleep. ⁷Then he appeared to James, then to all the apostles, ⁸and last of all he appeared to me also, as to one abnormally born.

⁹For I am the least of the apostles and do not even deserve to be called an apostle, because I persecuted the church of God. ¹⁰But by the grace of God I am what I am, and his grace to me was not without effect. No, I worked harder than all of them—yet not I, but the grace of God that was with me. ¹¹Whether, then, it was I or they, this is what we preach, and this is what you believed.

¹²But if it is preached that Christ has been raised from the dead, how can some of you say that there is no resurrection of the dead? ¹³If there is no resurrection of the dead, then not even Christ has been raised. ¹⁴And if Christ has not been raised, our preaching is useless and so is your faith. ¹⁵More than that, we are then found to be false witnesses about God, for we have testified about God that he raised Christ from the dead. But he did not raise him if in fact the dead are not raised. ¹⁶For if the dead are not raised, then Christ has not been raised either. ¹⁷And if Christ has not been raised, your faith is futile; you are still in your sins. ¹⁸Then those also who have fallen asleep in Christ are lost. ¹⁹If only for this life we have hope in Christ, we are to be pitied more than all men.

²⁰But Christ has indeed been raised from the dead, the firstfruits of those who have fallen asleep. ²¹For since death came through a man, the resurrection of the dead comes also through a man. ²²For as in Adam all die, so in Christ all will be made alive. ²³But each in his own turn: Christ, the firstfruits; then, when he comes, those who belong to him. ²⁴Then the end will come, when

⁰3 Or *you at the first*   ᵖ5 Greek *Cephas*

he hands over the kingdom to God the Father after he has destroyed all dominion, authority and power. 25For he must reign until he has put all his enemies under his feet. 26The last enemy to be destroyed is death. 27For he "has put everything under his feet." q Now when it says that "everything" has been put under him, it is clear that this does not include God himself, who put everything under Christ. 28When he has done this, then the Son himself will be made subject to him who put everything under him, so that God may be all in all.

29Now if there is no resurrection, what will those do who are baptized for the dead? If the dead are not raised at all, why are people baptized for them? 30And as for us, why do we endanger ourselves every hour? 31I die every day—I mean that, brothers—just as surely as I glory over you in Christ Jesus our Lord. 32If I fought wild beasts in Ephesus for merely human reasons, what have I gained? If the dead are not raised,

"Let us eat and drink,
    for tomorrow we die." r

33Do not be misled: "Bad company corrupts good character." 34Come back to your senses as you ought, and stop sinning; for there are some who are ignorant of God—I say this to your shame.

35But someone may ask, "How are the dead raised? With what kind of body will they come?" 36How foolish! What you sow does not come to life unless it dies. 37When you sow, you do not plant the body that will be, but just a seed, perhaps of wheat or of something else. 38But God gives it a body as he has determined, and to each kind of seed he gives its own body. 39All flesh is not the same: Men have one kind of flesh, animals have another, birds another and fish another. 40There are also heavenly bodies and there are earthly bodies; but the splendor of the heavenly bodies is one kind, and the splendor of the earthly bodies is another. 41The sun has one kind of splendor, the moon another and the stars another; and star differs from star in splendor.

42So will it be with the resurrection of the dead. The body that is sown is perishable, it is raised imperishable; 43it is sown in dishonor, it is raised in glory; it is sown in weakness, it is raised in power; 44it is sown a natural body, it is raised a spiritual body.

If there is a natural body, there is also a spiritual body. 45So it is written: "The first man Adam became a living being" s; the last Adam, a life-giving spirit. 46The spiritual did not come first, but the natural, and after that the spiritual. 47The first man was of the dust of the earth, the second man from heaven. 48As was the earthly man, so are those who are of the earth; and as is the man from heaven, so also are those who are of heaven. 49And just as we have borne the likeness of the earthly man, so shall we t bear the likeness of the man from heaven.

50I declare to you, brothers, that flesh and blood cannot inherit the kingdom of God, nor does the perishable inherit the imperishable. 51Listen, I tell you a mystery: We will not all sleep, but we will all be changed— 52in a flash, in the twinkling of an eye, at the last trumpet. For the trumpet will sound, the dead will be raised imperishable, and we will be changed. 53For the perishable must clothe itself with the imperishable, and the mortal with immortality. 54When the perishable has been clothed with the imperishable, and the mortal with immortality, then the saying that is written will come true: "Death has been swallowed up in victory." u

55"Where, O death, is your victory?
    Where, O death, is your sting?" v

56The sting of death is sin, and the power of sin is the law. 57But thanks be to God! He gives us the victory through our Lord Jesus Christ.

58Therefore, my dear brothers, stand firm. Let nothing move you. Always give yourselves fully to the work of the Lord, because you know that your labor in the Lord is not in vain.

16 Now about the collection for God's people: Do what I told the Galatian churches to do. 2On the first day of every week, each one of you should set aside a sum of money in keeping with his income, saving it up, so that when I come no collections will have to be made. 3Then, when I arrive, I will give letters of introduction to the men you approve and send them with your gift to Jerusalem. 4If it seems advisable for me to go also, they will accompany me.

5After I go through Macedonia, I will come to you—for I will be going through Macedonia. 6Perhaps I will stay with you awhile, or even spend the winter, so that you can help me on my journey, wherever I go. 7I do not want to see you

q27 Psalm 8:6   r32 Isaiah 22:13   s45 Gen. 2:7   t49 Some early manuscripts so let us   u54 Isaiah 25:8   v55 Hosea 13:14

now and make only a passing visit; I hope to spend some time with you, if the Lord permits. [8]But I will stay on at Ephesus until Pentecost, [9]because a great door for effective work has opened to me, and there are many who oppose me.

[10]If Timothy comes, see to it that he has nothing to fear while he is with you, for he is carrying on the work of the Lord, just as I am. [11]No one, then, should refuse to accept him. Send him on his way in peace so that he may return to me. I am expecting him along with the brothers.

[12]Now about our brother Apollos: I strongly urged him to go to you with the brothers. He was quite unwilling to go now, but he will go when he has the opportunity.

[13]Be on your guard; stand firm in the faith; be men of courage; be strong. [14]Do everything in love.

[15]You know that the household of Stephanas were the first converts in Achaia, and they have devoted themselves to the service of the saints. I urge you, brothers, [16]to submit to such as these and to everyone who joins in the work, and labors at it. [17]I was glad when Stephanas, Fortunatus and Achaicus arrived, because they have supplied what was lacking from you. [18]For they refreshed my spirit and yours also. Such men deserve recognition.

[19]The churches in the province of Asia send you greetings. Aquila and Priscilla[w] greet you warmly in the Lord, and so does the church that meets at their house. [20]All the brothers here send you greetings. Greet one another with a holy kiss.

[21]I, Paul, write this greeting in my own hand.

[22]If anyone does not love the Lord—a curse be on him. Come, O Lord[x]!

[23]The grace of the Lord Jesus be with you.

[24]My love to all of you in Christ Jesus. Amen.[y]

[w]19 Greek *Prisca*, a variant of *Priscilla* expression *Come, O Lord* is *Marana tha.*
[x]22 In Aramaic the [y]24 Some manuscripts do not have *Amen.*

 Discovering the Word 1. Paul reminds the Corinthians of the gospel he preached to them. What are the essential elements of the gospel (15:1–11)? 2. If there is no resurrection, what are the consequences for Christ, for Paul and for us (15:12–19)? 3. How does belief or disbelief in the resurrection affect a person's lifestyle (15:29–34)? 4. What illustrations does Paul use to explain why the resurrection is not illogical but makes good sense (15:35–41)? 5. Although the resurrection body is somehow related to the natural body, how is it also radically different (15:42–49)? 6. How does chapter 16 give several illustrations of "the work of the Lord" Paul referred to in 15:58?

Applying the Word 1. To which specific area of service will you give yourself this week, knowing that your labor in the Lord is not in vain? 2. What is the most substantial change that studying 1 Corinthians has brought about in your life?

Responding in Prayer Praise God for what you have learned in 1 Corinthians.

2 Corinthians

*L*ife is relational. We hope and hurt the most about relationships with people who matter to us. A special friend we are in danger of losing, an employer who misunderstands our actions, a spouse who seems distant and cold, a brother in Christ who has spoken behind our back, a family member long estranged are samples of the web of relationships that make up our lives. When a special relationship is hanging by a slender thread, we are often at a loss to know what to say or do. Should we tell the truth even if it hurts? Should we avoid confrontation? Should we share what is going on inside us even if it shows we are weak and struggling, far weaker than we would like others to know?

Second Corinthians is all about relationships—not perfect ones, but real ones. In this letter the apostle Paul reveals that he is struggling deeply in his relationship with the believers in Corinth. Though he founded this church, they have apparently rejected him. This letter is an attempt at reconciliation. What made Paul's relationship more complicated was the seeming contest between Paul and his converts. The Corinthians were enjoying charismatic ecstasy. They had their orators, theologians, super-saints and super-apostles. They were strong, wise and triumphant. Paul, in contrast, was weak, foolish and a seeming failure.

In similar circumstances most people try to use strength and wisdom to win their way back. They create just the right leadership image. But Paul chose to pour out his soul to them, trusting that in the process Christ would be revealed. In this letter Paul is both medium and message. This great Christian leader takes the enormous risk of telling how confused, upset and weak he is. In 1 Corinthians Paul lets us see inside a first-century church. But in 2 Corinthians Paul lets us see inside a first-century Christian, the apostle himself. Through his large heart we see into the heart of God and the heart of the Christian message.

Paul founded the church in Corinth about A.D. 50. It was a lively church composed of first-generation Christians but infected with many of the problems associated with a mission. Corinth was the Las Vegas of the Roman Empire. Some new believers polluted the church with their secular standards in business and sexuality. They argued that all things are permissible in Christ. Others got superspiritual and boasted about their visions, prophecies, words of knowledge and spiritual experiences. In the course of time they wrote Paul asking for advice. Paul write 1 Corinthians in about A.D. 55 to address these questions and various problems.

Then it seems the Corinthians turned against the founding apostle, a crucial fact to know in order to understand 2 Corinthians. This letter was born in hurt.

Paul paid a second "painful visit" (2Co 2:1) and wrote a sorrowful letter, now lost, from Ephesus (2:4). It is highly likely that Paul then came to Macedonia (2Co 7:5), modern Greece, where he was reunited with Titus from Corinth and from which he wrote 2 Corinthians, probably while in Philippi. Later in A.D. 56 Paul visited Corinth again to receive their gifts for the poor Christians in Jerusalem.

As 2 Corinthians was written, Paul had several problems with the Corinthians: he changed his travel plans and did not come when he said he would (2Co 1:12—2:4); they failed to discipline the person who caused a grievous offense (2:5–11); their contributions for his collection for the Jewish Christians had lapsed (2Co 8—9); he had accepted financial support from the Macedonians (Thessalonica and Philippi) but not from the Achaians, especially the Corinthians (11:7–11). Paul also conflicted with newly arrived ministers in Corinth who preached a different gospel, probably a return to a form of Judaism (2:14—7:4; 10:1—13:14). Some individual Corinthians criticized Paul because he was a powerful letter-writer but a weak speaker who was unimpressive in person.

This relational conflict becomes the medium for revealing the distinctive message of this book: Christ meets us at our point of desperate weakness, *not only before we are saved, but after*. Against the false triumphalism of his opponents, Paul proclaims a gospel in which God's power is demonstrated best in human weakness. We have the Christ-treasure in jars of clay or, as Phillips powerfully paraphrases, "in a common earthenware jar." In a day when authentic Christianity seems less attractive than superspirituality or the "gospel of health, wealth and prosperity," Paul's searing honesty offers exactly what the world so deeply hungers for: it tells us how to be really real. As we walk through Paul's relationship with the Corinthians step by step, we discover how God in Christ is prepared to meet our deepest relational needs just as we are and where we are.

Outline

1 / *2 Corinthians 1:1–11*
Our Comforting God

"LIFE IS DIFFICULT!" With these three words Scott Peck begins his bestselling book *The Road Less Traveled*. But in 2 Corinthians Paul says this and more. Just where life is difficult, where our relationships are strained, where our competence is questioned, where our health and security are threatened, God makes himself known in powerful comfort. We discover that one of the supreme greatnesses of Christianity is that it does not seek a supernatural escape from the difficulties of life. Instead it offers a supernatural use for them. Troubles become triumphs as God makes himself known in our weakness.

 Warming Up to God What comfort do you need from God today? Sit and wait for him to visit you with his peace and reassurance.

 Read 2 Corinthians 1:1–11.

1 Paul, an apostle of Christ Jesus by the will of God, and Timothy our brother,

To the church of God in Corinth, together with all the saints throughout Achaia:

²Grace and peace to you from God our Father and the Lord Jesus Christ.

³Praise be to the God and Father of our Lord Jesus Christ, the Father of compassion and the God of all comfort, ⁴who comforts us in all our troubles, so that we can comfort those in any trouble with the comfort we ourselves have received from God. ⁵For just as the sufferings of Christ flow over into our lives, so also through Christ our comfort overflows. ⁶If we are distressed, it is for your comfort and salvation; if we are comforted, it is for your comfort, which produces in you patient endurance of the same suf-

ferings we suffer. ⁷And our hope for you is firm, because we know that just as you share in our sufferings, so also you share in our comfort.

⁸We do not want you to be uninformed, brothers, about the hardships we suffered in the province of Asia. We were under great pressure, far beyond our ability to endure, so that we despaired even of life. ⁹Indeed, in our hearts we felt the sentence of death. But this happened that we might not rely on ourselves but on God, who raises the dead. ¹⁰He has delivered us from such a deadly peril, and he will deliver us. On him we have set our hope that he will continue to deliver us, ¹¹as you help us by your prayers. Then many will give thanks on our[a] behalf for the gracious favor granted us in answer to the prayers of many.

a11 Many manuscripts your

 Discovering the Word 1. After his customary greeting and "signature," Paul breaks into praise. What evokes this spontaneous worship (vv. 3–7)? 2. What is the connection between the sufferings of Christ and the comfort of Christ (vv. 5–6)? 3. Paul's hardships in the province of Asia (modern-day Turkey) are evidently life-threatening. What did he discover about the meaning of such sufferings in the Christian life (vv. 8–11)? 4. How do you think Paul's openness in sharing the realities of his Christian experience affected his relationship with the Corinthians?

Applying the Word 1. In what ways have you experienced God's comfort in a difficult situation? 2. How does your experience of God's comfort enable you to comfort others who are suffering? 3. Based on what you have learned in these first eleven verses, how can hardships draw you closer to God instead of driving you away from him?

Responding in Prayer Think of someone you know who needs to experience God's comfort. Ask God to comfort that person and to use you in offering comfort.

2 / *2 Corinthians 1:12—2:11*
Always Yes in Christ

CONTRARY TO WHAT some misguided Christian parents think, affirming children does not make them proud and self-centered. Rather, it meets a fundamental need of the human personality. But often our attempts to affirm each other backfire.

Such was Paul's experience with the Corinthians. Paul had promised to visit them again, twice, in fact; first as he made his way to Macedonia and then on his way back. But he changed his plans, delaying his visit and deciding to visit only once. This led his opponents to claim that he was unreliable or fickle. In the process of defending his actions, Paul pointed the Corinthians to the ultimate ground of our affirmation: the eternal yes spoken to us by God in Christ.

 Warming Up to God Recall an experience of being affirmed by another, possibly a parent or a good friend. What made that word or action especially upbuilding for you?

 Read 2 Corinthians 1:12—2:11.

---

¹²Now this is our boast: Our conscience testifies that we have conducted ourselves in the world, and especially in our relations with you, in the holiness and sincerity that are from God. We have done so not according to worldly wisdom but according to God's grace. ¹³For we do not write you anything you cannot read or understand. And I hope that, ¹⁴as you have understood us in part, you will come to understand fully that you can boast of us just as we will boast of you in the day of the Lord Jesus.

¹⁵Because I was confident of this, I planned to visit you first so that you might benefit twice. ¹⁶I planned to visit you on my way to Macedonia and to come back to you from Macedonia, and then to have you send me on my way to Judea. ¹⁷When I planned this, did I do it lightly? Or do I make my plans in a worldly manner so that in the same breath I say, "Yes, yes" and "No, no"?

¹⁸But as surely as God is faithful, our message to you is not "Yes" and "No." ¹⁹For the Son of God, Jesus Christ, who was preached among you by me and Silas*ᵇ* and Timothy, was not "Yes" and "No," but in him it has always been "Yes." ²⁰For no matter how many promises God has made, they are "Yes" in Christ. And so through him the "Amen" is spoken by us to the glory of God. ²¹Now it is God who makes both us and you stand firm in Christ. He anointed us, ²²set his seal of ownership on us, and put his Spirit in our hearts as a deposit, guaranteeing what is to come.

²³I call God as my witness that it was in order to spare you that I did not return to Corinth. ²⁴Not that we lord it over your faith, but we work with you for your joy, because it is by faith you stand firm. ¹So I made up my mind that I would not make another painful visit to you. ²For if I grieve you, who is left to make me glad but you whom I have grieved? ³I wrote as I did so that when I came I should not be distressed by those who ought to make me rejoice. I had confidence in all of you, that you would all share my joy. ⁴For I wrote you out of great distress and anguish of heart and with many tears, not to grieve you but to let you know the depth of my love for you.

⁵If anyone has caused grief, he has not so much grieved me as he has grieved all of you, to some extent—not to put it too severely. ⁶The punishment inflicted on him by the majority is sufficient for him. ⁷Now instead, you ought to forgive and comfort him, so that he will not be overwhelmed by excessive sorrow. ⁸I urge you, therefore, to reaffirm your love for him. ⁹The reason I wrote you was to see if you would stand the test and be obedient in everything. ¹⁰If you forgive anyone, I also forgive him. And what I have forgiven—if there was anything to forgive—I have forgiven in the sight of Christ for your sake, ¹¹in order that Satan might not outwit us. For we are not unaware of his schemes.

ᵇ19 Greek Silvanus, a variant of Silas

Discovering the Word 1. Based on 1:12–22, what do you think Paul's opponents were saying about his motives and ministry style? 2. What reasons does Paul give for maintaining that his change of itinerary was not a change of mind about the Corinthians (1:12, 17)? 3. Why do you think Paul directs their attention away for his travel plans to the unqualified yes or "amen" of the gospel (1:18–20)? 4. What further reason does Paul give for his change of travel plans (1:23—2:4)? 5. In 2:5–11 Paul refers to the discipline of a member of the church, possibly because of a gross sexual sin (see 1Co 5:1). How does Paul's handling of this problem affirm his love not only for the Corinthians but also for the man who had sinned?

 Applying the Word 1. What experiences have you had with church discipline? 2. How would Paul's approach to discipline be one that would still allow the person confronted to hear God's affirmation in Christ? 3. What have you learned about the conditions of receiving the affirmation Christ wants us to give?

Responding in Prayer Praise God for his faithful promises and his yes in Christ.

---

3 / 2 Corinthians 2:12—3:6
A Letter from Christ

CHRISTIANITY IS ESSENTIALLY a lay movement. But one would not think so while visiting the average church. Often the impression we get is that ministry is for the theologically trained, the polished and proficient. With the professionalism of ministry in our society, many of us question our ability to minister. Like Paul, we ask, "Who is equal to such a task?" (2:16). In this chapter Paul tells us why all believers are competent for ministry in Christ.

 Warming Up to God How do you feel about being told that becoming a Christian means becoming a minister? Talk to God about any fears you may have about being a minister.

 Read 2 Corinthians 2:12—3:6.

12Now when I went to Troas to preach the gospel of Christ and found that the Lord had opened a door for me, 13I still had no peace of mind, because I did not find my brother Titus there. So I said good-by to them and went on to Macedonia.

14But thanks be to God, who always leads us in triumphal procession in Christ and through us spreads everywhere the fragrance of the knowledge of him. 15For we are to God the aroma of Christ among those who are being saved and those who are perishing. 16To the one we are the smell of death; to the other, the fragrance of life. And who is equal to such a task? 17Unlike so many, we do not peddle the word of God for profit. On the contrary, in Christ we speak before God with sincerity, like men sent from God.

3 Are we beginning to commend ourselves again? Or do we need, like some people, letters of recommendation to you or from you? 2You yourselves are our letter, written on our hearts, known and read by everybody. 3You show that you are a letter from Christ, the result of our ministry, written not with ink but with the Spirit of the living God, not on tablets of stone but on tablets of human hearts.

4Such confidence as this is ours through Christ before God. 5Not that we are competent in ourselves to claim anything for ourselves, but our competence comes from God. 6He has made us competent as ministers of a new covenant—not of the letter but of the Spirit; for the letter kills, but the Spirit gives life.

 Discovering the Word 1. Because Paul had no peace of mind in Troas, he couldn't take full advantage of the "door" the Lord had opened for him. How was he able to speak of his triumph in Christ (2:14) in the same breath as confessing his weakness? 2. What do you think Paul means in saying we are "the smell of death" to some and "the fragrance of life" to others (2:15–16)? 3. In contrast to those who boasted about their letters of recommendation, Paul says the Corinthians are his letter (3:1–3). What sort of letter are they? 4. In 2:16 Paul asked, "Who is equal to such a task?" What answer does he give in 3:4–6? 5. According to Paul, how does our ministry under the New Covenant contrast with ministry under the Old (3:3–6)?

Applying the Word 1. When has Christ enabled you to triumph in the midst of a personal struggle? 2. How does the thought that Christianity spreads like a fragrance challenge your church or Christian group? 3. How has this passage encouraged you to feel competent to minister as a disciple of Jesus?

Responding in Prayer You are a letter from Christ. Pray that you would represent Christ to those around you.

4 / 2 Corinthians 3:7–18
Becoming Like Christ

IT SEEMS TO me that it ought to be that Christ is most revealed when we hide ourselves. But that is the Old Covenant with its fading glory, condemnation focus and death-dealing impact. The New Covenant ministry is paradoxically this: as I look at Christ and as I reveal myself, it is not I who am revealed but Christ. I am like a Kodachrome transparency. If I am looked *at,* one will see almost no image at all. But if I am held to the light and looked *through,* a beautiful image begins to appear. In this passage Paul celebrates the revelation that comes with the New Covenant.

Warming Up to God Ask God to reveal that part of himself which is in you. Spend some time seeing yourself through his eyes. Praise him for the beauty he reveals.

Read 2 Corinthians 3:7–18.

⁷Now if the ministry that brought death, which was engraved in letters on stone, came with glory, so that the Israelites could not look steadily at the face of Moses because of its glory, fading though it was, ⁸will not the ministry of the Spirit be even more glorious? ⁹If the ministry that condemns men is glorious, how much more glorious is the ministry that brings righteousness! ¹⁰For what was glorious has no glory now in comparison with the surpassing glory. ¹¹And if what was fading away came with glory, how much greater is the glory of that which lasts!

¹²Therefore, since we have such a hope, we are very bold. ¹³We are not like Moses, who would put a veil over his face to keep the Israelites from gazing at it while the radiance was fading away. ¹⁴But their minds were made dull, for to this day the same veil remains when the old covenant is read. It has not been removed, because only in Christ is it taken away. ¹⁵Even to this day when Moses is read, a veil covers their hearts. ¹⁶But whenever anyone turns to the Lord, the veil is taken away. ¹⁷Now the Lord is the Spirit, and where the Spirit of the Lord is, there is freedom. ¹⁸And we, who with unveiled faces all reflect*c* the Lord's glory, are being transformed into his likeness with ever-increasing glory, which comes from the Lord, who is the Spirit.

c18 Or contemplate

Discovering the Word 1. How does Paul demonstrate that ministry under the New Covenant is more glorious than under the Old (vv. 7–11)? 2. How are we contrasted with Moses (vv. 12–16)? 3. What does verse 18 reveal about the process and goal of our lives as Christians under the New Covenant? 4. Paul speaks of our boldness (v. 12) and freedom (v. 17). Why should each of these characterize our New Covenant ministry?

Applying the Word 1. What evidence do you see in your life of the glorious transformation (metamorphosis) described in verse 18? 2. Is it easy or difficult for you to recognize God's glory as it is revealed in you? Explain. 3. In what area would you like to be made more like Christ?

Responding in Prayer Praise God for the transformation he has worked and is working in you.

5 / *2 Corinthians 4:1—5:10*
This Treasure, These Jars of Clay

MARGERY WILLIAMS WROTE a delightful children's story about two nursery animals, a Velveteen Rabbit (after which the book is named) and a Skin Horse, who was very old and very wise. "What is real?" asked the Velveteen Rabbit. The Skin Horse said, "Real isn't how you are made, it is a thing that happens when you are loved for a long, long time. Generally, by the time you are real most of your hair has been loved off, and your eyes drop out and you get loose in the joints and very shabby. But these things don't matter at all, because once you are REAL you can't be ugly except to those who don't understand. Once you are real you can't become unreal again. It lasts for always" (Margery Williams, *The Velveteen Rabbit* [New York: Simon & Schuster, Inc., 1975]).

The gospel treasure is contained by people marked by weakness, frailty and a kind of living death. Paradoxically, as we shall see, this life situation serves to enhance the message we bring, not detract from it. Once real in Christ, you can't become ugly or unreal again.

 Warming Up to God Do you feel free to be real in your relationship with Christ? Talk to him about the parts of yourself you feel are shabby. Listen for his loving response.

 Read 2 Corinthians 4:1—5:10.

4 Therefore, since through God's mercy we have this ministry, we do not lose heart. ²Rather, we have renounced secret and shameful ways; we do not use deception, nor do we distort the word of God. On the contrary, by setting forth the truth plainly we commend ourselves to every man's conscience in the sight of God. ³And even if our gospel is veiled, it is veiled to those who are perishing. ⁴The god of this age has blinded the minds of unbelievers, so that they cannot see the light of the gospel of the glory of Christ, who is the image of God. ⁵For we do not preach ourselves, but Jesus Christ as Lord, and ourselves as your servants for Jesus' sake. ⁶For God, who said, "Let light shine out of darkness,"*ᵈ* made his light shine in our hearts to give us the light of the knowledge of the glory of God in the face of Christ.

⁷But we have this treasure in jars of clay to show that this all-surpassing power is from God and not from us. ⁸We are hard pressed on every side, but not crushed; perplexed, but not in despair; ⁹persecuted, but not abandoned; struck down, but not destroyed. ¹⁰We always carry around in our body the death of Jesus, so that the life of Jesus may also be revealed in our body. ¹¹For we who are alive are always being given over to death for Jesus' sake, so that his life may be revealed in our mortal body. ¹²So then, death is at work in us, but life is at work in you.

¹³It is written: "I believed; therefore I have spoken."*ᵉ* With that same spirit of faith we also believe and therefore speak, ¹⁴because we know that the one who raised the Lord Jesus from the dead will also raise us with Jesus and present us with you in his presence. ¹⁵All this is for your benefit, so that the grace that is reaching more and more people may cause thanksgiving to overflow to the glory of God.

¹⁶Therefore we do not lose heart. Though outwardly we are wasting away, yet inwardly we are being renewed day by day. ¹⁷For our light and momentary troubles are achieving for us an eternal glory that far outweighs them all. ¹⁸So we fix our eyes not on what is seen, but on what is unseen. For what is seen is temporary, but what is unseen is eternal.

5 Now we know that if the earthly tent we live in is destroyed, we have a building from God, an eternal house in heaven, not built by human hands. ²Meanwhile we groan, longing to be clothed with our heavenly dwelling, ³because when we are clothed, we will not be found naked. ⁴For while we are in this tent, we groan and are burdened, because we do not wish

ᵈ6 Gen. 1:3   *ᵉ13* Psalm 116:10

to be unclothed but to be clothed with our heavenly dwelling, so that what is mortal may be swallowed up by life. [5]Now it is God who has made us for this very purpose and has given us the Spirit as a deposit, guaranteeing what is to come.

[6]Therefore we are always confident and know that as long as we are at home in the body we are away from the Lord. [7]We live by faith, not by sight. [8]We are confident, I say, and would prefer to be away from the body and at home with the Lord. [9]So we make it our goal to please him, whether we are at home in the body or away from it. [10]For we must all appear before the judgment seat of Christ, that each one may receive what is due him for the things done while in the body, whether good or bad.

 Discovering the Word **1.** How does Paul's ministry contrast with the practices of evangelists who discredit the gospel (4:2)? **2.** What forces does Paul see at work behind those who reject and those who accept his gospel (4:4–6)? **3.** In what ways does Paul contrast the glory of the gospel with the weakness of those who preach it (4:7–18)? **4.** What images does Paul use to compare the shabbiness of life now with the glory of the life to come (5:1–5)? **5.** How does Paul's wonderful destiny in Christ affect his view of life and death (5:6–10)? **6.** Reviewing the entire passage, what do you now understand Paul to mean by saying, "we live by faith, not by sight" (5:7)?

 Applying the Word **1.** We often assume that our weakness will hinder the gospel and detract from it. On the contrary, how does our weakness reveal God's power? **2.** How can Paul's perspective help you come to terms with your own weaknesses and mortality?

 Responding in Prayer Praise God for what you have learned about yourself through this passage.

6 / 2 Corinthians 5:11—6:13
Ambassadors for Christ

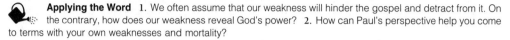

DIETRICH BONHOEFFER DESCRIBES the emergence of the super-leader under Hitler:
It is essential for the image of the Leader that the group does not see the face of the one who goes before, but sees him only from behind as the figure stepping ahead. His humanity is veiled in his Leader's form. (Quoted in Ray Anderson, *Minding God's Business* [Grand Rapids, Mich.: Eerdmans, 1986], p. 5.)

Warming Up to God Think of a time when you defended yourself in the context of a strained relationship. To what did you appeal?

Read 2 Corinthians 5:11—6:13.

[11]Since, then, we know what it is to fear the Lord, we try to persuade men. What we are is plain to God, and I hope it is also plain to your conscience. [12]We are not trying to commend ourselves to you again, but are giving you an opportunity to take pride in us, so that you can answer those who take pride in what is seen rather than in what is in the heart. [13]If we are out of our mind, it is for the sake of God; if we are in our right mind, it is for you. [14]For Christ's love compels us, because we are convinced that one died for all, and therefore all died. [15]And he died for all, that those who live should no longer live for themselves but for him who died for them and was raised again.

[16]So from now on we regard no one from a worldly point of view. Though we once regarded Christ in this way, we do so no longer. [17]Therefore, if anyone is in Christ, he is a new creation; the old has gone, the new has come! [18]All this is from God, who reconciled us to himself through Christ and gave us the ministry of reconciliation: [19]that God was reconciling the world to himself in Christ, not counting men's sins against them. And he has committed to us the message of reconciliation. [20]We are therefore Christ's ambassa-

dors, as though God were making his appeal through us. We implore you on Christ's behalf: Be reconciled to God. ²¹God made him who had no sin to be sin*ᶠ* for us, so that in him we might become the righteousness of God.

6 As God's fellow workers we urge you not to receive God's grace in vain. ²For he says,

"In the time of my favor I heard you,
    and in the day of salvation I helped you."*ᵍ*

I tell you, now is the time of God's favor, now is the day of salvation.

³We put no stumbling block in anyone's path, so that our ministry will not be discredited. ⁴Rather, as servants of God we commend ourselves in every way: in great endurance; in troubles, hardships and distresses; ⁵in beatings, imprisonments and riots; in hard work, sleepless nights and hunger; ⁶in purity, understanding, patience and kindness; in the Holy Spirit and in sincere love; ⁷in truthful speech and in the power of God; with weapons of righteousness in the right hand and in the left; ⁸through glory and dishonor, bad report and good report; genuine, yet regarded as impostors; ⁹known, yet regarded as unknown; dying, and yet we live on; beaten, and yet not killed; ¹⁰sorrowful, yet always rejoicing; poor, yet making many rich; having nothing, and yet possessing everything.

¹¹We have spoken freely to you, Corinthians, and opened wide our hearts to you. ¹²We are not withholding our affection from you, but you are withholding yours from us. ¹³As a fair exchange—I speak as to my children—open wide your hearts also.

ʄ21 Or *be a sin offering*   g2 Isaiah 49:8

 Discovering the Word 1. Paul defends his *ministry* and *message* of reconciliation in this passage. What accusations might Paul's opponents have made about his ministry (5:11–13)? 2. How does Paul explain his true motives and goals (5:11–14)? 3. In describing his message, Paul uses the words *reconciliation* and *reconciled* five times (5:18–20). What does it mean to be reconciled to God? 4. What would it mean for the Corinthians—or us today—to receive the grace of God in vain (6:1)? 5. To what further credentials does Paul point in order to commend himself to the Corinthians (6:3–10)?

 Applying the Word 1. How might Paul's example help you be a more effective ambassador, especially to people who are "turned off" by Christianity? 2. Who, specifically, would you like to be an ambassador to? 3. How could you reach that person?

Responding in Prayer Ask God to make you an effective ambassador.

---

7 / 2 Corinthians 6:14—7:16
Good Grief

A GREAT THEOLOGIAN once said, "To be a sinner is our distress, but to know it, is our hope!" Paul would say "Amen." We have nothing to lose and everything to gain if we are in Christ and walking into the light. But the Corinthians were tempted to cover up a scandal and not to call it sin. In response, Paul patiently and effectively ministered to the Corinthians, urging them not to cover up the problem. The result was what Paul calls godly sorrow.

 Warming Up to God Recall an experience of deep sorrow, possibly a significant loss, hurt or disappointment. What were some of the good things, if any, that came after the sorrow had passed? Praise God for what you learned from that experience.

Read 2 Corinthians 6:14—7:16.

¹⁴Do not be yoked together with unbelievers. For what do righteousness and wickedness have in common? Or what fellowship can light have with darkness? ¹⁵What harmony is there between Christ and Belial*ʰ*? What does a believer have in common with an unbeliever? ¹⁶What agreement is there between the temple of God and idols? For we are the temple of the living God. As God has said: "I will live with them and walk among them, and I will be their God, and they will be my people."*ⁱ*

¹⁷"Therefore come out from them
     and be separate,
                                        says the Lord.
   Touch no unclean thing,
     and I will receive you."*ʲ*
¹⁸"I will be a Father to you,
     and you will be my sons and daughters,
                              says the Lord Almighty."*ᵏ*

7 Since we have these promises, dear friends, let us purify ourselves from everything that contaminates body and spirit, perfecting holiness out of reverence for God.

²Make room for us in your hearts. We have wronged no one, we have corrupted no one, we have exploited no one. ³I do not say this to condemn you; I have said before that you have such a place in our hearts that we would live or die with you. ⁴I have great confidence in you; I take great pride in you. I am greatly encouraged; in all our troubles my joy knows no bounds.

⁵For when we came into Macedonia, this body of ours had no rest, but we were harassed at every turn—conflicts on the outside, fears within. ⁶But God, who comforts the downcast, comforted us by the coming of Titus, ⁷and not only by his com-

ing but also by the comfort you had given him. He told us about your longing for me, your deep sorrow, your ardent concern for me, so that my joy was greater than ever.

⁸Even if I caused you sorrow by my letter, I do not regret it. Though I did regret it—I see that my letter hurt you, but only for a little while— ⁹yet now I am happy, not because you were made sorry, but because your sorrow led you to repentance. For you became sorrowful as God intended and so were not harmed in any way by us. ¹⁰Godly sorrow brings repentance that leads to salvation and leaves no regret, but worldly sorrow brings death. ¹¹See what this godly sorrow has produced in you: what earnestness, what eagerness to clear yourselves, what indignation, what alarm, what longing, what concern, what readiness to see justice done. At every point you have proved yourselves to be innocent in this matter. ¹²So even though I wrote to you, it was not on account of the one who did the wrong or of the injured party, but rather that before God you could see for yourselves how devoted to us you are. ¹³By all this we are encouraged.

In addition to our own encouragement, we were especially delighted to see how happy Titus was, because his spirit has been refreshed by all of you. ¹⁴I had boasted to him about you, and you have not embarrassed me. But just as everything we said to you was true, so our boasting about you to Titus has proved to be true as well. ¹⁵And his affection for you is all the greater when he remembers that you were all obedient, receiving him with fear and trembling. ¹⁶I am glad I can have complete confidence in you.

ʰ15 Greek *Beliar,* a variant of *Belial*   *ⁱ16* Lev. 26:12; Jer. 32:38; Ezek. 37:27   *ʲ17* Isaiah 52:11; Ezek. 20:34,41   *ᵏ18* 2 Samuel 7:14; 7:8

Discovering the Word 1. This passage is usually understood to apply to marriages between believers and unbelievers. However, what other types of close relationships or partnerships might Paul have in mind? 2. What reasons does Paul give for avoiding such unions (6:14–16)? 3. Although we may forfeit certain relationships, what positive promises does the Lord give us (6:16—7:1)? 4. What difference should our relationship with God make when we contemplate marriage or other close relationships (6:17; 7:1)? 5. In 7:2–6 Paul recalls how comforted he was when he met Titus in Macedonia and heard news of the Corinthians. What makes Paul so "confident," "proud" and "encouraged" (7:4) about the Corinthians? 6. Referring to their response to his "sorrowful letter" (7:8), Paul compares worldly sorrow with godly sorrow (7:9–10). What are the positive indications and constructive results of godly sorrow (7:10–11)?

Applying the Word 1. It is often counterproductive to try to persuade someone not to marry a person they deeply love, even if the intended partner is unsuitable. What clues does this passage give us for ministering to someone who is tempted to marry outside the faith? 2. If godly sorrow is so beneficial, why do you think most Christians shrink from the relational work, discipline and tough love that are required to bring it about in others? **3.** In what areas of your life are you most in need of godly sorrow?

 Responding in Prayer Ask Christ to teach you more about godly sorrow.

8 / *2 Corinthians 8:1—9:15*
The Need to Give

THE PRIVACY OF the purse makes it extremely difficult for Christians to talk about their money. The fig leaf has slipped from the genitals to the wallet. The problem is compounded by hard-sell media evangelists raising funds for their personal empires. But Paul devotes two whole chapters to the grace of giving, because both he and the Corinthians have a problem in this area.

 Warming Up to God Reflect on your own pattern of giving. When is it hard for you?

 Read 2 Corinthians 8:1—9:15.

8 And now, brothers, we want you to know about the grace that God has given the Macedonian churches. ²Out of the most severe trial, their overflowing joy and their extreme poverty welled up in rich generosity. ³For I testify that they gave as much as they were able, and even beyond their ability. Entirely on their own, ⁴they urgently pleaded with us for the privilege of sharing in this service to the saints. ⁵And they did not do as we expected, but they gave themselves first to the Lord and then to us in keeping with God's will. ⁶So we urged Titus, since he had earlier made a beginning, to bring also to completion this act of grace on your part. ⁷But just as you excel in everything—in faith, in speech, in knowledge, in complete earnestness and in your love for us*ˡ*—see that you also excel in this grace of giving.

⁸I am not commanding you, but I want to test the sincerity of your love by comparing it with the earnestness of others. ⁹For you know the grace of our Lord Jesus Christ, that though he was rich, yet for your sakes he became poor, so that you through his poverty might become rich.

¹⁰And here is my advice about what is best for you in this matter: Last year you were the first not only to give but also to have the desire to do so. ¹¹Now finish the work, so that your eager willingness to do it may be matched by your completion of it, according to your means. ¹²For if the will-

ingness is there, the gift is acceptable according to what one has, not according to what he does not have.

¹³Our desire is not that others might be relieved while you are hard pressed, but that there might be equality. ¹⁴At the present time your plenty will supply what they need, so that in turn their plenty will supply what you need. Then there will be equality, ¹⁵as it is written: "He who gathered much did not have too much, and he who gathered little did not have too little."*ᵐ*

¹⁶I thank God, who put into the heart of Titus the same concern I have for you. ¹⁷For Titus not only welcomed our appeal, but he is coming to you with much enthusiasm and on his own initiative. ¹⁸And we are sending along with him the brother who is praised by all the churches for his service to the gospel. ¹⁹What is more, he was chosen by the churches to accompany us as we carry the offering, which we administer in order to honor the Lord himself and to show our eagerness to help. ²⁰We want to avoid any criticism of the way we administer this liberal gift. ²¹For we are taking pains to do what is right, not only in the eyes of the Lord but also in the eyes of men.

²²In addition, we are sending with them our brother who has often proved to us in many ways that he is zealous, and now even more so because of his great confidence in you. ²³As for Titus, he

ˡ7 Some manuscripts in our love for you   *ᵐ15 Exodus 16:18*

is my partner and fellow worker among you; as for our brothers, they are representatives of the churches and an honor to Christ. [24]Therefore show these men the proof of your love and the reason for our pride in you, so that the churches can see it.

9 There is no need for me to write to you about this service to the saints. [2]For I know your eagerness to help, and I have been boasting about it to the Macedonians, telling them that since last year you in Achaia were ready to give; and your enthusiasm has stirred most of them to action. [3]But I am sending the brothers in order that our boasting about you in this matter should not prove hollow, but that you may be ready, as I said you would be. [4]For if any Macedonians come with me and find you unprepared, we—not to say anything about you—would be ashamed of having been so confident. [5]So I thought it necessary to urge the brothers to visit you in advance and finish the arrangements for the generous gift you had promised. Then it will be ready as a generous gift, not as one grudgingly given.

[6]Remember this: Whoever sows sparingly will also reap sparingly, and whoever sows generously will also reap generously. [7]Each man should give what he has decided in his heart to give, not reluctantly or under compulsion, for God loves a cheerful giver. [8]And God is able to make all grace abound to you, so that in all things at all times, having all that you need, you will abound in every good work. [9]As it is written:

"He has scattered abroad his gifts to the poor;
his righteousness endures forever." [n]

[10]Now he who supplies seed to the sower and bread for food will also supply and increase your store of seed and will enlarge the harvest of your righteousness. [11]You will be made rich in every way so that you can be generous on every occasion, and through us your generosity will result in thanksgiving to God.

[12]This service that you perform is not only supplying the needs of God's people but is also overflowing in many expressions of thanks to God. [13]Because of the service by which you have proved yourselves, men will praise God for the obedience that accompanies your confession of the gospel of Christ, and for your generosity in sharing with them and with everyone else. [14]And in their prayers for you their hearts will go out to you, because of the surpassing grace God has given you. [15]Thanks be to God for his indescribable gift!

[n]9 Psalm 112:9

 Discovering the Word 1. In what ways are the Macedonians excellent examples of generosity (8:1–5)? 2. In both chapters Paul refrains from using the word *money*. Instead he speaks of *sharing* (8:4; 9:13), *service* (8:4, 18; 9:1, 12–13), *offering* (8:19), *grace* (8:6–7) and *gift* (8:12, 20; 9:5). What insights do these words give us into the nature of giving? 3. Paul never raised money for himself, for his own missionary organization or even for Corinth Community Church. What is the primary goal that governs his appeal for gifts (8:10–15)? 4. What care does Paul take to avoid any suspicion of dishonesty or self-interest as he handles this large gift (8:16–24)? 5. Some people teach that giving money to the Lord's work results in your getting more money yourself. What does Paul say about the personal benefits of giving (9:6–11)?

Applying the Word 1. What positive and negative feelings do you have about people raising money for a Christian cause? 2. Paul encourages *cheerful* giving (9:7). The word is the root of our English *hilarious*. It is the exact opposite of calculated giving under compulsion. According to these two chapters, how could you become a more cheerful giver? 3. What difference will this study make in the stewardship of your resources?

Responding in Prayer Pray for the needs of believers around the world, especially those who suffer persecution.

9 / *2 Corinthians 10*
Spiritual Warfare

SOMETIMES WHEN THINGS seem to be getting better we hear news that the situation is worse than we thought. While Paul was writing this letter, or after completing and sending chapters 1—9, he got fresh news that some outside leaders, some so-called super-apostles, had usurped his rightful place. Now Paul engages in spiritual warfare with principalities, powers and persons who oppose not only Paul but Christ himself. Unlike many of us, Paul wants to make peace, not keep the peace by covering over the problem.

 Warming Up to God In what area do you feel that you are currently battling evil? What help do you need from God?

 Read 2 Corinthians 10.

10 By the meekness and gentleness of Christ, I appeal to you—I, Paul, who am "timid" when face to face with you, but "bold" when away! ²I beg you that when I come I may not have to be as bold as I expect to be toward some people who think that we live by the standards of this world. ³For though we live in the world, we do not wage war as the world does. ⁴The weapons we fight with are not the weapons of the world. On the contrary, they have divine power to demolish strongholds. ⁵We demolish arguments and every pretension that sets itself up against the knowledge of God, and we take captive every thought to make it obedient to Christ. ⁶And we will be ready to punish every act of disobedience, once your obedience is complete.

⁷You are looking only on the surface of things.ᵒ If anyone is confident that he belongs to Christ, he should consider again that we belong to Christ just as much as he. ⁸For even if I boast somewhat freely about the authority the Lord gave us for building you up rather than pulling you down, I will not be ashamed of it. ⁹I do not want to seem to be trying to frighten you with my letters. ¹⁰For some say, "His letters are weighty and forceful, but in person he is unimpressive and his speaking amounts to nothing." ¹¹Such people should realize that what we are in our let-

ters when we are absent, we will be in our actions when we are present.

¹²We do not dare to classify or compare ourselves with some who commend themselves. When they measure themselves by themselves and compare themselves with themselves, they are not wise. ¹³We, however, will not boast beyond proper limits, but will confine our boasting to the field God has assigned to us, a field that reaches even to you. ¹⁴We are not going too far in our boasting, as would be the case if we had not come to you, for we did get as far as you with the gospel of Christ. ¹⁵Neither do we go beyond our limits by boasting of work done by others.ᵖ Our hope is that, as your faith continues to grow, our area of activity among you will greatly expand, ¹⁶so that we can preach the gospel in the regions beyond you. For we do not want to boast about work already done in another man's territory. ¹⁷But, "Let him who boasts boast in the Lord."�q ¹⁸For it is not the one who commends himself who is approved, but the one whom the Lord commends.

ᵒ7 Or *Look at the obvious facts*   ᵖ13-15 Or *¹³We, however, will not boast about things that cannot be measured, but we will boast according to the standard of measurement that the God of measure has assigned us—a measurement that relates even to you.* ¹⁴ . . . . *¹⁵Neither do we boast about things that cannot be measured in regard to the work done by others.*   q17 Jer. 9:24

Discovering the Word 1. What apparent disadvantages did Paul suffer in comparison to his opponents in Corinth? (See especially verses 1 and 9.) 2. Paul says he is not waging war "as the world does" (v. 3). What types of worldly weapons and strategies do you think he has in mind? 3. What is Paul's strategy in this spiritual warfare (vv. 4–6)? 4. Trace, in verses 7 and 10, the arguments of Paul's opponents. 5. What is wrong with the boasting of Paul's opponents (vv. 7–18)?

Applying the Word   1. In what situations are we tempted to use worldly weapons and strategies today?   2. What similar arguments and pretensions oppose the knowledge of God today?   3. Which of your own thoughts need to be "taken captive" (v. 5) to obedience to Christ?

 Responding in Prayer   Ask God to guard your words, that your boasting might be only in the Lord.

10 / *2 Corinthians 11*
Super-Apostles, Super-Leaders

IN HIS BOOK *Servant Leadership* Robert K. Greenleaf wrote, "We live in the age of the anti-leader, and our vast educational structure devotes little care to nurturing leaders or to understanding followership" (Robert K. Greenleaf, *Servant Leadership* [New York: Paulist Press, 1977], p. 4).

 Warming Up to God   Whose leadership are you under? Reflect before Christ on the positive or negative impact of that leadership in your life.

Read 2 Corinthians 11.

11 I hope you will put up with a little of my foolishness; but you are already doing that. ²I am jealous for you with a godly jealousy. I promised you to one husband, to Christ, so that I might present you as a pure virgin to him. ³But I am afraid that just as Eve was deceived by the serpent's cunning, your minds may somehow be led astray from your sincere and pure devotion to Christ. ⁴For if someone comes to you and preaches a Jesus other than the Jesus we preached, or if you receive a different spirit from the one you received, or a different gospel from the one you accepted, you put up with it easily enough. ⁵But I do not think I am in the least inferior to those "super-apostles." ⁶I may not be a trained speaker, but I do have knowledge. We have made this perfectly clear to you in every way.

⁷Was it a sin for me to lower myself in order to elevate you by preaching the gospel of God to you free of charge? ⁸I robbed other churches by receiving support from them so as to serve you. ⁹And when I was with you and needed something, I was not a burden to anyone, for the brothers who came from Macedonia supplied what I needed. I have kept myself from being a burden to you in any way, and will continue to do so. ¹⁰As surely as the truth of Christ is in me, nobody in the regions of Achaia will stop this boasting of mine. ¹¹Why? Because I do not love

you? God knows I do! ¹²And I will keep on doing what I am doing in order to cut the ground from under those who want an opportunity to be considered equal with us in the things they boast about.

¹³For such men are false apostles, deceitful workmen, masquerading as apostles of Christ. ¹⁴And no wonder, for Satan himself masquerades as an angel of light. ¹⁵It is not surprising, then, if his servants masquerade as servants of righteousness. Their end will be what their actions deserve.

¹⁶I repeat: Let no one take me for a fool. But if you do, then receive me just as you would a fool, so that I may do a little boasting. ¹⁷In this self-confident boasting I am not talking as the Lord would, but as a fool. ¹⁸Since many are boasting in the way the world does, I too will boast. ¹⁹You gladly put up with fools since you are so wise! ²⁰In fact, you even put up with anyone who enslaves you or exploits you or takes advantage of you or pushes himself forward or slaps you in the face. ²¹To my shame I admit that we were too weak for that!

What anyone else dares to boast about—I am speaking as a fool—I also dare to boast about. ²²Are they Hebrews? So am I. Are they Israelites? So am I. Are they Abraham's descendants? So am I. ²³Are they servants of Christ? (I am out of my mind to talk like this.) I am more. I have worked much harder, been in prison more frequently, been flogged more severely, and been exposed to death again and again. [24]Five times I received from the Jews the forty lashes minus one. [25]Three times I was beaten with rods, once I was stoned, three times I was shipwrecked, I spent a night and a day in the open sea, [26]I have been constantly on the move. I have been in danger from rivers, in danger from bandits, in danger from my own countrymen, in danger from Gentiles; in danger in the city, in danger in the country, in danger at sea; and in danger from false brothers. [27]I have labored and toiled and have often gone without sleep; I have known hunger and thirst and have often gone without food; I have been cold and naked. [28]Besides everything else, I face daily the pressure of my concern for all the churches. [29]Who is weak, and I do not feel weak? Who is led into sin, and I do not inwardly burn?

[30]If I must boast, I will boast of the things that show my weakness. [31]The God and Father of the Lord Jesus, who is to be praised forever, knows that I am not lying. [32]In Damascus the governor under King Aretas had the city of the Damascenes guarded in order to arrest me. [33]But I was lowered in a basket from a window in the wall and slipped through his hands.

 Discovering the Word 1. What are Paul's motives for challenging the so-called super-apostles who are winning over the Corinthians (vv. 1–6)? 2. Why do you think betrothal rather than marriage is such a good image of the goal of Christian ministry (vv. 2–3)? 3. Why do you think Paul's decision to "preach the gospel free of charge" was so important in defending his ministry (vv. 7–12)? 4. Looking at the whole chapter, what marks of the super-apostles justified Paul's description of them as *false, deceitful* and *masquerading*? 5. In contrast, what does Paul boast about as the mark of his own leadership (vv. 16–33)?

 Applying the Word 1. What kind of Christian leadership today might fall under the apostle's judgment? 2. What have you learned from this study about the marks of true Christian leadership? 3. What have you learned about being a healthy follower?

 Responding in Prayer Pray for your pastor and other Christian leaders.

---

11 / *2 Corinthians 12*
My Burden Carries Me

UNINTENTIONALLY, A GERMAN philosopher captured the genius of Paul's spirituality with these arresting words: "My burden carries me." Normally we think about the difficulty of carrying our burdens. But in reality our burdens carry us to Christ by convincing us that we are not self-sufficient. They are spiritual assets, not liabilities. "When I am weak, then I am strong" is Paul's final distinction between super-spirituality and the real thing.

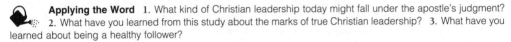 **Warming Up to God** What burdens are you carrying today? Turn them over to Christ one by one. Feel the weight lifted from you.

Read 2 Corinthians 12.

---

12 I must go on boasting. Although there is nothing to be gained, I will go on to visions and revelations from the Lord. [2]I know a man in Christ who fourteen years ago was caught up to the third heaven. Whether it was in the body or out of the body I do not know—God knows. [3]And I know that this man—whether in the body or apart from the body I do not know, but God knows—[4]was caught up to paradise. He heard inexpressible things, things that man is not permitted to tell. [5]I will boast about a man like that, but I will not boast about myself, except about my weaknesses. [6]Even if I should choose to boast, I would not be a fool, because I would be speaking the truth. But I refrain, so no one will think more of me than is warranted by what I do or say.

[7]To keep me from becoming conceited because

of these surpassingly great revelations, there was given me a thorn in my flesh, a messenger of Satan, to torment me. ⁸Three times I pleaded with the Lord to take it away from me. ⁹But he said to me, "My grace is sufficient for you, for my power is made perfect in weakness." Therefore I will boast all the more gladly about my weaknesses, so that Christ's power may rest on me. ¹⁰That is why, for Christ's sake, I delight in weaknesses, in insults, in hardships, in persecutions, in difficulties. For when I am weak, then I am strong.

¹¹I have made a fool of myself, but you drove me to it. I ought to have been commended by you, for I am not in the least inferior to the "super-apostles," even though I am nothing. ¹²The things that mark an apostle—signs, wonders and miracles—were done among you with great perseverance. ¹³How were you inferior to the other churches, except that I was never a burden to you? Forgive me this wrong!

¹⁴Now I am ready to visit you for the third time, and I will not be a burden to you, because what I want is not your possessions but you. After all, children should not have to save up for their parents, but parents for their children. ¹⁵So I will very gladly spend for you everything I have and expend myself as well. If I love you more, will you love me less? ¹⁶Be that as it may, I have not been a burden to you. Yet, crafty fellow that I am, I caught you by trickery! ¹⁷Did I exploit you through any of the men I sent you? ¹⁸I urged Titus to go to you and I sent our brother with him. Titus did not exploit you, did he? Did we not act in the same spirit and follow the same course?

¹⁹Have you been thinking all along that we have been defending ourselves to you? We have been speaking in the sight of God as those in Christ; and everything we do, dear friends, is for your strengthening. ²⁰For I am afraid that when I come I may not find you as I want you to be, and you may not find me as you want me to be. I fear that there may be quarreling, jealousy, outbursts of anger, factions, slander, gossip, arrogance and disorder. ²¹I am afraid that when I come again my God will humble me before you, and I will be grieved over many who have sinned earlier and have not repented of the impurity, sexual sin and debauchery in which they have indulged.

Discovering the Word 1. Paul describes his experience of being caught up to paradise by referring to "a man in Christ" (vv. 1–6). Why do you think he refrains from boasting about such an exalted experience? 2. Opinions concerning Paul's "thorn in my flesh" (v. 7) range from eye disease (Acts 9:9; Gal 4:15) to defective speech to his ever-present opponents. While no conclusive answer can be given about the details, what do we know about this bitter reality Paul faced? 3. How does Paul view Satan's part and God's part in his "thorn"? 4. In contrast to Paul's ecstatic experiences, the simple answer to his prayer (v. 9) is considered to be the summit from which we gain the most complete view of Paul's apostleship. What effect did this answer have on Paul himself? 5. To what credentials does Paul point while pleading for his rightful place in the Corinthians' hearts (vv. 11–21)?

Applying the Word 1. Reflecting on the whole chapter, what kind of weaknesses or problems can we legitimately expect God to transform into a means of grace? 2. What kinds of problems or weaknesses should we not expect God to transform? 3. How does this help you to understand an ongoing problem in your life?

Responding in Prayer Pray that you will be made strong even in your weak places, that you might serve Christ.

---

12 / *2 Corinthians 13*
Examine Yourselves

IMAGINE LIFE WITHOUT a final examination. At first it strikes us as a wonderful vacation, like school without tests and report cards. But without accountability life quickly loses its meaning. The whole Bible looks toward the final Day with vibrant hope. Those genuinely in Christ have nothing to fear and everything to anticipate. But what of those who are not sure, or who like the Corinthians might have false confidence about the outcome of the final exam? Paul deals with this matter in his final passionate plea.

Warming Up to God When is God's power real to you?

Read 2 Corinthians 13.

13 This will be my third visit to you. "Every matter must be established by the testimony of two or three witnesses."ʳ ²I already gave you a warning when I was with you the second time. I now repeat it while absent: On my return I will not spare those who sinned earlier or any of the others, ³since you are demanding proof that Christ is speaking through me. He is not weak in dealing with you, but is powerful among you. ⁴For to be sure, he was crucified in weakness, yet he lives by God's power. Likewise, we are weak in him, yet by God's power we will live with him to serve you.

⁵Examine yourselves to see whether you are in the faith; test yourselves. Do you not realize that Christ Jesus is in you—unless, of course, you fail the test? ⁶And I trust that you will discover that we have not failed the test. ⁷Now we pray to God that you will not do anything wrong. Not that people will see that we have stood the test but that you will do what is right even though we

may seem to have failed. ⁸For we cannot do anything against the truth, but only for the truth. ⁹We are glad whenever we are weak but you are strong; and our prayer is for your perfection. ¹⁰This is why I write these things when I am absent, that when I come I may not have to be harsh in my use of authority—the authority the Lord gave me for building you up, not for tearing you down.

¹¹Finally, brothers, good-by. Aim for perfection, listen to my appeal, be of one mind, live in peace. And the God of love and peace will be with you.

¹²Greet one another with a holy kiss. ¹³All the saints send their greetings.

¹⁴May the grace of the Lord Jesus Christ, and the love of God, and the fellowship of the Holy Spirit be with you all.

ʳ1 Deut. 19:15

Discovering the Word 1. What can the Corinthians expect from Paul's third visit (vv. 1–3, 10)? 2. Verse 4 sums up the whole book. Why does the cross represent the heart of what Paul has been saying to the Corinthians? 3. Paul asks them to examine themselves not so much in their doctrine as in their experience (vv. 5–6). How could the Corinthians know experientially that they truly belonged to Christ? 4. In what ways does Paul show that he cares more for *their* passing the test than for *his* seeming to pass the test in the eyes of others (vv. 7–9)? 5. In what specific ways does Paul pray they will be built up (vv. 11–14)?

Applying the Word 1. In what ways do you shrink from your daily cross and find your power elsewhere? 2. If you are unsure of your position in Christ, what can you do about it in light of this chapter?

Responding in Prayer Pray for courage to take up your cross and follow Christ.

Galatians

We all want to be accepted—by our family, by our friends and most of all by God. But so often people accept us only *if* we are attractive, smart, wealthy or powerful. So we work hard to project the right image and to conceal our faults. We often transfer this attitude to our relationship with God. We feel we must earn his acceptance. If we could only work harder, live better, pray longer, witness to more people—then we might get on God's good side.

In Galatians Paul challenges this kind of thinking. He exposes the futility of trying to earn God's acceptance when we are already accepted in Christ. His message frees us from living out of a sense of guilt. We find fresh assurance of God's love and renewed power to serve him.

Galatians was written by Paul sometime between A.D. 48–49. It was probably addressed to the churches in Antioch, Iconium, Lystra and Derbe, which were located in the Roman province of Galatia. Paul and Barnabas visited these cities during their first missionary journey. Their reception was unforgettable. Acts 13—14 tells us that they were driven out of Antioch, that they fled from Iconium and that Paul was stoned in Lystra! Yet in spite of the opposition against Paul and Barnabas, people believed the gospel and churches were formed.

The real threat arose shortly thereafter. Certain people infiltrated the new churches with a different message. "Paul omitted an important part of the gospel," they claimed. "You must also be circumcised and keep the law of Moses if you want to be saved" (see Acts 15:1). Their arguments were impressive and the religious zeal was undeniable. The Galatians were almost persuaded when Paul received word of what was happening. Quickly he dictated this letter and sent it to be read in each of the churches. Centuries later it still radiates the heat of Paul's anger. These preachers were impostors. Their gospel was perverted. The Galatians were in grave danger!

Outline

1 / *Galatians 1:1–10*
Good News and Bad

THE CHURCH HAS always been plagued by false teachers, heretics and followers of various cults. Usually such people have an aggressive program for winning new converts. How are we to respond to those who preach or accept a twisted gospel? Paul gives us an example in this passage.

 Warming Up to God Read and reflect on Galatians 1:3–5. Allow these verses to speak to you. Let them soak into your mind and heart. Praise God for what he has done in Christ.

 Read Galatians 1:1–10.

1 Paul, an apostle—sent not from men nor by man, but by Jesus Christ and God the Father, who raised him from the dead— ²and all the brothers with me,

To the churches in Galatia:

³Grace and peace to you from God our Father and the Lord Jesus Christ, ⁴who gave himself for our sins to rescue us from the present evil age, according to the will of our God and Father, ⁵to whom be glory for ever and ever. Amen.

⁶I am astonished that you are so quickly deserting the one who called you by the grace of Christ and are turning to a different gospel— ⁷which is really no gospel at all. Evidently some people are throwing you into confusion and are trying to pervert the gospel of Christ. ⁸But even if we or an angel from heaven should preach a gospel other than the one we preached to you, let him be eternally condemned! ⁹As we have already said, so now I say again: If anybody is preaching to you a gospel other than what you accepted, let him be eternally condemned!

¹⁰Am I now trying to win the approval of men, or of God? Or am I trying to please men? If I were still trying to please men, I would not be a servant of Christ.

 Discovering the Word 1. In three brief verses (3–5) Paul tells us an enormous amount about the gospel. What do we learn? 2. In verses 6–7 Paul summarizes the problem that caused him to write this letter. What was happening in the Galatian churches? 3. Verse 6 implies that if we desert the gospel, we also desert God. Why would this be true? 4. Why do you think Paul is so harsh in his judgment of those who preach a different gospel (vv. 8–9)? 5. How might the way we present the gospel be different if we were seeking the approval of people instead of God (v. 10)?

Applying the Word 1. What are some ways the gospel is being perverted today? 2. According to this passage, how can we ensure that the gospel we believe and preach is the true gospel? 3. What can you do to increase your understanding of the gospel?

Responding in Prayer Confess before God the ways in which you are seeking the approval of others before him. Ask God to help you turn your priorities around.

2 / *Galatians 1:11—2:10*
Why Believe the Gospel?

HAVE YOU EVER been talking with someone about the gospel when suddenly he or she says, "But that's just *your* opinion!"? This raises an important question. If the gospel is merely our opinion, then why should they listen to us? There are many other religions in the world, each one claiming to be a path to God. Who are we to assert that the gospel is the only true message of salvation? This objection isn't new. Paul's opponents questioned the authenticity of the gospel he preached.

 Warming Up to God We all struggle to believe at times. When is belief difficult for you? Don't be afraid to talk to God about it. Express your struggles and doubts to him.

 Read Galatians 1:11—2:10.

---

¹¹I want you to know, brothers, that the gospel I preached is not something that man made up. ¹²I did not receive it from any man, nor was I taught it; rather, I received it by revelation from Jesus Christ.

¹³For you have heard of my previous way of life in Judaism, how intensely I persecuted the church of God and tried to destroy it. ¹⁴I was advancing in Judaism beyond many Jews of my own age and was extremely zealous for the traditions of my fathers. ¹⁵But when God, who set me apart from birth*a* and called me by his grace, was pleased ¹⁶to reveal his Son in me so that I might preach him among the Gentiles, I did not consult any man, ¹⁷nor did I go up to Jerusalem to see those who were apostles before I was, but I went immediately into Arabia and later returned to Damascus.

¹⁸Then after three years, I went up to Jerusalem to get acquainted with Peter*b* and stayed with him fifteen days. ¹⁹I saw none of the other apostles—only James, the Lord's brother. ²⁰I assure you before God that what I am writing you is no lie. ²¹Later I went to Syria and Cilicia. ²²I was personally unknown to the churches of Judea that are in Christ. ²³They only heard the report: "The man who formerly persecuted us is now preaching the faith he once tried to destroy." ²⁴And they praised God because of me.

2 Fourteen years later I went up again to Jerusalem, this time with Barnabas. I took Titus along also. ²I went in response to a revelation and set before them the gospel that I preach among the Gentiles. But I did this privately to those who seemed to be leaders, for fear that I was running or had run my race in vain. ³Yet not even Titus, who was with me, was compelled to be circumcised, even though he was a Greek. ⁴⌐This matter arose⌐ because some false brothers had infiltrated our ranks to spy on the freedom we have in Christ Jesus and to make us slaves. ⁵We did not give in to them for a moment, so that the truth of the gospel might remain with you.

⁶As for those who seemed to be important— whatever they were makes no difference to me; God does not judge by external appearance— those men added nothing to my message. ⁷On the contrary, they saw that I had been entrusted with the task of preaching the gospel to the Gentiles,*c* just as Peter had been to the Jews.*d* ⁸For God, who was at work in the ministry of Peter as an apostle to the Jews, was also at work in my ministry as an apostle to the Gentiles. ⁹James, Peter*e* and John, those reputed to be pillars, gave me and Barnabas the right hand of fellowship when they recognized the grace given to me. They agreed that we should go to the Gentiles, and they to the Jews. ¹⁰All they asked was that we should continue to remember the poor, the very thing I was eager to do.

*a*15 Or *from my mother's womb*   *b*18 Greek *Cephas*   *c*7 Greek *uncircumcised*   *d*7 Greek *circumcised*; also in verses 8 and 9   *e*9 Greek *Cephas*; also in verses 11 and 14

Discovering the Word 1. In 1:11–12 Paul claims he received the gospel from Jesus Christ, not people. How does his brief autobiography in 1:13–24 confirm this claim? 2. Paul obviously did not need human authorization to preach the gospel. Why then did he present his gospel to the leaders in Jerusalem (2:1–2)? 3. Why was it significant that Titus (a Gentile) was not compelled to be circumcised (the sign of becoming a Jew) (2:3–5)? 4. Paul refused to give in to false brothers on the matter of circumcision "so that the truth of the gospel might remain with you" (2:5). How do you show your concern to preserve the gospel? 5. How did the leaders in Jerusalem respond to Paul's message and ministry (2:6–10)?

Applying the Word 1. The apostles were not simply zealous to preserve the gospel. They also felt called to proclaim the gospel (2:7–10). To whom do you feel called to bring the gospel? 2. What step can you take this week to bring the good news to someone? 3. How can Paul's testimony in this passage increase our confidence in the truth of the gospel?

Responding in Prayer Ask God to help you be a bearer of the good news.

3 / *Galatians 2:11–21*
Accepting Others

HAVE YOU EVER felt like avoiding certain types of Christians? Perhaps you don't like their theology. You may disapprove of their lifestyle. Or you may prefer to avoid people of their race, nationality or economic background. This passage helps us see why such attitudes conflict with the basic message of the gospel.

 Warming Up to God We have been justified by faith and are no longer under the law. In this way we have been accepted by God. How does God's acceptance help you feel good about who you are?

 Read Galatians 2:11–21.

¹¹When Peter came to Antioch, I opposed him to his face, because he was clearly in the wrong. ¹²Before certain men came from James, he used to eat with the Gentiles. But when they arrived, he began to draw back and separate himself from the Gentiles because he was afraid of those who belonged to the circumcision group. ¹³The other Jews joined him in his hypocrisy, so that by their hypocrisy even Barnabas was led astray.

¹⁴When I saw that they were not acting in line with the truth of the gospel, I said to Peter in front of them all, "You are a Jew, yet you live like a Gentile and not like a Jew. How is it, then, that you force Gentiles to follow Jewish customs?

¹⁵"We who are Jews by birth and not 'Gentile sinners' ¹⁶know that a man is not justified by observing the law, but by faith in Jesus Christ. So we, too, have put our faith in Christ Jesus that we may be justified by faith in Christ and not by observing the law, because by observing the law no one will be justified.

¹⁷"If, while we seek to be justified in Christ, it becomes evident that we ourselves are sinners, does that mean that Christ promotes sin? Absolutely not! ¹⁸If I rebuild what I destroyed, I prove that I am a lawbreaker. ¹⁹For through the law I died to the law so that I might live for God. ²⁰I have been crucified with Christ and I no longer live, but Christ lives in me. The life I live in the body, I live by faith in the Son of God, who loved me and gave himself for me. ²¹I do not set aside the grace of God, for if righteousness could be gained through the law, Christ died for nothing!"ʃ

ʃ21 Some interpreters end the quotation after verse 14.

 Discovering the Word 1. How were Peter and the other Jews not "acting in line with the truth of the gospel" (vv. 11–14)? 2. How might their actions have forced "Gentiles to follow Jewish customs" (v. 14)? 3. Why is it wrong to make such customs a basis for fellowship (vv. 15–16)? 4. How does Paul refute the accusation that Christ promotes sin (vv. 17–19)? 5. How has Christ enabled us to die to the law and to live for God (v. 20)?

Applying the Word 1. What nonessential customs do Christians sometimes force on each other? (For example, certain ways of praying, certain dress at worship, certain lifestyle habits and so on.) 2. Which of these are you most likely to be concerned about? 3. How can God's acceptance of you help you to be more accepting of others?

Responding in Prayer Pray for discernment about your own attitudes toward others, asking God to make you more accepting.

4 / *Galatians 3:1–14*
Why God Accepts Us

WE ALL WANT to be accepted. We do everything we can to win people's approval and avoid their rejection. But if we work so hard to please people, then what about God? How can we possibly meet his standards? The Galatians felt these inner struggles. They wanted to be fully accepted by God. But they seemed to forget that God had already accepted them. They also forgot *why*.

 Warming Up to God When have you felt unacceptable to God recently? Describe your feelings to God. Listen for his reassurance.

 Read Galatians 3:1–14.

3 You foolish Galatians! Who has bewitched you? Before your very eyes Jesus Christ was clearly portrayed as crucified. ²I would like to learn just one thing from you: Did you receive the Spirit by observing the law, or by believing what you heard? ³Are you so foolish? After beginning with the Spirit, are you now trying to attain your goal by human effort? ⁴Have you suffered so much for nothing—if it really was for nothing? ⁵Does God give you his Spirit and work miracles among you because you observe the law, or because you believe what you heard?

⁶Consider Abraham: "He believed God, and it was credited to him as righteousness."ᵍ ⁷Understand, then, that those who believe are children of Abraham. ⁸The Scripture foresaw that God would justify the Gentiles by faith, and announced the gospel in advance to Abraham: "All nations will be blessed through you."ʰ ⁹So those who have faith are blessed along with Abraham, the man of faith.

¹⁰All who rely on observing the law are under a curse, for it is written: "Cursed is everyone who does not continue to do everything written in the Book of the Law."ⁱ ¹¹Clearly no one is justified before God by the law, because, "The righteous will live by faith."ʲ ¹²The law is not based on faith; on the contrary, "The man who does these things will live by them."ᵏ ¹³Christ redeemed us from the curse of the law by becoming a curse for us, for it is written: "Cursed is everyone who is hung on a tree."ˡ ¹⁴He redeemed us in order that the blessing given to Abraham might come to the Gentiles through Christ Jesus, so that by faith we might receive the promise of the Spirit.

ᵍ6 Gen. 15:6   *ʰ8* Gen. 12:3; 18:18; 22:18   *ⁱ10* Deut. 27:26
ʲ11 Hab. 2:4   *ᵏ12* Lev. 18:5   *ˡ13* Deut. 21:23

 Discovering the Word 1. From verses 1–5 try to reconstruct in chronological order the Galatians' spiritual biography. 2. In what ways did the Galatians' behavior seem "bewitched" and "foolish" according to verses 1–5? 3. When we follow the example of Abraham's faith, what are the results (vv. 6–9)? 4. How does Abraham's experience contrast with that of the person who seeks to earn God's acceptance (vv. 10–12)? 5. How does the gift of the Spirit affirm that God accepts us completely in Christ?

Applying the Word 1. In what ways do we sometimes try to earn God's favor by what we do? 2. How can a vivid image of Christ's crucifixion (v. 1) guard us from this warped way of thinking? 3. How have you been blessed by the Spirit's presence in your life?

Responding in Prayer Spend some time thanking God for what Christ has done for us as described in these verses.

5 / Galatians 3:15–29
Exposing Our Needs

"HONEY," JILL CALLED out, "you'd better call the repairman. Our TV is on the blink again."

"Who needs a repairman!" Ron replied confidently. "I can fix this myself."

Four hours later. "There, that should do it." As he plugs it in, there's a loud buzzing noise, smoke rises from the TV, the lights begin to flicker, then darkness blacks out the room.

"Uh . . . maybe you're right, dear," Ron said sheepishly. "I suppose calling a repairman couldn't hurt."

People must admit they need help before they can receive it. Yet often this is very difficult. In Galatians 3:15–29 Paul tells us how God exposes our need for Christ.

 Warming Up to God What needs are pressing on you right now? Give them to God one by one.

 Read Galatians 3:15–29.

---

¹⁵Brothers, let me take an example from everyday life. Just as no one can set aside or add to a human covenant that has been duly established, so it is in this case. ¹⁶The promises were spoken to Abraham and to his seed. The Scripture does not say "and to seeds," meaning many people, but "and to your seed,"ᵐ meaning one person, who is Christ. ¹⁷What I mean is this: The law, introduced 430 years later, does not set aside the covenant previously established by God and thus do away with the promise. ¹⁸For if the inheritance depends on the law, then it no longer depends on a promise; but God in his grace gave it to Abraham through a promise.

¹⁹What, then, was the purpose of the law? It was added because of transgressions until the Seed to whom the promise referred had come. The law was put into effect through angels by a mediator. ²⁰A mediator, however, does not represent just one party; but God is one.

²¹Is the law, therefore, opposed to the promises of God? Absolutely not! For if a law had been given that could impart life, then righteousness would certainly have come by the law. ²²But the Scripture declares that the whole world is a prisoner of sin, so that what was promised, being given through faith in Jesus Christ, might be given to those who believe.

²³Before this faith came, we were held prisoners by the law, locked up until faith should be revealed. ²⁴So the law was put in charge to lead us to Christⁿ that we might be justified by faith. ²⁵Now that faith has come, we are no longer under the supervision of the law.

²⁶You are all sons of God through faith in Christ Jesus, ²⁷for all of you who were baptized into Christ have clothed yourselves with Christ. ²⁸There is neither Jew nor Greek, slave nor free, male nor female, for you are all one in Christ Jesus. ²⁹If you belong to Christ, then you are Abraham's seed, and heirs according to the promise.

ᵐ16 Gen. 12:7; 13:15; 24:7   ⁿ24 Or charge until Christ came

 Discovering the Word 1. Why is the law unable to set aside or add to the promises spoken to Abraham (vv. 15–18)? 2. If the law did not set aside or add to the promises given to Abraham, then why was it given (vv. 19–25)? 3. How does a clear grasp of God's law help us to realize our need for Christ (vv. 22–25)? 4. In verse 28 Paul lists several ways in which people have been categorized. How have these categories sometimes functioned as barriers? 5. In light of the context, how have these barriers been broken down in Christ?

Applying the Word 1. When is it difficult for you to admit to God that you have a need or problem? 2. When is it difficult for you to ask others for help? 3. What would help you allow both God and others to help you?

Responding in Prayer Ask God to help you put aside your pride and expose your needs to him and to your Christian friends and church family.

6 / *Galatians 4:1–20*
The Joys of Growing Up

HAVE YOU EVER longed to be a child again—to be free from work, mortgage payments, bills and taxes? Remember the carefree days, when from morning till night your job was to play? The Galatians did. They longed to return to the spiritual childhood of the law. But aren't we forgetting something? Just think of all the things we *couldn't* do as children. In Galatians 4:1–20 Paul reminds us of the joys of growing up.

 Warming Up to God What is frustrating you today? Take time to journal or talk to God about how you are feeling and why. Work at it until your mind is clear and you are ready to study.

 Read Galatians 4:1–20.

4What I am saying is that as long as the heir is a child, he is no different from a slave, although he owns the whole estate. ²He is subject to guardians and trustees until the time set by his father. ³So also, when we were children, we were in slavery under the basic principles of the world. ⁴But when the time had fully come, God sent his Son, born of a woman, born under law, ⁵to redeem those under law, that we might receive the full rights of sons. ⁶Because you are sons, God sent the Spirit of his Son into our hearts, the Spirit who calls out, *"Abba,º* Father." ⁷So you are no longer a slave, but a son; and since you are a son, God has made you also an heir.

⁸Formerly, when you did not know God, you were slaves to those who by nature are not gods. ⁹But now that you know God—or rather are known by God—how is it that you are turning back to those weak and miserable principles? Do you wish to be enslaved by them all over again? ¹⁰You are observing special days and months and seasons and years! ¹¹I fear for you, that somehow I have wasted my efforts on you.

¹²I plead with you, brothers, become like me, for I became like you. You have done me no wrong. ¹³As you know, it was because of an illness that I first preached the gospel to you. ¹⁴Even though my illness was a trial to you, you did not treat me with contempt or scorn. Instead, you welcomed me as if I were an angel of God, as if I were Christ Jesus himself. ¹⁵What has happened to all your joy? I can testify that, if you could have done so, you would have torn out your eyes and given them to me. ¹⁶Have I now become your enemy by telling you the truth?

¹⁷Those people are zealous to win you over, but for no good. What they want is to alienate you ⌐from us⌐, so that you may be zealous for them. ¹⁸It is fine to be zealous, provided the purpose is good, and to be so always and not just when I am with you. ¹⁹My dear children, for whom I am again in the pains of childbirth until Christ is formed in you, ²⁰how I wish I could be with you now and change my tone, because I am perplexed about you!

º6 Aramaic for *Father*

 Discovering the Word 1. How was life under the law like spiritual childhood (vv. 3–7)? 2. Verse 4 states, "When the time had fully come, God sent his Son." How did things change because of his coming (vv. 4–7)? 3. In view of Paul's discussion in verses 1–7, how does the Galatians' behavior seem incredible (vv. 8–11)? 4. How and why had the Galatians' attitude toward Paul changed (vv. 12–20)? 5. What do these verses reveal about Paul's feelings toward the Galatians? 6. How do verses 12–20 illustrate the care and concern we should have for other members of God's family?

 Applying the Word 1. In what ways do you sometimes act like a spiritual slave? 2. How can you begin acting more like God's beloved son or daughter?

Responding in Prayer Spend a few minutes of intimate prayer with the Father, thanking him for the privileges of being a member of his family.

7 / *Galatians 4:21—5:1*
Do-It-Yourself Religion

TRUSTING GOD CAN seem risky. What if he lets us down? Still worse, what if our faith is simply foolishness? When such thoughts enter our minds, it's easy to panic. We are tempted to take back what we have entrusted to God. We feel safer taking matters into our own hands. Abraham felt these struggles while waiting for God's promise of a son. He rushed God's plan and had a son through his slave Hagar. Later, even though he and Sarah were very old, the promised son was born. This story has become a timeless illustration of do-it-yourself religion versus trust in the promises of God.

Warming Up to God What promises has God kept with you? Spend time in reflection, thanksgiving and worship.

Read Galatians 4:21—5:1.

21Tell me, you who want to be under the law,
are you not aware of what the law says? 22For it
is written that Abraham had two sons, one by the
slave woman and the other by the free woman.
23His son by the slave woman was born in the
ordinary way; but his son by the free woman was
born as the result of a promise.
24These things may be taken figuratively, for
the women represent two covenants. One covenant is from Mount Sinai and bears children
who are to be slaves: This is Hagar. 25Now Hagar
stands for Mount Sinai in Arabia and corresponds
to the present city of Jerusalem, because she is in
slavery with her children. 26But the Jerusalem
that is above is free, and she is our mother. 27For
it is written:

"Be glad, O barren woman,
who bears no children;
break forth and cry aloud,
you who have no labor pains;
because more are the children of the desolate
woman
than of her who has a husband."[p]

28Now you, brothers, like Isaac, are children of
promise. 29At that time the son born in the ordinary way persecuted the son born by the power of
the Spirit. It is the same now. 30But what does the
Scripture say? "Get rid of the slave woman and
her son, for the slave woman's son will never
share in the inheritance with the free woman's
son."[q] 31Therefore, brothers, we are not children
of the slave woman, but of the free woman.

5 It is for freedom that Christ has set us free. Stand firm, then, and do not let yourselves be burdened again by a yoke of slavery.

p27 Isaiah 54:1 q30 Gen. 21:10

Discovering the Word 1. What does Paul mean when he says that the son of the slave woman was born the "ordinary way" but the son of the free woman was "the result of a promise" (v. 23; see also v. 29)? 2. In verse 24 Paul says that the story of Hagar and Sarah may be understood "figuratively." What do Hagar, the covenant from Sinai and "the present city of Jerusalem" have in common (vv. 24–25)? 3. How is Sarah (who, although unnamed, is the other woman in the story) similar to the new covenant and to the Jerusalem that is above (vv. 26–27)? 4. How does Paul describe the ultimate fate of the slave woman's and the free woman's spiritual descendants (v. 30)? 5. In 5:1 Paul states that Christ set us free so that we could experience freedom! Given the thrust of Galatians 1—4, what does Paul mean when he says we are free?

Applying the Word 1. The spiritual principle described in this passage has broad application. Throughout Scripture God promises to accomplish that which we cannot do on our own. Think of Abraham, Moses, Joshua, Gideon, the apostles and others. In what areas are you trusting in the promises of God and the power of the Spirit to accomplish the extraordinary? 2. What are some present-day threats to our spiritual freedom? 3. What are some practical ways we can "stand firm" against them?

Responding in Prayer Ask God to help you stand against any threat to spiritual freedom in society and in your life.

8 / *Galatians 5:2–15*
Heavenly Help

"HELP!" THE MAN cried as he dangled helplessly from the edge of a cliff. "Can anyone up there help me?"
"Yes," answered a heavenly voice, "I'll help you. But first you must let go."
"Let go!" gasped the man. "But then I'd fall!"
"I'll catch you," replied the voice.
There was a long pause, then the man cried out, "Can anyone *else* up there help me?"
If we want Christ to save us, we must let go of the idea that we can save ourselves—even a little.

 Warming Up to God In what area of your life are you ignoring the help that God is offering? Humble yourself before the Lord as you give him this area of concern.

 Read Galatians 5:2–15.

²Mark my words! I, Paul, tell you that if you let yourselves be circumcised, Christ will be of no value to you at all. ³Again I declare to every man who lets himself be circumcised that he is obligated to obey the whole law. ⁴You who are trying to be justified by law have been alienated from Christ; you have fallen away from grace. ⁵But by faith we eagerly await through the Spirit the righteousness for which we hope. ⁶For in Christ Jesus neither circumcision nor uncircumcision has any value. The only thing that counts is faith expressing itself through love.

⁷You were running a good race. Who cut in on you and kept you from obeying the truth? ⁸That kind of persuasion does not come from the one who calls you. ⁹"A little yeast works through the whole batch of dough." ¹⁰I am confident in the Lord that you will take no other view. The one who is throwing you into confusion will pay the penalty, whoever he may be. ¹¹Brothers, if I am still preaching circumcision, why am I still being persecuted? In that case the offense of the cross has been abolished. ¹²As for those agitators, I wish they would go the whole way and emasculate themselves!

¹³You, my brothers, were called to be free. But do not use your freedom to indulge the sinful nature*ʳ*; rather, serve one another in love. ¹⁴The entire law is summed up in a single command: "Love your neighbor as yourself."*ˢ* ¹⁵If you keep on biting and devouring each other, watch out or you will be destroyed by each other.

ʳ13 Or the flesh; also in verses 16, 17, 19 and 24   ˢ14 Lev. 19:18

 Discovering the Word 1. What were the Judaizers (those preaching against Paul) urging the Galatians to do and why (vv. 2–4)? 2. In verses 2–4 Paul gave stern warnings to those who desired to be circumcised. Now he says, "neither circumcision nor uncircumcision has any value" (v. 6). How can both of these views be true? 3. Paul compares the Galatians to runners in a race and to a batch of dough (vv. 7–9). How do these comparisons illustrate the nature and perils of the Christian life? 4. In verses 10–12 Paul makes some severe statements about those who are troubling the Galatians (especially v. 12!). Even by today's standards they are harsh. Why was he so upset? 5. What is the difference between the two concepts of freedom described in verses 13–14?

Applying the Word 1. Are you running the good race? In what area do you need to ask God to help you stay on track? 2. When have you "cut in on" someone and kept them from "obeying the truth" (v. 7)? 3. How can you encourage someone you know to stay in the race?

Responding in Prayer Ask God to help you be both a good runner and a good companion in the race.

9 / Galatians 5:16–26
Living by the Spirit

IF CHRIST HAS set us free, then why not live as we please? Why not grab all the money, sex and power we can get? Afterward, we can simply ask for forgiveness! Paul challenges this kind of thinking with the true meaning of Christian freedom.

 Warming Up to God Spend some time in quiet before the Lord, opening yourself to what he wants to say to you in prayer and through the Scripture.

 Read Galatians 5:16–26.

¹⁶So I say, live by the Spirit, and you will not gratify the desires of the sinful nature. ¹⁷For the sinful nature desires what is contrary to the Spirit, and the Spirit what is contrary to the sinful nature. They are in conflict with each other, so that you do not do what you want. ¹⁸But if you are led by the Spirit, you are not under law.

¹⁹The acts of the sinful nature are obvious: sexual immorality, impurity and debauchery; ²⁰idolatry and witchcraft; hatred, discord, jealousy, fits of rage, selfish ambition, dissensions, factions ²¹and envy; drunkenness, orgies, and the like. I warn you, as I did before, that those who live like this will not inherit the kingdom of God.

²²But the fruit of the Spirit is love, joy, peace, patience, kindness, goodness, faithfulness, ²³gentleness and self-control. Against such things there is no law. ²⁴Those who belong to Christ Jesus have crucified the sinful nature with its passions and desires. ²⁵Since we live by the Spirit, let us keep in step with the Spirit. ²⁶Let us not become conceited, provoking and envying each other.

 Discovering the Word 1. What does it mean to "live by the Spirit" (v. 16)? 2. How is being led by the Spirit different from living under law (v. 18)? 3. Why is it so easy to recognize the acts of the sinful nature (vv. 19–21)? 4. How can Paul's warning in verse 21 be reconciled with his emphasis on justification by faith? 5. Why is *fruit* a good description of the Spirit's work in us (vv. 22–23)?

 Applying the Word 1. Paul assumes that even though all Christians live by the Spirit, we do not always keep in step with the Spirit (vv. 25–26). In what ways do you struggle to keep in step with the Spirit? 2. In what ways do you see the Spirit's fruit ripening in your life? 3. What fruit would you like to cultivate more?

 Responding in Prayer Spend time thanking God for the Spirit's work in your life. Pray for the Spirit's help in those areas where you feel out of step.

10 / Galatians 6:1–10
The Law of Love

THE FRUIT OF the Spirit is most clearly demonstrated in our relationships with others. They are a visible and practical measure of our spirituality. In this passage Paul describes how we should relate to the family of believers and to all people.

 Warming Up to God This is a passage about relationships. Who are you having difficulty loving right now? Talk to God about it.

Read Galatians 6:1–10.

6 Brothers, if someone is caught in a sin, you who are spiritual should restore him gently. But watch yourself, or you also may be tempted. ²Carry each other's burdens, and in this way you will fulfill the law of Christ. ³If anyone thinks he is something when he is nothing, he deceives himself. ⁴Each one should test his own actions. Then he can take pride in himself, without comparing himself to somebody else, ⁵for each one should carry his own load.

⁶Anyone who receives instruction in the word must share all good things with his instructor.

⁷Do not be deceived: God cannot be mocked. A man reaps what he sows. ⁸The one who sows to please his sinful nature, from that nature ͭ will reap destruction; the one who sows to please the Spirit, from the Spirit will reap eternal life. ⁹Let us not become weary in doing good, for at the proper time we will reap a harvest if we do not give up. ¹⁰Therefore, as we have opportunity, let us do good to all people, especially to those who belong to the family of believers.

ͭ8 Or his flesh, from the flesh

Discovering the Word 1. What guidelines does Paul offer for dealing with a person who is "caught in a sin," and why is each important (v. 1)? 2. How does the law of Christ (v. 2) differ from the kind of law-keeping urged by Paul's opponents? 3. The sins or burdens of others can lead us to feel superior. How can proper methods of self-examination correct this attitude (vv. 3–5)? 4. What other application of the principle of sowing and reaping does Paul make in verses 9 and 10?

Applying the Word 1. What burdens are people you know carrying? 2. What are some ways you can help a friend carry these? 3. What are one or two new ways you could begin sowing to please the Spirit (a) personally, (b) in relationships with other Christians and (c) in relationships with non-Christians?

Responding in Prayer Ask God to help you "do good to all people," especially to those in the family of God.

---

11 / *Galatians 6:11–18*
Getting Motivated

PEER PRESSURE CAN exert a powerful influence on us. The style of our clothes, the kind of music we listen to, our vocabulary, even the soft drinks we buy are affected by what others do and say. We are often tempted to change our behavior so others will accept us. But such approval can have a high price tag. In this final passage Paul helps us to consider whose approval we desire most.

 Warming Up to God In what areas are you feeling cultural pressure? Consider work, family, Christian and non-Christian friendships, how you dress, what you do or don't buy and so on. Bring each of these pressures to God.

 Read Galatians 6:11–18.

---

¹¹See what large letters I use as I write to you with my own hand!

¹²Those who want to make a good impression outwardly are trying to compel you to be circumcised. The only reason they do this is to avoid being persecuted for the cross of Christ. ¹³Not even those who are circumcised obey the law, yet they want you to be circumcised that they may boast about your flesh. ¹⁴May I never boast except

in the cross of our Lord Jesus Christ, through which ͧ the world has been crucified to me, and I to the world. ¹⁵Neither circumcision nor uncircumcision means anything; what counts is a new creation. ¹⁶Peace and mercy to all who follow this rule, even to the Israel of God.

ͧ14 Or whom

¹⁷Finally, let no one cause me trouble, for I bear on my body the marks of Jesus.

¹⁸The grace of our Lord Jesus Christ be with your spirit, brothers. Amen.

 Discovering the Word 1. What do verses 12–13 reveal about the motives of Paul's opponents? 2. How will boasting in the cross affect our desire for the world's approval (v. 14)? 3. Why does the new creation have value in contrast to the worthlessness of circumcision or uncircumcision (v. 15)? 4. In Paul's closing blessing and benediction he mentions peace, mercy and the grace of our Lord Jesus Christ (vv. 16, 18). Why is each of these appropriate for those who follow the "rule" of verses 14–15?

Applying the Word 1. In what situations are you tempted to hide your Christianity in order to "make a good impression outwardly"? 2. Paul bore on his body the marks of Jesus (the evidence of faithful service). What are the "marks of Jesus" in your life? 3. How has this passage helped to purify your motives and goals in life?

Responding in Prayer Ask God to make the "marks of Jesus" more evident in your life.

Ephesians

L et's face it. Most of us are problem centered. How will I get all my work done on time? What can I do to be a better witness? Why do I get angry so easily?

Solving all these problems is good. But so often we lack a broader perspective. We put Band-Aids over gaping wounds instead of looking for long-term solutions. We lack vision, so we fail to ask why we are involved in certain activities at all.

I have enjoyed going back again and again to Paul's letter to the Ephesians because it communicates the Christian vision more powerfully and succinctly than any of his other letters. Most of Paul's other letters are directed to the particular problems of a given church. For example, he wrote to the Galatians about the threat of legalism. He addressed a variety of problems at the church at Corinth. But his letter to the Ephesians is blissfully free from turmoil.

Some believe the letter has this quality because it was not written solely for the church at Ephesus. Rather, it was probably a circular letter sent to the Christian communities of Asia and other provinces, especially where Paul was not personally known. While most of his letters are full of personal greetings, no individuals are mentioned here or greeted by name. In fact some early manuscripts even lack the words "in Ephesus" (1:1). They are addressed generally "to the saints who are also faithful in Christ Jesus." But at an early date the letter became associated with the Ephesian church, so most later manuscripts have "to the saints in Ephesus, the faithful in Christ Jesus."

Ultimately, however, this letter is written to us, whoever the original readers were. It enables us to see the full sweep of God's program from before creation to the ultimate union of everyone and everything in Jesus Christ. It puts our problems and our entire lives in the context of eternity.

May Ephesians expand your vision of what God is doing in history and give you wholeness in this broken world.

Outline

1 / *Ephesians 1:1–14*
The Purpose of God

WE HAVE A love-hate relationship with God's will. We dearly want to discover it and obey it, to be secure in knowing we are following the path he desires. On the other hand, we definitely don't want to find out what he wants, because deep down we suspect it may not be to our liking. In this study, we'll see what Paul says about God's will.

 Warming Up to God Reflect on the ways that God has revealed his will to you over the course of your life. What patterns do you see? Thank God for his guidance.

 Read Ephesians 1:1–14.

1 Paul, an apostle of Christ Jesus by the will of God,

To the saints in Ephesus,*a* the faithful*b* in Christ Jesus:

²Grace and peace to you from God our Father and the Lord Jesus Christ.

³Praise be to the God and Father of our Lord Jesus Christ, who has blessed us in the heavenly realms with every spiritual blessing in Christ. ⁴For he chose us in him before the creation of the world to be holy and blameless in his sight. In love ⁵he*c* predestined us to be adopted as his sons through Jesus Christ, in accordance with his pleasure and will— ⁶to the praise of his glorious grace, which he has freely given us in the One he loves. ⁷In him we have redemption through his blood, the forgiveness of sins, in accordance with the riches of God's grace ⁸that he lavished on us with all wisdom and understanding. ⁹And he*d*

made known to us the mystery of his will according to his good pleasure, which he purposed in Christ, ¹⁰to be put into effect when the times will have reached their fulfillment—to bring all things in heaven and on earth together under one head, even Christ.

¹¹In him we were also chosen,*e* having been predestined according to the plan of him who works out everything in conformity with the purpose of his will, ¹²in order that we, who were the first to hope in Christ, might be for the praise of his glory. ¹³And you also were included in Christ when you heard the word of truth, the gospel of your salvation. Having believed, you were marked in him with a seal, the promised Holy Spirit, ¹⁴who is a deposit guaranteeing our inheritance until the redemption of those who are God's possession—to the praise of his glory.

a1 Some early manuscripts do not have *in Ephesus.*   *b1* Or *believers who are*   *c4,5* Or *sight in love.* 5*He*   *d8,9* Or *us. With all wisdom and understanding,* 9*he*   *e11* Or *were made heirs*

 Discovering the Word 1. According to verses 3–6, what blessings are ours from the Father? 2. What other blessings, according to verses 7–12, do we have in Jesus Christ? 3. From the information given in 1:1–14 alone, try to formulate a clear statement of what it means to be chosen by God. 4. What additional blessings do we receive through the Holy Spirit (vv. 13–14)? 5. What does it mean to live "to the praise of his glory" (vv. 6, 12, 14)?

Applying the Word 1. How do you respond emotionally to knowing you are chosen by God? 2. How has this passage increased your sense of participation in God's total purpose for the universe? 3. How could your life be more in keeping with the phrase "to the praise of his glory"?

Responding in Prayer Spend time in praise to the God and Father of our Lord Jesus Christ who has blessed us with every spiritual blessing.

2 / Ephesians 1:15–23
"I Keep Asking"

SOMETIMES PRAYER CAN be like pushing a full wheelbarrow—with no wheel. At other times it's like rushing down the rapids of a mountain river. What makes the difference? In this passage, we'll see why Paul's prayers overflow with praise and thanksgiving.

 Warming Up to God Talk to God about the times prayer was hard for you. Describe your disappointment or pain. Take time to allow him to listen to you fully.

 Read Ephesians 1:15–23.

---

¹⁵For this reason, ever since I heard about your faith in the Lord Jesus and your love for all the saints, ¹⁶I have not stopped giving thanks for you, remembering you in my prayers. ¹⁷I keep asking that the God of our Lord Jesus Christ, the glorious Father, may give you the Spirit^f of wisdom and revelation, so that you may know him better. ¹⁸I pray also that the eyes of your heart may be enlightened in order that you may know the hope to which he has called you, the riches of his glorious inheritance in the saints, ¹⁹and his incomparably great power for us who believe. That power is like the working of his mighty strength, ²⁰which he exerted in Christ when he raised him from the dead and seated him at his right hand in the heavenly realms, ²¹far above all rule and authority, power and dominion, and every title that can be given, not only in the present age but also in the one to come. ²²And God placed all things under his feet and appointed him to be head over everything for the church, ²³which is his body, the fullness of him who fills everything in every way.

f17 Or *a spirit*

 **Discovering the Word** 1. How do Paul's prayers for his readers throughout this passage cover the past, the present and the future? 2. How does Paul emphasize the tremendous power available "for us who believe" (v. 19)? 3. How do verses 20–23 expand on Paul's discussion of Christ's headship begun in verses 9–10? 4. How is the church, the body of believers, central to God's plans for the universe (vv. 22–23)?

 Applying the Word 1. When you pray for fellow Christians, how do you usually pray for them? 2. In what ways would you like your prayers to be more like Paul's? 3. How could you make the church a more central part of your life?

 Responding in Prayer Pray for Christ's church and individuals in your church, following Paul's example.

---

3 / Ephesians 2:1–10
Amazing Grace

ONE OF THE best-known verses in the book of Ephesians is 2:8, "By grace you have been saved, through faith." Grace has often been defined by the acrostic God's Riches At Christ's Expense. With this passage, we'll consider some of the riches we have been given in Christ.

 Warming Up to God Focus on God's graciousness to you in the past days, weeks and months. Allow yourself to experience the depth of his goodness. Respond to him in prayer and praise.

Read Ephesians 2:1–10.

2 As for you, you were dead in your transgressions and sins, [2]in which you used to live when you followed the ways of this world and of the ruler of the kingdom of the air, the spirit who is now at work in those who are disobedient. [3]All of us also lived among them at one time, gratifying the cravings of our sinful natureᵍ and following its desires and thoughts. Like the rest, we were by nature objects of wrath. [4]But because of his great love for us, God, who is rich in mercy, [5]made us alive with Christ even when we were dead in transgressions—it is by grace you have been saved. [6]And God raised us up with Christ and seated us with him in the heavenly realms in Christ Jesus, [7]in order that in the coming ages he might show the incomparable riches of his grace, expressed in his kindness to us in Christ Jesus. [8]For it is by grace you have been saved, through faith—and this not from yourselves, it is the gift of God— [9]not by works, so that no one can boast. [10]For we are God's workmanship, created in Christ Jesus to do good works, which God prepared in advance for us to do.

ᵍ3 Or *our flesh*

Discovering the Word   1. In verse 1 Paul says, "You were dead in your transgressions and sins." How does sin kill?   2. In verses 2–3 Paul mentions three negative influences on our lives, which the church later put into the formula of "the world, the flesh and the devil." According to Paul, how did each of these affect our lives as non-Christians?   3. What does Paul mean when he says we have been "made alive," "raised" and "seated" with Christ (vv. 5–6)?   4. When Paul says that our salvation is not from ourselves (vv. 8–9), is he saying that we play no role in our salvation? Explain.   5. What do you learn about God's grace from verses 4–10?

Applying the Word   1. What good works has God prepared you to do?   2. What has hindered you from doing these?

Responding in Prayer   Thank God specifically for some of the many ways he has been gracious to you. Ask him to remove the barriers to the good works he has created for you to do.

---

4 / *Ephesians 2:11–22*
We Are One

MANY OF US have sung, "We are one in the Spirit; we are one in the Lord." But we also continue to find ourselves at odds with Christians who believe or live differently than we do. Such problems were just as common in Paul's day as in ours.

 Warming Up to God   Consider what groups of Christians you disagree with or have trouble getting along with. Reflect on what causes these tensions. Ask God to open your mind and heart so that you can develop understanding.

 Read Ephesians 2:11–22.

---

[11]Therefore, remember that formerly you who are Gentiles by birth and called "uncircumcised" by those who call themselves "the circumcision" (that done in the body by the hands of men)— [12]remember that at that time you were separate from Christ, excluded from citizenship in Israel and foreigners to the covenants of the promise, without hope and without God in the world. [13]But now in Christ Jesus you who once were far away have been brought near through the blood of Christ.

[14]For he himself is our peace, who has made the two one and has destroyed the barrier, the dividing wall of hostility, [15]by abolishing in his flesh the law with its commandments and regulations. His purpose was to create in himself one new man out of the two, thus making peace, [16]and in this one body to reconcile both of them

to God through the cross, by which he put to death their hostility. [17]He came and preached peace to you who were far away and peace to those who were near. [18]For through him we both have access to the Father by one Spirit.

[19]Consequently, you are no longer foreigners and aliens, but fellow citizens with God's people and members of God's household, [20]built on the foundation of the apostles and prophets, with Christ Jesus himself as the chief cornerstone. [21]In him the whole building is joined together and rises to become a holy temple in the Lord. [22]And in him you too are being built together to become a dwelling in which God lives by his Spirit.

Discovering the Word   1. Paul uses vivid imagery in this passage. What are some of these images?   2. What divided Gentiles from Jews (vv. 11–13)?   3. How are the two reconciliations Christ achieves related (vv. 14–18)?   4. How do the images Paul uses in verses 19–22 emphasize the unity Christians have with one another?

Applying the Word   1. What kinds of name-calling (perhaps even using biblical terms) do Christians in your church engage in?   2. What rules and requirements would you be inclined to enforce (like the law in verse 15) that might hinder people from coming into the kingdom?   3. What practical first step toward unity with another Christian can you take in the next week?

Responding in Prayer   Pray for unity in the church, that people would not be turned away from Christ by Christians who don't get along with each other.

---

5 / *Ephesians 3*
Prisoner and Preacher

WHAT DO YOU think of when you hear the word *church*? A building on the corner? A stuffy group of religious hypocrites? A vibrant fellowship? Paul's special ministry enables him to enlarge our conception of the church. In this passage he clarifies and exalts its place in God's plan.

Warming Up to God   When have you had a particularly powerful experience in the church? It might have been worship, teaching or fellowship. Reflect on what made it special and thank God for it.

Read Ephesians 3.

---

3 For this reason I, Paul, the prisoner of Christ Jesus for the sake of you Gentiles—

[2]Surely you have heard about the administration of God's grace that was given to me for you, [3]that is, the mystery made known to me by revelation, as I have already written briefly. [4]In reading this, then, you will be able to understand my insight into the mystery of Christ, [5]which was not made known to men in other generations as it has now been revealed by the Spirit to God's holy apostles and prophets. [6]This mystery is that through the gospel the Gentiles are heirs together with Israel, members together of one body, and sharers together in the promise in Christ Jesus.

[7]I became a servant of this gospel by the gift of God's grace given me through the working of his power. [8]Although I am less than the least of all God's people, this grace was given me: to preach to the Gentiles the unsearchable riches of Christ, [9]and to make plain to everyone the administration of this mystery, which for ages past was kept hidden in God, who created all things. [10]His intent was that now, through the church, the manifold wisdom of God should be made known to the rulers and authorities in the heavenly realms, [11]according to his eternal purpose which he accomplished in Christ Jesus our Lord. [12]In him and through faith in him we may approach God with freedom and confidence. [13]I ask you, therefore, not to be discouraged because of my sufferings for you, which are your glory.

¹⁴For this reason I kneel before the Father, ¹⁵from whom his whole family[h] in heaven and on earth derives its name. ¹⁶I pray that out of his glorious riches he may strengthen you with power through his Spirit in your inner being, ¹⁷so that Christ may dwell in your hearts through faith. And I pray that you, being rooted and established in love, ¹⁸may have power, together with all the saints, to grasp how wide and long and high and deep is the love of Christ, ¹⁹and to know this love that surpasses knowledge—that you may be filled to the measure of all the fullness of God.

²⁰Now to him who is able to do immeasurably more than all we ask or imagine, according to his power that is at work within us, ²¹to him be glory in the church and in Christ Jesus throughout all generations, for ever and ever! Amen.

[h]15 Or whom all fatherhood

Discovering the Word 1. What gifts of God's grace does Paul say he has received (vv. 2–3, 8)? 2. Explain the meaning of the mystery revealed to Paul (vv. 2–6). 3. How is the mystery connected with the ministry given to him (vv. 7–13)? 4. Three times in verses 14–21 Paul mentions "love" and "power." What do we learn about power and love in these verses? 5. How does the benediction in verses 20–21 tie together the main themes that have run through the first three chapters of Ephesians?

Applying the Word 1. What is your attitude toward the church? 2. What about your attitude matches Paul's? 3. What about your attitude would you like to change?

Responding in Prayer Choose at least one item from Paul's prayer and make it a prayer of your own, for yourself and your church.

---

6 / *Ephesians 4:1–16*
Unity and Uniqueness

WHILE EPHESIANS 1—3 provides a doctrinal foundation, Ephesians 4—6 shows in practical detail how to give glory to God in the church. Paul now considers the quality of life that is demanded of believers individually and in the fellowship of Christ's church.

 Warming Up to God Ephesians 4:2 reads, "Be completely humble and gentle; be patient, bearing with one another in love." Reflect on these words. Measure your recent behavior against them. Talk to God about what you discover.

 Read Ephesians 4:1–16.

---

4 As a prisoner for the Lord, then, I urge you to live a life worthy of the calling you have received. ²Be completely humble and gentle; be patient, bearing with one another in love. ³Make every effort to keep the unity of the Spirit through the bond of peace. ⁴There is one body and one Spirit—just as you were called to one hope when you were called— ⁵one Lord, one faith, one baptism; ⁶one God and Father of all, who is over all and through all and in all.

⁷But to each one of us grace has been given as Christ apportioned it. ⁸This is why it[i] says:

"When he ascended on high,

he led captives in his train
and gave gifts to men."[j]

⁹(What does "he ascended" mean except that he also descended to the lower, earthly regions[k]? ¹⁰He who descended is the very one who ascended higher than all the heavens, in order to fill the whole universe.) ¹¹It was he who gave some to be apostles, some to be prophets, some to be evangelists, and some to be pastors and teachers, ¹²to prepare God's people for works of service, so that the body of Christ may be built up ¹³until we all reach unity in the faith and in the knowledge

[i]8 Or God   [j]8 Psalm 68:18   [k]9 Or the depths of the earth

of the Son of God and become mature, attaining to the whole measure of the fullness of Christ.

¹⁴Then we will no longer be infants, tossed back and forth by the waves, and blown here and there by every wind of teaching and by the cunning and craftiness of men in their deceitful scheming. ¹⁵Instead, speaking the truth in love, we will in all things grow up into him who is the Head, that is, Christ. ¹⁶From him the whole body, joined and held together by every supporting ligament, grows and builds itself up in love, as each part does its work.

Discovering the Word 1. What are the characteristics of a life that is worthy of our calling (vv. 1–3)? 2. Paul says we have one body, one Spirit, one hope, one Lord, one faith, one baptism, and one God and Father of all. How do these seven "ones" contribute to actually living out true unity? 3. In verses 8–10 Christ is compared to a conquering hero whose victory parade fills "the whole universe," from the highest heaven to the lowest earth. He then generously distributes gifts (the spoils of victory) to his loyal followers. What is the nature and purpose of these gifts (vv. 11–13)? 4. How does spiritual infancy differ from spiritual maturity (vv. 14–16)?

Applying the Word 1. What spiritual gifts do you think you might have? 2. How do they fulfill the purposes described in verses 11–13? 3. In verse 16 Paul says that the body "grows and builds itself up in love, as each part does its work." What steps must you take to more fully work toward this goal?

Responding in Prayer Pray that your spiritual gifts will be used to help others grow in Christ and to build the church.

---

7 / *Ephesians 4:17–32*
Something Old, Something New

ALREADY AND NOT YET. That's how we experience Christ. Already we have come out of spiritual darkness and into his light. Already we have received his grace and come to know him. But not yet do we live completely the way God wants. We have not yet arrived. Still, Jesus is right beside us on this journey.

Warming Up to God When have you felt that you were lost in the darkness? What brought you into the light? Spend time praising God for his redemption.

Read Ephesians 4:17–32.

---

¹⁷So I tell you this, and insist on it in the Lord, that you must no longer live as the Gentiles do, in the futility of their thinking. ¹⁸They are darkened in their understanding and separated from the life of God because of the ignorance that is in them due to the hardening of their hearts. ¹⁹Having lost all sensitivity, they have given themselves over to sensuality so as to indulge in every kind of impurity, with a continual lust for more.

²⁰You, however, did not come to know Christ that way. ²¹Surely you heard of him and were taught in him in accordance with the truth that is in Jesus. ²²You were taught, with regard to your former way of life, to put off your old self, which is being corrupted by its deceitful desires; ²³to be made new in the attitude of your minds; ²⁴and to put on the new self, created to be like God in true righteousness and holiness.

²⁵Therefore each of you must put off falsehood and speak truthfully to his neighbor, for we are all members of one body. ²⁶"In your anger do not sin"ˡ: Do not let the sun go down while you are still angry, ²⁷and do not give the devil a foothold. ²⁸He who has been stealing must steal no longer, but must work, doing something useful with his own hands, that he may have something to share with those in need.

²⁹Do not let any unwholesome talk come out of your mouths, but only what is helpful for building others up according to their needs, that it may benefit those who listen. ³⁰And do not grieve the

ˡ26 Psalm 4:4

Holy Spirit of God, with whom you were sealed for the day of redemption. ³¹Get rid of all bitterness, rage and anger, brawling and slander, along with every form of malice. ³²Be kind and compassionate to one another, forgiving each other, just as in Christ God forgave you.

 Discovering the Word 1. How does Paul contrast the life of the Gentile (unbeliever) with that of a true believer throughout these verses? 2. What are the effects of hard-heartedness (vv. 17–19)? 3. What does it mean to put off the old self (v. 22)? 4. In verses 25–32 what does Paul tell us to put off, what does he say to put on and what reason does he give (or imply) for doing these things?

 Applying the Word 1. Which of the commands in verses 25–32 do you have the most difficulty following? Explain. 2. What practical steps could you take this week to improve your relationships with others in this area of difficulty? 3. Which of the commands in verses 25–32 have you seen God strengthen you to obey?

 Responding in Prayer Spend time praising God for his work in your life, and pray that he will give you grace in the areas needing improvement.

---

8 / *Ephesians 5:1–20*
Live in Love, Live in Light

NOT DOING WHAT is wrong is one thing. But sometimes it can be even more difficult to do what is right. In Ephesians 5 Paul continues to outline what it means "to live a life worthy of the calling you have received" (4:1). He does this by considering ways we shouldn't act and ways we should.

 Warming Up to God Spend some time singing and making music in your heart to the Lord with "psalms, hymns and spiritual songs" (5:19).

Read Ephesians 5:1–20.

---

5 Be imitators of God, therefore, as dearly loved children ²and live a life of love, just as Christ loved us and gave himself up for us as a fragrant offering and sacrifice to God.

³But among you there must not be even a hint of sexual immorality, or of any kind of impurity, or of greed, because these are improper for God's holy people. ⁴Nor should there be obscenity, foolish talk or coarse joking, which are out of place, but rather thanksgiving. ⁵For of this you can be sure: No immoral, impure or greedy person—such a man is an idolater—has any inheritance in the kingdom of Christ and of God.ᵐ ⁶Let no one deceive you with empty words, for because of such things God's wrath comes on those who are disobedient. ⁷Therefore do not be partners with them.

⁸For you were once darkness, but now you are light in the Lord. Live as children of light ⁹(for the fruit of the light consists in all goodness, righteousness and truth) ¹⁰and find out what pleases the Lord. ¹¹Have nothing to do with the fruitless deeds of darkness, but rather expose them. ¹²For it is shameful even to mention what the disobedient do in secret. ¹³But everything exposed by the light becomes visible, ¹⁴for it is light that makes everything visible. This is why it is said:

"Wake up, O sleeper,
  rise from the dead,
and Christ will shine on you."

¹⁵Be very careful, then, how you live—not as unwise but as wise, ¹⁶making the most of every opportunity, because the days are evil. ¹⁷Therefore do not be foolish, but understand what the Lord's will is. ¹⁸Do not get drunk on wine, which leads to debauchery. Instead, be filled with the Spirit. ¹⁹Speak to one another with psalms,

ᵐ5 Or *kingdom of the Christ and God*

hymns and spiritual songs. Sing and make music in your heart to the Lord, ²⁰always giving thanks to God the Father for everything, in the name of our Lord Jesus Christ.

 Discovering the Word 1. How is Christ the perfect example of what Paul asks of us (v. 2)? 2. How is thanksgiving an appropriate replacement for the behavior Paul condemns in verses 2–4? 3. Why will immoral, impure or greedy people be unable to inherit the kingdom (vv. 5–7)? 4. In verses 8–14 Paul contrasts light and darkness to say more about holy living. According to these verses, what does it mean to "live as children of light"? 5. Verses 19–20 describe several beneficial results of being filled with the Spirit. In your own words, explain the characteristics of those who are filled with the Spirit.

 Applying the Word 1. Look again at verses 1–2. What have you observed about God that you have begun or could begin to imitate? 2. Looking again at verses 3–4, how could you use thanksgiving to replace improper behavior in your life? 3. According to the characteristics in verses 15–17, how could you live more wisely?

 Responding in Prayer Talk to God as a child to a father. Tell him how you would like to imitate him.

9 / *Ephesians 5:21–33*
Wives and Husbands

A LOT OF emotion and misunderstanding surrounds the word *submit*. So try to come to this text as if you had never seen it before. Try to set aside your own biases and see what Paul really has to say on the subject of submission.

Warming Up to God How has God shown you that he is faithful and trustworthy? Express your thanksgiving for his care.

Read Ephesians 5:21–33.

²¹Submit to one another out of reverence for Christ.

²²Wives, submit to your husbands as to the Lord. ²³For the husband is the head of the wife as Christ is the head of the church, his body, of which he is the Savior. ²⁴Now as the church submits to Christ, so also wives should submit to their husbands in everything.

²⁵Husbands, love your wives, just as Christ loved the church and gave himself up for her ²⁶to make her holy, cleansing[n] her by the washing with water through the word, ²⁷and to present her to himself as a radiant church, without stain or wrinkle or any other blemish, but holy and blameless. ²⁸In this same way, husbands ought to love their wives as their own bodies. He who loves his wife loves himself. ²⁹After all, no one ever hated his own body, but he feeds and cares for it, just as Christ does the church— ³⁰for we are members of his body. ³¹"For this reason a man will leave his father and mother and be united to his wife, and the two will become one flesh."[o] ³²This is a profound mystery—but I am talking about Christ and the church. ³³However, each one of you also must love his wife as he loves himself, and the wife must respect her husband.

[n] 26 Or *having cleansed*   [o] 31 Gen. 2:24

 Discovering the Word 1. How does verse 21 set the tone for this passage? 2. Why is the church's submission to the Lord a helpful illustration of a wife's submission to her husband (vv. 22–24)? 3. How are husbands to show love for their wives (vv. 25–30)? 4. Why do you think Paul calls on wives to respect their husbands while he calls on husbands to love their wives (v. 33)? **5.** How do verses 31–33 summarize his teaching on the unity that is to exist between wives and husbands?

 Applying the Word 1. How do you react to the idea of being told to submit to someone? **2.** If you are married, how would you like to grow in your ability to love and submit to your spouse? **3.** Whether you are married or single, how would you like to grow in your submission to Christ?

 Responding in Prayer Tell Christ how you would like to more fully submit your life to him.

10 / *Ephesians 6:1–9*
Children, Parents, Slaves, Masters

HOW MUCH OUR parents mean to us—yet how difficult they can be! How much we love our children—yet how exasperating they are at times! In nine packed verses Paul delves not only into these important relationships but into those of the work world as well.

 Warming Up to God Reflect on the finest qualities of your parents (or of parenting in general). Consider which of these qualities you have experienced in your relationship with God and thank him.

 Read Ephesians 6:1–9.

6 Children, obey your parents in the Lord, for this is right. ²"Honor your father and mother"—which is the first commandment with a promise— ³"that it may go well with you and that you may enjoy long life on the earth."ᵖ

⁴Fathers, do not exasperate your children; instead, bring them up in the training and instruction of the Lord.

⁵Slaves, obey your earthly masters with respect and fear, and with sincerity of heart, just as you would obey Christ. ⁶Obey them not only to win their favor when their eye is on you, but like slaves of Christ, doing the will of God from your heart. ⁷Serve wholeheartedly, as if you were serving the Lord, not men, ⁸because you know that the Lord will reward everyone for whatever good he does, whether he is slave or free.

⁹And masters, treat your slaves in the same way. Do not threaten them, since you know that he who is both their Master and yours is in heaven, and there is no favoritism with him.

ᵖ3 Deut. 5:16

 Discovering the Word 1. What reasons are given for obeying and honoring parents (vv. 1–3)? **2.** Why does Paul contrast making children exasperated with bringing "them up in the training and instruction of the Lord" (v. 4)? **3.** What is implied about the way slaves normally worked for their masters (vv. 5–8)? **4.** Paul says masters should treat slaves the way slaves should treat masters because both have the same Master in heaven. Why should this make a difference in how slaves are treated? **5.** How do verses 1–9 contribute to the theme of the church glorifying God through visible unity?

 Applying the Word 1. What are some practical ways you can obey or honor your parents? **2.** If you are a parent, what can you do this week to follow verse 4 more closely? (If you are not a parent, how have you seen verse 4 in action?) **3.** How could the principles Paul considers in verses 5–9 be lived out in situations you have been in or are in?

 Responding in Prayer Pray that in all you do you would serve "wholeheartedly, as if you were serving the Lord."

11 / *Ephesians 6:10–24*
Prayer Wars

IN A WAR of bullets, careful aim and heavy armor win battles. In a war of words, eloquent speech and sharp pens overcome the opposition. But if the fight is outside the realm of sight, sound and touch, how are victories won?

 Warming Up to God How have you recently seen God protecting you as you face spiritual battles?

 Read Ephesians 6:10–24.

---

[10]Finally, be strong in the Lord and in his mighty power. [11]Put on the full armor of God so that you can take your stand against the devil's schemes. [12]For our struggle is not against flesh and blood, but against the rulers, against the authorities, against the powers of this dark world and against the spiritual forces of evil in the heavenly realms. [13]Therefore put on the full armor of God, so that when the day of evil comes, you may be able to stand your ground, and after you have done everything, to stand. [14]Stand firm then, with the belt of truth buckled around your waist, with the breastplate of righteousness in place, [15]and with your feet fitted with the readiness that comes from the gospel of peace. [16]In addition to all this, take up the shield of faith, with which you can extinguish all the flaming arrows of the evil one. [17]Take the helmet of salvation and the sword of the Spirit, which is the word of God. [18]And pray in the Spirit on all occasions with all kinds of prayers and requests. With this in mind, be alert and always keep on praying for all the saints.

[19]Pray also for me, that whenever I open my mouth, words may be given me so that I will fearlessly make known the mystery of the gospel, [20]for which I am an ambassador in chains. Pray that I may declare it fearlessly, as I should.

[21]Tychicus, the dear brother and faithful servant in the Lord, will tell you everything, so that you also may know how I am and what I am doing. [22]I am sending him to you for this very purpose, that you may know how we are, and that he may encourage you.

[23]Peace to the brothers, and love with faith from God the Father and the Lord Jesus Christ. [24]Grace to all who love our Lord Jesus Christ with an undying love.

 Discovering the Word 1. Four times in verses 10–14 Paul urges his readers to stand firm in the battle against the devil's stratagems. How are we as Christians susceptible to instability? 2. How does the "armor of God" (vv. 13–17) prepare us for spiritual battle? 3. In verses 18–20 Paul urges all kinds of prayers. How has he been a model prayer warrior throughout this letter?

Applying the Word 1. How do you sense a battle around you with more than physical forces and foes? 2. Which piece of armor do you need most to fight your spiritual battles? Explain. 3. What main obstacle do you face in fighting the battle of prayer more effectively?

Responding in Prayer Take time now to pray about your fight in spiritual warfare.

Philippians

"Rejoice in the Lord always," the author of Philippians exhorts us, "I will say it again: Rejoice!" Coming from most people, such words might sound trite and simplistic, but this is the apostle Paul speaking, a man who was not writing from a padded-leather office chair surrounded by books on how to be happy. On the contrary, he was a prisoner awaiting news that could result in his death. It isn't hard to get behind the words of Philippians and see the tension and uncertainty there. Yet through all this we see the example of a man whose life is filled with joy.

As we study Philippians, we discover Paul's secret: that a life lived for the glory of God will overflow with joy. What a message for our hurting world!

Philippi was an important city because it straddled the great east-west highway known as the Egnatian Way. The population of this city was cosmopolitan, being made up of Tracians, Greeks, Romans and a few Jews. In the center of the city was a large forum surrounded by temples, a library, fountains, monuments and public baths.

In 42 B.C. Antony and Octavian defeated Brutus and Cassius near Philippi. In honor of his victory, Antony made Philippi a Roman colony. This provided the Philippians with special rights and privileges as Roman citizens, and they responded with a great deal of pride and loyalty. Women enjoyed a high status in Philippi—taking an active part in both public and business life. Because of this, women also had important responsibilities in the Philippian church.

Paul founded this church sometime around the year A.D. 50, during his second missionary journey (Acts 16:12-40). From the letter to the Philippians we learn that this church was taking its share of suffering (1:29), it was in some danger of division (1:27; 2:2; 4:2), it may have been leaning toward a doctrine of perfectionism (3:12-13), and it was threatened by the teaching of Judaizers—a group which insisted that all Christians adhere to Jewish laws and customs. But despite these problems, Paul's love for this church was obvious. He sincerely rejoiced at the progress they were making.

We know that Paul was writing to the Philippians from prison (1:12-14). Unfortunately, it is not clear which prison he was writing from. If he was writing during his imprisonment in Rome, then the letter can be dated sometime between A.D. 61-63. However, many scholars have pointed out that the conditions which Paul describes seem much harsher than what we know of the Roman imprisonment (Acts 28:16, 30-31). It could be that there was an earlier imprisonment not recorded in Acts. A good case has been made for Ephesus. If this is true, Philippians would have been written about A.D. 54.

Paul had several reasons for writing this letter. He wanted to explain why he was sending a man named Epaphroditus back to Philippi. He also wanted to thank the Philippians for the gift of money they had sent and to reassure his friends of his condition. Also, the news Paul had received concerning the Philippians made him long to encourage and advise a church he loved.

I hope that these quiet times will help you learn and apply Paul's secret to joyful living.

Outline

1 / *Philippians 1:1–11*
A Church Is Born

HAVE ANY OF your good friends ever told you what they appreciate about you? Have you ever listened while others prayed for you? If so, you know what a warm feeling it is to be assured that others care. In Philippians 1:1–11 Paul prays and thanks God for his friends in Philippi. As you read the passage, try to imagine yourself sitting with the Philippian Christians as this letter is read for the first time. You might be meeting in the home of Lydia, a Christian businesswoman. Perhaps you would be seated next to the jailer who heard about Christ while guarding Paul and Silas.

 Warming Up to God When has someone encouraged you by praying for you?

 Read Philippians 1:1–11.

---

1 Paul and Timothy, servants of Christ Jesus,

To all the saints in Christ Jesus at Philippi, together with the overseers*a* and deacons:

²Grace and peace to you from God our Father and the Lord Jesus Christ.

³I thank my God every time I remember you. ⁴In all my prayers for all of you, I always pray with joy ⁵because of your partnership in the gospel from the first day until now, ⁶being confident of this, that he who began a good work in you will carry it on to completion until the day of Christ Jesus.

⁷It is right for me to feel this way about all of you, since I have you in my heart; for whether I am in chains or defending and confirming the gospel, all of you share in God's grace with me. ⁸God can testify how I long for all of you with the affection of Christ Jesus.

⁹And this is my prayer: that your love may abound more and more in knowledge and depth of insight, ¹⁰so that you may be able to discern what is best and may be pure and blameless until the day of Christ, ¹¹filled with the fruit of righteousness that comes through Jesus Christ—to the glory and praise of God.

*a*1 Traditionally *bishops*

 Discovering the Word 1. What are Paul's feelings toward the Philippians (vv. 3–8)? 2. Why does he feel this way about them? 3. What do verses 3–8 reveal about healthy Christian relationships? 4. What are Paul's prayer requests for the Philippians (vv. 9–11)? 5. Why would each of these qualities be essential to spiritual maturity?

 Applying the Word 1. How can your present relationships be strengthened to become more like what is described in verses 3–8? 2. What does Paul's prayer teach about how we should pray for others?

Responding in Prayer Using Paul's prayer as a model, spend a few minutes thanking God and praying for someone you love in Christ.

---

2 / *Philippians 1:12–30*
A Joyful Imprisonment

IN THIS PASSAGE we discover that Paul is writing to the Philippians from prison. This puts a whole new perspective on the joyful mood of the letter. While Paul is writing, he is experiencing what most of us would describe as awful circumstances. Yet even at a time like this, Paul's first concern is that Christ is praised. This passage can teach us how to honor Christ in a difficult situation.

 Warming Up to God What people or things in life bring you the greatest joy?

 Read Philippians 1:12–30.

¹²Now I want you to know, brothers, that what has happened to me has really served to advance the gospel. ¹³As a result, it has become clear throughout the whole palace guard^b and to everyone else that I am in chains for Christ. ¹⁴Because of my chains, most of the brothers in the Lord have been encouraged to speak the word of God more courageously and fearlessly.

¹⁵It is true that some preach Christ out of envy and rivalry, but others out of goodwill. ¹⁶The latter do so in love, knowing that I am put here for the defense of the gospel. ¹⁷The former preach Christ out of selfish ambition, not sincerely, supposing that they can stir up trouble for me while I am in chains.^c ¹⁸But what does it matter? The important thing is that in every way, whether from false motives or true, Christ is preached. And because of this I rejoice.

Yes, and I will continue to rejoice, ¹⁹for I know that through your prayers and the help given by the Spirit of Jesus Christ, what has happened to me will turn out for my deliverance.^d ²⁰I eagerly expect and hope that I will in no way be ashamed, but will have sufficient courage so that now as always Christ will be exalted in my body, whether by life or by death. ²¹For to me, to live is Christ and to die is gain. ²²If I am to go on living in the body, this will mean fruitful labor for me. Yet what shall I choose? I do not know! ²³I am torn between the two: I desire to depart and be with Christ, which is better by far; ²⁴but it is more necessary for you that I remain in the body. ²⁵Convinced of this, I know that I will remain, and I will continue with all of you for your progress and joy in the faith, ²⁶so that through my being with you again your joy in Christ Jesus will overflow on account of me.

²⁷Whatever happens, conduct yourselves in a manner worthy of the gospel of Christ. Then, whether I come and see you or only hear about you in my absence, I will know that you stand firm in one spirit, contending as one man for the faith of the gospel ²⁸without being frightened in any way by those who oppose you. This is a sign to them that they will be destroyed, but that you will be saved—and that by God. ²⁹For it has been granted to you on behalf of Christ not only to believe on him, but also to suffer for him, ³⁰since you are going through the same struggle you saw I had, and now hear that I still have.

^b13 Or *whole palace*   ^c16,17 Some late manuscripts have verses 16 and 17 in reverse order.   ^d19 Or *salvation*

 Discovering the Word 1. What does Paul say has happened as a result of his imprisonment (vv. 12–14)? 2. Compare the motives of the two groups described in verses 15–18. 3. What are Paul's considerations in choosing between life and death (vv. 20–26)? 4. What does it mean to conduct ourselves in a manner worthy of the gospel (vv. 27–30)?

Applying the Word 1. To what extent have you adopted Paul's attitude toward life and death? 2. What are the most difficult circumstances you are presently facing? 3. How can Christ be exalted in that situation?

Responding in Prayer Pray that you would learn to experience the joy that can emerge amidst sorrow.

3 / *Philippians 2:1–18*
The Path of Humility

IS IT POSSIBLE to have a good self-image and still be humble? Can a person want to be the best without being conceited? In Philippians 2:1–18 Paul directs us to Jesus Christ, a person equal with God yet whose incarnation and life are the supreme example of humility. This passage urges us to imitate Christ's attitude.

 Warming Up to God What is the difference between humility and a poor self-image?

 Read Philippians 2:1–18.

---

2 If you have any encouragement from being united with Christ, if any comfort from his love, if any fellowship with the Spirit, if any tenderness and compassion, ²then make my joy complete by being like-minded, having the same love, being one in spirit and purpose. ³Do nothing out of selfish ambition or vain conceit, but in humility consider others better than yourselves. ⁴Each of you should look not only to your own interests, but also to the interests of others.

⁵Your attitude should be the same as that of Christ Jesus:

⁶Who, being in very nature*e* God,
    did not consider equality with God
        something to be grasped,
⁷but made himself nothing,
    taking the very nature*f* of a servant,
    being made in human likeness.
⁸And being found in appearance as a man,
    he humbled himself
    and became obedient to death—
        even death on a cross!
⁹Therefore God exalted him to the highest
        place
and gave him the name that is above every
        name,

¹⁰that at the name of Jesus every knee should
        bow,
    in heaven and on earth and under the
        earth,
¹¹and every tongue confess that Jesus Christ is
        Lord,
    to the glory of God the Father.

¹²Therefore, my dear friends, as you have always obeyed—not only in my presence, but now much more in my absence—continue to work out your salvation with fear and trembling, ¹³for it is God who works in you to will and to act according to his good purpose.

¹⁴Do everything without complaining or arguing, ¹⁵so that you may become blameless and pure, children of God without fault in a crooked and depraved generation, in which you shine like stars in the universe ¹⁶as you hold out*g* the word of life—in order that I may boast on the day of Christ that I did not run or labor for nothing. ¹⁷But even if I am being poured out like a drink offering on the sacrifice and service coming from your faith, I am glad and rejoice with all of you. ¹⁸So you too should be glad and rejoice with me.

e6 Or in the form of   f7 Or the form   g16 Or hold on to

 Discovering the Word 1. How can our experience of Christ and his Spirit (v. 1) help us to achieve the unity Paul desires in verse 2? 2. How do verses 3–4 help us to understand the nature of humility? 3. How did each of Christ's actions illustrate humility and a concern for the interests of others (vv. 6–8)? 4. In your own words, describe God's response to Jesus' humility (vv. 9–11). 5. In verses 12–13 Paul says you are to "work out your salvation" because God "works in you." How are these ideas related?

 Applying the Word 1. Who might you be tempted to impress during the next few days? 2. What act of humble service could you do for this person instead?

Responding in Prayer Pray for the opportunity to serve others as Christ has served you.

4 / *Philippians 2:19–30*
Servants of Christ

WHEN THE PHILIPPIANS heard that Paul was in prison, they sent one of their members—a man named Epaphroditus—to Paul with a gift of money. It was his job to help Paul in any way necessary. Epaphroditus returned home carrying the letter to the Philippians.

In this section of the letter, Paul outlines his future plans and explains why he is sending Epaphroditus back. The passage gives several beautiful examples of Christian service as displayed in the lives of Timothy, Epaphroditus, Paul and the Philippians.

 Warming Up to God   What do you enjoy most and least about serving others?

 Read Philippians 2:19–30.

---

¹⁹I hope in the Lord Jesus to send Timothy to you soon, that I also may be cheered when I receive news about you. ²⁰I have no one else like him, who takes a genuine interest in your welfare. ²¹For everyone looks out for his own interests, not those of Jesus Christ. ²²But you know that Timothy has proved himself, because as a son with his father he has served with me in the work of the gospel. ²³I hope, therefore, to send him as soon as I see how things go with me. ²⁴And I am confident in the Lord that I myself will come soon.

²⁵But I think it is necessary to send back to you Epaphroditus, my brother, fellow worker and fellow soldier, who is also your messenger, whom you sent to take care of my needs. ²⁶For he longs for all of you and is distressed because you heard he was ill. ²⁷Indeed he was ill, and almost died. But God had mercy on him, and not on him only but also on me, to spare me sorrow upon sorrow. ²⁸Therefore I am all the more eager to send him, so that when you see him again you may be glad and I may have less anxiety. ²⁹Welcome him in the Lord with great joy, and honor men like him, ³⁰because he almost died for the work of Christ, risking his life to make up for the help you could not give me.

 Discovering the Word   1. Imagine that Timothy is being sent to visit your church or fellowship group. What might he do to help you?   2. Why is Paul sending Epaphroditus back to Philippi (vv. 25–28)?
3. How is Christ's attitude evident in the relationships among Paul, Epaphroditus and the Philippians (vv. 25–30)?
4. Why is it important to honor people like Epaphroditus, especially in light of Christ's exaltation (2:9–11)?

Applying the Word   1. Examine your plans and goals during the coming week. How can you bring your own interests into closer harmony with those of Jesus Christ?   2. What are some practical ways you can serve those around you during the coming week?

Responding in Prayer   Pray that Christ will continue to give you the heart of a servant.

---

5 / *Philippians 3*
Rejoice in the Lord

HAVE YOU EVER become excited about an idea only to be deflated by the realities of making it work? Sometimes trying to live a Christian life is like that. We start off very excited about knowing the Lord, but it isn't long before the pressure of keeping "all the right rules" drains us of our joy. Unfortunately, we can then swing too far in the other direction and decide, "I'm not going to be concerned about Christian conduct. If Jesus has saved me, then it doesn't matter how I live." This attitude will destroy our joy as quickly as the first. So what is the solution? Paul tells us in this passage.

 Warming Up to God What are some of your most important goals in life?

 Read Philippians 3.

3 Finally, my brothers, rejoice in the Lord! It is no trouble for me to write the same things to you again, and it is a safeguard for you.

²Watch out for those dogs, those men who do evil, those mutilators of the flesh. ³For it is we who are the circumcision, we who worship by the Spirit of God, who glory in Christ Jesus, and who put no confidence in the flesh— ⁴though I myself have reasons for such confidence.

If anyone else thinks he has reasons to put confidence in the flesh, I have more: ⁵circumcised on the eighth day, of the people of Israel, of the tribe of Benjamin, a Hebrew of Hebrews; in regard to the law, a Pharisee; ⁶as for zeal, persecuting the church; as for legalistic righteousness, faultless.

⁷But whatever was to my profit I now consider loss for the sake of Christ. ⁸What is more, I consider everything a loss compared to the surpassing greatness of knowing Christ Jesus my Lord, for whose sake I have lost all things. I consider them rubbish, that I may gain Christ ⁹and be found in him, not having a righteousness of my own that comes from the law, but that which is through faith in Christ—the righteousness that comes from God and is by faith. ¹⁰I want to know Christ and the power of his resurrection and the fellowship of sharing in his sufferings, becoming like him in his death, ¹¹and so, some-how, to attain to the resurrection from the dead.

¹²Not that I have already obtained all this, or have already been made perfect, but I press on to take hold of that for which Christ Jesus took hold of me. ¹³Brothers, I do not consider myself yet to have taken hold of it. But one thing I do: Forgetting what is behind and straining toward what is ahead, ¹⁴I press on toward the goal to win the prize for which God has called me heavenward in Christ Jesus.

¹⁵All of us who are mature should take such a view of things. And if on some point you think differently, that too God will make clear to you. ¹⁶Only let us live up to what we have already attained.

¹⁷Join with others in following my example, brothers, and take note of those who live according to the pattern we gave you. ¹⁸For, as I have often told you before and now say again even with tears, many live as enemies of the cross of Christ. ¹⁹Their destiny is destruction, their god is their stomach, and their glory is in their shame. Their mind is on earthly things. ²⁰But our citizenship is in heaven. And we eagerly await a Savior from there, the Lord Jesus Christ, ²¹who, by the power that enables him to bring everything under his control, will transform our lowly bodies so that they will be like his glorious body.

 Discovering the Word 1. How does rejoicing in the Lord (v. 1) differ from other reasons for joy? 2. Why were the people Paul warns against in verses 2–3 so dangerous? 3. Contrast Paul the Pharisee (vv. 4–6) with Paul the Christian (vv. 7–11). How have his reasons for confidence changed? 4. In verses 12–14 Paul compares himself to an athlete who is running a race. Why is this such an appropriate description of the Christian life? 5. In verses 17–21 Paul contrasts Christians with "enemies of the cross." What are the concerns and destiny of each group?

Applying the Word 1. Have you ever placed your confidence in something, thinking it would bring you closer to God, that you now consider to be rubbish? Explain. 2. In verse 6 Paul speaks of "legalistic righteousness." What legalisms are today's Christians pressured to keep? 3. How do these legalisms get in the way of knowing Christ and rejoicing in the Lord?

Responding in Prayer Reflect on Paul's words "We eagerly await . . . the Lord Jesus Christ." Worship Christ with your anticipation of his return.

6 / *Philippians 4:1–9*
Stand Firm in the Lord

TAKE A MOMENT to think of the people you care about most. What is your greatest desire for these people? As Paul thinks of the Philippians, his greatest desire is that they will stand firm in what they have been taught. But he is also aware of some problems which may cause their faith to weaken. He writes to warn them that in order to stand firm they must put an end to disagreements, rejoice always and fill their thoughts with good things.

 Warming Up to God Do you find your stand in the Lord to be firmer or weaker than it was a year ago? What has made the difference?

 Read Philippians 4:1–9.

4 Therefore, my brothers, you whom I love and long for, my joy and crown, that is how you should stand firm in the Lord, dear friends!

²I plead with Euodia and I plead with Syntyche to agree with each other in the Lord. ³Yes, and I ask you, loyal yokefellow,ʰ help these women who have contended at my side in the cause of the gospel, along with Clement and the rest of my fellow workers, whose names are in the book of life.

⁴Rejoice in the Lord always. I will say it again: Rejoice! ⁵Let your gentleness be evident to all. The Lord is near. ⁶Do not be anxious about any-thing, but in everything, by prayer and petition, with thanksgiving, present your requests to God. ⁷And the peace of God, which transcends all understanding, will guard your hearts and your minds in Christ Jesus.

⁸Finally, brothers, whatever is true, whatever is noble, whatever is right, whatever is pure, whatever is lovely, whatever is admirable—if anything is excellent or praiseworthy—think about such things. ⁹Whatever you have learned or received or heard from me, or seen in me—put it into practice. And the God of peace will be with you.

ʰ3 Or *loyal Syzygus*

 Discovering the Word 1. Paul opens this chapter with the statement "that is how you should stand firm in the Lord." Look back at 3:12–21. How are we to stand firm in the Lord? 2. In verse 2 Paul pleads with Euodia and Syntyche "to agree with each other in the Lord." Why do you think he is so concerned about their relationship? 3. How can each of the promises and commands listed in verses 4–7 help you to be joyful, peaceful and free from anxiety? 4. How can improper thoughts rob us of the peace God desires for us? 5. How can true, noble, right, pure, lovely, admirable, excellent or praiseworthy thoughts help to cleanse our minds and restore our tranquility (v. 8)?

 Applying the Word 1. What should be your response to disagreements within your church or fellowship group? 2. In verse 9 Paul tells us that the God of peace will be with us as we practice what we have learned. What have you learned in this passage that you need to put into practice?

Responding in Prayer Ask God to show you the thoughts and attitudes which are robbing you of joy and weakening your faith.

7 / *Philippians 4:10–23*
Paul's Thank-You Note

WE'VE ALL WRITTEN thank-you notes for gifts received for a birthday or for Christmas. Such notes usually include rather conventional phrases about the thankfulness of the recipient and the thoughtfulness of the giver. In Philippians 4 Paul thanks the Philippians for a gift of money they sent. However, it is a most unusual thank-you note. First he breaks the conventional rules by waiting until the very end of the letter to say thank you. Then he writes as though he didn't really need the gift!

 Warming Up to God Have you thanked God for his many gifts to you lately? Take time to do so before you begin.

 Read Philippians 4:10–23.

---

¹⁰I rejoice greatly in the Lord that at last you have renewed your concern for me. Indeed, you have been concerned, but you had no opportunity to show it. ¹¹I am not saying this because I am in need, for I have learned to be content whatever the circumstances. ¹²I know what it is to be in need, and I know what it is to have plenty. I have learned the secret of being content in any and every situation, whether well fed or hungry, whether living in plenty or in want. ¹³I can do everything through him who gives me strength.

¹⁴Yet it was good of you to share in my troubles. ¹⁵Moreover, as you Philippians know, in the early days of your acquaintance with the gospel, when I set out from Macedonia, not one church shared with me in the matter of giving and receiving, except you only; ¹⁶for even when I was in Thessalonica, you sent me aid again and again when I was in need. ¹⁷Not that I am looking for a gift, but I am looking for what may be credited to your account. ¹⁸I have received full payment and even more; I am amply supplied, now that I have received from Epaphroditus the gifts you sent. They are a fragrant offering, an acceptable sacrifice, pleasing to God. ¹⁹And my God will meet all your needs according to his glorious riches in Christ Jesus.

²⁰To our God and Father be glory for ever and ever. Amen.

²¹Greet all the saints in Christ Jesus. The brothers who are with me send greetings. ²²All the saints send you greetings, especially those who belong to Caesar's household.

²³The grace of the Lord Jesus Christ be with your spirit. Amen.ⁱ

ⁱ23 Some manuscripts do not have *Amen.*

 Discovering the Word 1. Paul thanks the Philippians not for the money but for the concern they have shown (v. 10). Why would this have been more important to Paul? 2. Many people believe they can only be content once they have reached a certain level of economic prosperity. How does their view differ from Paul's secret of contentment (vv. 11–13)? 3. How had the Philippians helped Paul both in the past and the present (vv. 14–18)? 4. What benefits does Paul expect the Philippians to receive from their giving (vv. 17–19)?

Applying the Word 1. Many people complain that missionaries are always asking for money. How does this passage provide a model for both missionaries and those who support them? 2. How will this passage affect your giving?

Responding in Prayer Pray for Christian workers you know, that they would have the emotional and financial support they need.

Colossians

"**M**ore! More!" urged our son John when I laid down the spoon after feeding him. "Again! Again!" pleaded our daughter Sara as I turned the last page in the book I was reading to her.

Their cries for more pudding or stories are echoed in our culture's search for more—more power, more money, more knowledge, more gadgets, more furniture, more clothes—more everything!

Books on self-improvement and success flood the market. Gurus gain eager followers by offering enlightenment, power and secret wisdom. Millions read horoscopes every day.

We cry for "more" not only in our society but also in the church. If only we had more wisdom, more maturity, more power, more faith. To fill these needs we attend seminars, go to concerts, hear celebrity speakers and read their latest books.

Colossians was written to Christians with similar longings. They didn't know who and what they already had. False teachers urged them to add rules, ascetic practices and new philosophies to their Christian faith. Then they would have fullness of life. Paul writes to satisfy their desire for more by showing that they already had fullness in Christ.

Paul never traveled to Colossae, a city in the Lycus River valley about a hundred miles east of Ephesus and twelve miles from Laodicea. But somehow he met Epaphras, the man who had taken the gospel to Colossae, and Philemon, the host for the local house church. While in prison in Rome, Paul learned from Epaphras about the Colossian church and the pressures threatening their peace and stability.

These "faithful brothers" had not turned away from faith in Christ. Paul's warm, friendly letter affirms their positive qualities and the changes in their lives. But he warns them against being deceived by "fine-sounding arguments" (2:4) or being captured by "hollow and deceptive philosophy, which depends on human tradition and on the basic principles of this world rather than on Christ" (2:8).

The temptation to add ascetic practices, regulations or "superior knowledge" threatened their dependence on Christ alone for the fullness of life they wanted. The early Gnostics boasted about a spiritual "fullness" not previously experienced. They promised to complete and perfect the simple and elementary faith introduced by Paul and Epaphras. They emphasized a deeper knowledge of God, reserved for a special few, and an experience of greater power.

Colossians is Paul's strongest declaration of the uniqueness and sufficiency of Christ, his full authority over all powers, and the fullness of life he gives. Paul spells out the implications of this fullness of life again and again in the letter.

Like the Colossians, we are bombarded by longings for something more. But Paul thunders in Colossians, You already have fullness in Christ. Enjoy it! "For in Christ all the fullness of the Deity lives in bodily form, and you have been given fullness in Christ" (2:9–10). The purpose of these quiet times is to help you discover the scope, reality and implications of the fullness of life you have in Christ. Paul's letter to Philemon gives principles for mending broken relationships that apply to us as well.

Outline

1 / *Colossians 1:1–14*
Thanks and Prayer

"GOD BLESS JENNIFER today" may be a typical prayer for a friend as she comes to mind. But what am I specifically asking for? How will I know if my prayer is answered? What difference would it make in Jennifer's life? Paul begins his letter by telling the Colossians why he is thankful for them and what he asks God to do in them. Paul's example gives us a model for encouraging and praying for one another.

 Warming Up to God How does it make you feel when a friend tells you the specific things he or she notices and appreciates about you?

 Read Colossians 1:1–14.

1 Paul, an apostle of Christ Jesus by the will of God, and Timothy our brother,

²To the holy and faithful*ᵃ* brothers in Christ at Colosse:

Grace and peace to you from God our Father.*ᵇ*

³We always thank God, the Father of our Lord Jesus Christ, when we pray for you, ⁴because we have heard of your faith in Christ Jesus and of the love you have for all the saints— ⁵the faith and love that spring from the hope that is stored up for you in heaven and that you have already heard about in the word of truth, the gospel ⁶that has come to you. All over the world this gospel is bearing fruit and growing, just as it has been doing among you since the day you heard it and understood God's grace in all its truth. ⁷You learned it from Epaphras, our dear fellow servant, who is a faithful minister of Christ on our*ᶜ* be-

half, ⁸and who also told us of your love in the Spirit.

⁹For this reason, since the day we heard about you, we have not stopped praying for you and asking God to fill you with the knowledge of his will through all spiritual wisdom and understanding. ¹⁰And we pray this in order that you may live a life worthy of the Lord and may please him in every way: bearing fruit in every good work, growing in the knowledge of God, ¹¹being strengthened with all power according to his glorious might so that you may have great endurance and patience, and joyfully ¹²giving thanks to the Father, who has qualified you*ᵈ* to share in the inheritance of the saints in the kingdom of light. ¹³For he has rescued us from the dominion of darkness and brought us into the kingdom of the Son he loves, ¹⁴in whom we have redemption,*ᶜ* the forgiveness of sins.

ᵃ2 Or believing   ᵇ2 Some manuscripts Father and the Lord Jesus Christ   ᶜ7 Some manuscripts your   ᵈ12 Some manuscripts us   ᶜ14 A few late manuscripts redemption through his blood

 Discovering the Word 1. What characteristics of the Colossians cause Paul to always be thankful for them (vv. 3–6)? 2. What impresses you about how the gospel was spreading (vv. 5–8)? 3. After affirming their strengths, Paul tells the Colossians what he prays for them. What are Paul's requests for how they think and act? 4. How might spiritual wisdom and understanding help us to understand God's will (v. 9)? 5. According to Paul, true knowledge leads to a "life worthy of the Lord" (v. 10). What qualities does such a life include (vv. 10–12)? How are these qualities related to each other?

Applying the Word 1. In what specific ways do you see the qualities in verses 10–12 developing in your life? 2. Reread verses 12–14, putting your name in each sentence. How would meditating on these verses help you to appreciate what God has done for you?

Responding in Prayer Take time to pray for your church or fellowship group, using verses 9–14 as your model.

2 / Colossians 1:15–23
Jesus Is Supreme

WE FREQUENTLY HEAR: "All roads lead to God. Everyone is trying to get to the same place. That belief is fine for you, but I don't buy it for myself. Only bigots and fanatics label belief *true* or *false*."

The Colossians heard, "Worship Jesus, but not exclusively. Jesus is just one spirit among many to be worshiped." In this passage we'll study Paul's adamant declaration of Christ's supremacy over every being and idea which invites our attention.

 Warming Up to God What problems have you encountered in helping someone understand why Jesus is the only way to God?

 Read Colossians 1:15–23.

---

¹⁵He is the image of the invisible God, the firstborn over all creation. ¹⁶For by him all things were created: things in heaven and on earth, visible and invisible, whether thrones or powers or rulers or authorities; all things were created by him and for him. ¹⁷He is before all things, and in him all things hold together. ¹⁸And he is the head of the body, the church; he is the beginning and the firstborn from among the dead, so that in everything he might have the supremacy. ¹⁹For God was pleased to have all his fullness dwell in him, ²⁰and through him to reconcile to himself all things, whether things on earth or things in heaven, by making peace through his blood, shed on the cross.

²¹Once you were alienated from God and were enemies in your minds because of⁄ your evil behavior. ²²But now he has reconciled you by Christ's physical body through death to present you holy in his sight, without blemish and free from accusation— ²³ if you continue in your faith, established and firm, not moved from the hope held out in the gospel. This is the gospel that you heard and that has been proclaimed to every creature under heaven, and of which I, Paul, have become a servant.

⁄21 Or *minds, as shown by*

Discovering the Word 1. Make as many statements as you can about why Jesus is supreme (vv. 15–18). Begin each with "Christ is . . ." 2. What does it mean that Christ is the "head of the body, the church" (v. 18)? 3. What actions was God pleased to take to reconcile us to himself (vv. 19–22)? 4. How does understanding God's actions help you explain why Jesus is the only way to God?

Applying the Word 1. How do the words *reconciled, holy in his sight, without blemish* and *free from accusation* (vv. 22–23) motivate you to continue firm in your faith in Christ? 2. How might those words appeal to unspoken needs of the friends you want to introduce to Jesus? 3. How did some recent choice you made about your time or money reflect Christ's supreme place in your life?

Responding in Prayer Spend some time worshiping Jesus Christ for who he is and what he has done for you and your friends who don't yet know him.

---

3 / Colossians 1:24—2:5
Struggles for Maturity

FOR A WHOLE year a young man lived in isolation on a remote Arctic mountain. He risked his life on the flight in and on trails over thin ice (which gave way when he struggled under a heavy backpack). He shared his cold tent with mice and mosquitoes. He experimented with a diet of boiled, fried or charred mice. Why would anyone willingly subject himself to such hardships? Farley Mowat had a goal. He wanted to learn the relationship between wolves and the diminishing caribou herds. In this study Paul describes his compelling goal, his struggles and his resources to reach it.

 Warming Up to God Recall a time when a goal was compelling enough to cause you to suffer for it. What helped you to keep going?

 Read Colossians 1:24—2:5.

²⁴Now I rejoice in what was suffered for you, and I fill up in my flesh what is still lacking in regard to Christ's afflictions, for the sake of his body, which is the church. ²⁵I have become its servant by the commission God gave me to present to you the word of God in its fullness— ²⁶the mystery that has been kept hidden for ages and generations, but is now disclosed to the saints. ²⁷To them God has chosen to make known among the Gentiles the glorious riches of this mystery, which is Christ in you, the hope of glory.

²⁸We proclaim him, admonishing and teaching everyone with all wisdom, so that we may present everyone perfect in Christ. ²⁹To this end I labor, struggling with all his energy, which so powerfully works in me.

2 I want you to know how much I am struggling for you and for those at Laodicea, and for all who have not met me personally. ²My purpose is that they may be encouraged in heart and united in love, so that they may have the full riches of complete understanding, in order that they may know the mystery of God, namely, Christ, ³in whom are hidden all the treasures of wisdom and knowledge. ⁴I tell you this so that no one may deceive you by fine-sounding arguments. ⁵For though I am absent from you in body, I am present with you in spirit and delight to see how orderly you are and how firm your faith in Christ is.

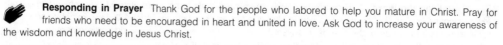 **Discovering the Word** 1. How does Paul define God's commission to him (1:24–29)? 2. In the New Testament the term *mystery* refers not to something mysterious but to something previously hidden which God now wishes to make clear. What is the mystery that represents the "word of God in its fullness" (1:26–27; 2:2–3)? 3. According to Paul, what are the marks of Christian maturity (2:2–5)? 5. The Gnostics taught that their secret knowledge was the key to salvation. How would Paul's description of Christ (2:3–4) protect the Colossians from the "fine-sounding arguments" of the Gnostics?

 Applying the Word 1. What "fine-sounding arguments" today lure us away from Christ and hinder our spiritual maturity? 2. What can you do to refocus your attention on Christ and on his goals for you?

Responding in Prayer Thank God for the people who labored to help you mature in Christ. Pray for friends who need to be encouraged in heart and united in love. Ask God to increase your awareness of the wisdom and knowledge in Jesus Christ.

4 / *Colossians 2:6–23*
No Additions Needed

KIM YENG AND his family celebrated the day they became American citizens. Now they were no longer refugees but free citizens with full privileges and endless opportunities. But soon the neighbors began to question Kim. "Why are you making your kids superpatriots? They don't have to wear flags on their shirts every day." "Why did you spend all that money installing a tall flagpole in your yard?" "Don't you know that making your family eat hamburgers instead of eggrolls doesn't make you a better citizen?" In this study Paul questions the Colossians about the foolish human additions they are trying to add to all they have in Christ.

Warming Up to God How would you finish the following sentence? "I would feel fulfilled if . . ."

Read Colossians 2:6–23.

6So then, just as you received Christ Jesus as Lord, continue to live in him, 7rooted and built up in him, strengthened in the faith as you were taught, and overflowing with thankfulness.

8See to it that no one takes you captive through hollow and deceptive philosophy, which depends on human tradition and the basic principles of this world rather than on Christ.

9For in Christ all the fullness of the Deity lives in bodily form, 10and you have been given fullness in Christ, who is the head over every power and authority. 11In him you were also circumcised, in the putting off of the sinful nature,*g* not with a circumcision done by the hands of men but with the circumcision done by Christ, 12having been buried with him in baptism and raised with him through your faith in the power of God, who raised him from the dead.

13When you were dead in your sins and in the uncircumcision of your sinful nature,*h* God made you*i* alive with Christ. He forgave us all our sins, 14having canceled the written code, with its regulations, that was against us and that stood opposed to us; he took it away, nailing it to the cross. 15And having disarmed the powers and authorities, he made a public spectacle of them, triumphing over them by the cross.*j*

16Therefore do not let anyone judge you by what you eat or drink, or with regard to a religious festival, a New Moon celebration or a Sabbath day. 17These are a shadow of the things that were to come; the reality, however, is found in Christ. 18Do not let anyone who delights in false humility and the worship of angels disqualify you for the prize. Such a person goes into great detail about what he has seen, and his unspiritual mind puffs him up with idle notions. 19He has lost connection with the Head, from whom the whole body, supported and held together by its ligaments and sinews, grows as God causes it to grow.

20Since you died with Christ to the basic principles of this world, why, as though you still belonged to it, do you submit to its rules: 21"Do not handle! Do not taste! Do not touch!"? 22These are all destined to perish with use, because they are based on human commands and teachings. 23Such regulations indeed have an appearance of wisdom, with their self-imposed worship, their false humility and their harsh treatment of the body, but they lack any value in restraining sensual indulgence.

g11 Or the flesh   h13 Or your flesh   i13 Some manuscripts us   j15 Or them in him

---

Discovering the Word 1. How do each of the images *rooted, built up, strengthened* and *overflowing* (v. 7) help us understand how we should continue to live in Christ? 2. In verse 8 we get the first real glimpse of the heresy being taught to the Colossians. What do we learn about it? 3. How would Paul's two statements about fullness in Christ (vv. 9–10) protect the Colossians from those deceptive ideas? 4. In verses 11–15 Paul describes some of what "fullness in Christ" includes. Which of our basic needs did Jesus' death, burial and resurrection meet? 5. What "shadows" were the Colossians adding to the "reality" they had found in Christ (vv. 16–17, 20–23)?

Applying the Word 1. Silently reread verses 9–15, inserting your name every time Paul says *you* or *us.* How do these facts affect your view of yourself? 2. What "shadows" are we tempted to add today?

Responding in Prayer Consider the fact that we are made complete in Christ. Allow your prayer and praise to arise out of that fact.

5 / *Colossians 3:1–11*
New Life, New Lifestyle (Part 1)

HAVE YOU SEEN pictures of marathon runners? Concentration and determination seem to ooze from every pore. These people set their hearts and minds on one thing—finish this race. They focus on the next step, the next checkpoint, until the race is complete. They shed pounds, unnecessary clothing or anything else that might slow them down. Attach their official number and they are ready to run.

As Christians, we are to live like marathon runners. We are to take off anything that slows us down and set our hearts and minds on the finish line.

 Warming Up to God As a child, how did setting your heart on a certain toy or gift affect how you acted and what you thought about?

 Read Colossians 3:1–11.

---

3 Since, then, you have been raised with Christ, set your hearts on things above, where Christ is seated at the right hand of God. ²Set your minds on things above, not on earthly things. ³For you died, and your life is now hidden with Christ in God. ⁴When Christ, who is your*ᵏ* life, appears, then you also will appear with him in glory.

⁵Put to death, therefore, whatever belongs to your earthly nature: sexual immorality, impurity, lust, evil desires and greed, which is idolatry. ⁶Because of these, the wrath of God is coming.*ˡ* ⁷You used to walk in these ways, in the life you once lived. ⁸But now you must rid yourselves of all such things as these: anger, rage, malice, slander, and filthy language from your lips. ⁹Do not lie to each other, since you have taken off your old self with its practices ¹⁰and have put on the new self, which is being renewed in knowledge in the image of its Creator. ¹¹Here there is no Greek or Jew, circumcised or uncircumcised, barbarian, Scythian, slave or free, but Christ is all, and is in all.

ᵏ4 Some manuscripts our   *ˡ6 Some early manuscripts coming on those who are disobedient*

Discovering the Word 1. What do you think Paul means by *things above* and *earthly things* (vv. 1–2)? 2. How can we set our hearts and minds on things above rather than on earthly things? 3. What do the things we are to "put to death" have in common (v. 5)? 4. Our old ways of reacting are compared to a garment we took off at conversion (vv. 8–10). Why is each type of behavior inconsistent with our new life in Christ? 5. Although we may still struggle with these sins, what resources for change do we now have (vv. 9–11)?

Applying the Word 1. How can we keep God's perspective on immorality and greed when our culture accepts them as the norm? 2. What has been the effect on you and others when you have fallen back into these old motives or actions (vv. 5, 8–9)? 3. In verse 11 Paul lists the distressing divisions between people in the Colossian culture. How would becoming aware of Christ in other Christians help us to eliminate our cultural divisions?

Responding in Prayer Paul has shown the necessary blending of our emotions, mind and will in order to live like people who have been raised with Christ. Pray for help in the area where you feel weak. Spend time thanking God for the changes he has already made in you.

6 / *Colossians 3:12–17*
New Life, New Lifestyle (Part 2)

MARATHON RUNNERS NOT only shed anything that might slow them down, they also dress carefully. They choose the best running shoes and the most comfortable shorts and shirt possible. After telling us what to get rid of, Paul now speaks about the new clothes we are to wear because of our new life in Christ.

 Warming Up to God When you were a child, what was one behavior your parents insisted on just because you were a member of their family?

 Read Colossians 3:12–17.

¹²Therefore, as God's chosen people, holy and dearly loved, clothe yourselves with compassion, kindness, humility, gentleness and patience. ¹³Bear with each other and forgive whatever grievances you may have against one another. Forgive as the Lord forgave you. ¹⁴And over all these virtues put on love, which binds them all together in perfect unity.

¹⁵Let the peace of Christ rule in your hearts, since as members of one body you were called to peace. And be thankful. ¹⁶Let the word of Christ dwell in you richly as you teach and admonish one another with all wisdom, and as you sing psalms, hymns and spiritual songs with gratitude in your hearts to God. ¹⁷And whatever you do, whether in word or deed, do it all in the name of the Lord Jesus, giving thanks to God the Father through him.

 Discovering the Word 1. Why does Paul begin by reminding us of who we are in God's sight (v. 12)? 2. Why is the description "God's chosen people, holy and dearly loved" (v. 12) not dependent on our feelings or efforts (1:12–14; 2:9–10)? 3. Paul recognizes that grievances occur even in the church. How are his instructions for handling grievances different from the way our culture handles them (vv. 13–14)? 4. Paul also recognizes that Christians conflict with each other. How could conflicts be better managed with peace ruling (literally, "functioning like an umpire") in our hearts (v. 15)? 5. What does it mean to let the word of Christ "dwell" in us richly (v. 16; see also Eph 5:18–20)?

 Applying the Word 1. What "new clothes" (v. 12) would you like to put on? 2. How would doing everything "in the name of the Lord Jesus" transform what you have to say and do today (v. 17)?

 Responding in Prayer Let your prayer grow out of the need to put on specific "new clothes." If there is someone you need to forgive, confess that and ask for power and determination to forgive.

7 / *Colossians 3:18—4:1*
At Home and On the Job

FACTORY WORKERS IN the Philippines had been meeting for months for a lunch-hour Bible study. One day the supervisor came to the leader and asked, "Could you start some more Bible studies in the factory? The men in the study have become the best workers on my shift."

That wouldn't have surprised the apostle Paul. In this section he instructs us about the distinctive attitudes and behavior that should mark Christians at home and on the job.

 Warming Up to God When is it easiest for you to have a "Christian" attitude toward your work?

Read Colossians 3:18—4:1.

18Wives, submit to your husbands, as is fitting in the Lord.

19Husbands, love your wives and do not be harsh with them.

20Children, obey your parents in everything, for this pleases the Lord.

21Fathers, do not embitter your children, or they will become discouraged.

22Slaves, obey your earthly masters in everything; and do it, not only when their eye is on you and to win their favor, but with sincerity of heart and reverence for the Lord. 23Whatever you do, work at it with all your heart, as working for the Lord, not for men, 24since you know that you will receive an inheritance from the Lord as a reward. It is the Lord Christ you are serving. 25Anyone who does wrong will be repaid for his wrong, and there is no favoritism.

4 Masters, provide your slaves with what is right and fair, because you know that you also have a Master in heaven.

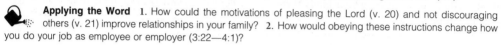

Discovering the Word 1. How do Paul's commands to wives/husbands, children/fathers and slaves/masters address our tendency to do the opposite? 2. The wife is to submit to the husband "as is fitting in the Lord" (v. 18). From what you learned in 3:5–17, what would that kind of submission include? What would it not include? 3. The husband is to love his wife and not be harsh with her (v. 19). How would 3:12–17 help him understand what that love should be like in actions and attitudes? 4. What attitudes and actions of parents embitter or discourage their children? 5. When and how are slaves to obey their masters (vv. 22–25)? With what motives? 6. What would it demand of a master to "provide your slaves with what is right and fair" (4:1)?

Applying the Word 1. How could the motivations of pleasing the Lord (v. 20) and not discouraging others (v. 21) improve relationships in your family? 2. How would obeying these instructions change how you do your job as employee or employer (3:22—4:1)?

Responding in Prayer Ask God to show you any attitudes or actions toward your family or at work that you need to change. Ask for grace to begin making one small change today.

---

8 / *Colossians 4:2–18*
Making the Most of Opportunities

NO ONE EVER becomes a Christian by just watching how a Christian lives. An observer might think the Christian is earning his way to heaven by trying to be good. How could anyone ever guess how to become a Christian? Debating if what we say or how we live is more important in witnessing is like asking which leg is more important for walking. In this study Paul shows that witnessing is an interplay between prayer, living and speaking. His closing greetings illustrate many ways Christians help and encourage each other.

Warming Up to God What one piece of advice about witnessing would you give to a younger Christian?

Read Colossians 4:2–18.

2Devote yourselves to prayer, being watchful and thankful. 3And pray for us, too, that God may open a door for our message, so that we may proclaim the mystery of Christ, for which I am in chains. 4Pray that I may proclaim it clearly, as I should. 5Be wise in the way you act toward outsiders; make the most of every opportunity. 6Let your conversation be always full of grace, sea- soned with salt, so that you may know how to answer everyone.

7Tychicus will tell you all the news about me. He is a dear brother, a faithful minister and fellow servant in the Lord. 8I am sending him to you for the express purpose that you may know about our^m circumstances and that he may encourage

m8 Some manuscripts *that he may know about your*

your hearts. 9He is coming with Onesimus, our faithful and dear brother, who is one of you. They will tell you everything that is happening here.

10My fellow prisoner Aristarchus sends you his greetings, as does Mark, the cousin of Barnabas. (You have received instructions about him; if he comes to you, welcome him.) 11Jesus, who is called Justus, also sends greetings. These are the only Jews among my fellow workers for the kingdom of God, and they have proved a comfort to me. 12Epaphras, who is one of you and a servant of Christ Jesus, sends greetings. He is always wrestling in prayer for you, that you may stand firm in all the will of God, mature and fully as-sured. 13I vouch for him that he is working hard for you and for those at Laodicea and Hierapolis. 14Our dear friend Luke, the doctor, and Demas send greetings. 15Give my greetings to the broth-ers at Laodicea, and to Nympha and the church in her house.

16After this letter has been read to you, see that it is also read in the church of the Laodiceans and that you in turn read the letter from Laodicea.

17Tell Archippus: "See to it that you complete the work you have received in the Lord."

18I, Paul, write this greeting in my own hand. Remember my chains. Grace be with you.

Discovering the Word 1. In verses 2–6 Paul teaches us how to speak to God about people and how to speak to people about God. Why would he tell us to *devote* ourselves to prayer (v. 2)? 2. Paul might have asked the church to pray for his release from prison. What requests does he make instead (vv. 3–4)? Why? 3. What advice does Paul give us about the way we live and converse with non-Christians (vv. 5–6)? 4. Paul concludes this letter with numerous personal messages and greetings. What qualities in people does Paul affirm, and why (vv. 7–18)?

Applying the Word 1. In what ways might you "be wise in the way you act toward outsiders" and "make the most of every opportunity" (v. 5)? 2. How could you encourage or comfort a fellow Christian this week by following the example of someone named here?

Responding in Prayer Use verses 3–4 to pray for yourself, your church leaders and missionaries. Ask God to make you aware of every opportunity to influence nonbelievers to consider Jesus.

1 Thessalonians

Conventional wisdom tells us that nothing is certain except death and taxes, but for most of us that is not enough. Wouldn't you like to be just as sure about where you stand with God? That's what the Thessalonians were looking for, and Paul's letters to them can help you find that assurance as well.

In the year A.D. 50, Paul entered Thessalonica while on his second missionary journey. He preached there for three weeks and was able to establish a church. However, a group of jealous Jews interpreted Paul's message to mean that he was proclaiming another ruler in opposition to the Roman emperor, and he was forced to leave town (Acts 17:1–10).

Because of Paul's concern for this young church, he sent his coworker, Timothy, to learn how the Thessalonians were doing. Timothy reported that the Christians' faith remained strong but that they continued to be persecuted by those who had banished Paul. Timothy also brought back questions which Paul had not had time to answer during his short stay.

First Thessalonians was Paul's first attempt at offering encouragement and answering questions—in fact it was probably the first of Paul's epistles. It was written from Corinth only a few months after Paul had left Thessalonica.

In 1 Thessalonians Paul offers encouragement in four major areas: (1) How can I be sure that I will be with Jesus after death? (2) How can I be sure that Jesus is coming again? (3) How can I be sure that Jesus hasn't forgotten me when I am suffering persecution? (4) How can I be sure that my life is pleasing to God?

Through your study of these letters, it is my hope that you will become sure of your faith and of your salvation and that, as a result, you will be able to "encourage each other with these words" (1Th 4:18).

Outline

1 / *1 Thessalonians 1*
Faith That Shows

A LIGHTHOUSE HAS become a common analogy for a church. Just as a lighthouse stands in a dark and dangerous spot flashing its message of warning and pointing to safe harbor, a church should also be a prominent and
unmistakable sign to the community in which it exists. How can you help your church or fellowship group become
such a shining light? This passage describes how the church in Thessalonica was able to do it.

 Warming Up to God What is the reputation of your church or fellowship group throughout the community?

 Read 1 Thessalonians 1.

1 Paul, Silas*ᵃ* and Timothy,

To the church of the Thessalonians in
God the Father and the Lord Jesus Christ:

Grace and peace to you.*ᵇ*

²We always thank God for all of you, mention-
ing you in our prayers. ³We continually remember before our God and Father your work produced by faith, your labor prompted by love, and
your endurance inspired by hope in our Lord
Jesus Christ.

⁴For we know, brothers loved by God, that he
has chosen you, ⁵because our gospel came to you
not simply with words, but also with power, with
the Holy Spirit and with deep conviction. You
know how we lived among you for your sake.

⁶You became imitators of us and of the Lord; in
spite of severe suffering, you welcomed the message with the joy given by the Holy Spirit. ⁷And
so you became a model to all the believers in
Macedonia and Achaia. ⁸The Lord's message rang
out from you not only in Macedonia and
Achaia—your faith in God has become known
everywhere. Therefore we do not need to say anything about it, ⁹for they themselves report what
kind of reception you gave us. They tell how you
turned to God from idols to serve the living and
true God, ¹⁰and to wait for his Son from heaven,
whom he raised from the dead—Jesus, who res-
cues us from the coming wrath.

*ᵃ1 Greek Silvanus, a variant of Silas   ᵇ1 Some early manuscripts you
from God our Father and the Lord Jesus Christ*

 Discovering the Word 1. Paul writes that he remembers the Thessalonians' "work produced by faith,"
"labor prompted by love" and "endurance inspired by hope" (v. 3). How do you think he could tell that faith,
love and hope were behind their actions? 2. What role has the Holy Spirit played in the Thessalonians' faith (vv.
5–6)? 3. What role did Paul, Silas and Timothy have in the Thessalonians' conversion (v. 6)? 4. When is it wise
and when is it unwise to imitate another Christian (vv. 6–7)? 5. What were the results of the Thessalonians' strong
faith (vv. 8–10)?

 Applying the Word 1. What do you think your reputation is with non-Christians? 2. How can your faith
(and the faith of your church or fellowship group) become more of a witness to others?

Responding in Prayer Ask to be made a genuine witness, and pray for the witness of your church.

2 / 1 Thessalonians 2:1–16
Gentle Evangelism

WHAT THOUGHTS COME to your mind when you hear the word *evangelism*? Pushy people trying to get you to see things their way? Guilt for not saying enough about your Savior? People swarming down the aisles at a gigantic rally? Or friends sharing the excitement of the good news with each other? For Paul, evangelism was always delightful and exciting. In this passage he tells us why talking about Christ is such a positive experience for him.

 Warming Up to God How do you feel about telling others about your faith? Talk with God about any fears or guilt you experience.

 Read 1 Thessalonians 2:1–16.

2 You know, brothers, that our visit to you was not a failure. ²We had previously suffered and been insulted in Philippi, as you know, but with the help of our God we dared to tell you his gospel in spite of strong opposition. ³For the appeal we make does not spring from error or impure motives, nor are we trying to trick you. ⁴On the contrary, we speak as men approved by God to be entrusted with the gospel. We are not trying to please men but God, who tests our hearts. ⁵You know we never used flattery, nor did we put on a mask to cover up greed—God is our witness. ⁶We were not looking for praise from men, not from you or anyone else.

As apostles of Christ we could have been a burden to you, ⁷but we were gentle among you, like a mother caring for her little children. ⁸We loved you so much that we were delighted to share with you not only the gospel of God but our lives as well, because you had become so dear to us. ⁹Surely you remember, brothers, our toil and hardship; we worked night and day in order not to be a burden to anyone while we preached the gospel of God to you.

¹⁰You are witnesses, and so is God, of how holy, righteous and blameless we were among you who believed. ¹¹For you know that we dealt with each of you as a father deals with his own children, ¹²encouraging, comforting and urging you to live lives worthy of God, who calls you into his kingdom and glory.

¹³And we also thank God continually because, when you received the word of God, which you heard from us, you accepted it not as the word of men, but as it actually is, the word of God, which is at work in you who believe. ¹⁴For you, brothers, became imitators of God's churches in Judea, which are in Christ Jesus: You suffered from your own countrymen the same things those churches suffered from the Jews, ¹⁵who killed the Lord Jesus and the prophets and also drove us out. They displease God and are hostile to all men ¹⁶in their effort to keep us from speaking to the Gentiles so that they may be saved. In this way they always heap up their sins to the limit. The wrath of God has come upon them at last.ᶜ

ᶜ16 Or *them fully*

 Discovering the Word 1. What excuses might Paul have had not to preach to the Thessalonians (vv. 1–2)? 2. What attitudes enable Paul to continue preaching despite opposition (vv. 3–6)? 3. What does this teach you about proper and improper reasons for witnessing to others? 4. Paul claims to have been "holy, righteous and blameless" (v. 10) among the Thessalonians. If this is important, how can imperfect people dare to do evangelism? 5. How is a father dealing with his children a good example of an evangelist (vv. 11–12)?

Applying the Word 1. In what specific ways can gentleness and caring become more a part of your evangelistic efforts? 2. In what ways have you found evangelism to be difficult? 3. What ideas and encouragement from this passage can help you to overcome these difficulties?

Responding in Prayer Ask God to give you encouragement to be a gentle evangelist.

3 / 1 Thessalonians 2:17—3:13
Unmistakable Love

STUDIES SHOW THAT more people leave their churches today for lack of love than for any other reason (Win Arn, Carroll Nyquist and Charles Arn, *Who Cares About Love?* [Pasadena, Calif.: Church Growth Press, 1986], p. 7). It is indeed sad that even those who are committed to the Lord of love are unable to offer that love to others. How can your church become a place where love will "increase and overflow for each other and for everyone else" (1Th 3:12)? This passage provides some practical examples.

 Warming Up to God On a scale of 1 to 10, how loved do you feel by the members of your church or fellowship group?

 Read 1 Thessalonians 2:17—3:13.

---

¹⁷But, brothers, when we were torn away from you for a short time (in person, not in thought), out of our intense longing we made every effort to see you. ¹⁸For we wanted to come to you—certainly I, Paul, did, again and again—but Satan stopped us. ¹⁹For what is our hope, our joy, or the crown in which we will glory in the presence of our Lord Jesus when he comes? Is it not you? ²⁰Indeed, you are our glory and joy.

3 So when we could stand it no longer, we thought it best to be left by ourselves in Athens. ²We sent Timothy, who is our brother and God's fellow worker[d] in spreading the gospel of Christ, to strengthen and encourage you in your faith, ³so that no one would be unsettled by these trials. You know quite well that we were destined for them. ⁴In fact, when we were with you, we kept telling you that we would be persecuted. And it turned out that way, as you well know. ⁵For this reason, when I could stand it no longer, I sent to find out about your faith. I was afraid that in some way the tempter might have tempted you and our efforts might have been useless.

⁶But Timothy has just now come to us from you and has brought good news about your faith and love. He has told us that you always have pleasant memories of us and that you long to see us, just as we also long to see you. ⁷Therefore, brothers, in all our distress and persecution we were encouraged about you because of your faith. ⁸For now we really live, since you are standing firm in the Lord. ⁹How can we thank God enough for you in return for all the joy we have in the presence of our God because of you? ¹⁰Night and day we pray most earnestly that we may see you again and supply what is lacking in your faith.

¹¹Now may our God and Father himself and our Lord Jesus clear the way for us to come to you. ¹²May the Lord make your love increase and overflow for each other and for everyone else, just as ours does for you. ¹³May he strengthen your hearts so that you will be blameless and holy in the presence of our God and Father when our Lord Jesus comes with all his holy ones.

ᵈ2 Some manuscripts *brother and fellow worker*; other manuscripts *brother and God's servant*

Discovering the Word 1. What evidence do you find in this passage that Paul really did love the Thessalonians (2:17, 20; 3:2, 5, 10)? 2. What phrases does Paul use to express his love (2:17–18; 3:5)? 3. What fears caused Paul to send Timothy to Thessalonica (3:2–5)? 4. What are Paul's desires for the Thessalonians (3:10–13)? 5. How do these desires reflect Paul's love and caring?

Applying the Word 1. How do you most often express your love for others? 2. What ideas from this passage can help you become even better at expressing love? 3. How can you (as an individual or group) help love increase within your church or fellowship group?

 Responding in Prayer Ask God to help you show love to someone in your church this week.

4 / *1 Thessalonians 4:1–12*
A Life That Pleases God

ALL OF US want to please the people we love the most. That is why a wife will surprise her husband with his favorite meal, a husband will plan a special evening at a concert he knows will excite his wife, or a child will pick a bouquet of dandelions to present to Mom and Dad. What can Christians do to please God, whom they love so dearly?

 Warming Up to God If a Christian brother or sister asked you for advice on how to make their life more pleasing to God, what is the first thing you would say?

 Read 1 Thessalonians 4:1–12.

4 Finally, brothers, we instructed you how to live in order to please God, as in fact you are living. Now we ask you and urge you in the Lord Jesus to do this more and more. ²For you know what instructions we gave you by the authority of the Lord Jesus.

³It is God's will that you should be sanctified: that you should avoid sexual immorality; ⁴that each of you should learn to control his own body*ᵉ* in a way that is holy and honorable, ⁵not in passionate lust like the heathen, who do not know God; ⁶and that in this matter no one should wrong his brother or take advantage of him. The Lord will punish men for all such sins, as we have already told you and warned you. ⁷For God did not call us to be impure, but to live a holy life.

⁸Therefore, he who rejects this instruction does not reject man but God, who gives you his Holy Spirit.

⁹Now about brotherly love we do not need to write to you, for you yourselves have been taught by God to love each other. ¹⁰And in fact, you do love all the brothers throughout Macedonia. Yet we urge you, brothers, to do so more and more.

¹¹Make it your ambition to lead a quiet life, to mind your own business and to work with your hands, just as we told you, ¹²so that your daily life may win the respect of outsiders and so that you will not be dependent on anybody.

ᵉ4 Or learn to live with his own wife; or learn to acquire a wife

 Discovering the Word 1. Why would Paul give these instructions on holy living to people whom he says are already living a life which pleases God (vv. 1,10)? 2. What clues does this passage give as to how Paul would define sexual immorality (vv. 3–6)? 3. How does sexual immorality "wrong" or "take advantage of" a brother (v. 6)? 4. Scholars agree that verses 11 and 12 were directed toward members of the church who had quit working and were relying on the kindness of their fellow Christians to provide them with necessities. Why would Paul have been concerned about the effect this attitude was having on outsiders?

Applying the Word 1. What work habits detract from your Christian witness? 2. How can this passage help you to resist sexual temptation? 3. Paul has given commands in this passage concerning sexual immorality, love for fellow Christians and work. What can you do this week to become more obedient in one of these areas?

Responding in Prayer Give your life to the Lord, praying that it will be made pleasing to him.

5 / 1 Thessalonians 4:13—5:11
The Hope of Christ's Coming

A CRISIS OCCURRED in the Thessalonian church when one of their members died. Since they had expected to all be alive when Christ returned, they were now confused. Did this mean their friend would miss out on Christ's coming? Had this person died because God was angry with them? How much longer would it be before Christ finally did return? Maybe you have fears about what will happen when you die or when Christ returns. In this passage, Paul seeks to calm our fears and encourage us to look forward to the day we meet our Maker.

 Warming Up to God What fears do you have about death?

 Read 1 Thessalonians 4:13—5:11.

---

¹³Brothers, we do not want you to be ignorant about those who fall asleep, or to grieve like the rest of men, who have no hope. ¹⁴We believe that Jesus died and rose again and so we believe that God will bring with Jesus those who have fallen asleep in him. ¹⁵According to the Lord's own word, we tell you that we who are still alive, who are left till the coming of the Lord, will certainly not precede those who have fallen asleep. ¹⁶For the Lord himself will come down from heaven, with a loud command, with the voice of the archangel and with the trumpet call of God, and the dead in Christ will rise first. ¹⁷After that, we who are still alive and are left will be caught up together with them in the clouds to meet the Lord in the air. And so we will be with the Lord forever. ¹⁸Therefore encourage each other with these words.

5 Now, brothers, about times and dates we do not need to write to you, ²for you know very well that the day of the Lord will come like a thief in the night. ³While peo-

ple are saying, "Peace and safety," destruction will come on them suddenly, as labor pains on a pregnant woman, and they will not escape.

⁴But you, brothers, are not in darkness so that this day should surprise you like a thief. ⁵You are all sons of the light and sons of the day. We do not belong to the night or to the darkness. ⁶So then, let us not be like others, who are asleep, but let us be alert and self-controlled. ⁷For those who sleep, sleep at night, and those who get drunk, get drunk at night. ⁸But since we belong to the day, let us be self-controlled, putting on faith and love as a breastplate, and the hope of salvation as a helmet. ⁹For God did not appoint us to suffer wrath but to receive salvation through our Lord Jesus Christ. ¹⁰He died for us so that, whether we are awake or asleep, we may live together with him. ¹¹Therefore encourage one another and build each other up, just as in fact you are doing.

 Discovering the Word 1. In what ways is grief different for a Christian than it is for a non-Christian (4:13)? 2. What sequence of events does Paul say will occur when Christ returns (4:16–17)? 3. Why are the examples of a thief (5:2) and labor pains (5:3) good analogies of what will happen on the day of the Lord? 4. What dangers are associated with living in darkness (5:5–7)? 5. What instructions does Paul give for living in the light (5:8)?

Applying the Word 1. How do Paul's words help you to face your own fears about death? 2. Paul tells us that our defensive weapons against darkness are faith, love and hope (v. 8). What are some practical ways in which these virtues can defend you?

Responding in Prayer Pray that you will be made ready for the day of the Lord.

6 / 1 Thessalonians 5:12–28
Life Among Friends

ANY GROUP OF people needs rules for getting along, and the church is no exception. Paul so wants the Thessalonians to "live in peace with each other" (1Th 5:13) that he closes his first letter to them with several instructions on how they can do this. These are instructions which have never gone out of date and can still be used to end the quarrels, hurt feelings and resentments in your church or fellowship group.

 Warming Up to God If you had the power to make one rule for helping people get along, what would it be?

 Read 1 Thessalonians 5:12–28.

---

¹²Now we ask you, brothers, to respect those who work hard among you, who are over you in the Lord and who admonish you. ¹³Hold them in the highest regard in love because of their work. Live in peace with each other. ¹⁴And we urge you, brothers, warn those who are idle, encourage the timid, help the weak, be patient with everyone. ¹⁵Make sure that nobody pays back wrong for wrong, but always try to be kind to each other and to everyone else.

¹⁶Be joyful always; ¹⁷pray continually; ¹⁸give thanks in all circumstances, for this is God's will for you in Christ Jesus.

¹⁹Do not put out the Spirit's fire; ²⁰do not treat prophecies with contempt. ²¹Test everything. Hold on to the good. ²²Avoid every kind of evil.

²³May God himself, the God of peace, sanctify you through and through. May your whole spirit, soul and body be kept blameless at the coming of our Lord Jesus Christ. ²⁴The one who calls you is faithful and he will do it.

²⁵Brothers, pray for us. ²⁶Greet all the brothers with a holy kiss. ²⁷I charge you before the Lord to have this letter read to all the brothers.

²⁸The grace of our Lord Jesus Christ be with you.

 Discovering the Word 1. What does it mean for someone to be "over you in the Lord" (v. 12)? 2. How can you warn a person about something they are doing wrong (v. 14) or prevent them from taking revenge (v. 15) and still live in peace with them? 3. What does it mean to be joyful "always," pray "continually" and give thanks "in all circumstances" (vv. 16–18)? 4. How can you test things like prophecy or teaching to find out if they are good or evil (vv. 19–22)? 5. Look through the passage again and pick out the actions and attitudes (stated or implied) which are displeasing to God. What are they?

 Applying the Word 1. When have you found God faithful in keeping you from sin (v. 24)? 2. In what way do you currently need God's faithfulness to keep you from sin?

Responding in Prayer Follow the discipline of giving thanks in all circumstances by finding as many things in your life as you can to be thankful for.

2 Thessalonians

S econd Thessalonians was written a short time after 1 Thessalonians to clear up misconceptions about the Second Coming that the first letter had failed to answer.

Although the letter was written to Gentiles, it assumes some knowledge of the Old Testament. According to Donald Guthrie, this was typical of early Christian teaching (*New Testament Introduction,* rev. ed. [Downers Grove, Ill.: InterVarsity Press, 1990], p. 596).

Paul most likely wrote the letter from Corinth. In addition to clarifying their understanding about Christ's return, Paul addressed some ongoing problems in the church in dealing with idleness. This book offered its readers comfort and insight about faith and end times, as well as a call to take responsibility. May it both challenge and encourage you as well.

Outline

1 / 2 Thessalonians 1
Evidence of Faith

CAN I KNOW for sure that I will go to heaven?

This is a question that plagued the Thessalonians to such an extent that even after the comfort of his first letter, Paul has to write again and give further encouragement. It was difficult for these young Christians to believe that the suffering of their present life would really be followed by the eternal joy of heaven. Perhaps you also wonder if heaven really exists and if you can be sure of going there. If so, you will find Paul writing this passage directly to you.

 Warming Up to God Have you ever met a person and gone away thinking, "They must be a Christian." What gave you that impression?

 Read 2 Thessalonians 1.

1 Paul, Silas^a and Timothy,

To the church of the Thessalonians in God our Father and the Lord Jesus Christ:

²Grace and peace to you from God the Father and the Lord Jesus Christ.

³We ought always to thank God for you, brothers, and rightly so, because your faith is growing more and more, and the love every one of you has for each other is increasing. ⁴Therefore, among God's churches we boast about your perseverance and faith in all the persecutions and trials you are enduring.

⁵All this is evidence that God's judgment is right, and as a result you will be counted worthy of the kingdom of God, for which you are suffering. ⁶God is just: He will pay back trouble to those who trouble you ⁷and give relief to you who are troubled, and to us as well. This will happen when the Lord Jesus is revealed from heaven in blazing fire with his powerful angels. ⁸He will punish those who do not know God and do not obey the gospel of our Lord Jesus. ⁹They will be punished with everlasting destruction and shut out from the presence of the Lord and from the majesty of his power ¹⁰on the day he comes to be glorified in his holy people and to be marveled at among all those who have believed. This includes you, because you believed our testimony to you.

¹¹With this in mind, we constantly pray for you, that our God may count you worthy of his calling, and that by his power he may fulfill every good purpose of yours and every act prompted by your faith. ¹²We pray this so that the name of our Lord Jesus may be glorified in you, and you in him, according to the grace of our God and the Lord Jesus Christ.^{b}

---

^{a}1 Greek *Silvanus*, a variant of *Silas* ^{b}12 Or *God and Lord, Jesus Christ*

 Discovering the Word 1. What good things does Paul notice about the lives of the Thessalonians (vv. 3–4)? 2. Why do you think that in times of persecution, some people's faith and love grow while others' fail (v. 4)? 3. Paul proclaims that "God is just." How does he describe God's justice (vv. 5–10)? 4. According to this passage, what makes a person "worthy of the kingdom" (v. 5) or "worthy of [God's] calling" (v. 11)? 5. In light of his teaching about God's judgment, why does Paul pray as he does in verses 11–12?

Applying the Word 1. How can God's justice encourage you when things are "just not fair"? 2. If someone were to pray for you as Paul did in verses 11–12, what is one specific way in which you would want God to change your life?

Responding in Prayer Pray that God's justice would be done in your life and throughout the world.

2 / 2 Thessalonians 2
Lawlessness on the Loose

HOW WILL THE world end? Will there be nuclear war? An evil empire? The destruction of civilization? Paul advises us that Satan has yet to attack us with the worst he has, and when he does, it will be a fearful time to be alive. However, Paul also promises that God will always be in control.

 Warming Up to God What potential threats to the safety of the world do you see right now (for example, attitudes, weapon building, warfare and so on)? What personal fears or concerns do you have about that?

 Read 2 Thessalonians 2.

2 Concerning the coming of our Lord Jesus Christ and our being gathered to him, we ask you, brothers, ²not to become easily unsettled or alarmed by some prophecy, report or letter supposed to have come from us, saying that the day of the Lord has already come. ³Don't let anyone deceive you in any way, for ˻that day will not come˼ until the rebellion occurs and the man of lawlessness*c* is revealed, the man doomed to destruction. ⁴He will oppose and will exalt himself over everything that is called God or is worshiped, so that he sets himself up in God's temple, proclaiming himself to be God.

⁵Don't you remember that when I was with you I used to tell you these things? ⁶And now you know what is holding him back, so that he may be revealed at the proper time. ⁷For the secret power of lawlessness is already at work; but the one who now holds it back will continue to do so till he is taken out of the way. ⁸And then the lawless one will be revealed, whom the Lord Jesus will overthrow with the breath of his mouth and destroy by the splendor of his coming. ⁹The coming of the lawless one will be in accordance with the work of Satan displayed in all kinds of coun-

terfeit miracles, signs and wonders, ¹⁰and in every sort of evil that deceives those who are perishing. They perish because they refused to love the truth and so be saved. ¹¹For this reason God sends them a powerful delusion so that they will believe the lie ¹²and so that all will be condemned who have not believed the truth but have delighted in wickedness.

¹³But we ought always to thank God for you, brothers loved by the Lord, because from the beginning God chose you*d* to be saved through the sanctifying work of the Spirit and through belief in the truth. ¹⁴He called you to this through our gospel, that you might share in the glory of our Lord Jesus Christ. ¹⁵So then, brothers, stand firm and hold to the teachings*e* we passed on to you, whether by word of mouth or by letter.

¹⁶May our Lord Jesus Christ himself and God our Father, who loved us and by his grace gave us eternal encouragement and good hope, ¹⁷encourage your hearts and strengthen you in every good deed and word.

---

c3 Some manuscripts sin   *d13 Some manuscripts* because God chose you as his firstfruits   *e15 Or* traditions

---

 Discovering the Word 1. In 1 Thessalonians 4:13–18 Paul responded to the fears of the Thessalonians that if they died before Christ returned, they would miss the joy Christ had for them. Apparently, after Paul sent the first letter, someone tried to convince the Thessalonians that the day of the Lord had already come. What is Paul's proof that the day of the Lord has not come (vv. 3, 9)? **2.** What can you learn about the "man of lawlessness" from this passage (vv. 3–4, 7–10)? **3.** In what ways have you noticed the "secret power of lawlessness" (v. 7) to be already at work? **4.** What contrasts do you find between those whom God condemns (vv. 10–12) and those whom he chooses for salvation (vv. 13–17)?

 Applying the Word 1. Even for Christians, the lawless one will bring fear and testing. What can you do to prepare yourself to withstand him? **2.** How can this passage encourage you about facing the future?

Responding in Prayer Talk openly with God about any fears or concerns you have regarding the future.

3 / 2 Thessalonians 3
Lazy Christians

MEMBERS OF THE Thessalonian church were refusing to take responsibility. Some had quit working because they thought Jesus would be back any moment and didn't see any reason to exert themselves. Others relaxed because there were plenty of wealthier members in the church who were always willing to share. Regardless of the reason, Paul was abhorred by such laziness, and set the rule "If a man will not work, he shall not eat." How can our laziness affect the work of Christ? What can we do about the laziness of others? Paul addresses those questions in this study.

 Warming Up to God When is it hard for you to feel motivated to do the work of your church?

 Read 2 Thessalonians 3.

3 Finally, brothers, pray for us that the message of the Lord may spread rapidly and be honored, just as it was with you. ²And pray that we may be delivered from wicked and evil men, for not everyone has faith. ³But the Lord is faithful, and he will strengthen and protect you from the evil one. ⁴We have confidence in the Lord that you are doing and will continue to do the things we command. ⁵May the Lord direct your hearts into God's love and Christ's perseverance.

⁶In the name of the Lord Jesus Christ, we command you, brothers, to keep away from every brother who is idle and does not live according to the teachingʲ you received from us. ⁷For you yourselves know how you ought to follow our example. We were not idle when we were with you, ⁸nor did we eat anyone's food without paying for it. On the contrary, we worked night and day, laboring and toiling so that we would not be a burden to any of you. ⁹We did this, not because we do not have the right to such help, but in order to make ourselves a model for you to follow. ¹⁰For even when we were with you, we gave you this rule: "If a man will not work, he shall not eat."

¹¹We hear that some among you are idle. They are not busy; they are busybodies. ¹²Such people we command and urge in the Lord Jesus Christ to settle down and earn the bread they eat. ¹³And as for you, brothers, never tire of doing what is right.

¹⁴If anyone does not obey our instruction in this letter, take special note of him. Do not associate with him, in order that he may feel ashamed. ¹⁵Yet do not regard him as an enemy, but warn him as a brother.

¹⁶Now may the Lord of peace himself give you peace at all times and in every way. The Lord be with all of you.

¹⁷I, Paul, write this greeting in my own hand, which is the distinguishing mark in all my letters. This is how I write.

¹⁸The grace of our Lord Jesus Christ be with you all.

ʲ6 Or *tradition*

Discovering the Word 1. In what ways did Paul expect that his ministry could be enhanced because of the Thessalonians' prayer (vv. 1–2)? 2. How is Paul's confidence in the Lord expressed in this request for prayer (vv. 3–5)? 3. How would you describe the problem the Thessalonian church was experiencing (v. 11)? 4. How did Paul make himself an example of the proper attitude toward work (vv. 7–9)? 5. What actions are to be taken against those who refuse to work (vv. 12–15)?

Applying the Word 1. What encouragement and ideas do these verses give you concerning your own prayer life? 2. In what ways do lazy Christians still continue to take advantage of the work of others? 3. What principles for discipline that could be applied in the church today do you find in this passage?

 Responding in Prayer Pray that like Paul you will be a good example to others in your attitude toward work.

1 Timothy

E phesus, a key seaport for Asia Minor, was a swinging commercial center. Without an army, it maintained its place in the world through deal-making. It was the crowded home of about 350,000 people.

Dominating the economy of Ephesus was the temple of Artemis, "goddess of the Ephesians." It was regarded as one of the seven wonders of the ancient world. A huge structure of solid marble, it was the largest temple in the world outside Egypt, and the biggest *bank* east of Rome! You can read in Acts 19 about the riot Paul's preaching triggered among the guilds that depended on temple business. Artemis herself was a 37-breasted fertility goddess who stood for bringing prosperity out of constant change.

And change there was.

Various cultures mixed in Ephesus. Its heritage was Greek, but Romans pushed in when it became part of the Empire. A sizeable Jewish community took root, as well as smaller communities of many ethnic groups. Different religions, philosophies and ethics coexisted while everybody sought some piece of the economic action.

Sports were a major entertainment. The Greeks had two gymnasia built for athletic contests, while the Romans built a stadium for gladiator combat. By the mid-second century, the Roman approach of spectacular violence won the day over the Greek ideal of simple competition.

Sex was also big business. Art depicting various sex acts adorned the garden walls of large villas. Bestiality and homosexuality were celebrated. The Romans built baths—a kind of ancient country club where the upper-class members of both sexes went nude. Prostitution, divorce, multiple marriages, abandoned children and neglect of the elderly were common. Religious opinion ranged from advocating deviant sex to shunning sex totally.

A confusing mix of religions existed in the shadow of the dominant Artemis. The large Jewish community coexisted with it. Smaller ethnic groups had their own religions but didn't seek prominence. The Romans argued the case to rename Artemis as Diana, while thinking Greeks argued over mystical experiences and whether the names of gods were just diverse labels for the "One Prime Mover."

Although Artemis ruled in the public square, magic influenced the personal lives of most people and invaded all of the formal religions. A striking example is the account in Acts

19:13–17, which involved even the family of the Jewish high priest. In magic, the Ephesian spirit of deal-making was applied to spirituality. Ephesian magic became famous throughout the Roman world.

Paul, for his part, saw Ephesus as a great place to preach the gospel. He began with preaching to his fellow Jews on his second missionary journey. On his third journey, he invested two solid years evangelizing and developing Christian leaders. Christian faith became so popular that the magic trade and temple business fell sharply.

Paul's farewell message (Acts 20), however, shows that he was bracing for a spiritual counterattack on the Christian community. He predicted even some of his converts would set themselves up as Christian "gurus" and carve out followings around their own blend of Scripture, the gospel and mystical teachings. The issue Paul saw as crucial was spiritual authority: When should we accept spiritual teachings? When should we reject them? How do we know if Christian teachers are trustworthy? This, in fact, was just the situation when Paul wrote his first letter to Timothy.

Paul had turned over the leadership of the church in Ephesus, the most strategic in Asia Minor, to Timothy, a bright, sensitive associate. Timothy was about forty years old at that time, which was considered young for such leadership. False teaching was coming from people within the church. Since some of these were leaders (see Acts 20:30), Paul could not write to the church at Ephesus directly, but instead went through Timothy whom he had confidence in (Gordon Fee, "Issues in Evangelical Hermeneutics," *Crux* 26, no. 4 [December 1990]). Timothy's mission was to deal with false teaching, and it seems he was a capable teacher.

From references in 1 and 2 Corinthians, Acts, and the letters to Timothy, we know Timothy was a committed, but very human, person with some insecurities. Hebrews 13:23 shows that he spent some time in prison for his faith. We don't know what finally happened to Timothy, but we do know that John became the leader of the church not too long after these letters were written.

In these letters we can see Paul coaching the younger leader. In the process he raises issues which bear on us all—leaders or not.

Outline

1 / *1 Timothy 1*
What Difference Does It Make?

"CHRIST CONSCIOUSNESS—MYSTICAL Teaching in the Bible," advertises a poster. "The mystical core of Christ's teaching has been obscured by centuries of dogma," it announces, inviting Christians to come to lectures by a young lady who follows a Hindu sect. And at the other extreme, some Christian leaders, dismayed by a low level of commitment, seek to create high-intensity groups with special teachings on top of the gospel and extra rules that regulate the social lives of their members. These modern examples are the kinds of thing that were rampant in the church at Ephesus; Paul sent Timothy to Ephesus to deal with them.

 Warming Up to God   How do you distinguish between true and false spirituality?

 Read 1 Timothy 1.

1 Paul, an apostle of Christ Jesus by the command of God our Savior and of Christ Jesus our hope,

²To Timothy my true son in the faith:

Grace, mercy and peace from God the Father and Christ Jesus our Lord.

³As I urged you when I went into Macedonia, stay there in Ephesus so that you may command certain men not to teach false doctrines any longer ⁴nor to devote themselves to myths and endless genealogies. These promote controversies rather than God's work—which is by faith. ⁵The goal of this command is love, which comes from a pure heart and a good conscience and a sincere faith. ⁶Some have wandered away from these and turned to meaningless talk. ⁷They want to be teachers of the law, but they do not know what they are talking about or what they so confidently affirm.

⁸We know that the law is good if one uses it properly. ⁹We also know that law*ᵃ* is made not for the righteous but for lawbreakers and rebels, the ungodly and sinful, the unholy and irreligious; for those who kill their fathers or mothers, for murderers, ¹⁰for adulterers and perverts, for slave traders and liars and perjurers—and for whatever else is contrary to the sound doctrine

¹¹that conforms to the glorious gospel of the blessed God, which he entrusted to me.

¹²I thank Christ Jesus our Lord, who has given me strength, that he considered me faithful, appointing me to his service. ¹³Even though I was once a blasphemer and a persecutor and a violent man, I was shown mercy because I acted in ignorance and unbelief. ¹⁴The grace of our Lord was poured out on me abundantly, along with the faith and love that are in Christ Jesus.

¹⁵Here is a trustworthy saying that deserves full acceptance: Christ Jesus came into the world to save sinners—of whom I am the worst. ¹⁶But for that very reason I was shown mercy so that in me, the worst of sinners, Christ Jesus might display his unlimited patience as an example for those who would believe on him and receive eternal life. ¹⁷Now to the King eternal, immortal, invisible, the only God, be honor and glory for ever and ever. Amen.

¹⁸Timothy, my son, I give you this instruction in keeping with the prophecies once made about you, so that by following them you may fight the good fight, ¹⁹holding on to faith and a good conscience. Some have rejected these and so have shipwrecked their faith. ²⁰Among them are Hymenaeus and Alexander, whom I have handed over to Satan to be taught not to blaspheme.

ᵃ9 Or that the law

Discovering the Word   1. How does Paul describe Timothy's job (vv. 3–5)?   2. Finding hidden meanings in the Old Testament was big business in first-century religion. False teachers here tried to mix these "secret teachings" with the gospel. What results were the false teachers getting for their efforts (vv. 4–6)?   3. From what Paul says about the proper use of the law, how does it seem that the false teachers use it (vv. 8–11)?   4. In what ways was Paul himself like the false teachers before his conversion (vv. 12–17)?   5. Note the places where the word *conscience* comes up (vv. 5, 19). When we speculate and theorize instead of dealing with our own issues of sin, what happens to conscience?

 Applying the Word 1. How can the kind of faith Paul shows in verse 15 help you face your own issues of conscience? 2. As in Paul's day, Christians can wander into groups that make unusual claims and demands. They may have impressive features, but engage in certain practices and pressures which make members feel uneasy. A lot of energy goes into keeping faith and conscience apart in these groups. Are you involved with some "spiritual" activities which bother your own conscience? (Be as honest as possible.)

Responding in Prayer Close in prayer by putting your own name in place of the general word *sinners* in verse 15. Now read verses 16–17 as your own prayer of thanks to God.

2 / 1 Timothy 2
Barriers to Renewal

DO YOU EVER have difficulty approaching God in prayer? The Christians in Ephesus did. The barriers to prayer described here are anger, an over-emphasis on appearance, and an inappropriate role for women. Having sized up the situation and reminded Timothy of his mission, Paul outlines first steps to dealing with the needs of the church.

 Warming Up to God When do you find prayer difficult?

 Read 1 Timothy 2.

2 I urge, then, first of all, that requests, prayers, intercession and thanksgiving be made for everyone— ²for kings and all those in authority, that we may live peaceful and quiet lives in all godliness and holiness. ³This is good, and pleases God our Savior, ⁴who wants all men to be saved and to come to a knowledge of the truth. ⁵For there is one God and one mediator between God and men, the man Christ Jesus, ⁶who gave himself as a ransom for all men—the testimony given in its proper time. ⁷And for this purpose I was appointed a herald and an apostle—I am telling the truth, I am not lying—and a teacher of the true faith to the Gentiles.

⁸I want men everywhere to lift up holy hands in prayer, without anger or disputing.

⁹I also want women to dress modestly, with decency and propriety, not with braided hair or gold or pearls or expensive clothes, ¹⁰but with good deeds, appropriate for women who profess to worship God.

¹¹A woman should learn in quietness and full submission. ¹²I do not permit a woman to teach or to have authority over a man; she must be silent. ¹³For Adam was formed first, then Eve. ¹⁴And Adam was not the one deceived; it was the woman who was deceived and became a sinner. ¹⁵But women*ᵇ* will be saved*ᶜ* through childbearing—if they continue in faith, love and holiness with propriety.

ᵇ15 Greek she   ᶜ15 Or restored

Discovering the Word 1. Find all the times Paul says "all" and "everyone" (vv. 1–6). What does the use of these terms communicate about God? 2. Why do you think Paul emphasizes the word *one* in verse 5? 3. This entire chapter deals with worship. The church in Ephesus was probably a network of house churches. Their worship may have been patterned after the Jewish synagogues which separated men and women. What problem hindered the worship by men (v. 8)? 4. What problem hindered the worship by women (v. 9)? 5. In verses 11–12, Paul forbids women to teach men. But in 1 Corinthians 11:5, he tells them how to dress when they preach (or prophesy). How do you reconcile these texts?

Applying the Word 1. According to this passage, what could hinder worship and sharing the gospel? 2. Consider which of those are problems for you. How can you better deal with them?

 Responding in Prayer Pray for your church's worship and for your personal worship.

3 / 1 Timothy 3
Who Can Lead?

SOME CHURCHES AND fellowships have a few people who are willing to lead. Those people may end up feeling burdened and alone. Other churches have people who are willing to lead, but not ready. If there are not enough leaders, however, the work of the church will not get done. The church of Ephesus was in the latter category. Those who were willing to lead were immature. And Timothy could not hope to carry out his mission against false teachers unless the leadership was healthy.

 Warming Up to God What have your experiences of Christian leadership been like?

 Read 1 Timothy 3.

---

3 Here is a trustworthy saying: If anyone sets his heart on being an overseer,[d] he desires a noble task. [2]Now the overseer must be above reproach, the husband of but one wife, temperate, self-controlled, respectable, hospitable, able to teach, [3]not given to drunkenness, not violent but gentle, not quarrelsome, not a lover of money. [4]He must manage his own family well and see that his children obey him with proper respect. [5](If anyone does not know how to manage his own family, how can he take care of God's church?) [6]He must not be a recent convert, or he may become conceited and fall under the same judgment as the devil. [7]He must also have a good reputation with outsiders, so that he will not fall into disgrace and into the devil's trap.

[8]Deacons, likewise, are to be men worthy of respect, sincere, not indulging in much wine, and not pursuing dishonest gain. [9]They must keep hold of the deep truths of the faith with a clear conscience. [10]They must first be tested; and then if there is nothing against them, let them serve as deacons.

[11]In the same way, their wives[e] are to be women worthy of respect, not malicious talkers but temperate and trustworthy in everything.

[12]A deacon must be the husband of but one wife and must manage his children and his household well. [13]Those who have served well gain an excellent standing and great assurance in their faith in Christ Jesus.

[14]Although I hope to come to you soon, I am writing you these instructions so that, [15]if I am delayed, you will know how people ought to conduct themselves in God's household, which is the church of the living God, the pillar and foundation of the truth. [16]Beyond all question, the mystery of godliness is great:

> He[f] appeared in a body,[g]
>   was vindicated by the Spirit,
> was seen by angels,
>   was preached among the nations,
> was believed on in the world,
>   was taken up in glory.

*d1 Traditionally bishop; also in verse 2   e11 Or way, deaconesses
f16 Some manuscripts God   g16 Or in the flesh*

Discovering the Word 1. Consider two categories of qualification—*character* and *ability*. How do the qualities mentioned in these verses divide into these two categories? 2. What do you think is Paul's reason for insisting that a leader's relationships must work in the spheres of both church and family (vv. 5–6)? 3. How have you seen the principle in verse 7 obeyed or disobeyed? 4. "Deacon" simply means "servant." In the passage it seems that deacons deal with the more practical affairs of church life, rather than with teaching. Given that, why do you think the point about doctrine in verse 9 is made with so much emphasis? **5.** What do verses 14–16 tell us about Paul's purpose in writing this letter?

 Applying the Word 1. Verse 16 was probably a hymn sung in the church at Ephesus. The word translated as "deep truths" in verse 9 is rendered "mystery" here. We can say that the result Paul wanted from good Christian leadership was that these truths would be revealed. Therefore, when people look at our fellowship, what should they see? **2.** How can you serve your church through leadership, or encourage others who lead?

 Responding in Prayer Pray for your pastor and church leaders.

4 / 1 Timothy 4
True and False Ministry

WITH THIS CHAPTER Paul's strategy for Timothy starts to emerge clearly. Timothy's mission was to deal with the false teachers. Paul sees, however, that fighting false teachers with ideology alone is fruitless. The real mission is that the church be healthy so that Jesus Christ is communicated through it. So he spoke of prayer and leadership first. With that foundation in place, Timothy will be able to turn his attention directly to the problems at hand.

 Warming Up to God Is there an older Christian in your family or church who has given you good advice? What was it?

Read 1 Timothy 4.

4 The Spirit clearly says that in later times some will abandon the faith and follow deceiving spirits and things taught by demons. ²Such teachings come through hypocritical liars, whose consciences have been seared as with a hot iron. ³They forbid people to marry and order them to abstain from certain foods, which God created to be received with thanksgiving by those who believe and who know the truth. ⁴For everything God created is good, and nothing is to be rejected if it is received with thanksgiving, ⁵because it is consecrated by the word of God and prayer.

⁶If you point these things out to the brothers, you will be a good minister of Christ Jesus, brought up in the truths of the faith and of the good teaching that you have followed. ⁷Have nothing to do with godless myths and old wives' tales; rather, train yourself to be godly. ⁸For physical training is of some value, but godliness has value for all things, holding promise for both the present life and the life to come.

⁹This is a trustworthy saying that deserves full acceptance ¹⁰(and for this we labor and strive), that we have put our hope in the living God, who is the Savior of all men, and especially of those who believe.

¹¹Command and teach these things. ¹²Don't let anyone look down on you because you are young, but set an example for the believers in speech, in life, in love, in faith and in purity. ¹³Until I come, devote yourself to the public reading of Scripture, to preaching and to teaching. ¹⁴Do not neglect your gift, which was given you through a prophetic message when the body of elders laid their hands on you.

¹⁵Be diligent in these matters; give yourself wholly to them, so that everyone may see your progress. ¹⁶Watch your life and doctrine closely. Persevere in them, because if you do, you will save both yourself and your hearers.

Discovering the Word 1. What is the nature of the teachings described in verses 2–3? **2.** Why is this teaching—which could seem to be "superspiritual"—really a doctrine of demons (vv. 3–4)? 3. When you think of "false teaching," do you think of teachers who are morally too loose or too strict? Explain. 4. What was Timothy's personal life to be like (vv. 7–16)? 5. How was it to differ from that of the false teachers?

Applying the Word 1. Why do you think you are motivated at some times and *not* motivated at other times for training in godliness (v. 7)? 2. Timothy's primary ministry was teaching. What in this passage encourages you to develop and use your ministry gifts?

Responding in Prayer Pray for those who might be under the hold of false teachers, that the truth would be revealed to them.

5 / *1 Timothy 5:1—6:2*
Implementing Spiritual Teaching

AT ONE TIME or another all of us have probably been in a situation in which we felt that someone in our church or fellowship was sinning. Whether or not we act on the situation and how we communicate to that person have a big effect on the outcome. Often when we rebuke others about their lifestyles, we come off as being judgmental and self-righteous. When Paul tells Timothy about specific persons and groups he needed to confront about certain issues, he is careful to show how to do so in love. Paul's teaching here gives us valuable guidance on being both direct and loving with other Christians.

Warming Up to God When have you found—or seen—rebuke to have a positive impact?

Read 1 Timothy 5:1—6:2.

5 Do not rebuke an older man harshly, but exhort him as if he were your father. Treat younger men as brothers, ²older women as mothers, and younger women as sisters, with absolute purity.

³Give proper recognition to those widows who are really in need. ⁴But if a widow has children or grandchildren, these should learn first of all to put their religion into practice by caring for their own family and so repaying their parents and grandparents, for this is pleasing to God. ⁵The widow who is really in need and left all alone puts her hope in God and continues night and day to pray and to ask God for help. ⁶But the widow who lives for pleasure is dead even while she lives. ⁷Give the people these instructions, too, so that no one may be open to blame. ⁸If anyone does not provide for his relatives, and especially for his immediate family, he has denied the faith and is worse than an unbeliever.

⁹No widow may be put on the list of widows unless she is over sixty, has been faithful to her husband,ʰ ¹⁰and is well known for her good deeds, such as bringing up children, showing hospitality, washing the feet of the saints, helping those in trouble and devoting herself to all kinds of good deeds.

¹¹As for younger widows, do not put them on such a list. For when their sensual desires overcome their dedication to Christ, they want to marry. ¹²Thus they bring judgment on themselves, because they have broken their first pledge. ¹³Besides, they get into the habit of being idle and going about from house to house. And not only do they become idlers, but also gossips and busybodies, saying things they ought not to. ¹⁴So I counsel younger widows to marry, to have children, to manage their homes and to give the enemy no opportunity for slander. ¹⁵Some have in fact already turned away to follow Satan.

¹⁶If any woman who is a believer has widows in her family, she should help them and not let the church be burdened with them, so that the church can help those widows who are really in need.

ʰ9 Or *has had but one husband*

¹⁷The elders who direct the affairs of the church well are worthy of double honor, especially those whose work is preaching and teaching. ¹⁸For the Scripture says, "Do not muzzle the ox while it is treading out the grain,"ⁱ and "The worker deserves his wages."ʲ ¹⁹Do not entertain an accusation against an elder unless it is brought by two or three witnesses. ²⁰Those who sin are to be rebuked publicly, so that the others may take warning.

²¹I charge you, in the sight of God and Christ Jesus and the elect angels, to keep these instructions without partiality, and to do nothing out of favoritism.

²²Do not be hasty in the laying on of hands, and do not share in the sins of others. Keep yourself pure.

²³Stop drinking only water, and use a little wine because of your stomach and your frequent illnesses.

²⁴The sins of some men are obvious, reaching the place of judgment ahead of them; the sins of others trail behind them. ²⁵In the same way, good deeds are obvious, and even those that are not cannot be hidden.

6 All who are under the yoke of slavery should consider their masters worthy of full respect, so that God's name and our teaching may not be slandered. ²Those who have believing masters are not to show less respect for them because they are brothers. Instead, they are to serve them even better, because those who benefit from their service are believers, and dear to them. These are the things you are to teach and urge on them.

ⁱ18 Deut. 25:4   ʲ18 Luke 10:7

 Discovering the Word 1. Paul touches on the different age and gender groups Timothy must lead. How is Timothy to regard the people he ministers to? 2. How is a godly widow to be distinguished from an ungodly one (vv. 3–8)? 3. What criteria did a widow need to meet to receive a place on the list of those who received financial aid from the church (vv. 9–10)? 4. Why do you think Paul gives these specific instructions about rebuking an elder in verses 19–20? 5. How have you found verses 24–25 to be true? 6. From 6:1–2 what do you think has been happening when slaves become believers?

 Applying the Word 1. How can you rebuke someone in ways that are clear but also affirm the other person as a member of God's family? 2. In affluent Ephesus, like twentieth-century America, many elderly people were evidently abandoned. What obligations do you have to your own parents? 3. What ideas does this passage give you for new areas of ministry?

 Responding in Prayer Pray for those in your church who are needy and who may be without family.

---

6 / *1 Timothy 6:3–20*
Find Your Riches in Christ

SOME WELL-KNOWN Christian teachers and authors tell us that being a Christian means success and prosperity. If we are faithful, God will bless us with wealth. Other Christians advocate a simple lifestyle without interest in material possessions. What does Scripture say about how we are to regard money? In this chapter Paul concludes his agenda of how to lead the powerful and the powerless by addressing the wealthy members of the church.

Warming Up to God What do you believe is the place of money in the life of a Christian?

Read 1 Timothy 6:3–20.

---

³If anyone teaches false doctrines and does not agree to the sound instruction of our Lord Jesus Christ and to godly teaching, ⁴he is conceited and understands nothing. He has an unhealthy interest in controversies and quarrels about words that result in envy, strife, malicious talk, evil suspi-

cions 5and constant friction between men of corrupt mind, who have been robbed of the truth and who think that godliness is a means to financial gain.

6But godliness with contentment is great gain. 7For we brought nothing into the world, and we can take nothing out of it. 8But if we have food and clothing, we will be content with that. 9People who want to get rich fall into temptation and a trap and into many foolish and harmful desires that plunge men into ruin and destruction. 10For the love of money is a root of all kinds of evil. Some people, eager for money, have wandered from the faith and pierced themselves with many griefs.

11But you, man of God, flee from all this, and pursue righteousness, godliness, faith, love, endurance and gentleness. 12Fight the good fight of the faith. Take hold of the eternal life to which you were called when you made your good confession in the presence of many witnesses. 13In the sight of God, who gives life to everything, and of Christ Jesus, who while testifying before Pontius Pilate made the good confession, I charge you 14to keep this command without spot or blame

until the appearing of our Lord Jesus Christ, 15which God will bring about in his own time— God, the blessed and only Ruler, the King of kings and Lord of lords, 16who alone is immortal and who lives in unapproachable light, whom no one has seen or can see. To him be honor and might forever. Amen.

17Command those who are rich in this present world not to be arrogant nor to put their hope in wealth, which is so uncertain, but to put their hope in God, who richly provides us with everything for our enjoyment. 18Command them to do good, to be rich in good deeds, and to be generous and willing to share. 19In this way they will lay up treasure for themselves as a firm foundation for the coming age, so that they may take hold of the life that is truly life.

20Timothy, guard what has been entrusted to your care. Turn away from godless chatter and the opposing ideas of what is falsely called knowledge, 21which some have professed and in so doing have wandered from the faith.

Grace be with you.

Discovering the Word 1. What do you think Paul means by an "unhealthy interest" (v. 4)? 2. According to verses 6–8, how are we to find contentment? 3. In your own words, how would you explain Paul's teaching on riches in verses 9–10? 4. What was Paul commanding Timothy to do in this context (vv. 11–14)? 5. How is Christ pictured in verses 13–16? 6. Why do you think Paul told Timothy to turn away from "godless chatter" (v. 20)?

Applying the Word 1. In what ways does your Christian life feel like a fight? 2. Describe how you have seen Christians use riches to do good work. 3. What has God entrusted to your care, and how do you guard it?

 Responding in Prayer Pray that you would be a good steward of what you have been given.

2 Timothy

Second Timothy is Paul's last letter. He is in prison in Rome again—under Nero. He is an older man and does not expect to get out, but to die in prison (contrast with Php 1:23–25).

Opposition to Paul both inside and outside the church has intensified. Many former associates have deserted him. His loneliness and desire to see Timothy come through clearly. Further, Nero's persecution is under way, and many Christians are facing the choice of suffering or leaving the faith. Much of what he has built is at risk. When Paul's personal resources are at their lowest, he faces the greatest test. In this context he reflects on his own life and gives his final counsel.

This letter has fantastic value for us. It gives us insight into facing persecution and supporting others who are persecuted. It also shows both how to give away leadership and how to assume it at the right time. Finally, it provides encouragement to us in facing our own death.

Outline

1 / *2 Timothy 1*
Rejected but Not Ashamed

SHAME MEANS BEING revealed to others as weak and inadequate. Rejection is always cause for shame unless we are quite sure of both our ideas and our approach. We are prone to believe what others say about us, especially if they are more successful or in authority. We often need support from our own friends to maintain our dignity even in the face of unjust charges.

It is remarkable but true that when Paul was imprisoned, the church in Rome did not come to Paul's defense. Only one believer came looking for him. The rest probably held back from fear or considered the imprisonment something shameful. But although he has been rejected, Paul tells us he is *not* ashamed.

 Warming Up to God When have non-Christian friends or pressures from the world caused you to feel ashamed of the gospel?

 Read 2 Timothy 1.

1 Paul, an apostle of Christ Jesus by the will of God, according to the promise of life that is in Christ Jesus,

²To Timothy, my dear son:

Grace, mercy and peace from God the Father and Christ Jesus our Lord.

³I thank God, whom I serve, as my forefathers did, with a clear conscience, as night and day I constantly remember you in my prayers. ⁴Recalling your tears, I long to see you, so that I may be filled with joy. ⁵I have been reminded of your sincere faith, which first lived in your grandmother Lois and in your mother Eunice and, I am persuaded, now lives in you also. ⁶For this reason I remind you to fan into flame the gift of God, which is in you through the laying on of my hands. ⁷For God did not give us a spirit of timidity, but a spirit of power, of love and of self-discipline.

⁸So do not be ashamed to testify about our Lord, or ashamed of me his prisoner. But join with me in suffering for the gospel, by the power of God, ⁹who has saved us and called us to a holy life—not because of anything we have done but because of his own purpose and grace. This grace was given us in Christ Jesus before the beginning of time, ¹⁰but it has now been revealed through the appearing of our Savior, Christ Jesus, who has destroyed death and has brought life and immortality to light through the gospel. ¹¹And of this gospel I was appointed a herald and an apostle and a teacher. ¹²That is why I am suffering as I am. Yet I am not ashamed, because I know whom I have believed, and am convinced that he is able to guard what I have entrusted to him for that day.

¹³What you heard from me, keep as the pattern of sound teaching, with faith and love in Christ Jesus. ¹⁴Guard the good deposit that was entrusted to you—guard it with the help of the Holy Spirit who lives in us.

¹⁵You know that everyone in the province of Asia has deserted me, including Phygelus and Hermogenes.

¹⁶May the Lord show mercy to the household of Onesiphorus, because he often refreshed me and was not ashamed of my chains. ¹⁷On the contrary, when he was in Rome, he searched hard for me until he found me. ¹⁸May the Lord grant that he will find mercy from the Lord on that day! You know very well in how many ways he helped me in Ephesus.

Discovering the Word 1. What information are we given about the relationship between Paul and Timothy (vv. 2–6)? 2. What is Paul's situation (vv. 1, 8, 11–12, 15–16)? 3. Find the references to shame (vv. 12, 16). Why would *shame* be a response to Paul's imprisonment? 4. How did Paul reject shame in this situation (vv. 3, 8–12)?

Applying the Word 1. Imprisonment can take many forms beyond the literal example here, such as chronic disease, financial collapse, abuse, or anything that severely restricts your freedom and separates you from people. How can we apply Paul's example of resisting the shame that arises from such situations?

2. Consider Timothy's situation: his mentor has been disgraced; many of his associates have deserted the ministry; many of his church's members are drifting from the faith or cowed by the threat of persecution. How have you struggled or are you struggling with similar situations?   **3.** How do you believe God is calling you to testify about him in your own situation?

 Responding in Prayer With your call to witness in mind, pray through what the text affirms about God in verses 8–12. As you pray, think especially about how you might be ashamed of sharing your faith, and ask for God's help.

2 / 2 Timothy 2
Pass It On

BARBARA BOYD ONCE said, "Paul had no dead-end disciples." The essence of Paul's ministry was to be certain that the gospel was handed on to other people in such a way that they came to regard this task as their own. This approach, which was very radical in its time, puts the "power" of the movement into the hands of thousands. Paul, having been deserted by many, wants to make sure the gospel won't die when he does—or when Timothy does.

 Warming Up to God Think of a time when an older Christian has entrusted some aspect of ministry to you. How did this create growth and maturity in your life?

 Read 2 Timothy 2.

2 You then, my son, be strong in the grace that is in Christ Jesus. ²And the things you have heard me say in the presence of many witnesses entrust to reliable men who will also be qualified to teach others. ³Endure hardship with us like a good soldier of Christ Jesus. ⁴No one serving as a soldier gets involved in civilian affairs—he wants to please his commanding officer. ⁵Similarly, if anyone competes as an athlete, he does not receive the victor's crown unless he competes according to the rules. ⁶The hardworking farmer should be the first to receive a share of the crops. ⁷Reflect on what I am saying, for the Lord will give you insight into all this.

⁸Remember Jesus Christ, raised from the dead, descended from David. This is my gospel, ⁹for which I am suffering even to the point of being chained like a criminal. But God's word is not chained. ¹⁰Therefore I endure everything for the sake of the elect, that they too may obtain the salvation that is in Christ Jesus, with eternal glory.

¹¹Here is a trustworthy saying:

If we died with him,
  we will also live with him;
¹²if we endure,
  we will also reign with him.

If we disown him,
  he will also disown us;
¹³if we are faithless,
  he will remain faithful,
  for he cannot disown himself.

¹⁴Keep reminding them of these things. Warn them before God against quarreling about words; it is of no value, and only ruins those who listen. ¹⁵Do your best to present yourself to God as one approved, a workman who does not need to be ashamed and who correctly handles the word of truth. ¹⁶Avoid godless chatter, because those who indulge in it will become more and more ungodly. ¹⁷Their teaching will spread like gangrene. Among them are Hymenaeus and Philetus, ¹⁸who have wandered away from the truth. They say that the resurrection has already taken place, and they destroy the faith of some. ¹⁹Nevertheless, God's solid foundation stands firm, sealed with this inscription: "The Lord knows those who are his,"ᵃ and, "Everyone who confesses the name of the Lord must turn away from wickedness."

²⁰In a large house there are articles not only of gold and silver, but also of wood and clay; some are for noble purposes and some for ignoble. ²¹If a man cleanses himself from the latter, he will be

ᵃ19 Num. 16:5 (see Septuagint)

an instrument for noble purposes, made holy, useful to the Master and prepared to do any good work.

22Flee the evil desires of youth, and pursue righteousness, faith, love and peace, along with those who call on the Lord out of a pure heart. 23Don't have anything to do with foolish and stupid arguments, because you know they produce quarrels. 24And the Lord's servant must not quarrel; instead, he must be kind to everyone, able to teach, not resentful. 25Those who oppose him he must gently instruct, in the hope that God will grant them repentance leading them to a knowledge of the truth, 26and that they will come to their senses and escape from the trap of the devil, who has taken them captive to do his will.

 Discovering the Word 1. Paul begins with the call to Timothy to "be strong in grace." Why does he give that instruction rather than "be strong in your gifts," "be strong in knowledge" or "be strong in willpower"? 2. What does each of the three images in verses 3–7 illustrate about the ministry of entrusting the gospel to others who can pass it on? 3. Why does Paul cite these specific aspects of Christ that Timothy should remember (v. 8)? 4. How does this explain Paul's own confidence even while he is imprisoned (v. 9)? 5. Why does Paul say he endures (vv. 10–13)? 6. What do verses 18–19 say is both the potential and the limitation of false teaching?

 Applying the Word 1. Which of the images in verses 3–7 seems most applicable to your life right now? Why? 2. How should the trustworthy saying in verses 11–13 motivate us?

Responding in Prayer Where is your own character being tested as you try to entrust the gospel to others? Pray that God will encourage you and strengthen you in those areas.

---

3 / 2 Timothy 3
How to Recognize God's Voice

MOST OF US go through stages in our lives where we are vulnerable to false teachers. Campus cults make their biggest outreaches during the opening days of school and during finals week—when students are under the greatest stress. Life crises are doors of change—for good or evil. In addition, guilt, greed and other lusts often distort judgment and give false teachers their opportunity.

Philetus and Hymanaeus represent a tradition of potent religious falsehood Timothy fought against his whole career. We can expect the same kind of struggle. In spite of the power and appeal of such groups, however, Paul had great confidence in both Scripture and those who live by it. In this chapter he encourages Timothy to have confidence in God's teaching as well.

 Warming Up to God What factors do you think would make a person particularly susceptible to heresy?

 Read 2 Timothy 3.

---

3 But mark this: There will be terrible times in the last days. 2People will be lovers of themselves, lovers of money, boastful, proud, abusive, disobedient to their parents, ungrateful, unholy, 3without love, unforgiving, slanderous, without self-control, brutal, not lovers of the good, 4treacherous, rash, conceited, lovers of pleasure rather than lovers of God— 5having a form of godliness but denying its power. Have nothing to do with them.

6They are the kind who worm their way into homes and gain control over weak-willed women, who are loaded down with sins and are swayed by all kinds of evil desires, 7always learning but never able to acknowledge the truth. 8Just as Jannes and Jambres opposed Moses, so also these men oppose the truth—men of depraved minds, who, as far as the faith is concerned, are rejected. 9But they will not get very far because, as in the case of those men, their folly will be clear to everyone.

10You, however, know all about my teaching,

my way of life, my purpose, faith, patience, love, endurance, [11]persecutions, sufferings—what kinds of things happened to me in Antioch, Iconium and Lystra, the persecutions I endured. Yet the Lord rescued me from all of them. [12]In fact, everyone who wants to live a godly life in Christ Jesus will be persecuted, [13]while evil men and impostors will go from bad to worse, deceiving and being deceived. [14]But as for you, continue in what you have learned and have become con-

vinced of, because you know those from whom you learned it, [15]and how from infancy you have known the holy Scriptures, which are able to make you wise for salvation through faith in Christ Jesus. [16]All Scripture is God-breathed and is useful for teaching, rebuking, correcting and training in righteousness, [17]so that the man of God may be thoroughly equipped for every good work.

 Discovering the Word 1. What evidence do we have here that these people are religious? 2. Notice the way those controlled by these religious leaders are described (v. 6). Why are we vulnerable to spiritual manipulation when we are "weak-willed," "loaded down with sins" and "swayed by evil desires"? 3. Why could Timothy trust Paul's spiritual influence (vv. 10–13)? 4. Paul does not expect blind faith from Timothy. What does he expect, and what two reasons does he give for it (vv. 14–15)? 5. Where does Scripture come from, and what is its power (vv. 15–17)?

Applying the Word 1. What would enhance your own trustworthiness among those you influence (children, students, coworkers or employees, and friends)? 2. In Hebrew (conceptually) to hear is to obey and do God's will. During this study, how have you sensed that God wants you to change in order to hear his voice more clearly?

Responding in Prayer Pray that you would hear God's voice and be kept safe from false teaching.

4 / 2 Timothy 4
It's Your Turn Now

THE STORY IS told of the umpire who called a strike on Babe Ruth. The Babe turned around and angrily shouted, "Hey, meathead! Me and 40,000 people here know that pitch was a ball!" The umpire replied, "Yeah, and mine is the only opinion that matters."

The gospel is not often popular. As he gears up for ministry, Timothy needs to know that only God's opinion matters. In this passage, the last written words of Paul we have, Paul instructs Timothy to think of eternity.

 Warming Up to God How do you respond (inwardly and outwardly) when you see friends turning away from the faith?

 Read 2 Timothy 4.

4 In the presence of God and of Christ Jesus, who will judge the living and the dead, and in view of his appearing and his kingdom, I give you this charge: [2]Preach the Word; be prepared in season and out of season; correct, rebuke and encourage—with great patience and careful instruction. [3]For the time will come when men will not put up with sound doctrine. Instead, to suit their own desires, they will gather around them a great number of teachers to

say what their itching ears want to hear. [4]They will turn their ears away from the truth and turn aside to myths. [5]But you, keep your head in all situations, endure hardship, do the work of an evangelist, discharge all the duties of your ministry.

[6]For I am already being poured out like a drink offering, and the time has come for my departure. [7]I have fought the good fight, I have finished the race, I have kept the faith. [8]Now there is in store

for me the crown of righteousness, which the Lord, the righteous Judge, will award to me on that day—and not only to me, but also to all who have longed for his appearing.

⁹Do your best to come to me quickly, ¹⁰for Demas, because he loved this world, has deserted me and has gone to Thessalonica. Crescens has gone to Galatia, and Titus to Dalmatia. ¹¹Only Luke is with me. Get Mark and bring him with you, because he is helpful to me in my ministry. ¹²I sent Tychicus to Ephesus. ¹³When you come, bring the cloak that I left with Carpus at Troas, and my scrolls, especially the parchments.

¹⁴Alexander the metalworker did me a great deal of harm. The Lord will repay him for what he has done. ¹⁵You too should be on your guard against him, because he strongly opposed our message.

¹⁶At my first defense, no one came to my support, but everyone deserted me. May it not be held against them. ¹⁷But the Lord stood at my side and gave me strength, so that through me the message might be fully proclaimed and all the Gentiles might hear it. And I was delivered from the lion's mouth. ¹⁸The Lord will rescue me from every evil attack and will bring me safely to his heavenly kingdom. To him be glory for ever and ever. Amen.

¹⁹Greet Priscilla*ᵇ* and Aquila and the household of Onesiphorus. ²⁰Erastus stayed in Corinth, and I left Trophimus sick in Miletus. ²¹Do your best to get here before winter. Eubulus greets you, and so do Pudens, Linus, Claudia and all the brothers.

²²The Lord be with your spirit. Grace be with you.

ᵇ19 Greek *Prisca*, a variant of *Priscilla*

 Discovering the Word 1. What charge was Timothy to keep (vv. 3–5)? 2. Paul is seeing a big part of what he labored so hard to build under God's power dissolve. How can he still feel such satisfaction about his life (vv. 6–8)? 3. What do verses 9–13 reveal about Paul's situation? 4. Rome had a big Christian community, but they shunned Paul when he came to trial (vv. 16–17, see also 1:8, 12, 16–18). Paul could have chosen to burn with resentment. What clues in the passage show why he was not bitter? 5. The names in verses 19–20 denote men, women, Romans, Greeks, nobles and commoners. What comfort would that fact give both Paul and Timothy?

 Applying the Word 1. What life tasks do you need to finish in order to share Paul's satisfaction? 2. Who is taking a public stand for the gospel in your community, and how can you support him or her?

Responding in Prayer Pray for the spread of the gospel locally and around the world.

Titus

T itus was no stranger to conflict. He was a long-term companion of Paul who was a valuable aid in two of Paul's greatest crises.

Titus first appears in the New Testament in Galatians 2:1, where Paul says he took Titus along on his trip to Jerusalem with Barnabas. Titus was a Gentile, and the issue at hand was whether Gentiles should have to comply with Jewish ceremonial rites (circumcision, diet restrictions and so on) in order to be full members of the Christian community. With the young Paul at one side and Barnabas at the other, he was essentially "tried" (and acquitted) by the leaders in Jerusalem.

Titus appears again in the middle of Paul's struggle with the church at Corinth. In that deeply divided church, he represented Paul. He had the unwelcome job of delivering what we call the "severe letter," which Paul refers to in 2 Corinthians 2:1–4 and 7:5–13, and then staying there for about a year. Then he delivered the letter we now call 2 Corinthians in which Paul takes on his critics and calls the church to honor an unfulfilled financial pledge.

Titus was in Crete at the time Paul wrote him. Crete was a seaport, a sleazy port of call for cargo ships traversing the Mediterranean. It had been socially backward for 1400 years since the Minoan civilization was destroyed by a devastating earthquake. We do not know exactly when Titus went with Paul to Crete, but one possible scenario places it after Paul's release from his first imprisonment in Rome.

Paul had preached in Crete and was giving Titus the job of following through with developing a healthy church. This letter was sent while he was in the midst of his task and reviews his assignment. It shows Titus as a forceful personality and skilled administrator. It seems he was made of tougher stuff than Timothy, but his assignments were shorter. By the time Paul had written 2 Timothy, the job in Crete was done, and Titus had been sent on to Dalmatia (part of modern Yugoslavia).

This letter gives us two very valuable things: (1) a showcase of Paul's strategy for leadership in the midst of chaos (Timothy was given a long-term assignment in an established church; Titus was sent to follow up an evangelistic movement and give the Christian body some coherence) (2) a model of hope in the face of a very messy situation (Paul's confidence in the power of the gospel shines throughout the letter).

Titus 1—3
Great Expectations

GREAT EXPECTATIONS IS the well-known title of a novel by Charles Dickens. It is the story of a young man's early experiences out in the "real world" as he seeks to gain the fortune he has inherited. Similarly, the book of Titus tells of Paul's expectations for Titus during his first ministry experience on his own. Paul's promise to Titus is that he will become an heir of eternity.

 Warming Up to God Think of a person in your life who expects great things from you. How do you feel about that person's expectations? Are they realistic?

 Read Titus 1—3.

---

1 Paul, a servant of God and an apostle of Jesus Christ for the faith of God's elect and the knowledge of the truth that leads to godliness— ²a faith and knowledge resting on the hope of eternal life, which God, who does not lie, promised before the beginning of time, ³and at his appointed season he brought his word to light through the preaching entrusted to me by the command of God our Savior,

⁴To Titus, my true son in our common faith:

Grace and peace from God the Father and Christ Jesus our Savior.

⁵The reason I left you in Crete was that you might straighten out what was left unfinished and appoint*ᵃ* elders in every town, as I directed you. ⁶An elder must be blameless, the husband of but one wife, a man whose children believe and are not open to the charge of being wild and disobedient. ⁷Since an overseer*ᵇ* is entrusted with God's work, he must be blameless—not overbearing, not quick-tempered, not given to drunkenness, not violent, not pursuing dishonest gain. ⁸Rather he must be hospitable, one who loves what is good, who is self-controlled, upright, holy and disciplined. ⁹He must hold firmly to the trustworthy message as it has been taught, so that he can encourage others by sound doctrine and refute those who oppose it.

¹⁰For there are many rebellious people, mere talkers and deceivers, especially those of the circumcision group. ¹¹They must be silenced, because they are ruining whole households by teaching things they ought not to teach—and that for the sake of dishonest gain. ¹²Even one of their own prophets has said, "Cretans are always liars, evil brutes, lazy gluttons." ¹³This testimony is true. Therefore, rebuke them sharply, so that

they will be sound in the faith ¹⁴and will pay no attention to Jewish myths or to the commands of those who reject the truth. ¹⁵To the pure, all things are pure, but to those who are corrupted and do not believe, nothing is pure. In fact, both their minds and consciences are corrupted. ¹⁶They claim to know God, but by their actions they deny him. They are detestable, disobedient and unfit for doing anything good.

2 You must teach what is in accord with sound doctrine. ²Teach the older men to be temperate, worthy of respect, self-controlled, and sound in faith, in love and in endurance.

³Likewise, teach the older women to be reverent in the way they live, not to be slanderers or addicted to much wine, but to teach what is good. ⁴Then they can train the younger women to love their husbands and children, ⁵to be self-controlled and pure, to be busy at home, to be kind, and to be subject to their husbands, so that no one will malign the word of God.

⁶Similarly, encourage the young men to be self-controlled. ⁷In everything set them an example by doing what is good. In your teaching show integrity, seriousness ⁸and soundness of speech that cannot be condemned, so that those who oppose you may be ashamed because they have nothing bad to say about us.

⁹Teach slaves to be subject to their masters in everything, to try to please them, not to talk back to them, ¹⁰and not to steal from them, but to show that they can be fully trusted, so that in every way they will make the teaching about God our Savior attractive.

¹¹For the grace of God that brings salvation has appeared to all men. ¹²It teaches us to say "No" to

ᵃ5 Or ordain   ᵇ7 Traditionally bishop

ungodliness and worldly passions, and to live self-controlled, upright and godly lives in this present age, ¹³while we wait for the blessed hope—the glorious appearing of our great God and Savior, Jesus Christ, ¹⁴who gave himself for us to redeem us from all wickedness and to purify for himself a people that are his very own, eager to do what is good.

¹⁵These, then, are the things you should teach. Encourage and rebuke with all authority. Do not let anyone despise you.

3 Remind the people to be subject to rulers and authorities, to be obedient, to be ready to do whatever is good, ²to slander no one, to be peaceable and considerate, and to show true humility toward all men.

³At one time we too were foolish, disobedient, deceived and enslaved by all kinds of passions and pleasures. We lived in malice and envy, being hated and hating one another. ⁴But when the kindness and love of God our Savior appeared, ⁵he saved us, not because of righteous things we had done, but because of his mercy. He saved us through the washing of rebirth and renewal by the Holy Spirit, ⁶whom he poured out on us generously through Jesus Christ our Savior, ⁷so that, having been justified by his grace, we might be-

come heirs having the hope of eternal life. ⁸This is a trustworthy saying. And I want you to stress these things, so that those who have trusted in God may be careful to devote themselves to doing what is good. These things are excellent and profitable for everyone.

⁹But avoid foolish controversies and genealogies and arguments and quarrels about the law, because these are unprofitable and useless. ¹⁰Warn a divisive person once, and then warn him a second time. After that, have nothing to do with him. ¹¹You may be sure that such a man is warped and sinful; he is self-condemned.

¹²As soon as I send Artemas or Tychicus to you, do your best to come to me at Nicopolis, because I have decided to winter there. ¹³Do everything you can to help Zenas the lawyer and Apollos on their way and see that they have everything they need. ¹⁴Our people must learn to devote themselves to doing what is good, in order that they may provide for daily necessities and not live unproductive lives.

¹⁵Everyone with me sends you greetings. Greet those who love us in the faith.

Grace be with you all.

Discovering the Word 1. Note all you can from the book about the social situation (family, public and private morality). 2. What do you learn about the economic situation (work, wealth and poverty)? 3. What is revealed about the religious situation (spirituality, doctrine, church life)? 4. Paul expected enormous things of Titus. And he wanted Titus to meet him in Nicopolis (3:12) in about eight months. When it comes to what others expect of us, our first response is often to question whether they are fair. How fair do you think Paul's expectations of Titus were? 5. Paul's expectations were built not only on his knowledge of Titus, but on solid theological grounds as well. What were they (see 1:1–3; 2:11–14; 3:3–7)? 6. Do you think Paul's expectations helped Titus to accomplish his mission? Why or why not?

Applying the Word 1. Do your own Christian leaders expect too much or too little of you? 2. What effect does that have on your own walk with Jesus Christ? 3. At work, home, school or church, whether you are a follower or a leader, you have a responsibility to communicate your expectations. Name one step you could take to do this more effectively.

Responding in Prayer What expectations are you wrestling with? Ask God for insight to know which come from him and which do not.

Philemon

T he little book of Philemon is the only surviving letter of Paul to an individual friend and convert about a private matter. In it we learn that Onesimus, one of Philemon's slaves, had stolen from his master and run away to Rome. In that great city he met Paul and became a Christian. Under Roman law, Philemon had the right to brand a returned slave and even kill him.

Paul applies what he wrote in Colossians: "Here there is no Greek or Jew . . . slave or free, but Christ is all, and is in all" (Col 3:11). Philemon and Onesimus are given the chance to participate in a revolutionary new process for reconciliation.

Philemon 1–25
Mending Fractured Relationships

DAVE AND ANDY enjoyed a prosperous business partnership for several years. Their families became closest friends, sharing vacations made possible by their growing computer business. Then one day Andy disappeared, along with the company bank account. Dave lost his friend, his business and his home. Three years later Andy returned, having squandered the money but having found Christ. Could Dave forgive him? Could they ever be friends again?

In Paul's letter to Philemon, you'll find principles for bringing reconciliation between two Christians who know the pain of wronging another and being wronged.

 Warming Up to God Recall a time when you wanted to restore a broken relationship. What were some of your fears in approaching the situation?

 Read Philemon 1–25.

---

[1]Paul, a prisoner of Christ Jesus, and Timothy our brother,

To Philemon our dear friend and fellow worker, [2]to Apphia our sister, to Archippus our fellow soldier and to the church that meets in your home:

[3]Grace to you and peace from God our Father and the Lord Jesus Christ.

[4]I always thank my God as I remember you in my prayers, [5]because I hear about your faith in the Lord Jesus and your love for all the saints. [6]I pray that you may be active in sharing your faith, so that you will have a full understanding of every good thing we have in Christ. [7]Your love has given me great joy and encouragement, because you, brother, have refreshed the hearts of the saints.

[8]Therefore, although in Christ I could be bold and order you to do what you ought to do, [9]yet I appeal to you on the basis of love. I then, as Paul—an old man and now also a prisoner of Christ Jesus— [10]I appeal to you for my son Onesimus,[a] who became my son while I was in chains. [11]Formerly he was useless to you, but now he has become useful both to you and to me. [12]I am sending him—who is my very heart—back to you. [13]I would have liked to keep him with me so that he could take your place in help-

ing me while I am in chains for the gospel. [14]But I did not want to do anything without your consent, so that any favor you do will be spontaneous and not forced. [15]Perhaps the reason he was separated from you for a little while was that you might have him back for good— [16]no longer as a slave, but better than a slave, as a dear brother. He is very dear to me but even dearer to you, both as a man and as a brother in the Lord.

[17]So if you consider me a partner, welcome him as you would welcome me. [18]If he has done you any wrong or owes you anything, charge it to me. [19]I, Paul, am writing this with my own hand. I will pay it back—not to mention that you owe me your very self. [20]I do wish, brother, that I may have some benefit from you in the Lord; refresh my heart in Christ. [21]Confident of your obedience, I write to you, knowing that you will do even more than I ask.

[22]And one thing more: Prepare a guest room for me, because I hope to be restored to you in answer to your prayers.

[23]Epaphras, my fellow prisoner in Christ Jesus, sends you greetings. [24]And so do Mark, Aristarchus, Demas and Luke, my fellow workers.

[25]The grace of the Lord Jesus Christ be with your spirit.

[a]10 Onesimus means useful.

Discovering the Word 1. Based on what you have read, how would you reconstruct the events that led up to this letter? 2. Having described Philemon's loving character, Paul appeals to him on the basis of love (v. 9). Why is love so essential for mending a fractured relationship? 3. In what ways has Onesimus changed since running away from Philemon (vv. 10–16)? 4. What will it require of Onesimus to return to Philemon? 5. What will it require of Philemon to do what Paul asks?

Applying the Word 1. What principles in this letter could you use for mending a fractured relationship? 2. Paul intervened to restore these two brothers in Christ. When might we need the help of a friend or counselor?

Responding in Prayer Pray for God's grace for you to follow these principles in a situation where you may be an Onesimus or Philemon or Paul.

Hebrews

A former Olympic distance runner and veteran missionary wrote the following letter of encouragement to a friend who was caught in the throes of a horrendous personal crisis:

> In this race . . . I suddenly hit a branch of a tree (and) . . . the blow almost knocked me out. . . . It knocked me out of my race, stopped me cold. . . . Somehow I staggered back on the track and stumbled along. . . . I remember one clear conclusion. I must keep going, even if I come in long behind. I must not quit. So I kept going. I won the race. . . . Whatever the difficulty, the blow, we must keep on. God will lead to the result that will glorify him. (Gordon MacDonald, *Rebuilding Your Broken World* [Nashville: Oliver-Nelson, 1988], p. 224.)

The sentence "Whatever . . . the blow, we must keep on" captures the theme of the letter to the Hebrews, which I have entitled "Race to Glory." The author of Hebrews states it very clearly: "Let us run with perseverance the race marked out for us" (12:1).

Throughout, the author emphasizes this chief concern for the readers—that they finish their faith-race with Jesus Christ gloriously and triumphantly. "Pay more careful attention," the author warns, "so that we do not drift away" (2:1). "Let us be careful that none of you be found to have fallen short of it [God's promised rest]" (4:1). "Let us leave the elementary teachings about Christ and go on to maturity," the writer appeals (6:1). "We want each of you to show this same diligence to the very end, in order to make your hope sure" (6:11).

After convincingly showing how Jesus Christ meets all of our needs, the writer cries out, "Let us draw near to God with a sincere heart in full assurance of faith. . . . Let us hold unswervingly to the hope we profess, for he who promised is faithful" (10:22–23). "Do not throw away your confidence. . . . You need to persevere so that when you have done the will of God, you will receive what he has promised" (10:35–36).

The author devotes an entire chapter (11) to drawing the readers to the stories of great heroes who finished the race to glory, people like Moses, Abraham, Noah, Jacob and Joseph. These witnesses are summoned to inspire us onward in our own faith-race.

A friend of mine loves to joke that when he gets to heaven he is going to find out who wrote Hebrews. The letter bears no byline, so scholars have had a field day speculating about its possible authors. Included in this list are Paul, Silas, Titus, Mark, Clement, Luke, Aquila, Priscilla and Barnabas. If you took a poll among these scholars, Luke, Barnabas and Apollos would be strongly favored. At any rate, whoever the author was, he or she knew the Hebrews very well.

The readers were knowledgeable Jews who had converted to faith in Jesus Christ. The entire scaffolding of the letter is Jewish history, theology and practice. These Jews were old enough in the faith to be teachers and to recall older leaders (5:12; 13:7). They had served one another and had suffered (6:10; 10:32–34). Their city can only be guessed at—possibly Jerusalem, Alexandria, Corinth, Ephesus or Rome.

What is completely clear about the audience is their spiritual peril. They were in danger of reverting to Judaism. The letter is chock full of warnings about it. They were being taunted by Jews as apostates from God and renegades from Moses. They were accused of abandoning their law and forfeiting the Old Testament promises.

So the writer goes to great lengths to prove that Jesus Christ is far superior to everything they had left behind for his sake. In that context, he warns them against neglect, unbelief, disobedience, immaturity and rejection. He stands in the grandstand, as it were, wildly cheering them on to stay on the track, not to quit, and to reach the finish line in the power of Jesus Christ.

Today's readers most likely will not have come to faith in Christ out of such a deeply embedded cultural and religious tradition. But every Christian at some time or other is tempted to quit and to ask, "What's the use?" As problems and roadblocks mount, as faith seems unproductive, as doors slam, we find it easy to think about quitting our personal faith-race.

We also need current reminders about the supremacy of Jesus Christ. There is no stronger enticement to stay in the race than to "fix our eyes on Jesus" (12:2). As the Pioneer of our salvation, he brings us to glory (2:10).

We run our faith-race in vital communion with God through prayer, by giving God's Word command of our lives, by faithfully worshiping him and loving fellow Christians, and by knowing and serving Jesus Christ better each day as our daily companion, guide and master.

Outline

1 / *Hebrews 1*
Starting the Race

WHEN THE ANCIENT church father John Chrysostom, bishop of Constantinople, was summoned by Emperor Arcadius and threatened with banishment, he responded, "You cannot banish me, for the whole world is my Father's kingdom."

"Then I will take away your life," said the emperor.

"You cannot," answered Chrysostom, "for my life is hid with Christ in God."

"I will take away your treasure," roared the emperor.

"You can't," replied Chrysostom, "for my treasure is in heaven, where my heart is."

"Then I will drive you away from all your friends," the emperor said.

"You cannot, for I have one friend from whom you can never separate me. I defy you," said Chrysostom, "because you can do me no harm."

Such conviction grows out of a firm grasp of who Jesus Christ really is. Hebrews 1 will get you started on the race with a look at the majesty, power and glory of Jesus Christ.

 Warming Up to God Focus on what you have experienced of the majesty, power and glory of Jesus Christ. Praise Jesus for who he is.

 Read Hebrews 1.

---

1 In the past God spoke to our forefathers through the prophets at many times and in various ways, ²but in these last days he has spoken to us by his Son, whom he appointed heir of all things, and through whom he made the universe. ³The Son is the radiance of God's glory and the exact representation of his being, sustaining all things by his powerful word. After he had provided purification for sins, he sat down at the right hand of the Majesty in heaven. ⁴So he became as much superior to the angels as the name he has inherited is superior to theirs.

⁵For to which of the angels did God ever say,

"You are my Son;
    today I have become your Father*a*"*b*?

Or again,

"I will be his Father,
    and he will be my Son"*c*?

⁶And again, when God brings his firstborn into the world, he says,

"Let all God's angels worship him."*d*

⁷In speaking of the angels he says,

"He makes his angels winds,
    his servants flames of fire."*e*

⁸But about the Son he says,

"Your throne, O God, will last for ever and
    ever,

and righteousness will be the scepter of
    your kingdom.
⁹You have loved righteousness and hated
    wickedness;
    therefore God, your God, has set you above
    your companions
    by anointing you with the oil of joy."*f*

¹⁰He also says,

"In the beginning, O Lord, you laid the
    foundations of the earth,
    and the heavens are the work of your
    hands.
¹¹They will perish, but you remain;
    they will all wear out like a garment.
¹²You will roll them up like a robe;
    like a garment they will be changed.
But you remain the same,
    and your years will never end."*g*

¹³To which of the angels did God ever say,

"Sit at my right hand
until I make your enemies
    a footstool for your feet"*h*?

¹⁴Are not all angels ministering spirits sent to serve those who will inherit salvation?

*a*5 Or *have begotten you*   *b*5 Psalm 2:7   *c*5 2 Samuel 7:14;
1 Chron. 17:13   *d*6 Deut. 32:43 (see Dead Sea Scrolls and Septuagint)
*e*7 Psalm 104:4   *f*9 Psalm 45:6,7   *g*12 Psalm 102:25-27
*h*13 Psalm 110:1

Discovering the Word   1. How do verses 1–3 reveal the essential truth of Christ's supremacy and sufficiency?   2. Based on what we learn in verses 2–3, how would you answer the question "Who is Jesus Christ?"   3. To drive his point home, the author uses seven Old Testament citations. What characteristics or attributes of Jesus does the writer find in the Old Testament to prove his claim that Jesus is superior to angels (vv. 4–14)?   4. Who is the source of all these astounding statements (vv. 5–8, 10, 13)?   5. What do you learn about angels from these verses?   6. Based on what you have observed in verses 5–14, how would you expand your answer to the question "Who is Christ?"

 Applying the Word   1. What needs in your life do these qualities of Jesus address?   2. What kind of life should you have because all this is true of Jesus?

Responding in Prayer   Pray that your life will reflect your knowledge of Jesus.

2 / Hebrews 2
Warning Signs

"WARNING!" A BLACK-and-white lettered sign that I encounter on the Fox River in St. Charles, Illinois, warns me of a dam ahead. In that placid stream it would be easy to drive over the dam. Cigarette packs, cans of weed killer, fences around nuclear power plants—they all carry impressive warnings designed to steer us from life-threatening perils. In Hebrews 2, the writer erects the first of six prominent warning signs in the letter. The first, in effect, alerts us to the danger of drifting off the course of our faith-race. It tells us to concentrate on staying in the race.

 Warming Up to God   What might cause you to "drive away" from Christ, or to let "such a great salvation" slip away like a loose ring that falls off your finger?

 Read Hebrews 2.

2 We must pay more careful attention, therefore, to what we have heard, so that we do not drift away. ²For if the message spoken by angels was binding, and every violation and disobedience received its just punishment, ³how shall we escape if we ignore such a great salvation? This salvation, which was first announced by the Lord, was confirmed to us by those who heard him. ⁴God also testified to it by signs, wonders and various miracles, and gifts of the Holy Spirit distributed according to his will.

⁵It is not to angels that he has subjected the world to come, about which we are speaking. ⁶But there is a place where someone has testified:

"What is man that you are mindful of him,
the son of man that you care for him?
⁷You made him a little[i] lower than the angels;
you crowned him with glory and honor
8 and put everything under his feet."[j]

In putting everything under him, God left noth-

ing that is not subject to him. Yet at present we do not see everything subject to him. ⁹But we see Jesus, who was made a little lower than the angels, now crowned with glory and honor because he suffered death, so that by the grace of God he might taste death for everyone.

¹⁰In bringing many sons to glory, it was fitting that God, for whom and through whom everything exists, should make the author of their salvation perfect through suffering. ¹¹Both the one who makes men holy and those who are made holy are of the same family. So Jesus is not ashamed to call them brothers. ¹²He says,

"I will declare your name to my brothers;
in the presence of the congregation I will
sing your praises."[k]

¹³And again,

"I will put my trust in him."[l]

And again he says,

[i]7 Or *him for a little while*; also in verse 9   [j]8 Psalm 8:4-6
[k]12 Psalm 22:22   [l]13 Isaiah 8:17

"Here am I, and the children God has given me."[m]

[14]Since the children have flesh and blood, he too shared in their humanity so that by his death he might destroy him who holds the power of death—that is, the devil—[15]and free those who all their lives were held in slavery by their fear of death. [16]For surely it is not angels he helps, but Abraham's descendants. [17]For this reason he had to be made like his brothers in every way, in order that he might become a merciful and faithful high priest in service to God, and that he might make atonement for[n] the sins of the people. [18]Because he himself suffered when he was tempted, he is able to help those who are being tempted.

[m]13 Isaiah 8:18   [n]17 Or *and that he might turn aside God's wrath, taking away*

 Discovering the Word 1. In verse 1 we read, "pay more careful attention . . . to," and in verse 3 we are told not to "ignore." What is it that we are to focus our lives on? 2. What logic does the writer use in verses 2–3 to further focus our attention on the peril of drifting away? 3. How does the writer strengthen the warning that God's salvation in Christ is well worth our most intense obedience (vv. 3–4)? 4. To prove that Jesus is too great and too valuable to neglect, the writer tells us more about him (vv. 5–9). What major facts does he cite here? 5. Why did Jesus have "to be made like his brothers [you and me] in every way" (vv. 16–18)?

 Applying the Word 1. How does Jesus help you when you are tempted? 2. What helps you to maintain a warm, life-changing relationship with Jesus? 3. "Be sure your seatbelts are securely fastened," the aircraft's captain warns you because of approaching turbulence. How can you help other believers to be "securely fastened" into Jesus?

 Responding in Prayer Ask God to keep you securely fastened to Jesus.

3 / *Hebrews 3*
Winning the Race

COACHES TELL US that what distinguishes average from superior athletes is the will to win. Endowed with equal physical strengths, one reaches the heights of stardom while the other slips into obscurity. In this chapter, the writer describes two equally endowed Christian runners in the faith-race. One succeeded and the other failed. What made the difference? The will to win. One held firmly to Christ, but the other fell by the wayside because of a hard heart.

Warming Up to God What makes the difference between vibrant, growing Christians you know and those who appear to be dull and uninterested in the implications of their profession of faith?

Read Hebrews 3.

3 Therefore, holy brothers, who share in the heavenly calling, fix your thoughts on Jesus, the apostle and high priest whom we confess. [2]He was faithful to the one who appointed him, just as Moses was faithful in all God's house. [3]Jesus has been found worthy of greater honor than Moses, just as the builder of a house has greater honor than the house itself. [4]For every house is built by someone, but God is the builder of everything. [5]Moses was faithful as a servant in all God's house, testifying to what would be said in the future. [6]But Christ is faithful as a son over God's house. And we are his house, if we hold on to our courage and the hope of which we boast.

[7]So, as the Holy Spirit says:

"Today, if you hear his voice,
[8]   do not harden your hearts
   as you did in the rebellion,
      during the time of testing in the desert,
[9]where your fathers tested and tried me

and for forty years saw what I did.
[10]That is why I was angry with that generation,
and I said, 'Their hearts are always going astray,
and they have not known my ways.'
[11]So I declared on oath in my anger,
'They shall never enter my rest.' "[o]

[12]See to it, brothers, that none of you has a
sinful, unbelieving heart that turns away from the
living God. [13]But encourage one another daily, as
long as it is called Today, so that none of you may
be hardened by sin's deceitfulness. [14]We have
come to share in Christ if we hold firmly till the
end the confidence we had at first. [15]As has just
been said:

"Today, if you hear his voice,
do not harden your hearts
as you did in the rebellion."[p]

[16]Who were they who heard and rebelled?
Were they not all those Moses led out of Egypt?
[17]And with whom was he angry for forty years?
Was it not with those who sinned, whose bodies
fell in the desert? [18]And to whom did God swear
that they would never enter his rest if not to those
who disobeyed[q]? [19]So we see that they were not
able to enter, because of their unbelief.

[o]11 Psalm 95:7-11 [p]15 Psalm 95:7,8 [q]18 Or *disbelieved*

Discovering the Word 1. What does the writer emphasize about Jesus in verses 1–6 that would encourage us to "fix [our] thoughts" on him (v. 1) and "hold on" to our courage and hope (v. 6)? 2. In verses 7–11 the writer hoists his second warning—unbelief and disobedience. These verses describe the nation of Israel after they crossed the Red Sea. They refused to obey God's command to take the Promised Land because they were afraid of the military might they would face. So they were forced to wander forty years till that whole generation died off. How does the psalmist describe God's perspective on the Israelites? 3. In what ways might Christians "test and try" God (v. 9)? Why? 4. How did God judge the Israelites whom Moses led out of Egypt (vv. 15–19)? 5. Why did he judge them in this way?

Applying the Word 1. Review the facts about the hardhearted (vv. 8, 10, 12–13, 15–18). Which aspects of this lifestyle come closest to your experience? 2. What are you doing to avoid the peril of "falling in the desert" (v. 17)?

Responding in Prayer Pray for your own salvation.

4 / *Hebrews 4:1–13*
Receiving God's Blessings

AMERICAN BUSINESS TYCOON Roger Babson once observed, "Opportunities are greater today than ever before in history. Young people have greater chances for health, happiness, and prosperity than had the children of any previous generation." The same is true for Christians in God's faith-race.

It was true for God's people, Israel, yet they missed the opportunity for living in God's land of blessing and perished in a wilderness of unbelief and disobedience. This chapter tells Christians in the race that there is something to fear, but also something to strive for—experiencing God's promised rest now.

Warming Up to God Do you need more times of rest in your life? In what areas?

Read Hebrews 4:1–13.

Therefore, since the promise of entering his rest still stands, let us be careful that none of you be found to have fallen short of it. ²For we also have had the gospel preached to us, just as they did; but the message they heard was of no value to them, because those who heard did not combine it with faith.ʳ ³Now we who have believed enter that rest, just as God has said,

"So I declared on oath in my anger,
'They shall never enter my rest.' "ˢ

And yet his work has been finished since the creation of the world. ⁴For somewhere he has spoken about the seventh day in these words: "And on the seventh day God rested from all his work."ᵗ ⁵And again in the passage above he says, "They shall never enter my rest."

⁶It still remains that some will enter that rest, and those who formerly had the gospel preached to them did not go in, because of their disobedience. ⁷Therefore God again set a certain day, calling it Today, when a long time later he spoke through David, as was said before:

"Today, if you hear his voice,
do not harden your hearts."ᵘ

⁸For if Joshua had given them rest, God would not have spoken later about another day. ⁹There remains, then, a Sabbath-rest for the people of God; ¹⁰for anyone who enters God's rest also rests from his own work, just as God did from his. ¹¹Let us, therefore, make every effort to enter that rest, so that no one will fall by following their example of disobedience.

¹²For the word of God is living and active. Sharper than any double-edged sword, it penetrates even to dividing soul and spirit, joints and marrow; it judges the thoughts and attitudes of the heart. ¹³Nothing in all creation is hidden from God's sight. Everything is uncovered and laid bare before the eyes of him to whom we must give account.

ʳ2 Many manuscripts *because they did not share in the faith of those who obeyed*   ˢ3 Psalm 95:11; also in verse 5   ᵗ4 Gen. 2:2
ᵘ7 Psalm 95:7,8

Discovering the Word 1. What do you think the promise of entering God's rest means in verse 1? 2. The tragic fate of the Israelites who perished in the desert serves as the basis of God's warning to those who have heard the gospel. Why did some who had the gospel preached to them miss their opportunity to receive God's rest (v. 2)? 3. From what you have observed in Hebrews thus far, how would you describe the faith which is required to receive God's rest? 4. We are told to do our best to reach God's rest (3:11, 18; 4:1, 3, 5–6, 9–11). How do you picture such rest? 5. Verses 6–8 refer to the Israelites. How did they refuse to receive God's rest? 6. The "word of God" that judges our thoughts and attitudes (vv. 12–13) is the specific promise of God's rest. How can God's Word show you the condition of your heart?

Applying the Word 1. God rested from all of his work (v. 4), and he offers us a "Sabbath-rest" on the seventh day of the week. What does it mean to you to rest from your work? 2. What role does Scripture have in your life right now? 3. How would you like to deepen or change that relationship?

Responding in Prayer Praise God for the gifts in this passage—of Scripture and of rest.

---

5 / *Hebrews 4:14—5:10*
Overcoming Weakness

THE PULITZER PRIZE-winning book *City of Joy* tells about the intense suffering of a Polish priest in a Calcutta slum. His superiors offered him a comfortable lodging, but he chose to live just like the slum-dwellers. By his suffering he learned what it was like to be a slum-dweller. He could not have learned that any other way. Likewise, the Hebrews needed to be reminded of their God-appointed, suffering high priest, Jesus Christ, so they would hold firmly to him.

Warming Up to God What experiences have you had that have helped you to better understand another person?

Read Hebrews 4:14—5:10.

14Therefore, since we have a great high priest who has gone through the heavens,ᵛ Jesus the Son of God, let us hold firmly to the faith we profess. 15For we do not have a high priest who is unable to sympathize with our weaknesses, but we have one who has been tempted in every way, just as we are—yet was without sin. 16Let us then approach the throne of grace with confidence, so that we may receive mercy and find grace to help us in our time of need.

5 Every high priest is selected from among men and is appointed to represent them in matters related to God, to offer gifts and sacrifices for sins. 2He is able to deal gently with those who are ignorant and are going astray, since he himself is subject to weakness. 3This is why he has to offer sacrifices for his own sins, as well as for the sins of the people.

4No one takes this honor upon himself; he must be called by God, just as Aaron was. 5So Christ also did not take upon himself the glory of becoming a high priest. But God said to him,

"You are my Son;
    today I have become your Father."ʷ "ˣ

6And he says in another place,

"You are a priest forever,
    in the order of Melchizedek."ʸ

7During the days of Jesus' life on earth, he offered up prayers and petitions with loud cries and tears to the one who could save him from death, and he was heard because of his reverent submission. 8Although he was a son, he learned obedience from what he suffered 9and, once made perfect, he became the source of eternal salvation for all who obey him 10and was designated by God to be high priest in the order of Melchizedek.

ᵛ14 Or gone into heaven   ʷ5 Or have begotten you   ˣ5 Psalm 2:7
ʸ6 Psalm 110:4

 Discovering the Word 1. What commands are given in 4:14 and 16? 2. What is there about the character of Jesus that encourages us to obey these commands? 3. Jesus, as our merciful and faithful high priest, made atonement for our sins. The writer reminds the Hebrews of their earthly high priest in Judaism. What was the high priest like (5:1–4)? 4. How would you compare Jesus' high appointment with the life he lived (5:7–8)? 5. What was the result of Christ's suffering (5:8–10)?

Applying the Word 1. When you are tempted, what difference does it make to know that Jesus was likewise tempted and therefore sympathizes with your weakness? 2. How does Christ's suffering help you to take a positive attitude toward suffering?

Responding in Prayer Pray that your life would reflect your high appointment as the adopted son or daughter of God.

---

6 / Hebrews 5:11—6:20
The Race to Maturity

PETER SNELL, FORMER Olympic gold medalist, said that the only way to win a race is to get in front and go flat out. Prior to that, he said, it takes a whole lot of hard training and self-discipline. The Hebrews were in desperate danger of quitting the race, so the writer urged them to go forward. This is a chapter with four strong appeals: "Let us go on to maturity" (v. 1). "Show diligence" (v. 11). "Do not become lazy" (v. 12). "Take hold of the hope " (v. 18).

 Warming Up to God When are you most tempted to drop out of the faith-race? Why?

 Read Hebrews 5:11—6:20.

¹¹We have much to say about this, but it is hard to explain because you are slow to learn. ¹²In fact, though by this time you ought to be teachers, you need someone to teach you the elementary truths of God's word all over again. You need milk, not solid food! ¹³Anyone who lives on milk, being still an infant, is not acquainted with the teaching about righteousness. ¹⁴But solid food is for the mature, who by constant use have trained themselves to distinguish good from evil.

6 Therefore let us leave the elementary teachings about Christ and go on to maturity, not laying again the foundation of repentance from acts that lead to death,ᶻ and of faith in God, ²instruction about baptisms, the laying on of hands, the resurrection of the dead, and eternal judgment. ³And God permitting, we will do so.

⁴It is impossible for those who have once been enlightened, who have tasted the heavenly gift, who have shared in the Holy Spirit, ⁵who have tasted the goodness of the word of God and the powers of the coming age, ⁶if they fall away, to be brought back to repentance, becauseᵃ to their loss they are crucifying the Son of God all over again and subjecting him to public disgrace.

⁷Land that drinks in the rain often falling on it and that produces a crop useful to those for whom it is farmed receives the blessing of God. ⁸But land that produces thorns and thistles is worthless and is in danger of being cursed. In the end it will be burned.

⁹Even though we speak like this, dear friends, we are confident of better things in your case—things that accompany salvation. ¹⁰God is not unjust; he will not forget your work and the love you have shown him as you have helped his people and continue to help them. ¹¹We want each of you to show this same diligence to the very end, in order to make your hope sure. ¹²We do not want you to become lazy, but to imitate those who through faith and patience inherit what has been promised.

¹³When God made his promise to Abraham, since there was no one greater for him to swear by, he swore by himself, ¹⁴saying, "I will surely bless you and give you many descendants."ᵇ ¹⁵And so after waiting patiently, Abraham received what was promised.

¹⁶Men swear by someone greater than themselves, and the oath confirms what is said and puts an end to all argument. ¹⁷Because God wanted to make the unchanging nature of his purpose very clear to the heirs of what was promised, he confirmed it with an oath. ¹⁸God did this so that, by two unchangeable things in which it is impossible for God to lie, we who have fled to take hold of the hope offered to us may be greatly encouraged. ¹⁹We have this hope as an anchor for the soul, firm and secure. It enters the inner sanctuary behind the curtain, ²⁰where Jesus, who went before us, has entered on our behalf. He has become a high priest forever, in the order of Melchizedek.

ᶻ1 Or from useless rituals   ᵃ6 Or repentance while
ᵇ14 Gen. 22:17

 Discovering the Word 1. How would you describe the failures of the Hebrews (5:11–14)? 2. In view of their resources and opportunities for growth, how do you account for their problems? 3. According to 6:6, why is it absolutely essential to develop Christian maturity? 4. What hope does the writer see for better things to come (vv. 9–10)? Why? 5. What essential part of God's nature encourages the Hebrews to be positive and hopeful about their future (vv. 13–18)?

Applying the Word 1. Two kinds of land production vividly portray the reason to go on to maturity (6:7–8). How does each characterize your life? 2. As you reflect on your track record, of both diligence and laziness (6:11–12), how can you improve? 3. In verses 19–20 the writer returns to the Hebrews' familiar religion of priests and their temple with its holy place curtained off. In other words, it was a picture of a more profound spiritual reality in Christ. How does Jesus fulfill your deepest aspirations and help you to go on to maturity in your faith-race?

Responding in Prayer Ask God to firmly anchor your soul with hope in Christ.

7 / *Hebrews 7*
Eternal Companion

IN THE OLD Testament, religion and priests go hand in hand. Moses had carefully laid out all the rules for the Levites, the priestly clan of Israel. But the Hebrew Christians had departed from their old religion that was centered on priestly functions. Yet some of them hankered to return to their old ways. "Don't turn back," the writer appeals. "You have something far better in Christ." In chapters 7—10 the author tells of Christ's superior priestly origin, his better covenant and his sufficient-for-all-time sacrifice of himself. Regardless of whether we have had to move away from old traditions to find Christ, we all need confidence builders like chapter 7 so that as we run our faith-race, we will stick with Jesus no matter what.

 Warming Up to God "He always makes me feel so strong," a church member said of his pastor after a sermon. What relationships strengthen your knowledge of Christ and build you up?

 Read Hebrews 7.

7 This Melchizedek was king of Salem and priest of God Most High. He met Abraham returning from the defeat of the kings and blessed him, ²and Abraham gave him a tenth of everything. First, his name means "king of righteousness"; then also, "king of Salem" means "king of peace." ³Without father or mother, without genealogy, without beginning of days or end of life, like the Son of God he remains a priest forever.

⁴Just think how great he was: Even the patriarch Abraham gave him a tenth of the plunder! ⁵Now the law requires the descendants of Levi who become priests to collect a tenth from the people—that is, their brothers—even though their brothers are descended from Abraham. ⁶This man, however, did not trace his descent from Levi, yet he collected a tenth from Abraham and blessed him who had the promises. ⁷And without doubt the lesser person is blessed by the greater. ⁸In the one case, the tenth is collected by men who die; but in the other case, by him who is declared to be living. ⁹One might even say that Levi, who collects the tenth, paid the tenth through Abraham, ¹⁰because when Melchizedek met Abraham, Levi was still in the body of his ancestor.

¹¹If perfection could have been attained through the Levitical priesthood (for on the basis of it the law was given to the people), why was there still need for another priest to come—one in the order of Melchizedek, not in the order of Aaron? ¹²For when there is a change of the priesthood, there must also be a change of the law. ¹³He of whom these things are said belonged to a different tribe, and no one from that tribe has ever served at the altar. ¹⁴For it is clear that our Lord descended from Judah, and in regard to that tribe Moses said nothing about priests. ¹⁵And what we have said is even more clear if another priest like Melchizedek appears, ¹⁶one who has become a priest not on the basis of a regulation as to his ancestry but on the basis of the power of an indestructible life. ¹⁷For it is declared:

"You are a priest forever,
    in the order of Melchizedek."ᶜ

¹⁸The former regulation is set aside because it was weak and useless ¹⁹(for the law made nothing perfect), and a better hope is introduced, by which we draw near to God.

²⁰And it was not without an oath! Others became priests without any oath, ²¹but he became a priest with an oath when God said to him:

"The Lord has sworn
    and will not change his mind:
'You are a priest forever.' "ᶜ

²²Because of this oath, Jesus has become the guarantee of a better covenant.

²³Now there have been many of those priests, since death prevented them from continuing in office; ²⁴but because Jesus lives forever, he has a permanent priesthood. ²⁵Therefore he is able to save completelyᵈ those who come to God through him, because he always lives to intercede for them.

²⁶Such a high priest meets our need—one who is holy, blameless, pure, set apart from sinners,

ᶜ17,21 Psalm 110:4   ᵈ25 Or *forever*

exalted above the heavens. 27Unlike the other high priests, he does not need to offer sacrifices day after day, first for his own sins, and then for the sins of the people. He sacrificed for their sins once for all when he offered himself. 28For the law appoints as high priests men who are weak; but the oath, which came after the law, appointed the Son, who has been made perfect forever.

Discovering the Word 1. Jesus is our high priest, not of the ancient Jewish line of Aaron but of the line of the pre-Aaronic Melchizedek. "Just think how great he [Melchizedek] was," commands the writer (v. 4). What was there about Melchizedek that made him so great (vv. 1–3)? 2. Great as his name and position were, there was one incident that proved Melchizedek's superiority to the Hebrews: Their patriarch Abraham tithed (gave one tenth of his income) to him (v. 4). According to verses 5–10, why does this prove that Jesus' high priesthood is superior to that of Levi (Aaron's son)? 3. Jesus inaugurated a new era and set aside the old because he was not of the priestly tribe (vv. 11–14). On what does his priestly authority rest (vv. 15–17)? 4. In what sense were the ancient rules of the Jews "weak and useless" (vv. 18–19)? 5. God's oath set aside Jesus as a distinctive high priest (vv. 20–21). How does Jesus guarantee our faith-agreement (covenant) with him (vv. 22–25)? 6. What about Christ's character and sacrifice sets him far above other earthly priests (vv. 26–28)?

Applying the Word 1. Twice the writer tells us to come to God through Christ's high priesthood (vv. 19, 25). Why do you need to do this? 2. How can you practice it in your faith-race?

Responding in Prayer Praise God for giving you a high priest over all in Jesus Christ.

8 / *Hebrews 8*
God's "New Deal"

BACK IN 1932, President Franklin Roosevelt sought to rescue the country from the pit of the Great Depression by launching the New Deal. The concept caught the imagination of the people. The time was ripe for a radically new economic and social program. In this chapter, the writer of Hebrews announces God's "new deal"—a covenant, or agreement, between God and humanity. It offers far superior promises to those of the "old deal" (Old Testament laws and regulations).

Warming Up to God What does knowing you are God's child mean to you?

Read Hebrews 8.

8 The point of what we are saying is this: We do have such a high priest, who sat down at the right hand of the throne of the Majesty in heaven, 2and who serves in the sanctuary, the true tabernacle set up by the Lord, not by man.

3Every high priest is appointed to offer both gifts and sacrifices, and so it was necessary for this one also to have something to offer. 4If he were on earth, he would not be a priest, for there are already men who offer the gifts prescribed by the law. 5They serve at a sanctuary that is a copy and shadow of what is in heaven. This is why Moses was warned when he was about to build the tabernacle: "See to it that you make everything according to the pattern shown you on the mountain."ᵉ 6But the ministry Jesus has received is as superior to theirs as the covenant of which he is mediator is superior to the old one, and it is founded on better promises.

7For if there had been nothing wrong with that first covenant, no place would have been sought for another. 8But God found fault with the people and said*f*:

"The time is coming, declares the Lord,
    when I will make a new covenant

ᵉ5 Exodus 25:40   f8 Some manuscripts may be translated fault and said to the people.

with the house of Israel
    and with the house of Judah.
⁹It will not be like the covenant
    I made with their forefathers
    when I took them by the hand
    to lead them out of Egypt,
because they did not remain faithful to my
        covenant,
    and I turned away from them,
                        declares the Lord.
¹⁰This is the covenant I will make with the
        house of Israel
    after that time, declares the Lord.
I will put my laws in their minds
    and write them on their hearts.

I will be their God,
    and they will be my people.
¹¹No longer will a man teach his neighbor,
    or a man his brother, saying, 'Know the
        Lord,'
because they will all know me,
    from the least of them to the greatest.
¹²For I will forgive their wickedness
    and will remember their sins no more."ᵍ

¹³By calling this covenant "new," he has made
the first one obsolete; and what is obsolete and
aging will soon disappear.

ᵍ12 Jer. 31:31-34

 Discovering the Word 1. "We do have such a high priest" (v. 1) refers to the description of Jesus in 7:23–28. What additional facts do you learn about him (vv. 1–2)? 2. What is Christ's heavenly ministry (vv. 3–6)? 3. Verse 6 looks back to prove Christ's superior ministry and ahead to prove that we have a superior covenant with God. The key is "better promises." What was the problem with the first covenant (vv. 7–12)? 4. What guarantees God's "new deal" (v. 12)? (See also vv. 1–3; 9:14.)

Applying the Word 1. Do you function better under external restraint (the law) or inner constraint (God's Spirit) (v. 10)? Why? 2. What happens to you when you say to God, "Thank you for forgiving and forgetting my sin"? 3. A magazine ad for dishwashers offers more power, more pizzazz and more performance. How could your understanding and application of God's "new deal" offer all of that to you in your walk with him?

Responding in Prayer Ask God to forgive your sins, naming those you can think of specifically.

---

9 / Hebrews 9
The Runner's Power

IN VIEW OF the colossal problems besetting us—drugs, divorce, depression, to name a few—it seems like a gross oversimplification to say that the blood of Jesus Christ is the solution. But, in a different context, the Hebrews faced similar problems of neglect, unbelief and immaturity. They were in danger of dropping out of the race and turning back to their old ways. Seemingly, they lacked the power and purpose to advance and press on in their faith-race. What was the solution given to them? The blood of Jesus. Only a full and perfect knowledge of what Jesus is and does for us can bring us to a full and perfect Christian life.

 Warming Up to God When do you feel like dropping out of the race?

 Read Hebrews 9.

---

9 Now the first covenant had regulations for worship and also an earthly sanctuary. ²A tabernacle was set up. In its first room were the lampstand, the table and the consecrated bread; this was called the Holy Place. ³Behind the second curtain was a room called the Most Holy Place, ⁴which had the golden altar of incense and the gold-covered ark of the covenant. This ark contained the gold jar of manna, Aaron's staff that had budded, and the stone tablets of the cov-

enant. [5]Above the ark were the cherubim of the Glory, overshadowing the atonement cover.[h] But we cannot discuss these things in detail now.

[6]When everything had been arranged like this, the priests entered regularly into the outer room to carry on their ministry. [7]But only the high priest entered the inner room, and that only once a year, and never without blood, which he offered for himself and for the sins the people had committed in ignorance. [8]The Holy Spirit was showing by this that the way into the Most Holy Place had not yet been disclosed as long as the first tabernacle was still standing. [9]This is an illustration for the present time, indicating that the gifts and sacrifices being offered were not able to clear the conscience of the worshiper. [10]They are only a matter of food and drink and various ceremonial washings—external regulations applying until the time of the new order.

[11]When Christ came as high priest of the good things that are already here,[i] he went through the greater and more perfect tabernacle that is not man-made, that is to say, not a part of this creation. [12]He did not enter by means of the blood of goats and calves; but he entered the Most Holy Place once for all by his own blood, having obtained eternal redemption. [13]The blood of goats and bulls and the ashes of a heifer sprinkled on those who are ceremonially unclean sanctify them so that they are outwardly clean. [14]How much more, then, will the blood of Christ, who through the eternal Spirit offered himself unblemished to God, cleanse our consciences from acts that lead to death,[j] so that we may serve the living God!

[15]For this reason Christ is the mediator of a new covenant, that those who are called may receive the promised eternal inheritance—now that he has died as a ransom to set them free from the sins committed under the first covenant.

[16]In the case of a will,[k] it is necessary to prove the death of the one who made it, [17]because a will is in force only when somebody has died; it never takes effect while the one who made it is living. [18]This is why even the first covenant was not put into effect without blood. [19]When Moses had proclaimed every commandment of the law to all the people, he took the blood of calves, together with water, scarlet wool and branches of hyssop, and sprinkled the scroll and all the people. [20]He said, "This is the blood of the covenant, which God has commanded you to keep."[l] [21]In the same way, he sprinkled with the blood both the tabernacle and everything used in its ceremonies. [22]In fact, the law requires that nearly everything be cleansed with blood, and without the shedding of blood there is no forgiveness.

[23]It was necessary, then, for the copies of the heavenly things to be purified with these sacrifices, but the heavenly things themselves with better sacrifices than these. [24]For Christ did not enter a man-made sanctuary that was only a copy of the true one; he entered heaven itself, now to appear for us in God's presence. [25]Nor did he enter heaven to offer himself again and again, the way the high priest enters the Most Holy Place every year with blood that is not his own. [26]Then Christ would have had to suffer many times since the creation of the world. But now he has appeared once for all at the end of the ages to do away with sin by the sacrifice of himself. [27]Just as man is destined to die once, and after that to face judgment, [28]so Christ was sacrificed once to take away the sins of many people; and he will appear a second time, not to bear sin, but to bring salvation to those who are waiting for him.

[h]5 Traditionally *the mercy seat*   [i]11 Some early manuscripts *are to come*   [j]14 Or *from useless rituals*   [k]16 Same Greek word as *covenant*; also in verse 17   [l]20 Exodus 24:8

Discovering the Word 1. Contrast what Jesus did (vv. 11–14) with the old system (vv. 1–10). 2. Why was the shedding of sacrificial blood required even under the old covenant (vv. 16–22)? 3. The writer explains why the offering of Jesus' blood is not only necessary, but also a superior sacrifice. Why is it important to direct our attention to "heavenly things" (v. 23)? 4. What difference would it make to those steeped in Old Testament religion to know that Jesus once-for-all offered his own blood, rather than offering animal blood (vv. 25–26)?

Applying the Word 1. How can you deepen your understanding of and appreciation for Christ's self-sacrifice? 2. Death and judgment are certain. In view of that, how would you encourage someone to face eternity with hope and peace, based on what you have learned in this chapter? 3. Also certain is Jesus' Second Coming (v. 28). In light of his blood offering, how should you spend your time waiting for him?

Responding in Prayer Pray that you will use your time to serve Jesus even as you wait for him.

10 / *Hebrews 10*
Staying in the Race

FACED WITH SEEMINGLY eternal years of schoolwork and a multitude of rules to obey, children get discouraged. When that happens, parents say, "Look at your great opportunities. Take advantage of what you have now. Don't throw it away."

The writer of Hebrews, in chapter 10, reaches the heights of Mt. Everest with a picture of Jesus that offers his readers encouragement. From those lofty heights he tells them to warm up to God, hold their faith in him, and stir up one another in Christian faith and practice.

 Warming Up to God Recall an opportunity you missed because it sounded too good. What did you miss by not believing the evidence?

 Read Hebrews 10.

10 The law is only a shadow of the good things that are coming—not the realities themselves. For this reason it can never, by the same sacrifices repeated endlessly year after year, make perfect those who draw near to worship. ²If it could, would they not have stopped being offered? For the worshipers would have been cleansed once for all, and would no longer have felt guilty for their sins. ³But those sacrifices are an annual reminder of sins, ⁴because it is impossible for the blood of bulls and goats to take away sins.

⁵Therefore, when Christ came into the world, he said:

"Sacrifice and offering you did not desire,
but a body you prepared for me;
⁶with burnt offerings and sin offerings
you were not pleased.
⁷Then I said, 'Here I am—it is written about me in the scroll—
I have come to do your will, O God.' "[m]

⁸First he said, "Sacrifices and offerings, burnt offerings and sin offerings you did not desire, nor were you pleased with them" (although the law required them to be made). ⁹Then he said, "Here I am, I have come to do your will." He sets aside the first to establish the second. ¹⁰And by that will, we have been made holy through the sacrifice of the body of Jesus Christ once for all.

¹¹Day after day every priest stands and performs his religious duties; again and again he offers the same sacrifices, which can never take away sins. ¹²But when this priest had offered for all time one sacrifice for sins, he sat down at the right hand of God. ¹³Since that time he waits for his enemies to be made his footstool, ¹⁴because by one sacrifice he has made perfect forever those who are being made holy.

¹⁵The Holy Spirit also testifies to us about this. First he says:

¹⁶"This is the covenant I will make with them
after that time, says the Lord.
I will put my laws in their hearts,
and I will write them on their minds."[n]

¹⁷Then he adds:

"Their sins and lawless acts
I will remember no more."[o]

¹⁸And where these have been forgiven, there is no longer any sacrifice for sin.

¹⁹Therefore, brothers, since we have confidence to enter the Most Holy Place by the blood of Jesus, ²⁰by a new and living way opened for us through the curtain, that is, his body, ²¹and since we have a great priest over the house of God, ²²let us draw near to God with a sincere heart in full assurance of faith, having our hearts sprinkled to cleanse us from a guilty conscience and having our bodies washed with pure water. ²³Let us hold

m7 Psalm 40:6-8 (see Septuagint)   *n16* Jer. 31:33   *o17* Jer. 31:34

unswervingly to the hope we profess, for he who promised is faithful. [24]And let us consider how we may spur one another on toward love and good deeds. [25]Let us not give up meeting together, as some are in the habit of doing, but let us encourage one another—and all the more as you see the Day approaching.

[26]If we deliberately keep on sinning after we have received the knowledge of the truth, no sacrifice for sins is left, [27]but only a fearful expectation of judgment and of raging fire that will consume the enemies of God. [28]Anyone who rejected the law of Moses died without mercy on the testimony of two or three witnesses. [29]How much more severely do you think a man deserves to be punished who has trampled the Son of God under foot, who has treated as an unholy thing the blood of the covenant that sanctified him, and who has insulted the Spirit of grace? [30]For we know him who said, "It is mine to avenge; I will repay,"[p] and again, "The Lord will judge his people."[q] [31]It is a dreadful thing to fall into the hands of the living God.

[32]Remember those earlier days after you had received the light, when you stood your ground in a great contest in the face of suffering. [33]Sometimes you were publicly exposed to insult and persecution; at other times you stood side by side with those who were so treated. [34]You sympathized with those in prison and joyfully accepted the confiscation of your property, because you knew that you yourselves had better and lasting possessions.

[35]So do not throw away your confidence; it will be richly rewarded. [36]You need to persevere so that when you have done the will of God, you will receive what he has promised. [37]For in just a very little while,

"He who is coming will come and will not
delay.
38 But my righteous one[r] will live by faith.
And if he shrinks back,
I will not be pleased with him."[s]

[39]But we are not of those who shrink back and are destroyed, but of those who believe and are saved.

p30 Deut. 32:35 *q30* Deut. 32:36; Psalm 135:14 *r38* One early manuscript *But the righteous* *s38* Hab. 2:3,4

Discovering the Word 1. The writer continues to discuss Jesus and the Old Testament offerings. How do verses 1–4 prove that the Old Testament system was a shadow, not the real thing? 2. Contrast Jesus' sacrifice (the reality) with the shadow (vv. 5–10). Why is his sacrifice better? 3. As you meditate on verses 11–18 and the awesome love and power of Jesus to take away your sins, what are the responses in your heart and mind? 4. In light of what God has done for us in Christ (vv. 19–21), what three commands does the writer feel compelled to issue (vv. 22–24)? 5. If we fail to draw near to God, hold fast our faith and stir up one another, what is likely to happen (vv. 25–26, 38–39)?

Applying the Word 1. How can you help hold someone you know "unswervingly" to faith? 2. What purposes could be achieved in your life by both this strong encouragement and this stern warning?

Responding in Prayer Pray for your church, that you would support and encourage one another.

11 / *Hebrews 11*
Models of Faith

PROBABLY NO SUBJECT is so glibly misunderstood as faith. Nearly everyone professes to have some of it. Many people would like to have more. The writer to the Hebrews takes faith out of religious theory and clothes it with flesh and blood. The author does this with what we today call *role models*. These models inspire us to go on believing in Jesus.

Warming Up to God Complete the sentence: "Faith is . . ."

Read Hebrews 11.

11 Now faith is being sure of what we hope for and certain of what we do not see. [2]This is what the ancients were commended for.

[3]By faith we understand that the universe was formed at God's command, so that what is seen was not made out of what was visible.

[4]By faith Abel offered God a better sacrifice than Cain did. By faith he was commended as a righteous man, when God spoke well of his offerings. And by faith he still speaks, even though he is dead.

[5]By faith Enoch was taken from this life, so that he did not experience death; he could not be found, because God had taken him away. For before he was taken, he was commended as one who pleased God. [6]And without faith it is impossible to please God, because anyone who comes to him must believe that he exists and that he rewards those who earnestly seek him.

[7]By faith Noah, when warned about things not yet seen, in holy fear built an ark to save his family. By his faith he condemned the world and became heir of the righteousness that comes by faith.

[8]By faith Abraham, when called to go to a place he would later receive as his inheritance, obeyed and went, even though he did not know where he was going. [9]By faith he made his home in the promised land like a stranger in a foreign country; he lived in tents, as did Isaac and Jacob, who were heirs with him of the same promise. [10]For he was looking forward to the city with foundations, whose architect and builder is God.

[11]By faith Abraham, even though he was past age—and Sarah herself was barren—was enabled to become a father because he[t] considered him faithful who had made the promise. [12]And so from this one man, and he as good as dead, came descendants as numerous as the stars in the sky and as countless as the sand on the seashore.

[13]All these people were still living by faith when they died. They did not receive the things promised; they only saw them and welcomed them from a distance. And they admitted that they were aliens and strangers on earth. [14]People who say such things show that they are looking for a country of their own. [15]If they had been thinking of the country they had left, they would

have had opportunity to return. [16]Instead, they were longing for a better country—a heavenly one. Therefore God is not ashamed to be called their God, for he has prepared a city for them.

[17]By faith Abraham, when God tested him, offered Isaac as a sacrifice. He who had received the promises was about to sacrifice his one and only son, [18]even though God had said to him, "It is through Isaac that your offspring[u] will be reckoned."[v] [19]Abraham reasoned that God could raise the dead, and figuratively speaking, he did receive Isaac back from death.

[20]By faith Isaac blessed Jacob and Esau in regard to their future.

[21]By faith Jacob, when he was dying, blessed each of Joseph's sons, and worshiped as he leaned on the top of his staff.

[22]By faith Joseph, when his end was near, spoke about the exodus of the Israelites from Egypt and gave instructions about his bones.

[23]By faith Moses' parents hid him for three months after he was born, because they saw he was no ordinary child, and they were not afraid of the king's edict.

[24]By faith Moses, when he had grown up, refused to be known as the son of Pharaoh's daughter. [25]He chose to be mistreated along with the people of God rather than to enjoy the pleasures of sin for a short time. [26]He regarded disgrace for the sake of Christ as of greater value than the treasures of Egypt, because he was looking ahead to his reward. [27]By faith he left Egypt, not fearing the king's anger; he persevered because he saw him who is invisible. [28]By faith he kept the Passover and the sprinkling of blood, so that the destroyer of the firstborn would not touch the firstborn of Israel.

[29]By faith the people passed through the Red Sea[w] as on dry land; but when the Egyptians tried to do so, they were drowned.

[30]By faith the walls of Jericho fell, after the people had marched around them for seven days.

[31]By faith the prostitute Rahab, because she welcomed the spies, was not killed with those who were disobedient.[x]

[32]And what more shall I say? I do not have time

---

[t]11 Or *By faith even Sarah, who was past age, was enabled to bear children because she*   [u]18 Greek *seed*   [v]18 Gen. 21:12
[w]29 That is, Sea of Reeds   [x]31 Or *unbelieving*

to tell about Gideon, Barak, Samson, Jephthah, David, Samuel and the prophets, ³³who through faith conquered kingdoms, administered justice, and gained what was promised; who shut the mouths of lions, ³⁴quenched the fury of the flames, and escaped the edge of the sword; whose weakness was turned to strength; and who became powerful in battle and routed foreign armies. ³⁵Women received back their dead, raised to life again. Others were tortured and refused to be released, so that they might gain a better resurrection. ³⁶Some faced jeers and flogging, while still others were chained and put in prison.

³⁷They were stoned*y*; they were sawed in two; they were put to death by the sword. They went about in sheepskins and goatskins, destitute, persecuted and mistreated— ³⁸the world was not worthy of them. They wandered in deserts and mountains, and in caves and holes in the ground.

³⁹These were all commended for their faith, yet none of them received what had been promised. ⁴⁰God had planned something better for us so that only together with us would they be made perfect.

y 37 Some early manuscripts stoned; they were put to the test;

 Discovering the Word 1. Look for both assured confidence and calm expectation (v. 1) in the role models of faith in this chapter. How did Abel, Enoch and Noah express their faith (vv. 4–7)? 2. Considering the foolishness of his choices by human standards, what do you think Abraham's emotions were like (vv. 8–10)? 3. How does the promise of a heavenly country help us to keep our faith, even when we don't see our hopes fulfilled immediately (vv. 13–16)? 4. Why do you think Abraham's faith triumphed when he was asked to give up Isaac (vv. 17–19)? 5. How would you compare the faith of the named heroes and heroines who achieved greatness (vv. 20–35) with those unnamed persons who suffered grievously (vv. 35–38)? 6. Some Christians believe that faith always leads to material and physical blessing. What does this passage tell you about the role of both blessing and suffering for the faithful?

 Applying the Word 1. In tough circumstances, what connection do you make between your faith and the certainty of resurrection (v. 35)? 2. What unseen certainties have guided you in making fundamental, life-changing decisions?

 Responding in Prayer Pray for the faith you need in your life right now to do God's will.

---

12 / *Hebrews 12*
The Runner's Discipline

WE OFTEN WONDER why thousands of marathoners seem to enjoy punishing themselves in grueling races. Certainly, for most, it's not the hope of winning. What is it then? Explaining it to his readers, writer Art Carey said, "The real joy of the Boston Marathon is just finishing, just winning the contest with yourself—doing what you have set out to do." That's the attitude the Hebrews were supposed to have: Stay in the faith-race to the end.

Warming Up to God Who has been a model of perseverance and endurance for you? Thank God for that person.

Read Hebrews 12.

---

12 Therefore, since we are surrounded by such a great cloud of witnesses, let us throw off everything that hinders and the sin that so easily entangles, and let us run with perseverance the race marked out for us. ²Let us fix our eyes on Jesus, the author and perfecter of our faith, who for the joy set before him endured the cross, scorning its shame, and sat down at the right hand of the throne of God. ³Consider him who endured such opposition from sinful men, so that you will not grow weary and lose heart.

⁴In your struggle against sin, you have not yet resisted to the point of shedding your blood. ⁵And you have forgotten that word of encouragement that addresses you as sons:

"My son, do not make light of the Lord's
    discipline,
  and do not lose heart when he rebukes
    you,
⁶because the Lord disciplines those he loves,
  and he punishes everyone he accepts as a
    son." ᶻ

⁷Endure hardship as discipline; God is treating you as sons. For what son is not disciplined by his father? ⁸If you are not disciplined (and everyone undergoes discipline), then you are illegitimate children and not true sons. ⁹Moreover, we have all had human fathers who disciplined us and we respected them for it. How much more should we submit to the Father of our spirits and live! ¹⁰Our fathers disciplined us for a little while as they thought best; but God disciplines us for our good, that we may share in his holiness. ¹¹No discipline seems pleasant at the time, but painful. Later on, however, it produces a harvest of righteousness and peace for those who have been trained by it.

¹²Therefore, strengthen your feeble arms and weak knees. ¹³"Make level paths for your feet," ᵃ so that the lame may not be disabled, but rather healed.

¹⁴Make every effort to live in peace with all men and to be holy; without holiness no one will see the Lord. ¹⁵See to it that no one misses the grace of God and that no bitter root grows up to cause trouble and defile many. ¹⁶See that no one is sexually immoral, or is godless like Esau, who for a single meal sold his inheritance rights as the oldest son. ¹⁷Afterward, as you know, when he wanted to inherit this blessing, he was rejected.

He could bring about no change of mind, though he sought the blessing with tears.

¹⁸You have not come to a mountain that can be touched and that is burning with fire; to darkness, gloom and storm; ¹⁹to a trumpet blast or to such a voice speaking words that those who heard it begged that no further word be spoken to them, ²⁰because they could not bear what was commanded: "If even an animal touches the mountain, it must be stoned." ᵇ ²¹The sight was so terrifying that Moses said, "I am trembling with fear." ᶜ

²²But you have come to Mount Zion, to the heavenly Jerusalem, the city of the living God. You have come to thousands upon thousands of angels in joyful assembly, ²³to the church of the firstborn, whose names are written in heaven. You have come to God, the judge of all men, to the spirits of righteous men made perfect, ²⁴to Jesus the mediator of a new covenant, and to the sprinkled blood that speaks a better word than the blood of Abel.

²⁵See to it that you do not refuse him who speaks. If they did not escape when they refused him who warned them on earth, how much less will we, if we turn away from him who warns us from heaven? ²⁶At that time his voice shook the earth, but now he has promised, "Once more I will shake not only the earth but also the heavens." ᵈ ²⁷The words "once more" indicate the removing of what can be shaken—that is, created things—so that what cannot be shaken may remain.

²⁸Therefore, since we are receiving a kingdom that cannot be shaken, let us be thankful, and so worship God acceptably with reverence and awe, ²⁹for our "God is a consuming fire." ᵉ

ᶻ6 Prov. 3:11,12   ᵃ13 Prov. 4:26   ᵇ20 Exodus 19:12,13
ᶜ21 Deut. 9:19   ᵈ26 Haggai 2:6   ᵉ29 Deut. 4:24

Discovering the Word 1. Of what value is it to keep your eyes on Jesus (vv. 2–3)? **2.** What discipline of the Hebrews do you think the writer alludes to (vv. 3–4, 7; 11:35–38)? **3.** How do the values of God's discipline cited here help us to respond positively to discipline (vv. 10–12)? **4.** Identify the writer's specific instructions in verses 14–17. On what principles are they based? **5.** How could you identify a "bitter root" or a "godless Esau" in your life (vv. 15–16)? **6.** We've all been tempted to drop out of the race. Why would the warning of verses 25–29 cause us to reconsider?

Applying the Word 1. What hindrances and entanglements get in the way of your Christian faith-race (v. 1)? Why? **2.** What encouragement do you find in verses 18–24 to run the faith-race with perseverance?

Responding in Prayer Let your prayer be one of worship for the God who is a "consuming fire."

13 / *Hebrews 13*
Running by the Rules

BEN JOHNSON OF Canada was stripped of the Olympic gold medals he won at Seoul in 1988 because he broke the rules about drug use. Similarly, the Christian's faith-race is much more than a sprint to the finish line. It's a race which brings glory to God by the way the runners behave. In the concluding chapter, the writer to the Hebrews sketches a variety of duties to God and humanity. Together they reveal an exalted level of personal morality and duty.

Warming Up to God Consider your attitude to God's law. At what times do you find it a burden? When does it help you?

Read Hebrews 13.

13 Keep on loving each other as brothers. ²Do not forget to entertain strangers, for by so doing some people have entertained angels without knowing it. ³Remember those in prison as if you were their fellow prisoners, and those who are mistreated as if you yourselves were suffering.

⁴Marriage should be honored by all, and the marriage bed kept pure, for God will judge the adulterer and all the sexually immoral. ⁵Keep your lives free from the love of money and be content with what you have, because God has said,

"Never will I leave you;
    never will I forsake you."*f*

⁶So we say with confidence,

"The Lord is my helper; I will not be afraid.
    What can man do to me?"*g*

⁷Remember your leaders, who spoke the word of God to you. Consider the outcome of their way of life and imitate their faith. ⁸Jesus Christ is the same yesterday and today and forever.

⁹Do not be carried away by all kinds of strange teachings. It is good for our hearts to be strengthened by grace, not by ceremonial foods, which are of no value to those who eat them. ¹⁰We have an altar from which those who minister at the tabernacle have no right to eat.

¹¹The high priest carries the blood of animals into the Most Holy Place as a sin offering, but the bodies are burned outside the camp. ¹²And so Jesus also suffered outside the city gate to make the people holy through his own blood. ¹³Let us, then, go to him outside the camp, bearing the disgrace he bore. ¹⁴For here we do not have an enduring city, but we are looking for the city that is to come.

¹⁵Through Jesus, therefore, let us continually offer to God a sacrifice of praise—the fruit of lips that confess his name. ¹⁶And do not forget to do good and to share with others, for with such sacrifices God is pleased.

¹⁷Obey your leaders and submit to their authority. They keep watch over you as men who must give an account. Obey them so that their work will be a joy, not a burden, for that would be of no advantage to you.

¹⁸Pray for us. We are sure that we have a clear conscience and desire to live honorably in every way. ¹⁹I particularly urge you to pray so that I may be restored to you soon.

²⁰May the God of peace, who through the blood of the eternal covenant brought back from the dead our Lord Jesus, that great Shepherd of the sheep, ²¹equip you with everything good for doing his will, and may he work in us what is pleasing to him, through Jesus Christ, to whom be glory for ever and ever. Amen.

²²Brothers, I urge you to bear with my word of exhortation, for I have written you only a short letter.

²³I want you to know that our brother Timothy has been released. If he arrives soon, I will come with him to see you.

²⁴Greet all your leaders and all God's people. Those from Italy send you their greetings.

²⁵Grace be with you all.

f5 Deut. 31:6   g6 Psalm 118:6,7

Discovering the Word 1. Verses 1–3 tie in with verse 16. In what sense should loving others, doing good, sharing, entertaining strangers, and helping the prisoners and the mistreated be considered "sacrifices" to God? 2. Sexual purity is one of God's absolutes (v. 4). How do you account for sexual impurity among professing Christians—some of them well-known public figures? 3. What facts about God help to keep you from loving money (vv. 5–6)? 4. Obligation to spiritual leaders are laid out in verses 7, 17–18. What is here that we should follow? 5. In what sense is our praise a sacrifice to God (v. 15)?

 Applying the Word 1. Which of these exhortations do you need to apply to yourself? 2. On the basis of your study of Hebrews, what do you think God would like to "work" in you that would please him?

Responding in Prayer Verses 20–21 are a benediction, a summary prayer. Make that your prayer for yourself.

James

What does James have to say to me? James is practical.

Take problems. James knows nobody's perfect. So he doesn't tell us how to live trouble-free. He tells us how to live when troubles hit. Do I complain? Or do I use difficulties as an opportunity for growth?

Take words. We all talk. And sometimes we say things we wish we hadn't. James helps us use words more carefully, more positively. Do my words hurt others? Do they advance God's kingdom? Are they truthful? Are they loving?

Take money. It flows around us (despite our complaints about tight budgets and taxes). Do I withhold my money when others are in need? Do I put more value on worldly things than on the things of God?

Take time. If we have enough money, we know we never have enough time. We do all we can to get the most out of each hour of each day, filling our calendars with activity. But am I missing God's will and perspective in the midst of schedule making?

James is practical—maybe too practical! So expect these quiet times to be challenging—not because they will be hard to understand but because they will be all too easy to understand.

Who is this fellow James? There are several people in the New Testament called James, including two apostles. Though they have never been completely certain, most church scholars have believed that a third man, James the brother of Jesus (Mt 13:55; Mk 6:3), wrote this letter. While he probably joined the others in Jesus' family in rejecting Jesus during his earthly ministry, James certainly started following Jesus after his resurrection. In fact, James soon became the head of the church in Jerusalem.

He probably led the first church council in Jerusalem (Acts 15), which decided that Gentiles did not have to become Jews before they could be saved. This is an important factor in assessing James's view of faith and works (which is to be noted in light of 2:14–16).

Yet James was aware of the very Jewish makeup of the church in Jerusalem and required Paul to squelch the rumor that he, Paul, was telling Jews to abandon the law of Moses. James himself apparently followed Jewish law closely, enough so that he was known as "James the Just." He died a martyr in A.D. 62.

James addresses his letter to "the twelve tribes scattered among the nations." "Twelve tribes" could refer to Jewish Christians who through exile, enslavement and trade were spread throughout the entire Mediterranean basin. More likely it refers simply to Christians, since the New Testament compares the church to Israel (Gal 6:16 RSV; 1Pe 2:9–10). In any case, the letter is not addressed to one specific congregation, as Paul's letters were. It is therefore called a general, or catholic, epistle.

These quiet times will help you face squarely James's call for a consistent Christian life, for a practical faith—a faith that works.

Outline

1 / James 1:1–18
Dependable or Double-minded?

NO PAIN, NO gain. Or so the saying goes. Athletes remind themselves of this to get their best possible performance. Sometimes they have to go through grueling training. Without it there is no improvement. James suggests it is the same for Christians.

 Warming Up to God Enduring pain is not pleasant! What fears do you have as you think about what it means to face trials? Be honest with yourself. Describe your fears to God. Allow him to comfort you.

 Read James 1:1–18.

1 James, a servant of God and of the Lord Jesus Christ,

To the twelve tribes scattered among the nations:

Greetings.

²Consider it pure joy, my brothers, whenever you face trials of many kinds, ³because you know that the testing of your faith develops perseverance. ⁴Perseverance must finish its work so that you may be mature and complete, not lacking anything. ⁵If any of you lacks wisdom, he should ask God, who gives generously to all without finding fault, and it will be given to him. ⁶But when he asks, he must believe and not doubt, because he who doubts is like a wave of the sea, blown and tossed by the wind. ⁷That man should not think he will receive anything from the Lord; ⁸he is a double-minded man, unstable in all he does.

⁹The brother in humble circumstances ought to take pride in his high position. ¹⁰But the one who is rich should take pride in his low position, because he will pass away like a wild flower. ¹¹For the sun rises with scorching heat and withers the plant; its blossom falls and its beauty is destroyed. In the same way, the rich man will fade away even while he goes about his business.

¹²Blessed is the man who perseveres under trial, because when he has stood the test, he will receive the crown of life that God has promised to those who love him.

¹³When tempted, no one should say, "God is tempting me." For God cannot be tempted by evil, nor does he tempt anyone; ¹⁴but each one is tempted when, by his own evil desire, he is dragged away and enticed. ¹⁵Then, after desire has conceived, it gives birth to sin; and sin, when it is full-grown, gives birth to death.

¹⁶Don't be deceived, my dear brothers. ¹⁷Every good and perfect gift is from above, coming down from the Father of the heavenly lights, who does not change like shifting shadows. ¹⁸He chose to give us birth through the word of truth, that we might be a kind of firstfruits of all he created.

 Discovering the Word 1. How are perseverance and maturity developed in us by enduring trials (vv. 3–4)? 2. Under pressure, how does the faithful Christian (described in vv. 5–6) contrast with the person described in verses 6–8? 3. In the context of trials and perseverance, why does James contrast rich and poor Christians (vv. 9–11)? 4. How are temptations different from trials (vv. 2–16)? 5. How is God the ultimate example of goodness and dependability (vv. 16–18)?

Applying the Word 1. What difficult experiences have increased your perseverance and maturity? 2. In what ways do you tend to rely on your possessions? 3. Think of trials or temptations you are currently facing. How can this passage encourage you to depend on God?

Responding in Prayer Take time now to talk to God about your needs. Ask him to help you be like him in his goodness and dependability.

2 / James 1:19–27
Words, Words, Words

WE ALL DO it. It's as common as flies around a horse. While someone else is talking, we're thinking about what we're going to say next instead of about what is being said to us. We know others are worth more care and attention. But the habit is hard to break.

God wants us to slow down and listen too. But even when we've really listened to him, we're still not done. This study gives us practical help on listening and more.

 Warming Up to God There's so much to listen to all around us. What different voices and messages are on your mind? Tell God about them and ask him to help you clear your mind and focus on his Word.

 Read James 1:19–27.

19My dear brothers, take note of this: Everyone should be quick to listen, slow to speak and slow to become angry, 20for man's anger does not bring about the righteous life that God desires. 21Therefore, get rid of all moral filth and the evil that is so prevalent and humbly accept the word planted in you, which can save you.

22Do not merely listen to the word, and so deceive yourselves. Do what it says. 23Anyone who listens to the word but does not do what it says is like a man who looks at his face in a mirror 24and, after looking at himself, goes away and immedi-ately forgets what he looks like. 25But the man who looks intently into the perfect law that gives freedom, and continues to do this, not forgetting what he has heard, but doing it—he will be blessed in what he does.

26If anyone considers himself religious and yet does not keep a tight rein on his tongue, he deceives himself and his religion is worthless. 27Religion that God our Father accepts as pure and faultless is this: to look after orphans and widows in their distress and to keep oneself from being polluted by the world.

Discovering the Word 1. How can being quick to listen and slow to speak help us to be slow to become angry (v. 19)? 2. James tells us that God's Word was planted in us. What weeds can choke that Word and keep it from growing (v. 21)? Explain. 3. In your own words explain how the person who merely listens to God's Word is different from the one who puts it into practice (vv. 22–25). 4. According to verses 26 and 27, how do people who think they are religious differ from those who are truly religious? 5. Based on what you've read in this chapter, do you think James would be satisfied with good works apart from our listening to and receiving God's Word? Explain.

Applying the Word 1. When is it hard for you to listen to God? 2. Sometimes we do listen to God's Word, but we still don't follow it. How is this true for you? 3. How would you like your religion to be more "pure and faultless"?

 Responding in Prayer Ask God to help you become a better listener and doer of his Word.

---

3 / James 2:1–13
Who's the Judge?

LABELS AREN'T JUST found on soup cans. We put them on people all the time. Funny or dull. Smart or thick-headed. Friendly or cold. There are all kinds of ways we can categorize people. And our categories can have a profound influence on the way we treat people. As you might suspect, James has a few words to say about favoritism.

Warming Up to God Reflect on judgmental words and thoughts you have had this week. Confess them to God. Allow yourself to experience his mercy.

Read James 2:1–13.

2 My brothers, as believers in our glorious Lord Jesus Christ, don't show favoritism. ²Suppose a man comes into your meeting wearing a gold ring and fine clothes, and a poor man in shabby clothes also comes in. ³If you show special attention to the man wearing fine clothes and say, "Here's a good seat for you," but say to the poor man, "You stand there" or "Sit on the floor by my feet," ⁴have you not discriminated among yourselves and become judges with evil thoughts?

⁵Listen, my dear brothers: Has not God chosen those who are poor in the eyes of the world to be rich in faith and to inherit the kingdom he promised those who love him? ⁶But you have insulted the poor. Is it not the rich who are exploiting you? Are they not the ones who are dragging you into court? ⁷Are they not the ones who are slan-dering the noble name of him to whom you belong?

⁸If you really keep the royal law found in Scripture, "Love your neighbor as yourself,"ᵃ you are doing right. ⁹But if you show favoritism, you sin and are convicted by the law as lawbreakers. ¹⁰For whoever keeps the whole law and yet stumbles at just one point is guilty of breaking all of it. ¹¹For he who said, "Do not commit adultery,"ᵇ also said, "Do not murder."ᶜ If you do not commit adultery but do commit murder, you have become a lawbreaker.

¹²Speak and act as those who are going to be judged by the law that gives freedom, ¹³because judgment without mercy will be shown to anyone who has not been merciful. Mercy triumphs over judgment!

ᵃ8 Lev. 19:18   ᵇ11 Exodus 20:14; Deut. 5:18   ᶜ11 Exodus 20:13; Deut. 5:17

Discovering the Word 1. How would you react if someone came into your church who wore sloppy clothes, was dirty or had body odor (vv. 2–4)? 2. Why is it wrong to give preferential treatment to those who have money (vv. 5–7)? 3. Verse 5 says God has chosen the poor to be rich in faith. Is God guilty of showing favoritism in this way? Explain. 4. How can "the royal law" (v. 8) guide our treatment of both poor and rich? 5. In what sense is violating one law as serious as breaking every law (vv. 9–11)?

Applying the Word 1. Toward what people or groups do you show favoritism? 2. How can you change your attitude and actions?

Responding in Prayer Ask God to work in your heart and mind to help you see beneath the surface as you relate to people.

4 / James 2:14–26
Just Works

"IT IS EASIER said than done" is a cliché that certainly applies to our Christian life. It is much easier to talk about God than to obey him. James said that even the demons believe there is one God. But that certainly does not make them Christians! That's why someone can have all his or her doctrine perfectly straight and still have missed out on God's will. James helps us stay on target.

Warming Up to God What has God been asking you to do that you have been ignoring? Talk to him about it.

Read James 2:14–26.

¹⁴What good is it, my brothers, if a man claims to have faith but has no deeds? Can such faith save him? ¹⁵Suppose a brother or sister is without clothes and daily food. ¹⁶If one of you says to him, "Go, I wish you well; keep warm and well fed," but does nothing about his physical needs, what good is it? ¹⁷In the same way, faith by itself, if it is not accompanied by action, is dead.

¹⁸But someone will say, "You have faith; I have deeds."

Show me your faith without deeds, and I will show you my faith by what I do. ¹⁹You believe that there is one God. Good! Even the demons believe that—and shudder.

²⁰You foolish man, do you want evidence that faith without deeds is useless^d? ²¹Was not our ancestor Abraham considered righteous for what he did when he offered his son Isaac on the altar? ²²You see that his faith and his actions were working together, and his faith was made complete by what he did. ²³And the scripture was fulfilled that says, "Abraham believed God, and it was credited to him as righteousness,"^e and he was called God's friend. ²⁴You see that a person is justified by what he does and not by faith alone.

²⁵In the same way, was not even Rahab the prostitute considered righteous for what she did when she gave lodging to the spies and sent them off in a different direction? ²⁶As the body without the spirit is dead, so faith without deeds is dead.

^d20 Some early manuscripts *dead*   ^e23 Gen. 15:6

 Discovering the Word 1. According to James, what good is faith without deeds (vv. 14–17)? Explain why he says this. 2. How does James answer the objection "You have faith; I have deeds" (vv. 18–19)? 3. James gives two Old Testament examples of faith in action. The first is the familiar story of God testing Abraham by asking him to sacrifice his son Isaac. Abraham obeyed but was stopped by an angel at the last minute. How was Abraham's faith made complete by what he did (vv. 21–24)? 4. The second Old Testament example is Rahab, the prostitute who hid two Israelite spies sent to Jericho before Israel's attack. How did Rahab's belief affect her (v. 25)? 5. How does James's closing analogy (v. 26) summarize his teaching on faith and actions?

 Applying the Word 1. How do your actions demonstrate the reality of your faith? 2. In what ways can you bring your actions more in line with your beliefs?

 Responding in Prayer Ask God to help you follow through with the works that will reveal your true faith.

---

5 / *James 3:1–12*
Preventing Forest Fires

ONE OF THE most distressing crises is a fire out of control. The pain of seeing the destruction can be almost unbearable. Personal belongings going up in smoke. The beauty of nature destroyed. Even loss of life itself. In this passage James compares the destructive power of the tongue to that of a forest fire.

 Warming Up to God How have you been hurt by someone's destructive words recently? Give your pain to God. Let him comfort you.

Read James 3:1–12.

3 Not many of you should presume to be teachers, my brothers, because you know that we who teach will be judged more strictly. ²We all stumble in many ways. If anyone is never at fault in what he says, he is a perfect man, able to keep his whole body in check.

³When we put bits into the mouths of horses to make them obey us, we can turn the whole animal. ⁴Or take ships as an example. Although they are so large and are driven by strong winds, they are steered by a very small rudder wherever the pilot wants to go. ⁵Likewise the tongue is a small part of the body, but it makes great boasts. Consider what a great forest is set on fire by a small

spark. 6The tongue also is a fire, a world of evil among the parts of the body. It corrupts the whole person, sets the whole course of his life on fire, and is itself set on fire by hell.

7All kinds of animals, birds, reptiles and creatures of the sea are being tamed and have been tamed by man, 8but no man can tame the tongue. It is a restless evil, full of deadly poison.

9With the tongue we praise our Lord and Fa-ther, and with it we curse men, who have been made in God's likeness. 10Out of the same mouth come praise and cursing. My brothers, this should not be. 11Can both fresh water and salt*f* water flow from the same spring? 12My brothers, can a fig tree bear olives, or a grapevine bear figs? Neither can a salt spring produce fresh water.

ʃ11 Greek *bitter* (see also verse 14)

Discovering the Word 1. James compares the tongue (the words we speak) to a bit and a rudder (vv. 3–4). Why do you think the tongue has such control over our lives? 2. James also compares the tongue to a fire and to a world of evil (vv. 5–6). What is the point of these two comparisons? 3. Verses 7–8 emphasize what a challenge it is to control the tongue. What makes this so difficult? 4. In what ways can the tongue poison people and relationships? 5. In verses 9–12 James uses a series of analogies from nature (springs, trees, vines). How do they highlight the inconsistencies of the tongue?

Applying the Word 1. What damage has your tongue done recently? 2. What in this text gives you added strength and motivation to be more careful with your words? 3. What can you do to give God more praise? Be specific. 4. How can you give more affirmation to those you come in contact with each day?

Responding in Prayer Ask God to help you to be self-controlled about the ways that you speak to others.

---

6 / *James 3:13—4:10*
Keeping the Peace

WHY DO PEOPLE who love each other the most often fight the most too? Husbands and wives, parents and children, brothers and sisters—it's all too common. James offers a valuable remedy for this sickness.

Warming Up to God How have you gotten caught up in fighting recently? If that conflict continues to be a concern to you, talk to God about it. Ask God to clear your mind of anger and distrust so that you can focus on his healing Word.

Read James 3:13—4:10.

13Who is wise and understanding among you? Let him show it by his good life, by deeds done in the humility that comes from wisdom. 14But if you harbor bitter envy and selfish ambition in your hearts, do not boast about it or deny the truth. 15Such "wisdom" does not come down from heaven but is earthly, unspiritual, of the devil. 16For where you have envy and selfish ambition, there you find disorder and every evil practice.

17But the wisdom that comes from heaven is first of all pure; then peace-loving, considerate, submissive, full of mercy and good fruit, impar-tial and sincere. 18Peacemakers who sow in peace raise a harvest of righteousness.

4 What causes fights and quarrels among you? Don't they come from your desires that battle within you? 2You want something but don't get it. You kill and covet, but you cannot have what you want. You quarrel and fight. You do not have, because you do not ask God. 3When you ask, you do not receive, because you ask with wrong motives, that you may spend what you get on your pleasures.

4You adulterous people, don't you know that friendship with the world is hatred toward God?

Anyone who chooses to be a friend of the world becomes an enemy of God. ⁵Or do you think Scripture says without reason that the spirit he caused to live in us envies intensely?ᵍ ⁶But he gives us more grace. That is why Scripture says:

"God opposes the proud
  but gives grace to the humble."ʰ

⁷Submit yourselves, then, to God. Resist the devil, and he will flee from you. ⁸Come near to God and he will come near to you. Wash your hands, you sinners, and purify your hearts, you double-minded. ⁹Grieve, mourn and wail. Change your laughter to mourning and your joy to gloom. ¹⁰Humble yourselves before the Lord, and he will lift you up.

g5 Or that God jealously longs for the spirit that he made to live in us; or that the Spirit he caused to live in us longs jealously   h6 Prov. 3:34

Discovering the Word 1. In 3:13–18 James discusses earthly and heavenly wisdom. What are the characteristics of each? 2. What does James say is the source of quarrels (4:1–2)? 3. What does James say is necessary to come to God in prayer (vv. 3–10)? 4. What does it mean to be humble, to submit to God (vv. 6–7)? 5. In verses 7–10 James gives several suggestions for humbling ourselves before God. How does each contribute to a humble spirit?

Applying the Word 1. As you look at 4:3, what might be examples of right and wrong motives in your prayer? 2. In what area are you an enemy of God (see v. 4 and consider your attitude toward material possessions, friends, study or work, and leisure time)? How can you restore your relationship to him? 3. In what situations could humility help you become a source of peace? Explain.

Responding in Prayer Take a few minutes to quietly humble yourself before God. Ask him to help you become a peacemaker.

---

7 / *James 4:11–17*
Getting Perspective

"I AM THE master of my fate. I am the captain of my soul." How subtly we convince ourselves that we control our lives. Sometimes only a crisis or even death itself convinces us otherwise. If we are truly wise and humble, we will listen carefully when James says, "You are a mist that appears for a little while and then vanishes."

Warming Up to God How have you been trying to control your life? Confess it to God and experience the freedom of giving him control.

Read James 4:11–17.

---

¹¹Brothers, do not slander one another. Anyone who speaks against his brother or judges him speaks against the law and judges it. When you judge the law, you are not keeping it, but sitting in judgment on it. ¹²There is only one Lawgiver and Judge, the one who is able to save and destroy. But you—who are you to judge your neighbor?

¹³Now listen, you who say, "Today or tomorrow we will go to this or that city, spend a year there, carry on business and make money." ¹⁴Why, you do not even know what will happen tomorrow. What is your life? You are a mist that appears for a little while and then vanishes. ¹⁵Instead, you ought to say, "If it is the Lord's will, we will live and do this or that." ¹⁶As it is, you boast and brag. All such boasting is evil. ¹⁷Anyone, then, who knows the good he ought to do and doesn't do it, sins.

Discovering the Word 1. Why does James say we shouldn't slander or speak against a Christian brother or sister (vv. 11–12)? 2. If we judge the law, what does this say about our attitude toward the lawgiver (v. 11)? 3. How can a proper attitude toward God (v. 12) enable us to have a proper attitude toward others? 4. How would you describe the two attitudes toward the future found in verses 13–17? 5. If our life is like a mist, what should be our attitude toward tomorrow?

Applying the Word 1. If you knew you were going to die tomorrow, how would your attitude toward life today be different? 2. What future plans do you often dwell on? 3. In what area of your life do you need to turn your plans over to God's will?

Responding in Prayer Ask God to help you love those around you rather than judge them. Humbly commit your future plans to the Lord.

8 / James 5:1–11
What Awaits

YOU HAVE PROBABLY heard of the young man who cried out, "Lord, I want patience and I want it now!" James encourages us in this passage to wait on God and to be patient, and warns us against wanting it all now.

 Warming Up to God God wants to know your concerns and frustrations. Tell God what has been making you impatient lately.

 Read James 5:1–11.

5 Now listen, you rich people, weep and wail because of the misery that is coming upon you. ²Your wealth has rotted, and moths have eaten your clothes. ³Your gold and silver are corroded. Their corrosion will testify against you and eat your flesh like fire. You have hoarded wealth in the last days. ⁴Look! The wages you failed to pay the workmen who mowed your fields are crying out against you. The cries of the harvesters have reached the ears of the Lord Almighty. ⁵You have lived on earth in luxury and self-indulgence. You have fattened yourselves in the day of slaughter.ⁱ ⁶You have condemned and murdered innocent men, who were not opposing you.

⁷Be patient, then, brothers, until the Lord's coming. See how the farmer waits for the land to yield its valuable crop and how patient he is for the autumn and spring rains. ⁸You too, be patient and stand firm, because the Lord's coming is near. ⁹Don't grumble against each other, brothers, or you will be judged. The Judge is standing at the door!

¹⁰Brothers, as an example of patience in the face of suffering, take the prophets who spoke in the name of the Lord. ¹¹As you know, we consider blessed those who have persevered. You have heard of Job's perseverance and have seen what the Lord finally brought about. The Lord is full of compassion and mercy.

ⁱ5 Or yourselves as in a day of feasting

Discovering the Word 1. James declares that misery awaits rich people. What crimes have they committed (vv. 1–6)? 2. Is James condemning all rich people? Explain. 3. James goes on to give three examples of patient people: a farmer, the prophets and Job. How is each an example of patience? 4. What different reactions would you expect the rich and those who suffer to have to the prospect of the Lord's return (vv. 7–9)? 5. How is piling up riches the opposite of patience that waits in faith for God to provide?

Applying the Word 1. When are you tempted to hoard rather than to give and wait on God? 2. In what areas of your life are you impatient? 3. What do you learn about patience from the examples James mentions?

Responding in Prayer Pray that God would make you a person who can wait for God to answer prayer.

9 / James 5:12–20
Making Others Whole

BROKEN HOMES, shattered relationships, damaged emotions—we live in a fragmented and hurting world. As we see all the wounded people around us, we long to help, to offer a healing touch. James gives us very practical suggestions for helping people become whole.

Warming Up to God God wants you to be whole. In what area are you struggling with emotional pain? Tell God how you want him to help you.

Read James 5:12–20.

¹²Above all, my brothers, do not swear—not by heaven or by earth or by anything else. Let your "Yes" be yes, and your "No," no, or you will be condemned.

¹³Is any one of you in trouble? He should pray. Is anyone happy? Let him sing songs of praise. ¹⁴Is any one of you sick? He should call the elders of the church to pray over him and anoint him with oil in the name of the Lord. ¹⁵And the prayer offered in faith will make the sick person well; the Lord will raise him up. If he has sinned, he will be forgiven. ¹⁶Therefore confess your sins to each other and pray for each other so that you may be healed. The prayer of a righteous man is powerful and effective.

¹⁷Elijah was a man just like us. He prayed earnestly that it would not rain, and it did not rain on the land for three and a half years. ¹⁸Again he prayed, and the heavens gave rain, and the earth produced its crops.

¹⁹My brothers, if one of you should wander from the truth and someone should bring him back, ²⁰remember this: Whoever turns a sinner from the error of his way will save him from death and cover over a multitude of sins.

Discovering the Word 1. What different types of prayer are mentioned in verses 13–18? 2. In verses 14–16 James discusses physical and spiritual healing. What are the steps in this process? 3. How is physical healing connected with the forgiveness of sins? 4. How does the Old Testament prophet Elijah illustrate the effectiveness of prayer (vv. 17–18)? 5. According to verses 19–20, how, if at all, are we our brother's keeper?

Applying the Word 1. Do you pray more when you are in trouble or when things are going well? Explain. 2. How could you make one of the types of prayer James describes more a part of your life? 3. How can you help others become whole physically, emotionally or spiritually?

Responding in Prayer Ask God for grace as you minister to others.

1 Peter

*I*t was a shaky time for Christians in the Roman Empire. In A.D. 68 Emperor Nero saw himself surrounded by political enemies and took the easy way out: suicide. In the next year three emperors, in rapid succession, took his place, but couldn't hold the job. So in A.D. 69 troops proclaimed the military leader Vespasian as emperor—and saw that he stayed there.

Vespasian hated Jews, and he counted Christians among them. Prior to becoming emperor, his goal had been to trample Judea and erase it from existence. As emperor, he sent his oldest son, Titus, to finish the job. Titus put Jerusalem under siege for three months. Then he tightened the noose. Troops leveled buildings to the ground. The temple became a crumble of stones. Jerusalem fell. Jews (and Christians) became Roman captives.

Aftershocks vibrated throughout the Roman Empire, blending with the general persecution against "atheists" (people who refused to worship Roman gods) that Nero had begun. Christians everywhere suffered. They were driven from their homes, deported to the outer borders of the empire, forbidden to worship openly and, worse yet, splintered by their own internal doctrinal disputes.

It is possible that the apostle Paul was martyred under Nero. And Peter was martyred as well—crucified upside-down, tradition says, because he felt unworthy to die in the same position as his Lord. It was a dark season for Christians.

How were they to endure?

Peter, through God's inspiration, sensed this coming darkness. If conservative scholars are correct, Peter's first letter can be dated about A.D. 64, written probably from the city of Rome —which Peter called Babylon in 5:13.

This is not a bleak letter. Indeed, it is full of hope and practical counsel on how to endure. It tells us to balance holy living with correct doctrine, to nurture spiritual growth, to work within existing authority structures, and to take care of each other.

This letter, sent with prophetic love to first-century Christians, still lives today. It provides a compass for our own dark road.

Outline

1 / *1 Peter 1:1–12*
Strangers in the World

A SMALL YOUNG man stood in the front of my classroom and spoke anxiously of home. He pointed to South Korean newspaper clippings that hinted of takeover by the North. He worried that the end was near: Ten years? Five? Two? If he is correct, Christians in South Korea have a right to feel nervous. Will they still have a church five years from now? Will they still have Bibles? Will they have to shutter their windows and lower their voices when they pray with their children?

How can a believer prepare for that kind of suffering? And what is it, anyway, that makes Christians strangers to the rest of the world?

 Warming Up to God If you knew you were about to enter a difficult set of circumstances that would test your faith, how would you prepare yourself?

 Read 1 Peter 1:1–12.

1 Peter, an apostle of Jesus Christ,

To God's elect, strangers in the world, scattered throughout Pontus, Galatia, Cappadocia, Asia and Bithynia, ²who have been chosen according to the foreknowledge of God the Father, through the sanctifying work of the Spirit, for obedience to Jesus Christ and sprinkling by his blood:

Grace and peace be yours in abundance.

³Praise be to the God and Father of our Lord Jesus Christ! In his great mercy he has given us new birth into a living hope through the resurrection of Jesus Christ from the dead, ⁴and into an inheritance that can never perish, spoil or fade—kept in heaven for you, ⁵who through faith are shielded by God's power until the coming of the salvation that is ready to be revealed in the last time. ⁶In this you greatly rejoice, though now for a little while you may have had to suffer grief in all kinds of trials. ⁷These have come so that your faith—of greater worth than gold, which perishes even though refined by fire—may be proved genuine and may result in praise, glory and honor when Jesus Christ is revealed. ⁸Though you have not seen him, you love him; and even though you do not see him now, you believe in him and are filled with an inexpressible and glorious joy, ⁹for you are receiving the goal of your faith, the salvation of your souls.

¹⁰Concerning this salvation, the prophets, who spoke of the grace that was to come to you, searched intently and with the greatest care, ¹¹trying to find out the time and circumstances to which the Spirit of Christ in them was pointing when he predicted the sufferings of Christ and the glories that would follow. ¹²It was revealed to them that they were not serving themselves but you, when they spoke of the things that have now been told you by those who have preached the gospel to you by the Holy Spirit sent from heaven. Even angels long to look into these things.

Discovering the Word 1. Study Peter's description of the people who were about to receive his letter (vv. 1–2). How does his description of them help explain why they were "strangers in the world"? 2. Peter says in verse 6, "Now for a little while you may have had to suffer grief in all kinds of trials." If you were to hear that kind of message, what information in this paragraph might help you through the suffering (vv. 3–9)? 3. What did Peter believe to be true of genuine faith (vv. 7–9)? 4. By what different routes did news of salvation come to the readers of Peter's letter (vv. 10–12)?

Applying the Word 1. How does the future, as Peter describes it here, offer you hope in your own setting? 2. When have you seen Jesus (through a person or event) in a way that increased your faith? 3. Peter refers to new birth, or salvation, throughout this passage as a central difference between Christians and the world. What tensions have you experienced because of this difference?

 Responding in Prayer Praise God for his gift of salvation that can help us cope with tensions with the world.

2 / 1 Peter 1:13–25
Called to Be Different

I GREW UP in a church of fervent Christians. We knelt to pray, carried Bibles to school, wore "modest" clothes—even to gym class—and talked a lot about Jesus. Needless to say, kids from our church never made the "most popular" lists at the local public high school. Instead, we feared the taunt "Holy Roller."

It's possible that our attempts to be separate and holy did more to close people out of our beliefs than to invite them in. Yet God does call his people to be different; different from what they would be if they did not believe in Jesus and different from the unbelievers around them.

  Warming Up to God Think of a Christian you admire. In what ways does that person resemble Christ? Praise God for what you learn about him through others.

Read 1 Peter 1:13–25.

---

¹³Therefore, prepare your minds for action; be self-controlled; set your hope fully on the grace to be given you when Jesus Christ is revealed. ¹⁴As obedient children, do not conform to the evil desires you had when you lived in ignorance. ¹⁵But just as he who called you is holy, so be holy in all you do; ¹⁶for it is written: "Be holy, because I am holy."[a]

¹⁷Since you call on a Father who judges each man's work impartially, live your lives as strangers here in reverent fear. ¹⁸For you know that it was not with perishable things such as silver or gold that you were redeemed from the empty way of life handed down to you from your forefathers, ¹⁹but with the precious blood of Christ, a lamb without blemish or defect. ²⁰He was chosen before the creation of the world, but was revealed in these last times for your sake. ²¹Through him you believe in God, who raised him from the dead and glorified him, and so your faith and hope are in God.

²²Now that you have purified yourselves by obeying the truth so that you have sincere love for your brothers, love one another deeply, from the heart.[b] ²³For you have been born again, not of perishable seed, but of imperishable, through the living and enduring word of God. ²⁴For,

"All men are like grass,
and all their glory is like the flowers of the field;
the grass withers and the flowers fall,
²⁵ but the word of the Lord stands forever."[c]

And this is the word that was preached to you.

[a]16 Lev. 11:44,45; 19:2; 20:7   [b]22 Some early manuscripts *from a pure heart*   [c]25 Isaiah 40:6-8

Discovering the Word 1. Peter lists several ways that followers of Jesus ought to respond to his gift of salvation. Define each of these responses more fully (vv. 13–16). 2. Select one of these responses. If you were to put that response on the "front burner" of your priorities, what changes would you have to make in your life? 3. What events from the past would help the recipients of Peter's letter to appreciate God's concern for them (vv. 18–21)? 4. How could the conditions that Peter describes in verses 21–25 promote sincere love among Christians? 5. Peter links the Word of God with salvation and new birth. (Compare verses 10, 12, 23 and 25.) What do you think Peter meant when he said that this Word is "enduring" and "stands forever"?

Applying the Word 1. How might an honest attempt to "be holy" improve your relationships with people close to you? 2. In what situations might it make you, as verse 17 says, more like a stranger? 3. Jot a quick list of all you have to do today (or tomorrow). How could you begin to tackle this list with the goal "Be holy in all you do"?

 Responding in Prayer Pray specifically from your list that you would be holy and would improve relationships with those around you.

3 / 1 Peter 2:1–12
Do I Want to Grow Up?

"WOULD YOU SEND me to school?" [Peter] inquired craftily.

"Yes . . ."

"I don't want to go to school and learn solemn things," he told her passionately. "I don't want to be a man. O Wendy's mother, if I was to wake up and feel there was a beard!"

"Peter," said Wendy the comforter, "I should love you in a beard." Mrs. Darling stretched out her arms to him.

"Keep back, lady, no one is going to catch me and make me a man." (James M. Barrie, *Peter Pan* [New York: Charles Scribner's Sons, 1911], p. 228.)

 Warming Up to God In what ways are you tempted to follow Peter Pan's approach to life?

 Read 1 Peter 2:1–12.

2 Therefore, rid yourselves of all malice and all deceit, hypocrisy, envy, and slander of every kind. ²Like newborn babies, crave pure spiritual milk, so that by it you may grow up in your salvation, ³now that you have tasted that the Lord is good.

⁴As you come to him, the living Stone—rejected by men but chosen by God and precious to him— ⁵you also, like living stones, are being built into a spiritual house to be a holy priesthood, offering spiritual sacrifices acceptable to God through Jesus Christ. ⁶For in Scripture it says:

"See, I lay a stone in Zion,
a chosen and precious cornerstone,
and the one who trusts in him
will never be put to shame."ᵈ

⁷Now to you who believe, this stone is precious. But to those who do not believe,

"The stone the builders rejected
has become the capstone,"ᵉ ᶠ

⁸and,

"A stone that causes men to stumble
and a rock that makes them fall."ᵍ

They stumble because they disobey the message—which is also what they were destined for.

⁹But you are a chosen people, a royal priesthood, a holy nation, a people belonging to God, that you may declare the praises of him who called you out of darkness into his wonderful light. ¹⁰Once you were not a people, but now you are the people of God; once you had not received mercy, but now you have received mercy.

¹¹Dear friends, I urge you, as aliens and strangers in the world, to abstain from sinful desires, which war against your soul. ¹²Live such good lives among the pagans that, though they accuse you of doing wrong, they may see your good deeds and glorify God on the day he visits us.

ᵈ6 Isaiah 28:16   ᵉ7 Or *cornerstone*   ᶠ7 Psalm 118:22
ᵍ8 Isaiah 8:14

 Discovering the Word 1. Peter speaks here of two aspects of Christian growth: individual and corporate. How might the five inner sins of verse 1 damage outer relationships with other believers? **2.** What does the metaphor in verses 2–3 contribute to your understanding of how to nurture spiritual growth? **3.** How does belief or unbelief influence the way a person understands Jesus, the "living Stone" (vv. 4–8)? **4.** What reasons do the people here have to praise God (vv. 9–10)? **5.** Verse 11 repeats a now familiar theme in 1 Peter—that Christians are aliens and strangers in the world. How might living up to the description of verse 9 cause a Christian to be alienated from the world?

 Applying the Word 1. The *New Bible Commentary* interprets verse 12, "the day [God] visits us," as "the day God will visit the earth and search out man's hearts in judgment." If this were to occur in your lifetime, what evidence would you want God to find of your own spiritual growth? **2.** How could today's passage help you overcome a tendency to become a spiritual Peter Pan?

Responding in Prayer Ask God to rid you of "all malice and all deceit, hypocrisy, envy, and slander of every kind."

4 / *1 Peter 2:13—3:7*
In His Steps

IN THE LATE 1800s a young social worker tramped the streets of Topeka, Kansas. Disguised as an unemployed printer, he begged for food, work, hope. The social-worker-turned-tramp was a believer in Jesus and knew the giving, caring moral code that Jesus lived and taught. So he assumed that fellow Christians, even though they could not see through his disguise, would be among the first to help. He was wrong. He found that a tramp's life was tough—and that Christians didn't make it any easier.

Charles Sheldon went home to write a book about his experience—a novel that introduced a dying tramp to the Reverend Henry Maxwell and his congregation. In it, a body of believers begins to see the submissive suffering of Jesus and what it means to walk *In His Steps*.

 Warming Up to God If you were to rate your natural inclination for being submissive on a scale of one to ten, where would you place yourself and why? (One is a mud-covered doormat; ten is a banner-waving firebrand.)

 Read 1 Peter 2:13—3:7.

---

¹³Submit yourselves for the Lord's sake to every authority instituted among men: whether to the king, as the supreme authority, ¹⁴or to governors, who are sent by him to punish those who do wrong and to commend those who do right. ¹⁵For it is God's will that by doing good you should silence the ignorant talk of foolish men. ¹⁶Live as free men, but do not use your freedom as a cover-up for evil; live as servants of God. ¹⁷Show proper respect to everyone: Love the brotherhood of believers, fear God, honor the king.

¹⁸Slaves, submit yourselves to your masters with all respect, not only to those who are good and considerate, but also to those who are harsh. ¹⁹For it is commendable if a man bears up under the pain of unjust suffering because he is conscious of God. ²⁰But how is it to your credit if you receive a beating for doing wrong and endure it? But if you suffer for doing good and you endure it, this is commendable before God. ²¹To this you were called, because Christ suffered for you, leaving you an example, that you should follow in his steps.

²²"He committed no sin,
    and no deceit was found in his mouth."ʰ

²³When they hurled their insults at him, he did not retaliate; when he suffered, he made no threats. Instead, he entrusted himself to him who

judges justly. ²⁴He himself bore our sins in his body on the tree, so that we might die to sins and live for righteousness; by his wounds you have been healed. ²⁵For you were like sheep going astray, but now you have returned to the Shepherd and Overseer of your souls.

3 Wives, in the same way be submissive to your husbands so that, if any of them do not believe the word, they may be won over without words by the behavior of their wives, ²when they see the purity and reverence of your lives. ³Your beauty should not come from outward adornment, such as braided hair and the wearing of gold jewelry and fine clothes. ⁴Instead, it should be that of your inner self, the unfading beauty of a gentle and quiet spirit, which is of great worth in God's sight. ⁵For this is the way the holy women of the past who put their hope in God used to make themselves beautiful. They were submissive to their own husbands, ⁶like Sarah, who obeyed Abraham and called him her master. You are her daughters if you do what is right and do not give way to fear.

⁷Husbands, in the same way be considerate as you live with your wives, and treat them with respect as the weaker partner and as heirs with you of the gracious gift of life, so that nothing will hinder your prayers.

ʰ22 Isaiah 53:9

Discovering the Word 1. According to Peter, why should Christians treat their governing leaders with respect (2:13–15)? 2. How could the teachings of 2:16–17 keep you from becoming a "muddy doormat" to your government? 3. How might being a Christian bring some meaning to the suffering that comes from being a slave (2:18–21)? 4. 2:23 says that in his suffering, Jesus "entrusted himself to him who judges justly." How might a similar trust in God help you to submit to the necessary suffering that has come into your own life?

Applying the Word 1. Finding a balance between responsible action for healthy change and submission to authority is a constant tension for the Christian who wants to obey this passage. How can you draw together both ends of this tension? (In what situations would you take action? At what point would you submit?) 2. How do you balance the tension of submission versus responsible action in your job? in your marriage? in other relationships?

Responding in Prayer Pray for courage to walk "in his steps" even in the face of suffering.

---

5 / 1 Peter 3:8–22
If I'm Living Right, Then Why Do I Hurt So Much?

WE OFTEN ASSUME a direct connection between "right living" and "easy living." It's an added pat on the back when life runs smoothly. But it is an unspoken accusation when trauma strikes. Peter contemplated this connection—even added a link or two to the chain. (Sure there are ways to live that will decrease our chances for unjust conflict.) But Peter made no promises of easy living. Sometimes suffering comes—whether or not we earn it. It came to Jesus.

Warming Up to God When in your life has suffering been hard to understand?

Read 1 Peter 3:8–22.

8Finally, all of you, live in harmony with one another; be sympathetic, love as brothers, be compassionate and humble. 9Do not repay evil with evil or insult with insult, but with blessing, because to this you were called so that you may inherit a blessing. 10For,

"Whoever would love life
   and see good days
must keep his tongue from evil
   and his lips from deceitful speech.
11He must turn from evil and do good;
   he must seek peace and pursue it.
12For the eyes of the Lord are on the righteous
   and his ears are attentive to their prayer,
but the face of the Lord is against those who
   do evil."[i]

13Who is going to harm you if you are eager to do good? 14But even if you should suffer for what is right, you are blessed. "Do not fear what they

fear[j]; do not be frightened."[k] 15But in your hearts set apart Christ as Lord. Always be prepared to give an answer to everyone who asks you to give the reason for the hope that you have. But do this with gentleness and respect, 16keeping a clear conscience, so that those who speak maliciously against your good behavior in Christ may be ashamed of their slander. 17It is better, if it is God's will, to suffer for doing good than for doing evil. 18For Christ died for sins once for all, the righteous for the unrighteous, to bring you to God. He was put to death in the body but made alive by the Spirit, 19through whom[l] also he went and preached to the spirits in prison 20who disobeyed long ago when God waited patiently in the days of Noah while the ark was being built. In it only a few people, eight in all, were saved through water, 21and this water symbolizes bap-

i12 Psalm 34:12-16   j14 Or *not fear their threats*   k14 Isaiah 8:12
l18,19 Or *alive in the spirit,* 19*through which*

tism that now saves you also—not the removal of dirt from the body but the pledge^m of a good conscience toward God. It saves you by the resurrection of Jesus Christ, ²²who has gone into heaven and is at God's right hand—with angels, authorities and powers in submission to him.

^m21 Or *response*

 Discovering the Word 1. Find as many phrases as you can in verses 8–12 that describe what a Christian ought to be and do. 2. What do you find difficult about the way of life described in verses 8–12? 3. In spite of godly living, Peter knew that Christians may encounter hardship. What counsel does Peter offer for coping with suffering (vv. 13–17)? 4. Why might unbelievers be willing to listen to reasons for hope from a person who is living the way Peter describes (vv. 15–17)? 5. Verse 18 is a "capsule" description of Christ's work and purpose. What all can you know from this verse about why Jesus came and what he accomplished?

Applying the Word 1. How could setting apart Christ as Lord, as verse 15 commands, help you endure suffering? 2. Our world is often unjust. Bring to mind some of your past or current sufferings. In the context of these sufferings, how can the picture of Christ portrayed by this passage bring you hope?

Responding in Prayer Thank God for the hope we have been given in Christ.

---

6 / 1 Peter 4
The Christian Path of Nails

SHUSAKO ENDO, THE Japanese novelist, tells the story of two missionary priests in *Silence*. The priests came from Portugal to Japan in the mid–1600s. At that time the Christian faith in Japan was one hundred years old. It had some 300,000 followers, a cluster of colleges, seminaries, hospitals and local clergy. But persecution had struck the church. A fragmented government united under a single cause: to become truly Japanese. And that meant erasing foreign religion, especially Christianity. Christians suffered horrible deaths. Endo's book asks why. Why the suffering? Why did God appear to sit through it in silence? And these questions are just as relevant for us today as we continue to suffer because of our beliefs.

 Warming Up to God When you learn of Christians suffering because of their faith, what questions come to your mind? Voice your questions to God.

 Read 1 Peter 4.

---

4 Therefore, since Christ suffered in his body, arm yourselves also with the same attitude, because he who has suffered in his body is done with sin. ²As a result, he does not live the rest of his earthly life for evil human desires, but rather for the will of God. ³For you have spent enough time in the past doing what pagans choose to do—living in debauchery, lust, drunkenness, orgies, carousing and detestable idolatry. ⁴They think it strange that you do not plunge with them into the same flood of dissipation, and they heap abuse on you. ⁵But they will have to give account to him who is ready to judge the living and the dead. ⁶For this is the reason the gospel was preached even to those who are now dead, so that they might be judged according to men in regard to the body, but live according to God in regard to the spirit.

⁷The end of all things is near. Therefore be clear minded and self-controlled so that you can pray. ⁸Above all, love each other deeply, because love covers over a multitude of sins. ⁹Offer hospitality to one another without grumbling. ¹⁰Each one should use whatever gift he has received to serve others, faithfully administering God's grace in its various forms. ¹¹If anyone speaks, he should do it as one speaking the very words of God. If anyone serves, he should do it with the strength God provides, so that in all things God may be

praised through Jesus Christ. To him be the glory and the power for ever and ever. Amen.

[12]Dear friends, do not be surprised at the painful trial you are suffering, as though something strange were happening to you. [13]But rejoice that you participate in the sufferings of Christ, so that you may be overjoyed when his glory is revealed. [14]If you are insulted because of the name of Christ, you are blessed, for the Spirit of glory and of God rests on you. [15]If you suffer, it should not be as a murderer or thief or any other kind of criminal, or even as a meddler. [16]However, if you suffer as a Christian, do not be ashamed, but praise God that you bear that name. [17]For it is

time for judgment to begin with the family of God; and if it begins with us, what will the outcome be for those who do not obey the gospel of God? [18]And,

> "If it is hard for the righteous to be saved,
>   what will become of the ungodly and the
>   sinner?" [n]

[19]So then, those who suffer according to God's will should commit themselves to their faithful Creator and continue to do good.

[n]18 Prov. 11:31

 Discovering the Word 1. According to this passage, how is a Christian different from a pagan (vv. 1–6)? (Note attitudes as well as actions.) 2. Our doubts may sometimes taunt us, "Of what use is your Christian faith? God does not protect you. When your time comes, you die like the rest." How might the information in verses 4–6 help us deal with those doubts? 3. What specific instructions does Peter give suffering Christians who are aware that the end of all things is coming (vv. 7–11)? 4. Of what spitirual and practical value are these instructions? 5. Verse 11 speaks of two forms of leadership in the early church: those who speak (teach) and those who serve. How would the purpose of church leadership as it is described here prevent a misuse of power between Christians? 6. According to verses 12–19, what are some right and wrong ways for a Christian to suffer?

Applying the Word 1. Think back to the questions you posed in question one. How do Peter's teachings help you deal with these questions? 2. How might verse 19 become both a comfort and a challenge to you when you suffer because of your faith?

Responding in Prayer Pray for Christians in many parts of the world who face suffering for their beliefs.

---

7 / 1 Peter 5
TLC for Trying Times

RELATIONSHIPS BRING COLOR to life. Sure, the mountaintop hermit has a spectacular view outside the window. But the colors inside the cabin are browns and grays. It is people who bring sparkle and fire to existence.

When Peter concluded his first letter, a work frequently pointing to suffering, he did not tell his readers to escape to the isolation of a spiritual or literal mountaintop. Instead, he pointed to their relationships and said, "Here's how to take care of each other."

 Warming Up to God What has been one of your most valuable relationships, and what made it valuable?

 Read 1 Peter 5.

---

5 To the elders among you, I appeal as a fellow elder, a witness of Christ's sufferings and one who also will share in the glory to be revealed: [2]Be shepherds of God's flock that is under your care, serving as overseers—not

because you must, but because you are willing, as God wants you to be; not greedy for money, but eager to serve; [3]not lording it over those entrusted to you, but being examples to the flock. [4]And when the Chief Shepherd appears, you will receive the crown of glory that will never fade away.

⁵Young men, in the same way be submissive to those who are older. All of you, clothe yourselves with humility toward one another, because,

"God opposes the proud
    but gives grace to the humble."ᵒ

⁶Humble yourselves, therefore, under God's mighty hand, that he may lift you up in due time. ⁷Cast all your anxiety on him because he cares for you.

⁸Be self-controlled and alert. Your enemy the devil prowls around like a roaring lion looking for someone to devour. ⁹Resist him, standing firm in the faith, because you know that your brothers

throughout the world are undergoing the same kind of sufferings.

¹⁰And the God of all grace, who called you to his eternal glory in Christ, after you have suffered a little while, will himself restore you and make you strong, firm and steadfast. ¹¹To him be the power for ever and ever. Amen.

¹²With the help of Silas,ᵖ whom I regard as a faithful brother, I have written to you briefly, encouraging you and testifying that this is the true grace of God. Stand fast in it.

¹³She who is in Babylon, chosen together with you, sends you her greetings, and so does my son Mark. ¹⁴Greet one another with a kiss of love.

Peace to all of you who are in Christ.

ᵒ5 Prov. 3:34   ᵖ12 Greek *Silvanus*, a variant of *Silas*

Discovering the Word 1. Peter speaks, in verse 1, to his fellow elders. In what ways did Peter see himself as like the elders he was writing to (vv. 1–4)? 2. When have you appreciated a person who acted toward you as a spiritual elder? 3. With what different beings or groups do these verses describe a Christian's relationships (vv. 5–11)? 4. What reasons did Peter give for following each of the commands in verses 5–9? 5. Peter points out three sets of relationships for all Christians—relationships with other believers, relationship with Satan, relationship with God. How would you summarize Peter's ideal for each of these?

Applying the Word 1. God's Word speaks to us in a variety of ways. What joy, comfort or warning do Peter's instructions in verses 5–11 point to in your own experience? 2. How could Peter's teachings about relationships in this chapter help you to "stand fast" in your own faith?

Responding in Prayer Ask God to comfort you, and wait before him to experience his care.

2 Peter

Peter's second letter refers appreciatively to Paul's letters in 3:15–16, but bears no hint that Paul is dead. On the other hand, Peter seems to anticipate his own death. Soon (see 1:13–14). Scholars therefore date this letter in the same decade of the sixties as 1 Peter—but closer to the end.

This letter does not tell us how to escape suffering, but instead to expect it. It shows us that throughout suffering we can enjoy our fellowship with other believers and look forward to a new heaven and a new earth, a "home of righteousness," with an end to pain.

Outline

1 / *2 Peter 1:1–11*
The Long Way Home

HOW DOES A person get to heaven? Is it by proper knowledge of Christian doctrines? Or by godly living? Is it by faith in Christ's gift of salvation? Or by working according to Christ's goals and principles? Is it by God's call to us to be his own? Or by our own endurance with God until the day we die? Weighty issues. And with them, Peter opens his second letter.

 Warming Up to God Reflect on your life. What qualities of godliness is God developing within you?

 Read 2 Peter 1:1–11.

1 Simon Peter, a servant and apostle of Jesus Christ,

To those who through the righteousness of our God and Savior Jesus Christ have received a faith as precious as ours:

²Grace and peace be yours in abundance through the knowledge of God and of Jesus our Lord.

³His divine power has given us everything we need for life and godliness through our knowledge of him who called us by his own glory and goodness. ⁴Through these he has given us his very great and precious promises, so that through them you may participate in the divine nature and escape the corruption in the world caused by evil desires.

⁵For this very reason, make every effort to add to your faith goodness; and to goodness, knowledge; ⁶and to knowledge, self-control; and to self-control, perseverance; and to perseverance, godliness; ⁷and to godliness, brotherly kindness; and to brotherly kindness, love. ⁸For if you possess these qualities in increasing measure, they will keep you from being ineffective and unproductive in your knowledge of our Lord Jesus Christ. ⁹But if anyone does not have them, he is nearsighted and blind, and has forgotten that he has been cleansed from his past sins.

¹⁰Therefore, my brothers, be all the more eager to make your calling and election sure. For if you do these things, you will never fall, ¹¹and you will receive a rich welcome into the eternal kingdom of our Lord and Savior Jesus Christ.

 Discovering the Word 1. In verses 1–2 we are told that we will receive the gifts of faith, grace and peace through Christ's righteousness and knowledge of God. How does your own spiritual well-being depend in part on Christ's righteousness and in part on your knowledge of God? 2. Verse 3 speaks of both knowledge and holy living as a part of the Christian life. Think of the balance between knowledge of Jesus and holy living that you have seen in Christians. What happens if one area or the other is weak? 3. Peter writes in verse 4 that because of God's promises, Christians "may participate in the divine nature and escape the corruption in the world." What does he then expect believers to do to nurture their own holy living (vv. 5–7)? 4. How are knowledge of Jesus and godly living related to each other (vv. 8–9)? 5. What do you think it means for a person to be called and elected by God (vv. 10–11)?

Applying the Word 1. Select one of the Christian qualities mentioned in verses 5–7 that you would like to become more prominent in your own life. If you were to practice this quality more faithfully, how would it help you escape the pollution of evil influences around you? 2. Verse 3 says that the divine power of Jesus has given us everything we need for godliness here and also for eternal life. If you were to draw more fully on this power that Jesus makes available to you, what changes would you hope to see in yourself?

Responding in Prayer Pray for the changes you think God is calling for within you.

2 / 2 Peter 1:12–21
If I Should Die . . .

IN 1976 JOE Bayly lay on a gurney outside an operating room at the Mayo Clinic's Methodist Hospital. He was scheduled for a minor operation. He'd probably be shuffling through the hospital hallway in a couple of days. But what if he just didn't wake up?

Joe's musings on that possibility left readers with a small thought-provoking book titled, appropriately, *Heaven*. In it he speaks of his faith in Jesus Christ and his hope here—and hereafter. It has influenced children and adults, believers and nonbelievers to follow Christ. Ten years later, Joe again lay on a gurney outside the operating room. The operation was a little more serious this time—his heart. But still, at Mayo, it was routine. But in 1986, when Joe woke up, it was hereafter.

  Warming Up to God As you think back over why you believe what you believe, who or what were the major influences in your life? Praise God for the privilege of knowing him.

Read 2 Peter 1:12–21.

---

¹²So I will always remind you of these things, even though you know them and are firmly established in the truth you now have. ¹³I think it is right to refresh your memory as long as I live in the tent of this body, ¹⁴because I know that I will soon put it aside, as our Lord Jesus Christ has made clear to me. ¹⁵And I will make every effort to see that after my departure you will always be able to remember these things.

¹⁶We did not follow cleverly invented stories when we told you about the power and coming of our Lord Jesus Christ, but we were eyewitnesses of his majesty. ¹⁷For he received honor and glory from God the Father when the voice came to him from the Majestic Glory, saying, "This is my Son, whom I love; with him I am well pleased."ᵃ ¹⁸We ourselves heard this voice that came from heaven when we were with him on the sacred mountain.

¹⁹And we have the word of the prophets made more certain, and you will do well to pay attention to it, as to a light shining in a dark place, until the day dawns and the morning star rises in your hearts. ²⁰Above all, you must understand that no prophecy of Scripture came about by the prophet's own interpretation. ²¹For prophecy never had its origin in the will of man, but men spoke from God as they were carried along by the Holy Spirit.

ᵃ17 Matt. 17:5; Mark 9:7; Luke 9:35

 Discovering the Word 1. What phrases here create a picture of Peter's view of death (vv. 13–15)? 2. Based on these phrases, how would you describe Peter's attitude about death? 3. What difference would it make to those who knew Peter that his teachings about Jesus came from an "eyewitness of his majesty" (v. 16)? 4. What do verses 19–21 show about the origin and purpose of Scripture?

Applying the Word 1. What do you hope will be your own feelings when you approach death? 2. What could you be doing during your lifetime to build toward a "good death"? 3. Peter did not want his readers to be so dependent on him that their faith would fall apart after his death. Who would you like to influence with your faith in your lifetime, and how can you best go about it?

Responding in Prayer Thank God for the gift of Scripture and the ways in which it increases our faith.

3 / *2 Peter 2*
Follow Which Leader?

"I HUGGED HER, and it was like hugging a statue. I looked into her eyes, and I felt that 'the lights were on, but no one was home.' She had been my best friend in a Christian college! What happened?"

For months my friend puzzled over this strange reunion with her college housemate. Later the puzzle pieces fell into place. A cult. "Someone got to her," she said later. "That person had to be very persuasive, and very tricky. My friend knew the Bible, and she wasn't dumb. I wish I knew what happened."

 Warming Up to God   Jesus Christ is always faithful to his promises. Reflect on that fact and allow praise to well up within you in response.

 Read 2 Peter 2.

---

2 But there were also false prophets among the people, just as there will be false teachers among you. They will secretly introduce destructive heresies, even denying the sovereign Lord who bought them—bringing swift destruction on themselves. ²Many will follow their shameful ways and will bring the way of truth into disrepute. ³In their greed these teachers will exploit you with stories they have made up. Their condemnation has long been hanging over them, and their destruction has not been sleeping.

⁴For if God did not spare angels when they sinned, but sent them to hell,*ᵇ* putting them into gloomy dungeons*ᶜ* to be held for judgment; ⁵if he did not spare the ancient world when he brought the flood on its ungodly people, but protected Noah, a preacher of righteousness, and seven others; ⁶if he condemned the cities of Sodom and Gomorrah by burning them to ashes, and made them an example of what is going to happen to the ungodly; ⁷and if he rescued Lot, a righteous man, who was distressed by the filthy lives of lawless men ⁸(for that righteous man, living among them day after day, was tormented in his righteous soul by the lawless deeds he saw and heard)— ⁹if this is so, then the Lord knows how to rescue godly men from trials and to hold the unrighteous for the day of judgment, while continuing their punishment.*ᵈ* ¹⁰This is especially true of those who follow the corrupt desire of the sinful nature*ᵉ* and despise authority.

Bold and arrogant, these men are not afraid to slander celestial beings; ¹¹yet even angels, although they are stronger and more powerful, do not bring slanderous accusations against such beings in the presence of the Lord. ¹²But these men blaspheme in matters they do not understand. They are like brute beasts, creatures of instinct, born only to be caught and destroyed, and like beasts they too will perish.

¹³They will be paid back with harm for the harm they have done. Their idea of pleasure is to carouse in broad daylight. They are blots and blemishes, reveling in their pleasures while they feast with you.*ᶠ* ¹⁴With eyes full of adultery, they never stop sinning; they seduce the unstable; they are experts in greed—an accursed brood! ¹⁵They have left the straight way and wandered off to follow the way of Balaam son of Beor, who loved the wages of wickedness. ¹⁶But he was rebuked for his wrongdoing by a donkey—a beast without speech—who spoke with a man's voice and restrained the prophet's madness.

¹⁷These men are springs without water and mists driven by a storm. Blackest darkness is reserved for them. ¹⁸For they mouth empty, boastful words and, by appealing to the lustful desires of sinful human nature, they entice people who are just escaping from those who live in error. ¹⁹They promise them freedom, while they themselves are slaves of depravity—for a man is a slave to whatever has mastered him. ²⁰If they have escaped the corruption of the world by knowing our Lord and Savior Jesus Christ and are again entangled in it and overcome, they are worse off at the end than they were at the beginning. ²¹It would have been better for them not to have

---

ᵇ4 Greek Tartarus   *ᶜ4 Some manuscripts into chains of darkness*
ᵈ9 Or unrighteous for punishment until the day of judgment   *ᵉ10 Or the flesh*   *ᶠ13 Some manuscripts in their love feasts*

known the way of righteousness, than to have known it and then to turn their backs on the sacred command that was passed on to them. ²²Of them the proverbs are true: "A dog returns to its vomit,"ᵍ and, "A sow that is washed goes back to her wallowing in the mud."

ᵍ22 Prov. 26:11

Discovering the Word 1. Why are false teachers dangerous (2:1–3, also 1:20–21)? 2. Study verses 4–9. What did Peter want his readers to learn from these Old Testament events? 3. What characteristics should alert us that we are encountering a false teacher (vv. 10–19)? 4. Why might some people be attracted to teachers with these characteristics? 5. Why might it be better if a false teacher had never known the truth (vv. 20–22)?

Applying the Word 1. How can you protect yourself from the influence of false teachers? 2. What cautions can you institute to keep from becoming a false teacher yourself?

Responding in Prayer Pray for those who are victims of false teachers.

---

4 / 2 *Peter 3*
The Fire Next Time

AS A TEEN and young adult, when someone mentioned the end of the world, I shuddered and hoped, "Not yet." I wanted to graduate, fall in love, get married, raise children, work at a career—not necessarily in that order. At the very least I wanted to see how the weekend's date turned out. My sunsets looked like sunrise. And God's promised end of the world seemed a cruel interruption.

But at this writing, my twenty-two-year-old daughter and her unborn child lie cold in a country cemetery, a teenage son struggles with severe depression in a nearby psychiatric ward, my husband's colleague of over twenty years just revealed a secret life that includes distributing drugs to teens. My sunrises long for sunset. And the end of the world promises welcome relief.

Warming Up to God When are you likely to wish the world would end? Explain.

Read 2 Peter 3.

---

3 Dear friends, this is now my second letter to you. I have written both of them as reminders to stimulate you to wholesome thinking. ²I want you to recall the words spoken in the past by the holy prophets and the command given by our Lord and Savior through your apostles.

³First of all, you must understand that in the last days scoffers will come, scoffing and following their own evil desires. ⁴They will say, "Where is this 'coming' he promised? Ever since our fathers died, everything goes on as it has since the beginning of creation." ⁵But they deliberately forget that long ago by God's word the heavens existed and the earth was formed out of water and by water. ⁶By these waters also the world of that time was deluged and destroyed. ⁷By the same word the present heavens and earth are reserved for fire, being kept for the day of judgment and destruction of ungodly men.

⁸But do not forget this one thing, dear friends: With the Lord a day is like a thousand years, and a thousand years are like a day. ⁹The Lord is not slow in keeping his promise, as some understand slowness. He is patient with you, not wanting anyone to perish, but everyone to come to repentance.

¹⁰But the day of the Lord will come like a thief. The heavens will disappear with a roar; the elements will be destroyed by fire, and the earth and everything in it will be laid bare.ʰ

ʰ10 Some manuscripts *be burned up*

¹¹Since everything will be destroyed in this way, what kind of people ought you to be? You ought to live holy and godly lives ¹²as you look forward to the day of God and speed its coming.ⁱ That day will bring about the destruction of the heavens by fire, and the elements will melt in the heat. ¹³But in keeping with his promise we are looking forward to a new heaven and a new earth, the home of righteousness.

¹⁴So then, dear friends, since you are looking forward to this, make every effort to be found spotless, blameless and at peace with him. ¹⁵Bear in mind that our Lord's patience means salvation, just as our dear brother Paul also wrote you with the wisdom that God gave him. ¹⁶He writes the same way in all his letters, speaking in them of these matters. His letters contain some things that are hard to understand, which ignorant and unstable people distort, as they do the other Scriptures, to their own destruction.

¹⁷Therefore, dear friends, since you already know this, be on your guard so that you may not be carried away by the error of lawless men and fall from your secure position. ¹⁸But grow in the grace and knowledge of our Lord and Savior Jesus Christ. To him be glory both now and forever! Amen.

ⁱ12 Or *as you wait eagerly for the day of God to come*

Discovering the Word 1. What reasons did Peter give his readers to pay attention to this writing? (Look especially at verses 1–3 and 15–18.) 2. What mistakes will the last-day scoffers make (vv. 4–7)? 3. What reasons does Peter offer for a delay in Christ's return (vv. 8–9, 15)? 4. Compare and contrast the use of fire and water in this passage. What is the significance of each? 5. Notice the question of verse 11, "What kind of people ought you to be?" What answers can you find through the remainder of the chapter?

Applying the Word 1. If the day of the Lord were to come in your lifetime, what would you like to accomplish first? 2. In what condition would you like God to find your work? 3. How would you like God to find your relationships?

Responding in Prayer Pray that you will be always ready for Christ's return.

1 John

T oday many people claim to be Christians. In fact, a 1986 Gallup Survey revealed that
ninety-four percent of adult Americans believe in God, and that seventy-six percent
believe that Jesus is either God or the Son of God. Furthermore, when the question
"Would you describe yourself as a 'born again' Christian or not?" was asked, thirty-three percent said yes.

The problem, of course, is that actions speak louder than words. The same survey revealed
that many of the mainline Protestant denominations have experienced sharp losses in
membership since the mid sixties. For example, only forty percent told Gallup that they had
attended church in the last week, and only ten percent claimed to read the Bible on a daily
basis.

This credibility problem is intensified when we move from the pew to the pulpit. A
shocking number of Christian leaders have been found guilty of sexual sin or financial
misconduct. Sadly, their moral failures have been brought to our national attention by the
secular news media, anxious to expose such blatant hypocrisy. If such leaders are representative of the church in general, it seems that we are indeed experiencing a period of
unprecedented moral decline.

How are we to respond to this kind of situation? How can we tell the difference between
genuine Christians and those who merely profess to know Christ?

John's letters were written for that very purpose. John writes to expose the false claims of
those whose conduct contradicts their claims. He also provides strong assurance to those
whose lifestyle is consistent with their Christian faith.

First John was written between A.D. 85 and 95 by the apostle John, the author of the
Gospel of John and Revelation. Evidently the letter was circulated among a number of
churches in Asia who were threatened by false teachers.

These false teachers embraced an early form of heresy known as Gnosticism. They taught
that matter was entirely evil and spirit was entirely good. This teaching resulted in two
fundamental errors:

A *"new" theology*. This centered in a denial of the incarnation. Since God could not be contaminated by a human body, these false teachers did not believe God became man in Jesus
Christ. Some taught that he merely seemed to have a body, a view known as Docetism. Others
claimed that the divine Christ descended on Jesus at his baptism but departed before the

crucifixion, a view known as Cerinthianism. This latter view seems to be in the background of much of 1 John.

A *"new" morality*. These false teachers also claimed "to have reached such an advanced stage in spiritual experience that they were 'beyond good and evil.' They maintained that they had no sin, not in the sense that they had attained moral perfection but in the sense that what might be sin for people at a less mature stage of inner development was no longer sin for the completely 'spiritual' man. For him ethical distinctions had ceased to be relevant" (F. F. Bruce, *The Epistles of John* [Grand Rapids, Mich.: Eerdmans, 1978], p. 26).

What intensified this problem was that these false teachers had once been an active part of the fellowship which John's readers were continuing to enjoy (see 2:19). But because their "new" teaching was so contrary to the apostolic truths of the gospel, they had to part company with the faithful. As you can well imagine, those who remained in the true fellowship were unsettled and shaken by the defection of these new teachers and needed to be reassured. But in the process, the others also needed to be exposed for what they truly were—unbelieving heretics.

In order to accomplish both purposes, John provides a series of tests for distinguishing between genuine Christians and those who falsely claim to know Christ. In response to the "new" theology, he provides us with a doctrinal test: What does the person believe about Christ? In response to the "new" morality, he provides us with a moral test: How does the person respond to the commandments of Christ? Finally, he provides us with a social test: Does the person love other Christians?

In fact, John's entire first letter is structured around these three tests, each of which appears in three separate groups, or cycles, in the letter. After the prologue (1:1–4), there is the first cycle (1:5—2:27), followed by the second (2:28—4:6) and third (4:7—5:12). Then in the conclusion (5:13–21) John again emphasizes his theme of Christian assurance.

In view of this purpose and structure, it is important to realize that the contrasts in John's letter are not between two types of Christians but between genuine Christians and those who merely claim to be Christians. For in the words of John Stott: "John's argument is double-edged. If he seeks to bring believers to the knowledge that they have eternal life, he is equally at pains to show that unbelievers have not. His purpose is to destroy the false assurance of the counterfeit as well as to confirm the right assurance of the genuine" (John Stott, *The Epistles of John* [Grand Rapids, Mich.: Eerdmans, 1964], p. 52).

Outline

1/ 1 John 1 ———————————— *Fellowship & Forgiveness*

2/ 1 John 2:1–11 ———————————— *Talking & Walking the Truth*

3/ 1 John 2:12–17 ———————————— *Encouragement & Warning*

4/ 1 John 2:18–27 ———————————— *How Important Is Theology?*

5/ 1 John 2:28—3:10 ———————————— *Like Father, Like Son*

6/ 1 John 3:11–24 ———————————— *Blessed Assurance*

7/ 1 John 4:1–12 ———————————— *Discernment & Devotion*

8/ 1 John 4:13–21 ———————————— *Fear's Remedy*

9/ 1 John 5:1–12 ———————————— *Faith Is the Victory*

10/ 1 John 5:13–21 ———————————— *What We Know as Christians*

1 / 1 John 1
Fellowship & Forgiveness

CHRISTIANS EVERYWHERE SEEM to be interested in fellowship. They gather in fellowship halls, attend fellowship dinners and participate in well-organized activities with fellow believers. But what really constitutes biblical fellowship? A covered-dish supper? Coffee and doughnuts? Social events and activities? Perhaps more than any other passage of Scripture, these opening verses of 1 John establish the basis of true fellowship that is to be enjoyed and experienced by all Christians. More importantly, they enable us to understand how we can know we have fellowship with God.

 Warming Up to God What thoughts and feelings come to your mind when you think of Christian fellowship?

 Read 1 John 1.

1 That which was from the beginning, which we have heard, which we have seen with our eyes, which we have looked at and our hands have touched—this we proclaim concerning the Word of life. ²The life appeared; we have seen it and testify to it, and we proclaim to you the eternal life, which was with the Father and has appeared to us. ³We proclaim to you what we have seen and heard, so that you also may have fellowship with us. And our fellowship is with the Father and with his Son, Jesus Christ. ⁴We write this to make our*ᵃ* joy complete.

⁵This is the message we have heard from him and declare to you: God is light; in him there is no darkness at all. ⁶If we claim to have fellowship with him yet walk in the darkness, we lie and do not live by the truth. ⁷But if we walk in the light, as he is in the light, we have fellowship with one another, and the blood of Jesus, his Son, purifies us from all*ᵇ* sin.

⁸If we claim to be without sin, we deceive ourselves and the truth is not in us. ⁹If we confess our sins, he is faithful and just and will forgive us our sins and purify us from all unrighteousness. ¹⁰If we claim we have not sinned, we make him out to be a liar and his word has no place in our lives.

ᵃ4 Some manuscripts your   ᵇ7 Or every

 Discovering the Word 1. John begins this chapter by announcing an apostolic message. What is the content of that message (vv. 1–2)? 2. What are John's reasons for announcing his message (vv. 3–4)? 3. John provides a test by which we can know if we have fellowship with God (vv. 5–10). 4. The first part of John's test concerns the way we live or "walk" (vv. 6–7). What is the relationship between our conduct and our claim to have fellowship with God? 5. The second part of John's test concerns our attitude toward sin (vv. 8–10). What does our denial or confession of sin reveal about the reality of our relationship with God? 6. Based on your study of this passage, what does it mean to have fellowship with God—and each other?

 Applying the Word 1. Does John's test strengthen or weaken your assurance of fellowship with God? Explain. 2. How can we enjoy a greater fellowship with those who know the Father and the Son?

 Responding in Prayer Pray that the level of fellowship in your church would be deepened and enriched.

2 / 1 John 2:1–11
Talking & Walking the Truth

FROM THE VERY beginning of Jesus' ministry, he emphasized that it is not what we profess but what we *possess* that counts for eternity. In his first major message he declared, "By their fruit you will recognize them." He then went on to teach, "Not everyone who says to me, 'Lord, Lord,' will enter the kingdom of heaven, but only he who does the will of my Father who is in heaven" (Mt 7:20–21). In the same way, John emphasizes that our claim to know Jesus must be backed by our conduct. This is necessary if we are to be certain about the reality of our faith.

 Warming Up to God When have you been impacted by someone saying one thing and doing another?

 Read 1 John 2:1–11.

2 My dear children, I write this to you so that you will not sin. But if anybody does sin, we have one who speaks to the Father in our defense—Jesus Christ, the Righteous One. ²He is the atoning sacrifice for our sins, and not only for ours but also for^c the sins of the whole world.

³We know that we have come to know him if we obey his commands. ⁴The man who says, "I know him," but does not do what he commands is a liar, and the truth is not in him. ⁵But if anyone obeys his word, God's love^d is truly made complete in him. This is how we know we are in him: ⁶Whoever claims to live in him must walk as Jesus did.

⁷Dear friends, I am not writing you a new command but an old one, which you have had since the beginning. This old command is the message you have heard. ⁸Yet I am writing you a new command; its truth is seen in him and you, because the darkness is passing and the true light is already shining.

⁹Anyone who claims to be in the light but hates his brother is still in the darkness. ¹⁰Whoever loves his brother lives in the light, and there is nothing in him^e to make him stumble. ¹¹But whoever hates his brother is in the darkness and walks around in the darkness; he does not know where he is going, because the darkness has blinded him.

^{c}2 Or *He is the one who turns aside God's wrath, taking away our sins, and not only ours but also* ^{d}5 Or *word, love for God* ^{e}10 Or it

---

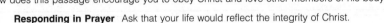 **Discovering the Word** 1. According to John, how can we tell whether we truly know Christ or merely claim to know him (vv. 3–6)? 2. Practically speaking, what does it mean to "walk as Jesus did" (v. 6)? 3. In verses 7–11, John focuses on one of the commands. How can this command be both old and new (vv. 7–8)? 4. Why would love for our brother rather than love for God serve as a test of being in the light (vv. 9–11)? 5. In view of the overall context of this passage, what does it mean to *live* in the light (v. 10)? to live in Christ (v. 6)?

 Applying the Word 1. Although John does not want us to sin, he knows that we sometimes do (vv. 1–2). How does the realization that Jesus speaks "in our defense" provide comfort and assurance when you sin? 2. How does this passage encourage you to obey Christ and love other members of his body?

Responding in Prayer Ask that your life would reflect the integrity of Christ.

3 / *1 John 2:12–17*
Encouragement & Warning

PILGRIM'S PROGRESS IS the classic tale of Christian's escape from the City of Destruction to the Heavenly City. It is true to experience because all of us can identify with his encounters along the way. In the Valley of Humiliation he enters into combat with Apollyon, his fiercest foe. At the Hill of Difficulty he meets Adam-the-First and his three daughters: Lust-of-the-Flesh, Lust-of-the-Eyes and Pride-of-Life. In the town of Folly he narrowly escapes its greatest attraction, Vanity Fair. These encounters are John Bunyan's well-known descriptions of the threefold arena of all Christian conflict—the world, the flesh and the devil. They are the same three foes that appear here in 1 John.

 Warming Up to God How far did you progress as a Christian before you became aware of these three foes? Explain.

 Read 1 John 2:12–17.

---

¹²I write to you, dear children,
  because your sins have been forgiven on
    account of his name.
¹³I write to you, fathers,
  because you have known him who is from
    the beginning.
 I write to you, young men,
  because you have overcome the evil one.
 I write to you, dear children,
  because you have known the Father.
¹⁴I write to you, fathers,
  because you have known him who is from
    the beginning.

I write to you, young men,
  because you are strong,
  and the word of God lives in you,
  and you have overcome the evil one.

¹⁵Do not love the world or anything in the world. If anyone loves the world, the love of the Father is not in him. ¹⁶For everything in the world—the cravings of sinful man, the lust of his eyes and the boasting of what he has and does—comes not from the Father but from the world. ¹⁷The world and its desires pass away, but the man who does the will of God lives forever.

 Discovering the Word 1. Who is represented by the three groups being addressed (vv. 12–14)? 2. What is the source of our victory over the evil one (vv. 13–14)? 3. Why can there be no middle ground between our love for God and love for the world (vv. 15–17)? 4. What are the reasons we are to resist such temptations (vv. 15–17)? 5. How does the realization that the world is passing away (v. 17) lessen its appeal in your life?

 Applying the Word 1. How does this passage help us gain a better understanding of our spiritual battle? 2. On a daily basis, how can that truth help us overcome the tactics and schemes of the evil one?

Responding in Prayer Praise God for giving you the strength you need to overcome the evil one.

---

4 / *1 John 2:18–27*
How Important Is Theology?

THERE IS AN increasingly popular mindset within the church today that seeks to divorce Christian teaching from Christian living. "We don't want more theology," we are told, "just more about Jesus." But how can we learn more about Jesus apart from a proper understanding of who he is and what he has accomplished? The fact is, there is nothing more basic to Christianity than the person and work of Christ. Apart from understanding Christ, there can be no real Christian living. That is why John goes to great lengths to protect his "dear children" from false views about Christ and to instruct them in the truth.

 Warming Up to God What have you been learning about the person and work of Christ recently?

 Read 1 John 2:18–27.

¹⁸Dear children, this is the last hour; and as you have heard that the antichrist is coming, even now many antichrists have come. This is how we know it is the last hour. ¹⁹They went out from us, but they did not really belong to us. For if they had belonged to us, they would have remained with us; but their going showed that none of them belonged to us.

²⁰But you have an anointing from the Holy One, and all of you know the truth.ʃ ²¹I do not write to you because you do not know the truth, but because you do know it and because no lie comes from the truth. ²²Who is the liar? It is the man who denies that Jesus is the Christ. Such a man is the antichrist—he denies the Father and the Son. ²³No one who denies the Son has the Father; whoever acknowledges the Son has the Father also.

²⁴See that what you have heard from the beginning remains in you. If it does, you also will remain in the Son and in the Father. ²⁵And this is what he promised us—even eternal life.

²⁶I am writing these things to you about those who are trying to lead you astray. ²⁷As for you, the anointing you received from him remains in you, and you do not need anyone to teach you. But as his anointing teaches you about all things and as that anointing is real, not counterfeit— just as it has taught you, remain in him.

ʃ20 Some manuscripts *and you know all things*

 Discovering the Word 1. What characteristics of false teachers and their teaching is John exposing in these verses? 2. All the New Testament authors viewed the first coming of Christ as the event which marked the beginning of the end—"the last hour." What are some of the signs of the last hour (vv. 18–19)? 3. To deny that "Jesus is the Christ" (v. 22) is to deny that the man Jesus is the eternal, divine Christ—the God-Man. Why is John so harsh toward those who believe and teach such a view (vv. 22–23)? 4. Why is remaining in the truth so important in the Christian life (vv. 24–25)? 5. How does his instruction (v. 27) help us understand what it means to remain in Christ?

 Applying the Word 1. What does this passage teach us about the Holy Spirit's ministry of *preserving* us from error? 2. What does it teach about our responsibility of *persevering* in the truth?

Responding in Prayer Ask God to fill your heart and mind with truth about himself.

5 / 1 John 2:28—3:10
Like Father, Like Son

A NUMBER OF years ago *Newsweek* featured an article on the increasing amount of people within our society who are claiming to be "born again." The article included the following report:

> According to a recent Gallup survey based on personal interviews with 1,553 Americans of voting age, half of all Protestants—and a third of all Americans—say they have been "born again." That figure comes to nearly 50 million adult American who claim to have experienced a turning point in their lives by making a personal commitment to Jesus Christ as their Savior. ("Born Again," *Newsweek*, October 25, 1976, p. 68.)

How would we go about discovering if the results of that survey were true? Where would we turn in God's Word to validate such a claim? Without question, 1 John 2:28—3:10 provides one of the clearest tests in Scripture for determining whether one who claims to be a Christian has truly been born of God.

Warming Up to God What do you think your local community would be like if one third of everyone who lived there was born again?

 Read 1 John 2:28—3:10.

---

²⁸And now, dear children, continue in him, so that when he appears we may be confident and unashamed before him at his coming.

²⁹If you know that he is righteous, you know that everyone who does what is right has been born of him.

3 How great is the love the Father has lavished on us, that we should be called children of God! And that is what we are! The reason the world does not know us is that it did not know him. ²Dear friends, now we are children of God, and what we will be has not yet been made known. But we know that when he appears,ᵍ we shall be like him, for we shall see him as he is. ³Everyone who has this hope in him purifies himself, just as he is pure.

⁴Everyone who sins breaks the law; in fact, sin is lawlessness. ⁵But you know that he appeared so that he might take away our sins. And in him is no sin. ⁶No one who lives in him keeps on sinning. No one who continues to sin has either seen him or known him.

⁷Dear children, do not let anyone lead you astray. He who does what is right is righteous, just as he is righteous. ⁸He who does what is sinful is of the devil, because the devil has been sinning from the beginning. The reason the Son of God appeared was to destroy the devil's work. ⁹No one who is born of God will continue to sin, because God's seed remains in him; he cannot go on sinning, because he has been born of God. ¹⁰This is how we know who the children of God are and who the children of the devil are: Anyone who does not do what is right is not a child of God; nor is anyone who does not love his brother.

ᵍ2 Or *when it is made known*

 Discovering the Word 1. Based on John's emphasis at the beginning and the end of the passage (2:28–29; 3:9–10), what test is he using to validate a person's claim of being born again? 2. Throughout this passage John teaches that God's children resemble their Father. In what ways does he reinforce this principle (2:29—3:10)? 3. How does John's definition of sin (v. 4) compare with some of the viewpoints people have today? 4. Although Christians can and do sin, how does knowing Christ change our relationship to sin (v. 6)? 5. Why does the new birth make it impossible for God's children to have a life characterized by sin (v. 9)?

 Applying the Word 1. As one who has been born of God, what are some ways you see the family traits of obedience and love developing in your life? 2. In what area would you like to be more obedient?

Responding in Prayer Pray that your family resemblance to God and to Christ would be increased.

---

6 / *1 John 3:11–24*
Blessed Assurance

IN HIS CLASSIC book *Holiness* J. C. Ryle expresses concern for believers who doubt: "I heartily wish that assurance was more sought after than it is. Too many among those who believe begin doubting and go on doubting, live doubting and die doubting, and go to heaven in a kind of mist" (J. C. Ryle, *Holiness* [Grand Rapids, Mich.: Baker, 1979], p. 158). He goes on to say:

> Doubts and fears have power to spoil much of the happiness of a true believer in Christ. Uncertainty and suspense are bad enough in any condition—in the matter of our health, our property, our families, our affections, our earthly callings—but never so bad as in the affairs of our souls. (Ryle, *Holiness*, p. 159.)

Without question, doubt and fear have robbed many of the joys of Christian assurance. That is why this passage is so important for Christian living. It overflows with the confidence and assurance that ought to characterize every member of God's family.

 Warming Up to God Have you ever questioned whether you were a member of God's family? Explain.

 Read 1 John 3:11–24.

11This is the message you heard from the beginning: We should love one another. 12Do not be like Cain, who belonged to the evil one and murdered his brother. And why did he murder him? Because his own actions were evil and his brother's were righteous. 13Do not be surprised, my brothers, if the world hates you. 14We know that we have passed from death to life, because we love our brothers. Anyone who does not love remains in death. 15Anyone who hates his brother is a murderer, and you know that no murderer has eternal life in him.

16This is how we know what love is: Jesus Christ laid down his life for us. And we ought to lay down our lives for our brothers. 17If anyone has material possessions and sees his brother in need but has no pity on him, how can the love of God be in him? 18Dear children, let us not love with words or tongue but with actions and in truth. 19This then is how we know that we belong to the truth, and how we set our hearts at rest in his presence 20whenever our hearts condemn us. For God is greater than our hearts, and he knows everything.

21Dear friends, if our hearts do not condemn us, we have confidence before God 22and receive from him anything we ask, because we obey his commands and do what pleases him. 23And this is his command: to believe in the name of his Son, Jesus Christ, and to love one another as he commanded us. 24Those who obey his commands live in him, and he in them. And this is how we know that he lives in us: We know it by the Spirit he gave us.

Discovering the Word 1. John begins this passage by talking about love and hate. How do Cain and Abel illustrate the two basic categories of humanity (vv. 11–15)? 2. Why is Christ's death on the cross the supreme example of love (v. 16)? 3. How can John's assurances in verses 19–20 help us deal with times of doubt? 4. Why would our obedience to God's commands affect our confidence in prayer (vv. 21–22)? 5. Why do you think John reduces the commandments to a single command to be obeyed (v. 23)?

Applying the Word 1. In verse 17 John mentions one specific way we can follow Christ's example. How have you and those in your church sought to love those with material needs? 2. In what other practical ways might we "lay down our lives" for each other? 3. Based on this passage, how would you counsel someone who lacked assurance that he or she was a Christian?

 Responding in Prayer Pray about the needs on your heart with confidence before God.

7 / 1 John 4:1–12
Discernment & Devotion

EVERY CHRISTIAN VIRTUE bears within itself the seeds of its own destruction. A zeal for the truth, for example, if not tempered by love and compassion can cause us to become arrogant, harsh and cold. Likewise, love for others if unchecked by the truth can cause us to be wishy-washy and even tolerant toward sin. If one of these virtues is not governed by the other, it can become a liability and not a strength. Like everything else, obtaining a proper balance is of utmost importance. In this passage, both doctrinal discernment and devotion to other Christians are held before us in perfect balance. They are not either/or, but both/and. One without the other is not enough.

Warming Up to God Which of these two aspects of the Christian life do you tend to emphasize above the other? Why?

Read 1 John 4:1–12.

4 Dear friends, do not believe every spirit, but test the spirits to see whether they are from God, because many false prophets have gone out into the world. ²This is how you can recognize the Spirit of God: Every spirit that acknowledges that Jesus Christ has come in the flesh is from God, ³but every spirit that does not acknowledge Jesus is not from God. This is the spirit of the antichrist, which you have heard is coming and even now is already in the world.

⁴You, dear children, are from God and have overcome them, because the one who is in you is greater than the one who is in the world. ⁵They are from the world and therefore speak from the viewpoint of the world, and the world listens to them. ⁶We are from God, and whoever knows God listens to us; but whoever is not from God does not listen to us. This is how we recognize the Spiritʰ of truth and the spirit of falsehood.

⁷Dear friends, let us love one another, for love comes from God. Everyone who loves has been born of God and knows God. ⁸Whoever does not love does not know God, because God is love. ⁹This is how God showed his love among us: He sent his one and only Sonⁱ into the world that we might live through him. ¹⁰This is love: not that we loved God, but that he loved us and sent his Son as an atoning sacrifice forʲ our sins. ¹¹Dear friends, since God so loved us, we also ought to love one another. ¹²No one has ever seen God; but if we love one another, God lives in us and his love is made complete in us.

ʰ6 Or *spirit*   ⁱ9 Or *his only begotten Son*   ʲ10 Or *as the one who would turn aside his wrath, taking away*

Discovering the Word 1. Why is there such a great need for Christians to be discerning (v. 1)? 2. What test does John give us for determining whether a person's teaching is from "the Spirit of God" or the "spirit of the antichrist" (vv. 2–3)? 3. As Christians, how can we overcome the doctrinal errors that continually confront us (vv. 4–6)? 4. Why must we be diligent in our devotion to one another (vv. 7–8)? 5. How does our love for each other make the invisible God visible in our midst (v. 12)?

Applying the Word 1. How does God's love for you motivate you to love others (v. 11)? 2. In what practical way can you show love this week to a brother or sister in Christ?

Responding in Prayer Ask that you would be filled with love.

8 / *1 John 4:13–21*
Fear's Remedy

IN THE SEQUEL to *Pilgrim's Progress*, Mr. Great-Heart and Father Honest engage in a conversation about an old friend, Mr. Fearing. At one point in the dialogue he is portrayed in the following way: "He was a man that had the root of the matter in him, but he was one of the most troublesome Pilgrims that I ever met with in all my days."

That is Bunyan's way of describing many who are on the road to heaven: thoroughly sincere (the root of the matter is in them) yet so overloaded with doubts and fears that their pilgrimage is indeed "troublesome." How is Mr. Fearing to fare in this life? How does he, and how do we, overcome this kind of problem? The answer, in part, lies within this passage in 1 John.

Warming Up to God In what ways do you feel burdened by fear? Pause to voice your fears to God and listen for his assurance.

Read 1 John 4:13–21.

13We know that we live in him and he in us, because he has given us of his Spirit. 14And we have seen and testify that the Father has sent his Son to be the Savior of the world. 15If anyone acknowledges that Jesus is the Son of God, God lives in him and he in God. 16And so we know and rely on the love God has for us.

God is love. Whoever lives in love lives in God, and God in him. 17In this way, love is made complete among us so that we will have confidence on the day of judgment, because in this world we are like him. 18There is no fear in love. But perfect love drives out fear, because fear has to do with punishment. The one who fears is not made perfect in love.

19We love because he first loved us. 20If anyone says, "I love God," yet hates his brother, he is a liar. For anyone who does not love his brother, whom he has seen, cannot love God, whom he has not seen. 21And he has given us this command: Whoever loves God must also love his brother.

Discovering the Word 1. What three tests does John give for determining whether "we live in him and he in us" (vv. 13–16)? 2. How is our experience of God's love related to our ability to love others (vv. 16, 19)? 3. What insights does verse 18 give us into why we sometimes fear God and others? 4. Why is it impossible to love God and yet hate one of the members of his family (vv. 19–21)?

Applying the Word 1. How can the principle "perfect love drives out fear" (v. 18) help you overcome your fears? 2. In what ways can this passage strengthen our confidence before God?

Responding in Prayer Ask God to fill you with love for someone whom you find difficult to love.

---

9 / *1 John 5:1–12*
Faith Is the Victory

CHRISTIANS WITH A variety of theological views have wholeheartedly sung the words to the well-known hymn:
    Faith is the victory! Faith is the victory!
    O glorious victory, That overcomes the world.
But in light of the daily battles in the Christian life, not all agree on what this victory is, when it is accomplished, or how we go about achieving it. In this passage John clears up some of our confusion. He focuses our attention on not only the victory we have in Christ, but also on Christ himself. For, first and foremost, an overcoming faith is one that is centered in a correct understanding of who Christ is.

Warming Up to God What spiritual battles are the focus of your attention?

Read 1 John 5:1–12.

---

5 Everyone who believes that Jesus is the Christ is born of God, and everyone who loves the father loves his child as well. 2This is how we know that we love the children of God: by loving God and carrying out his commands. 3This is love for God: to obey his commands. And his commands are not burdensome, 4for everyone born of God overcomes the world. This is the victory that has overcome the world, even our faith. 5Who is it that overcomes the world? Only he who believes that Jesus is the Son of God.

6This is the one who came by water and blood—Jesus Christ. He did not come by water only, but by water and blood. And it is the Spirit who testifies, because the Spirit is the truth. 7For there are three that testify: 8the^k Spirit, the water

^{k}7,8 Late manuscripts of the Vulgate *testify in heaven: the Father, the Word and the Holy Spirit, and these three are one.* 8*And there are three that testify on earth: the* (not found in any Greek manuscript before the sixteenth century)

and the blood; and the three are in agreement. ⁹We accept man's testimony, but God's testimony is greater because it is the testimony of God, which he has given about his Son. ¹⁰Anyone who believes in the Son of God has this testimony in his heart. Anyone who does not believe God has made him out to be a liar, because he has not believed the testimony God has given about his Son. ¹¹And this is the testimony: God has given us eternal life, and this life is in his Son. ¹²He who has the Son has life; he who does not have the Son of God does not have life.

 Discovering the Word 1. What are some inevitable results of the new birth (vv. 1–2)? 2. Why is obedience to God's commandments not burdensome for Christians (v. 3)? 3. How then can we explain the struggle we sometimes have to obey? 4. Reflect for a moment on the two major characteristics of the world described earlier (see 2:15–17; 4:1–6). What then does it mean for us to "overcome the world" (vv. 4–5)? 5. The heretics of John's day taught that the divine Christ descended on Jesus at his baptism but left *before* his death (v. 6). What is wrong with this view? 6. The Old Testament law required two or three witnesses to prove a claim. Who are John's three witnesses, and what do they testify (vv. 7–8)?

 Applying the Word 1. What evidence of the victory over the world do you see in your life? 2. How does your own experience confirm the truth that eternal life is found in Jesus (vv. 10–12)?

Responding in Prayer Take time to thank God for his son, and for the victory and eternal life we have in him.

10 / *1 John 5:13–21*
What We Know as Christians

ALMOST IMMEDIATELY AFTER his well-known conversion experience at Aldersgate Street, John Wesley struggled for months over the uncertainty of his own salvation. Receiving little help from his friends or his church, his thoughts began to turn inward. Focusing on his sinful failures, he became increasingly despondent and dejected. He sought relief by opening passages within the Bible at random, but when that also proved unfruitful he continued his downward spiral. Finally he sank to such depths of despair that he made the following shocking notation in his journal: "My friends affirm that I am mad because I said I was not a Christian a year ago. I affirm I am not a Christian now" (Arnold A. Dallimore, *George Whitefield*, Vol. I [Carlisle, Penn.: Banner of Truth, 1975], p. 196).

What was Wesley's problem? Unfortunately, it is the same problem that afflicts many sincere Christians today—a lack of knowledge. There are certain truths that all of us as Christians must know if we are to avoid an experience like his. Those truths are found in this passage.

 Warming Up to God How well can you relate to Wesley's experience? Explain.

 Read 1 John 5:13–21.

¹³I write these things to you who believe in the name of the Son of God so that you may know that you have eternal life. ¹⁴This is the confidence we have in approaching God: that if we ask anything according to his will, he hears us. ¹⁵And if we know that he hears us—whatever we ask—we know that we have what we asked of him.

¹⁶If anyone sees his brother commit a sin that does not lead to death, he should pray and God will give him life. I refer to those whose sin does not lead to death. There is a sin that leads to death. I am not saying that he should pray about that. ¹⁷All wrongdoing is sin, and there is sin that does not lead to death.

¹⁸We know that anyone born of God does not continue to sin; the one who was born of God keeps him safe, and the evil one cannot harm him. ¹⁹We know that we are children of God, and that the whole world is under the control of the

evil one. ²⁰We know also that the Son of God has come and has given us understanding, so that we may know him who is true. And we are in him who is true—even in his Son Jesus Christ. He is the true God and eternal life.

²¹Dear children, keep yourselves from idols.

 Discovering the Word 1. What assurance does John give us in these verses? 2. Verse 13 is a summary statement of purpose for the entire epistle. What then are those "things" which assure us we have eternal life? 3. How can we get to the point where we want what God wants (vv. 14–15)? 4. In light of the whole context of this epistle, what might be the distinction between the sin that does not lead to death and the one that does (vv. 16–17)? 5. How does the coming of God's Son enable us to know the true God in contrast to the false conceptions of God that continually surround us (vv. 20–21)?

 Applying the Word 1. What certainties in this passage are the most encouraging to you? 2. In what way do you need greater assurance from God?

Responding in Prayer Pray that God will make your desires his own will.

2 John

*L*ike 1 John, 2 John was written by the apostle John between A.D. 85 and 95. It was written to provide guidance about hospitality. During the first century, traveling evangelists relied on the hospitality of church members. Because inns were few and unsafe, believers would take such people into their homes and then give them provisions for their journey. Since Gnostic teachers also relied on hospitality, John warned his readers against taking such people into their homes lest they participate in spreading heresy.

2 John 1–13
Truth & Love

THERE ARE TWO equally extreme misconceptions many people have concerning what it means to be a Christian or to live the Christian life. One view says, "It doesn't matter what you believe as long as you are sincere and loving." The other one says, "It doesn't matter how you live as long as you believe the truth." The reason why both views are just as wrong is because the Word of God binds both truth and love inseparably together. They are friends, not enemies. Nowhere will you see this perspective more clearly than in John's second epistle. His major purpose is to demonstrate how love and truth are designed to support and complement one another as only good friends can.

 Warming Up to God Have you ever been in a situation where you felt you were torn between doing the right thing and the loving thing? Explain.

 Read 2 John 1–13.

---

¹The elder,

To the chosen lady and her children, whom I love in the truth—and not I only, but also all who know the truth— ²because of the truth, which lives in us and will be with us forever:

³Grace, mercy and peace from God the Father and from Jesus Christ, the Father's Son, will be with us in truth and love.

⁴It has given me great joy to find some of your children walking in the truth, just as the Father commanded us. ⁵And now, dear lady, I am not writing you a new command but one we have had from the beginning. I ask that we love one another. ⁶And this is love: that we walk in obedience to his commands. As you have heard from the beginning, his command is that you walk in love.

⁷Many deceivers, who do not acknowledge Jesus Christ as coming in the flesh, have gone out into the world. Any such person is the deceiver and the antichrist. ⁸Watch out that you do not lose what you have worked for, but that you may be rewarded fully. ⁹Anyone who runs ahead and does not continue in the teaching of Christ does not have God; whoever continues in the teaching has both the Father and the Son. ¹⁰If anyone comes to you and does not bring this teaching, do not take him into your house or welcome him. ¹¹Anyone who welcomes him shares in his wicked work.

¹²I have much to write to you, but I do not want to use paper and ink. Instead, I hope to visit you and talk with you face to face, so that our joy may be complete.

¹³The children of your chosen sister send their greetings.

 Discovering the Word 1. In the brief introductory address and greeting (vv. 1–3), notice how many times *truth* and *love* are mentioned together. What does it mean to love someone "in the truth" (v. 1)? 2. We tend to love only those Christians who agree with us or who we feel are compatible with us. But what does it mean to love them "because of the truth" (v. 2)? 3. In verses 4–6 the unity of truth and love is applied to our relationships within the church. What distinction is made between the *commandment* and the *commandments*? 4. In verses 7–11 the unity of truth and love is applied to our relationships outside the church. By denying that Christ had come in the flesh (v. 7), what fundamental truths were the false teachers rejecting? 5. Obtaining a future reward for faithful service was a strong motivation for John (v. 8). In what sense does the prospect of receiving a reward from Jesus Christ motivate you to walk in truth and love?

 Applying the Word 1. Would you identify yourself as someone whose truth needs to be balanced by love or whose love needs to be balanced by truth? Explain. 2. What can you do to gain a better balance?

Responding in Prayer Pray that your life would reveal an understanding of both truth and love.

3 John

L ike 2 John, 3 John was written to provide us with guidance about hospitality, but in a much more positive way. Whereas 2 John tells us what we are *not* to do, 3 John emphasizes what we *are* to do. For those genuine teachers who are totally dependent upon the body of Christ for all of their needs, we are to open not only our hearts but also our homes. This instruction is primarily found in John's commendation of Gaius, who has done this very thing, and in his denunciation of Diotrephes, who has refused. These two men become living examples of good and evil, truth and error.

It is my hope that these studies will encourage and assure you that you "walk in the truth."

3 John 1–14
Opening Our Hearts & Homes

IMAGINE LIVING IN a world where there were no bed-and-breakfasts, no hotels and headwaiters. If traveling evangelists and teachers were to come to your town, you would have the privilege of inviting them into your home for the night and giving them provisions for their journey. Such was the world of John and his readers. Their hospitality was one of the clearest testimonies of their love for the brethren and obedience to God.

The same is true today. For in the words of Helga Henry, wife of noted theologian Carl F. H. Henry, "Christian hospitality is not a matter of choice; it is not a matter of money; it is not a matter of age, social standing, sex, or personality. Christian hospitality is a matter of obedience to God" (V. A. Hall, *Be My Guest* [Chicago: Moody Press, 1979], p. 9). For that reason the instruction concerning hospitality in this letter takes on added significance.

 Warming Up to God When is showing hospitality difficult?

 Read 3 John 1–14.

¹The elder,

To my dear friend Gaius, whom I love in the truth.

²Dear friend, I pray that you may enjoy good health and that all may go well with you, even as your soul is getting along well. ³It gave me great joy to have some brothers come and tell about your faithfulness to the truth and how you continue to walk in the truth. ⁴I have no greater joy than to hear that my children are walking in the truth.

⁵Dear friend, you are faithful in what you are doing for the brothers, even though they are strangers to you. ⁶They have told the church about your love. You will do well to send them on their way in a manner worthy of God. ⁷It was for the sake of the Name that they went out, receiving no help from the pagans. ⁸We ought therefore to show hospitality to such men so that we may work together for the truth.

⁹I wrote to the church, but Diotrephes, who loves to be first, will have nothing to do with us. ¹⁰So if I come, I will call attention to what he is doing, gossiping maliciously about us. Not satisfied with that, he refuses to welcome the brothers. He also stops those who want to do so and puts them out of the church.

¹¹Dear friend, do not imitate what is evil but what is good. Anyone who does what is good is from God. Anyone who does what is evil has not seen God. ¹²Demetrius is well spoken of by everyone—and even by the truth itself. We also speak well of him, and you know that our testimony is true.

¹³I have much to write you, but I do not want to do so with pen and ink. ¹⁴I hope to see you soon, and we will talk face to face.

Peace to you. The friends here send their greetings. Greet the friends there by name.

Discovering the Word 1. Why is Gaius an especially good example for us to follow? 2. How are both love and faithfulness demonstrated in Christian hospitality (vv. 5–6)? 3. Why do you think Christian workers are to look to Christians for support and not to non-Christians (vv. 7–8)? 4. In addition to hospitality, how else can we "work together" with such people? 5. How are the actions of Diotrephes consistent with his true heart's desire (vv. 9–11)?

Applying the Word 1. In contrast to Diotrephes, Demetrius was "well spoken of by everyone" (v. 12). If those who know you best were asked about your love and hospitality, what might they say? 2. In light of this passage, what practical steps could you take to develop more of a ministry of hospitality?

 Responding in Prayer Pray for an open heart that will lead you to an open home.

Jude

J ude wrote in the same era as Peter. In fact, much of the information in Jude is found also
in 2 Peter 2.

Jude was the brother of James and the half-brother of Jesus. Both Matthew 13:55 and
Mark 6:3 speak of James and Jude (along with Joseph and Simon) as brothers of Jesus.
Though, according to John 7:5, Christ's brothers were not believers in him during his lifetime,
these two at least became converts after his death.

James became a leader in the early church. We see him in action in 1 Corinthians 15:7;
Acts 12:17 and 15:13; Galatians 1:19 and 2:9, 12; and Acts 21:18. We hear from Jude only in
this book, except perhaps in 1 Corinthians 9:5. It is interesting to note that while Jude claims
James as brother, both he and James refer to themselves as servants of Jesus.

The book of Jude was written to oppose false teachers who were sexually immoral and were
teaching arrogantly. This letter would have been used as a sermon in the writer's absence
(Craig S. Keener, *The IVP Bible Background Commentary: New Testament* [Downers Grove, Ill.:
InterVarsity Press, 1993], pp. 752–53).

Jude 1–25
The Twisted Fate of Twisted Faith

IN NOVEMBER OF 1978, in a jungle clearing in Guyana, more than nine hundred people committed suicide by drinking cyanide-treated punch. Those too young to act on their own were given the punch by their parents. The Jonestown massacre sends a shudder through all Christians—and well it should—because Jim Jones, who prescribed this "White Night" of death, at one time claimed to be among us. It's enough to cause Christians to take a hard, critical look at the life and faith of their leaders—and themselves. The book of Jude shows us how.

Warming Up to God   How do you think that people get tricked into perverted versions of the Christian faith?

Read Jude 1–25.

---

¹Jude, a servant of Jesus Christ and a brother of James,

To those who have been called, who are loved by God the Father and kept by*ª* Jesus Christ:

²Mercy, peace and love be yours in abundance.

³Dear friends, although I was very eager to write to you about the salvation we share, I felt I had to write and urge you to contend for the faith that was once for all entrusted to the saints. ⁴For certain men whose condemnation was written about*ᵇ* long ago have secretly slipped in among you. They are godless men, who change the grace of our God into a license for immorality and deny Jesus Christ our only Sovereign and Lord.

⁵Though you already know all this, I want to remind you that the Lord*ᶜ* delivered his people out of Egypt, but later destroyed those who did not believe. ⁶And the angels who did not keep their positions of authority but abandoned their own home—these he has kept in darkness, bound with everlasting chains for judgment on the great Day. ⁷In a similar way, Sodom and Gomorrah and the surrounding towns gave themselves up to sexual immorality and perversion. They serve as an example of those who suffer the punishment of eternal fire.

⁸In the very same way, these dreamers pollute their own bodies, reject authority and slander celestial beings. ⁹But even the archangel Michael, when he was disputing with the devil about the body of Moses, did not dare to bring a slanderous accusation against him, but said, "The Lord rebuke you!" ¹⁰Yet these men speak abusively against whatever they do not understand; and what things they do understand by instinct, like unreasoning animals—these are the very things that destroy them.

¹¹Woe to them! They have taken the way of Cain; they have rushed for profit into Balaam's error; they have been destroyed in Korah's rebellion.

¹²These men are blemishes at your love feasts, eating with you without the slightest qualm—shepherds who feed only themselves. They are clouds without rain, blown along by the wind; autumn trees, without fruit and uprooted—twice dead. ¹³They are wild waves of the sea, foaming up their shame; wandering stars, for whom blackest darkness has been reserved forever.

¹⁴Enoch, the seventh from Adam, prophesied about these men: "See, the Lord is coming with thousands upon thousands of his holy ones ¹⁵to judge everyone, and to convict all the ungodly of all the ungodly acts they have done in the ungodly way, and of all the harsh words ungodly sinners have spoken against him." ¹⁶These men are grumblers and faultfinders; they follow their own evil desires; they boast about themselves and flatter others for their own advantage.

¹⁷But, dear friends, remember what the apostles of our Lord Jesus Christ foretold. ¹⁸They said to you, "In the last times there will be scoffers who will follow their own ungodly desires." ¹⁹These are the men who divide you, who follow mere natural instincts and do not have the Spirit.

²⁰But you, dear friends, build yourselves up in your most holy faith and pray in the Holy Spirit. ²¹Keep yourselves in God's love as you wait for the mercy of our Lord Jesus Christ to bring you to eternal life.

ª1 Or for; or in   ᵇ4 Or men who were marked out for condemnation   ᶜ5 Some early manuscripts Jesus

²²Be merciful to those who doubt; ²³snatch others from the fire and save them; to others show mercy, mixed with fear—hating even the clothing stained by corrupted flesh.

²⁴To him who is able to keep you from falling and to present you before his glorious presence without fault and with great joy— ²⁵to the only God our Savior be glory, majesty, power and authority, through Jesus Christ our Lord, before all ages, now and forevermore! Amen.

Discovering the Word 1. What can you know of the circumstances of the people receiving this letter and of Jude's purpose in writing to them (vv. 3–4)? 2. Find as many words and phrases as you can in this letter that describe those "certain men" who have "secretly slipped in among you." 3. What harm could people like these do within a body of believers? 4. Jude used a series of six metaphors in verses 12–13. How does each illustrate the danger of teachers who have perverted the gospel? 5. In the face of this problem, Jude gives his readers two sets of instructions: "Remember" (v. 17) and "Build yourselves up" (v. 20). Notice the specific instructions under each of these. How would remembering, in the way Jude describes, help believers keep the essential ingredients of the Christian faith? 6. How would building ourselves up in the ways Jude outlines (vv. 17–23) help us keep on living in a way that is true to our faith?

Applying the Word 1. What errors in faith and life do you see as subtle dangers to today's Christians? 2. How can you protect yourself, and other believers whose lives you touch, from falling into these errors?

Responding in Prayer Pray that you and your church would be protected from false religion.

Revelation

T he human spirit is like a little child on a long journey asking, "Are we almost there?" Yet today many of us have stopped thinking about the future. Fear of the bomb and an unthinkable holocaust drives us to squeeze what we can from the present. We become obsessed with momentary gratification. This erodes our capacity to plan and build for the future—if there is one—and paralyzes us from living faithfully in the present.

Unlike people today, New Testament Christians eagerly awaited and longed for the future. They believed the complete reign of Christ on earth was a more certain reality than the seeming victory of evil. Jesus gave John the strangely beautiful vision recorded in the book of Revelation to give us hope. Of the three Christian virtues—faith, hope and love—the one most needing attention today is hope. Revelation touches us at the point of our despair, our world-weariness, our future shock, our fear of persecution, our collaboration with a sick (though friendly) society. It is quite possibly the most relevant book of the Bible for this moment in history.

But how are we to understand this highly symbolic book? Since Revelation was meant to be read at one sitting (1:3), we do well to put aside the charts, sermons and films we have seen that claim to unravel its mysteries. It is better just to read it. A child might understand Revelation better than adults who approach it with preconceived systems. If a child were to hear this as a story and were to conclude, "I'm so glad the Lamb won over the awful beast," he or she would have truly heard it and taken to heart what is written in it (1:3).

Two Common Misconceptions

Many people misunderstand the book because of two commonly held misconceptions. First, Revelation is not difficult to understand. Though it is highly symbolic, it is not a lock whose key has been lost. The major reason we have difficulty decoding the symbolism of this book is that, unlike the first readers, we are largely illiterate when it comes to the Bible.

The Old Testament provides the most important clues for decoding Revelation. Of the 404 verses in Revelation, 278 allude to the Old Testament (though not one direct citation is actually quoted). The book is a biblical implosion. Old Testament ideas, symbols, names and themes have been powerfully pulled together through the inspiration of the Spirit to form a collage, a kaleidoscopic effect in the message John brings.

For example, a phrase like "God will wipe away every tear from their eyes" (7:17) is a creative adaptation of Isaiah 25:8. Proper names like "Balaam," "Jerusalem" and "Sodom" and concepts like "the tree of life" are adapted from John's Bible. Numbers like "forty-two months" are used symbolically, as numbers like "seven" are in the Old Testament (Dan 9:27). This book above all others in the New Testament must be interpreted by Scripture.

Second, we misunderstand Revelation when we treat it as a book of predictions. It is not so much a prediction of future events as it is an exposé of spiritual realities that affect us now and will bring the events of history to a worthy end. John shows us how the world looks to someone in the Spirit.

John wrote Revelation between A.D. 90 and 95 from his place of exile on Patmos Island. Tradition tells us that prior to his exile John left Israel to live in Ephesus, capital of the Roman province of Asia. The seven churches to whom this book is addressed were visited by a courier traveling on the circular road through modern Turkey. His letter described John's vision of Christ as Lord of the churches (1:12–3:22), as the Lamb on the throne (5:1–14), as the liberating Word of God (19:11–16) and as the Leader in the new creation (21—22). This book is truly *the Revelation of Jesus Christ* (1:1).

John says, "Blessed is the one who reads the words of this prophecy, and blessed are those who hear it" (1:3). Look forward to this blessing as you study Revelation.

Outline

1 / *Revelation 1:1–8*
The Illustrated Letter

PERSECUTION, IMPRISONMENT, MARTYRDOM. These seem far removed from the lives of many Christians today. Yet we do suffer. Who can witness the breakup of families, the death of unborn children, the threat of war and the plight of the poor without crying out, "Come, Lord Jesus"? In this passage he does come in a vision to give us hope in a suffering world.

 Warming Up to God Following Jesus brings many benefits. It also causes new pressures and problems. In what ways have you found being a Christian difficult?

 Read Revelation 1:1–8.

1 The revelation of Jesus Christ, which God gave him to show his servants what must soon take place. He made it known by sending his angel to his servant John, ²who testifies to everything he saw—that is, the word of God and the testimony of Jesus Christ. ³Blessed is the one who reads the words of this prophecy, and blessed are those who hear it and take to heart what is written in it, because the time is near.

⁴John,

To the seven churches in the province of Asia:

Grace and peace to you from him who is, and who was, and who is to come, and from the seven spirits*ᵃ* before his throne, ⁵and from Jesus Christ, who is the faithful witness, the firstborn from the dead, and the ruler of the kings of the earth.

To him who loves us and has freed us from our sins by his blood, ⁶and has made us to be a kingdom and priests to serve his God and Father—to him be glory and power for ever and ever! Amen.

⁷Look, he is coming with the clouds,
    and every eye will see him,
even those who pierced him;
    and all the peoples of the earth will mourn
        because of him.
                              So shall it be! Amen.

⁸"I am the Alpha and the Omega," says the Lord God, "who is, and who was, and who is to come, the Almighty."

ᵃ4 Or the sevenfold Spirit

 Discovering the Word 1. The word *reveal* means "to bring to light what was formerly hidden, veiled and secret." Who and what will be unveiled by the revelation given to John (vv. 1–3)? 2. How would John's description of God be a comfort to his readers (vv. 4–5)? 3. Why would it help discouraged believers to know they are "a kingdom and priests to serve his God and Father" (v. 6)? 4. John presents a vision of Jesus as both coming (v. 7) and already and always here (v. 8). What would it be like to have only one of these two perspectives?

Applying the Word 1. In what ways has a knowledge of Christ's coming encouraged you in the midst of suffering? 2. John states that we will be blessed if we hear his message and take it to heart (v. 3). In what ways do you think he expects us to take this message to heart?

Responding in Prayer Ask God to fill your heart with hope.

2 / *Revelation 1:9–20*
Surprised by Magnificence

THE EXPERIENCE OF meeting a famous person is sometimes disconcerting. He or she may be less impressive than we had imagined. But when John sees Jesus face to face, he is overwhelmed with his magnificence. John's experience challenges us to ask whether we have ever met the same Person. Or do we follow a pale, distorted copy of the real Lord?

 Warming Up to God From all that you have read or experienced before opening Revelation, what images or pictures do you have of Jesus?

 Read Revelation 1:9–20.

⁹I, John, your brother and companion in the suffering and kingdom and patient endurance that are ours in Jesus, was on the island of Patmos because of the word of God and the testimony of Jesus. ¹⁰On the Lord's Day I was in the Spirit, and I heard behind me a loud voice like a trumpet, ¹¹which said: "Write on a scroll what you see and send it to the seven churches: to Ephesus, Smyrna, Pergamum, Thyatira, Sardis, Philadelphia and Laodicea."

¹²I turned around to see the voice that was speaking to me. And when I turned I saw seven golden lampstands, ¹³and among the lampstands was someone "like a son of man,"[b] dressed in a robe reaching down to his feet and with a golden sash around his chest. ¹⁴His head and hair were white like wool, as white as snow, and his eyes were like blazing fire. ¹⁵His feet were like bronze glowing in a furnace, and his voice was like the sound of rushing waters. ¹⁶In his right hand he held seven stars, and out of his mouth came a sharp double-edged sword. His face was like the sun shining in all its brilliance.

¹⁷When I saw him, I fell at his feet as though dead. Then he placed his right hand on me and said: "Do not be afraid. I am the First and the Last. ¹⁸I am the Living One; I was dead, and behold I am alive for ever and ever! And I hold the keys of death and Hades.

¹⁹"Write, therefore, what you have seen, what is now and what will take place later. ²⁰The mystery of the seven stars that you saw in my right hand and of the seven golden lampstands is this: The seven stars are the angels[c] of the seven churches, and the seven lampstands are the seven churches.

[b]13 Daniel 7:13   [c]20 Or *messengers*

Discovering the Word 1. John pictures the seven churches as seven golden lampstands (to hold oil lamps). What does John's picture tell us about the function of the churches? 2. How would Jesus' relationship to these churches (v. 13) encourage them to fulfill their function during hard times? 3. John's vision of Jesus is rich with biblical symbolism. Instead of trying to picture all these characteristics at once, allow them to impress you one at a time, like a slide presentation. Which images impress you most with the magnificence of Jesus, and why (vv. 13–16)? 4. Why do you think a godly person like John would be so powerfully overcome by the presence of the One he loved (v. 17)? 5. How would Jesus' words encourage John not to be fearful in his presence (vv. 17–18)?

Applying the Word 1. Revelation was written to churches persecuted under a totalitarian regime. Our society seems more friendly. Yet how is it hostile to us both morally and spiritually? 2. How has this passage enlarged your vision of who Jesus is? 3. How can this vision of Jesus encourage us to resist the seductions of our society?

 Responding in Prayer Praise Jesus for who he is and for what you have learned about him here.

3 / *Revelation 2*
Pardon My Speaking the Truth

WHAT CAN WE do to help a fellow Christian who is ready to cave in under pressure? Usually we wouldn't say that things are going to get worse before they get better! But that's what Christ does in the seven letters to churches in Asia (Rev 2—3). He confronts believers who have compromised morally and spiritually. But he also encourages them. This kind of tough love is essential for spiritual health.

 Warming Up to God   In what area of your life do you feel pressured (spiritually or otherwise)?

 Read Revelation 2.

2 "To the angel[d] of the church in Ephesus write:

These are the words of him who holds the seven stars in his right hand and walks among the seven golden lampstands: ²I know your deeds, your hard work and your perseverance. I know that you cannot tolerate wicked men, that you have tested those who claim to be apostles but are not, and have found them false. ³You have persevered and have endured hardships for my name, and have not grown weary.

⁴Yet I hold this against you: You have forsaken your first love. ⁵Remember the height from which you have fallen! Repent and do the things you did at first. If you do not repent, I will come to you and remove your lampstand from its place. ⁶But you have this in your favor: You hate the practices of the Nicolaitans, which I also hate.

⁷He who has an ear, let him hear what the Spirit says to the churches. To him who overcomes, I will give the right to eat from the tree of life, which is in the paradise of God.

⁸"To the angel of the church in Smyrna write:

These are the words of him who is the First and the Last, who died and came to life again. ⁹I know your afflictions and your poverty—yet you are rich! I know the slander of those who say they are Jews and are not, but are a synagogue of Satan. ¹⁰Do not be afraid of what you are about to suffer. I tell you, the devil will put some of you in prison to test you, and you will suffer persecution for ten

days. Be faithful, even to the point of death, and I will give you the crown of life.

¹¹He who has an ear, let him hear what the Spirit says to the churches. He who overcomes will not be hurt at all by the second death.

¹²"To the angel of the church in Pergamum write:

These are the words of him who has the sharp, double-edged sword. ¹³I know where you live—where Satan has his throne. Yet you remain true to my name. You did not renounce your faith in me, even in the days of Antipas, my faithful witness, who was put to death in your city—where Satan lives.

¹⁴Nevertheless, I have a few things against you: You have people there who hold to the teaching of Balaam, who taught Balak to entice the Israelites to sin by eating food sacrificed to idols and by committing sexual immorality. ¹⁵Likewise you also have those who hold to the teaching of the Nicolaitans. ¹⁶Repent therefore! Otherwise, I will soon come to you and will fight against them with the sword of my mouth.

¹⁷He who has an ear, let him hear what the Spirit says to the churches. To him who overcomes, I will give some of the hidden manna. I will also give him a white stone with a new name written on it, known only to him who receives it.

¹⁸"To the angel of the church in Thyatira write:

These are the words of the Son of God, whose eyes are like blazing fire and whose feet are like burnished bronze. ¹⁹I know your deeds, your love and faith, your service and

---

d1 Or *messenger*; also in verses 8, 12 and 18

perseverance, and that you are now doing more than you did at first.

²⁰Nevertheless, I have this against you: You tolerate that woman Jezebel, who calls herself a prophetess. By her teaching she misleads my servants into sexual immorality and the eating of food sacrificed to idols. ²¹I have given her time to repent of her immorality, but she is unwilling. ²²So I will cast her on a bed of suffering, and I will make those who commit adultery with her suffer intensely, unless they repent of her ways. ²³I will strike her children dead. Then all the churches will know that I am he who searches hearts and minds, and I will repay each of you according to your deeds. ²⁴Now I say to the rest of you in Thyatira, to you who do not hold to her teaching and have

not learned Satan's so-called deep secrets (I will not impose any other burden on you): ²⁵Only hold on to what you have until I come.

²⁶To him who overcomes and does my will to the end, I will give authority over the nations—

²⁷'He will rule them with an iron scepter;
        he will dash them to pieces like
                pottery'ᶜ—

just as I have received authority from my Father. ²⁸I will also give him the morning star. ²⁹He who has an ear, let him hear what the Spirit says to the churches.

ᶜ27 Psalm 2:9

Discovering the Word 1. Why would forsaking "your first love" (v. 4) be so tragic for the church at Ephesus? 2. Why do you think Christ's judgment would be so severe if they did not repent (v. 5)? 3. Smyrna was noted for emperor worship. Refusal to worship the emperor brought martyrdom to some Christians. What does Jesus know about the believers in Smyrna (vv. 8–11)? 4. The letter to Smyrna is the only one of the seven that mentions no problem and gives no warning. What role does affirmation play in helping Christians who are under spiritual pressure? 5. Pergamum was also a center of emperor worship. This may be why it is called the place "where Satan has his throne." In addition, temple prostitution was prevalent. How had the church responded to the lure of these temptations (vv. 12–17)? 6. Jezebel (v. 20) is an Old Testament character who symbolizes spiritual adultery (1 Kings 16:31). How was the so-called prophetess in Thyatira like her namesake (vv. 18–29)?

Applying the Word 1. Jesus charges the godly and loving church at Thyatira with being too tolerant of evil in their midst. In what areas are Christians today too tolerant? 2. Each of the letters (except the one to Smyrna) contains an affirmation, a problem, a warning and a promise. How might Jesus' example guide us as we care for a brother or sister ready to cave in under pressure?

Responding in Prayer Pray for someone you know who is under pressure to compromise.

---

4 / *Revelation 3*
My Dear Compromised People

EXPERTS TELL US we are exposed to fourteen hundred advertisements a day. It takes an enormous act of will not to be conformed to our environment, to be in but not of the world. The remaining three churches in the crownlike array of towns in Asia would be visited by a postal courier completing his circuit in the exact order of John's letters. Each letter helps us resist this powerful threat of being conformed to the world.

Warming Up to God In what ways do Christian groups and churches you know resemble the surrounding culture?

Read Revelation 3.

3 "To the angel[f] of the church in Sardis write:

These are the words of him who holds the seven spirits[g] of God and the seven stars. I know your deeds; you have a reputation of being alive, but you are dead. [2]Wake up! Strengthen what remains and is about to die, for I have not found your deeds complete in the sight of my God. [3]Remember, therefore, what you have received and heard; obey it, and repent. But if you do not wake up, I will come like a thief, and you will not know at what time I will come to you.

[4]Yet you have a few people in Sardis who have not soiled their clothes. They will walk with me, dressed in white, for they are worthy. [5]He who overcomes will, like them, be dressed in white. I will never blot out his name from the book of life, but will acknowledge his name before my Father and his angels. [6]He who has an ear, let him hear what the Spirit says to the churches.

[7]"To the angel of the church in Philadelphia write:

These are the words of him who is holy and true, who holds the key of David. What he opens no one can shut, and what he shuts no one can open. [8]I know your deeds. See, I have placed before you an open door that no one can shut. I know that you have little strength, yet you have kept my word and have not denied my name. [9]I will make those who are of the synagogue of Satan, who claim to be Jews though they are not, but are liars—I will make them come and fall down at your feet and acknowledge that I have loved you. [10]Since you have kept my command to endure patiently, I will also keep you from the hour of trial that is going to come upon the whole world to test those who live on the earth.

[11]I am coming soon. Hold on to what you have, so that no one will take your crown. [12]Him who overcomes I will make a pillar in the temple of my God. Never again will he leave it. I will write on him the name of my God and the name of the city of my God, the new Jerusalem, which is coming down out of heaven from my God; and I will also write on him my new name. [13]He who has an ear, let him hear what the Spirit says to the churches.

[14]"To the angel of the church in Laodicea write:

These are the words of the Amen, the faithful and true witness, the ruler of God's creation. [15]I know your deeds, that you are neither cold nor hot. I wish you were either one or the other! [16]So, because you are lukewarm—neither hot nor cold—I am about to spit you out of my mouth. [17]You say, 'I am rich; I have acquired wealth and do not need a thing.' But you do not realize that you are wretched, pitiful, poor, blind and naked. [18]I counsel you to buy from me gold refined in the fire, so you can become rich; and white clothes to wear, so you can cover your shameful nakedness; and salve to put on your eyes, so you can see.

[19]Those whom I love I rebuke and discipline. So be earnest, and repent. [20]Here I am! I stand at the door and knock. If anyone hears my voice and opens the door, I will come in and eat with him, and he with me.

[21]To him who overcomes, I will give the right to sit with me on my throne, just as I overcame and sat down with my Father on his throne. [22]He who has an ear, let him hear what the Spirit says to the churches."

f1 Or *messenger*; also in verses 7 and 14   *g1* Or *the sevenfold Spirit*

Discovering the Word 1. In the first century, Sardis exhibited a stark contrast between its past splendor as a Persian capital and its current decay. What indications does the Lord give that the church's reputation does not match its reality (vv. 1–6)? Why is this such a serious problem? **2.** Of the seven churches, only the church in Philadelphia received nothing but praise and promises. Why would a weak church be encouraged by Jesus' promise of an open door of opportunity (v. 8)? **3.** As the Philadelphian church faced opposition, how would Jesus' other promises encourage them (vv. 9–13)? **4.** Laodicea's northern neighbor, Hierapolis, had famous hot springs. Its southern neighbor, Colossae, had refreshing cool water. A six-mile aqueduct brought water to Laodicea, but by the time it arrived it was lukewarm. How does this help us understand Christ's statements in verses 14–16? **5.** Laodicea was so self-sufficient that when they suffered an earthquake in A.D. 60 they rejected help from Rome. How did this attitude affect them spiritually?

Applying the Word 1. Many churches today feel weak, insignificant and discouraged. What can we learn from Christ's words to the Philadelphians? **2.** As you review all seven letters (Rev 2—3), what has the Spirit taught you about being an overcomer?

 Responding in Prayer Pray that the church would be a powerful force in the world.

5 / *Revelation 4—5*
Worship the Omnipotent Lamb

IN A PLAY by George Bernard Shaw, Don Juan says, "Heaven is all right, of course, but for meeting old friends and acquaintances you can't beat hell." There is a powerful truth in this facetious remark. While most people *say* they want to go to heaven, they might prefer hell if heaven is like the picture given in these two chapters. People concerned only about themselves would find the ceaseless praise of God and the Lamb intolerable. Worship on earth, a foretaste of heaven, is just as unpalatable. But worship is the deepest need of the seven churches just described. And it is our deepest need too, as this study will show.

 Warming Up to God What was the most significant worship experience you have ever had, and what made it so special?

Read Revelation 4—5.

4 After this I looked, and there before me was a door standing open in heaven. And the voice I had first heard speaking to me like a trumpet said, "Come up here, and I will show you what must take place after this." ²At once I was in the Spirit, and there before me was a throne in heaven with someone sitting on it. ³And the one who sat there had the appearance of jasper and carnelian. A rainbow, resembling an emerald, encircled the throne. ⁴Surrounding the throne were twenty-four other thrones, and seated on them were twenty-four elders. They were dressed in white and had crowns of gold on their heads. ⁵From the throne came flashes of lightning, rumblings and peals of thunder. Before the throne, seven lamps were blazing. These are the seven spirits*ʰ* of God. ⁶Also before the throne there was what looked like a sea of glass, clear as crystal.

In the center, around the throne, were four living creatures, and they were covered with eyes, in front and in back. ⁷The first living creature was like a lion, the second was like an ox, the third had a face like a man, the fourth was like a flying eagle. ⁸Each of the four living creatures had six wings and was covered with eyes all around, even under his wings. Day and night they never stop saying:

"Holy, holy, holy
is the Lord God Almighty,
who was, and is, and is to come."

⁹Whenever the living creatures give glory, honor and thanks to him who sits on the throne and who lives for ever and ever, ¹⁰the twenty-four elders fall down before him who sits on the throne, and worship him who lives for ever and ever. They lay their crowns before the throne and say:

¹¹"You are worthy, our Lord and God,
to receive glory and honor and power,
for you created all things,
and by your will they were created
and have their being."

5 Then I saw in the right hand of him who sat on the throne a scroll with writing on both sides and sealed with seven seals. ²And I saw a mighty angel proclaiming in a loud voice, "Who is worthy to break the seals and open the scroll?" ³But no one in heaven or on earth or under the earth could open the scroll or even look inside it. ⁴I wept and wept because no one was found who was worthy to open the scroll or look inside. ⁵Then one of the elders said to me,

ʰ5 Or the sevenfold Spirit

"Do not weep! See, the Lion of the tribe of Judah, the Root of David, has triumphed. He is able to open the scroll and its seven seals."

⁶Then I saw a Lamb, looking as if it had been slain, standing in the center of the throne, encircled by the four living creatures and the elders. He had seven horns and seven eyes, which are the seven spirits[i] of God sent out into all the earth. ⁷He came and took the scroll from the right hand of him who sat on the throne. ⁸And when he had taken it, the four living creatures and the twenty-four elders fell down before the Lamb. Each one had a harp and they were holding golden bowls full of incense, which are the prayers of the saints. ⁹And they sang a new song:

"You are worthy to take the scroll
    and to open its seals,
because you were slain,
    and with your blood you purchased men
        for God
    from every tribe and language and people
        and nation.
¹⁰You have made them to be a kingdom and
    priests to serve our God,

and they will reign on the earth."

¹¹Then I looked and heard the voice of many angels, numbering thousands upon thousands, and ten thousand times ten thousand. They encircled the throne and the living creatures and the elders. ¹²In a loud voice they sang:

"Worthy is the Lamb, who was slain,
to receive power and wealth and wisdom and
    strength
and honor and glory and praise!"

¹³Then I heard every creature in heaven and on earth and under the earth and on the sea, and all that is in them, singing:

"To him who sits on the throne and to the
    Lamb
be praise and honor and glory and power,
    for ever and ever!"

¹⁴The four living creatures said, "Amen," and the elders fell down and worshiped.

ⁱ6 Or *the sevenfold Spirit*

Discovering the Word 1. Instead of trying to decode every part of the throne room of God, try to imagine what can be seen and heard. What are some of your initial impressions of God's glory as envisioned here (Rev 4)? 2. How do the four creatures and the twenty-four elders respond to God's glory (vv. 8, 10–11)? 3. How does their reaction help us define and practice worship? 4. While John leaves us in suspense about the contents of the scroll and its seals, there is no doubt about the central figure in the unfolding drama. Why do you think he superimposes the image of the Lamb on the image of the Lion (5:5–6)? 5. The heavenly choir gets larger and larger as the scene unfolds (5:8, 11, 13). What do we see in this vision of heavenly worship that is timelessly relevant?

Applying the Word 1. Worship is not an action but a reaction, a response evoked by a vision of God's glory. If we have difficulty worshiping God, what might we need to do? 2. If earthly worship is to be modeled after heavenly, what is most lacking in your experience of worship?

 Responding in Prayer Take time now to worship the Lamb and the One who sits on the throne.

---

6 / *Revelation 6*
The Beautiful Wrath of God

JUDGMENT IS NOT something we normally long for. But if we are suffering unjustly in an evil social system, God's judgment—far from being a dreaded prospect—is our only hope. Like a wood plane that is used against the grain rather than with it, so wrath is how people opposing the rule of God will experience his grace.

In Revelation 6—19 there is a complicated and rather confusing pattern of disaster and suffering. If we seek to unravel these pictures as a timetable for the future, we will be disappointed and perplexed. But if we want to learn how to live in the present and find hope for the future, there is much here to encourage us. These chapters inspire trust in a God who is faithful and just.

 Warming Up to God As you approach the subject of God's wrath, what thoughts and feelings do you have? Explain.

 Read Revelation 6.

6 I watched as the Lamb opened the first of the seven seals. Then I heard one of the four living creatures say in a voice like thunder, "Come!" ²I looked, and there before me was a white horse! Its rider held a bow, and he was given a crown, and he rode out as a conqueror bent on conquest.

³When the Lamb opened the second seal, I heard the second living creature say, "Come!" ⁴Then another horse came out, a fiery red one. Its rider was given power to take peace from the earth and to make men slay each other. To him was given a large sword.

⁵When the Lamb opened the third seal, I heard the third living creature say, "Come!" I looked, and there before me was a black horse! Its rider was holding a pair of scales in his hand. ⁶Then I heard what sounded like a voice among the four living creatures, saying, "A quart ʲ of wheat for a day's wages,ᵏ and three quarts of barley for a day's wages,ᵏ and do not damage the oil and the wine!"

⁷When the Lamb opened the fourth seal, I heard the voice of the fourth living creature say, "Come!" ⁸I looked, and there before me was a pale horse! Its rider was named Death, and Hades was following close behind him. They were given power over a fourth of the earth to kill by sword, famine and plague, and by the wild beasts of the earth.

⁹When he opened the fifth seal, I saw under the altar the souls of those who had been slain because of the word of God and the testimony they had maintained. ¹⁰They called out in a loud voice, "How long, Sovereign Lord, holy and true, until you judge the inhabitants of the earth and avenge our blood?" ¹¹Then each of them was given a white robe, and they were told to wait a little longer, until the number of their fellow servants and brothers who were to be killed as they had been was completed.

¹²I watched as he opened the sixth seal. There was a great earthquake. The sun turned black like sackcloth made of goat hair, the whole moon turned blood red, ¹³and the stars in the sky fell to earth, as late figs drop from a fig tree when shaken by a strong wind. ¹⁴The sky receded like a scroll, rolling up, and every mountain and island was removed from its place.

¹⁵Then the kings of the earth, the princes, the generals, the rich, the mighty, and every slave and every free man hid in caves and among the rocks of the mountains. ¹⁶They called to the mountains and the rocks, "Fall on us and hide us from the face of him who sits on the throne and from the wrath of the Lamb! ¹⁷For the great day of their wrath has come, and who can stand?"

ʲ6 Greek *a choinix* (probably about a liter)   ᵏ6 Greek *a denarius*

 Discovering the Word 1. The scene shifts back to earth as the Lamb opens the book of destiny. Summarize the events during the first four seals (vv. 1–8). 2. Are the events during the seals normal bad times (compare vv. 1–8 with vv. 12–14)? Explain. 3. How does the experience of the saints (vv. 9–11) contrast with that of the unbelievers (vv. 15–17) as they anticipate the impending wrath of God? 4. What evidence, if any, do you see of this contrast among people today?

Applying the Word 1. If we realize that the wrath of God will one day be fully expressed, what difference should it make in our attitude toward sin? 2. In our attitude toward unjust suffering? 3. In our attitude toward non-Christians?

Responding in Prayer Pray for non-Christians you know, that they would come to know the love of the Lord.

7 / *Revelation 7*
Living Faithfully Through the Holocaust

SOME PREACHERS SPEAK of the Christian life as one great success story. They say that if we attend church, live right, tithe and exercise faith, we will prosper financially and be free of illness and distress.

But the relative peace some of us enjoy at this moment is exceptional in the world and in history. From the ascension of Christ to his return, the normal lot of believers is tribulation.

Most of the Christians John pictures for us are martyrs. They are dead to the threats of this life but gloriously alive to God. Their experience reminds us that the call to discipleship is a call to radical obedience.

 Warming Up to God What feelings do you have when you hear of Christians today who lose their jobs, are thrown into prison or are martyred for Christ?

 Read Revelation 7.

7 After this I saw four angels standing at the four corners of the earth, holding back the four winds of the earth to prevent any wind from blowing on the land or on the sea or on any tree. ²Then I saw another angel coming up from the east, having the seal of the living God. He called out in a loud voice to the four angels who had been given power to harm the land and the sea: ³"Do not harm the land or the sea or the trees until we put a seal on the foreheads of the servants of our God." ⁴Then I heard the number of those who were sealed: 144,000 from all the tribes of Israel.

⁵From the tribe of Judah 12,000 were sealed,
from the tribe of Reuben 12,000,
from the tribe of Gad 12,000,
⁶from the tribe of Asher 12,000,
from the tribe of Naphtali 12,000,
from the tribe of Manasseh 12,000,
⁷from the tribe of Simeon 12,000,
from the tribe of Levi 12,000,
from the tribe of Issachar 12,000,
⁸from the tribe of Zebulun 12,000,
from the tribe of Joseph 12,000,
from the tribe of Benjamin 12,000.

⁹After this I looked and there before me was a great multitude that no one could count, from every nation, tribe, people and language, standing before the throne and in front of the Lamb. They were wearing white robes and were holding palm branches in their hands. ¹⁰And they cried out in a loud voice:

"Salvation belongs to our God,
who sits on the throne,
and to the Lamb."

¹¹All the angels were standing around the throne and around the elders and the four living creatures. They fell down on their faces before the throne and worshiped God, ¹²saying:

"Amen!
Praise and glory
and wisdom and thanks and honor
and power and strength
be to our God for ever and ever.
Amen!"

¹³Then one of the elders asked me, "These in white robes—who are they, and where did they come from?"

¹⁴I answered, "Sir, you know."

And he said, "These are they who have come out of the great tribulation; they have washed their robes and made them white in the blood of the Lamb. ¹⁵Therefore,

"they are before the throne of God
and serve him day and night in his temple;
and he who sits on the throne will spread his
tent over them.
¹⁶Never again will they hunger;
never again will they thirst.
The sun will not beat upon them,
nor any scorching heat.
¹⁷For the Lamb at the center of the throne will
be their shepherd;
he will lead them to springs of living water.
And God will wipe away every tear from their
eyes."

Discovering the Word 1. In verses 1–8 an angel seals 144,000 people. What do you think "the seal of the living God" means (7:2; 9:4)? 2. In verse 9 the scene shifts from earth to heaven. How did the great multitude in verse 9 come to stand before the Lamb? 3. Why does the multitude cry out with praise, worship and thanksgiving (vv. 10–12)? 4. How do the blessings these martyred Christians enjoy compare with the tribulations they suffered (vv. 13–17)? 5. How does their experience help us understand the ultimate benefit of being a faithful Christian?

Applying the Word 1. In the first century, persecution of Christians came from three basic sources: emperor worshipers, heretics and those whose commercial interests were threatened by the radical life-style of Christians. Why might faithful Christians suffer today? 2. This vision comes at the point of maximum dramatic intensity: between the sixth and seventh seals. How can the vision encourage us to be faithful no matter what happens in the world?

Responding in Prayer Pray for those who suffer for their faith.

---

8 / *Revelation 8—9*
The Message of the Angels

ANGELS ARE QUITE popular these days. We see them depicted on T-shirts, mugs and cards. You can get little pins picturing charming angels. And there's a growing category of books available to show you how to get in touch with your "inner angels" and other such things. None of this has much to do with the angels we meet in Scripture. In the next few passages you will meet some of God's angels—and you will be confronted with their terrible power.

 Warming Up to God What positive feelings or experiences have you had about angels?

 Read Revelation 8—9.

---

8 When he opened the seventh seal, there was silence in heaven for about half an hour.

²And I saw the seven angels who stand before God, and to them were given seven trumpets.

³Another angel, who had a golden censer, came and stood at the altar. He was given much incense to offer, with the prayers of all the saints, on the golden altar before the throne. ⁴The smoke of the incense, together with the prayers of the saints, went up before God from the angel's hand. ⁵Then the angel took the censer, filled it with fire from the altar, and hurled it on the earth; and there came peals of thunder, rumblings, flashes of lightning and an earthquake.

⁶Then the seven angels who had the seven trumpets prepared to sound them.

⁷The first angel sounded his trumpet, and there came hail and fire mixed with blood, and it was hurled down upon the earth. A third of the earth was burned up, a third of the trees were burned up, and all the green grass was burned up.

⁸The second angel sounded his trumpet, and something like a huge mountain, all ablaze, was thrown into the sea. A third of the sea turned into blood, ⁹a third of the living creatures in the sea died, and a third of the ships were destroyed.

¹⁰The third angel sounded his trumpet, and a great star, blazing like a torch, fell from the sky on a third of the rivers and on the springs of water— ¹¹the name of the star is Wormwood.[1] A third of the waters turned bitter, and many people died from the waters that had become bitter.

¹²The fourth angel sounded his trumpet, and a third of the sun was struck, a third of the moon, and a third of the stars, so that a third of them turned dark. A third of the day was without light, and also a third of the night.

¹³As I watched, I heard an eagle that was flying in midair call out in a loud voice: "Woe! Woe!

[1]11 That is, Bitterness

Woe to the inhabitants of the earth, because of the trumpet blasts about to be sounded by the other three angels!"

9 The fifth angel sounded his trumpet, and I saw a star that had fallen from the sky to the earth. The star was given the key to the shaft of the Abyss. [2]When he opened the Abyss, smoke rose from it like the smoke from a gigantic furnace. The sun and sky were darkened by the smoke from the Abyss. [3]And out of the smoke locusts came down upon the earth and were given power like that of scorpions of the earth. [4]They were told not to harm the grass of the earth or any plant or tree, but only those people who did not have the seal of God on their foreheads. [5]They were not given power to kill them, but only to torture them for five months. And the agony they suffered was like that of the sting of a scorpion when it strikes a man. [6]During those days men will seek death, but will not find it; they will long to die, but death will elude them.

[7]The locusts looked like horses prepared for battle. On their heads they wore something like crowns of gold, and their faces resembled human faces. [8]Their hair was like women's hair, and their teeth were like lions' teeth. [9]They had breastplates like breastplates of iron, and the sound of their wings was like the thundering of many horses and chariots rushing into battle. [10]They had tails and stings like scorpions, and in their tails they had power to torment people for five months. [11]They had as king over them the angel of the Abyss, whose name in Hebrew is Abaddon, and in Greek, Apollyon.[m]

[12]The first woe is past; two other woes are yet to come.

[13]The sixth angel sounded his trumpet, and I heard a voice coming from the horns[n] of the golden altar that is before God. [14]It said to the sixth angel who had the trumpet, "Release the four angels who are bound at the great river Euphrates." [15]And the four angels who had been kept ready for this very hour and day and month and year were released to kill a third of mankind. [16]The number of the mounted troops was two hundred million. I heard their number.

[17]The horses and riders I saw in my vision looked like this: Their breastplates were fiery red, dark blue, and yellow as sulfur. The heads of the horses resembled the heads of lions, and out of their mouths came fire, smoke and sulfur. [18]A third of mankind was killed by the three plagues of fire, smoke and sulfur that came out of their mouths. [19]The power of the horses was in their mouths and in their tails; for their tails were like snakes, having heads with which they inflict injury.

[20]The rest of mankind that were not killed by these plagues still did not repent of the work of their hands; they did not stop worshiping demons, and idols of gold, silver, bronze, stone and wood—idols that cannot see or hear or walk. [21]Nor did they repent of their murders, their magic arts, their sexual immorality or their thefts.

[m]11 Abaddon and Apollyon mean Destroyer.   [n]13 That is, projections

---

Discovering the Word 1. List the events that happen when each of the angels blows his trumpet. 2. What similarities do you note between all of these events? 3. The seventh seal (8:1–5) contains the seven trumpet judgments (8:6—11:15). What apparently is God's purpose in allowing these judgments to fall on the whole creation (9:20–21)? 4. Does such a response by God seem justified? Explain. 5. It is sometimes maintained that Christians are removed from the world before God's wrath falls. What alternate view is possibly suggested by 9:4 (see also 7:3)?

Applying the Word 1. Those mentioned in 9:20–21 did not repent. How do our sins today compare to theirs? 2. Where do you see yourself in this list of sins? 3. In what way do you feel that you need to be ready for the judgment that takes place here?

 Responding in Prayer Repent of your sins before God.

9 / *Revelation 10—11*
God's Messenger

IN THE OLD Testament, God often used specific persons to deliver a message to another person, or sometimes to entire groups. Sometimes these messages were positive and easy to hear. However, they were often condemnations of the way things were, and those who delivered the messages, the prophets, were often ridiculed or threatened. In chapter 10, John is given a message which is not easy to deliver.

In chapter 11, two of God's prophets have a life experience which roughly parallels Jesus' time on earth. Their example can give us hope that the God who calls us to be a light in the darkness is also the one who will vindicate us.

 Warming Up to God When has God used someone else to give you a message? How did you react to the message and the messenger?

 Read Revelation 10—11.

10 Then I saw another mighty angel coming down from heaven. He was robed in a cloud, with a rainbow above his head; his face was like the sun, and his legs were like fiery pillars. ²He was holding a little scroll, which lay open in his hand. He planted his right foot on the sea and his left foot on the land, ³and he gave a loud shout like the roar of a lion. When he shouted, the voices of the seven thunders spoke. ⁴And when the seven thunders spoke, I was about to write; but I heard a voice from heaven say, "Seal up what the seven thunders have said and do not write it down."

⁵Then the angel I had seen standing on the sea and on the land raised his right hand to heaven. ⁶And he swore by him who lives for ever and ever, who created the heavens and all that is in them, the earth and all that is in it, and the sea and all that is in it, and said, "There will be no more delay! ⁷But in the days when the seventh angel is about to sound his trumpet, the mystery of God will be accomplished, just as he announced to his servants the prophets."

⁸Then the voice that I had heard from heaven spoke to me once more: "Go, take the scroll that lies open in the hand of the angel who is standing on the sea and on the land."

⁹So I went to the angel and asked him to give me the little scroll. He said to me, "Take it and eat it. It will turn your stomach sour, but in your mouth it will be as sweet as honey." ¹⁰I took the little scroll from the angel's hand and ate it. It tasted as sweet as honey in my mouth, but when I had eaten it, my stomach turned sour. ¹¹Then I was told, "You must proph-

esy again about many peoples, nations, languages and kings."

11 I was given a reed like a measuring rod and was told, "Go and measure the temple of God and the altar, and count the worshipers there. ²But exclude the outer court; do not measure it, because it has been given to the Gentiles. They will trample on the holy city for 42 months. ³And I will give power to my two witnesses, and they will prophesy for 1,260 days, clothed in sackcloth." ⁴These are the two olive trees and the two lampstands that stand before the Lord of the earth. ⁵If anyone tries to harm them, fire comes from their mouths and devours their enemies. This is how anyone who wants to harm them must die. ⁶These men have power to shut up the sky so that it will not rain during the time they are prophesying; and they have power to turn the waters into blood and to strike the earth with every kind of plague as often as they want.

⁷Now when they have finished their testimony, the beast that comes up from the Abyss will attack them, and overpower and kill them. ⁸Their bodies will lie in the street of the great city, which is figuratively called Sodom and Egypt, where also their Lord was crucified. ⁹For three and a half days men from every people, tribe, language and nation will gaze on their bodies and refuse them burial. ¹⁰The inhabitants of the earth will gloat over them and will celebrate by sending each other gifts, because these two prophets had tormented those who live on the earth.

¹¹But after the three and a half days a breath of life from God entered them, and they stood on

their feet, and terror struck those who saw them. 12Then they heard a loud voice from heaven saying to them, "Come up here." And they went up to heaven in a cloud, while their enemies looked on.

13At that very hour there was a severe earthquake and a tenth of the city collapsed. Seven thousand people were killed in the earthquake, and the survivors were terrified and gave glory to the God of heaven.

14The second woe has passed; the third woe is coming soon.

15The seventh angel sounded his trumpet, and there were loud voices in heaven, which said:

"The kingdom of the world has become the
        kingdom of our Lord and of his Christ,
    and he will reign for ever and ever."

16And the twenty-four elders, who were seated on their thrones before God, fell on their faces and worshiped God, 17saying:

"We give thanks to you, Lord God Almighty,
    the One who is and who was,
because you have taken your great power
    and have begun to reign.
18The nations were angry;
    and your wrath has come.
The time has come for judging the dead,
    and for rewarding your servants the
        prophets
and your saints and those who reverence your
        name,
    both small and great—
and for destroying those who destroy the
        earth."

19Then God's temple in heaven was opened, and within his temple was seen the ark of his covenant. And there came flashes of lightning, rumblings, peals of thunder, an earthquake and a great hailstorm.

Discovering the Word 1. What are the actions of the "mighty angel" introduced in 10:1? 2. What is the significance of the mystery of God which will be revealed without further delay (10:6–7)? 3. What happens to the two witnesses empowered by God (11:3–14)? 4. Why do you think the witnesses caused such turmoil? 5. What happens when the seventh trumpet is blown (11:15–19)?

Applying the Word 1. The "little scroll" that John eats (10:8–11) probably refers to the gospel. When has the gospel tasted like honey or turned your stomach sour? 2. 11:10 says that the two witnesses had "tormented those who live on the earth." When have you felt that God was calling you to deliver a message of bad news? 3. What feelings about God and his actions do you have after reading the description of worship in 11:15–19?

Responding in Prayer Pray that you will be willing to be God's messenger to those around you.

---

10 / *Revelation 12*
Conflict with the Accuser

DRAGONS SYMBOLIZE ALL that is terrifying, evil and loathsome. In Revelation 12 Satan appears as an enormous red dragon, full of rage. Knowing that his time is short, he unleashes his fury as never before. During such dark moments of history, it seems as though God is absent and Satan is victorious. Yet in this passage John describes a heavenly vision that puts all earthly tribulation in proper perspective.

Warming Up to God In what ways are you experiencing the reality of spiritual warfare?

Read Revelation 12.

12

A great and wondrous sign appeared in heaven: a woman clothed with the sun, with the moon under her feet and a crown of twelve stars on her head. ²She was pregnant and cried out in pain as she was about to give birth. ³Then another sign appeared in heaven: an enormous red dragon with seven heads and ten horns and seven crowns on his heads. ⁴His tail swept a third of the stars out of the sky and flung them to the earth. The dragon stood in front of the woman who was about to give birth, so that he might devour her child the moment it was born. ⁵She gave birth to a son, a male child, who will rule all the nations with an iron scepter. And her child was snatched up to God and to his throne. ⁶The woman fled into the desert to a place prepared for her by God, where she might be taken care of for 1,260 days.

⁷And there was war in heaven. Michael and his angels fought against the dragon, and the dragon and his angels fought back. ⁸But he was not strong enough, and they lost their place in heaven. ⁹The great dragon was hurled down— that ancient serpent called the devil, or Satan, who leads the whole world astray. He was hurled to the earth, and his angels with him.

¹⁰Then I heard a loud voice in heaven say:

"Now have come the salvation and the power
    and the kingdom of our God,
  and the authority of his Christ.
For the accuser of our brothers,
who accuses them before our God day and
    night,
  has been hurled down.
¹¹They overcame him
    by the blood of the Lamb
    and by the word of their testimony;
they did not love their lives so much
    as to shrink from death.
¹²Therefore rejoice, you heavens
    and you who dwell in them!
But woe to the earth and the sea,
    because the devil has gone down to you!
He is filled with fury,
    because he knows that his time is short."

¹³When the dragon saw that he had been hurled to the earth, he pursued the woman who had given birth to the male child. ¹⁴The woman was given the two wings of a great eagle, so that she might fly to the place prepared for her in the desert, where she would be taken care of for a time, times and half a time, out of the serpent's reach. ¹⁵Then from his mouth the serpent spewed water like a river, to overtake the woman and sweep her away with the torrent. ¹⁶But the earth helped the woman by opening its mouth and swallowing the river that the dragon had spewed out of his mouth. ¹⁷Then the dragon was enraged at the woman and went off to make war against the rest of her offspring—those who obey God's commandments and hold to the testimony of Jesus.

Discovering the Word 1. Three of the characters in this chapter are the woman (perhaps the Lord's people or the Holy Spirit), the red dragon (Satan) and the male child (the Lord Jesus). What conflict does John observe among them (vv. 1–6)? **2.** In verses 7–9 John describes a war in heaven. What does the war reveal about the dragon? **3.** What does the dragon's defeat mean in heaven (vv. 10, 12) and on earth (vv. 12–17)? **4.** What does it mean to overcome Satan's accusations by the blood of the Lamb and the word of our testimony (v. 11)?

Applying the Word 1. How can we help a fellow Christian who is no longer under God's condemnation but who still feels condemned and defeated? **2.** In what other ways do we experience Satan's attacks? **3.** How can the victory of Christ help us face these battles and struggles of the Christian life?

Responding in Prayer Pray for those who are struggling against Satan.

11 / *Revelation 13*
The Beast

IN *BRAVE NEW World* Aldous Huxley described a future too close for comfort: "As political and economic freedom diminishes, sexual freedom tends compensatingly to increase. And the dictator will do well to encourage that freedom." Faithful Christianity inevitably involves conflict, tension and suffering for followers of Jesus. We cannot be fully at home in our own culture. Even where we do not face open hostility, we are pressured—indeed seduced—by a seemingly friendly society. Revelation 13 demonstrates that the church must always deal with radical evil. In these visions John unmasks the powers of darkness at work in everyday life and at the end of history.

Warming Up to God Why do you think it is so difficult for believers to make substantial changes in society? (For example, in the areas of justice, protection of the unborn or making peace.)

Read Revelation 13.

13 [1]And the dragon[o] stood on the shore of the sea.

And I saw a beast coming out of the sea. He had ten horns and seven heads, with ten crowns on his horns, and on each head a blasphemous name. [2]The beast I saw resembled a leopard, but had feet like those of a bear and a mouth like that of a lion. The dragon gave the beast his power and his throne and great authority. [3]One of the heads of the beast seemed to have had a fatal wound, but the fatal wound had been healed. The whole world was astonished and followed the beast. [4]Men worshiped the dragon because he had given authority to the beast, and they also worshiped the beast and asked, "Who is like the beast? Who can make war against him?"

[5]The beast was given a mouth to utter proud words and blasphemies and to exercise his authority for forty-two months. [6]He opened his mouth to blaspheme God, and to slander his name and his dwelling place and those who live in heaven. [7]He was given power to make war against the saints and to conquer them. And he was given authority over every tribe, people, language and nation. [8]All inhabitants of the earth will worship the beast—all whose names have not been written in the book of life belonging to the Lamb that was slain from the creation of the world.[p]

[9]He who has an ear, let him hear.

[10]If anyone is to go into captivity,
into captivity he will go.
If anyone is to be killed[q] with the sword,
with the sword he will be killed.

This calls for patient endurance and faithfulness on the part of the saints.

[11]Then I saw another beast, coming out of the earth. He had two horns like a lamb, but he spoke like a dragon. [12]He exercised all the authority of the first beast on his behalf, and made the earth and its inhabitants worship the first beast, whose fatal wound had been healed. [13]And he performed great and miraculous signs, even causing fire to come down from heaven to earth in full view of men. [14]Because of the signs he was given power to do on behalf of the first beast, he deceived the inhabitants of the earth. He ordered them to set up an image in honor of the beast who was wounded by the sword and yet lived. [15]He was given power to give breath to the image of the first beast, so that it could speak and cause all who refused to worship the image to be killed. [16]He also forced everyone, small and great, rich and poor, free and slave, to receive a mark on his right hand or on his forehead, [17]so that no one could buy or sell unless he had the mark, which is the name of the beast or the number of his name.

[18]This calls for wisdom. If anyone has insight, let him calculate the number of the beast, for it is man's number. His number is 666.

o1 Some late manuscripts *And I* p8 Or *written from the creation of the world in the book of life belonging to the Lamb that was slain*
q10 Some manuscripts *anyone kills*

Discovering the Word 1. In what ways is the beast a satanic imitation of Christ? 2. What is the mission of the beast (vv. 5–8)? 3. Why do you think John tells us about this formidable enemy of the soul? 4. What new powers are given to the second beast (vv. 11–18)? 5. How does this beast ensure that people worship the first beast?

 Applying the Word 1. John seems to be describing a conflict with Satan and his puppets that is going on now but will one day be fully realized (see 1Jn 2:18). How might we expect to see this satanic influence at work today? 2. How can we prepare ourselves to face this conflict?

 Responding in Prayer Pray that you will be equipped to face Satan.

12 / *Revelation 14—15*
Tale of Two Choices

AS YOU STRUGGLE to live according to God's laws, do you ever wonder if there will really be any reward? Will there be any difference between those who love God and those who live their lives in rebellion against God's love? In these chapters, John makes it clear that the choices we make now will have an impact on God's judgement on us in the future. These chapters are a tale of two choices.

Warming Up to God When have you really tried to do what is right, only to see those who didn't play by the rules seem to come out better than you? How did you feel about the outcome?

Read Revelation 14—15.

14 Then I looked, and there before me was the Lamb, standing on Mount Zion, and with him 144,000 who had his name and his Father's name written on their foreheads. ²And I heard a sound from heaven like the roar of rushing waters and like a loud peal of thunder. The sound I heard was like that of harpists playing their harps. ³And they sang a new song before the throne and before the four living creatures and the elders. No one could learn the song except the 144,000 who had been redeemed from the earth. ⁴These are those who did not defile themselves with women, for they kept themselves pure. They follow the Lamb wherever he goes. They were purchased from among men and offered as firstfruits to God and the Lamb. ⁵No lie was found in their mouths; they are blameless.

⁶Then I saw another angel flying in midair, and he had the eternal gospel to proclaim to those who live on the earth—to every nation, tribe, language and people. ⁷He said in a loud voice, "Fear God and give him glory, because the hour of his judgment has come. Worship him who made the heavens, the earth, the sea and the springs of water."

⁸A second angel followed and said, "Fallen! Fallen is Babylon the Great, which made all the nations drink the maddening wine of her adulteries."

⁹A third angel followed them and said in a loud voice: "If anyone worships the beast and his image and receives his mark on the forehead or on the hand, ¹⁰he, too, will drink of the wine of God's fury, which has been poured full strength into the cup of his wrath. He will be tormented with burning sulfur in the presence of the holy angels and of the Lamb. ¹¹And the smoke of their torment rises for ever and ever. There is no rest day or night for those who worship the beast and his image, or for anyone who receives the mark of his name." ¹²This calls for patient endurance on the part of the saints who obey God's commandments and remain faithful to Jesus.

¹³Then I heard a voice from heaven say, "Write: Blessed are the dead who die in the Lord from now on."

"Yes," says the Spirit, "they will rest from their labor, for their deeds will follow them."

¹⁴I looked, and there before me was a white cloud, and seated on the cloud was one "like a son of man"ʳ with a crown of gold on his head and a sharp sickle in his hand. ¹⁵Then another angel came out of the temple and called in a loud voice to him who was sitting on the cloud, "Take your sickle and reap, because the time to reap has come, for the harvest of the earth is ripe." ¹⁶So he who was seated on the cloud swung his sickle over the earth, and the earth was harvested.

¹⁷Another angel came out of the temple in heaven, and he too had a sharp sickle. ¹⁸Still another angel, who had charge of the fire, came from the altar and called in a loud voice to him who had the sharp sickle, "Take your sharp sickle and gather the clusters of grapes from the earth's vine, because its grapes are ripe." ¹⁹The angel swung his sickle on the earth, gathered its grapes and threw them into the great winepress of God's wrath. ²⁰They were trampled in the winepress outside the city, and blood flowed out of the press, rising as high as the horses' bridles for a distance of 1,600 stadia.ˢ

15 I saw in heaven another great and marvelous sign: seven angels with the seven last plagues—last, because with them God's wrath is completed. ²And I saw what looked like a sea of glass mixed with fire and, standing beside the sea, those who had been victorious over the beast and his image and over the number of his name. They held harps given them by God ³and sang the song of Moses the servant of God and the song of the Lamb:

"Great and marvelous are your deeds,
   Lord God Almighty.
Just and true are your ways,
   King of the ages.
⁴Who will not fear you, O Lord,
   and bring glory to your name?
For you alone are holy.
All nations will come
   and worship before you,
for your righteous acts have been revealed."

⁵After this I looked and in heaven the temple, that is, the tabernacle of the Testimony, was opened. ⁶Out of the temple came the seven angels with the seven plagues. They were dressed in clean, shining linen and wore golden sashes around their chests. ⁷Then one of the four living creatures gave to the seven angels seven golden bowls filled with the wrath of God, who lives for ever and ever. ⁸And the temple was filled with smoke from the glory of God and from his power, and no one could enter the temple until the seven plagues of the seven angels were completed.

ʳ14 Daniel 7:13   ˢ20 That is, about 180 miles (about 300 kilometers)

 Discovering the Word 1. What differences do you notice between the 144,000 who are with the Lamb (14:1–5) and Babylon (14:8), the beast and those who worship it (14:6–11)? 2. What harvest is reaped in 14:14–20? 3. What connections do you find between the angels who give warnings in 14:6–11 and the beings who reap the harvest? 4. Who sings the hymn to God in 15:1–4? 5. What are the righteous acts that have been revealed (15:4)?

Applying the Word 1. In 14:12 John states that this passage "calls for patient endurance on the part of the saints." How does this passage encourage you to endure in your faith? 2. The hymn beginning in 15:3 is called the song of Moses, which was sung by Moses after crossing the Red Sea. When have you been delivered by God from danger, spiritual or physical?

Responding in Prayer Thank God for the assurance you have of your salvation.

13 / *Revelation 16*
Who's to Blame?

WHEN SOMETHING GOES wrong, who do we blame? Often, God's name is among the first to come up. When we are inclined to blame God, we must ask ourselves what it is we expect out of life. Do we feel that we have an innate right to health, wealth and happiness? In understanding God's working in the world it's important that we learn to see beyond our private world to God's vast creation.

 Warming Up to God Be honest with yourself about your feelings toward God. When are you inclined to place blame on God for events in your life?

 Read Revelation 16.

16 Then I heard a loud voice from the temple saying to the seven angels, "Go, pour out the seven bowls of God's wrath on the earth."

²The first angel went and poured out his bowl on the land, and ugly and painful sores broke out on the people who had the mark of the beast and worshiped his image.

³The second angel poured out his bowl on the sea, and it turned into blood like that of a dead man, and every living thing in the sea died.

⁴The third angel poured out his bowl on the rivers and springs of water, and they became blood. ⁵Then I heard the angel in charge of the waters say:

"You are just in these judgments,
  you who are and who were, the Holy One,
  because you have so judged;
⁶for they have shed the blood of your saints
    and prophets,
  and you have given them blood to drink as
    they deserve."

⁷And I heard the altar respond:

"Yes, Lord God Almighty,
  true and just are your judgments."

⁸The fourth angel poured out his bowl on the sun, and the sun was given power to scorch people with fire. ⁹They were seared by the intense heat and they cursed the name of God, who had control over these plagues, but they refused to repent and glorify him.

¹⁰The fifth angel poured out his bowl on the throne of the beast, and his kingdom was plunged into darkness. Men gnawed their tongues in agony ¹¹and cursed the God of heaven because of their pains and their sores, but they refused to repent of what they had done.

¹²The sixth angel poured out his bowl on the great river Euphrates, and its water was dried up to prepare the way for the kings from the East. ¹³Then I saw three evil* spirits that looked like frogs; they came out of the mouth of the dragon, out of the mouth of the beast and out of the mouth of the false prophet. ¹⁴They are spirits of demons performing miraculous signs, and they go out to the kings of the whole world, to gather them for the battle on the great day of God Almighty.

¹⁵"Behold, I come like a thief! Blessed is he who stays awake and keeps his clothes with him, so that he may not go naked and be shamefully exposed."

¹⁶Then they gathered the kings together to the place that in Hebrew is called Armageddon.

¹⁷The seventh angel poured out his bowl into the air, and out of the temple came a loud voice from the throne, saying, "It is done!" ¹⁸Then there came flashes of lightning, rumblings, peals of thunder and a severe earthquake. No earthquake like it has ever occurred since man has been on earth, so tremendous was the quake. ¹⁹The great city split into three parts, and the cities of the nations collapsed. God remembered Babylon the Great and gave her the cup filled with the wine of the fury of his wrath. ²⁰Every island fled away and the mountains could not be found. ²¹From the sky huge hailstones of about a hundred pounds each fell upon men. And they cursed God on account of the plague of hail, because the plague was so terrible.

*13 Greek *unclean*

Discovering the Word 1. Note the similarity between these plagues and those brought on Egypt (blood, frogs, gnats, flies, livestock, boils, hail, locusts, darkness, firstborn). What might be meant by this comparison? 2. How could the same events lead to worship on the part of some (vv. 5–7) and cursing on the part of others (vv. 9, 21)? 3. How can we see this happening in our culture? 4. What is the result of the plagues (vv. 19–21)?

Applying the Word 1. When has God's judgment been a source of praise for you? 2. When has God's judgment caused you to curse or blame God?

Responding in Prayer Talk honestly with God about any feelings of blame and responsibility that have been revealed to you during this study.

14 / *Revelation 17—18*
Beneath the Surface

IN EVERY AGE there is at least one symbol for everything that goes against God. For several of the Old Testament writers it was Babylon, the beautiful city that held captive God's chosen people. Babylon represented everything that was evil and unsightly about humanity. John uses this powerful symbol to interpret his own age and the powers that opposed God in his generation. In these two chapters we see not only John's vision of how those powers opposed God, but the ultimate outcome of that opposition.

Warming Up to God When have you noticed someone or something that looked appealing, but upon closer scrutiny was unappealing or revolting?

Read Revelation 17—18.

17 One of the seven angels who had the seven bowls came and said to me, "Come, I will show you the punishment of the great prostitute, who sits on many waters. ²With her the kings of the earth committed adultery and the inhabitants of the earth were intoxicated with the wine of her adulteries."

³Then the angel carried me away in the Spirit into a desert. There I saw a woman sitting on a scarlet beast that was covered with blasphemous names and had seven heads and ten horns. ⁴The woman was dressed in purple and scarlet, and was glittering with gold, precious stones and pearls. She held a golden cup in her hand, filled with abominable things and the filth of her adulteries. ⁵This title was written on her forehead:

MYSTERY

BABYLON THE GREAT

THE MOTHER OF PROSTITUTES

AND OF THE ABOMINATIONS OF THE EARTH.

⁶I saw that the woman was drunk with the blood of the saints, the blood of those who bore testimony to Jesus.

When I saw her, I was greatly astonished. ⁷Then the angel said to me: "Why are you astonished? I will explain to you the mystery of the woman and of the beast she rides, which has the seven heads and ten horns. ⁸The beast, which you saw, once was, now is not, and will come up out of the Abyss and go to his destruction. The inhabitants of the earth whose names have not been written in the book of life from the creation of the world will be astonished when they see the beast, because he once was, now is not, and yet will come.

⁹"This calls for a mind with wisdom. The seven heads are seven hills on which the woman sits. ¹⁰They are also seven kings. Five have fallen, one is, the other has not yet come; but when he does come, he must remain for a little while. ¹¹The beast who once was, and now is not, is an eighth king. He belongs to the seven and is going to his destruction.

¹²"The ten horns you saw are ten kings who have not yet received a kingdom, but who for one hour will receive authority as kings along with the beast. ¹³They have one purpose and will give their power and authority to the beast. ¹⁴They

will make war against the Lamb, but the Lamb will overcome them because he is Lord of lords and King of kings—and with him will be his called, chosen and faithful followers."

¹⁵Then the angel said to me, "The waters you saw, where the prostitute sits, are peoples, multitudes, nations and languages. ¹⁶The beast and the ten horns you saw will hate the prostitute. They will bring her to ruin and leave her naked; they will eat her flesh and burn her with fire. ¹⁷For God has put it into their hearts to accomplish his purpose by agreeing to give the beast their power to rule, until God's words are fulfilled. ¹⁸The woman you saw is the great city that rules over the kings of the earth."

18

After this I saw another angel coming down from heaven. He had great authority, and the earth was illuminated by his splendor. ²With a mighty voice he shouted:

"Fallen! Fallen is Babylon the Great!
  She has become a home for demons
and a haunt for every evilᵘ spirit,
  a haunt for every unclean and detestable
    bird.
³For all the nations have drunk
  the maddening wine of her adulteries.
The kings of the earth committed adultery
  with her,
  and the merchants of the earth grew rich
    from her excessive luxuries."

⁴Then I heard another voice from heaven say:

"Come out of her, my people,
  so that you will not share in her sins,
  so that you will not receive any of her
    plagues;
⁵for her sins are piled up to heaven,
  and God has remembered her crimes.
⁶Give back to her as she has given;
  pay her back double for what she has done.
  Mix her a double portion from her own
    cup.
⁷Give her as much torture and grief
  as the glory and luxury she gave herself.
In her heart she boasts,
  'I sit as queen; I am not a widow,
  and I will never mourn.'
⁸Therefore in one day her plagues will
    overtake her:
  death, mourning and famine.

She will be consumed by fire,
  for mighty is the Lord God who judges her.

⁹"When the kings of the earth who committed adultery with her and shared her luxury see the smoke of her burning, they will weep and mourn over her. ¹⁰Terrified at her torment, they will stand far off and cry:

" 'Woe! Woe, O great city,
  O Babylon, city of power!
In one hour your doom has come!'

¹¹"The merchants of the earth will weep and mourn over her because no one buys their cargoes any more— ¹²cargoes of gold, silver, precious stones and pearls; fine linen, purple, silk and scarlet cloth; every sort of citron wood, and articles of every kind made of ivory, costly wood, bronze, iron and marble; ¹³cargoes of cinnamon and spice, of incense, myrrh and frankincense, of wine and olive oil, of fine flour and wheat; cattle and sheep; horses and carriages; and bodies and souls of men.

¹⁴"They will say, 'The fruit you longed for is gone from you. All your riches and splendor have vanished, never to be recovered.' ¹⁵The merchants who sold these things and gained their wealth from her will stand far off, terrified at her torment. They will weep and mourn ¹⁶and cry out:

" 'Woe! Woe, O great city,
  dressed in fine linen, purple and scarlet,
  and glittering with gold, precious stones
    and pearls!
¹⁷In one hour such great wealth has been
    brought to ruin!'

"Every sea captain, and all who travel by ship, the sailors, and all who earn their living from the sea, will stand far off. ¹⁸When they see the smoke of her burning, they will exclaim, 'Was there ever a city like this great city?' ¹⁹They will throw dust on their heads, and with weeping and mourning cry out:

" 'Woe! Woe, O great city,
  where all who had ships on the sea
  became rich through her wealth!
In one hour she has been brought to ruin!
²⁰Rejoice over her, O heaven!
  Rejoice, saints and apostles and prophets!

ᵘ2 Greek *unclean*

God has judged her for the way she treated
    you.'"

²¹Then a mighty angel picked up a boulder the
size of a large millstone and threw it into the sea,
and said:

"With such violence
    the great city of Babylon will be thrown
      down,
    never to be found again.
²²The music of harpists and musicians, flute
      players and trumpeters,
    will never be heard in you again.
No workman of any trade

will ever be found in you again.
The sound of a millstone
    will never be heard in you again.
²³The light of a lamp
    will never shine in you again.
The voice of bridegroom and bride
    will never be heard in you again.
Your merchants were the world's great men.
    By your magic spell all the nations were led
      astray.
²⁴In her was found the blood of prophets and
    of the saints,
    and of all who have been killed on the
      earth."

Discovering the Word 1. Who or what do you think John had in mind when he described the prostitute (17:3–6)? 2. What is the relationship between the prostitute and the beast, and how does it change (chapter 17)? 3. What are the crimes of the prostitute, identified as Babylon (17:3–6; 18:1–3)? 4. How does the prostitute see herself (18:7–8)? 5. What is the reaction of the kings (18:9–10), merchants (18:11–17a) and sea captains (18:17b–20) to the fall of Babylon?

Applying the Word 1. Who or what is a contemporary parallel to the prostitute? 2. In what ways is the modern "prostitute" a temptation to you? 3. How can you avoid this temptation?

Responding in Prayer Ask God for protection from the temptations of those who are prideful and oppose God.

---

15 / *Revelation 19*
Are You Going to the Wedding?

JOHN USES A metaphor that has lost much of its meaning in our generation—marriage. In this day of interchangeable marriage roles, five-year renewable relationships and serial monogamy, it is difficult to grasp the splendor of marriage as God intends it. John chooses a wedding to describe the consummation of the deepest longing of the human soul: Christ's coming to receive us. Our present engagement (betrothal) to Christ will be followed by the wedding service and a joyous feast. Then and only then can we experience complete unity with Christ. This vision seems a welcome relief after the long passage on tribulation and judgment (chapters 6—18). In fact, the marriage is the logical result of all that has gone before, as we shall see.

Warming Up to God In your opinion, what are some of the best things about marriage?

Read Revelation 19.

---

19 After this I heard what sounded like the roar of a great multitude in heaven shouting:

"Hallelujah!
Salvation and glory and power belong to our
    God,

² for true and just are his judgments.
He has condemned the great prostitute
    who corrupted the earth by her adulteries.
He has avenged on her the blood of his
      servants."

³And again they shouted:

"Hallelujah!
The smoke from her goes up for ever and
ever."

⁴The twenty-four elders and the four living
creatures fell down and worshiped God, who was
seated on the throne. And they cried:

"Amen, Hallelujah!"

⁵Then a voice came from the throne, saying:

"Praise our God,
all you his servants,
you who fear him,
both small and great!"

⁶Then I heard what sounded like a great multitude, like the roar of rushing waters and like loud
peals of thunder, shouting:

"Hallelujah!
For our Lord God Almighty reigns.
⁷Let us rejoice and be glad
and give him glory!
For the wedding of the Lamb has come,
and his bride has made herself ready.
⁸Fine linen, bright and clean,
was given her to wear."
(Fine linen stands for the righteous acts of the
saints.)

⁹Then the angel said to me, "Write: 'Blessed are
those who are invited to the wedding supper of
the Lamb!'" And he added, "These are the true
words of God."

¹⁰At this I fell at his feet to worship him. But he
said to me, "Do not do it! I am a fellow servant
with you and with your brothers who hold to the
testimony of Jesus. Worship God! For the testimony of Jesus is the spirit of prophecy."

¹¹I saw heaven standing open and there before

me was a white horse, whose rider is called Faithful and True. With justice he judges and makes
war. ¹²His eyes are like blazing fire, and on his
head are many crowns. He has a name written on
him that no one knows but he himself. ¹³He is
dressed in a robe dipped in blood, and his name
is the Word of God. ¹⁴The armies of heaven were
following him, riding on white horses and
dressed in fine linen, white and clean. ¹⁵Out of
his mouth comes a sharp sword with which to
strike down the nations. "He will rule them with
an iron scepter." ᵛ He treads the winepress of the
fury of the wrath of God Almighty. ¹⁶On his robe
and on his thigh he has this name written:

KING OF KINGS AND LORD OF LORDS.

¹⁷And I saw an angel standing in the sun, who
cried in a loud voice to all the birds flying in
midair, "Come, gather together for the great supper of God, ¹⁸so that you may eat the flesh of
kings, generals, and mighty men, of horses and
their riders, and the flesh of all people, free and
slave, small and great."

¹⁹Then I saw the beast and the kings of the
earth and their armies gathered together to make
war against the rider on the horse and his army.
²⁰But the beast was captured, and with him the
false prophet who had performed the miraculous
signs on his behalf. With these signs he had deluded those who had received the mark of the
beast and worshiped his image. The two of them
were thrown alive into the fiery lake of burning
sulfur. ²¹The rest of them were killed with the
sword that came out of the mouth of the rider on
the horse, and all the birds gorged themselves on
their flesh.

ᵛ15 Psalm 2:9

Discovering the Word 1. Why is the great multitude shouting praise in heaven? 2. John does not
describe the details of the marriage, he simply proclaims it. Why is marriage such a good image for the
believer's hope (vv. 7–9)? 3. Like a champion ready for battle, Jesus appears on horseback. What do we learn
about him (vv. 11–16)? 4. Why must this battle take place before the marriage can begin and the kingdom of God
can fully come (vv. 17–21)?

Applying the Word 1. In what ways would you like to see Christ triumph in your life or in the world around
you? 2. How can we confidently know we are invited to the "wedding supper of the Lamb"?

Responding in Prayer Allow praise for this future celebration to flow forth out of your prayer.

16 / *Revelation 20*
The Last Battle

FINALITY IS SOMETHING we crave and which God graciously provides. A relationship needs to be broken, an assignment needs to be completed, an extended friendship needs to become a committed marriage—all require closure. The previous study explored our inexpressible hope to be reunited with our Lord. This chapter enlarges our appreciation of God's master plan: his settled decision to be with us forever and to establish his glorious rule over everything.

 Warming Up to God What do you look forward to most about Christ's return?

 Read Revelation 20.

20 And I saw an angel coming down out of heaven, having the key to the Abyss and holding in his hand a great chain. ²He seized the dragon, that ancient serpent, who is the devil, or Satan, and bound him for a thousand years. ³He threw him into the Abyss, and locked and sealed it over him, to keep him from deceiving the nations anymore until the thousand years were ended. After that, he must be set free for a short time.

⁴I saw thrones on which were seated those who had been given authority to judge. And I saw the souls of those who had been beheaded because of their testimony for Jesus and because of the word of God. They had not worshiped the beast or his image and had not received his mark on their foreheads or their hands. They came to life and reigned with Christ a thousand years. ⁵(The rest of the dead did not come to life until the thousand years were ended.) This is the first resurrection. ⁶Blessed and holy are those who have part in the first resurrection. The second death has no power over them, but they will be priests of God and of Christ and will reign with him for a thousand years.

⁷When the thousand years are over, Satan will be released from his prison ⁸and will go out to deceive the nations in the four corners of the earth—Gog and Magog—to gather them for battle. In number they are like the sand on the seashore. ⁹They marched across the breadth of the earth and surrounded the camp of God's people, the city he loves. But fire came down from heaven and devoured them. ¹⁰And the devil, who deceived them, was thrown into the lake of burning sulfur, where the beast and the false prophet had been thrown. They will be tormented day and night for ever and ever.

¹¹Then I saw a great white throne and him who was seated on it. Earth and sky fled from his presence, and there was no place for them. ¹²And I saw the dead, great and small, standing before the throne, and books were opened. Another book was opened, which is the book of life. The dead were judged according to what they had done as recorded in the books. ¹³The sea gave up the dead that were in it, and death and Hades gave up the dead that were in them, and each person was judged according to what he had done. ¹⁴Then death and Hades were thrown into the lake of fire. The lake of fire is the second death. ¹⁵If anyone's name was not found written in the book of life, he was thrown into the lake of fire.

 Discovering the Word 1. This chapter, out of the whole book, has sparked the greatest controversy. Why is Satan, previously thrown to earth (12:9), now bound (20:1–3)? 2. The thousand-year reign of Christ (vv. 4–6) has been interpreted as referring to: (a) a period of righteousness and peace on earth *before* Christ's return; (b) Christ's reign in heaven *between* his First and Second Coming; (c) Christ's reign on earth *after* his return. Which view (if any) do you think best fits this passage and the book of Revelation? 3. What is the nature and outcome of Satan's last fling (vv. 7–10)? 4. Who will be judged at the great-white-throne judgment (vv. 11–15)? 5. What does it say about God's character that he should keep a record of each person's deeds?

Applying the Word 1. How can verses 4–6 help us to see life and death in proper perspective? 2. How should the ultimate judgment of evil and the reward of faithfulness affect the way we live now?

Responding in Prayer Pray that you will be made faithful in every way.

17 / *Revelation 21—22*
God Dwelling with His People

W. H. AUDEN said, "Nobody is ever sent to hell; he or she insists on going there." Could the same be said of heaven? Far from being "pie in the sky by and by" or a hedonistic longing for pleasure, John's vision of God dwelling with his people is the consummation of faith. Creation is renewed. Evil is finally excluded. The face of God is seen. But John's vision is, at the same time, unsettling to the normal view held by Christians about "last things." It goes beyond not only our imagination but even our faith.

 Warming Up to God What do you think about when you hear the word *heaven*?

 Read Revelation 21—22.

21 Then I saw a new heaven and a new earth, for the first heaven and the first earth had passed away, and there was no longer any sea. ²I saw the Holy City, the new Jerusalem, coming down out of heaven from God, prepared as a bride beautifully dressed for her husband. ³And I heard a loud voice from the throne saying, "Now the dwelling of God is with men, and he will live with them. They will be his people, and God himself will be with them and be their God. ⁴He will wipe every tear from their eyes. There will be no more death or mourning or crying or pain, for the old order of things has passed away."

⁵He who was seated on the throne said, "I am making everything new!" Then he said, "Write this down, for these words are trustworthy and true."

⁶He said to me: "It is done. I am the Alpha and the Omega, the Beginning and the End. To him who is thirsty I will give to drink without cost from the spring of the water of life. ⁷He who overcomes will inherit all this, and I will be his God and he will be my son. ⁸But the cowardly, the unbelieving, the vile, the murderers, the sexually immoral, those who practice magic arts, the idolaters and all liars—their place will be in the fiery lake of burning sulfur. This is the second death."

⁹One of the seven angels who had the seven bowls full of the seven last plagues came and said to me, "Come, I will show you the bride, the wife of the Lamb." ¹⁰And he carried me away in the Spirit to a mountain great and high, and showed me the Holy City, Jerusalem, coming down out of heaven from God. ¹¹It shone with the glory of God, and its brilliance was like that of a very precious jewel, like a jasper, clear as crystal. ¹²It had a great, high wall with twelve gates, and with twelve angels at the gates. On the gates were written the names of the twelve tribes of Israel. ¹³There were three gates on the east, three on the north, three on the south and three on the west. ¹⁴The wall of the city had twelve foundations, and on them were the names of the twelve apostles of the Lamb.

¹⁵The angel who talked with me had a measuring rod of gold to measure the city, its gates and its walls. ¹⁶The city was laid out like a square, as long as it was wide. He measured the city with the rod and found it to be 12,000 stadia[w] in length, and as wide and high as it is long. ¹⁷He measured its wall and it was 144 cubits[x] thick,[y] by man's measurement, which the angel was using. ¹⁸The wall was made of jasper, and the city of pure gold, as pure as glass. ¹⁹The foundations of the city walls were decorated with every kind of precious stone. The first foundation was jasper, the second sapphire, the third chalcedony, the fourth emerald, ²⁰the fifth sardonyx, the sixth carnelian, the

[w]16 That is, about 1,400 miles (about 2,200 kilometers)   [x]17 That is, about 200 feet (about 65 meters)   [y]17 Or *high*

seventh chrysolite, the eighth beryl, the ninth topaz, the tenth chrysoprase, the eleventh jacinth, and the twelfth amethyst.[z] 21The twelve gates were twelve pearls, each gate made of a single pearl. The great street of the city was of pure gold, like transparent glass.

22I did not see a temple in the city, because the Lord God Almighty and the Lamb are its temple. 23The city does not need the sun or the moon to shine on it, for the glory of God gives it light, and the Lamb is its lamp. 24The nations will walk by its light, and the kings of the earth will bring their splendor into it. 25On no day will its gates ever be shut, for there will be no night there. 26The glory and honor of the nations will be brought into it. 27Nothing impure will ever enter it, nor will anyone who does what is shameful or deceitful, but only those whose names are written in the Lamb's book of life.

22 Then the angel showed me the river of the water of life, as clear as crystal, flowing from the throne of God and of the Lamb 2down the middle of the great street of the city. On each side of the river stood the tree of life, bearing twelve crops of fruit, yielding its fruit every month. And the leaves of the tree are for the healing of the nations. 3No longer will there be any curse. The throne of God and of the Lamb will be in the city, and his servants will serve him. 4They will see his face, and his name will be on their foreheads. 5There will be no more night. They will not need the light of a lamp or the light of the sun, for the Lord God will give them light. And they will reign for ever and ever.

6The angel said to me, "These words are trustworthy and true. The Lord, the God of the spirits of the prophets, sent his angel to show his servants the things that must soon take place."

7"Behold, I am coming soon! Blessed is he who keeps the words of the prophecy in this book."

8I, John, am the one who heard and saw these things. And when I had heard and seen them, I fell down to worship at the feet of the angel who had been showing them to me. 9But he said to me,

"Do not do it! I am a fellow servant with you and with your brothers the prophets and of all who keep the words of this book. Worship God!"

10Then he told me, "Do not seal up the words of the prophecy of this book, because the time is near. 11Let him who does wrong continue to do wrong; let him who is vile continue to be vile; let him who does right continue to do right; and let him who is holy continue to be holy."

12"Behold, I am coming soon! My reward is with me, and I will give to everyone according to what he has done. 13I am the Alpha and the Omega, the First and the Last, the Beginning and the End.

14"Blessed are those who wash their robes, that they may have the right to the tree of life and may go through the gates into the city. 15Outside are the dogs, those who practice magic arts, the sexually immoral, the murderers, the idolaters and everyone who loves and practices falsehood.

16"I, Jesus, have sent my angel to give you[a] this testimony for the churches. I am the Root and the Offspring of David, and the bright Morning Star."

17The Spirit and the bride say, "Come!" And let him who hears say, "Come!" Whoever is thirsty, let him come; and whoever wishes, let him take the free gift of the water of life.

18I warn everyone who hears the words of the prophecy of this book: If anyone adds anything to them, God will add to him the plagues described in this book. 19And if anyone takes words away from this book of prophecy, God will take away from him his share in the tree of life and in the holy city, which are described in this book.

20He who testifies to these things says, "Yes, I am coming soon."

Amen. Come, Lord Jesus.

21The grace of the Lord Jesus be with God's people. Amen.

z20 The precise identification of some of these precious stones is uncertain.   a16 The Greek is plural.

Discovering the Word 1. What aspects of the "old order" must be eliminated before God can fully dwell with his people (21:1–5)? 2. What in the passage suggests that the new Jerusalem is nothing other than the church in its final, consummated life (21:10)? 3. Why do you think John gives such a detailed description of the splendor of the city (21:11–21)? 4. Why do you think a city (rather than a glorious garden like Eden) is used to describe our final home? 5. Taken together, chapters 21 and 22 describe a place of exquisite beauty. Yet what statements indicate that the real significance of the city lies in something else (22:1–21)? 6. What are the requirements for entering the city (21:6–7, 27; 22:12, 14)?

 Applying the Word 1. Why must the requirements for entering the city be met during the times of testing we experience in this life? 2. As you review what you have learned in Revelation, what new insight do you have into the early Christian prayer "Come, Lord Jesus!"?

Responding in Prayer Pray for Jesus' coming.

Psalms

People look into mirrors to see how they look; they look into the Psalms to find out who they are. With a mirror we detect a new wrinkle here, an old wart there. We use a mirror when shaving or applying makeup to improve, if we can, the face we present to the world. With the Psalms we bring into awareness an ancient sorrow, we release a latent joy. We use the Psalms to present ourselves before God as honestly and thoroughly as we are able. A mirror shows us the shape of our nose and the curve of our chin, things we otherwise know only through the reports of others. The Psalms show us the shape of our souls and the curve of our sin, realities deep within us, hidden and obscured, for which we need focus and names.

The Psalms are poetry and the Psalms are prayer. These two features, the poetry and the prayer, need to be kept in mind always. If either is forgotten the Psalms will not only be misunderstood but misused.

Poetry is language used with intensity. It is not, as so many suppose, decorative speech. Poets tell us what our eyes, blurred with too much gawking, and our ears, dulled with too much chatter, miss around and within us. Poets use words to drag us into the depths of reality itself, not by reporting on how life is but by pushing/pulling us into the middle of it. Poetry gets at the heart of existence. Far from being cosmetic language, it is intestinal. It is root language. Poetry doesn't so much tell us something we never knew as bring into recognition what was latent or forgotten or overlooked. The Psalms are almost entirely this kind of language. Knowing this, we will not be looking primarily for ideas about God in the Psalms or for direction in moral conduct. We will expect, rather, to find exposed and sharpened what it means to be human beings before God.

Prayer is language used in relation to God. It gives utterance to what we sense or want or respond to before God. God speaks to us; our answers are our prayers. The answers are not always articulate. Silence, sighs, groaning—these also constitute responses. But God is always involved, whether in darkness or light, whether in faith or despair. This is hard to get used to. Our habit is to talk *about* God, not to him. We love discussing God. But the Psalms resist such discussions. They are provided not to teach us about God but to train us in responding to him. We don't learn the Psalms until we are praying them.

Those two features, the poetry and the prayer, account for both the excitement and the difficulty in studying the Psalms. The *poetry* requires that we deal with our actual humanity—these words dive beneath the surfaces of prose and pretense straight into the depths. We are more comfortable with prose, the laid-back language of our ordinary discourse. The *prayer* requires that we deal with God—this God who is determined on nothing less than the total renovation of our lives. We would rather have a religious bull session.

One editorial feature of the Psalms helps to keep these distinctive qualities of the Psalms before us. The Psalms are arranged into five books. At the end of Psalms 41, 72, 89, 106 and 150 formula sentences indicate a conclusion. Because of these miniconclusions the Psalms are usually printed (in English translations) as Book I (Psalms 1—41), Book II (42—72), Book III (73—89), Book IV (90—106) and Book V (107—150).

This five-book arrangement matches the five-book beginning of the Bible, deeply embedded in our minds as the five books of Moses. The five books of Moses are matched by the five books of David like two five-fingered hands clasping one another in greeting. In the five books of Moses God addresses us by his word, calling us into being and shaping our salvation. In the five books of David we personally respond to this word that addresses us. Prayer is answering speech. Every word that God speaks to us must be answered by us. God's Word has not done its complete work until it evokes an answer from us. All our answers are prayers. The Psalms train us in this answering speech, this language that responds to all God's creating and saving words targeted to our lives.

It is important to notice this well, for it shifts our interpretive stance. Our usual approach to God's Word is to ask, What is God saying to me? That is almost always the correct question when reading Scripture. But in the Psalms the question is, How do I answer the God who speaks to me? In the Psalms we do not primarily learn what God *says* to us, but how to honestly, devoutly and faithfully *answer* his words to us. In the course of acquiring language we learn how to answer our parents, our teachers, our employers and our friends, but we do not get very much practice in answering God. The Psalms train us in answering God. And so we bring a somewhat different mindset to the Psalms than we do to the rest of Scripture—we are learning to *pray,* not study, although the two activities will always be interconnected.

We know almost nothing of the circumstances in which the 150 psalms were written. David is the most named author, but most are anonymous. But that hardly matters, for the settings of the Psalms are not geographical or cultural but *interior.* Calvin called them "an anatomy of all the parts of the soul." Everything that anyone can feel or experience in relation to God is in these prayers. You will find them the best place in Scripture to explore all the parts of your life and then to say who you are and what is in you—guilt, anger, salvation, praise—to the God who loves, judges and saves you in Jesus Christ.

Outline

1/ Psalm 1 ———————— *Praying Our Inattention*

2/ Psalm 2 ———————— *Praying Our Intimidation*

3/ Psalm 3 ———————— *Praying Our Trouble*

4/ Psalm 4 ———————— *Dealing with Anger*

5/ Psalm 5 ———————— *Relying on God*

6/ Psalm 6 ———————— *Praying Our Tears*

7/ Psalm 8 ———————— *Praying Our Creation*

1 / *Psalm 1*
Praying Our Inattention

PSALM 1 IS the biblical preparation for a life of prayer. Step by step it detaches us from activities and words that distract us from God so that we can be attentive before him. Most of us can't step immediately from the noisy, high-stimulus world into the quiet concentration of prayer. We need a way of transition. Psalm 1 provides a kind of entryway into the place of prayer.

 Warming Up to God Do you feel a gap (or chasm!) between "real life" (work, school, family) and your prayer life? Explain. Ask God to help you begin to make prayer a part of your life.

 Read Psalm 1.

BOOK I
Psalms 1–41

Psalm 1

¹Blessed is the man
　who does not walk in the counsel of the
　　wicked
　or stand in the way of sinners
　　or sit in the seat of mockers.
²But his delight is in the law of the LORD,
　and on his law he meditates day and night.
³He is like a tree planted by streams of water,
　which yields its fruit in season

and whose leaf does not wither.
　Whatever he does prospers.

⁴Not so the wicked!
　They are like chaff
　　that the wind blows away.
⁵Therefore the wicked will not stand in the
　　judgment,
　nor sinners in the assembly of the
　　righteous.

⁶For the LORD watches over the way of the
　　righteous,
　but the way of the wicked will perish.

 Discovering the Word 1. What contrasts do you notice in the psalm? 2. What significance do you see in the progression from *walk* to *stand* to *sit* (v. 1)? 3. "The law of the LORD" is contrasted with the words *counsel, way* and *seat*. What does this contrast bring out? 4. *Tree* is the central metaphor of the psalm (v. 3). Put your imagination to use. How are law-delighting people like trees? 5. In what ways are the wicked like chaff (vv. 4–6)?

Applying the Word 1. How do these two radically different portraits (the tree-righteous and the chaff-wicked) motivate you to delight in God's Word? 2. How does meditation—listening to God speak to us through Scripture—prepare us for prayer? 3. A *life* of prayer requires preparation, a procedure for moving from inattention to attention. The same procedure will not suit everyone. How can you develop a procedure that fits your circumstances and development?

Responding in Prayer As you turn to prayer, spend careful time in preparation.

---

2 / *Psalm 2*
Praying Our Intimidation

WE WAKE UP each day in a world noisy with boasting, violent with guns, arrogant with money. How can we avoid being intimidated? What use can prayer have in the face of governments and armies and millionaires? None, if God is not at work; all, if God is. God is as much at work in the public sphere as he is in the personal, and our prayers are as needful there as in our personal lives.

 Warming Up to God How do you feel when you consider the needs of our world and try to pray for them? Know that God is in control. Spend time reflecting on that fact before you begin.

 Read Psalm 2.

Psalm 2

¹Why do the nations conspire*a*
  and the peoples plot in vain?
²The kings of the earth take their stand
  and the rulers gather together
against the LORD
  and against his Anointed One.*b*
³"Let us break their chains," they say,
  "and throw off their fetters."

⁴The One enthroned in heaven laughs;
  the Lord scoffs at them.
⁵Then he rebukes them in his anger
  and terrifies them in his wrath, saying,
⁶"I have installed my King*c*
  on Zion, my holy hill."

⁷I will proclaim the decree of the LORD:

He said to me, "You are my Son*d*;

today I have become your Father.*e*
⁸Ask of me,
  and I will make the nations your
    inheritance,
  the ends of the earth your possession.
⁹You will rule them with an iron scepter*f*;
  you will dash them to pieces like pottery."

¹⁰Therefore, you kings, be wise;
  be warned, you rulers of the earth.
¹¹Serve the LORD with fear
  and rejoice with trembling.
¹²Kiss the Son, lest he be angry
  and you be destroyed in your way,
  for his wrath can flare up in a moment.
  Blessed are all who take refuge in him.

*a*1 Hebrew; Septuagint *rage*   *b*2 Or *anointed one*   *c*6 Or *king*
*d*7 Or *son; also in verse 12*   *e*7 Or *have begotten you*   *f*9 Or *will break them with a rod of iron*

 Discovering the Word 1. Compare the opening nouns and verbs in Psalm 1:1–3 with those in Psalm 2:1–3. What differences in orientation do they suggest between these two psalms? 2. How does the Lord view the vaunted power of nations (vv. 4–6)? 3. "Anointed One" in verse 2 is a translation of the Hebrew word *Messiah*. What in this psalm reminds you of Jesus? 4. The psalm begins and ends with references to kings and rulers (vv. 2–3, 10–12). How do they relate to the King enthroned by the Lord (v. 6)?

Applying the Word 1. It is always easier to pray for personal needs than political situations. But Psalm 2 is entirely political. Therefore, as citizens of Christ's kingdom, what responsibility do we have as citizens of an earthly nation? 2. How does Christ's relationship with kings and rulers impact your prayers for the world?

Responding in Prayer Think of three rulers (presidents, kings, prime ministers or dictators). Pray for them.

3 / *Psalm 3*
Praying Our Trouble

PRAYER BEGINS IN a realization that we cannot help ourselves, so we must reach out to God. "Help!" is the basic prayer. We are in trouble, deep trouble. If God cannot get us out, we are lost; if God can get us out, we are saved. If we don't know that we need help, prayer will always be peripheral to our lives, a matter of mood and good manners. But the moment we know we are in trouble, prayer is a life-or-death matter.

 Warming Up to God What is the worst trouble you were in this last week? Where did you go for help? Did you get help? God is your help. Talk to him about what you need today.

Read Psalm 3.

Psalm 3

A psalm of David. When he fled from his
son Absalom.

¹O Lᴏʀᴅ, how many are my foes!
How many rise up against me!
²Many are saying of me,
"God will not deliver him."   *Selah*ᵍ

³But you are a shield around me, O Lᴏʀᴅ;
you bestow glory on me and lift*ʰ* up my
head.
⁴To the Lᴏʀᴅ I cry aloud,
and he answers me from his holy
hill.   *Selah*

⁵I lie down and sleep;
I wake again, because the Lᴏʀᴅ sustains me.
⁶I will not fear the tens of thousands
drawn up against me on every side.

⁷Arise, O Lᴏʀᴅ!
Deliver me, O my God!
Strike all my enemies on the jaw;
break the teeth of the wicked.

⁸From the Lᴏʀᴅ comes deliverance.
May your blessing be on your
people.   *Selah*

ᵍ2 A word of uncertain meaning, occurring frequently in the Psalms;
possibly a musical term   *ʰ*3 Or Lᴏʀᴅ, / my Glorious One, who lifts

---

Discovering the Word 1. *Deliver/deliverance* is a key word in this psalm. What do we learn about the nature of deliverance through its various uses here? 2. David's prayer naturally divides into five sections: verses 1–2, 3–4, 5–6, 7 and 8. What progression do you see from each section to the next? 3. What actions is God described as taking in this psalm? 4. Are you used to thinking of God in these ways? Explain. 5. What actions is David described as taking in the psalm?

Applying the Word 1. David describes his foes in verses 1–2. Do you ever feel overwhelmed by threatening people or circumstances? Give an example. 2. What kind of trouble are you in right now? 3. What in this psalm do you think will help you to pray your trouble?

Responding in Prayer Take an image or phrase from Psalm 3 and use it to pray your trouble.

---

4 / *Psalm 4*
Dealing with Anger

ANGER IS AN emotion common to all people. Anger in itself is not sin. It is simply an emotion, a God-given part of life as a human being. It's a natural reaction to threats or injuries; yet anger is all too often expressed in ways that spread the harm around. The Old Testament is full of references to God's righteous anger or indignation against sin, and this emotional aspect of God's character also appears in the New Testament through Christ. How can we learn to "be angry, but sin not"?

Warming Up to God How do you generally respond when you are angry? (For example, do you talk about it or do you keep it to yourself?)

Read Psalm 4.

Psalm 4

For the director of music. With stringed
instruments. A psalm of David.

¹Answer me when I call to you,
    O my righteous God.
Give me relief from my distress;
    be merciful to me and hear my prayer.

²How long, O men, will you turn my glory
        into shameⁱ?
    How long will you love delusions and seek
        false godsʲ?   *Selah*
³Know that the LORD has set apart the godly
        for himself;
    the LORD will hear when I call to him.

⁴In your anger do not sin;

when you are on your beds,
    search your hearts and be silent.   *Selah*
⁵Offer right sacrifices
    and trust in the LORD.

⁶Many are asking, "Who can show us any
        good?"
    Let the light of your face shine upon us,
        O LORD.
⁷You have filled my heart with greater joy
    than when their grain and new wine
        abound.
⁸I will lie down and sleep in peace,
    for you alone, O LORD,
    make me dwell in safety.

ⁱ2 Or *you dishonor my Glorious One*   ʲ2 Or *seek lies*

 Discovering the Word 1. What is David angry about (v. 2)? 2. How does David deal with his anger (vv. 1, 3)? 3. In verse 4 David suggests that we can be angry and not sin. How do you think that could be possible? 4. What do you think David means by the phrase "search your hearts and be silent" (v. 4)?

 Applying the Word 1. How can reflecting on angry feelings be a healthy way of dealing with anger? 2. How can knowing the joy of the Lord (vv. 6–7) help you deal with anger?

Responding in Prayer Talk to God about any anger you are dealing with right now. Ask him to help you express it directly and not hold it in.

---

5 / *Psalm 5*
Relying on God

FEELING BETRAYED, PERSECUTED or fearful are common human experiences. Christians are not immune from such emotions. Indeed, because of the opposition of the fallen world to Christ, we will inevitably face them. How do we pray in these circumstances? Instead of allowing our fear or anger to dominate our thinking, we need to focus on God. Psalm 5 is one example of a prayer written in the face of opposition.

 Warming Up to God What happens to your relationship with God (especially your prayer life) when you find yourself facing opposition or persecution?

 Read Psalm 5.

Psalm 5

For the director of music. For flutes.
A psalm of David.

¹Give ear to my words, O LORD,
    consider my sighing.
²Listen to my cry for help,
    my King and my God,

for to you I pray.
³In the morning, O LORD, you hear my voice;
    in the morning I lay my requests before
        you
    and wait in expectation.

⁴You are not a God who takes pleasure in evil;
    with you the wicked cannot dwell.

⁵The arrogant cannot stand in your
        presence;
    you hate all who do wrong.
⁶You destroy those who tell lies;
    bloodthirsty and deceitful men
    the LORD abhors.

⁷But I, by your great mercy,
    will come into your house;
in reverence will I bow down
    toward your holy temple.
⁸Lead me, O LORD, in your righteousness
    because of my enemies—
    make straight your way before me.

⁹Not a word from their mouth can
        be trusted;
    their heart is filled with destruction.

Their throat is an open grave;
    with their tongue they speak deceit.
¹⁰Declare them guilty, O God!
    Let their intrigues be their downfall.
Banish them for their many sins,
    for they have rebelled against you.

¹¹But let all who take refuge in you
        be glad;
    let them ever sing for joy.
Spread your protection over them,
    that those who love your name may rejoice
        in you.
¹²For surely, O LORD, you bless the
        righteous;
    you surround them with your favor as with
        a shield.

Discovering the Word 1. List the characteristics of the wicked and the righteous from David's descriptions in the passage. 2. When we are opposed or persecuted by others, it is easy to want to take revenge or become aggressive toward them. What is David's strategy for dealing with opposition? 3. David appears confident of God hearing his prayer and shielding him. What grounds are there in the passage for such confidence? 4. What does the passage show us about David's relationship with God? 5. David is clearly accustomed to beginning his day with prayer (v. 3). What are the benefits of this model?

Applying the Word 1. The psalm gives us a clear picture of how God opposes the wicked and deals with them. How does this help in coping with opposition or persecution on a day-to-day basis? 2. Both Christians and non-Christians often blame God for the pain, suffering or persecution that they encounter. How does Psalm 5 help us to understand the pain, suffering and persecution from God's perspective? 3. What aspects of David's prayer in this passage are a helpful model for you?

Responding in Prayer Think of any situations that represent a threat or pressure for you. Spend some time praying about those situations, trying to focus particularly on God's power and supremacy over the situation (while being realistic about the difficulties!).

---

6 / *Psalm 6*
Praying Our Tears

TEARS ARE A biological gift of God. They are a physical means for expressing emotional and spiritual experience. But it is hard to know what to do with them. If we indulge our tears, we cultivate self-pity. If we suppress our tears, we lose touch with our feelings. But if we *pray* our tears, we enter into sadnesses that integrate our sorrows with our Lord's sorrows and discover both the source of and the relief from our sadness.

 Warming Up to God How do you feel about crying (is it always negative, positive or mixed)?

 Read Psalm 6.

Psalm 6

For the director of music. With stringed
instruments. According to *sheminith.*[k]
A psalm of David.

[1]O LORD, do not rebuke me in your anger
  or discipline me in your wrath.
[2]Be merciful to me, LORD, for I am faint;
  O LORD, heal me, for my bones are in
    agony.
[3]My soul is in anguish.
  How long, O LORD, how long?

[4]Turn, O LORD, and deliver me;
  save me because of your unfailing love.
[5]No one remembers you when he is dead.

Who praises you from the grave[l]?

[6]I am worn out from groaning;
  all night long I flood my bed with weeping
  and drench my couch with tears.
[7]My eyes grow weak with sorrow;
  they fail because of all my foes.

[8]Away from me, all you who do evil,
  for the LORD has heard my weeping.
[9]The LORD has heard my cry for mercy;
  the LORD accepts my prayer.
[10]All my enemies will be ashamed and
    dismayed;
  they will turn back in sudden disgrace.

[k]Title: Probably a musical term   [l]5 Hebrew *Sheol*

Discovering the Word 1. Compare the first verse with the last. Are the tears because of the Lord or the enemies? Explain. 2. What is the cumulative effect of the three verbs *turn, deliver* and *save* in verse 4? 3. The emotional center of this prayer is verses 6–7. How many different ways is weeping expressed? 4. Why the tears? (Go through the psalm and note every possible source.) 5. In verses 8–9 there are three phrases in parallel: *weeping, cry for mercy* and *prayer.* Are these aspects of one thing or three different things? Explain.

Applying the Word 1. "How long?" (v. 3) is a frequent question in prayer. Considering the frequency with which it is uttered in Scripture, God must welcome it. What in your life, past or present, evokes this question? 2. Tears are often considered a sign that something is wrong with us—depression, unhappiness, frustration—and are therefore to be either avoided or cured. But what if they are a sign of something right with us? What rightness could they be evidence of?

Responding in Prayer Who do you know who is in grief? Pray for them now, using phrases from Psalm 6 to express their sorrow.

Psalm 7

Psalm 7

A *shiggaion*[m] of David, which he sang to
the LORD concerning Cush, a Benjamite.

[1]O LORD my God, I take refuge in you;
  save and deliver me from all who pursue
    me,
[2]or they will tear me like a lion
  and rip me to pieces with no one to rescue
    me.

[3]O LORD my God, if I have done this
  and there is guilt on my hands—
[4]if I have done evil to him who is at peace
    with me
  or without cause have robbed my foe—
[5]then let my enemy pursue and overtake me;
  let him trample my life to the ground

and make me sleep in the dust.   *Selah*

[6]Arise, O LORD, in your anger;
  rise up against the rage of my enemies.
  Awake, my God; decree justice.
[7]Let the assembled peoples gather around you.
  Rule over them from on high;
[8] let the LORD judge the peoples.
Judge me, O LORD, according to my
    righteousness,
  according to my integrity, O Most High.
[9]O righteous God,
  who searches minds and hearts,
bring to an end the violence of the wicked
  and make the righteous secure.

[10]My shield[n] is God Most High,

[m]Title: Probably a literary or musical term   [n]10 Or *sovereign*

who saves the upright in heart.
11 God is a righteous judge,
a God who expresses his wrath every day.
12 If he does not relent,
he[o] will sharpen his sword;
he will bend and string his bow.
13 He has prepared his deadly weapons;
he makes ready his flaming arrows.

14 He who is pregnant with evil
and conceives trouble gives birth to
disillusionment.
15 He who digs a hole and scoops it out
falls into the pit he has made.
16 The trouble he causes recoils on himself;
his violence comes down on his own head.

17 I will give thanks to the LORD because of his
righteousness
and will sing praise to the name of the LORD
Most High.

[o] 12 Or *If a man does not repent, / God*

7 / *Psalm 8*
Praying Our Creation

DISORIENTATION IS A terrible experience. If we cannot locate our place, we are in confusion and anxiety. We are also in danger, for we are apt to act inappropriately. If we are among enemies and don't know it, we may lose our life. If we are among friends and don't know it, we may miss good relationships. If we are alongside a cliff and don't know it, we may lose our footing. In Psalm 8, we find out where we are and some important aspects of who we are.

Warming Up to God When traveling, have you ever awakened and not known where you were? The bed is unfamiliar; the room is strange; you look out the window and don't recognize anything. What does it feel like to be disoriented?

Read Psalm 8.

Psalm 8

For the director of music. According to *gittith.*[p] A psalm of David.

1 O LORD, our Lord,
how majestic is your name in all the earth!

You have set your glory
above the heavens.
2 From the lips of children and infants
you have ordained praise[q]
because of your enemies,
to silence the foe and the avenger.

3 When I consider your heavens,
the work of your fingers,
the moon and the stars,
which you have set in place,
4 what is man that you are mindful of him,
the son of man that you care for him?
5 You made him a little lower than the
heavenly beings[r]
and crowned him with glory and honor.

6 You made him ruler over the works of your
hands;
you put everything under his feet:
7 all flocks and herds,
and the beasts of the field,
8 the birds of the air,
and the fish of the sea,
all that swim the paths of the seas.

9 O LORD, our Lord,
how majestic is your name in all the earth!

[p] Title: Probably a musical term [q] 2 Or *strength* [r] 5 Or *than God*

Discovering the Word 1. Browse through the psalm and note every word that refers to what God has created. How do these things reveal God's glory? 2. Why do you think the psalmist contrasts what children and infants say with what foes and avengers say (v. 2)? 3. What evidence do we have that God is mindful of us, that he cares for us? 4. "Ruler" and "under his feet" (v. 6) can be twisted into excuses to exploit and pillage. What is there in this psalm to prevent such twisting?

Applying the Word 1. How does Psalm 8 compare with the way you view yourself? 2. What adjustments do you need to make to view yourself as God views you? 3. Some people think of themselves as "a little higher than the heavenly beings"; others think, "a little lower than the beasts of the field." In what area has Psalm 8 corrected your self-image?

Responding in Prayer Praise God and use this psalm as the basis for your praise.

Psalm 9

Psalm 9ˢ

For the director of music. To ⌊the tune of⌋ "The Death of the Son." A psalm of David.

¹I will praise you, O LORD, with all my heart;
  I will tell of all your wonders.
²I will be glad and rejoice in you;
  I will sing praise to your name, O Most
        High.

³My enemies turn back;
  they stumble and perish before you.
⁴For you have upheld my right and my cause;
  you have sat on your throne, judging
        righteously.
⁵You have rebuked the nations and destroyed
        the wicked;
  you have blotted out their name for ever
        and ever.
⁶Endless ruin has overtaken the enemy,
  you have uprooted their cities;
  even the memory of them has perished.

⁷The LORD reigns forever;
  he has established his throne for judgment.
⁸He will judge the world in righteousness;
  he will govern the peoples with justice.
⁹The LORD is a refuge for the oppressed,
  a stronghold in times of trouble.
¹⁰Those who know your name will trust in you,
  for you, LORD, have never forsaken those
        who seek you.

¹¹Sing praises to the LORD, enthroned in Zion;
  proclaim among the nations what he has
        done.
¹²For he who avenges blood remembers;
  he does not ignore the cry of the afflicted.

¹³O Lord, see how my enemies persecute me!
  Have mercy and lift me up from the gates
        of death,
¹⁴that I may declare your praises
  in the gates of the Daughter of Zion
  and there rejoice in your salvation.
¹⁵The nations have fallen into the pit they have
        dug;
  their feet are caught in the net they have
        hidden.
¹⁶The LORD is known by his justice;
  the wicked are ensnared by the work of
        their hands.   *Higgaion.ᵗ Selah*
¹⁷The wicked return to the grave,ᵘ
  all the nations that forget God.
¹⁸But the needy will not always be forgotten,
  nor the hope of the afflicted ever perish.

¹⁹Arise, O LORD, let not man triumph;
  let the nations be judged in your presence.
²⁰Strike them with terror, O LORD;
  let the nations know they are but men.
                                              Selah

ˢPsalms 9 and 10 may have been originally a single acrostic poem, the stanzas of which begin with the successive letters of the Hebrew alphabet. In the Septuagint they constitute one psalm.   ᵗ16 Or *Meditation*; possibly a musical notation   ᵘ17 Hebrew *Sheol*

8 / *Psalm 10*
A Prayer of Helplessness

HELPLESSNESS. IT IS an experience shared by everyone. There is no way out. There are no alternatives. It is an experience full of fear, rage and despair. Because our culture places such a high value on individualism and self-reliance, the experience of helplessness is full of shame for us. We expect that others will blame us for letting it happen. And we end up blaming ourselves. In times of helplessness, however, shame and blame are not helpful. What might be helpful is to know that God understands helplessness and that he hears our prayers.

 Warming Up to God   Recall a time when you felt helpless. Picture God in that situation with you as your protector and defender. How does that make you feel?

 Read Psalm 10.

Psalm 10ᵛ

¹Why, O LORD, do you stand far off?
  Why do you hide yourself in times of
    trouble?

²In his arrogance the wicked man hunts down
    the weak,
  who are caught in the schemes he
    devises.
³He boasts of the cravings of his heart;
  he blesses the greedy and reviles
    the LORD.
⁴In his pride the wicked does not seek him;
  in all his thoughts there is no room for
    God.
⁵His ways are always prosperous;
  he is haughty and your laws are far from
    him;
  he sneers at all his enemies.
⁶He says to himself, "Nothing will shake me;
  I'll always be happy and never have
    trouble."
⁷His mouth is full of curses and lies and
    threats;
  trouble and evil are under his tongue.
⁸He lies in wait near the villages;
  from ambush he murders the innocent,
  watching in secret for his victims.
⁹He lies in wait like a lion in cover;
  he lies in wait to catch the helpless;

he catches the helpless and drags them off
    in his net.
¹⁰His victims are crushed, they collapse;
  they fall under his strength.
¹¹He says to himself, "God has forgotten;
  he covers his face and never sees."

¹²Arise, LORD! Lift up your hand, O God.
  Do not forget the helpless.
¹³Why does the wicked man revile God?
  Why does he say to himself,
    "He won't call me to account"?
¹⁴But you, O God, do see trouble
      and grief;
  you consider it to take it in hand.
  The victim commits himself to you;
    you are the helper of the fatherless.
¹⁵Break the arm of the wicked and evil man;
  call him to account for his wickedness
    that would not be found out.

¹⁶The LORD is King for ever and ever;
  the nations will perish from his land.
¹⁷You hear, O LORD, the desire of the afflicted;
  you encourage them, and you listen to their
    cry,
¹⁸defending the fatherless and the oppressed,
  in order that man, who is of the earth, may
    terrify no more.

ᵛPsalms 9 and 10 may have been originally a single acrostic poem, the stanzas of which begin with the successive letters of the Hebrew alphabet. In the Septuagint they constitute one psalm.

 Discovering the Word   1. The prayer begins with the question "Why, God, do you hide yourself?" Why is this such an urgent question when you are feeling helpless?   2. How does the author describe the person who is attacking him (vv. 3–11)?   3. What is the attitude of the wicked person toward God (vv. 3–4, 11)? 4. How does the writer describe the victim (vv. 2, 10, 14)?   5. How does the writer describe God and his actions on behalf of people who have been abused (vv. 12, 14–18)?

Applying the Word 1. Notice the author's various perspectives of God. The prayer begins with an absent God: "Where are you, God?" In the middle the author risks asking God to respond on his behalf: "Arise, Lord!" The prayer ends with praise to the God who hears and defends the oppressed. Which of these perspectives of God have you experienced? 2. When you feel helpless, how would it help you if you experienced God as acting on your behalf?

Responding in Prayer How would you like God to respond to your feelings of helplessness?

Psalms 11—12

Psalm 11

For the director of music. Of David.

¹In the LORD I take refuge.
How then can you say to me:
"Flee like a bird to your mountain.
²For look, the wicked bend their bows;
they set their arrows against the
strings
to shoot from the shadows
at the upright in heart.
³When the foundations are being destroyed,
what can the righteous do*w*?"

⁴The LORD is in his holy temple;
the LORD is on his heavenly throne.
He observes the sons of men;
his eyes examine them.
⁵The LORD examines the righteous,
but the wicked*x* and those who love
violence
his soul hates.
⁶On the wicked he will rain
fiery coals and burning sulfur;
a scorching wind will be their lot.

⁷For the LORD is righteous,
he loves justice;
upright men will see his face.

Psalm 12

For the director of music. According to
sheminith.*y* A psalm of David.

¹Help, LORD, for the godly are no more;
the faithful have vanished from among
men.
²Everyone lies to his neighbor;
their flattering lips speak with deception.

³May the LORD cut off all flattering lips
and every boastful tongue
⁴that says, "We will triumph with our
tongues;
we own our lips*z*—who is our master?"

⁵"Because of the oppression of the weak
and the groaning of the needy,
I will now arise," says the LORD.
"I will protect them from those who malign
them."
⁶And the words of the LORD are flawless,
like silver refined in a furnace of clay,
purified seven times.

⁷O LORD, you will keep us safe
and protect us from such people forever.
⁸The wicked freely strut about
when what is vile is honored among men.

---

*w*3 Or *what is the Righteous One doing*   *x*5 Or *The LORD, the*
Righteous One, examines the wicked, /   *y*Title: Probably a musical term
*z*4 Or / *our lips are our plowshares*

9 / Psalm 13
A Prayer of Self-Doubt

PEOPLE ASK ABOUT God: "Why did God let this happen?" "Was he unable to respond to my prayers?" "Was it my fault?" "Was my faith too weak?" These painful questions and the doubts which they represent are difficult to discuss with other people. They can also be very difficult to share with God.

Fortunately, the Bible itself gives voice to these painful questions. God is not shocked by our struggles with doubt. May knowing that God is able to respond to doubt in helpful ways give you the courage to pray when your heart is full of unanswerable questions.

 Warming Up to God At what times in your life have you struggled with doubt? Talk openly with God about it; he wants to know your true feelings.

 Read Psalm 13.

Psalm 13

For the director of music. A psalm of David.

¹How long, O Lᴏʀᴅ? Will you forget me forever?
How long will you hide your face from me?
²How long must I wrestle with my thoughts
and every day have sorrow in my heart?
How long will my enemy triumph over me?

³Look on me and answer, O Lᴏʀᴅ my God.
Give light to my eyes, or I will sleep in death;
⁴my enemy will say, "I have overcome him,"
and my foes will rejoice when I fall.

⁵But I trust in your unfailing love;
my heart rejoices in your salvation.
⁶I will sing to the Lᴏʀᴅ,
for he has been good to me.

Discovering the Word 1. The author begins with two questions that express his doubts about God. What are his concerns? 2. In verse 2 what reasons does he give for his sorrow? 3. Why is it helpful to express our doubts to God? 4. The author not only has questions about God, he also has questions about himself. He asks, "How long must I wrestle with my thoughts and every day have sorrow in my heart?" What is it about the experience of doubt that causes people to question themselves? 5. The writer ends the prayer of doubt with a statement of trust (vv. 5–6). How is it possible to doubt and trust at the same time?

Applying the Word 1. When is it difficult for you to follow the writer's example in expressing your doubts about God? 2. How might it give you courage in your spiritual struggle to know that the Bible gives voice to doubts?

 Responding in Prayer What doubts would you like to express to God?

Psalm 14

Psalm 14

For the director of music. Of David.

¹The foolᵃ says in his heart,
"There is no God."
They are corrupt, their deeds are vile;
there is no one who does good.

²The Lᴏʀᴅ looks down from heaven
on the sons of men
to see if there are any who understand,
any who seek God.

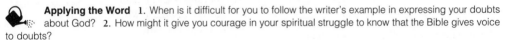

ᵃ1 The Hebrew words rendered *fool* in Psalms denote one who is morally deficient.

³All have turned aside,
  they have together become corrupt;
there is no one who does good,
  not even one.

⁴Will evildoers never learn—
  those who devour my people as men eat
  bread
  and who do not call on the Lᴏʀᴅ?
⁵There they are, overwhelmed with dread,

for God is present in the company of the
  righteous.
⁶You evildoers frustrate the plans of the poor,
  but the Lᴏʀᴅ is their refuge.

⁷Oh, that salvation for Israel would come out
  of Zion!
When the Lᴏʀᴅ restores the fortunes of his
  people,
  let Jacob rejoice and Israel be glad!

10 / *Psalm 15*
A Person of Honesty

A LIE CONTAMINATES everyone close to it. Worst of all, it rots the character of the person who tells the lie.

Warming Up to God Reflect on the past week. How have you failed to be honest? Take your failings to Christ. What does he have to say to you?

Read Psalm 15.

Psalm 15

A psalm of David.

¹Lᴏʀᴅ, who may dwell in your sanctuary?
  Who may live on your holy hill?

²He whose walk is blameless
  and who does what is righteous,
who speaks the truth from his heart
³ and has no slander on his tongue,
who does his neighbor no wrong

and casts no slur on his fellowman,
⁴who despises a vile man
  but honors those who fear the Lᴏʀᴅ,
who keeps his oath
  even when it hurts,
⁵who lends his money without usury
  and does not accept a bribe against the
  innocent.

He who does these things
  will never be shaken.

Discovering the Word 1. What must a person do to be worthy to approach the Lord ("dwell in your sanctuary") (vv. 2–5)? 2. What, according to this psalm, keeps a person from being shaken? 3. What would it be like to live "on the holy hill" of the Lord? 4. When is it hard to keep a promise (v. 4)?

Applying the Word 1. How might this psalm help you to make specific choices for honesty in your dealings with other people? 2. What forms of self-discipline would you recommend to someone who wanted to become more truthful? 3. What help in being honest do you need?

Responding in Prayer Ask God to help you to have a walk that is blameless.

11 / *Psalm 16*
Finding Balance in Life

JOE IS A Christian businessman. He has significant responsibility at work and puts in long hours. He enjoys his work and is productive. He is also active in his church, teaching Sunday school and serving as a deacon. His wife also works outside the home, so Joe often takes a turn cooking and cleaning. Additionally, he enjoys spending time with his family—playing a game of softball or going out to dinner together.

Joe is the Christian many of us strive to be. He is able to juggle many responsibilities and demands. He seems to be able to maintain a godly balance of values. But does he really exist? This study is about how we can discover God's values for our lives.

 Warming Up to God In what areas of your life do you struggle for balance?

 Read Psalm 16.

Psalm 16

A *miktam*[b] of David.

[1]Keep me safe, O God,
  for in you I take refuge.

[2]I said to the LORD, "You are my Lord;
  apart from you I have no good thing."
[3]As for the saints who are in the land,
  they are the glorious ones in whom is all
    my delight.[c]
[4]The sorrows of those will increase
  who run after other gods.
 I will not pour out their libations of blood
  or take up their names on my lips.

[5]LORD, you have assigned me my portion and
    my cup;
  you have made my lot secure.
[6]The boundary lines have fallen for me in
    pleasant places;

surely I have a delightful inheritance.

[7]I will praise the LORD, who counsels me;
  even at night my heart instructs me.
[8]I have set the LORD always before me.
  Because he is at my right hand,
  I will not be shaken.

[9]Therefore my heart is glad and my tongue
    rejoices;
  my body also will rest secure,
[10]because you will not abandon me to the
    grave,[d]
  nor will you let your Holy One[e] see decay.
[11]You have made[f] known to me the path of
    life;
  you will fill me with joy in your presence,
  with eternal pleasures at your right hand.

[b]Title: Probably a literary or musical term   [c]3 Or *As for the pagan priests who are in the land / and the nobles in whom all delight, I said:*
[d]10 Hebrew *Sheol*   [e]10 Or *your faithful one*   [f]11 Or *You will make*

 Discovering the Word 1. According to this passage, what has the Lord done for David? 2. What body imagery does David use to describe his relationship with God (vv. 5, 7–11)? 3. Describe the spirit of David's comments about the land in verses 5–6. 4. What is the significance of the Lord's being at David's right hand (vv. 8–11)? 5. Look back through the entire passage. What is important to people who follow God? 6. How do those values contrast with worldly values?

 Applying the Word 1. In what specific ways do you need to bring your values in line with God's values? 2. What would help you to do that?

Responding in Prayer Make thanking God for the "inheritance" he has given you a focus for prayer. Try to be aware of the different roles (counselor, protector, sustainer, refuge) God plays in your daily life.

Psalm 17

Psalm 17

A prayer of David.

¹Hear, O LORD, my righteous plea;
    listen to my cry.
Give ear to my prayer—
    it does not rise from deceitful lips.
²May my vindication come from you;
    may your eyes see what is right.

³Though you probe my heart and examine me
        at night,
    though you test me, you will find
        nothing;
    I have resolved that my mouth will
        not sin.
⁴As for the deeds of men—
    by the word of your lips
I have kept myself
    from the ways of the violent.
⁵My steps have held to your paths;
    my feet have not slipped.

⁶I call on you, O God, for you will
        answer me;
    give ear to me and hear my prayer.
⁷Show the wonder of your great love,
    you who save by your right hand
    those who take refuge in you from their
        foes.

⁸Keep me as the apple of your eye;
    hide me in the shadow of your wings
⁹from the wicked who assail me,
    from my mortal enemies who surround me.

¹⁰They close up their callous hearts,
    and their mouths speak with arrogance.
¹¹They have tracked me down, they now
        surround me,
    with eyes alert, to throw me to the
        ground.
¹²They are like a lion hungry for prey,
    like a great lion crouching in cover.

¹³Rise up, O LORD, confront them, bring them
        down;
    rescue me from the wicked by your sword.
¹⁴O LORD, by your hand save me from such
        men,
    from men of this world whose reward is in
        this life.

You still the hunger of those you cherish;
    their sons have plenty,
    and they store up wealth for their
        children.
¹⁵And I—in righteousness I will see
    your face;
    when I awake, I will be satisfied with
        seeing your likeness.

---

12 / *Psalm 18:1–24*
A Prayer for Justice

IT MAY COME as a surprise that God is angry at those who take advantage of others. God shares our anger at injustice. In the text for this study, the author suggests that God's response to the wicked is anger so intense that the earth itself trembles.

Warming Up to God When have you felt angry at injustice toward you or toward others?

Read Psalm 18:1–24.

Psalm 18

For the director of music. Of David the servant of the LORD. He sang to the LORD the words of this song when the LORD delivered him from the hand of all his enemies and from the hand of Saul. He said:

¹I love you, O LORD, my strength.

²The LORD is my rock, my fortress and my
    deliverer;
  my God is my rock, in whom I take refuge.
He is my shield and the horn*g* of my
    salvation, my stronghold.
³I call to the LORD, who is worthy of praise,
  and I am saved from my enemies.

⁴The cords of death entangled me;
  the torrents of destruction overwhelmed
    me.
⁵The cords of the grave*h* coiled around me;
  the snares of death confronted me.
⁶In my distress I called to the LORD;
  I cried to my God for help.
From his temple he heard my voice;
  my cry came before him, into his ears.

⁷The earth trembled and quaked,
  and the foundations of the mountains
    shook;
  they trembled because he was angry.
⁸Smoke rose from his nostrils;
  consuming fire came from his mouth,
  burning coals blazed out of it.
⁹He parted the heavens and came down;
  dark clouds were under his feet.
¹⁰He mounted the cherubim and flew;
  he soared on the wings of the wind.
¹¹He made darkness his covering, his canopy
    around him—
  the dark rain clouds of the sky.

¹²Out of the brightness of his presence clouds
    advanced,
  with hailstones and bolts of lightning.
¹³The LORD thundered from heaven;
  the voice of the Most High resounded.*i*
¹⁴He shot his arrows and scattered ⌊the
    enemies⌋,
  great bolts of lightning and routed them.
¹⁵The valleys of the sea were exposed
  and the foundations of the earth laid bare
at your rebuke, O LORD,
  at the blast of breath from your nostrils.

¹⁶He reached down from on high and took hold
    of me;
  he drew me out of deep waters.
¹⁷He rescued me from my powerful enemy,
  from my foes, who were too strong for me.
¹⁸They confronted me in the day of my disaster,
  but the LORD was my support.
¹⁹He brought me out into a spacious place;
  he rescued me because he delighted in me.

²⁰The LORD has dealt with me according to my
    righteousness;
  according to the cleanness of my hands he
    has rewarded me.
²¹For I have kept the ways of the LORD;
  I have not done evil by turning from my
    God.
²²All his laws are before me;
  I have not turned away from his decrees.
²³I have been blameless before him
  and have kept myself from sin.
²⁴The LORD has rewarded me according to my
    righteousness,
  according to the cleanness of my hands in
    his sight.

g2 Horn here symbolizes strength.   *h5* Hebrew *Sheol*   *i13* Some Hebrew manuscripts and Septuagint (see also 2 Samuel 22:14); most Hebrew manuscripts *resounded, / amid hailstones and bolts of lightning*

Discovering the Word **1.** How does David describe the distress he has experienced (vv. 4–6)? **2.** What does the text say God actually does to our enemies (vv. 7–15)? **3.** What does the Lord do to help David (vv. 16–19)? **4.** For what reasons does God deliver David (vv. 20–24)?

Applying the Word **1.** How do the author's feelings compare with your own? **2.** What thoughts and feelings do you have as you read this powerful description of God's response to a cry for help?

Responding in Prayer What would you like to say to the God who shares your anger about injustice and who delights in you?

13 / *Psalm 18:25–50*
A Prayer for Equipping

WRESTLERS, BOXERS AND fencers know that for every move there is an equal and opposite move meant to block it, counterpunch, or parry the thrust. So also God provides just the right protection and timely provision for his people. Here God enables David to alternately evade and thwart his enemies, particularly Saul, eventually overcoming and crushing them.

 Warming Up to God God is our fight coach too. The Lord does not guide where he does not also provide. Think about what battles God may be leading you into and what you need to emerge victorious. Thank God that he will make every provision to help you overcome enemies and obstacles along the way.

Read Psalm 18:25–50.

---

²⁵To the faithful you show yourself faithful,
   to the blameless you show yourself
      blameless,
²⁶to the pure you show yourself pure,
   but to the crooked you show yourself
      shrewd.
²⁷You save the humble
   but bring low those whose eyes are
      haughty.
²⁸You, O Lᴏʀᴅ, keep my lamp burning;
   my God turns my darkness into light.
²⁹With your help I can advance against a
      troopʲ;
   with my God I can scale a wall.

³⁰As for God, his way is perfect;
   the word of the Lᴏʀᴅ is flawless.
 He is a shield
   for all who take refuge in him.
³¹For who is God besides the Lᴏʀᴅ?
   And who is the Rock except our God?
³²It is God who arms me with strength
   and makes my way perfect.
³³He makes my feet like the feet of a deer;
   he enables me to stand on the heights.
³⁴He trains my hands for battle;
   my arms can bend a bow of bronze.
³⁵You give me your shield of victory,
   and your right hand sustains me;
   you stoop down to make me great.
³⁶You broaden the path beneath me,
   so that my ankles do not turn.

³⁷I pursued my enemies and overtook them;
   I did not turn back till they were destroyed.
³⁸I crushed them so that they could not rise;
   they fell beneath my feet.

³⁹You armed me with strength for battle;
   you made my adversaries bow at my feet.
⁴⁰You made my enemies turn their backs in
      flight,
   and I destroyed my foes.
⁴¹They cried for help, but there was no one to
      save them—
   to the Lᴏʀᴅ, but he did not answer.
⁴²I beat them as fine as dust borne on the wind;
   I poured them out like mud in the streets.

⁴³You have delivered me from the attacks of the
      people;
   you have made me the head of nations;
   people I did not know are subject to me.
⁴⁴As soon as they hear me, they obey me;
   foreigners cringe before me.
⁴⁵They all lose heart;
   they come trembling from their
      strongholds.

⁴⁶The Lᴏʀᴅ lives! Praise be to my Rock!
   Exalted be God my Savior!
⁴⁷He is the God who avenges me,
   who subdues nations under me,
⁴⁸ who saves me from my enemies.
 You exalted me above my foes;
   from violent men you rescued me.
⁴⁹Therefore I will praise you among the nations,
      O Lᴏʀᴅ;
   I will sing praises to your name.
⁵⁰He gives his king great victories;
   he shows unfailing kindness to his
      anointed,
   to David and his descendants forever.

J29 Or can run through a barricade

Discovering the Word 1. Previously, the psalmist noted that the earth trembled and quaked as an expression of God's anger (v. 7). Now it's the enemies of God's people who tremble or quake in their boots (v. 45). What has God done on David's behalf to bring this about? 2. What was David's part in securing this victory in cooperation with God (vv. 25–29)? 3. In what ways did God the Warrior specifically equip or provide for the warrior David (vv. 30–36)? 4. What reversal of fortune do David and the surrounding nations experience as a result of the Lord coming to his rescue (vv. 37–45)? 5. How does the conclusion of this psalm (vv. 46–50) compare with its beginning (vv. 1–6)? 6. What does that tell you about God the warrior?

Applying the Word 1. At what points (feelings, circumstances, outcomes) can you identify with David? 2. Think about the fights God may be preparing you for. What equipping do you need? (Where can God strengthen a particular weakness of yours? What can you praise him for already?)

Responding in Prayer Trust God to fight evil and avenge any wrongs done to you. If you have experienced God's justice in the face of evil, praise him. Recount the ways he has led you and equipped you every step of the way.

14 / *Psalm 19*
Comfort from Scripture

TOM WAS FRIGHTENED before going to surgery. I shared thoughts with him from Psalm 23 about our Shepherd who gives us all we need and goes with us through dark valleys. Tom didn't have to be afraid, because Jesus was with him. He seemed to be at peace. Sharing Scripture may not always be the right thing to help someone, but often it is. Psalm 19 describes what Scripture is like and how it can offer comfort.

Warming Up to God Reflect on some of your favorite words from Scripture. You may want to turn to the passage and reread it. Drink in the comfort those familiar words bring.

Read Psalm 19.

Psalm 19

For the director of music. A psalm of David.

¹The heavens declare the glory of God;
  the skies proclaim the work of his hands.
²Day after day they pour forth speech;
  night after night they display knowledge.
³There is no speech or language
  where their voice is not heard.ᵏ
⁴Their voiceˡ goes out into all the earth,
  their words to the ends of the world.

In the heavens he has pitched a tent for the sun,
5 which is like a bridegroom coming forth
    from his pavilion,
  like a champion rejoicing to run his course.
⁶It rises at one end of the heavens
  and makes its circuit to the other;
  nothing is hidden from its heat.

⁷The law of the LORD is perfect,
  reviving the soul.
The statutes of the LORD are trustworthy,
  making wise the simple.
⁸The precepts of the LORD are right,
  giving joy to the heart.
The commands of the LORD are radiant,
  giving light to the eyes.
⁹The fear of the LORD is pure,
  enduring forever.
The ordinances of the LORD are sure
  and altogether righteous.
¹⁰They are more precious than gold,
  than much pure gold;
they are sweeter than honey,
  than honey from the comb.
¹¹By them is your servant warned;
  in keeping them there is great reward.

¹²Who can discern his errors?

ᵏ3 Or *They have no speech, there are no words; / no sound is heard from them* ˡ4 Septuagint, Jerome and Syriac; Hebrew *line*

Forgive my hidden faults.
¹³Keep your servant also from willful sins;
    may they not rule over me.
Then will I be blameless,
    innocent of great transgression.

¹⁴May the words of my mouth and the
    meditation of my heart
be pleasing in your sight,
    O Lᴏʀᴅ, my Rock and my Redeemer.

Discovering the Word 1. What does creation reveal about God (vv. 1–6)? 2. The terms *law, statutes, precepts, commands* and *ordinances* in this passage are synonyms for Scripture. In verses 7–11, how are the Scriptures described? 3. What do they do? 4. What is the overall effect of the psalmist's encounter with God through nature and the Scriptures (vv. 12–14)?

Applying the Word 1. From which of the effects of Scripture listed in verses 7–11 have you benefited? 2. How has this psalm been helpful to you by offering insight or comfort? 3. Sharing Scripture can be done in three ways. The first and most obvious way is sharing a passage or verse directly. The second is sharing how we have been affected or changed by Scripture. The third is simply living out the principles of Scripture. How might you appropriately and effectively share Scripture with someone in need this week?

Responding in Prayer Ask God to make Scripture alive and active in you this week. Pray that he will help you share his Word, either directly or through actions, with someone in need.

Psalms 20—21

Psalm 20

For the director of music. A psalm
of David.

¹May the Lᴏʀᴅ answer you when you are in
    distress;
    may the name of the God of Jacob protect
      you.
²May he send you help from the sanctuary
    and grant you support from Zion.
³May he remember all your sacrifices
    and accept your burnt offerings.   *Selah*
⁴May he give you the desire of your heart
    and make all your plans succeed.
⁵We will shout for joy when you are victorious
    and will lift up our banners in the name of
      our God.
May the Lᴏʀᴅ grant all your requests.

⁶Now I know that the Lᴏʀᴅ saves his anointed;
    he answers him from his holy heaven
    with the saving power of his right hand.
⁷Some trust in chariots and some in horses,
    but we trust in the name of the Lᴏʀᴅ our
      God.
⁸They are brought to their knees and fall,
    but we rise up and stand firm.

⁹O Lᴏʀᴅ, save the king!
    Answer*ᵐ* us when we call!

Psalm 21

For the director of music. A psalm
of David.

¹O Lᴏʀᴅ, the king rejoices in your strength.
    How great is his joy in the victories you
      give!
²You have granted him the desire of his heart
    and have not withheld the request of his
      lips.   *Selah*
³You welcomed him with rich blessings
    and placed a crown of pure gold on his
      head.
⁴He asked you for life, and you gave it to
      him—
    length of days, for ever and ever.
⁵Through the victories you gave, his glory is
      great;
    you have bestowed on him splendor and
      majesty.
⁶Surely you have granted him eternal blessings
    and made him glad with the joy of your
      presence.
⁷For the king trusts in the Lᴏʀᴅ;
    through the unfailing love of the Most High
    he will not be shaken.

⁸Your hand will lay hold on all your enemies;

ᵐ9 Or save! / O King, answer

your right hand will seize your foes.
⁹At the time of your appearing
    you will make them like a fiery furnace.
In his wrath the Lᴏʀᴅ will swallow them up,
    and his fire will consume them.
¹⁰You will destroy their descendants from the
       earth,
    their posterity from mankind.

¹¹Though they plot evil against you
    and devise wicked schemes, they cannot
      succeed;
¹²for you will make them turn their backs
    when you aim at them with drawn bow.

¹³Be exalted, O Lᴏʀᴅ, in your strength;
    we will sing and praise your might.

15 / *Psalm 22*
A Prayer of Anguish

THIS PRAYER OF anguish parallels the experience of our Lord, who took Psalm 22 to heart and spoke it from the cross. No other psalm is quoted as often in the New Testament. Persecuted saints and lonely Christians ever since have used this prayer to draw near to their God at times when they feel most abandoned.

 Warming Up to God We jokingly refer to places we despise, or would never want to go near or visit again, as "Godforsaken." But being forsaken or abandoned by others is no laughing matter. Do you have a "Godforsaken place" in your past experience? What was that like?

 Read Psalm 22.

Psalm 22

For the director of music. To ⌊the tune of⌋
   "The Doe of the Morning." A psalm
      of David.

¹My God, my God, why have you forsaken
     me?
    Why are you so far from saving me,
    so far from the words of my groaning?
²O my God, I cry out by day, but you do not
     answer,
    by night, and am not silent.

³Yet you are enthroned as the Holy One;
    you are the praise of Israel.ⁿ
⁴In you our fathers put their trust;
    they trusted and you delivered them.
⁵They cried to you and were saved;
    in you they trusted and were not
      disappointed.

⁶But I am a worm and not a man,
    scorned by men and despised by the
      people.
⁷All who see me mock me;
    they hurl insults, shaking their heads:
⁸"He trusts in the Lᴏʀᴅ;

    let the Lᴏʀᴅ rescue him.
Let him deliver him,
    since he delights in him."

⁹Yet you brought me out of the womb;
    you made me trust in you
    even at my mother's breast.
¹⁰From birth I was cast upon you;
    from my mother's womb you have been my
      God.
¹¹Do not be far from me,
    for trouble is near
    and there is no one to help.

¹²Many bulls surround me;
    strong bulls of Bashan encircle me.
¹³Roaring lions tearing their prey
    open their mouths wide against me.
¹⁴I am poured out like water,
    and all my bones are out of joint.
My heart has turned to wax;
    it has melted away within me.
¹⁵My strength is dried up like a potsherd,
    and my tongue sticks to the roof of my
      mouth;

ⁿ3 Or *Yet you are holy, / enthroned on the praises of Israel*

you lay me *o* in the dust of death.
¹⁶Dogs have surrounded me;
 a band of evil men has encircled me,
 they have pierced *p* my hands and my feet.
¹⁷I can count all my bones;
 people stare and gloat over me.
¹⁸They divide my garments among them
 and cast lots for my clothing.

¹⁹But you, O Lᴏʀᴅ, be not far off;
 O my Strength, come quickly to help me.
²⁰Deliver my life from the sword,
 my precious life from the power of the
 dogs.
²¹Rescue me from the mouth of the lions;
 save *q* me from the horns of the wild oxen.

²²I will declare your name to my brothers;
 in the congregation I will praise you.
²³You who fear the Lᴏʀᴅ, praise him!
 All you descendants of Jacob, honor him!
 Revere him, all you descendants of Israel!
²⁴For he has not despised or disdained
 the suffering of the afflicted one;
he has not hidden his face from him
 but has listened to his cry for help.

²⁵From you comes the theme of my praise in
 the great assembly;
 before those who fear you *r* will I fulfill my
 vows.
²⁶The poor will eat and be satisfied;
 they who seek the Lᴏʀᴅ will praise him—
 may your hearts live forever!
²⁷All the ends of the earth
 will remember and turn to the Lᴏʀᴅ,
and all the families of the nations
 will bow down before him,
²⁸for dominion belongs to the Lᴏʀᴅ
 and he rules over the nations.

²⁹All the rich of the earth will feast and
 worship;
 all who go down to the dust will kneel
 before him—
 those who cannot keep themselves alive.
³⁰Posterity will serve him;
 future generations will be told about the
 Lord.
³¹They will proclaim his righteousness
 to a people yet unborn—
 for he has done it.

o 15 Or *I am laid*   *p 16* Some Hebrew manuscripts, Septuagint and
Syriac; most Hebrew manuscripts *like the lion,*   *q 21* Or *you have
heard*   *r 25* Hebrew *him*

Discovering the Word 1. David did not shrink back from asking tough "why" questions. Neither did Jesus in quoting verse 1 (Mt 27:46; Mk 15:34). What were David and Jesus experiencing at the time they prayed this prayer (vv. 1–2, 6–8)? **2.** Being abandoned by friends and surrounded by enemies can feel all the more stark in contrast to one's history of being close to God and his people. What kind of relationship have this psalmist and his people enjoyed with their God (vv. 3–5, 9–10)? **3.** What are his attackers like (vv. 12–18)? **4.** What does he pray for (vv. 11, 19–21)? **5.** In anticipation of God's sure deliverance, what does the psalmist vow (vv. 22, 25)? **6.** Who joins him in this chorus of praise and why (vv. 23, 26–31)?

Applying the Word 1. This psalm conjures up images of sword fights, bull fights, dog fights and a lion's den. What scenes of violence contemporary to your experience does this psalm conjure up for you? **2.** The Gospel writers applied this psalm to Jesus (see Mt 27:35, 39, 43 and 46). In what ways does Psalm 22 fit the circumstances of Jesus' crucifixion? **3.** At what points can you identify with the psalmist or with Jesus?

Responding in Prayer Pour out your anguish before God, as he will listen to your cry for help. Trust God to deliver you from physical circumstances and emotional moods that cause you to feel forsaken. Remember what God has done for you in the past, and join others in praising God for what he will do in the future.

16 / *Psalm 23*
Praying Our Fear

THE WORLD IS a fearsome place. If we manage with the help of parents, teachers and friends to survive the dangers of infancy and childhood, we find ourselves launched in an adult world that is ringed with terror—accident, assault, disease, violence, conflicts. Prayer brings fear into focus and faces it. But prayer does more than bravely face fear; it affirms God's presence in it.

 Warming Up to God Spend some time trying to bring your fears into focus. Know that God is with you in the midst of your fear.

 Read Psalm 23.

Psalm 23

A psalm of David.

¹The LORD is my shepherd, I shall not be in
        want.
² He makes me lie down in green pastures,
    he leads me beside quiet waters,
³ he restores my soul.
    He guides me in paths of righteousness
        for his name's sake.
⁴Even though I walk
        through the valley of the shadow of
            death,ˢ
    I will fear no evil,

for you are with me;
    your rod and your staff,
        they comfort me.

⁵You prepare a table before me
        in the presence of my enemies.
    You anoint my head with oil;
        my cup overflows.
⁶Surely goodness and love will follow me
        all the days of my life,
    and I will dwell in the house of the LORD
        forever.

ˢ4 *Or through the darkest valley*

Discovering the Word 1. There are two large metaphors in the psalm: the shepherd (vv. 1–4) and the host (vv. 5–6). Compare and contrast these two images. 2. Look carefully at the shepherd. How exactly does he care for his sheep (vv. 1–4)? 3. "I will fear no evil" (v. 4) is a bold statement. What does it mean for you to say that? 4. Look carefully at the host. How exactly does he provide for his guest (vv. 5–6)?

Applying the Word 1. Enemies are prominent in the psalm prayers and appear here. Who are your enemies? 2. What is the most comforting thing that you have experienced in the life of faith? 3. Psalm 23 is a weapon against fear. What fear in your life will you go to war against with this prayer as your cannon?

Responding in Prayer Name your fears and ask Christ the Shepherd and Christ the Host to relieve them.

---

17 / *Psalm 24*
A Prayer of Ascension

DAVID MAY HAVE composed this psalm on the occasion of bringing the Ark of the Covenant back to Jerusalem or in commemoration of that historic event. This prayer by worshipers ascending to Mount Zion has long been used by the church to celebrate Christ's ascension to the heavenly Jerusalem, paving the way for others to follow and stand in God's holy presence. Psalm 24 affirms that Jerusalem is the royal site for inaugurating the kingdom of God.

Warming Up to God What is the longest journey or pilgrimage you have made? What was arriving like for you?

 Read Psalm 24.

Psalm 24

Of David. A psalm.

¹The earth is the Lord's, and everything in it,
  the world, and all who live in it;
²for he founded it upon the seas
  and established it upon the waters.

³Who may ascend the hill of the Lord?
  Who may stand in his holy place?
⁴He who has clean hands and a pure heart,
  who does not lift up his soul to an idol
  or swear by what is false.ᵗ
⁵He will receive blessing from the Lord
  and vindication from God his Savior.
⁶Such is the generation of those who seek him,

who seek your face, O God of Jacob.ᵘ
                                    Selah

⁷Lift up your heads, O you gates;
  be lifted up, you ancient doors,
  that the King of glory may come in.
⁸Who is this King of glory?
  The Lord strong and mighty,
  the Lord mighty in battle.
⁹Lift up your heads, O you gates;
  lift them up, you ancient doors,
  that the King of glory may come in.
¹⁰Who is he, this King of glory?
  The Lord Almighty—
  he is the King of glory.   *Selah*

ᵗ4 Or *swear falsely*   ᵘ6 Two Hebrew manuscripts and Syriac (see also Septuagint); most Hebrew manuscripts *face, Jacob*

Discovering the Word 1. Verses 1–2 echo themes from creation in reference to the founding of a city and the temple. What feelings and images does that backdrop evoke for this worshiper? 2. What kind of person may enter the Lord's sanctuary (vv. 3–6)? 3. Do these restrictions render the temple accessible to the public, only to priests, or to the one and only King? 4. Who is this "King of glory," and how is he described? 5. What glorious things has he done as Lord of creation (vv. 1–2) and God of Jacob (v. 6)?

Applying the Word 1. This psalm raises the doors of our hearts and the standards of readiness for corporate worship. What steps in preparation for worship does this psalm conjure up for you? 2. Paul quotes verse 1, which had become a Jewish blessing at mealtimes, to underscore the believer's freedom to eat meat without a troubled conscience (1Co 10:25–26). What new freedoms does knowing the sovereignty of God, affirmed in Psalm 24, give you?

Responding in Prayer As you seek God's face, prepare to meet his standards of acceptance—pure motives, integrity, trusting totally in God to vindicate you. This may prompt you to confession. Then lift up the gates and doors of your life, with thanksgiving and praise, to let more of the King into your worship.

18 / *Psalm 25*
Integrity in Times of Doubt

IN PHILIP YANCEY'S thoughtful book, *Disappointment with God*, the writer speaks of Richard—a new and enthusiastic convert to the Christian faith. Richard studied the Bible with diligence and prayed every day. He transferred from a university to a Christian college, graduated, and went on to a Christian graduate school.

Then Richard's parents separated. Richard dropped out of school for a while to try to mend his family. He prayed constantly that God would bring his parents back together. His parents remained apart. Next Richard lost an important job. Then his fiancée jilted him. And his health began to deteriorate.

One night, Richard stayed up all night to pray. For four hours he pleaded with God to reveal himself. Nothing. Finally, Richard got up from his knees, gathered up his Bible and his theology textbooks, and went out to a backyard brick barbecue. There, in the last hours of darkness, Richard burned his books—and his faith.

Why? As Yancey said, "The theology he had learned in school and had written about in his book no longer *worked for him.*" He was disappointed with God. Is faith in God good only as long as it "works"?

 Warming Up to God When you are in a difficult situation, what kind of prayer are you likely to pray to God?

 Read Psalm 25.

Psalm 25[v]

Of David.

¹To you, O LORD, I lift up my soul;
² in you I trust, O my God.
Do not let me be put to shame,
    nor let my enemies triumph over me.
³No one whose hope is in you
    will ever be put to shame,
but they will be put to shame
    who are treacherous without excuse.

⁴Show me your ways, O LORD,
    teach me your paths;
⁵guide me in your truth and teach me,
    for you are God my Savior,
    and my hope is in you all day long.
⁶Remember, O LORD, your great mercy and
        love,
    for they are from of old.
⁷Remember not the sins of my youth
    and my rebellious ways;
according to your love remember me,
    for you are good, O LORD.

⁸Good and upright is the LORD;
    therefore he instructs sinners in
        his ways.
⁹He guides the humble in what is right
    and teaches them his way.
¹⁰All the ways of the LORD are loving and
        faithful

for those who keep the demands of his
        covenant.
¹¹For the sake of your name, O LORD,
    forgive my iniquity, though it is great.
¹²Who, then, is the man that fears the LORD?
    He will instruct him in the way chosen for
        him.
¹³He will spend his days in prosperity,
    and his descendants will inherit the land.
¹⁴The LORD confides in those who fear him;
    he makes his covenant known to them.
¹⁵My eyes are ever on the LORD,
    for only he will release my feet from the
        snare.

¹⁶Turn to me and be gracious to me,
    for I am lonely and afflicted.
¹⁷The troubles of my heart have multiplied;
    free me from my anguish.
¹⁸Look upon my affliction and my distress
    and take away all my sins.
¹⁹See how my enemies have increased
    and how fiercely they hate me!
²⁰Guard my life and rescue me;
    let me not be put to shame,
    for I take refuge in you.
²¹May integrity and uprightness protect me,
    because my hope is in you.

²²Redeem Israel, O God,
    from all their troubles!

[v]This psalm is an acrostic poem, the verses of which begin with the successive letters of the Hebrew alphabet.

 Discovering the Word 1. Psalm 25 divides into four stanzas. Give a topic-title to each (vv. 1–3, 4–7, 8–15, 16–22). 2. What does it mean to "lift up" your soul to God? 3. Study stanza 2. What all does David ask God to do? 4. Study stanza 3. David began his prayer by saying that he trusted God. In what ways does stanza 3 show that God has integrity—and therefore ought to be trusted? 5. Study stanza 4. What words and phrases here help you to understand David's current situation? 6. Compare David's position, described in stanza 4, with what he hopes from God in verses 12–13. In view of the differences, what does David's prayer say about his own integrity?

Applying the Word 1. Three times David uses the term *remember.* What would you want God to remember (and not remember) about you? 2. What do you count on God to do and to be?

Responding in Prayer Before you pray, meditate on God's character as David did. Ask God to make you a person of integrity.

Psalm 26

Psalm 26

Of David.

¹Vindicate me, O Lord,
  for I have led a blameless life;
I have trusted in the Lord
  without wavering.
²Test me, O Lord, and try me,
  examine my heart and my mind;
³for your love is ever before me,
  and I walk continually in your truth.
⁴I do not sit with deceitful men,
  nor do I consort with hypocrites;
⁵I abhor the assembly of evildoers
  and refuse to sit with the wicked.

⁶I wash my hands in innocence,
  and go about your altar, O Lord,
⁷proclaiming aloud your praise
  and telling of all your wonderful deeds.
⁸I love the house where you live, O Lord,
  the place where your glory dwells.

⁹Do not take away my soul along with sinners,
  my life with bloodthirsty men,
¹⁰in whose hands are wicked schemes,
  whose right hands are full of bribes.
¹¹But I lead a blameless life;
  redeem me and be merciful to me.

¹²My feet stand on level ground;
  in the great assembly I will praise the Lord.

19 / *Psalm 27*
Waiting for the Lord

ONE OF SAMUEL Beckett's most famous plays is entitled *Waiting for Godot*. Throughout the play the characters wait and wait for Godot to appear, but he never does. The play is Beckett's way of saying that hope is futile—especially hope in God.

In contrast to Beckett's despair, the Bible offers hope to the sufferer. When we feel overwhelmed and ready to give up, Psalm 27 encourages us to "wait for the Lord." When we see no possibility of relief, David assures us, "I am still confident of this: I will see the goodness of the Lord in the land of the living."

Warming Up to God In what kinds of situations do you find it hardest to wait?

Read Psalm 27.

Psalm 27

Of David.

¹The Lord is my light and my salvation—
  whom shall I fear?
The Lord is the stronghold of my life—
  of whom shall I be afraid?
²When evil men advance against me
  to devour my flesh,ʷ

when my enemies and my foes attack me,
  they will stumble and fall.
³Though an army besiege me,
  my heart will not fear;
though war break out against me,
  even then will I be confident.

⁴One thing I ask of the Lord,
  this is what I seek:

ʷ2 Or *to slander me*

that I may dwell in the house of the LORD
  all the days of my life,
to gaze upon the beauty of the LORD
  and to seek him in his temple.
⁵For in the day of trouble
  he will keep me safe in his dwelling;
he will hide me in the shelter of his
    tabernacle
  and set me high upon a rock.
⁶Then my head will be exalted
  above the enemies who surround me;
at his tabernacle will I sacrifice with shouts of
    joy;
  I will sing and make music to the LORD.

⁷Hear my voice when I call, O LORD;
  be merciful to me and answer me.
⁸My heart says of you, "Seek hisˣ face!"
  Your face, LORD, I will seek.
⁹Do not hide your face from me,
  do not turn your servant away in anger;

you have been my helper.
Do not reject me or forsake me,
  O God my Savior.
¹⁰Though my father and mother forsake me,
  the LORD will receive me.
¹¹Teach me your way, O LORD;
  lead me in a straight path
  because of my oppressors.
¹²Do not turn me over to the desire of my foes,
  for false witnesses rise up against me,
  breathing out violence.

¹³I am still confident of this:
  I will see the goodness of the LORD
  in the land of the living.
¹⁴Wait for the LORD;
  be strong and take heart
  and wait for the LORD.

ˣ8 Or *To you, O my heart, he has said, "Seek my*

 Discovering the Word 1. Why is David able to be fearless in the face of evil men, armies, and even war (vv. 1–3)? 2. What images of safety does David apply to the Lord in verses 1–2 and 5–6? 3. David seeks not only the Lord's protection but also the Lord himself (v. 4). How is David's intense desire for God revealed in this psalm (vv. 4, 8, 11)? 4. David's confident statements about the Lord (vv. 1–6) lead up to his prayer in verses 7–12. What is the substance of his prayer? 5. What real dangers does he seem to be facing? 6. Why must your hope not only be confident but also patient (v. 14)?

Applying the Word 1. How does it give you hope to know that the Lord is your stronghold (or "mighty fortress") during battle and your shelter from life's storms? 2. The psalm ends as it begins—with David's confidence in the Lord's help (vv. 13–14). How can David's view of God help you to "be strong and take heart" in the midst of suffering?

Responding in Prayer Ask God to strengthen your confidence in his promises and to make you patient as you wait for his answers.

Psalm 28

Psalm 28

Of David.

¹To you I call, O LORD my Rock;
  do not turn a deaf ear to me.
For if you remain silent,
  I will be like those who have gone down to
    the pit.
²Hear my cry for mercy
  as I call to you for help,
as I lift up my hands
  toward your Most Holy Place.

³Do not drag me away with the wicked,
  with those who do evil,
who speak cordially with their neighbors
  but harbor malice in their hearts.
⁴Repay them for their deeds
  and for their evil work;
repay them for what their hands have done
  and bring back upon them what they
    deserve.
⁵Since they show no regard for the works of
    the LORD
  and what his hands have done,
he will tear them down

and never build them up again.

⁶Praise be to the LORD,
    for he has heard my cry for mercy.
⁷The LORD is my strength and my shield;
    my heart trusts in him, and I am helped.
My heart leaps for joy

and I will give thanks to him in song.

⁸The LORD is the strength of his people,
    a fortress of salvation for his anointed one.
⁹Save your people and bless your inheritance;
    be their shepherd and carry them forever.

20 / *Psalm 29*
The Voice of the Lord

WHAT ARE THE ways that God chooses to speak to us? He uses the counsel of friends or the subtlety of our own conscience, and often he uses his own Word. But sometimes he speaks so that he can be heard loud and clear, and so that no one can be mistaken about what he is saying. This passage explores the ways we hear the voice of the Lord.

 Warming Up to God Recall a time in your life when you felt that God was speaking to you specifically. Thank him for coming to you, and ask him now to speak to your listening heart.

 Read Psalm 29.

Psalm 29

A psalm of David.

¹Ascribe to the LORD, O mighty ones,
    ascribe to the LORD glory and strength.
²Ascribe to the LORD the glory due his name;
    worship the LORD in the splendor of his ʸ
        holiness.

³The voice of the LORD is over the waters;
    the God of glory thunders,
    the LORD thunders over the mighty waters.
⁴The voice of the LORD is powerful;
    the voice of the LORD is majestic.
⁵The voice of the LORD breaks the cedars;
    the LORD breaks in pieces the cedars of
        Lebanon.

⁶He makes Lebanon skip like a calf,
    Sirion ᶻ like a young wild ox.
⁷The voice of the LORD strikes
    with flashes of lightning.
⁸The voice of the LORD shakes the desert;
    the LORD shakes the Desert of Kadesh.
⁹The voice of the LORD twists the oaks ᵃ
    and strips the forests bare.
And in his temple all cry, "Glory!"

¹⁰The LORD sits ᵇ enthroned over the flood;
    the LORD is enthroned as King forever.
¹¹The LORD gives strength to his people;
    the LORD blesses his people with peace.

ʸ2 Or *LORD with the splendor of*   ᶻ6 That is, Mount Hermon
ᵃ9 Or *LORD makes the deer give birth*   ᵇ10 Or *sat*

Discovering the Word 1. The psalmist addresses a specific audience in verse 1—"mighty ones." Why do you think he speaks to them? 2. David urges his audience to "ascribe to the Lord glory and strength" (v. 1). How does his psalm accomplish this? 3. What does "the voice of the Lord" do (vv. 3–9)? 4. What characteristics of God do these verses bring to mind? 5. What does verse 9 tell us about the proper response to hearing the voice of God? 6. Most of Psalm 29 describes the actions of God as a mighty and powerful rainstorm, inspiring not only awe, but even fear. However, the psalm ends (v. 11) describing the actions of God in quite a different fashion. How does this complete the picture of God that David has painted?

Applying the Word   1. How does observing the power of God in both nature and in his own actions help us understand the nature and role of worship in our lives?   2. Sometimes God uses a storm to draw our attention to him and cause us to fall before him in awe, but he also "blesses his people with peace." How can this passage help you to better understand the ways of God and his workings in your life?

Responding in Prayer   Take some time to "ascribe to the Lord" some of the marvelous deeds he has done for you.

21 / *Psalm 30*
Waiting for Security

MAJOR CORPORATIONS ARE laying off large numbers in the latest rage of downsizing. Those who have gotten a pink slip do their best to cover it, but you can see the pain in their eyes.

One of our basic human needs is security. In the end, if our security, in any area, is dependent on our own resources and abilities, then we must live in constant vigilance. How much better if the Creator of the universe were in charge of protecting us! In this psalm David relates the experience of looking to God for his security. He found it both a humbling and thrilling experience.

Warming Up to God   Imagine that you have turned off the radio that is blaring away inside you. Sit for a while in the quiet. You may find that there are protests inside. What are your thoughts and impressions?

Read Psalm 30.

Psalm 30

A psalm. A song. For the dedication of the
     temple.*c* Of David.

¹I will exalt you, O LORD,
     for you lifted me out of the depths
     and did not let my enemies gloat over me.
²O LORD my God, I called to you for help
     and you healed me.
³O LORD, you brought me up from the grave*d*;
     you spared me from going down into the
     pit.

⁴Sing to the LORD, you saints of his;
     praise his holy name.
⁵For his anger lasts only a moment,
     but his favor lasts a lifetime;
weeping may remain for a night,
     but rejoicing comes in the morning.

⁶When I felt secure, I said,
     "I will never be shaken."
⁷O LORD, when you favored me,

you made my mountain*e* stand firm;
but when you hid your face,
     I was dismayed.

⁸To you, O LORD, I called;
     to the Lord I cried for mercy:
⁹"What gain is there in my destruction,*f*
     in my going down into the pit?
Will the dust praise you?
     Will it proclaim your faithfulness?
¹⁰Hear, O LORD, and be merciful to me;
     O LORD, be my help."

¹¹You turned my wailing into dancing;
     you removed my sackcloth and clothed me
          with joy,
¹²that my heart may sing to you and not be
          silent.
     O LORD my God, I will give you thanks
          forever.

*c*Title: Or *palace*   *d*3 Hebrew *Sheol*   *e*7 Or *hill country*   *f*9 Or
there if I am silenced

Discovering the Word   1. No one knows for sure what the problem was, but from the words "depths," "healed," "enemies," "grave" and "pit" what possible dangers may David have been facing?   2. Read the whole psalm again. List the range of emotions that is described.   3. What insight into life does David gain by acknowledging that painful as well as pleasurable experiences come from God (v. 5)? **4.** How do verses 6–7 describe David's sense of dependence on God? **5.** What reasons does David present to God in favor of his deliverance (vv. 9–10)? **6.** Look over the entire psalm. How would you describe David's relationship with God?

 Applying the Word **1.** Difficult circumstances can cause us to reflect on the character of God. How have the circumstances of your life affected your relationship with God? **2.** David expresses some of the ups and downs of his life. Consider the last six months to year of your life and chart your ups and downs. **3.** Picture the Lord with you through the ups and downs of your life. How does it help you to know God is with you?

Responding in Prayer Give thanks to God for the ways he has been a help to you in the hard places of your life.

22 / *Psalm 31*
Rescued from Idolaters

WE LIVE IN a turbulent time. While the turbulence created by clashing belief systems seems new, the clash has been going on in different forms for thousands of years. In this psalm David affirms his choice to trust in the Lord rather than the popular idols of his age. In the current culture war we need to do the same.

 Warming Up to God Make a list of everything you have to do and give it over to God. If God blesses you with a sense of peace, just sit for a while and enjoy his presence before you move on to study.

 Read Psalm 31.

Psalm 31

For the director of music. A psalm of David.

¹In you, O Lord, I have taken refuge;
 let me never be put to shame;
 deliver me in your righteousness.
²Turn your ear to me,
 come quickly to my rescue;
 be my rock of refuge,
 a strong fortress to save me.
³Since you are my rock and my fortress,
 for the sake of your name lead and guide me.
⁴Free me from the trap that is set for me,
 for you are my refuge.
⁵Into your hands I commit my spirit;
 redeem me, O Lord, the God of truth.

⁶I hate those who cling to worthless idols;
 I trust in the Lord.
⁷I will be glad and rejoice in your love,
 for you saw my affliction
 and knew the anguish of my soul.
⁸You have not handed me over to the enemy
 but have set my feet in a spacious place.

⁹Be merciful to me, O Lord, for I am in distress;
 my eyes grow weak with sorrow,
 my soul and my body with grief.
¹⁰My life is consumed by anguish
 and my years by groaning;
 my strength fails because of my affliction,ᵍ
 and my bones grow weak.
¹¹Because of all my enemies,
 I am the utter contempt of my neighbors;
 I am a dread to my friends—
 those who see me on the street flee from me.
¹²I am forgotten by them as though I were dead;
 I have become like broken pottery.
¹³For I hear the slander of many;
 there is terror on every side;
 they conspire against me
 and plot to take my life.

¹⁴But I trust in you, O Lord;
 I say, "You are my God."
¹⁵My times are in your hands;
 deliver me from my enemies
 and from those who pursue me.

g10 Or guilt

¹⁶Let your face shine on your servant;
    save me in your unfailing love.
¹⁷Let me not be put to shame, O Lᴏʀᴅ,
    for I have cried out to you;
  but let the wicked be put to shame
    and lie silent in the grave.ʰ
¹⁸Let their lying lips be silenced,
    for with pride and contempt
    they speak arrogantly against the
      righteous.

¹⁹How great is your goodness,
    which you have stored up for those who
      fear you,
  which you bestow in the sight of men
    on those who take refuge in you.
²⁰In the shelter of your presence you
      hide them
    from the intrigues of men;

in your dwelling you keep them safe
    from accusing tongues.

²¹Praise be to the Lᴏʀᴅ,
    for he showed his wonderful love
      to me
    when I was in a besieged city.
²²In my alarm I said,
    "I am cut off from your sight!"
  Yet you heard my cry for mercy
    when I called to you for help.

²³Love the Lᴏʀᴅ, all his saints!
    The Lᴏʀᴅ preserves the faithful,
    but the proud he pays back in full.
²⁴Be strong and take heart,
    all you who hope in the Lᴏʀᴅ.

ʰ17 Hebrew *Sheol*

Discovering the Word   1. This is a psalm of urgency. What does David want from God (vv. 1–4)?
2. David feels threatened. What words does he use in these verses to describe his plight?   3. What words and ideas in verses 9–13 convey David's sense of isolation?   4. According to verses 14–18, what are several of the things David wants from God?   5. David's response to God's help is praise. What specific things does David praise God for?

Applying the Word   1. Consider a time in your life when you felt that others (perhaps non-Christians) held you in contempt and avoided you. How did it affect you?   2. What was your relationship with God like at that time?   3. What encouragement from God do you need to continue in a harsh world?

Responding in Prayer   Tell God that you trust him with the "times" of your life. Ask him to make himself known in new ways to you and your family.

---

23 / *Psalm 32*
Confession and Forgiveness

JUST AS CHOLESTEROL is the silent killer of the physical heart, guilt is the silent killer of our souls. Cholesterol accumulates slowly over the years, residue left by a poor diet, inadequate exercise and perhaps genetic malfunction. So it is with guilt. Little by little, with each act of envy, lust, anger, resentment or other sin, guilt accumulates around our spiritual hearts. The good news is that God won't let us succumb to guilt without many warnings. The exposure of guilt is not for the purpose of condemnation (as it is with Satan) but for cleansing our hearts and restoring the flow of his love.

Warming Up to God   What is causing you to feel frustrated or envious or resentful today? Give your feelings over to God one by one.

Read Psalm 32.

Psalm 32

Of David. A *maskil.*[i]

¹Blessed is he
  whose transgressions are forgiven,
  whose sins are covered.
²Blessed is the man
  whose sin the Lord does not count against
    him
  and in whose spirit is no deceit.

³When I kept silent,
  my bones wasted away
  through my groaning all day long.
⁴For day and night
  your hand was heavy upon me;
  my strength was sapped
  as in the heat of summer.   *Selah*
⁵Then I acknowledged my sin to you
  and did not cover up my iniquity.
I said, "I will confess
  my transgressions to the Lord"—
and you forgave
  the guilt of my sin.   *Selah*

⁶Therefore let everyone who is godly pray to
    you
  while you may be found;
surely when the mighty waters rise,
  they will not reach him.
⁷You are my hiding place;
  you will protect me from trouble
  and surround me with songs of deliverance.
                                              Selah

⁸I will instruct you and teach you in the way
    you should go;
  I will counsel you and watch over you.
⁹Do not be like the horse or the mule,
  which have no understanding
but must be controlled by bit and bridle
  or they will not come to you.
¹⁰Many are the woes of the wicked,
  but the Lord's unfailing love
  surrounds the man who trusts in him.

¹¹Rejoice in the Lord and be glad, you
    righteous;
  sing, all you who are upright in heart!

[i]Title: Probably a literary or musical term

   Discovering the Word 1. Verses 1 and 2 begin with the word *blessed*. How would you define *blessed* from the way David uses it in these verses?   2. David had a responsive conscience. How did his unexpressed sin affect him (vv. 3–4)?   3. It feels good to be forgiven. How does David respond in verses 6–11?   4. It is interesting that David experienced a sense of protection after receiving forgiveness (v. 7). How might unconfessed sin have made him feel vulnerable and exposed?   5. In verses 8–9 David records the Lord's promise of guidance. From these verses, what is the condition of receiving God's guidance?

   Applying the Word 1. Consider whether there are things in the past for which you are guilty but have never sought forgiveness. Name those things.   2. Are there things in the past for which you feel guilty but for which there was really no wrong done? Explain.

Responding in Prayer Ask God's forgiveness for what you have done wrong, and experience his grace.

---

24 / *Psalm 33*
Hoping in the Word

AFTER MY CONVERSION I was shocked at what happened when I picked up the Bible. I found myself enticed, confronted, spoken to and challenged. I couldn't get enough of it. Now almost thirty years later, I still can't get enough. The words that God has spoken are never outdated. In this psalm David meditates on the powerful Word of God by which he creates and sustains his world. Because of the nature of God's Word, we need to open our ears to hear as we read to understand.

Warming Up to God In order to spend time with God today—stop! Don't try to run your own life, and don't tell God what to do. Present your life to God. Ask God to bring in his order.

Read Psalm 33.

Psalm 33

¹Sing joyfully to the LORD, you righteous;
  it is fitting for the upright to praise him.
²Praise the LORD with the harp;
  make music to him on the ten-stringed
    lyre.
³Sing to him a new song;
  play skillfully, and shout for joy.

⁴For the word of the LORD is right and true;
  he is faithful in all he does.
⁵The LORD loves righteousness and justice;
  the earth is full of his unfailing love.

⁶By the word of the LORD were the heavens
    made,
  their starry host by the breath of his
    mouth.
⁷He gathers the waters of the sea into jars[j];
  he puts the deep into storehouses.
⁸Let all the earth fear the LORD;
  let all the people of the world revere him.
⁹For he spoke, and it came to be;
  he commanded, and it stood firm.
¹⁰The LORD foils the plans of the nations;
  he thwarts the purposes of the peoples.
¹¹But the plans of the LORD stand firm forever,
the purposes of his heart through all
    generations.

¹²Blessed is the nation whose God is the LORD,
  the people he chose for his inheritance.
¹³From heaven the LORD looks down
  and sees all mankind;
¹⁴from his dwelling place he watches
  all who live on earth—
¹⁵he who forms the hearts of all,
  who considers everything they do.
¹⁶No king is saved by the size of his army;
  no warrior escapes by his great strength.
¹⁷A horse is a vain hope for deliverance;
  despite all its great strength it cannot save.
¹⁸But the eyes of the LORD are on those who
    fear him,
  on those whose hope is in his unfailing
    love,
¹⁹to deliver them from death
  and keep them alive in famine.

²⁰We wait in hope for the LORD;
  he is our help and our shield.
²¹In him our hearts rejoice,
  for we trust in his holy name.
²²May your unfailing love rest upon us, O LORD,
  even as we put our hope in you.

j7 Or sea as into a heap

Discovering the Word 1. What is the emotional tone of this psalm? **2.** The word of the Lord is one of the themes of this psalm. What can you learn about God's word from verses 1–11? **3.** This psalm gives a big picture of God. Other nations thought of their god as a national deity with a limited realm of authority. Over what things does Israel's God have power (vv. 6–11)? **4.** According to verses 12–22, what is God's relationship to the world he created? **5.** What is his special relationship with "those who fear him" (vv. 18–22)?

Applying the Word 1. Imagine that God watched you conduct your day from beginning to end. What would he see about your actions? **2.** How do they express your priorities, values and commitments? **3.** What hopes for success do you have that are misdirected? (Consider whether you are trusting in your skills, your background, your education, your intelligence, your money, your influence, your friends . . . or a thousand other things.)

 Responding in Prayer After you have identified your false hopes, turn them over to God. Ask him to take them from you.

25 / *Psalm 34*
Deliverance from Trouble

DAVID WRITES THIS psalm for the spiritually immature, who need to be instructed in the ways of God. One thing David thinks we need to know is how to live in a way that brings the blessing of God. How do we face the hard times? When we hurt, we want to know: Have we done something wrong? Has God deserted us? What do we need to do to receive God's help? These are good questions. If we pay attention to David, we will get some answers.

 Warming Up to God It assaults our pride to acknowledge that there are things we don't know or problems we can't overcome. But when we stop trying to do it ourselves, we are in a position to receive the help God sends. List questions that you have for God. Don't tell him what to do, just ask. Then sit quietly for a while and listen.

Read Psalm 34.

Psalm 34ᵏ

Of David. When he pretended to be insane
before Abimelech, who drove him away,
and he left.

¹I will extol the Lord at all times;
his praise will always be on my lips.
²My soul will boast in the Lord;
let the afflicted hear and rejoice.
³Glorify the Lord with me;
let us exalt his name together.

⁴I sought the Lord, and he answered me;
he delivered me from all my fears.
⁵Those who look to him are radiant;
their faces are never covered with shame.
⁶This poor man called, and the Lord heard him;
he saved him out of all his troubles.
⁷The angel of the Lord encamps around those who fear him,
and he delivers them.

⁸Taste and see that the Lord is good;
blessed is the man who takes refuge in him.
⁹Fear the Lord, you his saints,
for those who fear him lack nothing.
¹⁰The lions may grow weak and hungry,
but those who seek the Lord lack no good thing.

¹¹Come, my children, listen to me;
I will teach you the fear of the Lord.

¹²Whoever of you loves life
and desires to see many good days,
¹³keep your tongue from evil
and your lips from speaking lies.
¹⁴Turn from evil and do good;
seek peace and pursue it.

¹⁵The eyes of the Lord are on the righteous
and his ears are attentive to their cry;
¹⁶the face of the Lord is against those who do evil,
to cut off the memory of them from the earth.

¹⁷The righteous cry out, and the Lord hears them;
he delivers them from all their troubles.
¹⁸The Lord is close to the brokenhearted
and saves those who are crushed in spirit.

¹⁹A righteous man may have many troubles,
but the Lord delivers him from them all;
²⁰he protects all his bones,
not one of them will be broken.

²¹Evil will slay the wicked;
the foes of the righteous will be condemned.
²²The Lord redeems his servants;
no one will be condemned who takes refuge in him.

ᵏ This psalm is an acrostic poem, the verses of which begin with the successive letters of the Hebrew alphabet.

Discovering the Word 1. What words does David use in verses 1–10 to express his feelings toward God? 2. What benefits are mentioned in verses 1–10 that come to those who seek God's help? 3. What do you think David means by inviting his readers to "taste and see that the Lord is good"? 4. From verses 11–22, describe a righteous person. **5.** According to what David writes, righteousness doesn't guarantee a trouble-free life. What assurances of comfort do the righteous have during times of pain?

 Applying the Word 1. How can the goodness of God be a means of strength in the problems that you face? **2.** *Fear of the Lord* is an Old Testament term for "respect and submission to God." We should be afraid of offending God with conscious acts of disobedience. What temptations are you facing now? **3.** How can learning the fear of the Lord keep you acting and thinking righteously?

 Responding in Prayer Ask God to increase your ability to "taste and see" that he is with you and that he is good.

26 / *Psalm 35*
Protection from My Enemies

YOU MIGHT BE tempted to look at this psalm as barbaric and primitive. It contains angry thoughts of revenge. When David feels hurt, the anger pours forth in an eloquent torrent. There is no sense of "I'm not supposed to feel this way." Christian maturity is not about reducing the highs and lows of emotions to a level plane, but of feeling deeply in a godly way. The issue is not how or what we feel, but what we do with our emotions. David shows the way.

 Warming Up to God Those who know God hunger for him. Before you begin your study, allow a desire for God to rise within you.

Read Psalm 35.

Psalm 35

Of David.

¹Contend, O Lord, with those who contend
  with me;
  fight against those who fight against me.
²Take up shield and buckler;
  arise and come to my aid.
³Brandish spear and javelin¹
  against those who pursue me.
Say to my soul,
  "I am your salvation."

⁴May those who seek my life
  be disgraced and put to shame;
  may those who plot my ruin
  be turned back in dismay.
⁵May they be like chaff before the wind,
  with the angel of the Lord driving them
    away;
⁶may their path be dark and slippery,
  with the angel of the Lord pursuing them.
⁷Since they hid their net for me without cause
  and without cause dug a pit for me,
⁸may ruin overtake them by surprise—

may the net they hid entangle them,
  may they fall into the pit, to their ruin.
⁹Then my soul will rejoice in the Lord
  and delight in his salvation.
¹⁰My whole being will exclaim,
  "Who is like you, O Lord?
You rescue the poor from those too strong for
    them,
  the poor and needy from those who rob
    them."

¹¹Ruthless witnesses come forward;
  they question me on things I know nothing
    about.
¹²They repay me evil for good
  and leave my soul forlorn.
¹³Yet when they were ill, I put on sackcloth
  and humbled myself with fasting.
When my prayers returned to me
    unanswered,
¹⁴ I went about mourning
  as though for my friend or brother.
I bowed my head in grief
  as though weeping for my mother.
¹⁵But when I stumbled, they gathered in glee;

13 Or and block the way

attackers gathered against me when I was
      unaware.
   They slandered me without ceasing.
¹⁶Like the ungodly they maliciously mocked ᵐ;
   they gnashed their teeth at me.
¹⁷O Lord, how long will you look on?
   Rescue my life from their ravages,
   my precious life from these lions.
¹⁸I will give you thanks in the great
      assembly;
   among throngs of people I will
      praise you.

¹⁹Let not those gloat over me
   who are my enemies without cause;
 let not those who hate me without reason
   maliciously wink the eye.
²⁰They do not speak peaceably,
   but devise false accusations
   against those who live quietly in
      the land.
²¹They gape at me and say, "Aha! Aha!
   With our own eyes we have seen it."

²²O Lord, you have seen this; be not silent.
   Do not be far from me, O Lord.

²³Awake, and rise to my defense!
   Contend for me, my God and Lord.
²⁴Vindicate me in your righteousness, O Lord
      my God;
   do not let them gloat over me.
²⁵Do not let them think, "Aha, just what we
      wanted!"
   or say, "We have swallowed him up."

²⁶May all who gloat over my distress
   be put to shame and confusion;
   may all who exalt themselves over me
   be clothed with shame and disgrace.
²⁷May those who delight in my vindication
   shout for joy and gladness;
   may they always say, "The Lord be
      exalted,
   who delights in the well-being of his
      servant."
²⁸My tongue will speak of your righteousness
   and of your praises all day long.

ᵐ16 Septuagint; Hebrew may mean *ungodly circle of mockers*.

Discovering the Word 1. In your own words describe the different kinds of misfortune David would like to see inflicted on those who have hurt him (vv. 4–6, 8, 26). 2. What reasons does David give for being so hurt and angry (vv. 4, 7, 11–16, 19–21)? 3. What do verses 11–16 reveal about David's enemies? 4. What does the cry "How long will you look on?" (v. 17) imply about David's sense of God's help? 5. David continues with the description of his adversaries' behavior. What have his enemies done in verses 19–28 to hurt him?

Applying the Word 1. We may not feel gracious toward those who hurt us, but we choose to act that way, not from feelings but from obedience to Jesus Christ. Who do you feel hostility and anger toward? 2. When we come through a trying experience with a sense of victory, it is natural to think about what a good job we have done and how cleverly we have faced our problems. David, however, avoids the temptation of personal boasting and gives praise to God. How does waiting on the Lord for help keep us from taking credit that belongs to God?

 Responding in Prayer Ask God to bless those who have hurt you.

27 / *Psalm 36*
The Fountain of the Lord's Love

I FIND LOVE difficult to talk about. For one thing, my need for love is embarrassing. When I acknowledge that I need love, it means that I am not complete in myself. To receive love, I must look to someone else. To make matters worse, I find that my need for love is inexhaustible. Yesterday's love is not enough for today.

Our need for love means we need people—friends, spouses, family members. However, our need for love is such that even if all those people loved us perfectly, we still wouldn't have enough love to meet our need. David celebrates the good news that God's supply of love is more than sufficient. God's love reaches to the heavens and has more substance than the biggest mountains.

 Warming Up to God Consider how open you are to receiving love from God, your family, friends and fellow Christians. Ask God to soften your heart as you prepare to spend time in his Word. Give over to God any hardening factors that you can discern.

 Read Psalm 36.

Psalm 36

For the director of music. Of David the servant of the LORD.

[1] An oracle is within my heart
    concerning the sinfulness of the
    wicked:[n]
There is no fear of God
    before his eyes.
[2] For in his own eyes he flatters himself
    too much to detect or hate his sin.
[3] The words of his mouth are wicked and
    deceitful;
    he has ceased to be wise and to do
    good.
[4] Even on his bed he plots evil;
    he commits himself to a sinful course
    and does not reject what is wrong.

[5] Your love, O LORD, reaches to the heavens,
    your faithfulness to the skies.
[6] Your righteousness is like the mighty
    mountains,

your justice like the great deep.
O LORD, you preserve both man and beast.
[7] How priceless is your unfailing love!
Both high and low among men
    find[o] refuge in the shadow of your
    wings.
[8] They feast on the abundance of your
    house;
    you give them drink from your river of
    delights.
[9] For with you is the fountain of life;
    in your light we see light.

[10] Continue your love to those who know you,
    your righteousness to the upright in heart.
[11] May the foot of the proud not come against
    me,
    nor the hand of the wicked drive me away.
[12] See how the evildoers lie fallen—
    thrown down, not able to rise!

[n]1 Or *heart: / Sin proceeds from the wicked.*   [o]7 Or *love, O God! / Men find; or love! / Both heavenly beings and men / find*

 Discovering the Word 1. Describe the character of a wicked person from verses 1–4. 2. Describe the dynamics of a wicked person's relationship to God. 3. What decisions does a wicked person make that lead to a sinful life (vv. 2–4)? 4. David observes that there is no fear of the Lord before the eyes of the wicked. From verses 5–9, what is it that they are blind to? 5. Initially David seems to jump without transition from musing on the wicked to writing on the love of God. However, in verses 10–12 he ties the two themes together. What do these verses tell you about David's experiences?

 Applying the Word 1. We all have sinful thoughts from time to time. The wicked, however, do not reject such thoughts. Instead they choose to entertain them and then make a commitment to act upon them. What are some thoughts you have chosen to reject recently because you knew they were wrong? 2. Consider your own ability to accept the Lord's love and his benefits. What hesitations do you have that the Lord loves you? 3. What would have to happen for you to be more open to his love?

Responding in Prayer After you have done that, give thanks to God that he has been so active in helping you choose what is right. If you find that you have let some ungodly ideas settle in your heart, reject them now and ask God to cleanse and redirect your thinking patterns.

28 / *Psalm 37:1–17*
The Peace of the Lord

COMING TO A narrow spot in the road during a Sunday afternoon ride, I got off and walked my bike. I'd gone only a short distance when a car swerved toward me. I dove for the ditch. As the car drove off, I was filled with indignation and rage. What the driver did was foolish, but I was surprised at the intensity of my fuming response. I wanted to yell and shake my fist. Something was out of place in my spirit. In my quiet time a couple of days later, I discovered a list of unresolved hurts and growing grudges. I set aside my Bible reading for the day and had a time of heart cleaning with the Lord.

David says that for us to enjoy peace in the land we have to "refrain from anger and turn from wrath." If you pay attention to what he says, then you will find a new way of coping with anger.

 Warming Up to God The first step in receiving God's peace is to stop shouting so loud. (If we aren't actually shouting out loud, we are usually doing so in our hearts.) Once we stop, he can sort things out. Put down the burdens and fights you face. Give them to God and allow him to speak peace to your heart.

Read Psalm 37:1–17.

Psalm 37*ᴾ*

Of David.

¹Do not fret because of evil men
  or be envious of those who do wrong;
²for like the grass they will soon wither,
  like green plants they will soon die away.

³Trust in the Lᴏʀᴅ and do good;
  dwell in the land and enjoy safe pasture.
⁴Delight yourself in the Lᴏʀᴅ
  and he will give you the desires of your
    heart.

⁵Commit your way to the Lᴏʀᴅ;
  trust in him and he will do this:
⁶He will make your righteousness shine like
    the dawn,
  the justice of your cause like the noonday
    sun.

⁷Be still before the Lᴏʀᴅ and wait patiently for
    him;
  do not fret when men succeed in their
    ways,
  when they carry out their wicked schemes.

⁸Refrain from anger and turn from wrath;
  do not fret—it leads only to evil.

⁹For evil men will be cut off,
  but those who hope in the Lᴏʀᴅ will inherit
    the land.

¹⁰A little while, and the wicked will be no
    more;
  though you look for them, they will not be
    found.
¹¹But the meek will inherit the land
  and enjoy great peace.

¹²The wicked plot against the righteous
  and gnash their teeth at them;
¹³but the Lord laughs at the wicked,
  for he knows their day is coming.

¹⁴The wicked draw the sword
  and bend the bow
  to bring down the poor and needy,
    to slay those whose ways are upright.
¹⁵But their swords will pierce their own hearts,
  and their bows will be broken.

¹⁶Better the little that the righteous have
  than the wealth of many wicked;
¹⁷for the power of the wicked will be broken,
  but the Lᴏʀᴅ upholds the righteous.

ᴾ This psalm is an acrostic poem, the stanzas of which begin with the successive letters of the Hebrew alphabet.

Discovering the Word 1. David gives an unusually extensive list of exhortations to his readers in verses 1–7. List them in your own words. 2. What benefits does God give to those who live this way? 3. We are not to worry when those who are evil succeed (v. 6). Why not? 4. What are the contrasts between the righteous and the wicked in verses 8–17? 5. Against the backdrop of the wicked, how is God's promise of peace and land an encouragement?

Applying the Word 1. David encourages you to "delight yourself in the Lord." What do you find delightful about knowing God? 2. What hesitations do you have that would keep you from delighting in God?

Responding in Prayer Pray for those who are angry at you. Ask God to bless them.

29 / *Psalm 37:18–40*
Our Inheritance

AS A NEW Christian, I was sure that life would be easier than it had been. I had been in deep trouble emotionally, spiritually and academically. My salvation brought visible, revolutionary changes to all those areas. Everyone knew that *something* had happened. Now looking back several decades, the changes were real. But I'm not so quick to say that becoming a Christian makes life easier. However, it is worth it. This psalm is written from David's perspective of knowing God for over eighty years. David affirms that God keeps his promises and brings rewards to those who trust him.

Warming Up to God Consider the staggering fact that the Creator of time and eternity loves you. Write down ten things you can think of about the love of God.

Read Psalm 37:18–40.

---

¹⁸The days of the blameless are known to the
　　LORD,
　　and their inheritance will endure forever.
¹⁹In times of disaster they will not wither;
　　in days of famine they will enjoy plenty.

²⁰But the wicked will perish:
　　The LORD's enemies will be like the beauty
　　　of the fields,
　　they will vanish—vanish like smoke.

²¹The wicked borrow and do not repay,
　　but the righteous give generously;
²²those the LORD blesses will inherit the land,
　　but those he curses will be cut off.

²³If the LORD delights in a man's way,
　　he makes his steps firm;
²⁴though he stumble, he will not fall,
　　for the LORD upholds him with his hand.

²⁵I was young and now I am old,
　　yet I have never seen the righteous forsaken
　　or their children begging bread.
²⁶They are always generous and lend freely;
　　their children will be blessed.

²⁷Turn from evil and do good;
　　then you will dwell in the land forever.
²⁸For the LORD loves the just
　　and will not forsake his faithful ones.

They will be protected forever,
　　but the offspring of the wicked will be cut
　　　off;
²⁹the righteous will inherit the land
　　and dwell in it forever.

³⁰The mouth of the righteous man utters
　　wisdom,
　　and his tongue speaks what is just.
³¹The law of his God is in his heart;
　　his feet do not slip.

³²The wicked lie in wait for the righteous,
　　seeking their very lives;
³³but the LORD will not leave them in their
　　　power
　　or let them be condemned when brought to
　　　trial.

³⁴Wait for the LORD
　　and keep his way.
He will exalt you to inherit the land;
　　when the wicked are cut off, you will see
　　　it.

³⁵I have seen a wicked and ruthless man
　　flourishing like a green tree in its native
　　　soil,
³⁶but he soon passed away and was no more;
　　though I looked for him, he could not be
　　　found.

37Consider the blameless, observe the upright;
    there is a future^q for the man of peace.
38But all sinners will be destroyed;
    the future^r of the wicked will be cut off.

39The salvation of the righteous comes from the
    LORD;

he is their stronghold in time of trouble.
40The LORD helps them and delivers them;
    he delivers them from the wicked and saves
      them,
because they take refuge in him.

^q37 Or *there will be posterity*   ^r38 Or *posterity*

 Discovering the Word 1. What are the contrasts between the blameless and the wicked in verses 18–24? 2. What can we know about the future of the wicked (vv. 20, 22, 28, 33–35)? 3. What are the benefits that come to the righteous in the end (vv. 18, 25, 28–29, 33, 37, 39–40)? 4. From verses 25–36, describe the character and actions of the righteous. 5. Describe the relationship between the wicked and the righteous in verses 32–40.

 Applying the Word 1. David emphasizes the theme of inheritance in these verses. How can the anticipation of a future inheritance affect the way you live today in your relationships and the way you use your money and your possessions? 2. Let's get more specific. If you knew that all you could want would be coming to you in five years, how would it affect your actions and decisions today?

 Responding in Prayer Pray for those you know who are facing hard times. Ask God to bring his comfort, protection and provision.

30 / *Psalm 38*
Rebuke and Judgment

IF I AM willing to acknowledge that God blesses me, I must be willing to acknowledge that he disciplines me as well. As the author of Hebrews writes, "the Lord disciplines those he loves." God refuses to let me go my own way. This is good news indeed! At the same time, when I talk about the blessing or the judgment of God, I must be careful. I don't understand all that the Lord does. What appears to be a blessing may not be, while what appears to be judgment may not be either. Let's see if we can gain a little light on this difficult issue from David.

Warming Up to God God is constantly rescuing us from tight spots. Some of those tight spots we are aware of; most we are not. Make a list of thank-yous to God for as many instances of his help as you can think of.

Read Psalm 38.

Psalm 38

A psalm of David. A petition.

1O LORD, do not rebuke me in your anger
    or discipline me in your wrath.
2For your arrows have pierced me,
    and your hand has come down upon me.
3Because of your wrath there is no health in
    my body;
    my bones have no soundness because of my
      sin.
4My guilt has overwhelmed me
    like a burden too heavy to bear.

5My wounds fester and are loathsome
    because of my sinful folly.
6I am bowed down and brought very low;
    all day long I go about mourning.
7My back is filled with searing pain;
    there is no health in my body.
8I am feeble and utterly crushed;
    I groan in anguish of heart.

9All my longings lie open before you, O Lord;
    my sighing is not hidden from you.
10My heart pounds, my strength fails me;
    even the light has gone from my eyes.

¹¹My friends and companions avoid me because
    of my wounds;
  my neighbors stay far away.
¹²Those who seek my life set their traps,
    those who would harm me talk of
    my ruin;
  all day long they plot deception.

¹³I am like a deaf man, who cannot
    hear,
  like a mute, who cannot open his
    mouth;
¹⁴I have become like a man who does
    not hear,
  whose mouth can offer no reply.
¹⁵I wait for you, O LORD;
  you will answer, O Lord my God.
¹⁶For I said, "Do not let them gloat

or exalt themselves over me when my foot
    slips."
¹⁷For I am about to fall,
  and my pain is ever with me.
¹⁸I confess my iniquity;
  I am troubled by my sin.
¹⁹Many are those who are my vigorous
    enemies;
  those who hate me without reason are
    numerous.
²⁰Those who repay my good with evil
  slander me when I pursue what is good.

²¹O LORD, do not forsake me;
  be not far from me, O my God.
²²Come quickly to help me,
  O Lord my Savior.

 Discovering the Word 1. David writes during a time of great pain. What images does he use to describe his situation (vv. 2–14)? 2. What reasons can you discover for his all-encompassing pain in these verses? 3. What physical, social and spiritual afflictions is David experiencing in these verses? 4. Describe David's attitude toward God in the midst of his afflictions. 5. What specific things does David want God to do to help him with his pain (vv. 15–16, 21–22)?

Applying the Word 1. What dangers and what benefits come from thinking of our physical, emotional and spiritual states as being the result of the discipline of God? 2. Although David is experiencing rejection and persecution, he acknowledges that he has sinned and shares in the responsibility for his affliction. When have you experienced pain that was at least partly your fault? How did you handle it? 3. What can you learn from David's example?

Responding in Prayer Pray for those whom you have offended this past year. Ask God's blessing on them.

---

31 / *Psalm 39*
Facing Life's End

JANE WALMSLEY, TELEVISION correspondent and commentator on American life, says that an essential element of the American psyche is the fervent belief and hope that somehow it is possible to elude death. That hope of eluding death flies in the face of reality. No one has. Life this side of the Fall is 100 percent fatal. There are some, and David would be among them, who would say that only those who have faced their death can really live life properly. In this psalm he asks God to help him take a long-term view of life, and as you shall read, that includes the impending prospect of death.

 Warming Up to God While we can never quite get our minds around this, the good news is that an eternal God can offer eternal life. Express praise and thanksgiving to our immortal God.

 Read Psalm 39.

Psalm 39

For the director of music. For Jeduthun.
A psalm of David.

¹I said, "I will watch my ways
  and keep my tongue from sin;
 I will put a muzzle on my mouth
  as long as the wicked are in my presence."
²But when I was silent and still,
  not even saying anything good,
  my anguish increased.
³My heart grew hot within me,
  and as I meditated, the fire burned;
  then I spoke with my tongue:

⁴"Show me, O LORD, my life's end
  and the number of my days;
  let me know how fleeting is my life.
⁵You have made my days a mere handbreadth;
  the span of my years is as nothing before
   you.
  Each man's life is but a breath.   *Selah*
⁶Man is a mere phantom as he goes to and fro:

He bustles about, but only in vain;
  he heaps up wealth, not knowing who will
   get it.

⁷"But now, Lord, what do I look for?
  My hope is in you.
⁸Save me from all my transgressions;
  do not make me the scorn of fools.
⁹I was silent; I would not open my mouth,
  for you are the one who has done this.
¹⁰Remove your scourge from me;
  I am overcome by the blow of your hand.
¹¹You rebuke and discipline men for their sin;
  you consume their wealth like a moth—
  each man is but a breath.   *Selah*

¹²"Hear my prayer, O LORD,
  listen to my cry for help;
  be not deaf to my weeping.
 For I dwell with you as an alien,
  a stranger, as all my fathers were.
¹³Look away from me, that I may rejoice again
  before I depart and am no more."

Discovering the Word 1. Remembering that the psalms combine life experience, knowledge of God and emotions, how would you describe David's mood and situation in this psalm? 2. David chooses to be silent in the presence of some hostile people. What effect does David's silence have on him in verses 1–6? 3. When David breaks his silence, he does so by offering a prayer to face his mortality. What does David know (vv. 5–6), and what does he want to know (v. 4)? 4. This is a psalm of judgment. In your own words describe God's approach toward sin in verses 7–13. 5. What does David desire from God for himself (vv. 8, 10)? 6. How does David seem to have come to terms with his death at the end of this passage?

Applying the Word 1. How does considering your own mortality affect the way you think of the present and the future, your possessions, and your relationships? 2. How does the knowledge of eternal life through Jesus Christ affect your reflections?

Responding in Prayer Following David's example, ask God to help you see as much about your own mortality as you can handle. Sit quietly and wait for the Lord's insight. Write down what benefits you can perceive from facing your own death.

---

32 / *Psalm 40*
Learning to Wait on the Lord

JUDY HAD A portable phone beside her. Her son's wife was expecting, and Judy was about to become a grandmother for the first time. During the entire Bible study, Judy contributed to our discussion. However, if that phone had rung with news of her daughter-in-law's labor, Judy would have been out of there in a minute. Just as Judy was prepared to receive a call and ready to respond when it came, so we should be waiting on the Lord.

Warming Up to God Jesus calls his disciples to deny themselves, take up their cross and follow him. Commit yourself, body and soul, to him. As reservations or objections rise to the surface, ask Jesus to take them from you.

Read Psalm 40.

Psalm 40

For the director of music. Of David.
A psalm.

¹I waited patiently for the LORD;
  he turned to me and heard my cry.
²He lifted me out of the slimy pit,
  out of the mud and mire;
he set my feet on a rock
  and gave me a firm place to stand.
³He put a new song in my mouth,
  a hymn of praise to our God.
Many will see and fear
  and put their trust in the LORD.

⁴Blessed is the man
  who makes the LORD his trust,
who does not look to the proud,
  to those who turn aside to false gods.ˢ
⁵Many, O LORD my God,
  are the wonders you have done.
The things you planned for us
  no one can recount to you;
were I to speak and tell of them,
  they would be too many to declare.

⁶Sacrifice and offering you did not desire,
  but my ears you have pierced t, u;
burnt offerings and sin offerings
  you did not require.
⁷Then I said, "Here I am, I have come—
  it is written about me in the scroll. ᵛ
⁸I desire to do your will, O my God;
  your law is within my heart."

⁹I proclaim righteousness in the great
    assembly;
  I do not seal my lips,

as you know, O LORD.
¹⁰I do not hide your righteousness in my heart;
  I speak of your faithfulness and salvation.
I do not conceal your love and your truth
  from the great assembly.

¹¹Do not withhold your mercy from me,
  O LORD;
  may your love and your truth always
    protect me.
¹²For troubles without number surround me;
  my sins have overtaken me, and I cannot
    see.
They are more than the hairs of my head,
  and my heart fails within me.

¹³Be pleased, O LORD, to save me;
  O LORD, come quickly to help me.
¹⁴May all who seek to take my life
  be put to shame and confusion;
may all who desire my ruin
  be turned back in disgrace.
¹⁵May those who say to me, "Aha! Aha!"
  be appalled at their own shame.
¹⁶But may all who seek you
  rejoice and be glad in you;
may those who love your salvation always
    say,
  "The LORD be exalted!"

¹⁷Yet I am poor and needy;
  may the Lord think of me.
You are my help and my deliverer;
  O my God, do not delay.

ˢ4 Or *to falsehood*   ᵗ6 Hebrew; Septuagint *but a body you have*
prepared for me (see also Symmachus and Theodotion)   ᵘ6 Or
opened   ᵛ7 Or *come / with the scroll written for me*

Discovering the Word 1. In response to God's help, David proclaims righteousness, doesn't seal his lips, doesn't hide God's righteousness and does not conceal God's love. From your reading of verses 1–10, what is he eager to make known? 2. Compare verses 1–10 with verses 11–17. How does the psalm's tone change in the second half? 3. Considering David's attitude in these verses, put into your own words David's description of life's dilemma. 4. What effect does it have on him? 5. David begins this psalm by saying he waited patiently. He concludes by asking that God would not delay. What do the elements of patience and the need for a speedy answer contribute to your understanding of what it means to wait on God?

Applying the Word 1. Waiting in a slimy pit—what a graphic picture of needing God's help! Imagine that you are in a slimy pit from which you need deliverance. What things in your life have placed you in that pit, and what makes it "slimy"? 2. As you call out for God to deliver you, what is it like to wait on God? 3. Imagine that you knew Jesus Christ was coming back in one week. How would you spend your week waiting?

Responding in Prayer Pray for your loved ones that don't yet have a relationship with Jesus Christ. Ask the Spirit to give them hungry hearts for his love.

Psalm 41

Psalm 41

For the director of music. A psalm of David.

¹Blessed is he who has regard for the weak;
the LORD delivers him in times of trouble.
²The LORD will protect him and preserve his life;
he will bless him in the land
and not surrender him to the desire of his foes.
³The LORD will sustain him on his sickbed
and restore him from his bed of illness.

⁴I said, "O LORD, have mercy on me;
heal me, for I have sinned against you."
⁵My enemies say of me in malice,
"When will he die and his name perish?"
⁶Whenever one comes to see me,
he speaks falsely, while his heart gathers slander;

then he goes out and spreads it abroad.

⁷All my enemies whisper together against me;
they imagine the worst for me, saying,
⁸"A vile disease has beset him;
he will never get up from the place where he lies."
⁹Even my close friend, whom I trusted,
he who shared my bread,
has lifted up his heel against me.

¹⁰But you, O LORD, have mercy on me;
raise me up, that I may repay them.
¹¹I know that you are pleased with me,
for my enemy does not triumph over me.
¹²In my integrity you uphold me
and set me in your presence forever.

¹³Praise be to the LORD, the God of Israel,
from everlasting to everlasting.
Amen and Amen.

33 / Psalms 42—43
Hoping in the Lord

THE AUTHOR OF Psalm 42 was a musician who used to lead the procession of worshipers to the temple in Jerusalem. But now the holy temple of God lay in ruins; the fields and vineyards were burned, and this former spiritual leader sat six hundred miles away—an exile in Babylon.

The psalmist grieved over his circumstances. Like the other holy people of his era, he had linked drawing near to God with going up to God's temple. How could he worship God now? And, as his taunters reminded him, where was God anyway?

 Warming Up to God When is it hard for you to worship God? Talk honestly with God about your struggles.

 Read Psalms 42—43.

BOOK II
Psalms 42–72

Psalm 42 [w]

For the director of music. A *maskil* [x] of the
Sons of Korah.

[1]As the deer pants for streams of water,
  so my soul pants for you, O God.
[2]My soul thirsts for God, for the living God.
  When can I go and meet with God?
[3]My tears have been my food
  day and night,
while men say to me all day long,
  "Where is your God?"
[4]These things I remember
  as I pour out my soul:
how I used to go with the multitude,
  leading the procession to the house of God,
with shouts of joy and thanksgiving
  among the festive throng.

[5]Why are you downcast, O my soul?
  Why so disturbed within me?
Put your hope in God,
  for I will yet praise him,
  my Savior and [6]my God.

My [y] soul is downcast within me;
  therefore I will remember you
from the land of the Jordan,
  the heights of Hermon—from Mount Mizar.
[7]Deep calls to deep
  in the roar of your waterfalls;
all your waves and breakers
  have swept over me.

[8]By day the LORD directs his love,
  at night his song is with me—
  a prayer to the God of my life.

[9]I say to God my Rock,

"Why have you forgotten me?
Why must I go about mourning,
  oppressed by the enemy?"
[10]My bones suffer mortal agony
  as my foes taunt me,
saying to me all day long,
  "Where is your God?"

[11]Why are you downcast, O my soul?
  Why so disturbed within me?
Put your hope in God,
  for I will yet praise him,
  my Savior and my God.

Psalm 43 [w]

[1]Vindicate me, O God,
  and plead my cause against an ungodly
    nation;
  rescue me from deceitful and wicked men.
[2]You are God my stronghold.
  Why have you rejected me?
Why must I go about mourning,
  oppressed by the enemy?
[3]Send forth your light and your truth,
  let them guide me;
let them bring me to your holy mountain,
  to the place where you dwell.
[4]Then will I go to the altar of God,
  to God, my joy and my delight.
I will praise you with the harp,
  O God, my God.

[5]Why are you downcast, O my soul?
  Why so disturbed within me?
Put your hope in God,
  for I will yet praise him,
  my Savior and my God.

[w] In many Hebrew manuscripts Psalms 42 and 43 constitute one psalm.
[x] Title: Probably a literary or musical term   [y] 5,6 A few Hebrew
manuscripts, Septuagint and Syriac; most Hebrew manuscripts *praise him
for his saving help.* / [6] *O my God, my*

Discovering the Word 1. 42:5 and 11 and 43:5 form a refrain for this psalm. What do you find in this refrain that makes it important enough to repeat? 2. The psalmist speaks honestly and openly to God. What words does he use to tell how he is feeling? 3. Why might the psalmist's honest words with God about his past and his present help to strengthen his faith? 4. Not all of what the psalmist says is about himself and his past. He also focuses on God. What aspects of God's character does he acknowledge (42:5, 8–9; 43:2, 3)? 5. How might a firm belief in a God of this character bring hope—even to an ancient Hebrew in exile?

Applying the Word 1. What kinds of things are likely to throw you into depression? 2. What do you talk about with God and with others when you are depressed? 3. Based on these psalms, when depression comes, what measures can you take to begin to cope with it?

Responding in Prayer Ask God to help you understand your own feelings of depression. Ask him to help you focus on him and to more readily turn to him, both with your own depression and with that of a troubled friend.

34 / *Psalm 44*
A Prayer When God Is Silent

"IS NOT GOD silent about Stalingrad? What do we hear above and under its ruins? Do we not hear the roar of artillery, the tumult of the world and the cries of the dying? But where is the voice of God? When we think of God, is it not suddenly so quiet, so terribly quiet, in the witch's kitchen of this hell, that one can hear a pin drop even though grenades are bursting around us? There is neither voice nor answer" (*The Silence of God*, Helmut Thielicke [Grand Rapids, Mich.: Eerdmans, 1962]). The silence of God is perhaps one of life's most frightening experiences. What do we do, how do we proceed when God is silent? Do we withdraw in fear? Do we give up all hope? This is certainly our temptation. This psalm shows us another way. It opens the way for us to pursue God even when he is silent.

Warming Up to God Think of a time when a friend did not respond to a letter or a phone message for a long time. What was your reaction to his or her silence?

Read Psalm 44.

Psalm 44

For the director of music. Of the Sons of
Korah. A *maskil.*[z]

¹We have heard with our ears, O God;
  our fathers have told us
what you did in their days,
  in days long ago.
²With your hand you drove out the nations
  and planted our fathers;
you crushed the peoples
  and made our fathers flourish.
³It was not by their sword that they won the
    land,
  nor did their arm bring them victory;
it was your right hand, your arm,
  and the light of your face, for you loved
    them.

⁴You are my King and my God,
  who decrees[a] victories for Jacob.
⁵Through you we push back our enemies;
  through your name we trample our foes.
⁶I do not trust in my bow,
  my sword does not bring me victory;
⁷but you give us victory over our enemies,
  you put our adversaries to shame.
⁸In God we make our boast all day long,

and we will praise your name forever. *Selah*

⁹But now you have rejected and humbled us;
  you no longer go out with our armies.
¹⁰You made us retreat before the enemy,
  and our adversaries have plundered us.
¹¹You gave us up to be devoured like sheep
  and have scattered us among the nations.
¹²You sold your people for a pittance,
  gaining nothing from their sale.

¹³You have made us a reproach to our
    neighbors,
  the scorn and derision of those around us.
¹⁴You have made us a byword among the
    nations;
  the peoples shake their heads at us.
¹⁵My disgrace is before me all day long,
  and my face is covered with shame
¹⁶at the taunts of those who reproach and revile
    me,
  because of the enemy, who is bent on
    revenge.

¹⁷All this happened to us,
  though we had not forgotten you
  or been false to your covenant.

---

[z] Title: Probably a literary or musical term   [a]4 Septuagint, Aquila and
Syriac; Hebrew *King, O God; / command*

18Our hearts had not turned back;
our feet had not strayed from your path.
19But you crushed us and made us a haunt for
jackals
and covered us over with deep darkness.

20If we had forgotten the name of our God
or spread out our hands to a foreign god,
21would not God have discovered it,
since he knows the secrets of the heart?
22Yet for your sake we face death all day long;

we are considered as sheep to be
slaughtered.

23Awake, O Lord! Why do you sleep?
Rouse yourself! Do not reject us forever.
24Why do you hide your face
and forget our misery and oppression?

25We are brought down to the dust;
our bodies cling to the ground.
26Rise up and help us;
redeem us because of your unfailing love.

 Discovering the Word 1. How does the writer contrast God in the past (vv. 1–8) with God in the present (vv. 9–16)? 2. The psalmist argues with God that the situation he and his people find themselves in is not fair. How does he express this (vv. 17–22)? 3. What is the significance of this plea for fairness and justice? 4. The psalmist summarizes his accusations of God in verses 23 and 24. What does he accuse God of? 5. In the final phrase of the psalm (v. 26), the writer appeals to God's unfailing love. This is a dramatic contrast to the accusations he has just made. How can these views of God be reconciled?

 Applying the Word 1. Think of a time when it seemed God was silent. How did your experience at that time compare with the experiences described in this psalm? 2. Think of a time when you experienced God's unfailing love. How would you describe that experience? 3. What encouragement does this psalm offer you for times when God seems silent?

 Responding in Prayer Ask God to help you to understand his ways and grant you peace when you are waiting for his voice.

---

35 / *Psalm 45*
A Wedding Song

THE EXCITEMENT OF a wedding day! Brides in beautiful gowns, an abundance of sweet-smelling flowers, nervous grooms and fathers waiting in the wings for the bride to make her entrance—and all are overflowing with a sense of expectancy that fills the air. The reason behind all of the extravagance, beyond the legal joining of two individuals together, is to celebrate a wonderful event and to capture it as something to remember for all time. This psalm is a celebration, both for the joy of the day and for the joy that is still to come.

Warming Up to God Reflect for a moment on the character of your God. He is the powerful judge and the Creator who flung the stars into space. But he is also the one who knows and loves you and became your Savior. Let this knowledge fill you with peace as you look to the words of God.

Read Psalm 45.

Psalm 45

For the director of music. To ⌊the tune of⌋
"Lilies." Of the Sons of Korah. A *maskil.*ᵇ
A wedding song.

1My heart is stirred by a noble theme
as I recite my verses for the king;
my tongue is the pen of a skillful writer.

2You are the most excellent of men
and your lips have been anointed with
grace,
since God has blessed you forever.
3Gird your sword upon your side, O mighty
one;
clothe yourself with splendor and majesty.

ᵇTitle: Probably a literary or musical term

⁴In your majesty ride forth victoriously
  in behalf of truth, humility and
    righteousness;
  let your right hand display awesome deeds.
⁵Let your sharp arrows pierce the hearts of the
    king's enemies;
  let the nations fall beneath your feet.
⁶Your throne, O God, will last for ever and
    ever;
  a scepter of justice will be the scepter of
    your kingdom.
⁷You love righteousness and hate wickedness;
  therefore God, your God, has set you above
    your companions
  by anointing you with the oil of joy.
⁸All your robes are fragrant with myrrh and
    aloes and cassia;
  from palaces adorned with ivory
  the music of the strings makes you glad.
⁹Daughters of kings are among your honored
    women;
  at your right hand is the royal bride in gold
    of Ophir.
¹⁰Listen, O daughter, consider and give ear:

  Forget your people and your father's house.
¹¹The king is enthralled by your beauty;
  honor him, for he is your lord.
¹²The Daughter of Tyre will come with a gift,ᶜ
  men of wealth will seek your favor.
¹³All glorious is the princess within ˻her
    chamber˼;
  her gown is interwoven with gold.
¹⁴In embroidered garments she is led to the
    king;
  her virgin companions follow her
  and are brought to you.
¹⁵They are led in with joy and gladness;
  they enter the palace of the king.

¹⁶Your sons will take the place of your fathers;
  you will make them princes throughout the
    land.
¹⁷I will perpetuate your memory through all
    generations;
  therefore the nations will praise you for
    ever and ever.

ᶜ12 Or *A Tyrian robe is among the gifts*

 Discovering the Word 1. Psalm 45 is a wedding song celebrating the marriage of a king of David's dynasty to a foreign princess. Twice in the psalm the poet refers to himself. What does he say are his purposes for writing (vv. 1, 17)? 2. What are the characteristics of this king? 3. How could these verses (particularly 6–7) refer to more than David's reign? 4. Verses 6 and 7 are quoted in Hebrews 1 and are used to describe the reign of Jesus Christ. How could the description of the king in this passage be applied to Christ? 5. What are the characteristics of the bride, and what is the attitude surrounding her coming (vv. 10–16)?

 Applying the Word 1. We are Christ's bride. What promises do you see for yourself in this passage? 2. What kind of a response does seeing the majesty of Christ cause in your own life?

 Responding in Prayer Thank God that your heart has been "stirred by a noble theme"—the promises of the King coming for his bride. Praise him for his majesty and the overwhelming awe that you feel because he has chosen *you* to be his bride.

---

36 / *Psalm 46*
Still Point in a Turning World

MARTIN LUTHER'S FAMOUS hymn "A Mighty Fortress Is Our God" is based on Psalm 46. This psalm celebrates Jerusalem as the city of God, the sure foundation for the kingdom of God. Today we can find spiritual strength and security in this psalm, especially when everything else is so topsy-turvy.

Warming Up to God Consider the times of loss, tragedy or high anxiety when you thought your world was falling apart. How were you able to find the strength to face the dawn of another day?

Read Psalm 46.

Psalm 46

For the director of music. Of the Sons of
Korah. According to *alamoth.*ᵈ A song.

¹God is our refuge and strength,
an ever-present help in trouble.
²Therefore we will not fear, though the earth
give way
and the mountains fall into the heart of the
sea,
³though its waters roar and foam
and the mountains quake with their
surging.   *Selah*

⁴There is a river whose streams make glad the
city of God,
the holy place where the Most High dwells.
⁵God is within her, she will not fall;
God will help her at break of day.

⁶Nations are in uproar, kingdoms fall;
he lifts his voice, the earth melts.
⁷The LORD Almighty is with us;
the God of Jacob is our fortress.   *Selah*

⁸Come and see the works of the LORD,
the desolations he has brought on the
earth.
⁹He makes wars cease to the ends of the earth;
he breaks the bow and shatters the spear,
he burns the shieldsᵉ with fire.
¹⁰"Be still, and know that I am God;
I will be exalted among the nations,
I will be exalted in the earth."

¹¹The LORD Almighty is with us;
the God of Jacob is our fortress.   *Selah*

ᵈTitle: Probably a musical term   ᵉ9 Or *chariots*

Discovering the Word 1. This psalm readily falls into three stanzas (vv. 1–3, 4–6 and 8–10) plus two refrains, or chorus lines (vv. 7, 11). What themes emerge in each section? 2. What images of a world falling apart do you see in these verses? 3. What truth about God is conveyed here in contrast to the world? 4. What effect does God's triumph over the nations have on the people who draw their strength from him (vv. 8–10)? 5. Where does one find stillness and security in the midst of violent forces unleashed all around (vv. 10–11)?

Applying the Word 1. What in your life is threatening or pounding away at your sense of security in God? 2. How can you remain still (v. 10) and know God's fortresslike strength (vv. 7, 11) in the midst of a world falling apart?

Responding in Prayer As God has triumphed, and will triumph, over all that wars against the city of Jerusalem and the soul of the believer, how can you exalt him among the nations? Spend some time being still and centering on him.

37 / *Psalm 47*
Being Devoted to God

THE SIGN OF a spiritually healthy heart is gratitude and affection. You will discover that after you have spent time with God, there rises from within your heart a deep sense of gratitude. Galatians 4:6 says, "Because you are sons, God sent the Spirit of his Son into our hearts, the Spirit who calls out, '*Abba,* Father.'" We can actually sense the Spirit within us as he cries, "Abba, Father."

Warming Up to God Make a list of things you are thankful for. While you may not be able to express gratitude right now, it will come in time if you continue to walk in this inner spiritual pilgrimage. If you do feel gratitude, sit for a while in heartfelt thanks to God.

 Read Psalm 47.

Psalm 47

For the director of music. Of the Sons of
Korah. A psalm.

¹Clap your hands, all you nations;
  shout to God with cries of joy.
²How awesome is the LORD Most High,
  the great King over all the earth!
³He subdued nations under us,
  peoples under our feet.
⁴He chose our inheritance for us,
  the pride of Jacob, whom he loved.   *Selah*

⁵God has ascended amid shouts of joy,
the LORD amid the sounding of trumpets.
⁶Sing praises to God, sing praises;
  sing praises to our King, sing praises.

⁷For God is the King of all the earth;
  sing to him a psalm*ᶠ* of praise.
⁸God reigns over the nations;
  God is seated on his holy throne.
⁹The nobles of the nations assemble
  as the people of the God of Abraham,
for the kings*ᵍ* of the earth belong to God;
  he is greatly exalted.

f7 Or a maskil (probably a literary or musical term)   g9 Or shields

---

Discovering the Word 1. What is the psalmist thankful for (vv. 2–4)? 2. How is God described in each
verse? 3. What is revealed about God's relationship with the people? 4. What actions of joy and gratitude do you see in these verses (vv. 1, 5–7)?

Applying the Word 1. How would you feel using the same outward expressions of joy as the psalmist?
2. The psalmist sings, claps, sacrifices and invites others to share in his joy in God. What ways can you
outwardly show your joy in the Lord? 3. The Holy Spirit within us is continually offering praise. If you can, allow
yourself to join the Spirit in praise. Try to write a psalm to the Lord, including in it reasons you enjoy knowing God.
If you haven't come to the place of heartfelt worship, don't try to generate what you don't feel. You might want to
sing a song or hymn that you can sing with meaning. Or perhaps play some recorded music that reflects your
mood.

Responding in Prayer Ask God to give you the courage to walk in honesty until he brings you into the
place of inner praise.

Psalms 48—49

Psalm 48

A song. A psalm of the Sons of Korah.

¹Great is the LORD, and most worthy of praise,
  in the city of our God, his holy mountain.
²It is beautiful in its loftiness,
  the joy of the whole earth.
Like the utmost heights of Zaphonʰ is Mount
    Zion,
  theⁱ city of the Great King.
³God is in her citadels;
  he has shown himself to be her fortress.

⁴When the kings joined forces,
  when they advanced together,
⁵they saw ⌐her⌐ and were astounded;
  they fled in terror.
⁶Trembling seized them there,
  pain like that of a woman in labor.

⁷You destroyed them like ships of Tarshish
  shattered by an east wind.

⁸As we have heard,
  so have we seen
in the city of the LORD Almighty,
  in the city of our God:
  God makes her secure forever.   *Selah*

⁹Within your temple, O God,
  we meditate on your unfailing love.
¹⁰Like your name, O God,
  your praise reaches to the ends of the earth;
  your right hand is filled with righteousness.
¹¹Mount Zion rejoices,
  the villages of Judah are glad
  because of your judgments.

¹²Walk about Zion, go around her,

h2 Zaphon can refer to a sacred mountain or the direction north.
i2 Or earth, / Mount Zion, on the northern side / of the

count her towers,
¹³consider well her ramparts,
    view her citadels,
    that you may tell of them to the next
        generation.
¹⁴For this God is our God for ever and ever;
    he will be our guide even to the end.

Psalm 49

For the director of music. Of the Sons of
    Korah. A psalm.

¹Hear this, all you peoples;
    listen, all who live in this world,
²both low and high,
    rich and poor alike:
³My mouth will speak words of wisdom;
    the utterance from my heart will give
        understanding.
⁴I will turn my ear to a proverb;
    with the harp I will expound my riddle:

⁵Why should I fear when evil days come,
    when wicked deceivers surround me—
⁶those who trust in their wealth
    and boast of their great riches?
⁷No man can redeem the life of another
    or give to God a ransom for him—
⁸the ransom for a life is costly,
    no payment is ever enough—
⁹that he should live on forever
    and not see decay.

¹⁰For all can see that wise men die;
    the foolish and the senseless alike perish
    and leave their wealth to others.

¹¹Their tombs will remain their houses[j]
        forever,
    their dwellings for endless generations,
    though they had[k] named lands after
        themselves.

¹²But man, despite his riches, does not endure;
    he is[l] like the beasts that perish.

¹³This is the fate of those who trust in
        themselves,
    and of their followers, who approve their
        sayings.   *Selah*
¹⁴Like sheep they are destined for the grave,[m]
    and death will feed on them.
The upright will rule over them in the
        morning;
    their forms will decay in the grave,[m]
    far from their princely mansions.
¹⁵But God will redeem my life[n] from the grave;
    he will surely take me to himself.   *Selah*

¹⁶Do not be overawed when a man grows rich,
    when the splendor of his house increases;
¹⁷for he will take nothing with him when he
        dies,
    his splendor will not descend with him.
¹⁸Though while he lived he counted himself
        blessed—
    and men praise you when you prosper—
¹⁹he will join the generation of his fathers,
    who will never see the light ⌊of life⌋.

²⁰A man who has riches without understanding
    is like the beasts that perish.

*j 11 Septuagint and Syriac; Hebrew In their thoughts their houses will
remain   k 11 Or l for they have   l 12 Hebrew; Septuagint and
Syriac read verse 12 the same as verse 20.   m 14 Hebrew Sheol; also
in verse 15   n 15 Or soul*

---

38 / *Psalm 50*
Offering Thanks

"HOW ARE YOU?" we ask, and the response generally comes back, "Fine." Often we follow that with the question
"Been busy?" and the answer is invariably yes. We live in a culture of busyness, and sometimes that overlaps into
our Christian lives. We can become so busy working for God, doing good deeds, that we don't have time to offer
him our praise and thanksgiving. This psalm helps us get our focus back to the fact that we are created to
worship God.

 Warming Up to God When have you gotten caught up in the things you *do* for God to the extent that you
neglected worshiping him?

Read Psalm 50.

Psalm 50

A psalm of Asaph.

¹The Mighty One, God, the Lord,
  speaks and summons the earth
  from the rising of the sun to the place
    where it sets.
²From Zion, perfect in beauty,
  God shines forth.
³Our God comes and will not be silent;
  a fire devours before him,
  and around him a tempest rages.
⁴He summons the heavens above,
  and the earth, that he may judge his
    people:
⁵"Gather to me my consecrated ones,
  who made a covenant with me by
    sacrifice."
⁶And the heavens proclaim his righteousness,
  for God himself is judge.   *Selah*

⁷"Hear, O my people, and I will speak,
  O Israel, and I will testify against you:
  I am God, your God.
⁸I do not rebuke you for your sacrifices
  or your burnt offerings, which are ever
    before me.
⁹I have no need of a bull from your stall
  or of goats from your pens,
¹⁰for every animal of the forest is mine,
  and the cattle on a thousand hills.
¹¹I know every bird in the mountains,
  and the creatures of the field are mine.
¹²If I were hungry I would not tell you,

for the world is mine, and all that is in it.
¹³Do I eat the flesh of bulls
  or drink the blood of goats?
¹⁴Sacrifice thank offerings to God,
  fulfill your vows to the Most High,
¹⁵and call upon me in the day of trouble;
  I will deliver you, and you will honor me."

¹⁶But to the wicked, God says:

"What right have you to recite my laws
  or take my covenant on your lips?
¹⁷You hate my instruction
  and cast my words behind you.
¹⁸When you see a thief, you join with him;
  you throw in your lot with adulterers.
¹⁹You use your mouth for evil
  and harness your tongue to deceit.
²⁰You speak continually against your brother
  and slander your own mother's son.
²¹These things you have done and I kept silent;
  you thought I was altogether*ᵒ* like you.
  But I will rebuke you
  and accuse you to your face.

²²"Consider this, you who forget God,
  or I will tear you to pieces, with none to
    rescue:
²³He who sacrifices thank offerings honors me,
  and he prepares the way
  so that I may show him*ᵖ* the salvation of
    God."

*ᵒ21 Or thought the 'I am' was   ᵖ23 Or and to him who considers his
way / I will show*

 Discovering the Word 1. How is God described in verses 1–6? 2. God does not say that sacrifices are wrong (v. 8), but what does he want the people to understand about their offerings to him (vv. 9–15)? 3. How does the tone of verses 16–22 change? 4. What evil deeds have the wicked done (vv. 16–22)? 5. How would "thank offerings" help them to understand salvation (vv. 14–15, 23)?

Applying the Word 1. What would a "thank offering" to God look like for you? 2. God promised that we can call upon him "in the day of trouble" and he will deliver us (v. 15). In what way would you like to call upon God today?

Responding in Prayer Make your prayers an offering of praise and thanksgiving for God's work in your life.

39 / *Psalm 51*
Praying Our Sin

ALONGSIDE THE BASIC fact that God made us good (Ps 8) is the equally basic fact that we have gone wrong. We pray our sins to get to the truth about ourselves and to find out how God treats sinners. Our experience of sin does not consist in doing some bad things but in being bad. It is a fundamental condition of our existence, not a temporary lapse into error. Praying our sin isn't resolving not to sin anymore; it is discovering what God has resolved to do with us as sinners.

Warming Up to God   As Christians, we know we are sinful. Why then is it so painful to be confronted with a specific sin? What sin have you been avoiding talking to God about? Take it to God and experience his forgiveness.

   Read Psalm 51.

Psalm 51

For the director of music. A psalm of David. When the prophet Nathan came to him after David had committed adultery with Bathsheba.

¹Have mercy on me, O God,
    according to your unfailing love;
according to your great compassion
    blot out my transgressions.
²Wash away all my iniquity
    and cleanse me from my sin.

³For I know my transgressions,
    and my sin is always before me.
⁴Against you, you only, have I sinned
    and done what is evil in your sight,
so that you are proved right when you speak
    and justified when you judge.
⁵Surely I was sinful at birth,
    sinful from the time my mother conceived
        me.
⁶Surely you desire truth in the inner parts*q*;
    you teach*r* me wisdom in the inmost
        place.

⁷Cleanse me with hyssop, and I will be clean;
    wash me, and I will be whiter than snow.
⁸Let me hear joy and gladness;
    let the bones you have crushed rejoice.
⁹Hide your face from my sins

and blot out all my iniquity.

¹⁰Create in me a pure heart, O God,
    and renew a steadfast spirit within me.
¹¹Do not cast me from your presence
    or take your Holy Spirit from me.
¹²Restore to me the joy of your salvation
    and grant me a willing spirit, to sustain me.

¹³Then I will teach transgressors your ways,
    and sinners will turn back to you.
¹⁴Save me from bloodguilt, O God,
    the God who saves me,
    and my tongue will sing of your
        righteousness.
¹⁵O Lord, open my lips,
    and my mouth will declare your praise.
¹⁶You do not delight in sacrifice, or I would
        bring it;
    you do not take pleasure in burnt offerings.
¹⁷The sacrifices of God are*s* a broken spirit;
    a broken and contrite heart,
    O God, you will not despise.

¹⁸In your good pleasure make Zion prosper;
    build up the walls of Jerusalem.
¹⁹Then there will be righteous sacrifices,
    whole burnt offerings to delight you;
    then bulls will be offered on your altar.

q6 The meaning of the Hebrew for this phrase is uncertain.   r6 Or you desired . . . ; / you taught   s17 Or My sacrifice, O God, is

---

Discovering the Word   **1.** List the different synonyms for sin in David's prayer.   **2.** What is God asked to do about sin? (Count and name the verbs.)   **3.** Verse 10 is the center sentence. How does it center the prayer?   **4.** Forgiveness is an internal action with external consequences. What are some of them (vv. 13–17)?   **5.** What do you understand a "broken and contrite heart" to be (v. 17)?   **6.** According to verses 18–19, what is the relationship between personal forgiveness and social righteousness?

Applying the Word 1. When have you had a "broken and contrite heart"? 2. Psalm 51 makes us aware of how sinful we are, and it makes us less actively sinful. How do you see it working that way in you?

Responding in Prayer Be quiet before God. In silence confess your sins to him. Accept his forgiveness and grace.

Psalms 52—54

Psalm 52

For the director of music. A *maskil*[t]
of David. When Doeg the Edomite had
gone to Saul and told him: "David has gone
to the house of Ahimelech."

¹Why do you boast of evil, you mighty man?
  Why do you boast all day long,
  you who are a disgrace in the eyes of God?
²Your tongue plots destruction;
  it is like a sharpened razor,
  you who practice deceit.
³You love evil rather than good,
  falsehood rather than speaking the truth.
                                    Selah
⁴You love every harmful word,
  O you deceitful tongue!

⁵Surely God will bring you down to everlasting
    ruin:
  He will snatch you up and tear you from
      your tent;
  he will uproot you from the land of the
      living.   *Selah*
⁶The righteous will see and fear;
  they will laugh at him, saying,
⁷"Here now is the man
  who did not make God his stronghold
 but trusted in his great wealth
  and grew strong by destroying others!"

⁸But I am like an olive tree
  flourishing in the house of God;
 I trust in God's unfailing love
  for ever and ever.
⁹I will praise you forever for what you have
    done;
  in your name I will hope, for your name is
      good.
 I will praise you in the presence of your
    saints.

Psalm 53

For the director of music. According to
  mahalath.[u] A *maskil*[t] of David.

¹The fool says in his heart,
  "There is no God."
They are corrupt, and their ways
    are vile;
  there is no one who does good.

²God looks down from heaven
  on the sons of men
to see if there are any who understand,
  any who seek God.
³Everyone has turned away,
  they have together become corrupt;
there is no one who does good,
  not even one.

⁴Will the evildoers never learn—
  those who devour my people as men eat
      bread
  and who do not call on God?
⁵There they were, overwhelmed with
      dread,
  where there was nothing to dread.
God scattered the bones of those who
      attacked you;
  you put them to shame, for God despised
      them.

⁶Oh, that salvation for Israel would come out
      of Zion!
  When God restores the fortunes of his
      people,
  let Jacob rejoice and Israel be glad!

[t]Title: Probably a literary or musical term   [u]Title: Probably a musical term

Psalm 54

For the director of music. With stringed instruments. A *maskil*ᵛ of David. When the Ziphites had gone to Saul and said, "Is not David hiding among us?"

¹Save me, O God, by your name;
    vindicate me by your might.
²Hear my prayer, O God;
    listen to the words of my mouth.

³Strangers are attacking me;
    ruthless men seek my life—
    men without regard for God.   *Selah*

⁴Surely God is my help;
    the Lord is the one who sustains me.

⁵Let evil recoil on those who slander me;
    in your faithfulness destroy them.

⁶I will sacrifice a freewill offering to you;
    I will praise your name, O LORD,
    for it is good.
⁷For he has delivered me from all my troubles,
    and my eyes have looked in triumph on my
        foes.

ᵛ Title: Probably a literary or musical term

40 / *Psalm 55*
Expressing Feelings to God

"I WISH I could talk to God about this. But I just can't. I can't get the words out. I feel so guilty because I can't trust him with the things that are most important to me."

Learning to express our feelings to God is not easy. The passionate, emotionally unrestrained prayers of the Bible may not be the kind we grew up with. We may find, in fact, that the prayers of the Bible make us anxious. We wonder how God would respond if we told him what we really felt.

Learning to express our feelings to God is a vital part of growing in intimacy with him. When we can tell him of our sorrow and anger and confusion and joy, we will experience his faithful love in new ways. In his Word we find many models of godly people who openly expressed their deepest feelings to God.

 Warming Up to God When you are sad or angry and you are talking to God, how do you expect him to respond? Talk to God about your concerns and fears.

 Read Psalm 55.

Psalm 55

For the director of music. With stringed instruments. A *maskil*ʷ of David.

¹Listen to my prayer, O God,
    do not ignore my plea;
² hear me and answer me.
My thoughts trouble me and I am distraught
³ at the voice of the enemy,
    at the stares of the wicked;
for they bring down suffering upon me
    and revile me in their anger.

⁴My heart is in anguish within me;
    the terrors of death assail me.
⁵Fear and trembling have beset me;
    horror has overwhelmed me.
⁶I said, "Oh, that I had the wings of a dove!

I would fly away and be at rest—
⁷I would flee far away
    and stay in the desert;   *Selah*
⁸I would hurry to my place of shelter,
    far from the tempest and storm."

⁹Confuse the wicked, O Lord, confound their
        speech,
    for I see violence and strife in the city.
¹⁰Day and night they prowl about on its walls;
    malice and abuse are within it.
¹¹Destructive forces are at work in the city;
    threats and lies never leave its streets.

¹²If an enemy were insulting me,
    I could endure it;
    if a foe were raising himself against me,

ʷ Title: Probably a literary or musical term

I could hide from him.
¹³But it is you, a man like myself,
my companion, my close friend,
¹⁴with whom I once enjoyed sweet fellowship
as we walked with the throng at the house
of God.

¹⁵Let death take my enemies by surprise;
let them go down alive to the grave,ˣ
for evil finds lodging among them.

¹⁶But I call to God,
and the Lᴏʀᴅ saves me.
¹⁷Evening, morning and noon
I cry out in distress,
and he hears my voice.
¹⁸He ransoms me unharmed
from the battle waged against me,
even though many oppose me.
¹⁹God, who is enthroned forever,
will hear them and afflict them—   *Selah*   ˣ15 Hebrew *Sheol*

men who never change their ways
and have no fear of God.

²⁰My companion attacks his friends;
he violates his covenant.
²¹His speech is smooth as butter,
yet war is in his heart;
his words are more soothing than oil,
yet they are drawn swords.

²²Cast your cares on the Lᴏʀᴅ
and he will sustain you;
he will never let the righteous fall.
²³But you, O God, will bring down the wicked
into the pit of corruption;
bloodthirsty and deceitful men
will not live out half their days.

But as for me, I trust in you.

Discovering the Word **1.** What feelings are described in each section of Psalm 55? **2.** Describe the image of God that you find in this passage. **3.** What seems to be causing the psalmist to suffer (vv. 12–15, 20–21)? **4.** What does the psalmist expect God to do for him (vv. 16–19, 22–23)?

Applying the Word **1.** We often have a negative response to our "negative" feelings. What thoughts do you typically have in response to your feelings of anger, depression or fear? **2.** How does it affect you to know that God is near to you when you are in pain?

Responding in Prayer How would you like God to help you to grow in your ability to express your feelings to him?

Psalm 56

Psalm 56

For the director of music. To ⌊the tune of⌋ "A Dove on Distant Oaks." Of David. A *miktam.ʸ* When the Philistines had seized him in Gath.

¹Be merciful to me, O God, for men hotly
pursue me;
all day long they press their attack.
²My slanderers pursue me all day long;
many are attacking me in their pride.

³When I am afraid,
I will trust in you.
⁴In God, whose word I praise,
in God I trust; I will not be afraid.
What can mortal man do to me?

⁵All day long they twist my words;
they are always plotting to harm me.
⁶They conspire, they lurk,
they watch my steps,
eager to take my life.

⁷On no account let them escape;
in your anger, O God, bring down the
nations.
⁸Record my lament;
list my tears on your scrollᶻ—
are they not in your record?

⁹Then my enemies will turn back
when I call for help.
By this I will know that God is for me.

ʸTitle: Probably a literary or musical term   ᶻ8 Or / *put my tears in your wineskin*

¹⁰In God, whose word I praise,
    in the L<small>ORD</small>, whose word I praise—
¹¹in God I trust; I will not be afraid.
    What can man do to me?

¹²I am under vows to you, O God;
    I will present my thank offerings to you.

¹³For you have delivered me^a from death
    and my feet from stumbling,
  that I may walk before God
    in the light of life.^b

^a13 Or *my soul*   ^b13 Or *the land of the living*

41 / *Psalm 57*
A Prayer of Distress

OUR NEED FOR God's presence and care in our lives is a daily reality. However, when life is good we may be unaware of our need. As C. S. Lewis wrote in *A Grief Observed*, sometimes "life is so good," we may be "tempted to forget our need of him." But there are times in our lives when we are acutely aware of our need of God. In times of distress, when we are threatened with loss or harm or even with death, we remember our need for God and we turn to him with great urgency. Some people feel that they cannot bring their troubles to God. I have often heard people say, "I can't turn to God when I am in distress if I haven't been doing this all along." And I have heard other people say, "I can't bother God with this. There are many people hurting more than I am." But God invites us to turn to him when we are in distress. Repeatedly in the Scriptures God says to us, "Call on me in the day of trouble and I will answer you." This is exactly what this psalm helps us to do.

 Warming Up to God What mental pictures does the word *distress* create for you?

 Read Psalm 57.

Psalm 57

For the director of music. ⌐To the tune of⌐
"Do Not Destroy." Of David. A *miktam.*^c
When he had fled from Saul into the cave.

¹Have mercy on me, O God, have mercy on
    me,
  for in you my soul takes refuge.
I will take refuge in the shadow of your wings
    until the disaster has passed.

²I cry out to God Most High,
    to God, who fulfills ⌐his purpose⌐ for me.
³He sends from heaven and saves me,
    rebuking those who hotly pursue me; *Selah*
  God sends his love and his faithfulness.

⁴I am in the midst of lions;
    I lie among ravenous beasts—
men whose teeth are spears and arrows,
    whose tongues are sharp swords.

⁵Be exalted, O God, above the heavens;
    let your glory be over all the earth.

⁶They spread a net for my feet—
    I was bowed down in distress.
They dug a pit in my path—
    but they have fallen into it themselves.
                      Selah

⁷My heart is steadfast, O God,
    my heart is steadfast;
  I will sing and make music.
⁸Awake, my soul!
    Awake, harp and lyre!
  I will awaken the dawn.

⁹I will praise you, O Lord, among the nations;
    I will sing of you among the peoples.
¹⁰For great is your love, reaching to the
          heavens;
  your faithfulness reaches to the skies.

¹¹Be exalted, O God, above the heavens;
    let your glory be over all the earth.

^cTitle: Probably a literary or musical term

Discovering the Word 1. The title and the introduction to this psalm suggest that this psalm was written by David when he fled into a cave, hiding from King Saul, who wanted to kill him. What image does David use in verse 1 to describe his experience of God as a safe shelter? 2. What metaphors does David use in verse 4 to describe the danger he found himself in? 3. In his time of distress David cried out to God (v. 2). What does it mean to "cry out" to God? 4. How did God intervene for David in his time of distress (vv. 3, 6)? 5. David responds to God's care in verse 7 by saying that his heart is steadfast. What is the significance of this response?

Applying the Word 1. Think of a time when you were in distress. What was your experience of God like during that time? 2. How might this psalm encourage you in times of distress?

Responding in Prayer David responds to God's care with praise in verses 9–11. Offer your praises to God for his work in your life.

Psalms 58—61

Psalm 58

For the director of music. ⌞To the tune of⌟ "Do Not Destroy." Of David. A *miktam.ᵈ*

¹Do you rulers indeed speak justly?
  Do you judge uprightly among men?
²No, in your heart you devise injustice,
  and your hands mete out violence on the earth.
³Even from birth the wicked go astray;
  from the womb they are wayward and speak lies.
⁴Their venom is like the venom of a snake,
  like that of a cobra that has stopped its ears,
⁵that will not heed the tune of the charmer,
  however skillful the enchanter may be.

⁶Break the teeth in their mouths, O God;
  tear out, O Lᴏʀᴅ, the fangs of the lions!
⁷Let them vanish like water that flows away;
  when they draw the bow, let their arrows be blunted.
⁸Like a slug melting away as it moves along,
  like a stillborn child, may they not see the sun.

⁹Before your pots can feel ⌞the heat of⌟ the thorns—
  whether they be green or dry—the wicked will be swept away.ᵉ
¹⁰The righteous will be glad when they are avenged,
  when they bathe their feet in the blood of the wicked.
¹¹Then men will say,
  "Surely the righteous still are rewarded;

surely there is a God who judges the earth."

Psalm 59

For the director of music. ⌞To the tune of⌟ "Do Not Destroy." Of David. A *miktam.ᵈ* When Saul had sent men to watch David's house in order to kill him.

¹Deliver me from my enemies, O God;
  protect me from those who rise up against me.
²Deliver me from evildoers
  and save me from bloodthirsty men.

³See how they lie in wait for me!
  Fierce men conspire against me
  for no offense or sin of mine, O Lᴏʀᴅ.
⁴I have done no wrong, yet they are ready to attack me.
  Arise to help me; look on my plight!
⁵O Lᴏʀᴅ God Almighty, the God of Israel,
  rouse yourself to punish all the nations;
  show no mercy to wicked traitors.   *Selah*

⁶They return at evening,
  snarling like dogs,
  and prowl about the city.
⁷See what they spew from their mouths—
  they spew out swords from their lips,
  and they say, "Who can hear us?"
⁸But you, O Lᴏʀᴅ, laugh at them;
  you scoff at all those nations.

⁹O my Strength, I watch for you;

ᵈTitle: Probably a literary or musical term   ᵉ9 The meaning of the Hebrew for this verse is uncertain.

you, O God, are my fortress, ¹⁰my loving
    God.

God will go before me
    and will let me gloat over those who
        slander me.
¹¹But do not kill them, O Lord our shield,ᶠ
    or my people will forget.
In your might make them wander about,
    and bring them down.
¹²For the sins of their mouths,
    for the words of their lips,
    let them be caught in their pride.
For the curses and lies they utter,
¹³   consume them in wrath,
    consume them till they are no more.
Then it will be known to the ends of the
        earth
    that God rules over Jacob.   *Selah*

¹⁴They return at evening,
    snarling like dogs,
    and prowl about the city.
¹⁵They wander about for food
    and howl if not satisfied.
¹⁶But I will sing of your strength,
    in the morning I will sing of your love;
for you are my fortress,
    my refuge in times of trouble.

¹⁷O my Strength, I sing praise to you;
    you, O God, are my fortress, my loving
        God.

Psalm 60

For the director of music. To ⌊the tune of⌋
    "The Lily of the Covenant." A *miktam*ᵍ of
    David. For teaching. When he fought Aram
    Naharaimʰ and Aram Zobah,ⁱ and when
    Joab returned and struck down twelve
    thousand Edomites in the Valley of Salt.

¹You have rejected us, O God, and burst forth
        upon us;
    you have been angry—now restore us!
²You have shaken the land and torn it open;
    mend its fractures, for it is quaking.
³You have shown your people desperate times;
    you have given us wine that makes us
        stagger.

⁴But for those who fear you, you have raised a
        banner
    to be unfurled against the bow.   *Selah*

⁵Save us and help us with your right hand,
    that those you love may be delivered.
⁶God has spoken from his sanctuary:
    "In triumph I will parcel out Shechem
    and measure off the Valley of Succoth.
⁷Gilead is mine, and Manasseh is mine;
    Ephraim is my helmet,
    Judah my scepter.
⁸Moab is my washbasin,
    upon Edom I toss my sandal;
    over Philistia I shout in triumph."

⁹Who will bring me to the fortified city?
    Who will lead me to Edom?
¹⁰Is it not you, O God, you who have rejected
        us
    and no longer go out with our armies?
¹¹Give us aid against the enemy,
    for the help of man is worthless.
¹²With God we will gain the victory,
    and he will trample down our enemies.

Psalm 61

For the director of music. With stringed
        instruments. Of David.

¹Hear my cry, O God;
    listen to my prayer.

²From the ends of the earth I call to you,
    I call as my heart grows faint;
    lead me to the rock that is higher than I.
³For you have been my refuge,
    a strong tower against the foe.

⁴I long to dwell in your tent forever
    and take refuge in the shelter of your
        wings.   *Selah*
⁵For you have heard my vows, O God;
    you have given me the heritage of those
        who fear your name.

⁶Increase the days of the king's life,
    his years for many generations.
⁷May he be enthroned in God's presence
        forever;
    appoint your love and faithfulness to
        protect him.

⁸Then will I ever sing praise to your name
    and fulfill my vows day after day.

ᶠ11 Or *sovereign*   ᵍTitle: Probably a literary or musical term
ʰTitle: That is, Arameans of Northwest Mesopotamia   ⁱTitle: That is,
Arameans of central Syria

42 / *Psalm 62*
A Prayer of Trust

HUMANS COME INTO the world as vulnerable creatures, completely dependent on their parents for their survival. For people to develop a healthy capacity to trust, they need to experience an emotional attachment with a nurturing parent. If children are not greeted with nurturing, empathic responses to their physical, emotional and social needs, or if the relationship with the parent is disrupted, the attachment will be threatened and the capacity to trust will be damaged. Later in life it will be difficult for them to trust God. Trust is based on a person's character, ability and truthfulness. It is an act of committing oneself to another's good intentions and care. This psalm invites us to risk trusting. It calls us to commit ourselves to God's care.

 Warming Up to God What makes a person trustworthy?

 Read Psalm 62.

Psalm 62

For the director of music. For Jeduthun.
A psalm of David.

¹My soul finds rest in God alone;
 my salvation comes from him.
²He alone is my rock and my salvation;
 he is my fortress, I will never be shaken.

³How long will you assault a man?
 Would all of you throw him down—
 this leaning wall, this tottering fence?
⁴They fully intend to topple him
 from his lofty place;
 they take delight in lies.
With their mouths they bless,
 but in their hearts they curse.   *Selah*

⁵Find rest, O my soul, in God alone;
 my hope comes from him.
⁶He alone is my rock and my salvation;
 he is my fortress, I will not be shaken.

⁷My salvation and my honor depend on God*ʲ*;
 he is my mighty rock, my refuge.
⁸Trust in him at all times, O people;
 pour out your hearts to him,
 for God is our refuge.   *Selah*

⁹Lowborn men are but a breath,
 the highborn are but a lie;
 if weighed on a balance, they are nothing;
 together they are only a breath.
¹⁰Do not trust in extortion
 or take pride in stolen goods;
though your riches increase,
 do not set your heart on them.

¹¹One thing God has spoken,
 two things have I heard:
 that you, O God, are strong,
¹² and that you, O Lord, are loving.
 Surely you will reward each person
 according to what he has done.

ʲ7 Or / God Most High is my salvation and my honor

 Discovering the Word 1. How does the writer contrast God and humanity? 2. The psalmist talks about resting in God. What pictures come to your mind with these words? 3. In verse 8, the psalmist draws a parallel between trusting in God and pouring out one's heart to God. How are these related? 4. Verse 10 warns against trusting in material wealth. Why is this such a strong temptation? 5. The last two verses depict God as strong and as loving. What images of a strong and loving God are presented in the psalm?

Applying the Word 1. Where else might you be tempted to place your trust, other than in God? 2. How does seeing God as strong help you to trust him? 3. How does seeing God as loving help you to trust him?

Responding in Prayer Express your hesitations and your desires to trust God.

43 / *Psalm 63*
A Prayer of Longing for God

SOMETIMES WE FEEL separated from God. During these times we may feel much like small children feel when they are separated from their parents—frightened, angry. And we may experience an intense longing for our Parent to return. Many things can create this sense of separation from God. It might come as a result of a loss or crisis in our life which leaves us feeling forgotten or uncared for by God. It might come during a time of personal sin or failure when we struggle with fear that God might condemn or reject us. It might come, as it did for this psalmist, as a result of being removed from our community of faith. Whatever the reason, a sense of separation from God can generate life's deepest pain, that of an intense longing for God. This psalm helps us express our longing for God in times when we feel separated from him.

 Warming Up to God Think of a time when you felt especially close to God. What was the experience like for you?

 Read Psalm 63.

Psalm 63

A psalm of David. When he was in the
     Desert of Judah.

¹O God, you are my God,
     earnestly I seek you;
my soul thirsts for you,
     my body longs for you,
in a dry and weary land
     where there is no water.

²I have seen you in the sanctuary
     and beheld your power and your glory.
³Because your love is better than life,
     my lips will glorify you.
⁴I will praise you as long as I live,
     and in your name I will lift up my hands.
⁵My soul will be satisfied as with the richest of
     foods;

with singing lips my mouth will praise you.

⁶On my bed I remember you;
     I think of you through the watches of the
          night.
⁷Because you are my help,
     I sing in the shadow of your wings.
⁸My soul clings to you;
     your right hand upholds me.

⁹They who seek my life will be destroyed;
     they will go down to the depths of the
          earth.
¹⁰They will be given over to the sword
     and become food for jackals.

¹¹But the king will rejoice in God;
     all who swear by God's name will praise
          him,
     while the mouths of liars will be silenced.

Discovering the Word 1. The psalmist describes his experience of longing for God in verse 1 with the strong physical metaphor of being thirsty in a desert with no sign of water. What does this image convey? 2. In verses 2 and 3 the psalmist describes how in the past he experienced God's presence. What did he experience of God? 3. Because of his longing for connection with God, the psalmist says he will seek God, he will remember God and he will cling to God. The first action he takes is to earnestly seek God. What does it mean to seek God? 4. The second action he takes is "remembering." Where, when, what and how does the psalmist say he "remembers" God? 5. The third action he describes is "clinging." In verse 8 he describes how he clings to God and how God holds him. What is your response to the image of clinging to God?

Applying the Word 1. Verse 1 describes a soul which is thirsty, with no chance of finding water. In stark contrast, verse 5 describes a soul which is satisfied with the richest of foods. These pictures contrast the experience of being separated from God and the experience of being close to God. What words or images would you use to describe times when you have felt separated from God? 2. What words or images would you use to describe times when you felt close to God? 3. As you think about the actions of seeking, remembering and clinging to God, which of these most closely describes what would be most helpful to you at this time? Explain.

Responding in Prayer Talk to God about your longing for him and your sense of deep satisfaction and joy in his presence.

Psalm 64

Psalm 64

For the director of music. A psalm of David.

¹Hear me, O God, as I voice my
  complaint;
  protect my life from the threat of the
  enemy.
²Hide me from the conspiracy of the
  wicked,
  from that noisy crowd of evildoers.

³They sharpen their tongues like swords
  and aim their words like deadly arrows.
⁴They shoot from ambush at the innocent
  man;
  they shoot at him suddenly, without
  fear.

⁵They encourage each other in evil plans,
  they talk about hiding their snares;
  they say, "Who will see them*k*?"

⁶They plot injustice and say,
  "We have devised a perfect plan!"
  Surely the mind and heart of man are
  cunning.

⁷But God will shoot them with arrows;
  suddenly they will be struck down.
⁸He will turn their own tongues against
  them
  and bring them to ruin;
  all who see them will shake their heads
  in scorn.

⁹All mankind will fear;
  they will proclaim the works of God
  and ponder what he has done.
¹⁰Let the righteous rejoice in the LORD
  and take refuge in him;
  let all the upright in heart praise
  him!

*k*5 Or *us*

44 / Psalm 65
A Prayer of Gratitude

BECAUSE I HAVE difficulty receiving gifts or compliments from others, I have had to remind myself to look people in the eyes when they offer me a gift or a compliment and say thank you. When we are unable to receive the good things that others offer us, we cheat ourselves, and we cheat them. When we are able to say thank you for gifts given, we are able to take the gift in, enjoy it and engage in a personal, intimate way with the giver of the gift. In the same way, when we express gratitude to God, we enter into a cycle of joyful relating with him. We take in his love, feel a deeper connection with him and experience joy. This psalm invites us to express gratitude to God for his good gifts.

 Warming Up to God What is it like for you to receive a gift or a compliment? What is it like for you to be on the receiving end of someone else's gratitude?

 Read Psalm 65.

Psalm 65

For the director of music. A psalm
of David. A song.

[1]Praise awaits[l] you, O God, in Zion;
  to you our vows will be fulfilled.
[2]O you who hear prayer,
  to you all men will come.
[3]When we were overwhelmed by sins,
  you forgave[m] our transgressions.
[4]Blessed are those you choose
  and bring near to live in your courts!
We are filled with the good things of your
    house,
  of your holy temple.

[5]You answer us with awesome deeds of
    righteousness,
  O God our Savior,
the hope of all the ends of the earth
  and of the farthest seas,
[6]who formed the mountains by your power,
  having armed yourself with strength,
[7]who stilled the roaring of the seas,
  the roaring of their waves,

and the turmoil of the nations.
[8]Those living far away fear your wonders;
  where morning dawns and evening fades
  you call forth songs of joy.

[9]You care for the land and water it;
  you enrich it abundantly.
The streams of God are filled with water
  to provide the people with grain,
  for so you have ordained it.[n]
[10]You drench its furrows
  and level its ridges;
you soften it with showers
  and bless its crops.
[11]You crown the year with your bounty,
  and your carts overflow with abundance.
[12]The grasslands of the desert overflow;
  the hills are clothed with gladness.
[13]The meadows are covered with flocks
  and the valleys are mantled with grain;
  they shout for joy and sing.

[l]1 Or *befits*; the meaning of the Hebrew for this word is uncertain.
[m]3 Or *made atonement for*   [n]9 Or *for that is how you prepare the*
land

Discovering the Word 1. God's great power is acknowledged in this psalm. How is God's power a gift
to us? 2. In verse 5 God is called "our Savior, the hope of all the ends of the earth and of the farthest
seas." In what ways is God the hope of all the earth and seas? 3. The psalmist mentions several of God's awesome
deeds in verses 6 and 7. What other awesome deeds might you add to the list? 4. Verse 8 offers a picture of the
fears and joys common to all people of the earth. How do God's wonders cause us to experience fear? 5. How
do God's wonders call forth songs of joy?

Applying the Word 1. Verses 9–13 describe the specific ways in which God tenderly loves and cares
for the earth. What thoughts and feelings does this description evoke for you? 2. What implications does
God's care for the earth have for the ways in which we treat the earth? 3. What personal value does expressing
gratitude to God have for you?

Responding in Prayer What are you grateful for today? Express your thanks to God.

---

45 / *Psalm 66*
A Prayer of Joy

LIFE WAS NOT intended by God to be a joyless ordeal. As much as it might surprise some of us, it is actually God's
desire for us to experience joy. Joy is an act of relating to God with vulnerable, unselfconscious gratitude for the
good gifts he gives. Joy comes when we experience and acknowledge God's love and care for us, when we allow
ourselves to express our gratitude for his love with great energy. This psalm invites us to experience joy.

Warming Up to God Think of a time when you experienced joy. What evoked this feeling in you?

Read Psalm 66.

Psalm 66

For the director of music. A song. A psalm.

¹Shout with joy to God, all the earth!
² Sing the glory of his name;
  make his praise glorious!
³Say to God, "How awesome are your deeds!
  So great is your power
  that your enemies cringe before you.
⁴All the earth bows down to you;
  they sing praise to you,
  they sing praise to your name." *Selah*

⁵Come and see what God has done,
  how awesome his works in man's behalf!
⁶He turned the sea into dry land,
  they passed through the waters on foot—
  come, let us rejoice in him.
⁷He rules forever by his power,
  his eyes watch the nations—
  let not the rebellious rise up against him.
                              Selah

⁸Praise our God, O peoples,
  let the sound of his praise be heard;
⁹he has preserved our lives
  and kept our feet from slipping.
¹⁰For you, O God, tested us;

you refined us like silver.
¹¹You brought us into prison
  and laid burdens on our backs.
¹²You let men ride over our heads;
  we went through fire and water,
  but you brought us to a place of
    abundance.

¹³I will come to your temple with burnt
    offerings
  and fulfill my vows to you—
¹⁴vows my lips promised and my mouth spoke
  when I was in trouble.
¹⁵I will sacrifice fat animals to you
  and an offering of rams;
  I will offer bulls and goats. *Selah*

¹⁶Come and listen, all you who fear God;
  let me tell you what he has done for me.
¹⁷I cried out to him with my mouth;
  his praise was on my tongue.
¹⁸If I had cherished sin in my heart,
  the Lord would not have listened;
¹⁹but God has surely listened
  and heard my voice in prayer.
²⁰Praise be to God,
  who has not rejected my prayer
  or withheld his love from me!

Discovering the Word 1. The writer calls us to action (vv. 1, 2, 3, 5, 8 and 16). What all does he call us to do? **2.** How are each of these behaviors related to the experience or the expression of joy? **3.** What does the section in the middle of this psalm (vv. 8–12) tell us about the cause for this particular expression of joy? **4.** How might this kind of experience lead to joy? **5.** Verses 16–20 are a more personal account of what the Lord has done. What does the writer say the Lord has done for him? **6.** How might this kind of experience lead to joy?

Applying the Word 1. What other ways of expressing joy to God would you add to the psalmist's list? **2.** Why is it important to allow ourselves to experience and express joy? **3.** How might this psalm help you to experience and express joy?

Responding in Prayer What joy would you like to express to God?

46 / *Psalm 67*
God's Love for All Creatures

Jesus loves the little children—
All the children of the world.
Red, brown, yellow, black, and white—
They are precious in his sight.
Jesus loves the little children of the world.

JESUS LOVES EVERY culture he created. Its members are his little children, and he longs for them to fully experience the healing of his compassion. That's what redemption is all about. Because some of our sincere attempts to bring others into this love have been clumsy and insulting to other cultures, we are bombarded with accusations of destroying other cultures with Christianity. Some of those accusations are true and worth listening to. Yet these mistakes are not the true picture of our ministry. The gospel is good news to all societies, and God has always called and is still calling his people to bear his redemptive love to every place and people group on the earth.

 Warming Up to God   How have you recently seen God's power being revealed in your nation?

 Read Psalm 67.

Psalm 67

For the director of music. With stringed
   instruments. A psalm. A song.

¹May God be gracious to us and bless us
   and make his face shine upon us,   *Selah*
²that your ways may be known on earth,
   your salvation among all nations.

³May the peoples praise you, O God;
   may all the peoples praise you.

⁴May the nations be glad and sing
      for joy,
   for you rule the peoples justly
   and guide the nations of the earth.   *Selah*
⁵May the peoples praise you, O God;
   may all the peoples praise you.

⁶Then the land will yield its harvest,
   and God, our God, will bless us.
⁷God will bless us,
   and all the ends of the earth will
      fear him.

 Discovering the Word   1. What words do you notice being repeated throughout this passage?   2. Identify the blessings the Lord wants to bring to the nations.   3. What does this reveal about how God regards the nations?

 Applying the Word   1. What would these blessings look like if they came to your own culture?   2. How would these blessings affect some other nation in the world (say, Bosnia or South Africa)?

Responding in Prayer   Thank God for his compassion for the nations.

Psalms 68—72

Psalm 68

For the director of music. Of David.
A psalm. A song.

1May God arise, may his enemies be scattered;
may his foes flee before him.
2As smoke is blown away by the wind,
may you blow them away;
as wax melts before the fire,
may the wicked perish before God.
3But may the righteous be glad
and rejoice before God;
may they be happy and joyful.

4Sing to God, sing praise to his name,
extol him who rides on the clouds[o]—
his name is the LORD—
and rejoice before him.
5A father to the fatherless, a defender of widows,
is God in his holy dwelling.
6God sets the lonely in families,[p]
he leads forth the prisoners with singing;
but the rebellious live in a sun-scorched land.

7When you went out before your people, O God,
when you marched through the wasteland, *Selah*
8the earth shook,
the heavens poured down rain,
before God, the One of Sinai,
before God, the God of Israel.
9You gave abundant showers, O God;
you refreshed your weary inheritance.
10Your people settled in it,
and from your bounty, O God, you provided for the poor.

11The Lord announced the word,
and great was the company of those who proclaimed it:
12"Kings and armies flee in haste;
in the camps men divide the plunder.
13Even while you sleep among the campfires,[q]
the wings of ⌊my⌋ dove are sheathed with silver,
its feathers with shining gold."
14When the Almighty[r] scattered the kings in the land,
it was like snow fallen on Zalmon.

15The mountains of Bashan are majestic mountains;
rugged are the mountains of Bashan.
16Why gaze in envy, O rugged mountains,
at the mountain where God chooses to reign,
where the LORD himself will dwell forever?
17The chariots of God are tens of thousands
and thousands of thousands;
the Lord ⌊has come⌋ from Sinai into his sanctuary.
18When you ascended on high,
you led captives in your train;
you received gifts from men,
even from[s] the rebellious—
that you,[t] O LORD God, might dwell there.

19Praise be to the Lord, to God our Savior,
who daily bears our burdens. *Selah*
20Our God is a God who saves;
from the Sovereign LORD comes escape from death.

21Surely God will crush the heads of his enemies,
the hairy crowns of those who go on in their sins.
22The Lord says, "I will bring them from Bashan;
I will bring them from the depths of the sea,
23that you may plunge your feet in the blood of your foes,
while the tongues of your dogs have their share."

24Your procession has come into view, O God,
the procession of my God and King into the sanctuary.
25In front are the singers, after them the musicians;
with them are the maidens playing tambourines.
26Praise God in the great congregation;

o4 Or / *prepare the way for him who rides through the deserts* p6 Or *the desolate in a homeland* q13 Or *saddlebags* r14 Hebrew *Shaddai* s18 Or *gifts for men, / even* t18 Or *they*

praise the LORD in the assembly of Israel.
27There is the little tribe of Benjamin, leading
    them,
    there the great throng of Judah's princes,
    and there the princes of Zebulun and of
        Naphtali.

28Summon your power, O God^u;
    show us your strength, O God, as you have
        done before.
29Because of your temple at Jerusalem
    kings will bring you gifts.
30Rebuke the beast among the reeds,
    the herd of bulls among the calves of the
        nations.
    Humbled, may it bring bars of silver.
    Scatter the nations who delight in war.
31Envoys will come from Egypt;
    Cush^v will submit herself to God.

32Sing to God, O kingdoms of the earth,
    sing praise to the Lord,   *Selah*
33to him who rides the ancient skies above,
    who thunders with mighty voice.
34Proclaim the power of God,
    whose majesty is over Israel,
    whose power is in the skies.
35You are awesome, O God, in your sanctuary;
    the God of Israel gives power and strength
        to his people.

Praise be to God!

Psalm 69

For the director of music. To ⌊the tune of⌋
        "Lilies." Of David.

1Save me, O God,
    for the waters have come up to my neck.
2I sink in the miry depths,
    where there is no foothold.
    I have come into the deep waters;
    the floods engulf me.
3I am worn out calling for help;
    my throat is parched.
    My eyes fail,
    looking for my God.
4Those who hate me without reason
    outnumber the hairs of my head;
many are my enemies without cause,
    those who seek to destroy me.
    I am forced to restore
    what I did not steal.

5You know my folly, O God;
    my guilt is not hidden from you.

6May those who hope in you
    not be disgraced because of me,
    O Lord, the LORD Almighty;
may those who seek you
    not be put to shame because of me,
    O God of Israel.
7For I endure scorn for your sake,
    and shame covers my face.
8I am a stranger to my brothers,
    an alien to my own mother's sons;
9for zeal for your house consumes me,
    and the insults of those who insult you fall
        on me.
10When I weep and fast,
    I must endure scorn;
11when I put on sackcloth,
    people make sport of me.
12Those who sit at the gate mock me,
    and I am the song of the drunkards.

13But I pray to you, O LORD,
    in the time of your favor;
in your great love, O God,
    answer me with your sure salvation.
14Rescue me from the mire,
    do not let me sink;
deliver me from those who hate me,
    from the deep waters.
15Do not let the floodwaters engulf me
    or the depths swallow me up
    or the pit close its mouth over me.
16Answer me, O LORD, out of the goodness of
        your love;
    in your great mercy turn to me.
17Do not hide your face from your servant;
    answer me quickly, for I am in trouble.
18Come near and rescue me;
    redeem me because of my foes.

19You know how I am scorned, disgraced and
        shamed;
    all my enemies are before you.
20Scorn has broken my heart
    and has left me helpless;
    I looked for sympathy, but there was none,
    for comforters, but I found none.
21They put gall in my food
    and gave me vinegar for my thirst.

---

^u28 Many Hebrew manuscripts, Septuagint and Syriac; most Hebrew
manuscripts *Your God has summoned power for you*   ^v31 That is, the
upper Nile region

²²May the table set before them become a snare;
  may it become retribution andᵂ a trap.
²³May their eyes be darkened so they cannot
    see,
  and their backs be bent forever.
²⁴Pour out your wrath on them;
  let your fierce anger overtake them.
²⁵May their place be deserted;
  let there be no one to dwell in their tents.
²⁶For they persecute those you wound
  and talk about the pain of those you hurt.
²⁷Charge them with crime upon crime;
  do not let them share in your salvation.
²⁸May they be blotted out of the book of life
  and not be listed with the righteous.

²⁹I am in pain and distress;
  may your salvation, O God, protect me.

³⁰I will praise God's name in song
  and glorify him with thanksgiving.
³¹This will please the LORD more than an ox,
  more than a bull with its horns and hoofs.
³²The poor will see and be glad—
  you who seek God, may your hearts live!
³³The LORD hears the needy
  and does not despise his captive people.

³⁴Let heaven and earth praise him,
  the seas and all that move in them,
³⁵for God will save Zion
  and rebuild the cities of Judah.
  Then people will settle there and possess it;
³⁶ the children of his servants will inherit it,
    and those who love his name will dwell
      there.

Psalm 70

For the director of music. Of David.
A petition.

¹Hasten, O God, to save me;
  O LORD, come quickly to help me.
²May those who seek my life
  be put to shame and confusion;
may all who desire my ruin
  be turned back in disgrace.
³May those who say to me, "Aha! Aha!"
  turn back because of their shame.
⁴But may all who seek you
  rejoice and be glad in you;
may those who love your salvation always
    say,

"Let God be exalted!"

⁵Yet I am poor and needy;
  come quickly to me, O God.
You are my help and my deliverer;
  O LORD, do not delay.

Psalm 71

¹In you, O LORD, I have taken refuge;
  let me never be put to shame.
²Rescue me and deliver me in your
    righteousness;
  turn your ear to me and save me.
³Be my rock of refuge,
  to which I can always go;
give the command to save me,
  for you are my rock and my fortress.
⁴Deliver me, O my God, from the hand of the
    wicked,
  from the grasp of evil and cruel men.

⁵For you have been my hope, O Sovereign
    LORD,
  my confidence since my youth.
⁶From birth I have relied on you;
  you brought me forth from my mother's
    womb.
  I will ever praise you.
⁷I have become like a portent to many,
  but you are my strong refuge.
⁸My mouth is filled with your praise,
  declaring your splendor all day long.

⁹Do not cast me away when I am old;
  do not forsake me when my strength is
    gone.
¹⁰For my enemies speak against me;
  those who wait to kill me conspire
    together.
¹¹They say, "God has forsaken him;
  pursue him and seize him,
  for no one will rescue him."
¹²Be not far from me, O God;
  come quickly, O my God, to help me.
¹³May my accusers perish in shame;
  may those who want to harm me
  be covered with scorn and disgrace.

¹⁴But as for me, I will always have hope;
  I will praise you more and more.
¹⁵My mouth will tell of your righteousness,
  of your salvation all day long,

ᵂ22 Or snare / and their fellowship become

though I know not its measure.
¹⁶I will come and proclaim your mighty acts,
  O Sovereign LORD;
  I will proclaim your righteousness, yours
    alone.
¹⁷Since my youth, O God, you have taught me,
  and to this day I declare your marvelous
    deeds.
¹⁸Even when I am old and gray,
  do not forsake me, O God,
  till I declare your power to the next
    generation,
  your might to all who are to come.

¹⁹Your righteousness reaches to the skies, O
    God,
  you who have done great things.
  Who, O God, is like you?
²⁰Though you have made me see troubles,
    many and bitter,
  you will restore my life again;
  from the depths of the earth
  you will again bring me up.
²¹You will increase my honor
  and comfort me once again.

²²I will praise you with the harp
  for your faithfulness, O my God;
  I will sing praise to you with the lyre,
  O Holy One of Israel.
²³My lips will shout for joy
  when I sing praise to you—
  I, whom you have redeemed.
²⁴My tongue will tell of your righteous acts
  all day long,
  for those who wanted to harm me
  have been put to shame and confusion.

Psalm 72

Of Solomon.

¹Endow the king with your justice, O God,
  the royal son with your righteousness.
²He will˟ judge your people in righteousness,
  your afflicted ones with justice.
³The mountains will bring prosperity to the
    people,
  the hills the fruit of righteousness.
⁴He will defend the afflicted among the people
  and save the children of the needy;
  he will crush the oppressor.

⁵He will endureʸ as long as the sun,
  as long as the moon, through all
    generations.
⁶He will be like rain falling on a mown field,
  like showers watering the earth.
⁷In his days the righteous will flourish;
  prosperity will abound till the moon is no
    more.

⁸He will rule from sea to sea
  and from the River˟ to the ends of the
    earth.ᵃ
⁹The desert tribes will bow before him
  and his enemies will lick the dust.
¹⁰The kings of Tarshish and of distant shores
  will bring tribute to him;
  the kings of Sheba and Seba
  will present him gifts.
¹¹All kings will bow down to him
  and all nations will serve him.

¹²For he will deliver the needy who cry out,
  the afflicted who have no one to help.
¹³He will take pity on the weak and the needy
  and save the needy from death.
¹⁴He will rescue them from oppression and
    violence,
  for precious is their blood in his sight.

¹⁵Long may he live!
  May gold from Sheba be given him.
  May people ever pray for him
  and bless him all day long.
¹⁶Let grain abound throughout the land;
  on the tops of the hills may it sway.
  Let its fruit flourish like Lebanon;
  let it thrive like the grass of the field.
¹⁷May his name endure forever;
  may it continue as long as the sun.

All nations will be blessed through him,
  and they will call him blessed.

¹⁸Praise be to the LORD God, the God of Israel,
  who alone does marvelous deeds.
¹⁹Praise be to his glorious name forever;
  may the whole earth be filled with his
    glory.
        Amen and Amen.

²⁰This concludes the prayers of David son of
    Jesse.

˟2 Or *May he*; similarly in verses 3-11 and 17   ʸ5 Septuagint;
Hebrew *You will be feared*   ᶻ8 That is, the Euphrates   ᵃ8 Or *the
end of the land*

47 / *Psalm 73*
Praying Our Doubt

DOUBT IS NOT a sin. It is an essential element in belief. Doubt is honesty. We see contradictions between what we believe and what we experience. What is going on here? Did God give us a bum steer? Why aren't things turning out the way we were taught to expect? No mature faith avoids or denies doubt. Doubt forces faith to bedrock.

 Warming Up to God What doubts have you had or do you have about the Christian life? Express them to God without fear.

 Read Psalm 73.

BOOK III
Psalms 73–89

Psalm 73

A psalm of Asaph.

¹Surely God is good to Israel,
   to those who are pure in heart.

²But as for me, my feet had almost slipped;
   I had nearly lost my foothold.
³For I envied the arrogant
   when I saw the prosperity of the wicked.

⁴They have no struggles;
   their bodies are healthy and strong.[b]
⁵They are free from the burdens common to man;
   they are not plagued by human ills.
⁶Therefore pride is their necklace;
   they clothe themselves with violence.
⁷From their callous hearts comes iniquity[c];
   the evil conceits of their minds know no limits.
⁸They scoff, and speak with malice;
   in their arrogance they threaten oppression.
⁹Their mouths lay claim to heaven,
   and their tongues take possession of the earth.
¹⁰Therefore their people turn to them
   and drink up waters in abundance.[d]
¹¹They say, "How can God know?
   Does the Most High have knowledge?"

¹²This is what the wicked are like—
   always carefree, they increase in wealth.

¹³Surely in vain have I kept my heart pure;

in vain have I washed my hands in innocence.
¹⁴All day long I have been plagued;
   I have been punished every morning.

¹⁵If I had said, "I will speak thus,"
   I would have betrayed your children.
¹⁶When I tried to understand all this,
   it was oppressive to me
¹⁷till I entered the sanctuary of God;
   then I understood their final destiny.

¹⁸Surely you place them on slippery ground;
   you cast them down to ruin.
¹⁹How suddenly are they destroyed,
   completely swept away by terrors!
²⁰As a dream when one awakes,
   so when you arise, O Lord,
   you will despise them as fantasies.

²¹When my heart was grieved
   and my spirit embittered,
²²I was senseless and ignorant;
   I was a brute beast before you.

²³Yet I am always with you;
   you hold me by my right hand.
²⁴You guide me with your counsel,
   and afterward you will take me into glory.
²⁵Whom have I in heaven but you?
   And earth has nothing I desire besides you.
²⁶My flesh and my heart may fail,
   but God is the strength of my heart
   and my portion forever.

²⁷Those who are far from you will perish;
   you destroy all who are unfaithful to you.
²⁸But as for me, it is good to be near God.
   I have made the Sovereign Lord my refuge;
   I will tell of all your deeds.

---

b4 With a different word division of the Hebrew; Masoretic Text
struggles at their death; / their bodies are healthy   *c7* Syriac (see also
Septuagint); Hebrew *Their eyes bulge with fat*   *d10* The meaning of
the Hebrew for this verse is uncertain.

Discovering the Word 1. How would you paraphrase the doubt expressed in verses 2–12? 2. Who do you know who is, as they say, "getting away with murder"? 3. The key word and the pivotal center of the psalm is the word *till* in verse 17. What takes place here in the sanctuary? 4. The *yet* in verse 23 links two contrasting statements. What are they? 5. The prosperity of the wicked occupied the first part of the psalm (vv. 1–16). The presence of the Lord occupies the second (vv. 17–28). What is more vivid to you, the wicked or the Lord? Explain.

Applying the Word 1. Self-pity is like a deadly virus. How would you express, in terms of your own life, what the psalmist says in verses 13–14? 2. The appearance of the wicked whom we envy is in utter and complete contrast to their reality (vv. 18–20). How do you discern between what you *see* (and are tempted to envy) and what *is* (and so is affirmed in obedience)? 3. Worship is the pivotal act in this prayer. The Christian consensus is that it is the pivotal act every week. How can worship become a more pivotal part of your experience?

Responding in Prayer In your time of prayer spend five minutes in silence, savoring God's presence, letting him restore your perspective. Then speak your praises.

Psalms 74—76

Psalm 74

A maskil[e] of Asaph.

¹Why have you rejected us forever, O God?
  Why does your anger smolder against the
    sheep of your pasture?
²Remember the people you purchased of old,
  the tribe of your inheritance, whom you
    redeemed—
Mount Zion, where you dwelt.
³Turn your steps toward these everlasting
    ruins,
  all this destruction the enemy has brought
    on the sanctuary.

⁴Your foes roared in the place where you met
    with us;
  they set up their standards as signs.
⁵They behaved like men wielding axes
  to cut through a thicket of trees.
⁶They smashed all the carved paneling
  with their axes and hatchets.
⁷They burned your sanctuary to the ground;
  they defiled the dwelling place of your
    Name.
⁸They said in their hearts, "We will crush
    them completely!"
  They burned every place where God was
    worshiped in the land.
⁹We are given no miraculous signs;
  no prophets are left,
  and none of us knows how long this will
    be.

¹⁰How long will the enemy mock you, O God?
  Will the foe revile your name forever?
¹¹Why do you hold back your hand, your right
    hand?
  Take it from the folds of your garment and
    destroy them!

¹²But you, O God, are my king from of old;
  you bring salvation upon the earth.
¹³It was you who split open the sea by your
    power;
  you broke the heads of the monster in the
    waters.
¹⁴It was you who crushed the heads of
    Leviathan
  and gave him as food to the creatures of
    the desert.
¹⁵It was you who opened up springs and
    streams;
  you dried up the ever flowing rivers.
¹⁶The day is yours, and yours also the night;
  you established the sun and moon.
¹⁷It was you who set all the boundaries of the
    earth;
  you made both summer and winter.

¹⁸Remember how the enemy has mocked you,
    O LORD,
  how foolish people have reviled your name.
¹⁹Do not hand over the life of your dove to
    wild beasts;
  do not forget the lives of your afflicted
    people forever.

---
e Title: Probably a literary or musical term

²⁰Have regard for your covenant,
because haunts of violence fill the dark
places of the land.
²¹Do not let the oppressed retreat in disgrace;
may the poor and needy praise your name.

²²Rise up, O God, and defend your cause;
remember how fools mock you all day
long.
²³Do not ignore the clamor of your adversaries,
the uproar of your enemies, which rises
continually.

Psalm 75

For the director of music. ⌐To the tune of⌐
"Do Not Destroy." A psalm of Asaph.
A song.

¹We give thanks to you, O God,
we give thanks, for your Name is near;
men tell of your wonderful deeds.

²You say, "I choose the appointed time;
it is I who judge uprightly.
³When the earth and all its people quake,
it is I who hold its pillars firm.   *Selah*
⁴To the arrogant I say, 'Boast no more,'
and to the wicked, 'Do not lift up your
horns.
⁵Do not lift your horns against heaven;
do not speak with outstretched neck.' "

⁶No one from the east or the west
or from the desert can exalt a man.
⁷But it is God who judges:
He brings one down, he exalts another.
⁸In the hand of the LORD is a cup
full of foaming wine mixed with spices;
he pours it out, and all the wicked of the
earth
drink it down to its very dregs.

⁹As for me, I will declare this forever;
I will sing praise to the God of Jacob.
¹⁰I will cut off the horns of all the wicked,

but the horns of the righteous will be lifted
up.

Psalm 76

For the director of music. With stringed
instruments. A psalm of Asaph. A song.

¹In Judah God is known;
his name is great in Israel.
²His tent is in Salem,
his dwelling place in Zion.
³There he broke the flashing arrows,
the shields and the swords, the weapons of
war.   *Selah*

⁴You are resplendent with light,
more majestic than mountains rich with
game.
⁵Valiant men lie plundered,
they sleep their last sleep;
not one of the warriors
can lift his hands.
⁶At your rebuke, O God of Jacob,
both horse and chariot lie still.
⁷You alone are to be feared.
Who can stand before you when you are
angry?
⁸From heaven you pronounced judgment,
and the land feared and was quiet—
⁹when you, O God, rose up to judge,
to save all the afflicted of the land.   *Selah*
¹⁰Surely your wrath against men brings you
praise,
and the survivors of your wrath are
restrained.ʃ

¹¹Make vows to the LORD your God and fulfill
them;
let all the neighboring lands
bring gifts to the One to be feared.
¹²He breaks the spirit of rulers;
he is feared by the kings of the earth.

ʃ10 Or *Surely the wrath of men brings you praise, / and with the
remainder of wrath you arm yourself*

48 / *Psalm 77*
Praying Our Discontent

"THE ROOM IS too cold. Why were we seated way back in the corner? You'd think a restaurant like this would have more selection on the menu. When is our food going to get here? I don't even think this waitress deserves a tip . . ."

Perhaps you've had a meal with a person who complains like this. Some people are never satisfied with what they are given. Such people are tiring to be with. In contrast, the person who is aware of God's never-ending good gifts (and a person who seems to have comparatively less) is a joy to be around. Where do you fall on this spectrum?

Warming Up to God Name three things you're grateful for. Reflect on your response. (How long did it take you to think of things you're grateful for? Did they come to mind quickly or slowly? How conscious are you of God's good gifts?) What did you learn about yourself?

 Read Psalm 77.

Psalm 77

For the director of music. For Jeduthun.
Of Asaph. A psalm.

¹I cried out to God for help;
I cried out to God to hear me.
²When I was in distress, I sought the Lord;
at night I stretched out untiring hands
and my soul refused to be comforted.

³I remembered you, O God, and I groaned;
I mused, and my spirit grew faint.   *Selah*
⁴You kept my eyes from closing;
I was too troubled to speak.
⁵I thought about the former days,
the years of long ago;
⁶I remembered my songs in the night.
My heart mused and my spirit inquired:

⁷"Will the Lord reject forever?
Will he never show his favor again?
⁸Has his unfailing love vanished forever?
Has his promise failed for all time?
⁹Has God forgotten to be merciful?
Has he in anger withheld his compassion?"
                                                          Selah

¹⁰Then I thought, "To this I will appeal:
the years of the right hand of the Most
High."

¹¹I will remember the deeds of the LORD;
yes, I will remember your miracles of long
ago.
¹²I will meditate on all your works
and consider all your mighty deeds.

¹³Your ways, O God, are holy.
What god is so great as our God?
¹⁴You are the God who performs miracles;
you display your power among the peoples.
¹⁵With your mighty arm you redeemed your
people,
the descendants of Jacob and Joseph.   *Selah*

¹⁶The waters saw you, O God,
the waters saw you and writhed;
the very depths were convulsed.
¹⁷The clouds poured down water,
the skies resounded with thunder;
your arrows flashed back and forth.
¹⁸Your thunder was heard in the whirlwind,
your lightning lit up the world;
the earth trembled and quaked.
¹⁹Your path led through the sea,
your way through the mighty waters,
though your footprints were not seen.

²⁰You led your people like a flock
by the hand of Moses and Aaron.

Discovering the Word 1. What words and phrases does the psalmist use to describe his emotion? 2. Why does he "groan" at the memory of God (vv. 3–9)? 3. How does the tone of the passage change in verses 10–15? 4. What is the source of the change? 5. How do verses 16–20 emphasize God's power?

Applying the Word 1. The psalmist's discontent makes him "too troubled to speak." When have you experienced this? 2. Sometimes our culture leads us to believe that material things and achievements, such as a promotion at work, social status, the right relationship, a new car or the perfect house, will bring contentment. What false sources of contentment do you put faith in? **3.** What in this passage could help you reform your thinking?

 Responding in Prayer The psalmist finds his source of contentment in who God is. Make God's character—rather than your needs—a focus of prayer.

Psalms 78—83

Psalm 78

A *maskil*ᵍ of Asaph.

¹O my people, hear my teaching;
   listen to the words of my mouth.
²I will open my mouth in parables,
   I will utter hidden things, things from of
       old—
³what we have heard and known,
   what our fathers have told us.
⁴We will not hide them from their children;
   we will tell the next generation
the praiseworthy deeds of the Lᴏʀᴅ,
   his power, and the wonders he has done.
⁵He decreed statutes for Jacob
   and established the law in Israel,
which he commanded our forefathers
   to teach their children,
⁶so the next generation would know them,
   even the children yet to be born,
   and they in turn would tell their children.
⁷Then they would put their trust in God
   and would not forget his deeds
   but would keep his commands.
⁸They would not be like their forefathers—
   a stubborn and rebellious generation,
whose hearts were not loyal to God,
   whose spirits were not faithful to him.

⁹The men of Ephraim, though armed with
       bows,
   turned back on the day of battle;
¹⁰they did not keep God's covenant
   and refused to live by his law.
¹¹They forgot what he had done,
   the wonders he had shown them.
¹²He did miracles in the sight of their fathers
   in the land of Egypt, in the region of Zoan.
¹³He divided the sea and led them through;
   he made the water stand firm like a wall.
¹⁴He guided them with the cloud by day
   and with light from the fire all night.

¹⁵He split the rocks in the desert
   and gave them water as abundant as the
       seas;
¹⁶he brought streams out of a rocky crag
   and made water flow down like rivers.

¹⁷But they continued to sin against him,
   rebelling in the desert against the Most
       High.
¹⁸They willfully put God to the test
   by demanding the food they craved.
¹⁹They spoke against God, saying,
   "Can God spread a table in the desert?
²⁰When he struck the rock, water gushed out,
   and streams flowed abundantly.
But can he also give us food?
   Can he supply meat for his people?"
²¹When the Lᴏʀᴅ heard them, he was very
       angry;
   his fire broke out against Jacob,
   and his wrath rose against Israel,
²²for they did not believe in God
   or trust in his deliverance.
²³Yet he gave a command to the skies above
   and opened the doors of the heavens;
²⁴he rained down manna for the people to eat,
   he gave them the grain of heaven.
²⁵Men ate the bread of angels;
   he sent them all the food they could eat.
²⁶He let loose the east wind from the heavens
   and led forth the south wind by his power.
²⁷He rained meat down on them like dust,
   flying birds like sand on the seashore.
²⁸He made them come down inside their camp,
   all around their tents.
²⁹They ate till they had more than enough,
   for he had given them what they craved.
³⁰But before they turned from the food they
       craved,
   even while it was still in their mouths,
³¹God's anger rose against them;
   he put to death the sturdiest among them,

ᵍTitle: Probably a literary or musical term

cutting down the young men of Israel.

³²In spite of all this, they kept on sinning;
　in spite of his wonders, they did not
　believe.
³³So he ended their days in futility
　and their years in terror.
³⁴Whenever God slew them, they would seek
　him;
　they eagerly turned to him again.
³⁵They remembered that God was their Rock,
　that God Most High was their Redeemer.
³⁶But then they would flatter him with their
　mouths,
　lying to him with their tongues;
³⁷their hearts were not loyal to him,
　they were not faithful to his covenant.
³⁸Yet he was merciful;
　he forgave their iniquities
　and did not destroy them.
Time after time he restrained his anger
　and did not stir up his full wrath.
³⁹He remembered that they were but flesh,
　a passing breeze that does not return.

⁴⁰How often they rebelled against him in the
　desert
　and grieved him in the wasteland!
⁴¹Again and again they put God to the test;
　they vexed the Holy One of Israel.
⁴²They did not remember his power—
　the day he redeemed them from the
　oppressor,
⁴³the day he displayed his miraculous signs in
　Egypt,
　his wonders in the region of Zoan.
⁴⁴He turned their rivers to blood;
　they could not drink from their streams.
⁴⁵He sent swarms of flies that devoured them,
　and frogs that devastated them.
⁴⁶He gave their crops to the grasshopper,
　their produce to the locust.
⁴⁷He destroyed their vines with hail
　and their sycamore-figs with sleet.
⁴⁸He gave over their cattle to the hail,
　their livestock to bolts of lightning.
⁴⁹He unleashed against them his hot anger,
　his wrath, indignation and hostility—
　a band of destroying angels.
⁵⁰He prepared a path for his anger;
　he did not spare them from death
　but gave them over to the plague.
⁵¹He struck down all the firstborn of Egypt,

the firstfruits of manhood in the tents of
　Ham.
⁵²But he brought his people out like a flock;
　he led them like sheep through the desert.
⁵³He guided them safely, so they were unafraid;
　but the sea engulfed their enemies.
⁵⁴Thus he brought them to the border of his
　holy land,
　to the hill country his right hand had
　taken.
⁵⁵He drove out nations before them
　and allotted their lands to them as an
　inheritance;
　he settled the tribes of Israel in their
　homes.

⁵⁶But they put God to the test
　and rebelled against the Most High;
　they did not keep his statutes.
⁵⁷Like their fathers they were disloyal and
　faithless,
　as unreliable as a faulty bow.
⁵⁸They angered him with their high places;
　they aroused his jealousy with their idols.
⁵⁹When God heard them, he was very angry;
　he rejected Israel completely.
⁶⁰He abandoned the tabernacle of Shiloh,
　the tent he had set up among men.
⁶¹He sent ⌐the ark of⌐ his might into captivity,
　his splendor into the hands of the enemy.
⁶²He gave his people over to the sword;
　he was very angry with his inheritance.
⁶³Fire consumed their young men,
　and their maidens had no wedding songs;
⁶⁴their priests were put to the sword,
　and their widows could not weep.

⁶⁵Then the Lord awoke as from sleep,
　as a man wakes from the stupor of wine.
⁶⁶He beat back his enemies;
　he put them to everlasting shame.
⁶⁷Then he rejected the tents of Joseph,
　he did not choose the tribe of Ephraim;
⁶⁸but he chose the tribe of Judah,
　Mount Zion, which he loved.
⁶⁹He built his sanctuary like the heights,
　like the earth that he established forever.
⁷⁰He chose David his servant
　and took him from the sheep pens;
⁷¹from tending the sheep he brought him
　to be the shepherd of his people Jacob,
　of Israel his inheritance.

⁷²And David shepherded them with integrity of
 heart;
 with skillful hands he led them.

Psalm 79

A psalm of Asaph.

¹O God, the nations have invaded your
 inheritance;
 they have defiled your holy temple,
 they have reduced Jerusalem to rubble.
²They have given the dead bodies of your
 servants
 as food to the birds of the air,
 the flesh of your saints to the beasts of the
 earth.
³They have poured out blood like water
 all around Jerusalem,
 and there is no one to bury the dead.
⁴We are objects of reproach to our neighbors,
 of scorn and derision to those around us.

⁵How long, O LORD? Will you be angry
 forever?
 How long will your jealousy burn like fire?
⁶Pour out your wrath on the nations
 that do not acknowledge you,
 on the kingdoms
 that do not call on your name;
⁷for they have devoured Jacob
 and destroyed his homeland.
⁸Do not hold against us the sins of the fathers;
 may your mercy come quickly to meet us,
 for we are in desperate need.

⁹Help us, O God our Savior,
 for the glory of your name;
 deliver us and forgive our sins
 for your name's sake.
¹⁰Why should the nations say,
 "Where is their God?"
 Before our eyes, make known among the
 nations
 that you avenge the outpoured blood of
 your servants.
¹¹May the groans of the prisoners come before
 you;
 by the strength of your arm
 preserve those condemned to die.

¹²Pay back into the laps of our neighbors seven
 times

the reproach they have hurled at you,
 O Lord.
¹³Then we your people, the sheep of your
 pasture,
 will praise you forever;
 from generation to generation
 we will recount your praise.

Psalm 80

For the director of music. To ⌊the tune of⌋
"The Lilies of the Covenant." Of Asaph.
A psalm.

¹Hear us, O Shepherd of Israel,
 you who lead Joseph like a flock;
 you who sit enthroned between the cherubim,
 shine forth
² before Ephraim, Benjamin and Manasseh.
Awaken your might;
 come and save us.

³Restore us, O God;
 make your face shine upon us,
 that we may be saved.

⁴O LORD God Almighty,
 how long will your anger smolder
 against the prayers of your people?
⁵You have fed them with the bread of tears;
 you have made them drink tears by the
 bowlful.
⁶You have made us a source of contention to
 our neighbors,
 and our enemies mock us.

⁷Restore us, O God Almighty;
 make your face shine upon us,
 that we may be saved.

⁸You brought a vine out of Egypt;
 you drove out the nations and planted it.
⁹You cleared the ground for it,
 and it took root and filled the land.
¹⁰The mountains were covered with its shade,
 the mighty cedars with its branches.
¹¹It sent out its boughs to the Sea,ʰ
 its shoots as far as the River.ⁱ

¹²Why have you broken down its walls
 so that all who pass by pick its grapes?
¹³Boars from the forest ravage it
 and the creatures of the field feed on it.
¹⁴Return to us, O God Almighty!

ʰ11 Probably the Mediterranean ⁱ11 That is, the Euphrates

Look down from heaven and see!
Watch over this vine,
¹⁵ the root your right hand has planted,
   the son^j you have raised up for yourself.

¹⁶Your vine is cut down, it is burned with fire;
   at your rebuke your people perish.
¹⁷Let your hand rest on the man at your right
     hand,
   the son of man you have raised up for
     yourself.
¹⁸Then we will not turn away from you;
   revive us, and we will call on your name.

¹⁹Restore us, O LORD God Almighty;
   make your face shine upon us,
   that we may be saved.

Psalm 81

For the director of music. According to
   gittith.^k Of Asaph.

¹Sing for joy to God our strength;
   shout aloud to the God of Jacob!
²Begin the music, strike the tambourine,
   play the melodious harp and lyre.

³Sound the ram's horn at the New Moon,
   and when the moon is full, on the day of
     our Feast;
⁴this is a decree for Israel,
   an ordinance of the God of Jacob.
⁵He established it as a statute for Joseph
   when he went out against Egypt,
   where we heard a language we did not
     understand.^l

⁶He says, "I removed the burden from their
     shoulders;
   their hands were set free from the basket.
⁷In your distress you called and I rescued you,
   I answered you out of a thundercloud;
   I tested you at the waters of Meribah. *Selah*

⁸"Hear, O my people, and I will warn you—
   if you would but listen to me, O Israel!
⁹You shall have no foreign god among you;
   you shall not bow down to an alien god.
¹⁰I am the LORD your God,
   who brought you up out of Egypt.
   Open wide your mouth and I will fill it.

¹¹"But my people would not listen to me;
   Israel would not submit to me.

¹²So I gave them over to their stubborn hearts
   to follow their own devices.

¹³"If my people would but listen to me,
   if Israel would follow my ways,
¹⁴how quickly would I subdue their enemies
   and turn my hand against their foes!
¹⁵Those who hate the LORD would cringe before
     him,
   and their punishment would last forever.
¹⁶But you would be fed with the finest of
     wheat;
   with honey from the rock I would satisfy
     you."

Psalm 82

A psalm of Asaph.

¹God presides in the great assembly;
   he gives judgment among the "gods":

²"How long will you^m defend the unjust
   and show partiality to the wicked?   *Selah*
³Defend the cause of the weak and fatherless;
   maintain the rights of the poor and
     oppressed.
⁴Rescue the weak and needy;
   deliver them from the hand of the wicked.

⁵"They know nothing, they understand
     nothing.
   They walk about in darkness;
   all the foundations of the earth are shaken.

⁶"I said, 'You are "gods";
   you are all sons of the Most High.'
⁷But you will die like mere men;
   you will fall like every other ruler."

⁸Rise up, O God, judge the earth,
   for all the nations are your inheritance.

Psalm 83

A song. A psalm of Asaph.

¹O God, do not keep silent;
   be not quiet, O God, be not still.
²See how your enemies are astir,
   how your foes rear their heads.
³With cunning they conspire against your
     people;

---

j 15 Or *branch*   ^kTitle: Probably a musical term   ^l5 Or *l and we
heard a voice we had not known*   ^m2 The Hebrew is plural.

they plot against those you cherish.
⁴"Come," they say, "let us destroy them as a
nation,
that the name of Israel be remembered no
more."

⁵With one mind they plot together;
they form an alliance against you—
⁶the tents of Edom and the Ishmaelites,
of Moab and the Hagrites,
⁷Gebal,ⁿ Ammon and Amalek,
Philistia, with the people of Tyre.
⁸Even Assyria has joined them
to lend strength to the descendants of Lot.
Selah

⁹Do to them as you did to Midian,
as you did to Sisera and Jabin at the river
Kishon,
¹⁰who perished at Endor
and became like refuse on the ground.
¹¹Make their nobles like Oreb and Zeeb,

all their princes like Zebah and Zalmunna,
¹²who said, "Let us take possession
of the pasturelands of God."

¹³Make them like tumbleweed, O my God,
like chaff before the wind.
¹⁴As fire consumes the forest
or a flame sets the mountains ablaze,
¹⁵so pursue them with your tempest
and terrify them with your storm.
¹⁶Cover their faces with shame
so that men will seek your name, O Lord.

¹⁷May they ever be ashamed and dismayed;
may they perish in disgrace.
¹⁸Let them know that you, whose name is the
Lord—
that you alone are the Most High over all
the earth.

ⁿ7 That is, Byblos

49 / *Psalm 84*
A Prayer of Yearning

CONTINUOUS ACCESS AND warm intimacy with God is sometimes difficult to maintain. Times of spiritual dryness, "busyness" and adversity may capture our attention more and rob us of regular meeting times with God. Psalm 84 reflects a time of spiritual dryness common to many believers experientially and to Israel historically. This psalmist laments his forced and prolonged separation from God (likely during the Babylonian exile), which has robbed him of the appointed duties, freedom of access and the warm intimacy he once enjoyed.

 Warming Up to God Think back to where you were living when you were twelve years old. What was the center of warmth in your home then?

 Read Psalm 84.

Psalm 84

For the director of music. According to
*gittith.*ᵒ Of the Sons of Korah. A psalm.

¹How lovely is your dwelling place,
O Lord Almighty!
²My soul yearns, even faints,
for the courts of the Lord;
my heart and my flesh cry out
for the living God.

³Even the sparrow has found a home,
and the swallow a nest for herself,

where she may have her young—
a place near your altar,
O Lord Almighty, my King and my God.
⁴Blessed are those who dwell in your house;
they are ever praising you.   *Selah*

⁵Blessed are those whose strength is in you,
who have set their hearts on pilgrimage.
⁶As they pass through the Valley of Baca,
they make it a place of springs;
the autumn rains also cover it with pools.ᵖ

ᵒTitle: Probably a musical term   ᵖ6 Or *blessings*

7 They go from strength to strength,
  till each appears before God in Zion.

8 Hear my prayer, O LORD God Almighty;
  listen to me, O God of Jacob. *Selah*
9 Look upon our shield,[q] O God;
  look with favor on your anointed one.

10 Better is one day in your courts
  than a thousand elsewhere;
I would rather be a doorkeeper in the house
    of my God
  than dwell in the tents of the wicked.
11 For the LORD God is a sun and shield;
  the LORD bestows favor and honor;
no good thing does he withhold
  from those whose walk is blameless.

12 O LORD Almighty,
  blessed is the man who trusts in you.

[q]9 Or *sovereign*

Discovering the Word 1. What is the psalmist yearning for (vv. 2–3, 10)? 2. What names and metaphors for God can you find in this psalm? 3. The "Valley of Baca" (v. 6) was an arid stretch of desert that brought tears of adversity to pilgrims who had to traverse it en route to Jerusalem. What does that valley symbolize—historically and spiritually? 4. What are the benefits or blessings of trusting God as this psalmist does (vv. 4–5, 11–12)?

Applying the Word 1. If you could have one wish come true regarding your Christian life, what one thing would you yearn for? 2. How do you usually address God in prayer? Why? 3. Try to visualize where and when God has been closest to you. Put yourself in that picture as a "doorkeeper." How do you feel at those intimate times?

Responding in Prayer Spend time with the Lord of the universe in prayer, fellowship and worship.

Psalm 85

Psalm 85

For the director of music. Of the Sons of Korah. A psalm.

1 You showed favor to your land, O LORD;
  you restored the fortunes of Jacob.
2 You forgave the iniquity of your people
  and covered all their sins. *Selah*
3 You set aside all your wrath
  and turned from your fierce anger.

4 Restore us again, O God our Savior,
  and put away your displeasure toward us.
5 Will you be angry with us forever?
  Will you prolong your anger through all
    generations?
6 Will you not revive us again,
  that your people may rejoice in you?
7 Show us your unfailing love, O LORD,
  and grant us your salvation.

8 I will listen to what God the LORD will say;
  he promises peace to his people, his
    saints—
  but let them not return to folly.
9 Surely his salvation is near those who fear
    him,
  that his glory may dwell in our land.

10 Love and faithfulness meet together;
  righteousness and peace kiss each other.
11 Faithfulness springs forth from the earth,
  and righteousness looks down from heaven.
12 The LORD will indeed give what is good,
  and our land will yield its harvest.
13 Righteousness goes before him
  and prepares the way for his steps.

50 / *Psalm 86*
A Prayer of Dependence

OUR RELATIONSHIP WITH God is that of children to a parent, sheep to a shepherd, creators to the Creator. We are dependent on him for life, for breath, for sustenance, for help in trouble, for love, for forgiveness, for mercy. We may like to think of ourselves as independent and self-sufficient. But we are not. We need God. It is vital that we acknowledge our need for him because it is the beginning place of our relationship with him. This psalm helps us give voice to our dependence on God.

 Warming Up to God   Think of a time when you needed to rely on someone for emotional or physical support. What feelings did you have about depending on them for help?

 Read Psalm 86.

Psalm 86

A prayer of David.

¹Hear, O Lᴏʀᴅ, and answer me,
    for I am poor and needy.
²Guard my life, for I am devoted to you.
    You are my God; save your servant
    who trusts in you.
³Have mercy on me, O Lord,
    for I call to you all day long.
⁴Bring joy to your servant,
    for to you, O Lord,
    I lift up my soul.

⁵You are forgiving and good, O Lord,
    abounding in love to all who call
      to you.
⁶Hear my prayer, O Lᴏʀᴅ;
    listen to my cry for mercy.
⁷In the day of my trouble I will call
      to you,
    for you will answer me.

⁸Among the gods there is none like you,
    O Lord;
    no deeds can compare with yours.
⁹All the nations you have made
    will come and worship before you, O Lord;
    they will bring glory to your name.
¹⁰For you are great and do marvelous deeds;
    you alone are God.

¹¹Teach me your way, O Lᴏʀᴅ,
    and I will walk in your truth;
    give me an undivided heart,
    that I may fear your name.
¹²I will praise you, O Lord my God, with all
      my heart;
    I will glorify your name forever.
¹³For great is your love toward me;
    you have delivered me from the depths of
      the grave.ʳ

¹⁴The arrogant are attacking me,
    O God;
    a band of ruthless men seeks
      my life—
    men without regard for you.
¹⁵But you, O Lord, are a compassionate and
      gracious God,
    slow to anger, abounding in love and
      faithfulness.
¹⁶Turn to me and have mercy on me;
    grant your strength to your servant
    and save the son of your maidservant.ˢ
¹⁷Give me a sign of your goodness,
    that my enemies may see it and be put to
      shame,
    for you, O Lᴏʀᴅ, have helped me and
      comforted me.

ʳ13 Hebrew Sheol   *ˢ16 Or save your faithful son*

Discovering the Word   1. What is the overall sense you get about the nature of the psalmist's relationship with God?   2. List the many requests the psalmist makes of God.   3. The psalmist sees God as loving, powerful and actively involved in caring for him. What are some of the specific statements he makes about God? 4. What impact would this view of God have on a person's ability to depend on God?   5. How does the psalmist show his dependence on God throughout this psalm?

Applying the Word 1. What reactions do you have to this kind of dependency on God? 2. How might the psalmist's dependency on God encourage you to depend more fully on God? 3. In what areas of your life do you need to acknowledge your dependence on God?

 Responding in Prayer Freely express your sense of need for God and your struggles to depend on him.

Psalm 87

Psalm 87

Of the Sons of Korah. A psalm. A song.

¹He has set his foundation on the holy
  mountain;
² the Lord loves the gates of Zion
  more than all the dwellings of Jacob.
³Glorious things are said of you,
  O city of God: *Selah*
⁴"I will record Rahab*ᵗ* and Babylon
  among those who acknowledge me—
Philistia too, and Tyre, along with
  Cush*ᵘ*—

and will say, 'This*ᵛ* one was born in
  Zion.' "

⁵Indeed, of Zion it will be said,
  "This one and that one were born in her,
  and the Most High himself will establish
  her."
⁶The Lord will write in the register of the
  peoples:
  "This one was born in Zion."   *Selah*
⁷As they make music they will sing,
  "All my fountains are in you."

*ᵗ4 A poetic name for Egypt   ᵘ4 That is, the upper Nile region
ᵛ4 Or "O Rahab and Babylon, / Philistia, Tyre and Cush, / I will record
concerning those who acknowledge me: / 'This*

51 / Psalm 88
A Prayer of Despair

"I GIVE UP," Nancy said as she buried her face in her hands. Nancy was not a passive person. She worked hard as a single mother to provide for her children. She had developed a good support system for herself. She was actively, compassionately engaged in life. But a series of losses had left her deeply shaken. Everything she had worked so hard for seemed to be gone. Nancy felt defeated. And without hope. Despair is giving up. Or, as the psalmist expresses it, despair is a time when "darkness" becomes our "closest friend."

 Warming Up to God What pictures come to mind when you think of a person who is experiencing despair?

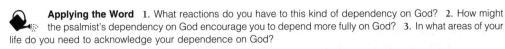 **Read Psalm 88.**

Psalm 88

A song. A psalm of the Sons of Korah. For
  the director of music. According to
  *mahalath leannoth.*ʷ A *maskil*ˣ of Heman
  the Ezrahite.

¹O Lord, the God who saves me,
  day and night I cry out before you.
²May my prayer come before you;

turn your ear to my cry.

³For my soul is full of trouble
  and my life draws near the grave.*ʸ*
⁴I am counted among those who go down to
  the pit;
  I am like a man without strength.
⁵I am set apart with the dead,

*ʷTitle: Possibly a tune, "The Suffering of Affliction"   ˣTitle: Probably a
literary or musical term   ʸ3 Hebrew Sheol*

like the slain who lie in the grave,
whom you remember no more,
who are cut off from your care.

⁶You have put me in the lowest pit,
in the darkest depths.
⁷Your wrath lies heavily upon me;
you have overwhelmed me with all your
waves.   *Selah*
⁸You have taken from me my closest friends
and have made me repulsive to them.
I am confined and cannot escape;
⁹   my eyes are dim with grief.

I call to you, O Lᴏʀᴅ, every day;
I spread out my hands to you.
¹⁰Do you show your wonders to the dead?
Do those who are dead rise up and praise
you?   *Selah*
¹¹Is your love declared in the grave,
your faithfulness in Destruction ᶻ?
¹²Are your wonders known in the place of
darkness,

or your righteous deeds in the land of
oblivion?

¹³But I cry to you for help, O Lᴏʀᴅ;
in the morning my prayer comes before
you.
¹⁴Why, O Lᴏʀᴅ, do you reject me
and hide your face from me?

¹⁵From my youth I have been afflicted and
close to death;
I have suffered your terrors and am in
despair.
¹⁶Your wrath has swept over me;
your terrors have destroyed me.
¹⁷All day long they surround me like a flood;
they have completely engulfed me.
¹⁸You have taken my companions and loved
ones from me;
the darkness is my closest friend.

ᶻ11 Hebrew *Abaddon*

 Discovering the Word 1. What evidence is there of despair in this psalm? 2. What emotional impact did you experience as you read this psalm? 3. Contrast the first and last verses of this psalm. Most psalms which express strong doubts end with hope or praise. This psalm ends with doubt and despair. What is it like to be left with unresolved questions? 4. The writer blames God for his desperate situation. What does he say in blaming God (vv. 6–9, 15–18)? 5. In spite of his sense that God has rejected him and hurt him, the psalmist continues to talk with God. What does this say about his relationship with God?

 Applying the Word 1. What reactions do you have to the psalmist blaming God? 2. Think of a time when it was difficult for you to talk to God. What was that experience like for you?

Responding in Prayer What would you like to say to God about the areas in life that feel "dark" or hopeless to you?

Psalm 89

Psalm 89

A *maskil*ᵃ of Ethan the Ezrahite.

¹I will sing of the Lᴏʀᴅ's great love
forever;
with my mouth I will make your
faithfulness known through all
generations.
²I will declare that your love stands firm
forever,
that you established your faithfulness in
heaven itself.

³You said, "I have made a covenant with my
chosen one,
I have sworn to David my servant,
⁴'I will establish your line forever
and make your throne firm through all
generations.' "   *Selah*

⁵The heavens praise your wonders, O Lᴏʀᴅ,
your faithfulness too, in the assembly of the
holy ones.
⁶For who in the skies above can compare with
the Lᴏʀᴅ?

ᵃTitle: Probably a literary or musical term

Who is like the LORD among the heavenly
   beings?
⁷In the council of the holy ones God is greatly
   feared;
   he is more awesome than all who surround
     him.
⁸O LORD God Almighty, who is like you?
   You are mighty, O LORD, and your
     faithfulness surrounds you.

⁹You rule over the surging sea;
   when its waves mount up, you still them.
¹⁰You crushed Rahab like one of the slain;
   with your strong arm you scattered your
     enemies.
¹¹The heavens are yours, and yours also the
     earth;
   you founded the world and all that is in it.
¹²You created the north and the south;
   Tabor and Hermon sing for joy at your
     name.
¹³Your arm is endued with power;
   your hand is strong, your right hand
     exalted.

¹⁴Righteousness and justice are the foundation
   of your throne;
   love and faithfulness go before you.
¹⁵Blessed are those who have learned to acclaim
   you,
   who walk in the light of your presence,
     O LORD.
¹⁶They rejoice in your name all day long;
   they exult in your righteousness.
¹⁷For you are their glory and strength,
   and by your favor you exalt our horn.ᵇ
¹⁸Indeed, our shieldᶜ belongs to the LORD,
   our king to the Holy One of Israel.

¹⁹Once you spoke in a vision,
   to your faithful people you said:
 "I have bestowed strength on a warrior;
   I have exalted a young man from among
     the people.
²⁰I have found David my servant;
   with my sacred oil I have anointed him.
²¹My hand will sustain him;
   surely my arm will strengthen him.
²²No enemy will subject him to tribute;
   no wicked man will oppress him.
²³I will crush his foes before him
   and strike down his adversaries.
²⁴My faithful love will be with him,

and through my name his hornᵈ will be
   exalted.
²⁵I will set his hand over the sea,
   his right hand over the rivers.
²⁶He will call out to me, 'You are my Father,
   my God, the Rock my Savior.'
²⁷I will also appoint him my firstborn,
   the most exalted of the kings of the earth.
²⁸I will maintain my love to him forever,
   and my covenant with him will never fail.
²⁹I will establish his line forever,
   his throne as long as the heavens endure.

³⁰"If his sons forsake my law
   and do not follow my statutes,
³¹if they violate my decrees
   and fail to keep my commands,
³²I will punish their sin with the rod,
   their iniquity with flogging;
³³but I will not take my love from him,
   nor will I ever betray my faithfulness.
³⁴I will not violate my covenant
   or alter what my lips have uttered.
³⁵Once for all, I have sworn by my holiness—
   and I will not lie to David—
³⁶that his line will continue forever
   and his throne endure before me like the
     sun;
³⁷it will be established forever like the moon,
   the faithful witness in the sky."   *Selah*

³⁸But you have rejected, you have spurned,
   you have been very angry with your
     anointed one.
³⁹You have renounced the covenant with your
     servant
   and have defiled his crown in the dust.
⁴⁰You have broken through all his walls
   and reduced his strongholds to ruins.
⁴¹All who pass by have plundered him;
   he has become the scorn of his neighbors.
⁴²You have exalted the right hand of his foes;
   you have made all his enemies rejoice.
⁴³You have turned back the edge of his sword
   and have not supported him in battle.
⁴⁴You have put an end to his splendor
   and cast his throne to the ground.
⁴⁵You have cut short the days of his youth;
   you have covered him with a mantle of
     shame.   *Selah*

ᵇ17 *Horn here symbolizes strong one.*   ᶜ18 Or *sovereign*
ᵈ24 *Horn here symbolizes strength.*

⁴⁶How long, O LORD? Will you hide yourself
    forever?
    How long will your wrath burn like fire?
⁴⁷Remember how fleeting is my life.
    For what futility you have created all
        men!
⁴⁸What man can live and not see death,
    or save himself from the power of the
        grave*?   *Selah*
⁴⁹O Lord, where is your former great love,
    which in your faithfulness you swore to
        David?

⁵⁰Remember, Lord, how your servant has*
    been mocked,
    how I bear in my heart the taunts of all the
        nations,
⁵¹the taunts with which your enemies have
    mocked, O LORD,
    with which they have mocked every step of
        your anointed one.

⁵²Praise be to the LORD forever!
    Amen and Amen.

48 Hebrew *Sheol*   *50* Or *your servants have*

52 / *Psalm 90*
Praying Our Death

DEATH IS NOT a popular subject. We live in a society characterized by the denial of death. This is unusual. Most people who have lived on this earth have given a great deal of attention to death. Preparing for a good death has been, in every century except our own, an accepted goal in life. Psalm 90 has been part of that preparation for millions of Christians.

 Warming Up to God   When you think about your own death, what do you think about? What do you feel?

 Read Psalm 90.

BOOK IV
Psalms 90–106

Psalm 90

A prayer of Moses the man of God.

¹Lord, you have been our dwelling place
    throughout all generations.
²Before the mountains were born
    or you brought forth the earth and the
        world,
    from everlasting to everlasting you are God.

³You turn men back to dust,
    saying, "Return to dust, O sons of men."
⁴For a thousand years in your sight
    are like a day that has just gone by,
    or like a watch in the night.
⁵You sweep men away in the sleep of death;
    they are like the new grass of the
        morning—
⁶though in the morning it springs up new,

by evening it is dry and withered.

⁷We are consumed by your anger
    and terrified by your indignation.
⁸You have set our iniquities before you,
    our secret sins in the light of your
        presence.
⁹All our days pass away under your wrath;
    we finish our years with a moan.
¹⁰The length of our days is seventy years—
    or eighty, if we have the strength;
    yet their span* is but trouble and sorrow,
    for they quickly pass, and we fly away.

¹¹Who knows the power of your anger?
    For your wrath is as great as the fear that is
        due you.
¹²Teach us to number our days aright,
    that we may gain a heart of wisdom.

¹³Relent, O LORD! How long will it be?
    Have compassion on your servants.

10 Or *yet the best of them*

¹⁴Satisfy us in the morning with your unfailing
love,
    that we may sing for joy and be glad all
    our days.
¹⁵Make us glad for as many days as you have
afflicted us,
    for as many years as we have seen trouble.
¹⁶May your deeds be shown to your servants,

your splendor to their children.

¹⁷May the favor[h] of the Lord our God rest
upon us;
    establish the work of our hands for us—
    yes, establish the work of our hands.

h 17 Or *beauty*

Discovering the Word 1. Read Psalm 90. Death sets a limit to our lives and stimulates reflection on the context of life, which is not death, but God. In verses 1–2 how does the psalmist set death within his view of God? 2. How does the psalmist describe God's anger and its effects on our lives (vv. 7–11)? 3. How do you integrate this view of God with John's well-known statement "God is love"? 4. Luther commented on verse 12: "Lord, teach us all to be such arithmeticians!" What does it mean to number our days aright? 5. Study the verbs in verses 14–17. What emerges as most important for you—what you do for the rest of your life or what God will do in your life? Explain.

Applying the Word 1. How long do you expect to live? 2. How do you plan to live the years left to you? 3. Plato believed that philosophy was nothing more than a study of death. In the Middle Ages pastoral care concentrated on preparing you for a good death. How does your meditation on death affect the way you live your life?

Responding in Prayer Express your awareness that you will die. In your prayers be conscious of Christ's death.

---

53 / *Psalm 91*
Angels Among Us

ANGEL STORIES ARE gaining wider acceptance today. People see angels taking various forms and functions—as messengers of glad tidings, spirits of people who have died, invisible guardians of our safety, angels in disguise as do-gooders or cherubs of romantic love. Many of the popular depictions of angels have nothing to do with the biblical perspective. The angels invoked in this psalm are heralds and harbingers of God's power. The psalm glows with testimony to the security of godly worshipers.

Warming Up to God In your mind's eye, what do angels look like? What do they spend their time doing?

Read Psalm 91.

Psalm 91

¹He who dwells in the shelter of the Most
High
    will rest in the shadow of the Almighty.[i]
²I will say[j] of the Lᴏʀᴅ, "He is my refuge and
my fortress,
    my God, in whom I trust."

³Surely he will save you from the fowler's
snare
    and from the deadly pestilence.

⁴He will cover you with his feathers,
    and under his wings you will find refuge;
    his faithfulness will be your shield and
    rampart.
⁵You will not fear the terror of night,
    nor the arrow that flies by day,
⁶nor the pestilence that stalks in the darkness,
    nor the plague that destroys at midday.
⁷A thousand may fall at your side,
    ten thousand at your right hand,

i 1 Hebrew *Shaddai*   j 2 Or *He says*

but it will not come near you.
⁸You will only observe with your eyes
and see the punishment of the wicked.

⁹If you make the Most High your dwelling—
even the LORD, who is my refuge—
¹⁰then no harm will befall you,
no disaster will come near your tent.
¹¹For he will command his angels concerning
you
to guard you in all your ways;
¹²they will lift you up in their hands,
so that you will not strike your foot against
a stone.

¹³You will tread upon the lion and the cobra;
you will trample the great lion and the
serpent.

¹⁴"Because he loves me," says the LORD, "I will
rescue him;
I will protect him, for he acknowledges my
name.
¹⁵He will call upon me, and I will answer him;
I will be with him in trouble,
I will deliver him and honor him.
¹⁶With long life will I satisfy him
and show him my salvation."

Discovering the Word 1. The psalm divides into two stanzas: vv. 1–8 and vv. 9–16. What theme is common to the opening couplet of each stanza (vv. 1–2, 9–10)? 2. What threatens the security of the believer, even those who take refuge in God (vv. 3–6, 13)? 3. Is the godly believer protected *from* calamity and sorrow, or is he promised God's presence *amidst* terrible circumstances? Explain your answer from the passage. 4. What is the basis for the psalmist's assurance that he will be safe and secure (vv. 9–12, 14–15)? 5. In this psalm, what does "my [God's] salvation" (v. 16) look like?

Applying the Word 1. What are you particularly anxious about these days, for which God is waiting on you to call his name and acknowledge your need? 2. How can you make God your dwelling place, your refuge, your shield in times of trouble?

Responding in Prayer God is waiting to hear from his people who love him and acknowledge their need of him. Tell him whatever is on your mind, whatever fears you have and whatever terrible circumstances you are facing. Trust him to answer.

Psalms 92—93

Psalm 92

A psalm. A song. For the Sabbath day.

¹It is good to praise the LORD
and make music to your name, O Most
High,
²to proclaim your love in the morning
and your faithfulness at night,
³to the music of the ten-stringed lyre
and the melody of the harp.

⁴For you make me glad by your deeds, O LORD;
I sing for joy at the works of your hands.
⁵How great are your works, O LORD,
how profound your thoughts!
⁶The senseless man does not know,
fools do not understand,
⁷that though the wicked spring up like grass
and all evildoers flourish,
they will be forever destroyed.

⁸But you, O LORD, are exalted forever.

⁹For surely your enemies, O LORD,
surely your enemies will perish;
all evildoers will be scattered.
¹⁰You have exalted my horn[k] like that of a
wild ox;
fine oils have been poured upon me.
¹¹My eyes have seen the defeat of my
adversaries;
my ears have heard the rout of my wicked
foes.

¹²The righteous will flourish like a palm tree,
they will grow like a cedar of Lebanon;
¹³planted in the house of the LORD,
they will flourish in the courts of our God.
¹⁴They will still bear fruit in old age,
they will stay fresh and green,

[k]10 *Horn* here symbolizes strength.

¹⁵proclaiming, "The LORD is upright;
   he is my Rock, and there is no wickedness
     in him."

Psalm 93

¹The LORD reigns, he is robed in majesty;
   the LORD is robed in majesty
   and is armed with strength.
The world is firmly established;
   it cannot be moved.
²Your throne was established long ago;
   you are from all eternity.

³The seas have lifted up, O LORD,
   the seas have lifted up their voice;
   the seas have lifted up their pounding
     waves.
⁴Mightier than the thunder of the great waters,
   mightier than the breakers of the sea—
   the LORD on high is mighty.

⁵Your statutes stand firm;
   holiness adorns your house
   for endless days, O LORD.

54 / *Psalm 94*
A Prayer of Anger

MIKE AND JOHN had something in common—they had both been ripped off by their business partners and they were both angry. Very angry. As they shared their experiences with each other, they discovered an important difference, however. Mike was baffled by what to do with his strong feelings. His anger frightened him and did not seem very spiritual, so most of the time he kept quiet about his sense of outrage at the unfairness of it all. John, on the other hand, had grown up in a church that prayed the psalms together. Together they had spoken the words of anger and outrage to God. As a result, John was able to talk to God about his anger. He knew he had been grievously wronged and that he was deeply angry. And he knew he could take his anger to God. This psalm is one of the psalms that can help us speak freely to God about our anger.

 Warming Up to God Is it difficult or relatively easy for you to tell God about your anger? Explain.

 Read Psalm 94.

Psalm 94

¹O LORD, the God who avenges,
   O God who avenges, shine forth.
²Rise up, O Judge of the earth;
   pay back to the proud what they deserve.
³How long will the wicked, O LORD,
   how long will the wicked be jubilant?

⁴They pour out arrogant words;
   all the evildoers are full of boasting.
⁵They crush your people, O LORD;
   they oppress your inheritance.
⁶They slay the widow and the alien;
   they murder the fatherless.
⁷They say, "The LORD does not see;
   the God of Jacob pays no heed."

⁸Take heed, you senseless ones among the
     people;

you fools, when will you become wise?
⁹Does he who implanted the ear not hear?
   Does he who formed the eye not see?
¹⁰Does he who disciplines nations not punish?
   Does he who teaches man lack knowledge?
¹¹The LORD knows the thoughts of man;
   he knows that they are futile.

¹²Blessed is the man you discipline, O LORD,
   the man you teach from your law;
¹³you grant him relief from days of trouble,
   till a pit is dug for the wicked.
¹⁴For the LORD will not reject his people;
   he will never forsake his inheritance.
¹⁵Judgment will again be founded on
     righteousness,
   and all the upright in heart will follow it.

¹⁶Who will rise up for me against the wicked?

Who will take a stand for me against
    evildoers?
[17]Unless the LORD had given me help,
    I would soon have dwelt in the silence of
    death.
[18]When I said, "My foot is slipping,"
    your love, O LORD, supported me.
[19]When anxiety was great within me,
    your consolation brought joy to my soul.

[20]Can a corrupt throne be allied with you—

one that brings on misery by its decrees?
[21]They band together against the righteous
    and condemn the innocent to death.
[22]But the LORD has become my fortress,
    and my God the rock in whom I take
    refuge.
[23]He will repay them for their sins
    and destroy them for their wickedness;
    the LORD our God will destroy them.

Discovering the Word 1. The psalmist addresses God as the Judge and as the one who avenges (vv. 1–2). What is the meaning of this for the psalmist? 2. In pleading his case before God, what does the psalmist say the wicked have done (vv. 4–7)? 3. In verses 8, 9 and 10 the psalmist asks several rhetorical questions of God. What statement is he making in these questions? 4. What hope does the psalmist express in verses 12–15? 5. Verse 16 captures the question the psalmist is wrestling with. What words would you use to express this question? 6. In verses 17 through 19 the psalmist expresses himself in vulnerable terms. How does he describe the experience of danger and fear that generated his anger?

Applying the Word 1. The psalmist concludes with statements that God will take care of justice, that God will judge. Why is this important to remember when we are feeling powerless and outraged in the face of injustice? 2. This psalm models several constructive ways we can behave when we are angry. It models honesty with ourselves and with God, stating our case to God, acknowledging our vulnerability, trusting God's care and letting God take care of justice. How might this example help you in times of anger? 3. Which of these behavioral examples might be especially important for you to follow when you are angry? Explain.

Responding in Prayer Talk to God about any feelings of anger—fresh or lingering—that you have.

---

55 / *Psalm 95*
A Psalm of Rest

SO OFTEN GOD gives us the consequences of our choices; other times he withholds or spares us the punishment our rebellion or hardheartedness deserves. That is an act of his mercy, for which this psalmist and all believers can give thanks. This psalm acknowledges God as Lord of the earth and Shepherd King of his people. The writer reflects on times of rebellion when the Israelites put God to the test and ended up missing out on God's rest.

 Warming Up to God Picture the place where you go to enjoy peace and serenity, rest from your labors, and listen to God. If you don't have a place like that, make one up. Where is that place? (Does it have mountain peaks, sandy beaches, desert calm, green pastures?)

 Read Psalm 95.

Psalm 95

[1]Come, let us sing for joy to the LORD;
    let us shout aloud to the Rock of our
    salvation.
[2]Let us come before him with thanksgiving
    and extol him with music and song.

[3]For the LORD is the great God,
    the great King above all gods.
[4]In his hand are the depths of the earth,
    and the mountain peaks belong to him.
[5]The sea is his, for he made it,
    and his hands formed the dry land.

⁶Come, let us bow down in worship,
 let us kneel before the Lord our Maker;
⁷for he is our God
 and we are the people of his pasture,
 the flock under his care.

Today, if you hear his voice,
⁸ do not harden your hearts as you did at
  Meribah,^l
 as you did that day at Massah^m in the
  desert,

⁹where your fathers tested and tried me,
 though they had seen what I did.
¹⁰For forty years I was angry with that
  generation;
 I said, "They are a people whose hearts go
  astray,
 and they have not known my ways."
¹¹So I declared on oath in my anger,
 "They shall never enter my rest."

^l8 *Meribah* means *quarreling*.   ^m8 *Massah* means *testing*.

Discovering the Word 1. Where does this psalmist envision God ruling as Lord and King (vv. 3–5)? 2. Meribah and Massah are places where the Israelites rebelled in the desert and tested the Lord about whether he was with them or not (vv. 8–9). What happened as a result of that testing (vv. 10–11)? 3. What is the "rest" from which the rebellious Israelites were banned with an oath of God, but which a later generation would enjoy (v. 11)? 4. Imagine life without God's promised rest. What must that have been like? 5. What warning does the psalmist derive from that experience as he contemplates "Meribah" and "Massah" recurring for the present generation of God's people?

Applying the Word 1. Imagine life for you without God's promised rest. If your life and well-being were constantly threatened with adversaries in the land where you live and work, what would you be praying for? 2. During those times in your past when your heart strayed from God's ways (v. 10), how did God bring you back to himself? 3. As you listen to God's voice "today" (v. 7), what is he saying to you?

Responding in Prayer Whatever the past or present circumstances of your relationship with him may be, this psalm invites you to come into God's presence today. Try kneeling in his presence, acknowledging him as Lord of your life, even during those times you have strayed. Soften your heart and give him the praise and thanksgiving he deserves.

---

56 / *Psalm 96*
Worldwide Worship

OUR GOD IS a missionary God. He wants all nations, every living thing, to bow down in worship of him. And God wants us to take that message—in word and deed, in song and praise—to the ends of the earth. The psalmist bids us to be most inclusive in our worship of the one true God.

Warming Up to God Think about the greatness of God. What hymns come to mind that prompt you with the melody, the lyrics and reasons to praise him for the great things he has done?

Read Psalm 96.

Psalm 96

¹Sing to the Lord a new song;
 sing to the Lord, all the earth.
²Sing to the Lord, praise his name;
 proclaim his salvation day after
  day.
³Declare his glory among the nations,
 his marvelous deeds among all peoples.

⁴For great is the Lord and most worthy of
  praise;
 he is to be feared above all gods.
⁵For all the gods of the nations are idols,
 but the Lord made the heavens.
⁶Splendor and majesty are before him;
 strength and glory are in his sanctuary.

⁷Ascribe to the Lord, O families of nations,

ascribe to the Lord glory and strength.
[8]Ascribe to the Lord the glory due his name;
bring an offering and come into his courts.
[9]Worship the Lord in the splendor of his[n]
holiness;
tremble before him, all the earth.

[10]Say among the nations, "The Lord reigns."
The world is firmly established, it cannot
be moved;
he will judge the peoples with equity.
[11]Let the heavens rejoice, let the earth be glad;

let the sea resound, and all that is in it;
[12] let the fields be jubilant, and everything in
them.
Then all the trees of the forest will sing for
joy;
[13] they will sing before the Lord, for he
comes,
he comes to judge the earth.
He will judge the world in righteousness
and the peoples in his truth.

[n]9 Or Lord with the splendor of

Discovering the Word   1. This psalm is divided up into four parts that are identifiable by repeated words or refrains: verses 1–3, 4–6, 7–9 and 10–13. What repetition do you see in each of these sections? **2.** What "marvelous deeds" (v. 3) come to mind that would prompt a believer to sing God's praises?   **3.** Why is the Lord "most worthy of" (entitled to) praise (vv. 4–6, 10, 13)?   **4.** Like an orchestra conductor that bids different sections to join in the ensemble, the psalmist bids different sections to join in the chorus of praise to God. How extensive or inclusive is this call to "ascribe glory to" (worship) God (vv. 7–13)?

Applying the Word   1. In light of this universal call to worship, think of those around you and on the other side of the globe. What does this psalmist prompt you to do about those who don't know God?   **2.** This psalm invites us to sing a "new song" declaring his glory to others (in witness) and ascribing glory directly to God (in worship). How would someone who is not musically inclined be creative in this kind of witness and worship? **3.** Let the joy of knowing God bubble up within you and burst forth in a "new song" of worship. Be spontaneous and let this psalm be the wellspring for singing out or jotting down words of praise. (Later see if you, or someone you know, could set those words to music.)

Responding in Prayer Pray for someone who does not yet know God. Pray about inviting that person to join you in worship.

Psalms 97—98

Psalm 97

[1]The Lord reigns, let the earth be glad;
let the distant shores rejoice.

[2]Clouds and thick darkness surround him;
righteousness and justice are the foundation
of his throne.
[3]Fire goes before him
and consumes his foes on every side.
[4]His lightning lights up the world;
the earth sees and trembles.
[5]The mountains melt like wax before the Lord,
before the Lord of all the earth.
[6]The heavens proclaim his righteousness,
and all the peoples see his glory.

[7]All who worship images are put to shame,

those who boast in idols—
worship him, all you gods!

[8]Zion hears and rejoices
and the villages of Judah are glad
because of your judgments, O Lord.
[9]For you, O Lord, are the Most High over all
the earth;
you are exalted far above all gods.

[10]Let those who love the Lord hate evil,
for he guards the lives of his faithful ones
and delivers them from the hand of the
wicked.
[11]Light is shed upon the righteous
and joy on the upright in heart.
[12]Rejoice in the Lord, you who are righteous,
and praise his holy name.

Psalm 98

A psalm.

[1]Sing to the LORD a new song,
    for he has done marvelous things;
his right hand and his holy arm
    have worked salvation for him.
[2]The LORD has made his salvation known
    and revealed his righteousness to the
        nations.
[3]He has remembered his love
    and his faithfulness to the house of Israel;
all the ends of the earth have seen
    the salvation of our God.

[4]Shout for joy to the LORD, all the earth,
    burst into jubilant song with music;
[5]make music to the LORD with the harp,
    with the harp and the sound of singing,
[6]with trumpets and the blast of the ram's
        horn—
    shout for joy before the LORD, the King.

[7]Let the sea resound, and everything in it,
    the world, and all who live in it.
[8]Let the rivers clap their hands,
    let the mountains sing together for joy;
[9]let them sing before the LORD,
    for he comes to judge the earth.
He will judge the world in righteousness
    and the peoples with equity.

57 / *Psalm 99*
Hail to the King of Kings

THE ATTRIBUTES AND actions of our holy God inspire praise, awe and obedience in those who call on his name. This psalm calls to mind the special relationship that he had with Moses, Aaron and Samuel—a relationship that is representative and possible for all of God's people.

 Warming Up to God Think about the holiness of God. What hymns come to mind that prompt you to praise God for his holiness, the justice and rightness of his ways? How do those hymns make you feel about approaching God?

 Read Psalm 99.

Psalm 99

[1]The LORD reigns,
    let the nations tremble;
he sits enthroned between the cherubim,
    let the earth shake.
[2]Great is the LORD in Zion;
    he is exalted over all the nations.
[3]Let them praise your great and awesome
        name—
    he is holy.

[4]The King is mighty, he loves justice—
    you have established equity;
in Jacob you have done
    what is just and right.
[5]Exalt the LORD our God
    and worship at his footstool;
    he is holy.

[6]Moses and Aaron were among his priests,
    Samuel was among those who called on his
        name;
they called on the LORD
    and he answered them.
[7]He spoke to them from the pillar of cloud;
    they kept his statutes and the decrees he
        gave them.

[8]O LORD our God,
    you answered them;
you were to Israel[o] a forgiving God,
    though you punished their misdeeds.[p]
[9]Exalt the LORD our God
    and worship at his holy mountain,
    for the LORD our God is holy.

*o*8 Hebrew *them*   *p*8 Or / *an avenger of the wrongs done to them*

Discovering the Word 1. This psalm speaks of the Lord in different ways a total of seven times. (Seven is a symbol of completeness.) What aspects or characteristics of this complete Lord does the psalmist affirm? 2. Study the verbs. How do or should others respond in relation to the exalted Lord? 3. Consider the causes and effects, also the actions and explanations, in this psalm. Why should God's people worship this Lord (vv. 4–8)? 4. Out of reverence for God's unapproachable holiness, the people went through intermediaries to God. Priests such as Moses, Aaron and Samuel were the go-betweens (v. 6). How did God speak with them (vv. 6–8)?

Applying the Word 1. God is terribly awesome and holy, forgiving and punishing. What does that say about the casual God-is-my-buddy approach or the presumptuous God-is-my-bellhop approach we often take in worship and prayer? 2. What does God expect you to do in response to his holy character and righteous decrees? 3. This psalm invites us to tremble, praise, exalt and worship this Lord. How do you do that each day?

Responding in Prayer Let the awe of knowing this holy God sink in. Pray for a desire to be and do and love the things that characterize this holy God.

58 / *Psalm 100*
Seeing Myself as Human

"IT MAKES ME nervous when people say, 'I'm only human,'" said Bob. "I'm afraid that if I give myself excuses like that I will let myself off the hook instead of doing my best. I don't know why, but I need to keep pushing myself beyond my limits or I become terribly anxious."

We may not consciously think that we are superhuman, but we often try to act that way in order to avoid our vulnerability and our neediness. We may not consciously think we are subhuman either, but we may feel that way about ourselves when we cannot escape our finitude and dependency. To be human, for us, is to be a long list of things we would rather avoid. We do not like the vulnerability, the limits, the dependency or the needs. And so, all too often, we defend ourselves against our fears by trying to be God. But, we are not God. The more we are able to embrace this most fundamental of realities—that we are creatures and God is our Creator—the freer our lives can become. The text for this study will help us to see ourselves as belonging to God.

 Warming Up to God God invites you to see yourself as a child of God. What obstacles might keep you from seeing yourself in this way?

 Read Psalm 100.

Psalm 100

A psalm. For giving thanks.

¹Shout for joy to the Lord, all the earth.
² Worship the Lord with gladness;
   come before him with joyful songs.
³Know that the Lord is God.
   It is he who made us, and we are his*q*;
   we are his people, the sheep of his pasture.

⁴Enter his gates with thanksgiving
   and his courts with praise;
   give thanks to him and praise his name.
⁵For the Lord is good and his love endures forever;
   his faithfulness continues through all generations.

q3 Or and not we ourselves

Discovering the Word 1. According to this psalm, who is God and what is he like? 2. This psalm also tells us about ourselves. According to this psalm, who are we? 3. The text instructs us to "know that Lord is God." What does it mean to "know that the Lord is God"? 4. What freedom might knowing this provide? 5. What things are we invited to do in response to God?

Applying the Word 1. In what area of your life do you need to quit trying to be superhuman? 2. How might it help you personally to "know that the LORD is God," that you are a creature, and "the sheep of his pasture"?

 Responding in Prayer We are invited by this psalm to worship the Lord with gladness. Offer a brief song or poem or prayer of worship or praise to God.

Psalm 101

Psalm 101

Of David. A psalm.

¹I will sing of your love and justice;
  to you, O LORD, I will sing praise.
²I will be careful to lead a blameless life—
  when will you come to me?

I will walk in my house
  with blameless heart.
³I will set before my eyes
  no vile thing.

The deeds of faithless men I hate;
  they will not cling to me.
⁴Men of perverse heart shall be far
    from me;
  I will have nothing to do with evil.

⁵Whoever slanders his neighbor in
    secret,

him will I put to silence;
whoever has haughty eyes and a proud
    heart,
  him will I not endure.

⁶My eyes will be on the faithful in the
    land,
  that they may dwell with me;
he whose walk is blameless
  will minister to me.

⁷No one who practices deceit
  will dwell in my house;
no one who speaks falsely
  will stand in my presence.

⁸Every morning I will put to silence
  all the wicked in the land;
I will cut off every evildoer
  from the city of the LORD.

59 / Psalm 102
A Prayer of Grief

AND GRIEF STILL feels like fear. Perhaps, more strictly, like suspense. Or like waiting; just hanging around waiting for something to happen. It gives life a permanently provisional feeling. . . . The act of living is different all through. Her absence is like the sky, spread over everything. (C. S. Lewis, *A Grief Observed*, [New York: Bantam, 1976], pp. 39, 13)

Grief is an experience of deep sorrow over a significant loss. Whether the loss we have suffered is the loss of a loved one, a job, our health or our home, the physical, emotional and spiritual suffering is intense. This psalm speaks our anguish to God in times of grief.

 Warming Up to God How would you describe the experience of grief?

 Read Psalm 102.

Psalm 102

A prayer of an afflicted man. When he is faint and pours out his lament before the LORD.

¹Hear my prayer, O LORD;
    let my cry for help come to you.
²Do not hide your face from me
    when I am in distress.
 Turn your ear to me;
    when I call, answer me quickly.

³For my days vanish like smoke;
    my bones burn like glowing embers.
⁴My heart is blighted and withered like grass;
    I forget to eat my food.
⁵Because of my loud groaning
    I am reduced to skin and bones.
⁶I am like a desert owl,
    like an owl among the ruins.
⁷I lie awake; I have become
    like a bird alone on a roof.
⁸All day long my enemies taunt me;
    those who rail against me use my name as
        a curse.
⁹For I eat ashes as my food
    and mingle my drink with tears
¹⁰because of your great wrath,
    for you have taken me up and thrown me
        aside.
¹¹My days are like the evening shadow;
    I wither away like grass.

¹²But you, O LORD, sit enthroned forever;
    your renown endures through all
        generations.
¹³You will arise and have compassion on Zion,
    for it is time to show favor to her;
    the appointed time has come.
¹⁴For her stones are dear to your servants;
    her very dust moves them to pity.
¹⁵The nations will fear the name of the LORD,

all the kings of the earth will revere your
    glory.
¹⁶For the LORD will rebuild Zion
    and appear in his glory.
¹⁷He will respond to the prayer of the
        destitute;
    he will not despise their plea.

¹⁸Let this be written for a future generation,
    that a people not yet created may praise the
        LORD:
¹⁹"The LORD looked down from his sanctuary on
        high,
    from heaven he viewed the earth,
²⁰to hear the groans of the prisoners
    and release those condemned to death."
²¹So the name of the LORD will be declared in
        Zion
    and his praise in Jerusalem
²²when the peoples and the kingdoms
    assemble to worship the LORD.

²³In the course of my life*ʳ* he broke my
        strength;
    he cut short my days.
²⁴So I said:
    "Do not take me away, O my God, in the
        midst of my days;
    your years go on through all generations.
²⁵In the beginning you laid the foundations of
        the earth,
    and the heavens are the work of your
        hands.
²⁶They will perish, but you remain;
    they will all wear out like a garment.
 Like clothing you will change them
    and they will be discarded.
²⁷But you remain the same,
    and your years will never end.
²⁸The children of your servants will live in your
        presence;
    their descendants will be established before
        you."

ʳ23 Or *By his power*

Discovering the Word 1. In verses 1–2 the psalmist pleads for God to hear him. Why is this need so urgent in times of grief and distress? 2. How does the psalmist describe his current physical and emotional state (vv. 2–11)? 3. The psalmist seems to be blaming God and pleading with God (vv. 1–2, 24) at the same time. What does he blame God for (vv. 8, 10, 23)? 4. The writer seems to have mixed feelings about God. What positive perspectives does he express about God (vv. 12–22, 25–28)? 5. Mixed feelings about God are common in times of suffering and grief. What is it about times of grief that might create these mixed feelings?

Applying the Word 1. How do the psalmist's descriptions compare with your experiences of grief? 2. What experience have you had with mixed feelings toward God in times of grief? 3. What grief are you aware of (over a loss you have suffered—recent or long past) that you need to express to God?

Responding in Prayer Express your feelings of grief to God, and pray for others you know who are grieving.

60 / *Psalm 103*
Praying Our Salvation

WHAT GOD HAS done for us far exceeds anything we have done for or against him. The summary word for this excessive, undeserved, unexpected act by God is *salvation*. Prayer explores the country of salvation, tramping the contours, smelling the flowers, touching the outcroppings. There is more to do than recognize the sheer fact of salvation and witness to it; there are unnumbered details of grace, of mercy, of blessing to be appreciated and savored. Prayer is the means by which we do this.

 Warming Up to God Reflect on the meaning of your salvation. Allow praise for God to arise from your joy.

 Read Psalm 103.

Psalm 103

Of David.

¹Praise the Lord, O my soul;
  all my inmost being, praise his holy
    name.
²Praise the Lord, O my soul,
  and forget not all his benefits—
³who forgives all your sins
  and heals all your diseases,
⁴who redeems your life from the pit
  and crowns you with love and
    compassion,
⁵who satisfies your desires with good things
  so that your youth is renewed like the
    eagle's.

⁶The Lord works righteousness
  and justice for all the oppressed.

⁷He made known his ways to Moses,
  his deeds to the people of Israel:
⁸The Lord is compassionate and gracious,
  slow to anger, abounding in love.
⁹He will not always accuse,
  nor will he harbor his anger forever;
¹⁰he does not treat us as our sins deserve

  or repay us according to our iniquities.
¹¹For as high as the heavens are above the
    earth,
  so great is his love for those who fear him;
¹²as far as the east is from the west,
  so far has he removed our transgressions
    from us.
¹³As a father has compassion on his children,
  so the Lord has compassion on those who
    fear him;
¹⁴for he knows how we are formed,
  he remembers that we are dust.
¹⁵As for man, his days are like grass,
  he flourishes like a flower of the field;
¹⁶the wind blows over it and it is gone,
  and its place remembers it no more.
¹⁷But from everlasting to everlasting
  the Lord's love is with those who fear
    him,
  and his righteousness with their children's
    children—
¹⁸with those who keep his covenant
  and remember to obey his precepts.

¹⁹The Lord has established his throne in
    heaven,
  and his kingdom rules over all.

²⁰Praise the LORD, you his angels,
  you mighty ones who do his bidding,
  who obey his word.
²¹Praise the LORD, all his heavenly hosts,
  you his servants who do his will.

²²Praise the LORD, all his works
  everywhere in his dominion.

Praise the LORD, O my soul.

Discovering the Word 1. Note the first and last sentences. How does this bracketing affect your understanding of the psalm's contents? 2. Salvation is more richly complex than we sometimes think. What five actions of God add up to salvation (vv. 3–5)? 3. How did God make his ways known to Moses and Israel (v. 7)? 4. What astounding statements about God does the psalmist make in verses 8–14? 5. Carefully observe the contrast between us (vv. 15–16) and God (vv. 17–19). Does this make you feel better or worse about yourself? Explain.

Applying the Word 1. How have you benefited from your salvation? 2. How do verses 8–14 show you ways in which you would like to expand your thinking about God?

Responding in Prayer Add your personal praise to the praise in this psalm.

61 / *Psalm 104*
Protecting God's Creation

ONE NIGHT LAST summer, I stretched flat on my back in the grass of Trail Ridge Camp Sherith in central Wisconsin. "The stars are great at camp," my kids had all said. I was there to find out.

They emerged slowly at first, a few in the central heavens, but none near the still-lighted horizon. Could I count them? Almost. Then more and more came out. The first ones glared trumpetlike against the inky black, while others danced a gentle harmony. Even the horizon forgot the glow of sun and took on hundreds of thousands of lesser lights. Constellations, those artificial lines connecting stars like so many games of dot-to-dot, followed the patterns of my schoolgirl memory. A shooting star streaked across the sky, as if to connect the dots for me in some new constellation. Should I wish upon it?

I prayed instead. But what could I say to a God who had made all this and had somehow created in me the ability to enjoy it? For a long time I lay silent. Perhaps silence was the most sensible part of my prayer.

Warming Up to God When have you felt that God's creation helped you to know him?

Read Psalm 104.

Psalm 104

¹Praise the LORD, O my soul.

O LORD my God, you are very great;
  you are clothed with splendor and majesty.
²He wraps himself in light as with a garment;
  he stretches out the heavens like a tent
³ and lays the beams of his upper chambers
    on their waters.
He makes the clouds his chariot
  and rides on the wings of the wind.
⁴He makes winds his messengers,ˢ

flames of fire his servants.

⁵He set the earth on its foundations;
  it can never be moved.
⁶You covered it with the deep as with a
    garment;
  the waters stood above the mountains.
⁷But at your rebuke the waters fled,
  at the sound of your thunder they took to
    flight;

ˢ4 Or *angels*

8they flowed over the mountains,
  they went down into the valleys,
  to the place you assigned for them.
9You set a boundary they cannot cross;
  never again will they cover the earth.

10He makes springs pour water into the ravines;
  it flows between the mountains.
11They give water to all the beasts of the field;
  the wild donkeys quench their thirst.
12The birds of the air nest by the waters;
  they sing among the branches.
13He waters the mountains from his upper
      chambers;
  the earth is satisfied by the fruit of his
      work.
14He makes grass grow for the cattle,
  and plants for man to cultivate—
  bringing forth food from the earth:
15wine that gladdens the heart of man,
  oil to make his face shine,
  and bread that sustains his heart.
16The trees of the LORD are well watered,
  the cedars of Lebanon that he planted.
17There the birds make their nests;
  the stork has its home in the pine trees.
18The high mountains belong to the wild goats;
  the crags are a refuge for the coneys.[t]

19The moon marks off the seasons,
  and the sun knows when to go down.
20You bring darkness, it becomes night,
  and all the beasts of the forest prowl.
21The lions roar for their prey
  and seek their food from God.
22The sun rises, and they steal away;
  they return and lie down in their dens.
23Then man goes out to his work,
  to his labor until evening.

24How many are your works, O LORD!
  In wisdom you made them all;

the earth is full of your creatures.
25There is the sea, vast and spacious,
  teeming with creatures beyond number—
  living things both large and small.
26There the ships go to and fro,
  and the leviathan, which you formed to
      frolic there.

27These all look to you
  to give them their food at the proper time.
28When you give it to them,
  they gather it up;
  when you open your hand,
  they are satisfied with good things.
29When you hide your face,
  they are terrified;
  when you take away their breath,
  they die and return to the dust.
30When you send your Spirit,
  they are created,
  and you renew the face of the earth.

31May the glory of the LORD endure forever;
  may the LORD rejoice in his works—
32he who looks at the earth, and it trembles,
  who touches the mountains, and they
      smoke.

33I will sing to the LORD all my life;
  I will sing praise to my God as long as I
      live.
34May my meditation be pleasing to him,
  as I rejoice in the LORD.
35But may sinners vanish from the earth
  and the wicked be no more.

Praise the LORD, O my soul.

Praise the LORD.[u]

---

*t18 That is, the hyrax or rock badger   u35 Hebrew Hallelu Yah; in
the Septuagint this line stands at the beginning of Psalm 105.*

  Discovering the Word 1. Study verses 1–4. How does the sky serve God? 2. Study verses 5–9. What elements of earth's creation show God at work? 3. Study verses 10–18. What relationships does this description of God's creation reveal? 4. Study verses 19–26. How do these verses express an orderliness to what God has made? 5. Study verses 27–30. How do these verses show that God not only created but also personally takes care of what he has made? 6. Study verses 31–35. What responses to God are triggered by the psalmist's meditation on creation?

  Applying the Word 1. When have you enjoyed some aspect of the natural rhythms described here? 2. As you meditate on what God has made, how would you like to respond to God?

Responding in Prayer Praise God for the glory of his creation.

Psalms 105—106

Psalm 105

¹Give thanks to the LORD, call on his name;
　　make known among the nations what he
　　　　has done.
²Sing to him, sing praise to him;
　　tell of all his wonderful acts.
³Glory in his holy name;
　　let the hearts of those who seek the LORD
　　　　rejoice.
⁴Look to the LORD and his strength;
　　seek his face always.

⁵Remember the wonders he has done,
　　his miracles, and the judgments he
　　　　pronounced,
⁶O descendants of Abraham his servant,
　　O sons of Jacob, his chosen ones.
⁷He is the LORD our God;
　　his judgments are in all the earth.

⁸He remembers his covenant forever,
　　the word he commanded, for a thousand
　　　　generations,
⁹the covenant he made with Abraham,
　　the oath he swore to Isaac.
¹⁰He confirmed it to Jacob as a decree,
　　to Israel as an everlasting covenant:
¹¹"To you I will give the land of Canaan
　　as the portion you will inherit."

¹²When they were but few in number,
　　few indeed, and strangers in it,
¹³they wandered from nation to nation,
　　from one kingdom to another.
¹⁴He allowed no one to oppress them;
　　for their sake he rebuked kings:
¹⁵"Do not touch my anointed ones;
　　do my prophets no harm."

¹⁶He called down famine on the land
　　and destroyed all their supplies of food;
¹⁷and he sent a man before them—
　　Joseph, sold as a slave.
¹⁸They bruised his feet with shackles,
　　his neck was put in irons,
¹⁹till what he foretold came to pass,
　　till the word of the LORD proved him true.
²⁰The king sent and released him,
　　the ruler of peoples set him free.
²¹He made him master of his household,

ruler over all he possessed,
²²to instruct his princes as he pleased
　　and teach his elders wisdom.

²³Then Israel entered Egypt;
　　Jacob lived as an alien in the land of Ham.
²⁴The LORD made his people very fruitful;
　　he made them too numerous for their foes,
²⁵whose hearts he turned to hate his people,
　　to conspire against his servants.
²⁶He sent Moses his servant,
　　and Aaron, whom he had chosen.
²⁷They performed his miraculous signs among
　　　　them,
　　his wonders in the land of Ham.
²⁸He sent darkness and made the land dark—
　　for had they not rebelled against his words?
²⁹He turned their waters into blood,
　　causing their fish to die.
³⁰Their land teemed with frogs,
　　which went up into the bedrooms of their
　　　　rulers.
³¹He spoke, and there came swarms of flies,
　　and gnats throughout their country.
³²He turned their rain into hail,
　　with lightning throughout their land;
³³he struck down their vines and fig trees
　　and shattered the trees of their country.
³⁴He spoke, and the locusts came,
　　grasshoppers without number;
³⁵they ate up every green thing in their land,
　　ate up the produce of their soil.
³⁶Then he struck down all the firstborn in their
　　　　land,
　　the firstfruits of all their manhood.

³⁷He brought out Israel, laden with silver and
　　　　gold,
　　and from among their tribes no one
　　　　faltered.
³⁸Egypt was glad when they left,
　　because dread of Israel had fallen on them.
³⁹He spread out a cloud as a covering,
　　and a fire to give light at night.
⁴⁰They asked, and he brought them quail
　　and satisfied them with the bread of
　　　　heaven.
⁴¹He opened the rock, and water gushed out;
　　like a river it flowed in the desert.

42For he remembered his holy promise
    given to his servant Abraham.
43He brought out his people with rejoicing,
    his chosen ones with shouts of joy;
44he gave them the lands of the nations,
    and they fell heir to what others had toiled
       for—
45that they might keep his precepts
    and observe his laws.

Praise the LORD.^v

Psalm 106

1Praise the LORD.^w

Give thanks to the LORD, for he is good;
    his love endures forever.
2Who can proclaim the mighty acts of the LORD
    or fully declare his praise?
3Blessed are they who maintain justice,
    who constantly do what is right.
4Remember me, O LORD, when you show favor
       to your people,
    come to my aid when you save them,
5that I may enjoy the prosperity of your
       chosen ones,
    that I may share in the joy of your nation
    and join your inheritance in giving praise.

6We have sinned, even as our fathers did;
    we have done wrong and acted wickedly.
7When our fathers were in Egypt,
    they gave no thought to your miracles;
    they did not remember your many kindnesses,
    and they rebelled by the sea, the Red Sea.^x
8Yet he saved them for his name's sake,
    to make his mighty power known.
9He rebuked the Red Sea, and it dried up;
    he led them through the depths as through
       a desert.
10He saved them from the hand of the foe;
    from the hand of the enemy he redeemed
       them.
11The waters covered their adversaries;
    not one of them survived.
12Then they believed his promises
    and sang his praise.

13But they soon forgot what he had done
    and did not wait for his counsel.
14In the desert they gave in to their craving;
    in the wasteland they put God to the test.
15So he gave them what they asked for,

but sent a wasting disease upon them.

16In the camp they grew envious of Moses
    and of Aaron, who was consecrated to the
       LORD.
17The earth opened up and swallowed Dathan;
    it buried the company of Abiram.
18Fire blazed among their followers;
    a flame consumed the wicked.

19At Horeb they made a calf
    and worshiped an idol cast from metal.
20They exchanged their Glory
    for an image of a bull, which eats grass.
21They forgot the God who saved them,
    who had done great things in Egypt,
22miracles in the land of Ham
    and awesome deeds by the Red Sea.
23So he said he would destroy them—
    had not Moses, his chosen one,
  stood in the breach before him
    to keep his wrath from destroying them.

24Then they despised the pleasant land;
    they did not believe his promise.
25They grumbled in their tents
    and did not obey the LORD.
26So he swore to them with uplifted hand
    that he would make them fall in the desert,
27make their descendants fall among the nations
    and scatter them throughout the lands.

28They yoked themselves to the Baal of Peor
    and ate sacrifices offered to lifeless gods;
29they provoked the LORD to anger by their
       wicked deeds,
    and a plague broke out among them.
30But Phinehas stood up and intervened,
    and the plague was checked.
31This was credited to him as righteousness
    for endless generations to come.

32By the waters of Meribah they angered the
       LORD,
    and trouble came to Moses because of
       them;
33for they rebelled against the Spirit of God,
    and rash words came from Moses' lips.^y

34They did not destroy the peoples
    as the LORD had commanded them,
35but they mingled with the nations

v45 Hebrew *Hallelu Yah*   w1 Hebrew *Hallelu Yah*; also in verse 48
x7 Hebrew *Yam Suph*; that is, Sea of Reeds; also in verses 9 and 22
y33 Or *against his spirit, / and rash words came from his lips*

and adopted their customs.
³⁶They worshiped their idols,
which became a snare to them.
³⁷They sacrificed their sons
and their daughters to demons.
³⁸They shed innocent blood,
the blood of their sons and daughters,
whom they sacrificed to the idols of Canaan,
and the land was desecrated by their blood.
³⁹They defiled themselves by what they did;
by their deeds they prostituted themselves.

⁴⁰Therefore the LORD was angry with his people
and abhorred his inheritance.
⁴¹He handed them over to the nations,
and their foes ruled over them.
⁴²Their enemies oppressed them
and subjected them to their power.
⁴³Many times he delivered them,

but they were bent on rebellion
and they wasted away in their sin.

⁴⁴But he took note of their distress
when he heard their cry;
⁴⁵for their sake he remembered his covenant
and out of his great love he relented.
⁴⁶He caused them to be pitied
by all who held them captive.

⁴⁷Save us, O LORD our God,
and gather us from the nations,
that we may give thanks to your holy name
and glory in your praise.

⁴⁸Praise be to the LORD, the God of Israel,
from everlasting to everlasting.
Let all the people say, "Amen!"

Praise the LORD.

62 / *Psalm 107*
The Goodness of God

PSALM 107 IS the classic exposition of God's goodness. J. I. Packer writes: "The whole psalm is a majestic panorama of the operations of divine goodness, transforming human lives" (*Knowing God* [Downers Grove, Ill.: InterVarsity Press, 1973], p. 148). God's actions reveal goodness in its highest and purest form. His goodness provides the standard for developing this fruit in our own lives.

 Warming Up to God Try to imagine what it would be like if God were to withdraw all his goodness from you. How would your life be changed? Respond to God with praise for his presence with you.

 Read Psalm 107.

BOOK V
Psalms 107–150

Psalm 107

¹Give thanks to the LORD, for he is good;
his love endures forever.
²Let the redeemed of the LORD say this—
those he redeemed from the hand of the foe,
³those he gathered from the lands,
from east and west, from north and south.ᶻ

⁴Some wandered in desert wastelands,
finding no way to a city where they could settle.

⁵They were hungry and thirsty,
and their lives ebbed away.
⁶Then they cried out to the LORD in their trouble,
and he delivered them from their distress.
⁷He led them by a straight way
to a city where they could settle.
⁸Let them give thanks to the LORD for his unfailing love
and his wonderful deeds for men,
⁹for he satisfies the thirsty
and fills the hungry with good things.

¹⁰Some sat in darkness and the deepest gloom,
prisoners suffering in iron chains,

ᶻ3 Hebrew *north and the sea*

¹¹for they had rebelled against the words of
        God
    and despised the counsel of the Most High.
¹²So he subjected them to bitter labor;
    they stumbled, and there was no one to
        help.
¹³Then they cried to the LORD in their trouble,
    and he saved them from their distress.
¹⁴He brought them out of darkness and the
        deepest gloom
    and broke away their chains.
¹⁵Let them give thanks to the LORD for his
        unfailing love
    and his wonderful deeds for men,
¹⁶for he breaks down gates of bronze
    and cuts through bars of iron.

¹⁷Some became fools through their rebellious
        ways
    and suffered affliction because of their
        iniquities.
¹⁸They loathed all food
    and drew near the gates of death.
¹⁹Then they cried to the LORD in their trouble,
    and he saved them from their distress.
²⁰He sent forth his word and healed them;
    he rescued them from the grave.
²¹Let them give thanks to the LORD for his
        unfailing love
    and his wonderful deeds for men.
²²Let them sacrifice thank offerings
    and tell of his works with songs of joy.

²³Others went out on the sea in ships;
    they were merchants on the mighty
        waters.
²⁴They saw the works of the LORD,
    his wonderful deeds in the deep.
²⁵For he spoke and stirred up a tempest
    that lifted high the waves.
²⁶They mounted up to the heavens and went
        down to the depths;
    in their peril their courage melted away.
²⁷They reeled and staggered like drunken men;
    they were at their wits' end.

²⁸Then they cried out to the LORD in their
        trouble,
    and he brought them out of their distress.
²⁹He stilled the storm to a whisper;
    the waves of the sea were hushed.
³⁰They were glad when it grew calm,
    and he guided them to their desired haven.
³¹Let them give thanks to the LORD for his
        unfailing love
    and his wonderful deeds for men.
³²Let them exalt him in the assembly of the
        people
    and praise him in the council of the elders.

³³He turned rivers into a desert,
    flowing springs into thirsty ground,
³⁴and fruitful land into a salt waste,
    because of the wickedness of those who
        lived there.
³⁵He turned the desert into pools of water
    and the parched ground into flowing
        springs;
³⁶there he brought the hungry to live,
    and they founded a city where they could
        settle.
³⁷They sowed fields and planted vineyards
    that yielded a fruitful harvest;
³⁸he blessed them, and their numbers greatly
        increased,
    and he did not let their herds diminish.

³⁹Then their numbers decreased, and they were
        humbled
    by oppression, calamity and sorrow;
⁴⁰he who pours contempt on nobles
    made them wander in a trackless waste.
⁴¹But he lifted the needy out of their affliction
    and increased their families like flocks.
⁴²The upright see and rejoice,
    but all the wicked shut their mouths.

⁴³Whoever is wise, let him heed these
        things
    and consider the great love of the LORD.

Discovering the Word   1. How do verses 1–3 introduce the major themes of the psalm?   2. The psalmist
gives four illustrations of God's goodness in verses 4–9, 10–16, 17–22 and 23–32. What do each of these
illustrations have in common?   3. What needs do the people have in each of these sections?   4. According to the
psalmist, what are some ways we should give thanks to God for his goodness and love (vv. 22, 32)?   5. What do
verses 33–42 reveal about the ups and downs of life?

Applying the Word 1. Are you likely to call out to God in the midst of your trouble as those in this passage did? Why or why not? 2. In what ways can we imitate the goodness of God displayed in this psalm?

Responding in Prayer Thank God for his goodness and unfailing love. Ask him to help you develop the fruit of goodness in your life.

Psalm 108

Psalm 108

A song. A psalm of David.

¹My heart is steadfast, O God;
  I will sing and make music with all my
    soul.
²Awake, harp and lyre!
  I will awaken the dawn.
³I will praise you, O Lord, among the nations;
  I will sing of you among the peoples.
⁴For great is your love, higher than the
    heavens;
  your faithfulness reaches to the skies.
⁵Be exalted, O God, above the heavens,
  and let your glory be over all the earth.

⁶Save us and help us with your right hand,
  that those you love may be delivered.
⁷God has spoken from his sanctuary:

"In triumph I will parcel out Shechem
  and measure off the Valley of Succoth.
⁸Gilead is mine, Manasseh is mine;
  Ephraim is my helmet,
  Judah my scepter.
⁹Moab is my washbasin,
  upon Edom I toss my sandal;
  over Philistia I shout in triumph."

¹⁰Who will bring me to the fortified city?
  Who will lead me to Edom?
¹¹Is it not you, O God, you who have rejected
    us
  and no longer go out with our armies?
¹²Give us aid against the enemy,
  for the help of man is worthless.
¹³With God we will gain the victory,
  and he will trample down our enemies.

63 / *Psalm 109*
Feeling Anger

FOR MOST OF us, anger is not a comfortable emotion. For some of us, it is a terrifying emotion. We know the damage that anger can do. We know the pain it can cause. We fear our own capacity for evil when we are angry. We recognize our desire for revenge. We know that we have been hurt, and we know that anger feeds our longing to hurt back. However, avoiding anger will not make it go away, but can instead allow it to grow into bitterness. Feeling anger and expressing it honestly to God and to others makes it possible for us to continue growing toward forgiveness. There are, of course, both helpful and unhelpful things we can do with our anger. Denying, avoiding, minimizing and blaming others for it are just a few of the many unhelpful ways of responding to anger.

Warming Up to God What do you usually do when you are angry with someone who is important to you?

Read Psalm 109.

Psalm 109

For the director of music. Of David.
A psalm.

¹O God, whom I praise,
do not remain silent,
²for wicked and deceitful men
have opened their mouths against me;
they have spoken against me with lying
tongues.
³With words of hatred they surround me;
they attack me without cause.
⁴In return for my friendship they accuse me,
but I am a man of prayer.
⁵They repay me evil for good,
and hatred for my friendship.

⁶Appoint*ᵃ* an evil man*ᵇ* to oppose him;
let an accuser*ᶜ* stand at his right hand.
⁷When he is tried, let him be found guilty,
and may his prayers condemn him.
⁸May his days be few;
may another take his place of leadership.
⁹May his children be fatherless
and his wife a widow.
¹⁰May his children be wandering beggars;
may they be driven*ᵈ* from their ruined
homes.
¹¹May a creditor seize all he has;
may strangers plunder the fruits of his
labor.
¹²May no one extend kindness to him
or take pity on his fatherless children.
¹³May his descendants be cut off,
their names blotted out from the next
generation.
¹⁴May the iniquity of his fathers be remembered
before the LORD;
may the sin of his mother never be blotted
out.
¹⁵May their sins always remain before the LORD,
that he may cut off the memory of them
from the earth.

¹⁶For he never thought of doing a kindness,
but hounded to death the poor

and the needy and the brokenhearted.
¹⁷He loved to pronounce a curse—
may it*ᵉ* come on him;
he found no pleasure in blessing—
may it be*ᶠ* far from him.
¹⁸He wore cursing as his garment;
it entered into his body like water,
into his bones like oil.
¹⁹May it be like a cloak wrapped about him,
like a belt tied forever around him.
²⁰May this be the LORD's payment to my
accusers,
to those who speak evil of me.

²¹But you, O Sovereign LORD,
deal well with me for your name's sake;
out of the goodness of your love, deliver
me.
²²For I am poor and needy,
and my heart is wounded within me.
²³I fade away like an evening shadow;
I am shaken off like a locust.
²⁴My knees give way from fasting;
my body is thin and gaunt.
²⁵I am an object of scorn to my accusers;
when they see me, they shake their heads.

²⁶Help me, O LORD my God;
save me in accordance with your love.
²⁷Let them know that it is your hand,
that you, O LORD, have done it.
²⁸They may curse, but you will bless;
when they attack they will be put to shame,
but your servant will rejoice.
²⁹My accusers will be clothed with disgrace
and wrapped in shame as in a cloak.

³⁰With my mouth I will greatly extol the LORD;
in the great throng I will praise him.
³¹For he stands at the right hand of the needy
one,
to save his life from those who condemn
him.

*ᵃ6 Or ⌊They say:⌋ "Appoint (with quotation marks at the end of verse
19)   ᵇ6 Or the Evil One   ᶜ6 Or let Satan   ᵈ10 Septuagint;
Hebrew sought   ᵉ17 Or curse, / and it has   ᶠ17 Or blessing, / and
it is*

Discovering the Word 1. To what painful experiences is the author reacting (vv. 2–5)? 2. The speaker is particularly outraged at the injustice of his accusers. "They repay me evil for good, and hatred for my friendship" (v. 5). How does this add to his sense of rage? 3. What does the author ask God to do to his enemies (vv. 6–20, 28–29)? 4. What does the author want God to do for him (vv. 20–26)?

Applying the Word 1. God is described in verse 31 as being on the side of the "needy" and "condemned." How could seeing God in this way be a practical help to you when you are angry? 2. How would expressing your anger to God be helpful to you? 3. How can other people be helpful to you in your struggle with anger?

Responding in Prayer What anger do you want to express to God today?

---

64 / *Psalm 110*
A Psalm of Submission

THINK ABOUT THE enemies you have. Bring to mind people you know who are opposed to Christianity. Picture them (and yourself) one day coming to Christ who will settle all disputes and rule with an iron hand. Psalm 110 acknowledges God as the eternal King-Priest who will, in fact, settle all disputes and judge all nations. This coronation hymn, although used for other kings of Israel, was viewed by Jews and Christians alike as clearly Messianic and forward-looking. Writers of the New Testament quote verses 1 and 4 on numerous occasions, making this psalm one of the most prophetic.

 Warming Up to God Just as you picture your enemies settling accounts with God the Supreme Justice, picture yourself doing the same. That means submitting any of your own behaviors and beliefs that are not conformed or submissive to the Lord. How do you feel as you consider this scene?

Read Psalm 110.

Psalm 110

Of David. A psalm.

¹The LORD says to my Lord:
  "Sit at my right hand
until I make your enemies
  a footstool for your feet."

²The LORD will extend your mighty scepter
    from Zion;
  you will rule in the midst of your enemies.
³Your troops will be willing
  on your day of battle.
Arrayed in holy majesty,
  from the womb of the dawn
you will receive the dew of your youth.ᵍ

⁴The LORD has sworn
  and will not change his mind:
"You are a priest forever,
  in the order of Melchizedek."

⁵The Lord is at your right hand;
  he will crush kings on the day of his wrath.
⁶He will judge the nations, heaping up the
    dead
  and crushing the rulers of the whole earth.
⁷He will drink from a brook beside the wayʰ;
  therefore he will lift up his head.

g 3 Or / your young men will come to you like the dew   h 7 Or / The One who grants succession will set him in authority

---

Discovering the Word 1. Who is the psalmist referring to as "my Lord" (v. 1; see Mt 22:41–45)? 2. How will that Lord rule, and over whom (vv. 1–3, 5, 6)? 3. What is significant about the Lord swearing with a covenant oath (v. 4; Heb 6:16–18; 7:20–22)? 4. Melchizedek was the original king-priest of the God Most High in Jerusalem, who received a tithe from Abraham. His priesthood was a prototype of Christ's eternal priesthood (v. 4). What is significant about a priesthood for God's people that is permanent and irrevocable? 5. What is significant about this Lord sitting at the right hand of God (vv. 1, 5)?

Applying the Word 1. The troops are freewill offerings (v. 3) in the service of their Lord. What is your sacrificial offering to the Lord? 2. The Lord rules over all the powers that be, even enemies of his kingdom, with an iron hand and the undiminished vigor of youth (vv. 2–3). How is that good news to you and the battles you face?

Responding in Prayer Whatever battles you are engaged in right now, rest assured that the Lord will ultimately triumph and that the Lord's army will attack those problems with you. What battles or problem areas can you turn over to him now for his intercession and judgment?

Psalms 111—114

Psalm 111[i]

[1]Praise the LORD.[j]

I will extol the LORD with all my heart
   in the council of the upright and in the
     assembly.

[2]Great are the works of the LORD;
   they are pondered by all who delight in
     them.
[3]Glorious and majestic are his deeds,
   and his righteousness endures forever.
[4]He has caused his wonders to be remembered;
   the LORD is gracious and compassionate.
[5]He provides food for those who fear him;
   he remembers his covenant forever.
[6]He has shown his people the power of his
     works,
   giving them the lands of other nations.
[7]The works of his hands are faithful and just;
   all his precepts are trustworthy.
[8]They are steadfast for ever and ever,
   done in faithfulness and uprightness.
[9]He provided redemption for his people;
   he ordained his covenant forever—
   holy and awesome is his name.

[10]The fear of the LORD is the beginning of
     wisdom;
   all who follow his precepts have good
     understanding.
   To him belongs eternal praise.

Psalm 112[i]

[1]Praise the LORD.[j]

Blessed is the man who fears the LORD,
   who finds great delight in his commands.

[2]His children will be mighty in the land;
   the generation of the upright will be
     blessed.
[3]Wealth and riches are in his house,
   and his righteousness endures forever.
[4]Even in darkness light dawns for the upright,

for the gracious and compassionate and
   righteous man.[k]
[5]Good will come to him who is generous and
     lends freely,
   who conducts his affairs with justice.
[6]Surely he will never be shaken;
   a righteous man will be remembered
     forever.
[7]He will have no fear of bad news;
   his heart is steadfast, trusting in the LORD.
[8]His heart is secure, he will have no fear;
   in the end he will look in triumph on his
     foes.
[9]He has scattered abroad his gifts to the poor,
   his righteousness endures forever;
   his horn[l] will be lifted high in honor.

[10]The wicked man will see and be vexed,
   he will gnash his teeth and waste away;
   the longings of the wicked will come to
     nothing.

Psalm 113

[1]Praise the LORD.[m]

Praise, O servants of the LORD,
   praise the name of the LORD.
[2]Let the name of the LORD be praised,
   both now and forevermore.
[3]From the rising of the sun to the place where
     it sets,
   the name of the LORD is to be praised.

[4]The LORD is exalted over all the nations,
   his glory above the heavens.
[5]Who is like the LORD our God,
   the One who sits enthroned on high,
[6]who stoops down to look
   on the heavens and the earth?

[7]He raises the poor from the dust
   and lifts the needy from the ash heap;

---

[i] This psalm is an acrostic poem, the lines of which begin with the successive letters of the Hebrew alphabet.   [j]1 Hebrew *Hallelu Yah* [k]4 Or / *for* ⌐*the* LORD⌐ *is gracious and compassionate and righteous* [l]9 *Horn* here symbolizes dignity.   [m]1 Hebrew *Hallelu Yah*; also in verse 9

8he seats them with princes,
    with the princes of their people.
9He settles the barren woman in her home
    as a happy mother of children.

Praise the LORD.

Psalm 114

1When Israel came out of Egypt,
    the house of Jacob from a people of foreign
        tongue,
2Judah became God's sanctuary,
    Israel his dominion.

3The sea looked and fled,
    the Jordan turned back;
4the mountains skipped like rams,
    the hills like lambs.

5Why was it, O sea, that you fled,
    O Jordan, that you turned back,
6you mountains, that you skipped like rams,
    you hills, like lambs?

7Tremble, O earth, at the presence of the Lord,
    at the presence of the God of Jacob,
8who turned the rock into a pool,
    the hard rock into springs of water.

65 / *Psalm 115*
A Psalm of Praise

THIS PSALM PRAISES God as the one true Lord and ridicules the many cheap imitations and pretenders to the throne that prevail in the surrounding culture. The liturgical exchange between people and priests in this psalm makes it a very appropriate lead-in for public worship. In this liturgy, the cares and snares of the world are left behind and the people are called to trust God, who will abundantly bless them and receive the praise of his people.

Warming Up to God When has God seemed distant or unresponsive to you (in the past or present)? Open yourself up to the possibilities of God blessing you and your family afresh.

Read Psalm 115.

Psalm 115

1Not to us, O LORD, not to us
    but to your name be the glory,
    because of your love and faithfulness.

2Why do the nations say,
    "Where is their God?"
3Our God is in heaven;
    he does whatever pleases him.
4But their idols are silver and gold,
    made by the hands of men.
5They have mouths, but cannot speak,
    eyes, but they cannot see;
6they have ears, but cannot hear,
    noses, but they cannot smell;
7they have hands, but cannot feel,
    feet, but they cannot walk;
    nor can they utter a sound with their
        throats.
8Those who make them will be like them,

and so will all who trust in them.
9O house of Israel, trust in the LORD—
    he is their help and shield.
10O house of Aaron, trust in the LORD—
    he is their help and shield.
11You who fear him, trust in the LORD—
    he is their help and shield.

12The LORD remembers us and will bless us:
    He will bless the house of Israel,
    he will bless the house of Aaron,
13he will bless those who fear the LORD—
    small and great alike.

14May the LORD make you increase,
    both you and your children.
15May you be blessed by the LORD,
    the Maker of heaven and earth.

16The highest heavens belong to the LORD,
    but the earth he has given to man.
17It is not the dead who praise the LORD,

those who go down to silence;
18it is we who extol the LORD,
both now and forevermore.

Praise the LORD.ⁿ

ⁿ18 Hebrew *Hallelu Yah*

 Discovering the Word 1. Note that this psalm divides into five parts: three stanzas spoken by the respondents—a taunt song (vv. 1–8), confession of trust (vv. 12–13) and the closing doxology (vv. 16–18)—interspersed with an invocation (vv. 9–11) and benediction (vv. 14–15) spoken by the priests. What does this response-and-revelation rhythm call forth from the worship participants and leaders? 2. How do the idols that others worship compare to the God that Israel worships (vv. 1–8)? 3. Why should anyone, but especially Israel, trust in the Lord (vv. 9–11)? 4. Who will the Lord bless, why and how (vv. 12–15)? 5. What is the reason for living granted to those who have survived the exile and a whole lot more (vv. 16–18)?

Applying the Word 1. The Lord is not the only person or object that people trust to get them through the day. What else do people trust in these days for their salvation or their guidance? 2. For what have you recently trusted God alone to provide? 3. How did God prove to be your help and shield?

Responding in Prayer Consider how vastly superior God is to all idols. Ask God to help you forsake the idols of your culture.

66 / *Psalm 116*
Talking to God

HONESTY IS A NECESSARY ingredient to all intimate relationships. If we are to grow in our intimacy with God, we will need to learn to be honest with him. This will require us to challenge our distorted images of God and to grow in our understanding of him. God invites us to talk to him. He has promised to pay attention. He does not require us to do any physical, mental or spiritual gymnastics to get his attention. He does not insist that we have our lives "together" before we can talk to him. We can talk to him even when we are in trouble. We will always find him interested and compassionate.

Warming Up to God Imagine yourself as one of the little children whom Jesus invited to come to him. Imagine yourself standing next to Jesus. Take a few minutes to close your eyes and experience his arm around your shoulder as you stand next to him. Tell him what you are thinking and feeling. What thoughts and feelings did you have during this meditation?

 Read Psalm 116.

Psalm 116

1I love the LORD, for he heard my voice;
he heard my cry for mercy.
2Because he turned his ear to me,
I will call on him as long as I live.

3The cords of death entangled me,
the anguish of the graveᵒ came upon me;
I was overcome by trouble and sorrow.
4Then I called on the name of the LORD:
"O LORD, save me!"

5The LORD is gracious and righteous;
our God is full of compassion.
6The LORD protects the simplehearted;
when I was in great need, he saved me.

7Be at rest once more, O my soul,
for the LORD has been good to you.

8For you, O LORD, have delivered my soul from death,

ᵒ3 Hebrew *Sheol*

my eyes from tears,
my feet from stumbling,
9 that I may walk before the LORD
in the land of the living.
10 I believed; therefore[p] I said,
"I am greatly afflicted."
11 And in my dismay I said,
"All men are liars."

12 How can I repay the LORD
for all his goodness to me?
13 I will lift up the cup of salvation
and call on the name of the LORD.
14 I will fulfill my vows to the LORD
in the presence of all his people.

15 Precious in the sight of the LORD
is the death of his saints.

16 O LORD, truly I am your servant;
I am your servant, the son of your
maidservant[q];
you have freed me from my chains.

17 I will sacrifice a thank offering to you
and call on the name of the LORD.
18 I will fulfill my vows to the LORD
in the presence of all his people,
19 in the courts of the house of the LORD—
in your midst, O Jerusalem.

Praise the LORD.[r]

p10 Or *believed even when* q16 Or *servant, your faithful son* r19 Hebrew *Hallelu Yah*

Discovering the Word 1. What images of God are presented here? 2. What did the author of the psalm experience when he called on God? 3. How does the psalmist respond to God (vv. 12–19)? 4. God invites us to talk to him about our troubles. He does not ask us to ignore them or minimize them or take care of them ourselves. How does this compare or contrast with your expectations of God?

Applying the Word 1. Think of a time when you had difficulty calling on God. What made it difficult for you? 2. Recall a time when you did call on God and he "answered you and showed you great and mighty things." What was this experience like for you?

Responding in Prayer What do you need to talk with God about today?

Psalm 117

Psalm 117

1 Praise the LORD, all you nations;
extol him, all you peoples.
2 For great is his love toward us,
and the faithfulness of the LORD endures
forever.

Praise the LORD.[s]

s2 Hebrew *Hallelu Yah*

67 / *Psalm 118*
Enduring Love

REMEMBER WHEN YOUR parents used to force you to write thank-you notes for the Christmas and birthday gifts you received from your out-of-town relatives? Although it may have been painful at the time, this discipline of thanksgiving helped you develop a grateful heart.

In like manner, the psalmist expresses thanks to God for delivering Israel from her many enemies. The historic occasion for Psalm 118 may have been Israel's defeat of a confederacy of nations or her deliverance from the Babylonian exile. In either event, the Israelites had much to thank God for, especially his love which endures forever. We who know the love of God in Christ have even more reason to give thanks through this psalm.

 Warming Up to God Think of all the things and relationships in your life that have passed on or proven temporary. Contrast that with the most enduring love relationship you know, or with the times that come to mind when you hum that ditty "Happy Days Are Here Again." How does that relationship or those days compare with the enduring love of God?

Read Psalm 118.

Psalm 118

¹Give thanks to the Lord, for he is good;
　　his love endures forever.

²Let Israel say:
　　"His love endures forever."
³Let the house of Aaron say:
　　"His love endures forever."
⁴Let those who fear the Lord say:
　　"His love endures forever."

⁵In my anguish I cried to the Lord,
　　and he answered by setting me free.
⁶The Lord is with me; I will not be afraid.
　　What can man do to me?
⁷The Lord is with me; he is my helper.
　　I will look in triumph on my enemies.

⁸It is better to take refuge in the Lord
　　than to trust in man.
⁹It is better to take refuge in the Lord
　　than to trust in princes.

¹⁰All the nations surrounded me,
　　but in the name of the Lord I cut them off.
¹¹They surrounded me on every side,
　　but in the name of the Lord I cut them off.
¹²They swarmed around me like bees,
　　but they died out as quickly as burning
　　　　thorns;
　　in the name of the Lord I cut them off.

¹³I was pushed back and about to fall,
　　but the Lord helped me.
¹⁴The Lord is my strength and my song;
　　he has become my salvation.

¹⁵Shouts of joy and victory
　　resound in the tents of the righteous:
　"The Lord's right hand has done mighty
　　　　things!

¹⁶　The Lord's right hand is lifted high;
　　the Lord's right hand has done mighty
　　　　things!"

¹⁷I will not die but live,
　　and will proclaim what the Lord has done.
¹⁸The Lord has chastened me severely,
　　but he has not given me over to death.

¹⁹Open for me the gates of righteousness;
　　I will enter and give thanks to the Lord.
²⁰This is the gate of the Lord
　　through which the righteous may enter.
²¹I will give you thanks, for you answered me;
　　you have become my salvation.

²²The stone the builders rejected
　　has become the capstone;
²³the Lord has done this,
　　and it is marvelous in our eyes.
²⁴This is the day the Lord has made;
　　let us rejoice and be glad in it.

²⁵O Lord, save us;
　　O Lord, grant us success.
²⁶Blessed is he who comes in the name of the
　　　　Lord.
　From the house of the Lord we bless you.ᵗ
²⁷The Lord is God,
　　and he has made his light shine upon us.
　With boughs in hand, join in the festal
　　　　procession
　　upᵘ to the horns of the altar.

²⁸You are my God, and I will give you thanks;
　　you are my God, and I will exalt you.
²⁹Give thanks to the Lord, for he is good;
　　his love endures forever.

ᵗ26 The Hebrew is plural.　　ᵘ27 Or *Bind the festal sacrifice with ropes / and take it*

Discovering the Word 1. Note that this psalm divides into five parts: a liturgical call to praise at the beginning (vv. 1–4) and end (v. 29)—which sandwiches the leader's song of thanksgiving (vv. 5–21), the people's response (vv. 22–27) and the leader's final prompting (v. 28). What indicators do you see that suggest a change of voice or speaker in each section? 2. What is the significance of the many double and triple repetitions found throughout this psalm? 3. What has the Lord done for the king and/or representatively for the people (vv. 5–21)? 4. As an Israelite prompted to give thanks on the occasion of this psalm, what redemptive occasions in the life of your people come to mind? 5. What is the significance of the stone-turned-capstone (v. 22), which is being celebrated on this festive day (v. 23)?

Applying the Word 1. The early church applied verse 22 to Jesus. How is Jesus like this stone-turned-capstone? 2. For what events in your life are you particularly grateful to God? 3. How did God prove to be your helper, your strength or your salvation?

Responding in Prayer Praise God for the day(s) he has given you to rejoice (v. 24).

68 / *Psalm 119:1–24*
Searching for God's Wisdom

FEW SITUATIONS BRING life to a grinding halt like losing a contact lens. Have you ever seen it happen to a major-league baseball pitcher? Frustration turns to comedy as fellow players trickle out from the dugout and hunch over the mound on hands and knees. Fans get restless. Commentators start reminiscing about recent games. The TV audience goes on commercial break.

If we are going to have the vision to see life from God's perspective, we will regularly have to stop everything, hunker down and find out just what that perspective is. Like finding a contact lens, finding God's wisdom is simply worth whatever inconveniences may come in its pursuit.

Warming Up to God In what area of your life do you need God's wisdom?

Read Psalm 119:1–24.

Psalm 119[v]

א Aleph

1 Blessed are they whose ways are blameless,
  who walk according to the law of the Lord.
2 Blessed are they who keep his statutes
  and seek him with all their heart.
3 They do nothing wrong;
  they walk in his ways.
4 You have laid down precepts
  that are to be fully obeyed.
5 Oh, that my ways were steadfast
  in obeying your decrees!
6 Then I would not be put to shame
  when I consider all your commands.
7 I will praise you with an upright heart
  as I learn your righteous laws.
8 I will obey your decrees;
  do not utterly forsake me.

ב Beth

9 How can a young man keep his way pure?
  By living according to your word.
10 I seek you with all my heart;
  do not let me stray from your commands.
11 I have hidden your word in my heart
  that I might not sin against you.
12 Praise be to you, O Lord;
  teach me your decrees.
13 With my lips I recount
  all the laws that come from your mouth.
14 I rejoice in following your statutes
  as one rejoices in great riches.
15 I meditate on your precepts
  and consider your ways.
16 I delight in your decrees;

[v] This psalm is an acrostic poem; the verses of each stanza begin with the same letter of the Hebrew alphabet.

I will not neglect your word.

ג   Gimel

¹⁷Do good to your servant, and I will live;
  I will obey your word.
¹⁸Open my eyes that I may see
  wonderful things in your law.
¹⁹I am a stranger on earth;
  do not hide your commands from me.

²⁰My soul is consumed with longing
  for your laws at all times.
²¹You rebuke the arrogant, who are cursed
  and who stray from your commands.
²²Remove from me scorn and contempt,
  for I keep your statutes.
²³Though rulers sit together and slander me,
  your servant will meditate on your decrees.
²⁴Your statutes are my delight;
  they are my counselors.

Discovering the Word 1. What different words does the psalmist use to describe God's Word? 2. What benefits of knowing and following God's Word does the psalmist mention in verses 1–8? 3. How does God's Word help us to deal with sin (vv. 9–16)? 4. How does God's Word enlighten us about God's ways (vv. 17–24)? 5. What are the consequences of *not* knowing or following God's Word (vv. 5–6, 9–11, 21–22)?

Applying the Word 1. What is a way you have experienced frustration in studying Scripture? 2. What in the psalmist's example can bring encouragement to us to meditate on and delight in God's Word?

Responding in Prayer Ask God to guide you as you turn to his Word for wisdom.

---

69 / *Psalm 119:25–40*
Seeking God

PRAYER AND MEDITATION are not easy disciplines. Many of us have used prayer as a magical device for controlling God or for acquiring God's favor. Similarly, many use meditation as a magical tool for control. But there is nothing magical about the spiritual disciplines of prayer and meditation. Both are ways to focus our attention on God. We can talk (pray) openly, honestly, vulnerably to God, and we can listen (meditate) with humility. It is this dynamic of speaking/listening, prayer/meditation that makes it possible for us to increase our contact with God. We can experience loving and being loved by our Creator.

 Warming Up to God What difficulties do you experience with prayer and meditation?

 Read Psalm 119:25–40.

ד   Daleth

²⁵I am laid low in the dust;
  preserve my life according to your word.
²⁶I recounted my ways and you answered me;
  teach me your decrees.
²⁷Let me understand the teaching of your
    precepts;
  then I will meditate on your wonders.
²⁸My soul is weary with sorrow;
  strengthen me according to your word.
²⁹Keep me from deceitful ways;
  be gracious to me through your law.

³⁰I have chosen the way of truth;
  I have set my heart on your laws.
³¹I hold fast to your statutes, O LORD;
  do not let me be put to shame.
³²I run in the path of your commands,
  for you have set my heart free.

ה   He

³³Teach me, O LORD, to follow your decrees;
  then I will keep them to the end.
³⁴Give me understanding, and I will keep your
    law

and obey it with all my heart.
³⁵Direct me in the path of your commands,
  for there I find delight.
³⁶Turn my heart toward your statutes
  and not toward selfish gain.
³⁷Turn my eyes away from worthless things;
  preserve my life according to your word.ʷ
³⁸Fulfill your promise to your servant,

so that you may be feared.
³⁹Take away the disgrace I dread,
  for your laws are good.
⁴⁰How I long for your precepts!
  Preserve my life in your righteousness.

ʷ37 Two manuscripts of the Masoretic Text and Dead Sea Scrolls; most manuscripts of the Masoretic Text *life in your way*

Discovering the Word 1. Restate in your own words the requests the psalmist makes of God. 2. What major needs and desires is the psalmist expressing in these requests? 3. How do these needs/desires compare with your own at this time? 4. How does the psalmist describe what he has done and what he desires to do in his pursuit of God? 5. What benefits does the psalmist suggest might come from prayer and meditation (vv. 32–40)?

Applying the Word 1. The psalmist describes himself as "laid low in the dust" and as "weary with sorrow." Describe a time when you experienced these feelings. 2. In your experience, how can prayer and meditation improve our contact with God?

Responding in Prayer Ask God to help you practice the disciplines of prayer and meditation.

Psalm 119:41—120:7

ו Waw

⁴¹May your unfailing love come to me, O Lᴏʀᴅ,
  your salvation according to your promise;
⁴²then I will answer the one who taunts me,
  for I trust in your word.
⁴³Do not snatch the word of truth from my
    mouth,
  for I have put my hope in your laws.
⁴⁴I will always obey your law,
  for ever and ever.
⁴⁵I will walk about in freedom,
  for I have sought out your precepts.
⁴⁶I will speak of your statutes before kings
  and will not be put to shame,
⁴⁷for I delight in your commands
  because I love them.
⁴⁸I lift up my hands toˣ your commands,
    which I love,
  and I meditate on your decrees.

ז Zayin

⁴⁹Remember your word to your servant,
  for you have given me hope.

⁵⁰My comfort in my suffering is this:
  Your promise preserves my life.
⁵¹The arrogant mock me without restraint,
  but I do not turn from your law.
⁵²I remember your ancient laws, O Lᴏʀᴅ,
  and I find comfort in them.
⁵³Indignation grips me because of the wicked,
  who have forsaken your law.
⁵⁴Your decrees are the theme of my song
  wherever I lodge.
⁵⁵In the night I remember your name, O Lᴏʀᴅ,
  and I will keep your law.
⁵⁶This has been my practice:
  I obey your precepts.

ח Heth

⁵⁷You are my portion, O Lᴏʀᴅ;
  I have promised to obey your words.
⁵⁸I have sought your face with all my heart;
  be gracious to me according to your
    promise.
⁵⁹I have considered my ways

ˣ48 Or *for*

and have turned my steps to your statutes.
⁶⁰I will hasten and not delay
　　to obey your commands.
⁶¹Though the wicked bind me with ropes,
　　I will not forget your law.
⁶²At midnight I rise to give you thanks
　　for your righteous laws.
⁶³I am a friend to all who fear you,
　　to all who follow your precepts.
⁶⁴The earth is filled with your love, O Lord;
　　teach me your decrees.

ט   Teth

⁶⁵Do good to your servant
　　according to your word, O Lord.
⁶⁶Teach me knowledge and good judgment,
　　for I believe in your commands.
⁶⁷Before I was afflicted I went astray,
　　but now I obey your word.
⁶⁸You are good, and what you do is good;
　　teach me your decrees.
⁶⁹Though the arrogant have smeared me with
　　lies,
　　I keep your precepts with all my heart.
⁷⁰Their hearts are callous and unfeeling,
　　but I delight in your law.
⁷¹It was good for me to be afflicted
　　so that I might learn your decrees.
⁷²The law from your mouth is more precious to
　　me
　　than thousands of pieces of silver and gold.

י   Yodh

⁷³Your hands made me and formed me;
　　give me understanding to learn your
　　　commands.
⁷⁴May those who fear you rejoice when they see
　　me,
　　for I have put my hope in your word.
⁷⁵I know, O Lord, that your laws are righteous,
　　and in faithfulness you have afflicted me.
⁷⁶May your unfailing love be my comfort,
　　according to your promise to your servant.
⁷⁷Let your compassion come to me that I may
　　live,
　　for your law is my delight.
⁷⁸May the arrogant be put to shame for
　　wronging me without cause;
　　but I will meditate on your precepts.
⁷⁹May those who fear you turn to me,
　　those who understand your statutes.

⁸⁰May my heart be blameless toward your
　　decrees,
　　that I may not be put to shame.

כ   Kaph

⁸¹My soul faints with longing for your
　　salvation,
　　but I have put my hope in your word.
⁸²My eyes fail, looking for your promise;
　　I say, "When will you comfort me?"
⁸³Though I am like a wineskin in the smoke,
　　I do not forget your decrees.
⁸⁴How long must your servant wait?
　　When will you punish my persecutors?
⁸⁵The arrogant dig pitfalls for me,
　　contrary to your law.
⁸⁶All your commands are trustworthy;
　　help me, for men persecute me without
　　　cause.
⁸⁷They almost wiped me from the earth,
　　but I have not forsaken your precepts.
⁸⁸Preserve my life according to your love,
　　and I will obey the statutes of your mouth.

ל   Lamedh

⁸⁹Your word, O Lord, is eternal;
　　it stands firm in the heavens.
⁹⁰Your faithfulness continues through all
　　generations;
　　you established the earth, and it endures.
⁹¹Your laws endure to this day,
　　for all things serve you.
⁹²If your law had not been my delight,
　　I would have perished in my affliction.
⁹³I will never forget your precepts,
　　for by them you have preserved my life.
⁹⁴Save me, for I am yours;
　　I have sought out your precepts.
⁹⁵The wicked are waiting to destroy me,
　　but I will ponder your statutes.
⁹⁶To all perfection I see a limit;
　　but your commands are boundless.

מ   Mem

⁹⁷Oh, how I love your law!
　　I meditate on it all day long.
⁹⁸Your commands make me wiser than my
　　enemies,
　　for they are ever with me.
⁹⁹I have more insight than all my teachers,

for I meditate on your statutes.
[100]I have more understanding than the elders,
for I obey your precepts.
[101]I have kept my feet from every evil path
so that I might obey your word.
[102]I have not departed from your laws,
for you yourself have taught me.
[103]How sweet are your words to my taste,
sweeter than honey to my mouth!
[104]I gain understanding from your precepts;
therefore I hate every wrong path.

ב   Nun

[105]Your word is a lamp to my feet
and a light for my path.
[106]I have taken an oath and confirmed it,
that I will follow your righteous laws.
[107]I have suffered much;
preserve my life, O LORD, according to your
word.
[108]Accept, O LORD, the willing praise of my
mouth,
and teach me your laws.
[109]Though I constantly take my life in my
hands,
I will not forget your law.
[110]The wicked have set a snare for me,
but I have not strayed from your precepts.
[111]Your statutes are my heritage forever;
they are the joy of my heart.
[112]My heart is set on keeping your decrees
to the very end.

ס   Samekh

[113]I hate double-minded men,
but I love your law.
[114]You are my refuge and my shield;
I have put my hope in your word.
[115]Away from me, you evildoers,
that I may keep the commands of my God!
[116]Sustain me according to your promise, and I
will live;
do not let my hopes be dashed.
[117]Uphold me, and I will be delivered;
I will always have regard for your decrees.
[118]You reject all who stray from your decrees,
for their deceitfulness is in vain.
[119]All the wicked of the earth you discard like
dross;
therefore I love your statutes.
[120]My flesh trembles in fear of you;
I stand in awe of your laws.

ע   Ayin

[121]I have done what is righteous and just;
do not leave me to my oppressors.
[122]Ensure your servant's well-being;
let not the arrogant oppress me.
[123]My eyes fail, looking for your salvation,
looking for your righteous promise.
[124]Deal with your servant according to your
love
and teach me your decrees.
[125]I am your servant; give me discernment
that I may understand your statutes.
[126]It is time for you to act, O LORD;
your law is being broken.
[127]Because I love your commands
more than gold, more than pure gold,
[128]and because I consider all your precepts
right,
I hate every wrong path.

פ   Pe

[129]Your statutes are wonderful;
therefore I obey them.
[130]The unfolding of your words gives light;
it gives understanding to the simple.
[131]I open my mouth and pant,
longing for your commands.
[132]Turn to me and have mercy on me,
as you always do to those who love your
name.
[133]Direct my footsteps according to your word;
let no sin rule over me.
[134]Redeem me from the oppression of men,
that I may obey your precepts.
[135]Make your face shine upon your servant
and teach me your decrees.
[136]Streams of tears flow from my eyes,
for your law is not obeyed.

צ   Tsadhe

[137]Righteous are you, O LORD,
and your laws are right.
[138]The statutes you have laid down are
righteous;
they are fully trustworthy.
[139]My zeal wears me out,
for my enemies ignore your words.
[140]Your promises have been thoroughly tested,
and your servant loves them.
[141]Though I am lowly and despised,
I do not forget your precepts.

142Your righteousness is everlasting
  and your law is true.
143Trouble and distress have come upon me,
  but your commands are my delight.
144Your statutes are forever right;
  give me understanding that I may live.

ק Qoph

145I call with all my heart; answer me, O LORD,
  and I will obey your decrees.
146I call out to you; save me
  and I will keep your statutes.
147I rise before dawn and cry for help;
  I have put my hope in your word.
148My eyes stay open through the watches of
    the night,
  that I may meditate on your promises.
149Hear my voice in accordance with your love;
  preserve my life, O LORD, according to your
    laws.
150Those who devise wicked schemes are near,
  but they are far from your law.
151Yet you are near, O LORD,
  and all your commands are true.
152Long ago I learned from your statutes
  that you established them to last forever.

ר Resh

153Look upon my suffering and deliver me,
  for I have not forgotten your law.
154Defend my cause and redeem me;
  preserve my life according to your promise.
155Salvation is far from the wicked,
  for they do not seek out your decrees.
156Your compassion is great, O LORD;
  preserve my life according to your laws.
157Many are the foes who persecute me,
  but I have not turned from your statutes.
158I look on the faithless with loathing,
  for they do not obey your word.
159See how I love your precepts;
  preserve my life, O LORD, according to your
    love.
160All your words are true;
  all your righteous laws are eternal.

ש Sin and Shin

161Rulers persecute me without cause,
  but my heart trembles at your word.
162I rejoice in your promise
  like one who finds great spoil.
163I hate and abhor falsehood

but I love your law.
164Seven times a day I praise you
  for your righteous laws.
165Great peace have they who love your law,
  and nothing can make them stumble.
166I wait for your salvation, O LORD,
  and I follow your commands.
167I obey your statutes,
  for I love them greatly.
168I obey your precepts and your statutes,
  for all my ways are known to you.

ת Taw

169May my cry come before you, O LORD;
  give me understanding according to your
    word.
170May my supplication come before you;
  deliver me according to your promise.
171May my lips overflow with praise,
  for you teach me your decrees.
172May my tongue sing of your word,
  for all your commands are righteous.
173May your hand be ready to help me,
  for I have chosen your precepts.
174I long for your salvation, O LORD,
  and your law is my delight.
175Let me live that I may praise you,
  and may your laws sustain me.
176I have strayed like a lost sheep.
  Seek your servant,
  for I have not forgotten your commands.

Psalm 120

A song of ascents.

1I call on the LORD in my distress,
  and he answers me.
2Save me, O LORD, from lying lips
  and from deceitful tongues.

3What will he do to you,
  and what more besides, O deceitful tongue?
4He will punish you with a warrior's sharp
    arrows,
  with burning coals of the broom tree.

5Woe to me that I dwell in Meshech,
  that I live among the tents of Kedar!
6Too long have I lived
  among those who hate peace.
7I am a man of peace;
  but when I speak, they are for war.

70 / *Psalm 121*
A Prayer of Assurance

THE JEWS WERE on an uphill journey to Jerusalem and the temple at Mount Zion. This psalm is among the many "songs of ascent" sung (or inwardly affirmed) by individuals in the caravan along the way. Any pilgrim facing an uphill climb of faith, and all of us on life's pilgrimage from this earthly existence to the heavenly glory, will find assurance in repeating the confession of this psalm.

Warming Up to God Imagine a battle of faith that you may be facing. Think of all helpful resources you may have turned to, or could be turning to, for help. Then face the Lord who watched you go to and fro. How do you imagine God making a difference in that situation?

Read Psalm 121.

Psalm 121

A song of ascents.

¹I lift up my eyes to the hills—
 where does my help come from?
²My help comes from the LORD,
 the Maker of heaven and earth.

³He will not let your foot slip—
 he who watches over you will not slumber;
⁴indeed, he who watches over Israel

will neither slumber nor sleep.

⁵The LORD watches over you—
 the LORD is your shade at your right hand;
⁶the sun will not harm you by day,
 nor the moon by night.

⁷The LORD will keep you from all harm—
 he will watch over your life;
⁸the LORD will watch over your coming and
 going
 both now and forevermore.

Discovering the Word 1. Judging from the words and phrases most often repeated in this psalm, what is its major theme? 2. How does the second verse in each of the four verse pairs (vv. 2, 4, 6, 8) expand on the minitheme of the introductory line in each pair (vv. 1, 3, 5, 7)? 3. What kind of help does the Lord provide his people along the journey (in contrast to those idols who may slumber or slouch on the job)? 4. In light of the assurances offered in this psalm, how do you account for the fact that some people do slip and fall into harm's way?

Applying the Word 1. Imagine you are an Israelite making this pilgrimage to Mount Zion and dialoguing your way through this psalm of confession and assurance. What parts do you find most reassuring for yourself? 2. What parts do you find most reassuring for a fellow pilgrim who you know is struggling along the way? 3. Consider one time, day or night, when you slipped badly and fell into harm's way. How was God watching over you in that situation?

Responding in Prayer Consider using Psalm 121 as an appropriate prayer for all your comings and goings. Offer it at mealtimes, office breaks and bedtimes. Let it influence the prayers and counsel you offer family, friends and work associates, especially anyone facing an uphill battle.

---

71 / *Psalm 122*
A Prayer for Peace

PRAYER FOR THE "peace of Jerusalem" (vv. 6–9) distinguished this Zion hymn. (For other Zion songs, see Ps 46, 48, 76, 84, 126, 129, 137.) This prayer is not just for fellow worshipers, but for the policies and programs that bring "peace and prosperity" to the city. This call to pray for the decision-makers in government confers a benediction on their work, the result of which would be shalom for the "City of Peace."

Warming Up to God When you think about doing good and seeking the welfare of others, who comes to mind? Mentally open up today's newspaper along with the Bible to see the people and the needs that God cares most about in your city.

Read Psalm 122.

Psalm 122

A song of ascents. Of David.

¹I rejoiced with those who said to me,
"Let us go to the house of the
LORD."
²Our feet are standing
in your gates, O Jerusalem.

³Jerusalem is built like a city
that is closely compacted together.
⁴That is where the tribes go up,
the tribes of the LORD,
to praise the name of the LORD

according to the statute given to
Israel.
⁵There the thrones for judgment stand,
the thrones of the house of David.

⁶Pray for the peace of Jerusalem:
"May those who love you be secure.
⁷May there be peace within your walls
and security within your citadels."
⁸For the sake of my brothers and friends,
I will say, "Peace be within you."
⁹For the sake of the house of the LORD our
God,
I will seek your prosperity.

Discovering the Word 1. What was it like for these worshipers to go to the house of the Lord in Jerusalem (Mount Zion)? 2. Describe the city of Jerusalem (vv. 3–5). 3. What things does the psalmist pray will be given to the city (vv. 6–9)? 4. What would this psalmist say to someone who wanted to first meet his own needs or those of his family before seeking the peace and prosperity of the city?

Applying the Word 1. Worship at Mount Zion was both a regular obligation (although a joyous event) and a bonding experience for temple-bound worshipers. What is "going to church" like for you? 2. Psalm 122 also evokes memories of how Jesus revered and wept over Jerusalem (Lk 9:51; 13:31–35; 19:41–44). By comparison, what tears have you shed over your beloved city? 3. "Peace within *your* walls" and "security within *your* citadels" (author's italics, v. 7) will also benefit believers, but the city itself is the end in view here, not believers. How do you go about working for the good of the city where you live and worship?

Responding in Prayer Scan the city news section of your newspaper for events and people that need God's "shalom" (peace and prosperity). Bring to God in prayer everyone you know in city hall and the key urban areas that need shalom.

Psalms 123—125

Psalm 123

A song of ascents.

¹I lift up my eyes to you,
to you whose throne is in heaven.
²As the eyes of slaves look to the hand of their
master,
as the eyes of a maid look to the hand of
her mistress,

so our eyes look to the LORD our God,
till he shows us his mercy.

³Have mercy on us, O LORD, have mercy
on us,
for we have endured much contempt.
⁴We have endured much ridicule from the
proud,
much contempt from the arrogant.

Psalm 124

A song of ascents. Of David.

¹If the LORD had not been on our side—
  let Israel say—
²if the LORD had not been on our side
  when men attacked us,
³when their anger flared against us,
  they would have swallowed us alive;
⁴the flood would have engulfed us,
  the torrent would have swept over us,
⁵the raging waters
  would have swept us away.

⁶Praise be to the LORD,
  who has not let us be torn by their
    teeth.
⁷We have escaped like a bird
  out of the fowler's snare;
the snare has been broken,
  and we have escaped.
⁸Our help is in the name of the LORD,
  the Maker of heaven and earth.

Psalm 125

A song of ascents.

¹Those who trust in the LORD are like Mount
    Zion,
  which cannot be shaken but endures
    forever.
²As the mountains surround Jerusalem,
  so the LORD surrounds his people
  both now and forevermore.

³The scepter of the wicked will not remain
  over the land allotted to the righteous,
for then the righteous might use
  their hands to do evil.

⁴Do good, O LORD, to those who are good,
  to those who are upright in heart.
⁵But those who turn to crooked ways
  the LORD will banish with the evildoers.

Peace be upon Israel.

72 / *Psalm 126*
A Song of Joy

ONE IMAGE OF happiness that sticks out in my mind is the suppertime dance that Snoopy does in the "Peanuts" comic strip. His head is flung back, his ears are flopping about, and his feet pound furiously. Have you ever felt like dancing for joy? In this passage the Israelites do.

 Warming Up to God What do you do when you are filled with joy?

 Read Psalm 126.

Psalm 126

A song of ascents.

¹When the LORD brought back the captives to*ᵃ*
    Zion,
  we were like men who dreamed.*ᵇ*
²Our mouths were filled with laughter,
  our tongues with songs of joy.
Then it was said among the nations,
  "The LORD has done great things for them."
³The LORD has done great things for us,

and we are filled with joy.

⁴Restore our fortunes,*ᶜ* O LORD,
  like streams in the Negev.
⁵Those who sow in tears
  will reap with songs of joy.
⁶He who goes out weeping,
  carrying seed to sow,
will return with songs of joy,
  carrying sheaves with him.

ᵃ1 Or LORD *restored the fortunes of*   *ᵇ1* Or *men restored to health*
ᶜ4 Or *Bring back our captives*

Discovering the Word 1. This is a song of celebration by the exiles who returned to Zion. What emotions do you see expressed throughout this psalm? 2. What imagery is used in verses 1–2 to describe the joy the writers feel? 3. How do verses 4–6 reflect a balance between cause and effect? 4. How are sadness and joy intertwined (vv. 5–6)?

 Applying the Word 1. The Israelites give God the credit for the "great things" that have happened. How do you do with giving God the credit? 2. When do you feel inhibited about freely expressing your joy?

Responding in Prayer What do you need to praise God for? Share your joy with him.

73 / *Psalm 127*
Worthwhile Work

WILL WE ALLOW technology and our society's definition of personhood to drive a wedge into our community? It can and does happen almost naturally—without our help.

As we respond to Jesus, there will be purpose in our lives and meaning within our relationships. It is the context of relationships with God and other persons that should give meaning to our work. Unfortunately, our culture elevates the possession of things and applauds compulsive work habits. We need to intervene where God's image in people is being destroyed by our society and structures. These passages encourage us to take the lead in bringing God's kingdom back into our relationships.

 Warming Up to God What challenges to faith are you currently facing in your workplace?

 Read Psalm 127.

Psalm 127

A song of ascents. Of Solomon.

¹Unless the LORD builds the house,
    its builders labor in vain.
Unless the LORD watches over the city,
    the watchmen stand guard in vain.
²In vain you rise early
    and stay up late,
toiling for food to eat—
    for he grants sleep to*d* those he loves.

³Sons are a heritage from the LORD,
    children a reward from him.
⁴Like arrows in the hands of a warrior
    are sons born in one's youth.
⁵Blessed is the man
    whose quiver is full of them.
They will not be put to shame
    when they contend with their enemies in
      the gate.

d2 Or eat— / for while they sleep he provides for

 Discovering the Word 1. What basis is offered in this passage for the worth of our work (v. 1)? 2. Why is it foolish to work long hours (v. 2)? 3. Children (v. 3) are a gift from God and are a sign of his favor on those who do worthwhile work. In what ways has God rewarded you for good work?

 Applying the Word 1. How does your attitude toward work shape how you view your personal relationships? 2. In what way do you need the rest that the Lord grants "to those he loves"?

Responding in Prayer Ask God to build in you the attitude toward work that he wants you to have.

Psalms 128—129

Psalm 128

A song of ascents.

¹Blessed are all who fear the LORD,
who walk in his ways.
²You will eat the fruit of your
labor;
blessings and prosperity will be
yours.
³Your wife will be like a fruitful
vine
within your house;
your sons will be like olive shoots
around your table.
⁴Thus is the man blessed
who fears the LORD.

⁵May the LORD bless you from Zion
all the days of your life;
may you see the prosperity of
Jerusalem,
6   and may you live to see your
children's children.

Peace be upon Israel.

Psalm 129

A song of ascents.

¹They have greatly oppressed me from my
youth—
let Israel say—
²they have greatly oppressed me from my
youth,
but they have not gained the victory over
me.
³Plowmen have plowed my back
and made their furrows long.
⁴But the LORD is righteous;
he has cut me free from the cords of the
wicked.

⁵May all who hate Zion
be turned back in shame.
⁶May they be like grass on the roof,
which withers before it can grow;
⁷with it the reaper cannot fill his hands,
nor the one who gathers fill his arms.
⁸May those who pass by not say,
"The blessing of the LORD be upon you;
we bless you in the name of the LORD."

74 / Psalm 130
A Prayer of Hope

HOPE IS NECESSARY. It gives us the strength to keep going through the tough times. It gives life joy and meaning in the good times. However, when hope has been repeatedly disappointed, it slips away. This psalm offers a picture of this struggle. The writer is without much hope. Yet he puts himself in a place of allowing for the possibility of hope. As we pray with him, we too can begin to wait with growing expectation. We too can nurture our hope.

 Warming Up to God How would you describe the experience of hope? How would you describe the experience of hopelessness?

 Read Psalm 130.

Psalm 130

A song of ascents.

¹Out of the depths I cry to you, O LORD;
2   O Lord, hear my voice.
Let your ears be attentive
to my cry for mercy.

³If you, O LORD, kept a record of sins,
O Lord, who could stand?
⁴But with you there is forgiveness;
therefore you are feared.

⁵I wait for the LORD, my soul waits,
and in his word I put my hope.
⁶My soul waits for the Lord

more than watchmen wait for the morning,
more than watchmen wait for the morning.

⁷O Israel, put your hope in the LORD,

for with the LORD is unfailing love
and with him is full redemption.
⁸He himself will redeem Israel
from all their sins.

Discovering the Word 1. The psalm begins with a cry to the Lord from "out of the depths" (v. 1). What pictures come to mind as you read this phrase? 2. The psalmist's distress seems to be related to a struggle with guilt. How can guilt lead to hopelessness? 3. Verses 3 and 4 tell us that God forgives. How does the promise of forgiveness contribute to hope? 4. Verse 5 says, "I wait, . . . my soul waits." What is the relationship between waiting and hope? 5. The psalmist then uses the metaphor of watchmen (v. 6) to describe the experience of hope. What does he convey with this image? 6. What reasons does the psalmist give for hoping in the Lord (vv. 7–8)?

Applying the Word 1. What area of life is it difficult for you to be hopeful about? 2. What reasons do you have for hoping in the Lord?

Responding in Prayer Thank God for being the source of hope. Pray for courage when you face hopelessness.

Psalms 131—132

Psalm 131

A song of ascents. Of David.

¹My heart is not proud, O LORD,
    my eyes are not haughty;
I do not concern myself with great matters
    or things too wonderful for me.
²But I have stilled and quieted my soul;
    like a weaned child with its mother,
    like a weaned child is my soul within me.

³O Israel, put your hope in the LORD
    both now and forevermore.

Psalm 132

A song of ascents.

¹O LORD, remember David
    and all the hardships he endured.

²He swore an oath to the LORD
    and made a vow to the Mighty One of
        Jacob:
³"I will not enter my house
    or go to my bed—
⁴I will allow no sleep to my eyes,
    no slumber to my eyelids,
⁵till I find a place for the LORD,
    a dwelling for the Mighty One of Jacob."

⁶We heard it in Ephrathah,

we came upon it in the fields of Jaar*ᵉ:ᶠ*
⁷"Let us go to his dwelling place;
    let us worship at his footstool—
⁸arise, O LORD, and come to your resting place,
    you and the ark of your might.
⁹May your priests be clothed with
        righteousness;
    may your saints sing for joy."

¹⁰For the sake of David your servant,
    do not reject your anointed one.

¹¹The LORD swore an oath to David,
    a sure oath that he will not revoke:
"One of your own descendants
    I will place on your throne—
¹²if your sons keep my covenant
    and the statutes I teach them,
then their sons will sit
    on your throne for ever and ever."

¹³For the LORD has chosen Zion,
    he has desired it for his dwelling:
¹⁴"This is my resting place for ever and ever;
    here I will sit enthroned, for I have desired
        it—
¹⁵I will bless her with abundant provisions;
    her poor will I satisfy with food.
¹⁶I will clothe her priests with salvation,
    and her saints will ever sing for joy.

ᵉ6 That is, Kiriath Jearim   ᶠ6 Or *heard of it in Ephrathah, / we found
it in the fields of Jaar.* (And no quotes around verses 7-9)

¹⁷"Here I will make a horn⁸ grow for David
    and set up a lamp for my anointed
    one.
¹⁸I will clothe his enemies with shame,

but the crown on his head will be
    resplendent."

75 / *Psalm 133*
Blessed Unity

THINK ABOUT THE many brother-to-brother and sister-to-sister loyalties and rivalries that are celebrated in our society—fraternities and sororities, sports teams, family corporations, class reunions, the Mafia (that is, "the Brotherhood"). In your mind's eye, or from your own experience, how do you picture those relationships? Do you envision any fraternal unity so blessed that it fairly oozes and drips with sweetness? David does. He waxes eloquent on this theme. Many contemporary songs which extol the blessedness of "mystic sweet communion" are based, in part, on this psalm.

Warming Up to God   How does the "mystic sweet communion" enjoyed by God's people compare to the kinds of unity that you have witnessed or experienced firsthand with others? As you get into this brief Bible study, surround yourself with images of warm Christian fellowship.

   Read Psalm 133.

Psalm 133

A song of ascents. Of David.

¹How good and pleasant it is
    when brothers live together in unity!
²It is like precious oil poured on the head,

running down on the beard,
running down on Aaron's beard,
    down upon the collar of his robes.
³It is as if the dew of Hermon
    were falling on Mount Zion.
For there the LORD bestows his blessing,
    even life forevermore.

Discovering the Word   1. What is so good or pleasant or blessed about brothers living together in unity (v. 1)?   2. To what is this blessedness compared (vv. 2–3)?   3. If the oil of anointing that saturated Aaron's beard and priestly robes was so precious and sanctifying (v. 2; Ex 29:7; Lev 21:10), what does that say about harmony running its course through the fellowship of God's people?   4. Mount Hermon rises 9,000 feet at three snow-covered peaks, its many glaciers stretching across 20 miles in northern Israel, watering the Jordan River valleys and cities below. However, during the summer, its snow and glaciers produce a heavy dew that envelops Mount Hermon, leaving much of the surroundings arid. For the "dew of Hermon" to fall on Mount Zion (v. 3) would be most unusual. What does that say about the blessing of brotherly unity?

Applying the Word   1. What does this psalm say to those who know only the brotherhood and sisterhood as it is portrayed in the media (consider fraternity hazing, sports teams that brawl, family corporations divided by sibling rivalry)?   2. Where are you experiencing strong brother-to-brother or sister-to-sister bonds and blessings that sanctify and sustain God's people, as does "oil" and "dew"?   3. In what way could you experience more of the priestly "oil" and Mount Hermon's "dew"?

Responding in Prayer   Think about the spiritual refreshment and moral accountability that strong fellowship provides you. Thank God for the brothers and sisters he has given you to sanctify and sustain you. Consider ways that you can live in harmony with your family of faith, and pray toward that end.

Psalms 134—136

Psalm 134

A song of ascents.

[1]Praise the LORD, all you servants of the LORD
who minister by night in the house of the
LORD.
[2]Lift up your hands in the sanctuary
and praise the LORD.

[3]May the LORD, the Maker of heaven and earth,
bless you from Zion.

Psalm 135

[1]Praise the LORD.[h]

Praise the name of the LORD;
praise him, you servants of the LORD,
[2]you who minister in the house of the LORD,
in the courts of the house of our God.

[3]Praise the LORD, for the LORD is good;
sing praise to his name, for that is pleasant.
[4]For the LORD has chosen Jacob to be his own,
Israel to be his treasured possession.

[5]I know that the LORD is great,
that our Lord is greater than all gods.
[6]The LORD does whatever pleases him,
in the heavens and on the earth,
in the seas and all their depths.
[7]He makes clouds rise from the ends of the
earth;
he sends lightning with the rain
and brings out the wind from his
storehouses.

[8]He struck down the firstborn of Egypt,
the firstborn of men and animals.
[9]He sent his signs and wonders into your
midst, O Egypt,
against Pharaoh and all his servants.
[10]He struck down many nations
and killed mighty kings—
[11]Sihon king of the Amorites,
Og king of Bashan
and all the kings of Canaan—
[12]and he gave their land as an inheritance,
an inheritance to his people Israel.

[13]Your name, O LORD, endures forever,
your renown, O LORD, through all
generations.
[14]For the LORD will vindicate his people

and have compassion on his servants.

[15]The idols of the nations are silver and gold,
made by the hands of men.
[16]They have mouths, but cannot speak,
eyes, but they cannot see;
[17]they have ears, but cannot hear,
nor is there breath in their mouths.
[18]Those who make them will be like them,
and so will all who trust in them.

[19]O house of Israel, praise the LORD;
O house of Aaron, praise the LORD;
[20]O house of Levi, praise the LORD;
you who fear him, praise the LORD.
[21]Praise be to the LORD from Zion,
to him who dwells in Jerusalem.

Praise the LORD.

Psalm 136

[1]Give thanks to the LORD, for he is good.
His love endures forever.
[2]Give thanks to the God of gods.
His love endures forever.
[3]Give thanks to the Lord of lords:
His love endures forever.

[4]to him who alone does great wonders,
His love endures forever.
[5]who by his understanding made the heavens,
His love endures forever.
[6]who spread out the earth upon the waters,
His love endures forever.
[7]who made the great lights—
His love endures forever.
[8]the sun to govern the day,
His love endures forever.
[9]the moon and stars to govern the night;
His love endures forever.

[10]to him who struck down the firstborn of
Egypt
His love endures forever.
[11]and brought Israel out from among them
His love endures forever.
[12]with a mighty hand and outstretched arm;
His love endures forever.
[13]to him who divided the Red Sea[i] asunder
His love endures forever.

[h]1 Hebrew *Hallelu Yah*; also in verses 3 and 21   [i]13 Hebrew *Yam Suph*; that is, Sea of Reeds; also in verse 15

¹⁴and brought Israel through the midst of it,
> *His love endures forever.*

¹⁵but swept Pharaoh and his army into the Red Sea;
> *His love endures forever.*

¹⁶to him who led his people through the desert,
> *His love endures forever.*

¹⁷who struck down great kings,
> *His love endures forever.*

¹⁸and killed mighty kings—
> *His love endures forever.*

¹⁹Sihon king of the Amorites
> *His love endures forever.*

²⁰and Og king of Bashan—
> *His love endures forever.*

²¹and gave their land as an inheritance,
> *His love endures forever.*

²²an inheritance to his servant Israel;
> *His love endures forever.*

²³to the One who remembered us in our low estate
> *His love endures forever.*

²⁴and freed us from our enemies,
> *His love endures forever.*

²⁵and who gives food to every creature.
> *His love endures forever.*

²⁶Give thanks to the God of heaven.
> *His love endures forever.*

76 / *Psalm 137*
Praying Our Hate

WE PUT ON our "Sunday best" in our prayers. But when we pray the prayers of God's people, the Psalms, we find that will not do. We must pray who we actually are, not who we think we should be. Here is a prayer that brings out not the best but the worst in us; vile, venomous, vicious hate.

Warming Up to God Everyone has hated at one time or another. It is one of the basic human experiences. Be honest before God. Whom have you hated? Why?

Read Psalm 137.

Psalm 137

¹By the rivers of Babylon we sat and wept
when we remembered Zion.
²There on the poplars
we hung our harps,
³for there our captors asked us for songs,
our tormentors demanded songs of joy;
they said, "Sing us one of the songs of Zion!"

⁴How can we sing the songs of the LORD
while in a foreign land?
⁵If I forget you, O Jerusalem,
may my right hand forget ⌞its skill⌟.
⁶May my tongue cling to the roof of my mouth
if I do not remember you,
if I do not consider Jerusalem
my highest joy.

⁷Remember, O LORD, what the Edomites did
on the day Jerusalem fell.
"Tear it down," they cried,
"tear it down to its foundations!"

⁸O Daughter of Babylon, doomed to destruction,
happy is he who repays you
for what you have done to us—
⁹he who seizes your infants
and dashes them against the rocks.

Discovering the Word **1.** This psalm combines the loveliest lyric we can sing with the ugliest emotion we can feel. What makes verses 1–6 lovely? **2.** What makes verses 7–9 ugly? **3.** Homesickness is understandable. Sometimes it is evidence of loyalty. Sometimes it is simply irresponsibility. Remembering your own experiences of this, how would you evaluate verses 4–6? **4.** The two dominant emotions in this prayer are self-pity

(vv. 1–6) and avenging hate (vv. 7–9), neither of them particularly commendable. Praying our sins doesn't, as such, launder them. What does it do?

 Applying the Word 1. Jesus said, "Love your enemies and pray for those who persecute you" (Mt 5:44). How can we possibly love and pray for such people? 2. Most of us suppress our negative emotions (unless, neurotically, we advertise them). The way of prayer is not to cover them up so we will appear respectable, but to expose them so we can be healed. What negative emotion would you like healed?

Responding in Prayer Take any hate or dislike that you have uncovered and give it voice as you pray.

Psalm 138

Psalm 138

Of David.

¹I will praise you, O Lord, with all my heart;
  before the "gods" I will sing your praise.
²I will bow down toward your holy temple
  and will praise your name
  for your love and your faithfulness,
for you have exalted above all things
  your name and your word.
³When I called, you answered me;
  you made me bold and stouthearted.

⁴May all the kings of the earth praise you,
  O Lord,

when they hear the words of your mouth.
⁵May they sing of the ways of the Lord,
  for the glory of the Lord is great.

⁶Though the Lord is on high, he looks upon
    the lowly,
  but the proud he knows from afar.
⁷Though I walk in the midst of trouble,
  you preserve my life;
you stretch out your hand against the anger
    of my foes,
  with your right hand you save me.
⁸The Lord will fulfill ⌐his purpose¬ for me;
  your love, O Lord, endures forever—
  do not abandon the works of your hands.

77 / *Psalm 139*
Wonderfully Made

A CRAFTSMAN IN medieval times would work for months on a special piece that displayed his finest artistic skill. Finally, when the work was finished, he would present it to the craftsmen's guild in hopes of achieving the rank of master. The work was called his masterpiece. In Psalm 139 we see God the master craftsman, lovingly at work on his masterpiece. The psalm can have a profound impact on the way we view ourselves.

 Warming Up to God Do you think of yourself as God's artwork, his masterpiece? Why or why not? Ask God to help you see yourself through his eyes as you begin this study.

 Read Psalm 139.

Psalm 139

For the director of music. Of David.
A psalm.

¹O Lord, you have searched me
  and you know me.

²You know when I sit and when I rise;
  you perceive my thoughts from afar.
³You discern my going out and my lying
    down;
  you are familiar with all my ways.
⁴Before a word is on my tongue
  you know it completely, O Lord.

⁵You hem me in—behind and before;
  you have laid your hand upon me.
⁶Such knowledge is too wonderful for me,
  too lofty for me to attain.

⁷Where can I go from your Spirit?
  Where can I flee from your presence?
⁸If I go up to the heavens, you are there;
  if I make my bed in the depths,ʲ you are
    there.
⁹If I rise on the wings of the dawn,
  if I settle on the far side of the sea,
¹⁰even there your hand will guide me,
  your right hand will hold me fast.

¹¹If I say, "Surely the darkness will hide me
  and the light become night around me,"
¹²even the darkness will not be dark to you;
  the night will shine like the day,
  for darkness is as light to you.

¹³For you created my inmost being;
  you knit me together in my mother's
    womb.
¹⁴I praise you because I am fearfully and
    wonderfully made;
  your works are wonderful,
  I know that full well.
¹⁵My frame was not hidden from you
  when I was made in the secret place.

When I was woven together in the depths of
    the earth,
¹⁶ your eyes saw my unformed body.
All the days ordained for me
  were written in your book
  before one of them came to be.

¹⁷How precious toᵏ me are your thoughts,
    O God!
  How vast is the sum of them!
¹⁸Were I to count them,
  they would outnumber the grains of sand.
When I awake,
  I am still with you.

¹⁹If only you would slay the wicked, O God!
  Away from me, you bloodthirsty men!
²⁰They speak of you with evil intent;
  your adversaries misuse your name.
²¹Do I not hate those who hate you, O Lᴏʀᴅ,
  and abhor those who rise up against you?
²²I have nothing but hatred for them;
  I count them my enemies.

²³Search me, O God, and know my heart;
  test me and know my anxious thoughts.
²⁴See if there is any offensive way in me,
  and lead me in the way everlasting.

ʲ8 Hebrew *Sheol*   ᵏ17 Or *concerning*

Discovering the Word 1. According to the psalmist, what specific things does the Lord know about us (vv. 1–6)? 2. The psalmist declares that God's knowledge of him is wonderful (v. 6). Yet why do you think he also feels an urge to flee from God's presence (vv. 7–12)? 3. What words are used to describe God's activity and artistry in making us (vv. 13–16)?

Applying the Word 1. How do you hide your true self from God? 2. When do you hide your true self from others? 3. How does this psalm help you to feel more loved and valued by God?

Responding in Prayer Take time to thank God for the fact that you are "fearfully and wonderfully made." Put verses 23–24 in your own words and express them to God in prayer.

Psalms 140—141

Psalm 140

For the director of music. A psalm
of David.

¹Rescue me, O Lᴏʀᴅ, from evil men;
  protect me from men of violence,
²who devise evil plans in their hearts
  and stir up war every day.

³They make their tongues as sharp as a
    serpent's;
  the poison of vipers is on their lips.   *Selah*

⁴Keep me, O Lᴏʀᴅ, from the hands of the
    wicked;
  protect me from men of violence
  who plan to trip my feet.
⁵Proud men have hidden a snare for me;

they have spread out the cords of their net
and have set traps for me along my path.
                                    Selah

⁶O Lᴏʀᴅ, I say to you, "You are my God."
   Hear, O Lᴏʀᴅ, my cry for mercy.
⁷O Sovereign Lᴏʀᴅ, my strong deliverer,
   who shields my head in the day of battle—
⁸do not grant the wicked their desires, O Lᴏʀᴅ;
   do not let their plans succeed,
   or they will become proud.   *Selah*

⁹Let the heads of those who surround me
   be covered with the trouble their lips have
      caused.
¹⁰Let burning coals fall upon them;
   may they be thrown into the fire,
   into miry pits, never to rise.
¹¹Let slanderers not be established in the land;
   may disaster hunt down men of violence.

¹²I know that the Lᴏʀᴅ secures justice for the
      poor
   and upholds the cause of the needy.
¹³Surely the righteous will praise your name
   and the upright will live before you.

Psalm 141

A psalm of David.

¹O Lᴏʀᴅ, I call to you; come quickly to me.
   Hear my voice when I call to you.
²May my prayer be set before you like incense;
   may the lifting up of my hands be like the
      evening sacrifice.

³Set a guard over my mouth, O Lᴏʀᴅ;
   keep watch over the door of my lips.
⁴Let not my heart be drawn to what is evil,
   to take part in wicked deeds
with men who are evildoers;
   let me not eat of their delicacies.

⁵Let a righteous manˡ strike me—it is a
      kindness;
   let him rebuke me—it is oil on my head.
   My head will not refuse it.

Yet my prayer is ever against the deeds of
      evildoers;
⁶   their rulers will be thrown down from the
      cliffs,
   and the wicked will learn that my words
      were well spoken.
⁷⌊They will say,⌋ "As one plows and breaks up
      the earth,
   so our bones have been scattered at the
      mouth of the grave.ᵐ"

⁸But my eyes are fixed on you, O Sovereign
      Lᴏʀᴅ;
   in you I take refuge—do not give me over
      to death.
⁹Keep me from the snares they have laid for
      me,
   from the traps set by evildoers.
¹⁰Let the wicked fall into their own nets,
   while I pass by in safety.

ˡ5 Or *Let the Righteous One*   ᵐ7 Hebrew *Sheol*

78 / *Psalm 142*
A Prayer of Desperation

"IT'S CANCER." THE words shattered the tension in the room. I had been waiting with my friend to find out the results of her biopsy. My friend was calm. She was probably too stunned to feel. I, however, felt desperate. I wanted to scream "No!" I felt frightened, powerless, outraged. Desperation is an experience of extreme need and helplessness. We feel desperate when life's circumstances overpower us. We feel desperate when our well-being is threatened and we feel unable to affect the outcome. This psalm gives voice to our experiences of desperation.

 Warming Up to God Think of a time when you felt desperate. What phrases or images would you use to describe the situation you faced?

 Read Psalm 142.

Psalm 142

A *maskil*[n] of David. When he was in the
   cave. A prayer.

[1]I cry aloud to the LORD;
   I lift up my voice to the LORD
     for mercy.
[2]I pour out my complaint before him;
   before him I tell my trouble.

[3]When my spirit grows faint within
     me,
   it is you who know my way.
In the path where I walk
   men have hidden a snare for me.
[4]Look to my right and see;
   no one is concerned for me.
I have no refuge;
   no one cares for my life.

[5]I cry to you, O LORD;
   I say, "You are my refuge,
   my portion in the land of the
     living."
[6]Listen to my cry,
   for I am in desperate need;
rescue me from those who pursue me,
   for they are too strong for me.
[7]Set me free from my prison,
   that I may praise your name.

Then the righteous will gather
   about me
   because of your goodness to me.

[n] Title: Probably a literary or musical term

 Discovering the Word 1. This psalm was written by David when he was in a cave, perhaps when he was hiding from Saul. How would you describe David's emotional state? 2. What phrases and images does David use to describe the situation he faces (vv. 3, 6 and 7)? 3. What contrast do you see between David's experiences with people and his experience with God? 4. How would you compare his view of his personal power with his view of God's power?

 Applying the Word 1. What is the significance of the contrast between our power and God's power when we feel desperate? 2. Are you able to pray with this kind of directness and urgency in times of personal need? Why or why not?

 Responding in Prayer Write a psalm of your own, allowing yourself to cry out to God on your own behalf or on behalf of someone else who faces a desperate situation.

79 / *Psalm 143*
Asking for Guidance

"THE WAY I was taught to pray," explained Sue, "was to list for God the things I wanted done. I would give God a long list of 'requests' that were really thinly disguised expectations or demands. It amazes me now, but I really felt I knew what everyone needed and that my job was to bring these needs to God's attention. I would decide what needed to be done and God would do it. Sound backwards? I think so. I was surprised to discover a humbler way to pray. I learned to say, 'show me your will today and give me the power to carry it out.' I stopped telling God what to do and started to ask for guidance and help. Now I pray with an awareness that I am talking to my Creator, who knows me better than I know me, who loves me more than I love me, and who is personally involved in my life."

Warming Up to God What fears might keep you from seeking to know and to do God's will?

Read Psalm 143.

Psalm 143

A psalm of David.

¹O LORD, hear my prayer,
    listen to my cry for mercy;
in your faithfulness and righteousness
    come to my relief.
²Do not bring your servant into judgment,
    for no one living is righteous before you.

³The enemy pursues me,
    he crushes me to the ground;
he makes me dwell in darkness
    like those long dead.
⁴So my spirit grows faint within me;
    my heart within me is dismayed.

⁵I remember the days of long ago;
    I meditate on all your works
    and consider what your hands have done.
⁶I spread out my hands to you;
    my soul thirsts for you like a parched land.
                          Selah

⁷Answer me quickly, O LORD;

my spirit fails.
Do not hide your face from me
    or I will be like those who go down to the
        pit.
⁸Let the morning bring me word of your
        unfailing love,
    for I have put my trust in you.
Show me the way I should go,
    for to you I lift up my soul.
⁹Rescue me from my enemies, O LORD,
    for I hide myself in you.
¹⁰Teach me to do your will,
    for you are my God;
may your good Spirit
    lead me on level ground.

¹¹For your name's sake, O LORD, preserve my
    life;
    in your righteousness, bring me out of
        trouble.
¹²In your unfailing love, silence my enemies;
    destroy all my foes,
    for I am your servant.

 Discovering the Word 1. What specifically does the psalmist say he longs for in this text (vv. 1, 7)? 2. What does the psalmist fear might happen (vv. 2, 7)? 3. Why does the psalmist need God's help (vv. 3–6)? 4. The psalmist asks for knowledge of God's will and the power to carry it out. What specifically does he ask for (vv. 8–12)? 5. The psalmist reminds God: "I have put my trust in you.... To you I lift up my soul.... I hide myself in you" (vv. 8–9). What do you think the psalmist is trying to communicate to God?

 Applying the Word 1. In what area of life do you feel a need for knowledge of God's will? 2. What knowledge of God's will have you received, but are hesitant and needing power to carry out?

Responding in Prayer What guidance would you like to ask God for today?

Psalm 144

Psalm 144

Of David.

¹Praise be to the LORD my Rock,
    who trains my hands for war,
    my fingers for battle.
²He is my loving God and my fortress,
    my stronghold and my deliverer,
my shield, in whom I take refuge,
    who subdues peoples° under me.

³O LORD, what is man that you care for him,
    the son of man that you think of him?

⁴Man is like a breath;
    his days are like a fleeting shadow.

⁵Part your heavens, O LORD, and come down;
    touch the mountains, so that they smoke.
⁶Send forth lightning and scatter ⌊the enemies⌋;
    shoot your arrows and rout them.
⁷Reach down your hand from on high;
    deliver me and rescue me
from the mighty waters,
    from the hands of foreigners

°2 Many manuscripts of the Masoretic Text, Dead Sea Scrolls, Aquila, Jerome and Syriac; most manuscripts of the Masoretic Text *subdues my people*

8 whose mouths are full of lies,
whose right hands are deceitful.

9 I will sing a new song to you, O God;
on the ten-stringed lyre I will make music to you,
10 to the One who gives victory to kings,
who delivers his servant David from the deadly sword.

11 Deliver me and rescue me
from the hands of foreigners
whose mouths are full of lies,
whose right hands are deceitful.

12 Then our sons in their youth
will be like well-nurtured plants,
and our daughters will be like pillars
carved to adorn a palace.
13 Our barns will be filled
with every kind of provision.
Our sheep will increase by thousands,
by tens of thousands in our fields;
14 our oxen will draw heavy loads.[p]
There will be no breaching of walls,
no going into captivity,
no cry of distress in our streets.

15 Blessed are the people of whom this is true;
blessed are the people whose God is the LORD.

[p] 14 Or *our chieftains will be firmly established*

80 / *Psalm 145*
Relying on God

PEOPLE WHO HAVE experienced repeated disappointments with parents or other significant people can develop an image of an unreliable God. He is seen as a God who cannot be counted on. He makes promises he may not keep. He may be loving one day and unaccountably angry the next. People who have experienced unreliable parents may ask: "How do I know God will keep his promises? How do I know he listens to me? How do I know he will answer me or help me?" The image of an unreliable God stands in stark contrast to biblical images of God. The God of the Bible is the Faithful One, the Rock, the Fortress. He is the same yesterday, today and forever.

Warming Up to God Think of a person whom you see as reliable. Describe the person and your response to his or her reliability.

Read Psalm 145.

Psalm 145[q]

A psalm of praise. Of David.

1 I will exalt you, my God the King;
I will praise your name for ever and ever.
2 Every day I will praise you
and extol your name for ever and ever.

3 Great is the LORD and most worthy of praise;
his greatness no one can fathom.
4 One generation will commend your works to another;
they will tell of your mighty acts.
5 They will speak of the glorious splendor of your majesty,
and I will meditate on your wonderful works.[r]
6 They will tell of the power of your awesome works,
and I will proclaim your great deeds.
7 They will celebrate your abundant goodness
and joyfully sing of your righteousness.

8 The LORD is gracious and compassionate,
slow to anger and rich in love.
9 The LORD is good to all;
he has compassion on all he has made.
10 All you have made will praise you, O LORD;
your saints will extol you.
11 They will tell of the glory of your kingdom
and speak of your might,
12 so that all men may know of your mighty acts

[q] This psalm is an acrostic poem, the verses of which (including verse 13b) begin with the successive letters of the Hebrew alphabet.
[r] 5 Dead Sea Scrolls and Syriac (see also Septuagint); Masoretic Text *On the glorious splendor of your majesty / and on your wonderful works I will meditate*

and the glorious splendor of your kingdom.
¹³Your kingdom is an everlasting kingdom,
and your dominion endures through all
generations.

The LORD is faithful to all his promises
and loving toward all he has made.^s
¹⁴The LORD upholds all those who fall
and lifts up all who are bowed down.
¹⁵The eyes of all look to you,
and you give them their food at the proper
time.
¹⁶You open your hand
and satisfy the desires of every living thing.

¹⁷The LORD is righteous in all his ways

and loving toward all he has made.
¹⁸The LORD is near to all who call on him,
to all who call on him in truth.
¹⁹He fulfills the desires of those who fear him;
he hears their cry and saves them.
²⁰The LORD watches over all who love him,
but all the wicked he will destroy.

²¹My mouth will speak in praise of the LORD.
Let every creature praise his holy name
for ever and ever.

^s13 One manuscript of the Masoretic Text, Dead Sea Scrolls and Syriac
(see also Septuagint); most manuscripts of the Masoretic Text do not
have the last two lines of verse 13.

 Discovering the Word 1. What descriptive words and phrases are used about God in this prayer? 2. What phrases suggest that God is reliable? 3. How does God help those who are in need (vv. 14–20)? 4. What image of God comes through to you most clearly?

 Applying the Word 1. How does the picture of God here compare or contrast with your image of God's reliability? 2. Why is it important for you to know that God is reliable?

 Responding in Prayer Offer God your thanks for his faithfulness.

81 / *Psalm 146*
The Source of Hope

"MY OWN MOM and Dad failed me," Linda said in her support group meeting. "Then my marriage fell apart. And then my health fell apart. Life has always been hard. I don't see why I should expect it to ever get any better. If anything, it will probably get worse. How is it possible for me to have hope?"

The Bible teaches that there is more to the story of our lives than our experiences of loss and disappointment. The planet may be fallen, but it is not forsaken by God. God is actively present in our lives, bringing gifts of life and joy into the midst of our darkness. We can dare to hope because of who God is.

 Warming Up to God In what area of life is it hard for you to find hope?

 Read Psalm 146.

Psalm 146

¹Praise the LORD.^t

Praise the LORD, O my soul.
² I will praise the LORD all my life;
I will sing praise to my God as long as I
live.

³Do not put your trust in princes,
in mortal men, who cannot save.

⁴When their spirit departs, they return to the
ground;
on that very day their plans come to
nothing.

⁵Blessed is he whose help is the God of Jacob,
whose hope is in the LORD his God,
⁶the Maker of heaven and earth,

^t1 Hebrew *Hallelu Yah*; also in verse 10

the sea, and everything in them—
   the LORD, who remains faithful forever.
⁷He upholds the cause of the oppressed
   and gives food to the hungry.
The LORD sets prisoners free,
8   the LORD gives sight to the blind,
the LORD lifts up those who are bowed down,
   the LORD loves the righteous.

⁹The LORD watches over the alien
   and sustains the fatherless and the widow,
   but he frustrates the ways of the wicked.

¹⁰The LORD reigns forever,
   your God, O Zion, for all generations.

   Praise the LORD.

Discovering the Word 1. How does this psalm contrast the experience of hoping in God with the experience of hoping in people? 2. The psalmist mentions eight kinds of circumstances that might seem hopeless. List these situations/conditions and the reasons why they might seem hopeless. 3. Describe how God responds to people in each of these situations. 4. What do these responses from God to people in hopeless situations suggest to you about God's character?

Applying the Word 1. Which of the eight images of hopelessness do you most strongly relate to at this time? Explain. 2. Take a few minutes and allow yourself to picture God responding to you in the way this text describes God's response. What thoughts and feelings do you have in response to this image of God's care for you?

Responding in Prayer What would you like to say to God who is the source of your hope?

Psalm 147

Psalm 147

¹Praise the LORD.ᵘ

How good it is to sing praises to our God,
   how pleasant and fitting to praise him!

²The LORD builds up Jerusalem;
   he gathers the exiles of Israel.
³He heals the brokenhearted
   and binds up their wounds.

⁴He determines the number of the stars
   and calls them each by name.
⁵Great is our Lord and mighty in power;
   his understanding has no limit.
⁶The LORD sustains the humble
   but casts the wicked to the ground.

⁷Sing to the LORD with thanksgiving;
   make music to our God on the harp.
⁸He covers the sky with clouds;
   he supplies the earth with rain
   and makes grass grow on the hills.
⁹He provides food for the cattle
   and for the young ravens when they call.

¹⁰His pleasure is not in the strength of the horse,

nor his delight in the legs of a man;
¹¹the LORD delights in those who fear him,
   who put their hope in his unfailing love.

¹²Extol the LORD, O Jerusalem;
   praise your God, O Zion,
¹³for he strengthens the bars of your gates
   and blesses your people within you.
¹⁴He grants peace to your borders
   and satisfies you with the finest of wheat.

¹⁵He sends his command to the earth;
   his word runs swiftly.
¹⁶He spreads the snow like wool
   and scatters the frost like ashes.
¹⁷He hurls down his hail like pebbles.
   Who can withstand his icy blast?
¹⁸He sends his word and melts them;
   he stirs up his breezes, and the waters flow.

¹⁹He has revealed his word to Jacob,
   his laws and decrees to Israel.
²⁰He has done this for no other nation;
   they do not know his laws.

   Praise the LORD.

ᵘ1 Hebrew *Hallelu Yah*; also in verse 20

82 / *Psalm 148*
A Symphony of Praise

THIS CALL TO praise, if heeded by all of creation, would make for quite a symphony of praise. Perhaps it would sound more like a cacophony than a symphony. Judging from the noises that all of God's creatures make individually, it boggles the mind (never mind the eardrums!) to imagine the concert called for in Psalm 148. Its location at the end of the book suggests that Psalm 148 is meant to wrap everything up on a high praise note.

 Warming Up to God Think about an exciting time of corporate praise that you have been a part of. How does seeing others engaged in worship inspire your worship?

 Read Psalm 148.

Psalm 148

¹Praise the LORD.ᵛ

Praise the LORD from the heavens,
  praise him in the heights above.
²Praise him, all his angels,
  praise him, all his heavenly hosts.
³Praise him, sun and moon,
  praise him, all you shining stars.
⁴Praise him, you highest heavens
  and you waters above the skies.
⁵Let them praise the name of the LORD,
  for he commanded and they were created.
⁶He set them in place for ever and ever;
  he gave a decree that will never pass away.

⁷Praise the LORD from the earth,
  you great sea creatures and all ocean
    depths,
⁸lightning and hail, snow and clouds,
  stormy winds that do his bidding,

⁹you mountains and all hills,
  fruit trees and all cedars,
¹⁰wild animals and all cattle,
  small creatures and flying birds,
¹¹kings of the earth and all nations,
  you princes and all rulers on earth,
¹²young men and maidens,
  old men and children.

¹³Let them praise the name of the LORD,
  for his name alone is exalted;
  his splendor is above the earth and the
    heavens.
¹⁴He has raised up for his people a horn,ʷ
  the praise of all his saints,
  of Israel, the people close to his heart.

Praise the LORD.

ᵛ1 Hebrew *Hallelu Yah*; also in verse 14   ʷ14 *Horn* here symbolizes strong one, that is, king.

 Discovering the Word 1. This psalm divides into two six-verse stanzas (vv. 1–6 and 7–12), with a recap that underscores the motivation to praise (vv. 13–14). What two major chorus groups are appealed to here? 2. Within those two major choral divisions, who joins in praising God? 3. Do you see this as mere figurative (symbolic or exaggerated) language used by the psalmist to call all things in heaven and on earth, or is there some way that all the various elements actually praise God? 4. Why praise God at all (vv. 5–6, 13–14)?

Applying the Word 1. What is the closest you have come, this side of heaven, to experiencing a worldwide worship service such as this psalm announces? 2. Do you look forward to heaven when this psalm finds its fulfillment, or does praising God all day long sound boring to you? 3. How does this psalm provide a new or fresh picture of praise for you?

Responding in Prayer Imagine what it would be like to have every man, woman and child—young and old alike—participating in your church's choir. Pray (and practice) toward that end.

Psalm 149

Psalm 149

¹Praise the LORD.ˣ

Sing to the LORD a new song,
  his praise in the assembly of the saints.

²Let Israel rejoice in their Maker;
  let the people of Zion be glad in their King.
³Let them praise his name with dancing
    and make music to him with tambourine
      and harp.
⁴For the LORD takes delight in his people;
  he crowns the humble with salvation.
⁵Let the saints rejoice in this honor

and sing for joy on their beds.

⁶May the praise of God be in their mouths
  and a double-edged sword in their hands,
⁷to inflict vengeance on the nations
  and punishment on the peoples,
⁸to bind their kings with fetters,
  their nobles with shackles of iron,
⁹to carry out the sentence written against
    them.
  This is the glory of all his saints.

  Praise the LORD.

ˣ1 Hebrew *Hallelu Yah*; also in verse 9

83 / Psalm 150
Praying Our Praise

ALL PRAYER FINALLY, in one way or another, becomes praise. Psalm 150 is deliberately placed as the concluding prayer of the church's book of prayers. No matter how much we suffer, no matter our doubts—everything finds its way into praise, the final consummating prayer.

 Warming Up to God What circumstances or feelings in the last year have, however momentarily, made a praising person out of you? Reflect on that again in joy, celebrating with Christ.

 Read Psalm 150.

Psalm 150

¹Praise the LORD.ʸ

Praise God in his sanctuary;
  praise him in his mighty heavens.
²Praise him for his acts of power;
  praise him for his surpassing greatness.
³Praise him with the sounding of the trumpet,
  praise him with the harp and lyre,

⁴praise him with tambourine and dancing,
  praise him with the strings and flute,
⁵praise him with the clash of cymbals,
  praise him with resounding cymbals.

⁶Let everything that has breath praise the LORD.

  Praise the LORD.

ʸ1 Hebrew *Hallelu Yah*; also in verse 6

Discovering the Word 1. How many times is the word *praise* used in the psalm? 2. Verse 1 tells us *where* the Lord is to be praised. What is the meaning of "in his sanctuary" and "in his mighty heavens"? 3. Verse 2 tells us *why* he is to be praised. What reasons does the psalmist give? 4. Verses 3–5 tell us *how* to praise the Lord. As you read these verses, what kind of scene do you imagine?

Applying the Word 1. Building on verse 2, what reasons can you give for praising God? 2. There are no shortcuts to praise. We can see this in many psalms that express pain. What difficult circumstances in your life have found their way into praise? 3. Augustine claimed that a "Christian should be a hallelujah from head to foot." What needs to be done to get to that point?

 Responding in Prayer Gather the reflections and insights that have come from your study and turn them into a time of concluding and celebrative praise.

ACKNOWLEDGMENTS

The following articles were revised and adapted from InterVarsity Press publications:

"Why Have a Quiet Time?" by John White, from pp. 136-43 of *The Race* © 1984 by InterVarsity Christian Fellowship of the United States of America.

"How to Have a Quiet Time" by Stephen D. Eyre, from pp. 3-12 and 28-31 of *Quiet Time Dynamics* © 1989 by InterVarsity Christian Fellowship of the United States of America.

"How to Study the Bible" by James F. Nyquist and Jack Kuhatschek, from pages 25-35 of *Leading Bible Discussions*, 2d ed. © 1985 by InterVarsity Christian Fellowship of the United States of America.

"Prayer and Journaling" by Bill Hybels, from pages 39-44 and 59-60 of *Too Busy Not to Pray* © 1988 by InterVarsity Christian Fellowship of the United States of America.

The New Testament quiet times were adapted from the following LifeGuide® Bible Studies:

Matthew © 1987 by Stephen and Jacalyn Eyre.

Mark by James Hoover © 1985 by InterVarsity Christian Fellowship of the United States of America.

Luke © 1992 by Ada Lum.

John © 1990 by Douglas Connelly.

Acts © 1992 by Phyllis J. Le Peau.

Romans by Jack Kuhatschek © 1986 by InterVarsity Christian Fellowship of the United States of America.

1 Corinthians © 1988 by Paul Stevens and Dan Williams.

2 Corinthians © 1990 by Paul Stevens.

Galatians by Jack Kuhatschek © 1986 by InterVarsity Christian Fellowship of the United States of America.

Ephesians by Andrew T. and Phyllis J. Le Peau © 1985 by InterVarsity Christian Fellowship of the United States of America.

Philippians by Donald Baker © 1985 by InterVarsity Christian Fellowship of the United States of America.

Colossians and Philemon © 1989 by Martha Reapsome.

1 & 2 Thessalonians © 1991 by Donald E. Baker.

1 & 2 Timothy and Titus © 1991 by Pete Sommer.

Hebrews © 1991 by James Reapsome.

James by Andrew T. and Phyllis J. Le Peau, rev. ed. © 1987.

1 & 2 Peter and Jude © 1992 by Carolyn Nystrom.

John's Letters © 1990 by Ron Blankley.

Revelation © 1987 by R. Paul Stevens.

Quiet times 9, 12 and 14 of Revelation are by Scott Hotaling.

Quiet times in the Psalms are from the following sources:

Quiet time 33 taken from *Caring for Emotional Needs* © 1991 by Phyllis J. Le Peau and NCF.

Quiet time 11 taken from *Created Male* © 1993 by Brian M. Wallace & Cindy Bunch.

Quiet time 68 taken from *Deciding Wisely* © 1992 by Bill Syrios.

Quiet time 37 taken from *Entering God's Presence* © 1992 by Stephen D. Eyre.

Quiet time 62 taken from *The Fruit of the Spirit* by Hazel Offner, rev. ed. © 1987.

Quiet time 4 taken from *Healing for Broken People* © 1990 by Dan Harrison.

Quiet time 61 taken from *Loving the World* © 1992 by Carolyn Nystrom.

Quiet times 34, 41-45, 50-51, 54, 59, 74 and 78 taken from *Psalms II* © 1994 by Juanita Ryan.

Quiet time 46 taken from *Multi-Ethnicity* © 1990 by Isaac Canales.

Quiet time 73 taken from *People and Technology* © 1990 by Mary Fisher.

Quiet times 1-3, 6-7, 16, 39, 47, 52, 60, 76 and 83 taken from *Psalms* © 1987 by Eugene H. Peterson.

Quiet time 5 taken from *Prayer* © 1994 by David Healey.

Quiet time 10 taken from *Pursuing Holiness* © 1992 by Carolyn Nystrom.

Quiet times 69 and 79 taken from *Recovery: A Lifelong Journey* © 1993 by Juanita and Dale Ryan.

Quiet times 8, 9 and 12 taken from *Recovery from Abuse* © 1990 by Dale and Juanita Ryan.

Quiet time 63 taken from *Recovery from Bitterness* © 1990 by Dale and Juanita Ryan.

Quiet time 81 taken from *Recovery from Depression* © 1993 by Juanita and Dale Ryan.

Quiet time 80 taken from *Recovery from Distorted Images of God* © 1990 by Dale and Juanita Ryan.

Quiet time 58 taken from *Recovery from Distorted Images of Self* © 1993 by Juanita and Dale Ryan.

Quiet times 40 and 66 taken from *Recovery from Family Dysfunctions* © 1990 by Dale and Juanita Ryan.

Quiet time 14 taken from *Resources for Caring People* © 1991 by Phyllis J. Le Peau and NCF.

Quiet time 77 taken from *Self-Esteem* © 1990 by Jack Kuhatschek.

Quiet time 19 taken from *Suffering* © 1992 by Jack Kuhatschek.

Quiet times 21-32 taken from *Waiting on the Lord* © 1994 by Stephen D. and Jacalyn Eyre.

Quiet time 48 taken from *Women Facing Temptation* © 1993 by Cindy Bunch.

Quiet times 38 and 72 are by Cindy Bunch.

Quiet times 29 and 45 are by Linda Gehrs.

Quiet times 13, 15, 17, 36, 49, 53, 55-57, 64-65, 67, 70-71, 75 and 82 are by Dietrich Gruen.

INDEX OF QUIET TIME SUBJECTS